CONTEMPORARY
Black
Biography

ISSN-1058-1316

CONTEMPORARY

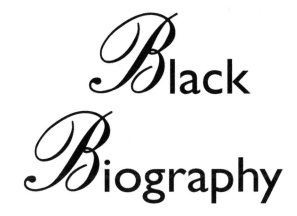

Black
Biography

Profiles from the International Black Community

Volume 136

 GALE
CENGAGE Learning

Farmington Hills, Mich • San Francisco • New York • Waterville, Maine
Meriden, Conn • Mason, Ohio • Chicago

Contemporary Black Biography, Volume 136

Kepos Media, Inc.: Deborah A. Ring, Derek Jacques, and Paula Kepos, editors

Project Editor: Margaret Mazurkiewicz

Image Research and Acquisitions: Ashley M. Maynard, Carissa Poweleit

Editorial Support Services: Nataliya Mikheyeva

Manufacturing: Dorothy Maki, Rita Wimberley

Composition and Prepress: Mary Beth Trimper, Gary Leach

Imaging: John Watkins

For product information and technology assistance, contact us at
Gale Customer Support, 1-800-877-4253.
For permission to use material from this text or product,
submit all requests online at **www.cengage.com/permissions**.
Further permissions questions can be emailed to
permissionrequest@cengage.com

Gale
27500 Drake Rd.
Farmington Hills, MI, 48331-3535

ISBN-13: 978-1-4103-1205-1

ISSN 1058-1316

This title is also available as an e-book.
ISBN 13: 978-1-4103-1216-7
Contact your Gale sales representative for ordering information.

Printed in Mexico
1 2 3 4 5 6 7 21 20 19 18 17

Advisory Board

Contents

Introduction ix

Cumulative Nationality Index 167

Cumulative Occupation Index 191

Cumulative Subject Index 223

Cumulative Name Index 275

Muhammad Ali 1
   Legendary boxer and humanitarian
Baby Laurence...6
   Pioneer of modern jazz dance in the 1940s
Charles Barron...8
   Outspoken New York City politician and activist
Inez Barron 11
   Longtime New York City educator and politician
Harold Battiste Jr. 14
   New Orleans jazzman who nurtured the city's musical heritage
Boris Berian 16
   U.S. middle-distance runner who competed at 2016 Summer Olympics
Chu Berry...19
   Jazz saxophonist of the swing era
Simone Biles...22
   Gold medal–winning American Olympic gymnast
Tom Browne...25
   Jazz, R&B, and gospel trumpeter
Cassandra Butts 27
   Former policy advisor to President Barack Obama
Vinnette Carroll 30
   Trailblazing director of Broadway musicals
Charlie Christian 33
   Pioneer of the amplified electric guitar
Margaret A. Dixon...37
   First black president of AARP

Malachi Favors 40
   Bassist who helped develop avant-garde jazz
Roxane Gay...43
   Contemporary feminist author
Yaa Gyasi 46
   Ghanaian-American writer who made literary debut in 2016
Michael S. Harper...48
   Poet who employed jazz rhythms
Oliver W. Harrington 51
   Satirist and political cartoonist
Jim Ray Hart...55
   Journeyman player for the Giants, Yankees in the 1960s and 1970s
Paula Hicks-Hudson 57
   Mayor of Toledo, Ohio
The Highway QC's...60
   Gospel group of the 1940s that featured Lou Rawls, Sam Cooke
Christopher Jackson 63
   Broadway actor who appeared in hit musical Hamilton
Joseph Jarman 66
   Avant-garde jazz saxophonist
Richard Jefferson...69
   NBA veteran who played on Cleveland Cavaliers championship team in 2016
Blind Willie Johnson 72
   Gospel-blues singer and guitarist
Leslie Jones...74
   Brash comedian who starred in Ghostbusters reboot
Loïs Mailou Jones...78
   Painter whose work spanned diverse styles
Howard N. Lee...82
   North Carolina politician who served in city, state government
Tyronn Lue...85
   Coach who led Cleveland Cavaliers to NBA championship in 2016

Shawn Marion..88

All-Star forward who played 16 seasons in the NBA

Oseola McCarty..91

Mississippi woman who gave her life savings for college scholarships

Famoudou Don Moye...95

Jazz percussionist and expert in African drumming

Julius Nyerere..97

Tanzania's first president and revered African leader

Anne-Marie Nzié..102

African singer known as the "Golden Voice of Cameroon"

Leslie Odom Jr...104

Actor who played Aaron Burr in the Broadway musical Hamilton

McKinley L. Price..107

Dentist and mayor of Newport News, Virginia

Prince Be..110

One-half of the hip-hop duo P.M. Dawn

Wallace Roney..112

Jazz trumpeter often compared to Miles Davis

Sean Rooks..115

NBA player and coach who died suddenly in 2016

Andre Royo..118

Actor best known for his role on HBO's The Wire

Marcus Scribner...121

Teen actor who stars on hit ABC series black-ish

Eddie Shaw..124

Chicago blues saxophonist

Moneta Sleet Jr..127

Photographer who captured Pulitzer Prize–winning image in 1968

Kimbo Slice...131

Mixed martial arts fighter who died at 42

Lee Smith...134

Versatile jazz bassist

S.O.S. Band...136

Popular R&B group of the 1980s

Thundercat..138

Eclectic bassist, singer, and producer

Bobby Timmons...141

Jazz pianist who contributed to the development of "soul jazz"

Karl-Anthony Towns...144

Minnesota Timberwolves center named 2016 NBA Rookie of the Year

Sylvester Turner...147

Longtime Texas legislator elected mayor of Houston in 2015

Jessie T. Usher..150

Young actor who starred in Independence Day: Resurgence

Lovely Warren...153

First black woman elected mayor of Rochester, New York

Ben Webster...156

Jazz master of the tenor saxophone

Robert F. Williams...159

Civil rights activist who advocated armed self-defense

Malik Yusef...164

Spoken word poet who has collaborated with Kanye West

Introduction

Contemporary Black Biography provides informative biographical profiles of the important and influential persons of African heritage who form the international black community: men and women who have changed today's world and are shaping tomorrow's. *Contemporary Black Biography* covers persons of various nationalities in a wide variety of fields, including architecture, art, business, dance, education, fashion, film, industry, journalism, law, literature, medicine, music, politics and government, publishing, religion, science and technology, social issues, sports, television, theater, and others. In addition to in-depth coverage of names found in today's headlines, *Contemporary Black Biography* provides coverage of selected individuals from earlier in this century whose influence continues to impact on contemporary life. *Contemporary Black Biography* also provides coverage of important and influential persons who are not yet household names and are therefore likely to be ignored by other biographical reference series. Each volume also includes listee updates on names previously appearing in *CBB* .

Designed for Quick Research and Interesting Reading

- **Attractive page design** incorporates textual subheads, making it easy to find the information you're looking for.

- **Easy-to-locate data sections** provide quick access to vital personal statistics, career information, major awards, and mailing addresses, when available.

- **Informative biographical essays** trace the subject's personal and professional life with the kind of in-depth analysis you need.

- **To further enhance your appreciation** of the subject, most entries include photographic portraits.

- **Sources for additional information** direct the user to selected books, magazines, and newspapers where more information on the individuals can be obtained.

Helpful Indexes Make It Easy to Find the Information You Need

Contemporary Black Biography includes cumulative Nationality, Occupation, Subject, and Name indexes that make it easy to locate entries in a variety of useful ways.

Available in Electronic Formats

Diskette/Magnetic Tape. Contemporary Black Biography is available for licensing on magnetic tape or diskette in a fielded format. Either the complete database or a custom selection of entries may be ordered. The database is available for internal data processing and nonpublishing purposes only. For more information, call (800) 877-GALE.

On-line. Contemporary Black Biography is available online through Mead Data Central's NEXIS Service in the NEXIS, PEOPLE and SPORTS Libraries in the GALBIO file and Gale's Biography Resource Center.

Disclaimer

Contemporary Black Biography uses and lists websites as sources and these websites may become obsolete.

We Welcome Your Suggestions

The editors welcome your comments and suggestions for enhancing and improving *Contemporary Black Biography*. If you would like to suggest persons for inclusion in the series, please submit these names to the editors. Mail comments or suggestions to:

The Editor

Contemporary Black Biography

Gale, Cengage Learning

27500 Drake Rd.

Farmington Hills, MI 48331-3535

Phone: (800) 347-4253

Muhammad Ali

1942–2016

Professional boxer, humanitarian

Ali, Muhammad, photograph. Paul Hawthorne/Getty Images.

Widely regarded as the greatest heavyweight boxer of all time, Muhammad Ali first achieved international fame at the 1960 Summer Olympics in Rome, when he won a gold medal in the light-heavyweight division as a member of the U.S. boxing team. Ali won his first professional heavyweight title in 1964 and later regained the world championship twice more over the next decade and a half. Known as much for his brash humor and outsized personality as for his dynamic, innovative fighting style, Ali influenced society and culture far beyond the boxing ring. As a young man, he was recruited by Malcolm X to join the Nation of Islam. He later refused to serve in the military during the Vietnam War, sacrificing his heavyweight crown for the sake of his political ideals. After retiring from boxing in 1981, Ali devoted himself to promoting diverse charities and causes, while his life and career became the subject of numerous books and film tributes. Despite being diagnosed with Parkinson's disease in 1982, Ali remained active in global political and athletic events until his death in 2016.

Discovered Early Passion for Boxing

Muhammad Ali was born Cassius Marcellus Clay Jr. on January 17, 1942, and raised in a clapboard house at 3302 Grand Avenue in middle-class Louisville, Kentucky. He began boxing at age 12. A Louisville patrolman named Joe Martin, who had an early television show called *Tomorrow's Champions,* started Ali working out in Louisville's Columbia Gym, but it was trainer Fred Stoner who taught him the science of boxing. Stoner taught Ali to move with the grace of a dancer and impressed on him the subtle skills necessary to move beyond good and into the realm of great.

After winning an Olympic gold medal at 18, Ali signed the most lucrative contract—a 50–50 split—ever negotiated by a beginning professional in the history of boxing with a 12-member group of millionaires called the Louisville Sponsoring Group. Later he worked his way into contention for a coveted heavyweight title shot by boasting and creating media interest at a time when, by his own admission, he was only ranked

At a Glance . . .

Born Cassius Marcellus Clay Jr. on January 17, 1942, in Louisville, KY; died on June 3, 2016, in Scottsdale, AZ; son of Cassius (a piano player) and Odessa Clay; married Sonji Roi, 1964 (divorced, 1966); married Belinda Boyd, 1967 (divorced); married Veronica Porche, 1977 (divorced, 1986); married Yolanda "Lonnie" Williams, 1986; children: Maryum Jamillah, Rasheda, Muhammad Ali Jr., Laila, Hana, Khaliah, Miya, Asaad Amin.

Career: Professional boxer, 1960–81.

Awards: Gold medal, boxing, Summer Olympics, 1960; six-time Kentucky Golden Gloves champion; two-time National Golden Gloves champion; world heavyweight champion, 1964–67, 1974–78, 1978–79; inducted into U.S. Olympic Hall of Fame, 1983; named Greatest Heavyweight Champion of All Time, *Ring Magazine,* 1987; inducted into International Boxing Hall of Fame, 1990; Jim Thorpe Pro Sports Award, Lifetime Achievement, 1992; Essence Award, 1997; ESPY Award, Arthur Ashe Award for Courage to All, 1997; Service to America Leadership Award, National Association of Broadcasters Foundation, 2001; Presidential Medal of Freedom, 2005.

number nine on the list of contenders. Even at the beginning of his career, it was clear that Ali was his own man—quick, strong-willed, original, and witty. In 1961 he told Gilbert Rogin *of Sports Illustrated,* "Boxing is dying because everybody's so quiet…. What boxing needs is more … Clays."

Ali knew that his personality and press-grabbing claims would infuse more interest and more money into the sport of boxing, and he was his own best public relations man. In February of 1964, he told readers of *Sports Illustrated,* "If I were like a lot of … heavyweight boxers … you wouldn't be reading this story right now. If you wonder what the difference between them and me is, I'll break the news: you never heard of them. I'm not saying they are not good boxers. Most of them … can fight almost as good as I can. I'm just saying you never heard of them. And the reason for that is because they cannot throw the jive. Cassius Clay is a boxer who can throw the jive better than anybody."

The following month Ali—then still known by the name Cassius Clay—fought Sonny Liston in a match of classic contenders for the heavyweight championship of the world. Clay had been chanting the war cry "Float

like a butterfly, sting like a bee" for weeks; he beat Liston in a display of beautiful, controlled boxing. Liston could hit with deadly power, but Ali utilized his skills and courage with forethought and aplomb to win the fight. At the tender age of 22, Ali knew that he was something above and beyond a great boxer: he had marketing sense, political finesse, and a feeling of noble purpose.

Became Committed to Political Ideals

Throughout his career and life, Ali always wanted to help other black Americans. When he returned from Italy, having just won an Olympic gold medal, he was so proud of his trophy that he wore it day and night and showed it to everyone, whether they wanted to see it or not. In the *Philadelphia Inquirer,* Ali's first wife remembered him saying, "I was young, black Cassius Marcellus Clay, who had won a gold medal for his country. I went to downtown Louisville to a five-and-dime store that had a soda fountain. I sat down at the counter to order a burger and soda pop. The waitress looked at me…. 'sorry, we don't serve coloreds,''she said. I was furious. I went all the way to Italy to represent my country, won a gold medal, and now I come back to America and can't even get served at a five-and-dime store. I went to a bridge, tore the medal off my neck and threw it into the river. That gold medal didn't mean a thing to me if my black brothers and sisters were treated wrong in a country I was supposed to represent."

While in Miami, at age 21, Ali was inspired by human rights activist Malcolm X to become a member of the Muslim faith. The following year Malcolm X said of Ali, as quoted by Houston Horn in *Sports Illustrated,* "[He] will mean more to his people than any athlete before him. He is more than [first black major-league baseball player] Jackie Robinson was, because Robinson is the white man's hero. But Cassius is the black man's hero. Do you know why? Because the white press wanted him to lose [his heavyweight championship bout] … because he is a Muslim. You notice nobody cares about the religion of other athletes. But their prejudice against Clay blinded them to his ability." Twelve years later, on *Face the Nation,* Ali said, "We don't have Black Muslims, that's a press word. We have white brothers, we have brown, red, and yellow, all colors can be Muslims…. I'm looking for peace one day with all people." He was given the name Muhammad Ali by the Muslim patriarch Elijah Muhammad; it was not just a name but a title meaning "beloved of Allah," deity of the Muslim faith.

Ali retained his world heavyweight champion title in June of 1965 by again knocking out Liston, this time with a stunning right-hand punch to the side of the head. The knockout blow was thrown with the astounding speed that separated Ali from other heavyweights:

it had sufficient force to lift Liston's left foot—upon which most of his weight was resting—clear off the canvas.

A conscientious objector because of his faith, Muhammad Ali refused to even consider going to Vietnam when he was drafted in 1966. His refusal brought a tremendous public outcry against him. According to Jack Olsen in *Sports Illustrated,* "The governor of Illinois found Clay 'disgusting,' and the governor of Maine said Clay 'should be held in utter contempt by every patriotic American.' An American Legion post in Miami asked people to 'join in condemnation of this unpatriotic, loudmouthed, bombastic individual.' The *Chicago Tribune* waged a choleric campaign against holding the next Clay fight in Chicago…. The noise became a din, the drumbeats of a holy war. TV and radio commentators, little old ladies … bookmakers, and parish priests, armchair strategists at the Pentagon and politicians all over the place joined in a crescendo of get-Cassius clamor."

Although Ali had not been charged or arrested for violating the Selective Service Act—much less convicted—the New York State Athletic Commission and World Boxing Association suspended his boxing license and stripped him of his heavyweight title in May of 1967, minutes after he officially announced that he would not submit to induction. Ali told *Sports Illustrated* contributor Edwin Shrake, "I'm giving up my title, my wealth, maybe my future. Many great men have been tested for their religious beliefs. If I pass this test, I'll come out stronger than ever." Eventually Ali was sentenced to five years in prison. He was released on appeal, and his conviction was overturned three years later.

Achieved Legendary Status in the Ring

In November of 1970, Ali fought Jerry Quarry in Atlanta and won. Ali had personally survived his vilification by much of the American public, but more than that, he had reclaimed his professional reputation and prominence. Four months later, he had the world as his audience when he went up against Joe Frazier at Madison Square Garden in New York City. There Ali fell from invincibility; suddenly Frazier reigned as heavyweight champ. Returning with a vengeance, Ali fought Frazier again in 1974 and won, resuming his place as the world heavyweight champion.

In October of that same year, he faced off against World Boxing Commission and World Boxing Association heavyweight champion George Foreman in Kinshasa, Zaire. Dubbed the "Rumble in the Jungle," the fight was among the most highly anticipated bouts of Ali's career. While the younger, stronger Foreman was favored to win, Ali won an upset victory with an eighth-round knockout. More than two decades later,

the Ali-Foreman fight would become the subject of the Academy Award–winning documentary *When We Were Kings* (1997). Ali fought Frazier again in October of 1975, in Manila, the Philippines. Ali won the "Thrilla in Manila" after Frazier's corner men asked the referee to stop the fight in the 14th round. At around this time, Ali cowrote his autobiography, *The Greatest: My Own Story* (1975). He fought 10 more bouts before retiring from boxing in 1981.

A year later, Dr. Dennis Cope, director of the Medical Ambulatory Care Center at the University of California, Los Angeles, began treating Ali for Parkinson's syndrome; the diagnosis was later modified to Parkinson's disease. Cope and colleague Dr. Stanley Fahn later theorized in the *Chicago Tribune* that Ali was suffering from Pugilistic Parkinsonism, brought on by repetitive trauma to the head. Under Dr. Cope's care, Ali was shortly restored to his previous level of energy and awareness; as long as he took his medication regularly, he was able to keep the disease in check. In 1988 Ali told *New York Times Magazine* contributor Peter Tauber, "I'm in no pain…. If I was in perfect health—if I had won my last two fights—if I had no problem, people would be afraid of me. Now they feel sorry for me. They thought I was Superman. Now they can say 'He's human, like us. He has problems.'"

Became Elder Statesman of Boxing

Toward the end of Ali's boxing career, and afterward, his ambitions turned toward statesmanship. In 1980 he cast his lot with the Democratic Party, supporting Presidential candidate Jimmy Carter. In August of that year, while in intense training for the Holmes fight, he found time to work the floor of the Democratic National Convention in New York City. He also functioned as something of a diplomat in February of 1985 when he attempted to secure the release of four kidnapped Americans in Lebanon. Unfortunately, he and his three advisors were not successful.

Although Parkinson's disease slowed Ali down, he remained active, raising money for the Muhammad Ali Foundation and frequently appearing at sports tributes and fund-raisers. As his wife Lonnie told *People,* "Muhammad knows he has this illness for a reason. It's not by chance. Parkinson's disease has made him a more spiritual person. Muhammad believes God gave it to him to bring him to another level, to create another destiny." During the 1996 Olympic Games in Atlanta, 3.5 billion people watched on television as three-time heavyweight champion Muhammad Ali slowly ascended the stadium steps with trembling hands to ignite the Olympic flame. Watchers were deeply touched, although no one more so than Ali himself. "He kept turning it [the torch] in his hands and looking at it. He knows now that people won't slight his message be-

cause of his impairment," his wife Lonnie told *People*.

During these years, Ali traveled frequently, meeting dignitaries from across the globe while performing missionary work and making public appearances. When not traveling, he spent time with his family in Berrien Springs, Michigan. When asked by *People* whether he had any regrets, Ali replied candidly: "My children, I never got to raise them because I was always boxing and because of divorce." Still, he never regretted his decision to become a professional fighter. "If I wasn't a boxer, I wouldn't be famous," he told *People*. "If I wasn't famous, I wouldn't be able to do what I'm doing now."

In 2004 he coauthored a memoir, *The Soul of a Butterfly: Reflection's on Life's Journey,* with his daughter, Hana Yasmeen Ali. A year later, after years of preparation, the Muhammad Ali Center opened in Louisville, Kentucky. The center served as both a museum celebrating Ali's life and career and a forum for sharing his ideals and beliefs, by promoting respect, hope, and understanding. In 2005 President George W. Bush awarded Ali the Medal of Freedom.

In his last decade, Ali traveled less frequently, as complications from Parkinson's and other health issues limited his mobility. He spent his final years at his home in Paradise Valley, Arizona. Ali died in a hospital in Scottsdale, Arizona, on June 3, 2016, after being admitted with respiratory problems. The official cause of death was septic shock. Ali's passing prompted an outpouring of memorials from around the world. In a statement issued after the great fighter's death, President Barack Obama cited a memorable passage from Ali's 1975 memoir *The Greatest*. "I am America," Obama quoted Ali declaring in the work. "'I am the part you won't recognize. But get used to me—black, confident, cocky; my name, not yours; my religion, not yours; my goals, my own. Get used to me.'" In his own words, Obama went on to add, "That's the Ali I came to know as I came of age—not just as skilled a poet on the mic as he was a fighter in the ring, but a man who fought for what was right. A man who fought for us."

Selected writings

(With Richard Durham) *The Greatest: My Own Story,* Random House, 1975.
Ali! Ali! The Words of Muhammad Ali, edited by Sultan Karim, Harcourt Brace Jovanovich, 1979.
(With Thomas Hauser) *Healing,* Collins Publishers San Francisco, 1996.
I Am the Greatest: The Best Quotations from Muhammad Ali, edited by Karl Evanzz, Andrews McMeel, 2002.

(With Hana Yasmeen Ali) *The Soul of a Butterfly: Reflections on Life's Journey,* Simon & Schuster, 2004.

Sources

Books

Early, Gerald, ed., *The Muhammad Ali Reader,* Ecco Press, 1998.
GOAT: A Tribute to Muhammad Ali, Taschen, 2003.
Kram, Mark, *Ghosts of Manila: The Fateful Blood Feud between Muhammad Ali and Joe Frazier,* HarperCollins, 2001.
Miller, Davis, *The Tao of Muhammad Ali,* Warner Books, 1996.
Muhammad Ali (photographs), Harry N. Abrams, 2004.
Myers, Walter Dean, *The Greatest: Muhammad Ali,* Scholastic, 2001.
Pacheco, Ferdie, *Muhammad Ali: A View from the Corner,* Birch Lane Press, 1992.
Remnick, David, *King of the World: Muhammad Ali and the Rise of an American Hero,* Random House, 1998.

Periodicals

Atlanta Journal and Constitution, December 13, 1988.
Boston Globe, October 1, 1984.
Chicago Tribune, October 9, 1984.
Ebony, April 1969.
Interview, February 1, 2004.
Jet, July 2, 2001.
Los Angeles Times, June 10, 2016.
Newsweek, June 22, 1987.
New York Daily News, February 2, 1989.
New Yorker, June 4, 2016.
New York Post, July 14, 1987.
New York Times, June 4, 2016.
New York Times Magazine, July 17, 1988.
People, January 13, 1997, p. 40.
Philadelphia Inquirer, August 12, 1990.
Spin, October 1991.
Sports Illustrated, December 20, 1976; April 25, 1988.
Time, December 13, 2004.
Washington Post, June 9, 1991; July 6, 2016.

Online

Muhammad Ali, http://muhammadali.com/ (accessed September 28, 2016).
"Statement from President Barack Obama and First Lady Michelle Obama on the Passing of Muhammad Ali," White House, Office of the Press Secretary, June 4, 2016, https://www.whitehouse.gov/the

-press-office/2016/06/04/statement-president-ba
rack-obama-and-first-lady-michelle-obama-passing
(accessed September 28, 2016).

Other

Face the Nation, CBS, May 2, 1976.

—B. Kimberly Taylor, Tom Pendergast,
and Stephen Meyer

Baby Laurence

1921–1974

Tap dancer

Tap dancer Baby Laurence is remembered as a pioneer of modern jazz dance, one of the first hoofers to incorporate the complex rhythms and improvisation of jazz into tap dancing during the 1940s. "Tap dancing is very much like jazz music," Laurence said in 1961, according to Marshall Stearns in *Jazz Dance: The Story of American Vernacular Dance.* "The dancer improvises his own solo and expresses himself." Influenced by jazzmen such as Charlie Parker, Art Tatum, and Max Roach, Laurence sought to duplicate with his feet what jazz musicians were doing with their instruments. In doing so, he created an entirely new genre of tap that had a profound influence on dancers in the second half of the 20th century.

Baby Laurence was born Laurence Donald Jackson on February 23, 1921, in Baltimore, Maryland. He first began performing at age 11 or 12, singing with McKinney's Cotton Pickers, an African-American jazz band. When bandleader Don Redman came through town, he heard Laurence sing and was so impressed that he asked Laurence's mother for permission to take him on the road. She agreed that he could go as long as he had a tutor. While performing on the Loew's vaudeville circuit with Redman, Laurence made his first trip to New York City and visited the famous Hoofers Club in Harlem, a hangout for the best tap dancers in the city. There he saw legendary tap dancers such as Charles "Honi" Coles, Raymond Winfield, Roland Holder, and Harold Mablin and began imitating their steps. "I had to develop a liking for it," he recalled to Stearns, "but after I saw them, I knew I wanted to dance."

Returning to Baltimore, Laurence found that both of his parents had been killed in a fire. Soon after he formed a vocal group called the Four Buds with his brother and went back to New York. While he was working in the nightclub owned by former dancer Dickie Wells, he earned the nickname "Baby" and thereafter became known professionally as Baby Laurence. In the late 1930s he performed with a group called the Six Merry Scotchmen (also known as the Harlem Highlanders), a song-and-dance group that wore kilts and performed Jimmie Lunceford arrangements in six-part harmony.

By 1940 Laurence was focusing on tap dance and performing as a soloist. During the following decade he performed with some of the great big bands of the era, including those of Duke Ellington and Count Basie. Laurence's style of tap was deeply influenced by jazz. Inspired by jazzmen such as saxophonist Charlie "Bird" Parker, drummer Max Roach, and pianist Art Tatum, he extended tap into jazz dancing, becoming one of the first dancers to adapt his tap technique to bebop, the highly improvisational style of jazz that was then emerging. Laurence sought to duplicate the sound and rhythm of jazz in dance, using the percussion of his feet the same way a drummer in a jazz combo would. "He wanted to create the varied tones and shifting accents with his feet that imply the polyrhythmic effect of the drums," Melinda Abern of the *Village Voice* noted in 1974, "and he had the impulse to move his feet as fast as Art Tatum moved his fingers on the keyboard."

Laurence's style of dance was meant to be heard as much as seen, and in fact he recorded an album,

At a Glance . . .

Born Laurence Donald Jackson on February 23, 1921, in Baltimore, MD; died on April 2, 1974, in New York, NY.

Career: Vaudeville performer, from 1930s; solo performer, 1940s–60s.

Awards: Inducted into Tap Dance Hall of Fame, 2002.

"Baby" Laurence Dancemaster (released on Classic Jazz in 1963), that showcased the interplay of jazz and tap. While dancing Laurence often kept his arms and torso relaxed while executing a flurry of intricate rhythms with his feet. He eschewed formal choreography, preferring instead to improvise, like a musician. "From my point of view, having a choreographer telling me what to do would ruin everything," he said, according to Stearns. "I wouldn't be able to improvise or interpret the music, and I couldn't express myself."

By the 1950s tap was waning in popularity, and Laurence stopped performing for a time as his addiction to drugs and alcohol got the better of him. By the next decade, however, he was back on the stage, performing mostly in small jazz clubs. In 1960 he performed with Charles Mingus at the Showplace jazz club in Greenwich Village, and that summer he danced with Mingus and Roach in Newport, Rhode Island. In 1962 Laurence made a comeback, joining with Honi Coles, Bunny Briggs, and Pete Nugent for a legendary performance at the Newport Jazz Festival that marked the beginning of a tap revival. By the late 1960s Laurence had faded from the spotlight once again, dancing on weekends at a restaurant in Gaithersburg, Maryland. In the last year of his life, he tap danced on Sunday afternoons at the Jazz Museum in Harlem, appeared at the Newport and Monterey jazz festivals, and performed with the singer Josephine Baker. He died of cancer on April 2, 1974, in a Manhattan hospital, at age 53. Laurence was posthumously inducted into the Tap Dance Hall of Fame in 2002.

Selected works

"Baby" Laurence Dancemaster (recorded 1959–60), Classic Jazz, 1963.

Sources

Books

Hill, Constance Valis, *Tap Dancing America: A Cultural History,* Oxford University Press, 2010.

Stearns, Marshall, and Jean Stearns, *Jazz Dance: The Story of American Vernacular Dance,* Da Capo Press, 1994.

Periodicals

New York Times, July 4, 1981; August 22, 2014.
Village Voice, May 23, 1974.

Online

"'Baby' Laurence Jackson," Library of Congress, http://memory.loc.gov/diglib/ihas/loc.music.tdab o.109/default.html (accessed September 25, 2016).

"'Baby Laurence' Jackson (1921–1974)," American Tap Dance Foundation, http://www.atdf.org/a wardslaurence.html (accessed September 25, 2016).

"Baby Laurence: Taps—Hollywood Palace 26.09. 1967," YouTube, https://www.youtube.com/watch ?v=gsfPQ8SwQvE (accessed September 25, 2016).

—Deborah A. Ring

Charles Barron

1950—

Politician, activist

Barron, Charles, photograph. Taylor Hill/FilmMagic/Getty Images.

Charles Barron is an outspoken and often polarizing New York City politician and activist. A former Black Panther, Barron served on the New York City Council for 12 years, representing East New York's 42nd District. After failed bids for mayor, governor, and congressman, in 2014 Barron was elected to the New York State Assembly. Over the course of his career, Barron, a Democrat, has alienated many of his fellow politicians by declaring his admiration for some of the world's most notorious dictators and accusing Israel of committing genocide against the Palestinian people, among other provocative remarks. Barron remains unapologetic about his stances. "I'm not in this to be careful," he told the *Village Voice* in a 2014 interview. "There's a lot of politicians—when they talk, they talk all slow and hesitantly, 'cause they're always thinking about who they might help or hurt or offend. I try to speak truth to power. Oftentimes, people aren't ready for that. I didn't come here to be a coward or a political punk." Barron is married to Inez Barron, a longtime educator who has also risen to prominence in New York politics.

Charles Barron was born on October 7, 1950, in Queens, New York. His father, Charles Sr., served as an artilleryman during World War II before joining the merchant marines; he later became an interior decorator. Barron's mother, Daisy, was an administrative worker. Neither parent was inclined toward political activism. The family lived in Queens until Barron was about six years old and then moved to the Lillian Wald housing project on the Lower East Side. Barron attended New York City public schools. He left Stewart Park High School in Floral Park without graduating but later obtained his high school equivalency diploma. In the years that followed, he earned an associate's degree from New York City Technical College and a bachelor's degree in sociology from Hunter College.

Barron's revolutionary consciousness was sparked in early adolescence when he read Patrice Lumumba's *Congo: My Country* (1962), a philosophical treatise about the liberation of the Congo from Belgian colonial rule. Joining the Harlem chapter of the Black Panther Party in 1969, Barron continued to learn about third-world struggles for political self-determination and the

At a Glance . . .

Born Charles Barron on October 7, 1950, in New York, NY; son of Charles Barron Sr. (a merchant marine) and Daisy Barron (an administrative worker); married Inez Smith (a politician); children: Jelani Johnson, Jawanza Barron. *Politics:* Democrat. *Religion:* Pentecostal. *Education:* New York City Technical College, AA; Hunter College, City University of New York, BA, sociology.

Career: Chief of Staff to the Reverend Herbert Daughtry, 1980–82; African Peoples' Christian Organization, secretary general, 1982–87; Dynamics of Leadership, Inc., cofounder and chief executive officer, 1985–2001; New York City Council, 42nd District representative, 2002–13; New York State Assembly, District 60 representative, 2015—.

Memberships: African Peoples' Christian Organization; National Black United Front; Operation POWER (People Organization and Working for Empowerment and Respect), cofounder.

Addresses: *District office*—669 Vermont St., Brooklyn, NY 11207. *Web*—http://assembly.state.ny.us/mem/Charles-Barron/.

heroism, as he saw it, of leaders such as Che Guevara and Fidel Castro of Cuba and Muammar Gaddafi of Libya. "All of my heroes were America's enemies," Barron recalled to the *Village Voice.*

In 1979 Barron went to work for the Reverend Herbert Daughtry, a Brooklyn-based community organizer and chairman of the National Black United Front, a prominent progressive black political organization. Barron soon became his chief of staff. In that role, he gained his first exposure to the workings of city government and traveled to Africa, witnessing firsthand and lending his support to anticolonial resistance movements that were active in Mozambique, Angola, and Zimbabwe. Barron also served as secretary general of Daughtry's African Peoples' Christian Organization from 1982 to 1987. During this period, he authored biographies of the pioneering Jamaican black nationalist Marcus Garvey for young readers: *Look for Me in the Whirlwind* (1987) and *Marcus Mosiah Garvey: Up You Mighty People, You Can Accomplish What You Will* (1988).

In 1983 Barron moved to East New York, one of Brooklyn's poorest neighborhoods. Around the same time, he married Inez Smith, a Brooklyn native and public school teacher. The couple was married by the Reverend Daughtry; both were active members of his congregation at the House of the Lord Church. Together the Barrons launched Dynamics of Leadership, Inc., a company that provided training in conflict resolution, team building, leadership skills, diversity awareness, and critical thinking. As the company's chief executive officer, Barron traveled across the United States, conducting seminars and workshops for churches, nonprofit organizations, schools, colleges, and other groups. During these years, Barron also became increasingly active as a community leader in East New York, organizing protests against local police brutality, apartheid in South African, and other social injustices.

In 1997, disillusioned by the actions of city councilwoman Priscilla Wooten, who had represented his East New York district for 15 years, Barron decided to run for her seat. He lost the election with only 38 percent of the vote. Later that same year, he and his wife founded Operation POWER (People Organizing and Working for Empowerment and Respect), an East New York–based political action group. Barron ran for City Council again in 2001, this time against Wooten's son, Donald Wooten, and won. He took office in 2002, introducing himself to the Council Chamber, according to the *Village Voice,* as a "black radical revolutionary anti-capitalist anti-imperialist elected official." Barron quickly became well known for his refusal to join his colleagues in reciting the Pledge of Allegiance at council meetings, rejecting the claim that the United States offers "liberty and justice for all" as "a damn lie."

Barron inflamed controversy from the outset of his tenure on the City Council, famously denouncing Thomas Jefferson as a "slave-holding pedophile" and hosting a city hall reception for Zimbabwean dictator Robert Mugabe. At the same time, Barron built a loyal following among his constituents and was twice reelected, remaining on the council through 2013. During that time, Barron helped orchestrate notable improvements for his East New York district, increasing significantly the number of city-subsidized affordable housing units, securing $80 million for public schools in the district, and overseeing the restoration and renewal of three public parks.

During his tenure on the council, however, Barron also was a thorn in the side of Council Speaker Christine Quinn, publicly referring to her as a "dictator" and twice challenging her leadership. Quinn retaliated against Barron directly by stripping him of his role as chairman of the Higher Education Committee in 2010 and indirectly by relegating his district to the bottom of the pile among recipients of discretionary funding.

Terms limits prevented Barron from running for reelection to the City Council in 2013. He was succeeded as the representative for East New York by his wife, Inez

Barron. The following year, Charles Barron won election to the New York State Assembly, taking over the seat that had just been vacated by his wife.

Although many speculated that Barron might be forced to tone down his rhetoric when he moved to the state legislature, the lifelong firebrand soon proved otherwise, announcing his intention to vote against the 20-year Speaker of the Assembly, Sheldon Silver, and to unify the legislature's African-American members. Never far from the political limelight, in January of 2016, Barron drew condemnation for heckling Governor Andrew Cuomo in the middle of his State of the State address, accusing him of failing to adequately address poverty and homelessness in New York City. That same year, Barron was on the front lines of public protests in East New York as police shootings of unarmed black men made headlines around the country. In July of that year, following the fatal police shooting of an unarmed 37-year-old black man named Delrawn Small, Barron drew applause from protesters on Brooklyn's Atlantic Avenue when he warned that violent retaliation would be "inevitable" if the New York City Police Department failed to hold officers accountable for their actions.

Selected writings

Look for Me in the Whirlwind: A Biographical Sketch of the Honorable Marcus Mosiah Garvey, African Peoples' Christian Organization, 1987.
Marcus Mosiah Garvey: Up You Mighty People, You Can Accomplish What You Will, Dynamics of Leadership, 1988.

Sources

Periodicals

New York Times, June 16, 2012.
Village Voice, January 22, 2014.

Online

"Biography, Assemblymember Charles Barron, Assembly District 60," New York State Assembly, http://nyassembly.gov/mem/Charles-Barron/bio/ (accessed July 29, 2016).
Bredderman, Will, "Mr. Barron Goes to Albany," Observer.com, October 23, 2014, http://observer.com/2014/10/mr-barron-goes-to-albany/ (accessed July 29, 2016).
Paybarah, Azi, "City Portraits: Charles Barron's East New York," Politico, August 18, 2010, http://www.politico.com/states/new-york/city-hall/story/2010/08/city-portraits-charles-barrons-east-new-york-000000 (accessed July 29, 2016).
Sommerfeldt, Chris, Murray Weiss, and Aidan Gardiner, "More Than 100 Mourners Protest Police over Death of Unarmed Brooklyn Man," DNA Info, July 7, 2016, https://www.dnainfo.com/new-york/20160707/east-new-york/more-than-100-mourners-protest-police-for-death-of-unarmed-brooklyn-man (accessed July 29, 2016).

—Erin Brown

Inez Barron

1946—

Educator, politician, activist

Inez Barron is a New York City politician and activist. A Democrat, she served in the New York State Assembly from 2008 to 2013 and subsequently was elected to the New York City Council representing East New York's 42nd District. Barron is widely respected as the less inflammatory, although no less principled or effective, political counterpart to her husband Charles Barron, the self-proclaimed radical socialist whose City Council seat she took over in 2014. Together, as founders of the community organization Operation POWER (People Organizing and Working for Empowerment and Respect), the Barrons have positioned themselves as East New York's foremost political power brokers and challengers to the local Democratic party establishment. Before she entered the political arena, Barron served for more than 30 years in the New York City public school system as an educator and administrator. A deeply religious woman, Barron avows that her commitment to social justice, and all of her leadership decisions, are informed by her relationship with God.

Barron was born in Brooklyn, New York, on February 16, 1946, the daughter of George and Margaret R. Smith. Raised in Brooklyn's Fort Greene housing projects, she attended New York City public schools. Her parents taught her to commit herself in service to God, to be proud of her African-American heritage, and to believe in the value of education. After earning her bachelor's degree in physiology from Hunter College in 1967, she began her career as a teacher in the New York City public schools. Over the next 18 years, Barron taught various subjects and grade levels, pro-

ceeding from a pedagogical philosophy, as stated in her New York City Council profile, that "children should be valued and motivated to achieve, and teachers have a responsibility not only to provide the skills necessary to be life-long learners and become productive and critical members of society, but also to challenge and stimulate children's thinking."

In the early 1970s, Barron had a son, Jelani Johnson. Still living in Brooklyn, she was an active member of the House of the Lord Church, whose pastor, the Reverend Herbert Daughtry, was a local community organizer and chairman of the National Black United Front, a prominent progressive black political organization. In the early 1980s, Barron met and married Charles Barron, who was also active in the House of the Lord Church and was Daughtry's chief of staff. Together, the Barrons had another son, Jawanza. During these years Barron, also continued to build her educational credentials, earning a master's degree in reading and special education from the Bank Street College of Education.

After nearly two decades as a classroom teacher, Barron shifted into supervisory and administrative roles in the New York City Department of Education. At the time of her retirement, after 36 years of service, she was principal of PS 81 Thaddeus Stevens school in the Bedford-Stuyvesant neighborhood of Brooklyn.

Barron was politically active throughout her adult life as a community organizer and a champion for racial and social justice causes. In addition to voicing her opposi-

At a Glance . . .

Born Inez Smith on February 16, 1946, in New York, NY; daughter of George and Margaret R. Smith; married Charles Barron; children: Jelani Johnson, Jawanza Barron. *Politics:* Democrat. *Religion:* Pentecostal. *Education:* Hunter College, City University of New York, BS, physiology, 1967; Bank Street College of Education, MS, reading and special education.

Career: New York City Department of Education, teacher, administrator, principal, 1970s–1990s; New York State Assembly, District 60 representative, 2008–13; New York City Council, 42nd District representative, 2014—.

Memberships: Operation POWER (People Organizing and Working for Empowerment and Respect.

Addresses: *District office*—718 Pennsylvania Ave., Brooklyn, NY 11207.

tion to South African apartheid, she also fought for diversity in New York's public school curriculum. In 1997 Barron and her husband founded Operation POWER (People Organizing and Working for Empowerment and Respect), an East New York–based political action group inspired by the black nationalist ideals of the Black Panther Party, to which Charles Barron had once belonged. In 2001 Charles Barron was elected to the New York City Council as the representative for East New York. He was reelected twice, remaining in the seat through 2013.

While Inez Barron served as an important advisor to her husband's campaigns, she did not consider running for elected office herself until 2008, when Diane Gordon, the New York State assemblywoman for East New York, was forced to resign after she was convicted on corruption charges. Barron campaigned on a platform that emphasized her expertise in education and her dedication to improving educational outcomes, particularly for African-American students. With strong name recognition and endorsements from the Working Families Party, labor organizations, and prominent local leaders such as Daughtry, Barron won the seat.

In Barron's first term in office, she quickly distinguished herself as a critic of the educational policies of New York City mayor Michael Bloomberg, charging that under his leadership, the Department of Education was failing to implement a sufficiently diverse curriculum, was criminalizing young people, and was "gentrifying the public school system," according to an article on the website Chalkbeat. Another of Barron's signature issues was the need for more affordable housing in her district. Barron was twice reelected, serving in the Assembly for five years.

In 2013, with her husband stepping down after serving the maximum 12 years on the City Council, Barron ran to replace him. She won the seat and was appointed to chair the Committee on Higher Education. The following year, in a rare political feat, Charles Barron was elected to fill the State Assembly seat that had just been vacated by his wife. The seat swap was a testament to the strong loyalty the Barrons had built among their constituency in East New York.

In her role as a City Council member, Barron was committed to building on her husband's legacy of bringing economic opportunity, affordable housing, and revitalization to East New York. A 2014 article in *City and State New York* quoted her as saying, "Having been married to Charles for over 30 years, I've learned from him how to get results without compromising my principles." At the outset of her term, her vision for the district included renovating the waterfront, establishing a science museum, and introducing a trade school. Barron also promised to continue fighting for her education reform agenda. Referring to her constituents, she said, "The people appreciate someone who's not namby-pamby, wishy-washy, but someone who is firm. That's what our community appreciates."

Barron and her husband continued to exert their considerable influence in local and state politics, not only through their elected offices but also through Operation POWER, which positioned itself markedly to the left of Brooklyn's Democratic Party establishment. A 2016 article in the New York *Observer* reported that Operation POWER "largely controls the Democratic Party in impoverished, predominantly black East New York."

Sources

Periodicals

Village Voice, January 22, 2014.

Online

"Biography," New York City Council, http://council.nyc.gov/d42/html/members/biography.shtml (accessed July 30, 2016).

Bredderman, Will, "Brooklyn Power Couple Go to War with Democratic Machine in State Senate Race," Observer, February 10, 2016, http://observer.com/2016/02/brooklyn-power-couple-go-to-war-with-democratic-machine-in-state-senate-race/ (accessed July 30, 2016).

Green, Elizabeth, "Meet Inez Barron, Wife of Charles, and a New Assembly Member," Chalkbeat, May 9,

2009 http://www.chalkbeat.org/posts/ny/2009/
05/04/meet-inez-barron-wife-of-charles-and-a-new
-assembly-member/#.V6jn_5grI2x (accessed August
8, 2016).
"Meet the City Council's New Members: Inez Barron,"
CityandStateNY.com, January 4, 2014 http://city
andstateny.com/articles/personality/interviews-and
-profiles/meet-the-city-council%E2%80%99s-new
-members-inez-barron.html#.V6kARZgrI2x
(accessed August 8, 2016).

—Erin Brown

Harold Battiste Jr.

1931–2015

Jazz, R&B, and pop musician, educator

An elder statesman of the New Orleans music scene, Harold Battiste Jr. dedicated his life to the preservation and enhancement of that city's unique heritage. In a distinguished career that stretched well over 60 years, he moved easily between a number of roles, serving at various times as an instrumentalist, arranger, producer, label executive, and educator. A mentor to dozens of leading musicians, from R&B crooner Sam Cooke to the pop duo Sonny & Cher, he won a host of honors in his later life, including the Governor's Arts Lifetime Achievement Award from the state of Louisiana (1995) and the Sidney Bechet Award for Innovation in New Orleans Music from the New Orleans International Music Colloquium (1999).

The son of a tailor, Harold Raymond Battiste Jr. was born in New Orleans on October 28, 1931. His interest in music developed steadily, particularly after he moved with his family to the city's Magnolia housing development in the early 1940s. Abutting that vast project was Lasalle Street, home of the Dew Drop Inn, a celebrated nightspot that regularly attracted some of the most prominent African-American stars in the country. So close to his home that he could hear its shows from his living room, the Inn played a critical role in Battiste's decision to become a musician. "I couldn't help but be drawn to that music," he later recalled in a widely quoted comment, "because it spoke directly to my spirit."

Like many of his peers, Battiste began his musical training in church, where he sang in the choir as a young boy. By his mid-teens he had picked up the clarinet and the saxophone, later adding the piano as well. His affinity for music was quickly apparent, and after high school he entered nearby Dillard University with plans to become a music educator. He earned his bachelor's degree in 1952.

In the early 1950s he also began to work steadily as a professional musician, most notably with a group called the American Jazz Quintet, with which he toured locally and made several recordings. However, most of these were unreleased at the time, and his earnings from live gigs were minimal. He soon turned to more stable employment, teaching music at a public school in Beauregard Parish in western Louisiana, several hours from New Orleans. Despite that distance he was able to maintain the professional contacts he had made in his hometown, and by the second half of the 1950s he was working regularly there as an arranger and talent scout. Battiste played a key role in Sam Cooke's transition from gospel music to pop, writing the arrangement for the vocalist's first pop song, "You Send Me" (1957), which became one of the biggest hits of the decade and a touchstone of its era.

As he gained experience behind the scenes of the music business, Battiste grew all too aware of the racial and economic disparities in that field: although African-American musicians were among the biggest stars in the country, virtually all record companies were owned and managed by whites. Musicians of all races, moreover, typically had little control over their work, as the standard contract of the day gave the label rights in perpetuity in exchange for a one-time fee. In a pioneer-

At a Glance . . .

Born Harold Raymond Battiste Jr. on October 28, 1931, in New Orleans, LA; died on June 19, 2015, in New Orleans, LA; son of Harold Battiste Sr. (a tailor) and Pearl Wilmer Bodar; married Alviette Dominique, 1950s (divorced, 1988), Berweda Hatch, 1995 (separated, 1997); children: four. *Education:* Dillard University, BA, music education, 1952.

Career: Independent musician and arranger, late 1940s–2015; Beauregard Parish Training School, music educator, 1950s; independent producer, early 1960s–2015; A.F.O. Records, founder, 1961; Colburn School, faculty member and director of jazz studies, 1980s; University of New Orleans, faculty member, 1989–2015; author, 2010–15.

Memberships: A.F.O. Foundation, founder, 1991.

Awards: Governor's Arts Lifetime Achievement Award, State of Louisiana, 1995; Sidney Bechet Award for Innovation in New Orleans Music, New Orleans International Music Colloquium, 1999.

ing effort to redress those imbalances, Battiste founded his own label, A.F.O. (All For One) Records, in New Orleans in 1961. Widely believed to be the first record company in the city to be owned and managed by an African-American musician, it released one major hit, vocalist Barbara George's 1961 classic "I Know (You Don't Love Me No More)." Financial problems, however, soon forced its closure.

In 1964 Battiste moved to Los Angeles, where he found a host of new opportunities. Soon after his arrival there, he began a long collaboration with Sonny & Cher. In addition to arranging and coproducing several of their biggest hits, including "I Got You Babe" (1965) and "The Beat Goes On" (1967), he served for more than a decade as their musical director. The latter role became increasingly important over the course of the 1970s, as Sonny & Cher became major television stars, appearing frequently on talk shows and hosting their own variety programs.

Amid his other projects Battiste also managed to continue his work as an educator. In the 1980s he won increasing recognition for his activities at the Colburn School, a major conservatory in Los Angeles. As a faculty member and director of the jazz studies program, he mentored dozens of young musicians, many of whom went on to distinguished careers. In 1989,

following a move back to Louisiana, he accepted a similar position at the University of New Orleans.

In his later years Battiste struggled with health issues, including a stroke in 1993 that forced him to curtail some of his instrumental work. By all accounts, however, he remained upbeat, focusing on projects including the establishment of a new nonprofit organization and a relaunch of the A.F.O. label. Under his direction the nonprofit, known as the A.F.O. Foundation, developed educational initiatives designed to preserve the music and cultural heritage of New Orleans.

As Battiste entered his late 70s his health continued to decline, and on June 19, 2015, five years after the publication of his autobiography, he died in New Orleans at age 83. News of his passing prompted dozens of tributes, many of which emphasized his kindness as well as his musicianship. "He was always encouraging," music educator Ed Anderson—one of his former students—told Keith Spera of the New Orleans *Times-Picayune.* "He motivated us to keep pushing forward, trying to get better. We all saw this old, wise man sitting there quietly. People love[d] to be around Harold."

Selected works

Singles

(Arranger) Sam Cooke, "You Send Me," 1957.
(Arranger and coproducer) Sonny & Cher, "I Got You Babe," 1965.
(Arranger and coproducer) Sonny & Cher, "The Beat Goes On," 1967.

Albums

American Jazz Quintet, *Gulf Coast Jazz, Volume One,* VSOP, 1989 (recorded 1959).

Books

(With Karen Celestan) *Unfinished Blues: Memories of a New Orleans Music Man,* Historic New Orleans Collection, 2010.

Sources

Periodicals

Los Angeles Times, June 21, 2015.
New York Times, June 28, 2015.
Times-Picayune (New Orleans, LA), June 22, 2015.

Online

"Harold R. Battiste, Jr.," AFO Foundation, http://www.afofoundation.org/hb/ (accessed October 1, 2016).

—R. Anthony Kugler

Boris Berian

1992—

Professional runner

Berian, Boris, photograph. Christian Petersen/Getty Images.

Boris Berian is middle-distance runner who first entered international competition in 2015 after dropping out of college and taking a job at McDonald's. A competitor in the 800 meters who is known for his front-leading racing style, Berian won the gold medal at the International Association of Athletics Federations (IAAF) World Indoor Championships in Portland, Oregon, in March of 2016 and then qualified for the Summer Olympic Games in Rio de Janeiro, Brazil, that summer. After performing strongly at the Olympic trials and semifinals, Berian turned in a disappointing time at the Rio Games, finishing in eighth place. Despite his poor showing in Rio, many observers agreed that Berian's quick rise from fast-food server to Olympic runner was remarkable. As Jonathan Lloyd of NBC4 in Los Angeles noted, Berian's "road to Rio symbolized the grit and dedication required of athletes determined to compete with the world's best, no matter what hurdles they face."

Discovered While Working at McDonald's

Berian was born in 1992 in Colorado Springs, Colo-rado, the son of a German mother and an African-American father. Colorado Springs provided an ideal training ground for the young runner. With an elevation of 6,035 feet and a thriving running community that hosts track and field competitions, festivals, and clubs, Colorado Springs is a known runner's mecca. The city is also home to the Olympic Training Center. Berian began running in junior high school, when he joined the track and field team as a sprinter. Soon he was going for longer distances, and by the time he joined the track team at Widefield High School, he was specializing in middle-distance events of 800 meters to 3,000 meters.

Berian thrived as a runner at Widefield, although his road was rocky. Facing personal struggles, he quit the track team during his sophomore year. His coach, Fred Marjerrison, convinced him to rejoin. That situation was repeated several times that year, with Berian quitting and Marjerrison talking him back. "We refused to let him quit," Marjerrison told Scott Reid of the *Orange County Register* in 2016. Berian concurred, explaining to Reid, "It was my high school coach year after year pushing me, yelling at me. It started becom-

At a Glance . . .

Born Boris Berian on December 19, 1992, in Colorado Springs, CO; son of Silvia Dean. *Education:* Attended Adams State University, 2012–14.

Career: Professional runner, 2015—.

Awards: Gold medal, 800 meters, International Association of Athletics Federations World Indoor Championships, 2016.

Addresses: *Home*—Big Bear Lake, CA. *Agent*—Merhawi Keflezighi, HAWI Sports Management, 10436 Prairie Fox Dr., Fishers, IN 46037. *Twitter*—@borisgump800.

ing something I was really interested in. It wasn't a hobby anymore."

Berian broke out during his junior year of high school, capturing the Colorado state title in the 400 meters (47.99 seconds) and the 800 meters (1:53.43). The following year, he again took the state titles in both events, trimming his times to 46.93 and 1:52.18, respectively. His accomplishments on the track, however, did not extend to academics, prompting most Division I schools to pass on offering Berian a scholarship. He enrolled at Division II Adams State University in Alamosa, Colorado, where, once again, he thrived on the track but not in the classroom. During his freshman year, he won the 2012 Division II 800-meter title in indoor and outdoor track and set a new personal best of 1:48.93 in the 800 meters. His grades left him ineligible to compete for most of his sophomore year, however, and during the spring semester of his junior year, Berian dropped out of school.

Back in Colorado Springs, Berian worked the morning shift at a McDonald's fast-food restaurant, trained every evening on the dirt track at a local high school, and slept on a friend's couch. His mother, dismayed, encouraged her son to pursue a career as a firefighter or police officer. As she recalled to Jere Longman of *New York Times* in July of 2016, she warned her son, "You're going to work there forever." She continued, "I was sure he would regret dropping out of college. He wanted to run. To a mother, that doesn't seem achievable." Berian gave himself until the end of 2015 to continue running. If did not achieved success by then, he would find another job or join the army. Five months later, Berian got a call from trainer Carlos Handler, and in December of 2014, he headed for the Big Bear Track Club in Big Bear Lake, California.

Sued by Nike for Contract Breach

Handler, a middle-distance coach at Big Bear, worked under legendary track coach Joe Vigil. The training at Big Bear was intense, but within a month Berian had gotten the hang of it. Although it had been two years since his last race, he set an ambitious goal: to cut his 800-meter time from under 1:49 to under 1:45. "Why have a goal if it's not going to be crazy?," Berian said in an interview with Sarah Barker for Deadspin. In his first race, he set a new 800-meter personal best of 1:48.53, and then at the 2015 Payton Jordan Invitational at Stanford, he won the event with a time of 1:45.30, just a fraction of a second from his goal. His performance in that race set a meet record and gave Berian a first-place U.S. ranking. At the Adidas Grand Prix in New York City a month later, as all eyes were on the newcomer, Berian did not disappoint. Placing second, behind Kenyan Olympic champion David Rudisha, Berian finished in 1:43.89 (just 0.15 second behind Rudisha), surpassing his original goal.

A couple of weeks later, Berian's performance at the 2015 USA Track & Field Outdoor Championships in Eugene, Oregon, was less successful. In the preliminaries, Berian finished second in his heat with a time of 1:48.47, qualifying him for the semifinals. However, his semifinal time of 1:46.28 was not fast enough to advance to the finals. The disappointment affected Berian for weeks. "It took something out of him," Handler recalled to Reid. "He was just sad." A fourth-place finish in the Monaco Diamond League the following month restored his spirits. Running the 800 meters in 1:43.34, he set a new personal best, ranking fifth fastest of all time for an American.

Berian signed a six-month sponsorship deal with Nike that year. Although the agreement was set to expire on December 31, 2015, the contract included a six-month counteroffer clause giving the company the right to match a competitor's offer. In January of 2016, Berian informed Nike that he planned to sign a three-year, $375,000 deal with New Balance, even though Nike had agreed to match the offer. Disputing Nike's claim, Berian and his agent pointed out that New Balance's contract differed from Nike's in that it came without any reduction clauses (which could reduce Berian's compensation under certain circumstances). Nike sued Berian for breach of contract, and the lawsuit quickly evolved into a highly public battle between the young runner and the corporate giant.

Competed at Summer Olympics in Rio

The lawsuit hung over Berian's head for months, and each time he raced wearing New Balance running shoes or promoted the company on social media, the

media quoted Nike's indignant response to the runner's "breach of contract." Although it was a distraction, the lawsuit did not prevent Berian from winning the 800-meter gold medal at the 2016 IAFF World Indoor Championships in Portland. As usual, Berian started the race out in front. During his final lap, he slowed somewhat but managed to hold the lead. Berian's win, and talks of his anticipated place at the upcoming Olympic Games in Rio de Janeiro, fueled Nike's legal efforts. In June of 2016, a judge upheld the company's request to temporarily ban Berian from competing in non-Nike gear. The announcement, however, bolstered public support for Berian, who seemed to become a spokesperson for athletes' rights. The attention prompted Nike to drop the lawsuit just before the Olympic trials began, and Berian soon signed with New Balance.

With the lawsuit behind him, Berian soared at the Olympic trials, dominating in the semifinals and, in the finals, finishing second with a time of 1:44.92. Ahead of Berian, with a time of 1:44.76, was Clayton Murphy, a junior from Akron University in Ohio. In Rio in August, Berian exited the semifinal qualifier with a time of 1:45.87 and a sixth-place ranking (Kenya's Rudisha was first, and Murphy advanced as the second-fastest nonautomatic qualifier). At the semifinals the next day, Berian took second place with a time of 1:44.56.

In the finals, however, Berian floundered. Starting the race at the front with Rudisha, Berian slowed in the final 200 meters. Berian crossed the finish line with a time of 1:46.16, for an eighth-place finish. Rudisha finished first in 1:42.15, trailed by Algeria's Taoufik Makhloufi (1:42.61) and Murphy (1:42.93). Speaking with Reid of the *Orange County Register* following the race, Berian expressed more gratitude than disappointment. "I guess I'm still inexperienced with rounds," he acknowledged. "But it's an Olympic final, it's the Olympics. I'm grateful to be here. I'm an Olympian forever more."

Sources

Periodicals

Denver Post, March 19, 2016.
New York Times, July 4, 2016.
Orange County (CA) Register, June 23, 2016; August 15, 2016.
Sports Illustrated, July 5, 2016.
Wall Street Journal, June 23, 2016.

Online

Barker, Sarah, "How An Implausible Runner and a Tiny Track Club Conquered the 800 Meters," Deadspin, June 19, 2015, http://fittish.deadspin.com/how-a-tiny-track-club-and-an-implausible-runner-conquer-1712584681 (accessed September 28, 2016).
Bernstein, Maxine, "Nike Seeks Order to Halt Olympic Hopeful Runner Boris Berian From Wearing New Balance Gear," OregonLive.com, June 6, 2016, http://www.oregonlive.com/business/index.ssf/2016/06/nike_seeks_court_order_to_halt.html (accessed September 28, 2016).
"Boris Berian: Athlete Profile," International Association of Athletics Federations, https://www.iaaf.org/athletes/united-states/boris-berian-279213 (accessed September 28, 2016).
Lloyd, Jonathan, "Boris Berian Turns Job at Fast-Food Counter into Super-Sized Success," NBC4 Los Angeles, August 16, 2016, http://www.nbclosangeles.com/news/sports/Rio-Olympics-800m-Track-Field-Boris-Berian-McDonalds-390314072.html (accessed September 28, 2016).

—Candice Mancini

Chu Berry

1908–1941

Jazz saxophonist

Leon "Chu" Berry was one of the most talented tenor saxophone players of the swing era. Although his daring solo improvisations and robust tone reminded many listeners of the most famous tenor sax player of the time, Coleman Hawkins, Berry's style was softer, more relaxed, and more reliant on vibrato. Hawkins himself said that Berry was "about the best." Berry played in several of the top jazz bands of the period, making his mark as the lead soloist in Cab Calloway's orchestra between 1937 and his untimely death in 1941. Berry's work is well represented on recordings, where he made the most of his brief solos in the middle of tightly arranged orchestral performances. Berry never led his own band but served as leader on a handful of recording sessions.

Chose Music over Football Career

Leon Brown Berry was born on September 13, 1908, in Wheeling, West Virginia. His parents, Brown Berry and Maggie Glasgow Berry, made sure their children received piano lessons and learned to appreciate music. Berry's brother, Nelson, learned to play the saxophone, while his half-sister played jazz piano with a small combo that sometimes rehearsed at the family home. One summer when he was a teenager, Berry saw a performance by the famous Fletcher Henderson Orchestra from New York, featuring Coleman Hawkins on the tenor sax, and he was inspired to pick up the instrument. At Lincoln High School he played the lighter alto sax but switched permanently to tenor while he was a student at West Virginia State College in

Charleston. Berry had a large, athletic build and was a talented enough college football player to consider playing professionally, but he decided to pursue music instead.

Berry's professional career began around 1928 when he played in Wheeling and toured the Ohio Valley with Perry Smith's Broadway Buddies. The following year he was playing with Phil Edwards' Collegians, a territory band out of Bluefield, West Virginia, when he was offered a spot in one of the nation's most successful African-American society orchestras, led by Sammy Stewart. When Berry got off the bus in Columbus, Ohio, to join the group, saxophone player Bill Stewart (no relation to the bandleader) thought that Berry's goatee made him look stereotypically Chinese and began calling him "Chu Chin Chow." The first part of the nickname stuck, and thereafter he was known as Chu Berry. In 1930 Stewart's orchestra went to New York for an engagement at the Savoy Ballroom in Harlem. Berry quit the group a few months later and remained in New York, where he began to make a name for himself.

Between 1930 and 1932, Berry played for short stints with groups led by Cecil Scott, saxophonist Otto Hardwick, and pianist Charlie Johnson, as well as drummer Kaiser Marshall's Czars of Harmony. His first experience in a recording studio came in 1932 as a member of saxophonist, composer, and arranger Benny Carter's band. A good friend of Carter's, record producer and jazz critic John Hammond, heard Berry play at a Harlem dance hall called the Dunbar Palace

At a Glance . . .

Born Leon Brown Berry on September 13, 1908, in Wheeling, WV; died on October 30, 1941, in Conneaut, OH; son of Brown Berry and Maggie Glasgow Berry. *Education:* Attended West Virginia State College.

Career: Professional musician, from 1929; recording artist, from 1932; played with orchestras led by Benny Carter, 1932–33, Teddy Hill, 1933–35, Fletcher Henderson, 1936–37, and Cab Calloway, 1937–41.

Awards: Named to *Metronome* magazine All-Stars, 1937–38; inducted into West Virginia Music Hall of Fame, 2007.

and subsequently invited him to take part in jam sessions on his short-lived radio program on WEVD. Hammond then hired the saxophonist, along with Hawkins and trumpeter Henry "Red" Allen, for several sessions in 1933 led by British musician Spike Hughes. These recordings are now considered jazz classics. In November of 1933, Berry accompanied the great blues singer Bessie Smith on her last recordings, also produced by Hammond.

Composed Theme for Fletcher Henderson Orchestra

In 1933 Berry won a spot as featured soloist with Teddy Hill's orchestra. He stayed with Hill for about two years, during which time the up-and-coming trumpet star Roy Eldridge, called "Little Jazz," joined the band. Eldridge and Berry developed a close friendship and musical partnership, which they honed by playing together in many "cutting contests" at after-hours clubs. The two men were intensely driven and devoted to refining their expressiveness in hot jazz improvisation. After leaving Hill's band, Berry freelanced for most of 1935, appearing on records in small-group sessions led by Red Norvo, Red Allen, Teddy Wilson, Gene Krupa, Putney Dandridge, and Mildred Bailey.

Early in 1936, Berry and Eldridge joined Fletcher Henderson's new orchestra for a long engagement at the Grand Terrace ballroom in Chicago. It was Berry who provided Henderson with his theme song and biggest hit, "Christopher Columbus," which originated from one of the sax player's riffs. Henderson's brother Horace developed the piece into a full orchestration, with a strikingly dissonant countermelody played by the brass. Berry got credit for the composition; the lyrics were penned by Andy Razaf. At least a dozen bands

recorded the tune in 1936, and the following year it was incorporated into Benny Goodman's eight-minute smash hit "Sing, Sing, Sing." With the Henderson band, Berry broke through as a soloist. His performances on the recording of "Christopher Columbus" and another tune recorded the same day, "Stealin' Apples," were among the best of his career to date. Many of the band's arrangements allowed him space to take a full chorus, usually 32 measures, solo. He also had his first opportunity to record as a leader in March of 1937, putting down four tracks under the name Chu Berry and His Stompy Stevedores.

Henderson's difficulties as a businessman limited prospects for his band's success. In the summer of 1937, Berry left the group and joined Cab Calloway's orchestra. Berry pushed the group to feature more instrumental pieces, periodically bringing in charts he felt would work well for the orchestra. According to the bassist Milt Hinton, Calloway appreciated the input. "Chu was very frank and Cab liked him," Hinton recalled. "He was very much responsible for us having good music in the band." Berry also performed in the Cab Jivers, Calloway's band-within-a-band, with Tyree Glenn on vibraphone and the group's sensational rhythm section of Hinton, Danny Barker on guitar, and Cozy Cole on drums.

Became a Star with Cab Calloway

Berry was now a prominent jazz figure, stepping out of Hawkins's shadow with his own captivating tone, outstanding breath control, keen harmonic sense, and explosive bursts of aggressive improvisation in brief solos. *Metronome* magazine named Berry a member of its All-Star band in 1937 and 1938. He reunited with Eldridge for a memorable November of 1938 session billed as Chu Berry and His "Little Jazz" Ensemble, producing intimate solos on "Stardust" and "Body and Soul"—a year before Hawkins released his classic version of the latter.

During the next few months, Berry recorded with Count Basie's orchestra, Teddy Wilson and Billie Holiday, the vibraphone star Lionel Hampton, and trumpeter and vocalist Wingy Manone. Calloway's orchestra, already one of the hardest swinging of the big bands, rose in stature when it added Dizzy Gillespie's trumpet in the summer of 1939. Berry, however, remained the group's most prized soloist. He was featured start to finish on Calloway's 1940 recording of "I Don't Stand a Ghost of a Chance With You," an effort to outdo Hawkins's "Body and Soul," and smoldered on Benny Carter's haunting "Lonesome Nights," recorded in August of 1940. "Chuberry Jam" was the name of another all-Berry showcase piece. Along with Gillespie, Berry frequented the after-hours spots such as Minton's Playhouse in Harlem, where the city's most cutting-edge jazzmen were setting the template

for the musical revolution that would soon emerge as bebop.

After playing a one-night engagement in Brookfield, Ohio, on October 26, 1941, Berry got into a car with bandmates Andy Brown and Lammar Wright en route to their next gig in Toronto. The car skidded in the misty evening and crashed into a bridge abutment. The other two passengers suffered only minor injuries, but Berry's skull was fractured, and he died October 30 in Conneaut, Ohio, at age 33. Calloway said that Berry's death was like losing a brother, and the band kept his chair empty for many weeks. Among the younger musicians Berry influenced, the most prominent was Charlie Parker, who named his first-born child, Leon, after him. Many of Berry's recordings have been preserved. Mosaic Records released a seven-volume box set of Berry's works in 2007. In the same year, he was posthumously inducted into the West Virginia Music Hall of Fame.

Selected discography

Chu Berry/Lucky Thompson, *Giants of the Tenor Sax* (recorded 1938–41), Commodore, 1988.
The Chronological Chu Berry, 1937–1941, Classics, 2000.
Classic Columbia and Victor Sessions (recorded 1932–41), Mosaic, 2007.

Sources

Books

Carr, Ian, Digby Fairweather, and Brian Priestley, *The Rough Guide to Jazz,* Rough Guides, 2004.
Chilton, John, *Who's Who of Jazz,* Time-Life Records, 1978.
McCarthy, Albert J., *Big Band Jazz,* Putnam, 1974.
Schuller, Gunther, *The Swing Era: The Development of Jazz, 1930–1945,* Oxford University Press, 1989.

Periodicals

Baltimore Afro American, November 8, 1941.
JazzTimes, July/August 2007.
New York Sun, May 22, 2007.

Online

Douglas, John, "Chu Berry," e-WV: The West Virginia Encyclopedia, http://www.wvencyclopedia.org/articles/468 (accessed August 22, 2016).
Evensmo, Jan, "The Tenorsax of Leon Berry 'Chu,'" Jazz Archeology, November 10, 2014, http://www.jazzarcheology.com/artists/chu_berry.pdf (accessed August 22, 2016).

Other

Schoenberg, Loren, liner notes to Chu Berry, *Classic Columbia and Victor Sessions,* Mosaic Records, 2007.

—Roger K. Smith

Simone Biles

1997—

Gymnast

American gymnast Simone Biles shined at the 2016 Olympic Games in Rio de Janeiro, winning four gold medals, in the vault, floor exercise, all-around, and team competition, and a bronze medal in the balance beam. Biles, a spitfire at four feet, nine inches who is regarded as one of the best gymnasts of all time, was among the biggest stars—in personality, if not stature—of the Rio Games, chosen by her teammates to be the U.S. flag-bearer at the closing ceremonies. Biles's four Olympic gold medals set a record for the most gold medals in gymnastics at a single Olympics. In all, Biles holds a total of 19 world championship and Olympic medals, making her the most decorated U.S. women's gymnast in the world.

Born in Columbus, Ohio, in 1997, Simone Biles and her younger sister Adria were raised by their maternal grandfather, Ronald Biles, and his wife Nellie in Spring, Texas, near Houston. Simone was three years old and Adria a newborn when the family moved to Texas; they were formally adopted by their grandparents three years later. The girls' biological father abandoned the family when they were young, and their mother, Shanon, relinquished custody of the girls as she struggled with drug and alcohol addiction. Two older siblings were adopted by Ron Biles's sister. Simone and her sister formed a strong relationship with their grandparents, whom they called "Mom" and "Dad." Speaking with Kelly Wallace of CNN in 2016, Simone said of Nellie Biles, "She encourages me and never lets me feel down about something for too long. If I've had a bad day in the gym or needed emotional support, she was always there."

Biles was first introduced to gymnastics at age six during a field trip to a gymnastics class. At home she began trying the tricks she had seen the gymnasts do, even teaching herself to do a back flip off the family mailbox. Soon after that, her parents signed her up for gymnastics classes. At age seven, Biles began training with Aimee Boorman (her coach to this day). Speaking with Lonnae O'Neal of the website The Undefeated in 2016, Boorman described Biles as having a natural "air sense," explaining, "You know how some people have incredible balance? Well, imagine having balance without your feet on the ground while flipping and twisting and knowing exactly when you have to bring your feet down to the floor so that you don't die."

At age 10, Biles began competing in women's artistic gymnastics through the USA Gymnastics Junior Olympic Program. A natural in all four of the sport's events—vault, uneven bars, balance beam, and floor—she moved quickly through the ranks and established herself as a fierce contender in the all-around (the combination of the four events). At age 14, Biles joined the international circuit and was thriving in national competitions. At the 2011 American Classic in Huntville, Texas, she won both the vault and the balance beam and took third in the all-around, fourth in floor, and eighth on bars. The finish qualified her for the 2011 Visa Championships, where she tied for seventh in the vault. She also competed at the CoverGirl Classic that year, where she placed 20th all-around and fifth on the beam. A high school freshman at the time, Biles's competition schedule had become too intense to continue unless she started homeschooling. Her choice to

At a Glance . . .

Born Simone Arianne Biles on March 14, 1997, in Columbus, OH; daughter of Ronald Biles (a former air-traffic control system installer) and Nellie Biles (a nurse). *Religion:* Roman Catholic.

Career: USA Gymnastics, junior gymnast, 2007–13, senior gymnast, 2013—.

Awards: American Cup: first place, all-around, 2013, 2015; World Championships: first place, all-around and floor exercise, 2013, first place, team, all-around, balance beam, and floor exercise, 2014, first place, team, all-around, balance beam, and floor exercise, 2015; Pacific Rim Championships: first place, team and all-around, 2016; Olympic Games: gold medal, team, all-around, vault, and floor exercise, bronze medal, balance beam, 2016.

Addresses: *Home*—Conroe, TX. *Agent*—Janey Miller, Octagon, 800 Connecticut Ave., 2nd Floor, Norwalk, CT 06854. *Twitter*—@Simone_Biles.

pursue gymnastics over staying in school was bittersweet. "I was just so lonely all the time," Biles told O'Neal. "I missed … all my friends at school … But I mean, in the end, it worked out."

In 2012, although Biles was considered strong enough to compete at the Olympic trials, she was two and a half months too young. (Gymnasts must be at least 16 years old to compete in senior-level events.) Continuing on the national circuit that year, she cemented her reputation as a formidable all-around opponent, taking first at both the American Classic and the Secret U.S. Classic and placing third at the 2012 Visa Championships in St. Louis, Missouri. During these competitions, she also earned a half-dozen top-three placements in her other events. The following year, Biles experienced a setback at the 2013 Secret U.S. Classic in Chicago, when Nellie Biles invited Simone's biological mother to attend the competition. Rattled by the situation, Biles stumbled on the balance beam, fell off the uneven bars, and hurt her ankle on the floor, requiring her to withdraw from the vault. In the end, she placed in just two events (seventh in beam and eighth in floor).

The slump did not last, and the rest of the season produced plenty of cause for celebration. At the 2013 City of Jesolo Trophy in Italy, she won five events—team, all-around, vault, beam, and floor. More significantly, Biles won her first world championship that year. In fact, at the 2013 World Championships in

Antwerp, Belgium, she won both the all-around and floor and took second in the vault, third on beam, and fourth on uneven bars. At the World Championships in 2014 and 2015, she finished first both years in team, all-around, beam, and floor (in vault she placed second in 2014 and third in 2015). By this time, Biles was considered unbeatable in the all-around, winning in all eight competitions that she took part in between 2014 and 2015.

By the time of the Olympic trials in July of 2016, it was clear that Biles would be a top contender. She easily advanced to the Summer Games in Rio de Janeiro, taking first in vault, floor, and all-around. Some predicted, however, that Biles would flop at the Games, citing the so-called Olympic jinx: before Biles, only three reigning world champions had gone on to win an Olympic title. Biles considered the jinx a challenge. "That's all the media cares about right now, whether I'm going to break some Olympic jinx that I've never even heard of," Biles told Michael Hardy of *Texas Monthly* in July of 2016, rolling her eyes. "It was never my deal to break that. But I guess I have to now, because you guys said I have to."

Biles followed through on her promise. Leaving Rio with four gold medals (all-around, vault, floor, and team) and one bronze (beam), she set an American gymnastics record for the most gold medals at a single Olympic Games. For the closing ceremony, Biles was chosen as the flag bearer for Team USA, the first female gymnast ever chosen.

Following the Olympics, Biles planned to join members of the 2012 and 2016 Olympic teams for the Kellogg's Gymnastics Tour of Gymnastics Champions, a 36-city national tour scheduled for the fall of 2016.

Sources

Periodicals

Los Angeles Times, August 11, 2016.
Texas Monthly, July 2016.
USA Today, August 22, 2016.
Wall Street Journal, August 10, 2016.

Online

"The Fine Line: What Makes Simone Biles the World's Best Gymnast," NYTimes.com, August 5, 2016, http://www.nytimes.com/interactive/2016/08/05/sports/olympics-gymnast-simone-biles.html (accessed September 28, 2016).

O'Neal, Lonnae, "The Difficulty of Being Simone Biles," The Undefeated, July 6, 2016, https://theundefeated.com/features/the-difficulty-of-being-simone-biles/ (accessed September 28, 2016).

"Simone Biles," USA Gymnastics, https://usagym.org/pages/athletes/athleteListDetail.html?id=164887 (accessed September 28, 2016).

Wallace, Kelly, "Olympic Gymnast Simone Biles' Lessons from Mom," CNN.com, August 9, 2016, http://www.cnn.com/2016/04/27/health/simone -biles-olympics-mom-100-days-until-rio/ (accessed September 28, 2016).

—Candice Mancini

Tom Browne

1954—

Jazz, R&B, and gospel trumpeter

Engaging, inventive, and highly skilled, trumpeter Tom Browne is adept at a variety of styles, moving easily from jazz to R&B to gospel. An industry veteran whose career stretches back to the early days of disco, he is best known for his work in the late 1970s and early 1980s, when he had a string of radio-friendly hits on both sides of the Atlantic. His work has been sampled by dozens of rappers and hip-hop artists, from Snoop Dogg to the Notorious B.I.G. Sampling "is surely one of the things that's keeping some of my earlier music alive," he told Kevin Goins of SoulMusic.com in a 2012 interview. "I surely appreciate it."

The son of an airport meteorologist, Browne was born on October 30, 1954, in Queens, New York, one of New York City's five boroughs. Raised there in the neighborhood of Jamaica, a socially and ethnically diverse area near the city's two main airports, he was drawn to aviation as well as music as a child. He later earned his pilot's license, balancing his music career with regular flying assignments for a variety of commercial firms. "I just fell in love with [aviation]," he told Goins, adding, "I just said, 'That's what I want to do.'"

That kind of determination also drove his involvement in music. He began with the piano, moving on to the trumpet around age 12. His progress on it was rapid, thanks in part to lessons from Murray Karpilovsky, the principal trumpet for several leading ensembles, including conductor Arturo Toscanini's renowned NBC Orchestra. Initially interested in classical music, Browne won admission to New York's High School of Music & Art and Performing Arts, one of the most competitive

arts magnet programs in the country. His enthusiasm for jazz developed rapidly around this time, and not long after graduation he was playing professionally in clubs around the city. Because many of these nightspots encouraged jam sessions and other forms of informal collaboration, he was able to work almost immediately with some of the genre's leading figures. Among them was the saxophonist Sonny Fortune, whom he backed on the album *Infinity Is,* released by Atlantic Records in 1978.

By that point he had also assembled a quintet of his own, and after a pivotal engagement at New York's Breezin' Lounge he signed a contract with GRP Records, a small but well-regarded label. Work on his first album, *Browne Sugar* (1979), began soon thereafter. A rousing collection of eight compositions, including "Throw Down" and "The Closer I Get to You," it gave ample evidence of his ability to blend styles. Drawing on the "jazz fusion" approach pioneered by his fellow trumpeter Miles Davis, he mixed relatively traditional chords and melodies with the rhythms and instrumentation of rock and roll and R&B. Both critics and the public responded favorably, and GRP lost little time in bringing him back into the studio for a follow-up.

Browne's second album, *Love Approach* (1980), made him an international star, thanks in large part to its best-known track, the infectious "Funkin' for Jamaica (N.Y.)." A tribute to the street culture of his childhood home, it featured a memorable contribution by vocalist Toni Smith. Driven by a pounding bass line he devised one day in his parents' attic, it drew heavily on funk,

At a Glance . . .

Born on October 30, 1954, in New York, NY. *Religion:* Evangelical Christian.

Career: Independent musician, 1970s—.

Addresses: *Agent*—Mark Green, Celebrity Talent Agency, Inc., 111 E. 14th St., Suite 249, New York, NY 10003. *Web*—http://www.TomBrowne.org. *Twitter*—@TomBrowne.

disco, and other forms of R&B. Audiences responded with enthusiasm, sending the song to the top of the Billboard R&B list, where it remained for about a month; it also broke the top 10 in the United Kingdom. The album as a whole, meanwhile, was certified gold, as was *Magic,* a 1981 follow-up that included "Thighs High (Grip Your Hips and Move)," another top-five R&B hit.

Browne had gradually moved from jazz into R&B, a shift he was not entirely comfortable with. Although danceable R&B typically sold much better than jazz, he was increasingly ill at ease with the risqué lyrics typical of dance songs, particularly in light of his newfound Christian faith and a move to Arista Records; like many of his peers, he found that larger labels tended to emphasize sales over personal preferences. While he continued for several more years to record music in the same vein, releasing solid but relatively undistinguished albums such as *Rockin' Radio* (1983) and *Tommy Gun* (1984), his devotion to evangelical Christianity helped spark his departure from Arista around 1985.

In the wake of that shift, a new phase in his career began. After signing with Malaco Records, a gospel-oriented label based in Mississippi, he released a Christian album called *No Longer I* (1986). While it won some strong reviews, its impact was limited, and it seemed likely that Browne's time in the spotlight was over. For much of the next decade, he focused on his flying career. Around 1994, however, he signed a new contract with Hip-Bop Records, a firm focused on blends of jazz and hip-hop. Over the next few years, he completed a string of albums for that innovative label, including *Mo' Jamaica Funk* (1994) and *Another Shade of Browne* (1996), the latter of which showcased his rapport with an excellent backing group that included bassist Ron Carter, drummer Idris Muham-

mad, and pianist Billy Childs. "Even with an occasional misstep," noted Scott Yanow of AllMusic.com in his review of *Another Shade,* "Tom Browne's playing in this setting is well worth hearing." Browne continued to perform regularly in the 2000s and 2010s.

Selected discography

Singles

"Funkin' for Jamaica (N.Y.)," 1980.
"Thighs High (Grip Your Hips and Move)," 1981.

Albums

Sonny Fortune, *Infinity Is,* Atlantic, 1978.
Browne Sugar (includes "Throw Down" and "The Closer I Get to You"), GRP, 1979.
Love Approach (includes "Funkin' for Jamaica [N.Y.]"), GRP, 1980.
Magic (includes "Thighs High [Grip Your Hips and Move]"), GRP, 1981.
Rockin' Radio, Arista, 1983.
Tommy Gun, Arista, 1984.
No Longer I, Malaco, 1986.
Mo' Jamaica Funk, Hip-Bop, 1994.
Another Shade of Browne, Hip-Bop, 1996.
S' Up, Pony Canyon, 2010.

Sources

Online

Goins, Kevin, "Tom Browne 2012 SoulMusic.com Interview: The Magic of Tom Browne," SoulMusic.com, May 3, 2012, http://www.soulmusic.com/index.asp?S=1&T=38&ART=2429 (accessed August 30, 2016).
"Tom Browne," SoulWalking.co.uk, http://www.soulwalking.co.uk/Tom%20Browne.html (accessed August 30, 2016).
Tom Browne: The Official Site of the Best Smooth Jazz Trumpet Artist, http://www.tombrowne.org (accessed August 30, 2016).
Yanow, Scott, "*Another Shade of Browne:* AllMusic Review by Scott Yanow," AllMusic.com, http://www.allmusic.com/album/another-shade-of-browne-mw0000079190 (accessed August 30, 2016).
———, "Tom Browne: Artist Biography by Scott Yanow," AllMusic.com, http://www.allmusic.com/artist/tom-browne-mn0000603091/biography (accessed August 30, 2016).

—R. Anthony Kugler

Cassandra Butts

1965–2016

Attorney

Cassandra Butts was an attorney and policy expert who served in the White House as deputy counsel during President Barack Obama's first term in office. A former law school classmate of the president and a longtime friend to him and his wife, Butts served as an advisor to Obama—in both formal and informal roles—throughout his career, beginning with his election to the U.S. Senate in 2004. Butts went on to advise Obama during his first presidential campaign in 2008 and then served on his transition team after his election and in his administration. During his second term, President Obama nominated Butts to serve as U.S. ambassador to the Bahamas. When she died unexpectedly in May of 2016, her nomination to the ambassadorship had been in limbo in the Senate for more than two years. In a statement released by the White House upon her death, President Obama described his friend and colleague as "someone who put her hands squarely on that arc of the moral universe, and never stopped doing whatever she could to bend it towards justice."

Embarked on a Public Service Career

Born in 1965 in Brooklyn, New York, Butts grew up in Durham, North Carolina, and enrolled at the nearby University of North Carolina at Chapel Hill following her high school graduation. She earned her undergraduate degree in political science in 1987. After working for a year as a researcher for the African News Service, Butts entered Harvard Law School in the same class as the future president Obama. The two met early

in their first year of law school while filling out financial aid forms and became part of the same circle of friends.

After completing her law degree in 1991, Butts held a series of public service jobs. During the early 1990s, she was an attorney for the Legal Defense and Educational Fund of the National Association for the Advancement of Colored People (NAACP) for three years, handling voting rights challenges and school desegregation cases for the civil rights organization. Thereafter, Butts served as counsel to Democratic senator Harris Wofford of Pennsylvania and then as senior advisor to Representative Dick Gephardt of Missouri. One of the ranking Democrats in the House, Gephardt was the party's minority leader for eight years; during that time, Butts advised the congressman on key policy matters, including the 1998 hearings on the impeachment of President Bill Clinton. Butts traveled overseas in 2000 as an international observer for the parliamentary elections in Zimbabwe. She later drafted a bill for Gephardt that created a compensation fund for victims of the terrorist attacks of September 11, 2001, against the United States.

In 2004, when Gephardt made a bid for the Democratic presidential nomination, Butts moved on to a position as senior vice president for domestic policy at the Center for American Progress, a Washington, DC, lobbying group. She also was tapped as an informal advisor to Obama when he was elected to the U.S. Senate. Speaking at her funeral, President Obama noted that "when I arrived here in Washington after winning my senate race, I was 99th in seniority. But I

At a Glance . . .

Born Cassandra Quin Butts on August 10, 1965, in New York, NY; died on May 25, 2016, in Washington, DC; daughter of Charles Norman Butts (a businessman) and Mae A. Karim (an accountant). *Politics:* Democrat. *Education:* University of North Carolina at Chapel Hill, BA, political science, 1987; Harvard Law School, JD, 1991.

Career: African News Service, researcher, 1987–88; Legal Defense and Educational Fund, National Association for the Advancement of Colored People, attorney, 1991–94; U.S. Senator Harris Wofford, counsel; U.S. Representative Dick Gephardt, senior advisor, 1997–2004; Center for American Progress, senior vice president for domestic policy, 2004–08; Barack Obama presidential campaign, senior policy advisor, 2008; President Obama transition team, general counsel, 2008–09; White House, deputy counsel for domestic policy and ethics, 2009; Millennium Challenge Corporation, senior advisor, 2009–16.

did have a secret weapon, and that was, I knew Cassandra." Drawing on her many personal and professional relationships in Washington, Butts helped Obama connect with experienced Senate staffers, including Pete Rouse, who had most recently served as chief of staff for longtime South Dakota Democratic senator Tom Daschle. Rouse became chief of staff for the freshman senator Obama and, with Butts, would later be part of Obama's presidential campaign and administration.

Joined Obama Campaign and Administration

Butts joined Obama's 2008 presidential campaign team in July of that year as a senior policy advisor. She was one of several advisors and longtime friends who would later be referred to as the "Obama Sisterhood" for their close ties with one another and with the president and First Lady Michelle Obama. Butts was also one of 20 former Harvard classmates who worked on the Obama campaign. Butts was deeply affected by the people she met on the campaign trail, who drove home for her the possibility of electing the nation's first black president. "You talk to African American voters who are baby boomers or older, and they never thought that they would see an African American who was a serious contender for the presidency of the United States," she recalled in a 2008 interview for PBS's *Frontline.* "Before I met Barack Obama, I never

thought I would see it in my lifetime. But I'm happy to be in the moment."

After Obama won the presidency in November of 2008, Butts was named to his official transition team as general counsel. In late December of that year, the president-elect named Butts as his deputy White House counsel with a focus on domestic policy and ethics. She served in that role for a year, during which time she worked to staff the U.S. Department of Justice with attorneys and helped craft the administration's ethics policies and earliest executive orders, all of which, in the president's words, "reflected both of our views that public service is a privilege; that it's not about advancing yourself or your friends … or some ideological agenda; it's about advancing the interests of every single American."

In 2009 Butts also played a role in recruiting Sonia Sotomayor as an Obama nominee to the U.S. Supreme Court. In his funeral remarks, Obama noted that his deputy counsel had convinced Sotomayor "to agree to undergo a difficult process," which eventually led to her appointment to the Court. Later that same year, President Obama appointed Butts to be a senior advisor to the Millennium Challenge Corporation, an independent government agency focused on making recommendations about how the United States can help reduce poverty in developing countries through targeted foreign aid programs.

Nominated for Bahamas Ambassadorship

In February of 2014, at age 48, Butts was nominated by President Obama to the post of U.S. ambassador to the Bahamas. She was excited about the prospect and looked forward to a new chapter in her life in public service. After an initial Senate hearing in May of 2014, however, no action was taken to fill the long-vacant ambassadorship. Two years later, in May of 2016, with her nomination still on hold in the Senate, Butts died of acute leukemia following a short illness; she had, in fact, consulted a physician only a few days earlier, feeling unwell, and died before tests could confirm her diagnosis.

Two weeks before her death, Butts spoke with *New York Times* columnist Frank Bruni about the status of her nomination, which was held up initially by Republican senator Ted Cruz of Texas as part of his senatorial "hold" on all U.S. State Department nominations made by President Obama. Later, Arkansas senator Tom Cotton, also a Republican, placed a hold on three ambassadorial nominees, including Butts, to pressure the president on an unrelated matter. Although Cotton eventually lifted his hold on the other two nominations, he refused to do so for Butts, telling her, according to Bruni's posthumous report in the *New York Times,* "that he knew that she was a close friend of Obama's

... and that blocking her was a way to inflict special pain on the president."

Although Butts had not expected an easy confirmation, in light of the partisan political rancor in Washington, she "never expected such an enduring limbo," she told Bruni. After Butts's death, Valerie Jarrett, another longtime Obama friend, confidant, and advisor, told Bruni, "All Cassandra wanted to do was serve her country," adding, "it is devastating to think that through no fault of her own, she spent the last 835 days of her life waiting for confirmation."

Despite her disappointment, Butts refused to withdraw from consideration for the diplomatic post, determined to wait out the opposition to her approval. While her official diplomatic status remained unresolved, she served as an advisor to the U.S. delegation to the United Nations and forged ahead on projects of personal interest, including a college arts scholarship program for underprivileged students. At her funeral, President Obama eulogized his longtime friend and former law school classmate, describing her as being "like a Swiss Army Knife—whatever you needed, you could find. Smart enough to do just about any project, thoughtful enough to help others step in, finding those who might add to our collective efforts." He recounted a list of admirable qualities exemplified by Butts, including "professionalism, decency, integrity, insight, smarts, humor, and a fundamental kindness," and praised her as someone who was "infinitely patient and forgiving of people's foibles."

Sources

Periodicals

New York, October 22, 2007, p. 32.
New Yorker, May 7, 2007, p. 48.
New York Times, November 24, 2008; June 7, 2016.
Washington Post, May 28, 2016.

Online

Beckwith, Ryan Teague, "Read President Obama's Eulogy for His Friend and Adviser," Time.com, June 7, 2016, http://time.com/4360811/barack-obama-eulogy-cassandra-butts/ (accessed September 30, 2016).

Brown, Carrie Budoff, "School Buds," Politico, December 5, 2008, http://www.politico.com/news/stories/1208/16224.html (accessed September 30, 2016).

"Former Deputy White House Counsel Cassandra Butts Dies at 50," The Root, May 28, 2016, http://www.theroot.com/articles/news/2016/05/cassandra-butts-dies-dead-at-50/ (accessed September 30, 2016).

"Interview: Cassandra Butts," *Frontline,* PBS, July 10, 2008, http://www.pbs.org/wgbh/pages/frontline/choice2008/interviews/butts.html (accessed September 30, 2016).

—Carol Brennan and Pamela Willwerth Aue

Vinnette Carroll

1922–2002

Actress, director, playwright

Vinnette Carroll was a trailblazing actress, director, and playwright in the 1960s and 1970s. Best known for her work as a director, Carroll was the first black woman ever to direct a production on Broadway, scoring hits with the exuberant, gospel-infused musicals *Don't Bother Me, I Can't Cope* (1972) and *Your Arms Too Short to Box with God* (1976), which together earned her three Tony Award nominations. Throughout her career, Carroll was dedicated to creating opportunities for African-American artists and promoting the work of black playwrights. "I want to show Black people that there is dignity and beauty in our art," she told Nelson George in a 1977 interview for the *New York Amsterdam News*. "That's my goal." To that end Carroll founded the Urban Arts Corps, a repertory company that provided a training ground for emerging minority artists in New York City from the 1960s to the 1980s, and later created the Vinnette Carroll Repertory Company in Fort Lauderdale, Florida. Carroll's work helped pave the way for future generations of black artists in the theater.

Traded Psychology for a Theatrical Career

Vinnette Justine Carroll was born on March 11, 1922, in New York City, the daughter of Dr. Edgar C. Carroll, a dentist, and Florence Morris Carroll. Her parents were Jamaican immigrants, and Carroll and her older sister Dorothy spent much of their childhood in Falmouth, Jamaica, with their maternal grandmother. When she was 10 years old Carroll and her sister returned from Jamaica to live with their parents in the well-to-do Sugar Hill neighborhood in Harlem. Carroll showed an early affinity for the arts, playing the violin and viola as a student at Wadleigh High School, an integrated school in Washington Heights. Although Carroll was inclined toward the arts, her father urged her to purse a medical career. Repelled by the sight of blood, however, she enrolled at Long Island University as a psychology major. After completing her undergraduate degree in 1944, went on to earn a master's degree in clinical psychology from New York University in 1946.

Carroll found a job as a clinical psychologist in the New York City public schools and was working toward a doctoral degree at Columbia University when she began to study acting, taking classes at night. Her love of drama eventually won out, and she abandoned psychology for a career in the theater. In 1948 Carroll won a scholarship to attend Erwin Piscator's Dramatic Workshop at the New School for Social Research, where she studied with Lee Strasberg and Stella Adler. That same year she made her professional acting debut in George Bernard Shaw's *Androcles and the Lion* at the Falmouth Playhouse in Massachusetts. She made her Broadway debut with a bit part in *A Streetcar Named Desire* in 1956 and then appeared the next year in *A Small War on Murray Hill,* whose run lasted only a week. In 1962 she won an Obie Award for her performance in Errol John's play *Moon on a Rainbow Shawl,* in which she appeared with James Earl Jones.

To supplement her income during this time, Carroll taught drama at New York's High School of the

At a Glance . . .

Born Vinnette Justine Carroll on March 11, 1922, in New York, NY; died on November 5, 2002, in Lauderhill, FL; daughter of Dr. Edgar C. Carroll (a dentist) and Florence Morris Carroll. *Education:* Long Island University, BA, 1944; New York University, MA, 1946.

Career: High School of the Performing Arts, drama teacher, 1953–64; Inner City Repertory Company, Los Angeles, associate director, 1967; Urban Arts Corps, founder and artistic director, 1967–1980s; Vinnette Carroll Repertory Company, founder and artistic director, 1985–2000.

Memberships: Actors' Equity Association; American Federation of Television and Radio Artists; Screen Actors Guild.

Awards: Obie Award, Distinguished Performance, Actress, 1962, for *Moon on a Rainbow Shawl;* Emmy Award, 1964, for *Beyond the Blues;* Los Angeles Drama Critics Circle Award, 1970, for *Don't Bother Me, I Can't Cope;* AUDELCO Achievement Award for outstanding contribution to black theater, 1975; inducted into Black Filmmakers Hall of Fame, 1979.

Performing Arts from 1953 to 1964, and it was there that she discovered a passion for directing, envisioning a different role for herself in the theater. "I learned for sure that I wanted most to direct and that I loved working with young people and I didn't want to act anymore," she said, according to Judith Katz. "Later on, I began to see that what I wanted was my own company." Carroll landed her first directing job in 1958, when she staged Howard Richardson and William Berney's *Dark of the Moon* at the Harlem YMCA; she revived the production two years later at the Equity Liberty Theatre off Broadway.

Her directorial breakthrough came in 1961, when she staged a production of the poet Langston Hughes's *Black Nativity,* a gospel "song-play," at the Forty-First Street Theatre. Two years later Carroll had her first hit with her own play *Trumpets of the Lord,* a musical revue that she wrote based on the poetry of James Weldon Johnson. The show, which featured Cicely Tyson, ran for 160 performances at the off-Broadway Astor Place Theatre and later had a short Broadway run in 1969. Carroll worked with Hughes again in 1965, when she directed and starred in his play *Prodigal Son,* another gospel-based production

adapted from the biblical parable that had 141 performances at the off-Broadway Greenwich Mews Theatre and then went on a successful European tour.

Directed Hit Broadway Shows

In 1967 Carroll briefly served as associate director of the Inner City Repertory Company in Los Angeles. Six months later she returned to New York and founded the Urban Art Corps (UAC), a pilot program of the Ghetto Arts Program that was funded by the New York Council on the Arts. Carroll served as the UAC's first artistic director. The UAC was intended to provide a training ground for young minority artists and to give them an opportunity to develop their craft. A long-term goal of the UAC was to establish a repertory company that would produce works by and about minorities. During its 1969–70 season, the UAC staged a production of Carroll's *Never Jam Today,* a musical adaptation of Lewis Carroll's *Alice's Adventures in Wonderland* and *Through the Looking Glass,* at the City Center of Music and Drama in New York City and gave performances across New York State.

While working with the UAC, Carroll met the lyricist, composer, and playwright Micki Grant, with whom she would collaborate on her most successful works. "Micki came in here and sang her songs, and I knew it was right," Carroll told Beth Fallon of the *Daily News* in 1972. "I heard those lyrics and knew she was special." Carroll directed and coauthored with Grant the musical revue *Don't Bother Me, I Can't Cope,* which was developed at the UAC before premiering at Ford's Theatre in Washington, DC, in 1971. The subsequent Broadway production, which opened in April of 1972, was a huge hit, running for more than 1,000 performances and earning Carroll a Tony Award nomination for best direction of a musical. A subsequent production at the Mark Taper Forum in Los Angeles earned Carroll a Los Angeles Drama Critics Circle Award.

Carroll and Grant followed up in 1975 with *Your Arms Too Short to Box with God,* a spirited musical based on the biblical Book of Matthew. Again developed by the UAC, the production was conceived and directed by Carroll, with music and lyrics by Alex Bradford and Grant. The show premiered in Italy at the Festival of Two Worlds in Spoleto and played at Ford's Theatre before opening on Broadway in December of 1976. *Your Arms Too Short* ran for 429 performances over two years. Carroll, who was the first black woman ever to direct a musical on Broadway, earned two Tony nominations, for best direction of a musical and best book of a musical. Carroll went on to stage several successful revivals of the musical: in 1980, starring actress Jennifer Holiday; in 1982, with Al Green and Patti LaBelle; and finally in 1996, with Teddy Pendergrass, Stephanie Mills, and BeBe Winans.

In the 1980s, Carroll, then in her 60s, bought a home in Fort Lauderdale and divided her time between New York and Florida. In 1985 she founded the Vinnette Carroll Repertory Company in Fort Lauderdale, through which she aimed, as she had done with the UAC, to promote the work of black playwrights. She served as artistic director of the theater until 2000, when she suffered a stroke. No longer able to lead the company, she asked that her name be removed; today the theater continues to operate as the Metropolitan Diversity Theatre Company. Carroll died at her home in Fort Lauderdale on November 5, 2002, at age 80.

Selected works

Theater (as a director and playwright)

Trumpets of the Lord, 1963.
But Never Jam Today, 1969.
Don't Bother Me, I Can't Cope, 1970.
Croesus and the Witch, 1971.
Step Lively, Boy, 1973.
The Ups and Downs of Theophilus Maitland, 1974.
All the King's Men, 1974.
Your Arms Too Short to Box with God, 1975.
I'm Laughin' but I Ain't Tickled, 1976.
What You Gonna Name That Pretty Little Baby?, 1978.
When Hell Freezes Over I'll Skate, 1979.

Sources

Books

Fliotsos, Anne, and Wendy Vierow, *American Women Stage Directors of the Twentieth Century,* University of Illinois Press, 2008.
Katz, Judith, *The Business of Show Business: A Guide to Career Opportunities Behind the Scenes in Theatre and Film,* Barnes, 1981.
Nelson, Emmanuel S., ed., *African American Dramatists: An A-to-Z Guide,* Greenwood Press, 2004.

Periodicals

New York Amsterdam News, March 5, 1977, p. D9.
New York Daily News, June 6, 1972, p. 42.
New York Times, December 19, 1976; November 7, 2002.

Online

"Remembering Vinnette Carroll: Pioneering African-American Director and Her Connection to Fords," Ford's Theatre Blog, December 11, 2015, https://blog.fords.org/2015/12/11/remembering-vinnette-carroll-pioneering-african-american-director-and-her-connection-to-fords/ (accessed September 26, 2016).
"Urban Arts Corps Records, 1955–1983," New York Public Library, http://archives.nypl.org/scm/21883 (accessed September 26, 2016).

—Deborah A. Ring

Charlie Christian

1916–1942

Jazz guitarist

Charlie Christian was the most important electric guitar player in the United States before World War II and a pioneer of the modern amplified guitar technique that came to dominate popular music in the following decades. Before Christian rose to prominence with the Benny Goodman Sextet in 1939, the guitar was rarely heard in orchestral settings except as a supporting player in the rhythm section, and the few guitarists who used amplification treated it as a novelty. Christian's prowess as a soloist—his blistering single-note arcs of fluent melodic invention, phrased like trumpet or saxophone riffs—revealed the guitar's potential as a lead instrument. Christian is also considered one of the founding figures of the modernist movement in jazz that developed into bebop during the 1940s. Christian pulled off these memorable achievements in a brief career: he died in 1942 at age 25 after just two years in the national spotlight.

Christian, Charlie, photograph. JP Jazz Archive/Redferns/Getty Images.

the cotton country of Bonham in northeastern Texas, the youngest of three sons of Clarence and Willie Mae Christian. Two years or so after Charlie's birth, Clarence Christian fell victim to an illness that robbed him of his sight. No longer employable as a waiter, he decided to use his musical skills to bring in income. The whole family had musical talent: Christian's mother played piano and sang, and his father could play just about any instrument; he, in turn, taught his sons to play the strings. The family relocated to Oklahoma City, Oklahoma, where Clarence Christian let his children guide him through the streets as a blind singing guitarist. Charlie began as "lead boy" and dancer on these "busts," as they called busking, while Edward, the eldest, played mandolin and Clarence Jr. the fiddle. They meandered through middle-class white neighborhoods or parked themselves in front of cafés, offering blues and light classics.

Grew Up Busking in Oklahoma City

Charles Henry Christian was born on July 29, 1916, in

Clarence Christian Sr. died when his youngest son was 10 years old. Like his father, Charlie loved baseball as much as music and was talented at both. He attended Frederick Douglass School through at least the seventh grade. There he was a student of Zelia N. Page Breaux,

At a Glance . . .

Born Charles Henry Christian on July 29, 1916, in Bonham, TX; died on March 2, 1942, in New York, NY; son of Clarence and Willie Mae Christian; children: Billie Jean Christian.

Career: Professional musician, 1930s–1940s; played with Alphonso Trent and Anna Mae Winburn orchestras; member of Benny Goodman Sextet, 1939–41.

Awards: Best Guitarist, *Metronome* and *DownBeat* magazine polls, 1939–42; inducted into Big Band and Jazz Hall of Fame, 1981; inducted into Rock and Roll Hall of Fame, 1990.

Oklahoma City's music supervisor for its African-American public schools, who taught music theory and appreciation. Breaux also was part owner of the local Aldridge Theater, the central entertainment venue on North East Second Street, also known as "Deep Deuce," the city's African-American thoroughfare. Christian wanted to learn to play the tenor saxophone in school, but Breaux instead gave him a trumpet, which he said hurt his lip. In shop class, he made a guitar out of a cigar box.

Christian's brother Ed, 10 years his senior, became a professional pianist in 1929, eventually leading bands in Oklahoma City. Before he was a teenager, Christian started hanging around Deep Deuce with his brothers and making friends with other musicians. At some point he got serious about the guitar and received help from a local guitar player named "Bigfoot" Ralph Hamilton and from horn player James Simpson. By 1930 or 1931, Christian was quite proficient—more than his oldest brother realized.

According to Peter Broadbent, the author of a biography of Christian, these musicians had the youngster practice improvisation three jazz tunes: "Sweet Georgia Brown," "Tea for Two," and "Rose Room." One night when the famous Don Redman Orchestra was in town, Hamilton and Ed Christian joined Redman's band at an after-hours jam session at Honey's. Charlie wanted to join in. His brother objected, but Hamilton insisted. The first tune was "Sweet Georgia Brown," and Christian surprised and delighted the crowd with his fine picking. When the audience demanded encores, Christian called the other two pieces he had practiced, again astonishing the crowd. By the time he returned home, his mother had already heard all about her son's debut.

Played with Territory Bands

Christian began playing in the dives of Deep Deuce and anywhere he could. When Lester Young came to town in 1932 as a member of the Blue Devils territory band, Christian was knocked over by the saxophonist's mellow tone and relaxed, swinging rhythm. The pair jammed together, and the guitarist tried to replicate Young's solos on his guitar. Despite his obsession with developing his musical acumen, he did have time for other pursuits: he was dating Margretta Downey, and in 1932, at age 16, the two had a daughter.

Still underage, Christian got his mother's permission to join a traveling territory band, one of the best in the Southwest, run by pianist Alphonso Trent. He played guitar and bass in Trent's orchestra for a year or more, and over the next few years, he worked with several other bands, including Leslie Sheffield's Rhythmaires and, briefly, his brother Ed Christian's band. With Anna Mae Winburn and Her Cotton Club Boys, he traveled to Kansas City and as far as Chicago and Minneapolis.

In working on his solo technique, he ran up against the difficulty of playing loudly enough to be heard over the brass and reeds. By the mid-1930s, some musicians were already playing the amplified steel guitar, notably, Bob Dunn with Milton Brown and His Musical Brownies and Leon McAuliffe with Bob Wills and His Texas Playboys, both Western swing bands. At some point, possibly in 1937, Christian crossed paths with Eddie Durham, a veteran who had played with Bennie Moten, Jimmie Lunceford, and Count Basie. Durham had been experimenting with pickups and resonator guitars for years, heard on the 1935 Lunceford recording of "Hittin' the Bottle." Christian is believed to have taken lessons from Durham.

In 1937 Christian purchased his first electric guitar, a Gibson model, and quickly adapted his solo style to playing with amplification. Instead of strumming chords, as he did when accompanying other players, he picked out lines of piercing single notes in phrases. The endlessly flowing streams of notes were filled with explosive interval jumps, funky riffs, and countermelodies. He made intricate use of advanced harmonies and aggressively exposed the chord changes in and out of the bridge of a standard pop tune. The raw talent of this unpretentious, somewhat naive young man attracted a fair amount of notice among musicians in the region.

Auditioned for Benny Goodman

Mary Lou Williams, the star pianist for Andy Kirk's band, heard Christian play when the Clouds of Joy came through Oklahoma City in July of 1939. A few weeks later, in a New York recording studio, Williams mentioned the guitarist to John Hammond. Hammond

was a well-known figure in the jazz world, a producer, critic, and talent scout who had already helped establish the careers of Billie Holiday, Benny Goodman, and pianist Teddy Wilson. Williams told Hammond that if wanted to hear the best electric guitar in jazz, he should find Christian at the Ritz Cafe in Oklahoma City. Hammond rearranged his travel plans to include a stop in Oklahoma, where six band members met him and took him first to the hotel where Willie Mae Christian worked as a maid, then to the Ritz.

Hammond recognized Christian's talent right away and concluded immediately that Benny Goodman should hire him for his small group. The Goodman Trio, with Wilson and drummer Gene Krupa, and the Goodman Quartet, adding Lionel Hampton on vibraphone, were the first integrated jazz groups to perform regularly and had achieved nationwide popularity. Days later, Hammond sent a wire inviting Christian to audition for Goodman in Los Angeles. With almost nothing packed, the musician boarded a train west.

On August 16, 1939, when Christian arrived at the studio where Goodman's band was recording for Columbia Records, the "King of Swing" was too preoccupied to deal with him. At Hammond's insistence, he let Christian chord him through a chorus of "Tea for Two" on acoustic guitar, then sent him away. It was a perfunctory audition, but Hammond devised a way to ensure Christian a full hearing. The story has become jazz lore. Goodman was opening that night at the Victor Hugo, a segregated restaurant in Beverly Hills. Hammond invited Christian to meet him in the kitchen. After Goodman's first set, the leader took a dinner break backstage before coming back with his quintet. That was when Hammond and Goodman's bassist, Artie Bernstein, hauled Christian's amplifier on stage. When Goodman walked onstage and saw the guitarist sitting there, he shot Hammond a ferocious glare, but decorum demanded that he let the guest play at least one tune. Goodman called out a song he expected Christian not to know, "Rose Room"—which happened to be one of the original three tunes in Christian's repertoire. The guitarist played such scorching improvisations that, in Hammond's recollection, the number went on for 45 minutes. Before they left the stage, Goodman's quintet had become a sextet.

Became a Jazz Sensation

Christian was an immediate sensation and helped bring about Goodman's return to the top of the crowded big band field. The sextet played the New York World's Fair in September of 1939 and was heard on the radio as part of the orchestra's weekly *Camel Caravan* broadcasts. Hammond inserted Christian into an all-star recording session on September 11 with Dizzy Gillespie, Benny Carter, Coleman Hawkins, Ben Web-

ster, Chu Berry, and Lionel Hampton. At its first recording date, the Goodman Sextet put down two classic tracks: one was "Rose Room," the other a piece reportedly created by Christian but released as a Goodman/Hampton composition, "Flying Home." The sextet played Carnegie Hall that Christmas Eve at Hammond's "From Spirituals to Swing" concert, where Christian also sat in with Lester Young and four other members of Count Basie's band as the Kansas City Six. In a survey conducted by *DownBeat* magazine at year's end, Goodman polled as the best big band, his sextet as best small group, and Christian as best guitar player. *Metronome* magazine gave Christian the same honor two or three years in a row.

The Goodman Sextet was one of the most innovative jazz combos of its era, and Christian was the spark that electrified the group. He helped compose some of the group's original pieces, such as "Seven Come Eleven," "AC-DC Current," and "A Smoo-o-o-th One." He also performed for a time with the full Goodman orchestra and was featured on the piece "Solo Flight." When he was done with his evening's work, he frequented after-hours clubs. He was especially fond of Minton's Playhouse on 118th Street in Harlem, where pianist Thelonious Monk and drummer Kenny Clarke were in the house band and Dizzy Gillespie was usually on the scene. The manager at Minton's, former bandleader Teddy Hill, even bought an amplifier so that Christian would not have to drag his uptown every night.

Despite his energy and productivity, it became increasingly clear that Christian was not well. It appears likely he contracted tuberculosis before leaving the Southwest. By the middle of 1940, his coughing fits were evident. Sickness did not slow him down; perhaps unwisely, Christian continued to stay out late at night, fueled by alcohol, marijuana, and music. In the summer of 1941, he collapsed while on tour with Goodman band's. After a few weeks at Bellevue Hospital in Manhattan, he was transferred to Seaview Sanitarium on Staten Island. Although he was expected to recover, after six months in the facility, he came down with pneumonia. Christian died there on March 2, 1942. After a funeral in Harlem, his body was shipped to Oklahoma City. Christian had many disciples among guitarists, not only jazz players such as Wes Montgomery and Les Paul but also blues stars such as B. B. King and rock-and-roll guitarists such as Chuck Berry. Christian was inducted into the Big Band and Jazz Hall of Fame in 1981 and the Rock and Roll Hall of Fame in 1990. In Oklahoma City, a street was named after him in 2006.

Selected discography

The Genius of the Electric Guitar, Columbia/Legacy, 2002.

Sources

Books

Broadbent, Peter, *Charlie Christian,* Ashley Mark, 1997.

Collier, James Lincoln, *Benny Goodman and the Swing Era,* Oxford University Press, 1989.

Gitler, Ira, *Swing to Bop,* Oxford University Press, 1985.

Goins, Wayne E., and Craig R. McKinney, *A Biography of Charlie Christian, Jazz Guitar's King of Swing,* Edwin Mellen Press, 2005.

Hammond, John, *John Hammond on Record,* Summit Books, 1977.

Prial, Dunstan, *The Producer: John Hammond and the Soul of American Music,* Farrar, Straus and Giroux, 2006.

Schuller, Gunther, *The Swing Era: The Development of Jazz, 1930–1945,* Oxford University Press, 1989.

Periodicals

New York Times, October 20, 2002.
Saturday Review, May 17, 1958.

Online

Gerard, Jim, "Eddie Durham: Genius in the Shadows," All About Jazz, November 12, 2012, https://www.allaboutjazz.com/eddie-durham-genius-in-the-shadows-eddie-durham-by-jim-gerard.php (accessed August 7, 2016).

—Roger K. Smith

Margaret A. Dixon

1923(?)–2011

Educator, administrator

Margaret A. Dixon was the first African American to serve as president of AARP (formerly the American Association of Retired Persons), a national advocacy organization for retired people. An educator by profession, Dixon worked for more than 25 years as a teacher and school administrator in the New York City public schools before beginning her second career as a leader of AARP. Dixon began working for the organization as a volunteer in the 1980s in retirement and quickly rose through the ranks to become president in 1996. In that position, she oversaw an association that then comprised some 30 million members, with 2,000 staffers and a budget of $300 million. Even after her final retirement in 1998, when she stepped down as AARP's president, Dixon continued to volunteer for the organization until her death in 2011.

Chose a Career in Education

Dixon was born in Columbia, South Carolina, in the early 1920s. She declined to reveal the exact year of her birth, telling the *Chicago Tribune* in a 1996 interview, "We're all aging, and it doesn't matter what step you're on—as long as you're hopeful and living a productive life a number doesn't matter." Dixon's parents died when she was a girl, and she was raised in Columbia by her grandparents, who instilled in her a great love of learning. She recalled to the *Chicago Tribune* that her grandfather's advice to her had been to "learn everything you can. Get it in your head, and nobody can take it away from you." Dixon grew up in a family of educators, and her grandparents' home was

always filled with books. Academic achievement was taken as a given. There was no celebration when Dixon brought home good grades, only a satisfaction that she was meeting expectations.

Upon graduating high school in the 1940s, Dixon saw that there were few career paths open to African-American women. She chose education as her profession because her race and gender would pose few problems in that field. Dixon attended Allen University, a historically black college in her hometown of Columbia, where she studied education. With her bachelor's degree in hand, Dixon headed for New York City, where she became a teacher in the public school system.

Over the course of 26 years with the New York City public schools, Dixon was a teacher of physically challenged students, director of a computer-assisted early learning program, and, for her final eight years in the system, principal of a large, urban elementary school, P.S. 345 in Brooklyn, for which she developed an innovative bilingual program. As a result of her leadership at P.S. 345, the school was chosen as a campus school for the Brooklyn College Teacher Education Program, for which Dixon served as supervising principal.

After Dixon retired from teaching in 1980, she and her husband, Octavius, returned to their native South Carolina. Back in her home state, Dixon took a position as associate professor and director of teacher education at her alma mater, Allen University, while

At a Glance . . .

Born in 1923(?) in Columbia, SC; died on September 17, 2011, in Clinton, MD; married Octavius Dixon, 1945; children: Kevin, Karen, and Edith. *Education:* Allen University, BA; Hunter College and New York University, MA; Nova Southeastern University, PhD, education; Fordham University, professional diploma in educational leadership.

Career: Educator in the New York City public school system, 1954–80, including teacher of physically challenged students, elementary school principal of P.S. 345, Brooklyn, director of a computer-assisted early learning program, supervising principal of Teacher Education Program at Brooklyn College; Allen University, associate professor and director of teacher education, 1981–86; South Carolina Department of Education, consultant, 1981–86; AARP, national secretary, 1990, vice president, 1992–94, president elect, 1994–96, president, 1996–98.

Awards: Delta Sigma Theta Living Legacy Award for Outstanding Community Service; Ford Foundation Fellowship for graduate study in education leadership; U.S. Office of Education graduate fellowship for study in education of people with disabilities; Women of Courage and Distinction Award, National Association of Colored Women's Clubs, Inc.; Outstanding Graduate Honor, Allen University; "100+ Most Influential Black Americans," *Ebony* magazine, 1997; Living Legacy Award, National Caucus and Center on Black Aged, 1997.

also serving as a consultant to the state's department of education. Along with her husband, Dixon also volunteered with a local literacy program and helped deliver meals to elderly and disabled neighbors.

Served as President of AARP

Dixon and her husband eventually relocated to Clinton, Maryland, a suburb of Washington, DC, to be closer to their three children. It was there that Dixon first became involved with AARP. "A friend said after church 'I volunteered you for a position at AARP as a spokesperson for the Minority Affairs Initiative.' That's how I started in 1988," she told the *Rocky Mountain News* in 1996. Dixon quickly moved up the ranks at AARP. She was elected vice president in 1992 and

then advanced to president-elect in 1994 and president in 1996, becoming the first African American ever to lead the organization. "We would like to think that Margaret Dixon becoming president of AARP—it's just coincidental that she is an African American," Dixon said of herself in an interview with the *Rocky Mountain News.* "However, I have found that we haven't reached that point yet. It is very significant. I have said let's play it down. But the media is playing it up. As I move about the country, I find people are so proud— African Americans, Hispanics, Asians, Native Americans—to see a minority person heading up AARP."

Dixon stepped into a hornet's nest during her tenure as president of AARP. During the 1990s, AARP drew fire, particularly from fiscal conservatives, for its opposition to Social Security and Medicare funding cuts, with some critics, accusing the organization of adhering to outdated "tax and spend" policies. "Far from being a do-gooder senior lobby, AARP is the field artillery in a liberal army dedicated to defending the welfare state," declared an editorial in the *Wall Street Journal.* While Dixon conceded that Social Security and Medicare reform was necessary, she sought to ensure that the programs would not be destroyed in the process. "AARP believes that there should be bipartisan discussions in Congress to come up with real and lasting solutions to preserve and strengthen both of these programs for our children and grandchildren," Dixon said.

AARP's nonprofit status also was questioned during Dixon's term of office. The organization generates revenue from insurance policies, mutual funds, mail-order pharmaceuticals, and other joint ventures with private companies. AARP's income for 1994 was reported as $383 million. In 1995 congressional hearings were initiated by Senator Alan Simpson, a Republican from Wyoming, to investigate AARP's use of a $86 million federal grant to set up a job training program for the elderly; there was some suspicion that funds from the grant had been spent on lobbying activities. The hearings uncovered no wrongdoing on the part of AARP, but the investigation prompted the organization to reform its record-keeping practices. Dixon told the *Chicago Tribune* in 1996 that she believed Simpson had used the hearings to divert AARP's attention from Medicare cuts and to "have us so busy talking about this lobbying thing that we wouldn't have time to pay attention to the Medicare cuts."

Retiring from the AARP presidency in 1998, Dixon told the *Washington Informer* that leading the large and influential organization was "an opportunity I never thought I'd have. It's a rare privilege to be in a position where I can get help for so many people." After Dixon left AARP, she devoted more time to her grandchildren and to hobbies including sewing and crafts, although she also continued to serve on AARP's Executive Committee, Board of Finance Committee,

and National Legislative Council and chaired the AARP Andrus Foundation Board of Trustees.

Dixon lived in Clinton for the rest of her life. After her husband died in 2003, Dixon moved into an assisted living center there. She died of a heart attack on September 17, 2011. Among the many honors that Dixon received during her long career was the Living Legacy Award from the National Caucus and Center on Black Aged, honoring "African Americans who have made and continue to make outstanding contributions to society," as Leonard Hughes reported in the *Washington Post.* Hughes went on to observe, "[Dixon] didn't set out to break any sort of color barrier, but she … discovered it … made her an inspiration to others."

Sources

Periodicals

Chicago Tribune, April 14, 1996, section 14, p. 6.
Consumer's Research, September 1996, p.15–18, 32.
Economist, May 13, 1995, p. 32.
Jet, May 6, 1996, p. 36.
Modern Maturity, March/April 1996, p. 83; May/June 1996, p. 9; July/August 1996, pp. 76–77, 79; September/October 1996, p. 87; November/December 1996, pp. 78–79.
National Review, September 11, 1995, pp. 44–48.
New Pittsburgh Courier, June 8, 1996, p. B6.
Newsweek, May 15, 1995, p. 27.
Philadelphia Tribune, June 7, 1996, p. A1.
Rocky Mountain News (Denver, CO), August 8, 1996, section S, pp. 2–4.
Wall Street Journal, May 25, 1995, p. A14.
Washington Informer, May 22, 1996, supplement, p. 8.
Washington Post, January 19, 1997, p. A23; December 11, 1997; October 4, 2011.

Other

Additional information for this article was provided by the AARP Media Relations Department.

—Mary C. Kalfatovic and J. Sydney Jones

Malachi Favors

1927–2004

Jazz bassist

Favors, Malachi, photograph. Frans Schellekens/Redferns/Getty Images.

An inventive and daringly original bassist, Malachi Favors played an important but widely underappreciated role in the development of avant-garde jazz. As a founding member of the pioneering Art Ensemble of Chicago (AEC), "he was an essential element of the group's artistic success," wrote Chris Kelsey of AllMusic.com, and "a solid team player—hard-swinging and possessing a large, rubbery bass sound in addition to a well-developed sense of his place in the ensemble." Ben Ratliff of the *New York Times* echoed that praise, calling him "concise, direct, and eloquent."

Favors, who as an adult sometimes appended "Magoustous" or, more commonly, "Maghostut" to his surname in a sign of his interest in the culture of ancient Egypt, was born on August 22, 1927, in the small town of Lexington, Mississippi. His birthplace has been the cause of some confusion over the years, with several sources pointing instead to Chicago, where he spent much of his childhood. Val Wilmer of the London *Guardian* traced the error to Favors himself: "like many black people born in the South during that hateful period of lynch-law," Wilmer wrote, "he would claim a northern birthplace." In later years, however,

he seemed to acknowledge the influence of the South on his development, writing, in a comment quoted on the website of jazz artist Kahil El-Zabar, that he "landed in Chicago by way of Lexington, Mississippi, for the purpose of serving my duty as a Music Messenger."

One of 10 children born to preacher Isaac Favors and Maggie Mayfield Favors, he grew up in a strict, churchgoing family that frowned on nonreligious music. In his early teens, however, he was drawn inexorably to jazz and to the bass, thanks in large part to the influence of the great bassist Oscar Pettiford, whom he saw in person at Chicago's famous Regal Theater. "I just like the bass," he recalled in a 1994 interview with Ted Panken of radio station WKCR. "But when I saw Oscar Pettiford with [bandleader] Duke [Ellington], that just blew me away. From then on, you know, I got a bass and tried to learn, and that's when I ran into Wilbur Ware." Ware was a native of Chicago whose self-taught, free-form approach to the bass proved a major influence on Favors.

Although he made rapid progress, Favors's music career did not begin immediately, thanks in part to

At a Glance . . .

Born on August 22, 1927, in Lexington, MS; died on January 30, 2004, in Chicago, IL; son of Isaac Favors (a preacher) and Maggie Mayfield Favors; children: one daughter. *Military service:* U.S. Army, 1950s. *Education:* Attended Woodrow Wilson Junior College, 1960s.

Career: Independent musician, 1950s–2004; toured and recorded with the Art Ensemble of Chicago, 1960s–2000s.

several years of service in the U.S. Army. On his return to Chicago in the mid-1950s, he began slowly, filling in for absent players at clubs around the city. As his reputation grew, he began to attract attention from more established figures, among them the pianist Andrew Hill, whom he backed on a fine album called *So in Love,* recorded around 1956 and released in 1960. He also collaborated extensively around this time with the bandleader and pianist King Fleming and the trumpeters Dizzy Gillespie and Freddie Hubbard. In the early 1960s he began working in the avant-garde style for which he is best known.

While there were undoubtedly a variety of reasons for Favors's move into experimental, free-form jazz, one major factor was his matriculation at Woodrow Wilson Junior College (later Kennedy-King College) around 1963. Soon after his arrival at that school, an important institution on Chicago's South Side, he met fellow students Roscoe Mitchell and Joseph Jarman, both saxophonists who later joined him in the AEC. Another important influence on him in this period was the pianist Muhal Richard Abrams, who served as an informal mentor to Wilson students and others interested in the avant-garde. After serving for a time in a group that Abrams called, fittingly, the Experimental Band, Favors became a founding member of the Association for the Advancement of Creative Musicians (AACM), an arts collective that combined cutting-edge jazz with a strong interest in theater, folklore, civil rights, and black nationalism.

It was under the auspices of the AACM that Favors helped complete *Sound* (1966), a landmark album often regarded as the informal debut of the AEC; although it was released under Mitchell's name, the personnel involved included three of that group's founding members (Favors, Mitchell, and trumpeter Lester Bowie). That trio, soon augmented by Jarman and drummer Phillip Wilson, went on to perform as the Roscoe Mitchell Art Ensemble until 1969, when, during an extended tour of Scandinavia and France, they renamed themselves the Art Ensemble of Chicago.

It was also during that trip to Europe that Favors and his bandmates came into their own, releasing a string of challenging, emotionally powerful albums such as *A Jackson in Your House* (1969) and *Go Home* (1970). On their return to the United States around 1972, they maintained that productivity, even as the activist spirit associated with the 1960s and avant-garde jazz began to recede around the country. Although some of their albums were, perhaps inevitably, better than others, their reputation for innovative, thought-provoking work grew steadily. Favors played a key role in that success, in part through his compositions. Throughout this period he also found time for side projects, most notably a joint album with Abrams called *Sightsong* in 1976 and a solo effort, *Natural & Spiritual,* two years later, but his primary focus remained the AEC. A magnetic presence on stage, he often wore costumes designed to reflect his intense interest in spirituality and early history. Those accouterments, however, did not overshadow his formidable technique on the bass and on several other instruments that he added to his repertoire over the years, including the balafon (a wooden xylophone from West Africa) and the harmonica.

Despite declining health, Favors remained active professionally until the last weeks of his life. Diagnosed with pancreatic cancer, he died in Chicago on January 30, 2004, at age 76. Less than a year before his passing, he completed a final album with the AEC. Titled *The Meeting* (2003), it prominently featured one of his own compositions, a haunting piece called "It's the Sign of the Times."

Selected discography

Roscoe Mitchell, *Sound,* Delmark, 1966.
Art Ensemble of Chicago, *A Jackson in Your House,* BYG, 1969.
Art Ensemble of Chicago, *Go Home,* Galloway, 1970.
(With Muhal Richard Abrams) *Sightsong,* Black Saint, 1976.
Natural & Spiritual, AECO, 1978.
Art Ensemble of Chicago, *Urban Bushmen,* ECM, 1982.
Art Ensemble of Chicago, *The Alternate Express,* DIW, 1989.
Art Ensemble of Chicago, *The Meeting* (includes "It's the Sign of the Times"), Pi, 2003.

Sources

Periodicals

Guardian (London), February 10, 2004.
New York Times, February 9, 2004.

Online

Kelsey, Chris, "Malachi Favors: Artist Biography by Chris Kelsey," AllMusic.com, http://www.allmusic

.com/artist/malachi-favors-mn0000668969/biography (accessed October 1, 2016).

"Malachi Favors Maghostut," KahilElZabar.net, http://www.kahilelzabar.net/favors.htm (accessed October 1, 2016).

Panken, Ted, "Lester Bowie & Malachi Favors: November 22, 1994, WKCR-FM, New York," Jazz House.org, http://www.jazzhouse.org/library/?read=panken8 (accessed October 1, 2016).

—R. Anthony Kugler

Roxane Gay

1974—

Writer, educator

Roxane Gay is an American writer of fiction and essays. Although she began publishing her work in the late 1990s, it was not until 2014 that she rose to literary prominence with the publication of her first novel, *An Untamed State,* and a collection of essays titled *Bad Feminist.* A survivor of childhood sexual assault, Gay is particularly concerned with writing about the experience of trauma and its aftermath. Her work also explores topics in contemporary popular culture as well as issues dealing with race, body image, sexuality, and desire. Gay's writing has appeared in publications such as *Bookforum,* the *Los Angeles Times,* the *New York Times, Time,* and *Virginia Quarterly Review.*

Found Solace in Writing and Reading

Roxane Gay was born on October 15, 1974, in Omaha, Nebraska, the eldest of three children of Haitian immigrants who had moved to the United States in their late teens. Her father was a civil engineer whose job required the family to move frequently, spending stints in Colorado, Illinois, Virginia, and New Jersey. Eventually they returned to Omaha and settled there. Gay's parents intentionally raised their children with a consciousness of their Haitian heritage, taking family trips to Haiti in the summers and building ties with Omaha's small Haitian-American community.

Growing up in a strict Catholic household, Gay was a self-professed "good girl." She recalled earning straight

As, respecting her elders, and doing as she was told. Although she was close with her two younger brothers, Gay was otherwise shy and socially awkward, preferring to lose herself in the pages of a book rather than try to make friends. In addition to being a voracious reader, she began writing at a young age, drawing little villages on paper napkins and writings stories about the people who lived there. In spite of her elaborate inner life, however, Gay recalled being a lonely child, plagued by a sense of longing for something or someone to fill the void that seemed to exist at her core.

It was this sense of loneliness that led Gay, at age 12, to entrust both her heart and her physical safety to a boy from school. He ended up betraying her, leading her to an abandoned hunting cabin in the woods where he and his friends held her against her will and sexually assaulted her. As Gay recalled in her essay "What We Hunger For," which appeared on the website The Rumpus in 2012, "They kept me there for hours. It was as bad as you might expect. The repercussions linger."

Indeed, Gay was deeply traumatized by the experience. For years she kept the truth of her victimization a secret from her family, her teachers, and everyone in her life, presenting a tough exterior in order to cover up her sense of being permanently defiled and broken inside. Among other defenses, Gay put on significant weight as a way to exert control over her body. Speaking with the London *Guardian* in 2014, she explained that the boys who assaulted her had taken away the body she had known and "ruined it. And so, when I ate, I got to

At a Glance . . .

Born Roxane Gay on October 15, 1974, in Omaha, NE. *Education:* University of Nebraska–Lincoln, MA, creative writing; Michigan Technological University, PhD, rhetoric and technical communication, 2010.

Career: *PANK,* founding editor, 2006; Tiny Hardcore Press, founder, 2010; Eastern Illinois University, assistant professor, 2010–14; Purdue University, associate professor of creative writing, 2014—.

Awards: Freedom to Write Award, PEN Center USA, 2015.

Addresses: *Literary agent*—Maria Massie, Lippincott Massie McQuilkin, 27 West 20th St., Suite 305, New York, NY 10011. *Web*—http://www.roxanegay.com. *Twitter*—@rgay.

make my body into what I wanted it to be, which is a fortress."

Discovered Her Literary Voice

In high school at Phillips Exeter Academy, a prestigious boarding school in New Hampshire, Gay was socially isolated and miserable. She channeled her pain into writing short stories that were filled with sexual violence. An English teacher, Rex McGuinn, recognized Gay's writing ability, as well as the emotional distress that resounded in her work. McGuinn helped Gay find a counselor and became an important mentor to her. As she told the *Guardian,* he encouraged her "to make these stories not just this purging of whatever ... He taught me craft, and he also taught me discipline. He told me to write *every day.* I was very impressionable, and so I write *every day.*"

After graduating from Exeter in 1992, Gay went on to Yale University, but she continued to struggle with the trauma of her sexual assault. At the outset of her second year, she abruptly abandoned her studies, traveling to Arizona with a man more than twice her age whom she had met online. When her parents finally tracked her down a year later, she returned to Nebraska and finished her undergraduate studies closer to home. Gay went on to earn a master's degree in English with an emphasis in creative writing from the University of Nebraska, Lincoln, followed by a doctorate in rhetoric and technical communication from Michigan Technological University in 2010. During her time at Michigan Tech, in collaboration with the poet M. Bartley Seigel, Gay cofounded *PANK,* an online literary magazine featuring new voices in experimental poetry and prose.

Much of Gay's early published writing was erotic fiction. In 2004 her story "A Cool Dry Place" was included in *The Best American Erotica,* an anthology edited by Susie Bright. In 2010 Gay earned her first book credit as editor of the anthology *Girl Crush: Women's Erotic Fantasies.* Her first book of her own writing, *Ayiti* (2010), is a collection of distinct, often brief, individual pieces depicting Haitian life and culture as it exists in Haiti and in the United States. Formally, *Ayiti* blurs the lines between poetry, fiction, and essay. Thematically, the book challenges the pervasive media stereotype of Haiti as a destitute, backward, and desperate country, even as many of its characters must recognize the reality that their beloved homeland is an untenable place for them to stay.

Although it was well-reviewed in *Necessary Fiction* and a number of other online magazines, *Ayiti* amounted to a quiet literary debut. In the next few years, Gay began her teaching career as assistant professor of English at Eastern Illinois University in Charleston. She continued to serve as coeditor of *PANK,* while writing prolifically and publishing her work widely in multiple online forums. During this time, Gay founded Tiny Hardcore Press, an independent "micropress," as she described it for the website The Lit Pub in 2011, dedicated to publishing pocket-sized books that are "small in stature but grand in reach and spirit."

Published First Novel

In 2014 Gay published her first novel, *An Untamed State* (2014), establishing herself as one of the most compelling voices in contemporary American fiction. The story is narrated in the first person by Mireille, a well-to-do Haitian-American woman who travels to Port-au-Prince with her husband and infant son to visit her wealthy parents. Upon their arrival, however, Mireille's seemingly charmed life takes a fateful turn when she is kidnapped at gunpoint by a gang of men seeking to extort a million-dollar ransom from her father. Contrary to her initial assumption that the situation will be quickly resolved as a business transaction, Mireille is held hostage for 13 days, during which time she is brutally raped and tortured, while her proud father refuses to give in to the kidnappers' demands. As the story unfolds, Gay chronicles her protagonist's physical and psychological ordeal with unflinching immediacy, forcing the reader to consider how it is possible to survive such a savage dismantling of the self. Ron Charles of the *Washington Post* described the novel as "horrible, hypnotic and perfectly constructed to frustrate any search for comfort or resolution," confessing that the power and precision of Gay's writing had made it "some of the most emotionally exhausting material I've ever read."

With the publication of Gay's essay collection, *Bad Feminist,* also in 2014, critics gained an even greater

appreciation for the range of her literary and intellectual agility. In her introduction to the collection, Gay explained that labeling herself a "bad feminist" is a reflection of her own ambivalence toward the limitations of conventional American feminism (especially its failure to adequately address issues of race, class, and sexual identity) and her sense that her own views and persuasions are perhaps too "messy" and imperfect to include her within its purist ranks. The essays that follow, many of them previously published, make a strong case for broadening the feminist umbrella, as Gay pivots back and forth between her personal experiences and her unique perspectives on race, gender, politics, and entertainment in our society. Writing for the *Guardian,* Kira Cochrane describes the title essay as "a clarion call to bad feminists everywhere—for pluralism, collective effort and mutual respect—and the most persuasive feminist recruitment drive in recent memory."

In 2014 Gay became associate professor of English at Purdue University in Indiana. The following year she received the PEN Center USA Freedom to Write Award, which recognizes "individuals and organizations that have produced notable work in the face of extreme adversity or demonstrated exceptional courage in the defense of free expression." In 2016 Gay was at work on her second novel, while the literary world awaited the release of her much-anticipate memoir, *Hunger.* She also was engaged in a collaboration with fellow black writers Ta-Nehisi Coates and Yona Harvey to create World of Wakanda, a companion to Marvel Comics' popular Black Panther series that will be centered on a female character. Speaking to the *New York Times,* Gay admitted that although her literary agent was apprehensive about her decision to add another project to her already full plate, it was a chance she could not pass up: "the opportunity to write black women and queer black women into the Marvel universe, there's no saying no to that."

Selected works

(Editor) *Girl Crush: Women's Erotic Fantasies,* Cleis Press, 2010.
Ayiti, Artistically Declined Press, 2011.
An Untamed State, Black Cat, 2014.
Bad Feminist: Essays, Harper Perennial, 2014.

Sources

Periodicals

Guardian (London), August 2, 2014.
New York Times, July 23, 2016.
Washington Post, May 27, 2014.

Online

Essmaker, Tina, "Roxane Gay" (interview), The Great Discontent, June 3, 2014, http://thegreatdiscontent.com/interview/roxane-gay (accessed August 9, 2016).
"Freedom to Write," PEN Center USA, https://penusa.org/programs/freedom-to-write (accessed September 13, 2016).
Gay, Roxane, "This Is Tiny Hardcore Press," The Lit Pub, July 5, 2011, http://thelitpub.com/this-is-tiny-hardcore-press/ (accessed August 10, 2016).
PANK, http://pankmagazine.com/ (accessed September 13, 2016).
Roxane Gay, http://www.roxanegay.com/ (accessed August 9, 2016).

—Erin Brown

Yaa Gyasi

1989—

Writer

Yaa Gyasi is a Ghanaian-American novelist who made her literary debut at age 26 with the publication of her highly anticipated novel, *Homegoing* (2016). The ambitious, sweeping narrative begins on the Gold Coast of Ghana during the 18th century and traces the impact of the transatlantic slave trade across seven generations to present-day America. The novel takes its title from a traditional African-American belief that dates to the era of slavery, whereby the soul of a deceased slave was liberated to return to his or her ancestral home in Africa in a spiritual journey known as a "homegoing." Written while Gyasi was in graduate school at the Iowa Writers' Workshop, the manuscript for *Homegoing* reportedly sparked a bidding war among 10 publishers at the 2015 London Book Fair, ultimately garnering the author a seven-figure advance. Reviews of *Homegoing* were overwhelmingly positive, announcing Gyasi as an important new voice in contemporary fiction.

Yaa Gyasi was born in 1989 in Mampong, a small town in the Ashanti region of Ghana. She was two years old when her family moved to the United States so that her father, a scholar of French and Francophone African literature, could finish his doctoral degree at Ohio State University. In the years that followed, as Gyasi's father embarked on his academic career, the family lived for periods in Illinois and Tennessee. Gyasi was 10 years old when the family finally settled in Huntsville, Alabama.

Raised in a Pentecostal Christian household, Gyasi was a very shy child. Her only close companions were her two brothers, with whom she shared the unique and often alienating experience of growing up Ghanaian in the American South. Her skin color set her apart from her mostly white classmates, but neither did she seem to belong among her black peers. As she recalled to Jennifer Maloney of the *Wall Street Journal,* "[O]ne of the things I found most difficult was trying to figure out where I fit in, particularly because while my family is black, obviously we aren't African-American." Further, she explained, "Because I grew up in predominantly white spaces, I think it could be difficult to figure out how to navigate America's racial tension."

An avid reader from an early age, Gyasi came of age with a particular love of Victorian literature, including the works of Charles Dickens, Charlotte Brontë, and George Eliot. It was not until she was 17 and a senior in high school that she encountered her first novel by a black woman, reading *Song of Solomon* by Toni Morrison. The experience was revelatory for Gyasi, as she recalled to *Vogue* in 2016: "That was the book that made me want to be a writer, not just because of how amazing the book is but because it was the first time I saw that a black woman was doing this, and at the top of her field. I felt like, oh, OK. This is a possible thing for me, and it can be intelligent and beautiful: all of the things that I love about fiction."

Gyasi studied English literature at Stanford University. In the summer of 2009, she was in Ghana on a research fellowship when she visited Cape Coast Castle, one of about 40 such "castles" (or fortresses) on the coast of what is now Ghana that served as commercial hubs for the transatlantic slave trade. Gyasi had

At a Glance . . .

Born Yaa Gyasi in 1989 in Mampong, Ghana. *Education:* Stanford University, BA, English literature, 2011; University of Iowa, MFA, creative writing, 2014.

Career: Novelist, 2016—.

Addresses: *Home*—Berkeley, CA. *Office*—c/o Eric Simonoff, William Morris Agency, 11 Madison Ave., 18th Floor, New York, NY 10010.

a profound and visceral experience at the castle, as she learned how the British colonial officers lived in luxury in the upper regions of the building, often taking African women as their wives, while thousands of kidnapped men, women, and children were held captive below, packed into sweltering underground dungeons before being shipped across the Atlantic Ocean to slavery in Americas. The young writer knew immediately that the Cape Coast Castle would serve as the point of origin for her novel.

After receiving her bachelor's degree from Stanford in 2011, Gyasi spent brief stint working for a start-up company in San Francisco before she began her graduate studies at the University of Iowa Writers' Workshop in 2012. The two-year master of fine arts program provided her the time and space she needed to devote herself to the research and writing of *Homegoing.* Graduating in 2014 with a completed manuscript in hand, she moved to Berkeley, California, with her boyfriend, who is also a writer. The following spring, with representation from Eric Simonoff of the William Morris Agency, she sold the novel to Alfred A. Knopf for a reported $1,000,000.

Homegoing begins in 18th-century Ghana, where the lives of two half-sisters dramatically diverge: the elder sister, Effia, is taken into marriage by a British officer and lives with him in the comfortable upper quarters of Cape Coast Castle; the younger sister, Esi, is kidnapped and, passing through the castle's horrific dungeon, sold into slavery in America. Gyasi traces the consequences and reverberations of the sisters' separate fates through their descendants over the course of 250 years, with each chapter devoted to a representa-

tive of the next generation in the lineage. As the narrative alternates between Ghana and the United States, Gyasi illustrates the ways in which history can act as a powerful determinant in people's lives, leaving them bereft of any real sense of agency or purpose.

Among the most distinguishing features of *Homegoing* is Gyasi's unflinching examination of the ways in which West Africans were complicit in the development and perpetuation of the transatlantic slave trade. The most prophetic summation of slavery's lingering curse comes from one of Effia's descendants, a wise old woman who tells her son, "There are people who have done wrong because they could not see the result of the wrong." Nonetheless, she continues, "Evil begets evil. It grows. It transmutes, so that sometimes you cannot see that the evil in the world began as the evil in your home."

Beyond the media sensation that accompanied the extraordinary price of the book's acquisition, *Homegoing* was widely hailed as a remarkable literary achievement. Ta-Nehisi Coates, winner of the National Book Award for his nonfiction examination of race in America, *Between the World and Me* (2015), drew attention to Gyasi's debut when he tweeted, "Finished Yaa Gyasi's 'Homegoing' yesterday. Thought it was a monster when I started. Felt it was a monster when I was done." In *Vogue,* Megan O'Grady noted the apparent influence of Toni Morrison in Gyasi's work, writing that "she shares Morrison's uncanny ability to crystalize, in a single event, slavery's moral and emotional fallout." At the same time O'Grady identified Gyasi's unique talent in "her ability to connect it so explicitly to the present day: No novel has better illustrated the way in which racism became institutionalized in this country."

Selected writings

Homegoing, Alfred A. Knopf, 2016.

Sources

Periodicals

New Yorker, May 30, 2016.
San Francisco Chronicle, June 28, 2016.
Time, June 6, 2016.
Vogue, May 25, 2016.
Wall Street Journal, May 26, 2016.

—Erin Brown

Michael S. Harper

1938–2016

Writer, educator

Michael S. Harper was regarded as one of the finest American poets during his lifetime; among African-American poets working in the academic world, he was the unquestioned dean. His complex works do not yield their deeper contents easily upon cursory reading, but Harper's poetry has been widely taught in literature classes and urged on readers by the many honors he received. Those who make the effort will find a body of work in which the African-American past is raised to a level of universal tragedy by virtue of Harper's unique style—one that weaves the personal, the historical, and the musical into a unique tapestry. As a professor at Brown University for more than 40 years, Harper fostered the careers of many younger African-American poets of various styles.

Encountered Racism in His Youth

Harper was born in Brooklyn, New York, on March 18, 1938; his father was a postal supervisor and his mother a medical secretary. One aspect of his childhood that had a lasting influence was his parents' large collection of jazz recordings; another was his family's move to Los Angeles in 1951. The previously segregated neighborhood in which they settled saw fire bombings when blacks began to move in.

Pressured by his parents to follow in the footsteps of his maternal grandfather and become a physician, Harper was an indifferent student at Dorsey High School. School staff who placed him in vocational-track classes did not help his motivation, although his father showed up at school to insist that his son be allowed to pursue

a college preparatory curriculum. Enrolling at Los Angeles State College (now California State University, Los Angeles), Harper took pre-med classes while holding down a full-time job at the post office. There he encountered well-educated African Americans whom the institutions of racism had robbed of the chance to utilize their talents; Harper seemed destined to suffer the same fate after a white zoology professor pressured him to give up his medical career, telling him that blacks were unable to survive the rigors of medical school.

Harper blossomed as a student for the first time in his English courses, where he was especially impressed by Ralph Ellison's 1952 novel *Invisible Man* and by the spiritually intense writings of the English Romantic poet John Keats. Harper's own interest in writing, which had first stirred while he was in high school, inspired him to enroll in the prestigious Iowa Writers' Workshop at the University of Iowa in 1961. There Harper was once again dispirited by discrimination in the form of segregated housing arrangements, but he began to focus seriously on poetry. He completed his master of fine arts degree in creative writing in 1963.

Published First Volume of Poetry

During the 1960s, Harper taught at schools on the West Coast—Pasadena City College, Contra Costa College, Lewis and Clark College, and California State College (now University) at Hayward. He had poems published in academic journals and other periodicals and began to bring together the materials that in 1970 would be published as his first book of poems, *Dear*

At a Glance . . .

Born Michael Steven Harper on March 18, 1938, in New York, NY; died on May 7, 2016, in Rhinebeck, NY; son of Walter Warren (a postal worker) and Katherine (Johnson) Harper (a secretary); married Shirley Ann Buffington, December 24, 1965 (divorced); children: Roland, Patrice, Rachel. *Education:* Los Angeles City College, AA, 1959; Los Angeles State College (now California State University, Los Angeles), BA, 1961, MA, 1963; University of Iowa, MFA, 1963.

Career: Pasadena City College, instructor in English, 1962; Contra Costa College, instructor in English, 1964–68; Lewis and Clark College, poet in residence, 1968–69; California State College (now University), Hayward, associate professor of English, 1968–69; Brown University, associate professor, 1970–73, full professor, 1973–2013.

Awards: Center for Advanced Study Fellowship, University of Illinois, 1970–71; Black Academy of Arts and Letters Award, 1972, for *History Is Your Own Heartbeat;* National Institute of Arts and Letters Award and American Academy Award in Literature, both 1972; Guggenheim Fellowship, 1976; National Endowment for the Arts Creative Writing Award, 1977; Melville Cane Award, Poetry Society of America, 1978, for *Images of Kin;* Robert Hayden Poetry Award, United Negro College Fund, 1990; Frost Medal, Poetry Society of America, 2008.

John, Dear Coltrane. Harper submitted the book to an annual competition sponsored by the University of Pittsburgh, and it was at that point that the U.S. poetry establishment realized that it had a major new talent on its hands.

Dear John, Dear Coltrane was inspired by Harper's friendship with the recently deceased jazz saxophonist John Coltrane, but the poems in the book address Coltrane and his music only obliquely. Instead, Coltrane serves as a reference point around which Harper connects personal and familial experiences with black history and with the American experience in general. In one widely quoted reflection on his status as an African-American poet, Harper said, "I don't believe in either/or. I believe in both/and. I'm not a Cartesian poet." *Dear John, Dear Coltrane* did not win the Pittsburgh prize, but in 1970, it earned Harper a professorship in the English Department at Brown University in Providence, Rhode Island, where he taught for the rest of his

career. *Dear John, Dear Coltrane* was nominated for a National Book Award in 1971.

Dear John, Dear Coltrane demonstrates several features of Harper's mature style, including a fascination with black music and an attempt to reproduce some of its qualities in words. Although he avoids the obviously rhythmic quality cultivated by other African-American poets (critic Amiri Baraka once dubbed him the "rhythmless Michael Harper"), his poems capture the subtleties of jazz—its capacity for allusion, for homage, and for wise commentary. The structure of the book—disparate poems united by a theme that has both personal and cultural resonance—was typical of Harper's later works.

In his next book, *History Is Your Own Heartbeat,* for example, Harper begins with a personal and seemingly everyday topic: his mother-in-law's suffering from gallstones. That subject is expanded into a range of symbolic meanings—the gallstones become symbolic of various kinds of American illness, both spiritual and physical, among whites as well as blacks. His *Images of Kin* (1977) and other books likewise address not only members of Harper's own family but also musicians and African-American leaders of the past. *Images of Kin* made explicit Harper's complex attempt to place himself within history: it is structured in reverse chronological order. *Images of Kin* earned Harper another National Book Award nomination in 1978.

Embraced "Modalities" in His Poetry

Harper was known for speaking in an unusual mixture of academic theoretical language and African-American vernacular speech. He used the term "modality" to describe aspects of his poetic technique, generating vigorous discussion among readers and critics as to what he meant by the word. In music, modality is the structuring of a composition around a certain selection of tones and melodic gestures, a subtle flavor that is imparted to a piece of music by its raw materials. Harper also drew contrasts between the idea of a poetic mode and the dualistic European philosophical outlook that divides the world into body and mind, life and spirit, and, for that matter, white and black; for Harper a mode was a unified way of looking at the world. "Our mode is our jam session / of tradition, / past in this present moment / articulated, blown through / with endurance, / an un-reaching extended/improvised love of past masters," Harper wrote in his poem "Corrected Review."

Harper continued to write, although not quite so prolifically, for many more years. His book *Healing Song for the Inner Ear* appeared in 1984, and *Honorable Amendments* in 1995. His volume of collected works, *Songlines in Michaeltree* (2000), also included new poems. During the 1990s, Harper edited

or coedited several collections of African-American poetry, including the *Vintage Book of African American Poetry* (2000). In 2009 he published *Use Trouble: Poems,* his first major collection in nearly a decade. Reviewing the volume for *Booklist,* Donna Seaman wrote, "This virtuosic, symphonic, embracive collection is a memoir, a reader's notebook, a professor's lesson plan, a family scrapbook, and a poet's book of gratitude.... Whether he is telling nuanced tales of friends or family, or celebrating the awakening power of art, Harper perceives life's interconnectivity and the perpetual cycle of sorrow and joy."

Harper served as the first poet laureate of the state of Rhode Island from 1988 to 1993. In 2008 the Poetry Society of America awarded him the prestigious Frost Medal for distinguished lifetime achievement in American poetry. Upon his retirement from teaching at Brown in 2013, he received many expressions of gratitude from the students and colleagues with whom he had worked. In an essay for the *Worcester Review,* George Makari summarized Harper's extraordinary influence, writing, "Over his august career, Michael S. Harper has taught hundreds of students literature, and for many others, myself included, he deeply entered our personal lives, challenged us to rethink who we thought we were, asked us to leave behind childhood and enter a kind of creative crisis. To take that step into our own underworlds required a guide. Michael provided that: he had been down there before, and he recognized who we were in a manner that predicted and created the future."

Harper died on May 7, 2016, at age 78, in Rhinebeck, New York.

Selected writings

Dear John, Dear Coltrane, University of Pittsburgh Press, 1970.
History Is Your Own Heartbeat, University of Illinois Press, 1971.
Song: I Want a Witness, University of Pittsburgh Press, 1972.
Debridement, Doubleday, 1973.
Nightmare Begins Responsibility, University of Illinois Press, 1974.
Images of Kin, University of Illinois Press, 1977.
Healing Song for the Inner Ear, University of Illinois Press, 1985.
Honorable Amendments, University of Illinois Press, 1995.
Songlines in Michaeltree, University of Illinois Press, 2000.
Selected Poems, Arc Publications, 2002.
Use Trouble: Poems, University of Illinois Press, 2009.

Sources

Periodicals

African American Review, Fall 2000, p. 501.
Booklist, February 15, 1994, p. 1054; February 15, 2001, p. 1102; February 1, 2009.
New York Times, May 10, 2016.
Publishers Weekly, November 27, 1995, p. 66; February 7, 2000, p. 72; August 28, 2000, p. 79.
Worcester Review, vol. 35, no. 1/2 (March 2014), pp. 123–128.

Online

"Michael S. Harper," Poetry Foundation, https://www.poetryfoundation.org/poems-and-poets/poets/detail/michael-s-harper (accessed September 19, 2016).
"Poet and Professor Emeritus Michael S. Harper," Brown University, May 11, 2016, https://news.brown.edu/articles/2016/05/harper (accessed September 19, 2016).

—James M. Manheim and Erin Brown

Oliver W. Harrington

1912–1995

Cartoonist, writer

Satirist and political cartoonist Oliver W. Harrington was little known in the United States during his lifetime except to readers of black newspapers of the 1930s and 1940s. After World War II, Harrington produced a large body of work, much of it dealing with issues of race and class, from his home base in Paris and later East Germany. Throughout his career, Harrington was a key figure in the African-American intellectual and artistic community, counting among his closest friends such luminaries as writers Richard Wright and Langston Hughes. Hughes once said that he considered Harrington to be America's greatest black cartoonist. During the 1990s, the publication of a book Harrington's essays and a book of his cartoons shed new light on Harrington's life and art, finally giving him the attention that those familiar with his work from his early days as a political cartoonist long believed he deserved.

Found Solace in Drawing

Harrington was born in Valhalla, New York, on Valentine's Day of 1912, the son of a black father and a white mother. His father had come to New York from North Carolina to seek work on the many construction projects that were then under way in the area; his mother was a Hungarian Jew from Budapest. Growing up in a multicultural household and in a diverse community where many different ethnic groups were represented, "Harrington grew up unable to remember which of his friends were white or black," M. Thomas

Inge wrote in his introduction to *Dark Laughter: The Satiric Art of Oliver W. Harrington.*

Harrington's first brushes with racism took place after his family, which included two brothers and a sister, moved to the South Bronx when he was about seven years old. Although his new neighborhood was as racially mixed as his old one, relations among ethnic groups were not as harmonious. An event that took place at school when Harrington was in the sixth grade helped shaped his views on racism and provided the spark for his career as an artist. One day, a teacher ordered Harrington and another boy, the only African Americans in the class, to stand at the front of the room. She pointed a finger at them and told the class, "Never, never forget these two belong in the trash." As the class erupted in laughter, Harrington was crushed. Over the following days, he found comfort in drawing. The drawings made him feel so much better that he began to think about becoming a cartoonist.

After graduating from DeWitt Clinton High School in 1929, Harrington moved to Harlem, where he made the acquaintance of some of the most important black writers of the day. He developed a close friendship with Langston Hughes, who served as a mentor to him. Harrington supported himself during this time by doing freelance art work while taking classes at the National Academy of Design. His first professional success came in 1932, when he placed several of his political cartoons in two black newspapers, the *National News* and the *New York State Contender.*

At a Glance . . .

Born Oliver Wendell Harrington on February 14, 1912, in Valhalla, NY; died on November 2, 1995, in Berlin, Germany; married Helma Richter (an economist and journalist); children: Oliver Jr. *Education:* Attended National Academy of Design; Yale University, BFA, 1940.

Career: Freelance political cartoonist, from 1932; *People's Voice,* art director, 1942–43; *Pittsburgh Courier,* war correspondent, 1944; National Association for the Advancement of Colored People (NAACP), director of public relations, 1946–47; illustrated *The Runaway Elephant,* 1950; contributor to several East German publications, from 1961; *Daily World,* contributor, 1968–late 1970s; Michigan State University, School of Journalism, artist-in-residence, 1994.

Awards: American Institute of Graphic Arts Award, 1951, for *The Runaway Elephant;* Award for Special Achievement, Swann Foundation, 1992.

Created the Character "Bootsie"

Harrington soon began landing steady assignments, becoming a regular contributor to many of the best-known black newspapers in the United States, including the *New York Amsterdam News, Pittsburgh Courier,* and *Baltimore Afro American.* In 1935 Harrington began drawing *Dark Laughter,* a single-panel cartoon, for the *Amsterdam News.* In December of that year, Harrington's most famous character, Bootsie, made his debut in that strip. Bootsie was an ordinary African-American man contending with racism in everyday American society. The character became immensely popular, and Harrington quickly was known as one of the top black cartoonists in the country. Bootsie appeared in various publications for nearly three decades, and the strip was the first black comic to receive recognition from a national audience.

Harrington enrolled in Yale University's School of the Fine Arts in 1936 to study painting and art history while continuing to support himself through his cartooning. He completed his bachelor of fine arts degree in 1940. Two years later Harrington landed his first full-time job, working as art director for the *People's Voice,* a progressive weekly newspaper founded by the Baptist clergyman and later congressman Adam Clayton Powell Jr. Harrington brought Bootsie and *Dark Laughter* with him and contributed editorial cartoons and other illustrations to the paper as well. The following year, Harrington left the *People's Voice* to work primarily for the *Pittsburgh Courier,* where his duties were more varied and challenging. At the *Courier* he introduced *Jive Gray,* an adventure comic strip that addressed World War II from an African-American perspective.

In January of 1944, the *Courier* sent Harrington abroad to cover the war in North Africa and Europe. While reporting from Italy, he met Walter White, and executive for the National Association for the Advancement of Colored People (NAACP). White was so impressed with Harrington's work that after the war, he invited the artist to develop a public relations department for the NAACP. Harrington took on the job in 1946, and later that same year, he debated U.S. Attorney General Tom Clark on the topic of "The Struggle for Justice as a World Force." During the debate, Harrington took Clark to task for failing to come up with a single conviction despite a massive, much-publicized federal investigation of a lynching of an African American in Monroe, Georgia.

Left the United States for Europe

Harrington left the NAACP in 1947 and returned to drawing full time. Over the next few years, he continued drawing Bootsie, as well as a steady stream of political and sports cartoons. He also tried his hand at book illustration, including the pictures for 1950's *The Runaway Elephant,* a well-received children's book by Ellen F. Tarry. Around this time, Harrington came under the scrutiny of Senator Joseph McCarthy's House Un-American Activities Committee, formed to investigate individuals and organizations suspected of having communist ties or engaging in subversive activities. Harrington's visibility as a spokesman for the NAACP—and the aggressive position on civil rights he had taken during his time with the organization—had drawn the committee's attention. To avoid discrediting the NAACP, Harrington chose to leave the United States for Paris in 1951.

At the time of Harrington's arrival, Paris was bustling with African-American expatriates. The community of black intellectuals and artists that gathered in the city included writers Richard Wright and Chester Himes and painter Beauford Delaney. In his autobiography, *My Life of Absurdity,* Himes described Harrington as "the center of the American community on the Left Bank in Paris, white and black." During his stay in Paris, Harrington supported himself primarily by contributing cartoons to the *Pittsburgh Courier* and *Chicago Defender,* sending his work through the mail. Despite his absence from the country, his cartoon anthology, *Bootsie and Others,* was published in the United States in 1958, with an admiring introduction by Langston Hughes.

In 1960 Wright—with whom Harrington had become extremely close—died suddenly; shortly thereafter,

Harrington wrote an article for *Ebony* titled "The Last Days of Richard Wright," in which he outlined the suspicious circumstances surrounding Wright's death. With Wright gone, Paris was no longer as appealing to Harrington, and in 1961 he traveled to East Berlin. There he considered an offer from the publisher Aufbau, which had invited Harrington to illustrate a series of English-language classics.

While Harrington was visiting East Berlin, the Berlin Wall dividing the city was erected, and he unexpectedly found himself trapped there without the proper paperwork to leave. Harrington soon realized that his prospects for work there were quite good, however, and so he settled in to stay. The communist audience in East Germany appreciated his political cartoons dealing with racism and poverty, and he became a regular contributor to some of East Germany's most popular magazines, including *Eulenspiegel* and *Das Magazine*. Harrington's take on U.S. affairs appealed especially to East German students and intellectuals, among whom he developed a loyal following. In 1964 Harrington met Helma Richter, a radio journalist. The two eventually were married and had a son, Oliver Jr. Bootsie finally was put into retirement in 1963, although Harrington continued creating political cartoons for a variety of publications.

Reflected on His Emigration

During the late 1960s, Harrington was invited to provide drawings and cartoons for the New York *Daily World,* a communist newspaper formerly known as the *Worker,* after a friend of his was named as its new editor. The *Daily World* published a collection of Harrington's work called *Soul Shots* in 1972. To celebrate the release of that book, Harrington made his first visit to the United States since leaving the country more than 20 years earlier. Upon his return to Europe, Harrington wrote "Look Homeward, Baby," a piece for *Freedomways* magazine in which he compared how America looked to him upon his return to his memories of Harlem in the 1940s.

During the rest of the 1970s and the 1980s, Harrington drew cartoons in East Germany while remaining little known in the United States. Harrington did not set foot on American soil again until 1991, when he was invited by Walter O. Evans, a Detroit surgeon and collector of African-American art. During that visit, Harrington delivered a speech at Detroit's Wayne State University called "Why I Left America," in he which he detailed the circumstances that had led him to emigrate 40 years earlier. Despite being an expatriate for so long, Harrington always considered himself an American.

Harrington's speech lent its title to a collection of nine of his essays that was published in 1993. That same year, *Dark Laughter: The Satiric Art of Oliver W. Harrington,* was issued, a collection of cartoons spanning his career. The publication of the two books led to Harrington's invitation to spend a semester at Michigan State University as an artist-in-residence in its school of journalism. During his time there, Harrington led a seminar focused on the role political cartoons play in journalism.

In his later years, Harrington found it difficult to continue working because of his declining health. Arthritis made it difficult for him to hold a pencil, which frustrated the artist, who still had ideas that he wanted to get onto paper. Harrington died of a heart attack in Berlin on November 2, 1995, at age 84. After his death, the Oliver Wendell Harrington Cartoon Art Collection was established at the Walter O. Evans Collection of African American Art in Savannah, Georgia.

Selected writings

Bootsie and Others (cartoon anthology), Dodd, Mead & Co., 1958.
Soul Shots (cartoon anthology), Daily World, 1972.
Dark Laughter: The Satiric Art of Oliver W. Harrington, University Press of Mississippi, 1993.
Why I Left America and Other Essays, University Press of Mississippi, 1993.

Sources

Books

Harrington, Oliver W., *Why I Left America and Other Essays,* University Press of Mississippi, 1993.
Inge, M. Thomas, "Introduction," in *Dark Laughter: The Satiric Art of Oliver W. Harrington,* University Press of Mississippi, 1993.

Periodicals

African American Review 44, no. 3 (Fall 2011), pp. 353–372.
Black Scholar 26, no. 1 (Winter/Spring 1996), p. 74.
Editor & Publisher, November 28, 1992, p. 28.
Emerge, May, 1994, p. 14.
New York Times, November 7, 1995.
New York Times Book Review, December 19, 1993, p. 20.
Publishers Weekly, September 6, 1993, p. 75.

Online

"The Museum of UnCut Funk Pays Tribute to Oliver Wendell Harrington's Dark Laughter Comic Strip Series," Museum of UnCut Funk, February 14, 2016, http://museumofuncutfunk.com/2016/02/14/oliver-w-harrington/ (accessed August 9, 2016).
"Oliver Harrington," The Civil Rights Struggle, African-American GIs, and Germany, http://www.aacvr-germany.org/index.php?option=com_con

tent&view=article&id=15&Itemid=17 (accessed August 11, 2016).

"Oliver Wendell Harrington (1912–1995)," PBS.org, http://www.pbs.org/blackpress/news_bios/harrington.html (accessed August 9, 2016).

"Oliver W. Harrington," Black History Now, September 9, 2011, http://blackhistorynow.com/oliver-w-harrington/ (accessed August 9, 2016).

—Robert R. Jacobson and Alana Joli Abbott

Jim Ray Hart

1941–2016

Professional baseball player

Hart, Jim Ray, photograph. Bettmann/Getty Images.

Third baseman Jim Ray Hart, a stalwart of the San Francisco Giants and New York Yankees lineups in the 1960s and early 1970s, never played in a World Series, and his statistics, although impressive, are unlikely to earn him a place in the Hall of Fame. Among baseball fans of that era, however, Hart was highly regarded for his tenacity and his ability to handle a variety of obstacles, many of them related to his health. A powerhouse in the batter's box, he struggled at times in the field, although typically with good humor. The trouble with his post at third base, he once said, in a comment quoted by Bruce Markusen for the website Hardball Times, was its location: "It's just too damn close to the hitters."

James Ray Hart was born October 30, 1941, in Hookerton, a tiny town in the farmlands of eastern North Carolina, roughly 75 miles east of Raleigh. Raised there in a tight-knit but racially segregated community, he was drawn to baseball at an early age. His talent, particularly when batting, was soon evident, and in 1960, when he was still in his late teens, he signed with the Giants as an amateur free agent. Over the next three years he made rapid progress through the franchise's minor league farm system, playing for a succession of teams around the country. By 1963 he had arrived at the San Francisco squad's AAA affiliate, the Tacoma Giants, where his brilliant performance over 83 games prompted his call to the majors. At his debut for San Francisco on July 7, 1963, he had two hits and batted in a run.

Soon after that auspicious beginning, however, Hart suffered the first of the injuries that would plague him throughout his career. One errant pitch caused a small fracture near the intersection of his collarbone and shoulder blade; another, just a few days later, hit him in the head and forced him to miss the rest of the year. Still considered a rookie on his return in 1964, he had one of the best seasons of his career, batting .286 with 31 home runs and 81 runs batted in. That performance led to a second-place finish in the National League's rookie of the year vote and several most valuable player nominations.

The seasons that immediately followed marked the peak of Hart's fame, as he emerged as one of the best-hitting infielders in the National League. In 1966 he earned an invitation to the All-Star Game with a fine performance that included a .285 batting average, 88

At a Glance . . .

Born James Ray Hart on October 30, 1941, in Hookerton, NC; died on May 19, 2016, in Acampo, CA; married Janet (divorced); children: four.

Career: Tacoma Giants and other minor-league teams, infielder, 1960–63; San Francisco Giants, third baseman, 1963–73; New York Yankees, designated hitter, 1973–74; Aguascalientes Rieleros, infielder, 1975–76.

Awards: All-Star selection, National League, 1966.

runs, 33 home runs, and 93 runs batted in. On July 8, 1970, he had what is widely considered the best game of his career, hitting a single, double, triple, and home run—a feat known as "hitting for the cycle"—and finished the game with seven runs batted in. Six of those came in just one inning, an achievement that tied what was then a long-standing major league record.

That brilliant day notwithstanding, it was clear by the early 1970s that Hart's performance was declining, particularly on defense, and in the spring of 1973, almost exactly a decade after his debut with the Giants, he was traded to the American League's New York Yankees, where he served as a designated hitter until his release a year later. His departure from the Yankees put an end to his major league career, although he went on to play for the Aguascalientes Rieleros, a team in the AAA-level Mexican League, for another two seasons.

Unlike many of his peers, Hart did not move easily into a life of quiet prosperity on his departure from baseball; on the contrary, his retirement exacerbated several long-standing problems, the largest of which by far was alcohol abuse. At a time when beer and hard liquor were staples in locker rooms, bullpens, and dugouts across the major leagues, many players routinely drank too much, and some, like Hart, became addicted. For most of his career he managed to hide the extent of the problem from all but a few friends, family members, and colleagues; to casual observers he was simply a convivial teammate who enjoyed parties and nightlife.

In retrospect, however, there is no doubt that his dependence on alcohol damaged his playing ability and his health. "If I hadn't been drinking, I'd have played another four, five years, no problem," he told Larry Stone of the *San Francisco Examiner*, as quoted by Markusen. "It got to the point where I didn't care about the game no more. What I was worrying about was the first and the 15th. That's when the checks came in. I just wanted to go out and have a drink or two. I mean, this was *every* day."

Hart's reliance on alcohol only deepened in his retirement, as he found himself with time on his hands and mounting bills. Drinking worsened his financial troubles, and he eventually lost his home to foreclosure; for a time he even struggled to pay for groceries. A turning point came when he became disoriented on an airplane, a frightening experience that inspired him to enter a treatment program, which he completed successfully. For the remainder of his life he lived quietly, balancing work in a warehouse with family activities. In the mid-2010s, when he was in his 70s, his health declined sharply, and on May 19, 2016, he died in Acampo, a small town in central California.

Sources

Periodicals

New York Times, May 23, 2016.

Online

"Blast from the Past: Jim Ray Hart," *When the Giants Come to Town …* (blog), January 9, 2010, http://whenthegiantscometotown.blogspot.com/2010/01/blast-from-past-jim-ray-hart.html (accessed October 2, 2016).

"Former Giants Third Baseman Jim Ray Hart Dies," SFGate.com, May 20, 2016, http://www.sfgate.com/giants/article/Former-Giants-third-baseman-Jim-Ray-Hart-dies-7873510.php (accessed October 2, 2016).

"Jim Ray Hart," Baseball-Reference.com, http://www.baseball-reference.com/register/player.cgi?id=hart–007jam (accessed October 2, 2016).

Markusen, Bruce, "Card Corner, 1973 Topps: Jim Ray Hart," Hardball Times, March 8, 2013, http://www.hardballtimes.com/card-corner-1973-topps-jim-ray-hart/ (accessed October 2, 2016).

—R. Anthony Kugler

Paula Hicks-Hudson

1951—

Attorney, politician

Paula Hicks-Hudson was elected mayor of Toledo, Ohio, in November of 2015, becoming the first African-American woman to hold the post. At the time of her election, Hicks-Hudson had already been Toledo's acting mayor for more than seven months, having succeeded Mayor D. Michael Collins after he died unexpectedly in February of that year; as president of the Toledo City Council, Hicks-Hudson filled the position until an election could be held. In the November race, she competed against a large field of candidates, including two former Toledo mayors and the widow of Mayor Collins. Hicks-Hudson prevailed with more than 35 percent of the vote in an election that split seven ways. During her campaign, Hicks-Hudson pointed to the stability she provided during the abrupt transition and to the substantive, future-oriented decisions that she made during the months preceding the election. At her victory party, Hicks-Hudson asserted, "Tonight, the citizens of Toledo voted to move toward a promising future to transform our dear Glass City into a safe and livable place."

Began Her Law Career

Paula Hicks-Hudson was born and raised in Hamilton, Ohio, near Cincinnati. Her parents juggled multiple jobs to raise their eight children. Her mother worked for the Hamilton City School system, as well as for various other employers, while her father worked in the streets department garage for the city of Hamilton. Together they also owned a small dry-cleaning business. Hicks-Hudson and her siblings were encouraged to excel in school and pursue higher education. She told the *Journal-News* in Hamilton that she had not planned on a career in politics, but, she explained, "[I] knew that I wanted to be a lawyer, and I wanted to make sure I got the best education possible." She also wanted to see more of the United States beyond southwest Ohio, so after graduating from high school in 1969, she left home to attend Spelman College in Atlanta, Georgia.

She graduated with a bachelor's degree in political science and journalism and married Freeman Hudson soon thereafter. The newlyweds moved to Colorado that year so that she could pursue a degree in communications development at Colorado State University. Although she loved the mountains there, as she told Tom Troy of the *Toledo Blade,* she had little time to enjoy the Colorado scenery; in addition to the rigors of her master's degree program, she became a mother during these years.

During the mid-1970s, Hicks-Hudson and her growing family returned to Ohio, this time to Wilberforce, about 60 miles from her hometown. There she worked with at-risk young people at Central State University in the Upward Bound program. She taught readiness skills to increase the possibility that underprepared students would someday be able to pursue higher education, but she also learned important lessons about the hurdles faced by young people in the American legal system. She told Troy, "We had kids who had challenges. I used to go to Juvenile Court to testify on how they did over the summer. I saw the need for vigorous representation

At a Glance . . .

Born Paula Sue Hicks in 1951 in Hamilton, OH; daughter of Clara Alberta Brooks Hicks (a business owner) and Pearlman David Hicks (a city worker); married Freeman Hudson (a maintenance worker), 1973; children: Patricia Hope Hudson, Leah Free Star Hudson. *Politics:* Democrat. *Religion:* Lutheran. *Education:* Spelman College, BA, political science and journalism, 1973; Colorado State University, MA, communications development, 1975; Iowa State University College of Law, JD, 1982.

Career: Central State University (Wilberforce, OH), Upward Bound instructor, 1970s; Toledo (OH) Legal Aid Society, attorney and director of senior legal services, 1982–84; Lucas County (OH) assistant prosecutor, 1985–89; worked as an assistant public defender and as assistant Ohio state attorney general, 1990s; Toledo City Council, legislative director, 1998–2002; Lucas County Board of Elections, director, 2004–05; Ohio Office of Budget and Management, 2007–11; Toledo City Council, member, 2011–15; City of Toledo, mayor, 2015–.

Memberships: Ohio State Bar Association; Toledo Bar Association; Toledo Women's Bar Association.

Awards: Sojourner Truth Award, National Association of Negro Business and Professional Women's Clubs, Inc., 2016.

Addresses: *Office*—Mayor's Office, One Government Center, Suite 2200, Toledo, Ohio 43604. *Twitter*—@phh4toledo.

for juveniles." Her next stop was law school at Iowa State University.

Put Down Roots in Toledo

In 1982, law degree in hand, Hicks-Hudson moved to Toledo, where she first worked with the Toledo Legal Aid Society. During the 1980s and 1990s, she worked in a variety of public law settings, serving as an assistant prosecutor and an assistant public defender and working in the state attorney general's office. She was the legislative director for the Toledo City Council for several years, and in 2008, during the administration of Democratic governor Ted Strickland, she became chief legal counsel for the Ohio Office of Budget and Man-

agement. She was active in local and county Democratic politics and in nonpartisan civic organizations as well.

Her rising profile in Democratic circles led to her first foray into elective politics in 2011. When Toledo's District 4 City Council representative was elected to the Ohio General Assembly, Hicks-Hudson was recruited and appointed to fill the spot in January. She won a special election in May of that year with nearly 71 percent of the vote, and she ran again and won in November, again gaining 71 percent of the vote. Two years later she was selected by her council colleagues as council president, setting the stage for yet another unexpected step in an unplanned political career.

In a 2015 interview with the *Toledo Blade*, Hicks-Hudson noted that the twists and turns of her varied career and educational paths had served her well, saying, "Each place, each life experience, if you pay attention, helps you learn lessons." Sensing that such a declaration to a newspaper writer might have sounded boastful, however, she quickly followed up with, "I don't want to say I'm all that and a bag of chips." Her ability to stay grounded, stable, self-aware, and adaptable would serve her well in what was to come.

Became Toledo's First Black Woman Mayor

On February 1, 2015, Mayor Collins collapsed while driving; the cause was cardiac arrest. As he lay unconscious at the hospital, Hicks-Hudson—as council president—was sworn in as acting mayor, as mandated by the city charter. Several days later, Collins died, and Hicks-Hudson became mayor of Toledo—albeit temporarily. In March of 2015 she announced that she would run in the election in November to officially fill the remainder of the late mayor's term of office. The Toledo city charter does not provide for a runoff election to fill a partial term, so seven candidates were on the general election ballot in the fall.

The campaign was notable for its civility, as was the immediate aftermath as the vote tallies came in. The *Toledo Blade's* Troy observed, "Having multiple candidates apparently discouraged direct attacks, out of concern that a negative campaign could backfire on the candidate doing it." Hicks-Hudson won the general election with 35.45 percent of the seven-way vote, while the second-place vote-getter—former mayor and former fire chief Mike Bell—received 17.39 percent. Hicks-Hudson is only the second woman to be elected mayor of the city, and she is the first Democrat in that office since 2006. Bell, a political independent, congratulated her publicly and told the *Toledo Blade*, "She has earned that position through trial by fire." Carty Finkbeiner, another former Toledo mayor, came in third, but acknowledged that if he could not win, he was glad that Hicks-Hudson had done so.

In her victory speech, Hicks-Hudson acknowledged that her candidacy had arisen from "the most unfortunate circumstances," and promised a "sensible and steadfast governing approach" to deal with community issues. In her first State of the City address, which was made almost a year to the day after she first stepped into the mayoral role, she declared, "We are a tenacious, tough city. We have challenges, and we have opportunities. We will not give up on either."

Sources

Periodicals

Journal News (Hamilton, OH), April 9, 2015.
Toledo (OH) Blade, February 2, 2015; February 8, 2015; November 4, 2015.

Online

Burns, Christopher, "Toledo Mayor Paula Hicks-Hudson delivers State of the City," NBC24.com, February 10, 2016, http://nbc24.com/news/election/candidates/toledo-mayor-paula-hicks-hudson-delivers-state-of-the-city (accessed August 2, 2016).
Mayor's Office, City of Toledo, http://toledo.oh.gov/government/mayors-office/ (accessed August 10, 2016).
Paula Hicks-Hudson, http://www.hickshudson4toledo.com/ (accessed August 2, 2016).
Paula Hicks-Hudson, LinkedIn, https://www.linkedin.com/in/paula-hicks-hudson-a369b16 (accessed August 2, 2016).

—Pamela Willwerth Aue

The Highway QC's

Gospel music group

In their influence, enthusiasm, and longevity, the group known as the Highways QC's have few peers in the history of recorded gospel music. A fixture on the concert circuit for more than 70 years, they are known for their ability to blend the spirit of traditional gospel with contemporary tones and rhythms. Led for most of their history by Spencer Taylor Jr., the group's alumni include Lou Rawls, Johnnie Taylor (no relation to Spencer), and Sam Cooke, all of whom went on to international fame in pop and R&B. By his own account, however, Spencer Taylor was never tempted to make that switch. "We're not going" into secular music, he told Noah Schaffer of the website ArtsFuse.org in 2014, "not as long as I live."

The Highway QC's, photograph. Gilles Petard/Redferns/Getty Images.

The Highway QC's (sometimes written as Q.C.s, QCs, Qc's, or Q.C.'s) originated in Chicago during the mid-1940s, a period that is now regarded as a golden age of gospel music. Swollen by waves of African-American migration from the rural South, Chicago and other northern cities each supported dozens of gospel acts during this time. Many of them were a cappella groups (vocals without musical accompaniment) sponsored by local congregations such as Chicago's Highway Baptist Church, where six young men—brothers Curtis and Lee Richardson, brothers Marvin and Charles Jones, Creadell Copeland, and Cooke—began singing together about 1945. The rapport among them grew quickly, and within months they were performing together in Chicago as The Highway QC's. The origin of their name, partly an homage to their home congregation, has been the subject of some mild debate over the years, as the abbreviation "QC" has defied easy explanation. According to one theory, it stood for "Qualified Christians."

Whatever the precise meaning of their name, The Highway QC's made rapid progress, although it would be another decade before they began recording. During that time they experienced a number of personnel changes, the most significant of which were Cooke's replacement by Rawls in the early 1950s and Johnnie Taylor's debut in place of Rawls several years later. Throughout these shifts and the many others that occurred in later decades, the group managed to maintain a consistent identity, thanks in large part to their reliance on close harmonizing and other techniques of traditional, church-based singing. Because that relatively conservative approach tended to emphasize the group over the individual, the disruption caused by a member's departure was minimized.

Their conservatism, however, was not all-encompassing. In contrast to some of their peers, who resisted

change so long that they began to sound old-fashioned, The Highway QC's were willing and able to react to shifts in public taste. During the early 1960s, for example, they brought in backing instrumentation, adding a guitar and then a bass. That relatively simple change modernized their sound and brought them new fans, many of whom were young people raised on R&B and rock and roll.

As they navigated the increasingly complex music business, The Highway QC's had assistance from several sources, including their first label, Vee-Jay Records. One of the only labels in the country at that time to be owned and managed by African Americans, Chicago-based Vee-Jay had a special insight into the gospel market. Under the direction of founders James and Vivian Bracken, The Highway QC's recorded their first singles in 1955, including an especially fine track called "Somewhere to Lay My Head." Roughly a year later, as they were working on follow-ups, Johnnie Taylor was replaced by Spencer Taylor, who soon emerged as the group's leader, both onstage and behind the scenes. Under his direction, The Highway QC's established themselves as one of Vee-Jay's core ensembles, completing a string of singles for that label through the first half of the 1960s, including "Child of God" (1959) and "Do You Love Him" (1961). They also began to record full-length albums, including *Jesus Is Waiting* (1960) and *The Highway QC's Sing from the Top of the Hill* (1964). By the time the latter appeared, however, Vee-Jay's finances were in severe disarray, forcing the QCs to find a new label.

By 1965 Taylor and his bandmates had signed with another gospel powerhouse, Peacock Records, where they completed a number of singles before moving on Nashboro, Savoy, and other labels over the following decade. It was at Savoy in 1976 that the group recorded "Oh How Wonderful," which was one of their biggest hits. "We started singing it [in concert] and … we found out that was a big song for us," Taylor recalled to Schaffer of ArtsFuse. A highlight of their album *Stay with God* (1976), it has become a staple of their live shows.

Gospel music, meanwhile, was changing rapidly, as the genre's production values caught up with those of rock and R&B. The Highway QC's gradually updated their approach with studio effects and other novelties. The result was a highly polished sound that contrasted sharply with the unadorned melodies characteristic of the 1940s and 1950s. Thanks to their skill in harmonizing—and to Taylor's distinctive and seemingly ageless voice—the group's links to the past were still evident. Significant albums during this period included 1983's *Something's on My Mind (That's Worrying Me)*, one of their last releases for Savoy; *Cry No More*, completed for the Meltone label in 1990; and *It Hasn't Always Been Easy*, released by Mississippi-based Malaco Records in 2007.

During the mid-2010s, as Spencer Taylor approached his 90th birthday, The Highway QC's remained an active presence on the gospel circuit. Based since the 1960s in Washington, DC, Taylor and his bandmates—among them two of his sons, Spencer Taylor III and Lynn "Fuzzy" Taylor—released a major new album, *The God Father* (sometimes rendered as *The Godfather*) on the Ophir Gospel label in 2014.

Selected discography

Singles

"Somewhere to Lay My Head," 1955.
"Child of God," 1959.
"Do You Love Him," 1961.
"Oh How Wonderful," 1976.

Albums

Jesus Is Waiting, Vee-Jay, 1960.
The Highway QC's Sing from the Top of the Hill (includes "Child of God" and "Do You Love Him"), Vee-Jay, 1964.
We Are the Highway QC's, Nashboro, 1973.
Stay with God (includes "Oh How Wonderful"), Savoy, 1976.
Something's on My Mind (That's Worrying Me), Savoy, 1983.
(As Spencer Taylor and the Highway QC's), *Cry No More,* Meltone, 1990.
(As Spencer Taylor and the Highway QC's) *It Hasn't Always Been Easy,* Malaco, 2007.
(As the Highway QC's Featuring Spencer Taylor) *The God Father,* Ophir Gospel, 2014.

Sources

Online

Ankeny, Jason, "The Highway Q.C.'s: Artist Biography," AllMusic.com, http://www.allmusic.com/artist/the-highway-qcs-mn0000609966/biography (accessed September 1, 2016).
Boyd, Libra, "Highway QCs' Spencer Taylor: 'If You're Gonna Sing Gospel, You Got to Know the Lord,'"

Gospel Music Fever (blog), 2014, http://gospelmu sicfever.blogspot.com/2014/03/highway-qcs-spen cer-taylor-if-youre.html (accessed September 1, 2016).

"The Highway QC's," Discogs.com, https://www .discogs.com/artist/1221681-The-Highway-QCs (accessed September 1, 2016).

"Highway Qc's Featuring Spencer Taylor," Facebook, https://www.facebook.com/lynntaylor594/ (accessed September 2, 2016).

Schaffer, Noah, "Fuse Music Interview: Spencer Taylor Jr.—Gospel's Grandfather Comes to Dorchester," ArtsFuse.org, December 3, 2014, http://artsfuse .org/118914/fuse-music-interview-spencer-taylor -jr-gospels-godfather-comes-to-dorchester/ (accessed September 1, 2016).

—R. Anthony Kugler

Christopher Jackson

1975—

Actor, singer, composer

Actor and singer Christopher Jackson is best known for originating the role of George Washington in the hit Broadway musical *Hamilton,* for which he earned a Tony Award nomination for best featured actor in a musical in 2016. A Broadway veteran and a close friend and colleague of *Hamilton* creator Lin-Manuel Miranda, Jackson made his Broadway debut in *The Lion King* in 1997 and went on to appear in Miranda's award-winning 2008 musical *In the Heights.* The incredible success of *Hamilton*—the hottest ticket of the 2015–16 theater season—provided Jackson with the biggest role of his career. An accomplished musician as well, Jackson has earned two Grammy Awards as well as an Emmy Award for music that he composed for the children's television series *Sesame Street.* His solo debut album, *In the Name of Love,* was released in 2011.

Jackson, Christopher, photograph. Helga Esteb/Shutterstock.com.

parents separated when he was young, he and his older sister were raised by their mother, a high school teacher, with help from their grandmother. Jackson grew up playing team sports, and as a boy his dream was to be a professional baseball player. He did not think about performing until he was a sophomore in high school, when a teacher handed him a copy of Arthur Miller's play *The Crucible.* "I'd never read a piece of classic theater. That changed my life," Jackson told Molly Parker of the *Southern Illinoisan* in 2016. "The more time I spent with it, the more I realized there was a world in which I could be an actor." Encouraged by the same teacher, Jackson auditioned for and won a place at the prestigious American Musical and Dramatic Academy in New York City, where he enrolled after graduating from high school in 1993.

Made Broadway Debut in Lion King

Jackson was born on September 30, 1975, in the small town of Cairo in southern Illinois. After his

The young actor got his first break in 1997, when he was cast in the Disney musical *The Lion King* on Broadway. Jackson started out as a member of the ensemble—cast only an hour before his first rehearsal—and eventually worked his way up to the role of Simba, staying with the show for three years. He landed his breakout role several years later, when he

At a Glance . . .

Born on September 30, 1975, in Cairo, IL; son of Jane Adams; married Veronica Vazquez, 2004; children: C. J., Jadelyn. *Education:* Attended American Music and Dramatic Academy.

Career: Stage actor, 1997—; recording artist, 2011—.

Awards: Drama Desk Award, Outstanding Ensemble Performance, 2007, for *In the Heights;* Daytime Emmy Award, Outstanding Original Song for a Children's Series, 2011, for "What I Am" (*Sesame Street*); Grammy Award, Best Musical Theater Album, 2008, for *In the Heights,* 2016, for *Hamilton.*

Addresses: *Twitter*—@ChrisisSingin.

was cast as Benny in the Broadway musical *In the Heights,* created by and starring Lin-Manuel Miranda. Set in the New York City neighborhood of Washington Heights and featuring a large and diverse cast (Jackson's was the only non-Spanish-speaking character), the hip-hop-inspired musical premiered at the Eugene O'Neill Theater in Waterford, Connecticut, in 2005 and then opened off Broadway in 2007 at the 37 Arts Theatre. *In the Heights* transferred to Broadway the following year, running for 1,184 performances; Jackson remained with the show for almost its entire run, until 2011. Jackson and his cast mates took home the Drama Desk Award for outstanding ensemble performance in 2007. *In the Heights* earned 13 Tony Award nominations the following year, winning four prizes, including best musical, and won the Grammy Award for best musical theater album that same year.

While working on *In the Heights,* Jackson formed a close personal and professional relationship with Miranda. When Miranda accepted the Tony Award for best musical score, he paid tribute to his friend, rapping, "I don't know about God, but I believe in Chris Jackson." Jackson also formed another important relationship during this time: he met his wife, actress and singer Veronica Vazquez, at an early reading of the play, and the two married a year later. The couple has two children, son C. J. and daughter Jadelyn.

After *In the Heights,* Jackson went on to appear in the Broadway musical *Memphis,* in the comic play *Lonely, I'm Not* at the off-Broadway Second Stage Theatre, and in the popular Jazz Age musical revue *Cotton Club Parade* at the New York City Center, all in 2012. The last-named play transferred to Broadway in November of 2013, where it was rechristened *After*

Midnight; Jackson joined the Broadway cast for a brief stint in the spring of the following year. Also in 2014 Jackson appeared in the short-lived baseball-themed play *Bronx Bombers,* playing Derek Jeter, and in the musical *Holler If Ya Hear Me,* based on the music of rapper Tupac Shakur.

Appeared in Hit Musical Hamilton

Jackson first heard about Miranda's next musical in 2009, when *Hamilton* was still a germ of an idea. "Lin came back from vacation and [said], 'I got the next thing,'" Jackson recalled in an interview with Deadline. "I said, 'What is it?' He said, 'It's about the first Treasury secretary.' I looked at him like he was crazy.... I said, 'Great, who do I get to play?' He got this look and said, 'Just wait, it's coming.'" A few days later Jackson saw Thomas Kail, the director of *In the Heights* and later *Hamilton,* who addressed him as "Mr. President." Jackson joined Miranda for a workshop performance of *Hamilton* at Vassar College in 2013, reading the part of George Washington, and has been with the show ever since.

Hamilton premiered off Broadway at the Joseph Papp Public Theater in February of 2015; the show was so popular that its run was extended twice. The production transferred to Broadway later that same year, opening at the Richard Rodgers Theatre in August. Jackson and most of the original cast joined the Broadway production. Although a hip-hop musical about founding father Alexander Hamilton might seem like an improbable hit, Hamilton was a hot ticket from the beginning, with advance sales of more than $30 million and a weekly gross of over $1 million. Audiences clamored for tickets, paying an average of $500 per seat; a daily lottery for $10 tickets (21 per show) had upwards of 10,000 entrants online. *Hamilton* also received rave reviews from critics. In the *New York Times,* Ben Brantley assured readers that the show lived up to the hype: "Yes, it really is that good," he wrote. "I am loath to tell people to mortgage their houses and lease their children to acquire tickets to a hit Broadway show. But 'Hamilton' ... might just about be worth it."

One of the most remarkable aspects of Miranda's retelling of the story of Alexander Hamilton was its casting of actors of color to play the founding fathers: in addition to Jackson as George Washington, the production also featured Miranda, of Puerto Rican heritage, as Hamilton and African-American actors Leslie Odom Jr. and Daveed Diggs as Aaron Burr and Thomas Jefferson, respectively. For Jackson, it was a special opportunity to be a part of such a groundbreaking production. "I know that when I was 11 years old, if I had seen a show like Hamilton, it would have changed everything for me," he said in an interview with *Playbill.* "It's really important to let people know that when they come to our show, they can have a life-changing moment. I think once you see characters

like us portrayed in real life, the power is [that] you can somehow *see* yourself in that."

Hamilton won the Pulitzer Prize for Drama in 2016 and was nominated for a record 16 Tony Award nominations, including a nod for Jackson for best featured actor in a musical (he lost to cast mate Daveed Diggs). Jackson won a second Grammy Award for best musical theater album for the cast recording of *Hamilton*.

In addition to performing on the stage, Jackson is also an accomplished composer and musician. With Miranda, he performs with Freestyle Love Supreme, an improv rap group that landed its own series on Pivot TV in 2016; each episode will be taped before a live audience. Jackson has also composed music for television. In 2011 he won an Emmy Award for outstanding original song for his lyrics to "What I Am," sung by will.i.am of the Black-Eyed Peas on *Sesame Street.* In 2016 Jackson appeared with *Sesame Street*'s Elmo for a video from the set of Hamilton that quickly went viral; Jackson also sang the original song "Puppet Man" for the 2011 documentary *Being Elmo: A Puppeteer's Journey* and composed music for the revival of PBS's *The Electric Company.* Jackson released his debut album, *In the Name of Love,* in 2011 on the Yellow Sound label.

Selected works

Theater

The Lion King, New Amsterdam Theatre, New York, 1997–2000.
In the Heights, Richard Rodgers Theatre, New York, 2008–11.
Memphis, Shubert Theatre, New York, 2012.
Lonely, I'm Not, Second Stage Theatre, New York, 2012.
Cotton Club Parade, New York City Center, 2012.
After Midnight, Brooks Atkinson Theatre, New York, 2014.
Bronx Bombers, Circle in the Square Theatre, New York, 2014.

Holler If Ya Hear Me, Palace Theatre, New York, 2014.
Hamilton, Richard Rodgers Theatre, New York, 2015—.

Albums

In the Name of Love, Yellow Sound, 2011.

Sources

Periodicals

New York Times, August 6, 2015; May 5, 2016.
Southern Illinoisan (Carbondale, IL), March 8, 2016.

Online

"Christopher Jackson: Connected to His Roots," ESME.com, https://esme.com/hall-of-fame/sons-daughters/christopher-jackson-connected-to-his-roots (accessed September 27, 2016).
Daniels, Karu F., "Broadway Audiences Hear Chris Jackson's *Holler:* Leading Man Plays Three Starring Roles in One Season," Playbill.com, July 8, 2014, http://www.playbill.com/article/broadway-audiences-hear-chris-jacksons-holler-leading-man-plays-three-starring-roles-in-one-season-com-323338 (accessed September 27, 2016).
Freestyle Love Supreme, http://www.freestylelovesupreme.com/ (accessed September 27, 2016).
Gerard, Jeremy, "Hamilton's Christopher Jackson: George Washington Shlepped Here," Deadline, April 27, 2016, http://deadline.com/2016/04/hamilton-christopher-jackson-q-and-a-1201745313/ (accessed September 27, 2016).
Purcell, Carey, "Chris Jackson Shares How Seeing *Hamilton* as a Child Would Have 'Changed Everything' for Him," Playbill.com, October 9, 2015, http://www.playbill.com/article/chris-jackson-shares-how-seeing-hamilton-as-a-child-would-have-changed-everything-for-him-com-366077 (accessed September 27, 2016).

—Deborah A. Ring

Joseph Jarman

1937—

Jazz saxophonist and educator

Jarmon, Joseph, photograph. Hiroyuki Ito/Getty Images.

A key figure in the world of avant-garde jazz, saxophonist Joseph Jarman has been inspiring audiences around the globe for more than half a century. A prominent member of three pioneering avant-garde organizations—the Experimental Band, the Association for the Advancement of Creative Musicians (AACM), and the Art Ensemble of Chicago (AEC)—he is known for his ability to incorporate elements of spirituality, theater, folklore, and poetry into his work. "We were doing performance art as far back as 1965," he said of the AACM in a 1999 interview with writer Jason Gross for the online music magazine Perfect Sound Forever, "just not calling it that." A longtime student of Buddhism, he has devoted an increasing proportion of his time since the early 1990s to meditation and other spiritual pursuits.

Born in Pine Bluff, Arkansas, on September 14, 1937, Jarman moved as a child to Chicago. As a student at DuSable High School, a landmark institution on Chicago's predominantly African-American South Side, he studied with a legendary—and notoriously demanding—band teacher, Captain Walter Dyett. A drummer initially, he switched to the saxophone after graduation, taking up that instrument while completing several years of service in Europe with the U.S. Army. Assigned to a military band, he had what he later described to writer Ted Panken as "a wonderful experience," adding, "I met a lot of musicians there who put me in the right direction." Discharged in 1958, he returned to Chicago and enrolled at Woodrow Wilson Junior College (later Kennedy-King College), where the next stage of his career began.

Valuable as his classroom training at Wilson was, it was not as significant to Jarman's career as the informal opportunities he found around campus and in his own neighborhood. "The music was everywhere," he told Panken. "It was available. You could go in a one-mile radius, and you could hear ten different bands." In that fertile environment he made rapid progress, and by the early 1960s he was playing regularly with a group of fellow students from Wilson, several of whom went on to join him in the pioneering ensemble known, fittingly, as the Experimental Band. Led by composer and multi-instrumentalist Muhal Richard Abrams, it was one of the first groups to focus on simultaneous improvisation. While improvised solos had been a crucial part of jazz since its start, group improvisations were new.

At a Glance . . .

Born on September 14, 1937, in Pine Bluff, AR. *Military service:* U.S. Army, 1950s. *Religion:* Buddhist. *Education:* Attended Woodrow Wilson Junior College, late 1950s–early 1960s.

Career: Independent musician, 1950s—; independent teacher of aikido and Buddhism, 1990s—.

Addresses: *Office*—Jikishinkan Aikido Dojo, 316 Dean St, 2nd Floor, Brooklyn, NY 11217.

They were also controversial, as their characteristic dissonance shocked many listeners used to traditional structures such as harmony and melody. In the hands of Jarman, Abrams, and the other members of the Experimental Band, dissonance became a powerful medium for self-expression and political activism. Over time those goals attracted growing notice, particularly after about 1965, when the Band developed into the AACM, which had strong ties to the civil rights and Black Power movements.

The next few years were a particularly active and vibrant period for Jarman. At workshops and theaters in Chicago, Detroit, and other cities, he joined other AACM members in presentations that were visually as well as musically intense, thanks in part to elaborate costumes and face paint. Also striking to observers was the versatility of the performers, as all involved played a variety of roles and instruments. Jarman's facility in that regard was particularly broad, ranging from the saxophone and vocal work to the clarinet, the flute, and the drums.

The theatrical nature of AACM performances was not especially well suited to audio recording, and many record companies hesitated to become involved with its members. Around 1966, however, Jarman assembled a new group and won a contract with Chicago's Delmark Records. That agreement soon resulted in the completion of two important albums, *Song For* (1967) and *As If It Were the Seasons* (1968). Completed with the help of fellow saxophonist Fred Anderson, bassist Charles Clark, and several other fine musicians, the two works did a great deal to increase awareness of the AACM beyond the upper Midwest.

Throughout this period Jarman also worked steadily as a backup musician, helping his friends and acquaintances complete projects of their own. One of these side gigs, a recording effort led by trumpeter Lester Bowie, led around this time to the emergence of the AEC, a quartet he formed with Bowie, saxophonist Roscoe Mitchell, and bassist Malachi Favors. Word of

the new group spread quickly, particularly after an extended sojourn in Scandinavia and France in the late 1960s and early 1970s. On their return the AEC enjoyed a warm reception, thanks in part to the strength of several albums they had recorded in Europe, including *A Jackson in Your House* (1969). Subsequent releases included *Live at Mandel Hall* (1972) and *Nice Guys* (1978).

In 1982, after roughly 15 years with the AEC, Jarman moved from Chicago to New York City, a shift that gave him, he told Gross, "more work" and "more opportunities." He continued to appear with the group for roughly another decade. In that span the AEC released some of their best-known albums, including *The Third Decade,* completed for Germany's ECM Records in 1984. In a glowing review for the *New York Times,* critic Don Palmer drew attention to Jarman's "gutbucket licks" on saxophone as well as to his abilities as a composer, calling his "Prayer for Jimbo Kwesi," the album's lead track, a "reverential composition" and "a near perfect vehicle for his nasal soprano [saxophone] and serene flute."

In the early 1990s Jarman began to shift his focus from music to Buddhism and aikido, a nonviolent martial art that, like meditation, requires breath control and the ability to put aside worldly pressures and desires. Ordained as a Buddhist priest on a trip to Japan in 1990, he left the AEC three years later to concentrate on the development of the Jikishinkan Aikido Dojo, an aikido training facility in Brooklyn, which became the center of his professional life. He also continued to perform with some regularity, particularly at music festivals on the East Coast.

Selected discography

Song For, Delmark, 1967.
As If It Were the Seasons, Delmark, 1968.
Art Ensemble of Chicago, *A Jackson in Your House,* BYG, 1969.
Art Ensemble of Chicago, *Live at Mandel Hall,* Delmark, 1972.
Art Ensemble of Chicago, *Nice Guys,* ECM, 1978.
Art Ensemble of Chicago, *The Third Decade* (includes "Prayer for Jimbo Kwesi"), ECM, 1984.

Sources

Periodicals

New York Times, April 14, 1985.

Online

Gross, Jason, "Joseph Jarman: Interview by Jason Gross (October 1999)," Perfect Sound Forever, October 1999, http://www.furious.com/perfect/jarman.html (accessed October 2, 2016).
Kelsey, Chris, "Joseph Jarman," AllMusic.com,

http://www.allmusic.com/artist/joseph-jarman-mn 0000827323/biography (accessed October 2, 2016).

Panken, Ted, "In Honor of Joseph Jarman's 74th Birthday, a WKCR Interview from 1987," Today Is the Question: Ted Panken on Music, Politics and the Arts, September 14, 2011, https://tedpanken .wordpress.com/2011/09/14/in-honor-of-joseph -jarmans-74th-birthday-a-wkcr-interview-from- 1987/ (accessed October 2, 2016).

—R. Anthony Kugler

Richard Jefferson

1980—

Professional basketball player

Jefferson, Richard, photograph. David Livingston/Getty Images.

Fifteen years and seven teams into his career in the National Basketball Association (NBA), Richard Jefferson won his first championship as a member of the Cleveland Cavaliers. Cleveland's 2016 win over the Golden State Warriors was history making on several levels. Led by superstar LeBron James, the Cavaliers claimed their first title in franchise history, in the process snapping a 52-year championship drought in Cleveland. Even more unlikely was the way they did it, rallying from an unprecedented 3–1 deficit. For the veteran Jefferson, the Cavaliers triumph seemed a way of turning back the clock. He tied the NBA record for going the longest time between NBA Finals appearances—13 years—having last found himself on basketball's biggest stage in 2003 as the starting small forward for the New Jersey Nets.

Practiced "Positive Confession"

Richard Allen Jefferson was born on June 21, 1980, in South Central Los Angeles. He and his two older brothers were raised by their single mother, Wanda Marshall, a born-again Christian who later changed her name to Meekness after a preacher called her that at a revival meeting. Struggling to get off welfare and wanting to escape the crack epidemic that plagued South Central L.A., Meekness married an old friend from her childhood, John LeCato, and they relocated to Phoenix, Arizona, with several other families from their church looking for a fresh start.

Meekness and John set a good example for their children. Meekness, a high school dropout, returned to school and eventually became a member of the English department faculty at South Mountain Community College in Phoenix. John worked as a security guard for many years. Together they started their own church; in the summers, when their jobs allowed, they traveled to East Africa as missionaries, on one occasion taking Richard with them on a trip to Kenya.

A rambunctious child with many friends, Jefferson liked to have fun, at the expense of his schoolwork. He spent the bulk of his time shooting baskets in the park or reading sports magazines. As an eighth grader at Desert Foot Hills Junior High, he was academically ineligible to play basketball. He was kicked off the

At a Glance . . .

Born Richard Allen Jefferson on June 21, 1980, in Los Angeles, CA; son of Meekness LeCato (an English teacher and Christian missionary); children: Richard.

Career: New Jersey Nets, 2001–08; Milwaukee Bucks, 2008–09; San Antonio Spurs, 2009–12; Golden State Warriors, 2012–13; Utah Jazz, 2013–14; Dallas Mavericks, 2014–15; Cleveland Cavaliers, 2015—.

Awards: McDonald's High School All-American Team, 1998; Arizona State 4A Player of the Year, 1998; All-Freshman Team, Pacific-10 Conference, 1998–99; All-NCAA Final Four selection, All-NCAA Midwest Regional Selection, 2001; NBA All-Rookie Second Team, 2002; bronze medal, men's basketball, Summer Olympics, 2004; inducted into Pac-12 Conference Men's Basketball Hall of Honor, 2012.

Addresses: *Office*—c/o Cleveland Cavaliers, Quicken Loans Arena, 1 Center Court, Cleveland, OH 44115–4001.

freshman team at Moon Valley High School for horsing around during practice. Bounced up to the varsity level as a result of his antics, Richard decided he needed to reestablish his priorities before his behavior got him into trouble with the older kids.

Jefferson hoped he could redirect his energies by following his mother's example. Meekness's mantra was "Speak and Believe." She claimed that she had brought her new life into existence by verbalizing the positive things she wanted to happen—a practice known as "positive confession" in charismatic Christianity circles. So, at age 14, Jefferson repeated two sentences into a tape recorder that he listened to every day: "My name is Richard Jefferson and by the time I reach my sophomore year, I will be All-State. By the time I reach my senior year, I will be All-American." In a 2004 interview with Chris Broussard of the *New York Times,* Jefferson recalled, "It was probably only a total of five or six minutes, but to put it on and work out or to put it on and watch TV made it something that stuck in your head. And apparently it happened."

Blossomed with the Nets

Jefferson's predictions for himself came true. With the help of a growth spurt that saw him sprout from six feet, one inch to six feet, six inches between his

freshman and sophomore years, he advanced to All-State, All-Regional, and All-American. In his junior year, he made the honor roll. In 1998, when he was a senior, he led his team to the Class 4A Arizona state championship. With more than respectable SAT scores and an affable personality in the bargain, Jefferson was recruited by several top colleges, including the University of Kansas and the University of Connecticut.

In the end, Jefferson decided to sign with Coach Lute Olson and the University of Arizona Wildcats. In 84 college games, Jefferson started 77, usually at the small forward position. As a junior, Jefferson helped lead the Wildcats to a 28–8 regular-season record and a nearly successful run for the 2001 national championship title. During the National Collegiate Athletic Association (NCAA) tournament, Arizona stormed through Eastern Illinois, Butler, Ole Miss, Illinois, and Michigan State before losing to Duke University in the final game, 82–72.

An All-NCAA Final Four and Midwest Regional selection, Jefferson was the 13th overall pick in the 2001 NBA draft. Originally selected by the Houston Rockets, he was almost immediately acquired by the New Jersey Nets, along with the draft rights of Jason Collins and Brandon Armstrong, in exchange for Eddie Griffin. In seven seasons with the Nets, Jefferson established himself as one of the best small forwards in the league. With his incredible athleticism, great defensive skills, and mid- and long-range shooting ability, Jefferson moved easily into the starting position left vacant by the departure of Keith Van Horn. Mentored by the no-nonsense point guard Jason Kidd, Jefferson reined in his cockiness and emerged as a key contributor in the team's back-to-back Eastern Conference championships in his first two seasons. The Nets were overmatched in both of their NBA Finals appearances, losing first to the Los Angeles Lakers and then to the San Antonio Spurs.

The Nets made it to the top of the Atlantic Division for the 2003–04 season, aided in no small part by Jefferson's team-high 18.5 points per game. In August of 2004, Jefferson was rewarded with a six-year, $78 million contract extension. Jefferson missed portions of the 2004–05 and 2006–07 seasons due to injury, but he remained a major contributor. In six consecutive playoff years, Jefferson made 78 appearances, averaging 15.1 points, 5.4 rebounds, and 2.5 assists. In his last season with the Nets, Jefferson played all 82 games, averaging a career-high 22.6 points, marking the first time he finished among the top 10 in the league in scoring.

Enjoyed Late-Career Resurgence

In June of 2008, Jefferson was traded to the Milwaukee Bucks in exchange for forwards Bobby Simmons

and Yi Jianlian. Jefferson was not happy about leaving the only team he had ever known, but he eventually got used to the idea, knowing that he would get a chance to play alongside another elite scorer, All-Star Michael Redd. Jefferson put up good numbers as a Buck and started every game, but he wound up being traded to the San Antonio Spurs after one season.

Jefferson spent two and a half years playing with big man Tim Duncan and the Spurs. Although he came to the Spurs billed as the missing piece in their championship puzzle, Jefferson proved a poor fit for the Spurs' style of offense. Traded in March of 2012, Jefferson began a stint as an NBA journeyman, recreating himself as a stationary three-point shooter in seasons with the Golden State Warriors, Utah Jazz, and Dallas Mavericks before singing with the Cleveland Cavaliers on August 5, 2015.

The 35-year-old Jefferson played a key role for the Cavs during their title run. A rotation stalwart, he played in 74 regular-season games, averaging 17.9 minutes and 5.5 points. In the finals against Golden State, Jefferson started in game 3 in place of the injured Kevin Love. He posted 9 points and 8 rebounds in 33 minutes, giving the Cavaliers the boost they needed to cut their series deficit to 2–1. Jefferson was integral to the remainder of the series as well, as Sean Costello observed in an article for the sports website FanSided: "Jefferson didn't go out there and score a plethora of points, dish out dimes or even dominate the boards but he gave Cleveland something more by allowing them to play small and play stretches where they actually were able to match up with Golden State." Jefferson had planned to retire after his one-year contract with Cleveland expired, but he soon had a change of heart and re-signed with Cavs, inking a two-year deal on July 6, 2016.

Sources

Periodicals

New York Times, May 6, 2004; June 4, 2016.
Sports Illustrated, August 4, 1997; May 10, 2004; March 8, 2010.
Tucson (AZ) Citizen, April 2, 2001.

Online

Citak, Matt, "13 Years Later, Richard Jefferson Returns to NBA Finals," SportsNet New York, June 2, 2016, https://www.sny.tv/nets/news/13-years -later-richard-jefferson-returns-to-nba-finals/ 181713510 (accessed August 10, 2016).
Costello, Sean, "Brooklyn Nets: Thank You Richard Jefferson," FanSided, June 21, 2016, http://nothin butnets.com/2016/06/21/brooklyn-nets-thank -richard-jefferson/ (accessed August 10, 2016).
Ogus, Simon, "NBA Finals Hero Richard Jefferson Decides to Return to the Cavaliers and Announces His New Contract on Snapchat," Forbes.com, July 7, 2016, http://www.forbes.com/sites/simonogus/ 2016/07/07/nba-finals-hero-richard-jefferson-de cides-to-return-to-the-cavaliers-and-announces-his -new-deal-on-snapchat/#1b57099c25e6 (accessed August 10, 2016).
"Richard Jefferson," Cleveland Cavaliers, http://www .nba.com/cavaliers/content/search/?query=richard %20jefferson (accessed August 10, 2016).
"Richard Jefferson," NBA.com, http://www.nba .com/search/?text=richard+jefferson (accessed August 10, 2016).
"Richard Jefferson: Player Profile," CBS Sports, http://www.cbssports.com/nba/players/player page/240295/richard-jefferson (accessed August 10, 2016).

—Janet Mullane

Blind Willie Johnson

1897(?)–1945

Guitarist, vocalist, preacher

While he was never a household name, even at the peak of his career, vocalist and guitarist Blind Willie Johnson had a sizable impact on the development of popular music. A prodigy whose work drew on gospel and the blues in equal measure, he recorded fewer than three dozen songs over the course of his career. Many of these, however, have become beloved standards, routinely covered by some of the biggest names in folk, pop, and rock and roll. In 1977 NASA included his harrowing 1927 track "Dark Was the Night—Cold Was the Ground" on a special recording packed aboard the *Voyager I* spacecraft as a demonstration of the achievements of human culture and the power of music. Guitarist and impresario Ry Cooder described the song, in a comment quoted by Tidal's Ryan Pinkard, as "the most soulful, transcendent piece in all American music."

The towns of Pendleton and Marlin have both been widely identified as Johnson's birthplace, but a death certificate unearthed by critic Michael Corcoran in 2000 points instead to an area just outside Brenham, Texas, roughly 100 miles to the south of those two communities. It also lends credence to the claim that Johnson was born in 1897 and not in 1902, as other writers have suggested. Johnson's early life was exceptionally difficult. When he was very small, he lost both his mother and his vision, and he was still a child when poverty forced him to begin working. As his blindness kept him from most of the jobs open to children, he turned to street corner performance, singing and playing guitar for the pocket change of passersby. Largely self-taught, he focused from the start on religious topics, relying on the Bible for lyrical inspiration and often preaching between songs. It was not gospel, however, but the blues that shaped his approach to the guitar. His ability to mix the two styles was unusual at the time, for blues songs were widely considered to be inappropriate for the churchgoers who constituted gospel's primary audience. Instrumental technique aside, Johnson himself seems to have agreed with that judgment, for by all accounts his songs were always focused on issues of faith and spiritual redemption; liquor, romance, heartbreak, and other staples of the blues had no place in his lyrics.

As a young man Johnson traveled frequently around central and eastern Texas, singing and preaching wherever he could find an audience. His break came around 1927, when a scout for Columbia Records brought him into the recording studio for the first time. That session resulted in several of his best-known tracks, including "Dark Was the Night—Cold Was the Ground," a moving reflection on the last hours of Jesus Christ; "Mother's Children Have a Hard Time" (often rendered as "Motherless Children Have a Hard Time"), a powerful evocation of grief, poverty, and untimely death; and "If I Had My Way," which focused on the Old Testament story of Samson and Delilah. While all of these sold well, "If I Had My Way" proved particularly popular, selling 15,000 copies by Corcoran's count. At a time when recordings by African Americans were not heavily promoted or widely broadcast, that was a remarkable achievement.

The next few years marked the height of his career. In 1928 and 1930 he returned to the recording studio,

At a Glance . . .

Born in 1897 in Texas; died on September 18, 1945, in Beaumont, TX; married Willie, Angeline; children: one daughter.

Career: Independent musician, 1920s–1945.

Awards: Inducted into Blues Hall of Fame, 1999, for "Dark Was the Night—Cold Was the Ground."

completing a string of powerful singles each time. Notable songs from these sessions included "Lord, I Just Can't Keep from Cryin'" (1928) and "John the Revelator" (1930). On many of these tracks he was accompanied by a female vocalist who was thought for many years to be his second wife, Angeline; subsequent research, however, has shown that it was in fact his first wife, Willie. The addition of a female voice enhanced his work considerably, as it offered an effective contrast to his loud and powerful bass; as Joslyn Layne of AllMusic.com has noted, he typically sang "with a volume meant to be heard over the sounds of the streets."

Despite the success of his singles, Johnson stopped recording in the early 1930s, as the worsening Great Depression devastated the music industry, and focused once again on street corner performance and on preaching. Based for many years in Beaumont, an industrial hub near Houston, he eventually established his own church there, the House of Prayer. A leader in his community, he also performed live on local radio from time to time, particularly during World War II. On September 18, 1945, just weeks after a fire that had left him homeless, he died in Beaumont of malarial fever.

In the decades since his passing, Johnson's status has risen significantly. In 1952 musicologist Harry Smith included "John the Revelator" in his landmark *Anthology of American Folk Music*. A favorite of folk singers and, later, rock guitarists, Smith's collection helped bring Johnson's work to the attention of new generations, as did *Blind Willie Johnson: His Story*, a compilation released by Folkways Records in 1957, and *The Complete Blind Willie Johnson*, a comprehensive box set issued by Sony Legacy in 1993. Together those posthumous releases have inspired dozens of musicians to record their own renditions of his songs, including folk icons Bob Dylan and Peter, Paul, and Mary; jazz and R&B diva Nina Simone; rockers Eric Clapton and Led Zeppelin; and the gospel group Blind Boys of Alabama.

Selected discography

"Dark Was the Night—Cold Was the Ground," 1927.
"Mother's Children Have a Hard Time," 1927.
"If I Had My Way," 1927.
"Lord, I Just Can't Keep from Cryin'," 1928.
"John the Revelator," 1930.

Sources

Periodicals

New Yorker, March 5, 2016.

Online

Corcoran, Michael, "He Left a Massive Imprint on the Blues, but Little Is Known about Blind Willie Johnson," Austin360.com, June 22, 2011, http://www.austin360.com/news/entertainment/arts-theater/he-left-a-massive-imprint-on-the-blues-but-little-/nRzPM/ (accessed October 2, 2016).

Layne, Joslyn, "Blind Willie Johnson," AllMusic.com, http://www.allmusic.com/artist/blind-willie-johnson-mn0000040137/biography (accessed October 2, 2016).

"1999 Blues Hall of Fame Inductees: Dark Was the Night—Blind Willie Johnson (Columbia, 1927)," Blues Foundation, http://blues.org/awards-search/?cat=hof (accessed October 2, 2016).

Pinkard, Ryan, "Dark Was the Night: The Legacy of Blind Willie Johnson," Tidal, February 26, 2016, http://read.tidal.com/article/dark-was-the-night-the-legacy-of-blind-willie-johnson-share http://read.tidal.com/article/dark-was-the-night-the-legacy-of-blind-willie-johnson-share</hyllink> (accessed October 2, 2016).

—R. Anthony Kugler

Leslie Jones

1967—

Comedian, actor

Jones, Leslie, photograph. DFree/Shutterstock.com.

In January of 2014, comedian Leslie Jones had been on the road, bouncing from club to club, for more than 20 years when she got the call that changed her life: it was Lorne Michaels, the creator and executive producer of NBC's long-running sketch-comedy series *Saturday Night Live* (*SNL*), inviting her to join the show's staff as a writer. Within months Jones had made the transition to on-air talent. Since then her career has exploded, and Jones seems to be everywhere—on talk shows, on magazine covers, in television commercials, and at red carpet events. She was the subject of an expansive *New Yorker* profile prepared by Andrew Marantz for the January 4, 2016, issue, the first such write-up on an *SNL* cast member to appear in the magazine since Virginia Heffernan's 2003 piece on Tina Fey. Jones got another breakout opportunity when she was cast in a lead role in *Ghostbusters* (2016), the highly anticipated all-female reboot of the 1984 film, costarring fellow comedian Melissa McCarthy and *SNL* veterans Kristen Wiig and Kate McKinnon.

A former college basketball player, Jones is six feet tall and big boned. Her imposing presence is integral to her stand-up routine. Brash, irreverent, and aggressive, she is known for her in-your-face crowd work and profanity-laden social observations on race, gender, and class. Despite her confident exterior, Jones is often the butt of her own jokes, particularly when it comes to the singles scene and her difficulty finding the right man. Nothing about Jones is subtle. Her comedy is boldly physical and unabashedly politically incorrect, and she offers no apologies for offending the squeamish.

Won College Comedy Contest

Jones was born in Memphis, Tennessee, on September 7, 1967. She moved to Los Angeles after her father, an electrical engineer, got a job as a studio technician at Stevie Wonder's radio station, KJLH. The family settled in Lynwood, a city that borders Compton to the north. Jones focused on basketball, but her older brother fell into the gang culture that was prevalent in the area during the 1980s, and he started selling crack cocaine out of their house.

Jones's basketball skills landed her a scholarship to Chapman University, a Christian college in Orange County, about 30 miles southeast of Lynwood. Before her sophomore year, her coach at Chapman, Brian

At a Glance . . .

Born Leslie Jones on September 7, 1967, in Memphis, TN.

Career: Stand-up comic, mid-1990s—; actor, late 1990s—.

Awards: Funniest Person on Campus, Colorado State University, 1987; Comedy Champion, Bacardi by Night Comedy Tour, 2000.

Addresses: *Talent agent*—Agency for the Performing Arts, 405 South Beverly Dr., Beverly Hills, CA 90212. *Twitter*—@Lesdoggg.

Berger, was hired to work for the women's basketball team at Colorado State University. Jones followed him there.

Jones's career at Colorado State was short-lived. Redshirted in her first year, she never played a game. Lacking an academic focus, she spent more time writing jokes than studying. A friend entered her into a contest for the "Funniest Person on Campus." Without preparation, Jones stepped onstage at a local bar and delivered a hilarious bit that won her the title. With only a 1.7 grade-point average, Jones could not keep her scholarship. She returned to Los Angeles, moved in with her boyfriend, and set out to become the next Eddie Murphy.

Jones's plans were derailed almost immediately. Within a month, she had bombed at the Comedy Store in Los Angeles and gotten booed off the stage opening on a bill with Jamie Foxx. Foxx took her out to dinner after the show, Jones recalled in her interview with Marantz, and offered her some advice: "You could be good, but you don't have shit to talk about yet. You need to get your heart broken, have some bad jobs—live life for a while."

Polished Her Stand-Up Routine

Jones took Foxx's words to heart. She quit performing for several years, vowing not to go back onstage until she was ready. In the meantime, she worked as a cook, waitress, cashier, justice of the peace, and receptionist. When she started performing again, she made ends meet by waiting tables and taking temporary jobs at UPS.

At the urging of two fellow comedians who were impressed by her talent, Mother Love and Dave Chappelle, Jones moved to New York to get more experi-

ence. It was in New York that she finally came into her own, as she explained to Jay Smith of *Pollstar* magazine: "I stayed there for about two-and-a-half years, got really good training and became a beast. I mean, I was already funny when I went there, but I became a beast when I got to New York.... I learned how to take care of hecklers in New York. I learned how to do crowds. I learned how to take on TV, how to write correctly, how to write jokes. I learned how to go for it and learned how to find out what it is that I'm about."

Once she returned to Los Angeles, Jones finally was able to make comedy her full-time job. She got regular gigs on BET's *ComicView* and *The Way We Do It*, became a fixture on the festival circuit, and received rave reviews for her work on HBO's *Def Comedy Jam*. Worried that she was not getting enough exposure with white audiences, Jones successfully argued for more prime-time slots at the Comedy Store. Jones caught her first big break in 2008 when Katt Williams invited her to be part of his now-legendary "It's Pimpin' Pimpin'" tour. The tour ran for six straight months, visiting 107 cities. Two years later, Jones landed her own Showtime comedy special, called *Problem Child*.

Hired at SNL

In 2012 Jones's most famous supporter, Chris Rock, saw her perform a set at the Comedy Store. After the show, as Jones told Marantz, Rock was full of praise, telling her, "You were always funny, but you're at a new level now." Rock cast Jones in his 2014 movie *Top Five*, where she appears in a scene in which a group of comedians, including Rock and Tracy Morgan, trade good-natured insults. Director Judd Apatow was so impressed by Jones's performance he created a part for her in the 2015 Amy Schumer vehicle *Trainwreck*. Jones was no stranger to acting, having appeared in television sitcoms and films since the late 1990s. However, she usually played unnamed characters or bit parts. Although she got the opportunity to work with Martin Lawrence in *National Security* (2003) and Ice Cube in *Lottery Ticket* (2010), most of her films to this point had gone straight to video.

It was Rock who pitched Jones to Lorne Michaels late in 2013. At the time, *SNL* was facing criticism for its lack of diversity. The show had not had a black female cast member since the departure of Maya Rudolph in 2007. When *SNL* held a casting call to address the problem, Jones auditioned. She was one of 12 finalists. In the end, the featured player spot went to 27-year-old Sasheer Zamata, a sketch performer with the Underground Citizens Brigade. However, Jones and another black woman, LaKendra Tookes, were hired as writers.

Jones got facetime on *SNL*, too. She set off an online firestorm with her on-air debut on the "Weekend Update" segment for May 3, 2014. In a sketch about slave rape that many viewers found offensive, Jones

talked about how much better her love life would have been during slavery, joking that her sturdy frame would have made her desirable as a breeder. Jones intended the bit as commentary on changing standards in black female beauty. Her immediate inspiration was *People*'s selection of Lupita Nyong'o as the "Most Beautiful Person" for 2014. Turning to "Weekend Update" coanchor Colin Jost, Jones said, "Let me ask you a question: If you walked in a club and you saw me and Lupita standing at the bar, who would you pick? ... You would pick Lupita. But let me ask you this: If we were in the parking lot and three Crips is about to whup your a**, who you gonna pick then?"

Starred in Ghostbusters

Jones was promoted to featured player on *SNL* in October of 2014. Paul Feig, the director of *Ghostbusters,* saw one of her "Weekend Update" skits and thought she would be perfect in the role of Patty Tolan, a New York subway worker who lends her knowledge of Manhattan history to a trio of eccentric scientists, played by McCarthy, Wiig, and McKinnon, who start a ghost-catching business. When news of Feig's feminist reboot broke, diehard fans took to the Internet to condemn the project, claiming that it defiled the memory of the original film starring Dan Aykroyd, Harold Ramis, and Bill Murray.

Ghostbusters was released on July 15, 2016. The domestic box-office take for its opening weekend was $46 million—solid but disappointing for a film with a production budget of $144 million. Reviews were mostly positive, with critics about equally divided over whether Jones or her costar MacKinnon, in the role of deadpan engineer Dr. Jillian Holtzmann, stole the show. Jake Coyle of the *Chicago Tribune* observed, "Jones, who plays a subway worker, might have been expected to be the broadest performer of the bunch, given the knockout punch of her 'sNL' appearances, but her character is impressively grounded. She's the best of the quartet, although Feig doesn't give her enough to do later in the film." Stephanie Zacharek of *Time* magazine praised the movie's energy and scolded nostalgia nuts for automatically condemning it: "No one has to love Paul Feig's new *Ghostbusters,* or even like it. But anyone who continues to stand against it on principle—'My childhood has been defiled! I don't like its stars! The trailer was bad!'—is ... unimaginative.... Because Feig's *Ghostbusters* is its own definitive creature, an affable, inventive riff on Ivan Reitman's proton-packing caper that exists not to score points but to make us laugh. For a summer comedy, there's no nobler purpose."

In addition to Rock, Jones counted among her comedic influences Richard Pryor, Eddie Murphy, Carol Burnett, Lucille Ball, Redd Foxx, and Buster Keaton. She cited Whoopi Goldberg as her greatest inspiration and role model. During a guest appearance on *The View* that aired July 14, 2016, Jones personally thanked her

longtime idol for pushing open the doors that made her career in comedy possible: "When I was young, my dad always let me listen to comedy albums and I always knew about comedy ... I always loved comedy. The day I saw Whoopi Goldberg on television, I cried so hard because I kept looking at my daddy going, 'Oh my God! There's somebody on TV who looks like me! She looks like me! Daddy! I can be on TV. I can be on TV, I can do it. Look at her. Look at her. She looks just like me.'"

Selected works

Films

Wrongfully Accused, Morgan Creek Productions, 1998.
National Security, Columbia Pictures, 2003.
Gangsta Rap: The Glockumentary, Big Business, 2007.
Lottery Ticket, Alcon Entertainment, 2010.
Something Like a Business, Swirl Films, 2010.
House Arrest, Josiah Films, 2012.
Top Five, IAC Films, 2014.
Trainwreck, Apatow Productions, 2015.
Ghostbusters, Columbia Pictures, 2016.

Television

Mermaid (television movie), Showtime, 2000.
Problem Child (comedy special), Showtime, 2010.
Saturday Night Live, NBC, 2014—.

Sources

Periodicals

Chicago Tribune, March 10, 2016; July 11, 2016.
Elle, July 2016.
New Yorker, January 4, 2016.
Time, July 25, 2016.
USA Today, July 15, 2016.

Online

Downs, Gordon, "Leslie Jones on the Craft of Comedy" (Interview), SanDiego.com, November 3, 2011, http://web.archive.org/web/20140109052827/http://www.sandiego.com/articles/2011–11-03/leslie-jones-craft-comedy (accessed July 22, 2016).
Lapin, Andrew, "I Ain't Afraid of No Fanboys: Quirky Performances Enliven New *Ghostbusters,*" National Public Radio, July 14, 2016, http://www.npr.org/2016/07/14/485261202/i-aint-afraid-of-no-fan boys-quirky-performances-enliven-new-ghostbusters (accessed July 22, 2016).
Lemieux, Jamilah, "Once Again, No One Is Laughing at 'sNL,'" Ebony.com, May 5, 2014, http://www.ebony.com/entertainment-culture/leslie-jones-week end-update-slavery-842 (accessed July 22, 2016).

"Leslie Jones," Internet Movie Database, http://www .imdb.com/name/nm0428656/ (accessed July 22, 2016).

Phifer, Tony, "Leslie Jones Found Her Funny at CSU," *The Magazine* (Colorado State University), July 2016, http://magazine.colostate.edu/issues/fall -2015/leslie-jones-found-her-funny-at-csu/ (accessed July 22, 2016).

Smith, Jay, "Leslie Jones: Comedian at Work," Poll star.com, March 19, 2010, http://www.pollstar .com/news_article.aspx?ID=714652 (accessed July 21, 2016).

Strohm, Emily, "Leslie Jones Talks Childhood Insecurities about Her Looks—and How She Found Her Confidence," People.com, July 14, 2016, http:// www.people.com/article/leslie-jones-talks-child hood-insecurities (accessed July 22, 2016).

—Janet Mullane

Loïs Mailou Jones

1905–1998

Artist, painter, educator

Jones, Loïs Mailou, photograph. Carol Guzy/The Washington Post/ Getty Images.

Loïs Mailou Jones was a groundbreaking painter who incorporated her African heritage and social issues of concern to African Americans into her artwork. Spanning eight decades, from the 1920s to her death in 1998, Jones's work was notable for its progression of artistic styles, from impressionism to cubism, realism, depictions of African sculpture, and political allegory. Jones also was a longtime professor of art at Howard University in Washington, DC, where she spent most of her career. Over the course of her nearly 50-year teaching career, Jones taught some 2,500 students, many of whom went on to successful careers as artists. Although recognition of her work was a long time coming, today the importance and impact of Jones's paintings is recognized by art historians, and her works are displayed in the collections of the Corcoran Gallery, the Museum of Fine Arts, Boston, and the Metropolitan Museum of Art.

Found Inspiration in Natural Landscapes

Jones was born in Boston, Massachusetts, in 1905.

Her father, Thomas Vreeland Jones, worked as the superintendent of their apartment building while continuing his education by taking night classes at Suffolk Law School, becoming the school's first African-American graduate when he was 40 years old. Her father's example showed Jones what a person could achieve through hard work. Jones's mother, Caroline, was a beautician who traveled to the homes of her clients, many of whom were wealthy white women. Jones sometimes accompanied her mother, and she was first exposed to fine art through the collections of her mother's clients.

Jones began experimenting with her own art at age seven. Her family traveled every summer to Martha's Vineyard, where Jones's grandmother worked for a wealthy family. For Jones, Martha's Vineyard was an ideal location to absorb the beauty of the natural landscape, which provided artistic inspiration. To encourage her artistic efforts in watercolor, Jones's mother hosted an informal art show when Jones was 15 years old, hanging her paintings from the clothesline. Jones also met a number of other artists on Martha's Vineyard, including National Academy of

At a Glance . . .

Born on November 3, 1905, in Boston, MA; died on June 9, 1998, in Washington, DC; daughter of Thomas Vreeland and Carolyn Dorinda (Adams) Jones; married Louis Vergniaud Pierre-Noël, 1953. *Education:* School of the Museum of Fine Arts, Boston, diploma, 1927; Boston Normal Art School, teaching certificate, 1928; attended Designers Art School, Boston, 1928, Académie Julian, Paris, 1938; Howard University, AB, 1945.

Career: Palmer Memorial Institute, teacher, 1928–30; Howard University, art instructor, 1930–45, professor, 1945–77, professor emeritus, 1977–98.

Awards: Nathaniel Thayer Prize for excellence in design, 1927; honorable mention, Harmon Foundation exhibition, 1930; first prize in oils, National Museum, 1940, 1947, 1960, 1963; Robert Woods Bliss Award, Corcoran Gallery, 1941; John Hope Award, Atlanta University, 1949; first place, National Museum of Art Competition, 1949, 1953, 1964; first prize in watercolors, Atlanta University, 1950, 1952; Decoration de l'Ordre National, Haiti, 1954; first place, Luban Watercolor Award, 1958; Franz Bader Award, 1962, for *Peasants on Parade;* first honorable mention, Salon des Artistes Français, 1966, for *Mediation;* Alumni Award of Howard University, 1978; Candace Award, Metropolitan Museum of Art, 1982; Women's Caucus Honor Award for Outstanding Achievement in Art, 1986; Living Legend Award, National Black Arts Festival, Atlanta Arts Festival, 1990; Artist Award, Studio Museum in Harlem, 1996.

Design president Jonas Lie and sculptor Meta Warrick Fuller, who advised Jones to study abroad.

Jones received a scholarship to attend Boston's High School for the Practical Arts; like her father, she continued her education in the evenings, taking additional courses at the Museum of Fine Arts in Boston. During this time she also worked as an apprentice to the dance costume designer Grace Ripley; for one production, Jones worked on masks, which she later considered her first exposure to African art. After graduating high school, Jones won a competitive Susan Minot Scholarship in Design to attend the School of the Museum Fine Arts, where she studied under artists Alice Morse and Anson Cross. Again Jones doubled up her studies, earning a teaching certificate in

art from the Boston Normal Art School (now the Massachusetts College of Art) at the same time. The internationally known designer Ludwig Frank, who was then teaching at the Designers Art School of Boston, was impressed with Jones's work and helped her secure a scholarship to study at that school as well.

After graduating with honors from the School of the Museum Fine Arts in 1927, Jones was disappointed to learn that she would not be hired to teach at the museum. Instead her teachers recommended that she apply for jobs in the South, where she could teach African-American students; one of her teachers helped her find a job at the Palmer Memorial Institute in Sedalia, North Carolina, one of the first black college preparatory schools in the United States. There Jones headed the art department, coached extracurricular activities including dance and basketball, and played the piano in church on Sundays. Jones invited James Vernon Herrin, the founder of Howard University's art program, to speak to her students; Herrin was so impressed with the achievements he saw in Jones's students that he offered her a job as an art instructor Howard. She took the position in 1930 and remained on the faculty at Howard until her retirement in 1977.

Influenced by Paris

Although she enjoyed teaching at Howard, Jones did not want to neglect her own art. She created illustrations, some for the *Negro History Bulletin*, and designed masks for dance companies. In 1937 Jones won a fellowship to go to Paris. The racially free environment of Paris, compared with that of Washington, DC, had a profound influence on Jones, and she was inspired to draw on her own African heritage in her work. When she first arrived in Paris, Jones was painting traditional street scenes of the beautiful boulevards, but in a city that accepted people of African descent so easily and appreciated African art, she began to see the value of her own artistic traditions. At the end of her time in Paris, Jones exhibited her groundbreaking painting *Les Fétiches* (1938). The oil painting, done in a modernist/cubist style, features five African masks. Perhaps her first masterpiece, *Les Fétiches* now hangs in the Smithsonian American Art Museum.

Upon her return to the United States, Jones had her first major solo exhibition at the Robert Vose Galleries in Boston. Critically acclaimed, that show led to a series of exhibitions throughout the 1940s. Jones often was the victim of prejudice, however, prevented from showing her work at some venues or entering competitions because of her race. Jones found creative ways to get around the racial restrictions. In 1941, for instance, she submitted her painting *Indian Shops, Gay Head* (1940) to the Corcoran Gallery's Robert Woods Bliss Competition, which was closed to blacks, under the name of a white friend. When she won the award, she declined to accept it in person, and it was not until

some time later that the painting was rightfully credited to Jones. In order to avoid being rejected by juries because of her race, she often submitted work to competitions out of town, where she was unknown.

Dealing with the strictures of racism after having experienced the freedom of Paris, Jones brought to her work a new social awareness that was evident in works such as *Mob Victim* (also known as *Mediation*), a 1944 piece depicting an African-American man who is about to be lynched. This new direction in Jones's painting drew the attention of Alain Locke, one of the most visible poets of the Harlem Renaissance. Locke encouraged Jones to deal not only with her African cultural heritage but also with the social and racial injustices that she saw in American society. Jones would later refer to her work during the 1940s as her "Locke period."

In 1953 Jones began a new phase of her life, both socially and artistically, when she married the Haitian graphic designer Louis Vergniaud Pierre-Noël. The couple honeymooned in Haiti, where Jones fell in love with the people and the activity of the market. Cubist elements remained in her work, but her paintings were imbued with a new sense of freedom, and she became bolder with color. In Haiti she found exuberance, which she expressed in works such as *Peasants on Parade,* produced 1962, some 10 years after her first visit to the island nation.

During the 1960s, even as Jones was considered a member of the art establishment by many radical students, she sought to reach out to a younger generation and continued to create issue-based art. Her 1963 collage *Challenge America,* for example, was based on her sketches of the historic March on Washington. In 1969 Howard University gave Jones a grant to go to Africa to photograph and archive the work of contemporary artists there. She brought back more than 1,000 slides for Howard's library. After returning home, Jones continued to combine clean lines and decorative elements with a brightly colored tendency toward abstraction.

Received Long-Overdue Recognition

During the 1970s, the art world finally began to acknowledge the impact and importance of Jones's art. In 1973 she became the first African-American artist to have a solo exhibition at the Museum of Fine Arts, Boston. Retrospectives of her work were held at the Museum of Fine Arts and at the Howard University Gallery. In 1980 President Jimmy Carter presented Jones with an award of international recognition.

Surveying her body of work, viewers can witness Jones's journey from classical, impressionistic styles, through her African-inspired period beginning in the 1930s, to a period in which the Haitian influence became dominant, and, in the 1980s, a return to some of the impressionistic elements she had left behind. Jones also produced a well-known montage of contemporary topics relevant to the African-American community in *We Shall Overcome,* a 1998 painting that included the figures of prominent sports figures, politicians, and other celebrities, alongside threatening images of drug abuse, apartheid, and the Ku Klux Klan.

Jones died of a heart attack in 1998 at age 92, just as she was beginning to see the recognition of her art that she had craved throughout her career. "It's all overdue," Jones said, as quoted in *Ebony.* "What's happening in my life should have happened 50 years ago, but because of my color everything has been slowed down." Since her death, Jones's work has continued to receive attention. In 2006 an exhibition of Jones's design work from the 1920s was mounted at the School of the Museum of Fine Arts in Boston; the Museum of Fine Arts showed a retrospective of her work in 2009, and 30 paintings and drawings "from every stage of the pioneering black woman artist's career," as the curators described it, were displayed there in 2013.

Selected exhibitions

Untitled solo exhibition, Vineyard Haven, MA, 1923.
Solo exhibition, Robert Vose Galleries, Boston, MA, 1938.
Solo exhibition featuring *Mob Victim,* Barnett Aden Gallery, Washington, DC, 1944.
Solo exhibition, Whyte Gallery and Howard University Gallery of Art, Washington, DC, 1948.
Solo exhibition, Centre d'Art, Port-au-Prince, Haiti.
Solo exhibition featuring Haitian works, Pan American Union Building, Washington, DC, 1955.
Solo exhibition, Galerie Internationale, New York, 1961.
Solo exhibition, Galerie Soulanges, Paris, 1966.
Retrospective, Howard University, Washington, DC, 1972.
Retrospective, Museum of Fine Arts, Boston, MA, 1972.
The Art of Loïs Mailou Jones, Bomani Art Gallery, San Francisco, CA, 1991.
Design work from the 1920s, School of the Museum of Fine Arts, Boston, MA, 2006.
Early Works, African American Museum, Philadelphia, PA, 2008.
Retrospective, Museum of Fine Arts, Boston, MA, 2009.
African American Art: Harlem Renaissance, Civil Rights Era, and Beyond, Smithsonian American Art Museum, Washington, DC, 2012.
Retrospective, Museum of Fine Arts, Boston, MA, 2013.

Sources

Books

Benjamin, Tritobia Hayse, *The Life and Art of Loïs Mailou Jones,* Pomegranate, 1994.

Periodicals

Ebony, January 1997; December 2005.
New York Times, June 13, 1998.
Washington Post, December 26, 1995.

Online

Loïs Mailou Jones, http://loismailoujones.com/ (accessed August 9, 2016).
"Loïs Mailou Jones," Museum of Fine Arts, Boston, http://www.mfa.org/exhibitions/lois-mailou-jones (accessed August 9, 2016).
Perry, Regenia A., "Loïs Mailou Jones," Smithsonian American Art Museum, http://americanart.si.edu/collections/search/artist/?id=5658 (accessed August 9, 2016).

—Alana Joli Abbott

Howard N. Lee

1934—

Politician, executive

In May of 1969, Howard N. Lee was sworn in as mayor of Chapel Hill, North Carolina, the first African American elected to that post in any majority-white southern U.S. city. Lee was motivated to run for office in large part by a desire to eliminate hostile housing policies that existed, even in that relatively progressive university town. Lee later become the first African American to serve in a North Carolina state cabinet position, appointed by Governor Jim Hunt, and he served in the North Carolina legislature as a senator between 1990 and 2003. Lee's personal and professional decisions frequently drew fire from African Americans—living in a white neighborhood or attending a church with very few black members, for example—yet he hewed to his own course and ignored the naysayers. He told the Durham, North Carolina, *Herald-Sun,* "To be called an Uncle Tom, as I was breaking down barriers, was hurtful.... But I decided to keep to a higher ground, and not be drawn into a racial divide. I weathered the storm."

Battled Racism in His Youth

In 1934 in a rural community outside Lithonia, Georgia, Howard Nathaniel Lee was born into a family of sharecroppers. Lee and his grandparents stayed on the farm when his parents left two years later to move into town, but by the time he was eight years old, they were all living together again in a small house in Lithonia. His best friend during childhood was Lukee, a white boy with whom he traded comic books and spent weekends and summers. When the boys were teenag-

ers, however, their friendship took a dark turn. Lukee told Lee that he was no longer allowed to spend time with him. He said that his father had set him straight on the "natural order of society": that white folks were to keep blacks in their place. Lukee also said that his father had advised him to start thinking about joining the Ku Klux Klan. Stunned, Lee asked whether he planned to do so. His friend seemed conflicted about the possibility but then shrugged and said it would probably happen because that was the way things were. In his 2008 book, *The Courage to Lead: One Man's Journey in Public Service,* Lee recalled his last words to his former friend: "Don't you ever mess with me.... If you do, make sure you destroy me the first time, because if you don't, I will die trying to destroy you."

Two years later Lee dared to use the white restroom at the Lithonia train station and was chased away by Klansmen. After escaping unharmed, he made two declarations: "The first was never to try to take on the system head-on but rather learn how to maneuver and use it to achieve my goals. The second was that no matter what, I would never leave the South. I ... had as much right to live, thrive, and enjoy the South as any other person and ... I would spend the rest of my life trying to make things better." As a high school student, Lee was gifted in oratory, but he was otherwise more interested in basketball than in academics. When he considered dropping out at age 16 to help support his family, his speech teacher persuaded him to stick it out and go as far as he could in school, so as to be ready for

any opportunity that might arise. He took the advice to heart and graduated high school in June of 1953.

After three lackluster years at Clark College in Atlanta, Lee's grade-point average was so low that he was told not to return for a fourth year. Feeling pressured not to fail, he managed to get accepted at Fort Valley State College in the fall of 1956. Believing this was likely his last chance to earn a college degree, Lee applied himself and ended the year on the honor roll. Meanwhile, his mother had also enrolled at Fort Valley. In June of 1959, Lee became the first member of his family to earn a college diploma, earning a degree in sociology. Two months later his mother graduated with a bachelor's degree in elementary education.

Elected Mayor of Chapel Hill

Shortly after graduation, Lee was drafted into the U.S. Army, landing in a unit in which he was the only college graduate and the only draftee in his barracks. Not happy, Lee wrote three letters: one to his congressional representative, one to a Georgia senator, and one to President Dwight D. Eisenhower. Under pressure from the recipients, Lee's captain assigned him to work as a social work technician in the mental health clinic. The next year, a few months after the civil rights sit-ins that took place in Greensboro, North Carolina, in February, Lee secretly plotted a sit-in at a restaurant in Killeen, Texas. His plan was thwarted when the Fort Hood general found out. Lee was summarily sent to Camp Casey in Korea for the remainder of his term of service.

In 1961 he left the army with an honorable discharge and moved to Savannah, Georgia, where he worked as a juvenile probation officer. There he met his future wife, Lillian Wesley, who was the mother of two children. They married in 1962, and barely two years later moved to Chapel Hill, where Lee completed a master's degree in social work at the University of North Carolina in 1966. Thereafter Lee took a position at Duke University, charged with designing and implementing a comprehensive educational program for disadvantaged children from birth through adolescence. Already the only black members of Chapel Hill's Binkley Memorial Baptist Church, the Lee family began to shop for a house. Lee's income was sufficient to purchase a home in any of the neighborhoods they liked, but with each inquiry, they were told that the house they were interested in had just been sold. They eventually did purchase a home, but not without intense pressure from the realty company, which offered them financial incentives not to buy the house. They rejected the bribe, and near the end of 1966, they moved into the all-white neighborhood.

Lee's unsuccessful efforts to get local officials to pass an open housing ordinance inspired his willingness to run for office three years later. In May of 1969, at age 34, Lee became the first African-American mayor to be elected in Chapel Hill, or any other majority-white city in the South. The campaign galvanized black and white activists and progressives in Chapel Hill, but there was resistance from some members of the black community. Lee worked hard to win voters from all parts of the city, visiting more than 300 homes for neighborhood coffee meetings and canvassing door to door with volunteer campaigners, including students from Duke and the University of North Carolina. During his first two-year term, Lee focused on many long-neglected concerns of the black community, particularly those related to discriminatory housing policies, the need for

affordable housing, and the desperate need for a comprehensive public transit system. The last did not come to fruition until well into Lee's third term, but it set the stage for a system that was still strong four decades later.

Sought New Opportunities in Public Service

In 1975 Lee handed off the mayoral gavel and sought new opportunities in public service. In 1976 he ran for lieutenant governor of North Carolina but lost a primary runoff election in September. Soon thereafter, Lee was named vice chairman of the state's Democratic Party, and in November, he was appointed by Governor-Elect Jim Hunt to the post of secretary of natural and economic resources, making him the first African American to be a cabinet member in North Carolina. Lee remained in the governor's administration until the summer of 1981. He returned to teaching, as an adjunct professor at North Carolina A&T State University, and to administrative work at the University of North Carolina's School of Social Work. He launched an unsuccessful run for Congress in 1984, and then, in 1987, Lee entered the world of business, opening restaurants at Raleigh-Durham Airport.

In 1990 Lee opened a new chapter in public life when he was elected to the North Carolina Senate. He would serve in this capacity until 2002, except for a one-term hiatus starting in 1994, when he lost his seat in the Republican congressional sweep that ousted many Democratic incumbents halfway through President Bill Clinton's first term in office. The district sent him back to Congress in 1996. During his years in the state legislature, Lee became a leader on education policy and education reform. In 2003 Governor Mike Easley tapped Lee to be his senior education advisor, and when a vacancy came up on the North Carolina State Board of Education, Easley named him to fill the unexpired term. The governor next asked Lee to fill a vacancy on the state's Utilities Commission, where he remained until newly elected governor Beverly Perdue named him executive director of the North Carolina governor's Education Cabinet.

Meanwhile, in the years following the terrorist attacks of September 11, 2001, Lee's airport concessions outlets suffered. By the mid-2000s he had sold his business interests and focused exclusively on his public service and personal interests. When he retired from state government work in 2011, Lee established the Howard N. Lee Institute, described by Matt Dees in *Chapel Hill Magazine* as an effort to help "high-potential students from low-income areas.... with a particular focus on math and science." On the institute's website, Lee explained, "I founded the Howard N. Lee Institute to organize and mobilize stakeholders and citizens in every community across North Carolina to muster the political will" needed to guarantee that every student has access to the resources needed for success. He added, "It is my hope that this movement will motivate and energize citizens of all ages, of all ethnic groups, of all education levels to work together." In November of 2015, Lee was recognized by Governor Pat McCrory for exemplary service public service with the North Carolina Award, the state's highest civilian honor.

Selected writings

The Courage to Lead, Cotton Patch Press, 2008.

Sources

Periodicals

Chapel Hill Magazine, November 9, 2015.
Herald-Sun (Durham, NC), October 29, 2008.
News & Observer (Raleigh, NC), October 17, 2015.

Online

"BAR Awards Profile—Howard N. Lee '66 (MSW)," University of North Carolina General Alumni Association, 2011, https://alumni.unc.edu/awards-pro file-howard-n-lee/ (accessed August 13, 2016).

Howard Lee Institute, http://www.howardleeinstitute .org/ (accessed August 5, 2016).

"Howard Lee: Timeline," UNCTV.org, http://www .unctv.org/content/biocon/howardlee/timeline (accessed August 2, 2016).

"Howard N. Lee," LinkedIn, https://www.linkedin .com/in/howard-n-lee-b7952317 (accessed August 2, 2016).

—Pamela Willwerth Aue

Tyronn Lue

1977—

Professional basketball player, coach

Lue, Tyronn, photograph. Bryan Steffy/Getty Images.

Tyronn Lue is head coach of the Cleveland Cavaliers in the National Basketball Association (NBA). Originally hired by the Cavaliers as an assistant, Lue was promoted in January of 2016 after the team fired head coach David Blatt. Despite having no head coaching experience, Lue helped guide Cleveland to a successful playoff run, culminating with an upset over the Golden State Warriors in the NBA Finals. With Cavs' dramatic victory in game 7 of the series, Lue helped deliver Cleveland its first NBA title in franchise history. Before joining the ranks of professional coaches, Lue enjoyed a long career as an NBA point guard. Playing for six franchises over 11 seasons, Lue is best known for his defensive effort against star point guard Allen Iverson in the 2001 NBA Finals, helping the Lakers defeat the Philadelphia 76ers in five games to win the championship.

Enjoyed Long Career as Player

Lue overcame considerable personal adversity on his path to an NBA career. He was born on May 3, 1977, in Mexico, Missouri. His father, Ron Lue, was a talented basketball player whose potential was cut short by drug addiction and crime. With their father largely absent from the household, Lue and his siblings were raised by their mother, Kim Miller. Lue showed exceptional talent on the basketball court at a young age, honing his skills at the Garfield Park playground in his hometown. He also exhibited a strong desire to prove himself against the older players in his neighborhood, sometimes refusing to leave the court until they allowed him to join their games. "I wouldn't move unless they'd let me play. But they said I was too little and I'd get mad," Lue told Brian Schmitz of the *Orlando Sentinel* in 2003. "My uncle, Jay Graves, would have to carry me off every time."

As he entered his teen years, Lue saw many of his friends become involved with petty crime, a development that was deeply concerning to his mother. To help her son stay out of trouble, Miller sent Lue to live with his aunt and uncle in Kansas City, where he enrolled at Raytown High School. Lue thrived at Raytown, earning a spot on the varsity basketball team as a sophomore and soon developing into one of the top point guard talents in the state. Although he was largely ignored by college scouts because of his small

stature, Lue eventually caught the attention of the University of Nebraska coaching staff, who offered him a scholarship to play for the Cornhuskers. The point guard quickly proved a valuable contributor to the Nebraska squad, logging 29.5 minutes per game during his freshman campaign while averaging 8.5 points, 4.1 assists, and 3.0 rebounds per contest. As a sophomore, Lue emerged as a serious offensive threat in the backcourt, scoring 18.8 points per game while finishing sixth in the Big 12 Conference with a .452 field goal percentage. Lue's performance during the 1996–97 National Collegiate Athletic Association (NCAA) season earned him a spot on the U.S. 22 and Under World Championship Team roster for 1997.

Lue continued to showcase his elite talent as a junior, pacing the Nebraska offense with 21.2 points and 4.8 assists per game while leading the Cornhuskers to their first NCAA tournament berth in four years. After earning All-Big 12 first-team honors for the 1997–98 season, Lue declared himself eligible for the NBA draft. After being selected by the Denver Nuggets with the 23rd overall pick, Lue was promptly traded to the Los Angeles Lakers. Lue played sparingly during his early tenure in Los Angeles, appearing in only 23 games over his first two NBA seasons. He proved himself a reliable role player during the 2000–01 campaign, appearing in 38 games while providing defensive energy off the bench. Lue's performance during the regular season earned him valuable minutes during the

playoffs, particularly during the NBA Finals, when his ability to help frustrate Iverson's offensive attack contributed to the Lakers' successful title run.

In July of 2001, Lue signed as a free agent with the Washington Wizards. Playing alongside future Hall of Famer Michael Jordan, Lue established himself as a consistent contributor on both sides of the ball, eventually earning a starting role toward the end of the 2002–03 season. During his stint in Washington, Lue also emerged as a clubhouse leader, impressing his teammates with his maturity and his ability to offer constructive criticism without offending his fellow players. "He'd just get his point across," Brendan Haywood, Lue's teammate with the Wizards, recalled to Dan Steinberg of the *Washington Post* in 2016. "And the way he did it, he might be joking, but there was still a little bit of truth to what he said. He did a great job of communicating with stars that seemed bigger than life, even back then."

After two seasons with the Wizards, Lue signed with the Orlando Magic. For the first time in his career, Lue was expected to assume starting point guard duties on a regular basis. "I'm ready for this role," Lue told Brian Schmitz prior to the 2003–04 regular season. "I've played behind a lot of great players. I've learned from a lot of great players. I think I'll be fine stepping into this role, being consistent and playing hard every night like I always do." During his one season in Orlando, Lue averaged 10.5 points and 4.2 assists per game, while logging 30.7 minutes per contest. He also formed a close relationship with head coach Doc Rivers, who would later give Lue his first opportunity to coach in the NBA.

Moved into the Coaching Ranks

In June of 2004, Lue was traded to the Houston Rockets as part of a multiplayer deal. He was subsequently dealt to the Atlanta Hawks, where he remained until February of 2008. After brief stops in Sacramento and Dallas, Lue signed a free agent deal with the Milwaukee Bucks before rejoining the Magic as a result of a trade midway through the 2008–09 season. Lue retired later that year. He soon reunited with Doc Rivers, who had taken over head coaching duties for the Boston Celtics. Lue spent the next two seasons working as director of basketball development, before joining Rivers on the bench as an assistant. He received his first opportunity to guide a team on his own during the 2012 off-season, when he coached the Celtics squad in the Las Vegas Summer League.

After joining Rivers for a year with the Los Angeles Clippers, Lue was hired as an assistant coach in Cleveland for the 2014–15 season. Lue quickly developed a strong rapport with the Cleveland players, notably LeBron James, whose own experience of being raised by a single mother helped foster a bond between the two men. After Blatt was fired, Lue

became the clear choice to succeed him. From the beginning, the young coach set out to change the culture within the Cavaliers locker room. Whereas the players had previously declined to participate in pregame introductions in Cleveland, Lue encouraged them to embrace the tradition as a way of building up enthusiasm among the fans. At the same time, Lue placed a new emphasis on physical fitness, insisting that endurance and stamina would be the key to the team's effectiveness on defense during the playoffs.

Lue's approach appeared to revitalize the Cavaliers. Under Lue, the team won its first 10 playoff games during the 2015–16 postseason, setting an NBA record for a first-time coach. Even after the Cavaliers went down three games to one against the Warriors in the finals, Lue's poise helped give his players the confidence they needed to mount a historic comeback. Upon winning game 7, Cleveland became the first team in NBA history to win a title after falling behind by a 3–1 deficit. Minutes after the game ended, television cameras showed Lue crying on the Cleveland bench. "I never cry. I've always been tough and never cried," Lue told Steve Aschburner for NBA.com. "It just all built up at one time. Then finally hearing that last horn go off, it was just unbelievable." Having helped deliver an NBA title to the city of Cleveland, Lue had certainly earned his moment of glory.

Sources

Periodicals

Boston Globe, February 4, 2016, p. D1; February 6, 2016, p. C1.

Lincoln (NE) Journal Star, April 1, 1998, p. 1; March 12, 2006, p. 2.

McClatchy-Tribune Business News, February 6, 2009.

Philadelphia Inquirer, June 6, 2001, p. S12.

TCA Regional News, May 11, 2015.

Orlando Sentinel, July 24, 2003, p. D1; October 5, 2003, p. D1.

Washington Post, January 25, 2016; May 21, 2016; June 6, 2016.

Online

Aschburner, Steve, "Cleveland's Tyronn Lue, Accidental Coach No More," NBA.com, June 20, 2016, http://www.nba.com/2016/news/features/steve_aschburner/06/20/tyronn-lue-accidental-coach-no-more-cleveland-cavaliers/ (accessed September 28, 2016).

Hall, Mia, and Ko Bragg, "7 Things You Need to Know about Cavs Head Coach Tyronn Lue," NBC News, June 20, 2016, http://www.nbcnews.com/news/nbcblk/7-things-you-need-know-about-cavs-head-coach-tyronn-n595631 (accessed September 28, 2016).

—Stephen Meyer

Shawn Marion

1978—

Professional basketball player

Marion, Shawn, photograph. s_bukley/Shutterstock.com.

Shawn Marion was an All-Star small forward who played for 16 seasons in the National Basketball Association (NBA). Nicknamed "The Matrix" because of his extraordinary speed and athleticism, Marion was among the most versatile offensive threats of his era, skilled at scoring on quick cuts to the basket while also possessing a reliable jump shot from outside. At the same time, he was a formidable defensive presence, frequently assuming the task of guarding an opponent's most prolific scorer. Marion remains best known as a member of the Phoenix Suns, where he was a key contributor to the team's fast-paced offensive attack. Although Marion was often overshadowed by star teammates Steve Nash and Amar'e Stoudemire, he was among the team's most explosive scorers and routinely finished among the top 10 in the league in steals and rebounds. During his later career, Marion developed into a valuable role player with the Dallas Mavericks and was instrumental in guiding the team to its first NBA title in 2010–11.

Shawn Marion was born on May 7, 1978, in Waukegan, Illinois. He was raised by a single mother, Elaine Marion, who gave birth to Marion and his twin sister, Shawnett, when she was only 14 years old. Marion spent his early years growing up in South Chicago before moving with his mother and siblings to Clarksville, Tennessee. He became a star basketball player at Clarksville High School, averaging 26.4 points and 13.1 rebounds per game as a senior while earning All-State first-team honors. After graduating, Marion entered Vincennes University, a junior college in Indiana. In his freshman season at Vincennes, Marion scored 23.3 points and hauled in 12.8 rebounds per game while shooting 56 percent from the field. The promising young forward continued to dominate the junior college ranks in 1997–98, when he averaged 23.5 points and 13.1 rebounds per contest while leading Vincennes to a berth in the National Junior College Athletic Association (NJCAA) tournament. That year Marion also earned most valuable player honors in the National Junior College All-Star Game, scoring 21 points while contributing 16 rebounds and nine assists. At season's end, he was named the NJCAA David Rowlands Male Student Athlete of the Year.

Upon leaving Vincennes, Marion continued his collegiate career at the University of Nevada, Las Vegas. Marion excelled during his stint in Las Vegas, leading

the Runnin' Rebels in points (18.7), rebounds (9.3), steals (2.5), and blocks (1.9) per game. For the 1998–99 season, he finished among the top 10 in the Western Athletic Conference in numerous statistical categories, including field goal percentage (.529, fifth in the conference) and points (543, eighth in the conference). Following his standout year at Las Vegas, the talented forward declared himself eligible for the NBA draft. Despite his limited experienced playing at the Division I level, Marion's combination of athleticism and skill caught the notice of professional scouts, and he was selected by the Phoenix Suns with the ninth overall pick of the 1999 draft. Marion made an immediate impact with the Suns, contributing 10.2 points and 6.5 rebounds per game during his rookie campaign. It was during this time that TNT basketball analyst Kenny Smith first dubbed Marion "The Matrix," in reference to his unparalleled quickness on the court.

By 2000–01 Marion had earned a permanent spot in the Suns starting lineup. He averaged 17.3 points and 10.7 rebounds per game that year while also gaining a reputation as an aggressive defender. Marion earned a spot on his first All-Star team in 2002–03, when he scored 21.2 points and grabbed 9.5 rebounds per game while establishing career-high averages in minutes (41.6) and steals (2.3). A year later, Marion led the NBA with 167 steals for the season while continuing his reliable production on the offensive end of the floor.

After the Suns signed All-Star point guard Steve Nash prior to the 2004–05 season, Marion found himself playing a key role in one of the most lethal offensive attacks in the league. Dubbed "Seven Seconds or Less"

because of its relentless pace, the Phoenix offense led the league in points for three straight years during the middle of the decade, as Marion enjoyed some of the most productive seasons of his career. His best performance as a professional came in 2005–06, when he set career-high marks with 21.8 points and 11.8 rebounds per game while earning All-Star honors for the third time in four years. Marion continued his strong play in the postseason, contributing 20.4 points and 11.7 rebounds per contest while helping lead the Suns to the Western Conference Finals for the second straight year.

Marion remained in Phoenix until midway through the 2007–08 season, when he was traded to the Miami Heat. Marion struggled to adapt to Miami's methodical, half-court offensive approach, however, and he was traded to the Toronto Raptors in February of 2009. The following off-season, Marion was sent to the Dallas Mavericks as part of a multiplayer deal. Although his overall production had declined since his peak years in Phoenix, Marion enjoyed a career revival in Dallas, as he joined a lineup that included perennial All-Stars Dirk Nowitzki and Jason Kidd. After averaging 12.5 points and 6.9 rebounds per game during the 2010–11 regular season, Marion continued to provide valuable contributions during the team's deep postseason run, both as a scorer and a defender. The forward delivered what was arguably the most impressive performance of his career during the NBA Finals against the Miami Heat, when his stout defense against LeBron James proved critical to helping Dallas win the title. For the series, Marion averaged 13.7 points and 6.3 rebounds per game.

Marion played three more seasons in Dallas before signing as a free agent with the Cleveland Cavaliers in September of 2014. The forward appeared in 57 games in 2014–15, 24 as a starter. Although his contributions were limited that season, Marion's veteran leadership played a role in Cleveland's deep playoff run, as he earned a visit to the NBA Finals for the fourth time in his career. Soon after the Cavaliers fell short of their title bid, losing to the Golden State Warriors in six games, Marion announced his retirement from the game. He ended his NBA career with 1,729 steals and 1,233 blocks, becoming only the fifth player in league history to eclipse 1,500 and 1,000 in the two statistical categories. Upon leaving professional basketball, Marion took time to focus on his personal life before turning his attention to a new career. "The biggest thing is I want to develop a full-time schedule with my son," Marion told Jared Zwerling in June of 2015, "but I'm slowly getting into the process of exploring some things. I definitely want to do something with the NBA, but I don't know what yet." In the meantime, Marion continued to run his youth basketball camp in his native Chicago, which had just entered its 10th year in 2015.

Sources

Periodicals

Dallas Morning News, July 9, 2009.
Knight Ridder Tribune News Service, March 11, 2005, p. 1.
Las Vegas Review-Journal, February 15, 2007, p. 2CC.
Las Vegas Sun, July 7, 2011.
Sun-Sentinel (South Florida), February 12, 2008; November 5, 2008; February 17, 2009; June 4, 2011.
Toronto Star, June 5, 2011, p. S2.
USA Today, April 24, 2007, p. C10; August 1, 2011.
Washington Post, June 18, 2015.

Online

Matrix 31, http://www.matrix31.com/home.php (accessed September 28, 2016).
"Shawn Marion," Basketball-Reference.com, http://www.basketball-reference.com/players/m/mariosh 01.html (accessed September 28, 2016).
"Shawn Marion," UNLV Rebels, http://www.unlvrebels.com/sports/m-baskbl/mtt/unlv-m-baskbl -marion.html (accessed September 28, 2016).
Zwerling, Jared, "The Matrix Reloaded: Retirement Won't End the Unique Versatility of Shawn Marion," Bleacher Report, June 13, 2015, http://bleach erreport.com/articles/2469873-the-matrix-reload ed-retirement-wont-end-the-unique-versatility-of -shawn-marion (accessed September 28, 2016).

—Stephen Meyer

Oseola McCarty

1908–1999

Philanthropist

Oseola McCarty spent 78 years of her life washing other people's laundry by hand, using a large pot over a wood fire and a scrub board. A private woman who dropped out of school in the sixth grade to care for her sick aunt and grandmother, she made international headlines in 1995 when, at age 87, she donated $150,000—most of the money that she had earned during her lifetime—to the University of Southern Mississippi (USM) to fund scholarships for black students who otherwise would not be able to afford to go to college.

McCarty never left the home she was raised in, never married or had children, and never learned to drive. The people of Hattiesburg referred to her incredible generosity simply as "The Gift." McCarty told the *New York Times* that the money was more than she could ever use and that she wanted to share her wealth with deserving young people so that they would not have to work as hard as she did. "I live where I want to live, and I live the way I want to live," she explained. "I couldn't drive a car if I had one. I'm too old to go to college. So I planned to do this."

Learned from Humble Beginnings

Born in Wayne County, Mississippi, near the small town of Shubuta on March 7, 1908, Oseola McCarty was raised by her mother, Lucy, who moved to Hattiesburg when McCarty was a girl. The household included McCarty's aunt and grandmother. The women worked long hours cooking or cleaning in white families' houses and taking in laundry, which was all washed by hand, dried on a clothesline outdoors, and ironed in the evening, no matter how hot and muggy the Mississippi weather may have been. McCarty took the lesson of hard work to heart at a young age. By the time she was eight years old, she was also working for an income, and she began stashing her hard-earned pay in a doll's buggy. "I would go to school and come home and iron," she told the *University of Southern Mississippi News.* "I'd put the money away and save it. When I got enough, I went to First Mississippi Bank and put it in. The teller told me it would be best to put it in a savings account." McCarty told Karl Zinsmeister of the Philanthropy Roundtable that she made her first trip to the bank on her own, with no input from her elders: "Didn't know how to do it. Went there myself. Didn't tell mama and them I was goin'." She added, "I commenced to save money. I never would take any of it out. I just put it in."

When McCarty was in the sixth grade at Eureka Elementary School in Hattiesburg, the aunt with whom she lived became ill. Instead of going to school, McCarty waited on her aunt in the hospital, as was the custom, and assumed her aunt's share of the laundry work at home. Once her aunt left the hospital, she continued as both her substitute and her caretaker. By the time her aunt was well enough for her young niece to return to school, McCarty recounted to the *University of Southern Mississippi News,* "All my classmates had gone off and left me, so I didn't go back. I just washed and ironed."

Indeed, that was what she did until she retired in 1994, well into her 80s. For most of those years she used only

At a Glance . . .

Born Oseola McCarty on March 7, 1908, in Wayne County, MS; died on September 26, 1999, in Hattiesburg, MS; daughter of Lucy McCarty. *Religion:* Baptist.

Career: Washed and ironed clothes, 1918–94.

Awards: Presidential Citizens Medal, Friends of the University of Southern Mississippi Award, National Urban League Community Heroes Award, Wallenberg Foundation Humanitarian Award, and UNESCO Avicenna Medal, all 1995; Harriett Tubman Award, Essence Award, Aetna Foundation Award, Black Expo Woman of the Year, AARP Andrus Award, and National Association of Black Journalists Newsmaker Award, all 1996; Turner Broadcasting Fifth Annual Trumpet Award, Black History Month Heroes recognition, National Council of Negro Women's Fannie Lou Hamer Award, Jackson State University honors, University of Southern Mississippi Phi Kappa Phi honors, and Mississippi Head Start Humanitarian Award, all 1997.

a pot of boiling water over a fire in the yard, plus a scrub board. Rinsing, "wrenching," and hanging wet clothes to dry was work best done by hand, she believed. She described for Zinsmeister what a typical day was like: "I would go outside and start a fire.... Then I would soak, wash, and boil a bundle of clothes. Then I would rub 'em, wrench 'em, rub 'em again, starch 'em, and hang 'em on the line. After I had all of the clean clothes on the line I would start on the next batch. I'd wash all day and in the evenin' I'd iron until 11:00." She added, "I loved the work. The bright fire. Wrenching the wet, clean cloth. White shirts shinin' on the line." She did all of her scrubbing with a "Maid Rite" scrub board and water from a fire hydrant in the neighborhood. She admitted to Zinsmeister that she had briefly tried using a washer and dryer during the 1960s, but the results did not meet her high standards. "The washing machine didn't rinse enough, and the dryer turned whites yellow," she said.

McCarty's grandmother died in 1944, her mother in 1964, and her aunt in 1967. The house they had once shared had been given to her by an uncle in 1947, so she stayed. The small sums of money left to her by her mother and aunt after their deaths were added to her savings account. Over the years, as her savings began to accumulate, McCarty was advised by bank personnel to put her money into certificates of deposit, conservative mutual funds, or other accounts that would generate more earnings. As she continued to work and live

frugally, her money continued to compound. She never bought anything she did not need. She had a black-and-white television on which she could only get one channel, but she did not care because she never watched it anyway. She bought an air conditioner only after she began receiving visitors from outside Hattiesburg in the mid-1990s; she wanted them to be comfortable when they came to meet her. She never used it for herself, though, because it ran up the cost of her electric bill.

Prepared to Leave a Legacy

After her aunt died, McCarty began thinking about what she might do with her savings at the end of her own life. She knew that she wanted to leave something to her cousins and her church. She thought about leaving the largest portion of her savings to the University of Southern Mississippi, but she did not know how to go about it. When she eventually she met with Trustmark Bank officers to discuss her estate and make arrangements for her own care should she become incapacitated, her assets totaled more than $250,000. McCarty said that she wanted to leave the bulk of her money to USM. In an effort to ensure that was what she wanted to do, Paul Laughlin, Trustmark's assistant vice president, first consulted with McCarty's attorney, Jimmy Frank McKenzie. He then helped her determine how she wanted the funds distributed.

Laughlin found a simple way to explain to McCarty how she could decide how much money she wanted to give and to whom. He laid out 10 dimes to represent percentages. On slips of paper, he wrote out the parties to whom she wanted to leave her money. He explained to her that she could decide how much money each party got by placing the dimes where she wanted them. She placed three dimes next to her cousins, one for her church, and six dimes next to the university. McCarty's gift was made in the form of an irrevocable trust agreement: the money, handled by her bank, gave her an income for life, but her gift itself would not go to the University of Southern Mississippi until after her death. Years later, the university renamed its planned giving program the McCarty Legacy Society for alumni who name the school as a beneficiary in their wills. The society's logo is a tree with six dimes at the end of its branches.

McCarty was asked by some why she chose to give her money to the University of Southern Mississippi, which did not even accept black students until the early 1960s, as opposed to a predominantly black college. Her reply exemplified her life. She said, "Because it's here; it's close." She also noted that while black students were now welcome, many could not afford to take advantage of the opportunity. McCarty's unselfish gift so stirred the business community of Hattiesburg that local businesses pledged to match her donation and raise the Oseola McCarty Scholarship Fund to $300,000. Before long, more than 600 individuals

from Hattiesburg and elsewhere had contributed enough to triple the original endowment, allowing the scholarships to begin immediately.

"I've been in the business 24 years now, in private fund raising," Bill Pace, executive director of the University's Foundation told the *New York Times* shortly after McCarty's gift was made public. "And this is the first time I've experienced anything like this from an individual who simply was not affluent, did not have the resources and yet gave substantially. In fact, she gave almost everything she had," he continued.

Became a Celebrity

When McCarty gave the University of Southern Mississippi $150,000 on July 26, 1995, she did not think that she was doing anything remarkable, but she quickly became a celebrity. The unassuming woman who wanted to help young black people get an education made front-page headlines in many major newspapers, including the *New York Times.* She was interviewed by every major television network and traveled across the United States for recognition ceremonies and speaking engagements. In 1996 she wrote a book—*Oseola McCarty's Simple Wisdom for Rich Living,* a collection of her views on work, faith, savings, relationships, and good living in her own words—and was invited to help carry the torch in advance of the Olympic Games in Atlanta, Georgia.

The awards and recognitions were many and varied. In September of 1995, taking her first trip out of the South since her visit to Niagara Falls 50 years earlier, McCarty boarded a train for Washington, DC, where she was honored by President Bill Clinton and the Congressional Black Caucus at a dinner at the White House. She received the Presidential Citizens Medal. McCarty, who had wanted to be a nurse before dropping out of school in the sixth grade, received a nurse's cap and an honorary diploma in nursing from Baptist Memorial Hospital in Memphis, Tennessee, and an honorary doctorate from Harvard University. She was a commencement speaker in 1997 at Alcorn State University in Mississippi.

McCarty's generosity inspired others to make donations. According to John Koten of the *Wall Street Journal,* media magnate Ted Turner was so moved that he pledged $1 billion to the United Nations. In 2014, nearly 15 years after her death, sixth-grade students in Tulare, California, learned about McCarty and decided to donate a fund-raising prize the class had won—a total of $40—to the McCarty Scholarship fund. Their choice to do so instead of spending the prize on themselves inspired contributions from their teacher, and then their principal, and their school librarian, until, in McCarty's spirit, the gift more than tripled, reaching $135.

Saw Scholarship Recipients Graduate

McCarty was most proud of the scholarships themselves and the prospective recipients, not the media attention and honors she received. She told Sharon Wertz of *University of Southern Mississippi News,* "I wanted to fix up a scholarship at USM so young people could get their education. You can't do nothing nowadays without an education. I don't regret one penny I gave. I just wish I had more to give."

Stephanie Bullock was at home when the call came advising her that she was the first recipient of the Oseola McCarty Scholarship at the University of Southern Mississippi. She quickly adopted McCarty as her honorary grandmother. Carletta Barnes of Hattiesburg was the second scholarship recipient. McCarty's dream was to live to see Bullock and Barnes graduate from the University of Southern Mississippi. During the last year of her life, McCarty underwent surgery for colon cancer, and then, three weeks before she died, she was diagnosed with liver cancer.

In December of 2013, the *Wall Street Journal* reported that Stephanie Bullock Ferguson, by then married and the mother of three, was working as a quality assurance analyst at Accenture, thanks in part to the master of business administration degree she earned at Southern Miss. Carletta Barnes-Ekunwe graduated magna cum laude in the late 1990s, attended medical school, and returned to her hometown to open a dental practice.

By January of 2014, the market value of the Oseola McCarty Endowed Scholarship Fund totaled well over $700,000, and scholarships worth more than $370,000 had been awarded to 44 students. The university is able to offer multiple full-tuition scholarships each year. A residence hall on the Southern Miss campus, just a few blocks from the modest home where a washerwoman boiled and "wrenched" dollar-fifty bundles of clothes for 78 years, bears the name of Oseola McCarty, a woman who never stepped foot on a college campus until she arrived one day in 1995 offering the gift of a lifetime. In 1996 McCarty told the *University of Southern Mississippi News,* "I can't do everything, but I can do something to help somebody. And what I can do I will do. I wish I could do more."

Selected writings

Oseola McCarty's Simple Wisdom for Rich Living, Longstreet Press, 1996.

Sources

Books

McCarty, Oseola, *Oseola McCarty's Simple Wisdom for Rich Living,* Longstreet Press, 1996.

Periodicals

Ebony, December 1995, p. 84.
New York Times, August 10, 1995; September 23, 1995; September 28, 1999.
University of Southern Mississippi News, July 1996.
Wall Street Journal, December 13, 2013.

Online

Arnold, Van, "California Students Make Donation to Oseola McCarty Scholarship Fund," University of Southern Mississippi, January 30, 2014, http://news.usm.edu/article/california-students-make-do nation-oseola-mccarty-scholarship-fund (accessed July 29, 2016).
Zinsmeister, Karl, "Oseola McCarty," Philanthropy Roundtable, http://www.philanthropyroundtable .org/almanac/hall_of_fame/oseola_mccarty (accessed August 2, 2016).

Other

Additional information for this profile was obtained from University of Southern Mississippi news releases on August 3, 1995; August 14, 1995; and September 21, 1995.

—Paula M. Morin and Pamela Willwerth Aue

Famoudou Don Moye

1946—

Jazz percussionist

Pioneering percussionist Famoudou Don Moye has been creating eclectic and emotionally powerful soundscapes for half a century. An expert in the drumming traditions of Africa, he is best known for his long tenure with the Art Ensemble of Chicago (AEC), one of the most influential groups in the history of avant-garde jazz. Largely self-taught and daringly original, he has also recorded extensively as a leader and coleader. Echoing critics around the globe, the website All About Jazz described him as a "drummer extraordinaire."

Born on May 23, 1946, in Rochester, New York, Moye grew up there in a musically oriented family. His passion for percussion developed at a young age, thanks in part to the influence of his father, who played the drums for several amateur ensembles based at the local Elks Club. Touring professionals, many of whom stopped regularly in Rochester on their way to larger cities, sparked his interest as well. Drum kits were notoriously expensive, however, and it was not until his early teens that he gained access to the necessary equipment and began to practice consistently. In an early sign of the eclecticism for which he later became well known, he studied a range of different drums in this period, from congas and bongos to the more common snares and tom-toms.

In 1965 Moye he moved to Detroit and enrolled at Wayne State University. By his own account, his percussion classes there did not influence him as much as the informal training he received at venues such as the Artists' Workshop, a collaborative that often sponsored concerts and discussion groups focused on the

avant-garde. "It was a whole scene," Moye later recalled in an interview with critic Ted Panken, "with a lot of people, you know, academics, creative types, and then some other people coming around." Among them were saxophonist Roscoe Mitchell and trumpeter Lester Bowie, both of whom he later joined in the AEC.

His drumming technique, meanwhile, was developing steadily, as he gained experience with a variety of groups. These included Detroit Free Jazz, a freewheeling ensemble that departed on a self-financed tour of Europe in 1968. When it was over, Moye traveled on his own, studying local percussion techniques in Morocco and working briefly for RAI, Italy's public broadcasting service. By 1970 he had made his way north to Paris, where he met Mitchell, Bowie, bassist Malachi Favors, and saxophonist Joseph Jarman, who were playing together there as the Art Ensemble of Chicago. The group was then in need of a drummer, and after a series of auditions he was offered the job. Within weeks he had become an integral member of the band, thanks in no small part to his insight and versatility. AEC performances often depended on unusual sounds, many of them percussive. While every member of the group made important contributions in this area, frequently creating new instruments from nontraditional materials, Moye's vast knowledge of drumming techniques made him invaluable.

After his arrival the AEC remained in Europe for about two more years, a span in which they recorded some of their most acclaimed albums, including *Certain Blacks* (1970) and *Phase One* (1971). On their return to the

At a Glance . . .

Born on May 23, 1946, in Rochester, NY; married; children: one son. *Education:* Attended Wayne State University, 1960s.

Career: Independent musician, 1960s—; Art Ensemble of Chicago, percussionist, 1970–2000s.

Addresses: *Office*—c/o Unit Records, St. Johanns-Vorstadt 41, CH-4056 Basel, Switzerland.

United States they continued to tour and record, while finding time for solo albums and other side projects. In 1975 Moye completed a solo album called *Sun Percussion, Volume One.* Released on the AEC's own label, AECO Records, it drew heavily on the traditional rhythms and instrumentation of West Africa; his skill with the xylophone-like balafon was particularly noted by critics. "Each [composition] is shaped by a certain idea, a certain family of instruments within which Moye extracts a wealth of complex rhythms and colors," noted AllMusic.com's Brian Olewnick in a glowing review. Olewnick was especially impressed by his "veritable arsenal of percussion, ranging from the smallest handheld clickers to massive gongs and African log drums." Critics around the world—including Stanley Crouch, a writer not generally known for avant-garde preferences—were equally enthusiastic, and the album became one of Moye's best-known works.

The decade that followed *Sun Percussion* was among the most active of Moye's long career, due in part to partnerships with his AEC bandmate Jarman, with whom he completed an album called *Egwu-Anwu* in 1978; bassist Cecil McBee, whom he backed on *Music from the Source,* also in 1978; and vibraphonist Jay Hoggard, whom he joined for *Mystic Winds, Tropic Breezes* in 1982. He then went on to join the Leaders, an all-star group that also included Bowie, trumpeter Don Cherry, pianist Kirk Lightsey, and saxophonists Chico Freeman and Arthur Blythe.

Amid these projects his work with the AEC continued. Increasingly recognized for their innovative stage theatrics as well as their music, the group's live shows were frequently more popular than their albums. Adorned with face paint and other accouterments that reflected their interest in folklore and history, Moye and his bandmates enjoyed a warm reception at theaters and music festivals around the world, especially in Europe. Most of their recordings, meanwhile, sold only modestly; while albums such as *Nice Guys* (1979) and *The Third Decade* (1984) won acclaim from critics, many of whom took care to highlight Moye's contributions, they failed to capture the visual features so important to the group's emotional power.

The AEC remained active off and on until the deaths of Bowie (1999) and Favors (2004) essentially brought the group to an end. Moye showed little sign of retiring, however, recording regularly with a variety of partners, including Lightsey and bassist Tibor Elekes, both of whom joined him on an album called *Le Corbu,* released by Unit Records in 2015. He also appeared with some frequency on the concert circuit, particularly in Europe.

Selected discography

Art Ensemble of Chicago, *Certain Blacks,* America, 1970.
Art Ensemble of Chicago, *Phase One,* America, 1971.
Sun Percussion, Volume One, AECO, 1975.
(With Joseph Jarman) *Egwu-Anwu,* India Navigation, 1978.
Cecil McBee, *Music from the Source,* Enja, 1978.
Art Ensemble of Chicago, *Nice Guys,* ECM, 1979.
Jay Hoggard, *Mystic Winds, Tropic Breezes,* India Navigation, 1982.
Art Ensemble of Chicago, *The Third Decade,* ECM, 1984.
Art Ensemble of Chicago, *The Meeting,* Pi, 2003.
(With Kirk Lightsey and Tibor Elekes) *Le Corbu,* Unit, 2015.

Sources

Online

"Famoudou Don Moye," All About Jazz, https://musicians.allaboutjazz.com/famoudoudonmoye (accessed October 3, 2016).
"Famoudou Don Moye," YouTube, https://www.youtube.com/results?q=famoudou+don+moye&sp=CAM%253D (accessed October 3, 2016).
Kelsey, Chris, "Famoudou Don Moye: Artist Biography," AllMusic.com, http://www.allmusic.com/artist/famoudou-don-moye-mn0000794972/biography (accessed October 3, 2016).
Kuntz, Henry, "Don Moye: An Interview," 1975, Bells Free Jazz Journal, http://bells.free-jazz.net/bells-part-one/don-moye-an-interview/ (accessed October 3, 2016).
Olewnick, Brian, "*Sun Percussion, Vol. 1:* AllMusic Review," AllMusic.com, http://www.allmusic.com/album/sun-percussion-vol-1-mw0000852605 (accessed October 3, 2016).
Panken, Ted, "A WKCR Interview with Lester Bowie (R.I.P.) and Don Moye (and Lester and Malachi Favors) on Lester's 70th Birthday," Today is the Question: Ted Panken on Music, Politics and the Arts, October 11, 2011, https://tedpanken.wordpress.com/category/don-moye/ (accessed October 3, 2016).

—R. Anthony Kugler

Julius Nyerere

1922–1999

Politician, educator

Nyerere, Julius, photograph. William F. Campbell/The LIFE Images Collection/Getty Images.

When he stepped down as president of Tanzania in 1985, one of the few African rulers ever to relinquish power voluntarily, Julius Nyerere cemented his reputation as one of the continent's greatest leaders. Nyerere spearheaded his nation's struggle for independence from Great Britain, becoming its first president in 1962. Known fondly as the "Father of the Nation," Nyerere was reelected to the presidency three times. His 24-year leadership was highlighted by the peaceful union of Tanganyika and neighboring Zanzibar to form Tanzania and his commitment to remake the nation into a self-sufficient, egalitarian, socialist society based on cooperative agriculture.

A major force behind the modern pan-African movement, Nyerere helped found the Organization of African Unity (OAU); united five African nations to successfully pressure the white supremacist government of Rhodesia into becoming black-ruled Zimbabwe; and ousted Idi Amin, the tyrannical dictator of Uganda, from power. This last feat in particular won him the respect of world leaders, including American president Jimmy Carter, Canadian prime minister Pierre Trudeau, West German chancellor Willy Brandt, and

Swedish prime minister Olof Palme. Nyerere's accomplishments led many to call him the "Conscience of Africa" and made him one of the developing world's most prominent statesmen. Although his economic policies fell short of his far-sighted goals, Nyerere nonetheless managed to introduce free and universal education, greatly raising the nation's literacy rate, and vastly improved health care for the majority of the population. He also instilled a sense of national pride among Tanzania's diverse tribes.

Raised in Colonial Tanganyika

It was raining so hard the day Nyerere was born that he was named Kambarage after an ancestral spirit who lived in the rain. His home was the village of Butiama, located southeast of Lake Victoria and west of the Serengeti Plain in the British colony of Tanganyika. Years later, when he was baptized in the Catholic Church, he took the first name Julius. He remained a devout, practicing Catholic throughout his life. Nyerere's father, Nyerere Burito, was village chief of the Zanaki, one of the smallest of Tanganyika's 126 tribes. Nyerere was sent away to school at age 12 for instruc-

At a Glance . . .

Born Kambarage Nyerere on April 13, 1922, in Butiama-Musoma, Mara Region, Tanzania; died on October 14, 1999, in London, England; son of Nyerere Burito (a village chief) and Mgaya Wanyang'ombe; married Maria Gabriel Magige (a teacher), January 24, 1953; children: Madaraka, Makongoro, Andrew, John, Majige, Rosemary, Anna. *Politics:* Chama cha Mapinduzi (Revolutionary Party). *Religion:* Catholic. *Education:* Makerere College, Uganda, graduated 1945; Edinburgh University, MA, 1952.

Career: St. Mary's College, Tabora, Tanganyika, biology and history teacher, 1946–49; St. Francis' College, Pugu, Tanganyika, history teacher, 1953–55; Tanganyika African Association (renamed Tanganyika African National Union), president, 1953–77; Tanganyika Legislative Council (TLC), temporary appointment, 1954, elected member, 1958–60, chief minister, 1960; prime minister of Tanganyika, 1961–62; Tanganyika Republic, president, 1962–64; United Republic of Tanzania, president, 1964–85; Chama cha Mapinduzi, founder and chairman, 1977–90.

Memberships: Organization of African Unity.

Awards: Order of Jose Marti, Cuba, 1974; Nehru Award for International Understanding, India, 1976; Third World Prize, India, 1982; Distinguished Son of Africa, 1988; UNESCO (United Nations Educational, Scientific and Cultural Organization) Simon Bolivar Prize, 1992; Gandhi Peace Prize, 1995.

attend Edinburgh University, becoming the first Tanganyikan to study at a British university. During his years abroad, he became enthralled with the socialist ideology of the British labor movement, and in 1952 he earned a master's degree in history and economics. He returned home and in 1953 married Maria Magige and began teaching history at St. Francis' College in Pugu, just outside Dar es Salaam, the colonial capital and largest city of Tanganyika.

Had he not found a significant role to play in seeking the independence of his country, observers surmise that Nyerere might have become a respected academic. Teaching was his first love, and throughout his career he preferred to be addressed by the humble honorific "Mwalimu," meaning "teacher." Throughout his public life, as well as in retirement, he wrote essays and poetry, compiled his essays and speeches into published thematic volumes, and translated works of literature, including several books of the Bible, into the Zanaki language. According to the *Dictionary of African Christian Biography*, many of Nyerere's own works were translated from Swahili into Arabic, English, French, and Portuguese, and numerous volumes were used as textbooks in Tanzania and elsewhere. During the last years of his life, Nyerere also composed spiritual songs and poems inspired by the four gospels of the New Testament and the Acts of the Apostles.

Entered Politics Eyeing Independence

Small, unpretentious, soft-spoken, and quick to laugh, Nyerere impressed his less educated countrymen with his willingness to talk and work with them as equals. In addition, he was a dynamic orator and unusually politically perceptive. Three months after arriving at St. Francis' College, Nyerere was elected president of the TAA. Shortly thereafter, in July of 1954, he transformed the TAA into a political party, the Tanganyika African National Union (TANU), and began agitating for Tanganyikan independence. Under his leadership, the organization espoused anticolonialism but stressed peaceful change, racial harmony, and social equality for all.

Tanganyika's British governor, Sir Edward Twining, appointed Nyerere to a temporary vacancy on the colony's Legislative Council in 1954. The following year, TANU sent Nyerere to New York to address the United Nations Trusteeship Council. Granted a hearing, he asked that the UN set a date for Tanganyikan independence and recognize the principle that the colony's future government be led by Africans. Although the British government rejected his demands, the debate established Nyerere as his country's preeminent nationalist spokesman.

Returning to Tanganyika, he recognized that he had to choose one path over another, and he decided to resign

tion in Catholicism, Swahili, and English. He scored first in the 1936 territorial examinations and was enrolled at the Tabora Governmental School, originally established for the sons of tribal chieftains.

Upon graduating, he entered Makerere College in neighboring Uganda, where he organized the campus chapter of the Tanganyika African Association (TAA), which had begun years earlier as a social group for African civil servants. After his graduation from Makerere in 1945, he taught history and biology by day at St. Mary's College, a Catholic school in Tabora, and taught English to the townspeople in the evenings. Many nights he stayed up late discussing politics and Tanganyika's future with his friends.

With a grant from St. Mary's and a government scholarship, Nyerere traveled to Scotland in 1949 to

his teaching post to devote himself fully to campaigning for independence. For the next several years, he tirelessly toured the countryside preaching anticolonialism without racial strife while building TANU into a powerful political organization whose membership grew from 100,000 in 1955 to a half million in 1957. This hard work paid off in 1958, when TANU candidates won all of the seats available to them on the Legislative Council in the colony's first free elections. In the unrestricted election of 1960, TANU candidates won 70 of the total 71 seats, and Nyerere became chief minister. The understanding and mutual trust that developed between Nyerere and the new British governor, Sir Richard Turnbull, during independence negotiations helped make the bloodless transition period one of the most peaceful of any African nation. Other key factors were the large number of tribes in Tanganyika, which made it difficult for any single tribe to dominate affairs, and the relatively small number of whites living in the colony.

Elected President, Sought Unity

Nyerere became prime minister in May of 1961 when Tanganyika achieved self-government; complete independence came in December of that year. Six weeks after independence, Nyerere resigned his post to devote himself to fortifying TANU to aid "the creation of a country in which the people take a full and active part in the fight against poverty, ignorance, and disease," he was quoted as saying in a biography by William Edgett Smith. Within six months, the new TANU-led government had abolished the powers and salaries of the country's hereditary chiefs.

But Nyerere could not stay away from politics for long. He was elected president of the new republic in November of 1962, receiving 98.1 percent of the vote. Pondering the meaning of a one-party democracy, he wrote a pamphlet, "Democracy and the Party System," explaining that parties such as the TANU "were not formed to challenge any ruling group of our own people; they were formed to challenge foreigners who ruled us. They were not, therefore, political parties, i.e., factions, but nationalist movements."

Following the election, TANU opened party membership to non-Africans and began the "Africanization" of the country's civil service. Several hundred British employees were cashiered with severance pay and left Tanganyika, so that by the end of 1963, roughly half of the senior- and middle-grade posts were held by Africans, many insufficiently trained. Western nations stepped up their criticism of Tanganyika's one-party system. "Africanization" officially ended in 1964.

The new president turned his attention to African affairs, seeking to unite the continent's newly independent nations. He was one of the founders of the Organization of African Unity in 1963 and the driving force behind Tanganyika, Kenya, and Uganda forming the East African Community in 1967, a common market and administrative union that operated a wide range of shared services for the three countries.

Oversaw Creation of a New Country

Meanwhile, trouble was brewing at home. Zanzibar, an island 24 miles off the coast of Tanganyika, achieved independence from Great Britain in December of 1963. One month later, the island's African majority revolted, seizing power from the traditional ruling Arab minority. Scarcely a week later, in January of 1964, a small group of Tanganyikan soldiers mutinied, causing Nyerere to flee the State House. Simultaneously, similar military coups erupted in neighboring Kenya and Uganda. All three governments immediately called on Great Britain for military assistance against their own armies. With British help, the attempted coups were quickly extinguished.

Zanzibar's continued instability worried Nyerere. Its new government quickly accepted aid from China, East Germany, and the Soviet Union, becoming, in the eyes of the West, the "Cuba of East Africa." In April of 1964, Tanganyika and Zanzibar merged to form a new country, the United Republic of Tanzania, with Nyerere as its president. The union was widely interpreted as a victory for Western interests in the region.

Nyerere was reelected president in 1965 with 96 percent of the vote. On a state visit to China that year, he was impressed by its progress since liberation and struck by the relevance of Chinese problems to those of Tanzania. Close relations ensued between the two countries, and the Chinese agreed to finance and build a new railroad to connect the Tanzanian capital and major seaport, Dar es Salaam, with the neighboring landlocked country of Zambia.

Nyerere's shift toward the East continued when he broke off diplomatic relations with England in 1965 over Rhodesia—Britain had allowed white settlers in that African colony to declare independence, thereby thwarting the wishes of the black majority. Nyerere organized five African nations to officially oppose white-minority rule in that runaway colony as well as in South Africa, Namibia, and the Portuguese colonies of Mozambique and Angola. To that end, Tanzania became the home base for nationalist freedom movements in those lands. By 1994, with the election of Nelson Mandela as president of South Africa, all of the countries on the continent were independent and governed by black leaders.

Condemning white racism, oppression, and misrule while ignoring similar actions by black rulers was not within Nyerere's conscience, however. In 1972 he denounced Uganda's Idi Amin when the brutal dictator

expelled all Asians from that country. When Ugandan troops invaded and annexed a small border area of Tanzania in 1978, Nyerere appealed to the OAU for action, without success. The *New York Times* recalled, after Nyerere's death, his blunt statement at the time: "There is this tendency in Africa to think that it does not matter if an African kills other Africans. Had Amin been white, free Africa would have passed many resolutions condemning him." The following year, 45,000 Tanzanian troops supported Ugandan exiles seeking to liberate their homeland. Within months Amin was toppled and former Ugandan president Milton Obote returned to power. Africa had successfully policed itself.

Pursued an Egalitarian, Socialist Society

From the beginning, Nyerere's goal had been to build his largely rural, impoverished country into an egalitarian socialist society based on cooperative agriculture. His 1967 Arusha Declaration set out the principles by which he meant to accomplish this. It collectivized village farmlands, established mass literacy programs, instituted free and universal education, and nationalized the country's banks, commerce, and major industries. At the same time, the declaration established a strict code of ethics for political leaders, prohibiting them from receiving more than one salary, owning rental property, or holding shares in private corporations. Nyerere also stressed that Tanzania must become economically self-sufficient, depending on its own peasant agricultural economy rather than foreign aid and investment.

Calling his experiment in African socialism *ujamaa* (Swahili for familyhood), Nyerere emphasized economic cooperation, racial and tribal harmony, and self-sacrifice. But his dream came at a cost: more than 13 million peasants were resettled, sometimes forcibly, into 8,000 cooperative villages so that medical services, water, and schools could be more easily provided. State-run corporations, called *parastatals,* set and controlled imports, exports, agricultural production, and ran the newly nationalized industries.

Results were discouraging. Agricultural production plummeted, with the yield of some crops such as sisal and cashews declining by 50 percent. Food became scarce, and agricultural imports skyrocketed in order to feed the growing population. Peasant farmers were never able to accept the new collective farms, and by 1985, nearly 85 percent of them had returned to subsistence farming. Of the 330 companies nationalized, in industries ranging from clothes to cloves, nearly half went bankrupt; the survivors were working at only 20 percent of capacity. Declining government revenues coupled with increasing expenditures caused inflation-producing budget deficits. The national currency fell in value, per capita income was $250—one

of the lowest in the world—and Tanzania's gross national product decreased annually. Only the infusion of $10 billion in foreign aid from 1970 to 1990 kept the economy afloat.

Critics blamed poor management and a bloated, inefficient state bureaucracy, which controlled the failed *parastatals,* for turning the country into "an economic basket case," according to an international banker quoted in a 1985 issue of *Time.* Supporters of Nyerere ascribed the failure of ujamaa to collapsing world market prices for Tanzanian agricultural exports like coffee, tea, tobacco, and cotton, while prices for the country's imports, including oil and machinery, rose sharply. The dissolution of the East African Community in 1977 and war with Uganda two years later also greatly taxed the national treasury.

Improved Literacy, Life Expectancy, Stability

In many ways, however, Nyerere's policies vastly improved the lives of his countrymen. At 70 percent, Tanzania had one of the highest adult-literacy rates in Africa; primary school enrollment jumped from 25 percent of the child population at independence to 95 percent; 55 percent of the population had clean water; the number of hospitals and rural health centers—as well as doctors—had risen significantly since colonial days; infant mortality declined; and life expectancy increased from 35 to 61 years. Tanzania's citizens possessed national pride, and the country remained politically stable, a rarity on the African continent, more than 30 years after Nyerere left office.

Although his dreams of a pan-African union and ujamaa did not materialize, Nyerere remained a popular figure in Tanzania and throughout Africa. Reelected president in 1970, 1975, and 1980, he retired in 1985 but continued as chairman of the Chama cha Mapinduzi (Revolutionary Party), created by the merger of TANU and Zanzibar's ruling party, until 1990. Being one of the few African rulers to voluntarily relinquish power only reinforced his moral stature and worldwide perception of his personal integrity. Typical of Nyerere's overriding commitment to Tanzania was his choice of successor, Ali Hassan Mwinyi, former president of Zanzibar, a move designed to preserve the unity of the nation. In his years of retirement, Nyerere continued to assist developing countries seek peaceful solutions to social, tribal, economic, and religious conflicts.

President Nyerere died of leukemia on October 14, 1999, at St. Thomas' Hospital in London, England. His 24-year rule was unsullied by scandal or corruption, and his devotion to egalitarian ideals was never seriously questioned. Apparently uninterested in seeking personal wealth, he maintained modest housing and, at never more than $8,000 per year, he earned a presidential salary lower than that of his cabinet ministers.

Michael T. Kaufman, writing in the *New York Times,* noted that Nyerere eschewed the typical visual symbols of power: "In contrast to many African leaders, who often raced through their capitals in motorcades with phalanxes of motorcycle outriders, he moved around Dar es Salaam in an old car with just his driver, who stopped for red lights." "He is above corruption," stated a political opponent quoted in *Time* on Nyerere's 1985 retirement. "He never sought power for power's sake. He is a real man of the people." Julian Marshall, writing for *The Guardian,* observed that Nyerere is "likely to be remembered for having provided a moral leadership to Tanzania, and indeed Africa, when the continent was taking its first shaky steps after independence."

Selected writings

Education for Self-Reliance, 1967.
Freedom and Socialism, 1969.
Ujamaa—Essays on Socialism, 1971.
Freedom and Development, 1974.
Man and Development, 1974.
Azimio la Arusha (The Arusha Declaration), 1976.
Crusade for Liberation, 1979.
(With Darcus Howe) *President Nyerere in Conversation with Darcus Howe and Tariq Ali,* 1986.
Africa's Development in a Global Perspective, 1994.
Our Leadership and the Destiny of Tanzania, 1995.

Sources

Books

Smith, William Edgett, *We Must Run While They Walk: A Portrait of Africa's Julius Nyerere,* Random House, 1971.

Periodicals

Christian Century, March 1, 1972.
Current History, April 1985; May 1988.
Economist, June 2, 1990; August 24, 1991.
Guardian (London), October 14, 1999.
Harper's, July 1981.
Newsweek, October 26, 1981.
New Yorker, March 3, 1986.
New York Times, October 15, 1999.
Time, November 4, 1985.
U.S. News & World Report, March 26, 1979.

Online

"Africa: Tanzania," CIA World Factbook, July 25, 2016, https://www.cia.gov/library/publications/the-world-factbook/geos/tz.html (accessed August 9, 2016).

Beverton, Alys, "Nyerere, Julius K. (1922–1999)," BlackPast.org, http://www.blackpast.org/gah/nyerere-julius-k-1922–1999 (accessed August 9, 2016).

Malambugi, Angolowisye Isakwisa, "Julius Kambarage Nyerere," Dictionary of African Christian Biography, 2007, http://www.dacb.org/stories/tanzania/nyerere.html (accessed August 9, 2016).

Nyerere Centre for Peace Research, http://www.juliusnyerere.org/ (accessed August 9, 2016).

—James J. Podesta and Pamela Willwerth Aue

Anne-Marie Nzié

1932–2016

Singer, songwriter, musician

Known as the "Golden Voice of Cameroon," Anne-Marie Nzié is famous for popularizing *bikutsi,* the folk song–based music of the indigenous Beti populations of that country. Characterized by a quick and intense 6/8 beat, bikutsi, which translates literally as "beat the earth," originated in the ancient war rhythms and tribal ceremonies of the Beti people native to the central and southern regions of the country. Modernized forms of bikutsi with electric guitars and keyboards began to gain mainstream popularity in the 1950s through the efforts of innovators like Nzié who succeeded in adapting the local idiom to foreign musical influences and multiple languages. During the independence era, Nzié was an important ambassador of national culture who won the favor of Cameroon's first president, Ahmadou Ahidjo (in office from 1960 to 1982), and his successor, Paul Biya (in office since 1982). Nzié's best-known song is "Liberté" (1984), an updated version of a patriotic song from the 1960s that has been embraced as the unofficial anthem of annual independence celebrations in Cameroon. Nzié died on May 24, 2016, at age 84. She was honored with a state funeral at Biya's decree.

The daughter of an evangelical preacher, Nzié was born in 1932 in Bibia, a village near the town of Lolodorf in southern Cameroon. When she was a child, Nzié was recruited to sing in the choir at her father's church. At age 12, Nzié was seriously injured when she fell from a mango tree. During her long stay in the hospital, she learned to play the guitar in the Hawaiian style, coached by her older brother, Moise, a rising musician who is better known by his stage name, Cromwell. Within a few years, Moise and Anne-Marie were performing together locally, and he hired her as a backup singer on his albums. The brother-and-sister duo recorded their first single, "Ma Ba Nze," in 1954 on the Congolese Opika label.

After a few years, Anne-Marie established herself as a solo singer, at that time a rare accomplishment for a woman in Cameroon. Blessed with a voice that has been compared with that of French chanteuse Edith Piaf, Nzié accompanied herself on the guitar, first in a duo with a banjo player and later with another guitarist, Emmanuel Ntonga. In 1958 Nzié married Ntonga's older brother, Franck Denis Nziou.

Beginning in the 1960s, bikutsi vied for prominence in the bars and clubs of Cameroon's biggest cities with another musical style, *makossa.* Tracing its origins to the ancestral traditions of the Douala ethnic group, makossa evolved into a bouncy dance music incorporating elements of rumba, highlife, and jazz. As the decade progressed, Nzié's live performances and radio appearances made her increasingly popular. She was the only woman invited to record for the local Africambiance label, which was principally associated with makossa greats Manu Dibango and Francis Bebey. In 1968 Nzié sang in Paris for the United Nations Food and Agriculture Organization and on the same trip signed with the French record label Pathé-Marconi.

President Ahidjo sent Nzié to represent Cameroon at various international music events, including the Pan-African Music Festival in Algiers in 1969 and FESTAC (Second World Black and African Festival of Arts and

At a Glance . . .

Born Anne-Marie Mvunga Nzié in 1932 in Bibia, Cameroon; died on May 24, 2016, in Yaoundé, Cameroon; married Franck Denis Nziou, 1958.

Career: Recording artist and stage performer, 1950s–2000s.

Awards: Chevalier de la Légion d'Honneur, French government, 2000.

Culture) in Nigeria in 1977. With her growing celebrity, Nzié equipped herself with a band and sometimes performed with the Cameroon National Orchestra.

Nzié planned on retiring to her village after the release of her 1984 album, *Liberté,* but the title track was so successful that she decided to keep performing. Dedicated to Biya and his Cameroon People's Democratic Movement, "Liberté" is an updated version of "Dieu Merci," a song that Nzié composed during the 1960s in celebration of postindependence Africa. Biya, a Beti from the village of Mvomeka'a, has been an ardent supporter of bikutsi in its ongoing rivalry with makossa for national dominance.

Nzié threatened to retire again in the 1990s, but, once again, her fans would not allow it. In 1996 a well-known radio personality lured her back onto the concert stage, and in 1998 she recorded another album, *Beza Ba Dzo,* which mixes traditional bikutsi rhythms with elements of jazz, blues, and Latin music. The album features backup vocals from up-and-coming Cameroonian talent Coco Mbassi. On one track, Manu Dibango sings and plays the saxophone. At close to 70 years old, Nzié went on a tour of France and Germany to promote her new album.

In 2000 Nzié was awarded the French Legion of Honor medal. The following year, the Cameroonian government honored her with a cash prize and a house in Yaoundé in recognition of her distinguished singing career and work on behalf of human rights. In 2008, at Biya's behest, Cameroon's Ministry of Culture sponsored a week of activities in Yaoundé to promote Nzié's music. Nzié made her last public appearance in 2010 with an emotional rendition of "Liberté" at celebrations in Buea marking the 50th anniversary of Cameroon's independence.

Nzié spent two weeks in the Yaoundé hospital in critical condition before her death on May 24, 2016. In July of that year, her remains were removed from the hospital mortuary, and she was buried in her home village of Bibia during a state funeral that spanned three days.

Selected works

Singles

(With Cromwell) "Ma Ba Nze," Opika, 1954.
"Ballade en Novembre," Pathé-Marconi, date unknown.
"O Mbina Ma Me," Pathé-Marconi, date unknown.

Albums

Anne-Marie Nzié, Le Kiosque d'Orphée, 1965.
Liberté (includes "Liberté"), Safari Ambiance, 1984.
Beza Ba Dzo, Indigo, 1998.

Sources

Books

Tenaille, Frank, *Music Is the Weapon of the Future: Fifty Years of African Popular Music,* Lawrence Hill Books, 2002.

Periodicals

African Affairs 104, no. 415 (2005), pp. 251–274.
Daily Herald (Chicago), May 25, 2016.

Online

Anne-Marie Nzié, Discogs, https://www.discogs.com/artist/1635063-Anne-Marie-Nzie (accessed July 27, 2016).
"Anne-Marie Nzié," Memim Encyclopedia, http://memim.com/anne-marie-nzie.html (accessed July 27, 2016).
Lavaine, Bertrand, "Cameroon: Land of Musical Contrasts: Makossa and Bikutsi," RFI Music, March 25, 2010, http://www.rfimusique.com/musiqueen/articles/123/article_8336.asp (accessed July 27, 2016).
Moki, Edwin Kindzeka, "Cameroon Mourns 'Queen Mother' of Bikutsi Music," Voice of America, June 1, 2016, http://www.voanews.com/content/cameroon-mourns-queen-mother-of-bikutsi-music/3349903.html (accessed July 27, 2016).
Ndi, Eugene Ndi, "Cameroonian Singer Anne Marie Nzie Dies at 84," AfricaReview.com, May 25, 2016, http://www.africareview.com/arts-and-culture/Cameroonian-singer-Anne-Marie-Nzie-dies/-/979194/3217914/-/w658djz/-/index.html (accessed July 27, 2016).
———, "Cameroonian Singer Anne Marie Nzie to Be Accorded State Funeral," AfricaReview.com, July 21, 2016, http://www.africareview.com/news/Cameroonian-singer-Anne-Marie-Nzie-to-be-accorded-state-funeral/-/979180/3304620/-/15ru530z/-/index.html (accessed July 27, 2016).

—Janet Mullane

Leslie Odom Jr.

1981—

Actor, singer

Odom, Leslie Jr., photograph. Helga Esteb/Getty Images.

Actor and singer Leslie Odom Jr. is best known for originating the role of Aaron Burr in the hit Broadway musical Hamilton, for which he earned a Tony Award for best actor in a musical in 2016. Odom had previously worked on Broadway—he made his debut there at age 17 in the musical *Rent*—and on television, but *Hamilton* gave the young actor his breakout role, making him a star. *Hamilton* was the biggest hit of the 2015–16 theater season, playing to sold-out houses every night and nabbing a record 16 Tony Award nominations. The role of Burr—the show's narrator and rival to Hamilton—provided an opportunity for Odom to showcase his vocal talents in show-stoppers such as his second-act number "The Room Where It Happens." After a run of more than 10 months, Odom left the award-winning show to pursue a career as a recording artist, releasing his self-titled debut album in the same month that he won the Tony Award.

Made Broadway Debut at 17

Odom was born on August 6, 1981, in Queens, New York, and grew up in Philadelphia, where his father was a salesman and his mother a recreation director at a nursing home. From an early age, he was enamored of the sound of his own voice. At age five he would sing into a tape recorder and play it back for himself; when he was nine, his parents bought him a karaoke machine, and he sang for hours. Odom gave his first performances at his family's church in Philadelphia, Canaan Baptist Church, where the pastor would sometimes call on him to sing during his sermons. "I had to get used to not being shy," Odom told Mary Louise Kelly of National Public Radio in 2016. "If he was inspired, if he looked in my eyes and he found a place in the sermon where it would make sense, he would call me up to sing something. And so I got used to singing on the spot."

In school a teacher helped Odom channel his energy into oratory competitions. When he was 13, he was awarded a scholarship to attend the Freedom Theater, which focused on African-American drama. After taking a few acting and movement classes, he was hooked, and he started performing in school plays thereafter. "People just kept pointing me to the stage," he recalled in an interview with the *New York Times*. In 1998, when Odom was in the 11th grade, he heard about the

At a Glance . . .

Born Leslie Odom Jr. on August 6, 1981, in New York, NY; married Nicolette Robinson, 2012. *Education:* Carnegie Mellon University, BA, 2003.

Career: Stage, television, and film actor, 1998—.

Awards: Princess Grace Award, Acting, 2002; Fred and Adele Astaire Award, Outstanding Male Dancer in a Broadway Show, 2012, for *Leap of Faith;* Drama Desk Award, Outstanding Featured Actor in a Musical, Lucille Lortel Award, Outstanding Lead Actor in a Musical, and Tony Award, Best Actor in a Musical, all 2016, for *Hamilton;* Grammy Award, Best Musical Theater Album, 2016, for *Hamilton.*

Addresses: *Talent agent*—Creative Artists Agency, 2000 Avenue of the Stars, Los Angeles, CA 90067. *Web*—http://www.leslieodomjr.com/. *Twitter*—@leslieodomjr.

Pulitzer Prize–winning musical *Rent* on Broadway and desperately wanted to be a part of it. Skipping school one day, he snuck off to an audition and, to his surprise, landed a small role as a replacement member in the ensemble, becoming the youngest actor ever cast in the show. At age 17, he was performing on Broadway.

Odom spent several months on Broadway with *Rent* and then returned to Philadelphia to finish high school. Although he had an offer to do another musical on Broadway, Disney's *Aida,* his parents urged him to go to college. Odom turned down the part and enrolled at Carnegie Mellon University in Pittsburgh to study acting. He chose the school because his idol Michael McElroy, a Broadway actor who had appeared with Odom in *Rent* and later was nominated for a Tony for his role in the musical *Big River,* had gone there. "I wanted to be him," Odom recalled in an interview with *Backstage* magazine. "And I learned while I was there that I couldn't be Michael McElroy! But in the process I found I could be myself."

After completing his undergraduate degree in 2003, Odom spent the next decade in Los Angeles, working mostly in television and singing in clubs. He landed his first recurring role in CBS's *CSI: Miami* in 2003 and went on to appear in the series *Vanished* and *Big Day* before returning to New York for a role in the NBC musical drama *Smash.* Odom finally returned to Broadway in 2012 in the short-lived musical *Leap of Faith,* based on the 1992 Steve Martin movie of the same title. Although the show ran for only 24 previews and 20 performances, it still earned a Tony nomination

for best musical of the year, and Odom won a Fred and Adele Astaire Award for best male dancer on Broadway. The following year Odom appeared in the off-Broadway musical *Venice* at the Joseph Papp Public Theater.

Landed Role in Hamilton

By 2013 Odom was feeling discouraged about the direction of his career, so much so that he began applying for jobs as a hotel clerk. As it happened, in the summer of that year, he received an e-mail from actor and composer Lin-Manuel Miranda, the creator and star of the 2008 hit Broadway musical *In the Heights,* inviting him to participate in a workshop of a new play that he was working on—a hip-hop musical about founding father Alexander Hamilton. Odom was unavailable, but he scored tickets to the presentation that Miranda and the cast gave at Vassar College in July. "I was on the edge of my seat the entire time—that's what falling in love feels like," Odom remembered in an interview with *Broadway Style Guide.* "I tweeted at Lin after I saw it. I said, 'Oh my God, if you're ever doing this again, tell me and I will be the biggest champion of this.'" A few months later Odom received another e-mail from Miranda—subject line: "Octoburrfest"—inviting him to a reading of the musical.

Odom accepted and read the part of Aaron Burr, the third vice president of the United States and the man who famously shot and killed Hamilton in a duel. Although Burr has been vilified in history, in Miranda's retelling, Burr, who also serves as the play's narrator, is presented as a brilliant but flawed man. Odom was deeply affected by the play and believed that he could bring something special to the role of Burr. He lobbied Manuel and the show's director, Thomas Kail, aggressively for the part. His persistence eventually paid off, and the role of Burr was Odom's.

Hamilton premiered off Broadway at the Joseph Papp Public Theater in February of 2015 before transferring to Broadway, where it opened at the Richard Rodgers Theatre in August. Odom and most of the original cast joined the Broadway production. From the beginning, *Hamilton* was a hot ticket, with advance sales reportedly topping $30 million; by September the show was sold out for most of its Broadway run, with tickets going for an average price of just under $500. Hamilton also received rave reviews from critics. In the *New York Times,* reviewer Ben Brantley assured readers that the show lived up to the hype: "Yes, it really is that good," he wrote. "I am loath to tell people to mortgage their houses and lease their children to acquire tickets to a hit Broadway show. But 'Hamilton' ... might just about be worth it."

Won Tony Award, Released Debut Album

One of the most notable facts about Hamilton was its

casting of actors of color to play the founding fathers: in addition to Odom as Burr, the production also featured Miranda, of Puerto Rican heritage, as Hamilton and African-American actors Christopher Jackson and Daveed Diggs as George Washington and Thomas Jefferson, respectively. This aspect of the production appealed strongly to Odom and made it a special opportunity. "As a black actor, I can just tell you that I saw the potential to turn what is expected of us so often on its head," he told the *New York Times*. "We're oftentimes asked to stop the show, or to make 'em laugh, but we're very rarely asked for vulnerability, very rarely asked for complication. And here was a role where he got to do 'Room Where It Happens' [Odom's second-act number] ... You just don't find parts like that."

In 2016 *Hamilton* was nominated for a record 16 Tony Award nominations and took home 11 awards, including best musical and best original score; it also won the Pulitzer Prize for Drama that year. Odom won the Tony Award for best actor in a musical, beating his costar Miranda, in addition to Lucille Lortel and Drama Desk awards for the original off-Broadway production of Hamilton. Odom and his cast mates also nabbed a Grammy Award for best musical theater album for their recording of *Hamilton*. In addition to his onstage duties, Odom also hosted the Broadway.com web series Aaron Burr, Sir, which provided a behind-the-scenes look at the popular musical.

Following the Tony Awards in June of 2016, Odom announced that he would leave the cast of *Hamilton* on July 9, along with Miranda and several other cast mates; Odom was replaced by Broadway veteran Brandon Victor Dixon. That same month Odom released his self-titled solo debut album, a collection of 10 jazz and cabaret standards such as "Look for the Silver Lining" and "The Party's Over." Odom originally recorded the album in 2014 with money raised from a Kickstarter crowdfunding campaign but then remade the record with new songs after signing with a label, S Curve. The actor had no immediate plans to return to Broadway but instead intended to focus on his work as a solo artist. Soon after leaving Hamilton, Odom embarked on a two-week residency at the McKittrick Hotel in New York City.

Selected works

Theater

Rent, Nederlander Theatre, New York, 1998.
Jersey Boys, La Jolla Playhouse, La Jolla, CA, 2004–05.
Being Alive, Philadelphia Theatre Company, Philadelphia, PA, 2007.
Leap of Faith, St. James Theatre, New York, 2012.

Venice, Joseph Papp Public Theater, New York, 2013.
Tick, Tick ... Boom!, New York City Center, 2014.
Hamilton, Richard Rodgers Theatre, New York, 2015–16.

Films

Red Tails, Twentieth Century Fox, 2012.

Television

CSI: Miami, CBS, 2003–06.
Vanished, Fox, 2006.
Big Day, ABC, 2006–07.
Smash, NBC, 2012–13.
Law & Order: Special Victims Unit, NBC, 2013–15.
Person of Interest, CBS, 2014–15.

Albums

Leslie Odom Jr., S-Curve, 2016.

Sources

Periodicals

Broadway Style Guide, March 2016.
New York Times, August 7, 2015; May 15, 2016.

Online

Evans, Suzy, "Leslie Odom Jr. on Leaving 'Hamilton,' Releasing Solo Album: 'I Have Not Come to Terms with All That Happened,'" Billboard.com, July 12, 2016, http://www.billboard.com/articles/news/7438042/leslie-odom-jr-album-solo-release (accessed August 23, 2016).
Kelly, Mary Louise, "Leslie Odom Jr.: 'I Want to Sing to the Moment That You're In,'" *Morning Edition,* National Public Radio, June 10, 2016, http://www.npr.org/2016/06/10/481282363/leslie-odom-jr-i-want-to-sing-to-the-moment-that-youre-in (accessed August 23, 2016).
Smart, Jack, "Leslie Odom Jr. Risks It All in 'Hamilton,'" Backstage.com, April 6, 2016, http://www.backstage.com/interview/leslie-odom-jr-risks-it-all-hamilton/ (accessed August 23, 2016).
Tyler-Ameen, Daoud, "Being Aaron Burr," National Public Radio, December 21, 2015, http://www.npr.org/sections/therecord/2015/12/21/460526573/being-aaron-burr (accessed August 23, 2016).
Whelan, Aubrey, "Leslie Odom Jr.: Being Burr in 'Hamilton' Like Falling in Love," Philly.com, December 28, 2015, http://articles.philly.com/2015–12-28/news/69337081_1_east-oak-lane-alvin-ailey-audition (accessed August 23, 2016).

—Deborah A. Ring

McKinley L. Price

1949—

Dentist, politician

McKinley L. Price opened a dental practice in his hometown of Newport News, Virginia, in 1977. Thirty-three years later, still working as a full-time dentist, he became the first African American to be elected mayor of that city. During his first term in office, Price managed his dual professional life by seeing patients in his office every day except Tuesday, which he reserved for city-related meetings and other mayoral activities. Price is able to stay connected with both offices by e-mail and smartphone, no matter where he may be working on a particular day. He told Alison Johnson of the online *Health Journal* that he does draw a line when it comes to overlapping one role with the other, saying, "We try not to have any politics in my office." He added, "When I'm there I'm a doctor and not the mayor. If people have political concerns, I ask them to schedule a time to talk through the mayor's office.... patients deserve my full attention as a doctor."

Returned to Hometown as a Dentist

From an early age, Price knew he wanted to enter the medical profession. After graduating from high school in 1967, he attended the nearby Hampton Institute (now Hampton University) on a tennis scholarship and earned a bachelor's degree in biology in 1971. He then spent a year in the U.S. Army, discharged in 1972 as a first lieutenant, and headed to Howard University to pursue a degree in dentistry. His professional role model was Dr. C. Waldo Scott, the father of one of his closest friends, who was his surgeon when an appen-

dectomy was required at age eight. In 1974 Price married Valerie Scott, the sister of his best friend and daughter of the man he had looked up to since childhood. It was Scott who counseled Price to consider dentistry as a career path, in part because the field offered more regular hours than he would likely experience as a general practitioner or in another medical specialty.

Following his general anesthesia residency in Baltimore, Maryland, Price returned to Newport News and opened a dental practice. He became involved in local civic and professional organizations, and, as his two children grew, he was an active participant in school, church, and community activities, as his father had been. As a child Price had participated in Little League, Boy Scouts, and the local recreation center then known as the Boys Club. His father, who worked for the Newport News Shipyard for more than 40 years, made it a point to attend games and other activities that he and his sisters were involved in; his future mother-in-law was the den leader for one of his early Scout troops. A desire to build a network of such role models for the children of Newport News motivated many of the choices Price made after returning to his hometown.

When Price married Valerie Scott, whom he had known since childhood, he joined "a family whose standards for service are high," as described by the *Daily Press* in a 2005 profile of Price, that year's *Daily Press* Citizen of the Year. In addition to being a much-loved local physician and surgeon, Dr. Scott was

a civil rights pioneer in Newport News who became chief of surgery at two hospitals and was the first African American appointed to the Newport News School Board in the 20th century. His son, U.S. Representative Robert C. "Bobby" Scott, was first elected to the Virginia state legislature in 1977, serving as both a delegate and a senator before being elected to

Congress in 1992. For many years Price was content to leave elective politics to his brother-in-law, preferring to make his contributions to the community through volunteer work and occasional appointments to public positions, such as the school board, on which he served from 1984 until 1992. In 2004 Price filled a temporary slot on the Newport News City Council when the seat was vacated by a councilor's election to another office. In 2005 he was appointed to the board of the Virginia Economic Development Partnership by Governor Mark Warner. He also served on board of Thomas Nelson Community College, volunteered at the Boys and Girls Club, and helped found the Hampton Roads chapter of 100 Black Men of America.

Elected Mayor of Newport News

One of his earliest civic contributions came as an organizer of a local group called People to People. In 1992 the all-white City Council made a number of decisions that alarmed the African-American residents of Newport News. To reduce tensions and improve communication and cooperation across racial and other divisions, local leaders created People to People, described in 2005 by the *Daily Press* as "a mechanism and an environment in which people on all sides of an issue can discuss it and come up with ways to solve it themselves. It tackles topics important to the city, cutting across education economics, race relations and, most recently, gangs."

Price's motivation to seek the office of mayor in 2010 arose, in part, from his desire to see the city do more to counter gang violence, not just through stepped-up police work but also by understanding—and applying resources to resolve—the community issues that contribute to gang involvement on the part of Newport News teens. Recalling his childhood and adolescence in the city, Price believed that the key to keeping kids out of gangs is to ensure that many recreational and mentoring opportunities are available for all, not just those who have a strong family support system.

While the position of Newport News mayor is, by charter, a nonpartisan office, and candidates are not officially endorsed by any political party, financial supporters and campaign volunteers may identify with a party. Price's opponent, Councilwoman Pat Woodbury, was backed primarily by those affiliated with local Republican politics; Price's support more typically came from those affiliated with the Democratic Party. Price prevailed in the May of 2010 election and became the first directly elected African-American mayor of Newport News. Until 1996 Newport News mayors were selected from among the city council members; under that system, Jessie M. Rattley, first elected to the city council in 1970, served as mayor from 1986 until 1990, the first woman and the first African American to hold the seat.

Focused on Community Concerns

During his first term in office, Price moved quickly to focus on community concerns, especially jobs, roads, gangs. On the issue of gangs, he and several council members disagreed on whether there was a need for the city to invest in its recreational infrastructure. The new mayor commissioned a study about ways to reduce gang activity. The findings indicated that the community needed a comprehensive approach that included recreation and job training programs. Both the cost of the study—which had been subsidized by federal funds—and the projected costs of building a new recreation center were publicly panned by some council members and citizens. Price defended the initiative, noting that the report provided a strategic plan for integrating many of the efforts that were already under way, and for incorporating additional programs that had been successful in other similar cities. He also promised that implementation of all proposals would rely on finding a workable combination of federal and state grants and private contributions, in addition to local funding.

Upgrading the recreational facility infrastructure across the city would remain a work in progress well into Price's second term as mayor. In 2015, however, the city successfully completed its second 10-week summer program known as STEP (Summer Training and Enrichment Program), under the auspices of the Youth and Gang Violence Prevention Initiative. The 2015 program provided 316 young people between 16 and 24 with "paid work experience, field trips, workshops, financial literacy training and GED preparation classes," as described by the city's Communication Department. Area businesses and nonprofit organizations partner with the city to offer on-the-job training, where participants work three or four days each week and engage in "Enrichment Days" the other one or two days. Participants are paid a weekly stipend that is higher if they have a GED or high school diploma. At the end of the 2015 session, jobs were offered to 21 participants who, prior to the program, didn't have the skills to apply for or maintain employment. The 2016 session was slated to serve as many as 600 participants, due to increased participation of businesses and greater interest in the community.

Commenting on this program, which would not have existed without his vision for improving the quality of life for all Newport News residents, Price noted, "Be-cause of our commitment to reducing and eliminating youth and gang violence, we are working tirelessly to help our young people connect to valuable resources and provide them with much needed training to make sure they are armed with tools that will help them to lead productive lives." Price's administration also worked with institutions including the University of Virginia and Virginia Tech to create new opportunities in higher education for the city's residents. In 2013 he presided over the opening of the University of Virginia-Virginia Tech Newport News Center, a collaboration intended to provide certificate programs, professional development, customized business programs, graduate degrees, and a business-focused bachelor's degree program in conjunction with the city's Thomas Nelson Community College.

Sources

Periodicals

Daily Press (Newport News, VA), March 5, 2001; July 4, 2010; September 28, 2011; August 13, 2013.

Online

Johnson, Alison, "Mayor McKinley Price, D.D.S.: Helping Others, through Patients and Politics," *Health Journal,* June 2012, http://www.the healthjournals.com/mayor-mckinley-price-d-d-s-help ing-others-through-patients-and-politics/ (accessed August 4, 2016).

"Mayor McKinley L. Price, DDS," City of Newport News, https://www.nngov.com/1012/Mayor-Price (accessed August 2, 2016).

"McKinley Price's Biography," VoteSmart.org,http:// votesmart.org/candidate/biography/132666/mc kinley-price#.V6X8mDU4vHE (accessed August 2, 2016).

"Newport News Prepares to Serve 600 Young Adults in Summer Training and Enrichment Program," Newport News Now, March 23, 2016, https:// www.nnva.gov/Blog.aspx?IID=22 (accessed August 13, 2016).

"2005 Citizen of the Year: McKinley Price," Daily-Press.com, 2005, http://www.dailypress.com/ news/newport-news/dp-coy-2005-mckinley-price -story.html (accessed August 2, 2016).

—Pamela Willwerth Aue

Prince Be

1970–2016

Rapper, songwriter, producer

Prince Be, photograph. Ebet Roberts/Redferns/Getty Images.

Prince Be was one-half of the hip-hop duo P.M. Dawn, formed in the late 1980s with his brother D.J. Minutemix. Heavyset and dreadlocked, Prince Be was the group's front man and songwriter, while his brother worked the turntable. P.M. Dawn became famous in the 1990s for their psychedelic blend of pop and rap, epitomized by their biggest hit, "Set Adrift on Memory Bliss," from their 1991 debut album, *Of the Heart, of the Soul, and of the Cross*. The single topped the Billboard Hot 100 pop chart in November of 1991, the first rap song by a black artist ever to do so. P.M. Dawn's debut and their 1993 follow-up, *The Bliss Album,* were critically acclaimed, and both went gold. Their subsequent records did not match that success, however, and the group's star had faded by the end of the 1990s. Prince Be, who was diagnosed with diabetes in 1992, suffered from complications of the disease until his death from renal failure in 2016 at age 46.

Prince Be was born Attrell Cordes on May 15, 1970, in Jersey City, New Jersey. His father died when Cordes was young, and he was raised by his mother, Janice, who was a gospel singer, and his stepfather, George Brown, a drummer who was a member of the group Kool and the Gang. Prince Be began deejaying parties as a teenager and eventually started writing songs. In the late 1980s, he and his younger brother Jarrell, known as D.J. Minutemix, formed a duo called P.M. Dawn. They made their first demo tape for $600, using money that Prince Be earned while working as a security guard at a homeless shelter. They released their first single, "Ode to a Forgetful Mind," on the Warlock label in 1989. The single attracted little notice in the United States but found greater success in the United Kingdom, where the track was released by the London-based Gee Street Records. The brothers signed with Gee Street in 1990 and were set to record their debut album when the label went bankrupt.

P.M. Dawn's contract was sold to the U.S. label Island Records, which released the group's debut album, *Of the Heart, of the Soul, and of the Cross: The Utopian Experience,* in August of 1991. The record was an immediate hit, rising to number 29 on the Billboard 200, fueled by the single "Set Adrift on Memory Bliss," which featured a lilting hook sampled from Spandau Ballet's 1983 new wave hit "True." The single topped the pop, R&B, and dance charts, and

At a Glance . . .

Born Attrell Cordes on May 15, 1970, in Jersey City, NJ; died on June 17, 2016, in Neptune City, NJ; son of Attrell Cordes Sr. and Janice Carr; married Mary Sierra; children: Mia, Christian, Brandon.

Career: Member of P.M. Dawn, 1980s–2016.

was the first rap single by black artists to reach number one on the Billboard Hot 100.

P.M. Dawn blazed a different trail in hip-hop, incorporating elements of R&B and pop, blurring the lines between rapping and singing, and employing mysticism and abstract imagery in their lyrics. The resulting sound contrasted sharply with the more aggressive gangsta rap of the West Coast. The brothers were hailed as pioneers of a new brand of "psychedelic rap" and earned comparisons to groups such as De La Soul and Arrested Development. Writing in the New Jersey *Star-Ledger* in 1998, critic Jay Lustig described P.M. Dawn as "philosophical instead of macho," noting that their music "described what was going on in their minds rather than in the streets." In the *Village Voice*, Robert Christgau wrote of P.M. Dawn's debut, "This is rap that's totally idiosyncratic, yet so lost in music it's got total outreach—moving effortlessly from speech to song … [a] quiet storm of sweet hooks and soft beats." In that newspaper's year-end list of the best albums, Christgau ranked *Of the Heart* third.

While the group's musical and lyrical experimentation drew praise from critics, it inspired negative reactions from some of their fellow rappers. After Prince Be made disparaging comments about the rapper KRS-One in an interview with *Details* magazine, KRS-One attacked the brothers at a January 1992 show in New York City, breaking the record that D.J. Minutemix had on the turntable and shoving Prince Be off the stage. The incident was captured and aired on *Yo! MTV Raps*, bolstering the group's image as unconventional rappers.

The group's sophomore album, *The Bliss Album … ? (Vibrations of Love and Anger and the Ponderance of Life and Existence)*, released in March of 1993, was an even greater success. The record reached number 23 on the Billboard R&B/Hip-Hop Albums chart and peaked at number 30 on the Billboard 200 pop chart. It produced two hit singles, "I'd Die Without You," which reached number three on the Billboard Hot 100 and appeared on the soundtrack for the Eddie Murphy film *Boomerang*, and "Looking through Patient Eyes," which rose to number six on the Hot 100. *The Bliss Album*, like *Of the Heart*, achieved gold status with more than half a million sold.

P.M. Dawn released two more albums in the 1990s—*Jesus Wept* (1995) and *Dearest Christian, I'm So Very Sorry for Bringing You Here. Love, Dad* (1998)—but neither achieved the success of their predecessors, and the group faded into obscurity. A greatest-hits compilation, *The Best of P.M. Dawn*, was issued in 2000.

Prince Be experienced a variety of health problems beginning in 1992, when he was diagnosed with diabetes after sinking into a three-day coma. In 2005 he suffered a massive stroke that left him paralyzed on his left side. Despite that, he and his brother competed on the NBC talent competition *Hit Me, Baby, One More Time* later that year; Prince Be performed sitting in a chair and had to be helped on and off the stage. P.M. Dawn won the competition and a $20,000 prize, which they donated to the Juvenile Diabetes Research Foundation. Prince Be had a second stroke in 2009 and later had to have a partial amputation of one leg; during his last years, he was confined to a nursing home. Prince Be died of renal failure at a New Jersey hospital on June 17, 2016, at age 46.

Selected discography

Of the Heart, of the Soul, and of the Cross: The Utopian Experience (includes "Set Adrift on Memory Bliss"), Gee Street/Island, 1991.
The Bliss Album … ? (Vibrations of Love and Anger and the Ponderance of Life and Existence) (includes "I'd Die without You," and "Looking through Patient Eyes"), Gee Street/Island, 1993.
Jesus Wept, Gee Street/Island, 1995
Dearest Christian, I'm So Very Sorry for Bringing You Here. Love, Dad, Gee Street/Island, 1998.
The Best of P.M. Dawn, V2, 2000.

Sources

Periodicals

Billboard, September 12, 1998, March 20, 1993.
New York Times, June 19, 2016.
Star-Ledger (Newark, NJ), October 4, 1998.
Vibe, November 1995, pp. 90–92.
Village Voice, January 28, 1992.

Online

Erlewine, Stephen Thomas, "P.M. Dawn: Artist Biography," AllMusic.com, http://www.allmusic.com/artist/pm-dawn-mn0000741718/biography (accessed September 27, 2016).
Kreps, Daniel, "Attrell 'Prince Be' Cordes, P.M. Dawn Rapper, Dead at 46," RollingStone.com, June 17, 2016, http://www.rollingstone.com/music/news/attrell-prince-be-cordes-p-m-dawn-rapper-dead-at-46-20160617 (accessed September 27, 2016).

—Deborah A. Ring

Wallace Roney

1960—

Jazz trumpeter

Roney, Wallace, photograph. David Redfern/Redferns/Getty Images.

One of the leading trumpeters of his generation, Grammy Award winner Wallace Roney has been playing with the biggest names in jazz since his mid-teens. Adept at a wide range of styles, from the classic bebop of the 1950s to the jazz-rock blend known as fusion, he has often been compared to the legendary Miles Davis, one of his mentors. As Stanley Crouch and others have noted, he is more than an imitator, although his debt to Davis and other predecessors is clear. "Wallace seems to be the only trumpet player who understands how Miles did what he did," bassist Ron Carter told Crouch for the *New York Times*. "He didn't just imitate the order of the notes; he understands why they are in that order. Because he understands the concept way past the imitator stage, he's able to develop it to the next level of harmony, space, phrasing and achieve his own individuality. It's time people began to recognize that."

Born in Philadelphia on May 25, 1960, Roney grew up there in a household devoted to jazz; "his father's favorite musician," noted Crouch, "was Miles Davis and his mother's was Thelonious Monk." His training on the trumpet began as early as the age of four, when he started lessons at the Settlement Music School, a Philadelphia landmark known for its innovative programs. By his mid-teens he had moved on to the Duke Ellington School of the Arts, a rigorous and highly regarded magnet program in Washington, DC. By the time his studies there were complete, he was playing professionally, appearing alongside much older musicians in clubs up and down the East Coast. He continued to do so as an undergraduate, balancing his coursework at the Berklee College of Music in Boston and Howard University in Washington with a number of prominent gigs, including a tour with drummer Art Blakey's Jazz Messengers, an ensemble renowned as an incubator of rising talent.

Despite that success Roney encountered some difficulties in the early 1980s, as he made the transition from college to full-time work. Jazz itself was struggling in this period; increasingly regarded as somewhat old-fashioned, it often lacked the vibrancy that had characterized it in the 1950s and 1960s. As jazz clubs around the country closed their doors, it became challenging for younger musicians—even those as talented as Roney—to find steady work. That situation, fortunately, proved relatively short-lived, thanks in

At a Glance . . .

Born on May 25, 1960, in Philadelphia, PA. *Education:* Attended Berklee College of Music, late 1970s(?)–early 1980s(?), Howard University, late 1970s(?)–early 1980s(?).

Career: Independent musician, 1970s—.

Awards: Grammy Award, Best Jazz Instrumental Performance, Individual or Group, 1994, for *A Tribute to Miles.*

Addresses: *Agent*—Ed Keane Associates, 1140 Saratoga St., Boston, MA 02128. *Web*—http://www.WallaceRoney.com. *Twitter*—@WallaceRoney.

large part to the emergence of several charismatic newcomers, all of them well versed in the jazz of decades past. While Roney was certainly an influential member of that group, he was not its most prominent figure, a role most likely filled by Wynton Marsalis, another trumpeter. Marsalis's efforts to reinvigorate the genre drew considerable media attention, and the situation began to improve. The turning point for Roney came around 1985, when he began an extended collaboration with drummer Tony Williams, whom he backed on two well-received albums, *Foreign Intrigue* (1985) and *Civilization* (1986). Soon thereafter Williams returned the favor, backing him on *Verses* (1987), his full-length debut as a leader.

In the early 1990s, as he continued to release his own albums, Roney received a major boost from Davis, who had been an admirer of his work since at least 1983, when they met at New York City's Carnegie Hall. In the months that followed their first encounter, they were often compared in the press, frequently in terms that were not especially favorable to Roney. With that criticism simmering in the background, Davis and his equally legendary producer, Quincy Jones, invited him to join them on stage in Montreux, Switzerland, the site of a famous jazz festival. Their performance there in 1991, memorialized in an album called *Miles & Quincy Live at Montreux* (1991), did a great deal to dispel the notion that Roney was simply an imitator of his mentor. A mercurial man who did not mince words, Davis was not shy about criticizing other musicians, particularly those he felt were trying to take advantage of his accomplishments. To Roney, however, he gave his full approval, a fact he made unmistakably clear at Montreux.

In the wake of that famous concert and Davis's death later the same year, Roney returned to the recording studio, completing albums with a variety of partners

and labels. In 1994 he joined Williams, Carter, saxophonist Wayne Shorter, and pianist Herbie Hancock for *A Tribute to Miles,* which won a Grammy Award as the year's best jazz instrumental performance by an individual or group.

On many of his albums in the 1990s and 2000s, Roney moved in a new direction, blending the complex melodies and chord progressions typical of classic jazz with the driving rhythms of hip-hop and soul. Particularly successful was *No Room for Argument,* a 2000 release for Stretch Records that featured several original compositions as well as new interpretations of Davis's "Filles de Kilimanjaro" and saxophonist John Coltrane's *A Love Supreme.* Interspersed throughout were clips of speeches by Malcolm X and Martin Luther King Jr. Those spoken-word passages, together with novel studio effects and powerful drumming by Lenny White, gave the album a rap-like feel that won him many new fans.

As of the mid-2010s, some 40 years since he burst onto the scene as a teenager, Roney remained an active presence on the international concert circuit, regularly drawing large crowds on both sides of the Atlantic. He was also involved in recording projects with a variety of groups, including his own ensembles and a new sextet called Powerhouse. Organized by producer Bob Belden, Powerhouse focused initially on radical reimaginings of Davis's compositions. In 2015 the group completed *In an Ambient Way,* a reworking of Davis's 1969 classic *In a Silent Way.*

Selected discography

Tony Williams, *Foreign Intrigue,* Blue Note, 1985.
Tony Williams, *Civilization,* Blue Note, 1986.
Verses, Muse, 1987.
Intuition, Muse, 1988.
Miles Davis and Quincy Jones, *Miles & Quincy Live at Montreux,* Warner Brothers, 1991.
(With Tony Williams, Ron Carter, Wayne Shorter, and Herbie Hancock) *A Tribute to Miles,* Qwest, 1994.
No Room for Argument (includes "Homage & Acknowledgement [Love Supreme/Filles de Kilimanjaro]"), Stretch, 2000.
Mystikal, HighNote, 2005.
If Only for One Night, HighNote, 2010.
Powerhouse, *In an Ambient Way,* Chesky, 2015.

Sources

Periodicals

New York Times, September 24, 2000.

Online

Collar, Matt, "Wallace Roney: Artist Biography by Matt Collar," AllMusic.com, http://www.allmusic.com/

artist/wallace-roney-mn0000813629/biography (accessed October 3, 2016).

"Wallace Roney," All About Jazz, https://musicians .allaboutjazz.com/wallaceroney (accessed October 3, 2016).

"Wallace Roney—Biography," http://www.wallacero ney.com/bio.php (accessed October 3, 2016).

—R. Anthony Kugler

Sean Rooks

1969–2016

Professional basketball player and coach

Rooks, Sean, photograph. Dave Eggen/NBAE via Getty Images.

Sean Rooks was a center who played for 13 seasons in the National Basketball Association (NBA). Although he was primarily a bench player, Rooks earned the admiration of his coaches and teammates for his professionalism and work ethic. "He was a big guy who understood how to play," Byron Scott, who played with Rooks on the Los Angeles Lakers during the mid-1990s, told Mark Medina of the *Los Angeles Daily News* in 2016. "He could make shots. He was a decent post-up player and a very good team defensive player." Rooks was also known for his positive attitude and generosity, devoting his free time to working with children at youth basketball camps. After retiring as a player, Rooks embarked on a new career as a coach, working with three NBA Development League (D-League) teams before eventually joining the player development staff of the Phoenix Suns. In June of 2016 Rooks was a strong candidate for an assistant coaching position with the New York Knicks until he unexpectedly died of heart disease at age 46.

Sean Rooks was born on September 9, 1969, in New York City. He later moved with his family to Fontana, California, where he starred on the Fontana High School basketball team. During these years, Rooks also briefly participated in football, earning a spot on the junior varsity roster. Although he was not a key contributor on the gridiron, Rooks proved to be a popular teammate, injecting his distinctive enthusiasm and energy into practices and games. Writing in the *Inland Valley Daily Bulletin* following Rooks's death, Louis Brewster quoted former Fontana High School athlete Brian Colbrunn, who played football with Rooks: "Sean was not the football player that he was a basketball player, but his heart and smile was as giant as his body…. We sang, we danced, we had a ball. Of course, we would never get away with that on the varsity bus. Sean is the reason I loved Thursdays. Sean the poet. Sean the giant personality."

It was on the basketball court that Rooks demonstrated his exceptional athletic abilities. As a senior, the standout center helped guide Fontana High School to a record of 24–4 while leading the Steelers to their first league title in school history. His performance that season attracted the notice of college recruiters, and after graduating from high school, Rooks earned the opportunity to continue playing at the University of

At a Glance . . .

Born Sean Lester Rooks on September 9, 1969, in New York, NY; died on June 7, 2016, in Philadelphia, PA; son of Deborah Brown; married Susanne O'Brien; children: Kameron, Khayla. *Education:* University of Arizona, BA, communications, 1992.

Career: Dallas Mavericks, center, 1992–94, 1999–2000; Minnesota Timberwolves, center, 1994–96; Atlanta Hawks, center, 1996; Los Angeles Lakers, center, 1996–99; Los Angeles Clippers, center, 2000–03; New Orleans Hornets (later Pelicans), center, 2003–04; Orlando Magic, center, 2004; Unicaja Malaga, Spanish Liga ACB, center, 2005; Joventut Badalona, Asociación de Clubs de Baloncesto, center, 2005; Bakersfield Jam, NBA Development League, assistant coach and interim head coach, 2007–08; New Mexico Thunderbirds, assistant coach, 2010–11; Los Angeles Slam, American Basketball Association (ABA), center, 2011–13; Sioux Falls Skyforce, assistant coach, 2012, 2013–14; Phoenix Suns, player development assistant, 2012–13; Philadelphia 76ers, player development coach, 2014–16.

Arizona. He spent the 1987–88 season as a redshirt freshman, participating in practices while maintaining his four-year playing eligibility. The following year, Rooks made the varsity roster, logging 11.3 minutes per game as a backup center, contributing 5.6 points and 2.8 rebounds per contest. Rooks continued to improve his performance during his sophomore campaign, scoring 12.7 points, collecting 4.9 rebounds, and blocking 1.6 shots and averaging 22.1 minutes of playing time per game. After posting similar numbers as a junior, Rooks established himself as the anchor of the Arizona frontcourt during his senior year, setting career-high averages in points (16.3), rebounds (6.9), and minutes (28.3) per game. The center's combination of size, strength, and skill eventually garnered notice from professional scouts. Following his senior season, Rooks was selected by the Dallas Mavericks in the second round of the 1992 NBA draft.

Rooks enjoyed his most productive year in the NBA during his rookie campaign in Dallas. During the 1992–93 season, Rooks started 68 games while setting career-high marks in points (13.5) and rebounds (7.4) per contest. After appearing in only 47 games in the 1993–94 season, Rooks was traded to the Minnesota Timberwolves. In his first year in Minnesota, Rooks appeared in 80 games, 70 as a starter, while logging a career-best 30.1 minutes per game. His production declined the following season, however,

and in February of 1996 he was traded to the Atlanta Hawks as part of a multiplayer deal. Rooks appeared in 10 playoff games for the Hawks that year, averaging 4.5 points and 2.7 rebounds in 14 minutes per contest. After Atlanta was eliminated by the Orlando Magic in the Eastern Conference Semifinals, Rooks became a free agent. In July of 1996, he signed a deal to join the Los Angeles Lakers.

Rooks spent the next three seasons in Los Angeles, where he served as a backup to star center Shaquille O'Neal. As Rooks told Theresa Smith of the *Orange County Register* in 1998, practicing every day against the player known as "Diesel" proved one of the biggest challenges of his NBA tenure. "It's hard," Rooks admitted to Smith. "The guy is so big and powerful, it's really not fair. I'm doing the best I can and he barely has to do anything to score." Despite the arduousness of his role, Rooks also conceded that all the time spent defending Shaq had made him into a more effective player. "When you go up against Diesel every day, who do you have to worry about?" Rooks asked Smith. "Any other center? Shoot, they can't do what Shaq can do."

Following the 1998–99 season, Rooks returned to Dallas as a result of a trade. He was dealt again the following year, when the Mavericks sent him to the Los Angeles Clippers. In three seasons with the Clippers, Rooks appeared in 213 games, 40 as a starter. In July of 2003 he signed a free agent deal with the New Orleans Hornets, who subsequently traded him to the Orlando Magic the following February. Rooks played 20 games off the bench for the Magic, before retiring from the NBA following the 2003–04 season. Rooks played briefly for two professional teams in Spain, then returned to the United States to take a job as an assistant coach with the Bakersfield Jam of the NBA Development League. Over the next half decade, Rooks coached for Development League squads in New Mexico and Sioux Falls, South Dakota, before joining the Phoenix Suns as a player development assistant in 2012.

After briefly returning to Sioux Falls for the 2013–14 Development League season, Rooks was hired to become a player development coach with the Philadelphia 76ers. Over the next two years, Rooks emerged as a top candidate for an NBA assistant coaching position. He received an opportunity in June of 2016, when he interviewed to join the New York Knicks as an assistant under new head coach Jeff Hornacek. On June 7, 2016, only hours after his interview in New York, Rooks collapsed and died in a Philadelphia restaurant. "This is just a horrible shock," Rooks's head coach in college, Lute Olson, wrote on the University of Arizona Athletics Twitter feed hours after his passing. "Sean was such a wonderful young man with a great disposition. During his time at Arizona, he was always one of the most pleasant individuals to be around. His positivity was something I'll always remem-

ber." In a statement issued the day after Rooks's death, 76ers head coach Brett Brown wrote: "He meant so much to so many people. We are all deeply saddened by his loss and extend our condolences to his family during this time. He will be missed."

Sources

Periodicals

Arizona Daily Star, June 7, 2016.
Daily Wildcat, July 11, 2006.
Inland Valley Daily Bulletin (Rancho Cucamonga, CA), January 23, 2015; June 8, 2016.
Los Angeles Daily News, June 7, 2016.
Los Angeles Times, June 8, 2016.
Newsday, June 8, 2016.
Orange County Register, January 4, 1998, p. C12.
Philadelphia Inquirer, June 8, 2016, p. D2.
Washington Post, June 8, 2016.

Online

"Head Coach Brett Brown Statement on Passing of Sean Rooks," Philadelphia 76ers, NBA.com, June 8, 2016, http://www.nba.com/sixers/head-coach-brett-brown-statement-passing-sean-rooks/ (accessed September 29, 2016).
"Sean Rooks," Basketball-Reference.com, http://www.basketball-reference.com/players/r/rooksse01.html (accessed September 29, 2016).
"Statements from Greg Byrne and Lute Olson on the Passing of Sean Rooks," Arizona Athletics, June 7, 2016, https://twitter.com/azathletics/status/740346663747735552 (accessed September 29, 2016).

—Stephen Meyer

Andre Royo

1968—

Actor

Royo, Andre, photograph. Santiago Felipe/Getty Images.

Andre Royo is best known for his role as the drug-addicted police informant "Bubbles" in HBO's critically acclaimed crime drama *The Wire,* appearing in all five seasons of the show from 2002 to 2008. Concerned with raising his character above stereotype, Royo sought to humanize Bubbles, portraying him as street smart and cunning but also well-intentioned, caring, and engaged in an honest struggle against his demons. Royo was thoroughly convincing as the bedraggled but ever-hopeful Bubbles, with his soiled clothes, yellowed teeth, and shopping basket full of wares to sell on the street—so much so that he was sometimes mistaken for a homeless man while he was on set. A little-known stage actor with only one major role before he landed the part of Bubbles, Royo now boasts a string of post-*Wire* film and television credits. In his best-known role since Bubbles, he plays Thirsty Rawlins, the shady lawyer on Fox's hit series *Empire,* which premiered in 2015.

Joined a Small Theater Company

Royo was born on July 18, 1968, in the Bronx, New York, the son of an African-American mother and a Cuban father. From 1982 to 1986, Royo attended an all-boys Catholic high school in the Bronx, Mount St. Michael Academy. Growing up he knew he wanted to be an actor, but he had only a vague idea of how to make his dream a reality.

After graduating high school, Royo settled in Manhattan, where he worked as stage actor for a number of years. He took a variety of odd jobs—construction worker, waiter, bathroom attendant, shop clerk—while studying his craft. Classes at HB Studios in Greenwich Village led Royo to a theater on the Lower East Side, Room 203, where he joined a small company that mostly performed sketch comedy and one-act plays. In an interview with Andrew Salomon of *Backstage* magazine, Royo recalled, "We had seven, eight actors, two writers, and it was like our version of The Little Rascals. We had to paint and do all the construction within the theatre, and the payback was they'd let us put up shows there."

As Royo's troupe and Room 203 came to be better known, he landed more auditions and a few small roles on television. He had trouble getting cast, however, as

At a Glance . . .

Born Andre Royo on July 18, 1968, in New York, NY; married Jane Choi; children: Stella.

Career: Stage actor, early 1990s—; television actor, 1998—; film actor, 2000—.

Awards: Special Jury Recognition, Best Actor, SXSW Film Festival, 2016, for *Hunter Gatherer*.

Addresses: *Twitter*—@AndreRoyo.

he explained to Salomon, because directors often felt he was not black enough for black roles or Spanish enough for Spanish roles. Royo got his first big break in 1999 when he was working the door at a popular New York City hip-hop hangout, the Cheetah Club. When a friend of Royo's arrived with the celebrated director John Singleton, Royo ushered them inside like royalty. "I just made sure when he got there I parted the Red Sea," Royo told Salomon. Singleton liked Royo's energy and invited him to audition for a small part in his new movie, *Shaft* (2000), a remake of the 1971 blaxploitation film of the same name. Singleton's version starred Samuel L. Jackson as private detective John Shaft, the role made famous by Richard Roundtree. Royo was cast as Tattoo, a henchman of the Dominican drug lord Peoples Hernandez, played by Jeffrey Wright.

Won Career-Making Role

Royo's appearance in *Shaft* led to the role that would make his career. Not long after the movie opened, Royo's manager told him he had an audition to play a junkie snitch on David Simon's new crime drama, *The Wire*. Royo was initially hesitant; he had played similar roles before and did not want to contribute to the stereotyping of blacks as drug dealers, convicts, and addicts. One look at his bank account, however, convinced him otherwise. Four auditions later, Simon and his producers offered Royo the role of Bubbles, the homeless heroin addict and police informant. Initially the series creators only guaranteed Royo seven episodes.

The Wire premiered in June of 2002. The creation of Simon, a former newspaper reporter known for his work on the earlier Baltimore crime drama *Homicide,* and Ed Burns, a former Baltimore homicide detective, *The Wire* was a mix of tough street life and police procedural, equal parts lawbreakers and law enforcers, told from both points of view. The program eschewed Hollywood formula in the name of authenticity. Most of the cast was African American, replicating Baltimore's

demographics, and shooting was done on location in the city's rundown neighborhoods, with local offices, restaurants, and public buildings as backdrops. Most of the actors on the series were relatively unknown, and some episodes even featured real-life figures in minor roles.

Despite critical kudos, *The Wire* failed to attract a large audience. Poor Nielsen ratings notwithstanding, *The Wire* ran for five seasons on HBO. Central to the show's ambitions was the realistic depiction of character, and in this area Royo did not disappoint. In fact, he was so convincing as Bubbles that workers at the food table on set thought he was a bum and turned him away. In interviews, Royo often told the story of his "street Oscar"—the day he was offered heroin by a real-life drug addict who thought he looked like he needed a fix. Desperately fighting his addiction, with a heart of gold and the wisdom of a philosopher, Bubbles emerged as one of the most likeable characters on the show. Bubbles provided an unexpected voice of morality, "the show's Greek chorus," as Michael Wilson of the *New York Times* called him. Royo's character persisted through all five seasons. When *The Wire* concluded in the spring of 2008, Royo had appeared in 49 of its 60 episodes.

Critics praised *The Wire* for its gritty realism and sociological significance. Jacob Weisberg of Slate went so far as to declare it the best show in the history of American television: "No other program has ever done anything remotely like what this one does, namely to portray the social, political, and economic life of an American city with the scope, observational precision, and moral vision of great literature." Although *The Wire* received no Emmys or any of the other awards typically bestowed on television's most popular programs, it nonetheless carried so much weight with Hollywood's creative types that it jump-started the careers of many actors, including, in addition to Royo, Idris Elba (drug kingpin Stringer Bell), Dominic West (Detective Jimmy McNulty), Michael Kenneth Williams (stick-up man Omar Little), and Wendell Pierce (Detective Bunk Moreland).

Landed First Lead Role

After *The Wire* wrapped in 2008, Royo began to land other small-screen credits, including recurring roles in the Fox science-fiction series *Fringe* (2010–11), the Amazon thriller *Hand of God* (2014–15), and the offbeat Showtime comedy *Happyish* (2015). Royo turned in a memorable performance as Spider Raymond in Marvel's *Agent Carter* series, but he is more famous as Thirsty Rawlins, the unethical defense attorney on Fox's popular hip-hop soap opera, *Empire* (2015—).

A supporting player in a string of independent films, Royo got his first lead role in *Calloused Hands* (2013),

cast as an abusive and broken stepfather to a 12-year-old boy with great promise. Royo also played the lead in *Hunter Gatherer* (2016), about a wily ex-convict trying to reconnect with his family and friends. The role won Royo best actor honors at the SXSW Film Festival in Austin, Texas, in March of 2016. Royo's best-known film is *The Spectacular Now,* a sensitive coming-of-age romance that debuted to positive reviews at the Sundance Film Festival in 2013. In that movie, Royo plays a geometry teacher, Mr. Aster, in a cast that also includes Miles Teller, Shailene Woodley, Brie Larson, Jennifer Jason Leigh, and Bob Odenkirk. Another film of note is *Red Tails* (2012), George Lucas's story about the exploits of the Tuskegee Airmen in World II, in which Royo plays chief mechanic Antwan "Coffee" Coleman opposite stars Terrence Howard and Cuba Gooding Jr.

Royo and his wife, Jane Choi, live in Los Angeles, where she is the co-owner of the restaurant Canelé. They are the parents of one child, a daughter named Stella, born in 1998. Even now, nearly a decade after *The Wire,* fans shout out the character's name whenever they see Royo on the street. Royo appreciates the recognition, although he worries about being pigeonholed as an actor. Interviewed by Chris Kaltenbach of the *Baltimore Sun* during the 2016 Maryland Film Festival, Royo reflected, "I've gotten into a lot of rooms because of Bubbles. It's just made for a different kind of challenge. I mean, I was typecast as unemployed a lot longer, so I can't complain."

Selected works

Television

The Wire, HBO, 2002–08.
Fringe, Fox, 2010–11.
Hand of God, Amazon, 2014–15.
Happyish, Showtime, 2015.
Empire, Fox, 2015—.

Films

Shaft, Scott Rudin Productions, 2000.
G, Andrew Lauren Productions, 2002.
Men without Jobs, Straphanger/No Work Films, 2004.
Jellysmoke, Mark Banning, 2005.
5up 2down, Screen Media Ventures, 2006.
All about Us, Faith Filmworks, 2007.
August, Original Media/Periscope, 2008.
The Mercy Man, Champawat, 2009.
Super, This Is That Productions, 2010.
Aftermath, Eastlake Films, 2012.
The Collection, Fortress Features, 2012.
Hellbenders, Circle of Confusion Productions, 2012.
Red Tails, Lucasfilm, 2012.
(And producer) *Calloused Hands,* Woolfcub, 2013.

A Miracle in Spanish Harlem, Vista Clara, 2013.
The Spectacular Now, Andrew Lauren Productions, 2013.
Of Mind and Music, Una Vida, 2014.
Lila & Eve, A+E Studios, 2015.
Hunter Gatherer, Mama Bear Studios, 2016.

Sources

Periodicals

Backstage, February 21, 2008.
Newsweek, January 14, 2008.
New Yorker, October 22, 2007.
New York Times, August 27, 2006.

Online

"Andre Royo: *The Wire*'s Bubbles on Baltimore, Free Drugs & Tarantino," Sabotage Times, September 12, 2013, http://sabotagetimes.com/life/andre-royo-the-wires-bubbles-on-baltimore-free-drugs-tarantino (accessed July 14, 2016).
"Andre Royo," Internet Movie Database, http://www.imdb.com/name/nm0747420/ (accessed July 14, 2016).
Daniels, Karu F., "From Bubbles to Thirsty: Andre Royo's Career Transcends Character," Man's Life, November 18, 2015, http://manslife.com/14012/andre-royo-the-wire-empire/ (accessed July 14, 2016).
Gulliver, Katrina, "*The Wire, Serial* and the Decline of the American Industrial Empire," Time.com, February 5, 2015, http://time.com/3691610/wire-serial-baltimore/ (accessed July 14, 2016).
HBO: *The Wire,* http://www.hbo.com/the-wire (accessed July 14, 2016).
Kaltenbach, Chris, "Andre Royo Moves Beyond Bubbles and *The Wire* at Maryland Film Festival," BaltimoreSun.com, May 7, 2016, http://www.baltimoresun.com/entertainment/movies/bs-ae-royo-20160507-story.html (accessed July 14, 2016).
Penrice, Ronda Racha, "Andre Royo: From Bubbles on *The Wire* to Thirsty on *Empire,*" The Root, September 30, 2015, http://www.theroot.com/articles/culture/2015/09/andre_royo_interview_from_bubbles_on_the_wire_to_thirsty_on_empire/ (accessed July 14, 2016).
"The 25 Greatest Characters of *The Wire,* Ranked," Esquire.com, June 10, 2015, http://www.esquire.com/entertainment/tv/a35609/wire-best-characters-ranking/ (accessed July 14, 2016).
Weisberg, Jacob, "*The Wire* on Fire," Slate, September 13, 2006, http://www.slate.com/articles/news_and_politics/the_big_idea/2006/09/the_wire_on_fire.html (accessed July 14, 2016).

—Janet Mullane

Marcus Scribner

2000—

Actor

Scribner, Marcus, photograph. DFree/Shutterstock.com.

Marcus Scribner is a teen actor who is best known for his role on the ABC series *black-ish*. Scribner first started acting at age seven, and over the next several years, he landed a handful of guest appearances on television sitcoms. Scribner got his first break at age 14, when he was cast in *black-ish* as the clumsy, nerdy, and likeable Andre Johnson Jr. Scribner nailed the role, earning an NAACP Image Award for his performance in 2016. That same year, Scribner appeared in his first big-screen film, the independent teen flick *Alexander IRL.*

The actor was born in 2000 in Los Angeles. Scribner's father, Troy, had been named for the classics, and he extended the tradition to his own children, Marcus (derived from the Roman god Mars) and Athena (the ancient Greek goddess). In an interview for the blog *5 Minutes for Mom,* Troy Scribner told Don Cullo that he had wanted his son to play sports, but that "didn't work out as well as we had wanted." Instead, when Scribner was seven years old, his mother enrolled him in acting classes. "I fell in love with it from the first day," he said in a 2016 interview with HNGN. In addition to teaching him acting skills, the classes helped Scribner overcome his shyness. Within a few years, he had landed his first role, a guest spot on the ABC series *Castle.* More roles came Scribner's way, and between 2010 and 2014, he made single-episode appearances on four television shows.

In 2014 Scribner's career took a dramatic turn when he landed a role the ABC comedy *black-ish.* Starring Tracee Ellis Ross, Laurence Fishburne, and Anthony Anderson, the show made an immediate impact on viewers and critics. Writing for Slate in 2014, Willa Paskin reflected widespread opinion when she called the show "proud, politically incorrect, and the fall's best new sitcom." Immediately compared with Bill Cosby's hit television show of the 1980s about the Huxtable family, many critics noted that *black-ish* shined a light on a gap in network television. "We can argue whether things have progressed, regressed, or simply gotten weirder since the Huxtables' day in American society overall," noted James Poniewozik in *Time.* "But the fact is, here we are, three decades later, and a major network premiering a comedy about an African American family is still news."

For his depiction of Andre Johnson Jr., Scribner was nominated for an NAACP Image Award in 2015.

Scribner's success stemmed, in part, from his ability to relate to the gullible and clumsy yet confident Andre. Speaking with Monique Jones of *Entertainment Weekly* in 2015, Scribner said that the similarities between the two included a love of video games and a clothing style that Scribner referred to as "pretty fly."

To stay grounded in Hollywood, Scribner turned to his parents, whom he credited with teaching him the value of hard work and helping him maintain his school routine. A high school freshman when he began work on *black-ish,* Scribner continued to play the clarinet, a hobby he began in fifth grade. He also remained in touch with his friends at home. Before long, however, his shooting schedule proved too demanding, and Scribner transferred to an online high school program. "It's a tough balance but when you do it for a while, I think you get it down pat," he told Tonya Pendleton in an interview for BlackAmericaWeb.com in 2015. "Now, it's a routine I do every day and it runs smoothly. I do an online school program, but I hang out with my friends sometime and I to go to parties and stuff. I have a pretty normal life."

In addition to his role in *black-ish,* in 2015 Scribner voiced the character of Buck in Pixar Animation Studio's *The Good Dinosaur.* Buck—an Apatosaurus trying to be as tough as his big brother—was significantly different from Andre, but it was a role Scribner embraced. "I was like ... Oh my gosh ... I get to play a dinosaur! My mind was blown," Scribner shared in a 2015 interview with the website Fanlala. "I didn't think this day would come. I grew up watching *Toy Story, Monsters Inc.,* all the Pixar classics, so I was very familiar with their work. But to be in one of their movies, well that's just incredible."

In 2016 Scribner won the NAACP Image Award for outstanding performance by a youth. It was presented at that year's Emmy Awards ceremony, which Scribner also cohosted. His was one of six Image Awards for *black-ish* that evening, including outstanding comedy series, an award that it also received in 2015. Since the show's premiere in 2014, *black-ish* has won 18 awards, including honors from the African-American Film Critics Association, Grace Allen Awards, Peabody Awards, Television Critics Association Awards, Young Artist Awards, and Image Awards.

Pegged as a young star to watch, Scribner made guest appearances on *Good Morning America, Jimmy Kimmel Live!, The Real,* and *The View.* In 2016 he made his big-screen debut as Darius in *Alexander IRL,* an independent comedy about teen coders, slated for release in October of 2016.

In 2016 Scribner partnered with the Sandals Foundation to help communities in need. As the organization's youth advocacy ambassador, Scribner visits schools and shelters in communities where the Sandals Foundation has resorts. In an interview with *Teen Vogue* while he was in Jamaica, Scribner noted, "Sometimes the problem can seem so big you don't know where to start, but it starts with one small action, and everyone can do something."

Selected works

Television

black-ish, ABC, 2014—.

Films

The Good Dinosaur, Pixar Animation Studios, 2015.

Sources

Periodicals

Teen Vogue, April 29, 2016.
Time, September 23, 2014.

Online

"Actor Marcus Scribner, Age 15, Thankful That His Parents Encourage Him and Keep Him Grounded," Hubmesh, December 21, 2015, http://hubmesh .com/actor-marcus-scribner-age-15-thankful-that-his -parents-encourage-him-and-keep-him-grounded .html (accessed September 28, 2016).

"'Black-ish' Star Marcus Scribner Talks Role Models, Using Comedy To Highlight Important Cultural Issues And Giving Back," HNGN, January 20, 2016, http://www.hngn.com/articles/169253/2016 0120/black-ish-star-marcus-scribner-talks-working -with-his-role-models-bringing-comedy-to-important -cultural-issues-and-giving-back-exclusive-interview -photos.htm (accessed September 28, 2016).

Cullo, Dawn, "Chatting with the Kids from ABC TV's 'Blackish,'" *5 Minutes for Mom* (blog), November

12, 2014, http://www.5minutesformom.com/98177/chatting-with-the-kids-from-abc-tvs-black-ish-abctvevent/ (accessed September 28, 2016).

Jones, Monique, "'Black-ish' Star Marcus Scribner Talks NAACP Image Award Nomination," EW.com, December 18, 2014, http://community.ew.com/2014/12/18/marcus-scribner-black-ish-naacp/ (accessed September 28, 2016).

Lipsitz, Jordana, "The 'Alexander IRL' Teaser Trailer Invites You to a Party You Just Can't Miss," Bustle, July 25, 2016, http://www.bustle.com/articles/174591-the-alexander-irl-teaser-trailer-invites-you-to-a-party-you-just-cant-miss-exclusive-video (accessed September 28, 2016).

"Marcus Scribner Talks 'The Good Dinosaur,' Out November 25th!," Fanlala, November 20, 2015, https://www.fanlala.com/news/marcus-scribner-talks-good-dinosaur-out-november-25th (accessed September 28, 2016).

Paskin, Willa, "Say it Loud," Slate, September 24, 2014, http://www.slate.com/articles/arts/television/2014/09/black_ish_review_abc_tv_show_about_black_family_is_the_best_new_sitcom_of.html (accessed September 28, 2016).

Pendleton, Tonya, "Marcus Scribner Of 'black-ish' Talks Fun on and off Set and How Education Is as Important as Acting," BlackAmericaWeb.com, November 11, 2015, http://blackamericaweb.com/2015/11/18/marcus-scribner-of-black-ish-talks-fun-on-and-off-set-and-how-education-is-as-important-as-acting/ (accessed September 28, 2016).

—Candice Mancini

Eddie Shaw

1937—

Blues saxophonist, vocalist

Shaw, Eddie, photograph. James Fraher/Redferns/Getty Images.

Saxophonist and vocalist Eddie Shaw has been a prominent figure on the Chicago blues scene for more than half a century. A protégé of two of the genre's biggest stars, Muddy Waters and Howlin' Wolf, Shaw has built a reputation both for his backup work and for his efforts as a bandleader, composer, and arranger. The winner of five Blues Music Awards (in 2006, 2007, 2011, 2013, and 2014) from the Blues Foundation, he was inducted into the Blues Hall of Fame in 2014. "Eddie Shaw continues to build upon his unparalleled career as a Chicago blues saxophonist/bandleader," noted the Blues Foundation on its website, "in a city where guitar, harmonica and piano players have long ruled the roost."

Like many of his peers and bandmates, Shaw grew up in the rural South and moved to Chicago at the beginning of his career. Born on March 20, 1937, on a farm in Stringtown, Mississippi, a hamlet located a few miles outside the town of Benoit, he spent much of his youth in the nearby communities of Rosedale and Greenville. At Coleman High School, a segregated school in Greenville, Shaw studied the trombone and clarinet before focusing on the saxophone. His prog-ress was rapid, and by the time he graduated he was performing professionally across the region, often in partnership with his band teacher, a local impresario named Winchester Davis.

Greenville's location in the heart of the Mississippi Delta, a region often regarded as the birthplace of the blues, ensured Shaw's continued progress, as he came face to face almost nightly with discerning and demanding fans as well as with a host of the genre's leading stars, many of whom he backed on stage. The pay he received for those gigs was modest, however, and for a time it was not clear that he would be able to support himself with music alone. After high school, therefore, he made alternative plans, taking courses at Mississippi Vocational College (later Mississippi Valley State University) in Itta Bena, a small town east of Greenville. His break came soon thereafter, when Waters heard him at an Itta Bena club. A shrewd judge of talent, the famed guitarist hired him on the spot and quickly brought him north to Chicago, where his career began in earnest about 1957.

Upon his arrival, Shaw adjusted quickly to Chicago's characteristic sound, which was harder and grittier than

the Delta blues of his youth. His reputation grew steadily, and after several years with Waters, he moved on to join Howlin' Wolf, with whom he remained until the latter's death in 1976. Over that time, Shaw emerged as one of the principal architects of Wolf's sound, regularly contributing new songs and arrangements as well as handling personnel issues within the guitarist's backing band, the Wolf Gang (sometimes rendered as Wolfgang).

Throughout this period, Shaw's career as a bandleader was progressing as well. A pivotal moment for him came in 1966, when he completed his first single, an instrumental called "Blues for the West Side." Joining him on that release was the revered guitarist Magic Sam, whom he backed two years later on a landmark album called *Black Magic*. Despite the success of both recordings, it was only in 1977 that Shaw's full-length debut, titled *Have Blues, Will Travel*, was ready for release. Issued by Simmons Records, a small Chicago-based label, the record was completed with the help of the Wolf Gang, whose leadership he had assumed after Wolf's death the previous year. Showcasing his abilities as a songwriter, arranger, and vocalist as well as a saxophonist, the album included a number of original compositions, including "I've Got to Tell Somebody," which soon become one of Shaw's signature pieces.

Have Blues, Will Travel brought Shaw a host of new fans, many of them in Europe. His popularity there was bolstered by several international tours and, in the early 1980s, by a recording contract with Isabel, a French label. That deal resulted in his second major album as a leader, *Movin' and Groovin' Man* (1982). Featuring a fresh rendition of "I've Got to Tell Somebody" as well as a guest appearance by fellow saxophonist Eddie "Cleanhead" Vinson, it was reissued by Evidence Music in 1993. By that time, Shaw had released several other albums, including *King of the Road* (1985), a compi-

lation by Rooster Blues Records, and *In the Land of the Crossroads*, a 1992 release for Flying Fish Records. The latter recording, reissued four years later by Rooster Blues, was one of Shaw's best-known albums. A roots-oriented collection recorded in his native Mississippi with the help of the Wolf Gang, it highlighted his penchant for dryly humorous lyrics, particularly on the tracks "Dunkin' Donut Woman" and "She Didn't Tell Me Everything," as well as his resonant voice and virtuosic technique on the saxophone.

By the time *In the Land of the Crossroads* was reissued, Shaw was increasingly recognized as one of the elder statesmen of the Chicago blues scene. A clear sign of his growing stature came in the mid-2000s, when he won the first of his Blues Music Awards. It was also around that time that he earned a small but memorable role in *Honeydripper* (2007), a Hollywood drama directed by John Sayles and set in the rural South. His string of albums, meanwhile, continued with releases like *Too Many Highways,* released by Austria's Wolf Records in 1999, and *Naked,* which appeared on the North Atlantic Blues imprint a decade later.

In addition his work in nightclubs and recording studios, Shaw is also the proprietor of a barbecue restaurant and a bar; the latter, a West Side landmark known as Eddie's Place, served for many years as one of the leading blues venues in Chicago.

Some 60 years after his fateful meeting with Waters in Itta Bena, Shaw remained an active and highly visible presence on the blues scene, performing regularly at blues clubs and music festivals around the country.

Selected discography

Singles

"Blues for the West Side," 1966.

Albums

Magic Sam, *Black Magic*, Delmark, 1968.
Have Blues, Will Travel (includes "I've Got to Tell Somebody"), Simmons, 1977.
Movin' and Groovin' Man (includes "I've Got to Tell Somebody"), Isabel/Evidence, 1982/1993.
King of the Road, Rooster Blues, 1985.
In the Land of the Crossroads (includes "Dunkin' Donut Woman" and "She Didn't Tell Me Everything"), Flying Fish/Rooster Blues, 1992/1996.
Too Many Highways, Wolf, 1999.
Naked, North Atlantic Blues, 2009.

Films

Honeydripper, Emerging Pictures, 2007.

Sources

Online

Dahl, Bill, "Eddie Shaw: Artist Biography," AllMusic .com, http://www.allmusic.com/artist/eddie-shaw -mn0000795387/biography (accessed August 8, 2016).

"Eddie Shaw," Mississippi Blues Commission, http:// msbluestrail.org/blues-trail-markers/eddie-shaw (accessed August 8, 2016).

"Eddie Shaw (2)," Discogs.com, https://www.discogs .com/artist/806501-Eddie-Shaw-2 (accessed August 8, 2016).

"2014 Blues Hall of Fame Inductees: Eddie Shaw," Blues Foundation, http://blues.org/awards-search/ ?cat=hof (accessed August 12, 2016).

"Where It All Started," EddieShawSax.com, http:// eddieshawsax.com/learn_more (accessed August 8, 2016).

—R. Anthony Kugler

Moneta Sleet Jr.

1926–1996

Photographer, journalist

Sleet, Moneta Jr., photograph. Bettmann/Getty Images.

Photographer Moneta Sleet Jr. is best known for the iconic photo that he took of Coretta Scott King—her face hidden behind a black veil, with her youngest daughter, Bernice, huddled in her lap—at the funeral of her husband, the Reverend Martin Luther King Jr., in 1968. "I considered myself fortunate to be there documenting everything," Sleet later recounted, according to a profile on the website of the Contemporary Art Center of Virginia. "If I wasn't there I knew I would be somewhere crying." The following year, Sleet became the first African American to win a Pulitzer Prize for feature photography for his moving homage to the fallen civil rights leader.

Throughout his long career, Sleet was a quiet and patient, if not always objective, observer of the American civil rights movement, documenting such landmark moments as the 1963 March on Washington and the voting rights marches of 1965 in Alabama for *Jet* and *Ebony* magazines, for which he was a staff photographer for more than 40 years. Photographing people from all walks of life, from celebrities and world leaders to ordinary people on the street, Sleet captured the exuberance, sorrow, steadfast determination, and in-

trospection of his subjects, depicting aspects of black life that otherwise might have gone unseen.

Transformed Hobby into a Career

Moneta J. Sleet Jr. was born on Valentine's Day of 1926 in Owensboro, Kentucky, where he attended segregated public schools. He first became interested in photography at age nine, when his parents gave him a box camera. He continued to pursue his hobby throughout high school—when he was the official photographer and editor of the school newspaper—and into his college years. At Kentucky State College in Frankfort, Sleet studied business and photography under the tutelage of the dean of the college. His college career was interrupted by World War II, when he served in the U.S. Army.

Although he finished in business degree in 1947, Sleet had already determined to pursue photography as a career. In 1948 he was invited to set up a department of photography at Maryland State College, but after a year he left to pursue postgraduate study in New York. Sleet briefly attended the School of Modern Photogra-

At a Glance . . .

Born Moneta J. Sleet Jr. on February 14, 1926, in Owensboro, KY; died on September 30, 1996, in New York, NY; son of Moneta J. Sleet Sr. and Ozetta L. Sleet; married Juanita Harris, 1950; children: Gregory, Michael, Lisa. *Military service:* U.S. Army, 1944–46. *Education:* Kentucky State College, BA, 1947; New York University, MA, 1950.

Career: Maryland State College, photography instructor, 1948–49; *New York Amsterdam News,* sportswriter, 1950; *Our World,* photographer, 1951–55; Johnson Publishing Company, staff photographer for *Ebony* and *Jet* magazines, 1955–96.

Memberships: Black Academy of Arts and Letters; National Association for the Advancement of Colored People.

Awards: Citation for Excellence, Overseas Press Club of America, 1957; Pulitzer Prize for Feature Photography, 1969; Photojournalism Award, National Urban League, 1969; Photojournalism Award, National Association of Black Journalists, 1978; inducted into Kentucky Journalism Hall of Fame, University of Kentucky, 1989.

phy and in 1950 received a master's degree in journalism from New York University.

Sleet began his career in journalism as a sportswriter for the *New York Amsterdam News,* a black newspaper, in 1950. Several months later, he secured a position with the black picture magazine *Our World* and worked there until it folded in 1955. That same year, he joined the staff of the Johnson Publishing Company and began shooting pictures for *Jet* and *Ebony* magazines. For the next 40 years, he would provide dramatic photographs from around the world for the two publications.

Documented American Civil Rights Movement

In his four decades as a staff photographer for Johnson Publishing, Sleet documented the struggles and triumphs of people of color throughout the world. In addition to traveling extensively in the United States, he visited Africa, Europe, South America, and the West Indies. He photographed many African heads of state, such as Ethiopian emperor Haile Selassie, Ghanaian leader Kwame Nkrumah, Liberian president William

Tubman, and Kenyan president Jomo Kenyatta. His celebrity photos included memorable shots of singers Billie Holiday and Patti LaBelle; jazz musician Thelonious Monk; actors Bill Cosby, Phylicia Rashad, and Sidney Poitier; and the late tennis great Arthur Ashe.

Sleet also took pictures of ordinary people in settings ranging from civil rights marches to beauty contests. He recorded the woes of the less fortunate in such places as a prison death row, a West Virginia mining town, and Miami, Florida, in the aftermath of a riot. Traveling was especially difficult on his family. As he told *Ebony,* "It's not an easy life, so it's important to have a family who understands. I have been very fortunate." His family included his wife, Juanita, whom he married in 1950, and three children: Gregory, Michael, and Lisa.

Sleet made his greatest contributions to history through his pictorial chronicles of the American civil rights movement and the emergence of independent African states. He recorded such major events as the 1963 March on Washington; the 1965 march for voting rights from Selma to Montgomery, Alabama; and the independence day celebrations in Nairobi, Kenya, a former British colony, in 1963.

Sleet brought his experience as an African American to his photography of black subjects, and his photographs illustrate a great sense of commitment to the events he was photographing: "I must say that I wasn't there [at major civil rights demonstrations] as an objective reporter," he told C. Gerald Fraser in the *New York Times.* "To be perfectly honest I had something to say, or, at least hoped that I did, and was trying to show one side of it—because we didn't have any problems finding the other side. So I was emotionally involved. That may not be a good school of journalism, but that's the way I felt."

Won the Pulitzer Prize

Sleet came to know the Reverend Martin Luther King Jr. well and produced one of the largest collections of candid shots of King and his family. He took one of his first photographs of the Kings in 1956—a photo of Dr. and Mrs. King with their infant daughter, Yolanda, on the steps of the Dexter Avenue Baptist Church in Montgomery, Alabama. Sleet later traveled with the family to Oslo, Norway, when King received the Nobel Peace Prize. Sleet grew close to the family over the years. "It's kind of a peculiar position to be in," he told Fraser, "because, on one hand, you are there as [a photographer], but people soon forgot that."

Following King's assassination in 1968, Sleet attended the slain leader's funeral, where he took his prize-winning picture of Coretta Scott King comforting her young daughter during the service. Initially Sleet was not to be included in the photography pool for the

funeral, which was made up of photographers from news magazines such as *Time, Life,* and *Newsweek.* When Sleet informed Mrs. King that no black photographers were to be included, she told those organizing the service that if there was no photographer from Johnson Publishing in the pool, there would be no pool. Sleet subsequently was invited to join the pool.

Sleet's image of Mrs. King holding her daughter was widely distributed by the Associated Press. The following year he was awarded the Pulitzer Prize for Feature Photography—the first photography prize awarded to an African American and the first given to anyone working for a black publication. Some critics—including Sleet himself—credited his success more to his sensitivity and patience as an observer than to his practical technique as a photographer. As Sleet explained to Fraser in the *New York Times,* "You've got to know when to intrude and when not to intrude and when to pull back. You have to be very patient, a thing that's good for me because I have a lot of patience and don't mind waiting." In *An Illustrated Bio-Bibliography of Black Photographers,* Sleet elaborated: "You try to develop the sensitivity and the 'eye' to see that very special mood of the moment. You develop the discipline to block out everything but you, the camera and the subject, and you develop the tenacity to stick with it, to have patience. The picture will happen—that very special picture will happen."

Served as Witness of a Generation

Although Sleet's photographs were shown at the Metropolitan Museum of Art in New York, he saw only one solo exhibition of his work during the height of the civil rights movement. That showing was sponsored by the Alpha Kappa Alpha sorority and toured St. Louis and Detroit in 1970. For more than a decade and a half after that, Sleet's works were not displayed in formal one-man exhibitions. In 1986 the Philip Morris Companies and Johnson Publishing Company cosponsored Sleet's a retrospective exhibit that opened at the New York Public Library.

Initially set to run for two years and visit four cities, the show received so much attention and so many requests for bookings that its schedule was extended. In addition to New York, the retrospective was shown in Chicago; Milwaukee, Wisconsin; Newark, New Jersey; Frankfort, Kentucky; and Washington, DC. Highlights of the exhibit included many of his most famous shots of the King family, other political leaders, and celebrities. The photographs ranged in mood from heart-rending sadness to triumph; included was a strikingly poignant photograph of the great blues singer Billie Holiday, wearily resting her head on her needle-scarred arms, as well as a shot of an unknown, exultant woman tramp-

ing and singing through the rain during the 1965 Selma march.

Meanwhile, Sleet continued his work in photojournalism for both *Jet* and *Ebony.* In 1996 he covered the Summer Olympics in Atlanta, Georgia. Upon returning to his home on Long Island, he was diagnosed with cancer. Sleet died shortly thereafter, on September 30, 1996, at age 70. Eulogizing his childhood friend, the Reverend Dr. Norman M. Rates observed, "While others of us see things through the naked eye, ... Sleet saw things through his soul," according to *Jet.* Writing in the *New York Times* in 1996 upon Sleet's death, Robert McG. Thomas Jr. noted that the photographer had "brought his camera to a revolution and ended up capturing many of the images that defined the struggle for racial equality in the United States and Africa." Quoting Sleet, Thomas commented on this photographer's desire for remembrance and commemoration as captured in his work: "A lot of people have forgotten those days and I don't think they ever should."

In 1998 Johnson Publishing issued *Special Moments in African-American History, 1955–1996: The Photographs of Moneta Sleet, Jr.,* a collection of Sleet's photographs spanning his career, including images from the civil rights era, Africa, and elsewhere in the world and images from the world of politics. An *Ebony* contributor noted of this publication: "If you lived any part of the last 50 years and if you expect to live any part of the next 50, you ought to read Moneta Sleet Jr.'s magnificent celebration of the images and people who created the new world of Black and White America." Similarly, Lerone Bennett Jr., Sleet's editor for decades, commented in *Jet,* "[Sleet] was a major witness, perhaps the greatest witness, of our greatest 50 years .... He was there, he had a camera and an eye, and he saw it all."

Selected works

Books

Special Moments in African-American History, 1955–1996: The Photographs of Moneta Sleet, Jr., Johnson Publishing Company, 1998.

Sources

Books

Crawford, Joe, ed., *The Black Photographers Annual: 1973,* Black Photographers Annual, 1972.
Willis-Thomas, Deborah, ed., *An Illustrated Bio-Bibliography of Black Photographers, 1940–1988,* Garland, 1989.

Periodicals

American Photographer, July 1988.

Chicago Defender, May 2, 1987.

Ebony, February 1969; June 1969; August 1971; January 1987; December 1998.

Jet, October 13, 1986; March 2, 1987; June 5, 1989; October 14, 1996; October 21, 1996; March 20, 2000.

New York Times, October 19, 1986; October 2, 1996.

Online

"Monet Sleet, Jr.: Pulitzer Prize Photojournalist," Contemporary Art Center of Virginia, http://www.virginiamoca.org/sites/default/files/38475_CAC_1.pdf (accessed July 16, 2016).

—Robin Armstrong and J. Sydney Jones

Kimbo Slice

1974–2016

Mixed martial arts fighter

Slice, Kimbo, photograph. Gregg DeGuire/FilmMagic/Getty Images.

Mixed martial arts (MMA) fighter Kimbo Slice made his name brawling in underground street fights, becoming famous for knocking down his opponents with a single brutal punch. When videos of those fights started turning up on YouTube, Slice quickly became an Internet sensation, prompting *Rolling Stone* magazine to call him the "undisputed online king of the underground bare-knuckle world" in 2006. Indeed, at 6 feet, two inches and 260 pounds, bald and bearded with gold teeth, Slice cut a menacing and unforgettable figure. Moving from the street to the cage in 2007, Slice became a star attraction of the professional MMA circuit. His career lasted only a few years, however, as his technical abilities fell short of his brute strength, and he was no match for the sport's top fighters. Slice made a brief comeback in 2015–16, going 5–2 before he died suddenly of heart failure at age 42.

Kimbo Slice was born Kevin Ferguson in Nassau, Bahamas, on February 8, 1974, the oldest son in a family of 11 children. Raised by his single mother, Rosemary Clarke, in Cutler Ridge, Florida, south of Miami, Ferguson attended Palmetto High School, where he was a star middle linebacker with hopes of playing college football. In August of 1992, Ferguson's senior year, Hurricane Andrew devastated South Florida. As the Category 5 storm barreled through the Miami area, Ferguson huddled under a mattress in his mother's home to shield himself from falling debris. The hurricane cut short Palmetto's football season and, with it, Ferguson's hopes of winning a scholarship.

Ferguson enrolled at Bethune-Cookman University in Daytona Beach as a criminal justice major, planning on a career as a police officer, but he flunked out after two semesters. By early 1994, with no college degree and no job prospects, Ferguson was on the streets, living out of his car. He first found work as a bouncer at a strip club, and then, with help from high school friend (and future manager) "Icey Mike" Ember, he took a job as a limousine driver and bodyguard for RK Netmedia, an online pornography company. His earnings were enough to get him off the street and into an apartment.

Ferguson found that he could earn even more by competing in street fights in alleys, parking lots, and backyards, netting $300 to $500 or more a for each brawl. "At first, it was to make a couple bucks—I'd

At a Glance . . .

Born Kevin Ferguson on February 8, 1974, in Nassau, Bahamas; died on June 6, 2016, in Margate, FL; son of Rosemary Clarke; partner of Antoinette Ray; children: Kevin Jr., Kevin II, Kevlar, Kassandra, Kiandra, Kevina. *Education:* Attended Bethune-Cookman University, University of Miami.

Career: ProElite, mixed martial arts fighter, 2007–08; Ultimate Fighting Championship, 2009–10; Bellator MMA, 2015–16.

Addresses: *Web*—http://www.kimbo305.com/home.htm.

rather fight than steal—but it came natural," Ferguson told the *Miami Herald* in 2008. A friend had the idea to film the fights, and soon crude videos were appearing on the Internet, attracting millions of viewers. In 20 fights, Slice lost only one, to Boston police officer Sean Gannon in 2003. Thereafter he became known as Kimbo Slice: "Kimbo" was a nickname he had had since childhood, while "Slice" was a moniker given to him by Internet fans after he tore a large gash in an opponent's face.

As the legend of Kimbo Slice grew, MMA promoters sought to draw him into the professional arena. Popularized in the 1990s, mixed martial arts is a full-contact sport that combines elements of boxing, wrestling, striking, and grappling with martial arts techniques from karate, judo, and jiu-jitsu. Bouts are organized by professional MMA organizations such as the Ultimate Fighting Championship (UFC) and Bellator. With fewer rules than professional boxing or wrestling, the sport tends toward extreme violence—so much so that until 2008, network television would not air MMA matchups, despite their increasing popularity.

Slice, who had no formal training in martial arts, began working with retired MMA champion Bas Rutten and boxing instructor Randy Shatami in Thousand Oaks, California. MMA insiders, however, doubted that Slice could compete at the pro level. Dana White, president of the UFC, told *ESPN: The Magazine* that Slice "wouldn't last two minutes in the Octagon," referring to the octagonal cage that MMA fighters spar in, while Ricco Rodriguez, a UFC heavyweight champ, told a radio station, "Kimbo is a tomato can. What has he done to prove himself? He hasn't fought anybody. He's a nobody. Kimbo Slice is just a clown," according to ESPN.

Slice made his sanctioned MMA debut in an exhibition match against former boxer Ray Mercer on June 23, 2007, in Atlantic City. He defeated Mercer with a guillotine choke just 72 seconds into the first round. The following November, in his first professional bout, Slice put down veteran cage fighter Bo Cantrell only 19 seconds into the first round by submission due to strikes. Then, in February of 2008, Slice pummeled David "Tank" Abbott, winning by knockout in 43 seconds. In the first MMA event to be shown live on network television, on May 31, 2008, Slice went three rounds against James "Colossus" Thompson. In the third round, he ruptured Thompson's ear and threw three unanswered punches, prompting the referee to stop the bout. The win brought Slice's pro record to 3–0.

In his most anticipated contest, Slice was scheduled to fight 44-year-old Ken Shamrock, known as "The World's Most Dangerous Man," on October 4, 2008, during a live broadcast on the CBS network's *Saturday Night Fights*. At the last minute, however, Shamrock was declared ineligible because of a cut on his eye, and fight officials chose Seth Petruzelli as his stand-in. In a stunning upset, Petruzelli defeated Slice by technical knockout just 14 seconds into the first round. In the aftermath of the fight, some fans and sportswriters cheered the loss, happy to see Slice get his comeuppance. A headline on Yahoo Sports declared, "Final Curtain for the Kimbo Show." In October of 2008, ProElite, the organizer of the fight, filed for bankruptcy, a move that was widely attributed to Slice's loss.

The following year Slice signed with UFC and competed on The Ultimate Fighter: Heavyweights. His UFC career lasted less than a year, however, as he was released in May of 2010 after losing by technical knockout in the second round to Matt Mitrione. Thereafter Slice tried to reinvent himself as a professional boxer, going undefeated in seven bouts between 2011 and 2013.

In 2015 Slice returned to the ring as a fighter with Bellator MMA. In his first fight in June of that year, he faced Shamrock again, defeating the 51-year-old with a knockout. A subsequent win over Dhafir Harris in February of the next year was later ruled a no contest when Slice tested positive for steroids. Slice had been scheduled to fight James Thompson in London in July of 2016, but on June 3 he was rushed to a hospital near his home in Coral Springs, Florida, where he was diagnosed with heart failure and a mass was found on his liver. He died a few days later, on June 6, 2016, at age 42. According to the *South Florida Sun-Sentinel*, at the time of his death, Slice was being prepared for transport to Cleveland, Ohio, where he was to be placed on an organ donor list for a heart transplant.

Sources

Periodicals

ESPN: The Magazine, May 20, 2008.
Miami Herald, October 2, 2008.

Rolling Stone, July 28, 2006.
Ventura County (CA) Star, May 10, 2008.

Online

"Kevin Ferguson," BoxRec.com, http://boxrec.com/boxer/575561 (accessed September 27, 2016).

"Kimbo Slice," Bellator MMA, http://bellator.spike.com/fighters/ps9qc5/kimbo-slice (accessed September 27, 2016).

O'Brien, Luke, "The Ultimate Fighter," Slate, June 8, 2016, http://www.slate.com/articles/sports/sports_nut/2016/06/kimbo_slice_died_at_age_42_his_street_fights_made_him_a_viral_video_star.html (accessed September 27, 2016).

Trischetta, Linda, and Wells Dusenbury, "Kimbo Slice Needed Heart Transplant before His Death," Sun-Sentinel.com, June 8, 2016, http://www.sun-sentinel.com/sports/fl-kimbo-slice-update-0608–20160607-story.html (accessed September 27, 2016).

Wetzel, Dan, "Final Curtain for the Kimbo Show," Yahoo Sports, October 5, 2008, https://ca.sports.yahoo.com/news/final-curtain-kimbo-show-085000091–mma.html (accessed September 27, 2016).

—Deborah A. Ring

Lee Smith

195(?)—

R&B and jazz bassist

A versatile, dynamic, and long underappreciated bassist, Lee Smith has been making important contributions to rhythm and blues and jazz for more than 40 years. Until the early 2010s, when he finally began to release his own albums, he was largely overlooked by the general public, both because of his natural reticence and because of the brilliant rise of his son Christian McBride, one of the most prominent bassists in the world. His own career, however, has been enviable, and he counts dozens of major stars, from R&B icon Billy Paul to jazz legend Mongo Santamaria, among his partners. "As a bassist," critic Bruce Klauber wrote, "Smith has it all, and 'all' includes a fierce sense of swing, formidable technique, exquisite taste and restraint, and an always-inventive ability as a soloist."

Born in Philadelphia in 1951 or 1952, Lee W. Smith grew up on the West Side of that city, long a hotbed of both R&B and jazz. His involvement in music began around age 10, when he took up the trumpet. While continuing with that instrument as a student at Philadelphia's Overbrook High School, he began to experiment in his spare time with an old bass guitar he had found at his grandparents' house. His progress on the bass was rapid, and by the time he entered nearby West Chester College (later West Chester University), he was playing professionally, backing a variety of R&B acts at gigs around the city. The late 1960s and early 1970s were a golden era in the history of Philadelphia R&B, as the lush, orchestral sound that came to be known as "Philly soul" attracted international attention. In that vibrant environment, the demand for skilled bassists was high, and after a few semesters he left West Chester to focus on music full time.

The next few years were a highlight of Smith's career, as he toured around the world with acts such as Brenda and the Tabulations, the Delfonics, and Billy Paul. As Philly soul was eclipsed by disco during the mid-1970s, however, Smith began to look for new opportunities. The break he needed came in the summer of 1977, when Alfred Williams, a friend from Overbrook who was managing Santamaria's band, asked him to audition for the percussionist, a pioneer in the development of Afro-Cuban jazz. Hired on the spot, he spent the next five years touring and recording with Santamaria's group. "This was Lee's first time playing Latin music," noted a brief biography on his website (LeeSmithMusic. com), "and was one of the most challenging musical experiences he had in his career." Notable recordings during his tenure include *Red Hot,* released by Tappan Zee Records in 1979, and *Summertime,* a joint project with trumpeter Dizzy Gillespie that appeared on the Pablo Live label two years later.

Soon after *Summertime*'s release, Smith's career shifted direction, as his mother's declining health forced him to leave Santamaria and return to Philadelphia, where the music scene had declined significantly in his absence. He recovered quickly from that setback, however, finding new opportunities in the resorts of Atlantic City, New Jersey, just a short drive away. Over the next few years, he became a familiar presence there, appearing regularly with pianist Milton Sealey and other jazz veterans. He also continued to work on

At a Glance . . .

Born Lee W. Smith in 195? in Philadelphia, PA; son of Leopold and Anne Smith; children: three. *Education:* Attended West Chester College, late 1960s or early 1970s.

Career: Independent musician, 1960s—; toured and recorded with Mongo Santamaria, 1977–82.

Addresses: *Office*—c/o Vectordisc Records, 2573 Clothier St., Coatesville, PA 19320. *Web*—http://www.LeeSmithMusic.com.

his technique, gradually shifting from an electrified bass guitar to an upright, acoustic model. The latter instrument, sometimes known as a double bass, gave him a new range of sounds and textures and helped introduce him to jazz fans who had missed his work with Santamaria.

His growing reputation notwithstanding, Smith hesitated for many years to release albums as a leader, preferring instead to remain in the background. "I always felt like the guys in the orchestra were the real heroes," he told Shaun Brady of the *Philadelphia City Paper.* "They're kind of anonymous, no one knows who they are, but yet they're producing this great music. That's what I related to. I never felt like I had a need to step out front." In the early 2010s, however, his attitude shifted, and he began preparations for his first album. Released on Philadelphia-based Vectordisc Records, Smith's debut, *Sittin' on a Secret,* was based on compositions he had written in his spare time. "I had this passion and this music that wants to come out, but for some reason it just hasn't yet," he told Brady in 2012, just as the album was being released. "I'm at a point in my life now where I felt like it needed to."

Completed with the help of an excellent band that included pianist Anthony Wonsey, trumpeter Terell Stafford, drummer Justin Faulkner, and saxophonist Tim Warfield, *Sittin' on a Secret* featured six original compositions as well as new arrangements of standards such as "Count Down," a piece written and made famous by saxophone legend John Coltrane. "Highlights abound," noted Klauber in a glowing review for

JazzTimes, adding, "Smith has been around long enough to know the importance of pacing, song and solo length. He's wisely edited same, making for great pacing and consistent interest. If that's a traditional point of view, then so be it, as Lee Smith personifies tradition. Make that 'today's tradition.'"

Amid such praise, Smith and Vectordisc lost little time in preparing a follow-up, *My Kind of Blues,* released in 2015. Featuring his own compositions as well as classics such as Santamaria's "Afro Blue," it, too, won accolades. In a review for the website All About Jazz, Victor L. Schermer called the album "a fine piece of craftsmanship that is also very listenable and accessible," adding, "Smith sticks to his roots and his heart, which is more than can be said for a lot of people these days."

By the summer of 2016, nearly half a century after his professional debut, Smith's profile was rising steadily, and he was increasingly recognized as an elder statesman of the Philadelphia music scene. A review of online sources in August of that year suggested, however, that he was not touring as widely as he once did.

Selected discography

Mongo Santamaria, *Red Hot,* Tappan Zee, 1979.
Mongo Santamaria and Dizzy Gillespie, *Summertime,* Pablo Live, 1981.
Sittin' on a Secret (includes "Count Down"), Vectordisc, 2012.
My Kind of Blues (includes "Afro Blue"), Vectordisc, 2015.

Sources

Periodicals

JazzTimes, September 13, 2012.
Philadelphia City Paper, October 2, 2012.

Online

"Biography," LeeSmithMusic.com, http://leesmithmusic.com/biography/ (accessed August 26, 2016).
Schermer, Victor L., "Lee Smith: *My Kind of Blues,*" All About Jazz, August 6, 2015, https://www.allaboutjazz.com/lee-smith-my-kind-of-blues-by-victor-l-schermer.php (accessed August 26, 2016).

—R. Anthony Kugler

S.O.S. Band

R&B group

One of the most highly regarded R&B groups to emerge in the 1980s, the S.O.S. Band has been entertaining audiences around the globe for more than 30 years. Led for much of its history by the brilliant vocalist Mary Davis, the ensemble has had an impressive string of hits, including 1980's "Take Your Time (Do It Right)"—arguably one of the era's most familiar songs—and 1986's "The Finest." Amid that success, however, Davis and her partners have also faced a number of obstacles, many of which they have overcome. As of the mid-2010s, they were still active, holding their own amid rapid changes in both public taste and the structure of the music business.

The S.O.S. Band began in Atlanta, Georgia, around 1977, when Davis had an extended singing engagement at a nightclub called the Royal Room. There she met an experienced and skilled keyboard player, Jason Bryant. "In just weeks," noted Mark C. Horn of the *Phoenix New Times,* "their two musical worlds collided." As their rapport grew, they began to lay the groundwork for a new group, recruiting saxophonist Willie "Sonny" Killebrew, guitarist Bruno Speight, bassist John Simpson, drummer James Earl Jones III, and saxophonist and flutist Billy Ellis. With the help of club owner Milton Lamar and manager Bunnie Jackson-Ransom, the new ensemble—originally named Santa Monica—recorded a demo tape and sent it to Tabu Records, a relatively new label based in Los Angeles. Tabu's founder, Clarence Avant, liked what he heard, and the next phase of the group's career began.

Before much work could be done in the recording studio, however, it was agreed that a new name was necessary. At the suggestion of a veteran producer named Sigidi Abdullah, Santa Monica became the S.O.S. Band; S.O.S. was taken to be an abbreviation for "Sounds of Success," but a variety of interpretations are possible.

Released in 1980, the S.O.S. Band's debut, titled simply *S.O.S.,* was a sensation, reaching number two on the R&B Albums chart; it was eventually certified gold, selling more than half a million copies. Its success owed a great deal to a single track, "Take Your Time (Do It Right)," which spent a month at the top of the R&B chart when released as a single. With an easy, catchy chorus, a strong bass line, and memorable instrumentation that included bells and a glockenspiel, "Take Your Time" soon became a template for other R&B acts. The rapid demise of disco in the late 1970s had shaken the world of R&B, and many performers were looking for a new sound. In that challenging environment, the new group from Atlanta seemed to offer a way forward.

Thrust into the national spotlight by the success of their debut, Davis and her partners had to adjust quickly to the pressures of publicity. Other changes came as well, the most significant of which was the addition of trumpeter, percussionist, and vocalist Abdul Ra'oof, who arrived just in time for the band's second album, *Too* (1981). While it had some strong moments, it failed to match the critical or commercial success of its predecessor and was widely considered a disappointment. As the lineup continued to adjust to Ra'oof's presence, however, the group's internal dynamics improved, and their next album, *III* (1982), showed marked improvement, as did their fourth, *On the Rise* (1983). The latter, in fact, rivaled the group's debut, breaking the top 10 on the R&B Albums chart and

At a Glance . . .

Members included Mary Davis, Jason Bryant, Willie Killebrew, Bruno Speight, John Simpson, James Earl Jones III, Billy Ellis, and Abdul Ra'oof.

Career: R&B group.

Addresses: *Office*—c/o Demon Music Group, BBC Television Centre, 101 Wood Ln., London W12 7FA, United Kingdom.

spawning two top-five R&B hits, "Just Be Good to Me" and "Tell Me If You Still Care." It, too, was eventually certified gold.

The months that followed marked the peak of the group's long career. After *On the Rise* they released two more albums in characteristically quick succession: *Just the Way You Like It* (1984) and *Sands of Time* (1986). The title track to the former was a major hit, peaking at number six on the R&B chart and sending the album to number six as well. In its wake came "The Finest," a number-two R&B hit and the highlight of *Sands of Time,* yet another gold record.

Amid this success, however, there were signs of trouble. The most serious issue was simple fatigue. While near-constant touring had an impact on every member of the group, Davis, by her own account, was particularly affected by it. "I couldn't maintain the rigorous schedule that we had," she told Horn, "and I had to take a break." Her departure about 1987 was followed by a period of convalescence and a solo album. The rest of the band soldiered on, recording two major albums, *Diamonds in the Raw* (1989) and *One of Many Nights* (1991) with Davis's replacement, Chandra Currelley. Both records included a significant hit; *Diamonds* had "I'm Still Missing Your Love," while "Sometimes I Wonder" was the highlight of *One of Many Nights.* Neither received as much airplay as the group's earlier hits, however. With the tragic death of Ellis and the continued absence of Davis, who was regarded as the heart of the band, a permanent breakup seemed likely.

Davis announced her return in 1994. With the help of Bryant and Ra'oof, she was able to re-form the group and bring it back into the limelight. After touring for roughly 15 years, however, differences arose, and the band split in two. As of the mid-2010s, both factions—one led by Davis and the other by Speight—were appearing regularly as the S.O.S. Band. Speight, for his part, seemed to take the situation in stride. "Anytime, man, you run into bands that are this old and older," he told Craig D. Lindsey of the Raleigh *News &*

Observer in 2014, "there are gonna be two of them—sometimes three."

Selected discography

Singles

"Take Your Time (Get It Right)," 1980.
"Just Be Good to Me," 1983.
"Tell Me If You Still Care," 1983.
"Just the Way You Like It," 1984.
"The Finest," 1986.
"I'm Still Missing Your Love," 1989.
"Sometimes I Wonder," 1991.

Albums

S.O.S. (includes "Take Your Time [Get It Right]"), Tabu, 1980.
Too, Tabu, 1981.
III, Tabu, 1982.
On the Rise (includes "Just Be Good to Me" and "Tell Me If You Still Care"), Tabu, 1983.
Just the Way You Like It (includes "Just the Way You Like It"), Tabu, 1984.
Sands of Time (includes "The Finest"), Tabu, 1986.
Diamonds in the Raw (includes "I'm Still Missing Your Love"), Tabu, 1989.
One of Many Nights (includes "Sometimes I Wonder"), Arista, 1991.

Sources

Online

Hogan, Ed, "The S.O.S. Band: Artist Biography," AllMusic.com, http://www.allmusic.com/artist/the-sos-band-mn0000495366/biography (accessed September 3, 2016).
Horn, Mark C., "The Timing Has Always Been Right for Mary Davis and the S.O.S. Band," PhoenixNew Times.com, April 9, 2015, http://www.phoenixnewtimes.com/music/the-timing-has-always-been-right-for-mary-davis-and-the-sos-band-7286782 (accessed September 3, 2016).
Lindsey, Craig D., "S.O.S. Band Brings the Funk to Raleigh," NewsObserver.com, December 11, 2914, http://www.newsobserver.com/entertainment/music-news-reviews/article10189271.html (accessed September 3, 2016).
"S.O.S. Band," SoulWalking.co.uk, http://www.soulwalking.co.uk/S.O.S%20Band.html (accessed September 3, 2016).
Williams, Chris, "Key Tracks: Jimmy Jam on the S.O.S. Band's *Just the Way You Like It,*" Red Bull Music Academy, January 11, 2015, http://daily.redbullmusicacademy.com/2015/01/key-tracks-jimmy-jam-sos-band (accessed September 3, 2016).

—R. Anthony Kugler

Thundercat

1984—

Bassist, singer, music producer

Thundercat, photograph. Anthony Pidgeon/Redferns/Getty Images.

Stephen "Thundercat" Bruner is a bass player, vocalist, and producer who is best known for his contributions to rapper Kendrick Lamar's Grammy Award–winning 2015 album *To Pimp a Butterfly,* one of the most critically acclaimed records of that year. A prodigy on the bass guitar, Thundercat began playing professionally while he was still in high school, and at the beginning of his career he was known primarily as a sideman for artists such as Erykah Badu and Snoop Dogg. Thundercat's musical collaboration with the electronic artist and producer Flying Lotus, beginning with the latter's 2010 album *Cosmogramma,* revealed the full range of the bassist's talents and marked the beginning of a period of prolific creativity. Over the next five years, he released three solo albums that showcased his virtuosity on the bass and his powerful vocals. Teaming with Lamar in 2015, Thundercat was credited with helping shape the sound of *To Pimp a Butterfly,* a groundbreaking album that earned 11 Grammy nominations. Thundercat's collaboration with jazz saxophonist Kamasi Washington on his album *The Epic* that same year, together with the release of his third solo album, *The Beyond/Where Giants Roam,* cemented his reputation for creating genre-bending, innovative music.

The musician was born Stephen Bruner on October 19, 1984, in Los Angeles and grew up in a musical family. His father, Ronald Bruner Sr., was a drummer who played with Diana Ross, Gladys Knight, and the Temptations. Thundercat, so called for his obsession with the *Thunder-Cats* cartoon of the 1980s, started playing the bass guitar at age four; he later studied the stand-up bass at the Colburn School of Music in Los Angeles and then was mentored by Reggie Williams, a legendary music teacher at L.A.'s Locke High School. His brother Ronald Jr. followed in their father's footsteps, picking up the drums at age two, while another brother, Jameel, took up the keyboards. As children the Bruner brothers—all three of whom would go on to become Grammy-nominated musicians—received a broad musical education, absorbing the diverse sounds of Motown, rhythm and blues, soul, funk, jazz, and gospel.

Thundercat was playing the bass professionally by the time he was a teenager. Already he was pushing the boundaries of genre, not limiting himself to a particular musical style. At age 15 he sang with a short-lived boy band called No Curfew. The next year he joined the

At a Glance . . .

Born Stephen Bruner on October 19, 1984, in Los Angeles, CA; son of Ronald Bruner Sr. and Pamela Bruner (both musicians).

Career: Bassist for Suicidal Tendencies, 2000s; bassist for artists such as Sa-Ra, Erykah Badu, Snoop Dogg; solo recording artist, 2011—.

Awards: Grammy Award, Best Rap/Sung Collaboration, 2016, for "These Walls" (with Kendrick Lamar).

Addresses: *Twitter*—@Thundercat.

L.A.-based thrash band Suicidal Tendencies, together with his brother Ronald. Thundercat played on three of the group's albums: *Year of the Cycos* (2008), *No Mercy Fool!/The Suicidal Family* (2010), and *13* (2013). During the same time, the two Bruner brothers joined with jazz saxophonist Kamasi Washington and pianist Cameron Graves to form the group Young Jazz Giants. In 1999 the group won the John Coltrane Music Competition, and in 2004 they released a self-titled album on Birdman Records.

Thundercat's virtuosic bass playing—quick, nimble, and heavy on grooves—quickly made him an in-demand session musician, and over the next decade he was known for his work as a sideman. Thundercat collaborated with the L.A. hip-hop collective Sa-Ra on the albums *The Hollywood Recordings* (2007) and *Nuclear Evolution: The Age of Love* (2009) and earned praise for his bass work on soul singer Erykah Badu's two-volume *New Amerykah* (2008, 2010). He also played bass in the studio and on tour for the rapper Snoop Dogg.

The bassist found his most productive musical partnership with the rapper, electronic musician, and producer Flying Lotus. After meeting at the South by Southwest music festival in 2009, the two quickly fell into a sonic kinship. Thundercat played bass on Flying Lotus's critically acclaimed 2010 album *Cosmogramma* and, for the first time, sang on the track "MmmHmm." The following year he stepped into the role of front man and released his own solo debut album, *The Golden Age of Apocalypse*, on Flying Lotus's Brainfeeder label. *Golden Age* received positive marks from critics for its brand of 1970s-inspired jazz fusion as well as for Thundercat's technical prowess on the bass. *LA Weekly* named it one of the top five Los Angeles jazz albums of the year.

Two years later Thundercat followed up with a second album, *Apocalypse*, executive produced by Flying Lo-tus. Recorded soon after the sudden death of jazz pianist and composer Austin Peralta, a frequent collaborator with Thundercat, the album is much darker than the first, reflecting the bassist's attempt to cope with the loss of a close friend and colleague. Writing in *Billboard*, Reggie Ugwu called *Apocalypse* Thundercat's "most fully realized statement as an artist yet," describing the record as "a funk-drenched, intermittently electronic record that borrows liberally from R&B, jazz, and Quincy Jones–era pop."

The next two years were a period of prolific creativity for the bassist, who seemed to be ubiquitous. In 2014 Thundercat appeared on Flying Lotus's avant-garde electronic album *You're Dead!*, contributing on bass, guitar, and vocals. In 2015 he appeared on one of the most acclaimed albums of the year, rapper Kendrick Lamar's *To Pimp a Butterfly*, released in March of 2015. Lamar initially invited Thundercat to play on a few tracks on *To Pimp a Butterfly*, but as the bassist began collaborating with the producer Sounwave, he helped shape the album's sound, pushing Lamar in new directions musically. "I don't think he was totally aware of what I was capable of bringing to the table until he started hearing the stuff that me and Sounwave were creating," Thundercat told Randall Roberts of the *Los Angeles Times*, speaking of his collaboration with Lamar. "I would … send Kendrick [music] as I would be creating it … just to try and keep him inspired." The resulting album was a critical and commercial success. *To Pimp a Butterfly* debuted at number one on the Billboard 200 chart and exceeded half a million in sales within a month. The album was ranked as the best album of the year by *Rolling Stone* and *Billboard* and won the Grammy Awards for album of the year and best rap album, in addition to best rap/sung collaboration for "These Walls" featuring Thundercat.

That same year Thundercat appeared, together with his brother Ronald, on Kamasi Washington's debut jazz album, *The Epic*, which was released in May of 2015 on Brainfeeder. A sprawling, three-volume record, *The Epic* reached number three on the Billboard Jazz Albums charts and was hailed as one of the most innovative jazz albums of the year. Just a month after *The Epic* was released, Thundercat dropped his third solo album, *The Beyond/Where Giants Roam.* Conceived at the same time the bassist was working on *You're Dead!* and *To Pimp a Butterfly*, the album drew creative inspiration from his collaborations with Flying Lotus and Lamar. "Everything was kind of symbiotic," Thundercat recalled to Jason Woodbury of the *Phoenix New Times*. "I feel like [the albums] worked and played off of each other. When I wasn't working on my album, I was working on Kendrick's, or Kamasi's, or Flying Lotus'[s]," all of which he characterized as "brainchildren of similar minds."

In August of 2016, Thundercat released a new single, "Bus in These Streets," produced by Flying Lotus. His fourth solo album was reported to be in the works that year.

Selected discography

Young Jazz Giants, *Young Jazz Giants,* Birdman, 2004.

Sa-Ra, *The Hollywood Recordings,* Babygrande, 2007.

Suicidal Tendencies, *Year of the Cycos,* Suicidal Records, 2008.

Erykah Badu, *New Amerykah Part One (4th World War),* Universal Motown, 2008.

Sa-Ra, *Nuclear Evolution: The Age of Love,* Ubiquity, 2009.

Erykah Badu, *New Amerykah Part Two (Return of the Ankh),* Universal Motown, 2010.

Suicidal Tendencies, *No Mercy Fool!/The Suicidal Family,* Suicidal Records, 2010.

Flying Lotus, *Cosmogramma,* Warp Records, 2010.

The Golden Age of Apocalypse, Brainfeeder, 2011.

Suicidal Tendencies, *13,* Suicidal Records, 2013.

Apocalypse, Brainfeeder, 2013.

Flying Lotus, *You're Dead!,* Warp Records, 2014.

Kendrick Lamar, *To Pimp a Butterfly,* Interscope, 2015.

Kamasi Washington, *The Epic,* Brainfeeder, 2015.

The Beyond/Where Giants Roam, Brainfeeder, 2015.

Sources

Periodicals

Guardian (London), July 22, 2015.
Phoenix New Times, September 15, 2015.

Online

Cohen, Ian, "Thundercat Emerges with His Debut, Co-Produced by Flying Lotus," LAWeekly.com, September 1, 2011, http://www.laweekly.com/music/thundercat-emerges-with-his-debut-co-produced-by-flying-lotus-2171825 (accessed September 27, 2016).

Kelley, Frannie, "Thundercat on Making Music Outside the Lines," *All Things Considered,* National Public Radio, July 20, 2013, http://www.npr.org/sections/therecord/2013/07/20/203347014/thundercat-on-making-music-outside-the-lines (accessed September 27, 2016).

O'Connell, Sean J., "Top 5 Los Angeles Jazz Albums of 2011," LAWeekly.com, December 20, 2011, http://www.laweekly.com/music/top-5-los-angeles-jazz-albums-of-2011–2405380 (accessed September 27, 2016).

Roberts, Randall, "Thundercat, One of Kendrick Lamar's Secret Weapons on 'To Pimp a Butterfly,' Emerges in Time for Grammys," LATimes.com, February 12, 2016, http://www.latimes.com/entertainment/la-ca-ms-grammys-thundercat-20160214-story.html (accessed September 27, 2016).

Thomas, Vincent, "Thundercat: Artist Biography," AllMusic.com, http://www.allmusic.com/artist/thundercat-mn0002424073/biography (accessed September 27, 2016).

Ugwu, Reggie, "Thundercat Q&A: Coping with Loss, Surprising Snoop, and the Jazz Roots of Mac Miller," Billboard.com, June 11, 2013, http://www.billboard.com/articles/columns/code/1566467/thundercat-qa-coping-with-loss-surprising-snoop-and-the-jazz-roots-of (accessed September 27, 2016).

Weiner, Natalie, "Thundercat Talks Surprise Album, Playing Jazz for Kendrick & Why Drake Is the Best," Billboard.com, June 22, 2015, http://www.billboard.com/articles/news/6605621/thundercat-inter view-kendrick-jazz-new-album-drake (accessed September 27, 2016).

Weiss, Jeff, "Meet Thundercat, the Jazz-Fusion Genius Behind Kendrick Lamar's 'Butterfly,'" RollingStone.com, April 2, 2015. http://www.rollingstone.com/music/features/meet-thundercat-the-mad-genius-behind-kendrick-lamar-pimp-a-butterfly-20150402 (accessed September 27, 2016).

—Deborah A. Ring

Bobby Timmons

1935–1974

Jazz pianist

Timmons, Bobby, photograph. Gilles Petard/Redferns/Getty Images.

Revered by his colleagues and jazz aficionados, pianist Bobby Timmons had a brilliant but relatively brief career. Although he is best known for his work with the bandleaders Art Blakey and Cannonball Adderley during the late 1950s and early 1960s, his own efforts as a leader were also well received. A primary developer of the rhythmic, gospel-laden style known as "soul jazz," he was "one of the seminal communicators of his generation," in the words of critic Ted Panken. "Timmons' music was relentlessly earthy and primal," Panken added. "He was anything but primitive, but a soulful perspective was in his bones."

Robert Henry Timmons was born on December 19, 1935, in Philadelphia. Raised on the South Side of the city by his grandfather, a minister, he was exposed to a wide variety of music from an early age. Philadelphia was known at the time as a center of jazz and the blues, and the sounds he heard on the streets there—particularly the highly rhythmic "stride" style pioneered by pianists James P. Johnson and Willie "The Lion" Smith—influenced him deeply, as did the hymns and spirituals he heard at his grandfather's church. His training on the piano began with lessons around age

six. He made rapid progress, and by the time he was a teenager, he was accompanying the vocalists at Sunday services. He was also playing jazz regularly with several of his friends, among them the brilliant drummer Albert "Tootie" Heath, who joined him on many of his first gigs. Their performances at house parties and other local events drew considerable attention, and after finishing high school he was able to focus on music full time.

His career developed quickly, particularly after 1954, when he moved north to New York City. Not yet 20 years old, he found work in New York's many clubs with a number of other rising stars, including trumpeter and vocalist Chet Baker, trumpeter Lee Morgan, and saxophonist Sonny Stitt. Those gigs led to his debut in 1958 with Blakey's group, the Jazz Messengers. A long-lived ensemble regarded as a finishing school for young performers, the Messengers had a soulful, gospel-infused sound that meshed well with Timmons's talents. Between 1958 and his departure roughly a year later, he made crucial contributions to several of the group's most famous pieces, including the track "Moanin'" (1958), which he wrote. That success prompted his recruitment by Adderley, for whom he wrote the

classic piece "This Here" (1959). The opening track on an important album called *The Cannonball Adderley Quintet in San Francisco* (1959), it quickly became a standard and a benchmark for soul jazz.

By that point Timmons, now in high demand, was on the verge of becoming a household name. After roughly a year with Adderley, he returned to Blakey and the Messengers, with whom he completed *A Night in Tunisia* (1961), one of that group's best-known albums. He also had fruitful collaborations with trumpeter Kenny Dorham, vibraphonist Johnny Lytle, and many others.

His career as a leader, meanwhile, was developing rapidly. In 1960 he completed his first major work, an album for Riverside Records called *This Here Is Bobby Timmons*. Completed with the help of drummers Heath and Jimmy Cobb and bassists Ron Carter and Sam Jones, it featured fresh renditions of "Moanin'" and "This Here" as well as a new piece called "Dat Dere," which enjoyed international success, particularly after singer Oscar Brown Jr. included a vocal version on his 1961 album *Sin & Soul*. Brown's witty, soulful rendition drew many new fans to *This Here Is Bobby Timmons*, which has come to be regarded as a classic of its era. One of several critics to describe it in glowing terms, Scott Yanow of AllMusic.com called it "essential music" from an artist "at the peak of his creativity."

Over the next decade, Timmons continued to record regularly as a leader for Capitol, Atlantic, and other labels. These releases generally did not receive as much attention as his earlier work with Blakey and Adderley or his own debut. Several, however, have since become collector's items, particularly *The Soul Man!* (1966). Released by Prestige Records, it was notable in part for the rapport evident between Timmons and his band, an excellent group that included saxophonist Wayne Shorter as well as Carter and Cobb.

In general, however, these years were increasingly challenging for him, due in large part to the public's rapidly changing tastes. By the mid-1960s, soul jazz was yielding quickly to other genres, including free jazz—the highly impressionistic and often discordant approach championed by saxophonists Ornette Coleman and Albert Ayler—and R&B, which was exploding

in popularity. While Timmons was adept at a variety of styles, the public associated him so closely with soul jazz that its decline did significant damage to his career, particularly outside New York. Within the city, however, his live performances at small clubs such as the Lion's Head, a Greenwich Village landmark, still drew crowds.

Meanwhile, there were signs of problems in Timmons's personal life. By far the most serious of these was his dependence on alcohol and narcotics. A heavy user of both for many years, he was eventually diagnosed with cirrhosis, a chronic and often fatal liver ailment. Treatment proved ineffective, and on March 1, 1974, Timmons died in New York at age 38.

In the decades since Timmons's passing, periodic reissues of his work have helped preserve his legacy, as have the recollections of many who worked with him. Bassist Reggie Workman, for example, gave Panken a vivid glimpse of Timmons as he was in his prime. "I remember Bobby as a young man, his brilliance, his jovial attitude, and his depth of soul—or depth of being, I should say," Workman noted. "He was always an ardent dresser, neat in his music and in his personality. He was also very witty. It all turned up in his music. No matter what he was doing, he always had his personal voice. You'd know that it was Bobby Timmons doing it."

Selected discography

Art Blakey and the Jazz Messengers, *Moanin'* (includes "Moanin'"), Blue Note, 1958.

Cannonball Adderley, *The Cannonball Adderley Quintet in San Francisco* (includes "This Here"), Riverside, 1959.

This Here Is Bobby Timmons (includes "Moanin'," "This Here," and "Dat Dere"), Riverside, 1960.

Art Blakey and the Jazz Messengers, *A Night in Tunisia,* Blue Note, 1961.

Kenny Dorham, *Matador,* United Artists, 1962.

Johnny Lytle, *Nice and Easy: The Soulful Vibes of Johnny Lytle,* Jazzland, 1962.

The Soul Man!, Prestige, 1966.

Sources

Online

"Bobby Timmons Discography," JazzDisco.org, http://www.jazzdisco.org/bobby-timmons/discography/ (accessed July 25, 2016).

Nadal, James, "Bobby Timmons: Biography," All About Jazz, https://musicians.allaboutjazz.com/bobbytimmons (accessed July 25, 2016).

Panken, Ted, "For the 78th Birthday Anniversary of Bobby Timmons (1945–1974), a Liner Note and Five Interviews Conducted for It," Today Is the Question: Ted Panken on Music, Politics and the Arts, December 19, 2013, https://tedpanken.wordpress

.com/2013/12/19/for-the-78th-birthday-anniver
sary-of-bobby-timmons-1935–1974-a-liner-note
-and-five-interviews-conducted-for-it/ (accessed July
25, 2016).

Yanow, Scott, "Bobby Timmons: Artist Biography,"
AllMusic.com, http://www.allmusic.com/artist/bob

by-timmons-mn0000765435/biography (accessed
August 7, 2016).

Yanow, Scott, "*This Here Is Bobby Timmons:* AllMusic Review," AllMusic.com, http://www.allmusic
.com/album/this-here-is-bobby-timmons-mw00
00192568 (accessed August 7, 2016).

—R. Anthony Kugler

Karl-Anthony Towns

1995—

Professional basketball player

Towns, Karl-Anthony, photograph. Allen Berezovsky/WireImage/ Getty Images.

Karl-Anthony Towns is star center with the Minnesota Timberwolves of the National Basketball Association (NBA). The number-one overall pick of the 2015 draft, Towns quickly established himself as one of the top big men in the league during his debut season, averaging 18.3 points and 10.5 rebounds per game en route to earning NBA Rookie of the Year honors. At seven feet, 244 pounds, Towns has the size and strength both to protect the rim on defense and to generate offense underneath the rim. At the same time, he possesses unusual ball handing and shooting skills for a center, enabling him to create scoring chances on the perimeter. In addition to his considerable skills on the court, Towns has also garnered early praise for his professionalism and maturity, impressing coaches and veteran players with his willingness to sacrifice personal achievements in order to help build a successful team. "I burn to be a winner," Towns told Steve Serby for the *New York Post* in 2015. "It's more about winning than being great. I think greatness comes with winning. And you have to win first to be considered great."

Karl-Anthony Towns was born on November 15, 1995, in Edison, New Jersey. His mother, Jacqueline Cruz-Towns, is of Dominican descent. As a child, Towns learned the fundamentals of the game from his father, Karl Towns Sr., who had been a star forward for Monmouth University during the 1980s and later enjoyed a brief career in the United States Basketball League. Throughout his early years, Towns hone his skills on the court at Piscataway Vocational and Technical High School, where his father was head basketball coach. He began to gain statewide recognition as a star player at St. Joseph's High School, a Catholic preparatory school in nearby Metuchen. As a sophomore, Towns helped lead St. Joe's to a New Jersey state title, while earning a spot on the Dominican Republic national team at the age of only 16. In addition to his dominating play beneath the basket, Towns demonstrated a deft shooting touch, making 127 three-pointers in his final three seasons. The standout center also excelled as a student during his time at St. Joseph's, compiling a cumulative grade-point average of 3.96 over four years.

By his senior campaign, Towns had emerged as one of the top high school recruits in the nation. That season, Towns averaged 20.9 points, 13.4 rebounds, and 6.2

blocks per game while shooting over 66 percent from the field and 82 percent from the free throw line. In 2014 Towns was named the Gatorade National Basketball Player of the Year and earned McDonald's All-American honors. After receiving scholarship offers from a number of major college programs, Towns elected to play at the University of Kentucky. Under head coach John Calipari, Towns devoted his time at Kentucky to developing his low-post game, despite his tendency to shoot and create plays from the outside. "He had no real post game. We forced him," Calipari recalled to Andy Greder of the *St. Paul Pioneer Press* in 2015, describing the freshman center's early tenure with the Wildcats. "You're going to be a post player that can play out on the floor. You're going to learn to play pick-and-roll defense. You have to have an idea of how to keep a quicker guard in front of you, block shots and still play that way. You will fly up and down this court."

Towns adapted quickly to Calipari's coaching philosophy, emerging as one of the most productive players on an exceptional Kentucky team during the 2014–15 National Collegiate Athletic Conference (NCAA) season. Despite logging a modest 21.1 minutes per game, Towns led the Wildcats with 261 rebounds for the year, fifth best in the Southeastern Conference, while also placing second on the team with 10.3 points per contest. In addition, Towns proved himself to be a formidable rim protector during his freshman season at Kentucky, finishing second in the SEC with 88 blocked shots. Towns also played a key role in leading the undefeated Wildcats deep into the 2015 NCAA Tournament. One of the best games of his collegiate career came in the Midwest Regional Final against Notre

Dame, when the star center led all scorers with 25 points, while contributing five rebounds and four assists in a dramatic 68–66 victory. In Kentucky's National Semifinal matchup against Wisconsin, Towns paced the team with 16 points and nine rebounds while logging 31 minutes of playing time; the Wildcats ultimately fell short of their title bid, however, as they fell to the Badgers 71–64.

Following his successful freshman campaign, the Kentucky center announced his intention to turn professional. Widely regarded to be one of the most promising collegiate players in the country, Towns was selected by the Minnesota Timberwolves with the first overall pick of the 2015 draft. Only three days before Towns was set to make his NBA debut, tragedy struck the Timberwolves organization, when head coach and president of team operations Flip Saunders died of cancer. He was replaced by interim coach Sam Mitchell. Despite this upheaval, Towns adjusted easily to the rigors of professional basketball, immediately earning a spot in the starting rotation while emerging as one of the team's most productive players on both sides of the court. During his first season in the league, Towns also forged a strong bond with veteran big man Kevin Garnett, whose unique ability to play both beneath the basket and along the perimeter provided a valuable model for the young center's own style of play.

During his inaugural season, Towns earned Western Conference Rookie of the Month honors six times, while starting all 82 regular-season games. He finished fourth in the NBA with 857 total rebounds and sixth in the league with 138 blocks. He also proved to be one of the most efficient scorers in professional basketball, as he shot .542 from the field, eighth best in the league. At year's end, Towns was a unanimous pick as NBA Rookie of the Year. His caliber of play particularly impressed incoming head coach Tom Thibodeau, who viewed Towns as a key part of the franchise's future. "We've got a lot of work to do and he's got a lot of room for improvement. But when you look at what he did his rookie year and at his age, that's pretty remarkable," Thibodeau told Jerry Zgoda for the Minneapolis *Star Tribune*. "He's hungry. He's driven. He's mentally tough. Those are qualities you look for. He has to be a leader. He has to help sell the vision to the team."

Although the Timberwolves finished with a disappointing 29–53 record in 2015–16, the emergence of Towns and other young stars such as Andrew Wiggins, Zach Levine, and Ricky Rubio gave the team reason for confidence heading into their first season under Thibodeau. Indeed, the poise and desire of their star center was critical to the team's long-term goals. "Absolutely without a problem I think we should be making the playoffs next year," Towns told Jorge Castillo for the *Washington Post* in 2016. "I think we have that kind of anticipation. We have that kind of talent. It's just up to us to put it all together."

Sources

Periodicals

Newsday, December 12, 2015.

New York Post, May 19, 2015, p. 60.

New York Times, March 6, 2016.

Saint Paul (MN) Pioneer Press, June 23, 2015; June 25, 2015; January 11, 2016.

Star Tribune (Minneapolis-St. Paul, MN), February 12, 2016, p. C2; May 17, 2016, p. C1.

Washington Post, March 15, 2015; July 27, 2015; May 19, 2016.

Online

Adams, Jonathan, "Jacqueline Cruz & Karl Towns, Sr., Karl-Anthony's Parents: 5 Fast Facts You Need to Know," Heavy.com, June 25, 2015, http://heavy .com/sports/2015/06/karl-anthony-towns-parents -father-mother-family-mom-dad-jacqueline-cruz-karl -towns-sr-coach-towns-bio-hometown-dominican-re public-national-team-coach-cal-interview-photos-new -jersey-hometown/ (accessed September 29, 2016).

Gomez, Jesus, "Karl-Anthony Towns Is Better than Every Rookie Big Man at Everything," SB Nation, March 7, 2016, http://www.sbnation.com/nba/ 2016/3/7/11155988/karl-anthony-towns-timber wolves-skills-so-many-skills (accessed September 29, 2016).

"Karl-Anthony Towns," Basketball-Reference.com, http://www.basketball-reference.com/players/t/ townska01.html (accessed September 29, 2016).

"Karl-Anthony Towns," University of Kentucky Basket ball, http://www.ukathletics.com/sport/m-baskbl/ 2015/roster/559d911ce4b01c7eefd5f22e (accessed September 29, 2016).

Parker, Brandon, "Towns Jr. Going Global," ESPN. com, June 18, 2012, http://espn.go.com/high -school/boys-basketball/story/_/id/8001784/new -jersey-native-karl-towns-jr-16-play-dominican-repub lic-olympic-qualifying (accessed September 29, 2016).

—Stephen Meyer

Sylvester Turner

1954—

Attorney, politician

Turner, Sylvester, photograph. Aaron M. Sprecher/Bloomberg via Getty Images.

Longtime Texas state representative Sylvester Turner was elected mayor of Houston on December 12, 2015, after narrowly winning a runoff contest in his third bid for city hall. First elected to the Texas House of Representatives in 1988, Turner represented a district that included some of the state's most disadvantaged neighborhoods. As a leader among Democrats in a Republican-dominated state house, Turner earned a reputation as a pragmatist, a coalition builder across partisan lines, and a passionate voice for the most economically challenged Texans. Turner's efforts to resist budget cuts for education, medical coverage for children, and mental health care services earned him the nickname "Conscience of the House." Turner's dedication to these causes was born of his own experience: the Harvard Law School alumnus told *Harvard Magazine* in 2016, "I came up in a household that was at the bottom of the economic ladder … so I know what I'm talking about when I talk about income inequality."

Raised with Determination and Vision

Sylvester Turner was born on September 27, 1954, in Houston and grew up in the semirural, predominantly black neighborhood of Acres Homes, sharing a bedroom with his nine siblings. Turner's mother, who worked as a maid at a local hotel, was left to raise her children alone when her husband died of cancer; Turner was 13 years old at the time. He told *Harvard Magazine* in 2016 that he did not think of himself or his family as poor "until people told me I was." He added, "My parents always found a way to make sure there was food on the table. I had a roof over my head. I had clothes." Turner was an academically talented student who, as a seventh grader, was among the first wave of African Americans to be bused to an all-white school. He recalled to *Harvard Magazine* that things were rough at first, but he surmised that much of the conflict was the result of black and white teens simply "responding to what adults were putting in their ears." He continued, "I tell everyone, if you leave kids to themselves, they find a way of getting along. After two or three years, things started to level out and improve."

Turner excelled as a member of his high school debate team, winning top honors all four years. He was also elected president of the student council and was the

At a Glance . . .

Born Sylvester Turner on September 27, 1954, in Houston, TX; son of Eddie Turner (an industrial painter) and Ruby May Turner (a hotel maid); married Cheryl Gillum, 1983 (divorced, 1991); children: Ashley Paige Turner. *Politics:* Democrat. *Religion:* Baptist. *Education:* University of Houston, BA, political science, 1977; Harvard Law School, JD, 1980.

Career: Fulbright & Jaworski, staff attorney, 1980–83; Barnes & Turner, partner, 1983–2016; Texas House of Representatives, District 139 representative, 1988–2015, speaker pro tempore, 2003–09; City of Houston, TX, mayor, 2016—.

Addresses: *Office*—City of Houston, 901 Bagby, Houston, TX 77002. *Twitter*—@SylvesterTurner.

valedictorian of his graduating class. He attended the University of Houston, where, again, he joined the debate team and was active in student government. He decided to pursue a career in law—a choice that was based largely on how he had seen the profession portrayed on television dramas, including *Perry Mason,* as he had never met any lawyers personally. He applied for and won admission to Harvard Law School, enrolling in 1977. Once again an outsider, Turner honed his ability to cultivate alliances with his peers, no matter how great the differences between them may have seemed.

Upon his graduation in 1980, Turner returned to Houston, where he joined Fulbright & Jaworski, a prestigious law firm in the city, and began working in corporate law. In 1983 he and attorneys Barry Barnes and Rosemarie Morse founded their own firm, which focused on providing legal services to small, black-owned companies. A year later, Turner made his first foray into Houston politics, running unsuccessfully for a position as a Harris County commissioner. Next he set his sights on the state legislature, and in 1988 he was elected to the Texas House of Representatives.

Ran Unsuccessfully for Mayor

Early in his career in the state house, Turner established a reputation as a progressive but pragmatic politician who could overcome partisanship to achieve legislative results. Turner had long dreamed of being the mayor of Houston, however, and in 1991 he campaigned to become the first African American to

hold the position. After the general election, the top two candidates—Turner and Bob Lanier—faced off in a December runoff. Just days before the election, however, a local television station, Channel 13, published a shocking story that purported to expose Turner as the mastermind of what *Houston Press* writer Jim Simmon termed "a bizarre insurance scam" involving a former client of Turner's who had, unbeknownst to Turner, faked his own death and turned up in prison in another country. The story also included salacious details suggesting that Turner was a closeted gay man. On the eve of the hotly contested election, in which Houston seemed to be on the verge of electing its first black mayor, Simmon noted, "The cumulative effect ... was to plant the idea in the minds of many voters that there was a different and darker side to Sylvester Turner than the one on the sparkling resume he had proudly presented to the public: the poor boy from Acres Homes made good, the Harvard law school grad and chairman of the legislative caucus."

Turner lost the runoff election and later sued Channel 13 for libel. He initially won a $5.5 million judgment against the station. The decision, however, was later overturned by the Texas Supreme Court, which ruled that the although story had been inaccurate, the station and the reporter who had broken the story had not acted with malicious intent.

For the next 12 years, Turner focused on his legal and legislative work, building a reputation as the "Conscience of the House" for repeatedly speaking out against legislation with significant consequences for the least advantaged members of society, including uninsured families and children whose educational opportunities were limited by lack of school funding. In 2003 Turner ran again for mayor but missed the runoff election, coming in third in a three-way race.

Won Election to City Hall

In 2015, after serving for more than 25 years in the state legislature, Turner saw another opportunity to run for city hall. As the general campaign neared its end in October of 2015, Rice University professor Robert Stein speculated in an article for the *Houston Chronicle* about why Turner would once again enter a race that had caused him such personal and professional anguish twice before. Asserting that he believed that Turner had been well qualified to be mayor the first time he ran, "When he ran the second time, he was even better-prepared." Stein added, "this ... isn't just about ambition. He sees this as a logical conclusion and, frankly, believes he's best-equipped to solve the problems of drainage, traffic, finance—even more capable than he was back then." Prior to the election, Turner told the *Houston Chronicle* that he continued to live by the advice of his mother, who had always told him never to give up. He said, "Life is not always fair,

but you still have to navigate it and believe tomorrow is going to be better than today." He added, "I've found that to be true more often than not …. When you no longer believe that, you have pretty much lost hope and things certainly won't get better."

Turner also told the *Chronicle* that one of the most important lessons he had learned through his legislative career is "that people want results. They may not care if the Republicans are in charge or if the Democrats are in charge, they want answers to their problems." When the votes were counted in the December of 2015 runoff, Turner had finally prevailed, winning a close contest with 51 percent of the vote. Following his inauguration in January of 2016, as described in *Harvard Magazine,* he went into the community and "donned work gloves and safety goggles, picked up a shovel, and spread hot, smoking asphalt over a gaping pothole … in West Houston." As he did so, he noted that the 936th pothole had been filled since he was elected mayor; people were getting results.

Sources

Periodicals

Harvard Magazine, May 2016.
Houston Chronicle, October 12, 2015.
Houston Press, September 1, 1994.
University of Houston Magazine, Spring 2016.

Online

"The Honorable Sylvester Turner," TheHistoryMakers.com, August 15, 2012, http://www.thehistorymakers.com/biography/honorable-sylvester-turner (accessed August 2, 2016).

"Mayor's Biography," Mayor's Office, City of Houston, http://www.houstontx.gov/mayor/bio.html (accessed August 2, 2016).

"Sylvester Turner's Biography," VoteSmart.org, http://votesmart.org/candidate/biography/8018/sylvester-turner#.V6vIJDU4vHE (accessed August 2, 2016).

—Pamela Willwerth Aue

Jessie T. Usher

1992—

Actor

Usher, Jessie T., photograph. Kobby Dagan/Shutterstock.com.

Actor Jessie T. Usher landed his first major film role in 2016, when he starred in *Independence Day: Resurgence.* Set 20 years after its predecessor, *Independence Day* (1996), which starred Will Smith in one of his own breakthrough roles, the sequel features Usher as the stepson of Smith's character. Usher also is known for his role as Cam Calloway, a basketball player who is suddenly thrust into stardom, in the LeBron James–produced Starz television series *Survivor's Guilt.* Usher has appeared in a number of other small-screen roles, including a long run on the Cartoon Network series *Level Up.*

Usher was born in Maryland on February 29, 1992. He was a precocious child, learning to read at age two. Usher's older sister began acting as a child; Usher, wanting to do everything that his older sister did, tagged along. He began performing himself at age four and filmed his first professional commercial, for Oscar Meyer, when he was five years old. When his family moved to Los Angeles in 2003, more opportunities became available, and in 2005 he appeared on an episode of the CBS crime drama *Without a Trace.*

Following a self-paced academic program in high school, Usher completed all of his requirements by age 15 and had to wait for months to graduate, as salutatorian, with the rest of his class. During his senior year, he performed on the Disney Channel series *Hannah Montana* alongside Miley Cyrus. The experience was Usher's first time shooting in front of a live studio audience; he credited Cyrus with teaching him "a lot in a very short period of time," he told Sara Stewart in *New York Post.* On top of his academic studies and his acting career, Usher also practiced archery, American Kenpo, and the Korean martial art of Tang Soo Do.

Usher continued to take small roles while he attended college, where he fell "in love with baking, more than anything," he told Andy Chan of the website Flaunt. He switched his major to culinary arts but ended up cutting his education short when he was offered a regular role on the Cartoon Network series *Level Up.*

After *Level Up* wrapped in 2013, Usher auditioned for *Survivor's Remorse,* a series produced by LeBron James about a young basketball player who is learning to cope with his sudden fame. The audition process

At a Glance . . .

Born on February 29, 1992, in Maryland.

Career: Film and television actor, 2012—.

Memberships: Alpha Gamma Sigma Honor Society.

Awards: Breakthrough Performer, Hamptons International Film Festival, 2015, for *Survivor's Remorse;* CinemaCon Award for Ensemble of the Universe, 2016, for *Independence Day: Resurgence.*

Addresses: *Talent agent*—Paradigm LA, 360 N. Crescent Dr., North Building, Beverly Hills, CA 90210. *Twitter*—@The_JessieT.

was grueling, taking place over nearly five months. Eventually Usher won the lead role of Cam Calloway in the series. Although the first two seasons of *Survivor's Remorse* did not receive much attention, Kenny Herzog of *Vulture* declared the show "premium cable's most refreshing half-hour" and praised its "cunning marriage of cutting cultural satire and edgy family sitcom." The show was renewed for a fourth season in the summer of 2016.

The casting process for *Independence Day: Resurgence* was much different from Usher's audition for *Survivor's Remorse:* he landed the role through his trainer, who counted among his clients the film's producer, Harold Kloser. Usher met Kloser at the gym a few times, and when Kloser mentioned the film, Usher jokingly asked to be involved. Kloser did not take the request as a joke, however; he convinced director Roland Emmerich that Usher was the man for the role of Dylan Hiller, the stepson of the late Captain Steven Hiller (played by Smith in the original film). Usher's character is a fighter pilot with the weight of the world on his shoulders: when aliens return to Earth, he feels he must rise to the occasion and live up to the legacy of his stepfather. "We wanted to create a new generation. Jessie ... had this honorable feel about him. He's this very, very refined person. And he has this great smile. We didn't want him to fill the shoes of Will Smith. We didn't make him too funny, either," Emmerich, who also cowrote and directed the original film, explained to Kelley L. Carter of the website The Undefeated. "We needed somebody who had a natural charm and feels the pressure of this famous 'father' he has." *Independence Day: Resurgence* premiered in June of 2016. The film received tepid reviews from critics, however, who criticized the overly complicated plot and overblown action sequences.

In addition to acting, Usher also hoped to become a producer. After his role in *Independence Day: Resurgence,* Usher began thinking seriously about forming his own production company. "To be able to create and produce and take ideas and make them real has always been a passion of mine," he told Brown. Usher also told Daniel Fienberg of *Hollywood Reporter* that his goal was "to have a company where I can produce and maybe even have some in-house writers and directors and just put together passion projects, things of my own that I can create myself."

After *Independence Day: Resurgence,* Usher had a small role in the ensemble comedy *Almost Christmas,* released later that same year. In 2017 the actor was slated to appear in the film *Stronghold,* for which he also was a producer.

Selected works

Films

Independence Day: Resurgence, Twentieth Century Fox, 2016.
Almost Christmas, Universal Pictures, 2016.

Television

Level Up, Cartoon Network, 2012–13.
Survivor's Remorse, Starz, 2014—.

Sources

Periodicals

Variety, October 6, 2015, p. 101.

Online

Brown, Emma, "Jessie T. Usher," Interview Magazine, June 24, 2016, http://www.interviewmagazine .com/film/jessie-t-usher#_ (accessed August 11, 2016).
Carter, Kelley L., "State of Independence," The Undefeated, June 21, 2016, http://theundefeated.com/ features/survivors-remorse-lebron-james-jessie-t-ush er-independence-day/ (accessed October 3, 2016).
Chan, Andy, "Jessie T. Usher Would Rather Be Baking," Flaunt, August 11, 2016, http://flaunt.com/ people/jessie-t-usher/ (accessed August 11, 2106).
Connley, Courtney, "Actor Jessie T. Usher Talks *Survivor's Remorse, Independence Day: Resurgence,* and How He Got His Start in Acting," BlackEnterprise.com, July 30, 2015, http://www.black enterprise.com/lifestyle/jessie-t-usher-talks-survi vors-remorse-independence-day/ (accessed August 11, 2016).
Fienberg, Daniel, "Next Gen 2015: Why 'survivor's Remorse' Star Jessie T. Usher Religiously Studies 'Fresh Prince of Bel Air,'" HollywoodReporter.com, November 4, 2015, http://www.hollywoodreporter

.com/news/next-gen-2015-why-survivors-836587 (accessed August 10, 2016).

Herzog, Kenny, "*Survivor's Remorse* Season Premiere Recap: Say Uncle," *Vulture,* July 25, 2016, http://www.vulture.com/2016/07/survivors-re morse-recap-season-3-episode-1.html (accessed October 3, 2016).

Lindsay, Benjamin, "How Jessie T. Usher Booked 'Independence Day: Resurgence,'" Backstage.com, June 28, 2016, http://www.backstage.com/inter view/how-jessie-usher-booked-independence-day -resurgence/ (accessed August 11, 2016).

Stewart, Sara, "Meet Jessie T. Usher, the New Hero of 'Independence Day: Resurgence,'" NYPost.com, June 24, 2016, http://nypost.com/2016/06/24/ meet-jessie-usher-the-new-hero-of-independence -day-resurgence/ (accessed August 11, 2016).

—Alana Joli Abbott

Lovely Warren

1977—

Politician, lawyer

Lovely Warren was elected mayor of Rochester, New York, in 2013, when she was just 36 years old. Warren, a Democrat, was the first woman and only the second African American to hold the post. During her tenure as mayor, Warren has sought to revitalize her native city through job creation, improved neighborhood safety and vibrancy, and better educational outcomes for children.

Lovely Ann Warren was born on July 1, 1977, in Rochester, where her father worked for the Xerox Corporation and her mother for Eastman Kodak. Growing up, Warren benefited from a strong support network through her mother's extended family, who lived close by. She was particularly influenced by her maternal grandfather, Cecil McClary, a former South Carolina sharecropper who never learned to read but knew much of the Bible by heart.

Warren was seven years old in 1984 when her grandfather, who was then working as a security guard at a Wegmans supermarket, was shot multiple times and critically injured by a shoplifter. The incident had a profound impact on Warren, and she has often cited it as the impetus for her to become a lawyer. Speaking to the *Rochester Business Journal* in 2012, Warren recalled, "I always thought I would be a prosecutor because my grandfather was shot while working at Wegmans. I always felt like I was going to make people pay for their crimes."

Warren's young life was significantly overshadowed by her father's addiction to crack cocaine. When she was

eight years old, the family moved to California in an attempt to remove her father from the environment where his drug habit had taken hold. Within two months of their arrival, however, Warren's mother realized that her husband's disease had simply followed them to the West Coast, and she returned with her daughters, Lovely and her older sister Yantise, to Rochester.

In the years that followed, Warren's father divided his time between California and Rochester, unable to break free of his addiction. Warren recalled that it was not unusual to come home and find the television gone—sold for the cash he needed to buy another fix. Warren's relationship with her once-attentive father deteriorated, although she did not realize that he was using drugs until her cousin told her when she was 13 years old.

As a student at Wilson Magnet High School, Warren struggled with an increasingly violent temper and was suspended repeatedly for fighting. At the same time, she became embroiled in a physically abusive relationship with an older man. Warren's ambition to study law might have gone unrealized without the mentorship of Bless Thomas, a teacher and administrator at Wilson Magnet, who recognized Warren's potential and helped her manage her anger. As Warren told the *Rochester Business Journal,* "[Mr. Thomas] saw the diamond in the rough."

During a turbulent period that was made more difficult when Warren's mother fell ill, Thomas was a steady

At a Glance . . .

Born Lovely Ann Warren on July 1, 1977, in Rochester, NY; married Timothy Granison; children: Taylor (daughter). *Politics:* Democrat. *Religion:* Christian. *Education:* John Jay College of Criminal Justice, BA, government, 2000; Albany Law School of Union University, JD, 2003.

Career: Office of New York State Assemblyman David F. Gantt, legislative assistant, deputy counsel, lead counsel, chief of staff, 2000–2013; Rochester City Council, member, 2007–13, president, 2010–13; City of Rochester, NY, mayor, 2014—.

Memberships: Rochester Black Bar Association.

Awards: Distinguished Alumni Award, John Jay College, 2016.

Addresses: *Office*—Rochester City Hall, 30 Church St., Rochester, NY 14614.

source of guidance and support, motivating Warren to focus on her schoolwork and her future. "He really gave that fatherly advice and love and compassion that I was searching for," she recalled. After graduating high school, Warren began her undergraduate studies at SUNY (State University of New York) College at Buffalo and then transferred to John Jay College of Criminal Justice in New York City. The summer after her junior year, she worked in Albany as an intern for New York State Democratic assemblyman David F. Gantt, who would become another significant influence in her life. Working in Gantt's office, Warren recalled, "I learned a different side of the law, that I could actually make laws and impact laws."

After receiving her bachelor's degree in 2000, Warren entered Albany Law School of Union University. At the same time, she was also battling a kidney disease that required her to undergo debilitating chemotherapy treatments. Refusing to delay her studies in spite of her doctor's recommendation, Warren persevered; the treatments worked, and the disease was eventually eradicated from her system. In her second year of law school, she was elected president of the Black Law Students Association. She completed her law degree in 2003 and was admitted to the New York State Bar the following year.

Warren had continued to work part time for Gantt while she was in law school and then joined the assemblyman's full-time legal staff immediately after graduation. In the years that followed, Warren rose through the ranks to become Gantt's lead counsel and chief of staff. At the same time, she began to pursue opportunities in Rochester city politics. Warren was elected to the Northeast District seat of the Rochester City Council in 2007 and became council president in 2010. That same year, she and her husband, Timothy Granison, had a daughter named Taylor.

From the outset of her political career, Warren focused her energies on creating economic and educational opportunities in Rochester, particularly for the city's underserved African-American community. According to the *Minority Reporter*, when Warren announced her candidacy for mayor in April of 2013, she asked, "How can we talk about our dreams for Rochester's future of that dream doesn't include all of us?" Indeed, Warren's mayoral campaign focused on the theme of "two Rochesters"—indicating a city that was conspicuously divided along economic and racial lines.

On November 5, 2013, Warren was elected mayor of Rochester, receiving 55 percent of the vote. Her grandfather, Cecil McClary, who had been a prominent figure in her campaign, was quoted by the *Democrat and Chronicle* as saying, "I'm so high, I'm still flying." In December of 2013, McClary suffered a stroke. Warren was sworn into office on January 1, 2014, standing at her grandfather's bedside in Strong Memorial Hospital. He died the following day.

Warren launched her first term in office with bold plans to reduce Rochester's unemployment and crime rates, increase the city's tax base, create more affordable housing, overhaul a failing public school system, and build a more unified and prosperous city. Even with her remarkable tenacity, however, the young mayor faced formidable challenges and an impatient constituency, as Rochester remained one of the poorest U.S. cities of its size in 2016.

Sources

Periodicals

Democrat and Chronicle (Rochester, NY), November 6, 2013; December 25, 2013; January 2, 2014.
Minority Reporter, April 1–7, 2013.
Rochester Business Journal, October 26, 2012.

Online

"About Mayor Lovely Warren," https://mayor lovelywarren.com/bio/ (accessed July 26, 2016).
"A Victory for Lovely Warren, and for Her Wily Mentor," Politico, November 6, 2013, http://www .politico.com/states/new-york/albany/story/2013/ 11/a-victory-for-lovely-warren-and-for-her-wily-men tor-000000 (accessed July 26, 2016).

"Office of the Mayor," City of Rochester, New York,
http://www.cityofrochester.gov/article.aspx?id=
8589934829 (accessed July 26, 2016).

—Erin Brown

Ben Webster

1909–1973

Jazz saxophonist

Ben Webster was one of the great jazz masters of the tenor saxophone. Jazz historians often place Webster alongside Coleman Hawkins and Lester Young in a triumvirate of saxophonists who came to prominence during the swing era of the 1930s and 1940s. Webster initially emulated Hawkins in the 1930s, the first decade of his career, when he played with many of the top big bands. By the next decade, he had settled into a distinctive style of his own while playing with Duke Ellington's orchestra: a gruff and growly tone on up-tempo

Webster, Ben, photograph. Michael Ochs Archives/Getty Images.

numbers and blues and a velvety lyricism on ballads. This musical profile matched Webster's personality. A big, strong man, he could be tenderly emotional and generous, but he also had a mean, violent streak that came out principally under alcohol's influence, a quality that led him to be nicknamed "The Brute."

Began Career as Stride Pianist

Benjamin Francis Webster was born on March 27, 1909, in Kansas City, Missouri. His temper and addiction to alcohol were clear inheritances from his father, a violent drunk who left the family before his son was

born. Webster's mother, Mayme, and great-aunt, Agnes Johnson, both churchgoing schoolteachers, raised him. They were responsible for his first music lessons, which they insisted take place on the violin. He came to detest the instrument; at age 12, he crushed one. As a teenager he taught himself to play the piano. He had a neighbor, Pete Johnson, a few years his senior, who taught him to play the blues and went on to become a celebrated boogie-woogie keyboardist. Webster wanted to become a professional "tickler" like the pianists he heard in the streets and jazz clubs of Kansas City. Growing to a prodigious size, he dove into the city's night life from an early age.

Webster enrolled in the college preparatory program at Wilberforce College in Ohio, but by 1925 he had dropped out of school to make his way as a musician. His first paid job as a pianist was in Oklahoma. He formed a band around this time called Rooster Ben and His Little Red Roosters. In 1927 he was employed playing at a silent movie house in Amarillo, Texas. It was there that he met fellow jazzman Budd Johnson, who taught him to make a tone on the saxophone. Next he spent several months with the Young Family

Band, a traveling act that played at carnivals and vaudeville houses. The father, W. H. (Billy) Young, gave Webster an alto sax and taught him alongside his own son, Lester, who was Webster's age.

In 1930 Webster began making the rounds of midwestern "territory bands," joining Gene Coy's Happy Black Aces out of Amarillo. While he was with Coy, he switched from alto to tenor sax, which had a bigger sound and allowed him to express himself more fully. A job with Jasper "Jap" Allen brought him back to Kansas City, but in 1932 he quit Allen's group to join Blanche Calloway, a talented singer and the older sister of Cab Calloway. His first of hundreds of recording sessions came as a member of Calloway's backing band. Later that year, he hooked up with one of Kansas City's premier orchestras, led by Bennie Moten. Count Basie, Walter Page, and Eddie Durham were in Moten's band at the time, and Webster arrived just in time to take part in a December of 1932 recording session that produced several influential sides, including "Moten Swing" and "Toby." From there he jumped to another successful Kansas City band, Andy Kirk and His Clouds of Joy. Webster was beginning to make a name for himself with his ferocious solos, but he was also developing a reputation as a troublesome employee, likely to start fights when he was drinking.

Reached Artistic Peak with Ellington

Webster's career advanced further when he was hired by one of the country's most acclaimed bandleaders, Fletcher Henderson. Hawkins had risen to stardom as Henderson's key soloist before going freelance in 1934. His immediate replacement, Lester Young, discovered quickly that his musical sense did not jibe with the New York–based swing unit, so Henderson and Kirk, who were good friends, traded tenor soloists. Webster contributed some fine solos to Henderson's September of 1934 recordings, such as "Wild Party" and "Rug Cutters Swing," but the group disbanded

shortly afterward. Webster went on to play with the bands of Benny Carter (one of his musical idols), Willie Bryant, and Cab Calloway. He made some freelance recordings in New York during the mid-1930s, including several sessions with Billie Holiday and pianist Teddy Wilson. The group he longed to play with was Ellington's, and he got a shot, temporarily, in 1935, when he substituted for the sax and clarinet player Barney Bigard, but the Duke had no permanent spot for him. After a stint with Henderson's new band, he joined Wilson's big band as its star soloist in 1939, but this group folded within a year.

Early in 1940, Webster's dream job came through: Ellington hired him as his first permanent tenor sax soloist. The band's arrangements had no dedicated parts for tenor sax, and the Duke encouraged Webster to improvise on many numbers. Ellington's specialty was knowing how to utilize and highlight the tonal colors of his sidemen. Quickly he had a standout feature for Webster in the tune "Cotton Tail." Webster took a prolonged, beautifully constructed solo and composed the number's saxophone ensemble chorus. The piece became an Ellington classic and the saxophonist's calling card. Musically, Webster had come into his own: he no longer reminded listeners inevitably of Hawkins. Absorbing the influence of his bandmate, Ellington veteran Johnny Hodges, Webster developed more robust control of his phrasing and dynamics and achieved a uniquely sensual, breathy tone on the slower pieces. Webster also had a strong rapport, on and off the bandstand, with the young bassist Jimmy Blanton, so much so that jazz buffs now refer to the 1940–42 Ellington orchestra as the Blanton-Webster band. (Blanton died of tuberculosis in July of 1942.)

Ellington said he had a "yen for Ben," but the two men ultimately failed to get along. According to one story—perhaps apocryphal—a drunken Webster burst into the Duke's dressing room and sliced up one of his fanciest suits. The maestro gave Webster his two weeks' notice in mid-1943. Webster's stature on the music scene, however, was such that he rarely lacked for work in clubs and the recording studio. In 1944 he did some jobs for the CBS radio orchestra under Raymond Scott, played with the popular John Kirby Sextet, and recorded with Harlem piano legend James P. Johnson and drummer "Big Sid" Catlett. He kept up this busy pace for several years, although he began to drink more heavily during this time. He rejoined Ellington for about a year starting in 1948.

Liquor brought out Webster's demons and made him unpredictable. When his addiction reached its nadir, he went home to Kansas City and dried out under the care of his mother and aunt. He played there with the veteran bandleader Jay McShann and others before moving to Los Angeles in the early 1950s. Around this time, Webster entered into a very productive partnership with producer Norman Granz that helped him mount a comeback. Granz employed him on many

recording sessions, backing singers such as Ella Fitzgerald, Dinah Washington, and Carmen McRae, and gave Webster star billing in his "Jazz at the Philharmonic" concert series. A number of albums on the Verve label paired Webster with other jazz stars such as Art Tatum, Coleman Hawkins, Oscar Peterson, and Gerry Mulligan. One memorable performance came in 1957 on the CBS television special *The Sound of Jazz,* where Webster, Hawkins, and Young jammed together for the first and only time.

Settled in Europe

By 1960, despite his esteemed critical reputation, Webster was having difficulty finding steady work. The jazz scene had constricted, and cool and modern jazz were on the rise. Webster remained in Los Angeles, caring for his mother and aunt, until both passed away. In 1964 he was offered a month-long engagement at Ronnie Scott's club in London. It was his first trip to Europe, and he ended up staying on the continent for the rest of his life. After seeing London and other parts of England, he found reverent audiences in Scandinavia and elsewhere in Europe. Still prone to drunken fits, he settled in Amsterdam and allowed himself to be taken care of by his landlady.

In 1969 Webster moved to Copenhagen, where he performed and recorded with European musicians and met up with visiting American players whenever he could. A recognizable figure with his hulking frame, dark suits, and too-small fedora, Webster often showed up drunk and hours late for gigs. He gained a great deal of weight and had to walk with a cane, but he still was capable of making majestic music. One well-known story from these years concerns the time he performed for the Crown Prince of Norway. In the receiving line, rather than observe the niceties of interacting with royalty, the big musician clapped the prince on the back familiarly and roared, "How do you do, Prince? Ben Webster, king of the tenors!"

Webster suffered a cerebral hemorrhage after a concert in Amsterdam and died there on September 20, 1973. He was buried in Copenhagen. On his instruction, his saxophone, which he called Betsy, was given to the Institute of Jazz Studies at Rutgers University. The Ben Webster Foundation, established in Denmark in 1976, gives a small but prestigious prize annually to a deserving jazz musician. Two book-length biographies on Webster have been published, and a documentary film, *The Brute and the Beautiful,* appeared in 1989.

Selected discography

King of the Tenors, Verve, 1953.
Music for Loving, Verve, 1954.
(With Billie Holiday) *Body and Soul,* Verve, 1957.
Ben Webster Meets Oscar Peterson, Verve, 1959.
Ben Webster Encounters Coleman Hawkins, Verve, 1959.
The Soul of Ben Webster, Verve, 1960.
The Warm Moods, Reprise, 1961.
(With Fletcher Henderson) *Fletcher Henderson and His Orchestra, 1934,* Ace of Hearts, 1963.
See You at the Fair, Impulse!, 1964.
Blue Light, Polydor, 1966.
Big Ben Time!, Fontana, 1967.
Ben Webster Meets Don Byas, Saba, 1968.
(With Billie Holiday) *The Billie Holiday Story* (recorded 1935–41), Columbia, 1969.
Webster's Dictionary, Philips, 1970.
(With Duke Ellington) *The Blanton-Webster Band* (recorded 1940–43), RCA, 1989.
(With Bennie Moten) *Bennie Moten's Kansas City Orchestra, 1930–1932,* Classics, 1994.
Cottontail: The Best of Ben Webster, 1931–1944, ASV Living Era, 1995.
The Chronological Ben Webster, 1944–1946, Classics, 1999.
The Chronological Ben Webster, 1946–1951, Classics, 2002.

Sources

Books

Buchmann-Moller, Frank, *Someone to Watch Over Me: The Life and Music of Ben Webster,* University of Michigan Press, 2006.
de Valk, Jeroen, *Ben Webster: His Life and Music,* Berkeley Hills Books, 2011.
Morgenstern, Dan, *Living with Jazz: A Reader,* Pantheon, 2004.
Russell, Ross, *Jazz Style in Kansas City and the Southwest,* University of California Press, 1971.
Stewart, Rex, *Jazz Masters of the 30s,* Macmillan, 1973.
Teachout, Terry, *Duke: A Life of Duke Ellington,* Gotham, 2013.

Periodicals

New Yorker, August 20, 2001.
New York Times, February 9, 1986.
Village Voice, June 18, 1986.

Online

Buchmann-Moller, Frank, "Ben Webster Biography," Ben Webster Foundation, http://www.benwebster.dk/9170/Ben%20Webster%20Biography (accessed July 30, 2016).

—Roger K. Smith

Robert F. Williams

1925–1996

Civil rights activist

Williams, Robert F., photograph. J. Wilds/Keystone/Getty Images.

Robert F. Williams was a civil rights leader whose rejection in 1959 of the doctrine of nonviolence espoused by the civil rights movement helped pave the way for the emergence of the Black Panther Party and the Black Power movement a decade after he first called for African Americans to engage in armed self-defense and resistance to racial violence. As president of the Monroe, North Carolina, branch of the National Association for the Advancement of Colored People (NAACP), Williams shocked both whites and conservative blacks when he advocated "meeting violence with violence." A former serviceman who had become disillusioned with the nonviolent tactics of the civil rights movement, Williams launched a campaign of armed self-defense in his hometown and later established a revolutionary black liberation front in the United States while living in exile, first in Cuba and then in China, during the 1960s. After returning to the United States in 1969, Williams made a living as a lecturer on civil rights, social justice, and contemporary Chinese society. He died in 1996, his place in the history of the American civil rights movement virtually forgotten.

Encountered Racism as a Child

Robert Franklin Williams was born on February 26, 1925, in Monroe, North Carolina, a once-thriving railroad town located 14 miles from the South Carolina border. The son of a railroad boilermaker's helper, Williams grew up in a seven-room, two-story home on Boyte Street. As a schoolboy he was interested in history, geography, and writing. He was awakened to the brutality of racism at age 10, when a policeman dragged a black woman down Monroe's main street. Williams was haunted by the laughter of white onlookers and the victim's screams. He recalled in his autobiography, *Negroes with Guns,* how "the cop was grinning as he pulled her by the heels, her dress up over her hips and her back being scraped by the concrete pavement."

At age 17 Williams left high school to train as a machinist with the National Youth Administration in 1942. After his education at a camp near Rocky Mount, North Carolina, he continued his studies at Elizabeth City State Teachers College (now Elizabeth

At a Glance . . .

Born Robert Franklin Williams on February 26, 1925, in Monroe, NC; died on October 15, 1996, in Grand Rapids, MI; son of John Lemuel Williams (a boilermaker's helper) and Emma (Carter) Williams; married Mabel R. Williams, 1947; children: Robert Franklin, John Chalmers. *Military service:* U.S. Army, 1943–46; U.S. Marine Corps, 1954–55. *Education:* Attended Elizabeth City State Teachers College (now Elizabeth City State University), 1942(?); West Virginia State College, 1949; North Carolina State College, 1951; Johnson C. Smith University, 1953.

Career: Ford Motor Company, Detroit, MI, machinist, 1943; Mare Island Navy Yard, San Francisco, CA, 1944; *Daily Worker,* contributor, 1947–48; worked as field laborer in upstate New York, 1952; launched local civil rights and self-defense campaign, 1955–61; *Crusader* magazine, founder and publisher, 1959–1960s; *Radio Free Dixie,* creator, 1962–65; Republic of New Africa (RNA), president, 1968; American Program Bureau, lecturer, 1969–73; University of Michigan, Ann Arbor, consultant, 1970–71; People's Association for Human Rights, Inc., organizer, legal advisor, 1974–96.

Memberships: National Association for the Advancement of Colored People (NAACP).

Awards: Malcolm X Black Manhood Award, Malcolm X Society, 1989; JB Gold Medal Award, John Brown Society, 1991; Outstanding Contributions, Association of Black Social Workers, 1987; Black Image Award, Lake/Newaygo NAACP, 1992.

City State University), an all-black teachers college. A year later, he moved to Detroit to seek employment in the city's thriving war industry. Living with his oldest brother, Edward, he worked at the Ford Motor Company as a mill operator. Williams also attended Communist Party meetings and read the organization's publication, the *Daily Worker.* Although he did not become a party member, Williams was drawn to the party's program of racial equality. Williams again faced the destructiveness of racial tensions when a race riot erupted in Detroit in 1943. Shortly thereafter, Williams took a six-month job at the Mare Island Navy Yard near San Francisco. Unable to tolerate the racial violence that occurred in the employee dormitories there, he quit and returned home to Monroe.

Soon after, Williams was drafted into the U.S. Army and sent to Fort Bragg, North Carolina. After earning high scores on a radio aptitude test, he was transferred to a Signal Corps battalion at Camp Crowder, Missouri, to be trained as a radio operator. To his disappointment, however, he was assigned to a school for telephone linesmen. Before completing his training, he became ill and was reassigned as a clerical typist. In the months following the end of the war, Williams experienced the effects of low morale that spread among Camp Crowder's segregated black troops. Defying the harsh treatment by white officers, Williams was confined in the camp stockade for insubordination. As Robert Carl Cohen noted in his book *Black Crusader: A Biography of Robert Franklin Williams,* "Williams was proud of being in the stockade because he felt he was there for resisting an unjust system—not for committing a crime." In 1946, after a six-month stay at Fort Lewis, Washington, Williams received an honorable discharge without a good conduct medal. He was married the next year.

Sought Education, Employment, and Social Justice

Back in Monroe, Williams earned his high school diploma and wrote poetry and prose as well as a weekly column for the *Monroe Enquirer.* During another stint as an autoworker in Detroit, his short story "Some Day I Am Going Back South" was published in the *Daily Worker.* Taking advantage of the education benefits of the GI Bill, he took courses in psychology and creative writing at West Virginia State College. During his year there, he joined the staff of the college newspaper, the *Quill.* He subsequently transferred to North Carolina College in Durham, where he studied literary classics and read the works of Karl Marx and Vladimir Lenin, which were introduced to him by a group of college communists. In the fall of 1950, he continued his study of literature at Johnson C. Smith College in Charlotte.

When his GI Bill benefits expired in 1952, Williams went to New York City to look for work. Living with an aunt in Harlem, he took a job at the Curtis-Wright aircraft plant across the river in New Jersey. In New York he befriended a group of white left-wing intellectuals, some of whom were active in the American Labor Party. With the reduction in postwar aircraft production, however, Williams soon lost this job and returned to Monroe. Desperate to support his family, he left North Carolina once again to work as a farm laborer in upstate New York. In *Black Crusader,* Cohen wrote, "Sharing the lot with those migrant farm workers proved to Williams that exploitation isn't limited to the cotton fields of Dixie or to blacks."

Nearly destitute, Williams raised bus fare and traveled to Los Angeles, hoping to work as a machinist in the city's aircraft plants. By the time of his arrival, however,

the post–Korean War recession had left few employment opportunities. Unable to find a job, he joined the U.S. Marine Corps in 1954 to be trained as an information specialist. Instead he underwent special combat training at Camp Pendleton, learning the use of rifles, machine guns, grenades, rocket launchers, and infantry weapons. After refusing to salute the flag at a parade ceremony, he was sentenced to 180 days in the brig. Upon his release, he underwent special mountain warfare training in Nevada. Shortly before he would have left the United States for a tour of duty in Korea, Williams was discharged. Once again he returned to Monroe.

In October of 1955, Williams joined the predominantly white local Unitarian Fellowship and the Human Relations Group, a coalition of Unitarians, Catholics, and Protestants. Williams's increasing civil rights activity prompted him to join the Monroe branch of the NAACP as well. A year later, the organization's dwindling membership had fallen to just six people. Rather than dissolve the branch and risk the appearance of submitting to local racists, the members held an election and voted Williams in as president and Dr. Albert Perry as vice president. To build up the strength of the branch, Williams recruited members from among black domestics, laborers in pool halls, and the ranks of the unemployed. In contrast to the NAACP's traditional membership of middle- and upper-class professionals and intellectuals, Monroe's branch had a distinct working-class composition. By the end of the decade, branch membership numbered in the hundreds, and Williams had cemented his popularity as the branch's leader.

Targeted by the Ku Klux Klan

Following the 1954 U.S. Supreme Court decision *Brown v. Board of Education,* which called for an end to the "separate but equal" doctrine, Williams sought to desegregate Monroe's Union County Library. Although he expected opposition, the board chairman agreed, without protest, to desegregate the library. After this victory, Williams moved to desegregate Monroe's municipal swimming pool. Outraged over the deaths of several black children in backwoods swimming holes and the use of their tax dollars to support a segregated public facility, a large number of Monroe's blacks supported the campaign. When city government officials ignored requests for equal swimming facilities, Williams suggested that blacks could use the pool one day a week. City officials argued that such an arrangement would prove too costly because the water would have to be drained each time black people used the facility. Determined to desegregate the pool, Williams led groups of black youths in sit-ins.

In retaliation for Williams's civil rights activity, the Ku Klux Klan, a white supremacist organization, held rallies in Monroe. After their evening gatherings, Klansmen rode by car through Monroe's black neighborhood of Newtown, honking horns, shouting obscenities, and firing pistols. Stepping up its campaign to quell the Monroe NAACP, the Klan launched a petition to drive Williams and Perry out of Union County. When the police refused to intervene against the Klan, Williams urged the black community to undertake a program of armed self-defense. Within a year of obtaining a gun club charter from the National Rifle Association, he recruited 60 members who armed themselves with military surplus weapons and mail-order firearms.

In response to death threats against Perry, Williams posted a 24-hour vigil outside the doctor's home. On October 5, 1959, while the Klan made a routine night ride through Newtown, they unexpectedly met the fire of Williams's defense guard. In *Making of Black Revolutionaries,* writer Julian Mayfield described the scene: "It was just another good time for the Klan .... Near Dr. Perry's home their revelry was suddenly shattered by the sustained fire of scores of men who had been instructed not to kill anyone if it were not necessary. The firing was blistering, disciplined, and frightening. The motorcade, of about 80 cars, which had begun in a spirit of good fellowship, disintegrated into chaos, with panicky, robed men fleeing in every direction. Some abandoned their automobiles and had to continue on foot."

Suspended by the NAACP

Williams became increasingly involved in the defense of blacks wrongly accused of crimes. In October of 1958, two black boys, James Hanover Thompson, age seven, and David "Fuzzy" Simpson, age nine, were arrested on a charge of rape for kissing a white girl on the cheek. Although Williams contacted U.S. president Dwight Eisenhower and the national NAACP in regard to the matter, both parties failed to come the boys' defense. Williams then brought in New York defense lawyer Conrad Lynn, whose involvement in the case, along with photographs of the convicted youths in the *New York Post* and the *London News Chronicle,* prompted the NAACP to intervene. The boys were released on February 13, 1959. Despite the victory, Williams was disappointed with the national NAACP office.

In the spring of 1959, a local white man was charged with the attempted rape of a pregnant young black woman. In keeping with the old South's double racial standard concerning attacks upon women, the white man was acquitted. Embittered by the court's decision, Williams turned to the crowd of black men and women on the steps of the courthouse and delivered his legendary statement: "Since the federal government will not bring a halt to lynching in the South, and since the so-called courts lynch our people legally, if it's necessary to stop lynching with lynching, then we must be willing to resort to that method. We must meet violence with violence."

Early the next day, NAACP executive director Roy Wilkins called Williams to confirm the statement. Williams informed Wilkins that he had not spoken on behalf of the NAACP and refused to retract the statement. A few hours later, the national office suspended Williams for six months. "I first heard that I was suspended," related Williams in *Negroes with Guns,* "when Southern radio stations announced and kept repeating every 30 minutes that the NAACP suspended me for advocating violence." Although he twice appealed his suspension, the decision was upheld both times.

In the weeks before appearing at the NAACP convention in New York City, Williams launched his newsletter, the *Crusader.* As Williams explained in *Negroes with Guns,* "Through my newsletter … I started appealing to readers everywhere to protest the U.S. government, to protest the Justice Department; to protest the fact that the 14th Amendment [providing all U.S. citizens with equal protection under the law] did not exist in Monroe." Williams won reelection as president of Monroe's NAACP chapter in 1960, the same year that lunch counter sit-ins occurred throughout the South, including Monroe. At this time, Williams chose to reinstate picket lines at the town's municipal swimming pool, a decision that nearly resulted in his death when an unidentified automobile ran his car off the road. Williams was not daunted, however. He retaliated by setting up an integrated picket line around Monroe's courthouse.

Accused of Kidnapping White Couple

In August of 1961, several Freedom Riders—members of the civil rights movement from the North who rode buses to carry out desegregation of public transit facilities in the South—arrived in Monroe to assist in a protest led by Williams. Among them were Martin Luther King Jr.'s representative, the Reverend Paul Brooks, and James Forman. In his book *The Making of Black Revolutionaries,* Forman described Williams as a "determined man" who "wanted the world to know that law and order had broken down here, and that he was going to protect his home and family by any means necessary." Under the supervision of Williams, Brooks and Forman drafted a 10-point petition and presented it to Monroe's city aldermen. The document even included demands for equal employment opportunities for Monroe's black citizens. The petition, like Williams's appeal to the U.S. Justice Department, proved unsuccessful.

In late August, amid threats on his life and the expectation of a Klan invasion of Newtown, Williams posted guards around his Boyte Street home. Around six o'clock in the evening, a white couple, the Steagalls, drove into Newtown. Entering Boyte Street, the Steagalls encountered several hundred blacks. Drawn out-

side his home by the sounds of shouting, Williams came upon the Steagalls surrounded by a crowd of blacks who sent up a cry of "Kill them, kill them!" Fearing for their lives, Williams led the Steagalls into his house. On the way to the front door, Mrs. Steagall was heard to shout, "We have been kidnapped!" Williams attempted to calm the couple, assuring them his motive was to protect them from the crowd. However, alerted that the police had blockaded both ends of Boyte Street, Williams decided to flee rather than face arrest by state troopers.

Around nine o'clock that evening, Williams left Monroe with his wife and two sons and traveled to New York City, where he learned of his indictment for kidnapping by a Union County grand jury. Although his indictment came after he crossed the North Carolina state line, Williams remained a fugitive wanted by the Federal Bureau of Investigation. He then fled to the Canadian cities of Toronto and Montreal. Aware that Canadian authorities were also seeking his arrest, Williams decided to seek refuge in Cuba, where he was welcomed by young revolutionary Fidel Castro.

Lived in Exile in Cuba, China

Through his Havana-based revolutionary radio program, *Radio Free Dixie,* and his Cuban edition of the *Crusader,* Williams called for black Americans to take up arms against their white oppressors. In 1962 he wrote his autobiography, *Negroes with Guns,* which became influential among organizers of the Black Panther Party, including Huey P. Newton, later in the decade. In his newsletter, Williams explained how to launch a guerilla self-defense campaign with the use of Molotov cocktails and other homemade weapons. In a 1964 issue, reprinted in *Black Protest Thought in the Twentieth Century,* he wrote, "The hour is fast approaching when our people must make a decision to meekly submit to fascist forces of terror and extermination or surge forth to the battle to liberate ourselves, save America and liquidate its domestic enemies."

In 1965 Williams left Cuba after an alleged falling-out with Castro and sought refuge in China, where he was treated as something of a celebrity by Communist leaders Mao Zedong and Zhou Enlai. He resumed publication of the *Crusader* and in 1968 published a pamphlet, "Listen Brother!," which implored African-American combat troops in Vietnam to stop fighting against their Asiatic "dark-skinned brothers." In March of 1968, a group of African Americans gathered at the Shrine of the Black Madonna in Detroit to found the Republic of New Africa (RNA)—a revolutionary Marxist-Leninist organization dedicated to establishing a separate black nation within five of the southern states in the United States. The RNA elected Williams as its president in exile.

Between 1968 and 1969, Williams twice visited Tanzania in East Africa. In the Tanzanian city of Dar es

Salaam, he met revolutionaries from across Africa. While he was there, the U.S. embassy granted Williams a passport to reenter the United States. Williams had negotiated this with the administration of President Richard M. Nixon, which was interested in his knowledge of the Chinese government, as efforts to open diplomatic relations with China had begun in secret. In the fall of 1969, Williams left London on a nearly empty jet chartered by the U.S. government and arrived in Detroit. After being taken to the federal building in downtown Detroit for a seven-minute hearing, Williams was released on a bond of $11,000.

Lectured on Injustice

Returning home, Williams was disillusioned by the RNA's organization's internal struggles, and he resigned as president in early December of 1969. He settled in a small town near Grand Rapids, Michigan. In exchange for his return to the United States with no federal consequences for having lived in exile in Cuba and China for eight years, Williams had agreed to advise the U.S. State Department on matter related to the normalization of relations with China. He also received a grant from the Ford Foundation to work as a research associate at the University of Michigan's Institute for Chinese Studies. In 1976 he was finally ordered to return to North Carolina in connection with the 15-year-old kidnapping case, but prosecutors soon dropped all charges against him.

During the last decades of his life, Williams lived in Michigan, where he was an occasional lecturer on civil rights and was frequently interviewed in scholarly publications and the news media. He and his wife formed the People's Association for Human Rights and became active in local social justice activities. Despite his earlier rocky relationship with the NAACP, Williams again worked for the organization as a member and vice president of the Lake/Newaygo (Michigan) branch; this earned him the chapter's Black Image Award in 1992. He died of Hodgkin's lymphoma in Grand Rapids, Michigan, in 1996. Civil rights icon Rosa Parks spoke at his funeral.

After Williams's death his son told David Stout of the *New York Times* that although his father had learned from and appreciated some of communism's goals, he never espoused the politics or identity of communism, considering himself instead a "revolutionary black nationalist" who remained pessimistic about the long-lasting results of the civil rights movement. In 2004 Williams was the subject of the PBS documentary film *Negroes with Guns: Rob Williams and Black Power.*

Selected writings

Negroes with Guns, Marzani & Munsell, 1962; Third World Press, 1973.
While God Lay Sleeping: The Autobiography of Robert F. Williams, unpublished.

Sources

Books

Cohen, Robert Carl, *Black Crusader: A Biography of Robert Franklin Williams,* Stuart, 1972.
Foner, Phillip S., *The Black Panthers Speak,* Da Capo, 1995.
Forman, James, *The Making of Black Revolutionaries,* Open Hand, 1985.
Geschwender, James A., *The Black Revolt: The Civil Rights Movement, Ghetto Uprisings, and Separatism,* Prentice Hall, 1971.
Lokos, Lionel, *The New Racism: Reverse Discrimination in America,* Arlington House, 1971.
Meier, August, Elliot Rudwick, and Francis L. Broderick, eds., *Black Protest Thought in the Twentieth Century,* Bobbs-Merrill, 1971.
Shapiro, Herbert, *White Violence and Black Response,* University of Massachusetts, 1988.
Tyson, Timothy B., *Radio Free Dixie: Robert F. Williams and the Roots of Black Power,* University of North Carolina Press, 1999.
Williams, Robert F., *Negroes With Guns,* Marzani & Munsell, 1962; repr., Third World Press, 1973.

Periodicals

New York Times, October 19, 1996.

Online

"Negroes with Guns: Rob Williams and Black Power," PBS.org, http://www.pbs.org/independentlens/negroeswithguns/rob.html (accessed August 2, 2016).
Tyson, Timothy B., "Robert Franklin Williams: A Warrior for Freedom, 1925–1996," http://www.ibiblio.org/Southern_Exposure/RFW.html (accessed August 2, 2016).

—John Cohassey and Pamela Willwerth Aue

Malik Yusef

1971—

Spoken word artist, poet, songwriter, producer

Yusef, Malik, photograph. Steve Granitz/WireImage/Getty Images.

Poet, songwriter, and producer Malik Yusef is best known as the right-hand man of rapper Kanye West. Friends since their early days in the Chicago rap community, the two began a serious collaboration after Yusef signed with West's record label, GOOD Music, in 2005. A product of the rough neighborhoods of Chicago's South Side, Yusef overcame street violence and dyslexia to become one of Chicago's most prominent spoken word artists, renowned for expressing the frustrations of inner-city life and demands for social reforms. It was not long before Yusef made the natural progression to hip-hop and rap. Television appearances on BET's *RAP City* and HBO's *Russell Simmons Def Poetry Jam* and a series of successful collaborations with other artists paved the way for Yusef's eventual pairing with West.

Composed Street Poetry

Born Malik Yusef Jones in Chicago on April 4, 1971, Yusef grew up in one of the city's most violent and drug-infested neighborhoods, the Wild 100's, so called for the three-digit streets on the city's South Side.

When he was 12 years old, Yusef was recruited into the notorious street gang the Blackstone Rangers. In an interview with Andre Sternberg of *Mother Jones* magazine, Yusef described his struggle to survive the streets: "At an early age I realized that if I wasn't a Blackstone in this community then I was going to fight every day. And no matter whether I was or not, when I went to school, they'd say, 'Oh, you're from 122nd street? You're a Stone.' So the only way I could stave off any of these assaults was to become a gang banger, and to excel, so I could quell the behavior. If I excelled, then I could call the shots. So I became a community leader from inside."

Yusef's evolution from street hustler to street poet began in the early 1990s, when he started performing spoken word poetry at open-mic nights. He got a lucky break in 1997 when Ted Witcher, director of *Love Jones,* hired him as the off-screen poetry coach for the film's lead actor, Larenz Tate. Within a few years, Yusef was carving out a niche for himself on the music scene. In an interview with Tamone Bacon of the American Society of Composers, Authors and Publishers (ASCAP), Yusef described the difference between being

At a Glance . . .

Born Malik Yusef Jones on April 4, 1971, in Chicago, IL.

Career: Chicago stage performer, early 1990s—; recording artist, late 1990s—; songwriter, early 2000s—.

Memberships: American Society of Composers, Authors and Publishers; Chicago youth organizations For Yourself Foundation and Girl Power, founder; Drop Squad, founder; Hip Hop Caucus, director, arts and culture; People's Climate Music.

Awards: Truth Awards, Spoken Word Artist of the Year, Truth Media/MidWest Gap, 2001–05; Chicago Music Awards, Best Poet, 2002–08; Independent Film Project Award, Chicago Production Fund, 2007, for *The Untimely Demise of Hollywood Jerome*; Grammy Award, Best Rap Song, 2011, for "All of the Lights."

Addresses: *Record company*—GOOD Music, 550 Madison Ave., New York, NY. *Web*—http://www.malikyusefjones.com/. *Twitter*—@malikyusef.

a poet and a rapper: "In poetry, you have to be more prolific. You have to use adjectives or what I like to call, 'brain words.' Being a rapper, you have to have musicality. In poetry, you have pauses and you can move around it. I would say rappers have a harder time because they have to focus on the beat."

Yusef was invited to perform on Common's album *One Day It'll All Make Sense* (1997) and on Channel Live's *Armaghetto* (2000), and he was featured on the debut album of R&B singer Carl Thomas, *Emotional* (2000). While he was on tour with Thomas, Yusef met the jazz saxophonist Mike Phillips. The two struck up a partnership in 2002 that resulted in the spoken word jazz song "This Is Not a Game." The track figured in the marketing campaign for Michael Jordan's new line of sneakers, the Air Jordan 17, and was picked to appear on a CD-ROM packaged along with each pair of shoes.

Yusef went into the studio in 2003 to cut his first solo album, *The Great Chicago Fire: A Cold Day in Hell*, which was released on the independent label Bungalo Records. Featuring guest appearances from an assortment of new and established Chicago artists, including West, Thomas, Common, Twista, and Chantay Savage, the album mixes laid-back, sensuous tunes with deeper subject matter on such tracks as "Conversations with God" and "Revolutionary Words." Yusef teamed with West and Common on the album's lead single,

"Wouldn't You Like to Ride," which was included in the soundtrack for the 2005 film *Coach Carter*. On one of his turns on the mic, Yusef introduces himself to his audience: "The most critically acclaimed wordsmith in the game / I give you words spit with flames / Stay to myself and let nerves mix with lames."

Collaborated with Kanye West

New opportunities opened up for Yusef after he signed with West's label, GOOD (Getting Our Dreams Out), in 2005. He assembled a large collection of high-profile talent for his second studio album, *G.O.O.D. Morning G.O.O.D. Night* (2009). Boasting contributions from the likes of West, Common, John Legend, Pharrell Williams, Adam Levine, and Jennifer Hudson, *G.O.O.D. Morning G.O.O.D. Night* comprises two CDs, titled *Dusk* and *Dawn*, each of which features 15 tracks. Yusef explained the concepts behind *Dusk* and *Dawn* for Jessie Smith of the website Rap Chronicle: "It's just basically a reflection of the cycles of life. I mean, from just being human, you have love, you have hate; you'll experience both frustration and adulation. You have night, and you have day. Yin and yang."

Already an integral part of West's musical sound, Yusef cowrote seven of the songs on West's Grammy-winning album *My Beautiful Dark Twisted Fantasy*, released in 2010. Yusef also made major contributions to West's next two albums, the platinum sellers *Yeezus* (2013) and *The Life of Pablo* (2016). In addition, he is credited as a writer and artist on the GOOD compilation album *Cruel Summer* (2012).

Yusef maintains a close connection with his Chicago roots. His unpublished book *Infrared Poetry* is a collection of what he calls "love letters" to the city. Yusef is also a longtime community activist. Inspired by his Blackstone years, he founded a youth literacy initiative, the For Yourself Foundation, and a nonprofit aimed at empowering young females, Girl Power. In 2007 Yusef paired with director Frey Hoffman on a short film addressing urban themes, *The Untimely Demise of Hollywood Jerome*. The winner of a $100,000 award from the IPF/Chicago Production Fund, the film is based on one of Yusef's spoken word poems and tells the story of a 14-year-old gang member from the South Side who idolizes classic Hollywood gangsters. Yusef also sponsors a group called Drop Squad, which works to rid inner-city streets of trash. In 2013 Yusef cowrote and recorded a song with Chicago students at Hearst Elementary as part of the ASCAP Songwriter Residency program for underresourced schools.

Yusef is also a leading voice in the Hip Hop Caucus, a nonprofit organization that leverages hip-hop culture to inspire civic action. He served as executive producer of the soundtrack for the 2015 documentary *HOME*, which tells the story of a grassroots environmental

movement, People's Climate Change, spearheaded by the Hip Hop Caucus.

Selected works

Albums

The Great Chicago Fire: A Cold Day in Hell (includes "Wouldn't You Like to Ride," "Conversations with God," and "Revolutionary Words"), Bungalo Records, 2003.
G.O.O.D. Morning G.O.O.D. Night, GOOD Music, 2009.

Films

(Cowriter) *The Untimely Demise of Hollywood Jerome,* Freydesign Productions/Salaam Shalom Productions, 2007.
(Executive producer) *HOME* (soundtrack), Hip Hop Caucus, 2015.

Sources

Periodicals

Mother Jones, April 1, 2008.

Online

Bacon, Tamone, "Malik Yusef Brings Chicago's Diversity to His Mix of Mediums," ASCAP, June 7, 2011, http://www.ascap.com/playback/2011/06/radar_report/malikyusef.aspx (accessed August 5, 2016).

Chandler, Justin, Review of *The Great Chicago Fire: A Cold Day in Hell,* Rap Reviews, February 3, 2009, http://www.rapreviews.com/archive/BTTL_greatchicagofire.html (accessed August 5, 2016).

Drea O, Interview with Malik Yusef, YouTube, April 26, 2016, https://www.youtube.com/watch?v=1CQx2RmcBho (accessed August 5, 2016).

"Malik Yusef," Hip Hop Caucus, http://www.hiphopcaucus.org/our-story/team/15-our-story/team/12-malik-yusef (accessed August 5, 2016).

Malik Yusef Jones (official website), http://www.malikyusefjones.com/ (accessed August 5, 2016).

Smith, Jessie, "Mallik Yusef Talks G.O.O.D. Music, 'Nobody's Smiling,' Upcoming Album, Fashion & Violence in Chicago," Rap Chronicle, 2014, http://rapchronicle.com/malik-yusef-talks-g-o-o-d-music-nobodys-smiling-upcoming-album-fashion-violence-in-chicago/ (accessed August 5, 2016).

—Janet Mullane

Cumulative Nationality Index

Volume numbers appear in **bold**

American

Aaliyah **30**
Aaron, Hank **5**
Aaron, Quinton **82**
Abbott, Robert Sengstacke **27**
Abdi, Barkhad **119**
Abdirahman, Abdi **126**
Abdul-Jabbar, Kareem **8**
Abdullah, Kazem **97**
Abdur-Rahim, Shareef **28**
Abele, Julian **55**
Abercrumbie, P. Eric **95**
Abernathy, Ralph David **1**
Aberra, Amsale **67**
Abraham, Kyle **116**
Abu-Jamal, Mumia **15**
Ace, Johnny **36**
Aces, The **117**
Ackerman, Arlene **108**
Acklin, Barbara Jean **107**
Adams, Alberta **133**
Adams, Alma **127**
Adams, Eric **133**
Adams, Eula L. **39, 120**
Adams, Floyd, Jr. **12, 122**
Adams, Jenoyne **60**
Adams, Johnny **39**
Adams, Leslie **39**
Adams, Oleta **18**
Adams, Osceola Macarthy **31**
Adams, Sheila J. **25**
Adams, Yolanda **17, 67**
Adams-Campbell, Lucille L. **60**
Adams Earley, Charity **13, 34**
Adams-Ender, Clara **40**
Adderley, Julian "Cannonball" **30**
Adderley, Nat **29**
Adebimpe, Tunde **75**
Adegbile, Debo P. **119**
Adkins, Rod **41**
Adkins, Rutherford H. **21**
Adkins, Terry **122**
Adu, Freddy **67**
Aduba, Uzo **122**
Agyeman, Jaramogi Abebe **10, 63**
Ailey, Alvin **8**
Akil, Mara Brock **60, 82**
Akinmusire, Ambrose **103**
Akon **68**
Al-Amin, Jamil Abdullah **6**
Albert, Octavia V. R. **100**
Albright, Gerald **23**
Alcorn, George Edward, Jr. **59**

Aldridge, Ira **99**
Aldridge, LaMarcus **125**
Alexander, Archie Alphonso **14**
Alexander, Arthur **131**
Alexander, Claudia **130**
Alexander, Clifford **26**
Alexander, Elizabeth **75**
Alexander, Joseph L. **95**
Alexander, Joyce London **18**
Alexander, Khandi **43**
Alexander, Kwame **98**
Alexander, Margaret Walker **22**
Alexander, Michelle **98**
Alexander, Sadie Tanner Mossell **22**
Alexander, Shaun **58**
Ali, Hana Yasmeen **52**
Ali, Laila **27, 63**
Ali, Mahershala **122**
Ali, Muhammad **2, 16, 52, 136**
Ali, Rashied **79**
Ali, Russlynn H. **92**
Ali, Tatyana **73**
Allah, Khalik **131**
Allain, Stephanie **49**
Allen, Betty **83**
Allen, Byron **3, 24, 97**
Allen, Claude **68**
Allen, Debbie **13, 42**
Allen, Dick **85**
Allen, Ethel D. **13**
Allen, Eugene **79**
Allen, Geri **92**
Allen, Larry **109**
Allen, Lucy **85**
Allen, Macon Bolling **104**
Allen, Marcus **20**
Allen, Ray **82**
Allen, Red **129**
Allen, Robert L. **38**
Allen, Samuel W. **38**
Allen, Tina **22, 75**
Allen, Will **74**
Allen-Buillard, Melba **55**
Allensworth, Allen **129**
Allison, Luther **111**
Alonso, Laz **87**
Als, Hilton **105**
Alston, Charles **33**
Altidore, Jozy **109**
Amaker, Norman **63**
Amaker, Tommy **62**
Amaki, Amalia **76**
Amerie **52**

Ames, Wilmer **27**
Ammons, Albert **112**
Ammons, Gene **112**
Ammons, James H. **81**
Amos, Emma **63**
Amos, John **8, 62**
Amos, Wally **9**
Amy, Curtis **114**
Anderson, Anthony **51, 77**
Anderson, Carl **48**
Anderson, Charles Edward **37**
Anderson, Eddie "Rochester" **30**
Anderson, Elmer **25**
Anderson, Ezzrett **95**
Anderson, Fred **87**
Anderson, Ivie **126**
Anderson, Jamal **22**
Anderson, Lauren **72**
Anderson, Maceo **111**
Anderson, Marcia **115**
Anderson, Marian **2, 33**
Anderson, Michael P. **40**
Anderson, Mike **63**
Anderson, Norman B. **45**
Anderson, Reuben V. **81**
Anderson, T. J. **119**
Anderson, William G(ilchrist) **57**
Andrews, Benny **22, 59**
Andrews, Bert **13**
Andrews, Inez **108**
Andrews, Raymond **4**
Andrews, Tina **74**
Angelou, Maya **1, 15, 122**
Ansa, Tina McElroy **14**
Anthony, Carmelo **46, 94**
Anthony, La La **122**
Anthony, Wendell **25**
apl.de.ap **84**
Aplin-Brownlee, Vivian **96**
Appiah, Kwame Anthony **67, 101**
Archer, Dennis **7, 36**
Archer, Lee, Jr. **79**
Archibald, Tiny **90**
Archie-Hudson, Marguerite **44**
Ardoin, Alphonse **65**
Arenas, Gilbert **84**
Arkadie, Kevin **17**
Armenteros, Chocolate **133**
Armstrong, Govind **81**
Armstrong, Henry **104**
Armstrong, Louis **2**
Armstrong, Robb **15**
Armstrong, Vanessa Bell **24**
Arnez J **53**

Arnold, Billy Boy **112**
Arnold, Kokomo **116**
Arnold, Tichina **63**
Arnwine, Barbara **28**
Arrington, Richard **24, 100**
Arrington, Steve **132**
Arroyo, Martina **30**
Artest, Ron **52**
Asante, Molefi Kete **3**
A$AP Rocky **109**
Ashanti **37, 96**
Ashe, Arthur **1, 18**
Ashford, Calvin, Jr. **74**
Ashford, Emmett **22**
Ashford, Evelyn **63**
Ashford, Nickolas **21, 97**
Ashley & JaQuavis **107**
Ashley-Ward, Amelia **23**
Ashong, Derrick **86**
Asim, Jabari **71**
Asomugha, Nnamdi **100**
Atkins, Cholly **40**
Atkins, Erica **34**
Atkins, Juan **50**
Atkins, Russell **45**
Atkins, Tina **34**
Atlantic Starr **122**
Attaway, William **102**
Aubert, Alvin **41**
Aubespin, Mervin **95**
Augusta, Alexander T. **111**
Auguste, Donna **29**
Austin, Bobby W. **95**
Austin, Gloria **63**
Austin, Jim **63**
Austin, Junius C. **44**
Austin, Lloyd **101**
Austin, Lovie **40**
Austin, Patti **24**
Austin, Wanda M. **94**
Autrey, Wesley **68**
Avant, Clarence **19, 86**
Avery, James **118**
Avant, Nicole A. **90**
Avery, Byllye Y. **66**
Ayers, Roy **16**
Ayler, Albert **104**
Babatunde, Obba **35**
Baby Laurence **136**
Babyface **10, 31, 82**
Bacon-Bercey, June **38**
Badu, Erykah **22, 114**
Bahati, Wambui **60**
Bailey, Buster **38**

Bailey, Chauncey 68
Bailey, Clyde 45
Bailey, DeFord 33
Bailey, Pearl 14
Bailey, Philip 63
Bailey, Radcliffe 19
Bailey, Xenobia 11
Baines, Harold 32
Baiocchi, Regina Harris 41
Baisden, Michael 25, 66
Baker, Anita 21, 48
Baker, Augusta 38
Baker, Delbert W. 110
Baker, Dusty 8, 43, 72, 110
Baker, Ella 5
Baker, Gwendolyn Calvert 9
Baker, Houston A., Jr. 6
Baker, Josephine 3
Baker, LaVern 26
Baker, Matt 76
Baker, Maxine B. 28
Baker, Mickey 95
Baker, Thurbert 22
Baker, Vernon Joseph 65, 87
Bakewell, Danny 99
Baldwin, Cynthia 74, 107
Baldwin, James 1
Ballance, Frank W. 41
Ballard, Allen Butler, Jr. 40
Ballard, Florence 112
Ballard, Hank 41
Ballard, John 95
Baltimore, Richard Lewis, III 71
Bambaataa, Afrika 34
Bambara, Toni Cade 10
Bandele, Asha 36
Banks, Azealia 107
Banks, Chico 134
Banks, Ernie 33, 126
Banks, Jeffrey 17
Banks, Lloyd 113
Banks, Michelle 59
Banks, Paula A. 68
Banks, Tyra 11, 50
Banks, William 11
Banneker, Benjamin 93
Banner, David 55
Bannister, Edward Mitchell 88
Baquet, Dean 63, 121
Baraka, Amiri 1, 38, 118
Baraka, Ras J. 121
Baraka, Sho 109
Barbee, Lloyd Augustus 71
Barber, Ronde 41
Barber, Tiki 57, 107
Barboza, Anthony 10
Barclay, Paris 37, 94, 133
Barden, Donald H. 9, 20, 89
Bar-Kays, The 118
Barker, Danny 32
Barkley, Charles 5, 66
Barksdale, Don 103
Barlow, Roosevelt 49
Barnes, Ernie 16, 78
Barnes, Katreese 97
Barnes, Melody 75
Barnes, Roosevelt "Booba" 33
Barnes, Steven 54
Barnett, Amy Du Bois 46
Barnett, Etta Moten 56
Barnett, Herman 112
Barnett, Marguerite 46
Barney, Lem 26

Barnhill, David 30
Barrax, Gerald William 45
Barrett, Andrew C. 12
Barrett, Sweet Emma 130
Barrett, Jacquelyn 28
Barrino, Fantasia 53, 94
Barris, Kenya 135
Barron, Charles 136
Barron, Inez 136
Barron, Kenny 128
Barrow, Willie T. 85, 128
Barry, Marion, Jr. 7, 44, 125
Barthé, Earl 78
Barthe, Richmond 15
Basie, Count 23
Baskett, James 102
Basquiat, Jean-Michel 5
Bass, Charlotta Spears 40
Bass, Fontella 104, 109
Bass, Holly 134
Bass, Karen 70
Bassett, Angela 6, 23, 62
Bassett, Ebenezer D. 132
Bassey, Offiong 119
Baszile, Jennifer 79
Batch, Charlie 120
Bates, Daisy 13, 135
Bates, Karen Grigsby 40
Bates, Peg Leg 14, 135
Bath, Patricia E. 37
Batiste, Alvin 66
Batiste, Jonathan 108, 130
Batiste, Lionel 105
Battiste, Harold, Jr. 136
Battle, Kathleen 70
Battle, Samuel J. 130
Batts, Anthony 128
Baugh, David 23
Baylor, Don 6
Baylor, Elgin 93
Baylor, Helen 36
Beach, Michael 26, 120
Beal, Bernard B. 46
Beals, Jennifer 12
Beals, Melba Pattillo 15, 94
Beard, Matthew 120
Bearden, Romare 2, 50
Beasley, Jamar 29
Beasley, Phoebe 34
Beatty, Joyce 117
Beatty, Talley 35
Beaty, Zelmo 115
Beauvais, Garcelle 29, 95
Bechet, Sidney 18
Beckford, Tyson 11, 68
Beckham, Barry 41
Beckham, Odell, Jr. 132
Beckwith, Naomi 101
Becton, Julius W., Jr. 110
Belafonte, Harry 4, 65
Belgrave, Cynthia 75
Belgrave, Marcus 77, 129
Bell, Carey 114
Bell, Carl C. 111
Bell, Darrin 77
Bell, Derrick 6, 98
Bell, James "Cool Papa" 36
Bell, James A. 50
Bell, James Madison 40
Bell, LeRoy 98
Bell, Le'Veon 132
Bell, Michael 40
Bell, Robert Mack 22

Bell, Thom 112
Bell, W. Kamau 107
Bell, William A., Sr. 122
Bellamy, Bill 12
Bellamy, Terry 58
Bellamy, Walt 119
Belle, Albert 10
Belle, Regina 1, 51
Belton, Sharon Sayles 9, 16
Benberry, Cuesta 65
Benét, Eric 28, 77
Benham, Robert 78
Ben-Israel, Ben Ami 11
Benjamin, Andre 45
Benjamin, Regina 20, 75
Benjamin, Steve 98
Benjamin, Tritobia Hayes 53
Bennett, Estelle 77
Bennett, George Harold "Hal" 45
Bennett, Gwendolyn B. 59
Bennett, Lerone, Jr. 5, 84
Bennett, Richard 97
Benson, Angela 34
Benson, Obie 96
Bentley, Lamont 53
Benton, Brook 121
Berian, Boris 136
Berrien, Jacqueline A. 93
Berry, Chu 136
Berry, Edwin C. 81
Berry, Eric 125
Berry, Halle 4, 19, 57, 91
Berry, Bertice 8, 55
Berry, Chuck 29
Berry, Fred "Rerun" 48
Berry, Mary Frances 7
Berry, Moses 84
Berry, Theodore 31
Berrysmith, Don Reginald 49
Bethune, Mary McLeod 4
Betsch, MaVynee 28
Bettis, Jerome 64
Betts, Keter 85
Betts, R. Dwayne 86
Bevel, James L. 75
Beverly, Frankie 25
Bey, Salome 134
Bey, Yasiin 30, 96
Beyoncé 39, 70, 105
Bibb, Eric 49, 123
Bibb, Henry and Mary 54
Bibb, Leon 132
Bickerstaff, Bernie 21, 133
Bickerstaff, Cydni L. 133
Bickerstaff, J. B. 133
Big Daddy Kane 79
Big Freedia 128
Big L 120
Big Maybelle 117
Big Sean 96
Big Time Sarah 45, 134
Biggers, John 20, 33
Biggers, Sanford 62
Bilal 101
Biles, Simone 136
Billops, Camille 82
Billy Ward and the Dominoes 105
bin Wahad, Dhoruba 85
Bing, Dave 3, 59, 78
Bingham, Howard 96
Bingham, Margot 135
Birch, Adolpho A., Jr. 85
Birch, Glynn R. 61

Birdman 110
Birdsong, Cindy 113
Bishop, Sanford D., Jr. 24, 111
Bishop, Stephen 95
Bivins, Michael 72
Blacc, Aloe 119
Black, Albert 51
Black, Barry C. 47
Black, Joe 75
Black, Keith Lanier 18, 84
Black Thought 63
Blackburn, Robert 28
Blackman, Toni 86
Blackmon, Brenda 58
Blackshear, Leonard 52
Blackwell, David 79
Blackwell, Gloria 127
Blackwell, Kenneth, Sr. 61
Blackwell, Otis 98
Blackwell, Robert D., Sr. 52
Blackwell, Unita 17
Blacque, Taurean 58
Blade, Brian 88
Blair, Jayson 50
Blair, Paul 36
Blake, Asha 26
Blake, Charles E. 82
Blake, Eubie 29
Blake, James 43, 131
Blake, John, Jr. 123
Blakely, Delois N. 122
Blakely, Edward J. 88
Blakey, Art 37
Blanchard, Shawn 129
Blanchard, Terence 43
Blanco, Mykki 106
Bland, Bobby 36, 113
Bland, Edward 111
Bland, Eleanor Taylor 39
Blanks, Billy 22
Blanks, Deborah K. 69
Blanton, Dain 29
Blanton, Jimmy 108
Blassingame, John Wesley 40
Blaylock, Ronald 86
Blayton, Jesse B., Sr. 55
Bleu, Corbin 65
Blige, Mary J. 20, 34, 60, 97
Blind Boys of Alabama, The 99
Blitz the Ambassador 115
Blockson, Charles L. 42
Bloomer, George 86
Blow, Charles M. 73
Blow, Kurtis 31, 122
Blue, Vida 122
Bluford, Guy 2, 35
Bluitt, Juliann S. 14
B.o.B. 91
Bobb, Robert C. 83
Bobo, Lawrence 60
Bogle, Donald 34
Bogues, Tyrone "Muggsy" 56
Bolden, Buddy 39
Bolden, Charles Frank, Jr. 7, 78
Bolden, Frank E. 44
Bolden, Tonya 32
Bolin, Jane 22, 59
Bolton, Terrell D. 25
Bolton-Holifield, Ruthie 28
Bond, Beverly 53
Bond, J. Max, Jr. 76
Bond, Julian 2, 35, 106, 130
Bonds, Barry 6, 34, 63, 99

Bonds, Bobby **43**
Bonds, Margaret **39**
Bonet, Lisa **58, 133**
Bonner, Leroy **113**
Bonney, Tabi **98**
Bontemps, Arna **8**
Booker, Cory Anthony **68**
Booker, Simeon **23**
Boozer, Bob **103**
Borders, James **9**
Borders, Marcy **131**
Borders, William Holmes **94**
Boseman, Chadwick **111**
Bosh, Chris **85**
Bosley, Freeman, Jr. **7**
Bostic, Earl **121**
Bostic, Joe **95**
Boston, Kelvin E. **25**
Boston, Lloyd **24**
Boulware, Harold R. **109**
Bow Wow **35**
Bowe, Riddick **6, 107**
Bowen, John W. E., Sr. **89**
Bowen, Ruth **83**
Bowles, Cephas **127**
Bowles, Todd **128**
Bowman, Bertie **71**
Bowser, Muriel **129**
Bowser, Yvette Lee **17, 133**
Boyd, Edward **70**
Boyd, Gerald M. **32, 59**
Boyd, Gwendolyn **49**
Boyd, John W., Jr. **20, 72**
Boyd, Melba Joyce **86**
Boyd, T. B., III **6**
Boykin, Keith **14**
Boykin, Otis **92**
Boykin, Phillip **102**
Boynton Robinson, Amelia **131**
Boyz II Men **82**
Bozella, Dewey **97**
Bradford, Alex **121**
Bradford, Mark **89**
Bradley, Adam **101**
Bradley, Charles **126**
Bradley, David Henry, Jr. **39**
Bradley, Ed **2, 59**
Bradley, J. Robert **65**
Bradley, Jennette B. **40**
Bradley, Thomas **2, 20**
Bradshaw, Tiny **102**
Brady, St. Elmo **107**
Brady, Wayne **32, 71**
Brae, C. Michael **61**
Braithwaite, William Stanley **52**
Bramlett, Joseph **91**
Branch, William Blackwell **39**
Brand, Elton **31**
Brandon, Barbara **3**
Brandon, Terrell **16**
Brandy **14, 34, 72**
Branham, George, III **50**
Branson, Herman **87**
Brashear, Carl **29**
Brashear, Donald **39**
Braugher, Andre **13, 58, 91**
Braun, Carol Moseley **4, 42**
Brawley, Benjamin **44**
Braxton, Anthony **128**
Braxton, Brad **77**
Braxton, Tamar **134**
Braxton, Toni **15, 61, 91**
Brazier, Arthur M. **115**

Brazile, Donna **25, 70**
Brewer, Rosalind **100**
Brewster, W. Herbert **128**
Bridgeman, Junior **132**
Bridges, Leon **126**
Bridges, Ruby **77**
Bridges, Sheila **36**
Bridges, Todd **37**
Bridgewater, Dee Dee **32, 92**
Bridgewater, Teddy **132**
Bridgforth, Glinda **36**
Briggs, Curtis **84**
Brim, John **117**
Brimm, Charles E. **105**
Brimmer, Andrew **2, 48, 106**
Briscoe, Connie **15**
Briscoe, Marlin **37**
Britt, Donna **28**
Broadbent, Hydeia **36**
Brock, Lou **18**
Brock, Roslyn McCallister **86**
Bromery, Randolph Wilson **85**
Broner, Adrien **109**
Bronner, Nathaniel H., Sr. **32**
Brooke, Edward W. **8, 88, 126**
Brookins, Hamel Hartford **102**
Brooks, Aaron **33**
Brooks, Avery **9, 98**
Brooks, Danielle **119**
Brooks, Derrick **43, 119**
Brooks, Golden **62**
Brooks, Gwendolyn **1, 28**
Brooks, Hadda **40**
Brooks, Mehcad **62**
Brooks, Roy **125**
Brooks, Tina **133**
Brooks, Tyrone **59**
Broonzy, Big Bill **82**
Brothers Johnson **130**
Brower, William **49**
Brown, Aja **115**
Brown, Alvin **96**
Brown, Angela M. **54**
Brown, Anne **76**
Brown, Anthony G. **72**
Brown, Antron **85**
Brown, Bobbi Kristina **130**
Brown, Bobby **58, 124**
Brown, Byrd **49**
Brown, Byron W. **72**
Brown, Cecil M. **46**
Brown, Charles **23**
Brown, Charlotte Hawkins **106**
Brown, Chris **74, 109**
Brown, Chuck **78, 102**
Brown, Clarence Gatemouth **59**
Brown, Claude **38**
Brown, Clifford **86**
Brown, Cora **33**
Brown, Corrine **24, 90**
Brown, Cupcake **63**
Brown, Donald **19**
Brown, Eddie C. **35**
Brown, Elaine **8**
Brown, Ernest **80**
Brown, Erroll M. **23**
Brown, Foxy **25**
Brown, Frederick J. **102**
Brown, George Leslie **62**
Brown, Hallie Quinn **100**
Brown, Homer S. **47**
Brown, James **15, 60**
Brown, James **22**

Brown, Jamie Foster **91**
Brown, Janice Rogers **43**
Brown, Jason **125**
Brown, Jerry **117**
Brown, Jesse **6, 41**
Brown, Jesse Leroy **31**
Brown, Jim **11, 95**
Brown, Joe **29**
Brown, Joyce F. **25**
Brown, Kwame R. **91**
Brown, Lee P. **1, 24, 109**
Brown, Les **5**
Brown, Lloyd Louis **42**
Brown, Marie Dutton **12**
Brown, Mike **77, 107**
Brown, Nappy **73**
Brown, Oliver Leon **94**
Brown, Oscar, Jr. **53**
Brown, Patrick "Sleepy" **50**
Brown, Raymond **102**
Brown, Robert **65**
Brown, Ron **5**
Brown, Ronald K. **91**
Brown, Ruth **90**
Brown, Shirley **132**
Brown, Sterling Allen **10, 64**
Brown, Tim **134**
Brown, Tony **3**
Brown, Uzee **42**
Brown, Vivian **27**
Brown, Warren **61**
Brown, Wesley **23**
Brown, Wesley A. **102**
Brown, Willa **40**
Brown, Willard **36**
Brown, William Wells **99**
Brown, Willie **7, 85**
Brown, Zora Kramer **12**
Browne, Richard **132**
Browne, Roscoe Lee **66**
Browne, Tom **136**
Brownlee, Lawrence **88**
Broyard, Anatole **68**
Broyard, Bliss **68**
Bruce, Blanche Kelso **33**
Bruce, Bruce **56**
Bruce, Isaac **26**
Brunson, Dorothy **1, 87**
Bryan, Ashley **41, 104**
Bryant, Cullen **81**
Bryant, Dez **116**
Bryant, Howard **130**
Bryant, Jamal **128**
Bryant, John **26**
Bryant, John R. **45**
Bryant, Kimberly **127**
Bryant, Kobe **15, 31, 71, 110**
Bryant, Paul **115**
Bryant, Ray **95**
Bryant, Wayne R. **6**
Bryant, William Benson **61**
Buchanan, Ray **32**
Buckley, Gail Lumet **39**
Buckley, Victoria **24**
Buckner, Milt **110**
Buckwheat Zydeco **132**
Budden, Joe **108**
Buery, Richard, Jr. **97**
Bullard, Eugene **12**
Bullard, Robert D. **121**
Bullins, Ed **25, 121**
Bullock, Steve **22**
Bully-Cummings, Ella **48**

Bumbry, Grace **5**
Bun B **123**
Bunch, Lonnie G., III **91**
Bunche, Ralph J. **5**
Bunkley, Anita Richmond **39**
Burbridge, Kofi **120**
Burbridge, Oteil **120**
Buress, Hannibal **101**
Burgess, John **46**
Burgess, Marjorie L. **55**
Burke, Clarence, Jr. **112**
Burke, Glenn **122**
Burke, Selma **16**
Burke, Solomon **31, 86, 129**
Burke, Yvonne Brathwaite **42**
Burkett, Ben **123**
Burks, Juanita P. **95**
Burks, Mary Fair **40**
Burleigh, Henry Thacker **56**
Burley, Dan **96**
Burnett, Charles **16, 68**
Burnim, Mickey L. **48**
Burns, Anthony **102**
Burns, Eddie **44**
Burns, Ursula **60**
Burnside, R. L. **56**
Burrell, Tom **21, 51**
Burris, Chuck **21**
Burris, Roland W. **25, 75**
Burroughs, Margaret Taylor **9, 134**
Burroughs, Nannie Helen **96**
Burrows, Stephen **31**
Burrus, William Henry "Bill" **45**
Burt-Murray, Angela **59**
Burton, Bill **96**
Burton, LeVar **8**
Burton, Tony **135**
Burwell, Bryan **83**
Busby, Jheryl **3, 74**
Bush, Charles Vernon **125**
Bush, Gordon **82**
Bush, Reggie **59, 88**
Butler, George, Jr. **70**
Butler, Henry **121**
Butler, Jerry **26**
Butler, Jimmy **135**
Butler, Leroy, III **17**
Butler, Louis **70**
Butler, Octavia **8, 43, 58**
Butler, Paul D. **17**
Butler, Selena Sloan **98**
Butts, Calvin O., III **9, 90**
Butts, Cassandra **78, 136**
Byas, Don **133**
Bynoe, Peter C. B. **40**
Bynum, Juanita **31, 71**
Byrd, Donald **10**
Byrd, Donald **109**
Byrd, Eugene **64**
Byrd, Marlon **112**
Byrd, Michelle **19**
Byrd, Robert **11**
Cabell, Enos **102**
Cables, George **125**
Cadillacs **107**
Cadoria, Sherian Grace **14**
Caesar, Adolph **133**
Caesar, Shirley **19**
Cage, Byron **53**
Cain, Herman **15, 92**
Cain, Lorenzo **128**
Calabrese, Karyn **89**
Caldwell, Benjamin **46**

Caldwell, Earl 60
Caldwell, Jim 81
Caldwell, Kirbyjon 55
Calhoun, Lillian Scott 87
Callender, Clive O. 3
Callender, Eugene 119
Callier, Terry 106
Calloway, Blanche 100
Calloway, Cab 14
Cameo 120
Cameron, James 80
Camp, Kimberly 19
Campanella, Roy 25
Campbell, Bebe Moore 6, 24, 59
Campbell, Bill 9, 76
Campbell, Dick 129
Campbell, Donald J.66
Campbell, E. Simms 13
Campbell, Earl 104
Campbell, Lucie E. 118
Campbell, Mary Schmidt 43
Campbell, Milt 113
Campbell, Roy, Jr. 118
Campbell-Martin, Tisha 8, 42
Cam'ron 104
Canada, Geoffrey 23
Canady, Alexa 28
Canedy, Dana 132
Cannon, Katie 10
Cannon, Nick 47, 73, 132
Cannon, Park 134
Cannon, Patrick 120
Cannon, Reuben 50
Cannon, Toronzo 135
Cara, Irene 77
Carney, William H. 104
Carr, James 117
Carr, Johnnie 69
Carr, Keela 74
Cardozo, Francis L. 33
Carew, Rod 20
Carey, Mariah 32, 53, 69
Cargill, Victoria A. 43
Carlos, John 97
Carmichael, Jerrod 124
Carolina Chocolate Drops 111
Carr, Kurt 56
Carr, Leroy 49
Carrington, Terri Lyne 132
Carroll, Diahann 9
Carroll, L. Natalie 44
Carroll, Rocky 74
Carroll, Vinnette 29, 136
Carruthers, George R. 40
Carson, André 69
Carson, Ben 1, 35, 76, 128
Carson, Candy 133
Carson, Johnnie 85
Carson, Julia 23, 69
Carson, Lisa Nicole 21
Carter, Anson 24
Carter, Benny 46
Carter, Betty 19
Carter, Butch 27
Carter, Cris 21, 109
Carter, Edward A., Jr. 104
Carter, Herbert E. 108
Carter, Jill P. 110
Carter, Joe 30
Carter, Joye Maureen 41
Carter, Kenneth 53
Carter, Majora 77
Carter, Mandy 11

Carter, Nell 39
Carter, Pamela Lynn 67
Carter, Regina 23, 131
Carter, Robert L. 51, 100
Carter, Ron 104
Carter, Rubin 26, 121
Carter, Stephen L. 4
Carter, Troy 98
Carter, Vince 26
Carter, Warrick L. 27
Cartey, Wilfred 47
Cartiér, Xam Wilson 41
Carver, George Washington 4
Cary, Lorene 3
Cary, Mary Ann Shadd 30
Casey, Dwane 135
Cash, Rosalind 28
Cash, Swin 59
Cashin, Sheryll 63
CasSelle, Malcolm 11
Castor, Jimmy 100
Catchings, Tamika 43
Cathey, Reg E. 122
Catlett, Elizabeth 2, 120
Catlett, Sid 133
Catlin, Mamie 131
Catto, Octavius V. 83
Cayton, Horace 26
Cedric the Entertainer 29, 60, 115
Celestin, Josaphat 101
Cenac, Wyatt 94
Chadiha, Jeffri 57
Chalmers, Mario 122
Chamberlain, Wilt 18, 47
Chambers, Ernie 130
Chambers, Julius 3
Chambers, Paul 121
Chambers Brothers, The 116
Chamillionaire 82
Chancellor, Kam 131
Chancler, Ndugu 115
Chandler, Gene 105
Chandler, Tyson 114
Chaney, Don 98
Chaney, John 67
Chantels, The 128
Chanticleer, Raven 91
Chapman, Nathan A., Jr. 21
Chapman, Susan E. 94
Chapman, Tracy 26
Chappell, Emma 18
Chappell, Roy M. 95
Chappelle, Dave 50, 115
Charles, Ezzard 95
Charles, Ray 16, 48
Charleston, Oscar 39
Chase, Debra Martin 49, 96
Chase, John Saunders, Jr. 99
Chase, Leah 57
Chase-Riboud, Barbara 20, 46
Chatard, Peter 44
Chavis, Benjamin 6
Che, Michael 123
Cheadle, Don 19, 52
Checker, Chubby 28
Cheeks, Julius 135
Cheeks, Maurice 47, 106
Chenault, John 40
Chenault, Kenneth 4, 36, 108
Chenier, C. J. 134
Chenier, Clifton 134
Cherry, Deron 40
Cherry, Don 119

Chesnutt, Charles 29
Chestnut, J. L., Jr. 73
Chestnut, Morris 31, 116
Chew, Robert F. 109
Chic 117
Chideya, Farai 14, 61
Chief Keef 112
Chiffons, The 129
Childers, Lulu Vere 95
Childress, Alice 15
Childress, Alvin 114
Chiles, Nick 98
Chineworth, Mary Alice 79
Chinn, May Edward 26
Chisholm, Daquan 93
Chisholm, Samuel 32
Chisholm, Shirley 2, 50
Christensen, Donna M. 17, 132
Christian, Barbara T. 44
Christian, Charlie 136
Christian, Jodie 103
Christian, Spencer 15
Christie, Angella 36
Christie, Ron 83
Chuck D 9
Church, Robert Reed, Sr. 132
Churchwell, Robert, Sr. 76
Ciara 56, 115
Ciara, Barbara 69
Clack, Zoanne 73
Claiborne, Loretta 34
Clarence 13X 126
Clark, Carl 101
Clark, Celeste 15
Clark, Joe 1
Clark, Kenneth B. 5, 52
Clark, Mamie Phipps 79
Clark, Mattie Moss 61
Clark, Patrick 14
Clark, Ray 122
Clark, Septima 7
Clark, Sharón 105
Clark, Sonny 128
Clark, Wahida 107
Clark, Yvonne Young 95
Clark-Cole, Dorinda 66
Clarke, Anna Mac 95
Clarke, Cheryl 32
Clarke, Hope 14
Clarke, John Henrik 20
Clarke, Kenny 27
Clarke, Stanley 115
Clarke, Yvette 92
Clark-Sheard, Karen 22, 114
Clash, Kevin 14, 93
Clay, Bryan 57, 74
Clay, Otis 112, 133
Clay, William Lacy 8
Clay, William Lacy, Jr. 95
Clayton, Constance 1
Clayton, Doctor 120
Clayton, Eva M. 20
Clayton, Gerald 111
Clayton, Mayme Agnew 62
Clayton, Merry 112
Clayton, Xernona 3, 45
Claytor, Helen 14, 52
Cleage, Pearl 17, 64
Cleaver, Eldridge 5
Cleaver, Emanuel 4, 45, 68, 107
Cleaver, Kathleen 29
Clemente, Rosa 74
Clement-Holmes, Linda 94

Clements, George 2
Clemmons, Reginal G. 41
Clemons, Clarence 41
Clemons, Michael "Pinball" 64
Clendenon, Donn 26, 56
Cleveland, James 19
Cliff, Michelle 42
Clifton, Lucille 14, 64, 91
Clifton, Nathaniel "Sweetwater" 47
Clinton, George 9, 93
Clovers, The 104
Clyburn, James E. 21, 71, 118
Clyburn, Mignon 78
C-Murder 99
Coachman, Alice 18, 123
Coasters, The 102
Coates, Dorothy Love 125
Coates, Ta-Nehisi 76, 131
Cobb, Arnett 114
Cobb, Jewel Plummer 42
Cobb, Jimmy 119
Cobb, W. Montague 39
Cobb, William Jelani 59, 121
Cobbs, Bill 101
Cobbs, Price M. 9
Cobbs, Tasha 114
Cobham, Billy 123
Cochran, Johnnie 11, 39, 52
Cockrel, Kenneth V., Jr. 79
Cockrel, Kenneth Vern, Sr. 79
CoCo Brother 93
Cody, Radmilla 99
Cohen, Anthony 15
Cohen, Cathy J. 88
Colbert, Tom 115
Colbert, Virgis William 17
Cole, Cozy 123
Cole, Freddy 128
Cole, J. 97
Cole, Johnnetta B. 5, 43
Cole, Keyshia 63, 107
Cole, Lorraine 48
Cole, Maria 104
Cole, Nat "King" 17
Cole, Natalie 17, 60, 84, 133
Cole, Rebecca 38
Cole, Teju 120
Coleman, Beatrice 120
Coleman, Bessie 9
Coleman, Chad L. 128
Coleman, Donald 24, 62
Coleman, Gary 35, 86
Coleman, George 106
Coleman, James E., Jr. 79
Coleman, Ken 2
Coleman, Leonard S., Jr. 12
Coleman, Mary 46
Coleman, Michael B. 28, 79
Coleman, Denardo 122
Coleman, Ornette 39, 69, 129
Coleman, Ronald S. 110
Coleman, Steve 124
Coleman, Vince 128
Coleman, Wanda 48, 119
Coleman, William F., III 61
Coleman, William T. 76
Colemon, Johnnie 11
Coles, Alice 80
Coles, Honi 128
Colescott, Robert 69
Collette, Buddy 119
Collins, Albert 12
Collins, Barbara-Rose 7, 87

Collins, Bootsy 31
Collins, Cardiss 10, 80, 120
Collins, Janet 33, 64
Collins, Jason 111
Collins, Lyn 53
Collins, Marva 3, 71
Collins, Patricia Hill 67
Collins, Paul 61
Colston, Hal 72
Colter, Cyrus J. 36
Coltrane, Alice 70
Coltrane, John 19
Coltrane, Ravi 71
Combs, Sean 17, 43, 92
Comer, James P. 6
Common 31, 63, 98
Compton-Rock, Malaak 86
Cone, James H. 3, 82
Coney, PonJola 48
Conley, Arthur 129
Connerly, Ward 14
Conrad, Barbara Smith 90
Conrad, Cecilia A. 94
Consolers, The 125
Contee, Cheryl 88
Contours, The 109
Conyers, John, Jr. 4, 45, 111
Conyers, Monica 85
Conyers, Nathan G. 24
Coogler, Ryan 114
Cook, Charles "Doc" 44
Cook, Junior 126
Cook, (Will) Mercer 40
Cook, Samuel DuBois 14
Cook, Suzan D. Johnson 22
Cook, Toni 23
Cook, Will Marion 40
Cooke, Marcia 60
Cooke, Marvel 31
Cooke, Sam 17
Cook-Parrish, Mary Virginia 95
Coolio 103
Cooper, Andrew W. 36
Cooper, Andy "Lefty" 63
Cooper, Anna Julia 20
Cooper, Barry 33
Cooper, Charles "Chuck" 47
Cooper, Chuck 75
Cooper, Edward S. 6
Cooper, Evern 40
Cooper, Helene 74
Cooper, J. California 12, 85, 125
Cooper, Jerome 129
Cooper, Lisa 73
Cooper, Margaret J. 46
Cooper, Mario 129
Cooper, Michael 31
Cooper, Tarzan 96
Cooper Cafritz, Peggy 43
Cooper-Dyke, Cynthia 17, 89
Copeland, Johnny 110
Copeland, Michael 47
Copeland, Misty 125
Copeland, Shemekia 110
Coppola, Imani Francesca 82
Corbi, Lana 42
Corbin, Tyrone 126
Corinealdi, Emayatzy 133
Corley, Tony 62
Cornelius, Don 4, 100
Cornish, Sam 50
Cornwell, Edward E., III 70
Correia, De'Jaun 93

Cortez, Jayne 43, 109
Corthron, Kia 43
Cortor, Eldzier 42
Cosby, Bill 7, 26, 59, 125
Cosby, Camille 14, 80
Cose, Ellis 5, 50, 118
Cosey, Pete 103
Cotter, Joseph Seamon, Sr. 40
Cotton, James 123
Cottrell, Comer 11
Counce, Curtis 127
Council, LaVerne 94
Counter, S. Allen 74
Cousin, Ertharin 115
Cousins, DeMarcus 108
Covay, Don 127
Cowans, Adger W. 20
Cowboy Troy 54
Cox, Bryan 83
Cox, Donald Lee 93
Cox, Elbert Frank 111
Cox, Ida 42
Cox, Joseph Mason Andrew 51
Cox, Laverne 122
Cox, Renée 67
Cox, William E. 68
Craig, Carl 31, 71
Craig-Jones, Ellen Walker 44
Crawford, Carl 90
Crawford, Hank 77
Crawford, Randy 19
Crawford, Terence 135
Cray, Robert 30, 132
Creagh, Milton 27
Crennel, Romeo 54, 107
Crenshaw, Kimberlé Williams 88
Crew, Rudy 16, 113
Crew, Spencer R. 55
Crews, Terry 123
Crichlow, Ernest 75
Crisp, Coco 109
Criss, Sonny 128
Crite, Allan Rohan 29
Croal, N'Gai 76
Crocker, Frankie 29
Crockett, George W., Jr. 10, 64
Cromartie, Antonio 115
Croom, Sylvester 50
Cross, Dolores E. 23
Crosthwait, David 93
Crothers, Scatman 19
Crouch, Andraé 27, 115, 126
Crouch, Hubert 95
Crouch, Stanley 11, 87
Crowder, Henry 16
Crowdy, William Saunders 109
Crown Heights Affair 132
Crudup, Arthur 115
Crum, George 101
Crump, Steven 96
Crumpler, Rebecca Lee 89
Crusaders, The 116
Cruse, Harold 54
Crutchfield, James N. 55
Cruz, Victor 107
Cuffe, Paul 98
Cullen, Countee 8
Cullers, Vincent T. 49
Culp, Curley 110
Culpepper, Daunte 32, 85
Cummings, Elijah E. 24, 102
Cuney, William Waring 44
Cunningham, Evelyn 23, 85

Cunningham, Randall 23
Curren$y 114
Currie, Betty 21
Currie, Ulysses 73
Curry, Dell 126
Curry, George E. 23
Curry, Mark 17
Curry, Michael 85
Curry, Stephen 110
Curson, Ted 108
Curtis, Christopher Paul 26, 113
Curtis-Hall, Vondie 17
Curvin, Robert 132
Da Don, Polow 86
Dabiri, John 93
DaCosta, YaYa 98
Daemyon, Jerald 64
Dailey, Ulysses Grant 87
Dale, Clamma 103
Daly, Marie Maynard 37, 134
Dameron, Tadd 103
Dandridge, Dorothy 3
Dandridge, Ray 36
Dandridge, Raymond Garfield 45
D'Angelo 27, 123
Daniels, Billy 124
Daniels, Lee 36, 76
Daniels, Mel 106
Daniels-Carter, Valerie 23
Danner, Margaret Esse 49
Danquah, Meri Nana Ama 93
Danticat, Edwidge 15, 68, 128
Dantley, Adrian 72
Dara, Olu 35
Darden, Calvin 38
Darden, Christopher 13
Dash, Damon 31, 113
Dash, Darien 29
Dash, Julie 4, 132
Dash, Leon 47
Datcher, Michael 60
Davenport, Cow Cow 115
David, Keith 27
Davidson, Jaye 5
Davidson, Tommy 21
Davis, Allison 12
Davis, Altovise 76
Davis, Angela 5, 114
Davis, Angela J. 88
Davis, Anthony 11
Davis, Anthony 120
Davis, Arthur Paul 41
Davis, Artur 41
Davis, Belva 61
Davis, Ben 115
Davis, Benjamin O., Jr. 2, 43
Davis, Benjamin O., Sr. 4
Davis, Bing 84
Davis, Carl 105
Davis, Charles T. 48
Davis, Chuck 33
Davis, Danny K. 24, 79
Davis, Doris A. 100
Davis, Ed 24
Davis, Eisa 68
Davis, Eric 116
Davis, Ernie 48
Davis, Erroll B., Jr. 57
Davis, Frank Marshall 47
Davis, Gary 41
Davis, George 36
Davis, Gordon J. 76
Davis, Guy 36

Davis, James E. 50
Davis, Mia Amber 94
Davis, Mike 41
Davis, Miles 4
Davis, Milt 74
Davis, Nolan 45
Davis, Ossie 5, 50
Davis, Phil 132
Davis, Piper 19
Davis, Rajai 135
Davis, Ruth 37
Davis, Shani 58, 84
Davis, Terrell 20
Davis, Thomas 132
Davis, Thornetta 131
Davis, Thulani 61
Davis, Tyrone 54
Davis, Vernon 133
Davis, Viola 34, 76, 100, 131
Davis, Wade, Jr. 103
Davis, Walter, Jr. 134
Davis, Wild Bill 114
Davis Sisters, The 119
Dawes, Dominique 11, 126
Dawes, Kwame 126
Dawkins, Darryl 131
Dawkins, Jimmy 111
Dawkins, Wayne 20
Dawn, Marpessa 75
Dawson, Andre 85
Dawson, Matel "Mat," Jr. 39
Dawson, Michael C. 63
Dawson, Rosario 72
Dawson, William L. 130
Dawson, William Levi 39
Day, Andra 132
Day, Leon 39
Days, Drew S., III 10
Dazz Band 116
De' Alexander, Quinton 57
De La Soul 119
de Lavallade, Carmen 78
de Passe, Suzanne 25
De Priest, Oscar Stanton 80
De Shields, André 72
De Veaux, Alexis 44
Dean, Fred 98
Dean, Mark E. 35
Dean, Phillip Hayes 122
Deas, Gerald 85
DeBaptiste, George 32
DeBarge, El 89
DeBerry, Lois M. 115
DeCarava, Roy 42, 81
Deconge-Watson, Lovenia 55
Dedeaux, Richard 119
Dee, Merri 55
Dee, Ruby 8, 50, 68, 122
Deep River Boys 131
Deezer D 53
DeFrantz, Anita 37
Deggans, Eric 71
DeJongh, John, Jr. 85
DeLaine, Joseph A. 110
Delaney, Beauford 19
Delaney, Joe 76
Delaney, Joseph 30
Delany, Bessie 12
Delany, Martin R. 27
Delany, Sadie 12
Delany, Samuel R., Jr. 9
Delco, Wilhelmina 33
DeLille, Henriette 30

Dells, The 109
Dellums, Ronald 2, 81
DeLoach, Nora 30
Delpit, Lisa 101
Delsarte, Louis 34
Delta Rhythm Boys 133
Demby, William 51
Dennard, Brazeal 37
Dennis, Gary C. 91
Dent, Richard 97
Dent, Thomas C. 50
DePreist, James 37, 109
DePrince, Michaela 104
DeRozan, DeMar 125
Derulo, Jason 93, 132
DeSanto, Sugar Pie 122
Detroit Emeralds, The 121
DeVard, Jerri 61
DeVaughn, Raheem 91
Devers, Gail 7, 87
Devine, Loretta 24
DeVore-Mitchell, Ophelia 120
Dewitty, Thelma 114
Dial, Thornton 114
Diamond, Lydia R. 101
Dickens, Helen Octavia 14, 64
Dickenson, Vic 38
Dickerson, Debra J. 60
Dickerson, Eric 27, 108
Dickerson, Ernest R. 6, 17
Dickey, Eric Jerome 21, 56
Diddley, Bo 39, 72
Diehl, Aaron 132
Diesel, Vin 29
Diggs, Charles C. 21
Diggs, Taye 25, 63
Diggs-Taylor, Anna 20
Dillard, Godfrey J. 45
Dillard, Ricky 134
Dillon, Leo 103
Dinkins, David 4
Divine, Father 7
Dixie Cups, The 109
Dixon, Bill 87
Dixon, Brandon Victor 134
Dixon, Dean 68
Dixon, Ivan 69
Dixon, Julian C. 24
Dixon, Margaret A. 14, 136
Dixon, Sharon Pratt 1
Dixon, Sheila 68
Dixon, Willie 4
DJ Clue? 111
DJ Jazzy Jeff 32
DJ Lance Rock 94
DJ Rashad 121
DJ Screw 110
DMX 28, 64
Dobbs, John Wesley 89
Dobbs, Mattiwilda 34
Dobson, Tamara 111
Doby, Lawrence Eugene, Sr. 16, 41
Dodson, Howard, Jr. 7, 52
Dodson, Owen Vincent 38
Dogan, Matthew Winifred 91
Doggett, Bill 124
Dokes, Michael 105
Doley, Harold, Jr. 26
Dollar, Creflo 106
Domingo, Colman 94
Domino, Fats 20
Donald, Arnold 36, 126
Donaldson, Jeff 46

Donegan, Dorothy 19
Dorham, Kenny 113
Dorn, Michael 112
Dorrell, Karl 52
Dorsey, Lee 65
Dorsey, Thomas Andrew 15
Dorsey, Thomas J. 90
Dortch, Thomas W., Jr. 45
Dougherty, Mary Pearl 47
Douglas, Aaron 7
Douglas, Bob 96
Douglas, Buster 127
Douglas, Derek 88
Douglas, Donya 97
Douglas, Emory 89
Douglass, Frederick 87
Dourdan, Gary 37
Dove, Rita 6, 78, 101
Dove, Ulysses 5
Downing, George T. 91
Downing, Will 19
Dr. Dre 10, 14, 30, 116
Drake, Hamid 121
Drake, Michael V. 122
Dramatics, The 106
Draper, Sharon Mills 16, 43
Drew, Alvin, Jr. 67
Drew, Charles Richard 7
Drew, Kenny 123
Drexler, Clyde 4, 61
Drifters, The 121
Driskell, David C. 7
Driver, David E. 11
Driver, Donald 99
Drummond, Andre 132
Drummond, William J. 40
Du Bois, David Graham 45, 135
Du Bois, W. E. B. 3
du Cille, Michel 74
DuBois, Joshua 88
DuBois, Shirley Graham 21
Ducksworth, Marilyn 12
Dudley, Edward R. 58
Dudley, Sherman H. 117
Due, Patricia Stephens 100
Due, Tananarive 30
Duerson, Dave 93
Duggins, George 64
Duke, Bill 3, 96
Duke, George 21, 113
Dukes, Hazel Nell 56
Dumars, Joe 16, 65, 126
Dumas, Henry 41
Dumpson, James R. 108
Dunbar, Paul Laurence 8
Dunbar-Nelson, Alice Ruth Moore 44
Duncan, Michael Clarke 26, 104
Duncan, Tim 20, 91
Duncan, Todd 76
Duncanson, Robert S. 127
Dungey, Channing 134
Dungey, Merrin 62
Dungy, Camille 86
Dungy, Tony 17, 42, 59, 118
Dunham, Katherine 4, 59
Dunlap, Ericka 55
Dunn, Jerry 27
Dunn, Warrick 90
Dunner, Leslie B. 45
Dunnigan, Alice Allison 41
Dunston, Georgia Mae 48
Duplechan, Larry 55

DuPree, Johnny 96
Dupri, Jermaine 13, 46
Durant, Kevin 76, 107
Durham, Bobby 73
Durham, James 90
Duthiers, Vladimir 109
Dutton, Charles S. 4, 22
DuVernay, Ava 98, 126
Dworkin, Aaron P. 52
Dwight, Edward 65
Dye, Jermaine 58
Dyett, Walter 113
Dyson, Michael Eric 11, 40, 128
E-40 125
Eagleson, William Lewis 90
Early, Gerald 15
Early, Norman S., Jr. 124
Earthquake 55
Easley, Annie J. 61
Easton, Hosea 91
Ebanks, Michelle 60
Eberhardt, Jennifer 124
Eckstine, Billy 28
Edelin, Ramona Hoage 19
Edelman, Marian Wright 5, 42
Edison, Harry 114
Edley, Christopher 2, 48
Edley, Christopher F., Jr. 48
Edmonds, Terry 17
Edmonds, Tracey 16, 64
Edmunds, Gladys 48
Edwards, David 122
Edwards, Donna 77
Edwards, Esther Gordy 43
Edwards, Harry 2
Edwards, Herman 51
Edwards, Lena Frances 76
Edwards, Melvin 22
Edwards, Teddy 123
Edwards, Teresa 14, 95
Edwards, Willarda V. 59
Edwards, Willis 104
El Wilson, Barbara 35
Elder, Larry 25, 120
Elder, Lee 6
Elder, Lonne, III 38
Elders, Joycelyn 6
Eldridge, Roy 37
Elie, Lolis Eric 97
Elise, Kimberly 32, 101
Ellerbe, Brian 22
Ellington, Duke 5
Ellington, E. David 11
Ellington, Mercedes 34
Ellington, Mercer 129
Elliott, Missy 31, 90
Elliott, Sean 26
Ellis, Aunjanue 108
Ellis, Charles H., III 79
Ellis, Clarence A. 38
Ellis, Dock 78
Ellis, Dorothy 131
Ellis, Jennifer 135
Ellis, Jimmy 44, 127
Ellis, Larry R. 110
Ellis, Nelsan 105
Ellis, Thomas Sayers 129
Ellis, Trey 97
Ellis-Lamkins, Phaedra 88
Ellison, Keith 59
Ellison, Ralph 7
Elmore, Ronn 21
Elzy, Ruby 119

Emanuel, James A. 46
Emeagwali, Dale 31
Emotions, The 125
En Vogue 100
Ephriam, Mablean 29
Epperson, Sharon 54
Epps, Archie C., III 45
Epps, Mike 60
Epps, Omar 23, 59
Ericsson-Jackson, Aprille 28
Ervin, Anthony 66
Ervin, Booker 106
Ervin, Clark Kent 82
Erving, Julius 18, 47
Escobar, Damien 56
Escobar, Tourie 56
Esposito, Giancarlo 9
Espy, Mike 6
Estes, Rufus 29
Estes, Simon 28
Estes, Sleepy John 33
Eubanks, Kevin 15, 108
Eugene-Richard, Margie 63
Europe, James Reese 10
Evans, Darryl 22
Evans, Etu 55
Evans, Faith 22
Evans, Harry 25
Evans, Mari 26
Evans, Melvin H. 88
Evans, Warren C. 76
Eve 29
Everett, Carl 103
Everett, Francine 23
Everett, Percival 93
Evers, Medgar 3
Evers, Myrlie 8
Ewing, Patrick 17, 73, 130
Fabio, Sarah Webster 48
Fabolous 93
Fabre, Shelton 71
Fagan, Garth 18, 98
Fair, Ronald L. 47
Fairbanks, Mabel 117
Faison, Donald 50
Faison, Frankie 55
Faison, George 16
Falana, Lola 42
Falconer, Etta Zuber 59
Falcons, The 128
Fales-Hill, Susan 88
Fargas, Antonio 50
Farley, Christopher John 54
Farley, James Conway 99
Farmer, Art 38
Farmer, Forest J. 1
Farmer, James 2, 64
Farmer, Ray 133
Farmer-Paellmann, Deadria 43
Farr, Mel 24
Farrakhan, Louis 2, 15
Farrell, Herman D., Jr. 81
Farris, Isaac Newton, Jr. 63
Fattah, Chaka 11, 70, 112, 130
Faulk, Marshall 35, 96
Faulkner, Harris 131
Fauntroy, Walter E. 11
Fauset, Crystal Dreda Bird 100
Fauset, Jessie 7
Favors, Malachi 136
Favors, Steve 23
Fax, Elton 48
Feelings, Muriel 44

Feelings, Tom 11, 47
Felix, Allyson 48, 98
Felix, Larry R. 64
Felix Da Housecat 110
Feemster, Herbert 72
Fennoy, Ilene 72
Fenty, Adrian 60, 88
Ferbos, Lionel 95
Ferguson, Roger W., Jr. 25, 112
Ferguson, Ronald F. 75
Ferguson, Vernice D. 108
Ferrell, Rachelle 29
Fetchit, Stepin 32
Fetty Wap 130
Fiasco, Lupe 64
Fielder, Cecil 2, 112
Fielder, Prince Semien 68
Fields, C. Virginia 25
Fields, Cleo 13
Fields, Evelyn J. 27
Fields, Felicia P. 60
Fields, Julia 45
Fields, Kim 36
50 Cent 46, 83
Files, Lolita 35
Fils-Aimé, Reggie 74
Fine, Sam 60
Finley, Ron 110
Finner-Williams, Paris Michele 62
Fishbone 101
Fishburne, Laurence 4, 22, 70
Fisher, Ada Lois Sipuel 76
Fisher, Ada M. 76
Fisher, Antwone 40
Fisher, Derek 97
Fisher, Gail 85
Fisher, Miles Mark 91
Fisk Jubilee Singers 112
Fitzgerald, Ella 1, 18
Fitzgerald, Larry 133
Five Keys, The 104
Flack, Roberta 19
Flake, Floyd H. 18, 110
Flamingos, The 108
Flanagan, Tommy 69
Flavor Flav 67
Fleming, Erik R. 75
Fleming, Raymond 48
Fletcher, Arthur A. 63
Fletcher, Benjamin 90
Fletcher, Bill, Jr. 41
Fletcher, Buddy 16, 108
Fletcher, Geoffrey 85
Flo Rida 78
Flood, Curt 10, 93
Flowers, Sylester 50
Flowers, Vonetta 35
Floyd, Eddie 127
Floyd, Elson S. 41
Flying Lotus 124
Forbes, Calvin 46
Forbes, James A., Jr. 71
Ford, Barney 90
Ford, Cheryl 45
Ford, Clyde W. 40
Ford, Harold E(ugene) 42
Ford, Harold E(ugene), Jr. 16, 70
Ford, Jack 39
Ford, Johnny 70
Ford, Nick Aaron 44
Ford, T-Model 91, 113
Ford, Wallace 58
Forman, James 7, 51

Forman, James, Jr. 89
Forrest, Leon 44
Forrest, Vernon 40, 79
Forté, John 74
Forte, Linda Diane 54
Fortune, James 92
Foster, Andrew 79
Foster, Arian 114
Foster, Ezola 28
Foster, Frank 97
Foster, George "Pops" 40
Foster, Henry W., Jr. 26
Foster, Jylla Moore 45
Foster, Marie 48
Foster, William P. 88
Fowler, Reggie 51
Fox, Donal 114
Fox, John R. 105
Fox, Vivica A. 15, 53
Foxx, Anthony 81, 123
Foxx, Jamie 15, 48
Foxx, Kim 134
Foxx, Redd 2
Foye, K'wan 97
Francis, Norman (C.) 60
Francis, Thais 93
Francis-McBarnette, Yvette Fay 135
Francois, Terry A. 106
Franklin, Aretha 11, 44, 115
Franklin, C. L. 68
Franklin, Hardy R. 9, 87
Franklin, J. E. 44
Franklin, John Hope 5, 77
Franklin, Kirk 15, 49, 97
Franklin, Shirley 34, 80
Franti, Michael 93
Fraser, Sarah Loguen 100
Frazer, Jendayi 68
Frazer, Victor O. 98
Frazier, E. Franklin 10
Frazier, Joe 19, 98
Frazier, Kenneth 97
Frazier, Kevin 58
Frazier, LaToya Ruby 131
Frazier, Oscar 58
Frazier, Ryan 89
Frazier, Walt 91
Frazier-Lyde, Jacqui 31
Freelon, Nnenna 32
Freeman, Aaron 52
Freeman, Al, Jr. 11, 105
Freeman, Charles 19
Freeman, Harold P. 23
Freeman, Leonard 27
Freeman, Marianna 23
Freeman, Morgan 2, 20, 62, 100
Freeman, Paul 39
Freeman, Von 104
Freeman, Yvette 27
Freestyle Fellowship 122
French, Albert 18
French, D. M. 94
Fresh, Doug E. 93
Friday, Jeff 24
Fryer, Roland G. 56
Fudge, Ann (Marie) 11, 55
Fudge, Marcia L. 76
Fuentes, Tito 123
Fulani, Lenora 11
Fuller, A. Oveta 43
Fuller, Arthur 27
Fuller, Blind Boy 86
Fuller, Charles 8

Fuller, Curtis 115
Fuller, Howard L. 37
Fuller, Hoyt 44
Fuller, Meta Vaux Warrick 27
Fuller, S. B. 13
Fuller, Solomon Carter, Jr. 15
Fuller, Thomas O. 90
Fuller, Vivian 33
Fulson, Lowell 118
Funches, Ron 121
Funderburg, I. Owen 38
Funnye, Capers C., Jr. 73
Fuqua, Antoine 35
Fuqua, Harvey 90
Futch, Eddie 33
Future 109
Gaines, Brenda 41
Gaines, Clarence E., Sr. 55
Gaines, Ernest J. 7
Gaines, Grady 38
Gaines, Lloyd 79
Gaines, Matthew 95
Gaines, Patrice 106
Gaiter, Dorothy J. 80
Gaither, Alonzo Smith (Jake) 14
Gaither, Israel L. 65
Gamble, Kenny 85
Gamble, Oscar 113
Gans, Joe 91
Gant, Richard 105
Gantt, Harvey 1
Gap Band, The 100
Gardere, Jeffrey 76
Gardner, Chris 65
Gardner, Edward G. 45
Garland, Red 115
Garner, Erroll 76
Garner, Tyron 99
Garnet, Henry Highland 100
Garnett, Kevin 14, 70, 118
Garrett, James F. 78
Garrett, Joyce Finley 59
Garrison, Jimmy 133
Garrison, Zina 2, 133
Garvin, Gerry 78
Gary, Willie E. 12, 117
Gaskins, Eric 64
Gaskins, Rudy 74
Gaspard, Patrick 84
Gaston, Arthur George 3, 38, 59
Gaston, Cito 71
Gaston, Marilyn Hughes 60
Gates, Henry Louis, Jr. 3, 38, 67
Gates, Sylvester James, Jr. 15, 130
Gates, Theaster 118
Gates, William 97
Gatlin, Justin 123
Gay, Roxane 136
Gay, Tyson 114
Gaye, Anna Gordy 121
Gaye, Marvin 2
Gaye, Nona 56
Gayle, Addison, Jr. 41
Gayle, Helene D. 3, 46
Gaynor, Gloria 36
Gentry, Alvin 23
George, Eddie 80
George, Nelson 12, 101
George, Paul 124
George, Zelma Watson 42
Gervin, George 80
Geto Boys 115
Ghostface Killah 90

Gibbons, Gary 107
Gibbs, Freddie 125
Gibbs, Marla 86
Gibbs, Mifflin W. 99
Gibson, Althea 8, 43
Gibson, Bob 33
Gibson, Donald Bernard 40
Gibson, John Trusty 87
Gibson, Johnnie Mae 23
Gibson, Josh 22
Gibson, Kenneth Allen 6
Gibson, Ted 66
Gibson, Truman K., Jr. 60
Gibson, Tyrese 27, 62, 134
Gibson, William F. 6
Giddings, Paula 11
Gidron, Richard D. 68
Gilbert, Christopher 50
Gilbert, John Wesley 91
Giles, Roscoe C. 93
Gill, Gerald 69
Gill, Johnny 51
Gill, Turner 83
Gilles, Ralph 61
Gillespie, Dizzy 1
Gilliam, Frank 23
Gilliam, Jim 122
Gilliam, Joe 31
Gilliam, Sam 16
Gilliard, Steve 69
Gillum, Andrew 128
Gilmore, Artis 101
Gilmore, Marshall 46
Gilpin, Charles Sidney 81
Ginuwine 35
Giovanni, Nikki 9, 39, 85
Gist, Carole 1
Gittens, Charles L. 124
Givens, Adele 62
Givens, Robin 4, 25, 58
Givhan, Robin Deneen 72
Glanville, Douglas Metunwa 82
Glasper, Robert 101
Glass, Ron 111
Glenn, Tyree 129
Gloster, Hugh Morris, Sr. 90
Glover, Anwan 123
Glover, Cedric B. 103
Glover, Corey 34
Glover, Danny 1, 24, 103
Glover, Donald 85
Glover, Keith 79
Glover, Nathaniel, Jr. 12
Glover, Savion 14
Goapele 55
Goggins, Juanita 127
Goines, Donald 19
Goings, Russell 59
Goldberg, Whoopi 4, 33, 69
Golden, Marita 19, 99
Golden, Thelma 10, 55
Golden Gate Quartet 104
Golding, Meta 135
Goldsberry, Ronald 18
Golson, Benny 37
Golston, Allan C. 55
Gomes, Peter J. 15, 93
Gomez, Jewelle 30
Gomez-Preston, Cheryl 9
Gomillion, Charles 90
Gonzales, Babs 134
Good, Meagan 117
Goode, Mal 13

Goode, W. Wilson 4
Gooden, Dwight 20
Gooden, Linda 94
Gooding, Cuba, Jr. 16, 62
Goodlett, Carlton B. 91
Goodman, Al 87
Goodman, Kim C. 94
Goodnight, Paul 32
Gorden, W. C. 71
Gordon, Bruce S. 41, 53, 82
Gordon, Carl 87
Gordon, Dee 130
Gordon, Dexter 25
Gordon, Ed 10, 53
Gordon, Josh 120
Gordon, Tom 130
Gordone, Charles 15
Gordon-Reed, Annette 74
Gordy, Berry, Jr. 1
Gore, Frank 117
Goss, Carol A. 55
Goss, Tom 23
Gossett, Louis, Jr. 7
Gotti, Irv 39
Gourdin, Edward O. 93
Gourdine, Meredith 33
Gourdine, Simon 11
Grace, George H. 48
Graham, Katerina 99
Graham, Lawrence Otis 12
Graham, Lorenz 48
Graham, Stedman 13
Graham, Trevor 84
Graham Central Station 123
Granderson, Curtis 66
Granderson, LZ 103
Granger, Lester B. 75
Grant, Augustus O. 71
Grant, Bernie 57
Grant, Frank 100
Grant, Gwendolyn Goldsby 28
Grant, Micki 125
Granville, Evelyn Boyd 36
Gravely, Samuel L., Jr. 5, 49
Graves, Butch 77
Graves, Denyce Antoinette 19, 57
Graves, Earl G. 1, 35
Graves, Milford 126
Gray, Ahuvah 130
Gray, Darius 69
Gray, Dobie 99
Gray, F. Gary 14, 49
Gray, Farrah 59
Gray, Fred 37
Gray, Ida 41
Gray, Macy 29
Gray, Vincent C. 88
Gray, Wardell 128
Gray, William H., III 3
Gray, Willie 46
Gray, Yeshimbra "Shimmy" 55
Greaves, R. B. 106
Greaves, William 38, 123
Greely, M. Gasby 27
Green, A. C. 32
Green, Al 13, 47, 74
Green, Al 118
Green, Bennie 131
Green, Cee Lo 70, 103
Green, Darrell 39, 74
Green, Dennis 5, 45
Green, Draymond 126
Green, Grant 56

Green, Hadiyah-Nicole 133
Green, Isaac H. 79
Green, Jonathan 54
Green, Nancy 112
Greene, Frank S., Jr. 101
Greene, Jimmy 74
Greene, Joe 10
Greene, Maurice 27, 77
Greene, Petey 65
Greene, Richard Thaddeus, Sr. 67
Greene, Travis 134
Greenfield, Elizabeth Taylor 116
Greenfield, Eloise 9
Greenhouse, Bunnatine "Bunny" 57
Greenlee, Sam 48
Greenwood, L. C. 115
Greenwood, Monique 38
Greer, Hal 92
Greer, Sonny 127
Gregory, Ann 63
Gregory, Dick 1, 54
Gregory, Frederick 8, 51
Gregory, Wilton 37
Grier, Bobby 95
Grier, David Alan 28
Grier, Eliza Ann 90
Grier, Mike 43
Grier, Pam 9, 31, 86
Grier, Roosevelt 13
Griffey, Dick 89
Griffey, Ken, Jr. 12, 73
Griffin, Anthony 71
Griffin, Bessie 135
Griffin, Bessie Blount 43, 135
Griffin, Blake 98
Griffin, Johnny 71
Griffin, LaShell 51
Griffin, Robert, III 107
Griffith, Emile 113
Griffith, Mark Winston 8
Griffith, Yolanda 25
Griffith-Joyner, Florence 28
Grillo, Evelio 95
Grimes, Henry 124
Grimké, Archibald H. 9
Griner, Brittney 128
Grist, Reri 84
Groff, Peter 96
Grooms, Henry R(andall) 50
Gryce, Gigi 124
Guillaume, Robert 3, 48
Guinier, Lani 7, 30
Guitar Slim 125
Gumbel, Bryant 14, 80
Gumbel, Greg 8
Gunn, Moses 10
Gurira, Danai 73
Guru 84
Guy, George "Buddy" 31
Guy, Jasmine 2
Guy, Rosa 5
Guyot, Lawrence 108
Guyse, Sheila 122
Guy-Sheftall, Beverly 13, 92
Guyton, Tyree 9, 94
Gwynn, Tony 18, 83, 122
Gyasi, Yaa 136
Haddon, Dietrick 55
Hageman, Hans 36
Hageman, Ivan 36
Hagler, Marvelous Marvin 102
Hailey, JoJo 22
Hailey, K-Ci 22

Hairston, Jester 88
Hairston, Sam 88
Hale, Clara 16
Hale, Lorraine 8
Haley, Alex 4
Haley, Charles 134
Haley, George 21, 129
Hall, Aaron 57
Hall, Adelaide 126
Hall, Alvin D. 86
Hall, Arsenio 58
Hall, Arthur 39
Hall, Elliott S. 24
Hall, Juanita 62
Hall, Katori 132
Hall, Kevan 61
Hall, Lloyd A. 8
Hall, Regina 135
Hall, Tamron 96
Halliburton, Warren J. 49
Ham, Cynthia Parker 58
Hamblin, Ken 10
Hamburg, Beatrix 84
Hamburg, Margaret 78
Hamer, Fannie Lou 6
Hamilton, Anthony 61
Hamilton, Bernie 117
Hamilton, Chico 117
Hamilton, Darryl 130
Hamilton, Lawrence 122
Hamilton, Leonard 100
Hamilton, Lisa Gay 71
Hamilton, Samuel C. 47
Hamilton, Vicki 95
Hamilton, Virginia 10
Hamlin, Larry Leon 49, 62
Hammon, Jupiter 124
Hammond, Fred 23
Hammond, Paula 119
Hammonds, Evelynn 69
Hammons, David 69
Hampton, Fred 18
Hampton, Henry 6
Hampton, Lionel 17, 41
Hancock, Herbie 20, 67
Hancock, Michael B. 123
Handy, John 131
Handy, W. C. 8
Haney, Lee 77
Hannah, Marc 10
Hansberry, Lorraine 6
Hansberry, Tony, II 93
Hansberry, William Leo 11
Hansen, Austin 88
Hardaway, Anfernee 13, 111
Hardaway, Tim 35
Harden, James 116
Harden, Monique 97
Hardin Armstrong, Lil 39
Harding, Vincent 67, 130
Hardison, Bethann 12
Hardison, Kadeem 22
Hardwick, Omari 122
Hardy, Greg 118
Hare, Nathan 44
Harewood, Dorian 104
Harkless, Necia Desiree 19
Harmon, Clarence 26
Harold, Erika 54
Harold Melvin & the Blue Notes 105
Harp, Toni 123
Harper, Ben 34, 62

Harper, Frances Ellen Watkins 11
Harper, Hill 32, 65, 97
Harper, Michael S. 34, 136
Harper, Rachel M. 92
Harrell, Andre 9, 30
Harrington, Oliver W. 9, 136
Harris, Alice 7
Harris, Barbara 12
Harris, Barry 68
Harris, Bernard A. 90
Harris, Bill 72
Harris, Carla A. 67
Harris, Corey 39, 73
Harris, Damon 110
Harris, E. Lynn 12, 33, 116
Harris, Eddy L. 18
Harris, Franco 97
Harris, Gary L. 87
Harris, James 79
Harris, Jay T. 19
Harris, Jessica B. 91
Harris, Kamala D. 64, 122
Harris, Kevin 120
Harris, Leslie 6
Harris, Lyle Ashton 83
Harris, Major 110
Harris, Marcelite Jordon 16
Harris, Mary Styles 31
Harris, Maya Lakshmi 88
Harris, Monica 18
Harris, Patricia Roberts 2
Harris, Rennie 120
Harris, Richard E. 61
Harris, Robin 7
Harris, Sylvia 70
Harris, Thurston 129
Harris, Wesley L. 92
Harris, Wood 114
Harris, Wynonie 102
Harris-Lacewell, Melissa 81
Harrison, Alvin 28
Harrison, Calvin 28
Harrison, Charles 72
Harrison, Marvin 134
Harris-Stewart, Lusia 90
Harry, Jackée 111
Harsh, Vivian Gordon 14
Hart, Alvin Youngblood 61, 132
Hart, Billy 126
Hart, Jim Ray 136
Hart, Kevin 103
Hart, Thomas A., Sr. 113
Hartman, Johnny 109
Harvard, Beverly 11
Harvey, Steve 18, 58
Harvey, William R. 42
Harvin, Percy 123
Haskins, Clem 23
Haskins, James 36, 54
Hassell, Leroy Rountree, Sr. 41, 116
Hastie, William H. 8
Hastings, Alcee 16, 119
Hatcher, Andrew T. 90
Hatcher, Richard G. 55
Hatchett, Glenda 32
Hathaway, Donny 18
Hathaway, Isaac Scott 33
Hathaway, Lalah 57, 88
Havens, Richie 111
Hawes, Hampton 121
Hawkins, Augustus F. 68
Hawkins, Coleman 9

Hawkins, Connie **91**
Hawkins, Edwin **113**
Hawkins, Erskine **14**
Hawkins, La-Van **17, 54**
Hawkins, Screamin' Jay **30**
Hawkins, Steven **14**
Hawkins, Tramaine **16**
Hawkins, Walter **87**
Hayden, Carla D. **47**
Hayden, Lewis **105**
Hayden, Palmer **13**
Hayden, Robert **12**
Hayes, Bob **77**
Hayes, Cecil N. **46**
Hayes, Dennis **54**
Hayes, Elvin **93**
Hayes, Isaac **20, 58, 73**
Hayes, James C. **10**
Hayes, Roland **4**
Hayes, Teddy **40**
Hayes, Terrance **124**
Haygood, Wil **83**
Haynes, Elizabeth Ross **102**
Haynes, George Edmund **8**
Haynes, Marques **22**
Haynes, Roy **87**
Haynes, Trudy **44**
Haynie, Sharon **94**
Haysbert, Dennis **42, 106**
Haysbert, Raymond V., Sr. **87**
Haywood, Gar Anthony **43**
Haywood, Jimmy **58**
Haywood, Margaret A. **24**
Haywood, Spencer **99**
Hazel, Darryl B. **50**
Hazzard, Walt **98**
Healy, James Augustine **30**
Healy, Michael **90**
Heard, Gar **25**
Heard, Nathan C. **45**
Hearns, Thomas **29**
Heath, Percy **100**
Heavy D **58, 98**
Hector, Jamie **98**
Hedgeman, Anna Arnold **22**
Hegamin, Lucille **120**
Height, Dorothy I. **2, 23, 78**
Hemingway, Anthony **107**
Hemphill, Essex **10**
Hemphill, Jessie Mae **33, 59**
Hemsley, Sherman **19, 104**
Henderson, Angelo **122**
Henderson, Cornelius Langston **26**
Henderson, David **53**
Henderson, Fletcher **32**
Henderson, George Washington **101**
Henderson, Gordon **5**
Henderson, Henry Fairfax, Jr. **89**
Henderson, Jeff **72**
Henderson, Joe **127**
Henderson, Rickey **28, 78**
Henderson, Stephen E. **45**
Henderson, Thelton E. **68**
Henderson, Wade J. **14**
Henderson, Zelma **71**
Hendrix, Jimi **10**
Hendryx, Nona **56**
Hendy, Francis **47**
Henries, A. Doris Banks **44**
Henry, Aaron **19**
Henry, Clarence "Frogman" **46**
Henry, Dwight **104**

Henry, Joshua **94**
Henry, Mark **116**
Henry, Troy **85**
Henson, Darrin **33**
Henson, Josiah **90**
Henson, Matthew **2**
Henson, Taraji P. **58, 77, 127**
Herbert, Bob **63, 96**
Hercules, Frank **44**
Herenton, Willie W. **24, 81**
Herman, Alexis M. **15**
Hernandez, Aileen Clarke **13**
Herndon, Alonzo Franklin **89**
Herndon, Angelo **90**
Hernton, Calvin C. **51**
Herzfeld, Will L. **132**
Heyward, Craig **131**
Hickman, Fred **11**
Hicks-Hudson, Paula **136**
Higginbotham, A. Leon, Jr. **13, 25**
Higginbotham, Jay C. **37**
Higginbotham, Joan **124**
Higginsen, Vy **65**
Hightower, Dennis F. **13**
Highway QC's, The **136**
Hill, Andrew **66**
Hill, Anita **5, 65**
Hill, Bonnie Guiton **20**
Hill, Calvin **19**
Hill, Candace **130**
Hill, Donna **32**
Hill, Dulé **29, 129**
Hill, Errol **40, 135**
Hill, Gil **135**
Hill, Grant **13, 94**
Hill, Hugh Morgan **83**
Hill, Janet **19**
Hill, Jemele **109**
Hill, Jesse, Jr. **13**
Hill, Lauryn **20, 53, 111**
Hill, Leslie Pinckney **44**
Hill, Marc Lamont **80, 128**
Hill, Michael **95**
Hill, Oliver W. **24, 63**
Hill, Peter **92**
Hill, Wyllstyne D. **94**
Hillard, Terry **25**
Hillary, Barbara **65**
Hilliard, Asa Grant, III **66**
Hilliard, David **7, 105**
Hilliard, Earl F. **24**
Hilliard, Wendy **53**
Hilson, Keri **84**
Himes, Chester **8**
Hinderas, Natalie **5**
Hine, Darlene Clark **24**
Hines, Earl "Fatha" **39**
Hines, Garrett **35**
Hines, Gregory **1, 42**
Hinton, Milt **30**
Hinton, William Augustus **8**
Hoagland, Everett H. **45**
Hobson, Julius W. **44**
Hobson, Mellody **40**
Hodge, Aldis **124**
Hodge, Derrick **114**
Hodges, Johnny **129**
Hogan, Beverly Wade **50**
Holden, Kip **120**
Holder, Eric, Jr. **9, 76, 104**
Holder, Geoffrey **78, 124**
Holder, Laurence **34**
Holdsclaw, Chamique **24, 110**

Holiday, Billie **1**
Holiday, Jrue **115**
Holland, Endesha Ida Mae **3, 57**
Holland, Kimberly N. **62**
Holland, Robert, Jr. **11**
Holland-Dozier-Holland **36**
Hollins, Lionel **133**
Holloway, Brenda **65**
Holloway, Loleatta **115**
Hollowell, Donald L. **57**
Holmes, Amy **69**
Holmes, Clint **57**
Holmes, Hamilton E. **82**
Holmes, Larry **20, 68**
Holmes, Santonio **87**
Holmes, Shannon **70**
Holmes, T. J. **98**
Holsey, Lucius Henry **92**
Holstein, Casper **89**
Holt, Lester **66**
Holt, Nora **38**
Holt Baker, Arlene **73**
Holton, Hugh, Jr. **39**
Holyfield, Evander **6**
Homesick James **124**
Honeywood, Varnette P. **54, 88**
Honoré, Russel L. **64**
Hood, James Walker **91**
Hooker, John Lee **30**
hooks, bell **5, 90**
Hooks, Benjamin L. **2, 85**
Hooks, Robert **76**
Hope, Elmo **135**
Hope, John **8**
Hope, Lugenia Burns **89**
Hopkins, Bernard **35, 69, 105**
Hopkins, Donald R. **89**
Hopkins, Lightnin' **83**
Horn, Shirley **32, 56**
Horne, Frank **44**
Horne, Lena **5, 86**
Horsford, Steven **88**
Horton, Andre **33**
Horton, Big Walter **115**
Horton, George Moses **124**
Horton, Gladys **92**
Horton, James Oliver **58**
Horton, Suki **33**
Horton, Willie **104**
Hoskins, Harold K. **103**
Houghton, Israel **92**
House, Son **8**
Houston, Charles Hamilton **4**
Houston, Cissy **20, 83**
Houston, Whitney **7, 28, 83, 100**
Howard, Ayanna **65**
Howard, Desmond **16, 58**
Howard, Dwight **113**
Howard, Elston **125**
Howard, Juwan **15**
Howard, M. William, Jr. **26**
Howard, Michelle **28, 125**
Howard, Perry Wilbon, Jr. **112**
Howard, Ryan **65, 113**
Howard, Sherri **36**
Howard, Terrence **59, 94**
Howell, Ayinde **91**
Howlin' Wolf **9**
Howroyd, Janice Bryant **42**
Hoyte, Lenon **50**
Hrabowski, Freeman A., III **22**
Hubbard, Arnette Rhinehart **38**
Hubbard, Freddie **75**

Hudlin, Reginald **9, 86**
Hudlin, Warrington **9**
Hudson, Cheryl **15**
Hudson, Ernie **72, 131**
Hudson, Jennifer **63, 83**
Hudson, Lou **121**
Hudson, Wade **15**
Huff, Leon **86**
Huggins, Edie **71**
Huggins, Larry **21**
Huggins, Nathan Irvin **52**
Hughes, Albert **7**
Hughes, Allen **7**
Hughes, Cathy **27**
Hughes, Dora **88**
Hughes, Ebony **57**
Hughes, Langston **4**
Hughley, D. L. **23, 76**
Hull, Akasha Gloria **45**
Humes, Helen **128**
Humphrey, Bobbi **20**
Humphrey, Claude **119**
Humphries, Frederick **20**
Hunt, Darnell **92**
Hunt, Richard **6**
Hunter, Alberta **42**
Hunter, Billy **22, 109**
Hunter, Clementine **45**
Hunter, Ivory Joe **106**
Hunter, Lindsey **110**
Hunter, Torii **43, 109**
Hunter-Gault, Charlayne **6, 31**
Hurd, Sam **116**
Hurst, Michelle **135**
Hurston, Zora Neale **3**
Hurt, Byron **61**
Hurt, Mississippi John **84**
Hurtt, Harold **46**
Hutch, Willie **62**
Hutcherson, Bobby **115**
Hutcherson, Hilda Yvonne **54**
Hutchinson, Earl Ofari **24**
Hutson, Jean Blackwell **16, 135**
Hutto, J. B. **129**
Hyde, Cowan F. "Bubba" **47**
Hyman, Earle **25, 79**
Hyman, Phyllis **19**
Ibrahim, Fuad **109**
Ice Cube **8, 30, 60**
Iceberg Slim **11**
Ice-T **6, 31, 96**
Ifill, Gwen **28**
Iglehart, James Monroe **129**
Iguodala, Andre **129**
Iman, Chanel **66**
Imani Winds **113**
Imes, Elmer Samuel **39**
Impressions, The **135**
India.Arie **34**
Ingram, James **84**
Ingram, Rex **5**
Ink Spots, The **102**
Innis, Niger **135**
Innis, Roy **5**
Intruders, The **119**
Irvin, Michael **64**
Irvin, Monte **31, 134**
Irvin, Vernon **65**
Irving, Barrington, Jr. **112**
Irving, Kyrie **102**
Irving, Larry, Jr. **12**
Irvis, K. Leroy **67**
Isaacs, Cheryl Boone **113**

Isaacs, John 76
Isley, Marvin 87
Isley, Ronald 25, 56
Iverson, Allen 24, 4, 129
Iverson, Johnathan Lee 22, 100
Ivey, Phil 72, 106
Iweala, Uzodinma 131
J Dilla 102
Ja Rule 35, 91
Jackson, Alexine Clement 22
Jackson, Alphonso R. 48
Jackson, Angela 134
Jackson, Bobby 119
Jackson, Brenda 87
Jackson, Bull Moose 130
Jackson, Christopher 136
Jackson, Deborah 94
Jackson, DeSean 120
Jackson, Earl 31
Jackson, Edison O. 67
Jackson, Eric 127
Jackson, Frank G. 76
Jackson, Fred James 25
Jackson, George 14
Jackson, George 19
Jackson, Hal 41, 104
Jackson, Hue 133
Jackson, Isaiah 3
Jackson, Jamea 64
Jackson, James A. 90
Jackson, Janet 6, 30, 68
Jackson, Jermaine 79
Jackson, Jesse 1, 27, 72
Jackson, Jesse, Jr. 14, 45, 81, 108
Jackson, Jimmie Lee 126
Jackson, Joe 78
Jackson, John 36
Jackson, Judith D. 57
Jackson, LaToya 95
Jackson, Lisa 77
Jackson, Mae 57
Jackson, Mahalia 5
Jackson, Mannie 14
Jackson, Mark 121
Jackson, Mary 73
Jackson, Maynard 2, 41
Jackson, Michael 19, 53, 76
Jackson, Millie 25
Jackson, Milt 26
Jackson, Phillip 115
Jackson, Rampage 83
Jackson, Randy 40
Jackson, Reggie 15
Jackson, Rickey 88
Jackson, Samuel L. 8, 19, 63, 102
Jackson, Sandi 108
Jackson, Sheneska 18
Jackson, Shirley Ann 12
Jackson, Stephen 118
Jackson, Tito 81
Jackson, Tom 70
Jackson, Vera 40
Jackson 5 103
Jackson Lee, Sheila 20
Jacob, John E. 2
Jacobs, George 118
Jacobs, Harriet 104
Jacobs, Regina 38
Jacquet, Illinois 49
Jagged Edge 117
Jaheim 58
Jakes, T. D. 17, 43, 116
Jamal, Ahmad 69

Jamerson, James 59
James, Charles H., III 62
James, Daniel, Jr. 16
James, Donna A. 51
James, Elmore 114
James, Etta 13, 52, 100
James, G. Larry 74
James, Juanita 13
James, LeBron 46, 78, 105
James, Leela 117
James, Nikki M. 94
James, Rick 19
James, Sharpe 23, 69
James, Skip 38
James, Sly 107
James & Bobby Purify 131
James Bracken and Vivian Bracken
    107
Jamison, Judith 7, 67, 96
Jarman, Joseph 136
Jarreau, Al 21, 65, 105
Jarrett, Valerie 73
Jarrett, Vernon D. 42, 135
Jarvis, Charlene Drew 21
Jarvis, Erich 67
Jarvis, Kristen 85
Jasper, John J. 91
Jasper, Kenji 39
Jay Electronica 125
Jay-Z 27, 69, 103
Jealous, Benjamin Todd 70, 113
Jean-Baptiste, Kyle 131
Jefferson, Blind Lemon 81
Jefferson, Denise 87
Jefferson, Margo 108
Jefferson, Mildred Fay 89
Jefferson, Richard 136
Jefferson, William J. 25, 72
Jeffries, Hakeem 118
Jeffries, Herb 122
Jeffries, Leonard 8
Jemison, Mae C. 1, 35, 129
Jemison, Major L. 48
Jemison, T. J. 119
Jenifer, Franklyn G. 2
Jenkins, Beverly 14
Jenkins, Chad 132
Jenkins, Ella 15
Jenkins, Kris 98
Jenkins, Ray 77
Jennings, Lyfe 56, 69
Jennings, Thomas L. 125
Jerkins, Rodney 31
Jeter, Claude 75
Jeter, Derek 27, 93, 124
Jimmy Jam 13
Jive Five 131
Joe, Yolanda 21
John, Daymond 23, 114
Johns, Vernon 38
Johnson, Al 119
Johnson, Alaya Dawn 129
Johnson, Andre 127
Johnson, Angela 52
Johnson, Anthony M. 92
Johnson, Avery 62
Johnson, Beverly 2, 102
Johnson, Blind Willie 136
Johnson, Buddy 36
Johnson, Bumpy 102
Johnson, Calvin 108
Johnson, Chad 108
Johnson, Charles 1, 82

Johnson, Charles S. 12
Johnson, Chris 92
Johnson, Clark 96
Johnson, Clifford "Connie" 52
Johnson, Conrad O. 97
Johnson, Dennis 89
Johnson, Eddie Bernice 8, 90
Johnson, Edward Austin 107
Johnson, Eunice W. 83
Johnson, Fenton 91
Johnson, George E. 29
Johnson, Georgia Douglas 41
Johnson, Gus 92
Johnson, Gus 132
Johnson, Hall 90
Johnson, Hank, Jr. 80
Johnson, Harry E. 57
Johnson, Harvey, Jr. 24, 82
Johnson, Henry 129
Johnson, J. J. 37
Johnson, J. Rosamond 121
Johnson, Jack 8
Johnson, James P. 134
Johnson, James Weldon 5
Johnson, Je'Caryous 63
Johnson, Jeh 76, 125
Johnson, Jeh Vincent 44
Johnson, Joe 94
Johnson, John H. 3, 54
Johnson, John Henry 96
Johnson, Johnnie 56
Johnson, Judy 105
Johnson, Katherine (Coleman
    Goble) 61
Johnson, Kevin 70, 132
Johnson, Keyshawn 91
Johnson, Larry 28
Johnson, Le'Andria 108
Johnson, Leroy R. 89
Johnson, Levi 48
Johnson, Lonnie 85
Johnson, Lonnie G. 32, 93
Johnson, Magic 3, 39, 101
Johnson, Mamie "Peanut" 40
Johnson, Marques 133
Johnson, Mat 31, 105
Johnson, Michael 13
Johnson, Mordecai Wyatt 79
Johnson, Norma H. 17, 97
Johnson, R. M. 36
Johnson, Rafer 33
Johnson, Robert 2
Johnson, Robert L. 3, 39, 121
Johnson, Robert T. 17
Johnson, Rodney Van 28
Johnson, Sandra K. 94
Johnson, Sheila Crump 48
Johnson, Shoshana 47
Johnson, Sterling, Jr. 124
Johnson, Syl 97
Johnson, Syleena 98
Johnson, Tommy 106
Johnson, Virginia 9
Johnson, William 91
Johnson, William Henry 3
Johnson-George, Tamara 79
Johnson-Powell, Gloria 107
Joiner, Charlie 102
Jolley, Willie 28
Jones, Absalom 52
Jones, Adam 103
Jones, Adam 114
Jones, Alex 64

Jones, Andruw 98
Jones, Bill T. 1, 46, 80
Jones, Bobby 20, 94
Jones, Bomani 121
Jones, Booker T. 84
Jones, Carl 7
Jones, Caroline 29
Jones, Clara Stanton 51
Jones, Clarence B. 114
Jones, Cobi N'Gai 18
Jones, Cullen 73
Jones, Deacon 92, 112
Jones, Donell 29
Jones, Doris W. 62
Jones, Dwight C. 122
Jones, E. Edward, Sr. 45
Jones, Ed "Too Tall" 46
Jones, Edith Mae Irby 65
Jones, Edward P. 43, 67
Jones, Elaine R. 7, 45
Jones, Elvin 14, 68
Jones, Emil, Jr. 74
Jones, Etta 35
Jones, Eugene Kinckle 79
Jones, Frederick McKinley 68
Jones, Gayl 37
Jones, Genevieve 101
Jones, Hank 57, 86
Jones, Ingrid Saunders 18
Jones, Jacoby 117
Jones, James Earl 3, 49, 79
Jones, John 89
Jones, Jon 121
Jones, Jonah 39
Jones, Julio 131
Jones, K. C. 83
Jones, Leslie 136
Jones, Loïs Mailou 13, 136
Jones, Lou 64
Jones, Marion 21, 66
Jones, Merlakia 34
Jones, Orlando 30
Jones, Papa Jo 99
Jones, Paul R. 76
Jones, Philly Joe 121
Jones, Quincy 8, 30
Jones, Randy 35
Jones, Rashida 101
Jones, Robbie 113
Jones, Robert Elijah 90
Jones, Robert G. 81
Jones, Roy, Jr. 22, 134
Jones, Sam 85
Jones, Sarah 39
Jones, Sharon 86
Jones, Tayari 96
Jones, Thad 68
Jones, Theodore T., Jr. 108
Jones, Thomas W. 41
Jones, Van 70
Jones, Walter 119
Jones, Wayne 53
Jones, William A., Jr. 61
Jones-Drew, Maurice 113
Joplin, Scott 6
Jordan, Barbara 4, 78
Jordan, Charles 122
Jordan, Deloris 108
Jordan, Duke 133
Jordan, Eddie 82
Jordan, Eddie 83
Jordan, June 7, 35
Jordan, Louis 104

Jordan, Michael **6, 21**
Jordan, Michael B. **97**
Jordan, Montell **23**
Jordan, Vernon E. **3, 35**
Joseph, Jamal **101**
Joseph, Kathie-Ann **56**
Josey, E. J. **10**
Joyce, Dru **81**
Joyner, Marjorie Stewart **26**
Joyner, Matilda Sissieretta **15**
Joyner, Tom **19, 90**
Joyner-Kersee, Jackie **5**
Juicy J **116**
Julian, Hubert **90**
Julian, Percy Lavon **6**
July, William **27**
Just, Ernest Everett **3**
Justice, David **18**
Juvenile **96**
Kaigler, Denise **63**
Kaiser, Cecil **42**
Kandi **83**
Kani, Karl **10**
Karenga, Maulana **10, 71**
Karim, Benjamin **61**
Kaufman, Bob **105**
Kaufman, Monica **66**
Kay, Connie **114**
Kay, Ulysses **37**
KB **122**
Kearney, Beverly **109**
Kearney, Janis **54**
Kearse, Amalya Lyle **12**
Keb' Mo' **36, 124**
Keckley, Elizabeth **90**
Kee, John P. **43, 116**
Keene, John **73**
Keflezighi, Meb **49, 121**
Keith, Damon J. **16, 74**
Keith, Floyd A. **61**
Kelela **132**
Kelis **58, 122**
Kelley, Cliff **75**
Kelley, Elijah **65**
Kelley, Malcolm David **59**
Kellogg, Clark **64**
Kelly, Jim **113**
Kelly, Patrick **3**
Kelly, R. **18, 44, 71, 117**
Kelly, Robin **114**
Kelly, Wynton **121**
KEM **47, 127**
Kemp, Herb **94**
Kendrick, Erika **57**
Kendricks, Eddie **22**
Kennedy, Adrienne **11**
Kennedy, Cortez **104**
Kennedy, Florynce **12, 33**
Kennedy, Randall **40**
Kennedy-Overton, Jayne Harris **46**
Kenney, John A., Jr. **48**
Kenoly, Ron **45**
Kenyatta, Robin **54**
Kerry, Leon G. **46**
Key & Peele **107**
Keyes, Alan **11, 105**
Keys, Alicia **32, 68**
Khalifa, Wiz **96**
Khan, Chaka **12, 50**
Khanga, Yelena **6**
Kid Cudi **83**
Kidd, Jason **86**
Kidd, Mae Street **39**

Killens, John O. **54**
Killer Mike **117**
Killings, Debra **57**
Killingsworth, Cleve, Jr. **54**
Kilpatrick, Carolyn Cheeks **16**
Kilpatrick, Kwame **34, 71, 116**
Kimbro, Dennis **10**
Kimbro, Henry A. **25**
Kimbro, Warren **76**
Kincaid, Bernard **28**
Kincaid, Jamaica **4, 109**
King, Alonzo **38**
King, B. B. **7, 129**
King, Barbara **22**
King, Ben E. **128**
King, Bernice **4, 81**
King, Chris Thomas **120**
King, Colbert I. **69**
King, Coretta Scott **3, 57**
King, Dexter **10**
King, Don **14, 128**
King, Evelyn **129**
King, Freddie **92**
King, Gayle **19, 99**
King, Martin Luther, III **20**
King, Martin Luther, Jr. **1**
King, Martin Luther, Sr. **89**
King, Preston **28**
King, Reatha Clark **65**
King, Regina **22, 45**
King, Robert Arthur **58**
King, Robert Hillary **84**
King, Rodney **103**
King, Teresa **80**
King, Woodie, Jr. **27**
King, Yolanda **6**
King Curtis **92**
Kingston, Sean **94**
Kirby, George **14**
Kirk, Andy **134**
Kirk, Clara **95**
Kirk, Ron **11, 75, 111**
Kirkland, Eddie **99**
Kitt, Eartha **16, 75**
Kitt, Sandra **23**
Kittles, Rick **51**
Kitwana, Bakari **86**
Klugh, Earl **59**
Knight, Etheridge **37**
Knight, Gladys **16, 66**
Knight, Marie **80**
Knight, Suge **11, 30, 102**
Knowles, Mathew **96**
Knowles, Tina **61**
Knowling, Robert E., Jr. **38**
Knox, Simmie **49**
Knuckles, Frankie **42, 120**
Komunyakaa, Yusef **9**
Kong, B. Waine **50**
Kool Moe Dee **37**
Koontz, Elizabeth Duncan **101**
Kotto, Yaphet **7**
Kountz, Samuel L. **10**
Kravitz, Lenny **10, 34**
Krigger, Kevin **111**
KRS-One **34**
K-Swift **73**
Kunjufu, Jawanza **3, 50**
Kweli, Talib **93**
La Roca, Pete **107**
La Salle, Eriq **12**
LaBelle, Patti **13, 30**
LaChanze **93**

Lacks, Henrietta **101**
Lacy, Marc **111**
Lacy, Sam **30, 46**
Ladd, Ernie **64**
Ladner, Joyce A. **42**
Ladson-Billings, Gloria **130**
Lafontant, Jewel Stradford **3, 51**
Lakeside **120**
Lamar, Jake **96**
Lamar, Kendrick **105**
Lampkin, Daisy **19**
Lampley, Oni Faida **43, 71**
Lancaster, Byard **105**
Lance, Major **111**
Land, Harold **125**
Lane, Charles **3**
Lane, Dick **92**
Lane, Lunsford **93**
Lane, Vincent **5**
Lane, William Henry **90**
Laneuville, Eric **123**
Langford, Larry P. **74**
Langhart Cohen, Janet **19, 60**
Langston, John Mercer **101**
Lanier, Bob **47**
Lanier, Willie **33**
Lankford, Ray **23**
Larkin, Barry **24**
Larrieux, Amel **63**
Lars, Byron **32**
Larsen, Nella **10**
Laryea, Thomas Davies, III **67**
LaSalle, Denise **111**
Lashley, Bobby **63**
Lassiter, Roy **24**
Lateef, Yusef **91, 117**
Lathan, Sanaa **27**
Latiker, Diane **132**
Latimer, Lewis H. **4**
Lattany, Kristin Hunter **88**
Lattimore, Kenny **35, 128**
LaVette, Bettye **85**
Lavizzo-Mourey, Risa **48**
Law, W. W. **121**
Lawless, Theodore K. **8**
Lawrence, Brenda **127**
Lawrence, Donald **99**
Lawrence, Jacob **4, 28**
Lawrence, Margaret Morgan **100**
Lawrence, Martin **6, 27**
Lawrence, Robert H., Jr. **16**
Lawrence-Lightfoot, Sara **10**
Laws, Hubert **90**
Lawson, James M., Jr. **90**
Lawson, Jennifer **1, 50**
Laymon, Kiese **113**
Layton, William **87**
Le1f **120**
Lea, Babatunde **124**
Leadbelly **82**
Leakes, NeNe **107**
Leary, Kathryn D. **10**
Leavell, Dorothy R. **17**
Lecrae **108**
Ledisi **73**
Lee, Annie Frances **22**
Lee, Barbara **25, 102**
Lee, Bertram M., Sr. **46**
Lee, Canada **8**
Lee, Consuela **84**
Lee, Debra L. **62**
Lee, Eric P. **79**
Lee, Howard N. **136**

Lee, Jarena **100**
Lee, Joe A. **45**
Lee, Joie **1**
Lee, Julia **130**
Lee, Leslie **85, 122**
Lee, Malcolm D. **75**
Lee, Raphael C. **87**
Lee, Robert **112**
Lee, Spike **5, 19, 86**
Lee Andrews & the Hearts **134**
Lee-Smith, Hughie **5, 22**
Leevy, Carroll M. **42**
Leffall, Lasalle, Jr. **3, 64**
LeFlore, Lyah Beth **96**
Legend, John **67, 116**
Leggs, Kingsley **62**
LeGrand, Eric **118**
LeGrand, Naquasia **126**
Leland, Mickey **2**
Lemmons, Kasi **20**
Lemon, Alton T. **112**
Lemon, Don **94**
Lennox, Betty **31**
Lenoir, J. B. **117**
LeNoire, Rosetta **37**
Lenox, Adriane **59**
Leon, Kenny **10, 98**
Leonard, Buck **67**
Leonard, Kawhi **122**
Leonard, Sugar Ray **15**
Leslie, Lisa **16, 73**
Lester, Bill **42, 85**
Lester, Julius **9, 115**
Lesure, James **64**
LeTang, Henry **66**
Letson, Al **39**
Levert, Eddie **70**
Levert, Gerald **22, 59**
Lewis, Ananda **28**
Lewis, Aubrey **133**
Lewis, Aylwin B. **51, 88**
Lewis, Butch **71, 99**
Lewis, Byron E. **13**
Lewis, Carl **4, 97**
Lewis, David Levering **9**
Lewis, Delano **7**
Lewis, Edmonia **10**
Lewis, Edward T. **21**
Lewis, Emmanuel **36**
Lewis, George **104**
Lewis, George **130**
Lewis, Henry **38**
Lewis, Jamal **115**
Lewis, John **2, 46, 83**
Lewis, Marvin **51, 87**
Lewis, Norman **39**
Lewis, Oliver **56**
Lewis, Ramsey **35, 70**
Lewis, Ray **33, 109**
Lewis, Reginald F. **6**
Lewis, Samella **25**
Lewis, Shirley A. R. **14**
Lewis, Terry **13**
Lewis, Thomas **19**
Lewis, William Henry **89**
Lewis, William M., Jr. **40**
Lewis-Hall, Freda **105**
Lewis-Thornton, Rae **32**
Liggins, Alfred, III **43**
Lighty, Chris **105**
Ligon, Glenn **82**
Lil B **121**
Lil Jon **124**

Lil' Kim 28
Lil Mama 117
Lil Wayne 66, 84
Liles, Kevin 42, 99
Lillard, Damian 117
Lincoln, Abbey 3, 88
Lincoln, C. Eric 38
Lindsay, Peta 100
Lindsey, Tommie 51
Lipscomb, Mance 49
LisaRaye 27
Lister, Marquita 65
Lister, Tommy 127
Liston, Melba 118
Liston, Sonny 33
Little, Benilde 21
Little, Booker 105
Little, Cleavon 117
Little, Floyd 86
Little, Larry 90
Little, Robert L. 2
Little Anthony & the Imperials 107
Little Eva 128
Little Milton 36, 54
Little Richard 15
Little Walter 36
Littlepage, Craig 35
LL Cool J 16, 49, 94
Llewellyn, J. Bruce 13, 85
Lloyd 99
Lloyd, Earl 26, 127
Lloyd, John Henry "Pop" 30
Lloyd, Reginald 64
Locke, Alain 10
Locke, Attica 85
Locke, Eddie 44
Lockwood, Robert, Jr. 120
Lofton, James 42
Lofton, Kenny 12
Logan, Onnie Lee 14
Logan, Rayford W. 40
Loguen, J. W. 91
Lomax, Louis E. 90
Lomax, Michael L. 58
Long, Eddie L. 29, 89
Long, Huey 79
Long, Loretta 58
Long, Nia 17, 95
Long, Richard Alexander 65
Lopes, Davey 92
Lopes, Lisa "Left Eye" 36
Lord Infamous 117
Lord Jamar 126
Lorde, Audre 6
Lott, Ronnie 9
Loueke, Lionel 88
Louis, Errol T. 8
Louis, Joe 5
Louis, Willie 113
Loury, Glenn 36
Love, Darlene 23, 92
Love, Ed 58
Love, Laura 50
Love, Loni 113
Love, Mia 96, 125
Love, Nat 9
Love, Reggie 77
Lovell, Whitfield 74
Lover, Ed 10
Loving, Alvin, Jr. 35, 53
Loving, Mildred 69
Lowe, Herbert 57
Lowe, Rick 124

Lowe, Sidney 64
Lowery, Evelyn Gibson 115
Lowery, Joseph 2
Lowery, Myron 80
Lowry, A. Leon 60
Lowry, Kyle 135
Lucas, Bill 97
Lucas, John 7
Lucie, Lawrence 80
Lucien, Jon 66
Luckett, Letoya 61
Lucy, William 50
Lucy Foster, Autherine 35
Ludacris 37, 60
Lue, Tyronn 136
Luke, Derek 61
Lumbly, Carl 47
Lumet, Jenny 80
Lumumba, Chokwe 118
Luna, Donyale 88
Lunceford, Jimmie 134
Luper, Clara 94
Lutcher, Nellie 130
Luter, Fred, Jr. 103
Lyle, Ron 125
Lyles, Lester Lawrence 31
Lymon, Frankie 22
Lynch, Loretta E. 103
Lynch, Marshawn 124
Lynch, Shola 61
Lynch, William, Jr. 115
Lynn, Barbara 126
Lynne, Gloria 115
Lyons, Henry 12, 118
Lyons, James E., Sr. 102
Lyttle, Hulda Margaret 14
Mabley, Moms 15
Mabon, Willie 119
Mabrey, Vicki 26
Mabry, Marcus 70
Mac, Bernie 29, 61, 72
Mac Daddy 111
Mack, Iris 105
Mack, Tony 104
Mack Maine 125
Mackey, Biz 82
Mackey, Nathaniel 75
Mackie, Anthony 102
Madame Sul-Te-Wan 95
Madhubuti, Haki 7, 85
Madison, Joseph E. 17
Madison, Paula 37, 99
Madison, Romell 45
Madlib 88
Magic Sam 131
Magic Slim 110
Magruder, Nilah 134
Mahal, Taj 39
Mahorn, Rick 60
Maitreya, Sananda 85
Majette, Denise 41
Major, Clarence 9
Majors, Jeff 41
Malco, Romany 71
Mallett, Conrad, Jr. 16
Mallory, Mark 62
Mallory, William L., Sr. 119
Malone, Annie 13
Malone, Karl 18, 51, 90
Malone, Maurice 32
Malone, Moses 79, 131
Malone Jones, Vivian 59
Malveaux, Floyd 54

Malveaux, Julianne 32, 70
Malveaux, Suzanne 88
Mance, Junior 132
Mandisa 119
Mane, Gucci 91
Manhattans, The 123
Manigault, Earl "The Goat" 15
Manley, Audrey Forbes 16
Manley, Dexter 116
Mann, Bob 126
Mann, Tamela 92
Manning, Frankie 78
Manuel, Jerry 94
Marable, Manning 10, 102
March, William Carrington 56
Marcille, Eva 97
Marian Anderson String Quartet 111
Mariner, Jonathan 41
Marino, Eugene Antonio 30
Mario 71
Marion, Shawn 136
Markham, Pigmeat 106
Marks, John R., III 123
Marrow, Queen Esther 24
Marsalis, Branford 34, 103
Marsalis, Delfeayo 41
Marsalis, Ellis 90
Marsalis, Wynton 16, 90
Marsh, Henry, III 32
Marshall, Bella 22
Marshall, Brandon 116
Marshall, Kerry James 59
Marshall, Paule 7, 77
Marshall, Thurgood 1, 44
Marshall, William 107
Marte, Starling 117
Martin, Cuonzo 121
Martin, Curtis 104
Martin, Darnell 43, 78
Martin, Duane 108
Martin, Helen 31
Martin, Jesse L. 31
Martin, Jonathan 119
Martin, Louis E. 16
Martin, Michel 97
Martin, Roberta 58
Martin, Roland S. 49, 84
Martin, Ruby Grant 49
Martin, Sallie 120
Martin, Sara 38
Martin, Trayvon 105
Martin-Green, Sonequa 133
Marvelettes, The 126
Mase 24
Masekela, Sal 106
Mason, Anthony 128
Mason, Biddy 89
Mason, Charles Harrison 107
Mason, Derek 120
Mason, Desmond 127
Mason, Felicia 31
Mason, Herman, Jr. 83
Mason, Judi Ann 112
Mason, Ronald 27
Massaquoi, Hans J. 30, 130
Massenburg, Kedar 23, 110
Massey, Brandon 40
Massey, Walter E. 5, 45
Massie, Samuel Proctor, Jr. 29
Masta Ace 118
Master P 21, 115
Matejka, Adrian 87
Mathabane, Mark 5, 99

Mathis, Greg 26
Mathis, Johnny 20
Mathis, Robert 121
Matson, Ollie 93
Matthews, Ameena 105
Matthews, Benjamin 93
Matthews, Mark 59
Matthews Shatteen, Westina 51
Matzeliger, Jan 93
Maupin, John E., Jr. 92
Maxey, Randall 46
Maxis, Theresa 62
Maxwell 20, 81
May, Brother Joe 123
May, Derrick 41
May, Mark 117
Mayberry-Stewart, Melodie 94
Maye, Lee 111
Mayfield, Curtis 2, 43
Mayhew, Martin R. 76
Mayhew, Richard 39
Maynard, Nancy Hicks 73
Maynard, Robert C. 7
Maynor, Dorothy 19
Mayo, Whitman 32
Mays, Benjamin E. 7
Mays, Leslie A. 41
Mays, William G. 34
Mays, Willie 3
Mayweather, Floyd 57, 104
MC Breed 75
M.C. Hammer 20, 80
MC Lyte 34, 108
McAdoo, Bob 75
McAlpin, Harry 121
McAnulty, William E., Jr. 66
McBay, Henry C. 91
McBee, Cecil 123
McBride, Bryant 18
McBride, Chi 73
McBride, Christian 134
McBride, James 35, 87
McCabe, Jewell Jackson 10
McCain, Franklin 119
McCall, H. Carl 27
McCall, Nathan 8
McCann, Renetta 44
McCarthy, Sandy 64
McCarty, Oseola 16, 136
McCauley, Gina 76
McClellan, George Marion 91
McClendon, Forrest 94
McClendon, Lisa 61
McClendon, Lloyd 123
McClinton, Marion Isaac 77
McClurkin, Donnie 25
McCoo, Marilyn 53
McCovey, Willie 103
McCoy, Elijah 8
McCoy, LeSean 123
McCoy, Van 123
McCracklin, Jimmy 108
McCraney, Tarell Alvin 116
McCrary, Darius 111
McCrary Anthony, Crystal 70
McCray, Chirlane 134
McCray, Nikki 18
McCullough, DeAndre 106
McCullough, Geraldine 58, 79
McCutchen, Andrew 116
McDaniel, Hattie 5
McDaniel, Randall Cornell 81
McDaniels, Ralph 79

McDonald, Audra 20, 62, 128
McDonald, Charles J. 120
McDonald, Erroll 1
McDonald, Gabrielle Kirk 20
McDougall, Gay J. 11, 43
McDuff, Jack 116
McDuffie, Dwayne 62
McEwen, Mark 5
McFadden, Bernice L. 39
McFarlan, Tyron 60
McFarland, Roland 49
McFerrin, Bobby 68
McFerrin, Robert, Sr. 94
McGee, Charles 10
McGee, James D. 74
McGee, James Madison 46
McGee, Vonetta 95
McGhee, Heather C. 106
McGhee, Howard 122
McGhee, Sharon K. 113
McGill, Anthony 76
McGlowan, Angela 64, 86
McGrady, Tracy 80
McGriff, Fred 24
McGriff, Jimmy 72
McGruder, Aaron 28, 56, 120
McGruder, Robert 22, 35
McGuire, Raymond J. 57
McHenry, Donald F. 83
McIntyre, Kalaparusha Maurice 117
McJunkin, George 93
McKay, Claude 6
McKay, Nellie Yvonne 17, 57
McKee, Lonette 12, 119
McKenzie, Vashti M. 29
Mckesson, DeRay 133
McKinney, Cynthia 11, 52, 74
McKinney, Nina Mae 40
McKinney-Whetstone, Diane 27
McKinnon, Isaiah 9
McKissack, Leatrice 80
McKissick, Floyd B. 3
McKnight, Brian 18, 34
McLean, Jackie 78
McLendon, John B., Jr. 89
McLeod, Gus 27
McMillan, Rosalynn A. 36
McMillan, Terry 4, 17, 53
McMillan, Tracy 93
McMurray, Georgia L. 36
McNabb, Donovan 29, 119
McNair, Ronald 3, 58
McNair, Steve 22, 47, 79
McNeil, Lori 1
McPhail, Sharon 2, 119
McPherson, David 32
McPherson, James Alan 70
McQueen, Butterfly 6, 54
McRae, Carmen 77
McRae, Hal 84
McShann, Jay 110
McTell, Blind Willie 89
McVea, Jack 135
McWhorter, John 35, 119
McWorter, Free Frank 91
Meadows, Tim 30
Meek, Barbara 131
Meek, Carrie 6, 36
Meek, Kendrick 41, 89
Meeks, Gregory W. 25, 117
Meeks, James T. 92
Mehretu, Julie 85
Mell, Patricia 49

Melton, Frank 81
Melton, Harold D. 79
Meminger, Dean 114
Memphis Jug Band 130
Memphis Minnie 33
Memphis Slim 105
Menard, John Willis 90
Mengestu, Dinaw 66, 114
Mercado-Valdes, Frank 43
Meredith, James H. 11
Merkerson, S. Epatha 47, 83
Merriweather, Big Maceo 109
Metcalfe, Ralph 26
Method Man 81
Meyers, Michael 131
Mfume, Kweisi 6, 41
Michaux, Solomon Lightfoot 91
Micheaux, Oscar 7
Michele, Michael 31
Mickelbury, Penny 28
Mickens, Ronald Elbert 105
Middleton, Reggie 105
Midnight Star 110
Mighty Clouds of Joy 110
Migos 126
Miguel 98
Miles, Buddy 69
Miles, Tiya 116
Miles, William 112
Miley, Bubber 120
Millender-McDonald, Juanita 21, 61
Miller, Bebe 3
Miller, Cheryl 10, 74
Miller, Clyde 113
Miller, Dorie 29
Miller, Larry G. 72
Miller, Lorraine C. 119
Miller, Marcus 84
Miller, Omar Benson 93
Miller, Patina 94
Miller, Pepper 96
Miller, Reggie 33
Miller, Tangi 116
Miller, Warren F., Jr. 53
Miller, Wentworth 75
Miller-Travis, Vernice 64
Millinder, Lucky 101
Millines Dziko, Trish 28
Millner, Denene 76
Mills, Florence 22
Mills, Joseph C. 51
Mills, Sam 33
Mills, Stephanie 36
Mills, Steve 47
Mills Brothers, The 99
Milner, Ron 39
Milton, DeLisha 31
Minaj, Nicki 86, 124
Ming, Mel 106
Ming, William Robert, Jr. 125
Mingo, Frank 32
Mingus, Charles 15
Minkins, Shadrach 104
Minner, D. C. 133
Minoso, Minnie 89, 127
Minor, DeWayne 32
Mississippi Sheiks 122
Mitchell, Arthur 2, 47
Mitchell, Arthur Wergs 91
Mitchell, Blue 126
Mitchell, Brian Stokes 21
Mitchell, Clarence M., Jr. 88
Mitchell, Corinne 8

Mitchell, Dwike 111
Mitchell, Elvis 67
Mitchell, Freddie 116
Mitchell, Juanita Jackson 128
Mitchell, Kel 66, 131
Mitchell, Leona 42
Mitchell, Loften 31
Mitchell, Nicole 66
Mitchell, Parren J. 42, 66
Mitchell, Roscoe 134
Mitchell, Russ 21, 73
Mitchell, Sam 82
Mitchell, Shireen 89
Mitchell, Stephanie 36
Mitchell, Willie 114
Moffett, Charnett 127
Mohammed, Nazr 64
Mohammed, W. Deen 27
Mokae, Zakes 80
Monáe, Janelle 86
Monica 21
Mo'Nique 35, 84
Monk, Art 38, 73
Monk, Thelonious 1
Monroe, Bryan 71
Monroe, Earl 89
Monroe, Mary 35
Montgomery, Isaiah T. 91
Montgomery, Little Brother 117
Montgomery, Robbie 101
Montgomery, Tim 41
Montgomery, Wes 88
Moody, Anne 127
Moody, James 83
Moody-Adams, Michele 76
Moon, Warren 8, 66
Moondog, Jemeel 119
Mooney, Paul 37, 120
Moonglows, The 108
Moore, Archie 120
Moore, Barbara C. 49
Moore, Chanté 26, 130
Moore, Davey 105
Moore, Dorothy Rudd 46
Moore, Gwendolynne S. 55
Moore, Harry T. 29
Moore, Jessica Care 30
Moore, Johnny B. 38
Moore, Juanita 83, 124
Moore, Kermit 116
Moore, LeRoi 72
Moore, Maya 94
Moore, Melba 21
Moore, Minyon 45
Moore, Shemar 21, 112
Moore, Tim 124
Moore, Undine Smith 28
Moore, Wes 86
Moorer, Michael 19, 132
Moose, Charles 40
Moran, Jason 89
Moreland, Mantan 117
Morgan, Garrett 1
Morgan, Gertrude 63
Morgan, Irene 65
Morgan, Joe 9, 96
Morgan, Lee 102
Morgan, Rose 11
Morgan, Tracy 61, 102, 131
Morial, Ernest "Dutch" 26
Morial, Marc H. 20, 51
Morón, Alonzo G. 91
Morris, Garrett 31, 133

Morris, Greg 28
Morris, Lamorne 135
Morris, Melvin 120
Morris, Mercury 114
Morris, Raheem 77
Morrison, Sam 50
Morrison, Toni 2, 15, 86
Morrison, Vanessa 84
Morrow, E. Frederic 100
Morton, Azie Taylor 48
Morton, Ferdinand Q. 90
Morton, Frederick A., Jr. 93
Morton, Jelly Roll 29
Morton, Joe 18
Mosby, Marilyn 128
Moses, Edwin 8
Moses, Gilbert 12
Moses, Robert Parris 11
Mosley, Shane 32
Mosley, Walter 5, 25, 68
Moss, Carlton 17
Moss, J. 64
Moss, Otis, Jr. 72
Moss, Otis, III 72
Moss, Preacher 63
Moss, Randy 23, 90
Mossell, Gertrude Bustill 40
Mossell, Nathan Francis 91
Moten, Bennie 135
Moten, Etta 18
Motley, Archibald, Jr. 30
Motley, Constance Baker 10, 55
Motley, Marion 26
Moton, Robert Russa 83
Mourning, Alonzo 17, 44, 131
Moutoussamy-Ashe, Jeanne 7
Mowry, Jess 7
Mowry, Tamera 79
Mowry, Tia 78
Moye, Famoudou Don 136
Moyo, Karega Kofi 36
Moyo, Yvette Jackson 36
Muhammad, Ava 31
Muhammad, Elijah 4
Muhammad, Ibtihaj 133
Muhammad, Jabir Herbert 72
Muhammad, Khallid Abdul 10, 31
Mullen, Harryette 34
Mullen, Nicole C. 45
Muncie, Chuck 112
Murphy, Charles 95
Murphy, Eddie 4, 20, 61
Murphy, John H. 42
Murphy, Laura M. 43
Murphy, Matt 117
Murphy, Taylonn 131
Murray, Albert L. 33
Murray, Cecil 12, 47
Murray, Eddie 12
Murray, Lenda 10
Murray, Pauli 38
Murray, Tai 47
Murrell, Sylvia Marilyn 49
Muse, Clarence Edouard 21
Musiq 37, 84
Mya 35
Myers, Lou 110
Myers, Walter Dean 8, 70, 123
Myles, Kim 69
Myles, Raymond Anthony 121
Nabrit, Samuel Milton 47
Nagin, Ray 42, 57, 88
Nail, John E. 92

Nance, Cynthia 71
Nanula, Richard D. 20
Napoleon, Benny N. 23
Nas 33, 111
Nash, Diane 72
Nash, Joe 55
Nash, Johnny 40
Nash, Niecy 66, 115
Nash, Shannon King 84
Nate Dogg 92
Naughton, Naturi 97
Naughty by Nature 124
Navarro, Fats 104
Naylor, Gloria 10, 42
Ndegeocello, Meshell 15, 83
Neal, Elise 29
Neal, Kenny 123
Neal, Larry 38
Neal, Mark Anthony 74
Neal, Raful 44, 121
Neals, Otto 73
Nell, William C. 128
Nelly 32, 90
Nelson, Jill 6, 54
Nelson, Kadir 115
Nelson, Oliver 113
Nelson, Sophia A. 93
Nelson, Stanley 92
Nelson Meigs, Andrea 48
Neville, Aaron 21
Neville, Arthel 53
New Birth 124
New Edition 101
Newborn, Phineas, Jr. 127
Newcombe, Don 24
Newkirk, Pamela 69
Newman, David 76
Newman, Lester C. 51
Newsome, Ozzie 26, 117
Newton, Cam 96
Newton, Huey 2
Ne-Yo 65
Ngaujah, Sahr 86
Nicholas, Denise 82
Nicholas, Fayard 20, 57
Nicholas, Harold 20
Nichols, Nichelle 11
Nighthawk, Robert 121
Nissel, Angela 42
Nix, Robert N. C., Jr. 51
Nixon, Edgar Daniel 100
Nixon, Otis 111
N'Namdi, George R. 17
Noble, Gil 76
Noble, Ronald 46
Noble Drew Ali 100
Norful, Smokie 127
Norman, Christina 47
Norman, Jessye 5
Norman, Maidie 20
Norman, Pat 10
Norris, Michele 83
Northup, Solomon 115
Norton, Eleanor Holmes 7, 93
Norton, Ken 101, 115
Norton, Meredith 72
Notorious B.I.G. 20
Nottage, Lynn 66
Nugent, Richard Bruce 39
Nunez, Elizabeth 62, 112
Nunn, Annetta 43
Nutter, Michael 69, 112
Obadele, Imari 84

Obama, Barack 49, 74, 91
Obama, Michelle 61, 90
O'Brien, Soledad 88
Ocean, Frank 100
Odetta 37, 74
Odom, Lamar 81
Odom, Leslie, Jr. 136
Ogden, Jonathan 110
Oglesby, Zena 12
Ogletree, Charles, Jr. 12, 47
O'Grady, Lorraine 73
Ojikutu, Bayo 66
Ojikutu, Bisola 65
Ol' Dirty Bastard 52
Olden, Georg(e) 44
O'Leary, Hazel 6
Oliver, Garrett 95
Oliver, Jerry 37
Oliver, Joe "King" 42
Oliver, John J., Jr. 48
Oliver, Kimberly 60
Oliver, Pam 54, 123
Oliver, Paul 115
Olusola, Kevin 133
Omalu, Bennet 132
Omarion 107
Omarosa 69, 110
O'Neal, Frederick 99
O'Neal, Patrice 99
O'Neal, Rodney 88
O'Neal, Ron 46
O'Neal, Shaquille 8, 30, 95
O'Neal, Stanley 38, 67
O'Neil, Buck 19, 59
Onyewu, Oguchi 60
Orange, James 74
Orioles, The 100
Orlandersmith, Dael 42
Orlons, The 130
Orman, Roscoe 55, 129
Ormes, Jackie 73
Orr, Kevyn 118
Ory, Kid 118
Osbey, Brenda Marie 102
Osborne, Jeffrey 26, 121
Osborne, Na'taki 54
Osman, Said 127
Otis, Clarence, Jr. 55
Otis, Clyde 67
Ouattara, Morou 74
Overton, Anthony 128
Owens, Brig 118
Owens, Clifford 129
Owens, Helen 48
Owens, Jack 38
Owens, Jesse 2
Owens, Jimmy 130
Owens, Major 6, 117
Owens, Terrell 53, 106
Ozanne, Ismael R. 129
Pace, Betty 59
Pace, Judy 119
Pace, Orlando 21, 134
Packer, Daniel 56
Packer, Will 71
Packer, Z. Z. 64
Page, Alan 7
Page, Clarence 4
Page, Greg 78
Page, Inman 82
Page, Walter 117
Paige, Rod 29
Paige, Satchel 7

Painter, Nell Irvin 24, 88
Palmer, Keke 68, 120
Palmer, Rissi 65
Palmer, Violet 59
Parham, Marjorie B. 71
Parham, Truck 124
Parish, Robert 43
Parker, Barrington D. 92
Parker, Candace 74
Parker, Charlie 20
Parker, Jim 64
Parker, Junior 116
Parker, Kellis E. 30
Parker, Maceo 72
Parker, Nicole Ari 52
Parker, Pat 19
Parker, Ray, Jr. 85
Parker, Star 70
Parker, Vernon 97
Parker, Willie J. 133
Parks, Bernard C. 17
Parks, Gordon 1, 35, 58
Parks, Henry Green, Jr. 89
Parks, Rosa 1, 35, 56
Parks, Suzan-Lori 34, 85
Parlan, Horace 108
Parr, Russ 51
Parris, Teyonah 131
Parsons, James 14
Parsons, Richard 11, 33, 124
Paterson, Basil A. 69, 122
Paterson, David A. 59
Patrick, Deval 12, 61, 127
Patterson, Chuck 124
Patterson, Don 135
Patterson, Floyd 19, 58
Patterson, Frederick Douglass 12
Patterson, Gilbert Earl 41
Patterson, J. O., Jr. 80
Patterson, Louise 25
Patterson, Mary Jane 54
Patterson, Orlando 4, 127
Patton, Antwan 45
Patton, Charley 107
Patton, Paula 62
Patton, Venetia K. 125
Paul, Billy 127, 135
Paul, Chris 84, 100
Paulk, Marcus T. 127
Payne, Allen 13
Payne, Donald M. 2, 57, 112
Payne, Donald M., Jr. 132
Payne, Ethel L. 28
Payne, Freda 58
Payne, Les 89
Payne, Ulice, Jr. 42
Payne, William D. 60
Payton, Benjamin F. 23
Payton, Gary 99
Payton, John 48, 124
Payton, Philip A., Jr. 88
Payton, Walter 11, 25
Pearson, Felicia 99
Peck, Carolyn 23
Peebles, Ann 114
Peete, Calvin 11
Peete, Holly Robinson 20
Peete, Rodney 60
Pena, Paul 58
Pendergrass, Teddy 22, 83
Penguins, The 107
Peoples, Dottie 22
Perez, Anna 1

Perkins, Carl 128
Perkins, Eddie 103
Perkins, Edward 5
Perkins, James, Jr. 55
Perkins, Marion 38
Perkins, Pinetop 70
Perkins, Tony 24
Perren, Freddie 60
Perrineau, Harold, Jr. 51
Perrot, Kim 23
Perry, Herman 89
Perry, James 83
Perry, Joe 95
Perry, Laval 64
Perry, Lowell 30
Perry, Matthew J., Jr. 96
Perry, Steve 98
Perry, Tyler 40, 54, 103
Perry, Warren 56
Person, Waverly 9, 51
Peters, Brock 96
Peters, Clarke 103
Peters, Jason 125
Peters, Margaret 43
Peters, Matilda 43
Petersen, Frank E. 31
Peterson, Adrian 109
Peterson, James 38
Peterson, James L. 81
Peterson, Jesse Lee 81
Peterson, Karen Carter 90
Peterson, Marvin "Hannibal" 27
Petioni, Muriel 99
Petry, Ann 19
Pettiford, Oscar 106
Pettigrew, Antonio 118
Pharcyde, The 127
Phife Dawg 134
Phifer, Mekhi 25, 103
Phillips, Brandon 116
Phillips, Carl 111
Phillips, Charles E., Jr. 57, 109
Phillips, Esther 107
Phillips, Helen L. 63
Phillips, Joseph C. 73
Phillips, Teresa L. 42
Phillips, Tony 135
Phipps, Wintley 59
Pickens, James, Jr. 59
Pickett, Bill 11
Pickett, Cecil 39
Pierce, Elijah 84
Pierce, Harold 75
Pierce, Paul 71
Pierce, Wendell 90
Pierre, Percy Anthony 46
Pierson, Katrina 134
Pilgrim Travelers, The 129
Pincham, R. Eugene, Sr. 69
Pinchback, P. B. S. 9
Pinckney, Clementa C. 130
Pinckney, Sandra 56
Pindell, Howardena 55
Pinder, Jefferson 77
Pinderhughes, John 47
Pineda, Michael 121
Pinkett, Randal 61
Pinkett Smith, Jada 10, 41, 95
Pinkney, Arnold R. 122
Pinkney, Bill 42
Pinkney, Fayette 80
Pinkney, Jerry 15, 124
Pinkston, W. Randall 24

Pinn, Vivian Winona **49**
Piper, Adrian **71**
Pippen, Scottie **15, 89**
Pippin, Horace **9**
Pitchford, Lonnie **133**
Pitts, Byron **71**
Pitts, Derrick **77**
Pitts, Leonard, Jr. **54, 85**
Pitts, Robb **84**
Pitts, Skip **103**
Plaskett, Stacey **127**
Platters, The **99**
Player, Willa B. **43**
Pleasant, Mary Ellen **9**
Pleasure P **84**
Plessy, Homer Adolph **31**
Plinton, James O., Jr. **98**
Plummer, Glenn **120**
P.M. Dawn **54**
Poindexter, Hildrus A. **87**
Poitier, Sidney **11, 36**
Poitier, Sydney Tamiia **65**
Polite, Carlene Hatcher **82**
Pollard, Fritz **53**
Pollard, William L. **91**
Pope.L, William **72**
Porter, Billy **112**
Porter, Bo **123**
Porter, David **127**
Porter, James A. **11**
Porter, Terry **75**
Porter, Tiran **133**
Portis, Clinton **130**
Potter, Myrtle **40**
Pough, Terrell **58**
Pounder, CCH **72**
Poussaint, Alvin F. **5, 67**
Poussaint, Renee **78**
Powell, Adam Clayton, Jr. **3**
Powell, Benny **87**
Powell, Bud **24**
Powell, Colin **1, 28, 75**
Powell, Debra A. **23**
Powell, Keith **101**
Powell, Kevin **31, 74**
Powell, Maxine **8, 115**
Powell, Michael **32**
Powell, Mike **7**
Powell, Renee **34**
Powell, William J. **82**
Power, Will **83**
Powers, Ben **132**
Pratt, Awadagin **31**
Pratt, Geronimo **18, 95**
Pratt, Kyla **57**
Preer, Evelyn **82**
Premice, Josephine **41**
Pressley, Condace L. **41**
Preston, Billy **39, 59**
Price, David **101**
Price, Florence **37**
Price, Frederick K. C. **21**
Price, Glenda **22**
Price, Hugh B. **9, 54**
Price, Kelly **23**
Price, Leontyne **1**
Price, Lisa **97**
Price, Lloyd **119**
Price, McKinley L. **136**
Price, Richard **51**
Pride, Charley **26**
Primas, Randy **106**
Primus, Pearl **6, 125**

Prince **18, 65, 134**
Prince, Richard E. **71**
Prince, Ron **64**
Prince, Tayshaun **68**
Prince Be **136**
Prince-Bythewood, Gina **31, 77**
Pritchard, Robert Starling **21**
Procope, Ernesta **23**
Procope, John Levy **56**
Proctor, Bernard Shaw **120**
Professor Longhair **109**
Proof **101**
Prophet, Nancy Elizabeth **42**
Prothrow-Stith, Deborah **10**
Pruitt, Wendell O. **106**
Pryce, Trevor **89**
Pryor, Rain **65**
Pryor, Richard **3, 24, 56**
Pryor, Snooky **119**
Prysock, Arthur **117**
Puckett, Kirby **4, 58**
Pugh, Charles **81**
Purdie, Bernard **77**
Purifoy, Noah **135**
Purnell, Silas **59**
Puryear, Martin **42, 101**
Pusha T **123**
Putney, Martha S. **75**
Pyfrom, Estella **127**
Quander, Nellie **102**
Quarles, Benjamin Arthur **18**
Quarles, Norma **25**
Quarterman, Lloyd Albert **4**
Queen Latifah **1, 16, 58, 119**
?uestlove **74**
Quigless, Helen G. **49**
Quince, Peggy A. **69**
Quivers, Robin **61**
Rabb, Maurice F., Jr. **58**
Rachell, Yank **129**
Radcliffe, Ted **74**
Rae Sremmurd **126**
Ragin, Derek Lee **84**
Rahman, Aishah **37**
Raines, Franklin **14, 107**
Raines, Tim **107**
Rainey, Ma **33**
Ralph, Sheryl Lee **18, 108**
Ramsey, Charles H. **21, 69**
Rand, A. Barry **6**
Randall, Alice **38**
Randall, Dudley **8, 55**
Randall, Vernellia R. **95**
Randle, John **87**
Randle, Theresa **16**
Randolph, A. Philip **3**
Randolph, Linda A. **52**
Randolph, Robert **132**
Randolph, Willie **53**
Rangel, Charles B. **3, 52, 85**
Ransome, James E. **88**
Raoul, Kwame **55**
Rapier, James T. **82**
Rare Essence **121**
Rashad, Ahmad **18**
Rashad, Phylicia **21**
Raspberry, William **2**
Ravens, The **103**
Raven-Symoné **44, 113**
Rawlings-Blake, Stephanie **93, 128**
Rawlinson, Johnnie B. **79**
Rawls, Johnny **135**
Rawls, Lou **17, 57**

Ray, Carline **113**
Ray, Charlotte E. **60**
Ray, Gene Anthony **47**
Ray, Goodman & Brown **131**
Ray J **86**
Razaf, Andy **19**
Reagins, Tony **94**
Reagon, Bernice Johnson **7**
Reagon, Toshi **76**
Reason, J. Paul **19**
Reaves, Donald J. **102**
Record, Eugene **60**
Red Alert, Kool DJ **33**
Redd, Dana **93**
Reddick, Lance **52, 128**
Reddick, Lawrence Dunbar **20**
Redding, Ann Holmes **77**
Redding, J. Saunders **26**
Redding, Louis L. **26**
Redding, Otis **16**
Redman **81**
Redman, Dewey **135**
Redman, Don **134**
Redman, Joshua **30**
Redmond, Eugene **23**
Redwood, John Henry **78**
Reece, Marcel **114**
Reed, A. C. **36**
Reed, Ishmael **8**
Reed, Jimmy **38**
Reed, Joe L. **110**
Reed, Kasim **82**
Reed, Natina **106**
Reed, Willis, Jr. **86**
Reed Hall, Alaina **83**
Reedy, Jessica **101**
Reems, Ernestine Cleveland **27**
Rees, Dee **100**
Reese, Della **6, 20, 96**
Reese, Jerry **103**
Reese, Milous J., Jr. **51**
Reese, Pokey **28**
Reese, Tracy **54**
Reeves, Bass **100**
Reeves, Carlton W. **129**
Reeves, Dianne **32, 119**
Reeves, Gregory **49**
Reeves, Martha **85**
Reeves, Rachel J. **23**
Reeves, Triette Lipsey **27**
Reid, Ira De A. **100**
Reid, Irvin D. **20**
Reid, L.A. **28, 129**
Reid, Rufus **130**
Reid, Senghor **55**
Reid, Tim **56**
Reid, Vernon **34**
Retta **131**
Revels, Hiram Rhoades **98**
Reverend Ike **79**
Revis, Darrelle **130**
Reyes, José **134**
Reynolds, Harold **77**
Reynolds, Star Jones **10, 27, 61**
Rhames, Ving **14, 50**
Rhimes, Shonda Lynn **67**
Rhoden, Dwight **40**
Rhoden, William C. **67**
Rhodes, Jewell Parker **84**
Rhodes, Ray **14**
Rhone, Sylvia **2**
Rhymefest **97**
Rhymes, Busta **31**

Rhyne, Melvin **109**
Ribbs, Willy T. **2**
Ribeau, Sidney **70**
Ribeiro, Alfonso **17**
Rice, Condoleezza **3, 28, 72**
Rice, Constance LaMay **60**
Rice, Emmett J. **94**
Rice, Jerry **5, 55, 89**
Rice, Jim **75**
Rice, Linda Johnson **9, 41**
Rice, Louise Allen **54**
Rice, Norm **8**
Rice, Ray **112**
Rice, Susan **74, 103**
Richard, Dawn **92**
Richard, J. R. **87**
Richards, Beah **30**
Richards, Hilda **49**
Richards-Ross, Sanya **66, 98**
Richardson, Desmond **39**
Richardson, Donna **39**
Richardson, Julieanna **81**
Richardson, LaTanya **71**
Richardson, Laura **81**
Richardson, Nolan **9**
Richardson, Rupert **67**
Richardson, Salli **68**
Richie, Leroy C. **18**
Richie, Lionel **27, 65, 114**
Richmond, Cedric **93**
Richmond, Mitch **19**
Rideau, Iris **46**
Ridley, John **69**
Riggins, Karriem **102**
Riggs, Marlon **5, 44**
Riles, Wilson C. **79**
Riley, Amber **97**
Riley, Ben **130**
Riley, Boots **89**
Riley, Helen Caldwell Day **13**
Riley, Rochelle **50**
Riley, Teddy **116**
Rillieux, Norbert **92**
Ringgold, Faith **4, 81**
Riperton, Minnie **32**
Rivers, Doc **25, 81**
Rivers, Eugene F., III **81**
Rivers, Sam **95**
Roach, Max **21, 63**
Roaf, Andrée Layton **106**
Roaf, Willie **106**
Roberts, Darryl **70**
Roberts, Dave **132**
Roberts, Deborah **35**
Roberts, Joseph Jenkins **125**
Roberts, Kimberly Rivers **72**
Roberts, Lillian **83**
Roberts, Marcus **19, 113**
Roberts, Michele **123**
Roberts, Mike **57**
Roberts, Robin **16, 54, 113**
Roberts, Roy S. **14**
Robertson, Gil L., IV **85**
Robertson, Oscar **26**
Robeson, Eslanda Goode **13**
Robeson, Paul **2**
Robey, Don **115**
Robinson, Aminah **50**
Robinson, Bill "Bojangles" **11**
Robinson, Bishop L. **66**
Robinson, Cleo Parker **38**
Robinson, Craig **103**
Robinson, Craig **107**

Robinson, Cynthia **132**
Robinson, Dave **110**
Robinson, David **24, 90**
Robinson, Eddie G. **10**
Robinson, Eugene **77**
Robinson, Fatima **34**
Robinson, Fenton **38**
Robinson, Flynn **112**
Robinson, Frank **9, 87**
Robinson, Ida B. **106**
Robinson, Jackie **6**
Robinson, Joann Gibson **100**
Robinson, LaVaughn **69**
Robinson, Malcolm S. **44**
Robinson, Matt **69**
Robinson, Max **3**
Robinson, Patrick **19, 71**
Robinson, Rachel **16**
Robinson, Randall **7, 46**
Robinson, Reginald R. **53**
Robinson, Sharon **22**
Robinson, Shaun **36**
Robinson, Smokey **3, 49**
Robinson, Spottswood W., III **22**
Robinson, Sugar Ray **18**
Robinson, Sylvia **79**
Robinson, Will **51, 69**
Robinson-Berry, Joan **94**
Roble, Abdi **71**
Roby, Kimberla Lawson **86**
Roche, Joyce M. **17**
Rochon, Lela **16**
Rochon, Stephen W. **78**
Rock, Chris **3, 22, 66**
Rock, John S. **113**
Rock, Pete **121**
Rock, The **29, 66**
Rock, Tony **108**
Rodgers, Johnathan **6, 51**
Rodgers, Rod **36**
Rodman, Dennis **12, 44, 96, 118**
Rodriguez, Cheryl **64**
Rodriguez, Jimmy **47**
Rogers, Alan G. **72**
Rogers, Bobby **110**
Rogers, Desirée **88**
Rogers, Jimmy **38**
Rogers, Joe **27**
Rogers, Joel Augustus **30**
Rogers, John W., Jr. **5, 52**
Rogers, Rodney Ray **106**
Roker, Al **12, 49**
Roker, Roxie **68**
Rolle, Esther **13, 21**
Rolle, Janet **97**
Rolle, Myron **98**
Rollins, Charlemae Hill **27**
Rollins, Howard E., Jr. **16**
Rollins, Jimmy **70**
Rollins, Sonny **37, 94**
Romanthony **115**
Romeo **98**
Rondo, Rajon **111**
Ronettes, The **132**
Roney, Wallace **136**
Rooks, Sean **136**
Roots, The **101**
Rose, Anika Noni **70**
Rose, Derrick **82**
Rose, Harold M. **134**
Rose, Jalen **108**
Rose Royce **120**
Roseboro, John **123**

Ross, Charles **27**
Ross, Diana **8, 27**
Ross, Don **27**
Ross, Isaiah "Doc" **40**
Ross, Rick **79, 104**
Ross, Tracee Ellis **35**
Ross-Lee, Barbara **67**
Rotimi **130**
Roundfield, Danny **109**
Roundtree, Dovey **80**
Roundtree, Richard **27**
Rouse, Cecilia **93**
Rouse, Charlie **130**
Rowan, Carl T. **1, 30**
Rowe-Adams, Jackie **109**
Rowell, Victoria **13, 68**
Rowland, Kelly **100**
Roy, Brandon **98**
Roy, Kenny **51**
Royce da 5'9" **134**
Royo, Andre **136**
Rubin, Chanda **37**
Rucker, Darius **34, 74, 108**
Rudolph, Maya **46, 106**
Rudolph, Wilma **4**
Ruffin, Jimmy **125**
Ruffin, Josephine St. Pierre **75**
Ruffins, Kermit **85**
Ruggles, David **126**
Ruley, Ellis **38**
Run **31, 73, 75**
RuPaul **17, 91**
Rush, Bobby **26, 76**
Rush, Bobby **78**
Rush, Otis **38**
Rushen, Patrice **12**
Rushing, Jimmy **37**
Russell, Bill **8**
Russell, Brenda **52**
Russell, Herman Jerome **17**
Russell, Nipsey **66**
Russell-McCloud, Patricia A. **17**
Russwurm, John Brown **100**
Rust, Art, Jr. **83**
Rustin, Bayard **4**
RZA **80, 128**
Saadiq, Raphael **125**
Saar, Alison **16**
Saar, Betye **80**
Sabathia, CC **74**
St. Jacques, Raymond **8**
Saint James, Synthia **12**
St. John, Kristoff **25**
St. Julien, Marlon **29**
St. Louis, David **126**
St. Patrick, Mathew **48**
Saldana, Zoe **72, 118**
Sales, Ruby **133**
Sallee, Charles **38**
Salter, Nikkole **73**
Salters, Lisa **71**
Sam, Michael **121**
Sam and Dave **102**
Samara, Noah **15**
Sample, Joe **51, 123**
Sampson, Charles **13**
Samuelsson, Marcus **53, 120**
Sanchez, Sonia **17, 51**
Sanders, Angelia **86**
Sanders, Barry **1, 53**
Sanders, Bob **72**
Sanders, Charlie **130**
Sanders, Deion **4, 31, 96**

Sanders, Joseph R., Jr. **11**
Sanders, Malika **48**
Sanders, Pharoah **64**
Sanders, Satch **77**
Sands, Diana **87**
Sanford, Isabel **53**
Sanneh, Kelefa **96**
Santamaria, Mongo **81**
Santana, Juelz **120**
Santiago-Hudson, Ruben **85**
Santigold **96**
Sapp, Marvin **74**
Sapp, Warren **38, 109**
Sapphire **14, 95**
Sarpong, Sam **132**
Sasser, Sean **113**
Satcher, David **7, 57, 111**
Savage, Augusta **12**
Sawyer, Eugene **81**
Sayers, Gale **28**
Sayles Belton, Sharon **9, 16**
Sbraga, Kevin **88**
Scantlebury-White, Velma **64**
Schiavocampo, Mara **97**
Schmoke, Kurt **1, 48**
ScHoolboyQ **117**
Schuyler, George Samuel **40**
Schuyler, Philippa **50**
Scott, Byron **125**
Scott, C(ornelius) A(dolphus) **29**
Scott, David **41, 117**
Scott, Dread **106**
Scott, George **55**
Scott, George **113**
Scott, Harold Russell, Jr. **61**
Scott, Hazel **66**
Scott, Jill **29, 83**
Scott, Jimmy **48, 122**
Scott, John T. **65**
Scott, Milton **51**
Scott, Robert C. **23**
Scott, Shirley **133**
Scott, Stuart **34, 126**
Scott, Tim **87, 125**
Scott, Wendell Oliver, Sr. **19**
Scott-Heron, Gil **94**
Scott-Young, Mona **101**
Scribner, Marcus **136**
Scurry, Briana **27**
Seals, Son **56**
Sealy, Lloyd G. **125**
Sealy, Malik **118**
Sears, Leah Ward **5, 79**
Sears, Stephanie **53**
Sebree, Charles **40**
Secada, Jon **97**
Seele, Pernessa **46**
Sengstacke, John **18**
Senna, Danzy **93**
Sermon, Erick **81**
Serrano, Andres **3**
Sessoms, Vivian **122**
Setmayer, Tara **130**
Sewell, Terri **93**
Seymour, Richard **101**
Seymour, Teddy **110**
Seymour, William J. **106**
Shabazz, Attallah **6**
Shabazz, Betty **7, 26**
Shabazz, Ilyasah **36**
Shabazz Palaces **123**
Shadd, Abraham D. **81**
Shakur, Afeni **67, 135**

Shakur, Assata **6**
Shakur, Tupac **14**
Shakur, Yusef **85**
Shamir **129**
Shange, Ntozake **8, 89**
Shanice **112**
Shank, Suzanne F. **77**
Shannon, Randy **82**
Shanté, Roxanne **33**
Sharp, Dee Dee **130**
Sharpe, Shannon **97**
Sharper, Darren **32, 118**
Sharpton, Al **21, 97**
Shavers, Charlie **131**
Shavers, Cheryl **31**
Shavers, Earnie **127**
Shaw, Bernard **2, 28**
Shaw, Brian **127**
Shaw, Eddie **136**
Shaw, Marlena **105**
Shaw, William J. **30**
Sheard, Kierra **61, 114**
Sheffield, Gary **16, 108**
Shell, Art **1, 66**
Shelton, Paula Young **86**
Shelton, Trent **122**
Shepherd, Sherri **55**
Shepp, Archie **101**
Sherman, Richard **118**
Sherrod, Clayton **17**
Sherrod, Shirley **87**
Shider, Garry **87**
Shines, Johnny **116**
Shinhoster, Earl **32**
Shipp, E. R. **15**
Shipp, Matthew **107**
Shippen, John **43**
Shirelles, The **111**
Shirley, Aaron **126**
Shirley, Donald **111**
Shirley, George **33**
Shmurda, Bobby **123**
Shockley, Ann Allen **84**
Shores, Arthur D. **99**
Short, Bobby **52**
Short, Columbus **79**
Shorter, Wayne **75**
Showers, Reggie **30**
Shropshire, Thomas B. **49**
Shuttlesworth, Fred **47, 98**
Sidat-Singh, Wilmeth **116**
Sidibe, Gabourey **84**
Sidner, Sara **105**
Sifford, Charlie **4, 49, 134**
Sigur, Wanda **44**
Silas, Paul **24, 129**
Silver, Horace **26, 122**
Siméus, Dumas M. **25, 110**
Simkins, Modjeska Monteith **112**
Simmons, Bob **29**
Simmons, E. Denise **79**
Simmons, Gary **58**
Simmons, Gwendolyn Zoharah **132**
Simmons, Henry **55**
Simmons, Jamal **72**
Simmons, Kimora Lee **51, 83**
Simmons, Russell **1, 30**
Simmons, Ruth J. **13, 38**
Simms, Margaret **94**
Simon, Joe **109**
Simon, Lateefah **95**
Simone, Nina **15, 41, 130**
Simpson, Carole **6, 30**

Simpson, Lorna **4, 36**
Simpson, Merton D. **110**
Simpson, O. J. **15, 100**
Simpson, Valerie **21, 97**
Simpson-Hoffman, N'kenge **52**
Sims, Danny **106**
Sims, Howard "Sandman" **48**
Sims, Lowery Stokes **27**
Sims, Naomi **29, 79**
Sinbad **1, 16**
Singletary, Mike **4, 76**
Singleton, John **2, 30, 122**
Sinkford, Jeanne C. **13**
Sir Mix-A-Lot **82**
Sisqo **30**
Sissle, Noble **29**
Sister Souljah **11, 100**
Sizemore, Barbara A. **26, 110**
Sizemore, Grady **96**
Skinner, Kiron K. **65**
Sklarek, Norma Merrick **25, 101**
Slater, Duke **125**
Slater, Rodney E. **15, 125**
Slaughter, John Brooks **53**
Sledge, Percy **39, 128**
Sleet, Gregory M. **109**
Sleet, Moneta, Jr. **5, 136**
Slice, Kimbo **73, 136**
Slick Rick **93**
Slim Harpo **120**
Slim Thug **86**
Slocumb, Jonathan **52**
Slyde, Jimmy **70**
Smalls, Robert **82**
Smaltz, Audrey **12**
Smiley, Rickey **59**
Smiley, Tavis **20, 68**
Smith, Amanda Berry **109**
Smith, Anna Deavere **6, 44**
Smith, B(arbara) **11**
Smith, Barbara **28**
Smith, Bessie **3**
Smith, Bruce **80**
Smith, Bruce W. **53**
Smith, Bubba **96**
Smith, Buster **116**
Smith, Cecilia **102**
Smith, Cladys "Jabbo" **32**
Smith, Clarence **113**
Smith, Clarence O. **21**
Smith, Damu **54**
Smith, Danyel **40**
Smith, DeMaurice **92**
Smith, Dr. Lonnie **49**
Smith, Emmitt **7, 87**
Smith, Gene **123**
Smith, Geno **118**
Smith, Greg **28**
Smith, Hale **118**
Smith, Hilton **29**
Smith, Ian **62**
Smith, Jaden **82**
Smith, Jane E. **24**
Smith, Jessie Carney **35**
Smith, Jimmy **127**
Smith, John L. **22**
Smith, Joshua **10**
Smith, Kemba **70**
Smith, Kenny **114**
Smith, LaQuan **113**
Smith, Lee **101**
Smith, Lee **136**
Smith, Lonnie Liston **49**

Smith, Lovie **66, 107**
Smith, Malcolm A. **75**
Smith, Mamie **32**
Smith, Marie F. **70**
Smith, Marvin **46**
Smith, Mary Carter **26, 134**
Smith, Michael **129**
Smith, Ming **100**
Smith, Morgan **46**
Smith, Myrna **92**
Smith, Nate **49**
Smith, Neil **109**
Smith, Ozzie **77**
Smith, Princella **86**
Smith, Randy **81**
Smith, Reggie **113**
Smith, Rick **72**
Smith, Roger Guenveur **12, 133**
Smith, Stephen A. **69**
Smith, Steve **120**
Smith, Stuff **37**
Smith, Tasha **73**
Smith, Tommie **102**
Smith, Trixie **34**
Smith, Tubby **18, 83**
Smith, Vincent D. **48**
Smith, Will **8, 18, 53**
Smith, Will **135**
Smith, Willi **8**
Smith, Willie **107**
Smith, Willow **92**
Smyre, Calvin **90**
Smythe Haith, Mabel **61**
Sneed, Paula A. **18**
Snipes, Wesley **3, 24, 67**
Snoop Dogg **35, 84**
Snow, Samuel **71**
Snow, Valaida **135**
Snowden, Frank M., Jr. **67**
Snowden, Gail **108**
Sohn, Sonja **100**
Solange **97**
Solomon, Jimmie Lee **38**
Somi **85**
Sommore **61**
Songz, Trey **88**
S.O.S. Band **136**
Soul Stirrers **127**
Southern, Eileen **56**
Southgate, Martha **58**
Sowell, Thomas **2, 99**
Spaniels, The **105**
Spann, Otis **107**
Sparks, Jordin **66**
Spaulding, Charles Clinton **9**
Spearman, Leonard H. O., Sr. **81**
Spears, Warren **52**
Spector, Ronnie **77**
Speech **82**
Spencer, Anne **27**
Spencer, Michael G. **87**
Spencer, Octavia **100**
Spencer, Peter **128**
Spencer, Vaino H. **99**
Spigner, Archie **81**
Spikes, Dolores **18**
Spiller, Bill **64**
Spivey, Victoria **119**
Sprewell, Latrell **23**
Spriggs, William **67**
Springer, Ashton, Jr. **115**
Stackhouse, Houston **122**
Stackhouse, Jerry **30**

Staley, Dawn **57**
Stallings, George A., Jr. **6**
Stallworth, John **102**
Stampley, Micah **54**
Stanford, John **20**
Stanford, Olivia Lee Dilworth **49**
Stanley, A. Knighton **117**
Stanton, Alysa **78**
Stanton, Robert **20**
Staples, Brent **8**
Staples, Cleotha **113**
Staples, Mavis **50, 88**
Staples, "Pops" **32**
Stargell, Willie **29**
Starks, Jabo **135**
Starr, Edwin **122**
Staton, Candi **27**
Staton, Dakota **62**
Staupers, Mabel K. **7**
Stearnes, Norman "Turkey" **31**
Steave-Dickerson, Kia **57**
Steele, Claude **13, 97**
Steele, Lawrence **28**
Steele, Michael **38, 73, 91**
Steele, Sage **115**
Steele, Shelby **13, 82**
Steinberg, Martha Jean "The
    Queen" **28**
Stephens, Charlotte Andrews **14**
Stephens, Sloane **105**
Stephenson, Lance **118**
Stevenson, Bryan **128**
Stew **69**
Steward, David L. **36**
Steward, Emanuel **18, 106**
Stewart, Alison **13**
Stewart, Amii **129**
Stewart, Billy **112**
Stewart, Dave **117**
Stewart, Ella **39**
Stewart, James, Jr. **60, 98**
Stewart, Kordell **21, 111**
Stewart, Maria W. Miller **19**
Stewart, Nzingha **89**
Stewart, Paul Wilbur **12**
Stewart, Slam **126**
Stewart, Tonea Harris **78**
Stewart, Tricky **98**
Stickney, Phyllis Yvonne **108**
Sticky Fingaz **86**
Still, William Grant **37**
Stingley, Darryl **69**
Stinson, Denise L. **59**
Stith, Charles R. **73**
Stith, James H. **116**
Stith, Tom **93**
Stokes, Carl **10, 73**
Stokes, Louis **3**
Stone, Angie **31**
Stone, Chuck **9, 120**
Stone, Jesse **98**
Stone, Sly **85**
Stone, Toni **15**
Stoney, Michael **50**
Storyboard P **118**
Stoudemire, Amar'e **59, 106**
Stout, Juanita Kidd **24**
Stout, Renee **63**
Stoute, Steve **38**
Stowers, Freddie **107**
Stradford, J. B. **101**
Strahan, Michael **35, 81, 135**
Strautmanis, Michael **87**

Strawberry, Darryl **22**
Strayhorn, Billy **31**
Street, John F. **24**
Street, Richard **110**
Streeter, Sevyn **115**
Stringer, C. Vivian **13, 66**
Stringer, Korey **35**
Stringer, Vickie **58**
Strode, Woody **111**
Strong, Barrett **89**
Strong, Charlie **118**
Stubblefield, Clyde **133**
Studdard, Ruben **46**
Sudarkasa, Niara **4**
Sudduth, Jimmy Lee **65**
Sugarhill Gang, The **79, 125**
Suggs, Terrell **108**
Sullivan, Jazmine **81**
Sullivan, Leon H. **3, 30**
Sullivan, Louis **8**
Sullivan, Maxine **37**
Sumlin, Hubert **101**
Summer, Donna **25, 102**
Summers, Myrna **129**
Sumner, Francis Cecil **112**
Sun Ra **60**
Sundiata, Sekou **66**
Sunnyland Slim **118**
Sutphen, Mona **77**
Suttles, Mule **108**
Sutton, Percy E. **42, 82**
Swallows, The **133**
Swan Silvertones, The **110**
Swann, Bettye **109**
Swann, Lynn **28**
Sweat, Keith **19**
Sweatman, Wilbur **125**
Sweatshirt, Earl **114**
Sweatt, Heman Marion **114**
Sweet, Ossian **68**
Sweet Honey in the Rock **106**
Swizz Beatz **108**
Swoopes, Sheryl **12, 56**
Swygert, H. Patrick **22**
Sykes, Roosevelt **20**
Sykes, Wanda **48, 81**
Syler, Rene **53**
Tacuma, Jamaaladeen **124**
Tademy, Lalita **36**
Tail Dragger **112**
Tait, Michael **57**
Take 6 **112**
Talbert, David E. **34, 93**
Talbert, Mary B. **77**
Talley, André Leon **56, 106**
Tamar-kali **63**
Tamia **24, 55**
Tampa Red **63**
Tancil, Gladys Quander **59**
Tanksley, Ann **37**
Tanner, Henry Ossawa **1**
Tanner, Jack E. **100**
Tapscott, Horace **126**
Taste of Honey, A **115**
Tate, Buddy **108**
Tate, Eleanora E. **20, 55**
Tate, Grady **106**
Tate, John **107**
Tate, Larenz **15**
Tatum, Art **28**
Tatum, Beverly Daniel **42, 84**
Tatum, Elinor R. **78**
Tatum, Jack **87**

Tatum, Reece 104
Tatum, Wilbert 76
Taulbert, Clifton Lemoure 19
Tavares 115
Taylor, Art 132
Taylor, Billy 23, 92
Taylor, Bo 72
Taylor, Cecil 70
Taylor, Charles 20
Taylor, Eddie 116
Taylor, Ephren W., II 61
Taylor, Gardner C. 76
Taylor, Helen (Lavon Hollingshed) 30
Taylor, Hound Dog 120
Taylor, Jason 70
Taylor, Jermain 60
Taylor, Koko 40, 80
Taylor, Kristin Clark 8
Taylor, Lawrence 25
Taylor, Lonzie Odie 96
Taylor, Marshall Walter "Major" 62
Taylor, Meshach 4
Taylor, Mildred D. 26
Taylor, Natalie 47
Taylor, Recy 92
Taylor, Regina 9, 46, 97
Taylor, Robert Robinson 80
Taylor, Robert Rochon 104
Taylor, Ron 35
Taylor, Susan C. 62
Taylor, Susan L. 10, 86
Taylor, Susie King 13
T-Boz 108
Tchicai, John 102
Teague, Bob 111
Teasley, Lisa 92
Teer, Barbara Ann 81
Temple, Collis, Jr. 119
Temple, Ed 109
Temple, Lewis 102
Terrell, Dorothy A. 24
Terrell, Ernie 118
Terrell, Jean 116
Terrell, Mary Church 9
Terrell, Tammi 32
Terrell-Kearney, Kim 83
Terrence J 108
Terry, Bryant 128
Terry, Clark 39, 127
Terry, Sonny 88
Tex, Joe 116
Tharpe, Rosetta 65
The-Dream 74
Thigpen, Ed 110
Thigpen, Lynne 17, 41
Thomas, Alma 14
Thomas, Arthur Ray 52
Thomas, Carla 96
Thomas, Clarence 2, 39, 65
Thomas, Claudia Lynn 64
Thomas, Debi 26
Thomas, Derrick 25
Thomas, Emmitt 71
Thomas, Frank 12, 51
Thomas, Franklin A. 5, 49
Thomas, Irma 29
Thomas, Isiah 7, 26, 65
Thomas, Jefferson 88
Thomas, Michael 69
Thomas, Mickalene 61
Thomas, Rozonda 34, 78
Thomas, Rufus 20, 96

Thomas, Sean Patrick 35
Thomas, Tabby 119
Thomas, Thurman 75
Thomas, Trisha R. 65
Thomas, Vivien 9
Thomas-Graham, Pamela 29
Thomas-Greenfield, Linda 99
Thompson, Bennie 26, 119
Thompson, Cynthia Bramlett 50
Thompson, Don 56, 108
Thompson, John Douglas 81
Thompson, John W. 26
Thompson, Ken 131
Thompson, Kenan 52
Thompson, Klay 126
Thompson, Larry D. 39
Thompson, Mychal 126
Thompson, Tazewell 13
Thompson, Tina 25, 75
Thompson, Tristan 131
Thompson, William C., Jr. 35, 114
Thoms, Tracie 61
Thornton, Big Mama 33
Thornton, Yvonne S. 69
Thrash, Dox 35
Threadgill, Henry 97
Thrower, Willie 35
Thundercat 136
Thurman, Howard 3
Thurman, Wallace 16
Thurmond, Nate 88
Thurston, Baratunde 79, 101
Thurston, Stephen J. 49
Tiant, Luis 102
Till, Emmett 7
Tillard, Conrad 47
Tillis, Frederick 40
Tillman, Deborah 98
Tillman, Dorothy 76
Tillman, George, Jr. 20
Timbaland 32
Timmons, Bobby 136
Tingling, Milton A. 110
Tinsley, Boyd 50
Tirico, Mike 68, 124
Tisdale, Wayman 50
Tobias, Channing H. 79
Tobin, Patricia 75
Todman, Terence A. 55
Tolbert, James L. 112
Tolbert, Mike 125
Tolbert, Terence 74
Toler, Burl 80
Tolliver, Mose 60
Tolliver, William 9
Tolson, Melvin 37
Tolton, Augustine 62
Tomlin, Mike 123
Tomlinson, LaDainian 65, 112
Tonex 54
Toney, James 89
Tony! Toni! Toné! 127
Tooks, Lance 62
Toomer, Jean 6
Toote, Gloria E. A. 64
Torres, Gina 52
Torry, Guy 31
Touré, Askia (Muhammad Abu Bakr el) 47
Touré, Faya Ora Rose 56
Toussaint, Allen 60, 132
Towles, Nat 128
Towns, Edolphus 19, 75

Towns, Karl-Anthony 136
Townsend, Robert 4, 23
T-Pain 73, 111
Trammps, The 108
Travis, Tracey T. 94
Treacherous Three 128
Tresvant, Ralph 57
Trethewey, Natasha 103
Tribbett, Tye 81
Tribble, Israel, Jr. 8
Trina 114
Trombone Shorty 97
Trotter, Donne E. 28
Trotter, Lloyd G. 56
Trotter, Monroe 9
Troupe, Quincy 83
Trouppe, Quincy Thomas, Sr. 84
True, Rachel 82
Trueheart, William E. 49
Truesdale, Yanic 133
Tubbs Jones, Stephanie 24, 72
Tubman, Harriet 9, 135
Tucker, C. Delores 12, 56
Tucker, Chris 13, 23, 62
Tucker, Cynthia 15, 61
Tucker, Rosina 14
Tucker, Tommy 127
Tuckson, Reed V. 71
Tuff, Antoinette 120
Tunie, Tamara 63
Tunnell, Emlen 54
Turman, Glynn 100
Turnbull, Charles Wesley 62
Turnbull, Walter 13, 60
Turner, Big Joe 92
Turner, Charles Henry 134
Turner, Henry McNeal 5
Turner, Ike 68
Turner, Mark 126
Turner, Morrie 122
Turner, Sylvester 136
Turner, Tina 6, 27
Turrentine, Stanley 129
Twiggs, Leo 127
Twilight, Alexander 125
Twitty, Michael 134
2 Chainz 105
Tyga 117
Tyler, Aisha N. 36
Tyler, Ollie 128
Tyler, the Creator 100
Tyner, McCoy 92
Tyree, Omar Rashad 21
Tyson, Andre 40
Tyson, Asha 39
Tyson, Cicely 7, 51, 112
Tyson, Mike 28, 44, 93
Tyson, Neil deGrasse 15, 65
Uggams, Leslie 23, 114
Ulmer, James 79
Underwood, Blair 7, 27, 76
Union, Gabrielle 31, 92
Unseld, Wes 23
Upshaw, Gene 18, 47, 72
Upton, Justin 124
Upton, Melvin, Jr. 124
Urschel, John 126
Usher 23, 56, 95
Usher, Jessie T. 136
Usry, James L. 23, 134
Ussery, Terdema, II 29
Utendahl, John 23
Valentino, Bobby 62

Van Lierop, Robert 53
Van Peebles, Mario 2, 51
Van Peebles, Melvin 7, 95
Vance, Courtney B. 15, 60
Vance, Jim 110
VanDerZee, James 6
Vandross, Luther 13, 48, 59
Vanzant, Iyanla 17, 47, 108
Vaughan, Sarah 13
Vaughn, Countess 53
Vaughn, Gladys Gary 47
Vaughn, Jacque 127
Vaughn, Mo 16
Vaughn, Viola 70
Vaughns, Cleopatra 46
Vega, Marta Moreno 61
Velez-Rodriguez, Argelia 56
Verdelle, A. J. 26
Vereen, Ben 4
Verrett, Shirley 66, 91
Vesey, Denmark 100
Via, Dennis 108
Vick, Michael 39, 65, 94
Villarosa, Clara 85
Vincent, Marjorie Judith 2
Vincent, Troy 91
Vinnegar, Leroy 124
Vinson, Eddie 112
Von Lipsey, Roderick K. 11
Waddles, Charleszetta "Mother" 10, 49
Wade, Dwyane 61, 103
Wade, Ernestine 126
Wade-Gayles, Gloria Jean 41
Wagner, Albert 78
Wagner, Annice 22
Wainwright, Joscelyn 46
Waka Flocka Flame 110
Walcott, Dennis M. 112
Walcott, Jersey Joe 102
Waldon, Alton R., Jr. 98
Waldron, Mal 109
Wale 92
Walker, Albertina 10, 58, 89
Walker, A'lelia 14
Walker, Alice 1, 43
Walker, Antoine 132
Walker, Arthur, II 87
Walker, Bernita Ruth 53
Walker, Cedric "Ricky" 19
Walker, Chet 106
Walker, Cora T. 68
Walker, David 129
Walker, Dianne 57
Walker, George 37
Walker, George 129
Walker, Herschel 1, 69
Walker, Hezekiah 34
Walker, Joe Louis 118
Walker, John T. 50
Walker, Joseph Edison 111
Walker, Kara 16, 80
Walker, LeRoy T. 106
Walker, Lucius, Jr. 88
Walker, Madame C. J. 7
Walker, Maggie Lena 17
Walker, Margaret 29
Walker, Ray 109
Walker, Rebecca 50
Walker, T. J. 7
Walker, T-Bone 111
Walker, Teshima 114
Walker, Tristan 98

Walker, Wyatt Tee 80
Wall, John 129
Wall, Orindatus S. B. 92
Wallace, Ben 54
Wallace, Joaquin 49
Wallace, Michele Faith 13
Wallace, Perry E. 47
Wallace, Phyllis A. 9
Wallace, Rasheed 56
Wallace, Sippie 1
Wallace, William 75
Waller, Fats 29
Wallis, Quvenzhané 109
Walters, Ronald 83
Walton, Cedar 114
Walton, Lester Aglar 134
Wanz 116
Ward, Andre 62
Ward, Anita 118
Ward, Benjamin 68
Ward, Douglas Turner 42
Ward, Hines 84
Ward, Lloyd 21, 46
Ward, Willa 105
Ward, William E. 107
Ware, Andre 37
Ware, Carl H. 30
Ware, David S. 106
Ware, DeMarcus 92
Warfield, Marsha 2
Warfield, William 94
Waring, Laura Wheeler 99
Warner, Malcolm-Jamal 22, 36, 110
Warren, Butch 116
Warren, Lovely 136
Warren, Michael 27
Warwick, Dionne 18, 111
Washington, Alonzo 29
Washington, Booker T. 4
Washington, Denzel 1, 16, 93
Washington, Dinah 22
Washington, Ebonya 79
Washington, Elsie B. 78
Washington, Fredi 10
Washington, Gene 63
Washington, Grover, Jr. 17, 44
Washington, Harold 6
Washington, Harriet A. 69
Washington, Hayma 86
Washington, Isaiah 62
Washington, James, Jr. 38
Washington, James Melvin 50
Washington, Kamasi 134
Washington, Karen 117
Washington, Kenny 50
Washington, Kenny 107
Washington, Kerry 46, 107
Washington, Laura S. 18
Washington, MaliVai 8
Washington, Margaret Murray 119
Washington, Mary T. 57
Washington, Ora Mae 115
Washington, Patrice Clarke 12
Washington, Pauletta Pearson 86
Washington, Regynald G. 44
Washington, Ron 119
Washington, Val 12
Washington, Walter 45
Washington-Williams, Essie Mae 118
Wasow, Omar 15
Waters, Benny 26
Waters, Ethel 7

Waters, Maxine 3, 67, 103
Waters, Muddy 34
Watkins, Craig 97
Watkins, Donald 35
Watkins, Joe 86
Watkins, Levi, Jr. 9
Watkins, Perry 12
Watkins, Shirley R. 17
Watkins, Ted 104
Watkins, Walter C. 24
Watley, Jody 54
Watson, Benjamin 126
Watson, Bob 25
Watson, Carlos 50
Watson, Diane 41
Watson, Johnny "Guitar" 18
Watson Coleman, Bonnie 127
Watt, Garland W. 113
Watt, Mel 26, 105
Wattleton, Faye 9
Watts, André 42, 101
Watts, J. C., Jr. 14, 38
Watts, Reggie 52, 102
Watts, Rolonda 9
Wayans, Damien 78
Wayans, Damon 8, 41
Wayans, Keenen Ivory 18
Wayans, Kim 80
Wayans, Marlon 29, 82
Wayans, Shawn 29
Wayne, Reggie 131
Weathers, Carl 10, 117
Weaver, Afaa Michael 37
Weaver, Karen 134
Weaver, Mike 109
Weaver, Robert C. 8, 46
Webb, Chick 105
Webb, Veronica 10, 95
Webb, Wellington 3, 81
Webb-Christburg, Sheyann 110
Webber, Chris 15, 30, 59, 118
Webber, Ben 136
Webster, Katie 29
Wedgeworth, Robert W. 42
Weeks, Thomas, III 70
Weems, Carrie Mae 63, 116
Weems, Renita J. 44
Wein, Joyce 62
Welburn, Edward T. 50
Welch, Elisabeth 52
Welcome, Verda Freeman 112
Wellington, Valerie 118
Wells, Henrietta Bell 69
Wells, James Lesesne 10
Wells, Junior 102
Wells, Mary 28
Wells, Vernon 91
Wells, Willie 105
Wells-Barnett, Ida B. 8
Welsing, Frances Cress 5
Wesley, Dorothy Porter 19
Wesley, Richard 73
Wesley, Rutina 97
Wesley, Valerie Wilson 18
Wess, Frank 116
West, Allen 89
West, Cornel 5, 33, 80
West, Dorothy 12, 54
West, James E. 87
West, Kanye 52, 93
West, Togo D., Jr. 16
Westbrook, Kelvin 50
Westbrook, Peter 20

Westbrook, Russell 116
Westbrooks, Bobby 51
Whack, Rita Coburn 36
Whalum, Kirk 37, 64
Wharton, A. C., Jr. 110
Wharton, Clifton R., Jr. 7
Wharton, Clifton Reginald, Sr. 36
Wheat, Alan 14
Wheaton, James 103
Whispers, The 124
Whitaker, Forest 2, 49, 67
Whitaker, Mark 21, 47
Whitaker, Pernell 10, 89
White, Armond 80, 118
White, Augustus, III 100
White, Barry 13, 41
White, Bill 1, 48
White, Bukka 120
White, Charles 39
White, Dondi 34
White, Frank 95
White, James L. 130
White, Jesse 22, 75
White, Jessica 83
White, Jo Jo 112
White, John H. 27
White, Josh 86
White, Josh, Jr. 52
White, Lillias 120
White, Linda M. 45
White, Lois Jean 20
White, Maurice 29
White, Michael Jai 71, 117
White, Michael R. 5
White, Reggie 6, 50
White, Sylvain 96
White, Terri 82
White, Walter F. 4
White, Willye 67
White-Hammond, Gloria 61
Whitehead, Colson 77
Whiteside, Hassan 127
Whitfield, Fred 23
Whitfield, LeRoy 84
Whitfield, Lynn 18
Whitfield, Mal 60
Whitfield, Norman 73
Whitfield, Van 34
Whitlock, Jason 78, 130
Whitmore, George 106
Whitney, Davey L. 110
Whitney, Marva 109
Wideman, John Edgar 5, 87
Widener, Warren 99
Wiggins, Andrew 128
Wiggins, Gerald 128
Wilbekin, Emil 63
Wilbon, Michael 68, 132
Wilder, Deontay 121
Wilder, L. Douglas 3, 48
Wiley, Kehinde 62
Wiley, Ralph 8, 78
Wiley, Samira 131
Wilfork, Vince 124
Wilkens, Lenny 11, 88
Wilkerson, Isabel 71
Wilkins, David 77
Wilkins, Dominique 74
Wilkins, J. Ernest, Jr. 43
Wilkins, Ray 47
Wilkins, Roger 2, 84
Wilkins, Roy 4
Wilkins, Thomas Alphonso 71

will.i.am 64
Williams, Ann Claire 82
Williams, Anthony 21
Williams, Armstrong 29
Williams, Bernie 128
Williams, Bert 18
Williams, Billy 86
Williams, Billy Dee 8, 105
Williams, Buster 131
Williams, Camilla 116
Williams, Cecil 130
Williams, Clarence 33
Williams, Clarence 70
Williams, Clarence, III 26
Williams, Claude 80
Williams, Cootie 114
Williams, Daniel Hale 2
Williams, Darrent 116
Williams, David Rudyard 50
Williams, David W. 110
Williams, Deniece 36
Williams, Dennis P. 123
Williams, Deron 92
Williams, Doug 22, 112
Williams, Dudley 60
Williams, Eddie N. 44
Williams, Evelyn 10
Williams, Fannie Barrier 27
Williams, Frederick (B.) 63
Williams, George Washington 18
Williams, Gregory 11
Williams, Hosea 15, 31, 123
Williams, J. Mayo 83
Williams, Jody 113
Williams, Joe 5, 25
Williams, John A. 27
Williams, Juan 35, 80
Williams, Ken 68
Williams, Larry 118
Williams, Lauryn 58, 127
Williams, Lil' Ed 135
Williams, Lindsey 75
Williams, Maggie 7, 71
Williams, Malinda 57
Williams, Marco 53
Williams, Mary Lou 15
Williams, Michael Kenneth 97
Williams, Michael L. 86
Williams, Michelle 73
Williams, Montel 4, 57
Williams, Monty 125
Williams, Nat D. 91
Williams, Natalie 31
Williams, O. S. 13
Williams, Patricia 11, 54
Williams, Paul 112
Williams, Paul R. 9
Williams, Pharrell 47, 82, 119
Williams, Preston Warren, II 64
Williams, Rhonda Y. 86
Williams, Richard 130
Williams, Richard 131
Williams, Ricky 85
Williams, Robert F. 11, 136
Williams, Ronald A. 57
Williams, Russell, II 70
Williams, Samm-Art 21
Williams, Saul 31
Williams, Serena 20, 41, 73, 129
Williams, Sherley Anne 25
Williams, Spencer 126
Williams, Stanley "Tookie" 29, 57
Williams, Stevie 71

Williams, Ted **91**
Williams, Terrie M. **35**
Williams, Tony **67**
Williams, Vanessa A. **32, 66**
Williams, Vanessa L. **4, 17**
Williams, Venus **17, 34, 62**
Williams, Walt **133**
Williams, Walter E. **4, 133**
Williams, Wendy **62**
Williams, William T. **11**
Williams, Willie L. **4**
Williams Brothers **135**
Williamson, Fred **67**
Williamson, Mykelti **22**
Williamson, Patrice **134**
Williamson, Sonny Boy **84**
Williamson, Sonny Boy **134**
Willie, Louis, Jr. **68**
Willingham, Tyrone **43**
Willis, Bill **68**
Willis, Chuck **132**
Willis, Deborah **85**
Willis, Dontrelle **55**
Willis, Patrick **99**
Williston, David Augustus **99**
Wills, Harry **80**
Wills, Maury **73**
Wilmore, Larry **121**
Wilson, Abram **104**
Wilson, Ajee' **129**
Wilson, August **7, 33, 55**
Wilson, Brian Courtney **94**
Wilson, Cassandra **16**
Wilson, Chandra **57**
Wilson, Charlie **31, 77, 135**
Wilson, David **123**
Wilson, Debra **38**
Wilson, Demond **102**
Wilson, Donald E. **88**
Wilson, Dorien **55**
Wilson, Ellis **39**
Wilson, Flip **21**
Wilson, Frank **106**
Wilson, Frederica **92**
Wilson, Gerald **49, 123**
Wilson, Jackie **60**
Wilson, Jimmy **45**
Wilson, John **109**
Wilson, Lionel **99**
Wilson, Margaret Bush **79**
Wilson, Mary **28**
Wilson, Nancy **10, 98**
Wilson, Natalie **38**
Wilson, Phill **9, 104**
Wilson, Reggie **116**
Wilson, Russell **119**
Wilson, Stephanie **72**
Wilson, Sunnie **7, 55**
Wilson, Teddy **134**
Wilson, Tracey Scott **777**
Wilson, William Julius **20**
Winans, Angie **36**
Winans, BeBe **14**
Winans, CeCe **14, 43**
Winans, David **77**
Winans, Debbie **36**
Winans, Marvin L. **17, 127**
Winans, Ronald **54**
Winans, Vickie **24**
Winburn, Anna Mae **135**
Winfield, Dave **5, 91**
Winfield, Paul **2, 45**
Winfrey, Oprah **2, 15, 61, 106**

Winkfield, Jimmy **42**
Winslow, Kellen **83**
Wisdom, Kimberlydawn **57**
Withers, Bill **61**
Withers, Ernest C. **68, 88**
Withers-Mendes, Elisabeth **64**
Witherspoon, Jimmy **113**
Witherspoon, John **38**
Witt, Edwin T. **26**
Wolfe, Ann **82**
Wolfe, George C. **6, 43, 127**
Womack, Bobby **60, 92, 123**
Wonder, Stevie **11, 53, 121**
Wood, Willie **111**
Woodard, Alfre **9, 108**
Woodard, Lynette **67**
Woodruff, Hale **9**
Woodruff, John **68**
Woods, Abraham, Jr. **74**
Woods, Belita **103**
Woods, Cheyenne **103**
Woods, Georgie **57**
Woods, Granville T. **5**
Woods, Jacqueline **52**
Woods, Mattiebelle **63**
Woods, Renn **110**
Woods, Scott **55**
Woods, Sylvia **34, 104**
Woods, Teri **69**
Woods, Tiger **14, 31, 81**
Woodson, Ali Ollie **89**
Woodson, Carter G. **2**
Woodson, Jacqueline **125**
Woodson, Mike **78**
Woodson, Robert L. **10**
Woodson, Rod **79**
Woolard, Jamal **102**
Wooten, Victor **131**
Work, John Wesley, III **133**
Workman, Reggie **131**
Worrill, Conrad **12**
Worthy, James **49**
Worthy, Kym **84**
Wray, Noble **114**
Wright, Antoinette **60**
Wright, Beverly **97**
Wright, Bruce McMarion **3, 52**
Wright, Chalky **103**
Wright, Charles H. **35**
Wright, Deborah C. **25**
Wright, Eugene **125**
Wright, Jeffrey **54, 111**
Wright, Jeremiah A., Jr. **45, 69, 103**
Wright, Leo **131**
Wright, Lewin **43**
Wright, Louis Tompkins **4**
Wright, Nathan, Jr. **56**
Wright, O. V. **114**
Wright, Rayfield **70**
Wright, Richard **5**
Wright, Richard Robert, Sr. **100**
Wright, Sarah E. **95**
Wright, Timothy **74**
Wyatt, Addie L. **56**
Wyllie, Tony **131**
Wynn, Albert R. **25, 77**
X, Malcolm **1**
X, Marvin **45**
Xuma, Madie Hall **59**
Xzibit **78**
Yancey, Jimmy **116**
Yancy, Dorothy Cowser **42**
Yarber, Tony **129**

Yarbrough, Camille **40**
Yarbrough, Cedric **51**
Yarbrough & Peoples **132**
Yates, Jack **114**
Yayo, Tony **113**
Yearwood, Lennox, Jr. **112**
Yerby, Frank **96**
Yergan, Max **123**
Yette, Samuel F. **63**
YG **122**
Ying Yang Twins **112**
Yoba, Malik **11**
York, Dwight D. **71**
York, Vincent **40**
Young, Al **82**
Young, Andrew **3, 48, 110**
Young, Charles **77**
Young, Coleman **1, 20**
Young, Darren **114**
Young, Donald, Jr. **57**
Young, Jean Childs **14**
Young, Jimmy **54**
Young, John **111**
Young, Johnny **120**
Young, Lee **72**
Young, Lee Thompson **114**
Young, Lester **37**
Young, Perry H. **100**
Young, Roger Arliner **29**
Young, Rosa J. **129**
Young, Whitney M., Jr. **4**
Young, Zora **129**
Young Jeezy **63**
Youngblood, Johnny Ray **8**
Youngblood, Shay **32**
Yusef, Malik **136**
Zane **71**
Zollar, Alfred **40**
Zollar, Jawole Willa Jo **28**
Zook, Kristal Brent **62**
Z-Ro **109**

Angolan
Bonga, Kuenda **13**
dos Santos, Isabel **114**
dos Santos, José Eduardo **43, 114**
Lopes, Leila **99**
Neto, António Agostinho **43**
Roberto, Holden **65**
Savimbi, Jonas **2, 34**

Antiguan and Barbudan
Ashe, John **131**
Kincaid, Jamaica **4, 109**
McGuire, George Alexander **80**
Spencer, Winston Baldwin **68**
Williams, Denise **40**

Aruban
Williams, David Rudyard **50**

Australian
Freeman, Cathy **29**
Irving, Kyrie **102**
Mundine, Anthony **56**
Rose, Lionel **56**

Austrian
Kodjoe, Boris **34, 89**

Bahamian
Christie, Perry Gladstone **53**
Ferguson, Amos **81**
Ingraham, Hubert A. **19**
Munroe, Myles **125**

Pindling, Lynden **81**
Spence, Joseph **49**
Thompson, Mychal **126**

Barbadian
Adams, Grantley **82**
Arthur, Owen **33**
Brathwaite, Kamau **36**
Clarke, Austin C. **32**
Foster, Cecil **32**
Fresh, Doug E. **93**
Grandmaster Flash **33, 60**
Kamau, Kwadwo Agymah **28**
Lamming, George **35**
Rihanna **65, 102**

Belgian
Kompany, Vincent **132**
Stromae **121**

Belizean
Barrow, Dean **69**
Jones, Marion **21, 66**
Palacio, Andy **96**
Shyne **101**

Beninese
Gantin, Bernardin **70**
Hounsou, Djimon **19, 45**
Joachim, Paulin **34**
Kérékou, Mathieu **1, 131**
Kidjo, Angelique **50**
Loueke, Lionel **88**
Soglo, Nicéphore **15**
Yayi, Boni T. **84**

Bermudian
Cameron, Earl **44**
Gordon, Pamela **17**
Smith, Jennifer **21**

Bissau-Guinean
Cabral, Amílcar **104**
Sanhá Malam Bacai **84, 101**
Vieira, João Bernardo **14, 84**

Botswanan
Dow, Unity **104**
Khama, Ian **95**
Masire, Quett **5**
Mogae, Festus Gontebanye **19, 79**

Brazilian
Alves, Dani **121**
Brown, Carlinhos **81**
Caymmi, Dorival **72**
da Silva, Benedita **5**
dos Santos, Manuel Francisco **65**
Gil, Gilberto **53**
Jorge, Seu **73**
Leônidas **96**
Machado de Assis **74**
Mello, Breno **73**
Moura, Paulo **87**
Nascimento, Abdias do **93**
Nascimento, Milton **2, 64**
Pelé **7**
Pitta, Celso **17**
Querino, Manuel Raimundo **84**
Ronaldinho **69**
Silva, Anderson **96**
Silva, Marina **80**

British
Abbott, Diane **9, 132**
Abrahams, Zaraah **127**

Abudu, Mo 121
Adjaye, David 38, 78
Adoboli, Kweku 106
Akinnuoye-Agbaje, Adewale 56
Akomfrah, John 37
Amos, Valerie 41
Anderson, Ho Che 54
Anderson, Jacob 128
Anthony, Trey 63
Appiah, Kwame Anthony 67, 101
Armah, Esther 87
Armatrading, Joan 32, 133
Bailey Rae, Corinne 83
Barnes, John 53
Bassey, Shirley 25
Berry, James 41
Blackwood, Maureen 37
Boateng, Ozwald 35, 113
Boateng, Paul Yaw 56
Boyega, John 133
Breeze, Jean "Binta" 37
Brown, Melanie 73
Campbell, Naomi 1, 31, 120
Carby, Hazel 27
Charles, John 108
Christie, Linford 8
Cole, Ashley 106
Coleridge-Taylor, Samuel 75
Crooks, Garth 53
Cruz, Taio 104
D'Aguiar, Fred 50
Danjah, Terror 91
David, Craig 31, 53
Davidson, Jaye 5
DeGale, James 74
Dexter, Felix 129
Dunn, Jourdan 130
Edwards, Trevor 54
Ejiofor, Chiwetel 67, 116
Ejogo, Carmen 126
Elba, Idris 49, 89, 116
Emmanuel, Alphonsia 38
Equiano, Olaudah 78
Erivo, Cynthia 133
Estelle 75, 133
Evans, Diana 72
Farah, Mo 104
Fenton, Kevin 87
Ferdinand, Rio 82
FKA Twigs 123
Forna, Aminatta 95
Garrett, Sean 57
Gladwell, Malcolm 62
Griffin, Angela 80
Hall, Adelaide 126
Hall, Stuart 78
Hamilton, Lewis 66
Harewood, David 52
Harris, Naomie 55, 116
Haye, David 82
Henriques, Julian 37
Henry, Lenny 9, 52
Hill, Darryl 128
Holmes, Kelly 47
Ibrahim, Mo 67, 115
Ince, Paul 83
Jamelia 51
James, David 84
Jean-Baptiste, Marianne 17, 46
Johnson, Ken 106
Jordan, Ronny 26
Joseph, Paterson 126
Julien, Isaac 3

Kay, Jackie 37
Kinch, Soweto 108
King, Oona 27
Kiwanuka, Michael 126
Kwei-Armah, Kwame 84
Labrinth 135
Lester, Adrian 46
Lewis, Denise 33
Lewis, Lennox 27
Lewis, Leona 75
Lindo, Delroy 18, 45
Markham, E. A. 37
Mbatha-Raw, Gugu 89
McGrath, Pat 72
McKinney Hammond, Michelle 51
McQueen, Steve 84
Miller, Wentworth 75
Ming, Mel 106
Morris, William "Bill" 51
Muamba, Fabrice 104
Mvula, Laura 110
Negga, Ruth 135
Newton, Thandie 26, 114
Ofili, Chris 124
Okonedo, Sophie 67
Oyelowo, David 82, 126
Oyeyemi, Helen 135
Pitt, David Thomas 10
Rascal, Dizzee 82
Regis, Cyrille 51
Roberts, Norwell 134
Sade 15, 92
Sancho, Ignatius 133
Sandé, Emeli 113
Sarpong, Sam 132
Scantlebury, Janna 47
Seacole, Mary 54
Seal 14, 75
Selasi, Taiye 125
Sesay, Isha 107
Siji 56
Slash 75
Slick Rick 93
Smalling, Chris 118
Smith, Anjela Lauren 44
Smith, Richard 51
Smith, Zadie 51
Stoutt, H. Lavity 83
Stuart, Moira 82
Sturridge, Daniel 120
Taylor, John (David Beckett) 16
Thomason, Marsha 47
Tinie Tempah 115
Tricky 98
Walker, Eamonn 37
Williams, Roy 89

Burkinabé
Compaore, Blaise 87
Kaboré, Roch Marc Christian 132
Kafando, Michel 131
Sankara, Thomas 17
Somé, Malidoma Patrice 10

Burundian
Bigirimana, Gael 115
Ndadaye, Melchior 7
Nkurunziza, Pierre 78, 130
Ntaryamira, Cyprien 8

Cameroonian
Ahidjo, Ahmadou 81
Bebey, Francis 45
Beti, Mongo 36

Biya, Chantal 89
Biya, Paul 28, 114
Eto'o, Samuel 73
Fosso, Samuel 116
Kotto, Yaphet 7
Milla, Roger 2
Njawe, Pius 87
Nteff, Alain 127
Nzié, Anne-Marie 136
Oyono, Ferdinand 38
Song, Alex 105

Canadian
Alexander, Lincoln 106
Auguste, Arnold A. 47
Augustine, Jean 53
Bannister, Edward Mitchell 88
Bell, Ralph S. 5
Best, Carrie 80
Boyd, Suzanne 52
Brand, Dionne 32
Brathwaite, Fred 35
Brown, Rosemary 62
Brown, Sean 52
Carnegie, Herbert 25
Chanté, Keshia 50
Chong, Rae Dawn 62
Clarke, Austin 32
Clarke, George 32
Cools, Anne 64
Cooper, Afua 53
Cox, Deborah 28
Croal, N'Gai 76
Curling, Alvin 34
Dixon, George 52
Doig, Jason 45
Drake 86
Edugyan, Esi 98
Elliot, Lorris 37
Fiona, Melanie 84
Foster, Cecil 32
Fox, Rick 27
Fuhr, Grant 1, 49
Grand-Pierre, Jean-Luc 46
Hammond, Lenn 34
Harris, Claire 34
Henry, Joshua 94
Iginla, Jarome 35
Isaac, Julius 34
James, Vanessa 84
Jean, Michaëlle; 70
Jenkins, Fergie 46
Johnson, Ben 1
Johnson, Clark 96
Kane, Evander 97
K'naan 76
Laraque, Georges 48
Lewis, Daurene 72
Mayers, Jamal 39
McKegney, Tony 3
Mollel, Tololwa 38
Neale, Haydain 52
O'Ree, Willie 5
Peterson, Oscar 52
Philip, Marlene Nourbese 32
Reuben, Gloria 15
Richards, Lloyd 2
Rodrigues, Percy 68
Ruth B 135
Sadlier, Rosemary 62
Salvador, Bryce 51
Scarlett, Millicent 49
Senior, Olive 37

Simmonds, Wayne 121
Sparks, Corinne Etta 53
Stiverne, Bermane 128
Subban, P. K. 121
Truesdale, Yanic 133
Vanity 67, 134
Verna, Gelsy 70
Ward, Joel 129
Weekes, Kevin 67
Weeknd, The 131
Williams, Denise 40

Cape Verdean
Antunes, Lúcio 109
Évora, Cesária 12, 99
Grace, Sweet Daddy 104
Pereira, Aristides 30, 97

Caymanian
Ebanks, Selita 67

Central African
Bozizé, François 96, 117
Djotodia, Michel 117

Chadian
Déby, Idriss 30, 125
Habré, Hissène 6, 104

Colombian
Pomare, Eleo 72

Congolese (Democratic Republic of the Congo)
Kabila, Joseph 30, 126
Kabila, Laurent 20
Katumbi, Moïse 135
Kintaudi, Leon 62
Kolosoy, Wendo 73
Lubanga, Thomas 104
Mobutu Sese Seko 1, 56
Muamba, Fabrice 104
Mudimbe, V. Y. 61
Mutombo, Dikembe 7, 107
Nkunda, Laurent 75
Ntaganda, Bosco 111
Papa Wemba 135
Rochereau, Tabu Ley 117

Congolese (Republic of the Congo)
Lumumba, Patrice 33
Sassou-Nguesso, Denis 103

Costa Rican
McDonald, Erroll 1

Cuban
Armenteros, Chocolate 133
Chapman, Aroldis 132
Dihigo, Martín 103
Ferrer, Ibrahim 41
Fuentes, Tito 123
Güines, Tata 69
Hernández, Orlando 96
León, Tania 13
Maceo, Antonio 82
Minoso, Minnie 89, 127
Ortiz, Luis 134
Portuondo, Omara 53
Puig, Yasiel 113
Quirot, Ana 13
Rodríguez, Arsenio 87
Santamaria, Mongo 81
Savón, Félix 105

Secada, Jon 97
Stevenson, Teófilo 103
Tiant, Luis 102
Valdés, Chucho 89
Velez-Rodriguez, Argelia 56

Curaçaoan
Jones, Andruw 98

Danish
Tchicai, John 102

Dominican (from Dominica)
Charles, Mary Eugenia 10, 55
Charles, Pierre 52
Skerrit, Roosevelt 72

Dominican (from Dominican Republic)
Cano, Robinson 97
Cueto, Johnny 130
Horford, Al 107
Martínez, Pedro 81, 126
Ortiz, David 52, 82
Perez, Pascual 108
Ramírez, Hanley 135
Reyes, José 134
Sosa, Sammy 21, 44
Uribe, Juan 122
Virgil, Ozzie 48

Dutch
Ali, Ayaan Hirsi 58, 92
Brigitha, Enith 126
Davids, Edgar 106
Liberia-Peters, Maria Philomena 12
Seedorf, Clarence 121

Ecuadoran
Benítez, Christian 113

Equatorial Guinean
Moussambani, Eric 105
Obiang, Teodoro 103

Eritrean
Afewerki, Isaias 98
Keflezighi, Meb 49, 121
Teklehaimanot, Daniel 130

Ethiopian
Aberra, Amsale 67
Abune Paulos 105
Afro, Teddy 78
Ahmed, Mahmoud 130
Astatke, Mulatu 81
Bekele, Kenenisa 75
Birra, Ali 113
Desalegn, Hailemariam 105
Dibaba, Genzebe 130
Dibaba, Mare 131
Dibaba, Tirunesh 73, 109
Gabre-Medhin, Tsegaye 64
Gebrselassie, Haile 70
Gerima, Haile 38, 80
Haile Selassie 7
Ibrahim, Fuad 109
Kebede, Liya 59
Mèkurya, Gétatchèw 135
Mengistu, Haile Mariam 65
Negga, Ruth 135
Samuelsson, Marcus 53, 120
Yirga, Samuel 126

Zenawi, Meles 3, 99

Filipino
apl.de.ap 84

Finnish
Toivola, Jani 118

French
Anelka, Nicolas 118
Baker, Josephine 3
Baldwin, James 1
Baugé, Grégory 86
Bebey, Francis 45
Bonaly, Surya 7
Boulogne, Joseph, Chevalier de Saint-Georges 94
Chase-Riboud, Barbara 20, 46
Diaw, Boris 122
Drogba, Didier 78, 132
Dieudonné 67, 118
Evra, Patrice 102
Fanon, Frantz 44
Henry, Thierry 66, 127
James, Vanessa 84
Kanouté, Fred 68
Noah, Yannick 4, 60, 121
Parker, Tony 75
Song, Alex 105
Sy, Omar 109
Tanner, Henry Ossawa 1
Taubira, Christiane 117
Thiam, Tidjane 104
White, Sylvain 96

Gabonese
Bongo, Ali Ben 80
Bongo, Omar 1, 79

Gambian
Bensouda, Fatou 103
Jammeh, Yahya 23, 104
Peters, Lenrie 43
Sanneh, Kelefa 96

German
Ayim, May 126
Massaquoi, Hans J. 30, 130

Ghanaian
Adoboli, Kweku 106
Adu, Freddy 67
Aidoo, Ama Ata 38
Ali, Mohammed Naseehu 60
Annan, Kofi Atta 15, 48
Appiah, Kwame Anthony 67, 101
Armah, Ayi Kwei 49
Atta Mills, John 75
Awoonor, Kofi 37, 115
Awuah, Patrick 111, 131
Balotelli, Mario 104
Bartels, Peggielene 80
Blitz the Ambassador 115
Danquah, Meri Nana Ama 93
Dawuni, Rocky 94
DuBois, Shirley Graham 21
Gyan, Asamoah 87
Gyasi, Yaa 136
Jawara, Dawda Kairaba 11
Kufuor, John Agyekum 54, 82
Lee, Robert 112
Mahama, John Dramani 103
Mensah, John 87
Mensah, Thomas 48
Nkrumah, Kwame 3

Pelé, Abedi 122
Rawlings, Jerry 9
Rawlings, Nana Konadu Agyeman 13
Yeboah, Emmanuel Ofosu 53

Grenadian
Bishop, Maurice 39
Gairy, Eric Matthew 83
Isaac, Julius 34
Mitchell, Keith 82

Guinean
Camara, Moussa Dadis 76
Condé, Alpha 95, 131
Conté, Lansana 7, 76
Diallo, Amadou 27
Diawara, Djeli Moussa 111
Niane, Katoucha 70
Touré, Sekou 6
Youla, Mamady 133

Guyanese
Amos, Valerie 41
Beaton, Norman 14
Burnham, Forbes 66
Carter, Martin 49
Dabydeen, David 48
D'Aguiar, Fred 50
Damas, Léon-Gontran 46
Dathorne, O. R. 52
DoHarris, Brenda 116
Griffith, Patrick A. 64
Jagan, Cheddi 16
Lefel, Edith 41
van Sertima, Ivan 25

Haitian
Aristide, Jean-Bertrand 6, 45
Auguste, Rose-Anne 13
Beauvais, Garcelle 29, 95
Beauvoir, Max 74
Beken 111
Celestin, Josaphat 101
Charlemagne, Manno 11
Christophe, Henri 9
Danticat, Edwidge 15, 68, 128
Delice, Ronald 48
Delice, Rony 48
Duvalier, François 124
Duvalier, Jean-Claude 124
Hector, Jamie 98
Jean, Wyclef 20, 86
Jean-Juste, Gérard 78
Jean-Louis, Jimmy 76
Jeune, Vitolio 98
Laferriere, Dany 33
Lamothe, Laurent 122
Laraque, Paul 67
Laroche, Joseph Philippe Lemercier 85
Magloire, Paul Eugène 68
Manigat, Mirlande 90
Martelly, Michel 90
Pape, Jean William 126
Pascal-Trouillot, Ertha 3
Paul, Evans 129
Peck, Raoul 32
Pierre, Andre 17
Pierre-Louis, Michèle 75
Préval, René 87
Siméus, Dumas M. 25, 110
Stiverne, Bermane 128
Verna, Gelsy 70

Villard-Appolon, Malya 106

Hungarian
Watts, André 42, 101

Irish
Adebari, Rotimi 83
Mumba, Samantha 29

Italian
Balotelli, Mario 104
Esposito, Giancarlo 9
Kyenge, Cécile 113

Ivorian
Bedie, Henri Konan 21
Blondy, Alpha 30
Dadié, Bernard 34
De Bankolé, Isaach 78
Drogba, Didier 78, 132
Gbagbo, Laurent 43, 90
Guéï, Robert 66
Houphouët-Boigny, Félix 4, 64
Ouattara 43
Ouattara, Alassane 90
Ouattara, Morou 74
Thiam, Tidjane 104
Touré, Yaya 99

Jamaican
Ashley, Maurice 15, 47
Atkinson, Alia 126
Banton, Buju 93
Barnes, John 53
Barnes, Lloyd 77
Barrett, Lindsay 43
Beenie Man 32
Belafonte, Harry 4, 65
Bennett, Louise 69
Bennett, Richard 97
Berry, James 41
Big Youth 107
Bolt, Usain 73, 104
Brown, Dennis 99
Burning Spear 79
Campbell-Brown, Veronica 102
Channer, Colin 36
Chronixx 123
Cliff, Jimmy 28, 92
Cliff, Michelle 42
Coke, Christopher 108
Cooper, Afua 53
Cox, Renée 67
Curling, Alvin 34
Dawes, Kwame 126
Dekker, Desmond 104
Dodd, Coxsone 99
Dunbar, Sly 34
Ellis, Alton 74
Ellis, Hortense 97
Ewing, Patrick 17, 73, 130
Fagan, Garth 18, 98
Fenton, Kevin 87
Figueroa, John J. 40
Ford, Vincent 75
Fraser-Pryce, Shelly-Ann 113
Garvey, Marcus 1
Golding, Bruce 78
Goodison, Lorna 71
Graham, Trevor 84
Griffiths, Marcia 29
Hamilton, Tanya 93
Hammond, Lenn 34
Hearne, John Edgar Caulwell 45

Heavy D **58, 98**
Hibbert, Toots **103**
Holness, Andrew **99**
Irving, Barrington, Jr. **112**
Isaacs, Gregory **89**
James, Marlon **85, 124**
Johnson, Ben **1**
Johnson, Linton Kwesi **37**
Joseph, Kathie-Ann **56**
Kingston, Sean **94**
Kong, B. Waine **50**
Manley, Edna **26**
Manley, Ruth **34**
Marks, Audrey **99**
Marley, Bob **5**
Marley, Rita **32, 70**
Marley, Stephen **100**
Marley, Ziggy **41**
McGregor, Stephen **99**
McKay, Claude **6**
McKenzie, Jaunel **73**
Minott, Sugar **86**
Moody, Ronald **30**
Morrison, Keith **13**
Mowatt, Judy **38**
Palmer, Everard **37**
Patterson, Orlando **4, 127**
Patterson, P. J. **6, 20**
Perry, Lee **19, 103**
Perry, Ruth **19**
Ranglin, Ernest **78**
Reece, E. Albert **63**
Rhoden, Wayne **70**
Rhone, Trevor **80**
Rogers, Joel Augustus **30**
Russwurm, John Brown **100**
Senior, Olive **37**
Shaggy **31**
Shakespeare, Robbie **34**
Sharpe, Samuel **103**
Shearer, Hugh **107**
Simpson, Sherone **120**
Simpson Miller, Portia **62, 100**
Sinclair, Madge **78**
Steely **80**
Taylor, Karin **34**
Tosh, Peter **9**
White, Willard **53**
Yabby You **83**

Kenyan
Cheruiyot, Robert **69**
Hayanga, Jeremiah **118**
Jeptoo, Rita **121**
Juma, Calestous **57**
Kahora, Billy **125**
Kamworor, Geoffrey **134**
Kariuki, J. M. **67**
Kenyatta, Jomo **5**
Kenyatta, Uhuru **110**
Kibaki, Mwai **60**
Kimetto, Dennis **125**
Kipchoge, Eliud **124**
Kipsang, Wilson **115**
Kobia, Samuel **43**
Loroupe, Tegla **59**
Maathai, Wangari **43, 97**
Mazrui, Ali **12, 124**
Mboya, Tom **107**
Moi, Daniel Arap **1, 35**
Mutu, Wangechi **44**
Mwangi, Meja **40**
Ngilu, Charity **58**

Ngugi wa Thiong'o **29, 61, 101**
Nyong'o, Lupita **127**
Odinga, Raila **67, 110**
Osman, Said **127**
Otunga, Maurice Michael **55**
Rudisha, David **112**
Tergat, Paul **59**
Wambugu, Florence **42**
Wanjiru, Sammy **94**

Korean
Ward, Hines **84**

Lesotho
Le Loka, Tsidii **116**
Mofolo, Thomas **37**
Mosisili, Pakalitha **96**
Thabane, Thomas **123**

Liberian
Conneh, Sekou Damate, Jr. **51**
Cooper, Lisa **73**
Doe, Samuel K. **100**
Fuller, Solomon Carter, Jr. **15**
Gbowee, Leymah **76**
Keith, Rachel Boone **63**
Perry, Ruth **15**
Roberts, Joseph Jenkins **125**
Sawyer, Amos **2, 123**
Sirleaf, Ellen Johnson **71**
Taylor, Charles **20**
Tolbert, William R. **100**
Tubman, William **99**
Weah, George **58**

Malagasy (from Madagascar)
Jaojoby, Eusèbe **130**

Malawian
Banda, Hastings Kamuzu **6, 54**
Banda, Joyce **101**
Chikoti, Shadreck **125**
Kayira, Legson **40**
Malawi Mouse Boys **114**
Muluzi, Bakili **14, 76**

Malian
Amadou & Mariam **113**
Diabaté, Toumani **129**
Diawara, Fatoumata **114**
Keïta, Ibrahim Boubacar **113**
Keita, Salif **83**
Keïta, Seydou **124**
Sangare, Oumou **18, 99**
Sangho, Awa **127**
Sidibé, Malick **124**
Sidibé, Michel **133**
Songhoy Blues **135**
Souleymane, Mahamane **78**
Touré, Amadou Toumani **18**
Traore, Dioncounda **103**

Martinican
Césaire, Aimé **48, 69**
Palcy, Euzhan **94**

Mauritanian
Sissako, Abderrahmane **127**

Mexican
Catlett, Elizabeth **2, 120**
Nyong'o, Lupita **127**

Mozambican
Chissano, Joaquim **7, 55, 67**
Couto, Mia **45**

Diogo, Luisa Dias **63**
Eusebio **118**
Guebuza, Armando **81**
Machel, Graça **16, 102**
Machel, Samora Moises **8**
Mutola, Maria **12**

Namibian
Mbuende, Kaire **12**
Nujoma, Samuel **10**
Pohamba, Hifikepunye **95**

Nigerian
Abacha, Sani **11, 70**
Abani, Chris **77**
Abiola, Moshood **70**
Abiola-Costello, Hafsat **108**
Abubakar, Abdulsalami **66**
Abudu, Mo **121**
Achebe, Chinua **6, 99, 111**
Ade, King Sunny **41**
Adichie, Chimamanda Ngozi **64, 121**
Aire, Chris **117**
Ake, Claude **30**
Akinola, Peter Jasper **65**
Akpan, Uwem **70**
Akunyili, Dora Nkem **58**
Allen, Tony **117**
Amadi, Elechi **40**
Amata, Jeta **111**
Arinze, Francis **19**
Azikiwe, Nnamdi **13**
Babangida, Ibrahim **4**
Babatunde, Rotimi **104**
Bandele, Biyi **68, 121**
Buhari, Muhammadu **128**
Clark-Bekedermo, J. P. **44**
Cole, Teju **120**
Dangote, Aliko **124**
Darego, Agbani **52**
D'banj **107**
Ekwensi, Cyprian **37**
Elumelu, Tony **116**
Emeagwali, Philip **30**
Emecheta, Buchi **30**
Fela **1, 42**
Jalade-Ekeinde, Omotola **118**
Jonathan, Goodluck **83**
Kuti, Femi **47, 110**
Lawal, Kase L. **45**
Muhammed, Murtala **119**
Obasanjo, Olusegun **5, 22**
Obasanjo, Stella **32, 56**
Ogunlesi, Adebayo O. **37**
Ojukwu, Odumegwu **99**
Okara, Gabriel **37**
Okigbo, Christopher **102**
Okocha, Jay Jay **99**
Okonjo-Iweala, Ngozi **101**
Okosuns, Sonny **71**
Olagundoye, Toks **113**
Olajuwon, Hakeem **2, 72**
Olatunji, Babatunde **36, 126**
Olojede, Dele **59**
Olopade, Olufunmilayo Falusi **58**
Omalu, Bennet **132**
Omolewa, Michael **119**
Onwueme, Tess Osonye **23**
Onwurah, Ngozi **38**
Osotimehin, Babatunde **107**
Prince Twins Seven-Seven **95**
Rotimi, Ola **1, 130**

Sade **15, 92**
Saro-Wiwa, Kenule **39**
Siji **56**
Sowande, Fela **39**
Soyinka, Wole **4, 93**
Tutuola, Amos **30**
Ujiri, Masai **107**
Ukpabio, Helen **86**
Wiwa, Ken **67**
Yar'Adua, Umaru **69, 89**

Nigerien
Bombino **112**
Issoufou, Mahamadou **102**
Tandja, Mamadou **33, 78**

Norwegian
Brown, Anne **76**

Panamanian
Bailey, Preston **64**
Cobham, Billy **123**
Williams, Juan **35, 80**

Peruvian
Baca, Susana **80**

Polish
Bridgetower, George **78**

Portuguese
Souza, Carmen **111**

Puerto Rican
Cepeda, Orlando **98**
Schomburg, Arthur Alfonso **9**

Russian
Khanga, Yelena **6**

Rwandan
Bizimungu, Pasteur **19**
Habyarimana, Juvenal **8**
Ilibagiza, Immaculée **66**
Kabera, Eric **104**
Kagame, Paul **54**
Mbabazi, Esther **122**
Mushikiwabo, Louise **88**
Rusesabagina, Paul **60**

St. Kitts and Nevis
Douglas, Bob **96**
Douglas, Denzil Llewellyn **53**

Saint Lucian
Compton, John **65**

Saudi
Amoudi, Mohammed al- **88**
Kalbani, Adil **77**

Senegalese
Acogny, Germaine **55**
Akon **68**
Ba, Mariama **30**
Boye, Madior **30**
Diop, Birago **53**
Diop, Cheikh Anta **4**
Diouf, Abdou **3**
Evra, Patrice **102**
Maal, Baaba **66**
Mbaye, Mariétou **31**
Mboup, Souleymane **10**
Ndiaye, Iba **74**
N'Dour, Youssou **1, 53, 79**
Paris, Adama **120**
Sall, Macky **101**

Sané, Pierre Gabriel 21
Sembène, Ousmane 13, 62
Senghor, Augustin Diamancoune 66
Senghor, Léopold Sédar 12, 66
Sy, Oumou 65
Wade, Abdoulaye 66

Sierra Leonean
Beah, Ishmael 69
Cheney-Coker, Syl 43
DePrince, Michaela 104
Jones, Monty 66
Kabbah, Ahmad Tejan 23
Koroma, Ernest Bai 84
Sankoh, Foday 74
Sesay, Isha 107
Yumkella, Kandeh 105

Somali
Abdirahman, Abdi 126
Ahmed, Sharif 80
Ali, Ayaan Hirsi 58, 92
Ali Mahdi Mohamed 5
Dirie, Waris 56
Farah, Mo 104
Farah, Nuruddin 27
Iman 4, 33, 87
K'naan 76
Mohamud, Hassan Sheikh 105
Omar, Samia Yusuf 107
Roble, Abdi 71

South African
Abrahams, Peter 39
Adams, Paul 50
Biko, Steven 4
Brutus, Dennis 38
Buthelezi, Mangosuthu Gatsha 9
Butler, Jonathan 28
Chaka Chaka, Yvonne 112
Chweneyagae, Presley 63
Cole, Ernest 123
Dandala, Mvume 77
Dlamini-Zuma, Nkosazana 34, 105
Dube, John Langalibalele 119
Dube, Lucky 77
Grae, Jean 51
Hani, Chris 6
Head, Bessie 28
Ibrahim, Abdullah 131
Jansen, Jonathan 102
Jim, Songezo 111
Johanneson, Albert 129
Ka Dinizulu, Mcwayizeni 29
Kaka, Luthando 118
Kente, Gibson 52
Khumalo, Leleti 51
Khumalo, S'manga 119
Kuzwayo, Ellen 68
Ladysmith Black Mambazo 103

LaGuma, Alex 30
Lebo M 109
Luthuli, Albert 13
Mabuza, Lindiwe 18
Mabuza-Suttle, Felicia 43
Madikizela-Mandela, Winnie 2, 35, 112
Mahlasela, Vusi 65
Makeba, Miriam 2, 50, 74
Malema, Julius 98
Mandela, Nelson 1, 14, 77, 117
Maponya, Maishe 101
Maponya, Richard 101
Masekela, Barbara 18
Masekela, Hugh 1, 106
Mathabane, Mark 5, 99
Matshikiza, Pumeza 115
Mbeki, Govan A. 80
Mbeki, Thabo 14, 73
Meyiwa, Senzo 124
Mhlaba, Raymond 55
Mokae, Zakes 80
Motlanthe, Kgalema 74
Mphahlele, Es'kia 40
Nakasa, Nat 123
Naki, Hamilton 63
Ngubane, Ben 33
Nkoli, Simon 60
Nkosi, Lewis 46
Noah, Trevor 128
Ntshona, Winston 52
Nyanda, Siphiwe 21
Nzo, Alfred 15
Petersen, Neal 96
Plaatje, Sol T. 80
Ramaphosa, Cyril 3, 117
Ramphele, Mamphela 29
Rapelang Rabana 112
Sisulu, Albertina 57, 95
Sisulu, Sheila Violet Makate 24
Sisulu, Walter 47
Sono, Jomo 86
Tau, Mpho Parks 124
Thugwane, Josia 21
Tutu, Desmond (Mpilo) 6, 44
Tutu, Nontombi Naomi 57
Uys, Ashley 125
Yende, Pretty 124
Zuma, Jacob 33, 75
Zwelithini, Goodwill 128

South Sudanese
Kiir, Salva Mayardit 85, 103
Machar, Riek 117
Wek, Alek 18, 63, 105

Spanish
Alves, Dani 121
Buika 120

Eto'o, Samuel 73

Sudanese
Bashir, Halima 73
Bashir, Omar al- 77
Bol, Manute 1
Cham, Adongo Agada Akway 77
Elbagir, Nima 121
Garang, John 105
Hussein, Lubna 80
Nour, Nawal M. 56
Salih, Al-Tayyib 37

Swazi
Mswati III 56

Swedish
Hendricks, Barbara 3, 67
Valdés, Bebo 75

Swiss
Sefolosha, Thabo 121

Tanzanian
Kikwete, Jakaya Mrisho 73
Mkapa, Benjamin W. 16, 77
Mollel, Tololwa 38
Mongella, Gertrude 11
Mwinyi, Ali Hassan 1, 77
Nyerere, Julius 5, 136
Ongala, Remmy 9, 91
Rugambwa, Laurean 20
Thabeet, Hasheem 123

Togolese
Eyadéma, Gnassingbé 7, 52
Gnassingbé, Faure 67
Olympio, Sylvanus 126
Soglo, Nicéphore 15

Trinidadian
Anthony, Michael 29
Auguste, Arnold A. 47
Brand, Dionne 32
Carmichael, Stokely 5, 26
Cartey, Wilfred 47
Dymally, Mervyn 42
Francis, Thais 93
Guy, Rosa 5
Harris, Claire 34
Hendy, Francis 47
Hercules, Frank 44
Hill, Errol 40, 135
Holder, Geoffrey 78, 124
Julian, Hubert 90
London, Theophilus 95
Lord Invader 117
Lord Kitchener 110
Lushington, Augustus Nathaniel 56
Nakhid, David 25
Nunez, Elizabeth 62, 112

Petioni, Muriel 99
Primus, Pearl 6, 125
Rudder, David 79
Shorty, Ras, I 47
Toussaint, Lorraine 32
Williams, Eric Eustace 65

Tunisian
Memmi, Albert 37

Ugandan
Amin, Idi 42
Arac de Nyeko, Monica 66
Atim, Julian 66
Atyam, Angelina 55
Kato, David 103
Kisekka, Samson 112
Kony, Joseph 101
Mugisha, Frank 119
Mupuya, Andrew 118
Museveni, Yoweri 4, 119
Mutebi, Ronald 25
Nabagesera, Kasha Jacqueline 130
Obote, Milton 63
Oboth, Isaac 117
Okaalet, Peter 58
Sentamu, John 58

Venezuelan
Escobar, Alcides 130

West Indian
Césaire, Aimé 48, 69
Coombs, Orde M. 44
Innis, Roy 5
Knight, Gwendolyn 63
Pitt, David Thomas 10
Rojas, Don 33
Staupers, Mabel K. 7
Taylor, Susan L. 10, 86
Walcott, Derek 5, 94

Zambian
Chiluba, Frederick 56, 80
Chitalu, Godfrey 108
Kaunda, Kenneth 2
Moyo, Dambisa 76
Mwanawasa, Levy 72
Sata, Michael 102, 125
Zulu, Princess Kasune 54

Zimbabwean
Bulawayo, NoViolet 125
Chideya, Farai 14
Marechera, Dambudzo 39
Moyo, Lovemore 76
Mtukudzi, Oliver 109
Mugabe, Robert 10, 71
Mukoko, Jestina 75
Muzorewa, Abel 85
Nkomo, Joshua 4, 65
Tsvangirai, Morgan 26, 72
Vera, Yvonne 32

Cumulative Occupation Index

Volume numbers appear in **bold**

Art and design

Abele, Julian **55**
Aberra, Amsale **67**
Adjaye, David **38, 78**
Adkins, Terry **122**
Allah, Khalik **131**
Allen, Tina **22, 75**
Alston, Charles **33**
Amaki, Amalia **76**
Amos, Emma **63**
Anderson, Ho Che **54**
Andrews, Benny **22, 59**
Andrews, Bert **13**
Armstrong, Robb **15**
Ashford, Calvin, Jr. **74**
Bailey, Preston **64**
Bailey, Radcliffe **19**
Bailey, Xenobia **11**
Baker, Matt **76**
Bannister, Edward Mitchell **88**
Barboza, Anthony **10**
Barnes, Ernie **16, 78**
Barthé, Earl **78**
Barthe, Richmond **15**
Basquiat, Jean-Michel **5**
Bass, Holly **134**
Bearden, Romare **2, 50**
Beasley, Phoebe **34**
Beckwith, Naomi **101**
Bell, Darrin **77**
Benberry, Cuesta **65**
Benjamin, Tritobia Hayes **53**
Biggers, John **20, 33**
Biggers, Sanford **62**
Billops, Camille **82**
Bingham, Howard **96**
Blackburn, Robert **28**
Bond, J. Max, Jr. **76**
Bradford, Mark **89**
Brandon, Barbara **3**
Bridges, Sheila **36**
Brown, Donald **19**
Brown, Frederick J. **102**
Brown, Robert **65**
Bryan, Ashley **41, 104**
Burke, Selma **16**
Burroughs, Margaret Taylor **9, 134**
Camp, Kimberly **19**
Campbell, E. Simms **13**
Campbell, Mary Schmidt **43**
Catlett, Elizabeth **2, 120**
Chanticleer, Raven **91**
Chase, John Saunders, Jr. **99**

Chase-Riboud, Barbara **20, 46**
Cole, Ernest **123**
Colescott, Robert **69**
Collins, Paul **61**
Cortor, Eldzier **42**
Cowans, Adger W. **20**
Cox, Renée **67**
Crichlow, Ernest **75**
Crite, Allan Rohan **29**
Davis, Bing **84**
De Veaux, Alexis **44**
DeCarava, Roy **42, 81**
Delaney, Beauford **19**
Delaney, Joseph **30**
Delsarte, Louis **34**
Dial, Thornton **114**
Dillon, Leo **103**
Donaldson, Jeff **46**
Douglas, Aaron **7**
Douglas, Emory **89**
Driskell, David C. **7**
du Cille, Michel **74**
Duncanson, Robert S. **127**
Dwight, Edward **65**
Edwards, Melvin **22**
El Wilson, Barbara **35**
Farley, James Conway **99**
Fax, Elton **48**
Feelings, Tom **11, 47**
Ferguson, Amos **81**
Fine, Sam **60**
Fosso, Samuel **116**
Frazier, LaToya Ruby **131**
Freeman, Leonard **27**
Fuller, Meta Vaux Warrick **27**
Gantt, Harvey **1**
Garvin, Gerry **78**
Gates, Theaster **118**
Gilles, Ralph **61**
Gilliam, Sam **16**
Golden, Thelma **10, 55**
Goodnight, Paul **32**
Green, Jonathan **54**
Guyton, Tyree **9, 94**
Hammons, David **69**
Hansen, Austin **88**
Harkless, Necia Desiree **19**
Harrington, Oliver W. **9, 136**
Harris, Lyle Ashton **83**
Harrison, Charles **72**
Hathaway, Isaac Scott **33**
Hayden, Palmer **13**
Hayes, Cecil N. **46**
Holder, Geoffrey **78, 124**

Honeywood, Varnette P. **54, 88**
Hope, John **8**
Hudson, Cheryl **15**
Hudson, Wade **15**
Hunt, Richard **6**
Hunter, Clementine **45**
Jackson, Earl **31**
Jackson, Mary **73**
Jackson, Vera **40**
Johnson, Jeh Vincent **44**
Johnson, William Henry **3**
Jones, Loïs Mailou **13, 136**
Jones, Paul R. **76**
Keïta, Seydou **124**
King, Robert Arthur **58**
Kitt, Sandra **23**
Knight, Gwendolyn **63**
Knox, Simmie **49**
Lawrence, Jacob **4, 28**
Lee, Annie Frances **22**
Lee-Smith, Hughie **5, 22**
Lewis, Edmonia **10**
Lewis, Norman **39**
Lewis, Samella **25**
Ligon, Glenn **82**
Lovell, Whitfield **74**
Loving, Alvin, Jr. **35, 53**
Lowe, Rick **124**
Magruder, Nilah **134**
Manley, Edna **26**
Marshall, Kerry James **59**
Mason, Desmond **127**
Mayhew, Richard **39**
McCullough, Geraldine **58, 79**
McDuffie, Dwayne **62**
McGee, Charles **10**
McGruder, Aaron **28, 56, 120**
McQueen, Steve **84**
Mehretu, Julie **85**
Mitchell, Corinne **8**
Moody, Ronald **30**
Morrison, Keith **13**
Motley, Archibald, Jr. **30**
Moutoussamy-Ashe, Jeanne **7**
Mutu, Wangechi **44**
Myles, Kim **69**
Nascimento, Abdias do **93**
Nelson, Kadir **115**
Ndiaye, Iba **74**
Neals, Otto **73**
N'Namdi, George R. **17**
Nugent, Richard Bruce **39**
Ofili, Chris **124**
O'Grady, Lorraine **73**

Olden, Georg(e) **44**
Ormes, Jackie **73**
Ouattara **43**
Owens, Clifford **129**
Perkins, Marion **38**
Pierce, Elijah **84**
Pierre, Andre **17**
Pindell, Howardena **55**
Pinder, Jefferson **77**
Pinderhughes, John **47**
Pinkney, Jerry **15, 124**
Piper, Adrian **71**
Pippin, Horace **9**
Pope.L, William **72**
Porter, James A. **11**
Prince Twins Seven-Seven **95**
Prophet, Nancy Elizabeth **42**
Purifoy, Noah **135**
Puryear, Martin **42, 101**
Querino, Manuel Raimundo **84**
Ransome, James E. **88**
Reid, Senghor **55**
Ringgold, Faith **4, 81**
Roble, Abdi **71**
Ruley, Ellis **38**
Saar, Alison **16**
Saar, Betye **80**
Saint James, Synthia **12**
Sallee, Charles **38**
Sanders, Joseph R., Jr. **11**
Savage, Augusta **12**
Scott, Dread **106**
Scott, John T. **65**
Sebree, Charles **40**
Serrano, Andres **3**
Shabazz, Attallah **6**
Shonibare, Yinka **58**
Sidibé, Malick **124**
Simmons, Gary **58**
Simpson, Lorna **4, 36**
Simpson, Merton D. **110**
Sims, Lowery Stokes **27**
Sklarek, Norma Merrick **25, 101**
Sleet, Moneta, Jr. **5, 136**
Smith, Bruce W. **53**
Smith, Marvin **46**
Smith, Ming **100**
Smith, Morgan **46**
Smith, Vincent D. **48**
Steave-Dickerson, Kia **57**
Stout, Renee **63**
Sudduth, Jimmy Lee **65**
Tanksley, Ann **37**
Tanner, Henry Ossawa **1**

Taylor, Lonzie Odie 96
Taylor, Robert Robinson 80
Thomas, Alma 14
Thrash, Dox 35
Tolliver, Mose 60
Tolliver, William 9
Tooks, Lance 62
Turner, Morrie 122
Twiggs, Leo 127
VanDerZee, James 6
Verna, Gelsy 70
Wagner, Albert 78
Wainwright, Joscelyn 46
Walker, A'lelia 14
Walker, Kara 16, 80
Waring, Laura Wheeler 99
Washington, Alonzo 29
Washington, James, Jr. 38
Weems, Carrie Mae 63, 116
Wells, James Lesesne 10
White, Charles 39
White, Dondi 34
White, John H. 27
Wiley, Kehinde 62
Williams, Clarence 70
Williams, O. S. 13
Williams, Paul R. 9
Williams, William T. 11
Willis, Deborah 85
Williston, David Augustus 99
Wilson, Ellis 39
Wilson, John 109
Withers, Ernest C. 68, 88
Woodruff, Hale 9

Business

Abbott, Robert Sengstacke 27
Abiola, Moshood 70
Abudu, Mo 121
Adams, Eula L. 39, 120
Adams, Jenoyne 60
Adkins, Rod 41
Adoboli, Kweku 106
Aire, Chris 117
Akil, Mara Brock 60, 82
Alexander, Archie Alphonso 14
Allen-Buillard, Melba 55
Amos, Wally 9
Amoudi, Mohammed al- 88
Archer, Lee, Jr. 79
Armstrong, Govind 81
Auguste, Donna 29
Austin, Gloria 63
Austin, Jim 63
Austin, Wanda M. 94
Avant, Clarence 19, 86
Avant, Nicole A. 90
Baker, Ella 5
Baker, Maxine 28
Bakewell, Danny 99
Banks, Paula A. 68
Banks, William 11
Barden, Donald H. 9, 20, 89
Barrett, Andrew C. 12
Bates, Daisy 13, 135
Beal, Bernard B. 46
Beamon, Bob 30
Beasley, Phoebe 34
Bell, James A. 50
Bennett, Richard 97
Bickerstaff, Cydni L. 133
Bing, Dave 3, 59, 78
Blackshear, Leonard 52

Blackwell, Robert D., Sr. 52
Blaylock, Ronald 86
Blayton, Jesse B., Sr. 55
Bolden, Frank E. 44
Boston, Kelvin E. 25
Boston, Lloyd 24
Bowen, Ruth 83
Bowles, Cephas 127
Boyd, Edward 70
Boyd, Gwendolyn 49
Boyd, John W., Jr. 20, 72
Boyd, T. B., III 6
Bradley, Jennette B. 40
Brae, C. Michael 61
Brewer, Rosalind 100
Bridgeman, Junior 132
Bridgforth, Glinda 36
Briggs, Curtis 84
Brimmer, Andrew 2, 48, 106
Bronner, Nathaniel H., Sr. 32
Brown, Eddie C. 35
Brown, Jamie Foster 91
Brown, Les 5
Brown, Marie Dutton 12
Brunson, Dorothy 1, 87
Bryant, John 26
Bryant, Kimberly 127
Burgess, Marjorie L. 55
Burks, Juanita P. 95
Burns, Ursula 60
Burrell, Tom 21, 51
Burrus, William Henry 45
Bush, Charles Vernon 125
Burt-Murray, Angela 59
Butler, George, Jr. 70
Cain, Herman 15, 92
Calabrese, Karyn 89
Caldwell, Earl 60
Cameron, James 80
Carter, Pamela Lynn 67
CasSelle, Malcolm 11
Chamberlain, Wilt 18, 47
Chapman, Nathan A., Jr. 21
Chapman, Susan E. 94
Chappell, Emma 18
Chase, Leah 57
Chenault, Kenneth 4, 36, 108
Cherry, Deron 40
Chisholm, Samuel J. 32
Church, Robert Reed, Sr. 132
Clark, Celeste 15
Clark, Patrick 14
Clay, William Lacy 8
Clayton, Xernona 3, 45
Clement-Holmes, Linda 94
Clyburn, Mignon 78
Cobbs, Price M. 9
Coke, Christopher 108
Colbert, Virgis William 17
Coleman, Donald 24, 62
Coleman, Ken 57
Compton-Rock, Malaak 86
Conyers, Nathan G. 24
Cooper, Barry 33
Cooper, Evern 40
Corbi, Lana 42
Cornelius, Don 4, 100
Cottrell, Comer 11
Council, LaVerne 94
Cox, William E. 68
Creagh, Milton 27
Crum, George 101
Cuffe, Paul 98

Cullers, Vincent T. 49
Dangote, Aliko 124
Daniels-Carter, Valerie 23
Darden, Calvin 38
Dash, Darien 29
Davis, Belva 61
Davis, Ed 24
Davis, Erroll B., Jr. 57
Dawson, Matel, Jr. 39
de Passe, Suzanne 25
Dean, Mark 35
Dee, Merri 55
Delany, Bessie 12
Delany, Martin R. 27
Delany, Sadie 12
DeVard, Jerri 61
Diallo, Amadou 27
Doley, Harold, Jr. 26
Donald, Arnold 36, 126
Dorsey, Thomas J. 90
dos Santos, Isabel 114
Downing, George T. 91
Driver, David E. 11
Ducksworth, Marilyn 12
Duerson, Dave 93
Easley, Annie J. 61
Ebanks, Michelle 60
Edelin, Ramona Hoage 19
Edmonds, Tracey 16, 64
Edmunds, Gladys 48
Edwards, Trevor 54
El Wilson, Barbara 35
Ellington, E. David 11
Elumelu, Tony 116
Evans, Darryl 22
Farmer, Forest J. 1
Farr, Mel 24
Fauntroy, Walter E. 11
Ferguson, Roger W., Jr. 25, 112
Ferdinand, Rio 82
Fils-Aimé, Reggie 74
Fletcher, Buddy 16, 108
Flowers, Sylester 50
Ford, Barney 90
Ford, Harold E(ugene), Jr. 16, 70
Forte, Linda Diane 54
Foster, Jylla Moore 45
Fowler, Reggie 51
Frazier, Kenneth 97
Friday, Jeff 24
Fryer, Roland G. 56
Fudge, Ann 11, 55
Fuller, S. B. 13
Funderburg, I. Owen 38
Gaines, Brenda 41
Gardner, Chris 65
Gardner, Edward G. 45
Garrett, James F. 78
Gaskins, Rudy 74
Gaston, Arthur George 3, 38, 59
Gibbs, Mifflin W. 99
Gibson, John Trusty 87
Gibson, Kenneth Allen 6
Gibson, Ted 66
Gidron, Richard D. 68
Gilles, Ralph 61
Goings, Russell 59
Goldsberry, Ronald 18
Golston, Allan C. 55
Gooden, Linda 94
Goodman, Kim C. 94
Gordon, Bruce S. 41, 53, 82
Gordon, Pamela 17

Gordy, Berry, Jr. 1
Goss, Carol A. 55
Grace, George H. 48
Graham, Stedman 13
Graves, Butch 77
Graves, Earl G. 1, 35
Gray, Farrah 59
Greely, M. Gasby 27
Green, Isaac H. 79
Green, Nancy 112
Greene, Richard Thaddeus, Sr. 67
Greenwood, Monique 38
Griffith, Mark Winston 8
Grooms, Henry R(andall) 50
Hale, Lorraine 8
Hall, Alvin D. 86
Ham, Cynthia Parker 58
Hamilton, Samuel C. 47
Handy, W. C. 8
Hannah, Marc 10
Hardison, Bethann 12
Harrell, Andre 9, 30
Harris, Alice 7
Harris, Carla A. 67
Harris, Monica 18
Harris, Richard E. 61
Hart, Thomas A., Sr. 113
Harvey, Steve 18, 58
Harvey, William R. 42
Hawkins, La-Van 17, 54
Haysbert, Raymond V., Sr. 87
Hazel, Darryl B. 50
Henderson, Gordon 5
Henderson, Henry Fairfax, Jr. 89
Henry, Dwight 104
Henry, Lenny 9, 52
Henry, Troy 85
Herndon, Alonzo Franklin 89
Hightower, Dennis F. 13
Hill, Bonnie Guiton 20
Hill, Calvin 19
Hill, Janet 19
Hill, Jesse, Jr. 13
Hill, Peter 92
Hobson, Mellody 40
Holland, Kimberly N. 62
Holland, Robert, Jr. 11
Holmes, Larry 20, 68
Holstein, Casper 89
Howell, Ayinde 91
Howroyd, Janice Bryant 42
Hudlin, Warrington 9
Hudson, Cheryl 15
Hudson, Wade 15
Huggins, Larry 21
Hughes, Cathy 27
Ibrahim, Mo 67, 115
Irvin, Vernon 65
Jackson, George 19
Jackson, Hal 41, 104
Jackson, Joe 78
Jackson, Mannie 14
Jackson, Michael 19, 53, 76
James, Charles H., III 62
James, Donna A. 51
James, Juanita 13
Jenkins, Ray 77
Jennings, Thomas L. 125
Johnson, Bumpy 102
Johnson, Eunice W. 83
Johnson, George E. 29
Johnson, John H. 3, 54
Johnson, Robert L. 3, 39, 121

Johnson, Sheila Crump 48
Johnson, William 91
Jolley, Willie 28
Jones, Carl 7
Jones, Caroline 29
Jones, Ingrid Saunders 18
Jones, John 89
Jones, Thomas W. 41
Jones, Wayne 53
Jordan, Michael 6, 21
Jordan, Montell 23
Joyner, Marjorie Stewart 26
Julian, Percy Lavon 6
Kaigler, Denise 63
Katumbi, Moïse 135
Keith, Floyd A. 61
Kemp, Herb 94
Kendrick, Erika 57
Kidd, Mae Street 39
Killingsworth, Cleve, Jr. 54
King, Dexter 10
Knowles, Tina 61
Knowling, Robert E., Jr. 38
Lamothe, Laurent 122
Lane, Vincent 5
Langhart Cohen, Janet 19, 60
Lanier, Willie 33
Laryea, Thomas Davies, III 67
Lawal, Kase L. 45
Lawless, Theodore K. 8
Lawson, Jennifer 1, 50
Leary, Kathryn D. 10
Leavell, Dorothy R. 17
Lee, Annie Frances 22
Lee, Bertram M., Sr. 46
Lee, Debra L. 62
Leonard, Sugar Ray 15
Lewis, Aubrey 133
Lewis, Aylwin B. 51, 88
Lewis, Byron E. 13
Lewis, Delano 7
Lewis, Edward T. 21
Lewis, Reginald F. 6
Lewis, William M., Jr. 40
Liggins, Alfred, III 43
Llewellyn, J. Bruce 13, 85
Long, Eddie L. 29, 89
Louis, Errol T. 8
Lucas, John 7
Lucy, William 50
Mack, Iris 105
Malone, Annie 13
Maponya, Richard 101
March, William Carrington 56
Marks, Audrey 99
Matthews Shatteen, Westina 51
Matzeliger, Jan 93
Mayberry-Stewart, Melodie 94
Maynard, Robert C. 7
Mays, Leslie A. 41
Mays, William G. 34
McCabe, Jewell Jackson 10
McCann, Renetta 44
McCoy, Elijah 8
McDonald, Erroll 1
McGee, James Madison 46
McGuire, Raymond J. 57
McKissack, Leatrice 80
McLeod, Gus 27
McPherson, David 32
McWorter, Free Frank 91
Middleton, Reggie 105
Miller, Larry G. 72

Miller, Pepper 96
Millines Dziko, Trish 28
Mills, Steve 47
Mingo, Frank 32
Mitchell, Shireen 89
Monk, Art 38, 73
Monroe, Bryan 71
Montgomery, Isaiah T. 91
Montgomery, Robbie 101
Moore, Wes 86
Morgan, Garrett 1
Morgan, Rose 11
Morris, William 51
Moyo, Karega Kofi 36
Moyo, Yvette Jackson 36
Muhammad, Jabir Herbert 72
Mupuya, Andrew 118
Nail, John E. 92
Nanula, Richard D. 20
Nash, Diane 72
Nelson Meigs, Andrea 48
Norman, Christina 47
Ogunlesi, Adebayo O. 37
Oliver, Garrett 95
Olojede, Dele 59
O'Neal, Rodney 88
O'Neal, Stanley 38, 67
Otis, Clarence, Jr. 55
Ouattara, Morou 74
Overton, Anthony 128
Packer, Daniel 56
Parham, Marjorie B. 71
Parks, Henry Green, Jr. 89
Parsons, Richard 11, 33, 124
Payton, Philip A., Jr. 88
Peck, Carolyn 23
Perez, Anna 1
Perkins, James, Jr. 55
Perry, Laval 64
Perry, Lowell 30
Phillips, Charles E., Jr. 57, 109
Pierce, Harold 75
Pinkett, Randal 61
Pleasant, Mary Ellen 9
Plinton, James O., Jr. 98
Potter, Myrtle 40
Price, Frederick K. C. 21
Price, Hugh B. 9, 54
Price, Lisa 97
Procope, Ernesta 23
Procope, John Levy 56
Raines, Franklin 14, 107
Rand, A. Barry 6
Reeves, Rachel J. 23
Rhone, Sylvia 2
Rice, Linda Johnson 9, 41
Rice, Norm 8
Richardson, Donna 39
Richie, Leroy C. 18
Rideau, Iris 46
Roberts, Mike 57
Roberts, Roy S. 14
Robertson, Oscar 26
Robinson, Randall 7, 46
Roche, Joyce M. 17
Rodgers, Johnathan 6, 51
Rodriguez, Jimmy 47
Rogers, Desirée 88
Rogers, John W., Jr. 5, 52
Rojas, Don 33
Rolle, Janet 97
Ross, Charles 27
Ross, Diana 8, 27

Russell, Bill 8
Russell, Herman Jerome 17
Russell-McCloud, Patricia 17
Saint James, Synthia 12
Samara, Noah 15
Samuelsson, Marcus 53, 120
Sanders, Angelia 86
Sanders, Dori 8
Sbraga, Kevin 88
Scott, C. A. 29
Scott, Milton 51
Sengstacke, John 18
Shank, Suzanne F. 77
Shropshire, Thomas B. 49
Siméus, Dumas M. 25, 110
Simmons, Kimora Lee 51, 83
Simmons, Russell 1, 30
Sims, Naomi 29, 79
Smith, B(arbara) 11
Smith, Clarence O. 21
Smith, Jane E. 24
Smith, Joshua 10
Sneed, Paula A. 18
Snowden, Gail 108
Spaulding, Charles Clinton 9
Staley, Dawn 57
Stanford, Olivia Lee Dilworth 49
Steinberg, Martha Jean "The
    Queen" 28
Steward, David L. 36
Stewart, Ella 39
Stewart, Paul Wilbur 12
Stinson, Denise L. 59
Stradford, J. B. 101
Stringer, Vickie 58
Sullivan, Leon H. 3, 30
Sutton, Percy E. 42, 82
Taylor, Ephren W., II 61
Taylor, Karin 34
Taylor, Kristin Clark 8
Taylor, Natalie 47
Taylor, Robert Rochon 104
Taylor, Susan L. 10, 86
Temple, Lewis 102
Terrell, Dorothy A. 24
Thiam, Tidjane 104
Thomas, Franklin A. 5, 49
Thomas, Jefferson 88
Thomas-Graham, Pamela 29
Thompson, Cynthia Bramlett 50
Thompsson, Don 56, 108
Thompson, John W. 26
Tobin, Patricia 75
Travis, Tracey T. 94
Tribble, Israel, Jr. 8
Trotter, Lloyd G. 56
Trotter, Monroe 9
Tuckson, Reed V. 71
Tyson, Asha 39
Ussery, Terdema, II 29
Utendahl, John 23
Uys, Ashley 125
VanDerZee, James 6
Vaughn, Gladys Gary 47
Vaughns, Cleopatra 46
Villarosa, Clara 85
Walker, A'lelia 14
Walker, Cedric 19
Walker, Joseph Edison 111
Walker, Madame C. J. 7
Walker, Maggie Lena 17
Walker, Ray 109
Walker, T. J. 7

Walker, Tristan 98
Ward, Lloyd 21, 46
Ware, Carl H. 30
Washington, Alonzo 29
Washington, Mary T. 57
Washington, Regynald G. 44
Washington, Val 12
Wasow, Omar 15
Watkins, Donald 35
Watkins, Walter C., Jr. 24
Wein, Joyce 62
Welburn, Edward T. 50
Wells-Barnett, Ida B. 8
Westbrook, Kelvin 50
White, Linda M. 45
White, Walter F. 4
Wilkins, Ray 47
Williams, Armstrong 29
Williams, Lindsey 75
Williams, O. S. 13
Williams, Paul R. 9
Williams, Ronald A. 57
Williams, Terrie 35
Williams, Wendy 62
Willie, Louis, Jr. 68
Wilson, Sunnie 7, 55
Woods, Jacqueline 52
Woods, Sylvia 34, 104
Woodson, Robert L. 10
Wright, Antoinette 60
Wright, Charles H. 35
Wright, Deborah C. 25
Wright, Rayfield 70
Wright, Richard Robert, Sr. 100
Yoba, Malik 11
Young, Perry H. 100
Zollar, Alfred 40

Dance
Abraham, Kyle 116
Acogny, Germaine 55
Adams, Jenoyne 60
Ailey, Alvin 8
Allen, Debbie 13, 42
Anderson, Lauren 72
Anderson, Maceo111
Atkins, Cholly 40
Babatunde, Obba 35
Baby Laurence 136
Baker, Josephine 3
Bates, Peg Leg 14, 135
Beatty, Talley 35
Brown, Ernest 80
Brown, Ronald K. 91
Byrd, Donald 10
Chanticleer, Raven 91
Clarke, Hope 14
Coles, Honi 128
Collins, Janet 33, 64
Copeland, Misty 125
Davis, Chuck 33
de Lavallade, Carmen 78
DePrince, Michaela 104
Dove, Ulysses 5
Dunham, Katherine 4, 59
Ellington, Mercedes 34
Fagan, Garth 18, 98
Falana, Lola 42
Glover, Savion 14
Hall, Arthur 39
Harris, Rennie 120
Henson, Darrin 33
Hines, Gregory 1, 42

Jamison, Judith **7, 67, 96**
Jefferson, Denise **87**
Jeune, Vitolio **98**
Johnson, Ken **106**
Johnson, Virginia **9**
Jones, Bill T. **1, 46, 80**
Jones, Doris W. **62**
King, Alonzo **38**
Lane, William Henry **90**
LeTang, Henry **66**
Manning, Frankie **78**
Miller, Bebe **3**
Mills, Florence **22**
Mitchell, Arthur **2, 47**
Moten, Etta **18**
Nash, Joe **55**
Nicholas, Fayard **20, 57**
Nicholas, Harold **20**
Nichols, Nichelle **11**
Polite, Carlene Hatcher **82**
Pomare, Eleo **72**
Premice, Josephine **41**
Primus, Pearl **6, 125**
Ray, Gene Anthony **47**
Rhoden, Dwight **40**
Ribeiro, Alfonso **17**
Richardson, Desmond **39**
Robinson, Bill "Bojangles" **11**
Robinson, Cleo Parker **38**
Robinson, Fatima **34**
Robinson, LaVaughn **69**
Rodgers, Rod **36**
Sims, Howard "Sandman" **48**
Slyde, Jimmy **70**
Spears, Warren **52**
Storyboard P **118**
Tyson, Andre **40**
Vereen, Ben **4**
Walker, Dianne **57**
Washington, Fredi **10**
Williams, Dudley **60**
Wilson, Reggie **116**
Zollar, Jawole Willa Jo **28**

Education

Abani, Chris **77**
Abercrumbie, P. Eric **95**
Ackerman, Arlene **108**
Adams, Alma **127**
Adams, Leslie **39**
Adams-Ender, Clara **40**
Adkins, Rutherford H. **21**
Aidoo, Ama Ata **38**
Ake, Claude **30**
Albert, Octavia V. R. **100**
Alexander, Margaret Walker **22**
Alexander, Michelle **98**
Allen, Robert L. **38**
Allen, Samuel W. **38**
Allen-Buillard, Melba **55**
Alston, Charles **33**
Amadi, Elechi **40**
Ammons, James H. **81**
Anderson, Charles Edward **37**
Appiah, Kwame Anthony **67, 101**
Archie-Hudson, Marguerite **44**
Asante, Molefi Kete **3**
Aubert, Alvin **41**
Austin, Bobby W. **95**
Awuah, Patrick **111, 131**
Bacon-Bercey, June **38**
Bahati, Wambui **60**
Baiocchi, Regina Harris **41**

Baker, Augusta **38**
Baker, Delbert W. **110**
Baker, Gwendolyn Calvert **9**
Baker, Houston A., Jr. **6**
Baldwin, Cynthia **74, 107**
Ballard, Allen Butler, Jr. **40**
Barbee, Lloyd Augustus **71**
Barboza, Anthony **10**
Barnett, Marguerite **46**
Barron, Inez **136**
Barthé, Earl **78**
Bath, Patricia E. **37**
Batiste, Alvin **66**
Beals, Melba Pattillo **15, 94**
Beckham, Barry **41**
Belgrave, Marcus **77, 129**
Bell, Derrick **6, 98**
Benberry, Cuesta **65**
Benjamin, Tritobia Hayes **53**
Berry, Bertice **8, 55**
Berry, Mary Frances **7**
Bethune, Mary McLeod **4**
Biggers, John **20, 33**
Black, Albert **51**
Blackwell, David **79**
Blackwell, Gloria **127**
Blakely, Edward J. **88**
Blanchard, Shawn **129**
Blassingame, John Wesley **40**
Blockson, Charles L. **42**
Bluitt, Juliann S. **14**
Bobo, Lawrence **60**
Bogle, Donald **34**
Bolden, Tonya **32**
Bosley, Freeman, Jr. **7**
Boyd, Melba Joyce **86**
Boyd, T. B., III **6**
Bradley, Adam **101**
Bradley, David Henry, Jr. **39**
Branch, William Blackwell **39**
Brathwaite, Kamau **36**
Braun, Carol Moseley **4, 42**
Braxton, Anthony **128**
Briscoe, Marlin **37**
Bromery, Randolph Wilson **85**
Brown, Claude **38**
Brown, Hallie Quinn **100**
Brown, Joyce F. **25**
Brown, Sterling Allen **10, 64**
Brown, Uzee **42**
Brown, Wesley **23**
Brown, Willa **40**
Bruce, Blanche Kelso **33**
Brutus, Dennis **38**
Bunch, Lonnie G., III **91**
Burke, Selma **16**
Burks, Mary Fair **40**
Burnim, Mickey L. **48**
Burroughs, Margaret Taylor **9, 134**
Burroughs, Nannie Helen **96**
Butler, Paul D. **17**
Butler, Selena Sloan **98**
Butts, Calvin O., III **9, 90**
Callender, Clive O. **3**
Campbell, Mary Schmidt **43**
Cannon, Katie **10**
Carby, Hazel **27**
Cardozo, Francis L. **33**
Carnegie, Herbert **25**
Carruthers, George R. **40**
Carter, Herbert E. **108**
Carter, Joye Maureen **41**
Carter, Kenneth **53**

Carter, Warrick L. **27**
Cartey, Wilfred **47**
Carver, George Washington **4**
Cary, Lorene **3**
Cary, Mary Ann Shadd **30**
Cayton, Horace **26**
Chaney, John **67**
Cheney-Coker, Syl **43**
Childers, Lulu Vere **95**
Clark, Joe **1**
Clark, Kenneth B. **5, 52**
Clark, Septima **7**
Clark, Yvonne Young **95**
Clarke, Cheryl **32**
Clarke, George **32**
Clarke, John Henrik **20**
Clayton, Constance **1**
Cleaver, Kathleen Neal **29**
Clements, George **2**
Clemmons, Reginal G. **41**
Cobb, Jewel Plummer **42**
Cobb, W. Montague **39**
Cobb, William Jelani **59, 121**
Cobbs, Price M. **9**
Cohen, Anthony **15**
Cohen, Cathy J. **88**
Cole, Johnnetta B. **5, 43**
Coleman, Beatrice **120**
Coleman, Steve **124**
Coleman, William F., III **61**
Colescott, Robert **69**
Collette, Buddy **119**
Collins, Janet **33, 64**
Collins, Marva **3, 71**
Collins, Patricia Hill **67**
Comer, James P. **6**
Coney, PonJola **48**
Conrad, Cecilia A. **94**
Cook, Mercer **40**
Cook, Samuel DuBois **14**
Cook, Toni **23**
Cooper, Afua **53**
Cooper, Anna Julia **20**
Cooper, Edward S. **6**
Cooper Cafritz, Peggy **43**
Copeland, Michael **47**
Cotter, Joseph Seamon, Sr. **40**
Cottrell, Comer **11**
Counter, S. Allen **74**
Cox, Elbert Frank **111**
Cox, Joseph Mason Andrew **51**
Cox, William E. **68**
Creagh, Milton **27**
Crenshaw, Kimberlé Williams **88**
Crew, Rudy **16, 113**
Crew, Spencer R. **55**
Cross, Dolores E. **23**
Crouch, Hubert **95**
Cruse, Harold **54**
Cullen, Countee **8**
Dathorne, O. R. **52**
Davis, Allison **12**
Davis, Angela J. **88**
Davis, Arthur P. **41**
Davis, Charles T. **48**
Davis, Erroll B., Jr. **57**
Davis, George **36**
Davis, Milt **74**
Dawson, William Levi **39**
Days, Drew S., III **10**
Deconge-Watson, Lovenia **55**
Delany, Sadie **12**
Delany, Samuel R., Jr. **9**

Delco, Wilhelmina R. **33**
Delpit, Lisa **101**
Delsarte, Louis **34**
Dennard, Brazeal **37**
Dewitty, Thelma **114**
Dickens, Helen Octavia **14, 64**
Dixon, Margaret A. **14, 136**
Dodson, Howard, Jr. **7, 52**
Dodson, Owen Vincent **38**
Dogan, Matthew Winifred **91**
Donaldson, Jeff **46**
Dove, Ulysses **5**
Drake, Michael V. **122**
Draper, Sharon Mills **16, 43**
Drummond, William J. **40**
Du Bois, David Graham **45, 135**
Dube, John Langalibalele **119**
Dumas, Henry **41**
Dunbar-Nelson, Alice Ruth Moore **44**
Dunnigan, Alice Allison **41**
Dunston, Georgia Mae **48**
Dymally, Mervyn **42**
Dyson, Michael Eric **11, 40, 128**
Early, Gerald **15**
Edelin, Ramona Hoage **19**
Edelman, Marian Wright **5, 42**
Edley, Christopher **2, 48**
Edley, Christopher F., Jr. **48**
Edwards, Harry **2**
Elders, Joycelyn **6**
Elliot, Lorris **37**
Ellis, Clarence A. **38**
Ellison, Ralph **7**
Epps, Archie C., III **45**
Evans, Mari **26**
Everett, Percival **93**
Falconer, Etta Zuber **59**
Fauset, Jessie **7**
Favors, Steve **23**
Feelings, Muriel **44**
Ferguson, Ronald F. **75**
Figueroa, John J. **40**
Fleming, Raymond **48**
Fletcher, Bill, Jr. **41**
Floyd, Elson S. **41**
Ford, Jack **39**
Forman, James, Jr. **89**
Foster, Ezola **28**
Foster, Henry W., Jr. **26**
Foster, William P. **88**
Francis, Norman (C.) **60**
Franklin, John Hope **5, 77**
Franklin, Robert M. **13**
Frazier, E. Franklin **10**
Fryer, Roland G. **56**
Fuller, A. Oveta **43**
Fuller, Arthur **27**
Fuller, Howard L. **37**
Fuller, Solomon Carter, Jr. **15**
Futrell, Mary Hatwood **33**
Gaines, Ernest J. **7**
Gates, Henry Louis, Jr. **3, 38, 67**
Gates, Sylvester James, Jr. **15, 130**
Gayle, Addison, Jr. **41**
George, Zelma Watson **42**
Gerima, Haile **38, 80**
Gibson, Donald Bernard **40**
Giddings, Paula **11**
Gilbert, John Wesley **91**
Gill, Gerald **69**
Gloster, Hugh Morris, Sr. **90**
Gomes, Peter J. **15, 93**

Gomez, Jewelle 30
Gomillion, Charles 90
Goodison, Lorna 71
Granville, Evelyn Boyd 36
Graves, Milford 126
Greenfield, Eloise 9
Groff, Peter 96
Guinier, Lani 7, 30
Guy-Sheftall, Beverly 13, 92
Hageman, Hans and Ivan 36
Hale, Lorraine 8
Hall, Stuart 78
Halliburton, Warren J. 49
Hamburg, Beatrix 84
Hammonds, Evelynn 69
Handy, W. C. 8
Hansberry, William Leo 11
Harkless, Necia Desiree 19
Harris, Alice 7
Harris, Barry 68
Harris, Bill 72
Harris, Gary L. 87
Harris, Jay T. 19
Harris, Jessica B. 91
Harris, Kevin 120
Harris, Patricia Roberts 2
Harris-Lacewell, Melissa 81
Harvey, William R. 42
Haskins, James 36, 54
Hathaway, Isaac Scott 33
Hayden, Robert 12
Haynes, George Edmund 8
Henderson, George Washington
101
Henderson, Stephen E. 45
Henries, A. Doris Banks 44
Herenton, Willie W. 24, 81
Hill, Andrew 66
Hill, Anita 5, 65
Hill, Bonnie Guiton 20
Hill, Leslie Pinckney 44
Hill, Marc Lamont 80, 128
Hilliard, Asa Grant, III 66
Hine, Darlene Clark 24
Hinton, William Augustus 8
Hoagland, Everett H. 45
Hogan, Beverly Wade 50
Holland, Endesha Ida Mae 3, 57
Holt, Nora 38
Hope, John 8
Horton, James Oliver 58
Houston, Charles Hamilton 4
Hoyte, Lenon 50
Hrabowski, Freeman A., III 22
Huggins, Nathan Irvin 52
Hughes, Ebony 57
Hull, Akasha Gloria 45
Humphries, Frederick 20
Hunt, Darnell 92
Hunt, Richard 6
Hutcherson, Hilda Yvonne 54
Imes, Elmer Samuel 39
Jackson, Edison O. 67
Jackson, Fred James 25
Jackson, Vera 40
Jansen, Jonathan 102
Jarvis, Charlene Drew 21
Jarvis, Erich 67
Jefferson, Denise 87
Jefferson, Margo 108
Jeffries, Leonard 8
Jenifer, Franklyn G. 2
Jenkins, Ella 15

Johns, Vernon 38
Johnson, Anthony M. 92
Johnson, Conrad O. 97
Johnson, Hazel 22
Johnson, James Weldon 5
Johnson, Katherine 61
Johnson, Mordecai Wyatt 79
Jones, Edward P. 43, 67
Jones, Gayl 37
Jones, Ingrid Saunders 18
Joplin, Scott 6
Jordan, June 7, 35
Joseph, Jamal 101
Just, Ernest Everett 3
Karenga, Maulana 10, 71
Kay, Ulysses 37
Keith, Damon J. 16, 74
Kennedy, Florynce 12, 33
Kennedy, Randall 40
Kimbro, Dennis 10
King, Preston 28
King, Reatha Clark 65
Kittles, Rick 51
Komunyakaa, Yusef 9
Koontz, Elizabeth Duncan 101
Kunjufu, Jawanza 3, 50
Ladner, Joyce A. 42
Ladson-Billings, Gloria 130
Lawrence, Jacob 4, 28
Lawrence-Lightfoot, Sara 10
Lee, Annie Frances 22
Lee, Joe A. 45
Leevy, Carroll M. 42
Leffall, Lasalle 3, 64
Lewis, David Levering 9
Lewis, Norman 39
Lewis, Samella 25
Lewis, Shirley A. R. 14
Lewis, Thomas 19
Liberia-Peters, Maria Philomena 12
Lincoln, C. Eric 38
Lindsey, Tommie 51
Locke, Alain 10
Logan, Rayford W. 40
Lomax, Michael L. 58
Long, Loretta 58
Long, Richard Alexander 65
Lorde, Audre 6
Loury, Glenn 36
Loving, Alvin, Jr. 35, 53
Lowry, A. Leon 60
Lucy Foster, Autherine 35
Luper, Clara 94
Lyons, James E., Sr. 102
Lyttle, Hulda Margaret 14
Mackey, Nathaniel 75
Major, Clarence 9
Malveaux, Floyd 54
Mance, Junior 132
Manley, Audrey Forbes 16
Marable, Manning 10, 102
Markham, E. A. 37
Marsalis, Ellis 90
Marshall, Paule 7, 77
Masekela, Barbara 18
Mason, Herman, Jr. 83
Mason, Ronald 27
Massey, Walter E. 5, 45
Massie, Samuel P., Jr. 29
Matejka, Adrian 87
Maupin, John E., Jr. 92
Mayhew, Richard 39
Maynard, Robert C. 7

Maynor, Dorothy 19
Mayo, Whitman 32
Mays, Benjamin E. 7
Mazrui, Ali 12, 124
McBay, Henry C. 91
McCarty, Oseola 16, 136
McCullough, Geraldine 58, 79
McDaniel, Randall Cornell 81
McKay, Nellie Yvonne 17, 57
Mckesson, DeRay 133
McLendon, John B., Jr. 89
McMurray, Georgia L. 36
McPherson, James Alan 70
McWhorter, John 35, 119
Mell, Patricia 49
Memmi, Albert 37
Meredith, James H. 11
Millender-McDonald, Juanita 21, 61
Ming, William Robert, Jr. 125
Mitchell, Corinne 8
Mitchell, Nicole 66
Mitchell, Sharon 36
Mofolo, Thomas Mokopu 37
Mollel, Tololwa 38
Mongella, Gertrude 11
Moody-Adams, Michele 76
Moore, Barbara C. 49
Moore, Harry T. 29
Morón, Alonzo G. 91
Morrison, Keith 13
Morrison, Toni 2, 15, 86
Moses, Robert Parris 11
Moton, Robert Russa 83
Mphahlele, Es'kia 40
Mudimbe, V. Y. 61
Mullen, Harryette 34
Murray, Pauli 38
Nabrit, Samuel Milton 47
Nance, Cynthia 71
Naylor, Gloria 10, 42
Neal, Larry 38
Neal, Mark Anthony 74
Newkirk, Pamela 69
Newman, Lester C. 51
N'Namdi, George R. 17
Norman, Maidie 20
Nour, Nawal M. 56
Obadele, Imari 84
Ogletree, Charles, Jr. 12, 47
Ojikutu, Bisola 65
Oliver, Kimberly 60
Omolewa, Michael 119
Onwueme, Tess Osonye 23
Onwurah, Ngozi 38
Owens, Helen 48
Owens, Jimmy 130
Page, Alan 7
Page, Inman 82
Paige, Rod 29
Painter, Nell Irvin 24, 88
Palmer, Everard 37
Parker, Kellis E. 30
Patterson, Frederick Douglass 12
Patterson, Mary Jane 54
Patterson, Orlando 4, 127
Patton, Venetria K. 125
Payton, Benjamin F. 23
Perry, Steve 98
Perry, Warren 56
Peters, Margaret 43
Peters, Matilda 43
Peterson, James 81
Pickett, Cecil 39

Pindell, Howardena 55
Pinkney, Bill 42
Piper, Adrian 71
Player, Willa B. 43
Pollard, William L. 91
Porter, James A. 11
Poussaint, Alvin F. 5, 67
Powell, Benny 87
Price, Florence 37
Price, Glenda 22
Price, Richard 51
Proctor, Bernard Shaw 120
Prophet, Nancy Elizabeth 42
Purnell, Silas 59
Putney, Martha S. 75
Pyfrom, Estella 127
Quarles, Benjamin Arthur 18
Querino, Manuel Raimundo 84
Quigless, Helen G. 49
Rahman, Aishah 37
Ramphele, Mamphela 29
Randall, Vernellia R. 95
Reaves, Donald J. 102
Reddick, Lawrence Dunbar 20
Redding, J. Saunders 26
Redmond, Eugene 23
Reid, Ira De A. 100
Reid, Irvin D. 20
Reid, Rufus 130
Rhodes, Jewell Parker 84
Ribeau, Sidney 70
Rice, Condoleezza 3, 28, 72
Rice, Louise Allen 54
Richards, Hilda 49
Riles, Wilson C. 79
Robinson, Joann Gibson 100
Robinson, Sharon 22
Robinson, Spottswood W., III 22
Rodriguez, Cheryl 64
Rogers, Joel Augustus 30
Ross-Lee, Barbara 67
Rouse, Cecilia 93
Russell-McCloud, Patricia 17
Russwurm, John Brown 100
Salih, Al-Tayyib 37
Sallee, Charles Louis, Jr. 38
Schomburg, Arthur Alfonso 9
Sears, Stephanie 53
Senior, Olive 37
Shabazz, Betty 7, 26
Shange, Ntozake 8, 89
Shelton, Paula Young 86
Shipp, E. R. 15
Shirley, George 33
Simkins, Modjeska Monteith 112
Simmons, Ruth J. 13, 38
Sinkford, Jeanne C. 13
Sisulu, Sheila Violet Makate 24
Sizemore, Barbara A. 26, 110
Smith, Anna Deavere 6
Smith, Barbara 28
Smith, Gene 123
Smith, John L. 22
Smith, Tubby 18, 83
Snowden, Frank M., Jr. 67
Southern, Eileen 56
Sowande, Fela 39
Spearman, Leonard H. O., Sr. 81
Spears, Warren 52
Spikes, Dolores 18
Spriggs, William 67
Stanford, John 20
Steele, Claude 13, 97

Steele, Shelby **13, 82**
Stephens, Charlotte Andrews **14**
Stewart, Maria W. Miller **19**
Stewart, Tonea Harris **78**
Stone, Chuck **9, 120**
Sudarkasa, Niara **4**
Sullivan, Louis **8**
Swygert, H. Patrick **22**
Talbert, Mary B. **77**
Tancil, Gladys Quander **59**
Tanksley, Ann **37**
Tatum, Beverly Daniel **42, 84**
Taylor, Helen (Lavon Hollingshed) **30**
Taylor, Susie King **13**
Terrell, Mary Church **9**
Thomas, Alma **14**
Thomas, Michael **69**
Thurman, Howard **3**
Tillis, Frederick **40**
Tillman, Deborah **98**
Tobias, Channing H. **79**
Toler, Burl **80**
Tolson, Melvin **37**
Tribble, Israel, Jr. **8**
Trueheart, William E. **49**
Tucker, Rosina **14**
Tuff, Antoinette **120**
Turnbull, Charles Wesley **62**
Turnbull, Walter **13, 60**
Turner, Charles Henry **134**
Tutu, Nontombi Naomi **57**
Tutuola, Amos **30**
Twilight, Alexander **125**
Tyler, Ollie **128**
Tyson, Andre **40**
Tyson, Asha **39**
Tyson, Neil deGrasse **15, 65**
van Sertima, Ivan **25**
Vaughn, Viola **70**
Vega, Marta Moreno **61**
Velez-Rodriguez, Argelia **56**
Verna, Gelsy **70**
Wade-Gayles, Gloria Jean **41**
Walcott, Dennis M. **112**
Walcott, Derek **5, 94**
Walker, George **37**
Wallace, Michele Faith **13**
Wallace, Perry E. **47**
Wallace, Phyllis A. **9**
Walters, Ronald **83**
Washington, Booker T. **4**
Washington, Margaret Murray **119**
Watkins, Shirley R. **17**
Wattleton, Faye **9**
Weaver, Afaa Michael **37**
Wells, Henrietta Bell **69**
Wells, James Lesesne **10**
Wells-Barnett, Ida B. **8**
Welsing, Frances Cress **5**
Wesley, Richard **73**
West, Cornel **5, 33, 80**
Wharton, Clifton R., Jr. **7**
White, Charles **39**
White, Lois Jean **20**
Wilkins, J. Ernest, Jr. **43**
Wilkins, Roger **2, 84**
Williams, David Rudyard **50**
Williams, Fannie Barrier **27**
Williams, Gregory **11**
Williams, Patricia **11, 54**
Williams, Rhonda Y. **86**
Williams, Sherley Anne **25**

Williams, Walter E. **4, 133**
Wilson, Donald E. **88**
Wilson, William Julius **22**
Woodruff, Hale **9**
Woodson, Carter G. **2**
Wooten, Victor **131**
Worrill, Conrad **12**
Wright, Antoinette **60**
Wright, Richard Robert, Sr. **100**
Xuma, Madie Hall **59**
Yancy, Dorothy Cowser **42**
Young, Jean Childs **14**
Zook, Kristal Brent **62**

Fashion
Aberra, Amsale **67**
Banks, Jeffrey **17**
Banks, Tyra **11, 50**
Barboza, Anthony **10**
Beals, Jennifer **12**
Beauvais, Garcelle **29, 95**
Beckford, Tyson **11, 68**
Boateng, Ozwald **35, 113**
Bond, Beverly **53**
Bonney, Tabi **98**
Boyd, Suzanne **52**
Brown, Joyce F. **25**
Burrows, Stephen **31**
Campbell, Naomi **1, 31, 120**
Chanticleer, Raven **91**
DaCosta, YaYa **98**
Darego, Agbani **52**
Davidson, Jaye **5**
Davis, Mia Amber **94**
De' Alexander, Quinton **57**
Delice, Ronald **48**
Delice, Rony **48**
DeVore-Mitchell, Ophelia **120**
Dirie, Waris **56**
Dobson, Tamara **111**
Dunn, Jourdan **130**
Ebanks, Selita **67**
Evans, Etu **55**
Finley, Ron **110**
Gaskins, Eric **64**
Gibson, Ted **66**
Givhan, Robin Deneen **72**
Hall, Kevan **61**
Harold, Erika **54**
Henderson, Gordon **5**
Hendy, Francis **47**
Iman **4, 33, 87**
Iman, Chanel **66**
John, Daymond **23, 114**
Johnson, Beverly **2, 102**
Johnson, Eunice W. **83**
Jones, Carl **7**
Jones, Genevieve **101**
Kani, Karl **10**
Kebede, Liya **59**
Keckley, Elizabeth **90**
Kelly, Patrick **3**
Kodjoe, Boris **34, 89**
Lars, Byron **32**
Lopes, Leila **99**
Luna, Donyale **88**
Malone, Maurice **32**
Marcille, Eva **97**
McGrath, Pat **72**
McKenzie, Jaunel **73**
Michele, Michael **31**
Niane, Katoucha **70**
Onwurah, Ngozi **38**

Paris, Adama **120**
Powell, Maxine **8, 115**
Reese, Tracy **54**
Rhymes, Busta **31**
Robinson, Patrick **19, 71**
Rochon, Lela **16**
Rowell, Victoria **13, 68**
Sarpong, Sam **132**
Simmons, Kimora Lee **51, 83**
Sims, Naomi **29, 79**
Smaltz, Audrey **12**
Smith, B(arbara) **11**
Smith, LaQuan **113**
Smith, Willi **8**
Smythe Haith, Mabel **61**
Steele, Lawrence **28**
Stoney, Michael **50**
Sy, Oumou **65**
Talley, André Leon **56, 106**
Taylor, Karin **34**
Walker, T. J. **7**
Webb, Veronica **10, 95**
Wek, Alek **18, 63, 105**
White, Jessica **83**

Film
Aaliyah **30**
Aaron, Quinton **82**
Abrahams, Zaraah **127**
Adebimpe, Tunde **75**
Abdi, Barkhad **119**
Akinnuoye-Agbaje, Adewale **56**
Akomfrah, John **37**
Ali, Tatyana **73**
Allah, Khalik **131**
Allain, Stephanie **49**
Allen, Debbie **13, 42**
Alonso, Laz **87**
Amata, Jeta **111**
Amos, John **8, 62**
Anderson, Anthony **51, 77**
Anderson, Eddie "Rochester" **30**
Anderson, Jacob **128**
Andrews, Tina **74**
Anthony, La La **122**
Armah, Esther **87**
Babatunde, Obba **35**
Babyface **10, 31, 82**
Baker, Josephine **3**
Banks, Michelle **59**
Banks, Tyra **11, 50**
Barclay, Paris **37, 94, 133**
Barnett, Etta Moten **56**
Baskett, James **102**
Bassett, Angela **6, 23, 62**
Beach, Michael **26, 120**
Beals, Jennifer **12**
Beard, Matthew **120**
Beckford, Tyson **11, 68**
Belafonte, Harry **4, 65**
Bellamy, Bill **12**
Bennett, Louise **69**
Bentley, Lamont **53**
Berry, Fred "Rerun" **48**
Berry, Halle **4, 19, 57, 91**
Bey, Yasiin **30, 96**
Bibb, Leon **132**
Billops, Camille **82**
Bingham, Margot **135**
Bivins, Michael **72**
Blackwood, Maureen **37**
Bleu, Corbin **65**
Bogle, Donald **34**

Bonet, Lisa **58, 133**
Boseman, Chadwick **111**
Boyega, John **133**
Brady, Wayne **32, 71**
Brandy **14, 34, 72**
Breeze, Jean "Binta" **37**
Brooks, Golden **62**
Brooks, Hadda **40**
Brown, Jim **11, 95**
Brown, Tony **3**
Browne, Roscoe Lee **66**
Burnett, Charles **16, 68**
Burton, Tony **135**
Byrd, Michelle **19**
Byrd, Robert **11**
Caesar, Adolph **133**
Calloway, Cab **14**
Campbell-Martin, Tisha **8, 42**
Cannon, Nick **47, 73, 132**
Cannon, Reuben **50**
Cara, Irene **77**
Carmichael, Jerrod **124**
Carroll, Diahann **9**
Carroll, Rocky **74**
Carson, Lisa Nicole **21**
Cash, Rosalind **28**
Cathey, Reg E. **122**
Cedric the Entertainer **29, 60, 115**
Chase, Debra Martin **49, 96**
Cheadle, Don **19, 52**
Chestnut, Morris **31, 116**
Chong, Rae Dawn **62**
Chweneyagae, Presley **63**
Cobbs, Bill **101**
Common **31, 63, 98**
Coogler, Ryan **114**
Corinealdi, Emayatzy **133**
Crump, Steven **96**
Curtis-Hall, Vondie **17**
DaCosta, YaYa **98**
Dandridge, Dorothy **3**
Daniels, Lee **36, 76**
Dash, Julie **4, 132**
David, Keith **27**
Davidson, Jaye **5**
Davidson, Tommy **21**
Davis, Eisa **68**
Davis, Guy **36**
Davis, Ossie **5, 50**
Davis, Sammy, Jr. **18**
Davis, Viola **34, 76, 100, 131**
Dawn, Marpessa **75**
Dawson, Rosario **72**
De Bankolé, Isaach **78**
de Passe, Suzanne **25**
De Shields, André **72**
Dee, Ruby **8, 50, 68, 122**
Delta Rhythm Boys **133**
Devine, Loretta **24**
Dickerson, Ernest **6, 17**
Diesel, Vin **29**
Dieudonné **67, 118**
Diggs, Taye **25, 63**
Dixon, Ivan **69**
DMX **28, 64**
Dobson, Tamara **111**
Domingo, Colman **94**
Duke, Bill **3, 96**
Duncan, Michael Clarke **26, 104**
Dutton, Charles S. **4, 22**
DuVernay, Ava **98, 126**
Ejiofor, Chiwetel **67, 116**
Ejogo, Carmen **126**

Elba, Idris **49, 89, 116**
Elder, Lonne, III **38**
Elie, Lolis Eric **97**
Elise, Kimberly **32, 101**
Ellis, Aunjanue **108**
Ellis, Nelsan **105**
Ellis, Trey **97**
Elzy, Ruby **119**
Emmanuel, Alphonsia **38**
Epps, Omar **23, 59**
Esposito, Giancarlo **9**
Evans, Darryl **22**
Everett, Francine **23**
Faison, Donald **50**
Faison, Frankie **55**
Fetchit, Stepin **32**
Fishburne, Laurence **4, 22, 70**
Fisher, Antwone **40**
Fisher, Gail **85**
Fletcher, Geoffrey **85**
Fox, Rick **27**
Fox, Vivica A. **15, 53**
Foxx, Jamie **15, 48**
Franklin, Carl **11**
Freeman, Al, Jr. **11, 105**
Freeman, Morgan **2, 20, 62, 100**
Freeman, Yvette **27**
Friday, Jeff **24**
Fuller, Charles **8**
Fuqua, Antoine **35**
Gant, Richard **105**
Gaye, Nona **56**
Gerima, Haile **38, 80**
Gibbs, Marla **86**
Gibson, Tyrese **27, 62, 134**
Givens, Adele **62**
Glover, Danny **1, 24, 103**
Glover, Donald **85**
Glover, Savion **14**
Goldberg, Whoopi **4, 33, 69**
Golding, Meta **135**
Good, Meagan **117**
Gooding, Cuba, Jr. **16, 62**
Gordon, Dexter **25**
Gossett, Louis, Jr. **7**
Gray, F. Gary **14, 49**
Greaves, William **38, 123**
Grier, David Alan **28**
Grier, Pam **9, 31, 86**
Gunn, Moses **10**
Gurira, Danai **73**
Guyse, Sheila **122**
Hairston, Jester **88**
Hall, Juanita **62**
Hall, Regina **135**
Hamilton, Bernie **117**
Hamilton, Lisa Gay **71**
Hamilton, Tanya **93**
Hampton, Henry **6**
Hardwick, Omari **122**
Harewood, David **52**
Harewood, Dorian **104**
Harper, Hill **32, 65, 97**
Harris, Leslie **6**
Harris, Naomie **55, 116**
Harris, Robin **7**
Hart, Kevin **103**
Hayes, Teddy **40**
Hector, Jamie **98**
Henriques, Julian **37**
Henry, Dwight **104**
Henry, Lenny **9, 52**
Henson, Darrin **33**

Henson, Taraji P. **58, 77, 127**
Hill, Darryl **128**
Hill, Gil **135**
Hines, Gregory **1, 42**
Hodge, Aldis **124**
Hooks, Robert **76**
Horne, Lena **5, 86**
Hounsou, Djimon **19, 45**
Howard, Sherri **36**
Howard, Terrence **59, 94**
Howell, Ayinde **91**
Hudlin, Reginald **9, 86**
Hudlin, Warrington **9**
Hudson, Ernie **72, 131**
Hudson, Jennifer **63, 83**
Hughes, Albert **7**
Hughes, Allen **7**
Hurt, Byron **61**
Ice Cube **8, 30, 60**
Ice-T **6, 31, 96**
Ingram, Rex **5**
Isaacs, Cheryl Boone **113**
Jackson, George **19**
Jackson, Janet **6, 30, 68**
Jackson, Rampage **83**
Jackson, Samuel L. **8, 19, 63, 102**
Jalade-Ekeinde, Omotola **118**
Jean, Michaëlle; **70**
Jean-Baptiste, Marianne **17, 46**
Jean-Louis, Jimmy **76**
Jeffries, Herb **122**
Johnson, Clark **96**
Jones, James Earl **3, 49, 79**
Jones, Leslie **136**
Jones, Orlando **30**
Jones, Quincy **8, 30**
Jones, Rashida **101**
Jones, Robbie **113**
Jones, Roy, Jr. **22, 134**
Jordan, Michael B. **97**
Jorge, Seu **73**
Joseph, Paterson **126**
Julian, Hubert **90**
Julien, Isaac **3**
Kabera, Eric **104**
Kelley, Elijah **65**
Kelly, Jim **113**
Keys, Alicia **32, 68**
Khumalo, Leleti **51**
King, Regina **22, 45**
King, Woodie, Jr. **27**
Kirby, George **14**
Kitt, Eartha **16, 75**
Kodjoe, Boris **34, 89**
Kool Moe Dee **37**
Kotto, Yaphet **7**
Kunjufu, Jawanza **3, 50**
Lane, Charles **3**
Laneuville, Eric **123**
Lathan, Sanaa **27**
Lawrence, Martin **6, 27, 60**
Lebo M **109**
Lee, Joie **1**
Lee, Malcolm D. **75**
Lee, Spike **5, 19, 86**
Lemmons, Kasi **20**
LeNoire, Rosetta **37**
Lester, Adrian **46**
Lewis, Samella **25**
Lil' Kim **28**
Lincoln, Abbey **3, 88**
Lindo, Delroy **18, 45**
LisaRaye **27**

Lister, Tommy **127**
Little, Cleavon **117**
LL Cool J **16, 49, 94**
Long, Nia **17, 95**
Love, Loni **113**
Lover, Ed **10**
Luke, Derek **61**
Lumet, Jenny **80**
Luna, Donyale **88**
Lynch, Shola **61**
Mac, Bernie **29, 61, 72**
Mackie, Anthony **102**
Madame Sul-Te-Wan **95**
Malco, Romany **71**
Mann, Tamela **92**
Marcille, Eva **97**
Marshall, William **107**
Martin, Darnell **43, 78**
Martin, Duane **108**
Martin, Helen **31**
Martin-Green, Sonequa **133**
Mason, Judi Ann **112**
Mbatha-Raw, Gugu **89**
McBride, Chi **73**
McDaniel, Hattie **5**
McGee, Vonetta **95**
McKee, Lonette **12, 119**
McKinney, Nina Mae **40**
McQueen, Butterfly **6, 54**
McQueen, Steve **84**
Meadows, Tim **30**
Mello, Breno **73**
Micheaux, Oscar **7**
Miles, William **7**
Miller, Omar Benson **93**
Miller, Tangi **116**
Miller, Wentworth **75**
Mitchell, Kel **66, 131**
Mokae, Zakes **80**
Mo'Nique **35, 84**
Moore, Juanita **83, 124**
Moore, Melba **21**
Moore, Tim **124**
Moreland, Mantan **117**
Morris, Lamorne **135**
Morrison, Vanessa **84**
Morton, Joe **18**
Moses, Gilbert **12**
Moss, Carlton **17**
Murphy, Charles **95**
Murphy, Eddie **4, 20, 61**
Murphy, Matt **117**
Muse, Clarence Edouard **21**
Nash, Johnny **40**
Naughton, Naturi **97**
Neal, Elise **29**
Negga, Ruth **135**
Nelson, Stanley **92**
Newton, Thandie **26, 114**
Nicholas, Fayard **20, 57**
Nicholas, Harold **20**
Nichols, Nichelle **11**
Norman, Maidie **20**
Nyong'o, Lupita **127**
Oboth, Isaac **117**
Okonedo, Sophie **67**
O'Neal, Ron **46**
O'Neal, Shaquille **8, 30, 95**
Onwurah, Ngozi **38**
Oyelowo, David **82, 126**
Pace, Judy **119**
Packer, Will **71**
Palcy, Euzhan **94**

Palmer, Keke **68, 120**
Parker, Nicole Ari **52**
Parks, Gordon **1, 35, 58**
Parris, Teyonah **131**
Patterson, Chuck **124**
Patton, Paula **62**
Paulk, Marcus T. **127**
Payne, Allen **13**
Peck, Raoul **32**
Perrineau, Harold, Jr. **51**
Perry, Tyler **40, 54, 103**
Peters, Brock **96**
Peters, Clarke **103**
Pierce, Wendell **90**
Pinkett Smith, Jada **10, 41, 95**
Plummer, Glenn **120**
Poitier, Sidney **11, 36**
Poitier, Sydney Tamiia **65**
Pounder, CCH **72**
Powers, Ben **132**
Pratt, Kyla **57**
Preer, Evelyn **82**
Prince-Bythewood, Gina **31, 77**
Pryor, Richard **3, 24, 56**
Queen Latifah **1, 16, 58, 119**
Ralph, Sheryl Lee **18, 108**
Randle, Theresa **16**
Reddick, Lance **52, 128**
Reed, Natina **106**
Rees, Dee **100**
Retta **131**
Reuben, Gloria **15**
Rhames, Ving **14, 50**
Rhimes, Shonda Lynn **67**
Rhymes, Busta **31**
Richards, Beah **30**
Richardson, LaTanya **71**
Richardson, Salli **68**
Ridley, John **69**
Riggs, Marlon **5, 44**
Riley, Amber **97**
Roberts, Darryl **70**
Roberts, Kimberly Rivers **72**
Robinson, Craig **103**
Robinson, Matt **69**
Robinson, Shaun **36**
Rochon, Lela **16**
Rock, Chris **3, 22, 66**
Rock, The **29, 66**
Rodrigues, Percy **68**
Rollins, Howard E., Jr. **16**
Rose, Anika Noni **70**
Ross, Diana **8, 27**
Rotimi **130**
Roundtree, Richard **27**
Rowell, Victoria **13, 68**
Royo, Andre **136**
Rudolph, Maya **46, 106**
St. Jacques, Raymond **8**
St. John, Kristoff **25**
Saldana, Zoe **72, 118**
Salter, Nikkole **73**
Sands, Diana **87**
Sarpong, Sam **132**
Schultz, Michael A. **6**
Scott, Hazel **66**
Scott, Jill **29, 83**
Sembène, Ousmane **13, 62**
Shakur, Tupac **14**
Shepherd, Sherri **55**
Short, Columbus **79**
Sidibe, Gabourey **84**
Sinbad **1, 16**

Sinclair, Madge 78
Singleton, John 2, 30, 122
Sisqo 30
Sissako, Abderrahmane 127
Smith, Anjela Lauren 44
Smith, Anna Deavere 6, 44
Smith, Bubba 96
Smith, Jaden 82
Smith, Roger Guenveur 12, 133
Smith, Tasha 73
Smith, Will 8, 18, 53
Smith, Willow 92
Snipes, Wesley 3, 24, 67
Solange 97
Souleymane, Mahamane 78
Spencer, Octavia 100
Strode, Woody 111
Sullivan, Maxine 37
Sy, Omar 109
Sykes, Wanda 48, 81
Tate, Larenz 15
Taylor, Meshach 4
Taylor, Regina 9, 46, 97
Terrence J 108
Thigpen, Lynne 17, 41
Thomas, Sean Patrick 35
Thompson, Kenan 52
Thurman, Wallace 16
Tillman, George, Jr. 20
Torres, Gina 52
Torry, Guy 31
Toussaint, Lorraine 32
Townsend, Robert 4, 23
True, Rachel 82
Tucker, Chris 13, 23, 62
Tunie, Tamara 63
Turman, Glynn 100
Turner, Tina 6, 27
Tyler, Aisha N. 36
Tyson, Cicely 7, 51, 112
Underwood, Blair 7, 27, 76
Union, Gabrielle 31, 92
Usher 23, 56, 95
Usher, Jessie T. 136
Van Lierop, Robert 53
Van Peebles, Mario 2, 51
Van Peebles, Melvin 7, 95
Vance, Courtney B. 15, 60
Vereen, Ben 4
Walker, Eamonn 37
Wallace, William 75
Wallis, Quvenzhané 109
Ward, Douglas Turner 42
Washington, Denzel 1, 16, 93
Washington, Fredi 10
Washington, Kerry 46, 107
Waters, Ethel 7
Wayans, Damien 78
Wayans, Damon 8, 41
Wayans, Keenen Ivory 18
Wayans, Kim 80
Wayans, Marlon 29, 82
Wayans, Shawn 29
Weathers, Carl 10, 117
Wesley, Richard 73
Wesley, Rutina 97
Wheaton, James 103
Whitaker, Forest 2, 49, 67
White, Armond 80, 118
White, James L. 130
White, Lillias 120
White, Michael Jai 71, 117
White, Sylvain 96

Whitfield, Lynn 18
Wiley, Samira 131
Williams, Billy Dee 8, 105
Williams, Clarence, III 26
Williams, Marco 53
Williams, Michael Kenneth 97
Williams, Russell, II 70
Williams, Samm-Art 21
Williams, Saul 31
Williams, Spencer 126
Williams, Vanessa A. 32, 66
Williams, Vanessa L. 4, 17
Williamson, Fred 67
Williamson, Mykelti 22
Wilson, Debra 38
Wilson, Dorien 55
Winfield, Paul 2, 45
Witherspoon, John 38
Woodard, Alfre 9, 108
Woolard, Jamal 102
Wright, Jeffrey 54, 111
Yarbrough, Cedric 51
Yoba, Malik 11

**Government and politics--
international**
Abacha, Sani 11, 70
Abbott, Diane 9, 132
Abiola, Moshood 70
Abubakar, Abdulsalami 66
Adebari, Rotimi 83
Afewerki, Isaias 98
Ahidjo, Ahmadou 81
Akunyili, Dora Nkem 58
Alexander, Lincoln 106
Ali Mahdi Mohamed 5
Amadi, Elechi 40
Amin, Idi 42
Amos, Valerie 41
Annan, Kofi Atta 15, 48
Aristide, Jean-Bertrand 6, 45
Arthur, Owen 33
Ashe, John 131
Atta Mills, John 75
Augustine, Jean 53
Avant, Nicole A. 90
Azikiwe, Nnamdi 13
Babangida, Ibrahim 4
Baker, Gwendolyn Calvert 9
Banda, Hastings Kamuzu 6, 54
Banda, Joyce 101
Barnes, Melody 75
Barrow, Dean 69
Bartels, Peggielene 80
Bashir, Omar al- 77
Bedie, Henri Konan 21
Berry, Mary Frances 7
Biko, Steven 4
Bishop, Maurice 39
Biya, Chantal 89
Biya, Paul 28, 114
Bizimungu, Pasteur 19
Boateng, Paul Yaw 56
Bongo, Ali Ben 80
Bongo, Omar 1, 79
Boye, Madior 30
Bozizé, François 96, 117
Brown, Rosemary 62
Buhari, Muhammadu 128
Bunche, Ralph J. 5
Burnham, Forbes 66
Buthelezi, Mangosuthu Gatsha 9
Cabral, Amílcar 104

Camara, Moussa Dadis 76
Césaire, Aimé 48, 69
Cham, Adongo Agada Akway 77
Charlemagne, Manno 11
Charles, Mary Eugenia 10, 55
Charles, Pierre 52
Chiluba, Frederick 56, 80
Chissano, Joaquim 7, 55, 67
Christie, Perry Gladstone 53
Christophe, Henri 9
Compaore, Blaise 87
Compton, John 65
Condé, Alpha 95, 131
Conneh, Sekou Damate, Jr. 51
Conté, Lansana 7, 76
Cools, Anne 64
Cousin, Ertharin 115
Curling, Alvin 34
da Silva, Benedita 5
Dadié, Bernard 34
Dandala, Mvume 77
Davis, Ruth 37
Déby, Idriss 30, 125
Desalegn, Hailemariam 105
Diogo, Luisa Dias 63
Diouf, Abdou 3
Djotodia, Michel 117
Dlamini-Zuma, Nkosazana 34, 105
Doe, Samuel K. 100
dos Santos, José Eduardo 43, 114
Douglas, Denzil Llewellyn 53
Dube, John Langalibalele 119
Duvalier, François 124
Duvalier, Jean-Claude 124
Ekwensi, Cyprian 37
Eyadéma, Gnassingbé 7, 52
Fela 1, 42
Gairy, Eric Matthew 83
Garang, John 105
Gbagbo, Laurent 43, 90
Gnassingbé, Faure 67
Golding, Bruce 78
Gordon, Pamela 17
Grant, Bernie 57
Guebuza, Armando 81
Habré, Hissène 6, 104
Habyarimana, Juvenal 8
Haile Selassie 7
Hani, Chris 6
Holness, Andrew 99
Houphouët-Boigny, Félix 4, 64
Hussein, Lubna 80
Ifill, Gwen 28
Ingraham, Hubert A. 19
Isaac, Julius 34
Issoufou, Mahamadou 102
Jagan, Cheddi 16
Jammeh, Yahya 23, 104
Jawara, Dawda Kairaba 11
Jean, Michaëlle; 70
Jean, Wyclef 20, 86
Jonathan, Goodluck 83
Ka Dinizulu, Mcwayizeni 29
Kabbah, Ahmad Tejan 23
Kabila, Joseph 30, 126
Kabila, Laurent 20
Kaboré, Roch Marc Christian 132
Kabunda, Kenneth 2
Kafando, Michel 131
Kagame, Paul 54
Kariuki, J. M. 67
Katumbi, Moïse 135
Keïta, Ibrahim Boubacar 113

Kenyatta, Jomo 5
Kenyatta, Uhuru 110
Kérékou, Mathieu 1, 131
Khama, Ian 95
Kibaki, Mwai 60
Kiir, Salva Mayardit 85, 103
Kikwete, Jakaya Mrisho 73
King, Oona 27
Kisekka, Samson 112
Kony, Joseph 101
Koroma, Ernest Bai 84
Kufuor, John Agyekum 54, 82
Kyenge, Cécile 113
Laraque, Paul 67
Lewis, Daurene 72
Liberia-Peters, Maria Philomena 12
Lubanga, Thomas 104
Lumumba, Patrice 33
Luthuli, Albert 13
Maathai, Wangari 43, 97
Mabuza, Lindiwe 18
Machar, Riek 117
Machel, Graça 16, 102
Machel, Samora Moises 8
Magloire, Paul Eugène 68
Mahama, John Dramani 103
Malema, Julius 98
Mandela, Nelson 1, 14, 77, 117
Mandela, Winnie 2, 35, 112
Manigat, Mirlande 90
Marks, Audrey 99
Martelly, Michel 90
Masekela, Barbara 18
Masire, Quett 5
Mbeki, Govan A. 80
Mbeki, Thabo 14, 73
Mboya, Tom 107
Mbuende, Kaire 12
Mengistu, Haile Mariam 65
Mhlaba, Raymond 55
Mitchell, Keith 82
Mkapa, Benjamin W. 16, 77
Mobutu Sese Seko 1, 56
Mogae, Festus Gontebanye 19, 79
Mohamud, Hassan Sheikh 105
Moi, Daniel Arap 1, 35
Mongella, Gertrude 11
Mosisili, Pakalitha 96
Motlanthe, Kgalema 74
Moyo, Dambisa 76
Moyo, Lovemore 76
Mswati III 56
Mugabe, Robert 10, 71
Muhammed, Murtala 119
Mukoko, Jestina 75
Muluzi, Bakili 14, 76
Museveni, Yoweri 4, 119
Mushikiwabo, Louise 88
Mutebi, Ronald 25
Muzorewa, Abel 85
Mwanawasa, Levy 72
Mwinyi, Ali Hassan 1, 77
Nascimento, Abdias do 93
Ndadaye, Melchior 7
Nelson, Sophia A. 93
Neto, António Agostinho 43
Ngilu, Charity 58
Ngubane, Ben 33
Nkoli, Simon 60
Nkomo, Joshua 4, 65
Nkrumah, Kwame 3
Nkurunziza, Pierre 78, 130
Ntaryamira, Cyprien 8

Nujoma, Samuel **10**
Nyanda, Siphiwe **21**
Nyerere, Julius **5, 136**
Nzo, Alfred **15**
Obasanjo, Olusegun **5, 22**
Obasanjo, Stella **32, 56**
Obiang, Teodoro **103**
Obote, Milton **63**
Odinga, Raila **67, 110**
Okara, Gabriel **37**
Okonjo-Iweala, Ngozi **101**
Olympio, Sylvanus **126**
Ouattara, Alassane **90**
Oyono, Ferdinand **38**
Pascal-Trouillot, Ertha **3**
Patterson, P. J. **6, 20**
Paul, Evans **129**
Pereira, Aristides **30, 97**
Perkins, Edward **5**
Perry, Ruth **15**
Pierre-Louis, Michèle **75**
Pindling, Lynden **81**
Pitt, David Thomas **10**
Pitta, Celso **17**
Pohamba, Hifikepunye **95**
Préval, René **87**
Ramaphosa, Cyril **3, 117**
Rawlings, Jerry **9**
Rawlings, Nana Konadu Agyeman **13**
Roberto, Holden **65**
Roberts, Joseph Jenkins **125**
Robinson, Randall **7, 46**
Rochereau, Tabu Ley **117**
Russwurm, John Brown **100**
Sall, Macky **101**
Sampson, Edith S. **4**
Sanhá Malam Bacai **84, 101**
Sankara, Thomas **17**
Sankoh, Foday **74**
Sassou-Nguesso, Denis **103**
Sata, Michael **102, 125**
Savimbi, Jonas **2, 34**
Sawyer, Amos **2, 123**
Senghor, Augustin Diamacoune **66**
Senghor, Léopold Sédar **12, 66**
Shearer, Hugh **107**
Silva, Marina **80**
Simpson Miller, Portia **62, 100**
Sirleaf, Ellen Johnson **71**
Sisulu, Walter **47**
Skerrit, Roosevelt **72**
Skinner, Kiron K. **65**
Smith, Jennifer **21**
Soglo, Nicephore **15**
Spencer, Winston Baldwin **68**
Tandja, Mamadou **33, 78**
Tau, Mpho Parks **124**
Taubira, Christiane **117**
Taylor, Charles **20**
Taylor, John (David Beckett) **16**
Thabane, Thomas **123**
Thiam, Tidjane **104**
Todman, Terence A. **55**
Toivola, Jani **118**
Tolbert, William R. **100**
Touré, Amadou Toumani **18**
Touré, Sekou **6**
Traore, Dioncounda **103**
Tsvangirai, Morgan **26, 72**
Tubman, William **99**
Tutu, Desmond **6, 44**
Van Lierop, Robert **53**

Vieira, João Bernardo **14, 84**
Wade, Abdoulaye **66**
Walton, Lester Aglar **134**
Weah, George **58**
Wharton, Clifton R., Jr. **7**
Wharton, Clifton Reginald, Sr. **36**
Williams, Eric Eustace **65**
Wiwa, Ken **67**
Yar'Adua, Umaru **69, 89**
Yarber, Tony **129**
Yayi, Boni T. **84**
Youla, Mamady **133**
Yumkella, Kandeh **105**
Zenawi, Meles **3, 99**
Zuma, Jacob G. **33, 75**
Zwelithini, Goodwill **128**

Government and politics--U.S.
Adams, Alma **127**
Adams, Eric **133**
Adams, Floyd, Jr. **12, 122**
Adams, Grantley **82**
Adegbile, Debo P. **119**
Ahmed, Sharif **80**
Alexander, Archie Alphonso **14**
Alexander, Clifford **26**
Allen, Claude **68**
Allen, Ethel D. **13**
Allen, Eugene **79**
Archer, Dennis **7, 36**
Arrington, Richard **24, 100**
Avant, Clarence **19, 86**
Baker, Thurbert **22**
Ballance, Frank W. **41**
Baltimore, Richard Lewis, III **71**
Baraka, Ras J. **121**
Barbee, Lloyd Augustus **71**
Barrett, Andrew C. **12**
Barrett, Jacqueline **28**
Barron, Charles **136**
Barron, Inez **136**
Barry, Marion, Jr. **7, 44, 125**
Bass, Karen **70**
Bassett, Ebenezer D. **132**
Beatty, Joyce **117**
Becton, Julius W., Jr. **110**
Bell, Michael **40**
Bell, William A., Sr. **122**
Bellamy, Terry **58**
Belton, Sharon Sayles **9, 16**
Benjamin, Steve **98**
Berrien, Jacqueline A. **93**
Berry, Edwin C. **81**
Berry, Mary Frances **7**
Berry, Theodore M. **31**
Bethune, Mary McLeod **4**
Bing, Dave **3, 59, 78**
Bishop, Sanford D., Jr. **24, 111**
Blackwell, Kenneth, Sr. **61**
Blackwell, Unita **17**
Bobb, Robert C. **83**
Bond, Julian **2, 35, 106, 130**
Booker, Cory Anthony **68**
Bosley, Freeman, Jr. **7**
Bowman, Bertie **71**
Bowser, Muriel **129**
Boykin, Keith **14**
Bradley, Jennette B. **40**
Bradley, Thomas **2**
Braun, Carol Moseley **4, 42**
Brazile, Donna **25, 70**
Brimmer, Andrew **2, 48, 106**
Brooke, Edward W. **8, 88, 126**

Brookins, Hamel Hartford **102**
Brooks, Tyrone **59**
Brown, Aja **115**
Brown, Alvin **96**
Brown, Anthony G. **72**
Brown, Byrd **49**
Brown, Byron W. **72**
Brown, Cora **33**
Brown, Corrine **24, 90**
Brown, Elaine **8**
Brown, George Leslie **62**
Brown, Jesse **6, 41**
Brown, Kwame R. **91**
Brown, Les **5**
Brown, Ron **5**
Brown, Willie **7, 85**
Bruce, Blanche K. **33**
Bryant, Wayne R. **6**
Buckley, Victoria (Vicki) **24**
Bunche, Ralph J. **5**
Burke, Yvonne Brathwaite **42**
Burris, Chuck **21**
Burris, Roland W. **25, 75**
Burton, Bill **96**
Bush, Gordon **82**
Butler, Jerry **26**
Butts, Cassandra **78, 136**
Caesar, Shirley **19**
Campbell, Bill **9, 76**
Cannon, Park **134**
Cannon, Patrick **120**
Cardozo, Francis L. **33**
Carson, André **69**
Carson, Ben **1, 35, 76, 128**
Carson, Johnnie **85**
Carson, Julia **23, 69**
Carter, Jill P. **110**
Carter, Pamela Lynn **67**
Celestin, Josaphat **101**
Chambers, Ernie **130**
Chavis, Benjamin **6**
Christensen, Donna M. **17, 132**
Christie, Ron **83**
Clarke, Yvette **92**
Clay, William Lacy **8**
Clay, William Lacy, Jr. **95**
Clayton, Eva M. **20**
Cleaver, Eldridge **5**
Cleaver, Emanuel **4, 45, 68, 107**
Clemente, Rosa **74**
Clyburn, James E. **21, 71, 118**
Clyburn, Mignon **78**
Cockrel, Kenneth V., Jr. **79**
Cockrel, Kenneth Vern, Sr. **79**
Coleman, Mary **46**
Coleman, Michael B. **28, 79**
Coleman, William T. **76**
Collins, Barbara-Rose **7, 87**
Collins, Cardiss **10, 80, 120**
Colter, Cyrus J. **36**
Connerly, Ward **14**
Conyers, John, Jr. **4, 45, 111**
Conyers, Monica **85**
Cook, Mercer **40**
Craig-Jones, Ellen Walker **44**
Crockett, George W., Jr. **10, 64**
Cummings, Elijah E. **24, 102**
Cunningham, Evelyn **23, 85**
Currie, Betty **21**
Currie, Ulysses **73**
Davis, Artur **41**
Davis, Benjamin O., Jr. **2, 43**

Davis, Benjamin O., Sr. **4**
Davis, Danny K. **24, 79**
Davis, Doris A. **100**
Davis, Gordon J. **76**
Davis, James E. **50**
Dawson, William L. **130**
Days, Drew S., III **10**
De Priest, Oscar Stanton **80**
DeBerry, Lois M. **115**
DeJongh, John, Jr. **85**
Delany, Martin R. **27**
Delco, Wilhelmina R. **33**
Dellums, Ronald **2, 81**
Diggs, Charles R. **21**
Dinkins, David **4**
Dixon, Julian C. **24**
Dixon, Sharon Pratt **1**
Dixon, Sheila **68**
Dougherty, Mary Pearl **47**
Douglas, Derek **88**
Du Bois, W. E. B. **3**
Dudley, Edward R. **58**
Dukes, Hazel Nell **56**
Dunbar-Nelson, Alice Ruth Moore **44**
DuPree, Johnny **96**
Dymally, Mervyn **42**
Easley, Annie J. **61**
Edmonds, Terry **17**
Edwards, Donna **77**
Edwards, Willis **104**
Ellison, Keith **59**
Ervin, Clark Kent **82**
Espy, Mike **6**
Evans, Melvin H. **88**
Farmer, James **2, 64**
Farrakhan, Louis **2**
Farrell, Herman D., Jr. **81**
Fattah, Chaka **11, 70, 112, 130**
Fauntroy, Walter E. **11**
Fauset, Crystal Dreda Bird **100**
Felix, Larry R. **64**
Fenty, Adrian **60, 88**
Fields, C. Virginia **25**
Fields, Cleo **13**
Fisher, Ada M. **76**
Flake, Floyd H. **18, 110**
Fleming, Erik R. **75**
Fletcher, Arthur A. **63**
Flipper, Henry O. **3**
Ford, Harold E(ugene) **42**
Ford, Harold E(ugene), Jr. **16, 70**
Ford, Jack **39**
Ford, Johnny **70**
Fortune, T. Thomas **6**
Foster, Ezola **28**
Foxx, Anthony **81, 123**
Francois, Terry A. **106**
Franklin, Shirley **34, 80**
Franks, Gary **2**
Frazer, Jendayi **68**
Frazer, Victor O. **98**
Frazier, Ryan **89**
Fudge, Marcia L. **76**
Fulani, Lenora **11**
Fuller, Thomas O. **90**
Gaines, Matthew **95**
Gantt, Harvey **1**
Garrett, Joyce Finley **59**
Garvey, Marcus **1**
Gaspard, Patrick **84**
Gibbs, Mifflin W. **99**
Gibson, Johnnie Mae **23**

Gibson, Kenneth Allen 6
Gibson, William F. 6
Gillum, Andrew 128
Glover, Cedric B. 103
Goggins, Juanita 127
Goode, W. Wilson 4
Gravely, Samuel L., Jr. 5, 49
Gray, Vincent C. 88
Gray, William H., III 3
Green, Al 118
Grillo, Evelio 95
Grimké, Archibald H. 9
Groff, Peter 96
Guinier, Lani 7, 30
Haley, George 21, 129
Hamer, Fannie Lou 6
Hancock, Michael B. 123
Harmon, Clarence 26
Harp, Toni 123
Harris, Alice 7
Harris, Kamala D. 64, 122
Harris, Patricia Roberts 2
Harvard, Beverly 11
Hastie, William H. 8
Hastings, Alcee 16, 119
Hatcher, Andrew T. 90
Hatcher, Richard G. 55
Hawkins, Augustus F. 68
Hayes, James C. 10
Henderson, Thelton E. 68
Henry, Aaron 19
Herenton, Willie W. 24, 81
Herman, Alexis M. 15
Hernandez, Aileen Clarke 13
Hicks-Hudson, Paula 136
Hill, Bonnie Guiton 20
Hill, Gil 135
Hilliard, Earl F. 24
Hobson, Julius W. 44
Holden, Kip 120
Holder, Eric H., Jr. 9, 76, 104
Holmes, Amy 69
Holt Baker, Arlene 73
Horsford, Steven 88
Howard, Perry Wilbon, Jr. 112
Hughes, Dora 88
Ifill, Gwen 28
Innis, Niger 135
Irving, Larry, Jr. 12
Irvis, K. Leroy 67
Jackson, Alphonso R. 48
Jackson, Eric 127
Jackson, Frank G. 76
Jackson, George 14
Jackson, Jesse 1, 27, 72
Jackson, Jesse, Jr. 14, 45, 81, 108
Jackson, Lisa 77
Jackson, Mae 57
Jackson, Maynard 2, 41
Jackson, Sandi 108
Jackson, Shirley Ann 12
Jackson Lee, Sheila 20
Jacob, John E. 2
James, Sharpe 23, 69
James, Sly 107
Jarrett, Valerie 73
Jarvis, Charlene Drew 21
Jarvis, Kristen 85
Jefferson, William J. 25, 72
Jeffries, Hakeem 118
Johnson, Eddie Bernice 8, 90
Johnson, Edward Austin 107
Johnson, Hank, Jr. 80

Johnson, Harvey, Jr. 24, 82
Johnson, James Weldon 5
Johnson, Jeh 76, 125
Johnson, Katherine (Coleman Goble) 61
Johnson, Kevin 70, 132
Johnson, Leroy R. 89
Johnson, Norma H. 17, 97
Johnson, Robert T. 17
Jones, Dwight C. 122
Jones, Elaine R. 7, 45
Jones, Emil, Jr. 74
Jones, John 89
Jordan, Barbara 4, 78
Jordan, Charles 122
Jordan, Vernon 3, 35
Kelley, Cliff 75
Kelly, Robin 114
Kennard, William Earl 18
Keyes, Alan 11, 105
Kidd, Mae Street 39
Kilpatrick, Carolyn Cheeks 16
Kilpatrick, Kwame 34, 71, 116
Kincaid, Bernard 28
King, Martin Luther, III 20
Kirk, Ron 11, 75, 111
Lafontant, Jewel Stradford 3, 51
Lamothe, Laurent 122
Langford, Larry P. 74
Langston, John Mercer 101
Lawrence, Brenda 127
Layton, William 87
Lee, Barbara 25, 102
Lee, Howard N. 136
Leland, Mickey 2
Lewis, Delano 7
Lewis, John 2, 46, 83
Lewis, William Henry 89
Lindsay, Peta 100
Love, Mia 96, 125
Love, Reggie 77
Lowery, Myron 80
Lumumba, Chokwe 118
Lynch, William, Jr. 115
Mack, Tony 104
Majette, Denise 41
Mallett, Conrad, Jr. 16
Mallory, Mark 62
Mallory, William L., Sr. 119
Marks, John R., III 123
Marsh, Henry, III 32
Marshall, Bella 22
Marshall, Thurgood 1, 44
Martin, Louis E. 16
Martin, Ruby Grant 49
McCall, H. Carl 27
McCray, Chirlane 134
McGee, James D. 74
McGee, James Madison 46
McGlowan, Angela 64, 86
McHenry, Donald F. 83
McKinney, Cynthia 11, 52, 74
McKissick, Floyd B. 3
McPhail, Sharon 2, 119
Meek, Carrie 6, 36
Meek, Kendrick 41, 89
Meeks, Gregory T. 25, 117
Meeks, James T. 92
Melton, Frank 81
Menard, John Willis 90
Meredith, James H. 11
Metcalfe, Ralph 26
Mfume, Kweisi 6, 41

Millender-McDonald, Juanita 21, 61
Miller, Lorraine C. 119
Mitchell, Arthur Wergs 91
Mitchell, Parren J. 42, 66
Moore, Gwendolynne S. 55
Moore, Minyon 45
Morial, Ernest "Dutch" 26
Morial, Marc H. 20, 51
Morrow, E. Frederic 100
Morton, Azie Taylor 48
Morton, Ferdinand Q. 90
Mosby, Marilyn 128
Moses, Robert Parris 11
Murrell, Sylvia Marilyn 49
Nagin, Ray 42, 57, 88
Nix, Robert N. C., Jr. 51
Norton, Eleanor Holmes 7, 93
Nutter, Michael 69, 112
Obama, Barack 49, 74, 91
Obama, Michelle 61, 90
O'Leary, Hazel 6
Owens, Major 6, 117
Page, Alan 7
Paige, Rod 29
Parker, Vernon 97
Paterson, Basil A. 69, 122
Paterson, David A. 59
Patrick, Deval 12, 61, 127
Patterson, J. O., Jr. 80
Patterson, Louise 25
Payne, Donald M. 2, 57, 112
Payne, Donald M., Jr. 132
Payne, William D. 60
Perez, Anna 1
Perkins, Edward 5
Perkins, James, Jr. 55
Perry, James 83
Perry, Lowell 30
Peterson, Karen Carter 90
Pierson, Katrina 134
Pinchback, P. B. S. 9
Pinckney, Clementa C. 130
Pinkney, Arnold R. 122
Pitts, Robb 84
Plaskett, Stacey 127
Powell, Adam Clayton, Jr. 3
Powell, Colin 1, 28, 75
Powell, Debra A. 23
Powell, Michael 32
Price, McKinley L. 136
Primas, Randy 106
Pugh, Charles 81
Randolph, A. Philip 3
Rangel, Charles B. 3, 52, 85
Raoul, Kwame 55
Rapier, James T. 82
Rawlings-Blake, Stephanie 93, 128
Redd, Dana 93
Reed, Joe L. 110
Reed, Kasim 82
Reeves, Gregory 49
Reeves, Martha 85
Reeves, Triette Lipsey 27
Revels, Hiram Rhoades 98
Rice, Condoleezza 3, 28, 72
Rice, Emmett J. 94
Rice, Norm 8
Rice, Susan 74, 103
Richardson, Laura 81
Richardson, Rupert 67
Richmond, Cedric 93
Riles, Wilson C. 79
Roberts, Lillian 83

Robinson, Bishop L. 66
Robinson, Randall 7, 46
Rochon, Stephen W. 78
Rogers, Desirée 88
Rogers, Joe 27
Ross, Don 27
Rouse, Cecilia 93
Rush, Bobby 26, 76
Rustin, Bayard 4
Sampson, Edith S. 4
Sanders, Malika 48
Sawyer, Eugene 81
Sayles Belton, Sharon 9
Schmoke, Kurt I. 48
Scott, David 41, 117
Scott, Robert C. 23
Scott, Tim 87, 125
Setmayer, Tara 130
Sewell, Terri 93
Shakur, Assata 6
Shavers, Cheryl 31
Shelton, Paula Young 86
Sherrod, Shirley 87
Simmons, E. Denise 79
Simmons, Jamal 72
Simpson, Carole 6, 30
Sisulu, Sheila Violet Makate 24
Slater, Rodney E. 15, 125
Smith, Malcolm A. 75
Smith, Nate 49
Smith, Princella 86
Smyre, Calvin 90
Smythe Haith, Mabel 61
Spearman, Leonard H. O., Sr. 81
Spencer, Vaino H. 99
Spigner, Archie 81
Stanton, Robert 20
Staupers, Mabel K. 7
Steele, Michael 38, 73, 91
Stewart, Nzingha 89
Stokes, Carl 10, 73
Stokes, Louis 3
Stoutt, H. Lavity 83
Strautmanis, Michael 87
Street, John F. 24
Sullivan, Louis 8
Sutphen, Mona 77
Sutton, Percy E. 42, 82
Taylor, Robert Rochon 104
Thomas, Clarence 2, 39, 65
Thomas-Greenfield, Linda 99
Thompson, Bennie 26, 119
Thompson, Larry D. 39
Thompson, William C., Jr. 35, 114
Tillman, Dorothy 76
Todman, Terence A. 55
Tolbert, Terence 74
Toote, Gloria E. A. 64
Towns, Edolphus 19, 75
Tribble, Israel, Jr. 8
Trotter, Donne E. 28
Tubbs Jones, Stephanie 24, 72
Tucker, C. Delores 12, 56
Turnbull, Charles Wesley 62
Turner, Henry McNeal 5
Turner, Sylvester 136
Twilight, Alexander 125
Tyler, Ollie 128
Usry, James L. 23, 134
Vaughn, Gladys Gary 47
Von Lipsey, Roderick K. 11
Waldon, Alton R., Jr. 98
Wallace, Phyllis A. 9

Warren, Lovely **136**
Washington, Harold **6**
Washington, Val **12**
Washington, Walter **45**
Waters, Maxine **3, 67, 103**
Watkins, Craig **97**
Watkins, Joe **86**
Watkins, Shirley R. **17**
Watson, Diane **41**
Watson Coleman, Bonnie **127**
Watt, Mel **26, 105**
Watts, J. C., Jr. **14, 38**
Weaver, Karen **134**
Weaver, Robert C. **8, 46**
Webb, Wellington **3, 81**
Welcome, Verda Freeman **112**
West, Allen **89**
Wharton, A. C., Jr. **110**
Wharton, Clifton R., Jr. **7**
Wharton, Clifton Reginald, Sr. **36**
Wheat, Alan **14**
White, Jesse **22, 75**
White, Michael R. **5**
Widener, Warren **99**
Wilder, L. Douglas **3, 48**
Williams, Anthony **21**
Williams, Dennis P. **123**
Williams, Eddie N. **44**
Williams, George Washington **18**
Williams, Hosea **15, 31, 123**
Williams, Maggie **7, 71**
Williams, Michael L. **86**
Wilson, Frederica **92**
Wilson, Lionel **99**
Wilson, Margaret Bush **79**
Woods, Abraham, Jr. **74**
Wynn, Albert **25, 77**
Young, Andrew **3, 48, 110**

Law
Adegbile, Debo P. **119**
Alexander, Clifford **26**
Alexander, Joyce London **18**
Alexander, Michelle **98**
Alexander, Sadie Tanner Mossell **22**
Ali, Russlynn H. **92**
Allen, Macon Bolling **104**
Allen, Samuel W. **38**
Amaker, Norman **63**
Anderson, Reuben V. **81**
Archer, Dennis **7, 36**
Arnwine, Barbara **28**
Bailey, Clyde **45**
Baldwin, Cynthia **74, 107**
Banks, William **11**
Barbee, Lloyd Augustus **71**
Barrett, Andrew C. **12**
Barrett, Jacqueline **28**
Battle, Samuel J. **130**
Batts, Anthony **128**
Baugh, David **23**
Benham, Robert **78**
Benjamin, Steve **98**
Bensouda, Fatou **103**
Berrien, Jacqueline A. **93**
Berry, Theodore M. **31**
Birch, Adolpho A., Jr. **85**
Bolin, Jane **22, 59**
Bolton, Terrell D. **25**
Booker, Cory Anthony **68**
Bosley, Freeman, Jr. **7**
Boulware, Harold R. **109**

Boykin, Keith **14**
Bradley, Thomas **2**
Brown, Byrd **49**
Brown, Cora **33**
Brown, Cupcake **63**
Brown, Homer S. **47**
Brown, Janice Rogers **43**
Brown, Joe **29**
Brown, Lee P. **1, 24, 109**
Brown, Ron **5**
Bryant, Wayne R. **6**
Bryant, William Benson **61**
Buery, Richard, Jr. **97**
Bully-Cummings, Ella **48**
Burris, Roland W. **25, 75**
Butler, Louis **70**
Butler, Paul D. **17**
Bynoe, Peter C. B. **40**
Campbell, Bill **9, 76**
Carter, Pamela Lynn **67**
Carter, Robert L. **51, 100**
Carter, Stephen L. **4**
Cashin, Sheryll **63**
Chambers, Julius **3**
Chestnut, J. L., Jr. **73**
Clark, Ray **122**
Cleaver, Kathleen Neal **29**
Clendenon, Donn **26, 56**
Cochran, Johnnie **11, 39, 52**
Colbert, Tom **115**
Coleman, James E., Jr. **79**
Coleman, William T. **76**
Colter, Cyrus J. **36**
Crenshaw, Kimberlé Williams **88**
Darden, Christopher **13**
Davis, Angela J. **88**
Davis, Artur **41**
Davis, Gordon J. **76**
Days, Drew S., III **10**
DeFrantz, Anita **37**
Dillard, Godfrey J. **45**
Dow, Unity **104**
Early, Norman S., Jr. **124**
Edley, Christopher **2, 48**
Edley, Christopher F., Jr. **48**
Ellington, E. David **11**
Ephriam, Mablean **29**
Ervin, Clark Kent **82**
Evans, Warren C. **76**
Farmer-Paellmann, Deadria **43**
Feemster, Herbert **72**
Fenty, Adrian **60, 88**
Fields, Cleo **13**
Finner-Williams, Paris Michele **62**
Fisher, Ada Lois Sipuel **76**
Ford, Wallace **58**
Forman, James, Jr. **89**
Foxx, Anthony **81, 123**
Foxx, Kim **134**
Frazer, Victor O. **98**
Freeman, Charles **19**
Gaines, Lloyd **79**
Gary, Willie E. **12, 117**
Gibson, Johnnie Mae **23**
Gittens, Charles L. **124**
Glover, Nathaniel, Jr. **12**
Gomez-Preston, Cheryl **9**
Gordon-Reed, Annette **74**
Gourdin, Edward O. **93**
Graham, Lawrence Otis **12**
Gray, Fred **37**
Gray, Willie **46**

Greenhouse, Bunnatine **57**
Grimké, Archibald H. **9**
Guinier, Lani **7, 30**
Haley, George **21, 129**
Hall, Elliott S. **24**
Harden, Monique **97**
Harris, Kamala D. **64, 122**
Harris, Maya Lakshmi **88**
Harris, Patricia Roberts **2**
Harvard, Beverly **11**
Hassell, Leroy Rountree, Sr. **41, 116**
Hastie, William H. **8**
Hatcher, Richard G. **55**
Hatchett, Glenda **32**
Hawkins, Augustus F. **68**
Hawkins, Steven **14**
Hayes, Dennis **54**
Haywood, Margaret A. **24**
Henderson, Thelton E. **68**
Higginbotham, A. Leon, Jr. **13, 25**
Hill, Anita **5, 65**
Hill, Gil **135**
Hillard, Terry **25**
Hills, Oliver W. **24**
Holder, Eric H., Jr. **9, 76, 104**
Hollowell, Donald L. **57**
Holton, Hugh, Jr. **39**
Hooks, Benjamin L. **2, 85**
Houston, Charles Hamilton **4**
Howard, Perry Wilbon, Jr. **112**
Hubbard, Arnette Rhinehart **38**
Hurtt, Harold **46**
Isaac, Julius **34**
Jackson, Maynard **2, 41**
Jackson Lee, Sheila **20**
Johnson, Edward Austin **107**
Johnson, Harry E. **57**
Johnson, James Weldon **5**
Johnson, Leroy R. **89**
Johnson, Norma H. **17, 97**
Johnson, Sterling, Jr. **124**
Jones, Clarence B. **114**
Jones, Elaine R. **7, 45**
Jones, Theodore T., Jr. **108**
Jones, Van **70**
Jordan, Eddie **82**
Jordan, Vernon E. **3, 35**
Kearse, Amalya Lyle **12**
Keith, Damon J. **16, 74**
Kennard, William Earl **18**
Kennedy, Florynce **12, 33**
Kennedy, Randall **40**
Kibaki, Mwai **60**
La Roca, Pete **107**
Lafontant, Jewel Stradford **3, 51**
Lewis, Aubrey **133**
Lewis, Delano **7**
Lewis, William Henry **89**
Lloyd, Reginald **64**
Lynch, Loretta E. **103**
Majette, Denise **41**
Mallett, Conrad, Jr. **16**
Marks, John R., III **123**
Marsh, Henry, III **32**
Marshall, Thurgood **1, 44**
Mathis, Greg **26**
McAnulty, William E., Jr. **66**
McCrary Anthony, Crystal **70**
McDonald, Gabrielle Kirk **20**
McDougall, Gay J. **11, 43**
McGhee, Heather C. **106**
McKinnon, Isaiah **9**

McPhail, Sharon **2, 119**
Melton, Harold D. **79**
Ming, William Robert, Jr. **125**
Mitchell, Arthur Wergs **91**
Mitchell, Clarence M., Jr. **88**
Mitchell, Juanita Jackson **128**
Moose, Charles **40**
Morial, Ernest "Dutch" **26**
Morton, Ferdinand Q. **90**
Morton, Frederick A., Jr. **93**
Mosby, Marilyn **128**
Motley, Constance Baker **10, 55**
Muhammad, Ava **31**
Murray, Pauli **38**
Nance, Cynthia **71**
Napoleon, Benny N. **23**
Nash, Shannon King **84**
Nelson, Sophia A. **93**
Nix, Robert N. C., Jr. **51**
Noble, Ronald **46**
Nunn, Annetta **43**
Obama, Michelle **61, 90**
Ogletree, Charles, Jr. **12, 47**
Ogunlesi, Adebayo O. **37**
Oliver, Jerry **37**
Orr, Kevyn **118**
Ozanne, Ismael R. **129**
Page, Alan **7**
Parker, Barrington D. **92**
Parker, Kellis E. **30**
Parks, Bernard C. **17**
Parsons, James **14**
Pascal-Trouillot, Ertha **3**
Paterson, Basil A. **69, 122**
Patrick, Deval **12**
Payne, Ulice, Jr. **42**
Payton, John **48, 124**
Perry, Lowell **30**
Perry, Matthew J., Jr. **96**
Philip, Marlene Nourbese **32**
Pincham, R. Eugene, Sr. **69**
Powell, Michael **32**
Quince, Peggy A. **69**
Ramsey, Charles H. **21, 69**
Raoul, Kwame **103**
Rawlinson, Johnnie B. **79**
Ray, Charlotte E. **60**
Redding, Louis L. **26**
Reed, Kasim **82**
Reeves, Bass **100**
Reeves, Carlton W. **129**
Reynolds, Star Jones **10, 27, 61**
Rice, Constance LaMay **60**
Richie, Leroy C. **18**
Roaf, Andrée Layton **106**
Roberts, Michele **123**
Roberts, Norwell **134**
Robinson, Bishop L. **66**
Robinson, Malcolm S. **44**
Robinson, Randall **7, 46**
Rock, John S. **113**
Roundtree, Dovey **80**
Russell-McCloud, Patricia **17**
Sampson, Edith S. **4**
Schmoke, Kurt I, **48**
Sealy, Lloyd G. **125**
Sears, Leah Ward **5, 79**
Shores, Arthur D. **99**
Slater, Duke **125**
Sleet, Gregory M. **109**
Smith, DeMaurice **92**
Solomon, Jimmie Lee **38**
Sparks, Corinne Etta **53**

Stevenson, Bryan **128**
Stokes, Louis **3**
Stout, Juanita Kidd **24**
Strautmanis, Michael **87**
Sutton, Percy E. **42, 82**
Tanner, Jack E. **100**
Taylor, John (David Beckett) **16**
Thomas, Arthur Ray **52**
Thomas, Clarence **2, 39, 65**
Thomas, Franklin A. **5, 49**
Thompson, Ken **131**
Thompson, Larry D. **39**
Tingling, Milton A. **110**
Tolbert, James L. **112**
Touré, Faya Ora Rose **56**
Tubbs Jones, Stephanie **24, 72**
Van Lierop, Robert **53**
Wagner, Annice **22**
Wainwright, Joscelyn **46**
Waldon, Alton R., Jr. **98**
Walker, Cora T. **68**
Wallace, Perry E. **47**
Ward, Benjamin **68**
Washington, Harold **6**
Watkins, Craig **97**
Watkins, Donald **35**
Watt, Garland W. **113**
Watt, Melvin **26**
Wharton, Clifton Reginald, Sr. **36**
Widener, Warren **99**
Wilder, L. Douglas **3, 48**
Wilkins, David **77**
Williams, Ann Claire **82**
Williams, David W. **110**
Williams, Evelyn **10**
Williams, Gregory **11**
Williams, Patricia **11, 54**
Williams, Willie L. **4**
Wilson, Jimmy **45**
Worthy, Kym **84**
Wray, Noble **114**
Wright, Bruce McMarion **3, 52**
Wynn, Albert **25, 77**

Military
Abacha, Sani **11, 70**
Adams Early, Charity **13, 34**
Adams-Ender, Clara **40**
Alexander, Margaret Walker **22**
Allensworth, Allen **129**
Amin, Idi **42**
Anderson, Marcia **115**
Archer, Lee, Jr. **79**
Austin, Lloyd **101**
Babangida, Ibrahim **4**
Baker, Vernon Joseph **65, 87**
Bashir, Omar al- **77**
Becton, Julius W., Jr. **110**
Bennett, Richard **97**
Black, Barry C. **47**
Bolden, Charles Frank, Jr. **7, 78**
Brashear, Carl **29**
Brown, Anthony G. **72**
Brown, Erroll M. **23**
Brown, Jesse **6, 41**
Brown, Jesse Leroy **31**
Brown, Wesley A. **102**
Brown, Willa **40**
Bullard, Eugene **12**
Bush, Charles Vernon **125**
Cadoria, Sherian Grace **14**
Carney, William H. **104**
Carter, Edward A., Jr. **104**

Chappell, Roy M. **95**
Chissano, Joaquim **7, 55, 67**
Christophe, Henri **9**
Clark, Carl **101**
Clarke, Anna Mac **95**
Clemmons, Reginal G. **41**
Coleman, Ronald S. **110**
Compaore, Blaise **87**
Conté, Lansana **7, 76**
Cooke, Marcia **60**
Davis, Benjamin O., Jr. **2, 43**
Davis, Benjamin O., Sr. **4**
Drew, Alvin, Jr. **67**
Duggins, George **64**
Ellis, Larry R. **110**
Europe, James Reese **10**
Eyadéma, Gnassingbé **7, 52**
Fields, Evelyn J. **27**
Flipper, Henry O. **3**
Fox, John R. **105**
Gravely, Samuel L., Jr. **5, 49**
Gregory, Frederick **8, 51**
Guéï, Robert **66**
Habré, Hissène **6, 104**
Habyarimana, Juvenal **8**
Harris, Marcelite Jordan **16**
Healy, Michael **90**
Honoré, Russel L. **64**
Hoskins, Harold K. **103**
Howard, Michelle **28, 125**
Jackson, Fred James **25**
James, Daniel, Jr. **16**
Johnson, Hazel **22**
Johnson, Henry **129**
Johnson, Shoshana **47**
Julian, Hubert **90**
Kagame, Paul **54**
Khama, Ian **95**
King, Teresa **80**
Kony, Joseph **101**
Laraque, Paul **67**
Lawrence, Robert H., Jr. **16**
Lubanga, Thomas **104**
Lyles, Lester **31**
Maceo, Antonio **82**
Magloire, Paul Eugène **68**
Matthews, Mark **59**
Miller, Dorie **29**
Morris, Melvin **120**
Muhammed, Murtala **119**
Nkunda, Laurent **75**
Ntaganda, Bosco **111**
Nyanda, Siphiwe **21**
Obasanjo, Olusegun **5, 22**
Ojukwu, Odumegwu **99**
Perry, Herman **89**
Petersen, Frank E. **31**
Plinton, James O., Jr. **98**
Powell, Colin **1, 28, 75**
Pruitt, Wendell O. **106**
Rawlings, Jerry **9**
Reason, J. Paul **19**
Rochon, Stephen W. **78**
Rogers, Alan G. **72**
Scantlebury, Janna **47**
Smalls, Robert **82**
Snow, Samuel **71**
Stanford, John **20**
Staupers, Mabel K. **7**
Stokes, Louis **3**
Stowers, Freddie **107**
Touré, Amadou Toumani **18**
Via, Dennis **108**

Von Lipsey, Roderick K. **11**
Ward, William E. **107**
Watkins, Perry **12**
West, Togo D., Jr. **16**
Wilson, Jimmy **45**
Wright, Lewin **43**
Young, Charles **77**

Music
Aaliyah **30**
Abdullah, Kazem **97**
Ace, Johnny **36**
Aces, The **117**
Acklin, Barbara Jean **107**
Adams, Alberta **133**
Adams, Johnny **39**
Adams, Leslie **39**
Adams, Oleta **18**
Adams, Yolanda **17, 67**
Adderley, Julian "Cannonball" **30**
Adderley, Nat **29**
Ade, King Sunny **41**
Adebimpe, Tunde **75**
Afro, Teddy **78**
Ahmed, Mahmoud **130**
Akinmusire, Ambrose **103**
Akon **68**
Albright, Gerald **23**
Alexander, Arthur **131**
Ali, Rashied **79**
Allen, Betty **83**
Allen, Geri **92**
Allen, Red **129**
Allen, Tony **117**
Allison, Luther **111**
Amadou & Mariam **113**
Amerie **52**
Ammons, Albert **112**
Ammons, Gene **112**
Amy, Curtis **114**
Anderson, Carl **48**
Anderson, Fred **87**
Anderson, Ivie **126**
Anderson, Jacob **128**
Anderson, Marian **2, 33**
Anderson, T. J. **119**
Andrews, Inez **108**
apl.de.ap **84**
Ardoin, Alphonse **65**
Armatrading, Joan **32, 133**
Armenteros, Chocolate **133**
Armstrong, Louis **2**
Armstrong, Vanessa Bell **24**
Arnold, Billy Boy **112**
Arnold, Kokomo **116**
Arrington, Steve **132**
Arroyo, Marina **30**
A$AP Rocky **109**
Ashanti **37, 96**
Ashford, Nickolas **21, 97**
Ashong, Derrick **86**
Astatke, Mulatu **81**
Atkins, Juan **50**
Atlantic Starr **122**
Attaway, William **102**
Austin, Lovie **40**
Austin, Patti **24**
Avant, Clarence **19, 86**
Avant, Nicole A. **90**
Ayers, Roy **16**
Ayler, Albert **104**
Babyface **10, 31, 82**
Baca, Susana **80**

Badu, Erykah **22, 114**
Bailey, Buster **38**
Bailey, DeFord **33**
Bailey, Pearl **14**
Bailey, Philip **63**
Bailey Rae, Corinne **83**
Baiocchi, Regina Harris **41**
Baker, Anita **21, 48**
Baker, Josephine **3**
Baker, LaVern **26**
Baker, Mickey **95**
Ballard, Florence **112**
Ballard, Hank **41**
Bambaataa, Afrika **34**
Banks, Azealia **107**
Banks, Chico **134**
Banks, Lloyd **113**
Banner, David **55**
Banton, Buju **93**
Baraka, Sho **109**
Bar-Kays, The **118**
Barker, Danny **32**
Barnes, Katreese **97**
Barnes, Lloyd **87**
Barnes, Roosevelt "Booba" **33**
Barrett, Sweet Emma **130**
Barrino, Fantasia **53, 94**
Barron, Kenny **128**
Basie, Count **23**
Bass, Fontella **104, 109**
Bassey, Offiong **119**
Bassey, Shirley **25**
Batiste, Alvin **66**
Batiste, Jon **108, 130**
Batiste, Lionel **105**
Battiste, Harold, Jr. **136**
Battle, Kathleen **70**
Baylor, Helen **36**
Bebey, Francis **45**
Bechet, Sidney **18**
Beenie Man **32**
Beken **111**
Belafonte, Harry **4, 65**
Belgrave, Marcus **77, 129**
Bell, Carey **114**
Bell, LeRoy **98**
Bell, Thom **112**
Belle, Regina **1, 51**
Benét, Eric **28, 77**
Benjamin, Andre **45**
Bennett, Estelle **77**
Benson, Obie **96**
Bentley, Lamont **53**
Benton, Brook **121**
Berry, Chu **136**
Berry, Chuck **29**
Betts, Keter **85**
Beverly, Frankie **25**
Bey, Salome **134**
Bey, Yasiin **30, 96**
Beyoncé **39, 70, 105**
Bibb, Eric **49, 123**
Bibb, Leon **132**
Big Daddy Kane **79**
Big Freedia **128**
Big L **120**
Big Maybelle **117**
Big Sean **96**
Big Time Sarah **45, 134**
Big Youth **107**
Bilal **101**
Billy Ward and the Dominoes **105**
Bingham, Margot **135**

Birdman **110**
Birdsong, Cindy **113**
Birra, Ali **113**
Bivins, Michael **72**
Blacc, Aloe **119**
Black Thought **63**
Blackman, Toni **86**
Blackwell, Otis **98**
Blade, Brian **88**
Blake, Eubie **29**
Blake, John, Jr. **123**
Blakey, Art **37**
Blanchard, Terence **43**
Blanco, Mykki **106**
Bland, Bobby **36, 113**
Bland, Edward **111**
Blanton, Jimmy **108**
Bleu, Corbin **65**
Blige, Mary J. **20, 34, 60, 97**
Blind Boys of Alabama, The **99**
Blitz the Ambassador **115**
Blondy, Alpha **30**
Blow, Kurtis **31, 122**
B.o.B. **91**
Bolden, Buddy **39**
Bombino **112**
Bond, Beverly **53**
Bonds, Margaret **39**
Boney M. **133**
Bonga, Kuenda **13**
Bonner, Leroy **113**
Bonney, Tabi **98**
Bostic, Earl **121**
Boulogne, Joseph, Chevalier de
    Saint-Georges **94**
Bow Wow **35**
Boykin, Phillip **102**
Boyz II Men **82**
Bradford, Alex **121**
Bradley, Charles **126**
Bradley, J. Robert **65**
Bradshaw, Tiny **102**
Brae, C. Michael **61**
Brandy **14, 34, 72**
Braxton, Anthony **128**
Braxton, Tamar **134**
Braxton, Toni **15, 61, 91**
Brewster, W. Herbert **128**
Bridges, Leon **126**
Bridgetower, George **78**
Bridgewater, Dee Dee **32, 92**
Brim, John **117**
Brooks, Hadda **40**
Brooks, Roy **125**
Brooks, Tina **133**
Broonzy, Big Bill **82**
Brothers Johnson **130**
Brown, Angela M. **54**
Brown, Anne **76**
Brown, Bobby **58, 124**
Brown, Carlinhos **81**
Brown, Charles **23**
Brown, Chris **74, 109**
Brown, Chuck **78, 102**
Brown, Clarence Gatemouth **59**
Brown, Clifford **86**
Brown, Dennis **99**
Brown, Foxy **25**
Brown, James **15, 60**
Brown, Melanie **73**
Brown, Nappy **73**
Brown, Oscar, Jr. **53**
Brown, Patrick "Sleepy" **50**

Brown, Ruth **90**
Brown, Shirley **132**
Brown, Uzee **42**
Browne, Tom **136**
Brownlee, Lawrence **88**
Bryant, Paul **115**
Bryant, Ray **95**
Buckner, Milt **110**
Buckwheat Zydeco **132**
Budden, Joe **108**
Buika **120**
Bumbry, Grace **5**
Bun B **123**
Burbridge, Kofi **120**
Burbridge, Oteil **120**
Burke, Clarence, Jr. **112**
Burke, Solomon **31, 86, 129**
Burleigh, Henry Thacker **56**
Burley, Dan **96**
Burning Spear **79**
Burns, Eddie **44**
Burnside, R. L. **56**
Busby, Jheryl **3, 74**
Butler, George, Jr. **70**
Butler, Henry **121**
Butler, Jerry **26**
Butler, Jonathan **28**
Byas, Don **133**
Byrd, Donald **109**
Cables, George **125**
Cadillacs **107**
Caesar, Shirley **19**
Cage, Byron **53**
Callier, Terry **106**
Calloway, Blanche **100**
Calloway, Cab **1**
Cameo **120**
Campbell, Lucie E. **118**
Campbell, Roy, Jr. **118**
Campbell-Martin, Tisha **8, 42**
Cam'ron **104**
Cannon, Nick **47, 73, 132**
Cannon, Toronzo **135**
Carey, Mariah **32, 53, 69**
Carolina Chocolate Drops **111**
Carr, James **117**
Carr, Kurt **56**
Carr, Leroy **49**
Carrington, Terri Lyne **132**
Carter, Benny **46**
Carter, Betty **19**
Carter, Nell **39**
Carter, Regina **23, 131**
Carter, Ron **104**
Carter, Troy **98**
Carter, Warrick L. **27**
Cartiér, Xam Wilson **41**
Castor, Jimmy **100**
Catlett, Sid **133**
Caymmi, Dorival **72**
Chaka Chaka, Yvonne **112**
Chambers, Paul **121**
Chambers Brothers, The **116**
Chamillionaire **82**
Chancler, Ndugu **115**
Chandler, Gene **105**
Chanté, Keshia **50**
Chantels, The **128**
Chapman, Tracy **26**
Charlemagne, Manno **11**
Charles, Ray **16, 48**
Cheatham, Doc **17**
Checker, Chubby **28**

Cheeks, Julius **135**
Chenault, John **40**
Chenier, C. J. **134**
Chenier, Clifton **134**
Cherry, Don **119**
Chic **117**
Chief Keef **112**
Chiffons, The **129**
Childers, Lulu Vere **95**
Chi-Lites **106**
Christian, Charlie **136**
Christian, Jodie **103**
Christie, Angella **36**
Chronixx **123**
Chuck D **9**
Ciara **56, 115**
Clark, Mattie Moss **61**
Clark, Sharón **105**
Clark, Sonny **128**
Clark-Cole, Dorinda **66**
Clarke, Kenny **27**
Clarke, Stanley **115**
Clark-Sheard, Karen **22, 114**
Clay, Otis **112, 133**
Clayton, Doctor **120**
Clayton, Gerald **111**
Clayton, Merry **112**
Clemons, Clarence **41**
Cleveland, James **19**
Cliff, Jimmy **28, 92**
Clinton, George **9, 93**
Clovers, The **104**
C-Murder **99**
Coasters, The **102**
Coates, Dorothy Love **125**
Cobb, Arnett **114**
Cobb, Jimmy **119**
Cobbs, Tasha **114**
Cobham, Billy **123**
Cody, Radmilla **99**
Cole, Cozy **123**
Cole, Freddy **128**
Cole, J. **97**
Cole, Keyshia **63, 107**
Cole, Maria **104**
Cole, Nat "King" **17**
Cole, Natalie **17, 60, 84, 133**
Coleman, Denardo **122**
Coleman, George **106**
Coleman, Ornette **39, 69, 129**
Coleman, Steve **124**
Coleridge-Taylor, Samuel **75**
Collette, Buddy **119**
Collins, Albert **21**
Collins, Bootsy **31**
Collins, Lyn **53**
Coltrane, Alice **70**
Coltrane, John **19**
Coltrane, Ravi **71**
Combs, Sean **17, 43, 92**
Commodores, The **118**
Common **31, 63, 98**
Conley, Arthur **129**
Conrad, Barbara Smith **90**
Consolers, The **125**
Contours, The **109**
Cook, Charles "Doc" **44**
Cook, Junior **126**
Cook, Will Marion **40**
Cooke, Sam **17**
Coolio **103**
Cooper, Jerome **129**
Copeland, Johnny **110**

Copeland, Shemekia **110**
Coppola, Imani Francesca **82**
Cosey, Pete **103**
Cotton, James **123**
Counce, Curtis **127**
Count Basie **23**
Covay, Don **127**
Cowboy Troy **54**
Cox, Deborah **28**
Cox, Ida **42**
Craig, Carl **31, 71**
Crawford, Hank **77**
Crawford, Randy **19**
Cray, Robert **30, 132**
Creagh, Milton **27**
Criss, Sonny **128**
Crocker, Frankie **29**
Crothers, Scatman **19**
Crouch, Andraé **27, 115, 126**
Crowder, Henry **16**
Crown Heights Affair **132**
Crudup, Arthur **115**
Crusaders, The **116**
Cruz, Taio **104**
Curren$y **114**
Curson, Ted **108**
Da Don, Polow **86**
Daemyon, Jerald **64**
Dale, Clamma **103**
Dameron, Tadd **103**
D'Angelo **27, 123**
Daniels, Billy **124**
Danjah, Terror **91**
Dara, Olu **35**
Dash, Damon **31, 113**
Dash, Darien **29**
Davenport, Cow Cow **115**
David, Craig **31, 53**
Davis, Anthony **11**
Davis, Carl **105**
Davis, Gary **41**
Davis, Guy **36**
Davis, Miles **4**
Davis, Sammy, Jr. **18**
Davis, Thornetta **131**
Davis, Tyrone **54**
Davis, Walter, Jr. **134**
Davis, Wild Bill **114**
Davis Sisters, The **119**
Dawkins, Jimmy **111**
Dawson, William Levi **39**
Dawuni, Rocky **94**
Day, Andra **132**
Dazz Band **116**
D'banj **107**
De La Soul **119**
de Passe, Suzanne **25**
DeBarge, El **89**
Dedeaux, Richard **119**
Deep River Boys **131**
Deezer D **53**
Dekker, Desmond **104**
Dells, The **109**
Delta Rhythm Boys **133**
Dennard, Brazeal **37**
DePreist, James **37, 109**
Derulo, Jason **93, 132**
DeSanto, Sugar Pie **122**
Detroit Emeralds, The **121**
DeVaughn, Raheem **91**
Diabaté, Toumani **129**
Diawara, Djeli Moussa **111**
Diawara, Fatoumata **114**

Dickenson, Vic 38
Diddley, Bo 39, 72
Diehl, Aaron 132
Dillard, Ricky 134
Dixie Cups, The 109
Dixon, Bill 87
Dixon, Dean 68
Dixon, Willie 4
DJ Clue? 111
DJ Jazzy Jeff 32
DJ Lance Rock 94
DJ Rashad 121
DJ Screw 110
DMX 28, 64
Dobbs, Mattiwilda 34
Dodd, Coxsone 99
Doggett, Bill 124
Domino, Fats 20
Donegan, Dorothy 19
Dorham, Kenny 113
Dorsey, Lee 65
Dorsey, Thomas 15
Downing, Will 19
Dr. Dre 10, 14, 30, 116
Drake 86
Drake, Hamid 121
Dramatics, The 106
Drew, Kenny 123
Drifters, The 121
Dube, Lucky 77
Duke, George 21, 113
Dumas, Henry 41
Duncan, Todd 76
Dunner, Leslie B. 45
Duplechan, Larry 55
Dupri, Jermaine 13, 46
Durham, Bobby 73
Dworkin, Aaron P. 52
Dyett, Walter 113
E-40 125
Earth, Wind & Fire 98
Earthquake 55
Eckstine, Billy 28
Edison, Harry 114
Edmonds, Tracey 16, 64
Edwards, David 122
Edwards, Esther Gordy 43
Edwards, Teddy 123
Eldridge, Roy 37
Ellington, Duke 5
Ellington, Mercer 129
Elliott, Missy 31, 90
Ellis, Alton 74
Ellis, Dorothy 131
Ellis, Hortense 97
Elzy, Ruby 119
Emotions, The 125
En Vogue 100
Ervin, Booker 106
Escobar, Damien 56
Escobar, Tourie 56
Estelle 75, 133
Estes, Simon 28
Estes, Sleepy John 33
Eubanks, Kevin 15, 108
Europe, James Reese 10
Evans, Faith 22
Eve 29
Évora, Cesária 12, 99
Fabolous 93
Falana, Lola 42
Falcons, The 128
Farmer, Art 38

Fat Boys 92
Favors, Malachi 136
Feemster, Herbert 72
Fela 1, 42
Felix Da Housecat 110
Ferbos, Lionel 95
Ferrell, Rachelle 29
Ferrer, Ibrahim 41
Fetty Wap 130
Fiasco, Lupe 64
50 Cent 46, 83
Fiona, Melanie 84
Fishbone 101
Fisk Jubilee Singers 112
Fitzgerald, Ella 8, 18
Five Keys, The 104
FKA Twigs 123
Flack, Roberta 19
Flamingos, The 108
Flanagan, Tommy 69
Flavor Flav 67
Flo Rida 78
Floyd, Eddie 127
Flying Lotus 124
Ford, T-Model 91, 113
Ford, Vincent 75
Forté, John 74
Fortune, James 92
Foster, Frank 97
Foster, George "Pops" 40
Foster, William P. 88
Fox, Donal 114
Franklin, Aretha 11, 44, 115
Franklin, Kirk 15, 49, 97
Franti, Michael 93
Freelon, Nnenna 32
Freeman, Paul 39
Freeman, Von 104
Freeman, Yvette 27
Freestyle Fellowship 122
Fresh, Doug E. 93
Fugees 129
Fuller, Blind Boy 86
Fuller, Curtis 115
Fulson, Lowell 118
Fuqua, Antoine 35
Fuqua, Harvey 90
Future 109
Gaines, Grady 38
Gamble, Kenny 85
Gap Band, The 100
Garland, Red 115
Garner, Erroll 76
Garrett, Sean 57
Garrison, Jimmy 133
Gaye, Anna Gordy 121
Gaye, Marvin 2
Gaye, Nona 56
Gaynor, Gloria 36
George, Zelma Watson 42
Geto Boys 115
Ghostface Killah 90
Gibbs, Freddie 125
Gibson, Althea 8, 43
Gil, Gilberto 53
Gill, Johnny 51
Gillespie, Dizzy 1
Ginuwine 35
Glasper, Robert 101
Glenn, Tyree 129
Glover, Corey 34
Goapele 55
Golden Gate Quartet 104

Golson, Benny 37
Gonzales, Babs 134
Goodman, Al 87
Gordon, Dexter 25
Gordy, Berry, Jr. 1
Gotti, Irv 39
Grae, Jean 51
Graham, Katerina 99
Graham Central Station 123
Grandmaster Flash 33, 60
Grant, Micki 125
Graves, Denyce Antoinette 19, 57
Graves, Milford 126
Gray, Dobie 99
Gray, F. Gary 14, 49
Gray, Macy 29
Gray, Wardell 128
Greaves, R. B. 106
Greely, M. Gasby 27
Green, Al 13, 47, 74
Green, Bennie 131
Green, Cee Lo 70, 103
Green, Grant 56
Greene, Jimmy 74
Greene, Travis 134
Greenfield, Elizabeth Taylor 116
Greer, Sonny 127
Griffey, Dick 89
Griffin, Bessie 135
Griffin, Johnny 71
Griffin, LaShell 51
Griffiths, Marcia 29
Grimes, Henry 124
Grist, Reri 84
Gryce, Gigi 124
Güines, Tata 69
Guitar Slim 125
Guru 84
Guy, Buddy 31
Guyse, Sheila 122
Haddon, Dietrick 55
Hailey, JoJo 22
Hailey, K-Ci 22
Hairston, Jester 88
Hall, Aaron 57
Hall, Adelaide 126
Hall, Juanita 62
Hamilton, Anthony 61
Hamilton, Chico 117
Hammond, Fred 23
Hammond, Lenn 34
Hampton, Lionel 17, 41
Hancock, Herbie 20, 67
Handy, John 131
Handy, W. C. 8
Hardin Armstrong, Lil 39
Harold Melvin & the Blue Notes 105
Harper, Ben 34, 62
Harrell, Andre 9, 30
Harris, Barry 68
Harris, Corey 39, 73
Harris, Damon 110
Harris, Kevin 120
Harris, Major 110
Harris, Thurston 129
Harris, Wynonie 102
Hart, Alvin Youngblood 61, 132
Hart, Billy 126
Hartman, Johnny 109
Hathaway, Donny 18
Hathaway, Lalah 57, 88
Havens, Richie 111

Hawes, Hampton 121
Hawkins, Coleman 9
Hawkins, Edwin 113
Hawkins, Erskine 14
Hawkins, Screamin' Jay 30
Hawkins, Tramaine 16
Hawkins, Walter 87
Hayes, Isaac 20, 58, 73
Hayes, Roland 4
Hayes, Teddy 40
Haynes, Roy 87
Heath, Percy 100
Heavy D 58, 98
Hegamin, Lucille 120
Hemphill, Jessie Mae 33, 59
Henderson, Fletcher 32
Henderson, Joe 127
Hendricks, Barbara 3, 67
Hendrix, Jimi 10
Hendryx, Nona 56
Henry, Clarence "Frogman" 46
Hibbert, Toots 103
Higginbotham, J. C. 37
Higginsen, Vy 65
Highway QC's, The 136
Hill, Andrew 66
Hill, Darryl 128
Hill, Lauryn 20, 53, 111
Hilson, Keri 84
Hinderas, Natalie 5
Hines, Earl "Fatha" 39
Hinton, Milt 30
Hodge, Derrick 114
Hodges, Johnny 129
Holiday, Billie 1
Holland-Dozier-Holland 36
Holloway, Brenda 65
Holloway, Loleatta 115
Holmes, Clint 57
Holt, Nora 38
Homesick James 124
Hooker, John Lee 30
Hope, Elmo 135
Hopkins, Lightnin' 83
Horn, Shirley 32, 56
Horne, Lena 5, 86
Horton, Big Walter 115
Horton, Gladys 92
Houghton, Israel 92
House, Son 8
Houston, Cissy 20, 83
Houston, Whitney 7, 28, 83, 100
Howell, Ayinde 91
Howlin' Wolf 9
Hubbard, Freddie 75
Hudson, Jennifer 63, 83
Huff, Leon 86
Humes, Helen 128
Humphrey, Bobbi 20
Hunter, Alberta 42
Hunter, Ivory Joe 106
Hurt, Mississippi John 84
Hutch, Willie 62
Hutcherson, Bobby 115
Hutto, J. B. 129
Hyman, Phyllis 19
Ibrahim, Abdullah 131
Ice Cube 8, 30, 60
Ice-T 6, 31, 96
Iglehart, James Monroe 129
Imani Winds 113
Impressions, The 135
India.Arie 34

Ingram, James **84**
Ink Spots, The **102**
Intruders, The **119**
Isaacs, Gregory **89**
Isley, Marvin **87**
Isley, Ronald **25, 56**
J Dilla **102**
Ja Rule **35, 91**
Jackson, Bobby **119**
Jackson, Bull Moose **130**
Jackson, Fred James **25**
Jackson, George **19**
Jackson, Hal **41, 104**
Jackson, Isaiah **3**
Jackson, Janet **6, 30, 68**
Jackson, Jermaine **79**
Jackson, John **36**
Jackson, LaToya **95**
Jackson, Mahalia **5**
Jackson, Michael **19, 53, 76**
Jackson, Millie **25**
Jackson, Milt **26**
Jackson, Randy **40**
Jackson, Tito **81**
Jackson 5 **103**
Jacquet, Illinois **49**
Jagged Edge **117**
Jaheim **58**
Jamal, Ahmad **69**
Jamelia **51**
Jamerson, James **59**
James, Elmore **114**
James, Etta **13, 52, 100**
James, Leela **117**
James, Rick **17**
James, Skip **38**
James & Bobby Purify **131**
James Bracken and Vivian Bracken **107**
Jaojoby **130**
Jarman, Joseph **136**
Jarreau, Al **21, 65, 105**
Jay Electronica **125**
Jay-Z **27, 69, 103**
Jean, Wyclef **20, 86**
Jefferson, Blind Lemon **81**
Jeffries, Herb **122**
Jenkins, Ella **15**
Jennings, Lyfe **56, 69**
Jerkins, Rodney **31**
Jeter, Claude **75**
Jimmy Jam **13**
Jive Five **131**
Johnson, Al **119**
Johnson, Blind Willie **136**
Johnson, Buddy **36**
Johnson, Conrad O. **97**
Johnson, Gus **132**
Johnson, Hall **90**
Johnson, J. J. **37**
Johnson, J. Rosamond **121**
Johnson, James P. **134**
Johnson, James Weldon **5**
Johnson, Johnnie **56**
Johnson, Ken **106**
Johnson, Le'Andria **108**
Johnson, Lonnie **85**
Johnson, Robert **2**
Johnson, Syl **97**
Johnson, Syleena **98**
Johnson, Tommy **106**
Johnson-George, Tamara **79**
Jones, Bobby **20, 94**

Jones, Booker T. **84**
Jones, Donell **29**
Jones, Elvin **14, 68**
Jones, Etta **35**
Jones, Hank **57, 86**
Jones, Jonah **39**
Jones, Papa Jo **99**
Jones, Philly Joe **121**
Jones, Quincy **8, 30**
Jones, Robert G. **81**
Jones, Roy, Jr. **22, 134**
Jones, Sharon **86**
Jones, Thad **68**
Joplin, Scott **6**
Jordan, Duke **133**
Jordan, Louis **104**
Jordan, Montell **23**
Jordan, Ronny **26**
Jorge, Seu **73**
Joyner, Matilda Sissieretta **15**
Juicy J **116**
Juvenile **96**
Kandi **83**
Kay, Connie **114**
Kay, Ulysses **37**
KB **122**
Keb'Mo' **36, 124**
Kee, John P. **43, 116**
Keita, Salif **83**
Kelela **132**
Kelis **58, 122**
Kelley, Elijah **65**
Kelly, R. **18, 44, 71, 117**
Kelly, Wynton **121**
KEM **47, 127**
Kendricks, Eddie **22**
Kenoly, Ron **45**
Kenyatta, Robin **54**
Keys, Alicia **32, 68**
Khalifa, Wiz **96**
Khan, Chaka **12, 50**
Kid Cudi **83**
Kidjo, Angelique **50**
Killer Mike **117**
Killings, Debra **57**
Kinch, Soweto **108**
King, B. B. **7, 129**
King, Ben E. **128**
King, Chris Thomas **120**
King, Evelyn **129**
King, Freddie **92**
King Curtis **92**
Kingston, Sean **94**
Kirk, Andy **134**
Kirkland, Eddie **99**
Kitt, Eartha **16, 75**
Kiwanuka, Michael **126**
Klugh, Earl **59**
K'naan **76**
Knight, Gladys **16, 66**
Knight, Marie **80**
Knight, Suge **11, 30, 102**
Knowles, Mathew **96**
Knowles, Tina **61**
Knuckles, Frankie **42, 120**
Kolosoy, Wendo **73**
Kool Moe Dee **37**
Kravitz, Lenny **10, 34**
KRS-One **34**
K-Swift **73**
Kuti, Femi **47, 110**
Kweli, Talib **93**
La Roca, Pete **107**

LaBelle, Patti **13, 30**
Labrinth **135**
Ladysmith Black Mambazo **103**
Lakeside **120**
Lamar, Kendrick **105**
Lancaster, Byard **105**
Lance, Major **111**
Land, Harold **125**
Larrieux, Amel **63**
LaSalle, Denise **111**
Lateef, Yusef **91, 117**
Lattimore, Kenny **35, 128**
LaVette, Bettye **85**
Lawrence, Donald **99**
Laws, Hubert **90**
Le Loka, Tsidii **116**
Le1f **120**
Lea, Babatunde **124**
Leadbelly **82**
Lebo M **109**
Lecrae **108**
Ledisi **73**
Lee, Consuela **84**
Lee, Julia **130**
Lee Andrews & the Hearts **134**
Lefel, Edith **41**
Legend, John **67, 116**
Lenoir, J. B. **117**
León, Tania **13**
Levert, Eddie **70**
Levert, Gerald **22, 59**
Lewis, Ananda **28**
Lewis, Butch **71, 99**
Lewis, George **104**
Lewis, George **130**
Lewis, Henry **38**
Lewis, Leona **75**
Lewis, Ramsey **35, 70**
Lewis, Terry **13**
Lighty, Chris **105**
Lil B **121**
Lil Jon **124**
Lil' Kim **28**
Lil Mama **117**
Lil Wayne **66, 84**
Liles, Kevin **42, 99**
Lincoln, Abbey **3, 88**
Lipscomb, Mance **49**
Lister, Marquita **65**
Liston, Melba **118**
Little, Booker **105**
Little Anthony & the Imperials **107**
Little Eva **128**
Little Milton **36, 54**
Little Richard **15**
Little Walter **36**
LL Cool J **16, 49, 94**
Lloyd **99**
Locke, Eddie **44**
Lockwood, Robert, Jr. **120**
London, Theophilus **95**
Long, Huey **79**
Lopes, Lisa "Left Eye" **36**
Lord Infamous **117**
Lord Invader **117**
Lord Jamar **126**
Lord Kitchener **110**
Loueke, Lionel **88**
Love, Darlene **23, 92**
Love, Ed **58**
Love, Laura **50**
Lover, Ed **10**
Lucie, Lawrence **80**

Lucien, Jon **66**
Luckett, Letoya **61**
Ludacris **37, 60**
Lunceford, Jimmie **134**
Lutcher, Nellie **130**
Lymon, Frankie **22**
Lynn, Barbara **126**
Lynne, Gloria **115**
Maal, Baaba **66**
Mabon, Willie **119**
Mac Daddy **111**
Mack Maine **125**
Madlib **88**
Magic Sam **131**
Magic Slim **110**
Mahal, Taj **39**
Mahlasela, Vusi **65**
Maitreya, Sananda **85**
Majors, Jeff **41**
Makeba, Miriam **2, 50, 74**
Malawi Mouse Boys **114**
Mance, Junior **132**
Mandisa **119**
Mane, Gucci **91**
Manhattans, The **123**
Mann, Tamela **92**
Marian Anderson String Quartet **111**
Mario **71**
Marley, Bob **5**
Marley, Rita **32, 70**
Marley, Stephen **100**
Marley, Ziggy **41**
Marrow, Queen Esther **24**
Marsalis, Branford **34, 103**
Marsalis, Delfeayo **41**
Marsalis, Ellis **90**
Marsalis, Wynton **16, 90**
Martelly, Michel **90**
Martin, Roberta **58**
Martin, Sallie **120**
Martin, Sara **38**
Marvelettes, The **126**
Mary Mary **34, 92**
Mase **24**
Masekela, Hugh **1, 106**
Massenburg, Kedar **23, 110**
Masta Ace **118**
Master P **21, 115**
Mathis, Johnny **20**
Matshikiza, Pumeza **115**
Matthews, Benjamin **93**
Maxwell **20, 81**
May, Brother Joe **123**
May, Derrick **41**
Maye, Lee **111**
Mayfield, Curtis **2, 43**
Maynor, Dorothy **19**
MC Breed **75**
M.C. Hammer **20, 80**
MC Lyte **34, 108**
McBee, Cecil **123**
McBride, Christian **134**
McClendon, Lisa **61**
McClurkin, Donnie **25**
McCoo, Marilyn **53**
McCoy, Van **123**
McCracklin, Jimmy **108**
McDaniel, Hattie **5**
McDuff, Jack **116**
McFerrin, Bobby **68**
McFerrin, Robert, Sr. **94**
McGhee, Howard **122**
McGill, Anthony **76**

McGregor, Stephen 99
McGriff, Jimmy 72
McIntyre, Kalaparusha Maurice 117
McKinney, Nina Mae 40
McKnight, Brian 18, 34
McLean, Jackie 78
McPherson, David 32
McRae, Carmen 77
McShann, Jay 110
McTell, Blind Willie 89
McVea, Jack 135
Mèkurya, Gétatchèw 135
Memphis Jug Band 130
Memphis Minnie 33
Memphis Slim 105
Merriweather, Big Maceo 109
Meters, The 118
Method Man 81
Midnight Star 110
Mighty Clouds of Joy 110
Migos 126
Miguel 98
Miles, Buddy 69
Miley, Bubber 120
Miller, Marcus 84
Millinder, Lucky 101
Mills, Stephanie 36
Mills Brothers, The 99
Minaj, Nicki 86, 124
Mingus, Charles 15
Minner, D. C. 133
Minott, Sugar 86
Mississippi Sheiks 122
Mitchell, Blue 126
Mitchell, Dwike 111
Mitchell, Leona 42
Mitchell, Nicole 66
Mitchell, Roscoe 134
Mitchell, Willie 114
Moffett, Charnett 127
Monáe, Janelle 86
Monica 21
Monk, Thelonious 1
Montgomery, Little Brother 117
Montgomery, Robbie 101
Montgomery, Wes 88
Moody, James 83
Moondoc, Jemeel 119
Moonglows, The 108
Moore, Chanté 26, 130
Moore, Dorothy Rudd 46
Moore, Johnny B. 38
Moore, Kermit 116
Moore, LeRoi 72
Moore, Melba 21
Moore, Undine Smith 28
Moran, Jason 89
Morgan, Lee 102
Morton, Jelly Roll 29
Moses, Gilbert 12
Moss, J 64
Moten, Bennie 135
Moten, Etta 18
Moura, Paulo 87
Mowatt, Judy 38
Moye, Famoudou Don 136
Mtukudzi, Oliver 109
Mullen, Nicole C. 45
Mumba, Samantha 29
Murphy, Eddie 4, 20, 61
Murphy, Matt 117
Murray, Tai 47
Musiq 37, 84

Mvula, Laura 110
Mya 35
Myles, Raymond Anthony 121
Nas 33, 111
Nascimento, Milton 2, 64
Nash, Johnny 40
Nate Dogg 92
Naughton, Naturi 97
Naughty by Nature 124
Navarro, Fats 104
Ndegeocello, Meshell 15, 83
N'Dour, Youssou 1, 53, 79
Neal, Kenny 123
Neal, Raful 44, 121
Neale, Haydain 52
Nelly 32, 90
Nelson, Oliver 113
Neville, Aaron 21
New Birth 124
New Edition 101
Newborn, Phineas, Jr. 127
Newman, David 76
Ne-Yo 65
Nicholas, Fayard 20, 57
Nicholas, Harold 20
Nighthawk, Robert 121
Noah, Yannick 4, 60, 121
Norful, Smokie 127
Norman, Jessye 5
Notorious B.I.G. 20
Nzié, Anne-Marie 136
Ocean, Frank 100
Odetta 37, 74
O'Jays, The 98
Okosuns, Sonny 71
Ol' Dirty Bastard 52
Olatunji, Babatunde 36, 126
Oliver, Joe "King" 42
Olusola, Kevin 133
Omarion 107
O'Neal, Shaquille 8, 30, 95
Ongala, Remmy 9, 91
Orioles, The 100
Orlons, The 130
Ory, Kid 118
Osborne, Jeffrey 26, 121
Otis, Clyde 67
OutKast 35
Owens, Jack 38
Owens, Jimmy 130
Page, Walter 117
Palacio, Andy 96
Palmer, Keke 68, 120
Palmer, Rissi 65
Papa Wemba 135
Parham, Truck 124
Parker, Charlie 20
Parker, Junior 116
Parker, Maceo 72
Parker, Ray, Jr. 85
Parks, Gordon 1, 35, 58
Parlan, Horace 108
Patterson, Don 135
Patton, Antwan 45
Patton, Charley 107
Paul, Billy 127, 135
Payne, Freda 58
Peebles, Ann 114
Pena, Paul 58
Pendergrass, Teddy 22, 83
Penguins, The 107
Peoples, Dottie 22
Perkins, Carl 128

Perkins, Pinetop 70
Perren, Freddie 60
Perry, Lee 19, 103
Perry, Ruth 19
Peterson, James 38
Peterson, Marvin "Hannibal" 27
Peterson, Oscar 52
Pettiford, Oscar 106
Pharcyde, The 127
Phife Dawg 134
Phillips, Esther 107
Phillips, Helen L. 63
Phipps, Wintley 59
Pilgrim Travelers, The 129
Pinkney, Fayette 80
Pitchford, Lonnie 133
Pitts, Skip 103
Platters, The 99
Pleasure P 84
P.M. Dawn 54
Porter, David 127
Porter, Tiran 133
Portuondo, Omara 53
Powell, Benny 87
Powell, Bud 24
Pratt, Awadagin 31
Premice, Josephine 41
Preston, Billy 39, 59
Price, Florence 37
Price, Kelly 23
Price, Leontyne 1
Price, Lloyd 119
Pride, Charley 26
Prince 18, 65, 134
Prince Be 136
Pritchard, Robert Starling 21
Professor Longhair 109
Proof 101
Pryce, Trevor 89
Pryor, Rain 65
Pryor, Snooky 119
Prysock, Arthur 117
Public Enemy 98
Purdie, Bernard 77
Pusha T 123
Queen Latifah 1, 16, 58, 119
?uestlove 74
Rachell, Yank 129
Rae Sremmurd 126
Ragin, Derek Lee 84
Rainey, Ma 33
Randall, Alice 38
Randolph, Robert 132
Ranglin, Ernest 78
Rare Essence 121
Rascal, Dizzee 82
Ravens, The 103
Rawls, Johnny 135
Rawls, Lou 17, 57
Ray, Carline 113
Ray, Goodman & Brown 131
Ray J 86
Razaf, Andy 19
Reagon, Bernice Johnson 7
Reagon, Toshi 76
Record, Eugene 60
Red Alert, Kool DJ 33
Redman 81
Redman, Dewey 135
Redman, Don 134
Redman, Joshua 30
Reed, A. C. 36
Reed, Jimmy 38

Reed, Natina 106
Reedy, Jessica 101
Reese, Della 6, 20, 96
Reeves, Dianne 32, 119
Reeves, Martha 85
Reid, L.A. 28, 129
Reid, Rufus 130
Reid, Vernon 34
Rhoden, Wayne 70
Rhone, Sylvia 2
Rhymefest 97
Rhymes, Busta 31
Rhyne, Melvin 109
Richard, Dawn 92
Richie, Lionel 27, 65, 114
Riggins, Karriem 102
Rihanna 65, 102
Riley, Ben 130
Riley, Boots 89
Riley, Teddy 116
Riperton, Minnie 32
Rivers, Sam 95
Roach, Max 21, 63
Roberts, Kimberly Rivers 72
Roberts, Marcus 19, 113
Robeson, Paul 2
Robey, Don 115
Robinson, Cynthia 132
Robinson, Fenton 38
Robinson, Reginald R. 53
Robinson, Smokey 3, 49
Robinson, Sylvia 79
Rochereau, Tabu Ley 117
Rock, Pete 121
Rodríguez, Arsenio 87
Rogers, Bobby 110
Rogers, Jimmy 38
Rollins, Sonny 37, 94
Romanthony 115
Romeo 98
Ronettes, The 132
Roney, Wallace 136
Roots, The 101
Rose Royce 120
Ross, Diana 8, 27
Ross, Isaiah "Doc" 40
Ross, Rick 79, 104
Rotimi 130
Rouse, Charlie 130
Rowland, Kelly 100
Royce da 5'9" 134
Rucker, Darius 34, 74, 108
Rudder, David 79
Ruffin, Jimmy 125
Ruffins, Kermit 85
Run 31, 73
Run-DMC 31, 75
RuPaul 17, 91
Rush, Bobby 78
Rush, Otis 38
Rushen, Patrice 12
Rushing, Jimmy 37
Russell, Brenda 52
Ruth B 135
RZA 80, 128
Saadiq, Raphael 125
Sade 15, 92
Sam and Dave 102
Sample, Joe 51, 123
Sandé, Emeli 113
Sanders, Angelia 86
Sanders, Pharoah 64
Sangare, Oumou 18, 99

Sangho, Awa 127
Santamaria, Mongo 81
Santana, Juelz 120
Santigold 96
Sapp, Marvin 74
Sarpong, Sam 132
Scarlett, Millicent 49
ScHoolboyQ 117
Schuyler, Philippa 50
Scott, George 55
Scott, Hazel 66
Scott, Jill 29, 83
Scott, Jimmy 48, 122
Scott, Shirley 133
Scott-Heron, Gil 94
Scott-Young, Mona 101
Seal 14, 75
Seals, Son 56
Secada, Jon 97
Sermon, Erick 81
Sessoms, Vivian 122
Shabazz Palaces 123
Shaggy 31
Shakur, Afeni 67, 135
Shakur, Tupac 14
Shamir 129
Shanice 112
Shanté, Roxanne 33
Sharp, Dee Dee 130
Shavers, Charlie 131
Shaw, Eddie 136
Shaw, Marlena 105
Sheard, Kierra 61, 114
Shepp, Archie 101
Shider, Garry 87
Shines, Johnny 116
Shipp, Matthew 107
Shirelles, The 111
Shirley, Donald 111
Shirley, George 33
Shmurda, Bobby 123
Short, Bobby 52
Shorter, Wayne 75
Shorty, Ras, I 47
Shyne 101
Siji 56
Silver, Horace 26, 122
Simmons, Russell 1, 30
Simon, Joe 109
Simone, Nina 15, 41, 130
Simpson, Valerie 21, 97
Simpson-Hoffman, N'kenge 52
Sims, Danny 106
Sir Mix-A-Lot 82
Sisqo 30
Sissle, Noble 29
Sister Souljah 11, 100
Slash 75
Sledge, Percy 39, 128
Slick Rick 93
Slim Harpo 120
Slim Thug 86
Sly & Robbie 34
Smith, Bessie 3
Smith, Buster 116
Smith, Cecilia 102
Smith, Cladys "Jabbo" 32
Smith, Clarence 113
Smith, Dr. Lonnie 49
Smith, Hale 118
Smith, Jimmy 127
Smith, Lee 136
Smith, Lonnie Liston 49

Smith, Mamie 32
Smith, Myrna 92
Smith, Stuff 37
Smith, Trixie 34
Smith, Will 8, 18, 53
Smith, Willie 107
Smith, Willow 92
Snoop Dogg 35, 84
Snow, Valaida 135
Solange 97
Somi 85
Songhoy Blues 135
Songz, Trey 88
S.O.S. Band 136
Soul Stirrers 127
Southern, Eileen 56
Souza, Carmen 111
Sowande, Fela 39
Spaniels, The 105
Spann, Otis 107
Sparks, Jordin 66
Spector, Ronnie 77
Speech 82
Spence, Joseph 49
Spivey, Victoria 119
Stackhouse, Houston 122
Stampley, Micah 54
Stanford, Olivia Lee Dilworth 49
Staples, Cleotha 113
Staples, Mavis 50, 88
Staples, "Pops" 32
Starks, Jabo 135
Starr, Edwin 122
Staton, Candi 27
Staton, Dakota 62
Steely 80
Steinberg, Martha Jean "The
    Queen" 28
Stew 69
Stewart, Amii 129
Stewart, Billy 112
Stewart, Slam 126
Stewart, Tricky 98
Sticky Fingaz 86
Still, William Grant 37
Stone, Angie 31
Stone, Jesse 98
Stone, Sly 85
Stoute, Steve 38
Strayhorn, Billy 31
Street, Richard 110
Streeter, Sevyn 115
Stromae 121
Strong, Barrett 89
Stubblefield, Clyde 133
Studdard, Ruben 46
Sugarhill Gang, The 79, 125
Sullivan, Jazmine 81
Sullivan, Maxine 37
Sumlin, Hubert 101
Summer, Donna 25, 102
Summers, Myrna 129
Sun Ra 60
Sundiata, Sekou 66
Sunnyland Slim 118
Supremes, The 33
Swallows, The 133
Swan Silvertones, The 110
Swann, Bettye 109
Sweat, Keith 19
Sweatman, Wilbur 125
Sweatshirt, Earl 114
Sweet Honey in the Rock 106

Swizz Beatz 108
Sykes, Roosevelt 20
Tacuma, Jamaaladeen 124
Tail Dragger 112
Tait, Michael 57
Take 6 112
Tamar-kali 63
Tamia 24, 55
Tampa Red 63
Tapscott, Horace 126
Taste of Honey, A 115
Tate, Buddy 108
Tate, Grady 106
Tatum, Art 28
Tavares 115
Taylor, Art 132
Taylor, Billy 23, 92
Taylor, Cecil 70
Taylor, Eddie 116
Taylor, Hound Dog 120
Taylor, Koko 40, 80
T-Boz 108
Tchicai, John 102
Temptations, The 33
Terrell, Jean 116
Terrell, Tammi 32
Terry, Clark 39, 127
Terry, Sonny 88
Tex, Joe 116
Tharpe, Rosetta 65
The-Dream 74
Thigpen, Ed 110
Thomas, Carla 96
Thomas, Irma 29
Thomas, Rozonda 34, 78
Thomas, Rufus 20, 96
Thomas, Tabby 119
Thornton, Big Mama 33
Threadgill, Henry 97
Three Mo' Tenors 35
Thundercat 136
Thurston, Stephen J. 49
Tillis, Frederick 40
Timbaland 32
Timmons, Bobby 136
Tinie Tempah 115
Tinsley, Boyd 50
Tisdale, Wayman 50
TLC 34
Tonex 54
Tony! Toni! Toné! 127
Tosh, Peter 9
Toussaint, Allen 60, 132
Towles, Nat 128
T-Pain 73, 111
Trammps, The 108
Treacherous Three 128
Tresvant, Ralph 57
Tribbett, Tye 81
Tricky 98
Trina 114
Trombone Shorty 97
Tucker, Tommy 127
Turnbull, Walter 13, 60
Turner, Big Joe 92
Turner, Ike 68
Turner, Tina 6, 27
Turrentine, Stanley 129
2 Chainz 105
Tyga 117
Tyler, the Creator 100
Tyner, McCoy 92
Uggams, Leslie 23, 114

Ulmer, James 79
Usher 23, 56, 95
Valdés, Bebo 75
Valdés, Chucho 89
Valentino, Bobby 62
Vandross, Luther 13, 48, 59
Vanity 67, 134
Vaughan, Sarah 13
Vereen, Ben 4
Verrett, Shirley 66, 91
Vinnegar, Leroy 124
Vinson, Eddie 112
Waka Flocka Flame 110
Waldron, Mal 109
Wale 92
Walker, Albertina 10, 58, 89
Walker, Cedric 19
Walker, George 37
Walker, Hezekiah 34
Walker, Joe Louis 118
Walker, T-Bone 111
Wallace, Sippie 1
Waller, Fats 29
Walton, Cedar 114
Wanz 116
Ward, Anita 118
Ward, Willa 105
Ware, David S. 106
Warfield, William 94
Warren, Butch 116
Warwick, Dionne 18, 111
Washington, Dinah 22
Washington, Grover, Jr. 17, 44
Washington, Kamasi 134
Washington, Kenny 107
Waters, Benny 26
Waters, Ethel 7
Waters, Muddy 34
Watley, Jody 54
Watson, Johnny "Guitar" 18
Watts, André 42, 101
Watts, Reggie 52, 102
Webb, Chick 105
Webster, Ben 136
Webster, Katie 29
Weeknd, The 131
Wein, Joyce 62
Welch, Elisabeth 52
Wellington, Valerie 118
Wells, Junior 102
Wells, Mary 28
Wess, Frank 116
West, Kanye 52, 93
Whalum, Kirk 37, 64
Whispers, The 124
White, Barry 13, 41
White, Bukka 120
White, Josh 86
White, Josh, Jr. 52
White, Maurice 29
White, Willard 53
Whitfield, Norman 73
Whitney, Marva 109
Wiggins, Gerald 128
Wilkins, Thomas Alphonso 71
will.i.am 64
Williams, Bert 18
Williams, Buster 131
Williams, Camilla 116
Williams, Clarence 33
Williams, Claude 80
Williams, Cootie 114
Williams, Deniece 36

Williams, Denise 40
Williams, J. Mayo 83
Williams, Jody 113
Williams, Joe 5, 25
Williams, Larry 118
Williams, Lil' Ed 135
Williams, Mary Lou 15
Williams, Michelle 73
Williams, Nat D. 91
Williams, Paul 112
Williams, Pharrell 47, 82, 119
Williams, Richard 130
Williams, Saul 31
Williams, Tony 67
Williams, Vanessa L. 4, 17
Williams Brothers 135
Williamson, Patrice 134
Williamson, Sonny Boy 84
Williamson, Sonny Boy 134
Willis, Chuck 132
Wilson, Abram 104
Wilson, Brian Courtney 94
Wilson, Cassandra 16
Wilson, Charlie 31, 77, 135
Wilson, Frank 106
Wilson, Gerald 49, 123
Wilson, Jackie 60
Wilson, Mary 28
Wilson, Nancy 10, 98
Wilson, Natalie 38
Wilson, Teddy 134
Winans, Angie 36
Winans, BeBe 14
Winans, CeCe 14, 43
Winans, David 77
Winans, Debbie 36
Winans, Marvin L. 17, 127
Winans, Ronald 54
Winans, Vickie 24
Winburn, Anna Mae 135
Withers, Bill 61
Withers-Mendes, Elisabeth 64
Witherspoon, Jimmy 113
Womack, Bobby 60, 92, 123
Wonder, Stevie 11, 53, 121
Woods, Belita 103
Woods, Georgie 57
Woods, Scott 55
Woodson, Ali Ollie 89
Woolard, Jamal 102
Wooten, Victor 131
Work, John Wesley, III 133
Workman, Reggie 131
Wright, Eugene 125
Wright, Leo 131
Wright, O. V. 114
Wright, Timothy 74
Xzibit 78
Yabby You 83
Yancey, Jimmy 116
Yarbrough, Camille 40
Yarbrough & Peoples 132
Yayo, Tony 113
Yende, Pretty 124
YG 122
Ying Yang Twins 112
Yoba, Malik 11
York, Vincent 40
Young, Johnny 120
Young, Lee 72
Young, Lester 37
Young, Zora 129
Young Jeezy 63

Yusef, Malik 136
Z-Ro 109

Religion

Abernathy, Ralph David 1
Abune Paulos 105
Adams, Yolanda 17, 67
Agyeman, Jaramogi Abebe 10, 63
Akinola, Peter Jasper 65
Akpan, Uwem 70
Al-Amin, Jamil Abdullah 6
Allensworth, Allen 129
Anthony, Wendell 25
Arinze, Francis 19
Aristide, Jean-Bertrand 6, 45
Armstrong, Vanessa Bell 24
Austin, Junius C. 44
Baker, Delbert W. 110
Banks, William 11
Barrow, Willie T. 85, 128
Baylor, Helen 36
Beauvoir, Max 74
Bell, Ralph S. 5
Ben-Israel, Ben Ami 11
Berry, Moses 84
Black, Barry C. 47
Blake, Charles E. 82
Blanks, Deborah K. 69
Bloomer, George 86
Blow, Kurtis 31, 122
Borders, William Holmes 94
Bowen, John W. E., Sr. 89
Boyd, T. B., III 6
Braxton, Brad 77
Brazier, Arthur M. 115
Brewster, W. Herbert 128
Brookins, Hamel Hartford 102
Bryant, Jamal 128
Bryant, John R. 45
Burgess, John 46
Butts, Calvin O., III 9, 90
Bynum, Juanita 31, 71
Caesar, Shirley 19
Cage, Byron 53
Caldwell, Kirbyjon 55
Callender, Eugene 119
Cannon, Katie 10
Cardozo, Francis L. 33
Carr, Kurt 56
Chavis, Benjamin 6
Chineworth, Mary Alice 79
Clarence 13X 126
Cleaver, Emanuel 4, 45, 68, 107
Clements, George 2
Cleveland, James 19
Colemon, Johnnie 11
Collins, Janet 33, 64
Coltrane, Alice 70
Cone, James H. 3, 82
Cook, Suzan D. Johnson 22
Crouch, Andraé 27, 115, 126
Crowdy, William Saunders 109
Dandala, Mvume 77
DeLille, Henriette 30
Dillard, Ricky 134
Divine, Father 7
Dollar, Creflo 106
DuBois, Joshua 88
Easton, Hosea 91
Ellis, Charles H., III 79
Elmore, Ronn 21
Fabre, Shelton 71
Farrakhan, Louis 2, 15

Fauntroy, Walter E. 11
Fisher, Miles Mark 91
Flake, Floyd H. 18, 110
Forbes, James A., Jr. 71
Franklin, C. L. 68
Franklin, Robert M. 13
Fuller, Thomas O. 90
Funnye, Capers C., Jr. 73
Gaither, Israel L. 65
Gantin, Bernardin 70
Gilmore, Marshall 46
Gomes, Peter J. 15, 93
Grace, Sweet Daddy 104
Gray, Ahuvah 130
Gray, Darius 69
Gray, William H., III 3
Green, Al 13, 47, 74
Greene, Travis 134
Gregory, Wilton 37
Grier, Roosevelt 13
Haddon, Dietrick 55
Harding, Vincent 67, 130
Harris, Barbara 12
Hawkins, Tramaine 16
Hawkins, Walter 87
Hayes, James C. 10
Healy, James Augustine 30
Herzfeld, Will L. 132
Holsey, Lucius Henry 92
Hood, James Walker 91
Hooks, Benjamin L. 2, 85
Howard, M. William, Jr. 26
Jackson, Jesse 1, 27, 72
Jakes, T. D. 17, 43, 116
Jasper, John J. 91
Jean-Juste, Gérard 78
Jemison, Major L. 48
Jemison, T. J. 119
Johns, Vernon 38
Jones, Absalom 52
Jones, Alex 64
Jones, Dwight C. 122
Jones, E. Edward, Sr. 45
Jones, Robert Elijah 90
Jones, William A., Jr. 61
Kalbani, Adil 77
Karim, Benjamin 61
Kelly, Leontine 33
King, Barbara 22
King, Bernice 4, 81
King, Martin Luther, Jr. 1
King, Martin Luther, Sr. 89
Kobia, Samuel 43
Lawson, James M., Jr. 90
Lee, Eric P. 79
Lee, Jarena 100
Lewis-Thornton, Rae 32
Lincoln, C. Eric 38
Little Richard 15
Loguen, J. W. 91
Long, Eddie L. 29, 89
Lowery, Joseph 2
Lowry, A. Leon 60
Luter, Fred, Jr. 103
Lyons, Henry 12, 118
Majors, Jeff 41
Marino, Eugene Antonio 30
Mason, Charles Harrison 107
Maxis, Theresa 62
Mays, Benjamin E. 7
McClellan, George Marion 91
McClurkin, Donnie 25
McGuire, George Alexander 80

McKenzie, Vashti M. 29
Meeks, James T. 92
Michaux, Solomon Lightfoot 91
Miller, Clyde 113
Morgan, Gertrude 63
Moss, J 64
Moss, Otis, Jr. 72
Moss, Otis, III 72
Muhammad, Ava 31
Muhammad, Elijah 4
Muhammad, Jabir Herbert 72
Muhammad, Khallid Abdul 10, 31
Muhammed, W. Deen 27
Munroe, Myles 125
Murray, Cecil 12, 47
Muzorewa, Abel 85
Noble Drew Ali 100
Norful, Smokie 127
Okaalet, Peter 58
Otunga, Maurice Michael 55
Patterson, Gilbert Earl 41
Patterson, J. O., Jr. 80
Peterson, Jesse Lee 81
Phipps, Wintley 59
Pierre, Andre 17
Pinckney, Clementa C. 130
Powell, Adam Clayton, Jr. 3
Price, Frederick K. C. 21
Redding, Ann Holmes 77
Reems, Ernestine Cleveland 27
Reese, Della 6, 20, 96
Reverend Ike 79
Riley, Helen Caldwell Day 13
Rivers, Eugene F., III 81
Robinson, Ida B. 106
Rogers, Alan G. 72
Roundtree, Dovey 80
Rugambwa, Laurean 20
Sapp, Marvin 74
Scott, George 55
Senghor, Augustin Diamancoune 66
Sentamu, John 58
Seymour, William J. 106
Shabazz, Betty 7, 26
Sharpe, Samuel 103
Sharpton, Al 21, 97
Shaw, William J. 30
Shelton, Trent 122
Shuttlesworth, Fred 47, 98
Simmons, Gwendolyn Zoharah 132
Slocumb, Jonathan 52
Smith, Amanda Berry 109
Spencer, Peter 128
Stallings, George A., Jr. 6
Stampley, Micah 54
Stanley, A. Knighton 117
Stanton, Alysa 78
Steinberg, Martha Jean "The
    Queen" 28
Stith, Charles R. 73
Sullivan, Leon H. 3, 30
Taylor, Gardner C. 76
Taylor, Lonzie Odie 96
Thurman, Howard 3
Tillard, Conrad 47
Tolton, Augustine 62
Tonex 54
Tribbett, Tye 81
Turner, Henry McNeal 5
Tutu, Desmond 6, 44
Ukpabio, Helen 86
Vanzant, Iyanla 17, 47, 108

Waddles, Charleszetta "Mother" 10, 49
Walker, Hezekiah 34
Walker, John T. 50
Walker, Lucius, Jr. 88
Walker, Wyatt Tee 80
Washington, James Melvin 50
Waters, Ethel 7
Watkins, Joe 86
Weeks, Thomas, III 70
Weems, Renita J. 44
White, Reggie 6, 50
White-Hammond, Gloria 61
Williams, Cecil 130
Williams, Frederick (B.) 63
Williams, Preston Warren, II 64
Wilson, Frank 106
Wilson, Natalie 38
Winans, BeBe 14
Winans, CeCe 14, 43
Winans, Marvin L. 17, 127
Winans, Ronald 54
Woods, Abraham, Jr. 74
Wright, Jeremiah A., Jr. 45, 69, 103
Wright, Nathan, Jr. 56
Wright, Timothy 74
Wyatt, Addie L. 56
X, Malcolm 1
Yarber, Tony 129
Yates, Jack 114
Yearwood, Lennox, Jr. 112
York, Dwight D. 71
Young, Rosa J. 129
Youngblood, Johnny Ray 8

Science and technology

Adams-Campbell, Lucille L. 60
Adkins, Rod 41
Adkins, Rutherford H. 21
Alcorn, George Edward, Jr. 59
Alexander, Archie Alphonso 14
Alexander, Claudia 130
Alexander, Joseph L. 95
Allen, Ethel D. 13
Allen, Will 74
Anderson, Charles Edward 37
Anderson, Michael P. 40
Anderson, Norman B. 45
Anderson, William G(ilchrist) 57
Atim, Julian 66
Augusta, Alexander T. 111
Auguste, Donna 29
Auguste, Rose-Anne 13
Austin, Wanda M. 94
Bacon-Bercey, June 38
Banda, Hastings Kamuzu 6, 54
Banneker, Benjamin 93
Barnett, Herman 112
Bashir, Halima 73
Bath, Patricia E. 37
Bell, Carl C. 111
Benjamin, Regina 20, 75
Benson, Angela 34
Bishop, Stephen 95
Black, Keith Lanier 18, 84
Blackwell, David 79
Bluford, Guy 2, 35
Bluitt, Juliann S. 14
Bolden, Charles Frank, Jr. 7, 78
Boykin, Otis 92
Brady, St. Elmo 107
Branson, Herman 87
Brimm, Charles E. 105

Brown, Vivian 27
Brown, Willa 40
Bullard, Eugene 12
Bullard, Robert D. 121
Callender, Clive O. 3
Campbell, Donald J. 66
Canady, Alexa 28
Cargill, Victoria A. 43
Carroll, L. Natalie 44
Carruthers, George R. 40
Carson, Ben 1, 35, 76, 128
Carter, Joye Maureen 41
Carter, Majora 77
Carver, George Washington 4
CasSelle, Malcolm 11
Chatard, Peter 44
Chinn, May Edward 26
Christensen, Donna M. 17, 132
Christian, Spencer 15
Clack, Zoanne 73
Clark, Mamie Phipps 79
Clark, Yvonne Young 95
Cobb, W. Montague 39
Cobbs, Price M. 9
Cole, Rebecca 38
Coleman, Bessie 9
Coleman, Ken 57
Comer, James P. 6
Coney, PonJola 48
Cooper, Edward S. 6
Cooper, Lisa 73
Cornwell, Edward E., III 70
Counter, S. Allen 74
Crosthwait, David 93
Crouch, Hubert 95
Crumpler, Rebecca Lee 89
Dabiri, John 93
Dailey, Ulysses Grant 87
Daly, Marie Maynard 37, 134
Davis, Allison 12
Dean, Mark 35
Deas, Gerald 85
Deconge-Watson, Lovenia 55
Delany, Bessie 12
Delany, Martin R. 27
Dennis, Gary C. 91
Dickens, Helen Octavia 14, 64
Douglas, Donya 97
Drake, Michael V. 122
Drew, Alvin, Jr. 67
Drew, Charles Richard 7
Dunham, Katherine 4, 59
Dunston, Georgia Mae 48
Durham, James 90
Eberhardt, Jennifer 124
Edwards, Lena Frances 76
Edwards, Willarda V. 59
Elders, Joycelyn 6
Ellington, E. David 11
Ellis, Clarence A. 38
Ellis, Jennifer 135
Emeagwali, Dale 31
Emeagwali, Philip 30
Ericsson-Jackson, Aprille 28
Fennoy, Ilene 72
Fenton, Kevin 87
Ferguson, Vernice D. 108
Fields, Evelyn J. 27
Fisher, Ada M. 76
Fisher, Rudolph 17
Flipper, Henry O. 3
Flowers, Sylester 50
Foster, Henry W., Jr. 26

Francis-McBarnette, Yvette Fay 135
Franklin, Hardy R. 9, 87
Fraser, Sarah Loguen 100
Freeman, Harold P. 23
French, D. M. 94
Fulani, Lenora 11
Fuller, A. Oveta 43
Fuller, Arthur 27
Fuller, Solomon Carter, Jr. 15
Gardere, Jeffrey 76
Gaston, Marilyn Hughes 60
Gates, Sylvester James, Jr. 15, 130
Gayle, Helene D. 3, 46
Gibbons, Gary 107
Gibson, Kenneth Allen 6
Gibson, William F. 6
Giles, Roscoe C. 93
Gilliard, Steve 69
Goodlett, Carlton B. 91
Gourdine, Meredith 33
Grant, Augustus O. 71
Granville, Evelyn Boyd 36
Gray, Ida 41
Green, Hadiyah-Nicole 133
Greene, Frank S., Jr. 101
Gregory, Frederick 8, 51
Grier, Eliza Ann 90
Griffin, Anthony 71
Griffin, Bessie Blount 43, 135
Griffith, Patrick A. 64
Hall, Lloyd A. 8
Hamburg, Margaret 78
Hamilton, Vicki 95
Hammond, Paula 119
Hammonds, Evelynn 69
Hannah, Marc 10
Hansberry, Tony, II 93
Harris, Bernard A. 90
Harris, Gary L. 87
Harris, Mary Styles 31
Harris, Wesley L. 92
Harsh, Vivian Gordon 14
Hayanga, Jeremiah 118
Hayden, Carla D. 47
Haynie, Sharon 94
Haywood, Jimmy 58
Henderson, Cornelius Langston 26
Henderson, Henry Fairfax, Jr. 89
Henson, Matthew 2
Higginbotham, Joan 124
Hill, Wyllstyne D. 94
Hillary, Barbara 65
Hinton, William Augustus 8
Holmes, Hamilton E. 82
Hopkins, Donald R. 89
Howard, Ayanna 65
Hutcherson, Hilda Yvonne 54
Hutson, Jean Blackwell 16, 135
Imes, Elmer Samuel 39
Irving, Barrington, Jr. 112
Irving, Larry, Jr. 12
Jackson, Deborah 94
Jackson, Lisa 77
Jackson, Shirley Ann 12
Jarvis, Erich 67
Jawara, Dawda Kairaba 11
Jefferson, Mildred Fay 89
Jemison, Mae C. 1, 35, 129
Jenifer, Franklyn G. 2
Jenkins, Chad 132
Johnson, Anthony M. 92
Johnson, Lonnie G. 32, 93

Johnson, Sandra K. 94
Johnson-Powell, Gloria 107
Jones, Clara Stanton 51
Jones, Edith Mae Irby 65
Jones, Frederick McKinley 68
Jones, Monty 66
Jones, Randy 35
Jones, Wayne 53
Joseph, Kathie-Ann 56
Josey, E. J. 10
Julian, Hubert 90
Julian, Percy Lavon 6
Juma, Calestous 57
Just, Ernest Everett 3
Keith, Rachel Boone 63
Kenney, John A., Jr. 48
King, Reatha Clark 65
Kintaudi, Leon 62
Kittles, Rick 51
Knowling, Robert E., Jr. 38
Kong, B. Waine 50
Kountz, Samuel L. 10
Kyenge, Cécile 113
Lacks, Henrietta 101
Laroche, Joseph Philippe Lemercier 85
Laryea, Thomas Davies, III 67
Latimer, Lewis H. 4
Lavizzo-Mourey, Risa 48
Lawless, Theodore K. 8
Lawrence, Margaret Morgan 100
Lawrence, Robert H., Jr. 16
Lee, Raphael C. 87
Lee, Robert 112
Leevy, Carroll M. 42
Leffall, Lasalle 3, 64
Lewis, Daurene 72
Lewis, Delano 7
Lewis-Hall, Freda 105
Logan, Onnie Lee 14
Lushington, Augustus Nathaniel 56
Lyttle, Hulda Margaret 14
Madison, Romell 45
Malveaux, Floyd 54
Manley, Audrey Forbes 16
Massey, Walter E. 5, 45
Massie, Samuel P., Jr. 29
Maupin, John E., Jr. 92
Maxey, Randall 46
Mays, William G. 34
Mbabazi, Esther 122
Mboup, Souleymane 10
McBay, Henry C. 91
McCain, Franklin 119
McCoy, Elijah 8
McDonald, Charles J. 120
McJunkin, George 93
McNair, Ronald 3, 58
Mensah, Thomas 48
Mickens, Ronald Elbert 105
Miller, Warren F., Jr. 53
Millines Dziko, Trish 28
Mills, Joseph C. 51
Morgan, Garrett 1
Morrison, Sam 50
Mossell, Nathan Francis 91
Murray, Pauli 38
Nabrit, Samuel Milton 47
Naki, Hamilton 63
Neto, António Agostinho 43
Nour, Nawal M. 56
Nteff, Alain 127
Ojikutu, Bisola 65

Olopade, Olufunmilayo Falusi 58
Omalu, Bennet 132
Osborne, Na'taki 54
Osman, Said 127
Pace, Betty 59
Pape, Jean William 126
Parker, Willie J. 133
Perry, Warren 56
Person, Waverly 9, 51
Peters, Lenrie 43
Petioni, Muriel 99
Pickett, Cecil 39
Pierre, Percy Anthony 46
Pinn, Vivian Winona 49
Pitt, David Thomas 10
Pitts, Derrick 77
Poindexter, Hildrus A. 87
Poussaint, Alvin F. 5, 67
Price, Richard 51
Prothrow-Stith, Deborah 10
Quarterman, Lloyd Albert 4
Rabb, Maurice F., Jr. 58
Randolph, Linda A. 52
Rapelang Rabana 112
Reece, E. Albert 63
Reese, Milous J., Jr. 51
Riley, Helen Caldwell Day 13
Rillieux, Norbert 92
Robinson-Berry, Joan 94
Roker, Al 12, 49
Rollins, Charlemae Hill 27
Ross-Lee, Barbara 67
Samara, Noah 15
Satcher, David 7, 57, 111
Schiavocampo, Mara 97
Seacole, Mary 54
Shabazz, Betty 7, 26
Shavers, Cheryl 31
Shirley, Aaron 126
Shockley, Ann Allen 84
Sigur, Wanda 44
Sinkford, Jeanne C. 13
Slaughter, John Brooks 53
Smith, Ian 62
Smith, Jessie Carney 35
Smith, Richard 51
Spencer, Michael G. 87
Staples, Brent 8
Staupers, Mabel K. 7
Stewart, Ella 39
Stith, James H. 116
Sullivan, Louis 8
Sumner, Francis Cecil 112
Sweet, Ossian 68
Taylor, Susan C. 62
Terrell, Dorothy A. 24
Thomas, Vivien 9
Thornton, Yvonne S. 69
Tuckson, Reed V. 71
Turner, Charles Henry 134
Tyson, Neil deGrasse 15, 65
Uys, Ashley 125
Walker, Arthur, II 87
Walker, Joseph Edison 111
Walker, Tristan 98
Wambugu, Florence 42
Washington, Patrice Clarke 12
Watkins, Levi, Jr. 9
Wedgeworth, Robert W. 42
Wein, Joyce 62
Welsing, Frances Cress 5
Wesley, Dorothy Porter 19
West, James E. 87

Westbrooks, Bobby 51
White, Augustus, III 100
White-Hammond, Gloria 61
Wilkins, J. Ernest, Jr. 43
Williams, Daniel Hale 2
Williams, David Rudyard 50
Williams, O. S. 13
Wilson, Donald E. 88
Wilson, Stephanie 72
Wisdom, Kimberlydawn 57
Witt, Edwin T. 26
Woods, Granville T. 5
Wright, Louis Tompkins 4
Young, Roger Arliner 29

Social issues
Abbott, Robert Sengstacke 27
Abernathy, Ralph David 1
Abiola-Costello, Hafsat 108
Abu-Jamal, Mumia 15
Adams, Sheila J. 25
Agyeman, Jaramogi Abebe 10, 63
Ake, Claude 30
Al-Amin, Jamil Abdullah 6
Alexander, Clifford 26
Alexander, Sadie Tanner Mossell 22
Allen, Lucy 85
Allen, Will 74
Ali, Muhammad 2, 16, 52, 136
Allen, Ethel D. 13
Amaker, Norman 63
Andrews, Benny 22, 59
Annan, Kofi Atta 15, 48
Anthony, Wendell 25
Appiah, Kwame Anthony 67, 101
Arac de Nyeko, Monica 66
Aristide, Jean-Bertrand 6, 45
Arnwine, Barbara 28
Asante, Molefi Kete 3
Ashe, Arthur 1, 18
Atyam, Angelina 55
Auguste, Rose-Anne 13
Austin, Bobby W. 95
Autrey, Wesley 68
Avery, Byllye Y. 66
Ayim, May 126
Azikiwe, Nnamdi 13
Ba, Mariama 30
Baisden, Michael 25, 66
Baker, Ella 5
Baker, Gwendolyn Calvert 9
Baker, Houston A., Jr. 6
Baker, Josephine 3
Baker, Thurbert 22
Baldwin, James 1
Ballard, John 95
Banks, Paula A. 68
Barbee, Lloyd Augustus 71
Barlow, Roosevelt 49
Barnett, Etta Moten 56
Barrow, Willie T. 85, 128
Bass, Charlotta Spears 40
Bates, Daisy 13, 135
Bell, Derrick 6, 98
Bell, Ralph S. 5
Berry, Bertice 8, 55
Berry, Edwin C. 81
Berry, Mary Frances 7
Berrysmith, Don Reginald 49
Bethune, Mary McLeod 4
Betsch, MaVynee 28
Betts, R. Dwayne 86

Bevel, James L. 75
Bibb, Henry and Mary 54
Biko, Steven 4
bin Wahad, Dhoruba 85
Birch, Glynn R. 61
Black, Albert 51
Blackwell, Gloria 127
Blackwell, Unita 17
Blakely, Delois N. 122
Blakely, Edward J. 88
Bobo, Lawrence 60
Bolin, Jane 22, 59
Bond, Julian 2, 35, 106, 130
Bonga, Kuenda 13
Booker, Cory Anthony 68
Borders, Marcy 131
Bosley, Freeman, Jr. 7
Boyd, Gwendolyn 49
Boyd, John W., Jr. 20, 72
Boyd, T. B., III 6
Boykin, Keith 14
Boynton Robinson, Amelia 131
Bozella, Dewey 97
Bradley, David Henry, Jr. 39
Braun, Carol Moseley 4, 42
Brazier, Arthur M. 115
Bridges, Ruby 77
Broadbent, Hydeia 36
Brock, Roslyn McCallister 86
Brown, Byrd 49
Brown, Charlotte Hawkins 106
Brown, Cora 33
Brown, Eddie C. 35
Brown, Elaine 8
Brown, Homer S. 47
Brown, Jesse 6, 41
Brown, Jim 11, 95
Brown, Les 5
Brown, Lloyd Louis 10 42
Brown, Oliver Leon 94
Brown, Oscar, Jr. 53
Brown, Tony 3
Brown, Willa 40
Brown, Zora Kramer 12
Brutus, Dennis 38
Bryant, Jamal 128
Bryant, Wayne R. 6
Buery, Richard, Jr. 97
Bullard, Robert D. 121
Bullock, Steve 22
Bunch, Lonnie G., III 91
Bunche, Ralph J. 5
Burkett, Ben 123
Burks, Mary Fair 40
Burns, Anthony 102
Burroughs, Nannie Helen 96
Butler, Paul D. 17
Butler, Selena Sloan 98
Butts, Calvin O., III 9, 90
Callender, Eugene 119
Cameron, James 80
Campbell, Bebe Moore 6, 24, 59
Canada, Geoffrey 23
Cannon, Park 134
Carby, Hazel 27
Carlos, John 97
Carmichael, Stokely 5, 26
Carr, Johnnie 69
Carr, Keela 74
Carson, Candy 133
Carter, Majora 77
Carter, Mandy 11
Carter, Rubin 26, 121

Carter, Stephen L. 4
Cary, Lorene 3
Cary, Mary Ann Shadd 30
Catlin, Mamie 131
Catto, Octavius V. 83
Cayton, Horace 26
Chambers, Ernie 130
Chavis, Benjamin 6
Chestnut, J. L., Jr. 73
Chideya, Farai 14, 61
Childress, Alice 15
Chisholm, Daquan 93
Chissano, Joaquim 7, 55, 67
Christophe, Henri 9
Church, Robert Reed, Sr. 132
Clark, Joe 1
Clark, Kenneth B. 5, 52
Clark, Septima 7
Clay, William Lacy 8
Clayton, Mayme Agnew 62
Claytor, Helen 14, 52
Cleaver, Eldridge 5
Cleaver, Kathleen Neal 29
Clements, George 2
Cobbs, Price M. 9
Cole, Johnnetta B. 5, 43
Cole, Lorraine 48
Coles, Alice 80
Collins, Patricia Hill 67
Colston, Hal 72
Comer, James P. 6
Compton-Rock, Malaak 86
Connerly, Ward 14
Cook, Toni 23
Cooke, Marvel 31
Cook-Parrish, Mary Virginia 95
Cooper, Anna Julia 20
Cooper, Edward S. 6
Cooper, Margaret J. 46
Cooper, Mario 129
Correia, De'Jaun 93
Cosby, Camille 14, 80
Cox, Donald Lee 93
Creagh, Milton 27
Crew, Spencer R. 55
Cruse, Harold 54
Cuffe, Paul 98
Curvin, Robert 132
da Silva, Benedita 5
Davis, Angela 5, 114
Davis, Artur 41
Davis, Danny K. 24
Dawson, Matel, Jr. 39
Dawson, Michael C. 63
DeBaptiste, George 32
DeLaine, Joseph A. 110
Delany, Martin R. 27
Dellums, Ronald 2, 81
Dent, Thomas C. 50
Diallo, Amadou 27
Dickerson, Ernest 6
Diop, Cheikh Anta 4
Dirie, Waris 56
Divine, Father 7
Dobbs, John Wesley 89
Dodson, Howard, Jr. 7, 52
Dortch, Thomas W., Jr. 45
Douglas, Derek 88
Douglass, Frederick 87
Drew, Charles Richard 7
Du Bois, W. E. B. 3
DuBois, Shirley Graham 21
Due, Patricia Stephens 100

Duggins, George 64
Dukes, Hazel Nell 56
Dumas, Henry 41
Dumpson, James R. 108
Dunham, Katherine 4, 59
Dyson, Michael Eric 11, 40, 128
Eagleson, William Lewis 90
Early, Gerald 15
Easton, Hosea 91
Eberhardt, Jennifer 124
Edelman, Marian Wright 5, 42
Edley, Christopher 2, 48
Edwards, Harry 2
Edwards, Lena Frances 76
Elder, Larry 25, 120
Ellis-Lamkins, Phaedra 88
Ellison, Ralph 7
Esposito, Giancarlo 9
Espy, Mike 6
Eugene-Richard, Margie 63
Europe, James Reese 10
Evers, Medgar 3
Evers, Myrlie 8
Farmer, James 2, 64
Farrakhan, Louis 15
Farris, Isaac Newton, Jr. 63
Fauntroy, Walter E. 11
Fauset, Jessie 7
Fela 1, 42
Fields, C. Virginia 25
Finley, Ron 110
Finner-Williams, Paris Michele 62
Fletcher, Benjamin 90
Fletcher, Bill, Jr. 41
Forbes, James A., Jr. 71
Forman, James 7, 51
Fortune, T. Thomas 6
Foster, Marie 48
Foxx, Kim 134
Franklin, Hardy R. 9
Franklin, John Hope 5, 77
Franklin, Robert M. 13
Frazier, E. Franklin 10
French, D. M. 94
Fulani, Lenora 11
Fuller, Arthur 27
Fuller, Charles 8
Gaines, Ernest J. 7
Gamble, Kenny 85
Gardner, Chris 65
Garner, Tyron 99
Garnet, Henry Highland 100
Garvey, Marcus 1
Gates, Henry Louis, Jr. 3, 38, 67
Gayle, Helene D. 3
Gbowee, Leymah 76
George, Nelson 12, 101
George, Zelma Watson 42
Gibson, Kenneth Allen 6
Gibson, William F. 6
Gilbert, Christopher 50
Gist, Carole 1
Golston, Allan C. 55
Gomez, Jewelle 30
Gomez-Preston, Cheryl 9
Gomillion, Charles 90
Goss, Carol A. 55
Gossett, Louis, Jr. 7
Graham, Lawrence Otis 12
Granger, Lester B. 75
Gray, Fred 37
Greene, Petey 65
Gregory, Dick 1, 54

Gregory, Wilton 37
Grier, Roosevelt 13
Griffith, Mark Winston 8
Grimké, Archibald H. 9
Guy, Rosa 5
Guyot, Lawrence 108
Hale, Lorraine 8
Haley, Alex 4
Hall, Elliott S. 24
Hall, Stuart 78
Hamblin, Ken 10
Hamer, Fannie Lou 6
Hampton, Fred 18
Hampton, Henry 6
Hani, Chris 6
Hansberry, William Leo 11
Harden, Monique 97
Harding, Vincent 67, 130
Harper, Frances Ellen Watkins 11
Harris, Alice 7
Harris, Leslie 6
Harris, Marcelite Jordan 16
Harris, Patricia Roberts 2
Hawkins, Augustus F. 68
Hawkins, Steven 14
Hayden, Lewis 105
Hayes, Dennis 54
Haynes, Elizabeth Ross 102
Haynes, George Edmund 8
Hedgeman, Anna Arnold 22
Height, Dorothy I. 2, 23, 78
Henderson, Thelton E. 68
Henderson, Wade J. 14
Henderson, Zelma 71
Henry, Aaron Edd 19
Henry, Lenny 9, 52
Henson, Josiah 90
Hernandez, Aileen Clarke 13
Herndon, Angelo 90
Hernton, Calvin C. 51
Hill, Anita 5, 65
Hill, Jesse, Jr. 13
Hill, Oliver W. 24, 63
Hilliard, Asa Grant, III 66
Hilliard, David 7, 105
Holland, Endesha Ida Mae 3, 57
Holt Baker, Arlene 73
Hood, James Walker 91
Hooks, Benjamin L. 2, 85
Hope, Lugenia Burns 89
Houston, Charles Hamilton 4
Howard, M. William, Jr. 26
Hoyte, Lenon 50
Hubbard, Arnette Rhinehart 38
Huggins, Nathan Irvin 52
Hughes, Albert 7
Hughes, Allen 7
Hughes, Langston 4
Hunt, Darnell 92
Hunter-Gault, Charlayne 6, 31
Hutchinson, Earl Ofari 24
Ingram, Rex 5
Innis, Roy 5
Irvis, K. Leroy 67
Jackson, Edison O. 67
Jackson, Fred James 25
Jackson, George 14
Jackson, Jesse 1, 27, 72
Jackson, Jimmie Lee 126
Jackson, Judith D. 57
Jackson, Phillip 115
Jacob, John E. 2
Jagan, Cheddi 16

James, Daniel, Jr. 16
Jansen, Jonathan 102
Jarrett, Vernon D. 42, 135
Jealous, Benjamin Todd 70, 113
Jean, Wyclef 20, 86
Jeffries, Leonard 8
Jemison, T. J. 119
Jenkins, Ray 77
Johnson, Charles S. 12
Johnson, James Weldon 5
Jolley, Willie 28
Jones, Clarence B. 114
Jones, Cullen 73
Jones, Elaine R. 7, 45
Jones, Eugene Kinckle 79
Jones, John 89
Jones, Van 70
Jones, William A., Jr. 61
Jordan, June 7, 35
Jordan, Vernon E. 3, 35
Joseph, Kathie-Ann 56
Josey, E. J. 10
Joyner, Marjorie Stewart 26
Joyner, Tom 19, 90
Julian, Percy Lavon 6
Karim, Benjamin 61
Kato, David 103
Kaunda, Kenneth 2
Keita, Salif 83
Kelley, Cliff 75
Kennedy, Florynce 12, 33
Khanga, Yelena 6
Kidd, Mae Street 39
Kimbro, Warren 76
King, Bernice 4, 81
King, Coretta Scott 3, 57
King, Dexter 10
King, Martin Luther, III 20
King, Martin Luther, Jr. 1
King, Martin Luther, Sr. 89
King, Preston 28
King, Robert Hillary 84
King, Rodney 103
King, Yolanda 6
Kirk, Clara 95
Kitwana, Bakari 86
Koontz, Elizabeth Duncan 101
Kuzwayo, Ellen 68
Ladner, Joyce A. 42
LaGuma, Alex 30
Lampkin, Daisy 19
Lane, Charles 3
Lane, Vincent 5
Langston, John Mercer 101
Laraque, Paul 67
Latiker, Diane 132
Law, W. W. 121
Lawson, James M., Jr. 90
Lee, Canada 8
Lee, Eric P. 79
LeGrand, Naquasia 126
Leland, Mickey 2
Lemon, Alton T. 112
Lewis, Ananda 28
Lewis, Delano 7
Lewis, Thomas 19
Lewis-Thornton, Rae 32
Little, Robert L. 2
Logan, Rayford W. 40
Loguen, J. W. 91
Louis, Errol T. 8
Louis, Willie 113
Loving, Mildred 69

Lowe, Rick 124
Lowery, Evelyn Gibson 115
Lowery, Joseph 2
Lowry, A. Leon 60
Lucas, John 7
Lucy, William 50
Lucy Foster, Autherine 35
Luper, Clara 94
Maathai, Wangari 43, 97
Mabuza-Suttle, Felicia 43
Madison, Joseph E. 17
Makeba, Miriam 2, 50, 74
Malone Jones, Vivian 59
Malveaux, Julianne 32, 70
Mandela, Nelson 1, 14, 77, 117
Mandela, Winnie 2, 35, 112
Manley, Audrey Forbes 16
Maponya, Maishe 101
Marable, Manning 10, 102
Marshall, Paule 7, 77
Marshall, Thurgood 1, 44
Martin, Louis E. 16
Martin, Trayvon 105
Masekela, Barbara 18
Mason, Biddy 89
Mason, Ronald 27
Matthews, Ameena 105
Maynard, Robert C. 7
Mays, Benjamin E. 7
Mbeki, Thabo 14, 73
McCabe, Jewell Jackson 10
McCain, Franklin 119
McCray, Chirlane 134
McDougall, Gay J. 11, 43
McKay, Claude 6
McKenzie, Vashti M. 29
Mckesson, DeRay 133
McKinney Hammond, Michelle 51
McKissick, Floyd B. 3
McMurray, Georgia L. 36
McQueen, Butterfly 6, 54
McWhorter, John 35, 119
McWorter, Free Frank 91
Meredith, James H. 11
Meyers, Michael 131
Mfume, Kweisi 6, 41
Mhlaba, Raymond 55
Micheaux, Oscar 7
Millender-McDonald, Juanita 21, 61
Miller, Clyde 113
Miller-Travis, Vernice 64
Millines Dziko, Trish 28
Minkins, Shadrach 104
Mitchell, Clarence M., Jr. 88
Mitchell, Juanita Jackson 128
Mkapa, Benjamin W. 16, 77
Mongella, Gertrude 11
Moody, Anne 127
Moore, Gwendolynne S. 55
Moore, Harry T. 29
Morgan, Irene 65
Morial, Ernest "Dutch" 26
Moses, Robert Parris 11
Moss, Otis, Jr. 72
Mossell, Gertrude Bustill 40
Motley, Constance Baker 10, 55
Moton, Robert Russa 83
Moutoussamy-Ashe, Jeanne 7
Mowry, Jess 7
Mugisha, Frank 119
Muhammad, Elijah 4
Muhammad, Khallid Abdul 10, 31
Mukoko, Jestina 75

Murphy, Laura M. 43
Murphy, Taylonn 131
Murray, Pauli 38
Nabagesera, Kasha Jacqueline 130
Nash, Diane 72
Ndadaye, Melchior 7
Nell, William C. 128
Nelson, Jill 6, 54
Newton, Huey 2
Niane, Katoucha 70
Nixon, Edgar Daniel 100
Nkoli, Simon 60
Nkrumah, Kwame 3
Noble, Gil 76
Norman, Pat 10
Nour, Nawal M. 56
Nzo, Alfred 15
Obasanjo, Olusegun 5
Oglesby, Zena 12
Ojikutu, Bisola 65
O'Neal, Frederick 99
Orange, James 74
Ormes, Jackie 73
Osborne, Na'taki 54
Osotimehin, Babatunde 107
Page, Alan 7
Page, Clarence 4
Parker, Kellis E. 30
Parker, Pat 19
Parks, Rosa 1, 35, 56
Parr, Russ 51
Patterson, Frederick Douglass 12
Patterson, Louise 25
Patterson, P. J. 6, 20
Perkins, Edward 5
Perry, James 83
Perry, Matthew J., Jr. 96
Peterson, Jesse Lee 81
Pitt, David Thomas 10
Pleasant, Mary Ellen 9
Plessy, Homer Adolph 31
Pough, Terrell 58
Poussaint, Alvin F. 5, 67
Powell, Adam Clayton, Jr. 3
Powell, Kevin 31, 74
Pratt, Geronimo 18, 95
Pressley, Condace L. 41
Price, Hugh B. 9, 54
Pritchard, Robert Starling 21
Prothrow-Stith, Deborah 10
Pyfrom, Estella 127
Quander, Nellie 102
Quarles, Benjamin Arthur 18
Quigless, Helen G. 49
Ramphele, Mamphela 29
Ramsey, Charles H. 21, 69
Rand, A. Barry 6
Randolph, A. Philip 3
Randolph, Linda A. 52
Rawlings, Nana Konadu Agyeman 13
Reed, Ishmael 8
Reid, Ira De A. 100
Rice, Louise Allen 54
Rice, Norm 8
Richards, Hilda 49
Richardson, Julieanna 81
Richardson, Rupert 67
Riley, Boots 89
Riley, Helen Caldwell Day 13
Rivers, Eugene F., III 81
Roberts, Lillian 83
Robeson, Eslanda Goode 13

Robeson, Paul 2
Robinson, Jackie 6
Robinson, Rachel 16
Robinson, Randall 7, 46
Robinson, Sharon 22
Robinson, Spottswood W., III 22
Roble, Abdi 71
Rock, John S. 113
Rodriguez, Cheryl 64
Rolle, Myron 98
Rose, Harold M. 134
Rowan, Carl T. 1, 30
Rowe-Adams, Jackie 109
Rowell, Victoria 13, 68
Ruffin, Josephine St. Pierre 75
Ruggles, David 126
Rusesabagina, Paul 60
Russwurm, John Brown 100
Rustin, Bayard 4
Sampson, Edith S. 4
Sanders, Malika 48
Sales, Ruby 133
Sané, Pierre Gabriel 21
Sapphire 14, 95
Saro-Wiwa, Kenule 39
Sasser, Sean 113
Savimbi, Jonas 2, 34
Sayles Belton, Sharon 9, 16
Scantlebury-White, Velma 64
Seacole, Mary 54
Seale, Bobby 3
Sears, Stephanie 53
Seele, Pernessa 46
Senghor, Léopold Sédar 12
Shabazz, Attallah 6
Shabazz, Betty 7, 26
Shadd, Abraham D. 81
Shakur, Afeni 67, 135
Shakur, Assata 6
Shakur, Yusef 85
Sharpe, Samuel 103
Sharpton, Al 21, 97
Sherrod, Shirley 87
Shinhoster, Earl 32
Shuttlesworth, Fred 47, 98
Sidibé, Michel 133
Simkins, Modjeska Monteith 112
Simmons, Gwendolyn Zoharah 132
Simms, Margaret 94
Simon, Lateefah 95
Sisulu, Albertina 57, 95
Sisulu, Sheila Violet Makate 24
Smith, Anna Deavere 6
Smith, Barbara 28
Smith, Damu 54
Smith, Greg 28
Smith, Kemba 70
Smith, Marie F. 70
Smith, Nate 49
Smith, Tommie 102
Snowden, Frank M., Jr. 67
Sohn, Sonja 100
Spriggs, William 67
Stallings, George A., Jr. 6
Staupers, Mabel K. 7
Steele, Claude 13, 97
Steele, Shelby 13, 82
Stevenson, Bryan 128
Stewart, Alison 13
Stewart, Ella 39
Stewart, Maria W. Miller 19
Sullivan, Leon H. 3, 30
Sweatt, Heman Marion 114

Sweet, Ossian 68
Talbert, Mary B. 77
Tate, Eleanora E. 20, 55
Tatum, Wilbert 76
Taulbert, Clifton Lemoure 19
Taylor, Bo 72
Taylor, Mildred D. 26
Taylor, Recy 92
Taylor, Robert Rochon 104
Terrell, Mary Church 9
Thomas, Arthur Ray 52
Thomas, Franklin A. 5, 49
Thomas, Jefferson 88
Thompson, Cynthia Bramlett 50
Thurman, Howard 3
Thurman, Wallace 16
Till, Emmett 7
Tobias, Channing H. 79
Toomer, Jean 6
Tosh, Peter 9
Touré, Askia (Muhammad Abu Bakr el) 47
Touré, Faya Ora Rose 56
Tribble, Israel, Jr. 8
Trotter, Donne E. 28
Trotter, Monroe 9
Tsvangirai, Morgan 26, 72
Tubman, Harriet 9, 135
Tucker, C. Delores 12, 56
Tucker, Cynthia 15, 61
Tucker, Rosina 14
Turner, Charles Henry 134
Tutu, Desmond 6, 44
Tyree, Omar Rashad 21
Vaughn, Viola 70
Vega, Marta Moreno 61
Velez-Rodriguez, Argelia 56
Vesey, Denmark 100
Villard-Appolon, Malya 106
Vincent, Marjorie Judith 2
Waddles, Charleszetta "Mother" 10, 49
Walcott, Derek 5, 94
Walker, A'lelia 14
Walker, Alice 1, 43
Walker, Bernita Ruth 53
Walker, David 129
Walker, Lucius, Jr. 88
Wall, Orindatus S. B. 92
Wallace, Joaquin 49
Wallace, Michele Faith 13
Wallace, Phyllis A. 9
Wallace, William 75
Washington, Booker T. 4
Washington, Ebonya 79
Washington, Fredi 10
Washington, Harold 6
Washington, Karen 117
Washington, Pauletta Pearson 86
Watkins, Ted 104
Wattleton, Faye 9
Webb-Christburg, Sheyann 110
Wells, Henrietta Bell 69
Wells, James Lesesne 10
Wells-Barnett, Ida B. 8
Welsing, Frances Cress 5
West, Cornel 5, 33, 80
White, Michael R. 5
White, Reggie 6, 50
White, Walter F. 4
White, Willye 67
White-Hammond, Gloria 61
Whitmore, George 106

Wilkins, Roy 4
Williams, Armstrong 29
Williams, Cecil 130
Williams, Evelyn 10
Williams, Fannie Barrier 27
Williams, George Washington 18
Williams, Hosea 15, 31, 123
Williams, Maggie 7, 71
Williams, Montel 4, 57
Williams, Patricia 11, 54
Williams, Robert F. 11, 136
Williams, Stanley "Tookie" 29, 57
Williams, Willie L. 4
Wilson, August 7, 33, 55
Wilson, Margaret Bush 79
Wilson, Phill 9, 104
Wilson, Sunnie 7, 55
Wilson, William Julius 22
Withers, Ernest C. 68, 88
Wiwa, Ken 67
Woodson, Robert L. 10
Worrill, Conrad 12
Wright, Beverly 97
Wright, Charles H. 35
Wright, Louis Tompkins 4
Wright, Nathan, Jr. 56
Wright, Richard 5
Wyatt, Addie L. 56
X, Malcolm 1
Xuma, Madie Hall 59
Yancy, Dorothy Cowser 42
Yarbrough, Camille 40
Yearwood, Lennox, Jr. 112
Yeboah, Emmanuel Ofosu 53
Yergan, Max 123
Yoba, Malik 11
Young, Jean Childs 14
Young, Whitney M., Jr. 4
Youngblood, Johnny Ray 8
Yumkella, Kandeh 105
Zulu, Princess Kasune 54

Sports
Aaron, Hank 5
Abdirahman, Abdi 126
Abdul-Jabbar, Kareem 8
Abdur-Rahim, Shareef 28
Adams, Paul 50
Adu, Freddy 67
Aldridge, LaMarcus 125
Alexander, Shaun 58
Ali, Laila 27, 63
Ali, Muhammad 2, 16, 52, 136'
Allen, Dick 85
Allen, Larry 109
Allen, Marcus 20
Allen, Ray 82
Altidore, Jozy 109
Alves, Dani 121
Amaker, Tommy 62
Amos, John 8, 62
Anderson, Elmer 25
Anderson, Ezzrett 95
Anderson, Jamal 22
Anderson, Mike 63
Anderson, Viv 58
Anelka, Nicolas 118
Anthony, Carmelo 46, 94
Antunes, Lúcio 109
Archibald, Tiny 90
Arenas, Gilbert 84
Armstrong, Henry 104
Artest, Ron 52

Ashe, Arthur **1, 18**
Ashford, Emmett **22**
Ashford, Evelyn **63**
Ashley, Maurice **15, 47**
Asomugha, Nnamdi **100**
Atkinson, Alia **126**
Baines, Harold **32**
Baker, Dusty **8, 43, 72, 110**
Balotelli, Mario **104**
Banks, Ernie **33, 126**
Barber, Ronde **41**
Barber, Tiki **57, 107**
Barkley, Charles **5, 66**
Barksdale, Don **103**
Barnes, Ernie **16, 78**
Barnes, John **53**
Barnes, Steven **54**
Barney, Lem **26**
Barnhill, David **30**
Batch, Charlie **120**
Baugé, Grégory **86**
Baylor, Don **6**
Baylor, Elgin **93**
Beamon, Bob **30**
Beasley, Jamar **29**
Beaty, Zelmo **115**
Beckham, Odell, Jr. **132**
Bekele, Kenenisa **75**
Bell, James "Cool Papa" **36**
Bell, Le'Veon **132**
Bellamy, Walt **119**
Belle, Albert **10**
Benítez, Christian **113**
Berian, Boris **136**
Berry, Eric **125**
Bettis, Jerome **64**
Bickerstaff, Bernie **21, 133**
Bickerstaff, J. B. **133**
Bigirimana, Gael **115**
Biles, Simone **136**
Bing, Dave **3, 59, 78**
Bivins, Michael **72**
Black, Joe **75**
Blair, Paul **36**
Blake, James **43, 131**
Blanks, Billy **22**
Blanton, Dain **29**
Blue, Vida **122**
Bogues, Tyrone "Muggsy" **56**
Bol, Manute **1**
Bolt, Usain **73, 104**
Bolton-Holifield, Ruthie **28**
Bonaly, Surya **7**
Bonds, Barry **6, 34, 63, 99**
Bonds, Bobby **43**
Bonheur, Yannick **84**
Boozer, Bob **103**
Bosh, Chris **85**
Bostic, Joe **95**
Bowe, Riddick **6, 107**
Bowles, Todd **128**
Bozella, Dewey **97**
Bramlett, Joseph **91**
Brand, Elton **31**
Brandon, Terrell **16**
Branham, George, III **50**
Brashear, Donald **39**
Brathwaite, Fred **35**
Bridgeman, Junior **132**
Bridgewater, Teddy **132**
Brigitha, Enith **126**
Briscoe, Marlin **37**
Brock, Lou **18**

Broner, Adrien **109**
Brooks, Aaron **33**
Brooks, Derrick **43, 119**
Brown, Antron **85**
Brown, James **22**
Brown, Jason **125**
Brown, Jerry **117**
Brown, Jim **11, 95**
Brown, Mike **77, 107**
Brown, Raymond **102**
Brown, Tim **134**
Browne, Richard **132**
Brown, Sean **52**
Brown, Willard **36**
Bruce, Isaac **26**
Bryant, Cullen **81**
Bryant, Dez **116**
Bryant, Kobe **15, 31, 71, 110**
Buchanan, Ray **32**
Burke, Glenn **122**
Burton, Tony **135**
Bush, Reggie **59, 88**
Butler, Jimmy **135**
Butler, Leroy, III **17**
Bynoe, Peter C. B. **40**
Byrd, Marlon **112**
Cabell, Enos **102**
Cain, Lorenzo **128**
Caldwell, Jim **81**
Campanella, Roy **25**
Campbell, Earl **104**
Campbell, Milt **113**
Campbell-Brown, Veronica **102**
Cano, Robinson **97**
Carew, Rod **20**
Carlos, John **97**
Carnegie, Herbert **25**
Carter, Anson **24**
Carter, Butch **27**
Carter, Cris **21, 109**
Carter, Joe **30**
Carter, Kenneth **53**
Carter, Rubin **26, 121**
Carter, Vince **26**
Casey, Dwane **135**
Cash, Swin **59**
Catchings, Tamika **43**
Cepeda, Orlando **98**
Chalmers, Mario **122**
Chamberlain, Wilt **18, 47**
Chancellor, Kam **131**
Chandler, Tyson **114**
Chaney, Don **98**
Chaney, John **67**
Chapman, Aroldis **132**
Charles, Ezzard **95**
Charles, John **108**
Charleston, Oscar **39**
Cheeks, Maurice **47, 106**
Cherry, Deron **40**
Cheruiyot, Robert **69**
Chitalu, Godfrey **108**
Christie, Linford **8**
Claiborne, Loretta **34**
Clay, Bryan **57, 74**
Clemons, Michael "Pinball" **64**
Clendenon, Donn **26, 56**
Clifton, Nathaniel "Sweetwater" **47**
Coachman, Alice **18, 123**
Cole, Ashley **106**
Coleman, Leonard S., Jr. **12**
Coleman, Vince **128**
Collins, Jason **111**

Cooper, Andy "Lefty" **63**
Cooper, Charles "Chuck" **47**
Cooper, Michael **31**
Cooper, Tarzan **96**
Cooper-Dyke, Cynthia **17, 89**
Copeland, Michael **47**
Corbin, Tyrone **126**
Corley, Tony **62**
Cottrell, Comer **11**
Cousins, DeMarcus **108**
Cox, Bryan **83**
Crawford, Carl **90**
Crawford, Terence **135**
Crennel, Romeo **54, 107**
Crisp, Coco **109**
Cromartie, Antonio **115**
Crooks, Garth **53**
Croom, Sylvester **50**
Cruz, Victor **107**
Cueto, Johnny **130**
Culp, Curley **110**
Culpepper, Daunte **32, 85**
Cunningham, Randall **23**
Curry, Dell **126**
Curry, Michael **85**
Curry, Stephen **110**
Dandridge, Ray **36**
Daniels, Mel **106**
Dantley, Adrian **72**
Davids, Edgar **106**
Davis, Anthony **120**
Davis, Ben **115**
Davis, Eric **116**
Davis, Ernie **48**
Davis, Mike **41**
Davis, Milt **74**
Davis, Phil **132**
Davis, Piper **19**
Davis, Rajai **135**
Davis, Shani **58, 84**
Davis, Terrell **20**
Davis, Thomas **132**
Davis, Vernon **133**
Davis, Wade, Jr. **103**
Dawes, Dominique **11, 126**
Dawkins, Darryl **131**
Dawson, Andre **85**
Day, Leon **39**
Dean, Fred **98**
DeFrantz, Anita **37**
DeGale, James **74**
Delaney, Joe **76**
Dent, Richard **97**
DeRozan, DeMar **125**
Devers, Gail **37, 87**
Diaw, Boris **122**
Dibaba, Genzebe **130**
Dibaba, Mare **131**
Dibaba, Tirunesh **73, 109**
Dickerson, Eric **27, 108**
Dihigo, Martín **103**
Dixon, George **52**
Doby, Lawrence Eugene, Sr. **16, 41**
Doig, Jason **45**
Dokes, Michael **105**
Dorrell, Karl **52**
dos Santos, Manuel Francisco **65**
Douglas, Bob **96**
Douglas, Buster **127**
Drew, Charles Richard **7**
Drexler, Clyde **4, 61**
Driver, Donald **99**
Drogba, Didier **78, 132**

Drummond, Andre **132**
Duerson, Dave **93**
Dumars, Joe **16, 65, 126**
Duncan, Tim **20, 91**
Dungy, Tony **17, 42, 59, 118**
Dunn, Jerry **27**
Dunn, Warrick **90**
Durant, Kevin **76, 107**
Dye, Jermaine **58**
Edwards, Harry **2**
Edwards, Herman **51**
Edwards, Teresa **14, 95**
Elder, Lee **6**
Ellerbe, Brian **22**
Elliott, Sean **26**
Ellis, Dock **78**
Ellis, Jimmy **44, 127**
Ervin, Anthony **66**
Erving, Julius **18, 47**
Escobar, Alcides **130**
Eto'o, Samuel **73**
Eusebio **118**
Everett, Carl **103**
Evra, Patrice **102**
Ewing, Patrick **17, 73, 130**
Fairbanks, Mabel **117**
Farah, Mo **104**
Farmer, Ray **133**
Farr, Mel **24**
Faulk, Marshall **35, 96**
Felix, Allyson **48, 98**
Ferdinand, Rio **82**
Fielder, Cecil **2, 112**
Fielder, Prince **68**
Fisher, Derek **87**
Fitzgerald, Larry **133**
Flood, Curt **10, 93**
Flowers, Vonetta **35**
Ford, Cheryl **45**
Foreman, George **1, 15**
Forrest, Vernon **40, 79**
Foster, Andrew **79**
Foster, Arian **114**
Fowler, Reggie **51**
Fox, Rick **27**
Fraser-Pryce, Shelly-Ann **113**
Frazier, Joe **19, 98**
Frazier, Walt **91**
Frazier-Lyde, Jacqui **31**
Freeman, Cathy **29**
Freeman, Marianna **23**
Fuentes, Tito **123**
Fuhr, Grant **1, 49**
Fuller, Vivian **33**
Futch, Eddie **33**
Gaines, Clarence E., Sr. **55**
Gaither, Alonzo Smith (Jake) **14**
Gamble, Oscar **113**
Gans, Joe **91**
Garnett, Kevin **14, 70, 118**
Garrison, Zina **2, 133**
Gaston, Cito **71**
Gates, William **97**
Gatlin, Justin **123**
Gay, Tyson **114**
Gebrselassie, Haile **70**
Gentry, Alvin **23**
George, Eddie **80**
George, Paul **124**
Gervin, George **80**
Gibson, Althea **8, 43**
Gibson, Bob **33**
Gibson, Josh **22**

Gibson, Truman K., Jr. 60
Gill, Turner 83
Gilliam, Frank 23
Gilliam, Jim 122
Gilliam, Joe 31
Gilmore, Artis 101
Glanville, Douglas Metunwa 82
Gooden, Dwight 20
Gorden, W. C. 71
Gordon, Dee 130
Gordon, Josh 120
Gordon, Tom 130
Gore, Frank 117
Goss, Tom 23
Gourdine, Meredith 33
Gourdine, Simon 11
Graham, Trevor 84
Granderson, Curtis 66
Grand-Pierre, Jean-Luc 46
Grant, Frank 100
Gray, Yeshimbra "Shimmy" 55
Green, A. C. 32
Green, Darrell 39, 74
Green, Dennis 5, 45
Green, Draymond 126
Greene, Joe 10
Greene, Maurice 27, 77
Greenwood, L. C. 115
Greer, Hal 92
Gregg, Eric 16
Gregory, Ann 63
Grier, Bobby 95
Grier, Mike 43
Grier, Roosevelt 1
Griffey, Ken, Jr. 12, 73
Griffin, Blake 98
Griffin, Robert, III 107
Griffith, Emile 113
Griffith, Yolanda 25
Griffith-Joyner, Florence 28
Griner, Brittney 128
Gumbel, Greg 8
Gwynn, Tony 18, 83, 122
Gyan, Asamoah 87
Hagler, Marvelous Marvin 102
Hairston, Sam 88
Haley, Charles 134
Hamilton, Darryl 130
Hamilton, Leonard 100
Hamilton, Lewis 66
Haney, Lee 77
Hardaway, Anfernee 13, 111
Hardaway, Tim 35
Harden, James 116
Hardy, Greg 118
Harris, Franco 97
Harris, James 79
Harris, Sylvia 70
Harrison, Alvin 28
Harrison, Calvin 28
Harrison, Marvin 134
Harris-Stewart, Lusia 90
Hart, Jim Ray 136
Hart, Thomas A., Sr. 113
Harvin, Percy 123
Haskins, Clem 23
Hawkins, Connie 91
Haye, David 82
Hayes, Bob 77
Hayes, Elvin 93
Haywood, Spencer 99
Hazzard, Walt 98
Heard, Gar 25

Hearns, Thomas 29
Henderson, Rickey 28, 78
Henry, Mark 116
Henry, Thierry 66, 127
Hernández, Orlando 96
Heyward, Craig 131
Hickman, Fred 11
Hill, Calvin 19
Hill, Candace 130
Hill, Grant 13, 94
Hill, Michael 95
Hillary, Barbara 65
Hilliard, Wendy 53
Hines, Garrett 35
Holdsclaw, Chamique 24, 110
Holiday, Jrue 115
Holland, Kimberly N. 62
Hollins, Lionel 133
Holmes, Kelly 47
Holmes, Larry 20, 68
Holmes, Santonio 87
Holyfield, Evander 6
Hopkins, Bernard 35, 69, 105
Horford, Al 107
Horton, Andre 33
Horton, Suki 33
Horton, Willie 104
Howard, Desmond 16, 58
Howard, Dwight 113
Howard, Elston 125
Howard, Juwan 15
Howard, Ryan 65, 113
Howard, Sherri 36
Hudson, Lou 121
Humphrey, Claude 119
Hunter, Billy 22, 109
Hunter, Lindsey 110
Hunter, Torii 43, 109
Hurd, Sam 116
Hyde, Cowan F. "Bubba" 47
Ibrahim, Fuad 109
Iginla, Jarome 35
Iguodala, Andre 129
Ince, Paul 83
Irvin, Michael 64
Irvin, Monte 31, 134
Irving, Kyrie 102
Isaacs, John 76
Iverson, Allen 24, 46, 129
Ivey, Phil 72, 106
Jackson, DeSean 120
Jackson, Hue 133
Jackson, Jamea 64
Jackson, Mannie 14
Jackson, Mark 121
Jackson, Rampage 83
Jackson, Reggie 15
Jackson, Rickey 88
Jackson, Stephen 118
Jackson, Tom 70
Jacobs, Regina 38
James, David 84
James, G. Larry 74
James, LeBron 46, 78, 105
James, Vanessa 84
Jefferson, Richard 136
Jenkins, Fergie 46
Jenkins, Kris 98
Jeptoo, Rita 121
Jeter, Derek 27, 93, 124
Jim, Songezo 111
Johanneson, Albert 129
Johnson, Andre 127

Johnson, Avery 62
Johnson, Ben 1
Johnson, Calvin 108
Johnson, Chad 108
Johnson, Chris 92
Johnson, Clifford "Connie" 52
Johnson, Dennis 89
Johnson, Gus 92
Johnson, Jack 8
Johnson, Joe 94
Johnson, John Henry 96
Johnson, Judy 105
Johnson, Kevin 70, 132
Johnson, Keyshawn 91
Johnson, Larry 28
Johnson, Levi 48
Johnson, Magic 3, 39, 101
Johnson, Mamie "Peanut" 40
Johnson, Marques 133
Johnson, Michael 13
Johnson, Rafer 33
Johnson, Rodney Van 28
Joiner, Charlie 102
Jones, Adam 103
Jones, Adam 114
Jones, Andruw 98
Jones, Cobi N'Gai 18
Jones, Cullen 73
Jones, Deacon 92, 112
Jones, Ed "Too Tall" 46
Jones, Jacoby 117
Jones, Jon 121
Jones, Julio 131
Jones, K. C. 83
Jones, Lou 64
Jones, Marion 21, 66
Jones, Merlakia 34
Jones, Randy 35
Jones, Robbie 113
Jones, Roy, Jr. 22, 134
Jones, Sam 85
Jones, Walter 119
Jones-Drew, Maurice 113
Jordan, Eddie 83
Jordan, Michael 6, 21
Joyce, Dru 81
Joyner-Kersee, Jackie 5
Justice, David 18
Kaiser, Cecil 42
Kaka, Luthando 118
Kamworor, Geoffrey 134
Kane, Evander 97
Kanouté, Fred 68
Kearney, Beverly 109
Keflezighi, Meb 49, 121
Keith, Floyd A. 61
Kellogg, Clark 64
Kelly, Jim 113
Kennedy, Cortez 104
Kennedy-Overton, Jayne Harris 46
Kerry, Leon G. 46
Khumalo, S'manga 119
Kidd, Jason 86
Kimbro, Henry A. 25
Kimetto, Dennis 125
King, Don 14, 128
Kipchoge, Eliud 124
Kipsang, Wilson 115
Kompany, Vincent 132
Krigger, Kevin 111
Lacy, Sam 30, 46
Ladd, Ernie 64
Lane, Dick 92

Lanier, Bob 47
Lanier, Willie 33
Lankford, Ray 23
Laraque, Georges 48
Larkin, Barry 24
Lashley, Bobby 63
Lassiter, Roy 24
Lee, Canada 8
LeGrand, Eric 118
Lennox, Betty 31
Leonard, Buck 67
Leonard, Kawhi 122
Leonard, Sugar Ray 15
Leônidas 96
Leslie, Lisa 16, 73
Lester, Bill 42, 85
Lewis, Aubrey 133
Lewis, Butch 71, 99
Lewis, Carl 4, 97
Lewis, Denise 33
Lewis, Jamal 115
Lewis, Lennox 27
Lewis, Marvin 51, 87
Lewis, Oliver 56
Lewis, Ray 33, 109
Lillard, Damian 117
Lister, Tommy 127
Liston, Sonny 33
Little, Floyd 86
Little, Larry 90
Littlepage, Craig 35
Lloyd, Earl 26, 127
Lloyd, John Henry "Pop" 30
Lofton, James 42
Lofton, Kenny 12
Lopes, Davey 92
Loroupe, Tegla 59
Lott, Ronnie 9
Louis, Joe 5
Love, Nat 9
Love, Reggie 77
Lowe, Sidney 64
Lowry, Kyle 135
Lucas, Bill 97
Lucas, John 7
Lue, Tyronn 136
Lyle, Ron 125
Lynch, Marshawn 124
Mackey, Biz 82
Madison, Paula 37, 99
Mahorn, Rick 60
Malone, Karl 18, 51, 90
Malone, Moses 79, 131
Manigault, Earl "The Goat" 15
Manley, Dexter 116
Mann, Bob 126
Manuel, Jerry 94
Mariner, Jonathan 41
Marion, Shawn 136
Marshall, Brandon 116
Marte, Starling 117
Martin, Cuonzo 121
Martin, Curtis 104
Martin, Jonathan 119
Martínez, Pedro 81, 126
Masekela, Sal 106
Mason, Anthony 128
Mason, Derek 120
Mason, Desmond 127
Mathis, Robert 121
Matson, Ollie 93
May, Mark 117
Maye, Lee 111

Mayers, Jamal **39**
Mayhew, Martin R. **76**
Mays, Willie **3**
Mayweather, Floyd **57, 104**
McAdoo, Bob **75**
McBride, Bryant **18**
McCarthy, Sandy **64**
McClendon, Lloyd **123**
McCovey, Willie **103**
McCoy, LeSean **123**
McCray, Nikki **18**
McCutchen, Andrew **116**
McDaniel, Randall Cornell **81**
McGrady, Tracy **80**
McGriff, Fred **24**
McKegney, Tony **3**
McLendon, John B., Jr. **89**
McNabb, Donovan **29, 119**
McNair, Steve **22, 47, 79**
McNeil, Lori **1**
McRae, Hal **84**
Mello, Breno **73**
Meminger, Dean **114**
Mensah, John **87**
Metcalfe, Ralph **26**
Meyiwa, Senzo **124**
Milla, Roger **2**
Miller, Cheryl **10, 74**
Miller, Larry G. **72**
Miller, Reggie **33**
Mills, Sam **33**
Milton, DeLisha **31**
Minor, DeWayne **32**
Minoso, Minnie **89, 127**
Mitchell, Freddie **116**
Mitchell, Sam **82**
Mohammed, Nazr **64**
Monk, Art **38, 73**
Monroe, Earl **89**
Montgomery, Tim **41**
Moon, Warren **8, 66**
Moore, Archie **120**
Moore, Davey **105**
Moore, Maya **94**
Moorer, Michael **19, 132**
Morgan, Joe **9, 96**
Morris, Mercury **114**
Morris, Raheem **77**
Moses, Edwin **8**
Mosley, Shane **32**
Moss, Randy **23, 90**
Motley, Marion **26**
Mourning, Alonzo **17, 44, 131**
Moussambani, Eric **105**
Muamba, Fabrice **104**
Muhammad, Ibtihaj **133**
Muhammad, Jabir Herbert **72**
Muncie, Chuck **112**
Mundine, Anthony **56**
Murray, Eddie **12**
Murray, Lenda **10**
Mutola, Maria **12**
Mutombo, Dikembe **7, 107**
Nakhid, David **25**
Newcombe, Don **24**
Newsome, Ozzie **26, 117**
Newton, Cam **96**
Nixon, Otis **111**
Noah, Yannick **4, 60, 121**
Norton, Ken **101, 115**
Odom, Lamar **81**
Ogden, Jonathan **110**
Okocha, Jay Jay **99**

Olajuwon, Hakeem **2, 72**
Oliver, Pam **54, 123**
Oliver, Paul **115**
Omar, Samia Yusuf **107**
O'Neal, Shaquille **8, 30, 95**
O'Neil, Buck **19, 59**
Onyewu, Oguchi **60**
O'Ree, Willie **5**
Ortiz, David **52, 82**
Ortiz, Luis **134**
Owens, Brig **118**
Owens, Jesse **2**
Owens, Terrell **53, 106**
Pace, Orlando **21, 134**
Page, Alan **7**
Page, Greg **78**
Paige, Satchel **7**
Palmer, Violet **59**
Parish, Robert **43**
Parker, Candace **74**
Parker, Jim **64**
Parker, Tony **75**
Patterson, Floyd **19, 58**
Paul, Chris **84, 100**
Payton, Gary **99**
Payton, Walter **11, 25**
Peck, Carolyn **23**
Peete, Calvin **11**
Peete, Rodney **60**
Pelé **7**
Pelé, Abedi **122**
Perez, Pascual **108**
Perkins, Eddie **103**
Perrot, Kim **23**
Perry, Joe **95**
Perry, Lowell **30**
Peters, Jason **125**
Peters, Margaret **43**
Peters, Matilda **43**
Petersen, Neal **96**
Peterson, Adrian **109**
Pettigrew, Antonio **118**
Phillips, Brandon **116**
Phillips, Teresa L. **42**
Phillips, Tony **135**
Pickett, Bill **11**
Pierce, Paul **71**
Pineda, Michael **121**
Pippen, Scottie **15, 89**
Pollard, Fritz **53**
Porter, Bo **123**
Porter, Terry **75**
Portis, Clinton **130**
Powell, Mike **7**
Powell, Renee **34**
Powell, William J. **82**
Price, David **101**
Pride, Charley **26**
Prince, Ron **64**
Prince, Tayshaun **68**
Pryce, Trevor **89**
Puckett, Kirby **4, 58**
Puig, Yasiel **113**
Quirot, Ana **13**
Radcliffe, Ted **74**
Raines, Tim **107**
Ramírez, Hanley **135**
Randle, John **87**
Randolph, Willie **53**
Rashad, Ahmad **18**
Ready, Stephanie **33**
Reagins, Tony **94**
Reece, Marcel **114**

Reed, Willis, Jr. **86**
Reese, Jerry **103**
Reese, Pokey **28**
Regis, Cyrille **51**
Revis, Darrelle **130**
Reyes, José **134**
Reynolds, Harold **77**
Rhoden, William C. **67**
Rhodes, Ray **14**
Ribbs, Willy T. **2**
Rice, Jerry **5, 55, 89**
Rice, Jim **75**
Rice, Ray **112**
Richard, J. R. **87**
Richards-Ross, Sanya **66, 98**
Richardson, Donna **39**
Richardson, Nolan **9**
Richmond, Mitch **19**
Rivers, Doc **25, 81**
Roaf, Willie **106**
Roberts, Dave **132**
Robertson, Oscar **26**
Robinson, Craig **107**
Robinson, Dave **110**
Robinson, David **24, 90**
Robinson, Eddie G. **10, 61**
Robinson, Flynn **112**
Robinson, Frank **9, 87**
Robinson, Jackie **6**
Robinson, Sugar Ray **18**
Robinson, Will **51, 69**
Rodman, Dennis **12, 44, 96, 118**
Rogers, Rodney Ray **106**
Rolle, Myron **98**
Rollins, Jimmy **70**
Ronaldinho **69**
Rondo, Rajon **111**
Rooks, Sean **136**
Rose, Derrick **82**
Rose, Jalen **108**
Rose, Lionel **56**
Roseboro, John **123**
Roundfield, Danny **109**
Roy, Brandon **98**
Rudisha, David **112**
Rudolph, Wilma **4**
Russell, Bill **8**
Sabathia, CC **74**
St. Julien, Marlon **29**
Salvador, Bryce **51**
Sam, Michael **121**
Sampson, Charles **13**
Sanders, Barry **1, 53**
Sanders, Bob **72**
Sanders, Charlie **130**
Sanders, Deion **4, 31, 96**
Sanders, Satch **77**
Sapp, Warren **38, 109**
Savón, Félix **105**
Sayers, Gale **28**
Scott, Byron **125**
Scott, George **113**
Scott, Stuart **34, 126**
Scott, Wendell Oliver, Sr. **19**
Scurry, Briana **27**
Sealy, Malik **118**
Seedorf, Clarence **121**
Sefolosha, Thabo **121**
Seymour, Richard **101**
Seymour, Teddy **110**
Shannon, Randy **82**
Sharpe, Shannon **97**

Sharper, Darren **32, 118**
Shavers, Earnie **127**
Shaw, Brian **127**
Sheffield, Gary **16, 108**
Shell, Art **1, 66**
Shelton, Trent **122**
Sherman, Richard **118**
Shippen, John **43**
Showers, Reggie **30**
Sidat-Singh, Wilmeth **116**
Sifford, Charlie **4, 49, 134**
Silas, Paul **24, 129**
Silva, Anderson **96**
Simmonds, Wayne **121**
Simmons, Bob **29**
Simpson, O. J. **15, 100**
Simpson, Sherone **120**
Singletary, Mike **4, 76**
Sizemore, Grady **96**
Slater, Duke **125**
Slice, Kimbo **73, 136**
Smalling, Chris **118**
Smith, Bruce **80**
Smith, Bubba **96**
Smith, Emmitt **7, 87**
Smith, Gene **123**
Smith, Geno **118**
Smith, Hilton **29**
Smith, Kenny **114**
Smith, Lee **101**
Smith, Lovie **66, 107**
Smith, Neil **109**
Smith, Ozzie **77**
Smith, Randy **81**
Smith, Reggie **113**
Smith, Rick **72**
Smith, Stephen A. **69**
Smith, Steve **120**
Smith, Tommie **102**
Smith, Tubby **18, 83**
Smith, Will **135**
Solomon, Jimmie Lee **38**
Song, Alex **105**
Sono, Jomo **86**
Sosa, Sammy **21, 44**
Spiller, Bill **64**
Sprewell, Latrell **23**
Stackhouse, Jerry **30**
Staley, Dawn **57**
Stallworth, John **102**
Stargell, Willie **29**
Stearns, Norman "Turkey" **31**
Steele, Sage **115**
Stephens, Sloane **105**
Stephenson, Lance **118**
Stevenson, Teófilo **103**
Steward, Emanuel **18, 106**
Stewart, Dave **117**
Stewart, James, Jr. **60, 98**
Stewart, Kordell **21, 111**
Stingley, Darryl **69**
Stith, Tom **93**
Stiverne, Bermane **128**
Stone, Toni **15**
Stoudemire, Amar'e **59, 106**
Strahan, Michael **35, 81, 135**
Strawberry, Darryl **22**
Stringer, C. Vivian **13, 66**
Stringer, Korey **35**
Strode, Woody **111**
Strong, Charlie **118**
Sturridge, Daniel **120**
Subban, P. K. **121**

Suggs, Terrell 108
Suttles, Mule 108
Swann, Lynn 28
Swoopes, Sheryl 12, 56
Tate, John 107
Tatum, Jack 87
Tatum, Reece 104
Taylor, Jason 70
Taylor, Jermain 60
Taylor, Lawrence 25
Taylor, Marshall Walter "Major" 62
Teklehaimanot, Daniel 130
Temple, Collis, Jr. 119
Temple, Ed 109
Tergat, Paul 59
Terrell, Ernie 118
Terrell-Kearney, Kim 83
Thabeet, Hasheem 123
Thomas, Debi 26
Thomas, Derrick 25
Thomas, Emmitt 71
Thomas, Frank 12, 51
Thomas, Isiah 7, 26, 65
Thomas, Thurman 75
Thompson, Klay 126
Thompson, Mychal 126
Thompson, Tina 25, 75
Thompson, Tristan 131
Thrower, Willie 35
Thugwane, Josia 21
Thurmond, Nate 88
Tiant, Luis 102
Tirico, Mike 68, 124
Tisdale, Wayman 50
Tolbert, Mike 125
Toler, Burl 80
Tomlin, Mike 123
Tomlinson, LaDainian 65, 112
Toney, James 89
Touré, Yaya 99
Towns, Karl-Anthony 136
Trouppe, Quincy Thomas, Sr. 84
Tunnell, Emlen 54
Turman, Glynn 100
Turner, Mark 126
Tyson, Mike 28, 44, 93
Ujiri, Masai 107
Unseld, Wes 23
Upshaw, Gene 18, 47, 72
Upton, Justin 124
Upton, Melvin, Jr. 124
Uribe, Juan 122
Urschel, John 126
Ussery, Terdema, II 29
Vanessa James and Yannick Bon-
   heur 84
Vaughn, Jacque 127
Vick, Michael 39, 65, 94
Vincent, Troy 91
Virgil, Ozzie 48
Wade, Dwyane 61, 103
Walcott, Jersey Joe 102
Walker, Antoine 132
Walker, Chet 106
Walker, Herschel 1, 69
Walker, LeRoy T. 106
Wall, John 129
Wallace, Ben 54
Wallace, Perry E. 47
Wallace, Rasheed 56
Wanjiru, Sammy 94
Ward, Andre 62
Ward, Hines 84

Ward, Joel 129
Ware, Andre 37
Ware, DeMarcus 92
Washington, Gene 63
Washington, Kenny 50
Washington, MaliVai 8
Washington, Ora Mae 115
Washington, Ron 119
Watson, Benjamin 126
Watson, Bob 25
Watts, J. C., Jr. 14, 38
Wayne, Reggie 131
Weah, George 58
Weaver, Mike 109
Webber, Chris 15, 30, 59, 118
Weekes, Kevin 67
Wells, Vernon 91
Wells, Willie 105
Westbrook, Peter 20
Westbrook, Russell 116
Whitaker, Pernell 10, 89
White, Bill 1, 48
White, Frank 95
White, Jesse 22, 75
White, Jo Jo 112
White, Reggie 6, 50
White, Willye 67
Whiteside, Hassan 127
Whitfield, Fred 23
Whitfield, Mal 60
Whitney, Davey L. 110
Wiggins, Andrew 128
Wilbon, Michael 68, 132
Wilder, Deontay 121
Wilfork, Vince 124
Wilkens, Lenny 11, 88
Wilkins, Dominique 74
Williams, Bernie 128
Williams, Billy 86
Williams, Darrent 116
Williams, Deron 92
Williams, Doug 22, 112
Williams, J. Mayo 83
Williams, Ken 68
Williams, Lauryn 58, 127
Williams, Monty 125
Williams, Natalie 31
Williams, Richard 131
Williams, Ricky 85
Williams, Serena 20, 41, 73, 129
Williams, Stevie 71
Williams, Venus 17, 34, 62
Williams, Walt 133
Williamson, Fred 67
Willingham, Tyrone 43
Willis, Bill 68
Willis, Dontrelle 55
Willis, Patrick 99
Wills, Harry 80
Wills, Maury 73
Wilson, Ajee' 129
Wilson, David 123
Wilson, Russell 119
Winfield, Dave 5, 91
Winkfield, Jimmy 42
Winslow, Kellen 83
Wolfe, Ann 82
Wood, Willie 111
Woodard, Lynette 67
Woodruff, John 68
Woods, Cheyenne 103
Woods, Tiger 14, 31, 81
Woodson, Mike 78

Woodson, Rod 79
Worthy, James 49
Wright, Chalky 103
Wright, Rayfield 70
Wyllie, Tony 131
Yeboah, Emmanuel Ofosu 53
Yirga, Samuel 126
Young, Darren 114
Young, Donald, Jr. 57
Young, Jimmy 54
Young, John 111

Television

Abrahams, Zaraah 127
Abudu, Mo 121
Aduba, Uzo 122
Akil, Mara Brock 60, 82
Akinnuoye-Agbaje, Adewale 56
Alexander, Khandi 43
Ali, Mahershala 122
Ali, Tatyana 73
Allen, Byron 3, 24, 97
Allen, Debbie 13, 42
Allen, Marcus 20
Alonso, Laz 87
Amos, John 8, 62
Anderson, Anthony 51, 77
Anderson, Eddie "Rochester" 30
Anderson, Jacob 128
Andrews, Tina 74
Anthony, La La 122
Arkadie, Kevin 17
Arnez J 53
Arnold, Tichina 63
Avery, James 118
Babatunde, Obba 35
Banks, Michelle 59
Banks, William 11
Barclay, Paris 37, 94, 133
Barris, Kenya 135
Bassett, Angela 6, 23, 62
Batiste, Jon 108, 130
Beach, Michael 26, 120
Beard, Matthew 120
Beaton, Norman 14
Beauvais, Garcelle 29, 95
Bell, LeRoy 98
Bell, W. Kamau 107
Bellamy, Bill 12
Bennett, Louise 69
Bentley, Lamont 53
Berry, Bertice 8, 55
Berry, Fred "Rerun" 48
Bey, Yasiin 30, 96
Big Freedia 128
Bingham, Margot 135
Blackmon, Brenda 58
Blackwood, Maureen 37
Blacque, Taurean 58
Blake, Asha 26
Bleu, Corbin 65
Bonet, Lisa 58, 133
Boseman, Chadwick 111
Boston, Kelvin E. 25
Bowser, Yvette Lee 17, 133
Boyega, John 133
Bradley, Ed 2, 59
Brady, Wayne 32, 71
Brandy 14, 34, 72
Braugher, Andre 13, 58, 91
Braxton, Tamar 134
Bridges, Todd 37
Brooks, Avery 9, 98

Brooks, Danielle 119
Brooks, Golden 62
Brooks, Hadda 40
Brooks, Mehcad 62
Brown, Bobbi Kristina 130
Brown, James 22
Brown, Joe 29
Brown, Les 5
Brown, Tim 134
Brown, Tony 3
Brown, Vivian 27
Brown, Warren 61
Browne, Roscoe Lee 66
Bruce, Bruce 56
Buress, Hannibal 101
Burnett, Charles 16, 68
Burton, LeVar 8
Byrd, Eugene 64
Byrd, Robert 11
Caldwell, Benjamin 46
Cameron, Earl 44
Campbell, Naomi 1, 31, 120
Campbell-Martin, Tisha 8, 42
Cannon, Nick 47, 73, 132
Cannon, Reuben 50
Cara, Irene 77
Carmichael, Jerrod 124
Carroll, Rocky 74
Carroll, Diahann 9
Carson, Lisa Nicole 21
Carter, Nell 39
Cash, Rosalind 28
Cathey, Reg E. 122
Cedric the Entertainer 29, 60, 115
Cenac, Wyatt 94
Chappelle, Dave 50, 115
Chase, Debra Martin 49, 96
Che, Michael 123
Cheadle, Don 19, 52
Chestnut, Morris 31, 116
Chew, Robert F. 109
Chideya, Farai 14, 61
Childress, Alvin 114
Christian, Spencer 15
Ciara, Barbara 69
Clack, Zoanne 73
Clash, Kevin 14, 93
Clayton, Xernona 3, 45
Cobbs, Bill 101
CoCo Brother 93
Cole, Keyshia 63, 107
Cole, Nat "King" 17
Coleman, Chad L. 128
Coleman, Gary 35, 86
Common 31, 63, 98
Coolio 103
Corbi, Lana 42
Corinealdi, Emayatzy 133
Cornelius, Don 4, 100
Cosby, Bill 7, 26, 59, 125
Cox, Laverne 122
Crews, Terry 123
Crothers, Scatman 19
Crump, Steven 96
Curry, Dell 126
Curry, Mark 17
Curtis-Hall, Vondie 17
DaCosta, YaYa 98
Daniels, Billy 124
Davidson, Tommy 21
Davis, Eisa 68
Davis, Mia Amber 94
Davis, Ossie 5, 50

Davis, Viola **34, 76, 100, 131**
de Passe, Suzanne **25**
De Shields, André **72**
Dee, Ruby **8, 50, 68, 122**
Deezer D **53**
Devine, Loretta **24**
Dexter, Felix **129**
Dickerson, Ernest **6**
Diggs, Taye **25, 63**
Dixon, Ivan **69**
DJ Lance Rock **94**
Dorn, Michael **112**
Dourdan, Gary **37**
Drake **86**
Duke, Bill **3, 96**
Dungey, Channing **134**
Dungey, Merrin **62**
Duthiers, Vladimir **109**
Dutton, Charles S. **4, 22**
Earthquake **55**
Ejogo, Carmen **126**
Elba, Idris **49, 89, 116**
Elbagir, Nima **121**
Elder, Larry **25, 120**
Elie, Lolis Eric **97**
Elise, Kimberly **32, 101**
Ellis, Aunjanue **108**
Ellis, Trey **97**
Emmanuel, Alphonsia **38**
Ephriam, Mablean **29**
Epperson, Sharon **54**
Erving, Julius **18, 47**
Esposito, Giancarlo **9**
Eubanks, Kevin **15, 108**
Evans, Harry **25**
Faison, Donald **50**
Faison, Frankie **55**
Falana, Lola **42**
Fales-Hill, Susan **88**
Fargas, Antonio **50**
Faulkner, Harris **131**
Fields, Kim **36**
Fishburne, Laurence **4, 22, 70**
Fisher, Gail **85**
Fox, Rick **27**
Foxx, Jamie **15, 48**
Foxx, Redd **2**
Frazier, Kevin **58**
Freeman, Aaron **52**
Freeman, Morgan **2, 20, 62, 100**
Freeman, Yvette **27**
Funches, Ron **121**
Gaines, Ernest J. **7**
Gant, Richard **105**
Gardere, Jeffrey **76**
Garvin, Gerry **78**
Gibbs, Marla **86**
Gibson, Tyrese **27, 62, 134**
Givens, Adele **62**
Givens, Robin **4, 25, 58**
Glass, Ron **111**
Glover, Anwan **123**
Glover, Danny **1, 24, 103**
Glover, Donald **85**
Glover, Savion **14**
Goldberg, Whoopi **4, 33, 69**
Golding, Meta **135**
Good, Meagan **117**
Goode, Mal **13**
Gooding, Cuba, Jr. **16, 62**
Gordon, Carl **87**
Gordon, Ed **10, 53**
Gossett, Louis, Jr. **7**

Graham, Katerina **99**
Gray, Darius **69**
Greely, M. Gasby **27**
Greene, Petey **65**
Grier, David Alan **28**
Grier, Pam **9, 31, 86**
Griffin, Angela **80**
Guillaume, Robert **3, 48**
Gumbel, Bryant **14, 80**
Gumbel, Greg **8**
Gunn, Moses **10**
Gurira, Danai **73**
Guy, Jasmine **2**
Hairston, Jester **88**
Haley, Alex **4**
Hall, Arsenio **58**
Hall, Regina **135**
Hall, Tamron **96**
Hamilton, Bernie **117**
Hamilton, Lisa Gay **71**
Hampton, Henry **6**
Hardison, Kadeem **22**
Hardwick, Omari **122**
Harewood, David **52**
Harewood, Dorian **104**
Harper, Hill **32, 65, 97**
Harrell, Andre **9, 30**
Harris, Naomie **55, 116**
Harris, Robin **7**
Harris, Wood **114**
Harry, Jackée **111**
Hart, Kevin **103**
Harvey, Steve **18, 58**
Hatchett, Glenda **32**
Hayes, Isaac **20, 58, 73**
Haynes, Trudy **44**
Haysbert, Dennis **42, 106**
Hector, Jamie **98**
Hemingway, Anthony **107**
Hemsley, Sherman **19, 104**
Henderson, Jeff **72**
Henriques, Julian **37**
Henry, Lenny **9, 52**
Henson, Darrin **33**
Henson, Taraji P. **58, 77, 127**
Hickman, Fred **11**
Hill, Darryl **128**
Hill, Dulé **29, 129**
Hinderas, Natalie **5**
Hines, Gregory **1, 42**
Hodge, Aldis **124**
Holmes, Amy **69**
Holmes, T. J. **98**
Holt, Lester **66**
Hooks, Robert **76**
Hounsou, Djimon **19, 45**
Howard, Sherri **36**
Howard, Terrence **59, 94**
Hudson, Ernie **72, 131**
Huggins, Edie **71**
Hughley, D. L. **23, 76**
Hunter-Gault, Charlayne **6, 31**
Hurst, Michelle **135**
Hyman, Earle **25, 79**
Ice-T **6, 31, 96**
Ifill, Gwen **28**
Ingram, Rex **5**
Jackson, George **19**
Jackson, Janet **6, 30, 68**
Jackson, Randy **40**
Jackson, Tom **70**
Jenkins, Kris **98**
Joe, Yolanda **21**

Johnson, Clark **96**
Johnson, Linton Kwesi **37**
Johnson, Robert L. **3, 39**
Johnson, Rodney Van **28**
Jones, Bomani **121**
Jones, James Earl **3, 49, 79**
Jones, Leslie **136**
Jones, Orlando **30**
Jones, Quincy **8, 30**
Jones, Rashida **101**
Jones, Robbie **113**
Jordan, Michael B. **97**
Joseph, Paterson **126**
Kandi **83**
Kaufman, Monica **66**
Kelley, Malcolm David **59**
Kennedy-Overton, Jayne Harris **46**
Key & Peele **107**
Keys, Alicia **32, 68**
Kid Cudi **83**
King, Gayle **19, 99**
King, Regina **22, 45**
King, Woodie, Jr. **27**
Kirby, George **14**
Kitt, Eartha **16, 75**
Knight, Gladys **16, 66**
Kodjoe, Boris **34, 89**
Kotto, Yaphet **7**
Kwei-Armah, Kwame **84**
La Salle, Eriq **12**
LaBelle, Patti **13, 30**
Laneuville, Eric **123**
Langhart Cohen, Janet **19, 60**
Lathan, Sanaa **27**
Lawrence, Martin **6, 27, 60**
Lawson, Jennifer **1, 50**
Leakes, NeNe **107**
LeFlore, Lyah Beth **96**
Lemmons, Kasi **20**
Lemon, Don **94**
Lesure, James **64**
Lewis, Ananda **28**
Lewis, Byron E. **13**
Lewis, Emmanuel **36**
Lil' Kim **28**
Lindo, Delroy **18, 45**
LisaRaye **27**
Little, Cleavon **117**
LL Cool J **16, 49, 94**
Lofton, James **42**
Long, Loretta **58**
Long, Nia **17, 95**
Love, Loni **113**
Lover, Ed **10**
Luke, Derek **61**
Lumbly, Carl **47**
Mabrey, Vicki **26**
Mabuza-Suttle, Felicia **43**
Mac, Bernie **29, 61, 72**
Madison, Paula **37, 99**
Malco, Romany **71**
Malveaux, Suzanne **88**
Mann, Tamela **92**
Marcille, Eva **97**
Marshall, William **107**
Markham, Pigmeat **106**
Martin, Duane **108**
Martin, Helen **31**
Martin, Jesse L. **31**
Martin, Michel **97**
Martin-Green, Sonequa **133**
Masekela, Sal **106**
Mason, Judi Ann **112**

Mathis, Greg **26**
Mayo, Whitman **32**
Mbatha-Raw, Gugu **89**
McBride, Chi **73**
McCrary, Darius **111**
McCrary Anthony, Crystal **70**
McCullough, DeAndre **106**
McDaniel, Hattie **5**
McDaniels, Ralph **79**
McDonald, Audra **20, 62, 128**
McEwen, Mark **5**
McFarland, Roland **49**
McGee, Vonetta **95**
McGlowan, Angela **64, 86**
McKee, Lonette **12, 119**
McKenzie, Vashti M. **29**
McKinney, Nina Mae **40**
McQueen, Butterfly **6, 54**
Meadows, Tim **30**
Mello, Breno **73**
Melton, Frank **81**
Mercado-Valdes, Frank **43**
Merkerson, S. Epatha **47, 83**
Michele, Michael **31**
Mickelbury, Penny **28**
Miles, William **112**
Miller, Omar Benson **93**
Miller, Tangi **116**
Miller, Wentworth **75**
Ming, Mel **106**
Mitchell, Brian Stokes **21**
Mitchell, Kel **66, 131**
Mitchell, Russ **21, 73**
Mokae, Zakes **80**
Mo'Nique **35, 84**
Montgomery, Robbie **101**
Mooney, Paul **37, 120**
Moore, Melba **21**
Moore, Shemar **21, 112**
Moore, Tim **124**
Morgan, Tracy **61, 102, 131**
Morris, Garrett **31, 133**
Morris, Greg **28**
Morris, Lamorne **135**
Morton, Frederick A., Jr. **93**
Morton, Joe **18**
Moses, Gilbert **12**
Moss, Carlton **17**
Mowry, Tamera **79**
Mowry, Tia **78**
Murphy, Charles **95**
Murphy, Eddie **4, 20, 61**
Muse, Clarence Edouard **21**
Myers, Lou **110**
Myles, Kim **69**
Nash, Johnny **40**
Nash, Niecy **66, 115**
Naughton, Naturi **97**
Neal, Elise **29**
Negga, Ruth **135**
Nicholas, Denise **82**
Nichols, Nichelle **11**
Nissel, Angela **42**
Neville, Arthel **53**
Noah, Trevor **128**
Noble, Gil **76**
Norman, Christina **47**
Norman, Maidie **20**
O'Brien, Soledad **88**
Okonedo, Sophie **67**
Olagundoye, Toks **113**
Oliver, Pam **54, 123**
Omarosa **69, 110**

O'Neal, Patrice 99
Onwurah, Ngozi 38
Orman, Roscoe 55, 129
Pace, Judy 119
Palcy, Euzhan 94
Palmer, Keke 68, 120
Parker, Nicole Ari 52
Parr, Russ 51
Parris, Teyonah 131
Patterson, Chuck 124
Paulk, Marcus T. 127
Payne, Allen 13
Pearson, Felicia 99
Peete, Holly Robinson 20
Peete, Rodney 60
Perkins, Tony 24
Perrineau, Harold, Jr. 51
Perry, Lowell 30
Perry, Tyler 40, 54, 103
Peters, Brock 96
Peters, Clarke 103
Phifer, Mekhi 25, 103
Phillips, Joseph C. 73
Pickens, James, Jr. 59
Pierce, Wendell 90
Pinckney, Sandra 56
Pinkett Smith, Jada 10, 41, 95
Pinkston, W. Randall 24
Pitts, Byron 71
Plummer, Glenn 120
Poitier, Sydney Tamiia 65
Pounder, CCH 72
Poussaint, Renee 78
Powell, Keith 101
Powers, Ben 132
Price, Frederick K. C. 21
Price, Hugh B. 9, 54
Prince-Bythewood, Gina 31, 77
Pugh, Charles 81
Quarles, Norma 25
Queen Latifah 1, 16, 58, 119
Quivers, Robin 61
Ralph, Sheryl Lee 18, 108
Randle, Theresa 16
Rashad, Ahmad 18
Rashad, Phylicia 21
Raven-Symoné 44, 113
Ray, Gene Anthony 47
Ray J 86
Reddick, Lance 52, 128
Reed Hall, Alaina 83
Reese, Della 6, 20, 96
Reid, Tim 56
Retta 131
Reuben, Gloria 15
Reynolds, Star Jones 10, 27, 61
Rhimes, Shonda Lynn 67
Ribeiro, Alfonso 17
Richards, Beah 30
Richardson, Donna 39
Richardson, LaTanya 71
Richardson, Salli 68
Ridley, John 69
Riley, Amber 97
Roberts, Deborah 35
Roberts, Robin 16, 54, 113
Robinson, Craig 103
Robinson, Matt 69
Robinson, Max 3
Robinson, Shaun 36
Rochon, Lela 16
Rock, Chris 3, 22, 66
Rock, Tony 108

Rodgers, Johnathan 6, 51
Rodrigues, Percy 68
Roker, Al 12, 49
Roker, Roxie 68
Rolle, Esther 13, 21
Rollins, Howard E., Jr. 16
Romeo 98
Roots, The 101
Rose, Jalen 108
Ross, Tracee Ellis 35
Rotimi 130
Roundtree, Richard 27
Rowell, Victoria 13, 68
Rowland, Kelly 100
Royo, Andre 136
Rudolph, Maya 46, 106
Run 31, 73
RuPaul 17, 91
Russell, Bill 8
Russell, Nipsey 66
Rust, Art, Jr. 83
St. Jacques, Raymond 8
St. John, Kristoff 25
St. Patrick, Mathew 48
Salters, Lisa 71
Sands, Diana 87
Sanford, Isabel 53
Santiago-Hudson, Ruben 85
Sarpong, Sam 132
Sasser, Sean 113
Schiavocampo, Mara 97
Schultz, Michael A. 6
Scott, Hazel 66
Scott, Jill 29, 83
Scott, Stuart 34, 126
Scott-Young, Mona 101
Scribner, Marcus 136
Shaw, Bernard 2, 28
Sesay, Isha 107
Setmayer, Tara 130
Shepherd, Sherri 55
Sidner, Sara 105
Simmons, Henry 55
Simmons, Jamal 72
Simmons, Kimora Lee 51, 83
Simpson, Carole 6, 30
Sinbad 1, 16
Sinclair, Madge 78
Smiley, Tavis 20, 68
Smith, Anjela Lauren 44
Smith, B(arbara) 11
Smith, Ian 62
Smith, Michael 129
Smith, Roger Guenveur 12, 133
Smith, Tasha 73
Smith, Will 8, 18, 53
Sohn, Sonja 100
Spencer, Octavia 100
Stewart, Alison 13
Stewart, Nzingha 89
Stickney, Phyllis Yvonne 108
Stokes, Carl 10, 73
Strahan, Michael 35, 81, 135
Stuart, Moira 82
Sykes, Wanda 48, 81
Syler, Rene 53
Swann, Lynn 28
Tate, Larenz 15
Taylor, Jason 70
Taylor, Karin 34
Taylor, Meshach 4
Taylor, Regina 9, 46, 97
Teague, Bob 111

Terrence J 108
Thigpen, Lynne 17, 41
Thomas-Graham, Pamela 29
Thomason, Marsha 47
Thompson, Kenan 52
Thoms, Tracie 61
Thurston, Baratunde 79, 101
Tillman, Deborah 98
Tirico, Mike 68, 124
Torres, Gina 52
Torry, Guy 31
Toussaint, Lorraine 32
Townsend, Robert 4, 23
True, Rachel 82
Truesdale, Yanic 133
Tucker, Chris 13, 23, 62
Tunie, Tamara 63
Turman, Glynn 100
Tyler, Aisha N. 36
Tyson, Cicely 7, 51, 112
Uggams, Leslie 23, 114
Underwood, Blair 7, 27, 76
Union, Gabrielle 31, 92
Usher 23, 56, 95
Usher, Jessie T. 136
Van Peebles, Mario 2, 51
Vance, Jim 110
Vaughn, Countess 53
Vereen, Ben 4
Wade, Ernestine 126
Walker, Chet 106
Walker, Eamonn 37
Ware, Andre 37
Warfield, Marsha 2
Warner, Malcolm-Jamal 22, 36, 110
Warren, Michael 27
Washington, Denzel 1, 16, 93
Washington, Hayma 86
Washington, Isaiah 62
Washington, Kerry 46, 107
Watson, Carlos 50
Watts, Rolonda 9
Wayans, Damien 78
Wayans, Damon 8, 41
Wayans, Kim 80
Wayans, Keenen Ivory 18
Wayans, Marlon 29, 82
Wayans, Shawn 29
Weathers, Carl 10, 117
Wesley, Richard 73
Wesley, Rutina 97
Whack, Rita Coburn 36
Wheaton, James 103
White, Lillias 120
White, Michael Jai 71, 117
Whitfield, Lynn 1, 18
Whitlock, Jason 78, 130
Wilbon, Michael 68, 132
Wiley, Samira 131
Williams, Armstrong 29
Williams, Clarence, III 26
Williams, Juan 35, 80
Williams, Malinda 57
Williams, Michael Kenneth 97
Williams, Montel 4, 57
Williams, Russell, II 70
Williams, Samm-Art 21
Williams, Spencer 126
Williams, Vanessa A. 32, 66
Williams, Vanessa L. 4, 17
Williams, Wendy 62
Williamson, Mykelti 22
Wills, Maury 73

Wilmore, Larry 121
Wilson, Chandra 57
Wilson, Debra 38
Wilson, Demond 102
Wilson, Dorien 55
Wilson, Flip 21
Winfield, Paul 2, 45
Winfrey, Oprah 2, 15, 61, 106
Witherspoon, John 38
Woodard, Alfre 9, 108
Wright, Jeffrey 54, 111
Yarbrough, Cedric 51
Yoba, Malik 11
Young, Lee Thompson 114

Theater
Adams, Osceola Macarthy 31
Aldridge, Ira 99
Allen, Debbie 13, 42
Anderson, Carl 48
Andrews, Bert 13
Anthony, Trey 63
Arkadie, Kevin 17
Armstrong, Vanessa Bell 24
Arnez J 53
Babatunde, Obba 35
Babatunde, Rotimi 104
Bandele, Biyi 68, 121
Barnett, Etta Moten 56
Barrett, Lindsay 43
Baskett, James 102
Beach, Michael 26, 120
Beaton, Norman 14
Belgrave, Cynthia 75
Bennett, Louise 69
Bey, Salome 134
Bibb, Leon 132
Blanco, Mykki 106
Borders, James 9
Boseman, Chadwick 111
Boykin, Phillip 102
Branch, William Blackwell 39
Braugher, Andre 13, 58, 91
Brooks, Avery 9, 98
Brown, Oscar, Jr. 53
Brown, Ruth 90
Bruce, Bruce 56
Caesar, Adolph 133
Caldwell, Benjamin 46
Calloway, Cab 14
Cameron, Earl 44
Campbell, Dick 129
Cara, Irene 77
Carroll, Rocky 74
Carroll, Vinnette 29, 136
Carter, Nell 39
Cash, Rosalind 28
Cheadle, Don 19, 52
Chenault, John 40
Childress, Alice 15
Clarke, Hope 14
Cleage, Pearl 17, 64
Cook, Will Marion 40
Cooper, Chuck 75
Corthron, Kia 43
Curtis-Hall, Vondie 17
Dadié, Bernard 34
David, Keith 27
Davis, Altovise 76
Davis, Eisa 68
Davis, Ossie 5, 50
Davis, Sammy, Jr. 18
Davis, Viola 34, 76, 100, 131

Dawn, Marpessa 75
De Shields, André 72
Dean, Phillip Hayes 122
Dee, Ruby 8, 50, 68, 122
Delta Rhythm Boys 133
Devine, Loretta 24
Diamond, Lydia R. 101
Dieudonné 67, 118
Diggs, Taye 25, 63
Dixon, Brandon Victor 134
Dixon, Ivan 69
Dodson, Owen Vincent 38
Dudley, Sherman H. 117
Dunham, Katherine 4, 59
Dutton, Charles S. 4, 22
Ejiofor, Chiwetel 67, 116
Elder, Lonne, III 38
Ellis, Nelsan 105
Elzy, Ruby 119
Emmanuel, Alphonsia 38
Epps, Mike 60
Erivo, Cynthia 133
Esposito, Giancarlo 9
Europe, James Reese 10
Faison, Frankie 55
Falana, Lola 42
Fargas, Antonio 50
Fields, Felicia P. 60
Fishburne, Laurence 4, 22, 70
Francis, Thais 93
Franklin, J. E. 44
Freeman, Aaron 52
Freeman, Al, Jr. 11, 105
Freeman, Yvette 27
Fuller, Charles 8
Gibson, John Trusty 87
Gilpin, Charles Sidney 81
Givens, Adele 62
Glover, Danny 1, 24, 103
Glover, Keith 79
Glover, Savion 14
Goldberg, Whoopi 4, 33, 69
Gordone, Charles 15
Gossett, Louis, Jr. 7
Graves, Denyce Antoinette 19, 57
Guillaume, Robert 3, 48
Gunn, Moses 10
Gurira, Danai 73
Guyse, Sheila 122
Hall, Juanita 62
Hall, Katori 132
Hamilton, Lawrence 122
Hamilton, Lisa Gay 71
Hamlin, Larry Leon 49, 62
Hansberry, Lorraine 6
Harewood, David 52
Harris, Bill 72
Harris, Robin 7
Hayes, Teddy 40
Henry, Joshua 94
Higginsen, Vy 65
Hill, Errol 40, 135
Hill, Hugh Morgan 83
Hines, Gregory 1, 42
Holder, Geoffrey 78, 124
Holder, Laurence 34
Holland, Endesha Ida Mae 3, 57
Hooks, Robert 76
Hyman, Earle 25, 79
Hyman, Phyllis 19
Iglehart, James Monroe 129
Ingram, Rex 5

Iverson, Johnathan Lee 22, 100
Jackson, Angela 134
Jackson, Christopher 136
Jackson, Millie 25
James, Nikki M. 94
Jamison, Judith 7, 67, 96
Jean-Baptiste, Kyle 131
Jean-Baptiste, Marianne 17, 46
Johnson, Je'Caryous 63
Jones, James Earl 3, 49, 79
Jones, Sarah 39
Joseph, Paterson 126
Joyner, Matilda Sissieretta 15
Kente, Gibson 52
Khumalo, Leleti 51
King, Woodie, Jr. 27
Kitt, Eartha 16, 75
Kotto, Yaphet 7
Kwei-Armah, Kwame 84
La Salle, Eriq 12
LaChanze 93
Lacy, Marc 111
Lampley, Oni Faida 43, 71
Lathan, Sanaa 27
Le Loka, Tsidii 116
Lee, Canada 8
Lee, Leslie 85, 122
Leggs, Kingsley 62
Lemmons, Kasi 20
LeNoire, Rosetta 37
Lenox, Adriane 59
Leon, Kenny 10, 98
Lester, Adrian 46
Letson, Al 39
Lindo, Delroy 18, 45
Lister, Marquita 65
Little, Cleavon 117
Mackie, Anthony 102
Mann, Tamela 92
Maponya, Maishe 101
Marrow, Queen Esther 24
Martin, Helen 31
Martin, Jesse L. 31
Mason, Judi Ann 112
Mbatha-Raw, Gugu 89
McClendon, Forrest 94
McClinton, Marion Isaac 77
McCraney, Tarell Alvin 116
McDaniel, Hattie 5
McDonald, Audra 20, 62, 128
McFarlan, Tyron 60
McQueen, Butterfly 6, 54
Meek, Barbara 131
Merkerson, S. Epatha 47, 83
Mickelbury, Penny 28
Miller, Patina 94
Mills, Florence 22
Milner, Ron 39
Mitchell, Brian Stokes 21
Mokae, Zakes 80
Mollel, Tololwa 38
Moore, Melba 21
Moore, Tim 124
Moses, Gilbert 12
Moss, Carlton 17
Moss, Preacher 63
Moten, Etta 18
Muse, Clarence Edouard 21
Nascimento, Abdias do 93
Ngaujah, Sahr 86
Nicholas, Fayard 20, 57
Nicholas, Harold 20
Norman, Maidie 20

Nottage, Lynn 66
Ntshona, Winston 52
Odom, Leslie, Jr. 136
Okonedo, Sophie 67
O'Neal, Frederick 99
Orlandersmith, Dael 42
Patterson, Chuck 124
Payne, Allen 13
Perrineau, Harold, Jr. 51
Perry, Tyler 40, 54, 103
Peters, Brock 96
Peters, Clarke 103
Pierce, Wendell 90
Porter, Billy 112
Pounder, CCH 72
Powell, Keith 101
Power, Will 83
Preer, Evelyn 82
Premice, Josephine 41
Pryor, Rain 65
Randle, Theresa 16
Rashad, Phylicia 21
Redwood, John Henry 78
Richards, Beah 30
Richards, Lloyd 2
Richardson, Desmond 39
Richardson, LaTanya 71
Robeson, Paul 2
Rolle, Esther 13, 21
Rollins, Howard E., Jr. 16
Rose, Anika Noni 70
Rotimi, Ola 1, 130
Royo, Andre 136
St. Jacques, Raymond 8
St. Louis, David 126
Salter, Nikkole 73
Sands, Diana 87
Sanford, Isabel 53
Santiago-Hudson, Ruben 85
Schultz, Michael A. 6
Scott, Harold Russell, Jr. 61
Shabazz, Attallah 6
Slocumb, Jonathan 52
Smiley, Rickey 59
Smith, Anjela Lauren 44
Smith, Anna Deavere 6, 44
Smith, Roger Guenveur 12, 133
Snipes, Wesley 3, 24, 67
Snow, Valaida 135
Sommore 61
Soyinka, Wole 4, 93
Springer, Ashton, Jr. 115
Stew 69
Stewart, Tonea Harris 78
Sundiata, Sekou 66
Talbert, David E. 34, 93
Taylor, Meshach 4
Taylor, Regina 9, 46, 97
Taylor, Ron 35
Teer, Barbara Ann 81
Thigpen, Lynne 17, 41
Thompson, John Douglas 81
Thompson, Tazewell 13
Thurman, Wallace 16
Torres, Gina 52
Toussaint, Lorraine 32
Townsend, Robert 4, 23
Turman, Glynn 100
Uggams, Leslie 23, 114
Underwood, Blair 7, 27, 76
Vance, Courtney B. 15, 60
Vereen, Ben 4
Walcott, Derek 5, 94

Walker, Eamonn 37
Walker, George 129
Ward, Douglas Turner 42
Warfield, William 94
Washington, Fredi 10
Waters, Ethel 7
Wesley, Rutina 97
Wheaton, James 103
Whitaker, Forest 2, 49, 67
White, Lillias 120
White, Terri 82
White, Willard 53
Whitfield, Lynn 18
Williams, Bert 18
Williams, Clarence, III 26
Williams, Michelle 73
Williams, Samm-Art 21
Williamson, Mykelti 22
Wilson, August 7, 33, 55
Wilson, Dorien 55
Wilson, Tracey Scott 777
Winfield, Paul 2, 45
Withers-Mendes, Elisabeth 64
Wolfe, George C. 6, 43, 127
Woods, Renn 110
Wright, Jeffrey 54, 111
Yarbrough, Cedric 51

Writing
Abani, Chris 77
Abrahams, Peter 39
Abu-Jamal, Mumia 15
Achebe, Chinua 6, 99, 111
Adams, Jenoyne 60
Adichie, Chimamanda Ngozi 64, 121
Aidoo, Ama Ata 38
Akpan, Uwem 70
Alexander, Elizabeth 75
Alexander, Kwame 98
Alexander, Margaret Walker 22
Ali, Ayaan Hirsi 58, 92
Ali, Hana Yasmeen 52
Ali, Mohammed Naseehu 60
Als, Hilton 105
Amadi, Elechi 40
Ames, Wilmer 27
Anderson, Ho Che 54
Andrews, Raymond 4
Andrews, Tina 74
Angelou, Maya 1, 15, 122
Ansa, Tina McElroy 14
Anthony, Michael 29
Aplin-Brownlee, Vivian 96
Arac de Nyeko, Monica 66
Aristide, Jean-Bertrand 6, 45
Arkadie, Kevin 17
Armah, Ayi Kwei 49
Armah, Esther 87
Asante, Molefi Kete 3
Ashley & JaQuavis 107
Ashley-Ward, Amelia 23
Asim, Jabari 71
Atkins, Cholly 40
Atkins, Russell 45
Attaway, William 102
Aubert, Alvin 41
Aubespin, Mervin 95
Auguste, Arnold A. 47
Awoonor, Kofi 37, 115
Ayim, May 126
Azikiwe, Nnamdi 13
Ba, Mariama 30

Babatunde, Rotimi 104
Bahati, Wambui 60
Bailey, Chauncey 68
Baiocchi, Regina Harris 41
Baisden, Michael 25, 66
Baker, Augusta 38
Baker, Houston A., Jr. 6
Baldwin, James 1
Ballard, Allen Butler, Jr. 40
Bambara, Toni Cade 10
Bandele, Asha 36
Bandele, Biyi 68, 121
Baquet, Dean 63, 121
Baraka, Amiri 1, 38, 118
Barnes, Steven 54
Barnett, Amy Du Bois 46
Barrax, Gerald William 45
Barrett, Lindsay 43
Barris, Kenya 135
Bashir, Halima 73
Bass, Charlotta Spears 40
Baszile, Jennifer 79
Bates, Daisy 13, 135
Bates, Karen Grigsby 40
Beah, Ishmael 69
Beals, Melba Pattillo 15, 94
Bebey, Francis 45
Beckham, Barry 41
Bell, James Madison 40
Benberry, Cuesta 65
Bennett, George Harold 45
Bennett, Gwendolyn B. 59
Bennett, Lerone, Jr. 5, 84
Bennett, Louise 69
Benson, Angela 34
Berry, James 41
Berry, Mary Frances 7
Best, Carrie 80
Beti, Mongo 36
Betts, R. Dwayne 86
Bishop, Maurice 39
Blackman, Toni 86
Blair, Jayson 50
Bland, Eleanor Taylor 39
Blassingame, John Wesley 40
Blockson, Charles L. 42
Blow, Charles M. 73
Bluitt, Juliann S. 14
Bolden, Tonya 32
Bontemps, Arna 8
Booker, Simeon 23
Bostic, Joe 95
Boston, Lloyd 24
Boyd, Gerald M. 32, 59
Boyd, Melba Joyce 86
Boyd, Suzanne 52
Bradley, Adam 101
Bradley, David Henry, Jr. 39
Braithwaite, William Stanley 52
Branch, William Blackwell 39
Brand, Dionne 32
Brathwaite, Kamau 36
Brawley, Benjamin 44
Breeze, Jean "Binta" 37
Briscoe, Connie 15
Britt, Donna 28
Brooks, Gwendolyn 1, 28
Brower, William 49
Brown, Cecil M. 46
Brown, Claude 38
Brown, Elaine 8
Brown, Lloyd Louis 10, 42
Brown, Marie Dutton 12

Brown, Sterling Allen 10, 64
Brown, Tony 3
Brown, Wesley 23
Brown, William Wells 99
Broyard, Anatole 68
Broyard, Bliss 68
Brutus, Dennis 38
Bryan, Ashley 41, 104
Bryant, Howard 130
Buckley, Gail Lumet 39
Bulawayo, NoViolet 125
Bullins, Ed 25, 121
Bunche, Ralph J. 5
Bunkley, Anita Richmond 39
Burgess, Marjorie L. 55
Burley, Dan 96
Burwell, Bryan 83
Butler, Octavia 8, 43, 58
Bynum, Juanita 31, 71
Caldwell, Earl 60
Calhoun, Lillian Scott 87
Campbell, Bebe Moore 6, 24, 59
Canedy, Dana 132
Carby, Hazel 27
Carmichael, Stokely 5, 26
Carter, Joye Maureen 41
Carter, Martin 49
Carter, Stephen L. 4
Cartey, Wilfred 47
Cartiér, Xam Wilson 41
Cary, Lorene 3
Cary, Mary Ann Shadd 30
Cayton, Horace 26
Cenac, Wyatt 94
Césaire, Aimé 48, 69
Chadiha, Jeffri 57
Channer, Colin 36
Chase-Riboud, Barbara 20, 46
Chenault, John 40
Cheney-Coker, Syl 43
Chesnutt, Charles 29
Chideya, Farai 14, 61
Chikoti, Shadreck 125
Childress, Alice 15
Chiles, Nick 98
Christian, Barbara T. 44
Churchwell, Robert, Sr. 76
Clack, Zoanne 73
Clark, Kenneth B. 5, 52
Clark, Septima 7
Clark, Wahida 107
Clark-Bekederemo, J. P. 44
Clarke, Austin C. 32
Clarke, Cheryl 32
Clarke, George 32
Cleage, Pearl 17, 64
Cleaver, Eldridge 5
Cliff, Michelle 42
Clifton, Lucille 14, 64, 91
Coates, Ta-Nehisi 76, 131
Cobb, William Jelani 59, 121
Cobbs, Price M. 9
Cohen, Anthony 15
Cole, Johnnetta B. 5, 43
Cole, Teju 120
Coleman, Wanda 48, 119
Collins, Patricia Hill 67
Colter, Cyrus J. 36
Comer, James P. 6
Contee, Cheryl 88
Cook, Suzan D. Johnson 22
Cooke, Marvel 31
Cook-Parrish, Mary Virginia 95

Coombs, Orde M. 44
Cooper, Afua 53
Cooper, Andrew W. 36
Cooper, Anna Julia 20
Cooper, Helene 74
Cooper, J. California 12, 85, 125
Cornish, Sam 50
Cortez, Jayne 43, 109
Cose, Ellis 5, 50, 118
Cotter, Joseph Seamon, Sr. 40
Couto, Mia 45
Cox, Joseph Mason Andrew 51
Creagh, Milton 27
Croal, N'Gai 76
Crouch, Stanley 11, 87
Cruse, Harold 54
Crutchfield, James N. 55
Cullen, Countee 8
Cuney, William Waring 44
Cunningham, Evelyn 23, 85
Curry, George E. 23
Curtis, Christopher Paul 26, 113
Curvin, Robert 132
Dabydeen, David 48
Dadié, Bernard 34
D'Aguiar, Fred 50
Damas, Léon-Gontran 46
Dandridge, Raymond Garfield 45
Danner, Margaret Esse 49
Danquah, Meri Nana Ama 93
Danticat, Edwidge 15, 68, 128
Dash, Leon 47
Datcher, Michael 60
Dathorne, O. R. 52
Davis, Allison 12
Davis, Charles T. 48
Davis, Eisa 68
Davis, Frank Marshall 47
Davis, George 36
Davis, Nolan 45
Davis, Thulani 61
Dawes, Kwame 126
Dawkins, Wayne 20
de Passe, Suzanne 25
De Veaux, Alexis 44
Dedeaux, Richard 119
Deggans, Eric 71
Delany, Martin R. 27
Delany, Samuel R., Jr. 9
DeLoach, Nora 30
Demby, William 51
Dent, Thomas C. 50
Dickerson, Debra J. 60
Dickey, Eric Jerome 21, 56
Diop, Birago 53
Diop, Cheikh Anta 4
Dodson, Howard, Jr. 7, 52
Dodson, Owen Vincent 38
DoHarris, Brenda 116
Douglass, Frederick 87
Dove, Rita 6, 78, 101
Draper, Sharon Mills 16, 43
Driver, David E. 11
Drummond, William J. 40
Du Bois, David Graham 45, 135
Du Bois, W. E. B. 3
DuBois, Shirley Graham 21
Due, Tananarive 30
Dumas, Henry 41
Dunbar, Paul Laurence 8
Dunbar-Nelson, Alice Ruth Moore 44
Dungy, Camille 86

Dunnigan, Alice Allison 41
Duplechan, Larry 55
Dyson, Michael Eric 11, 40, 128
Eagleson, William Lewis 90
Edmonds, Terry 17
Edugyan, Esi 98
Ekwensi, Cyprian 37
Elder, Larry 25, 120
Elder, Lonne, III 38
Elie, Lolis Eric 97
Elliot, Lorris 37
Ellis, Thomas Sayers 129
Ellis, Trey 97
Ellison, Ralph 7
Elmore, Ronn 21
Emanuel, James A. 46
Emecheta, Buchi 30
Equiano, Olaudah 78
Estes, Rufus 29
Evans, Diana 72
Evans, Mari 26
Everett, Percival 93
Fabio, Sarah Webster 48
Fair, Ronald L. 47
Fales-Hill, Susan 88
Fanon, Frantz 44
Farah, Nuruddin 27
Farley, Christopher John 54
Fauset, Jessie 7
Feelings, Muriel 44
Feelings, Tom 11, 47
Fields, Julia 45
Figueroa, John J. 40
Files, Lolita 35
Finner-Williams, Paris Michele 62
Fisher, Antwone 40
Fisher, Rudolph 17
Fleming, Raymond 48
Fletcher, Bill, Jr. 41
Fletcher, Geoffrey 85
Forbes, Calvin 46
Ford, Clyde W. 40
Ford, Nick Aaron 44
Ford, Wallace 58
Forman, James 7, 51
Forna, Aminatta 95
Forrest, Leon 44
Fortune, T. Thomas 6
Foster, Cecil 32
Foster, Jylla Moore 45
Foye, K'wan 97
Franklin, John Hope 5, 77
Franklin, Robert M. 13
Frazier, E. Franklin 10
Frazier, Oscar 58
French, Albert 18
Fuller, Charles 8
Fuller, Hoyt 44
Gabre-Medhin, Tsegaye 64
Gaines, Ernest J. 7
Gaines, Patrice 106
Gaiter, Dorothy J. 80
Gardner, Chris 65
Gaston, Marilyn Hughes 60
Gates, Henry Louis, Jr. 3, 38, 67
Gay, Roxane 136
Gayle, Addison, Jr. 41
George, Nelson 12, 101
Gibson, Donald Bernard 40
Giddings, Paula 11
Gilbert, Christopher 50
Gilliard, Steve 69
Giovanni, Nikki 9, 39, 85

Givhan, Robin Deneen 72
Gladwell, Malcolm 62
Gloster, Hugh Morris, Sr. 90
Glover, Donald 85
Goines, Donald 19
Golden, Marita 19, 99
Gomez, Jewelle 30
Goodison, Lorna 71
Goodlett, Carlton B. 91
Gordon-Reed, Annette 74
Graham, Lawrence Otis 12
Graham, Lorenz 48
Granderson, LZ 103
Grant, Gwendolyn Goldsby 28
Gray, Ahuvah 130
Gray, Darius 69
Greenfield, Eloise 9
Greenlee, Sam 48
Greenwood, Monique 38
Griffith, Mark Winston 8
Grimké, Archibald H. 9
Guy, Rosa 5
Guy-Sheftall, Beverly 13, 92
Gyasi, Yaa 136
Haley, Alex 4
Halliburton, Warren J. 49
Hamblin, Ken 10
Hamilton, Virginia 10
Hammon, Jupiter 124
Hansberry, Lorraine 6
Hare, Nathan 44
Harkless, Necia Desiree 19
Harper, Frances Ellen Watkins 11
Harper, Hill 32, 65, 97
Harper, Michael S. 34, 136
Harper, Rachel M. 92
Harrington, Oliver W. 9, 136
Harris, Bill 72
Harris, Claire 34
Harris, E. Lynn 12, 33, 116
Harris, Eddy L. 18
Harris, Jay 19
Harris, Jessica B. 91
Harris, Leslie 6
Harris, Monica 18
Harrison, Alvin 28
Harrison, Calvin 28
Haskins, James 36, 54
Hayden, Robert 12
Hayes, Teddy 40
Hayes, Terrance 124
Haygood, Wil 83
Haywood, Gar Anthony 43
Head, Bessie 28
Heard, Nathan C. 45
Hearne, John Edgar Caulwell 45
Hemphill, Essex 10
Henderson, Angelo 122
Henderson, David 53
Henderson, Stephen E. 45
Henries, A. Doris Banks 44
Henriques, Julian 37
Henry, Lenny 9, 52
Henson, Josiah 90
Henson, Matthew 2
Herbert, Bob 63, 96
Hercules, Frank 44
Herndon, Angelo 90
Hernton, Calvin C. 51
Hill, Donna 32
Hill, Jemele 109
Hill, Leslie Pinckney 44
Hill, Marc Lamont 80, 128

Hilliard, David 7, 105
Hoagland, Everett H. 45
Hobson, Julius W. 44
Holland, Endesha Ida Mae 3, 57
Holmes, Shannon 70
Holt, Nora 38
Holton, Hugh, Jr. 39
hooks, bell 5, 90
Horne, Frank 44
Horton, George Moses 124
Hrabowski, Freeman A., III 22
Hudlin, Reginald 9, 86
Hudson, Cheryl 15
Hudson, Wade 15
Hughes, Langston 4
Hull, Akasha Gloria 45
Hunter-Gault, Charlayne 6, 31
Hurston, Zora Neale 3
Iceberg Slim 11
Ifill, Gwen 28
Ilibagiza, Immaculée 66
Iweala, Uzodinma 131
Jackson, Angela 134
Jackson, Brenda 87
Jackson, Fred James 25
Jackson, George 14
Jackson, James A. 90
Jackson, Sheneska 18
Jacobs, George 118
Jacobs, Harriet 104
James, Marlon 85, 124
Jarrett, Vernon D. 42, 135
Jasper, Kenji 39
Jefferson, Margo 108
Jenkins, Beverly 14
Joachim, Paulin 34
Joe, Yolanda 21
Johnson, Alaya Dawn 129
Johnson, Angela 52
Johnson, Charles 1, 82
Johnson, Charles S. 12
Johnson, Fenton 91
Johnson, Georgia Douglas 41
Johnson, James Weldon 5
Johnson, John H. 3, 54
Johnson, Linton Kwesi 37
Johnson, Mat 31, 105
Johnson, R. M. 36
Johnson, Sandra K. 94
Johnson, William 91
Jolley, Willie 28
Jones, Bomani 121
Jones, Edward P. 43, 67
Jones, Gayl 37
Jones, Orlando 30
Jones, Sarah 39
Jones, Tayari 96
Jordan, Deloris 108
Jordan, June 7, 35
Joseph, Jamal 101
Josey, E. J. 10
July, William 27
Just, Ernest Everett 3
Kahora, Billy 125
Kamau, Kwadwo Agymah 28
Karenga, Maulana 10, 71
Kariuki, J. M. 67
Kaufman, Bob 105
Kay, Jackie 37
Kayira, Legson 40
Kearney, Janis 54
Keckley, Elizabeth 90
Keene, John 73

Kendrick, Erika 57
Kennedy, Adrienne 11
Kennedy, Florynce 12, 33
Kennedy, Randall 40
Khanga, Yelena 6
Killens, John O. 54
Kimbro, Dennis 10
Kincaid, Jamaica 4, 109
King, Colbert I. 69
King, Coretta Scott 3, 57
King, Preston 28
King, Woodie, Jr. 27
Kitt, Sandra 23
Kitwana, Bakari 86
Knight, Etheridge 37
Kobia, Samuel 43
Komunyakaa, Yusef 9
Kunjufu, Jawanza 3, 50
Lacy, Marc 111
Lacy, Sam 30, 46
Ladner, Joyce A. 42
Laferriere, Dany 33
LaGuma, Alex 30
Lamar, Jake 96
Lamming, George 35
Lampley, Oni Faida 43, 71
Lane, Lunsford 93
Larsen, Nella 10
Lattany, Kristin Hunter 88
Lawrence, Martin 6, 27, 60
Lawrence-Lightfoot, Sara 10
Laymon, Kiese 113
Lee, Jarena 100
LeFlore, Lyah Beth 96
Lemon, Don 94
Lester, Julius 9, 115
Letson, Al 39
Lewis, David Levering 9
Lewis, Samella 25
Lincoln, C. Eric 38
Little, Benilde 21
Locke, Alain 10
Locke, Attica 85
Lomax, Louis E. 90
Lorde, Audre 6
Louis, Errol T. 8
Loury, Glenn 36
Lowe, Herbert 57
Mabry, Marcus 70
Mabuza-Suttle, Felicia 43
Machado de Assis 74
Mackey, Nathaniel 75
Madhubuti, Haki 7, 85
Major, Clarence 9
Makeba, Miriam 2, 50, 74
Malveaux, Julianne 32, 70
Manley, Ruth 34
Marechera, Dambudzo 39
Markham, E. A. 37
Marshall, Paule 7, 77
Martin, Michel 97
Martin, Roland S. 49, 84
Mason, Felicia 31
Mason, Herman, Jr. 83
Massaquoi, Hans J. 30, 130
Matejka, Adrian 87
Mathabane, Mark 5, 99
Maynard, Nancy Hicks 73
Maynard, Robert C. 7
Mays, Benjamin E. 7
Mazrui, Ali 12, 124
Mbaye, Mariétou 31
McAlpin, Harry 121

McBride, James 35, 87
McCall, Nathan 8
McCauley, Gina 76
McClellan, George Marion 91
McCrary Anthony, Crystal 70
McCray, Chirlane 134
McDuffie, Dwayne 62
McFadden, Bernice L. 39
McGhee, Sharon K. 113
McGruder, Aaron 28, 56, 120
McGruder, Robert 22, 35
McKay, Claude 6
McKinney Hammond, Michelle 51
McKinney-Whetstone, Diane 27
McMillan, Rosalynn A. 36
McMillan, Terry 4, 17, 53
McMillan, Tracy 93
McPherson, James Alan 70
McWhorter, John 35, 119
Memmi, Albert 37
Menard, John Willis 90
Mengestu, Dinaw 66, 114
Meredith, James H. 11
Mickelbury, Penny 28
Miles, Tiya 116
Miller, Pepper 96
Millner, Denene 76
Milner, Ron 39
Mitchell, Elvis 67
Mitchell, Loften 31
Mitchell, Russ 21, 73
Mitchell, Sharon 36
Mofolo, Thomas Mokopu 37
Mollel, Tololwa 38
Monroe, Bryan 71
Monroe, Mary 35
Moore, Jessica Care 30
Moore, Wes 86
Morrison, Toni 2, 15, 86
Mosley, Walter 5, 25, 68
Moss, Carlton 17
Mossell, Gertrude Bustill 40
Moutoussamy-Ashe, Jeanne 7
Mowry, Jess 7
Mphahlele, Es'kia 40
Mudimbe, V. Y. 61
Mugo, Micere Githae 32
Mullen, Harryette 34
Murphy, John H. 42
Murray, Albert L. 33
Murray, Pauli 38
Mwangi, Meja 40
Myers, Walter Dean 8, 70, 123
Nakasa, Nat 123
Nash, Shannon King 84
Naylor, Gloria 10, 42
Neal, Larry 38
Neal, Mark Anthony 74
Nell, William C. 128
Nelson, Jill 6, 54
Nelson, Kadir 115
Neto, António Agostinho 43
Newkirk, Pamela 69
Newton, Huey 2
Ngugi wa Thiong'o 29, 61, 101
Nissel, Angela 42
Njawe, Pius 87
Nkosi, Lewis 46
Norris, Michele 83
Northup, Solomon 115
Norton, Meredith 72
Nugent, Richard Bruce 39
Nunez, Elizabeth 62, 112

Ojikutu, Bayo 66
Okara, Gabriel 37
Okigbo, Christopher 102
Oliver, John J., Jr. 48
Onwueme, Tess Osonye 23
Orlandersmith, Dael 42
Osbey, Brenda Marie 102
Oyeyemi, Helen 135
Oyono, Ferdinand 38
Packer, Z. Z. 64
Page, Clarence 4
Painter, Nell Irvin 24, 88
Palmer, Everard 37
Parker, Pat 19
Parker, Star 70
Parks, Suzan-Lori 34, 85
Patton, Venetria K. 125
Payne, Ethel L. 28
Payne, Les 89
Pearson, Felicia 99
Peters, Lenrie 43
Petersen, Neal 96
Petry, Ann 19
Philip, Marlene Nourbese 32
Phillips, Carl 111
Phillips, Joseph C. 73
Piper, Adrian 71
Pitts, Leonard, Jr. 54, 85
Plaatje, Sol T. 80
Polite, Carlene Hatcher 82
Poussaint, Alvin F. 5, 67
Poussaint, Renee 78
Powell, Kevin 31, 74
Power, Will 83
Pressley, Condace L. 41
Prince, Richard E. 71
Pryce, Trevor 89
Quarles, Benjamin Arthur 18
Rahman, Aishah 37
Randall, Alice 38
Randall, Dudley 8, 55
Rapier, James T. 82
Raspberry, William 2
Reddick, Lawrence Dunbar 20
Redding, J. Saunders 26
Redmond, Eugene 23
Reed, Ishmael 8
Reid, Ira De A. 100
Rhimes, Shonda Lynn 67
Rhoden, William C. 67
Rhodes, Jewell Parker 84
Rhone, Trevor 80
Richards, Beah 30
Ridley, John 69
Riley, Rochelle 50
Ringgold, Faith 4, 81
Robertson, Gil L., IV 85
Robeson, Eslanda Goode 13
Robinson, Aminah 50
Robinson, Eugene 77

Robinson, Matt 69
Roby, Kimberla Lawson 86
Rogers, Joel Augustus 30
Rollins, Charlamae Hill 27
Rowan, Carl T. 1, 30
Ruffin, Josephine St. Pierre 75
Run 31, 73
Russwurm, John Brown 100
Rust, Art, Jr. 83
Sadlier, Rosemary 62
Saint James, Synthia 12
St. John, Kristoff 25
Salih, Al-Tayyib 37
Sanchez, Sonia 17, 51
Sancho, Ignatius 133
Sanders, Dori 8
Sanneh, Kelefa 96
Sapphire 14, 95
Saro-Wiwa, Kenule 39
Shelton, Paula Young 86
Schomburg, Arthur Alfonso 9
Schuyler, George Samuel 40
Scott-Heron, Gil 94
Seale, Bobby 3
Selasi, Taiye 125
Sembène, Ousmane 13, 62
Senghor, Léopold Sédar 12, 66
Sengstacke, John 18
Senior, Olive 37
Senna, Danzy 93
Shabazz, Attallah 6
Shabazz, Ilyasah 36
Shakur, Assata 6
Shakur, Yusef 85
Shange, Ntozake 8, 89
Shaw, Bernard 2, 28
Shipp, E. R. 15
Shockley, Ann Allen 84
Simpson, Carole 6, 30
Singletary, Mike 4, 76
Sister Souljah 11, 100
Skinner, Kiron K. 65
Smiley, Tavis 20, 68
Smith, Anna Deavere 6
Smith, B(arbara) 11
Smith, Barbara 28
Smith, Bruce W. 53
Smith, Danyel 40
Smith, Jessie Carney 35
Smith, Mary Carter 26, 134
Smith, Michael 129
Smith, Stephen A. 69
Smith, Zadie 51
Snowden, Frank M., Jr. 67
Somé, Malidoma Patrice 10
Southgate, Martha 58
Sowell, Thomas 2, 99
Soyinka, Wole 4, 93
Spencer, Anne 27
Spriggs, William 67

Staples, Brent 8
Stewart, Alison 13
Stone, Chuck 9, 120
Stringer, Vickie 58
Sundiata, Sekou 66
Tademy, Lalita 36
Talbert, David E. 34, 93
Tate, Eleanora E. 20, 55
Tatum, Beverly Daniel 42, 84
Tatum, Elinor R. 78
Tatum, Wilbert 76
Taulbert, Clifton Lemoure 19
Taylor, Kristin Clark 8
Taylor, Mildred D. 26
Taylor, Susan C. 62
Taylor, Susan L. 10, 86
Teasley, Lisa 92
Terry, Bryant 128
Thomas, Michael 69
Thomas, Trisha R. 65
Thomas-Graham, Pamela 29
Thornton, Yvonne S. 69
Thurman, Howard 3
Thurston, Baratunde 79, 101
Tillis, Frederick 40
Tolson, Melvin 37
Toomer, Jean 6
Touré, Askia 47
Townsend, Robert 4
Trethewey, Natasha 103
Trotter, Monroe 9
Troupe, Quincy 83
Tucker, Cynthia 15, 61
Turner, Henry McNeal 5
Tutuola, Amos 30
Twitty, Michael 134
Tyree, Omar Rashad 21
Tyson, Asha 39
van Sertima, Ivan 25
Vanzant, Iyanla 17, 47, 108
Vega, Marta Moreno 61
Vera, Yvonne 32
Verdelle, A. J. 26
Wade-Gayles, Gloria Jean 41
Walcott, Derek 5, 94
Walker, Alice 1, 43
Walker, Margaret 29
Walker, Rebecca 50
Walker, Teshima 114
Wallace, Michele Faith 13
Wallace, Phyllis A. 9
Walters, Ronald 83
Walton, Lester Aglar 134
Ward, Douglas Turner 42
Washington, Booker T. 4
Washington, Elsie B. 78
Washington, Harriet A. 69
Washington, James, Jr. 38
Washington, Laura S. 18

Washington-Williams, Essie Mae 118
Weaver, Afaa Michael 37
Weems, Renita J. 44
Wells-Barnett, Ida B. 8
Wesley, Dorothy Porter 19
Wesley, Richard 73
Wesley, Valerie Wilson 18
West, Cornel 5, 33, 80
West, Dorothy 12, 54
Whack, Rita Coburn 36
Wharton, Clifton R., Jr. 7
Whitaker, Mark 21, 47
White, Walter F. 4
Whitehead, Colson 77
Whitfield, LeRoy 84
Whitfield, Van 34
Whitlock, Jason 78, 130
Wideman, John Edgar 5, 87
Wilbekin, Emil 63
Wilbon, Michael 68, 132
Wiley, Ralph 8, 78
Wilkerson, Isabel 71
Wilkins, Roger 2, 84
Wilkins, Roy 4
Williams, Armstrong 29
Williams, George Washington 18
Williams, John A. 27
Williams, Juan 35, 80
Williams, Patricia 11, 54
Williams, Robert F. 11, 136
Williams, Roy 89
Williams, Saul 31
Williams, Sherley Anne 25
Williams, Walter E. 4, 133
Williams, Wendy 62
Wilmore, Larry 121
Wilson, August 7, 33, 55
Wilson, Mary 28
Wilson, William Julius 22
Wiwa, Ken 67
Woods, Mattiebelle 63
Woods, Scott 55
Woods, Teri 69
Woodson, Carter G. 2
Woodson, Jacqueline 125
Worrill, Conrad 12
Wright, Bruce McMarion 3, 52
Wright, Richard 5
Wright, Sarah E. 95
X, Marvin 45
Yarbrough, Camille 40
Yerby, Frank 96
Yette, Samuel F. 63
Young, Al 82
Young, Whitney M., Jr. 4
Youngblood, Shay 32
Zane 71
Zook, Kristal Brent 62

Cumulative Subject Index

Volume numbers appear in **bold**

A cappella
Cooke, Sam 17
Fisk Jubilee Singers 112
Ladysmith Black Mambazo 103
Olusola, Kevin 133
Pilgrim Travelers, The 129
Reagon, Bernice Johnson 7
Swan Silvertones, The 110
Sweet Honey in the Rock 106
Take 6 112

AA
See Alcoholics Anonymous

AAAS
See American Association for the Advancement of Science

AARP
Dixon, Margaret A. 14, 136
Smith, Marie F. 70

ABC
See American Broadcasting Company

Abstract expressionism
Alston, Charles 33
Bearden, Romare 2, 50
Delaney, Beauford 19
Lewis, Norman 39
Simpson, Merton D. 110
Thomas, Alma 14
Woodruff, Hale 9

Academy Awards
Berry, Halle 4, 19, 57, 91
Cara, Irene 77
Fletcher, Geoffrey 85
Foxx, Jamie 15, 48
Freeman, Morgan 2, 20, 62, 100
Goldberg, Whoopi 4, 33, 69
Gooding, Cuba, Jr. 16, 62
Gossett, Louis, Jr. 7
Hancock, Herbie 20, 67
Hayes, Isaac 20, 58, 73
Hudson, Jennifer 63, 83
McDaniel, Hattie 5
Mo'Nique 35, 84
Nyong'o, Lupita 127
Poitier, Sidney 11, 36
Prince 18, 65, 134
Richie, Lionel 27, 65, 114
Spencer, Octavia 100
Washington, Denzel 1, 16, 93
Whitaker, Forest 2, 49, 67

Williams, Russell, II 70
Wonder, Stevie 11, 53, 121

Accordion
Buckwheat Zydeco 132

ACLU
See American Civil Liberties Union

Acquired immune deficiency syndrome (AIDS)
Ashe, Arthur 1, 18
Atim, Julian 66
Broadbent, Hydeia 36
Cargill, Victoria A. 43
Cooper, Mario 129
Fenton, Kevin 87
Gayle, Helene D. 3, 46
Hale, Lorraine 8
Lewis-Thornton, Rae 32
Mboup, Souleymane 10
Moutoussamy-Ashe, Jeanne 7
Norman, Pat 10
Ojikutu, Bisola 65
Okaalet, Peter 58
Pickett, Cecil 39
Sasser, Sean 113
Seele, Pernessa 46
Whitfield, LeRoy 84
Wilson, Phill 9, 104
Zulu, Princess Kasune 54

Acting
Aaliyah 30
Aaron, Quinton 82
Abdi, Barkhad 119
Abrahams, Zaraah 127
Adams, Osceola Macarthy 31
Adebimpe, Tunde 75
Aduba, Uzo 122
Akinnuoye-Agbaje, Adewale 56
Aldridge, Ira 99
Alexander, Khandi 43
Ali, Mahershala 122
Ali, Tatyana 73
Allen, Debbie 13, 42
Alonso, Laz 87
Amos, John 8, 62
Anderson, Anthony 51, 77
Anderson, Carl 48
Anderson, Eddie "Rochester" 30
Anderson, Jacob 128
Andrews, Tina 74
Armstrong, Vanessa Bell 24
Arnold, Tichina 63

Ashanti 37, 96
Avery, James 118
Babatunde, Obba 35
Bahati, Wambui 60
Bailey, Pearl 14
Baker, Josephine 3
Banks, Michelle 59
Barnett, Etta Moten 56
Baskett, James 102
Bassett, Angela 6, 23, 62
Beach, Michael 26, 120
Beals, Jennifer 12
Beard, Matthew 120
Beaton, Norman 14
Beauvais, Garcelle 29, 95
Belgrave, Cynthia 75
Bennett, Louise 69
Bentley, Lamont 53
Berry, Fred "Rerun" 48
Berry, Halle 4, 19, 57, 91
Bey, Yasiin 30, 96
Bibb, Leon 132
Bivins, Michael 72
Blacque, Taurean 58
Blanks, Billy 22
Bonet, Lisa 58, 133
Borders, James 9
Boseman, Chadwick 111
Bow Wow 35
Boyega, John 133
Boykin, Phillip 102
Brady, Wayne 32, 71
Branch, William Blackwell 39
Braugher, Andre 13, 58, 91
Bridges, Todd 37
Brooks, Avery 9, 98
Brooks, Danielle 119
Brooks, Golden 62
Brooks, Mehcad 62
Brown, Jim 11, 95
Browne, Roscoe Lee 66
Byrd, Eugene 64
Caesar, Adolph 133
Caesar, Shirley 19
Calloway, Cab 14
Cameron, Earl 44
Campbell-Martin, Tisha 8, 42
Cannon, Nick 47, 73, 132
Cara, Irene 77
Carroll, Diahann 9
Carroll, Rocky 74
Carson, Lisa Nicole 21
Carey, Mariah 32, 53, 69
Carter, Nell 39

Cash, Rosalind 28
Cathey, Reg E. 122
Cedric the Entertainer 29, 60, 115
Cheadle, Don 19, 52
Chestnut, Morris 31, 116
Chew, Robert F. 109
Childress, Alice 15
Childress, Alvin 114
Chong, Rae Dawn 62
Chweneyagae, Presley 63
Clarke, Hope 14
Cobbs, Bill 101
Coleman, Chad L. 128
Coleman, Gary 35, 86
Combs, Sean 17, 43, 92
Common 31, 63, 98
Cooper, Chuck 75
Corinealdi, Emayatzy 133
Cox, Laverne 122
Crews, Terry 123
Crothers, Scatman 19
Curry, Mark 17
Curtis-Hall, Vondie 17
DaCosta, YaYa 98
Dandridge, Dorothy 3
Daniels, Billy 124
David, Keith 27
Davidson, Jaye 5
Davis, Altovise 76
Davis, Eisa 68
Davis, Guy 36
Davis, Ossie 5, 50
Davis, Sammy, Jr. 18
Davis, Viola 34, 76, 100, 131
Dawn, Marpessa 75
Dawson, Rosario 72
De Bankolé, Isaach 78
De Shields, André 72
Dee, Ruby 8, 50, 68, 122
Derulo, Jason 93, 132
Devine, Loretta 24
Dexter, Felix 129
Diesel, Vin 29
Diggs, Taye 25, 63
Dixon, Brandon Victor 134
Dixon, Ivan 69
DMX 28, 64
Dobson, Tamara 111
Domingo, Colman 94
Dorn, Michael 112
Dourdan, Gary 37
Duke, Bill 3, 96
Duncan, Michael Clarke 26, 104
Dungey, Merrin 62

Dutton, Charles S. **4, 22**
Ejiofor, Chiwetel **67, 116**
Ejogo, Carmen **126**
Elba, Idris **49, 89, 116**
Elise, Kimberly **32, 101**
Ellis, Aunjanue **108**
Ellis, Nelsan **105**
Emmanuel, Alphonsia **38**
Epps, Mike **60**
Epps, Omar **23, 59**
Erivo, Cynthia **133**
Esposito, Giancarlo **9**
Everett, Francine **23**
Faison, Donald **50**
Faison, Frankie **55**
Fargas, Antonio **50**
Fetchit, Stepin **32**
Fields, Felicia P. **60**
Fields, Kim **36**
Fishburne, Laurence **4, 22, 70**
Fisher, Gail **85**
Fox, Rick **27**
Fox, Vivica A. **15, 53**
Foxx, Jamie **15, 48**
Foxx, Redd **2**
Francis, Thais **93**
Freeman, Al, Jr. **11, 105**
Freeman, Morgan **2, 20, 62, 100**
Freeman, Yvette **27**
Gant, Richard **105**
Gaye, Nona **56**
Gibbs, Marla **86**
Gibson, Tyrese **27, 62, 134**
Gilpin, Charles Sidney **81**
Ginuwine **35**
Givens, Adele **62**
Givens, Robin **4, 25, 58**
Glass, Ron **111**
Glover, Anwan **123**
Glover, Danny **1, 24, 103**
Glover, Donald **85**
Goldberg, Whoopi **4, 33, 69**
Good, Meagan **117**
Gooding, Cuba, Jr. **16, 62**
Gossett, Louis, Jr. **7**
Graham, Katerina **99**
Grant, Micki **125**
Grier, David Alan **28**
Grier, Pam **9, 31, 86**
Griffin, Angela **80**
Guillaume, Robert **3, 48**
Gunn, Moses **10**
Gurira, Danai **73**
Guy, Jasmine **2**
Guyse, Sheila **122**
Hairston, Jester **88**
Hamilton, Bernie **117**
Hamilton, Lawrence **122**
Hamilton, Lisa Gay **71**
Hamlin, Larry Leon **49, 62**
Hammond, Fred **23**
Hardison, Kadeem **22**
Hardwick, Omari **122**
Harewood, David **52**
Harewood, Dorian **104**
Harper, Hill **32, 65, 97**
Harris, Naomie **55, 116**
Harris, Robin **7**
Harris, Wood **114**
Harry, Jackée **111**
Harvey, Steve **18, 58**
Hawkins, Screamin' Jay **30**
Hayes, Isaac **20, 58, 73**

Haysbert, Dennis **42, 106**
Hector, Jamie **98**
Hemsley, Sherman **19, 104**
Henry, Dwight **104**
Henry, Joshua **94**
Henry, Lenny **9, 52**
Henson, Taraji P. **58, 77, 127**
Hill, Darryl **128**
Hill, Dulé **29, 129**
Hines, Gregory **1, 42**
Hodge, Aldis **124**
Holder, Geoffrey **78, 124**
Hooks, Robert **76**
Horne, Lena **5, 86**
Hounsou, Djimon **19, 45**
Houston, Whitney **7, 28, 83, 100**
Howard, Sherri **36**
Howard, Terrence **59, 94**
Howell, Ayinde **91**
Hudson, Ernie **72, 131**
Hudson, Jennifer **63, 83**
Hughley, D. L. **23, 76**
Hyman, Earle **25, 79**
Ice Cube **8, 30, 60**
Ice-T **6, 31, 96**
Iglehart, James Monroe **129**
Ingram, Rex **5**
Jackson, Christopher **136**
Jackson, Millie **25**
Jackson, Samuel L. **8, 19, 63, 102**
Jalade-Ekeinde, Omotola **118**
James, Nikki M. **94**
Jean-Baptiste, Kyle **131**
Jean-Baptiste, Marianne **17, 46**
Jean-Louis, Jimmy **76**
Jeffries, Herb **122**
Johnson, Clark **96**
Johnson, Rodney Van **28**
Jones, James Earl **3, 49, 79**
Jones, Leslie **136**
Jones, Orlando **30**
Jones, Rashida **101**
Jones, Robbie **113**
Jones, Roy, Jr. **22, 134**
Jordan, Michael B. **97**
Jorge, Seu **73**
Joseph, Paterson **126**
Kelley, Elijah **65**
Kelley, Malcolm David **59**
Kelly, Jim **113**
Kennedy-Overton, Jayne Harris **46**
Khumalo, Leleti **51**
Kid Cudi **83**
King, Regina **22, 45**
King, Woodie, Jr. **27**
Kirby, George **14**
Kitt, Eartha **16, 75**
Knight, Gladys **16, 66**
Kodjoe, Boris **34, 89**
Kotto, Yaphet **7**
La Salle, Eriq **12**
LaBelle, Patti **13, 30**
LaChanze **93**
Lampley, Oni Faida **43, 71**
Lane, Charles **3**
Laneuville, Eric **123**
Lassiter, Roy **24**
Lathan, Sanaa **27**
Lawrence, Martin **6, 27, 60**
Le Loka, Tsidii **116**
Leakes, NeNe **107**
Lee, Canada **8**
Lee, Joie **1**

Leggs, Kingsley **62**
Lemmons, Kasi **20**
LeNoire, Rosetta **37**
Lenox, Adriane **59**
Lester, Adrian **46**
Lesure, James **64**
Lewis, Emmanuel **36**
Lincoln, Abbey **3, 88**
Lindo, Delroy **18, 45**
LisaRaye **27**
Lister, Tommy **127**
Little, Cleavon **117**
LL Cool J **16, 49, 94**
Long, Nia **17, 95**
Luke, Derek **61**
Lumbly, Carl **47**
Mabley, Jackie "Moms" **15**
Mac, Bernie **29, 61, 72**
Mackie, Anthony **102**
Madame Sul-Te-Wan **95**
Malco, Romany **71**
Mann, Tamela **92**
Maponya, Maishe **101**
Marcille, Eva **97**
Mario **1**
Marrow, Queen Esther **24**
Marshall, William **107**
Martin, Duane **108**
Martin, Helen **31**
Martin, Jesse L. **31**
Martin-Green, Sonequa **133**
Mayo, Whitman **32**
Mbatha-Raw, Gugu **89**
M.C. Hammer **20, 80**
McBride, Chi **51**
McClendon, Forrest **94**
McClinton, Marion Isaac **77**
McCrary, Darius **111**
McCullough, DeAndre **106**
McDaniel, Hattie **5**
McDonald, Audra **20, 62, 128**
McGee, Vonetta **95**
McKee, Lonette **12, 119**
McKinney, Nina Mae **40**
McQueen, Butterfly **6, 54**
Meadows, Tim **30**
Meek, Barbara **131**
Mello, Breno **73**
Merkerson, S. Epatha **47, 83**
Michele, Michael **31**
Miller, Omar Benson **93**
Miller, Patina **94**
Miller, Tangi **116**
Miller, Wentworth **75**
Mitchell, Brian Stokes **21**
Mitchell, Kel **66, 131**
Mokae, Zakes **80**
Mo'Nique **35, 84**
Moore, Juanita **83, 124**
Moore, Shemar **21, 112**
Moreland, Mantan **117**
Morgan, Tracy **61, 102, 131**
Morris, Garrett **31, 133**
Morris, Greg **28**
Morton, Joe **18**
Moten, Etta **18**
Mowry, Tamera **79**
Mowry, Tia **78**
Murphy, Charles **95**
Murphy, Eddie **4, 20, 61**
Muse, Clarence Edouard **21**
Myers, Lou **110**
Nash, Johnny **40**

Nash, Niecy **66, 115**
Naughton, Naturi **97**
Neal, Elise **29**
Newton, Thandie **26, 114**
Ngaujah, Sahr **86**
Nicholas, Denise **82**
Nicholas, Fayard **20, 57**
Nicholas, Harold **20**
Nichols, Nichelle **11**
Norman, Maidie **20**
Notorious B.I.G. **20**
Ntshona, Winston **52**
Nyong'o, Lupita **127**
Odom, Leslie, Jr. **136**
Okonedo, Sophie **67**
Olagundoye, Toks **113**
O'Neal, Frederick **99**
O'Neal, Ron **46**
O'Neal, Shaquille **8, 30, 95**
Orlandersmith, Dael **42**
Orman, Roscoe **55, 129**
Oyelowo, David **82, 126**
Pace, Judy **119**
Palmer, Keke **68, 120**
Parker, Nicole Ari **52**
Parris, Teyonah **131**
Patterson, Chuck **124**
Patton, Paula **62**
Paulk, Marcus T. **127**
Payne, Allen **13**
Payne, Freda **58**
Pearson, Felicia **99**
Peete, Holly Robinson **20**
Perrineau, Harold, Jr. **51**
Peters, Brock **96**
Peters, Clarke **103**
Phifer, Mekhi **25, 103**
Phillips, Joseph C. **73**
Pickens, James, Jr. **59**
Pierce, Wendell **90**
Pinkett Smith, Jada **10, 41, 95**
Plummer, Glenn **120**
Poitier, Sidney **11, 36**
Poitier, Sydney Tamiia **65**
Porter, Billy **112**
Pounder, CCH **72**
Powers, Ben **132**
Pratt, Kyla **57**
Preer, Evelyn **82**
Premice, Josephine **41**
Pryor, Rain **65**
Pryor, Richard **3, 24, 56**
Queen Latifah **1, 16, 58, 119**
Ralph, Sheryl Lee **18, 108**
Randle, Theresa **16**
Rashad, Phylicia **21**
Raven-Symoné **44, 113**
Ray, Gene Anthony **47**
Reddick, Lance **52, 128**
Reed, Natina **106**
Reed Hall, Alaina **83**
Reese, Della **6, 20, 96**
Reid, Tim **56**
Retta **131**
Reuben, Gloria **15**
Rhames, Ving **14, 50**
Rhymes, Busta **31**
Ribeiro, Alfonso **17**
Richards, Beah **30**
Richards, Lloyd **2**
Richardson, LaTanya **71**
Richardson, Salli **68**
Riley, Amber **97**

Robeson, Paul **2**
Robinson, Craig **103**
Robinson, Shaun **36**
Rock, Chris **3, 22, 66**
Rock, The **29 66**
Rodgers, Rod **36**
Rodrigues, Percy **68**
Roker, Roxie **68**
Rolle, Esther **13, 21**
Rollins, Howard E., Jr. **17**
Romeo **98**
Rose, Anika Noni **70**
Ross, Diana **8, 27**
Ross, Tracee Ellis **35**
Rotimi **130**
Roundtree, Richard **27**
Rowell, Victoria **13, 68**
Rowland, Kelly **100**
Royo, Andre **136**
Rudolph, Maya **46, 106**
RZA **80, 128**
St. Jacques, Raymond **8**
St. John, Kristoff **25**
St. Louis, David **126**
St. Patrick, Mathew **48**
Saldana, Zoe **72, 118**
Salter, Nikkole **73**
Sands, Diana **87**
Sanford, Isabel **53**
Santiago-Hudson, Ruben **85**
Sarpong, Sam **132**
Scott, Hazel **66**
Scott, Jill **29, 83**
Scribner, Marcus **136**
Shakur, Tupac **14**
Short, Columbus **79**
Sidibe, Gabourey **84**
Simmons, Henry **55**
Sinbad **1, 16**
Sinclair, Madge **78**
Sisqo **30**
Smith, Anjela Lauren **44**
Smith, Anna Deavere **6, 44**
Smith, B(arbara) **11**
Smith, Bubba **96**
Smith, Jaden **82**
Smith, Roger Guenveur **12, 133**
Smith, Tasha **73**
Smith, Will **8, 18, 53**
Smith, Willow **92**
Snipes, Wesley **3, 24, 67**
Snoop Dogg **35, 84**
Sohn, Sonja **100**
Sommore **61**
Spencer, Octavia **100**
Stewart, Tonea Harris **78**
Sticky Fingaz **86**
Strode, Woody **111**
Sy, Omar **109**
Sykes, Wanda **48, 81**
Tamia **24, 55**
Tate, Larenz **15**
Taylor, Meshach **4**
Taylor, Regina **9, 46, 97**
Taylor, Ron **35**
Terrence J **108**
Thigpen, Lynne **17, 41**
Thomas, Sean Patrick **35**
Thomason, Marsha **47**
Thompson, John Douglas **81**
Thompson, Kenan **52**
Thompson, Tazewell **13**
Thoms, Tracie **61**

Toivola, Jani **118**
Torres, Gina **52**
Torry, Guy **31**
Toussaint, Lorraine **32**
Townsend, Robert **4, 23**
True, Rachel **82**
Truesdale, Yanic **133**
Tucker, Chris **13, 23, 62**
Tunie, Tamara **63**
Turman, Glynn **100**
Turner, Tina **6, 27**
Tyler, Aisha N. **36**
Tyson, Cicely **7, 51, 112**
Uggams, Leslie **23, 114**
Underwood, Blair **7, 27, 76**
Union, Gabrielle **31, 92**
Usher **23, 56, 95**
Usher, Jessie T. **136**
Van Peebles, Mario **2, 51**
Van Peebles, Melvin **7, 95**
Vance, Courtney B. **15, 60**
Vereen, Ben **4**
Wade, Ernestine **126**
Walker, Eamonn **37**
Wallis, Quvenzhané **109**
Ward, Douglas Turner **42**
Warfield, Marsha **2**
Warfield, William **94**
Warner, Malcolm-Jamal **22, 36, 110**
Warren, Michael **27**
Washington, Denzel **1, 16, 93**
Washington, Fredi **10**
Washington, Isaiah **62**
Washington, Kerry **46, 107**
Waters, Ethel **7**
Wayans, Damon **8, 41**
Wayans, Keenen Ivory **18**
Wayans, Kim **80**
Wayans, Marlon **29, 82**
Wayans, Shawn **29**
Weathers, Carl **10**
Wesley, Rutina **97**
Wheaton, James **103**
Whitaker, Forest **2, 49, 67**
White, Lillias **120**
White, Michael Jai **71, 117**
White, Terri **82**
Whitfield, Lynn **18**
Wiley, Samira **131**
Williams, Bert **18**
Williams, Billy Dee **8, 105**
Williams, Clarence, III **26**
Williams, Joe **5, 25**
Williams, Malinda **57**
Williams, Michael Kenneth **97**
Williams, Samm-Art **21**
Williams, Saul **31**
Williams, Spencer **126**
Williams, Vanessa A. **32, 66**
Williams, Vanessa L. **4, 17**
Williamson, Fred **67**
Williamson, Mykelti **22**
Wilson, Chandra **57**
Wilson, Debra **38**
Wilson, Demond **102**
Wilson, Dorien **55**
Wilson, Flip **21**
Winfield, Paul **2, 45**
Winfrey, Oprah **2, 15, 61, 106**
Withers-Mendes, Elisabeth **64**
Witherspoon, John **38**
Woodard, Alfre **9, 108**
Woods, Renn **110**

Woodson, Ali Ollie **89**
Wright, Jeffrey **54, 111**
Yarbrough, Cedric **51**
Yoba, Malik **11**
Young, Lee Thompson **114**

Adoption and foster care
Clements, George **2**
Hale, Clara **16**
Hale, Lorraine **8**
Oglesby, Zena **12**
Rowell, Victoria **13, 68**

Advertising
Barboza, Anthony **10**
Boyd, Edward **70**
Burrell, Tom **21, 51**
Campbell, E. Simms **13**
Chisholm, Samuel J. **32**
Coleman, Donald **24, 62**
Cullers, Vincent T. **49**
Gaskins, Rudy **74**
Green, Nancy **112**
Jones, Caroline R. **29**
Jordan, Montell **23**
Kemp, Herb **94**
Lewis, Byron E. **13**
McKinney Hammond, Michelle **51**
Mingo, Frank **32**
Olden, Georg(e) **44**
Pinderhughes, John **47**
Roche, Joyce M. **17**

Aeronautical/aerospace engineering
Harris, Wesley L. **92**
Williams, O. S. **13**

Affirmative action
Arnwine, Barbara **28**
Coleman, William T. **76**
Edley, Christopher F., Jr. **48**

AFL-CIO
See American Federation of Labor and Congress of Industrial Organizations

African American art
Burroughs, Margaret Taylor **9, 134**
Jones, Paul R. **76**
Twiggs, Leo **127**
Wainwright, Joscelyn **46**

African American folklore
Bailey, Xenobia **11**
Brown, Sterling Allen **10, 64**
Dial, Thornton **114**
Driskell, David C. **7**
Ellison, Ralph **7**
Gaines, Ernest J. **7**
Hamilton, Virginia **10**
Hurston, Zora Neale **3**
Lester, Julius **9, 115**
Tillman, George, Jr. **20**
Williams, Bert **18**
Yarbrough, Camille **40**

African American history
Benberry, Cuesta **65**
Bennett, Lerone, Jr. **5, 84**
Berry, Mary Frances **7**
Blackshear, Leonard **52**
Blockson, Charles L. **42**
Camp, Kimberly **19**

Chase-Riboud, Barbara **20, 46**
Clarke, John Henrik **20**
Clayton, Mayme Agnew **62**
Cobb, William Jelani **59, 121**
Coombs, Orde M. **44**
Cooper, Anna Julia **20**
Dodson, Howard, Jr. **7, 52**
DuBois, Shirley Graham **21**
Dyson, Michael Eric **11, 40, 128**
Feelings, Tom **11, 47**
Franklin, John Hope **5, 77**
Gaines, Ernest J. **7**
George, Nelson **12, 101**
Gill, Gerald **69**
Gordon-Reed, Annette **74**
Haley, Alex **4**
Halliburton, Warren J. **49**
Harkless, Necia Desiree **19**
Harris, Richard E. **61**
Hine, Darlene Clark **24**
Lewis, David Levering **9**
Marable, Manning **10, 102**
Mason, Herman, Jr. **83**
Miles, Tiya **116**
Nell, William C. **128**
Painter, Nell Irvin **24, 88**
Pritchard, Robert Starling **21**
Putney, Martha S. **75**
Quarles, Benjamin Arthur **18**
Richardson, Julieanna **81**
Schomburg, Arthur Alfonso **9**
Shadd, Abraham D. **81**
Southern, Eileen **56**
Tancil, Gladys Quander **59**
Twitty, Michael **134**
Woodson, Carter G. **2**
Yarbrough, Camille **40**

African American literature
Andrews, Raymond **4**
Angelou, Maya **1, 15, 122**
Baisden, Michael **25, 66**
Baker, Houston A., Jr. **6**
Baldwin, James **1**
Bambara, Toni Cade **1**
Bennett, George Harold "Hal" **45**
Bontemps, Arna **8**
Briscoe, Connie **15**
Brooks, Gwendolyn **1, 28**
Brown, Claude **38**
Brown, Wesley **23**
Brown, William Wells **99**
Campbell, Bebe Moore **6, 24, 59**
Cary, Lorene **3**
Childress, Alice **15**
Cleage, Pearl **17, 64**
Cullen, Countee **8**
Davis, Arthur P. **41**
Davis, Nolan **45**
Dickey, Eric Jerome **21, 56**
Du Bois, W. E. B. **3**
Dunbar, Paul Laurence **8**
Ellison, Ralph **7**
Evans, Mari **26**
Fair, Ronald L. **47**
Fauset, Jessie **7**
Feelings, Tom **11, 47**
Fisher, Rudolph **17**
Ford, Nick Aaron **44**
Fuller, Charles **8**
Gaines, Ernest J. **7**
Gates, Henry Louis, Jr. **3, 38, 67**
Gay, Roxane **136**

Gayle, Addison, Jr. 41
Gibson, Donald Bernard 40
Giddings, Paula 11
Giovanni, Nikki 9, 39, 85
Goines, Donald 19
Golden, Marita 19, 99
Guy, Rosa 5
Gyasi, Yaa 136
Haley, Alex 4
Hansberry, Lorraine 6
Harper, Frances Ellen Watkins 11
Heard, Nathan C. 45
Himes, Chester 8
Holland, Endesha Ida Mae 3, 57
Holmes, Shannon 70
Hughes, Langston 4
Hull, Akasha Gloria 45
Hurston, Zora Neale 3
Iceberg Slim 11
Joe, Yolanda 21
Johnson, Charles 1, 82
Johnson, James Weldon 5
Jones, Gayl 37
Jordan, June 7, 35
July, William 27
Kitt, Sandra 23
Larsen, Nella 10
Little, Benilde 21
Lorde, Audre 6
Madhubuti, Haki 7, 85
Major, Clarence 9
Marshall, Paule 7, 77
McKay, Claude 6
McKay, Nellie Yvonne 17, 57
McKinney-Whetstone, Diane 27
McMillan, Terry 4, 17, 53
McPherson, James Alan 70
Morrison, Toni 2, 15, 86
Mowry, Jess 7
Naylor, Gloria 10, 42
Patton, Venetria K. 125
Petry, Ann 19
Rahman, Aishah 37
Randall, Dudley 8, 55
Redding, J. Saunders 26
Redmond, Eugene 23
Reed, Ishmael 8
Ringgold, Faith 4, 81
Sanchez, Sonia 17, 51
Schomburg, Arthur Alfonso 9
Schuyler, George Samuel 40
Shange, Ntozake 8, 89
Smith, Mary Carter 26, 134
Taylor, Mildred D. 26
Thomas, Trisha R. 65
Thurman, Wallace 16
Toomer, Jean 6
Tyree, Omar Rashad 21
Verdelle, A. J. 26
Villarosa, Clara 85
Walker, Alice 1, 43
Wesley, Valerie Wilson 18
Wideman, John Edgar 5, 87
Williams, John A. 27
Williams, Sherley Anne 25
Wilson, August 7, 33, 55
Wright, Richard 5
Wright, Sarah E. 95
Yarbrough, Camille 40

African American studies
Alexander, Elizabeth 75
Baszile, Jennifer 79

Brawley, Benjamin 44
Carby, Hazel 27
Christian, Barbara T. 44
De Veaux, Alexis 44
Ford, Nick Aaron 44
Hare, Nathan 44
Harris-Lacewell, Melissa 81
Henderson, Stephen E. 45
Huggins, Nathan Irvin 52
Long, Richard Alexander 65
Neal, Mark Anthony 74
Peterson, James 81
West, Cornel 5, 33, 80

African art
Simpson, Merton D. 110

African Canadian literature
Elliott, Lorris 37
Foster, Cecil 32
Senior, Olive 37

African dance
Acogny, Germaine 55
Adams, Jenoyne 60
Ailey, Alvin 8
Davis, Chuck 33
Primus, Pearl 6, 125

African history
Chase-Riboud, Barbara 20, 46
Clarke, John Henrik 20
Counter, S. Allen 74
Diop, Cheikh Anta 4
Dodson, Howard, Jr. 7, 52
DuBois, Shirley Graham 21
Feelings, Muriel 44
Halliburton, Warren J. 49
Hansberry, William Leo 11
Harkless, Necia Desiree 19
Henries, A. Doris Banks 44
Hilliard, Asa Grant, III 66
Jawara, Dawda Kairaba 11
Marshall, Paule 7, 77
van Sertima, Ivan 25

African literature
Abrahams, Peter 39
Achebe, Chinua 6, 99, 111
Aidoo, Ama Ata 38
Akpan, Uwem 70
Amadi, Elechi 40
Arac de Nyeko, Monica 66
Armah, Ayi Kwei 49
Awoonor, Kofi 37, 115
Babatunde, Rotimi 104
Bandele, Biyi 68, 121
Barrett, Lindsay 43
Beti, Mongo 36
Brutus, Dennis 38
Cartey, Wilfred 47
Cheney-Coker, Syl 43
Chikoti, Shadreck 125
Couto, Mia 45
Dadié, Bernard 34
Dathorne, O. R. 52
Ekwensi, Cyprian 37
Farah, Nuruddin 27
Gabre-Medhin, Tsegaye 64
Head, Bessie 28
Kahora, Billy 125
Kayira, Legson 40
Mazrui, Ali 12, 124
Memmi, Albert 37

Mofolo, Thomas 37
Mphahlele, Es'kia 40
Mwangi, Meja 40
Ngugi wa Thiong'o 29, 61, 101
Okigbo, Christopher 102
Onwueme, Tess Osonye 23
Oyono, Ferdinand 38
Peters, Lenrie 43
Rotimi, Ola 1, 130
Salih, Al-Tayyib 37
Saro-Wiwa, Kenule 39
Selasi, Taiye 125
Soyinka, Wole 4, 93

African Methodist Episcopal
Church (AME)
Blanks, Deborah K. 69
Blow, Kurtis 31, 122
Brookins, Hamel Hartford 102
Bryant, Jamal 128
Bryant, John R. 45
Flake, Floyd H. 18, 110
Lee, Jarena 100
Loguen, J. W. 91
McKenzie, Vashti M. 29
Mudimbe, V. Y. 61
Murray, Cecil 12, 47
Pinckney, Clementa C. 130
Roundtree, Dovey 80
Turner, Henry McNeal 5
Youngblood, Johnny Ray 8

African music
Ade, King Sunny 41
Afro, Teddy 78
Ahmed, Mahmoud 130
Allen, Tony 117
Amadou & Mariam 113
Ashong, Derrick 86
Bassey, Offiong 119
Birra, Ali 113
Bombino 112
Chaka Chaka, Yvonne 112
Diawara, Djeli Moussa 111
Diawara, Fatoumata 114
Fela 1, 42
Ibrahim, Abdullah 131
Jaojoby 130
Keita, Salif 83
Kidjo, Angelique 50
Kolosoy, Wendo 73
Kuti, Femi 47, 110
Maal, Baaba 66
Mahlasela, Vusi 65
Makeba, Miriam 2, 50, 74
Malawi Mouse Boys 114
Nascimento, Milton 2 64
Nzié, Anne-Marie 136
Olatunji, Babatunde 36, 126
Rochereau, Tabu Ley 117
Sangare, Oumou 18, 99
Sangho, Awa 127
Somi 85

African National Congress
(ANC)
Dlamini-Zuma, Nkosazana 34, 105
Dube, John Langalibalele 119
Hani, Chris 6
Ka Dinizulu, Mcwayizeni 29
Kaunda, Kenneth 2
Kuzwayo, Ellen 68
Luthuli, Albert 13

Madikizela-Mandela, Winnie 2, 35,
112
Malema, Julius 98
Mandela, Nelson 1, 14, 77, 117
Masekela, Barbara 18
Mbeki, Govan A. 80
Mbeki, Thabo 14, 73
Mhlaba, Raymond 55
Motlanthe, Kgalema 74
Nkomo, Joshua 4, 65
Nyanda, Siphiwe 21
Nzo, Alfred 15
Ramaphosa, Cyril 3, 117
Sisulu, Albertina 57, 95
Sisulu, Walter 47
Tutu, Desmond Mpilo 6, 44
Weems, Renita J. 44
Xuma, Madie Hall 59
Zuma, Jacob 33, 75

African Union
Dlamini-Zuma, Nkosazana 34, 105
Haile Selassie 7
Kaunda, Kenneth 2
Kenyatta, Jomo 5
Nkrumah, Kwame 3
Nujoma, Samuel 10
Nyerere, Julius 5, 136
Sassou-Nguesso, Denis 103
Touré, Sekou 6

Afro-Brazilian music
Brown, Carlinhos 81
Caymmi, Dorival 72
Gil, Gilberto 53
Jorge, Seu 73
Moura, Paulo 87

Afrocentricity
Asante, Molefi Kete 3
Biggers, John 20, 33
Diop, Cheikh Anta 4
Hansberry, William Leo 11
Sanchez, Sonia 17, 51
Turner, Henry McNeal 5

Afro-Cuban music
Lefel, Edith 41
Rodríguez, Arsenio 87
Santamaria, Mongo 81
Secada, Jon 97

Afro-Peruvian music
Baca, Susana 80

Agriculture
Allen, Will 74
Boyd, John W., Jr. 20, 72
Brown, Jason 125
Burkett, Ben 123
Carver, George Washington 4
Finley, Ron 110
Hall, Lloyd A. 8
Jones, Monty 66
Sanders, Dori 8
Wambugu, Florence 42
Washington, Karen 117

AHA
See American Heart Association

AIDS
See Acquired immune deficiency
syndrome

ALA
See American Library Association

Alabama state government
Davis, Artur 41
Ford, Johnny 70
Gray, Fred 37
Rapier, James T. 82

Alcoholics Anonymous (AA)
Lucas, John 7

All Afrikan People's Revolutionary Party
Carmichael, Stokely 5, 26
Moses, Robert Parris 11

Alpha & Omega Ministry
White, Reggie 6, 50

Alpha Kappa Alpha Sorority
Quander, Nellie 102
White, Linda M. 45

Alternative music
Santigold 96

Alvin Ailey American Dance Theater
Ailey, Alvin 8
Clarke, Hope 14
Dove, Ulysses 5
Faison, George 16
Jamison, Judith 7, 67, 96
Jefferson, Denise 87
Rhoden, Dwight 40
Richardson, Desmond 39
Spears, Warren 52
Tyson, Andre 40
Williams, Dudley 60

Ambassadors
Avant, Nicole A. 90
Awoonor, Kofi 37, 115
Bassett, Ebenezer D. 132
Braun, Carol Moseley 4, 42
Carson, Johnnie 85
Cook, Mercer 40
Davis, Ruth 37
Dudley, Edward R. 58
Dymally, Mervyn 42
Frazer, Jendayi 68
Haley, George 21, 129
Mbuende, Kaire 12
Perkins, Edward 5
Smythe Haith, Mabel 61
Spearman, Leonard H. O., Sr. 81
Stith, Charles R. 73
Todman, Terence A. 55
Watson, Diane 41
Wharton, Clifton Reginald, Sr. 36
Whitfield, Mal 60

AME
See African Methodist Episcopal Church

American Association for the Advancement of Science (AAAS)
Cobb, W. Montague 39
Massey, Walter E. 5, 45
Pickett, Cecil 39

American Ballet Theatre
Copeland, Misty 125
Dove, Ulysses 5

Richardson, Desmond 39

American Bar Association
Archer, Dennis 7, 36
Pincham, R. Eugene, Sr. 69
Thompson, Larry D. 39
Walker, Cora T. 68

American Book Awards
Baraka, Amiri 1, 38, 118
Bates, Daisy 13, 135
Bradley, David Henry, Jr. 39
Clark, Septima 7
Danticat, Edwidge 15, 68, 128
Dyson, Michael Eric 11, 40, 128
Ellis, Trey 97
Gates, Henry Louis, Jr. 3, 38, 67
Jackson, Angela 134
Lorde, Audre 6
Loury, Glenn 36
Marshall, Paule 7, 77
Sanchez, Sonia 17, 51
Troupe, Quincy 83
Walker, Alice 1, 43

American Broadcasting Company (ABC)
Christian, Spencer 15
Dungey, Channing 134
Goode, Mal 13
Martin, Michel 97
Mickebury, Penny 28
Reynolds, Star Jones 10, 27, 61
Roberts, Robin 16, 54, 113
Robinson, Max 3
Simpson, Carole 6, 30

American Civil Liberties Union (ACLU)
Baugh, David 23
Harris, Maya Lakshmi 88
Murphy, Laura M. 43
Murray, Pauli 38
Pincham, R. Eugene, Sr. 69

American Civil War
Augusta, Alexander T. 111
Carney, William H. 104
Tubman, Harriet 9, 135

American Enterprise Institute
Woodson, Robert L. 10

American Express Company
Adams, Eula L. 39, 120
Chapman, Susan E. 94
Chenault, Kenneth 4, 36, 108
Goodman, Kim C. 94

American Federation of Labor and Congress of Industrial Organizations (AFL-CIO)
Fletcher, Bill, Jr. 41
Holt Baker, Arlene 73
O'Neal, Frederick 99
Randolph, A. Philip 3

American Heart Association (AHA)
Cooper, Edward S. 6
Grant, Augustus O. 71
Richardson, Donna 39

American Idol
Barrino, Fantasia 53, 94
Hudson, Jennifer 63, 83

Jackson, Randy 40

American Library Association (ALA)
Franklin, Hardy R. 9, 87
Hayden, Carla D. 47
Jones, Clara Stanton 51
Josey, E. J. 10
McFadden, Bernice L. 39
Rollins, Charlamae Hill 27
Wedgeworth, Robert W. 42

American Negro Theater
Martin, Helen 31
O'Neal, Frederick 99

American Psychological Association (APA)
Anderson, Norman B. 45

American Red Cross
Bullock, Steve 22
Drew, Charles Richard 7

American Society of Magazine Editors
Curry, George E. 23

American Tennis Association
Gibson, Althea 8, 43
Peters, Margaret and Matilda 43

American Writers Association
Schuyler, George Samuel 40

Amsterdam News
Bostic, Joe 95
Burley, Dan 96
Cooper, Andrew W. 36
Holt, Nora 38
Tatum, Elinor R. 78
Tatum, Wilbert 76

ANA
See American Nurses Association

ANC
See African National Congress

Anglican Church
Akinola, Peter Jasper 65
Tutu, Desmond Mpilo 6, 44

Angola government
dos Santos, José Eduardo 43, 114
Neto, António Agostinho 43

Anheuser-Busch distribution
Cherry, Deron 40

Anthropology
Asante, Molefi Kete 3
Cole, Johnnetta B. 5, 43
Davis, Allison 12
Diop, Cheikh Anta 4
Dunham, Katherine 4, 59
Hansberry, William Leo 11
Primus, Pearl 6, 125
Robeson, Eslanda Goode 13
Rodriguez, Cheryl 64

Antoinette Perry Awards
See Tony Awards

APA
See American Psychological Association

Apartheid
Abrahams, Peter 39
Ashe, Arthur 18

Biko, Steven 4
Brutus, Dennis 38
Butler, Jonathan 28
Cole, Ernest 123
Howard, M. William, Jr. 26
Jansen, Jonathan 102
Ka Dinizulu, Mcwayizeni 29
Kuzwayo, Ellen 68
LaGuma, Alex 30
Luthuli, Albert 13
Madikizela-Mandela, Winnie 2, 35, 112
Mahlasela, Vusi 65
Makeba, Miriam 2, 50, 74
Mandela, Nelson 1, 14, 77, 117
Maponya, Maishe 101
Masekela, Hugh 1, 106
Mbeki, Thabo 14, 73
McDougall, Gay J. 11, 43
Mhlaba, Raymond 55
Nkoli, Simon 60
Ntshona, Winston 52
Nyanda, Siphiwe 21
Nzo, Alfred 15
Plaatje, Sol T. 80
Ramaphosa, Cyril 3, 117
Ramphele, Mamphela 29
Robinson, Randall 7, 46
Sisulu, Albertina 57, 95
Sisulu, Walter 47
Sullivan, Leon H. 13, 30
Tau, Mpho Parks 124
Tutu, Desmond Mpilo 6, 44

Apollo Theater
Sims, Howard 48
Sutton, Percy E. 42, 82

Archaeology
Gilbert, John Wesley 91
McJunkin, George 93
Perry, Warren 56

Architecture
Abele, Julian 55
Adjaye, David 38, 78
Bond, J. Max, Jr. 76
Chase, John Saunders, Jr. 99
Gantt, Harvey 1
Johnson, Jeh Vincent 44
King, Robert Arthur 58
Lowe, Rick 124
McKissack, Leatrice 80
Sklarek, Norma Merrick 25, 101
Taylor, Robert Robinson 80
Williams, Paul R. 9

Argonne National Laboratory
Massey, Walter E. 5, 45
Quarterman, Lloyd Albert 4

Arkansas state government
Elders, Joycelyn 6

Arkansas Supreme Court
Roaf, Andrée Layton 106

Art history
Amaki, Amalia 76
Benjamin, Tritobia Hayes 53
Campbell, Mary Schmidt 43

Astronauts
Anderson, Michael P. 40
Bluford, Guy 2, 35

Bolden, Charles Frank, Jr. **7, 78**
Gregory, Frederick **8, 51**
Harris, Bernard A. **90**
Jemison, Mae C. **1, 35, 129**
Lawrence, Robert H., Jr. **16**
McNair, Ronald **3, 58**
Wilson, Stephanie **72**

Astronomy
Banneker, Benjamin **93**
Pitts, Derrick **77**

Astrophysics
Alcorn, George Edward, Jr. **59**
Carruthers, George R. **40**
Walker, Arthur, II **87**

Atlanta Baptist College
See Morehouse College

Atlanta Board of Education
Mays, Benjamin E. **7**

Atlanta Braves baseball team
Aaron, Hank **5**
Jones, Andruw **98**
Justice, David **18**
Lucas, Bill **97**
McGriff, Fred **24**

Atlanta city government
Campbell, Bill **9, 76**
Franklin, Shirley **34, 80**
Jackson, Maynard **2, 41**
Pitts, Robb **84**
Reed, Kasim **82**
Williams, Hosea **15, 31, 123**
Young, Andrew **3, 48, 110**

Atlanta Police Department
Harvard, Beverly **11**

Authors Guild
Schuyler, George Samuel **40**

Authors League of America
Abrahams, Peter **39**
Cotter, Joseph Seamon, Sr. **40**

Automobile dealership
Farr, Mel **24**
Gidron, Richard D. **68**
Parker, Jim **64**

Aviation
Brown, Jesse Leroy **31**
Brown, Willa **40**
Bullard, Eugene **12**
Coleman, Bessie **9**
Irving, Barrington, Jr. **112**
Julian, Hubert **90**
Mbabazi, Esther **122**
McLeod, Gus **27**
Petersen, Frank E. **31**
Plinton, James O., Jr. **98**
Roy, Kenny **51**
Turner, Henry McNeal **5**
Young, Perry H. **100**

Bahamas government
Christie, Perry Gladstone **53**
Pindling, Lynden **81**

Ballet
Ailey, Alvin **8**
Allen, Debbie **13, 42**
Anderson, Lauren **72**

Collins, Janet **33, 64**
DePrince, Michaela **104**
Dove, Ulysses **5**
Faison, George **16**
Jamison, Judith **7, 67, 96**
Johnson, Virginia **9**
Jones, Doris W. **62**
Mitchell, Arthur **2, 47**
Nichols, Nichelle **11**
Parks, Gordon **1, 35, 58**
Rhoden, Dwight **40**
Richardson, Desmond **39**
Rowell, Victoria **13, 68**
Tyson, Andre **40**

Baltimore city government
Dixon, Sheila **68**
Rawlings-Blake, Stephanie **93, 128**
Robinson, Bishop L. **66**
Schmoke, Kurt **1, 48**

Baltimore Orioles baseball team
Baylor, Don **6**
Blair, Paul **36**
Carter, Joe **30**
Jackson, Reggie **15**
Robinson, Frank **9, 87**

Banking
Blaylock, Ronald **86**
Boyd, T. B., III **6**
Bradley, Jennette B. **40**
Bridgforth, Glinda **36**
Bryant, John **26**
Chapman, Nathan A., Jr. **21**
Chappell, Emma **18**
Elumelu, Tony **116**
Forte, Linda Diane **54**
Funderburg, I. Owen **38**
Greene, Richard Thaddeus, Sr. **67**
Griffith, Mark Winston **8**
Harris, Carla A. **67**
Lawless, Theodore K. **8**
Louis, Errol T. **8**
March, William Carrington **56**
McGuire, Raymond J. **57**
Morgan, Rose **11**
Overton, Anthony **128**
Snowden, Gail **108**
Taylor, Robert Rochon **104**
Utendahl, John **23**
Walker, Maggie Lena **17**
Watkins, Donald **35**
Watkins, Walter C. **24**
Willie, Louis, Jr. **68**
Wright, Deborah C. **25**
Wright, Richard Robert, Sr. **100**

Baptist
Allensworth, Allen **129**
Austin, Junius C. **44**
Borders, William Holmes **94**
Bradley, J. Robert **65**
Braxton, Brad **77**
Brewster, W. Herbert **128**
Butts, Calvin O., III **9, 90**
Davis, Gary **41**
Forbes, James A., Jr. **71**
Franklin, C. L. **68**
Fuller, Thomas O. **90**
Gomes, Peter J. **15, 93**
Hooks, Benjamin L. **2, 85**
Jasper, John J. **91**

Jemison, Major L. **48**
Jones, Dwight C. **122**
Jones, E. Edward, Sr. **45**
King, Martin Luther, Sr. **89**
Long, Eddie L. **29, 89**
Luter, Fred, Jr. **103**
Meeks, James T. **92**
Moss, Otis, Jr. **72**
Rogers, Alan G. **72**
Sharpe, Samuel **103**
Sharpton, Al **21, 97**
Shuttlesworth, Fred **47, 98**
Taylor, Gardner C. **76**
Taylor, Lonzie Odie **96**
Thurston, Stephen J. **49**
Walker, Lucius, Jr. **88**
Walker, Wyatt Tee **80**
Yates, Jack **114**
Yergan, Max **123**

Barbados government
Adams, Grantley **82**
Arthur, Owen **33**

Baseball
Aaron, Hank **5**
Allen, Dick **85**
Anderson, Elmer **25**
Ashford, Emmett **22**
Baines, Harold **32**
Baker, Dusty **8, 43, 72, 110**
Banks, Ernie **33, 126**
Barnhill, David **30**
Baylor, Don **6**
Bell, James "Cool Papa" **36**
Belle, Albert **10**
Black, Joe **75**
Blair, Paul **36**
Blue, Vida **122**
Bonds, Barry **6, 34, 63, 99**
Bonds, Bobby **43**
Brock, Lou **18**
Brown, Raymond **102**
Brown, Willard **36**
Burke, Glenn **122**
Byrd, Marlon **112**
Cabell, Enos **102**
Cain, Lorenzo **128**
Campanella, Roy **25**
Cano, Robinson **97**
Carew, Rod **20**
Carter, Joe **30**
Cepeda, Orlando **98**
Chapman, Aroldis **132**
Charleston, Oscar **39**
Clendenon, Donn **26, 56**
Coleman, Leonard S., Jr. **12**
Coleman, Vince **128**
Cooper, Andy "Lefty" **63**
Cottrell, Comer **11**
Crawford, Carl **90**
Crisp, Coco **109**
Cueto, Johnny **130**
Dandridge, Ray **36**
Davis, Eric **116**
Davis, Piper **19**
Dawson, Andre **85**
Day, Leon **39**
Dihigo, Martín **103**
Doby, Lawrence Eugene, Sr. **16**
Dye, Jermaine **58**
Ellis, Dock **78**
Escobar, Alcides **130**

Everett, Carl **103**
Fielder, Cecil **2, 112**
Fielder, Prince **68**
Flood, Curt **10, 93**
Foster, Andrew **79**
Fuentes, Tito **123**
Gamble, Oscar **113**
Gaston, Cito **71**
Gibson, Bob **33**
Gibson, Josh **22**
Gilliam, Jim **122**
Glanville, Douglas Metunwa **82**
Gooden, Dwight **20**
Gordon, Dee **130**
Gordon, Tom **130**
Granderson, Curtis **66**
Grant, Frank **100**
Gregg, Eric **16**
Griffey, Ken, Jr. **12, 73**
Gwynn, Tony **18, 83, 122**
Hairston, Sam **88**
Hamilton, Darryl **130**
Hart, Jim Ray **136**
Henderson, Rickey **28, 78**
Hernández, Orlando **96**
Horton, Willie **104**
Howard, Elston **125**
Howard, Ryan **65, 113**
Hunter, Torii **43, 109**
Hyde, Cowan F. "Bubba" **47**
Irvin, Monte **31, 134**
Jackson, Reggie **15**
Jenkins, Fergie **46**
Jeter, Derek **27, 93, 124**
Johnson, Clifford "Connie" **52**
Johnson, Judy **105**
Johnson, Mamie "Peanut" **40**
Jones, Adam **114**
Jones, Andruw **98**
Justice, David **18**
Kaiser, Cecil **42**
Kimbro, Henry A. **25**
Lacy, Sam **30, 46**
Lankford, Ray **23**
Larkin, Barry **24**
Lloyd, John Henry "Pop" **30**
Lofton, Kenny **12**
Lopes, Davey **92**
Lucas, Bill **97**
Mackey, Biz **82**
Manuel, Jerry **94**
Mariner, Jonathan **41**
Marte, Starling **117**
Martínez, Pedro **81, 126**
Maye, Lee **111**
Mays, Willie **3**
McClendon, Lloyd **123**
McCovey, Willie **103**
McCutchen, Andrew **116**
McGriff, Fred **24**
McRae, Hal **84**
Minoso, Minnie **89, 127**
Morgan, Joe **9, 96**
Murray, Eddie **12**
Newcombe, Don **24**
Nixon, Otis **111**
O'Neil, Buck **19, 59**
Ortiz, David **52, 82**
Paige, Satchel **7**
Perez, Pascual **108**
Phillips, Brandon **116**
Pineda, Michael **121**
Porter, Bo **123**

Price, David **101**
Pride, Charley **26**
Puckett, Kirby **4, 58**
Puig, Yasiel **113**
Radcliffe, Ted **74**
Raines, Tim **107**
Randolph, Willie **53**
Reagins, Tony **94**
Reese, Pokey **28**
Reyes, José **134**
Reynolds, Harold **77**
Rice, Jim **75**
Richard, J. R. **87**
Roberts, Dave **132**
Robinson, Frank **9, 87**
Robinson, Jackie **6**
Robinson, Sharon **22**
Rollins, Jimmy **70**
Roseboro, John **123**
Sabathia, CC **74**
Sanders, Deion **4, 31, 96**
Scott, George **113**
Sheffield, Gary **16, 108**
Sizemore, Grady **96**
Smith, Hilton **29**
Smith, Lee **101**
Smith, Ozzie **77**
Smith, Reggie **113**
Sosa, Sammy **21, 44**
Stargell, Willie **29**
Stearnes, Norman "Turkey" **31**
Stewart, Dave **117**
Stone, Toni **15**
Strawberry, Darryl **22**
Suttles, Mule **108**
Thomas, Frank **12, 51**
Tiant, Luis **102**
Trouppe, Quincy Thomas, Sr. **84**
Upton, Justin **124**
Upton, Melvin, Jr. **124**
Uribe, Juan **122**
Vaughn, Mo **16**
Virgil, Ozzie **48**
Washington, Ron **119**
Watson, Bob **25**
Wells, Vernon **91**
Wells, Willie **105**
White, Bill **1, 48**
White, Frank **95**
Whitney, Davey L. **110**
Williams, Bernie **128**
Williams, Billy **86**
Williams, Ken **68**
Williams, Walt **133**
Willis, Dontrelle **55**
Wills, Maury **73**
Winfield, Dave **5, 91**

Baseball Hall of Fame
Banks, Ernie **33, 126**
Bell, James "Cool Papa" **36**
Brown, Raymond **102**
Brown, Willard **36**
Campanella, Roy **25**
Cepeda, Orlando **98**
Charleston, Oscar **39**
Dandridge, Ray **36**
Dawson, Andre **85**
Day, Leon **39**
Dihigo, Martín **103**
Doby, Lawrence Eugene, Sr. **16, 41**
Foster, Andrew **79**
Gibson, Josh **22**

Gwynn, Tony **18, 83, 122**
Henderson, Rickey **28, 78**
Irvin, Monte **31, 134**
Johnson, Judy **105**
Leonard, Buck **67**
Lloyd, John Henry "Pop" **30**
Mackey, Biz **82**
Martínez, Pedro **81, 126**
McCovey, Willie **103**
Morgan, Joe **9, 96**
Paige, Satchel **7**
Rice, Jim **75**
Robinson, Frank **9, 87**
Robinson, Jackie **6**
Smith, Hilton **29**
Smith, Ozzie **77**
Stearnes, Norman "Turkey" **31**
Wells, Willie **105**
Williams, Billy **86**
Winfield, Dave **5, 91**

Basket making
Jackson, Mary **73**

Basketball
Abdul-Jabbar, Kareem **8**
Abdur-Rahim, Shareef **28**
Aldridge, LaMarcus **125**
Allen, Ray **82**
Amaker, Tommy **62**
Anderson, Mike **63**
Anthony, Carmelo **46, 94**
Archibald, Tiny **90**
Arenas, Gilbert **84**
Artest, Ron **52**
Barkley, Charles **5, 66**
Barksdale, Don **103**
Baylor, Elgin **93**
Beaty, Zelmo **115**
Bellamy, Walt **119**
Bickerstaff, Bernie **21, 133**
Bickerstaff, J. B. **133**
Bing, Dave **3, 59, 78**
Bogues, Tyrone "Muggsy" **56**
Bol, Manute **1**
Bolton-Holifield, Ruthie **28**
Bosh, Chris **85**
Brand, Elton **31**
Brandon, Terrell **16**
Bridgeman, Junior **132**
Brown, Mike **77, 107**
Bryant, Kobe **15, 31, 71, 110**
Bynoe, Peter C. B. **40**
Carter, Butch **27**
Carter, Kenneth **53**
Carter, Vince **26**
Catchings, Tamika **43**
Chalmers, Mario **122**
Chamberlain, Wilt **18, 47**
Chandler, Tyson **114**
Chaney, Don **98**
Chaney, John **67**
Cheeks, Maurice **47, 106**
Clifton, Nathaniel "Sweetwater" **47**
Collins, Jason **111**
Cooper, Charles "Chuck" **47**
Cooper, Michael **31**
Cooper, Tarzan **96**
Cooper-Dyke, Cynthia **17, 89**
Corbin, Tyrone **126**
Cousins, DeMarcus **108**
Curry, Dell **126**
Curry, Michael **85**

Curry, Stephen **110**
Daniels, Mel **106**
Dantley, Adrian **72**
Davis, Anthony **120**
Davis, Mike **41**
Dawkins, Darryl **131**
DeRozan, DeMar **125**
Diaw, Boris **122**
Douglas, Bob **96**
Drexler, Clyde **4, 61**
Drummond, Andre **132**
Dumars, Joe **16, 65, 126**
Duncan, Tim **20, 91**
Dunn, Jerry **27**
Durant, Kevin **76, 107**
Edwards, Teresa **14, 95**
Ellerbe, Brian **22**
Elliott, Sean **26**
Erving, Julius **18, 47**
Ewing, Patrick **17, 73, 130**
Fisher, Derek **97**
Fox, Rick **27**
Frazier, Walt **91**
Freeman, Marianna **23**
Gaines, Clarence E., Sr. **55**
Garnett, Kevin **14, 70, 118**
Gates, William **97**
Gentry, Alvin **23**
George, Paul **124**
Gilmore, Artis **101**
Gourdine, Simon **11**
Gray, Yeshimbra "Shimmy" **55**
Green, A. C. **32**
Green, Draymond **126**
Greer, Hal **92**
Griffin, Blake **98**
Griffith, Yolanda **25**
Griner, Brittney **128**
Hamilton, Leonard **100**
Hardaway, Anfernee **13, 111**
Hardaway, Tim **35**
Harden, James **116**
Harris-Stewart, Lusia **90**
Haskins, Clem **23**
Hawkins, Connie **91**
Hayes, Elvin **93**
Haynes, Marques **22**
Haywood, Spencer **99**
Hazzard, Walt **98**
Heard, Gar **25**
Hill, Grant **13, 94**
Holdsclaw, Chamique **24, 110**
Holiday, Jrue **115**
Hollins, Lionel **133**
Horford, Al **107**
Howard, Dwight **113**
Howard, Juwan **15**
Hudson, Lou **121**
Hunter, Billy **22, 109**
Hunter, Lindsey **110**
Iguodala, Andre **129**
Irving, Kyrie **102**
Isaacs, John **76**
Iverson, Allen **24, 46, 129**
Jackson, Mark **121**
Jackson, Stephen **118**
James, LeBron **46, 78, 105**
Jefferson, Richard **136**
Johnson, Avery **62**
Johnson, Dennis **89**
Johnson, Gus **92**
Johnson, Joe **94**
Johnson, Kevin **70, 132**

Johnson, Larry **28**
Johnson, Magic **3, 39, 101**
Johnson, Marques **133**
Jones, K. C. **83**
Jones, Merlakia **34**
Jones, Robbie **113**
Jones, Sam **85**
Jordan, Eddie **83**
Jordan, Michael **6, 21**
Joyce, Dru **81**
Justice, David **18**
Kellogg, Clark **64**
Kidd, Jason **86**
Lanier, Bob **47**
Lennox, Betty **31**
Leonard, Kawhi **122**
Leslie, Lisa **16, 73**
Lillard, Damian **117**
Lloyd, Earl **26, 127**
Lowe, Sidney **64**
Lucas, John **7**
Lue, Tyronn **136**
Mahorn, Rick **60**
Malone, Karl **18, 51, 90**
Malone, Moses **79, 131**
Manigault, Earl "The Goat" **15**
Marion, Shawn **136**
Martin, Cuonzo **121**
Mason, Anthony **128**
Mason, Desmond **127**
McAdoo, Bob **75**
McGrady, Tracy **80**
McLendon, John B., Jr. **89**
Meminger, Dean **114**
Miller, Cheryl **10, 74**
Milton, DeLisha **31**
Mitchell, Sam **82**
Mohammed, Nazr **64**
Monroe, Earl **89**
Mourning, Alonzo **17, 44, 131**
Mutombo, Dikembe **7, 107**
Odom, Lamar **81**
Olajuwon, Hakeem **2, 72**
O'Neal, Shaquille **8, 30, 95**
Palmer, Violet **59**
Parish, Robert **43**
Parker, Candace **74**
Parker, Tony **75**
Paul, Chris **84, 100**
Payton, Gary **99**
Peck, Carolyn **23**
Phillips, Teresa L. **42**
Pierce, Paul **71**
Pippen, Scottie **15, 89**
Porter, Terry **75**
Prince, Tayshaun **68**
Reed, Willis, Jr. **86**
Richardson, Nolan **9**
Richmond, Mitch **19**
Rivers, Doc **25, 81**
Robertson, Oscar **26**
Robinson, Craig **107**
Robinson, David **24, 90**
Robinson, Flynn **112**
Robinson, Will **51, 69**
Rodman, Dennis **12, 44, 96, 118**
Rogers, Rodney Ray **106**
Rondo, Rajon **111**
Rooks, Sean **136**
Rose, Derrick **82**
Rose, Jalen **108**
Roundfield, Danny **109**
Roy, Brandon **98**

Russell, Bill 8
Sanders, Satch 77
Scott, Byron 125
Sealy, Malik 118
Sefolosha, Thabo 121
Shaw, Brian 127
Sidat-Singh, Wilmeth 116
Silas, Paul 24, 129
Smith, Kenny 114
Smith, Randy 81
Smith, Stephen A. 69
Smith, Tubby 18, 83
Sprewell, Latrell 23
Stackhouse, Jerry 30
Staley, Dawn 57
Stephenson, Lance 118
Stith, Tom 93
Stoudemire, Amar'e 59, 106
Stringer, C. Vivian 13, 66
Swoopes, Sheryl 12, 56
Tatum, Reece 104
Temple, Collis, Jr. 119
Thabeet, Hasheem 123
Thomas, Isiah 7, 26, 65
Thompson, Klay 126
Thompson, Mychal 126
Thompson, Tina 25, 75
Thompson, Tristan 131
Thurmond, Nate 88
Tisdale, Wayman 50
Towns, Karl-Anthony 136
Ujiri, Masai 107
Unseld, Wes 23
Usry, James L. 23, 134
Ussery, Terdema, II 29
Vaughn, Jacque 127
Wade, Dwyane 61, 103
Walker, Antoine 132
Walker, Chet 106
Wall, John 129
Wallace, Ben 54
Wallace, Perry E. 47
Wallace, Rasheed 56
Washington, Ora Mae 115
Webber, Chris 15, 30, 59, 118
Westbrook, Russell 116
White, Jo Jo 112
Whiteside, Hassan 127
Whitney, Davey L. 110
Wiggins, Andrew 128
Wilkens, Lenny 11, 88
Williams, Deron 92
Williams, Monty 125
Williams, Natalie 31
Woodard, Lynette 67
Woodson, Mike 78
Worthy, James 49

Basketball Hall of Fame
Abdul-Jabbar, Kareem 8
Archibald, Tiny 90
Barkley, Charles 5, 66
Barksdale, Don 103
Baylor, Elgin 93
Bellamy, Walt 119
Bing, Dave 3, 59, 78
Boozer, Bob 103
Chamberlain, Wilt 18, 47
Chaney, John 67
Cooper, Tarzan 96
Cooper-Dyke, Cynthia 17, 89
Daniels, Mel 106
Dantley, Adrian 72

Douglas, Bob 96
Drexler, Clyde 4, 61
Dumars, Joe 16, 65, 126
Edwards, Teresa 14, 95
Ewing, Patrick 17, 73, 130
Frazier, Walt 91
Gaines, Clarence E., Sr. 55
Gates, William 97
Gervin, George 80
Gilmore, Artis 101
Greer, Hal 92
Harris-Stewart, Lusia 90
Hawkins, Connie 91
Hayes, Elvin 93
Haynes, Marques 22
Johnson, Dennis 89
Johnson, Gus 92
Johnson, Magic 3, 39, 101
Jones, K. C. 83
Jones, Sam 85
Lanier, Bob 47
Lloyd, Earl 26, 127
Malone, Karl 18, 51, 90
Malone, Moses 79, 131
McAdoo, Bob 75
McLendon, John B., Jr. 89
Miller, Cheryl 10, 74
Monroe, Earl 89
Mourning, Alonzo 17, 44, 131
Olajuwon, Hakeem 2, 72
Parish, Robert 43
Pippen, Scottie 15, 89
Reed, Willis, Jr. 86
Robertson, Oscar 26
Robinson, David 24, 90
Rodman, Dennis 12, 44, 96, 118
Russell, Bill 8
Sanders, Satch 77
Thomas, Isiah 7, 26, 65
Thurmond, Nate 88
Unseld, Wes 23
Walker, Chet 106
Wilkens, Lenny 11, 88
Wilkins, Dominique 74
Woodard, Lynette 67
Worthy, James 49

Bass
Blanton, Jimmy 108
Burbridge, Oteil 120
Carter, Ron 104
Chambers, Paul 121
Clarke, Stanley 115
Counce, Curtis 127
Foster, George "Pops" 40
Garrison, Jimmy 133
Grimes, Henry 124
Isley, Marvin 87
Jamerson, James 59
McBee, Cecil 123
McBride, Christian 134
Moffett, Charnett 127
Page, Walter 117
Parham, Truck 124
Pettiford, Oscar 106
Porter, Tiran 133
Reid, Rufus 130
Smith, Lee 136
Stewart, Slam 126
Tacuma, Jamaaladeen 124
Towles, Nat 128
Vinnegar, Leroy 124
Warren, Butch 116

Williams, Buster 131
Wooten, Victor 131
Workman, Reggie 131
Wright, Eugene 125

BBC
See British Broadcasting Company

Beatrice International
See TLC Beatrice International
    Holdings, Inc.

Beauty salons and products
Cottrell, Comer 11
Fine, Sam 60
Fuller, S. B. 13
Gardner, Edward G. 45
Gibson, Ted 66
Johnson, George E. 29
Johnson, William 91
Joyner, Marjorie Stewart 26
Malone, Annie 13
Price, Lisa 97
Roche, Joyce M. 17
Stanford, Olivia Lee Dilworth 49
Walker, Madame C. J. 7

Bebop
Carter, Betty 19
Clarke, Kenny 27
Coltrane, John 19
Dameron, Tadd 103
Davis, Miles 4
Eckstine, Billy 28
Fitzgerald, Ella 8, 18
Freeman, Von 104
Gillespie, Dizzy 1
Gordon, Dexter 25
Hancock, Herbie 20, 67
Harris, Barry 68
Hawkins, Coleman 9
Jackson, Milt 26
McGhee, Howard 122
Navarro, Fats 104
Parker, Charlie 20
Powell, Bud 24
Roach, Max 21, 63
Vaughan, Sarah 13

Benin government
Kérékou, Mathieu 1, 131
Soglo, Nicéphore 15
Yayi, Boni T. 84

Bermuda government
Gordon, Pamela 17

BET
See Black Entertainment Television

Bethune-Cookman College
Bethune, Mary McLeod 4

**Bill and Melinda Gates Foun-
dation**
Golston, Allan C. 55

Biology
Cobb, Jewel Plummer 42
Crouch, Hubert 95
Emeagwali, Dale 31
Jarvis, Erich 67
Malveaux, Floyd 54

Pickett, Cecil 39

Biotechnology
Dabiri, John 93
Donald, Arnold 36, 126
Haynie, Sharon 94
Juma, Calestous 57
Uys, Ashley 125
Wambugu, Florence 42

**Birmingham (AL) city govern-
ment**
Arrington, Richard 24, 100
Bell, William A., Sr. 122
Kincaid, Bernard 28
Langford, Larry P. 74
Nunn, Annetta 43

**Birmingham (AL) Police De-
partment**
Nunn, Annetta 43
Woods, Abraham, Jr. 74

Bishop College
Cottrell, Comer 11

**Black Alliance for Educational
Options**
Fuller, Howard L. 37

Black American West Museum
Stewart, Paul Wilbur 12

Black arts movement
Baraka, Amiri 1, 38, 118
Barrett, Lindsay 43
Caldwell, Benjamin 46
Cornish, Sam 50
Cortez, Jayne 43, 109
Cortor, Eldzier 42
Cruse, Harold 54
Dent, Thomas C. 50
Donaldson, Jeff 46
Dumas, Henry 41
Gayle, Addison, Jr. 41
Giovanni, Nikki 9, 39, 85
Henderson, David 53
Hoagland, Everett H. 45
Neal, Larry 38
Pomare, Eleo 72
Sebree, Charles 40
Smith, Vincent D. 48
Touré, Askia 47
X, Marvin 45

**Black Coaches Association
(BCA)**
Freeman, Marianna 23
Keith, Floyd A. 61

**Black Consciousness move-
ment**
Biko, Steven 4
Fanon, Frantz 44
Fuller, Hoyt 44
Muhammad, Elijah 4
Ramphele, Mamphela 29

Black Enterprise magazine
Graves, Butch 77
Graves, Earl G. 1, 35
Wallace, Phyllis A. 9

**Black Entertainment Televi-
sion (BET)**
Gordon, Ed 10, 53
Greely, M. Gasby 27

Holmes, T. J. **98**
Johnson, Robert L. **3, 39, 121**
Johnson, Sheila Crump **48**
Jones, Bobby **20, 94**
Lee, Debra L. **62**
McCrary Anthony, Crystal **70**
Rolle, Janet **97**
Smiley, Tavis **20, 68**

Black Filmmakers Hall of Fame
Barnett, Etta Moten **18, 56**
Blake, Eubie **29**
Browne, Roscoe Lee **66**
Carroll, Diahann **9**
Carroll, Vinnette **29, 136**
Carter, Benny **46**
Cash, Rosalind **28**
Crothers, Scatman **19**
Davis, Sammy, Jr. **18**
de Passe, Suzanne **25**
Dee, Ruby **8, 50, 68, 122**
Dixon, Ivan **69**
Dunham, Katherine **4, 59**
Fetchit, Stepin **32**
Glover, Danny **1, 24, 103**
Greaves, William **38, 123**
Johnson, Hall **90**
Lincoln, Abbey **3, 88**
Madame Sul-Te-Wan **95**
McDaniel, Hattie **5**
McKinney, Nina Mae **40**
McQueen, Butterfly **6, 54**
Micheaux, Oscar **7**
Miles, William **112**
Muse, Clarence Edouard **21**
Nicholas, Fayard **20, 57, 61**
Nicholas, Harold **20**
Norman, Maidie **20**
Parks, Gordon **1, 35, 58**
Peters, Brock **96**
Poitier, Sidney **11, 36**
Robeson, Paul **2**
Schultz, Michael A. **6**
Tyson, Cicely **7, 51, 112**
Van Peebles, Melvin **7, 95**
Washington, Fredi **10**
Williams, Billy Dee **8, 105**
Wilson, August **7, 33, 55**

Black History Month
Woodson, Carter G. **2**

Black nationalism
Caldwell, Benjamin **46**
Carmichael, Stokely **5, 26**
Cuffe, Paul **98**
Donaldson, Jeff **46**
Farrakhan, Louis **2**
Forman, James **7, 51**
Garvey, Marcus **1**
Heard, Nathan C. **45**
Innis, Roy **5**
Muhammad, Elijah **4**
Obadele, Imari **84**
Turner, Henry McNeal **5**
X, Malcolm **1**
York, Dwight D. **71**

Black Panther Party (BPP)
Abu-Jamal, Mumia **15**
Al-Amin, Jamil Abdullah **6**
bin Wahad, Dhoruba **85**
Brown, Elaine **8**

Carmichael, Stokely **5**
Cleaver, Eldridge **5**
Cleaver, Kathleen Neal **29**
Cox, Donald Lee **93**
Davis, Angela **5, 114**
Douglas, Emory **89**
Forman, James **7, 51**
Hampton, Fred **18**
Hilliard, David **7, 105**
Jackson, George Lester **14**
Joseph, Jamal **101**
Kimbro, Warren **76**
Neal, Larry **38**
Newton, Huey **2**
Pratt, Geronimo **18, 95**
Rush, Bobby **26, 76**
Seale, Bobby **3**
Shakur, Afeni **67, 135**
Shakur, Assata **6**

Black Power movement
Al-Amin, Jamil Abdullah **6**
Brown, Elaine **8**
Carmichael, Stokely **5, 26**
Dodson, Howard, Jr. **7, 52**
Donaldson, Jeff **46**
Dumas, Henry **41**
Hare, Nathan **44**
McKissick, Floyd B. **3**

Black Think Tank
Hare, Nathan **44**

Blackvoices.com
Cooper, Barry **33**

Black World magazine
See *Negro Digest* magazine

Blogging
Contee, Cheryl **88**
Twitty, Michael **134**

Blues
Ace, Johnny **36**
Aces, The **117**
Adams, Alberta **133**
Allison, Luther **111**
Amy, Curtis **114**
Arnold, Billy Boy **112**
Arnold, Kokomo **116**
Austin, Lovie **40**
Banks, Chico **134**
Barnes, Roosevelt "Booba" **33**
Bell, Carey **114**
Bibb, Eric **49, 123**
Big Maybelle **117**
Big Time Sarah **45, 134**
Bland, Bobby **36, 113**
Bombino **112**
Brim, John **117**
Broonzy, Big Bill **82**
Brown, Charles **23**
Brown, Nappy **73**
Burbridge, Kofi **120**
Burns, Eddie **44**
Burnside, R. L. **56**
Carr, Leroy **49**
Chambers Brothers, The **116**
Chenier, C. J. **134**
Chenier, Clifton **134**
Clark, Sharón **105**
Clarke, Kenny **27**
Clayton, Doctor **120**
Collins, Albert **12**

Copeland, Johnny **110**
Copeland, Shemekia **110**
Cotton, James **123**
Cox, Ida **42**
Cray, Robert **30, 132**
Crudup, Arthur **115**
Davis, Gary **41**
Davis, Guy **36**
Davis, Tyrone **54**
Dawkins, Jimmy **111**
Dixon, Willie **4**
Dorsey, Thomas **15**
Edwards, David **122**
Ellis, Dorothy **131**
Estes, Sleepy John **33**
Évora, Cesária **12, 99**
Ford, T-Model **91, 113**
Freeman, Yvette **27**
Fuller, Blind Boy **86**
Fulson, Lowell **118**
Gaines, Grady **38**
Guitar Slim **125**
Guy, Buddy **31**
Handy, W. C. **8**
Harris, Corey **39, 73**
Harris, Wynonie **102**
Hart, Alvin Youngblood **61, 132**
Hegamin, Lucille **120**
Hemphill, Jessie Mae **33, 59**
Holiday, Billie **1**
Homesick James **124**
Hooker, John Lee **30**
Hopkins, Lightnin' **83**
House, Son **8**
Howlin' Wolf **9**
Humes, Helen **128**
Hunter, Alberta **42**
Hurt, Mississippi John **84**
Hutto, J. B. **129**
Jackson, John **36**
James, Elmore **114**
James, Skip **38**
Jefferson, Blind Lemon **81**
Johnson, Blind Willie **136**
Johnson, Buddy **36**
Johnson, Lonnie **85**
Johnson, Syl **97**
Johnson, Tommy **106**
Keb' Mo' **36, 124**
King, B. B. **7, 129**
King, Chris Thomas **120**
King, Freddie **92**
Kirkland, Eddie **99**
LaVette, Bettye **85**
Leadbelly **82**
Lenoir, J. B. **117**
Lipscomb, Mance **49**
Little Milton **36**
Little Walter **36**
Lockwood, Robert, Jr. **120**
Magic Sam **131**
Magic Slim **110**
Mahal, Taj **39**
Martin, Sara **38**
McCracklin, Jimmy **108**
McGriff, Jimmy **72**
McShann, Jay **110**
McTell, Blind Willie **89**
Memphis Slim **105**
Merriweather, Big Maceo **109**
Minner, D. C. **133**
Mississippi Sheiks **122**
Montgomery, Little Brother **117**

Moore, Johnny B. **38**
Murphy, Matt **117**
Muse, Clarence Edouard **21**
Neal, Kenny **123**
Neal, Raful **44, 121**
Nighthawk, Robert **121**
Odetta **37, 74**
Owens, Jack **38**
Parker, Charlie **20**
Parker, Junior **116**
Patton, Charley **107**
Peebles, Ann **114**
Pena, Paul **58**
Perkins, Pinetop **70**
Peterson, James **38**
Pitchford, Lonnie **133**
Professor Longhair **109**
Pryor, Snooky **119**
Rachell, Yank **129**
Rawls, Lou **17, 57**
Reed, A. C. **36**
Reed, Jimmy **38**
Robinson, Fenton **38**
Rogers, Jimmy **38**
Ross, Isaiah "Doc" **40**
Rush, Bobby **78**
Rush, Otis **38**
Seals, Son **56**
Shaw, Eddie **136**
Shines, Johnny **116**
Slim Harpo **120**
Smith, Bessie **3**
Smith, Clarence **113**
Smith, Mamie **32**
Smith, Trixie **34**
Spann, Otis **107**
Spivey, Victoria **119**
Stackhouse, Houston **122**
Sumlin, Hubert **101**
Sunnyland Slim **118**
Sykes, Roosevelt **20**
Tail Dragger **112**
Tampa Red **63**
Taylor, Eddie **116**
Taylor, Hound Dog **120**
Taylor, Koko **40, 80**
Terry, Sonny **88**
Thomas, Tabby **119**
Tucker, Tommy **127**
Turner, Big Joe **92**
Turner, Ike **68**
Walker, Joe Louis **118**
Walker, T-Bone **111**
Wallace, Sippie **1**
Washington, Dinah **22**
Waters, Ethel **7**
Waters, Muddy **34**
Watson, Johnny "Guitar" **18**
Webster, Katie **29**
Wellington, Valerie **118**
Wells, Junior **102**
White, Bukka **120**
White, Josh, Jr. **52**
Williams, Jody **113**
Williams, Joe **5, 25**
Williamson, Sonny Boy **84**
Williamson, Sonny Boy **134**
Witherspoon, Jimmy **113**
Young, Johnny **120**
Young, Zora **129**

Blues Hall of Fame
Allison, Luther **111**
Bland, Bobby **36, 113**
Broonzy, Big Bill **82**
Chenier, Clifton **134**
Clay, Otis **112, 133**
Cotton, James **123**
Cray, Robert **30, 132**
Crudup, Arthur **115**
Edwards, David **122**
Fulson, Lowell **118**
Guitar Slim **125**
Hopkins, Lightnin' **83**
Hunter, Alberta **42**
Hurt, Mississippi John **84**
Hutto, J. B. **129**
Johnson, Blind Willie **136**
King, B. B. **7, 129**
Lenoir, J. B. **117**
Little Milton **36**
Lockwood, Robert, Jr. **120**
Nighthawk, Robert **121**
Parker, Junior **116**
Shaw, Eddie **136**
Shines, Johnny **116**
Slim Harpo **120**
Sunnyland Slim **118**
Taylor, Eddie **116**
Taylor, Hound Dog **120**
Toussaint, Allen **60, 132**
Walker, Joe Louis **118**
White, Bukka **120**
Williamson, Sonny Boy **84**
Williamson, Sonny Boy **134**

Bobsledding
Flowers, Vonetta **35**
Hines, Garrett **35**
Jones, Randy **35**
Moses, Edwin **8**
Williams, Lauryn **58, 127**

Bodybuilding
Haney, Lee **77**
Murray, Lenda **10**

Boeing Company, The
Bell, James A. **50**
Grooms, Henry R(andall) **50**
Mills, Joseph C. **51**
Robinson-Berry, Joan **94**

Boogie-woogie music
Brooks, Hadda **40**
Smith, Clarence **113**

Boston Celtics basketball team
Allen, Ray **82**
Chaney, Don **98**
Cooper, Charles "Chuck" **47**
Fox, Rick **27**
Parish, Robert **43**
Pierce, Paul **71**
Rivers, Doc **25, 81**
Russell, Bill **8**
Sanders, Satch **77**
White, Jo Jo **112**

Boston Red Sox baseball team
Baylor, Don **6**
Martínez, Pedro **81, 126**
Ortiz, David **52, 82**

Rice, Jim **75**
Tiant, Luis **102**
Vaughn, Mo **16**

Botswana government
Khama, Ian **95**
Masire, Quett **5**
Mogae, Festus Gontebanye **19, 79**

Bowling
Branham, George, III **50**
Terrell-Kearney, Kim **83**

Boxing
Ali, Laila **27, 63**
Ali, Muhammad **2, 16, 52, 136**
Armstrong, Henry **104**
Bowe, Riddick **6, 107**
Bozella, Dewey **97**
Broner, Adrien **109**
Carter, Rubin **26, 121**
Charles, Ezzard **95**
DeGale, James **74**
Dixon, George **52**
Dokes, Michael **105**
Douglas, Buster **127**
Ellis, Jimmy **44, 127**
Foreman, George **1, 15**
Forrest, Vernon **40, 79**
Frazier, Joe **19, 98**
Frazier-Lyde, Jacqui **31**
Futch, Eddie **33**
Gans, Joe **91**
Gibson, Truman K., Jr. **60**
Griffith, Emile **113**
Hagler, Marvelous Marvin **102**
Haye, David **82**
Hearns, Thomas **29**
Holmes, Larry **20, 68**
Holyfield, Evander **6**
Hopkins, Bernard **35, 69, 105**
Johnson, Jack **8**
Jones, Roy, Jr. **22, 134**
King, Don **14, 128**
Lee, Canada **8**
Leonard, Sugar Ray **15**
Lewis, Butch **71, 99**
Lewis, Lennox **27**
Louis, Joe **5**
Lyle, Ron **125**
Mayweather, Floyd **57, 104**
Moore, Archie **120**
Moore, Davey **105**
Moorer, Michael **19, 132**
Mosley, Shane **32**
Muhammad, Jabir Herbert **72**
Mundine, Anthony **56**
Norton, Ken **101, 115**
Ortiz, Luis **134**
Page, Greg **78**
Patterson, Floyd **19, 58**
Perkins, Eddie **103**
Robinson, Sugar Ray **18**
Rose, Lionel **56**
Savón, Félix **105**
Shavers, Earnie **127**
Stevenson, Teófilo **103**
Steward, Emanuel **18, 106**
Stiverne, Bermane **128**
Tate, John **107**
Taylor, Jermain **60**
Terrell, Ernie **118**
Toney, James **89**
Tyson, Mike **28, 44, 93**

Walcott, Jersey Joe **102**
Ward, Andre **62**
Weaver, Mike **109**
Whitaker, Pernell **10, 89**
Wilder, Deontay **121**
Wills, Harry **80**
Wolfe, Ann **82**
Wright, Chalky **103**
Young, Jimmy **54**

Boys Choir of Harlem
Turnbull, Walter **13, 60**

BPP
See Black Panther Party

Brazil government
da Silva, Benedita **5**
Nascimento, Abdias do **93**
Silva, Marina **80**

Breast cancer awareness
Brown, Zora Kramer **12**
Norton, Meredith **72**
Riperton, Minnie **32**

British Broadcasting Company (BBC)
Armah, Esther **87**
Figueroa, John J. **40**
Stuart, Moira **82**

British Film Institute
Akomfrah, John **37**

British government
Abbott, Diane **9, 132**
Amos, Valerie **41**
Boateng, Paul Yaw **56**
Grant, Bernie **57**
King, Oona **27**
Pitt, David Thomas **10**

British Virgin Islands government
Stoutt, H. Lavity **83**

Broadcasting
Abudu, Mo **121**
Allen, Byron **3, 24, 97**
Ashley, Maurice **15, 47**
Bettis, Jerome **64**
Blackmon, Brenda **58**
Bostic, Joe **95**
Bradley, Ed **2, 59**
Branch, William Blackwell **39**
Brown, Les **5**
Brown, Tony **3**
Brown, Vivian **27**
Brunson, Dorothy **1, 87**
Bryant, Howard **130**
Clayton, Xernona **3, 45**
Cornelius, Don **4, 100**
Crump, Steven **96**
Curry, Dell **126**
Dee, Merri **55**
Evans, Harry **25**
Figueroa, John J. **40**
Freeman, Aaron **52**
Fuentes, Tito **123**
Garrison, Zina **2, 133**
Goode, Mal **13**
Gumbel, Bryant **14, 80**
Gumbel, Greg **8**
Hall, Tamron **96**

Hamblin, Ken **10**
Hickman, Fred **11**
Holt, Lester **66**
Hunter-Gault, Charlayne **6, 31**
Jackson, Hal **41, 104**
Jackson, Mark **121**
Johnson, Rafer **33**
Joyner, Tom **19, 90**
Kellogg, Clark **64**
Kennedy-Overton, Jayne Harris **46**
King, Gayle **19, 99**
Langhart Cohen, Janet **19, 60**
Lawson, Jennifer **1, 50**
Lemon, Don **94**
Lewis, Delano **7**
Lomax, Louis E. **90**
Mabrey, Vicki **26**
Madison, Joseph E. **17**
McEwen, Mark **5**
McFarland, Roland **49**
Melton, Frank **81**
Mickelbury, Penny **28**
Miller, Cheryl **10, 74**
Ming, Mel **106**
Mitchell, Russ **21, 73**
Morgan, Joe **9, 96**
Morton, Frederick A., Jr. **93**
Neville, Arthel **53**
Peete, Rodney **60**
Pinckney, Sandra **56**
Pinkston, W. Randall **24**
Quarles, Norma **25**
Reynolds, Star Jones **10, 27, 61**
Roberts, Deborah **35**
Roberts, Robin **16, 54, 113**
Rodgers, Johnathan **6, 51**
Rose, Jalen **108**
Russell, Bill **8**
Sanders, Deion **4, 31, 96**
Setmayer, Tara **130**
Shaw, Bernard **2, 28**
Simmons, Jamal **72**
Simpson, Carole **6, 30**
Smiley, Tavis **20, 68**
Smith, Michael **129**
Steele, Sage **115**
Stewart, Alison **13**
Strahan, Michael **35, 81, 135**
Swann, Lynn **28**
Syler, Rene **53**
Thompson, Mychal **126**
Watts, Rolonda **9**
White, Bill **1, 48**
Whitlock, Jason **78, 130**
Williams, Armstrong **29**
Williams, Juan **35, 80**
Williams, Montel **4, 57**
Winfrey, Oprah **2, 15, 61, 106**

Brookings Institute
Ladner, Joyce A. **42**

Brooklyn Dodgers baseball team
Black, Joe **75**
Campanella, Roy **25**
Gilliam, Jim **122**
Newcombe, Don **24**
Robinson, Jackie **6**

Brotherhood of Sleeping Car Porters
Randolph, A. Philip **3**
Tucker, Rosina **14**

Brown University
Beckham, Barry **41**
Simmons, Ruth **13, 38**

Brown v. Board of Education of Topeka
Boulware, Harold R. **109**
Brown, Oliver Leon **94**
Carter, Robert L. **51, 100**
Clark, Kenneth B. **5, 52**
Franklin, John Hope **5, 77**
Henderson, Zelma **71**
Hill, Oliver W. **24, 63**
Houston, Charles Hamilton **4**
Malone Jones, Vivian **59**
Marshall, Thurgood **1, 44**
Motley, Constance Baker **10, 55**
Redding, Louis L. **26**
Robinson, Spottswood W., III **22**
Simkins, Modjeska Monteith **112**

Buffalo Bills football team
Simpson, O. J. **15, 100**
Smith, Bruce **80**
Thomas, Thurman **75**

Bull-riding
Sampson, Charles **13**

Burkina Faso government
Kaboré, Roch Marc Christian **132**
Kafando, Michel **131**

Burundi government
Ndadaye, Melchior **7**
Nkurunziza, Pierre **78, 130**
Ntaryamira, Cyprien **8**

Cabinet
See U.S. Cabinet

Cable News Network (CNN)
Chideya, Farai **14, 61**
Hickman, Fred **11**
Malveaux, Suzanne **88**
O'Brien, Soledad **88**
Quarles, Norma **25**
Rolle, Janet **97**
Shaw, Bernard **2, 28**
Sidner, Sara **105**
Watson, Carlos **50**

Caldecott medal
Dillon, Leo **103**
Pinkney, Jerry **15, 124**

California Angels baseball team
See Los Angeles Angels baseball team

California state government
Bass, Karen **70**
Brown, Janice Rogers **43**
Brown, Willie **7, 85**
Dixon, Julian C. **24**
Dymally, Mervyn **42**
Harris, Kamala D. **64, 122**
Hawkins, Augustus F. **68**
Lee, Barbara **25, 102**
Millender-McDonald, Juanita **21, 61**
Richardson, Laura **81**
Riles, Wilson C. **79**
Waters, Maxine **3, 67, 103**

Watson, Diane **41**

California State University
Cobb, Jewel Plummer **42**
Karenga, Maulana **10, 71**

California Supreme Court
Brown, Janice Rogers **43**

Calypso
Belafonte, Harry **4, 65**
Lord Invader **117**
Lord Kitchener **110**
Premice, Josephine **41**
Rhoden, Wayne **70**
Rudder, David **79**

Cameroon government
Ahidjo, Ahmadou **81**
Biya, Paul **28, 114**
Oyono, Ferdinand **38**

Canadian Football League (CFL)
Anderson, Ezzrett **95**
Clemons, Michael "Pinball" **64**
Gilliam, Frank **23**
Moon, Warren **8, 66**
Thrower, Willie **35**
Weathers, Carl **10**

Canada government
Alexander, Lincoln **106**
Augustine, Jean **53**
Brown, Rosemary **62**
Cools, Anne **64**
Jean, Michaëlle; **70**
Lewis, Daurene **72**
Sparks, Corinne Etta **53**

Cancer research
Adams-Campbell, Lucille L. **60**
Chinn, May Edward **26**
Clark, Celeste **15**
Daly, Marie Maynard **37, 134**
Dunston, Georgia Mae **48**
Freeman, Harold P. **23**
Green, Hadiyah-Nicole **133**
Leffall, Lasalle **3, 64**
Olopade, Olufunmilayo Falusi **58**

Capital punishment
Correia, De'Jaun **93**
Hawkins, Steven **14**
Stevenson, Bryan **128**

Caribbean dance
Ailey, Alvin **8**
Dunham, Katherine **4, 59**
Fagan, Garth **18, 98**
Nichols, Nichelle **11**

Caribbean literature/West Indian literature
Beken **111**
Breeze, Jean "Binta" **37**
Carter, Martin **49**
Cartey, Wilfred **47**
Channer, Colin **36**
Coombs, Orde M. **44**
Dabydeen, David **48**
Guy, Rosa **5**
Hearne, John Edgar Caulwell **45**
Hill, Errol **40, 135**
Markham, E. A. **37**
Marshall, Paule **7, 77**

McKay, Claude **6**
Nunez, Elizabeth **62, 112**
Walcott, Derek **5, 94**

Caribbean music
Ellis, Alton **74**
Ellis, Hortense **97**
Lefel, Edith **41**
Ranglin, Ernest **78**

Casting
Cannon, Reuben **50**

Carolina Panthers
Davis, Thomas **132**
Smith, Steve **120**

Cartoonists/Comics artists
Armstrong, Robb **15**
Bell, Darrin **77**
Brandon, Barbara **3**
Brown, Robert **65**
Campbell, E. Simms **13**
Fax, Elton **48**
Harrington, Oliver W. **9, 136**
Magruder, Nilah **134**
McDuffie, Dwayne **62**
McGruder, Aaron **28, 56, 120**
Ormes, Jackie **73**
Smith, Bruce W. **53**
Turner, Morrie **122**

Catering
See Restaurants/Catering/Cooking

Catholicism
See Roman Catholic Church

CBS
See Columbia Broadcasting System

CDC
See Centers for Disease Control and Prevention

CDF
See Children's Defense Fund

Celebrity
Brown, Bobbi Kristina **130**

Censorship
Butts, Calvin O., III **9, 90**

Centers for Disease Control and Prevention (CDC)
Fenton, Kevin **87**
Gayle, Helene D. **3**
Satcher, David **7, 57, 111**
Wisdom, Kimberlydawn **57**

Central African Republic government
Bozizé, François **96, 117**
Djotodia, Michel **117**

Certified public accountant
Jones, Thomas W. **41**
Washington, Mary T. **57**

CFL
See Canadian Football League

Chad government
Déby, Idriss **30, 125**
Habré, Hissène **6, 104**

Chemistry
Brady, St. Elmo **107**
Daly, Marie Maynard **37, 134**

Hall, Lloyd A. **8**
Hammond, Paula **119**
Haynie, Sharon **94**
Humphries, Frederick **20**
Julian, Percy Lavon **6**
King, Reatha Clark **65**
Massie, Samuel Proctor, Jr. **29**
Mays, William G. **34**
McBay, Henry C. **91**
McCain, Franklin **119**
Mensah, Thomas **48**
Quarterman, Lloyd Albert **4**

Chess
Ashley, Maurice **15, 47**

Chicago Bears football team
Dent, Richard **97**
Page, Alan **7**
Payton, Walter **11, 25**
Sayers, Gale **28**
Singletary, Mike **4, 76**
Thrower, Willie **35**

Chicago Bulls basketball team
Brand, Elton **31**
Jordan, Michael **6, 21**

Chicago city government
Berry, Edwin C. **81**
De Priest, Oscar Stanton **80**
Foxx, Kim **134**
Jackson, Sandi **108**
Jones, Emil, Jr. **74**
Jones, John **89**
Kelley, Cliff **75**
Lane, Vincent **5**
Metcalfe, Ralph **26**
Sawyer, Eugene **81**
Taylor, Robert Rochon **104**
Tillman, Dorothy **76**
Washington, Harold **6**

Chicago Cubs baseball team
Banks, Ernie **33, 126**
Carter, Joe **30**
Sosa, Sammy **21, 44**
Williams, Billy **86**

Chicago Defender
Abbott, Robert Sengstacke **27**
Burley, Dan **96**
Holt, Nora **38**
Martin, Roland S. **49, 84**
Ormes, Jackie **73**
Payne, Ethel L. **28**

Chicago Eight
Seale, Bobby **3**

Chicago Negro Chamber of Commerce
Fuller, S. B. **13**

Chicago Police Department
Hillard, Terry **25**
Holton, Hugh, Jr. **39**

Chicago Reporter
Calhoun, Lillian Scott **87**
Washington, Laura S. **18**

Chicago Tribune
Page, Clarence **4**

Chicago White Sox baseball team
Baines, Harold **32**
Doby, Lawrence Eugene, Sr. **16, 41**

Johnson, Clifford "Connie" 52
Minoso, Minnie 89, 127
Thomas, Frank 12, 51
Williams, Ken 68

Child care
Tillman, Deborah 98

Children's Defense Fund (CDF)
Edelman, Marian Wright 5, 42
Williams, Maggie 7, 71

Children's literature
Asim, Jabari 71
Berry, James 41
Bryan, Ashley 41, 104
Curtis, Christopher Paul 26, 113
De Veaux, Alexis 44
Feelings, Muriel 44
Graham, Lorenz 48
Greenfield, Eloise 9
Haskins, James 36, 54
Johnson, Angela 52
Jordan, Deloris 108
Lester, Julius 9, 115
Magruder, Nilah 134
Mollel, Tololwa 38
Myers, Walter Dean 8, 20, 123
Nelson, Kadir 115
Okara, Gabriel 37
Palmer, Everard 37
Pinkney, Jerry 15, 124
Shelton, Paula Young 86
Woodson, Jacqueline 125
Yarbrough, Camille 40

Chi-Lites
Record, Eugene 60

Chiropractics
Ford, Clyde W. 40
Reese, Milous J., Jr. 51
Westbrooks, Bobby 51

Choreography
Abraham, Kyle 116
Acogny, Germaine 55
Ailey, Alvin 8
Alexander, Khandi 43
Allen, Debbie 13, 42
Atkins, Cholly 40
Babatunde, Obba 35
Bass, Holly 134
Beatty, Talley 35
Brown, Ronald K. 91
Byrd, Donald 10
Collins, Janet 33, 64
Davis, Chuck 33
de Lavallade, Carmen 78
de Passe, Suzanne 25
De Shields, André 72
Dove, Ulysses 5
Dunham, Katherine 4, 59
Ellington, Mercedes 34
Fagan, Garth 18, 98
Faison, George 16
Glover, Savion 14
Hall, Arthur 39
Harris, Rennie 120
Henson, Darrin 33
Jamison, Judith 7, 67, 96
Jeune, Vitolio 98
Johnson, Virginia 9
Jones, Bill T. 1, 46, 80

King, Alonzo 38
LeTang, Henry 66
Manning, Frankie 78
Miller, Bebe 3
Mitchell, Arthur 2, 47
Nicholas, Fayard 20, 57
Nicholas, Harold 20
Pomare, Eleo 72
Primus, Pearl 6, 125
Rhoden, Dwight 40
Richardson, Desmond 39
Robinson, Cleo Parker 38
Robinson, Fatima 34
Rodgers, Rod 36
Spears, Warren 52
Storyboard P 118
Tyson, Andre 40
Wilson, Reggie 116
Zollar, Jawole 28

Chrysler Corporation
Colbert, Virgis William 17
Farmer, Forest 1
Gilles, Ralph 61
Richie, Leroy C. 18

Cincinnati city government
Berry, Theodore M. 31
Mallory, Mark 62

Cincinnati Reds baseball team
Blair, Paul 36
Davis, Eric 116
Larkin, Barry 24
Morgan, Joe 9, 96
Phillips, Brandon 116
Reese, Pokey 28
Robinson, Frank 9, 87

Cinematography
Dickerson, Ernest 6, 17

Circus
Iverson, Johnathan Lee 22, 100
McFarlan, Tyron 60
Walker, Cedric "Ricky" 19

Citigroup
Gaines, Brenda 41
Jones, Thomas W. 41
McGuire, Raymond J. 57
Parsons, Richard 11, 33, 124

City government--U.S.
Adams, Floyd, Jr. 12, 122
Bell, Michael 40
Bellamy, Terry 58
Benjamin, Steve 98
Bobb, Robert C. 83
Bradley, Jennette B. 40
Brown, Aja 115
Brown, Alvin 96
Brown, Willie 7, 85
Burris, Chuck 21
Bush, Gordon 82
Caesar, Shirley 19
Cannon, Patrick 120
Celestin, Josaphat 101
Clayton, Constance 1
Cleaver, Emanuel 4, 45, 68, 107
Coleman, Michael 28, 79
Craig-Jones, Ellen Walker 44
Davis, Doris A. 100
Dellums, Ronald 2, 81
DuPree, Johnny 96

Ford, Jack 39
Ford, Johnny 70
Foxx, Anthony 81, 123
Francois, Terry A. 106
Gibbs, Mifflin W. 99
Gillum, Andrew 128
Glover, Cedric B. 103
Harp, Toni 123
Hatcher, Richard G. 55
Hayes, James C. 10
Herenton, Willie W. 24, 81
Hicks-Hudson, Paula 136
Holden, Kip 120
Jackson, Eric 127
James, Sly 107
Johnson, Harvey, Jr. 24, 82
Johnson, Kevin 70, 132
Jones, Dwight C. 122
Jordan, Charles 122
Lee, Howard N. 136
Love, Mia 96, 125
Lowery, Myron 80
Lumumba, Chokwe 118
Mack, Tony 104
Mallett, Conrad, Jr. 16
Marks, John R., III 123
Marsh, Henry 32
Melton, Frank 81
Morial, Ernest "Dutch" 26
Morial, Marc H. 20, 51
Murrell, Sylvia Marilyn 49
Parker, Vernon 97
Patterson, J. O., Jr. 80
Perkins, James, Jr. 55
Powell, Adam Clayton, Jr. 3
Powell, Debra A. 23
Price, McKinley L. 136
Primas, Randy 106
Redd, Dana 93
Turner, Sylvester 136
Tyler, Ollie 128
Usry, James L. 23, 134
Warren, Lovely 136
Weaver, Karen 134
Wharton, A. C., Jr. 110
Widener, Warren 99
Williams, Dennis P. 123
Wilson, Lionel 99
Yarber, Tony 129

City government--international
Tau, Mpho Parks 124

Civil rights
Abernathy, Ralph 1
Agyeman, Jaramogi Abebe 10, 63
Al-Amin, Jamil Abdullah 6
Alexander, Clifford 26
Alexander, Michelle 98
Amaker, Norman 63
Anthony, Wendell 25
Aristide, Jean-Bertrand 6, 45
Arnwine, Barbara 28
Baker, Ella 5
Baker, Josephine 3
Ballance, Frank W. 41
Ballard, John 95
Barbee, Lloyd Augustus 71
Barrow, Willie T. 85, 128
Bashir, Halima 73
Bass, Charlotta Spears 40
Bates, Daisy 13, 135
Baugh, David 23

Beals, Melba Pattillo 15, 94
Bell, James Madison 40
Berry, Theodore M. 31
Bevel, James L. 75
Bibb, Leon 132
Biko, Steven 4
Blackwell, Gloria 127
Bond, Julian 2, 35, 106, 130
Booker, Simeon 23
Borders, William Holmes 94
Boyd, John W., Jr. 20, 72
Boynton Robinson, Amelia 131
Bradle, David Henry, Jr. 39
Bridges, Ruby 77
Brock, Roslyn McCallister 86
Brooks, Tyrone 59
Brown, Byrd 49
Brown, Charlotte Hawkins 106
Brown, Elaine 8
Brown, Homer S. 47
Brown, Tony 3
Brown, Wesley 23
Brown, Willa 40
Burks, Mary Fair 40
Caldwell, Earl 60
Cameron, James 80
Carmichael, Stokely 5, 26
Carr, Johnnie 69
Carter, Mandy 11
Carter, Rubin 26, 121
Cary, Mary Ann Shadd 30
Catto, Octavius V. 83
Cayton, Horace 26
Chambers, Julius 3
Chavis, Benjamin 6
Chestnut, J. L., Jr. 73
Clark, Septima 7
Clay, William Lacy 8
Cleaver, Eldridge 5
Cleaver, Kathleen Neal 29
Cobb, W. Montague 39
Cobbs, Price M. 9
Coleman, James E., Jr. 79
Cooper, Anna Julia 20
Cunningham, Evelyn 23, 85
Curvin, Robert 132
Davis, Angela 5, 114
Davis, Artur 41
Davis, James E. 50
Dent, Thomas C. 50
Diallo, Amadou 27
Diggs, Charles C. 21
Divine, Father 7
Dobbs, John Wesley 89
Dodson, Howard, Jr. 7, 52
Douglass, Frederick 87
Du Bois, W. E. B. 3
Dudley, Edward R. 58
Due, Patricia Stephens 100
Dukes, Hazel Nell 56
Dumas, Henry 41
Eagleson, William Lewis 90
Edwards, Willis 104
Ellison, Ralph 7
Evers, Medgar 3
Evers, Myrlie 8
Farmer, James 2, 64
Farmer-Paellmann, Deadria 43
Fisher, Ada Lois Sipuel 76
Forman, James 7, 51
Fortune, T. Thomas 6
Foster, Marie 48
Franklin, C. L. 68

French, D. M. **94**
Gaines, Ernest J. **7**
Gaines, Lloyd **79**
Gibson, William F. **6**
Gomillion, Charles **90**
Granger, Lester B. **75**
Gray, Fred **37**
Gregory, Dick **1, 54**
Grillo, Evelio **95**
Grimké, Archibald H. **9**
Guinier, Lani **7, 30**
Guyot, Lawrence **108**
Hall, Elliott S. **24**
Hamer, Fannie Lou **6**
Hampton, Fred **18**
Hampton, Henry **6**
Harding, Vincent **67, 130**
Harper, Frances Ellen Watkins **11**
Hastie, William H. **8**
Hatcher, Richard G. **55**
Hawkins, Augustus F. **68**
Hawkins, Steven **14**
Hayes, Dennis **54**
Hedgeman, Anna Arnold **22**
Height, Dorothy I. **2, 23, 78**
Henderson, Thelton E. **68**
Henry, Aaron **19**
Higginbotham, A. Leon, Jr. **13, 25**
Hill, Jesse, Jr. **13**
Hill, Oliver W. **24, 63**
Hilliard, David **7, 105**
Hobson, Julius W. **44**
Holland, Endesha Ida Mae **3, 57**
Hollowell, Donald L. **57**
Hooks, Benjamin L. **2, 85**
Hope, Lugenia Burns **89**
Houston, Charles Hamilton **4**
Howard, M. William, Jr. **26**
Irvis, K. Leroy **67**
Jackson, Alexine Clement **22**
Jackson, Jesse **1, 27, 72**
Jackson, Jimmie Lee **126**
James, Daniel, Jr. **16**
Jemison, T. J. **119**
Jenkins, Ray **77**
Johns, Vernon **38**
Johnson, Georgia Douglas **41**
Johnson, James Weldon **5**
Johnson, Norma H. **17, 97**
Jones, Clarence B. **114**
Jones, Elaine R. **7, 45**
Jones, John **89**
Jones, William A., Jr. **61**
Jordan, Barbara **4, 78**
Jordan, June **7, 35**
Jordan, Vernon E. **3, 35**
Julian, Percy Lavon **6**
Karim, Benjamin **61**
Kennedy, Florynce **12, 33**
Kenyatta, Jomo **5**
Kidd, Mae Street **39**
King, Bernice **4, 81**
King, Coretta Scott **3, 57**
King, Martin Luther, III **20**
King, Martin Luther, Jr. **1**
King, Martin Luther, Sr. **89**
King, Preston **28**
King, Robert Hillary **84**
King, Rodney **103**
King, Yolanda **6**
Ladner, Joyce A. **42**
Lampkin, Daisy **19**
Lawson, James M., Jr. **90**

Lewis, William Henry **89**
Logan, Rayford W. **40**
Louis, Willie **113**
Loving, Mildred **69**
Lowery, Evelyn Gibson **115**
Lowery, Joseph **2**
Lowry, A. Leon **60**
Lucy Foster, Autherine **35**
Luper, Clara **94**
Madikizela-Mandela, Winnie **2, 35, 112**
Makeba, Miriam **2, 50, 74**
Malone Jones, Vivian **59**
Mandela, Nelson **1, 14, 77, 117**
Martin, Louis E. **16**
Martin, Ruby Grant **49**
Mays, Benjamin E. **7**
Mbeki, Thabo **14, 73**
McCain, Franklin **119**
McDonald, Gabrielle Kirk **20**
McDougall, Gay J. **11, 43**
McKissick, Floyd B. **3**
Meredith, James H. **11**
Metcalfe, Ralph **26**
Miller, Clyde **113**
Mitchell, Clarence M., Jr. **88**
Mitchell, Juanita Jackson **128**
Morgan, Irene **65**
Moody, Anne **127**
Moore, Barbara C. **49**
Moore, Harry T. **29**
Morial, Ernest "Dutch" **26**
Moses, Robert Parris **11**
Moss, Otis, Jr. **72**
Motley, Constance Baker **10, 55**
Mowry, Jess **7**
Murphy, Laura M. **43**
Murray, Pauli **38**
Nash, Diane **72**
Ndadaye, Melchior **7**
Nelson, Jill **6, 54**
Newton, Huey **2**
Nixon, Edgar Daniel **100**
Nkoli, Simon **60**
Nkomo, Joshua **4, 65**
Noble, Gil **76**
Nunn, Annetta **43**
Nzo, Alfred **15**
Orange, James **74**
Parker, Kellis E. **30**
Parks, Rosa **1, 35, 56**
Patterson, Louise **25**
Perry, Matthew J., Jr. **96**
Pincham, R. Eugene, Sr. **69**
Pinchback, P. B. S. **9**
Player, Willa B. **43**
Pleasant, Mary Ellen **9**
Plessy, Homer Adolph **31**
Poitier, Sidney **11, 36**
Powell, Adam Clayton, Jr. **3**
Price, Hugh B. **9, 54**
Randolph, A. Philip **3**
Redding, Louis L. **26**
Rivers, Eugene F., III **81**
Robeson, Paul **2**
Robinson, Jackie **6**
Robinson, Joann Gibson **100**
Robinson, Rachel **16**
Robinson, Randall **7, 46**
Robinson, Sharon **22**
Robinson, Spottswood W., III **22**
Roundtree, Dovey **80**
Rush, Bobby **26, 76**

Rustin, Bayard **4**
Sadlier, Rosemary **62**
Sales, Ruby **133**
Sanders, Malika **48**
Sané, Pierre Gabriel **21**
Saro-Wiwa, Kenule **39**
Seale, Bobby **3**
Shabazz, Attallah **6**
Shabazz, Betty **7, 26**
Shakur, Assata **6**
Sharpton, Al **21, 97**
Shelton, Paula Young **86**
Shinhoster, Earl **32**
Shores, Arthur D. **99**
Shuttlesworth, Fred **47, 98**
Simkins, Modjeska Monteith **112**
Simmons, Gwendolyn Zoharah **132**
Simon, Lateefah **95**
Simone, Nina **15, 41, 130**
Sisulu, Albertina **57, 95**
Sisulu, Sheila Violet Makate **24**
Sleet, Moneta, Jr. **5, 136**
Smith, Barbara **28**
Staupers, Mabel K. **7**
Sullivan, Leon H. **3, 30**
Sutton, Percy E. **42, 82**
Sweet, Ossian **68**
Taylor, Recy **92**
Taylor, Robert Rochon **104**
Thurman, Howard **3**
Till, Emmett **7**
Tillman, Dorothy **76**
Tolson, Melvin B. **37**
Touré, Faya Ora Rose **56**
Trotter, Monroe **9**
Tsvangirai, Morgan **26, 72**
Turner, Henry McNeal **5**
Walker, Rebecca **50**
Washington, Booker T. **4**
Washington, Fredi **10**
Webb-Christburg, Sheyann **110**
Wells, James Lesesne **10**
Wells-Barnett, Ida B. **8**
White, Walter F. **4**
Whitmore, George **106**
Wilkins, Roy **4**
Williams, Cecil **130**
Williams, Evelyn **10**
Williams, Fannie Barrier **27**
Williams, Hosea **15, 31, 123**
Williams, Robert F. **11, 136**
Wilson, William Julius **22**
Woods, Abraham, Jr. **74**
Woodson, Robert L. **10**
Wright, Nathan, Jr. **56**
X, Malcolm **1**
Yoba, Malik **11**
Young, Jean Childs **14**
Young, Whitney M., Jr. **4**

Clarinet
Bechet, Sidney **18**
Lewis, George **130**
McGill, Anthony **76**
Sweatman, Wilbur **125**

Classical music
Abdullah, Kazem **97**
Adams, Leslie **39**
Baiocchi, Regina Harris **41**
Bonds, Margaret **39**
Brown, Uzee **42**
Burleigh, Henry Thacker **56**

Coleridge-Taylor, Samuel **75**
Cook, Will Marion **40**
Dawson, William Levi **39**
DePreist, James **37, 109**
Dixon, Dean **68**
Dunner, Leslie B. **45**
Fox, Donal **114**
Freeman, Paul **39**
Imani Winds **113**
Kay, Ulysses **37**
Lewis, Henry **38**
Marian Anderson String Quartet **111**
McFerrin, Bobby **68**
McGill, Anthony **76**
Moore, Dorothy Rudd **46**
Moore, Kermit **116**
Murray, Tai **47**
Pratt, Awadagin **31**
Price, Florence **37**
Schuyler, Philippa **50**
Smith, Hale **118**
Sowande, Fela **39**
Still, William Grant **37**
Tillis, Frederick **40**
Walker, George **37**
Wilkins, Thomas Alphonso **71**
Williams, Denise **40**

Classical singers
Anderson, Marian **2, 33**
Battle, Kathleen **70**
Bumbry, Grace **5**
Burleigh, Henry Thacker **56**
Hayes, Roland **4**
Hendricks, Barbara **3, 67**
Lister, Marquita **65**
Norman, Jessye **5**
Price, Leontyne **1**
Three Mo' Tenors **35**
Williams, Denise **40**

Clergy
Abune Paulos **105**
Agyeman, Jaramogi Abebe **10, 63**
Anthony, Wendell **25**
Baker, Delbert W. **110**
Bell, Ralph S. **5**
Ben-Israel, Ben Ami **11**
Berry, Moses **84**
Black, Barry C. **47**
Bloomer, George **86**
Bowen, John W. E., Sr. **89**
Burgess, John **46**
Bynum, Juanita **31, 71**
Caesar, Shirley **19**
Caldwell, Kirbyjon **55**
Clarence 13X **126**
Cleveland, James **19**
Cook, Suzan D. Johnson **22**
Crowdy, William Saunders **109**
Dollar, Creflo **106**
Easton, Hosea **91**
Ellis, Charles H., III **79**
Falana, Lola **42**
Gilmore, Marshall **46**
Grace, Sweet Daddy **104**
Greene, Travis **134**
Gregory, Wilton **37**
Henson, Josiah **90**
Holsey, Lucius Henry **92**
Hood, James Walker **91**
Howard, M. William, Jr. **26**
Jakes, T. D. **17, 43, 116**

James, Skip 38
Jemison, Major L. 48
Johns, Vernon 38
Jones, Absalom 52
Jones, Alex 64
Jones, Robert Elijah 90
Jones, William A., Jr. 61
Karim, Benjamin 61
Kelly, Leontine 33
King, Barbara 22
King, Bernice 4, 81
Kobia, Samuel 43
Lee, Eric P. 79
Lincoln, C. Eric 38
Maxis, Theresa 62
McClurkin, Donnie 25
McGuire, George Alexander 80
McKenzie, Vashti M. 29
Michaux, Solomon Lightfoot 91
Morgan, Gertrude 63
Noble Drew Ali 100
Norful, Smokie 127
Okaalet, Peter 58
Otunga, Maurice Michael 55
Peterson, Jesse Lee 81
Phipps, Wintley 59
Reems, Ernestine Cleveland 27
Reese, Della 6, 20, 96
Reverend Ike 79
Robinson, Ida B. 106
Sentamu, John 58
Smith, Amanda Berry 109
Spencer, Peter 128
Taylor, Gardner C. 76
Thurman, Howard 3
Thurston, Stephen J. 49
Tillard, Conrad 47
Tolton, Augustine 62
Twilight, Alexander 125
Ukpabio, Helen 86
Walker, John T. 50
Washington, James Melvin 50
Watkins, Joe 86
Weeks, Thomas, III 70
Weems, Renita J. 44
White-Hammond, Gloria 61
Williams, David Rudyard 50
Williams, Frederick (B.) 63
Williams, Preston Warren, II 64
Wright, Nathan, Jr. 56
Yarber, Tony 129

Cleveland Browns football team
Brown, Jim 11, 95
Hill, Calvin 19
Motley, Marion 26
Newsome, Ozzie 26, 117
Willis, Bill 68

Cleveland city government
Jackson, Frank G. 76
Stokes, Carl 10, 73
White, Michael R. 5

Cleveland Indians baseball team
Belle, Albert 10
Carter, Joe 30
Doby, Lawrence Eugene, Sr. 16, 41
Justice, David 18
Lofton, Kenny 12
Murray, Eddie 12
Paige, Satchel 7

Robinson, Frank 9, 87
Sabathia, CC 74
Sizemore, Grady 96

CLIO Awards
Lewis, Emmanuel 36

Clothing design
Aberra, Amsale 67
Bailey, Xenobia 11
Bonney, Tabi 98
Burrows, Stephen 31
DeVore-Mitchell, Ophelia 120
Gaskins, Eric 64
Henderson, Gordon 5
Jones, Carl 7
Kani, Karl 10
Kelly, Patrick 3
Lars, Byron 32
Malone, Maurice 32
Paris, Adama 120
Robinson, Patrick 19, 71
Smith, Willi 8
Walker, T. J. 7
Williams, Serena 20, 41, 73, 129

CNBC
Epperson, Sharon 54
Thomas-Graham, Pamela 29

CNN
See Cable News Network

Coaching/Managing, Sports
Amaker, Tommy 62
Anderson, Mike 63
Ashley, Maurice 15, 47
Baker, Dusty 8, 43, 72, 110
Baylor, Don 6
Bickerstaff, Bernie 21, 133
Bickerstaff, J. B. 133
Bonds, Bobby 43
Bowles, Todd 128
Brown, Mike 77, 107
Caldwell, Jim 81
Campanella, Roy 25
Carter, Butch 27
Carter, Kenneth 53
Chaney, Don 98
Chaney, John 67
Cheeks, Maurice 47, 106
Cooper, Michael 31
Cox, Bryan 83
Crennel, Romeo 54, 107
Curry, Michael 85
Davis, Mike 41
Dorrell, Karl 52
Dungy, Tony 17, 42, 59, 118
Dunn, Jerry 27
Edwards, Herman 51
Ellerbe, Brian 22
Ewing, Patrick 17, 73, 130
Freeman, Marianna 23
Gaines, Clarence E., Sr. 55
Gaither, Alonzo Smith (Jake) 14
Gaston, Cito 71
Gates, William 97
Gentry, Alvin 23
Gibson, Bob 33
Gill, Turner 83
Gilliam, Jim 122
Gorden, W. C. 71
Graham, Trevor 84
Gray, Yeshimbra "Shimmy" 55

Green, Dennis 5, 45
Greene, Joe 10
Hamilton, Leonard 100
Hart, Thomas A., Sr. 113
Haskins, Clem 23
Hazzard, Walt 98
Heard, Gar 25
Hollins, Lionel 133
Jackson, Hue 133
Johnson, Avery 62
Jordan, Eddie 83
Joyce, Dru 81
Kearney, Beverly 109
Keith, Floyd A. 61
Lewis, Marvin 51, 87
Lloyd, Earl 26, 127
Lofton, James 42
Lue, Tyronn 136
Manuel, Jerry 94
Martin, Cuonzo 121
Mason, Derek 120
McClendon, Lloyd 123
Miller, Cheryl 10, 74
Mitchell, Sam 82
Morris, Raheem 77
O'Neil, Buck 19, 59
Parish, Robert 43
Phillips, Teresa L. 42
Porter, Bo 123
Rhodes, Ray 14
Richardson, Nolan 9
Rivers, Doc 25, 81
Roberts, Dave 132
Robinson, Craig 107
Robinson, Eddie G. 10, 61
Robinson, Frank 9, 87
Robinson, Will 51, 69
Rooks, Sean 136
Russell, Bill 8
Sanders, Satch 77
Scott, Byron 125
Shannon, Randy 82
Shaw, Brian 127
Shell, Art 1, 66
Silas, Paul 24, 129
Simmons, Bob 29
Singletary, Mike 4, 76
Smith, Lovie 66, 107
Smith, Tubby 18, 83
Stringer, C. Vivian 13, 66
Thomas, Emmitt 71
Tomlin, Mike 123
Tunnell, Emlen 54
Vaughn, Jacque 127
Washington, Ron 119
White, Frank 95
White, Jesse 22, 75
Whitney, Davey L. 110
Williams, Doug 22, 112
Williams, Monty 125
Williams, Richard 131
Willingham, Tyrone 43
Wills, Maury 73

Coca-Cola Company
Llewellyn, J. Bruce 13, 85
Ware, Carl T. 30

Coca-Cola Foundation
Jones, Ingrid Saunders 18

Collage
Andrews, Benny 22, 59
Bearden, Romare 2, 50

Bradford, Mark 89
Driskell, David C. 7
Pindell, Howardena 55
Pinder, Jefferson 77
Robinson, Aminah 50
Saar, Betye 80
Thomas, Mickalene 61
Verna, Gelsy 70

College and university administration
Abercrumbie, P. Eric 95
Ammons, James H. 81
Archie-Hudson, Marguerite 44
Austin, Bobby W. 95
Awuah, Patrick 111, 131
Baker, Delbert W. 110
Ballard, Allen Butler, Jr. 40
Barnett, Marguerite 46
Becton, Julius W., Jr. 110
Bromery, Randolph Wilson 85
Burnim, Mickey L. 48
Christian, Barbara T. 44
Cole, Johnnetta B. 5, 43
Cook, Samuel DuBois 14
Crew, Rudy 16, 113
Cross, Dolores E. 23
Davis, Erroll B., Jr. 57
Dogan, Matthew Winifred 91
Drake, Michael V. 122
Favors, Steve 23
Floyd, Elson S. 41
Ford, Nick Aaron 44
Francis, Norman (C.) 60
Gilbert, John Wesley 91
Harvey, William R. 42
Hill, Leslie Pinckney 44
Hogan, Beverly Wade 50
Horne, Frank 44
Jackson, Edison O. 67
Jarvis, Charlene Drew 21
King, Reatha Clark 65
Lee, Joe A. 45
Lewis, Shirley A. R. 14
Lomax, Michael L. 58
Lyons, James E., Sr. 102
Mason, Ronald 27
Massey, Walter E. 5, 45
Maupin, John E., Jr. 92
Mell, Patricia 49
Moody-Adams, Michele 76
Morón, Alonzo G. 91
Nance, Cynthia 71
Newman, Lester C. 51
Page, Inman 82
Pollard, William L. 91
Proctor, Bernard Shaw 120
Reaves, Donald J. 102
Ribeau, Sidney 70
Sizemore, Barbara A. 26, 110
Smith, Gene 123
Trueheart, William E. 49

Colorado Rockies baseball team
Baylor, Don 6

Colorado state government
Brown, George Leslie 62
Buckley, Victoria (Vikki) 24
Groff, Peter 96

Rogers, Joe 27

Columbia Broadcasting System (CBS)
Bradley, Ed 2, 59
Kellogg, Clark 64
Mabrey, Vicki 26
McEwen, Mark 5
Mitchell, Russ 21, 73
Olden, Georg(e) 44
Pinkston, W. Randall 24
Pitts, Byron 71
Rodgers, Johnathan 6, 51
Ware, Andre 37

Columbia Records
Jackson, Randy 40
Knowles, Tina 61

Columbia University
Huggins, Nathan Irvin 52
Joseph, Jamal 101
Marable, Manning 10, 102
Moody-Adams, Michele 76
Steele, Claude 13, 97

Comedy
Allen, Byron 3, 24, 97
Amos, John 8, 62
Anderson, Anthony 51, 77
Anderson, Eddie "Rochester" 30
Anthony, Trey 63
Arnez J 53
Beaton, Norman 14
Bell, W. Kamau 107
Bellamy, Bill 12
Berry, Bertice 8, 55
Brady, Wayne 32, 71
Bruce, Bruce 56
Buress, Hannibal 101
Cannon, Nick 47, 73, 132
Carmichael, Jerrod 124
Cedric the Entertainer 29, 60, 115
Cenac, Wyatt 94
Chappelle, Dave 50, 115
Che, Michael 123
Cosby, Bill 7, 26, 59, 125
Curry, Mark 17
Davidson, Tommy 21
Davis, Sammy, Jr. 18
Dexter, Felix 129
Dieudonné 67, 118
Earthquake 55
Epps, Mike 60
Foxx, Jamie 15, 48
Foxx, Redd 2
Freeman, Aaron 52
Funches, Ron 121
Givens, Adele 62
Glover, Donald 85
Goldberg, Whoopi 4, 33, 69
Harris, Robin 7
Hart, Kevin 103
Harvey, Steve 18, 58
Henry, Lenny 9, 52
Hughley, D. L. 23, 76
Jones, Leslie 136
Key & Peele 107
Kirby, George 14
Lawrence, Martin 6, 27, 60
Love, Loni 113
Mabley, Jackie "Moms" 15
Mac, Bernie 29, 61, 72
Markham, Pigmeat 106

Mayo, Whitman 32
McEwen, Mark 5
Meadows, Tim 30
Mitchell, Kel 66, 131
Mooney, Paul 37, 120
Moore, Tim 124
Morgan, Tracy 61, 102, 131
Morris, Garrett 31, 133
Moss, Preacher 63
Murphy, Charles 95
Murphy, Eddie 4, 20, 61
Nash, Niecy 66, 115
Noah, Trevor 128
O'Neal, Patrice 99
Powell, Keith 101
Pryor, Richard 3, 24, 56
Retta 131
Robinson, Craig 103
Rock, Chris 3, 22, 66
Rock, Tony 108
Russell, Nipsey 66
Schultz, Michael A. 6
Slocumb, Jonathan 52
Smiley, Rickey 59
Sommore 61
Stickney, Phyllis Yvonne 108
Sykes, Wanda 48, 81
Thompson, Kenan 52
Thurston, Baratunde 79, 101
Torry, Guy 31
Townsend, Robert 4, 23
Tucker, Chris 13, 23, 62
Tyler, Aisha N. 36
Walker, George 129
Watts, Reggie 52, 102
Wayans, Damon 8, 41
Wayans, Keenen Ivory 18
Wayans, Kim 80
Wayans, Marlon 29, 82
Wayans, Shawn 29
Wilson, Debra 38
Wilson, Flip 21
Witherspoon, John 38
Yarbrough, Cedric 51

Comerica Bank
Forte, Linda Diane 54

Commercial art
Freeman, Leonard 27

Communist Party
Brown, Lloyd Louis 42
Davis, Angela 5, 114
Herndon, Angelo 90
Patterson, Louise 25
Wright, Richard 5

Community activism
Blakely, Delois N. 122
Brazier, Arthur M. 115
Bryant, Jamal 128
Buery, Richard, Jr. 97
Catlin, Mamie 131
Cooper, Mario 129
Harden, Monique 97
Kimbro, Warren 76
Latiker, Diane 132
LeGrand, Naquasia 126
Matthews, Ameena 105
Mckesson, DeRay 133
Meyers, Michael 131
Murphy, Taylonn 131
Rowe-Adams, Jackie 109

Shakur, Yusef 85
Simon, Lateefah 95
Tapscott, Horace 126
Washington, Karen 117
Watkins, Ted 104
Yearwood, Lennox, Jr. 112

Computer science
Adkins, Rod 41
Auguste, Donna 29
Bryant, Kimberly 127
Coleman, Ken 57
Dean, Mark 35
Easley, Annie J. 61
Ellis, Clarence 38
Emeagwali, Philip 30
Hannah, Marc 10
Irvin, Vernon 65
Jenkins, Chad 132
Laryea, Thomas Davies, III 67
Mensah, Thomas 48
Millines Dziko, Trish 28
Pyfrom, Estella 127
Zollar, Alfred 40

Conceptual art
Allen, Tina 22, 75
Bailey, Xenobia 11
Bass, Holly 134
Blanco, Mykki 106
Cortez, Jayne 43, 109
Gates, Theaster 118
Harris, Lyle Ashton 83
London, Theophilus 95
O'Grady, Lorraine 73
Owens, Clifford 129
Piper, Adrian 71
Pope.L, William 72
Robinson, Aminah 50
Scott, Dread 106
Shonibare, Yinka 58
Simpson, Lorna 4, 36

Conductors
Abdullah, Kazem 97
Calloway, Blanche 100
Calloway, Cab 14
Cook, Will Marion 40
Dawson, William Levi 39
DePreist, James 37, 109
Dixon, Dean 68
Dunner, Leslie B. 45
Foster, William P. 88
Freeman, Paul 39
Hairston, Jester 88
Jackson, Isaiah 3
León, Tania 13
Lewis, Henry 38

Congo, Democratic Republic of the, government
Kabila, Joseph 30, 126
Kabila, Laurent 20
Mobutu Sese Seko 1, 56
Rochereau, Tabu Ley 117

Congo, Republic of the, government
Lumumba, Patrice 33
Sassou-Nguesso, Denis 103

Congress of Racial Equality (CORE)
Curvin, Robert 132
Farmer, James 2, 64

Hobson, Julius W. 44
Innis, Roy 5
Jackson, Jesse 1, 27, 72
McKissick, Floyd B. 3
Rustin, Bayard 4

Construction industry
Bennett, Richard 97
Russell, Herman Jerome 17

Contemporary Christian music
Baraka, Sho 109
Griffin, LaShell 51
KB 122
Lecrae 108
Tait, Michael 57

Continental Basketball Association (CBA)
Davis, Mike 41
Thomas, Isiah 7, 26, 65
Ussery, Terdema, II 29

Cooking
See Restaurants/Catering/Cooking

CORE
See Congress of Racial Equality

Coretta Scott King Awards
Bryan, Ashley 41, 104
Clifton, Lucille 14, 64, 91
Curtis, Christopher Paul 26, 113
Dillon, Leo 103
Draper, Sharon Mills 16, 43
Fax, Elton 48
Greenfield, Eloise 9
Hamilton, Virginia 10
Haskins, James 36, 54
Johnson, Angela 52
Lester, Julius 9, 115
Myers, Walter Dean 8, 20, 123
Morrison, Toni 2, 15, 86
Nelson, Kadir 115
Rollins, Charlemae Hill 27
Taylor, Mildred D. 26
Woodson, Jacqueline 125

Coronet
Oliver, Joe "King" 42

Corporate executive
Brewer, Rosalind 100
Coleman, Ken 57
Cottrell, Comer 11
Donald, Arnold 36, 126
Dortch, Thomas W., Jr. 45
Frazier, Kenneth 97
Hannah, Marc 10
Hill, Wyllstyne D. 94
Holland, Robert, Jr. 11
Jackson, Mannie 14
James, Donna A. 51
Johnson, George E. 29
Knowling, Robert 38
Lawal, Kase L. 45
Lewis, Aubrey 133
Lewis, William M., Jr. 40
Lewis-Hall, Freda 105
Mays, Leslie A. 41
Ogunlesi, Adebayo 37
Phillips, Charles E., Jr. 57, 109
Rand, A. Barry 6
Scott, Milton 51

Siméus, Dumas M. **25, 110**
Smith, Joshua **10**
Thompson, Cynthia Bramlett **50**
Walker, Joseph Edison **111**
Westbrook, Kelvin **50**

Corporation for Public Broadcasting (CPB)
Brown, Tony **3**

Cosmetology
Cottrell, Comer **11**
Fuller, S. B. **13**
McGrath, Pat **72**
Morgan, Rose **11**
Powell, Maxine **8, 115**
Roche, Joyce M. **17**
Walker, A'lelia **14**
Walker, Madame C. J. **7**

Council on Legal Education Opportunities (CLEO)
Henderson, Wade J. **14**
Henry, Aaron **19**

Count Basie Orchestra
Count Basie **23**
Dickenson, Vic **38**
Eldridge, Roy **37**
Foster, Frank **97**
Jacquet, Illinois **49**
Johnson, J. J. **37**
Jones, Papa Jo **99**
Jones, Thad **68**
Powell, Benny **87**
Rushing, Jimmy **37**
Terry, Clark **39, 127**
Williams, Joe **5, 25**
Young, Lester **37**

Country music
Bailey, DeFord **33**
Carolina Chocolate Drops **111**
Cowboy Troy **54**
Gray, Dobie **99**
Palmer, Rissi **65**
Pride, Charley **26**
Randall, Alice **38**
Rucker, Darius **34, 74, 108**

Cowboys
Jeffries, Herb **122**
Love, Nat **9**
Pickett, Bill **11**

CPB
See Corporation for Public Broadcasting

Craftwork
Hill, Peter **92**

Creative Artists Agency
Nelson Meigs, Andrea **48**

Creole music
Ardoin, Alphonse **65**

Cricket
Adams, Paul **50**

Critical race theory
Crenshaw, Kimberlé Williams **88**
Williams, Patricia **11, 54**

Crusader
Williams, Robert F. **11, 136**

Cuban League
Charleston, Oscar **39**
Day, Leon **39**

Cuban military
Maceo, Antonio **82**

Cuban music
Ferrer, Ibrahim **41**
Portuondo, Omara **53**
Valdés, Bebo **75**
Valdés, Chucho **89**

Cubism
Bearden, Romare **2, 50**
Green, Jonathan **54**

Culinary arts
Allen, Eugene **79**
Brown, Warren **61**
Calabrese, Karyn **89**
Chase, Leah **57**
Clark, Patrick **14**
Estes, Rufus **29**
Evans, Darryl **22**
Garvin, Gerry **78**
Henderson, Jeff **72**
Ouattara, Morou **74**
Samuelsson, Marcus **53, 120**
Sasser, Sean **113**
Twitty, Michael **134**

Cultural pluralism
Locke, Alain **10**
Vega, Marta Moreno **61**

Curator/exhibition designer
Amaki, Amalia **76**
Beckwith, Naomi **101**
Camp, Kimberly **19**
Campbell, Mary Schmidt **43**
Golden, Thelma **10, 55**
Hoyte, Lenon **50**
Pindell, Howardena **55**
Sanders, Joseph R., Jr. **11**
Sims, Lowery Stokes **27**
Stewart, Paul Wilbur **12**

Cy Young Awards
Blue, Vida **122**
Gibson, Bob **33**
Gooden, Dwight **20**
Jenkins, Fergie **46**
Martínez, Pedro **81, 126**
Newcombe, Don **24**
Price, David **101**
Sabathia, CC **74**

Cycling
Baugé, Grégory **86**
Jim, Songezo **111**
Kaka, Luthando **118**
Taylor, Marshall Walter "Major" **62**
Teklehaimanot, Daniel **130**
Yeboah, Emmanuel Ofosu **53**

Dallas city government
Kirk, Ron **11, 75, 111**

Dallas Cowboys football team
Allen, Larry **109**
Hayes, Bob **77**
Hill, Calvin **19**
Irvin, Michael **64**
Jones, Ed "Too Tall" **46**
Smith, Emmitt **7, 87**

Wright, Rayfield **70**

Dallas Police Department
Bolton, Terrell D. **25**

Dance Theatre of Harlem
DePrince, Michaela **104**
Johnson, Virginia **9**
King, Alonzo **38**
Mitchell, Arthur **2, 47**
Nicholas, Fayard **20, 57**
Nicholas, Harold **20**
Peters, Brock **96**

Daytona Institute
See Bethune-Cookman College

D.C. sniper
Moose, Charles **40**

Def Jam Records
Jay-Z **27, 69, 103**
Liles, Kevin **42, 99**
LL Cool J **16, 49, 94**
Simmons, Russell **1, 30**

Defense Communications Agency
Gravely, Samuel L., Jr. **5, 49**

Delaware state government
Williams, Dennis P. **123**

Delta Sigma Theta Sorority
Rice, Louise Allen **54**

Dentistry
Bluitt, Juliann S. **14**
Delany, Bessie **12**
Gray, Ida **41**
Lee, Robert **112**
Madison, Romell **45**
Maupin, John E., Jr. **92**
Rock, John S. **113**
Sinkford, Jeanne C. **13**

Denver Broncos football team
Barnes, Ernie **16, 78**
Briscoe, Marlin **37**
Davis, Terrell **20**
Jackson, Tom **70**
Little, Floyd **86**
Sharpe, Shannon **97**

Denver city government
Early, Norman S., Jr. **124**
Hancock, Michael B. **123**
Webb, Wellington **3, 81**

Denver Nuggets basketball team
Bynoe, Peter C. B. **40**
Hardaway, Tim **35**
Lee, Bertram M., Sr. **46**

Depression/The Great Depression
Hampton, Henry **6**

Dermatology
McDonald, Charles J. **120**
Taylor, Susan C. **62**

Destiny's Child
Beyoncé **39, 70, 105**
Luckett, Letoya **61**
Rowland, Kelly **100**

Williams, Michelle **73**

Detective fiction
See Mystery/detective fiction

Detroit city government
Archer, Dennis **7, 36**
Bing, Dave **3, 59, 78**
Cockrel, Kenneth V., Jr. **79**
Cockrel, Kenneth Vern, Sr. **79**
Collins, Barbara-Rose **7, 87**
Conyers, Monica **85**
Crockett, George W., Jr. **10, 64**
Evans, Warren C. **76**
Garrett, Joyce Finley **59**
Kilpatrick, Kwame **34, 71, 116**
Marshall, Bella **22**
McPhail, Sharon **2, 119**
Orr, Kevyn **118**
Pugh, Charles **81**
Reeves, Martha **85**
Young, Coleman **1, 20**

Detroit Lions football team
Barney, Lem **26**
Farr, Mel **24**
Johnson, Levi **48**
Mayhew, Martin R. **76**
Sanders, Barry **1, 53**
Sanders, Charlie **130**
Ware, Andre **37**

Detroit Pistons basketball team
Bing, Dave **3, 59, 78**
Dumars, Joe **16, 65, 126**
Gentry, Alvin **23**
Hill, Grant **13, 94**
Hunter, Lindsey **110**
Lanier, Bob **47**
Lloyd, Earl **26, 127**
Lowe, Sidney **64**
Mahorn, Rick **60**
Mohammed, Nazr **64**
Prince, Tayshaun **68**
Robinson, Will **51, 69**
Rodman, Dennis **12, 44, 96, 118**
Stackhouse, Jerry **30**
Thomas, Isiah **7, 26, 65**
Wallace, Ben **54**

Detroit Police Department
Bully-Cummings, Ella **48**
Gomez-Preston, Cheryl **9**
McKinnon, Isaiah **9**
Napoleon, Benny N. **23**

Detroit Tigers baseball team
Fielder, Cecil **2, 112**
Horton, Willie **104**
Virgil, Ozzie **48**

Diabetes
Fennoy, Ilene **72**
Wisdom, Kimberlydawn **57**

Dictators
Abacha, Sani **11, 70**
Afewerki, Isaias **98**
Ahidjo, Ahmadou **81**
Amin, Idi **42**
Bashir, Omar al- **77**
Biya, Paul **28, 114**
Compaore, Blaise **87**
Conté, Lansana **7, 76**

Eyadéma, Gnassingbé **7, 52**
Gbagbo, Laurent **43, 90**
Habré, Hissène **6, 104**
Kabila, Laurent **20**
Mengistu, Haile Mariam **65**
Moi, Daniel Arap **1, 35**
Mswati III **56**
Mugabe, Robert **10, 71**
Obiang, Teodoro **103**
Sassou-Nguesso, Denis **103**
Traore, Dioncounda **103**
Touré, Sekou **6**
Zenawi, Meles **3, 99**

Diner's Club
Gaines, Brenda **41**

Diplomatic Corps
See U.S. Department of State

Disco
Boney M. **133**
Chic **117**
Crown Heights Affair **132**
Gaynor, Gloria **36**
Holloway, Loleatta **115**
Payne, Freda **58**
Perren, Freddie **60**
Rose Royce **120**
Shaw, Marlena **105**
Staton, Candi **27**
Stewart, Amii **129**
Summer, Donna **25, 102**
Tavares **115**
Trammps, The **108**
Ward, Anita **118**

Distance running
Abdirahman, Abdi **126**
Cheruiyot, Robert **69**
Dibaba, Genzebe **130**
Dibaba, Mare **131**
Jeptoo, Rita **121**
Kamworor, Geoffrey **134**
Keflezighi, Meb **49, 121**
Kimetto, Dennis **125**
Kipchoge, Eliud **124**
Kipsang, Wilson **115**
Loroupe, Tegla **59**
Tergat, Paul **59**
Wanjiru, Sammy **94**

Diving
Brashear, Carl **29**

DJ
Atkins, Juan **50**
Bond, Beverly **53**
DJ Clue? **111**
DJ Jazzy Jeff **32**
DJ Lance Rock **94**
DJ Screw **110**
Felix Da Housecat **110**
Grandmaster Flash **33, 60**
Knuckles, Frankie **42, 120**
Love, Ed **58**
Red Alert, Kool DJ **32**

Documentary film
Allah, Khalik **131**
Billops, Camille **82**
Blackwood, Maureen **37**
Branch, William Blackwell **39**
Byrd, Robert **11**
Crump, Steven **96**

Dash, Julie **4, 132**
DuVernay, Ava **98, 126**
Elie, Lolis Eric **97**
Gray, Darius **69**
Greaves, William **38, 123**
Hampton, Henry **6**
Henry, Lenny **9, 52**
Hudlin, Reginald **9, 86**
Hudlin, Warrington **9**
Hurt, Byron **61**
Jean, Michaëlle; **70**
Julien, Isaac **3**
Kabera, Eric **104**
Lynch, Shola **61**
Miles, William **112**
Nelson, Stanley **92**
Peck, Raoul **32**
Rees, Dee **100**
Riggs, Marlon **5, 44**
Roberts, Kimberly Rivers **72**
Whack, Rita Coburn **36**
Williams, Marco **53**

Dollmaking
El Wilson, Barbara **35**

Dominica government
Charles, Mary Eugenia **10, 55**
Charles, Pierre **52**
Skerrit, Roosevelt **72**

Drama Desk Awards
Caesar, Adolph **133**
Carter, Nell **39**
Coles, Honi **128**
Holder, Geoffrey **78, 124**
Jackson, Christopher **136**
McDonald, Audra **20, 62, 128**
Odom, Leslie, Jr. **136**
Taylor, Ron **35**
Wesley, Richard **73**
Wolfe, George C. **6, 43, 127**

Drug abuse prevention
Clements, George **2**
Creagh, Milton **27**
Hale, Lorraine **8**
Harris, Alice **7**
Lucas, John **7**

Drums
Ali, Rashied **79**
Allen, Tony **117**
Arrington, Steve **132**
Batiste, Lionel **105**
Blade, Brian **88**
Blakey, Art **37**
Brooks, Roy **125**
Brown, Carlinhos **81**
Carrington, Terri Lyne **132**
Catlett, Sid **133**
Chancler, Ndugu **115**
Cobb, Jimmy **119**
Cobham, Billy **123**
Cole, Cozy **123**
Coleman, Denardo **122**
Cooper, Jerome **129**
Drake, Hamid **121**
Durham, Bobby **73**
Graves, Milford **126**
Greer, Sonny **127**
Günes, Tata **69**
Haynes, Roy **87**
Hamilton, Chico **117**

Hart, Billy **126**
Johnson, Gus **132**
Jones, Elvin **14, 68**
Jones, Philly Joe **121**
Kay, Connie **114**
La Roca, Pete **107**
Lea, Babatunde **124**
Locke, Eddie **44**
Miles, Buddy **69**
Moye, Famoudou Don **136**
Purdie, Bernard **77**
Riley, Ben **130**
Rodríguez, Arsenio **87**
Stubblefield, Clyde **133**
Tate, Grady **106**
Taylor, Art **132**
Thigpen, Ed **110**
Washington, Kenny **107**
Webb, Chick **105**
Williams, Tony **67**
Young, Lee **72**

Dunham Dance Company
Dunham, Katherine **4, 59**

E Street Band
Clemons, Clarence **41**

East Harlem School at Exodus House
Hageman, Hans **36**
Hageman, Ivan **36**

Ebonics
Cook, Toni **23**

***Ebony* magazine**
Bennett, Lerone, Jr. **5, 84**
Branch, William Blackwell **39**
Cullers, Vincent T. **49**
Fuller, Hoyt **44**
Johnson, Eunice W. **83**
Johnson, John H. **3, 54**
Massaquoi, Hans J. **30, 130**
Rice, Linda Johnson **9, 41**

Ebony Museum of African American History
See DuSable Museum of African American History

Economics
Ake, Claude **30**
Arthur, Owen **33**
Boyd, T. B., III **6**
Brimmer, Andrew **2, 48, 106**
Brown, Tony **3**
Conrad, Cecilia A. **94**
Fryer, Roland G. **56**
Gibson, William F. **6**
Hampton, Henry **6**
Juma, Calestous **57**
Malveaux, Julianne **32, 70**
Moyo, Dambisa **76**
Okonjo-Iweala, Ngozi **101**
Pitta, Celso **17**
Raines, Franklin **14, 107**
Robinson, Randall **7, 46**
Simms, Margaret **94**
Sowell, Thomas **2, 99**
Spriggs, William **67**
Sullivan, Leon H. **3, 30**
Wallace, Phyllis A. **9**
Washington, Ebonya **79**
Wharton, Clifton R., Jr. **7**

White, Michael R. **5**
Williams, Walter E. **4, 133**
Woodson, Robert L. **10**

Editing
Abani, Chris **77**
Aubert, Alvin **41**
Bass, Charlotta Spears **40**
Brown, Lloyd Louis **42**
Curry, George E. **23**
Delany, Martin R. **27**
Dumas, Henry **41**
Murphy, John H. **42**
Schuyler, George Samuel **40**

Edmonton Oilers hockey team
Fuhr, Grant **1, 49**
Grier, Mike **43**
Laraque, Georges **48**

EEOC
See Equal Employment Opportunity Commission

Electronic music
Atkins, Juan **50**
Craig, Carl **31, 71**
DJ Rashad **121**
Felix Da Housecat **110**
May, Derrick **41**
Romanthony **115**

Emmy Awards
Aduba, Uzo **122**
Allen, Debbie **13, 42**
Amos, John **8, 62**
Ashe, Arthur **1, 18**
Barclay, Paris **37, 94, 133**
Barnes, Katreese **97**
Belafonte, Harry **4, 65**
Bradley, Ed **2, 59**
Branch, William Blackwell **39**
Brown, James **22**
Brown, Les **5**
Browne, Roscoe Lee **66**
Carroll, Vinnette **29, 136**
Carter, Nell **39**
Clayton, Xernona **3, 45**
Coleman, Wanda **48, 119**
Cosby, Bill **7, 26, 59, 125**
Curtis-Hall, Vondie **17**
Davis, Viola **34, 76, 100, 131**
Dawes, Kwame **126**
De Shields, André **72**
Dee, Ruby **8, 50, 68, 122**
Fisher, Gail **85**
Foxx, Redd **2**
Freeman, Al, Jr. **11, 105**
Goldberg, Whoopi **4, 33, 69**
Gossett, Louis, Jr. **7**
Guillaume, Robert **3, 48**
Gumbel, Greg **8**
Hunter-Gault, Charlayne **6, 31**
Jackson, Christopher **136**
Jones, James Earl **3, 49, 79**
Kitt, Eartha **16, 75**
La Salle, Eriq **12**
Mabrey, Vicki **26**
Martin, Michel **97**
McQueen, Butterfly **6, 54**
Moore, Shemar **21, 112**
Parks, Gordon **1, 35, 58**
Pinkston, W. Randall **24**
Quarles, Norma **25**

Richards, Beah 30
Robinson, Max 3
Rock, Chris 3, 22, 66
Rolle, Esther 13, 21
St. John, Kristoff 25
Schiavocampo, Mara 97
Strahan, Michael 35, 81, 135
Taylor, Billy 23, 92
Thigpen, Lynne 17, 41
Tyson, Cicely 7, 51, 112
Uggams, Leslie 23, 114
Washington, Hayma 86
Wayans, Damon 8, 41
Whack, Rita Coburn 36
Whitfield, Lynn 18
Williams, Montel 4, 57
Williams, Russell, II 70
Williams, Sherley Anne 25
Wilmore, Larry 121
Winfrey, Oprah 2, 15, 61, 106
Woodard, Alfre 9, 108

Endocrinology
Fennoy, Ilene 72

Engineering
Alexander, Archie Alphonso 14
Anderson, Charles Edward 37
Auguste, Donna 29
Austin, Wanda M. 94
Benson, Angela 34
Boyd, Gwendolyn 49
Boykin, Otis 92
Burns, Ursula 60
Clark, Yvonne Young 95
Crosthwalt, David 93
Dabiri, John 93
Douglas, Donya 97
Emeagwali, Philip 30
Ericsson-Jackson, Aprille 28
Gibson, Kenneth Allen 6
Gourdine, Meredith 33
Greene, Frank S., Jr. 101
Grooms, Henry R(andall) 50
Hammond, Paula 119
Harris, Gary L. 87
Henderson, Cornelius Langston 26
Henderson, Henry Fairfax, Jr. 89
Howard, Ayanna 65
Jenkins, Chad 132
Johnson, Anthony M. 92
Johnson, Sandra K. 94
Jones, Wayne 53
Laroche, Joseph Philippe Lemercier 85
Laryea, Thomas Davies, III 67
McCoy, Elijah 8
Miller, Warren F., Jr. 53
Mills, Joseph C. 51
Nteff, Alain 127
O'Neal, Rodney 88
Pierre, Percy Anthony 46
Price, Richard 51
Rillieux, Norbert 92
Robinson-Berry, Joan 94
Sigur, Wanda 44
Slaughter, John Brooks 53
Spencer, Michael G. 87
Trotter, Lloyd G. 56
West, James E. 87

Entertainment promotion
Bowen, Ruth 83
Carter, Troy 98

Isaacs, Cheryl Boone 113
Lewis, Butch 71, 99

Entrepreneur
Aire, Chris 117
Bakewell, Danny 99
Barden, Donald H. 9, 20, 89
Bickerstaff, Cydni L. 133
Bridgeman, Junior 132
Burks, Juanita P. 95
Dangote, Aliko 124
Dash, Damon 31, 113
Dash, Darien 29
Downing, George T. 91
Fletcher, Buddy 16, 108
Fudge, Ann (Marie) 11, 55
Gardner, Edward G. 45
Gaston, Arthur George 3, 38, 59
Gordy, Berry, Jr. 1
Graves, Earl G. 1, 35
Henderson, Henry Fairfax, Jr. 89
Herndon, Alonzo Franklin 89
Howroyd, Janice Bryant 42
Jennings, Thomas L. 125
John, Daymond 23, 114
Johnson, John H. 3, 54
Jones, Carl 7
Lamothe, Laurent 122
Lewis, Reginald F. 6
Maponya, Richard 101
McCann, Renetta 44
Middleton, Reggie 105
Mupuya, Andrew 118
Nteff, Alain 127
Oboth, Isaac 117
Otis, Clarence, Jr. 55
Overton, Anthony 128
Parks, Henry Green, Jr. 89
Payton, Philip A., Jr. 88
Perry, Tyler 40, 54, 103
Rapelang Rabana 112
Roberts, Mike 57
Spaulding, Charles Clinton 9
Steward, David L. 36
Uys, Ashley 125
Walker, Madame C. J. 7
Walker, Maggie Lena 17
Walker, T. J. 7
Winfrey, Oprah 2, 15, 61, 106
Woods, Granville T. 5

Employment agencies
Howroyd, Janice Bryant 42

Environmental issues
Betsch, MaVynee 28
Bullard, Robert D. 121
Carter, Majora 77
Ellis-Lamkins, Phaedra 88
Eugene-Richard, Margie 63
Harden, Monique 97
Hill, Bonnie Guiton 20
Jackson, Lisa 77
Jones, Van 70
Jordan, Charles 122
Maathai, Wangari 43, 97
Miller-Travis, Vernice 64
Osborne, Na'taki 54
Saro-Wiwa, Kenule 39
Wright, Beverly 97

Epidemiology
Fenton, Kevin 87
Gayle, Helene D. 3

Poindexter, Hildrus A. 87

Episcopalian
Burgess, John 46
Harris, Barbara 12
Jones, Absalom 52
Redding, Ann Holmes 77
Walker, John T. 50
Williams, Frederick (B.) 63

Equal Employment Opportunity Commission (EEOC)
Alexander, Clifford 26
Berrien, Jacqueline A. 93
Hill, Anita 5, 65
Lewis, Delano 7
Norton, Eleanor Holmes 7, 93
Thomas, Clarence 2, 39, 65
Wallace, Phyllis A. 9

Equatorial Guinea government
Obiang, Teodoro 103

Eritrea government
Afewerki, Isaias 98

ESPN
Jackson, Tom 70
Lewis, Ray 33, 109
Masekela, Sal 106
Roberts, Robin 16, 54, 113
Salters, Lisa 71
Scott, Stuart 34, 126
Smith, Michael 129
Smith, Stephen A. 69
Tirico, Mike 68, 124
Wilbon, Michael 68, 132

Essence magazine
Bandele, Asha 36
Burt-Murray, Angela 59
De Veaux, Alexis 44
Ebanks, Michelle 60
Grant, Gwendolyn Goldsby 28
Greenwood, Monique 38
Lewis, Edward T. 21
Parks, Gordon 1, 35, 58
Smith, Clarence O. 21
Taylor, Susan L. 10, 86
Wesley, Valerie Wilson 18

Ethiopia government
Desalegn, Hailemariam 105
Haile Selassie 7
Mengistu, Haile Mariam 65
Zenawi, Meles 3, 99

Etiquette
Bates, Karen Grigsby 40

Event planning
Bailey, Preston 64
Bickerstaff, Cydni L. 133
Williams, Lindsey 75

Exiled heads of state
Amin, Idi 42
Aristide, Jean-Bertrand 6, 45
Mengistu, Haile Mariam 65
Mobutu Sese Seko 1, 56

Exploration
Bishop, Stephen 95
Henson, Matthew 2

Famine relief
See World hunger

Fannie Mae
Jackson, Maynard 2, 41
Raines, Franklin 14, 107

Fashion
Biya, Chantal 89
Boateng, Ozwald 35, 113
Boyd, Suzanne 52
Chanticleer, Raven 91
DaCosta, YaYa 98
Delice, Ronald 48
Delice, Rony 48
Evans, Etu 55
Fine, Sam 60
Finley, Ron 110
Givhan, Robin Deneen 72
Hall, Kevan 61
Hendy, Francis 47
Jones, Genevieve 101
Keckley, Elizabeth 90
Knowles, Tina 61
Luna, Donyale 88
McGrath, Pat 72
Reese, Tracy 54
Simmons, Kimora Lee 51, 83
Smaltz, Audrey 12
Smith, LaQuan 113
Steele, Lawrence 28
Stoney, Michael 50
Sy, Oumou 65
Talley, André Leon 56, 106
White, Jessica 83

Fashion Institute of Technology (FIT)
Brown, Joyce F. 25

FCC
See Federal Communications Commission

Federal Bureau of Investigation (FBI)
Gibson, Johnnie Mae 23
Harvard, Beverly 11
Lewis, Aubrey 133

Federal Communications Commission (FCC)
Barrett, Andrew C. 12
Clyburn, Mignon 78
Hughes, Cathy 27
Kennard, William Earl 18
Powell, Michael 32
Russell-McCloud, Patricia A. 17

Federal Court of Canada
Isaac, Julius 34

Federal Emergency Management Agency
Becton, Julius W., Jr. 110

Federal Reserve Bank
Brimmer, Andrew 2, 48, 106
Ferguson, Roger W., Jr. 25, 112
Layton, William 87
Rice, Emmett J. 94

Fencing
Boulogne, Joseph, Chevalier de Saint-Georges 94
Muhammad, Ibtihaj 133

Westbrook, Peter **20**

Fiction
Adams, Jenoyne **60**
Adichie, Chimamanda Ngozi **64, 121**
Alexander, Margaret Walker **22**
Ali, Mohammed Naseehu **60**
Amadi, Elechi **40**
Anthony, Michael **29**
Ansa, Tina McElroy **14**
Armah, Ayi Kwei **49**
Ashley & JaQuavis **107**
Attaway, William **102**
Ba, Mariama **30**
Baiocchi, Regina Harris **41**
Baisden, Michael **25, 66**
Beckham, Barry **41**
Benson, Angela **34**
Berry, James **41**
Bolden, Tonya **32**
Bradley, David Henry, Jr. **39**
Brand, Dionne **32**
Briscoe, Connie **15**
Brown, Cecil M. **46**
Brown, Lloyd Louis **42**
Bulawayo, NoViolet **125**
Bunkley, Anita Richmond **39**
Butler, Octavia **8, 43, 58**
Campbell, Bebe Moore **6, 24, 59**
Cartiér, Xam Wilson **41**
Chase-Riboud, Barbara **20, 46**
Cheney-Coker, Syl **43**
Chesnutt, Charles **29**
Clark, Wahida **107**
Clarke, Austin **32**
Cleage, Pearl **17, 64**
Cliff, Michelle **42**
Cole, Teju **120**
Colter, Cyrus J. **36**
Cooper, J. California **12, 85, 125**
Creagh, Milton **27**
Danticat, Edwidge **15, 68, 128**
Dathorne, O. R. **52**
Demby, William **51**
Diop, Birago **53**
DoHarris, Brenda **116**
Draper, Sharon Mills **16, 43**
Due, Tananarive **30**
Dumas, Henry **41**
Dunbar-Nelson, Alice Ruth Moore **44**
Duplechan, Larry **55**
Edugyan, Esi **98**
Ellis, Trey **97**
Emecheta, Buchi **30**
Evans, Diana **72**
Everett, Percival **93**
Fair, Ronald L. **47**
Fales-Hill, Susan **88**
Farah, Nuruddin **27**
Farley, Christopher John **54**
Files, Lolita **35**
Ford, Nick Aaron **44**
Ford, Wallace **58**
Forna, Aminatta **95**
Forrest, Leon **44**
Foye, K'wan **97**
Gomez, Jewelle **30**
Gray, Darius **69**
Greenlee, Sam **48**
Harper, Rachel M. **92**
Harris, E. Lynn **12, 33, 116**

Haywood, Gar Anthony **43**
Hercules, Frank **44**
Hill, Donna **32**
Holton, Hugh, Jr. **39**
Horne, Frank **44**
Iweala, Uzodinma **131**
Jackson, Angela **134**
Jackson, Sheneska **18**
Jakes, T. D. **17, 43, 116**
James, Marlon **85, 124**
Jasper, Kenji **39**
Jenkins, Beverly **14**
Johnson, Georgia Douglas **41**
Jones, Edward P. **43, 67**
Jones, Gayl **37**
Jones, Tayari **96**
Kamau, Kwadwo Agymah **28**
Kay, Jackie **37**
Kayira, Legson **40**
Keene, John **73**
Kendrick, Erika **57**
Killens, John O. **54**
Kincaid, Jamaica **4, 109**
Laferriere, Dany **33**
LaGuma, Alex **30**
Lamar, Jake **96**
Lamming, George **35**
Lattany, Kristin Hunter **88**
Laymon, Kiese **113**
LeFlore, Lyah Beth **96**
Locke, Attica **85**
Machado de Assis **74**
Marechera, Dambudzo **39**
Markham, E. A. **37**
Mason, Felicia **31**
Mathabane, Mark **5, 99**
Mbaye, Mariétou **31**
McCrary Anthony, Crystal **70**
McFadden, Bernice L. **39**
McKinney-Whetstone, Diane **27**
McMillan, Rosalynn A. **36**
McMillan, Terry **4, 17, 53**
Memmi, Albert **37**
Mengestu, Dinaw **66, 114**
Mitchell, Sharon **36**
Monroe, Mary **35**
Mosley, Walter **5, 25, 68**
Mossell, Gertrude Bustill **40**
Mwangi, Meja **40**
Nkosi, Lewis **46**
Nugent, Richard Bruce **39**
Okara, Gabriel **37**
Ojikutu, Bayo **66**
Packer, Z. Z. **64**
Peters, Lenrie **43**
Philip, Marlene Nourbese **32**
Polite, Carlene Hatcher **82**
Randall, Alice **38**
Ridley, John **69**
Roby, Kimberla Lawson **86**
Sapphire **14, 95**
Schuyler, George Samuel **40**
Senior, Olive **37**
Senna, Danzy **93**
Smith, Danyel **40**
Smith, Zadie **51**
Southgate, Martha **58**
Tate, Eleanora E. **20, 55**
Taylor, Mildred D. **26**
Teasley, Lisa **92**
Thomas, Michael **69**
Thomas-Graham, Pamela **29**

Tutuola, Amos **30**
Vera, Yvonne **32**
Verdelle, A. J. **26**
Walker, Margaret **29**
Weaver, Afaa Michael **37**
Whitehead, Colson **77**
Whitfield, Van **34**
Williams, Sherley Anne **25**
Williams, Stanley "Tookie" **29, 57**
Woods, Teri **69**
Yarbrough, Camille **40**
Yerby, Frank **96**
Young, Al **82**
Youngblood, Shay **32**
Zane **71**

Figure skating
Bonaly, Surya **7**
Bonheur, Yannick **84**
Fairbanks, Mabel **117**
James, Vanessa **84**
Thomas, Debi **26**
Vanessa James and Yannick Bonheur **84**

Film criticism
Mitchell, Elvis **67**
White, Armond **80, 118**

Film direction/video direction
Akomfrah, John **37**
Allain, Stephanie **49**
Barclay, Paris **37, 94, 133**
Blackwood, Maureen **37**
Bonney, Tabi **98**
Burnett, Charles **16, 68**
Byrd, Robert **11**
Coogler, Ryan **114**
Daniels, Lee **36, 76**
Dash, Julie **4, 132**
Dickerson, Ernest **6, 17**
Duke, Bill **3, 96**
DuVernay, Ava **98, 126**
Franklin, Carl **11**
Fuqua, Antoine **35**
Gerima, Haile **38, 80**
Gray, Darius **69**
Gray, F. Gary **14, 49**
Hamilton, Tanya **93**
Harris, Leslie **6**
Hayes, Teddy **40**
Henriques, Julian **37**
Hudlin, Reginald **9, 86**
Hudlin, Warrington **9**
Hughes, Albert **7**
Hughes, Allen **7**
Hurt, Byron **61**
Jackson, George **19**
Johnson, Clark **96**
Julien, Isaac **3**
Lane, Charles **3**
Lee, Malcolm D. **75**
Lee, Spike **5, 19, 86**
Lemmons, Kasi **20**
Lewis, Samella **25**
Martin, Darnell **43, 78**
McQueen, Steve **84**
Micheaux, Oscar **7**
Morton, Joe **18**
Moses, Gilbert **12**
Moss, Carlton **17**
Mwangi, Meja **40**
Onwurah, Ngozi **38**
Palcy, Euzhan **94**

Peck, Raoul **32**
Perry, Tyler **40, 54, 103**
Prince-Bythewood, Gina **31, 77**
Rees, Dee **100**
Riggs, Marlon **5, 44**
Roberts, Darryl **70**
RZA **80, 128**
St. Jacques, Raymond **8**
Schultz, Michael A. **6**
Sembène, Ousmane **13, 62**
Singleton, John **2, 30, 122**
Sissako, Abderrahmane **127**
Souleymane, Mahamane **78**
Tillman, George, Jr. **20**
Townsend, Robert **4, 23**
Tyler, Aisha N. **36**
Underwood, Blair **7, 27, 76**
Van Peebles, Mario **2, 51**
Van Peebles, Melvin **7, 95**
Wallace, William **75**
Ward, Douglas Turner **42**
Wayans, Damon **8, 41**
Wayans, Keenen Ivory **18**
White, Sylvain **96**
Whitaker, Forest **2, 49, 67**
Williams, Spencer **126**

Film production
Allain, Stephanie **49**
Amata, Jeta **111**
Chase, Debra Martin **49, 96**
Daniels, Lee **36, 76**
Gerima, Haile **38, 80**
Isaacs, Cheryl Boone **113**
Julian, Hubert **90**
McKee, Lonette **12, 119**
Morrison, Vanessa **84**
Onwurah, Ngozi **38**
Packer, Will **71**
Patton, Paula **62**
Robinson, Matt **69**
Stewart, Nzingha **89**
Tyler, Aisha N. **36**
Van Lierop, Robert **53**
Walker, Chet **106**
Ward, Douglas Turner **42**
Wayans, Damien **78**
Whitaker, Forest **2, 49, 67**
Williams, Marco **53**
Williams, Russell, II **70**
Williamson, Fred **67**

Film scores
Blanchard, Terence **43**
Crouch, Andraé **27, 115, 126**
Hancock, Herbie **20, 67**
Jones, Quincy **8, 30**
Lebo M **109**
RZA **80, 128**

Finance
Adoboli, Kweku **106**
Banks, Jeffrey **17**
Bell, James A. **50**
Boston, Kelvin E. **25**
Brown, Eddie C. **35**
Bryant, John **26**
Chapman, Nathan A., Jr. **21**
Chapman, Susan E. **94**
Doley, Harold, Jr. **26**
Epperson, Sharon **54**
Ferguson, Roger W., Jr. **25, 112**
Fletcher, Buddy **16, 108**
Funderburg, I. Owen **38**

Gaines, Brenda 41
Griffith, Mark Winston 8
Hall, Alvin D. 86
Harris, Carla A. 67
Hobson, Mellody 40
Jones, Thomas W. 41
Lawless, Theodore K. 8
Lewis, William M., Jr. 40
Louis, Errol T. 8
Mack, Iris 105
Marshall, Bella 22
Moyo, Dambisa 76
Nash, Shannon King 84
O'Neal, Stanley 38, 67
Rogers, John W., Jr. 5, 52
Ross, Charles 27
Shank, Suzanne F. 77
Taylor, Ephren W., II 61
Travis, Tracey T. 94

Finland government
Toivola, Jani 118

Firefighters
Barlow, Roosevelt 49
Bell, Michael 40

Fisk University
Imes, Elmer Samuel 39
Johnson, Charles S. 12
Phillips, Teresa L. 42
Smith, John L. 22
Work, John Wesley, III 133

Fitness
Richardson, Donna 39
Smith, Ian 62

Florida A & M University
Ammons, James H. 81
Foster, William P. 88
Gaither, Alonzo Smith (Jake) 14
Humphries, Frederick 20

Florida Marlins baseball team
Hill, Michael 95
Mariner, Jonathan 41

Florida state government
Brown, Corrine 24, 90
Meek, Carrie 6, 36
Meek, Kendrick 41, 89
Menard, John Willis 90
Tribble, Israel, Jr. 8
Wilson, Frederica 92

Florida Supreme Court
Quince, Peggy A. 69

Flute
Collette, Buddy 119
Laws, Hubert 90
Wess, Frank 116
Wright, Leo 131

Folk music
Beken 111
Bibb, Leon 132
Broonzy, Big Bill 82
Callier, Terry 106
Carolina Chocolate Drops 111
Chambers Brothers, The 116
Chapman, Tracy 26
Charlemagne, Manno 11
Cody, Radmilla 99
Cuney, William Waring 44

Davis, Gary 41
Dawson, William Levi 39
Handy, W. C. 8
Harper, Ben 34, 62
Havens, Richie 111
House, Son 8
Jenkins, Ella 15
King, Chris Thomas 120
Love, Laura 50
Memphis Jug Band 130
Nascimento, Milton 2, 64
Odetta 37, 74
Reagon, Toshi 76
Southern, Eileen 56
Spence, Joseph 49
White, Josh 86
Williams, Denise 40
Work, John Wesley, III 133

Food products
Amos, Wally 9
Briggs, Curtis 84
Oliver, Garrett 95
Parks, Henry Green, Jr. 89
Siméus, Dumas M. 25, 110

Football
Buchanan, Ray 32
Clemons, Michael "Pinball" 64
Davis, Ernie 48
Dorrell, Karl 52
Gaither, Alonzo Smith 14
Gill, Turner 83
Gorden, W. C. 71
Grier, Bobby 95
Grier, Roosevelt 13
Jones, Ed "Too Tall" 46
Keith, Floyd A. 61
Lanier, Willie 33
Lewis, Aubrey 133
Lewis, Marvin 51, 87
Lewis, William Henry 89
Mason, Derek 120
Perry, Lowell 30
Pollard, Fritz 53
Prince, Ron 64
Robinson, Eddie G. 10, 61
Shannon, Randy 82
Simmons, Bob 29
Smith, Lovie 66, 107
Strong, Charlie 118
Watts, J. C., Jr. 14, 38
Williams, Doug 22, 112
Willingham, Tyrone 43
Willis, Bill 68
Woodson, Rod 79

Football Hall of Fame, professional
Allen, Larry 109
Allen, Marcus 20
Barney, Lem 26
Briscoe, Marlin 37
Brooks, Derrick 43, 119
Brown, Jim 11, 95
Brown, Tim 134
Campbell, Earl 104
Carter, Cris 21, 109
Culp, Curley 110
Dean, Fred 98
Dent, Richard 97
Dickerson, Eric 27, 108
Faulk, Marshall 35, 96
Green, Darrell 39, 74

Greene, Joe 10
Haley, Charles 134
Harris, Franco 97
Harrison, Marvin 134
Hayes, Bob 77
Humphrey, Claude 119
Irvin, Michael 64
Jackson, Rickey 88
Johnson, John Henry 96
Joiner, Charlie 102
Jones, Deacon 92, 112
Jones, Walter 119
Kennedy, Cortez 104
Lane, Dick 92
Lanier, Willie 33
Little, Floyd 86
Little, Larry 90
Lofton, James 42
Lott, Ronnie 9
Martin, Curtis 104
Matson, Ollie 93
McDaniel, Randall Cornell 81
Monk, Art 38, 73
Moon, Warren 8, 66
Motley, Marion 26
Newsome, Ozzie 26, 117
Ogden, Jonathan 110
Pace, Orlando 21, 134
Page, Alan (Cedric) 7
Parker, Jim 64
Payton, Walter (Jerry) 11, 25
Perry, Joe 95
Pollard, Fritz 53
Randle, John 87
Rice, Jerry 5, 55, 89
Roaf, Willie 106
Robinson, Dave 110
Sanders, Barry 1, 53
Sanders, Charlie 130
Sanders, Deion 4, 31, 96
Sapp, Warren 38, 109
Sayers, Gale 28
Sharpe, Shannon 97
Shell, Art 1, 66
Simpson, O. J. 15, 100
Singletary, Mike 4, 76
Smith, Bruce 80
Smith, Emmitt 7, 87
Stallworth, John 102
Swann, Lynn 28
Taylor, Lawrence 25
Thomas, Derrick 25
Thomas, Emmitt 71
Thomas, Thurman 75
Tunnell, Emlen 54
Upshaw, Gene 18, 47, 72
White, Reggie 6, 50
Willis, Bill 68
Winslow, Kellen 83
Wood, Willie 111
Woodson, Rod 79
Wright, Rayfield 70

Ford Motor Company
Cherry, Deron 40
Dawson, Matel, Jr. 39
Goldsberry, Ronald 18
Hazel, Darryl B. 50
McMillan, Rosalynn A. 36

Foreign investment
Amoudi, Mohammed al- 88
dos Santos, Isabel 114

Forensic science
Griffin, Bessie Blount 43, 135
Omalu, Bennet 132

Fox Broadcasting Company
Corbi, Lana 42
Faulkner, Harris 131
McFarland, Roland 49
Oliver, Pam 54, 123

Fraternities/sororities
Thomas, Arthur Ray 52

Freddie Mac
Baker, Maxine 28

French Guiyana government
Taubira, Christiane 117

Funeral homes
March, William Carrington 56

Funk music
Arrington, Steve 132
Ayers, Roy 16
Bar-Kays, The 118
Bonner, Leroy 113
Brown, James 15, 60
Cameo 120
Castor, Jimmy 100
Clinton, George 9, 93
Collins, Bootsy 31
Collins, Lyn 53
Crown Heights Affair 132
Gap Band, The 100
Johnson, Conrad O. 97
Love, Laura 50
Midnight Star 110
Monáe, Janelle 86
New Birth 124
Parker, Maceo 72
Parker, Ray, Jr. 85
Purdie, Bernard 77
Randolph, Robert 132
Shider, Garry 87
Stone, Sly 85
Watson, Johnny "Guitar" 18
Wilson, Charlie 31, 77, 135
Woods, Belita 103

Fusion
Davis, Miles 4
Jones, Quincy 8, 30
Williams, Tony 67

Gabon government
Bongo, Ali Ben 80
Bongo, Omar 1, 79

Gambian government
Jammeh, Yahya 23, 104
Jawara, Dawda Kairaba 11

Gambling
Ivey, Phil 72, 106

Gangs
Coke, Christopher 108
Matthews, Ameena 105
Shakur, Yusef 85
Taylor, Bo 72
Williams, Stanley "Tookie" 29, 57

Garifuna music
Palacio, Andy 96

Gay and lesbian issues
Boykin, Keith 14
Cannon, Park 134

Carter, Mandy 11
Clarke, Cheryl 32
Collins, Jason 111
Davis, Wade, Jr. 103
De Veaux, Alexis 44
Garner, Tyron 99
Griner, Brittney 128
Hemphill, Essex 10
Julien, Isaac 3
Kato, David 103
Mugisha, Frank 119
Nabagesera, Kasha Jacqueline 130
Norman, Pat 10
Riggs, Marlon 5, 44
Wilson, Phill 9, 104

Genealogy
Allen, Lucy 85
Blockson, Charles L. 42
Haley, Alex 4

General Motors Corporation
O'Neal, Stanley 38, 67
Roberts, Roy S. 14
Welburn, Edward T. 50

Genetics
Dunston, Georgia Mae 48
Harris, Mary Styles 31
Kittles, Rick 51
Olopade, Olufunmilayo Falusi 58

Geography
Rose, Harold M. 134

Geophysics
Person, Waverly 9, 51

George Foster Peabody Awards
Bradley, Ed 2, 59
Hunter-Gault, Charlayne 6, 31
Mac, Bernie 29, 61, 72
Shaw, Bernard 2
Wilmore, Larry 121

Georgia state government
Baker, Thurbert 22
Bishop, Sanford D., Jr. 24, 111
Bond, Julian 2, 35, 106, 130
Brooks, Tyrone 59
Cannon, Park 134
Johnson, Hank, Jr. 80
Johnson, Leroy R. 89
Majette, Denise 41
McKinney, Cynthia 11, 52, 74
Reed, Kasim 82
Scott, David 41, 117
Smyre, Calvin 90
Williams, Hosea 15, 31, 123

Georgia Supreme Court
Benham, Robert 78
Melton, Harold D. 79
Sears, Leah Ward 5, 79

Ghana government
Atta Mills, John 75
Bartels, Peggielene 80
Kufuor, John Agyekum 54, 82
Lee, Robert 112
Mahama, John Dramani 103
Nkrumah, Kwame 3

Rawlings, Jerry 9

Girl Scouts of the USA
Thompson, Cynthia Bramlett 50

Goddard Space Flight Center
Douglas, Donya 97
Ericsson-Jackson, Aprille 28

Golden Globes
Allen, Debbie 13, 42
Bassett, Angela 6, 23, 62
Cara, Irene 77
Carroll, Diahann 9
Cosby, Bill 7, 26, 59, 125
Fisher, Gail 85
Freeman, Morgan 2, 20, 62, 100
Prince 18, 65, 134
Ross, Diana 8, 27
Spencer, Octavia 100
Taylor, Regina 9, 46, 97

Golf
Bramlett, Joseph 91
Davis, Ben 115
Elder, Lee 6
Gibson, Althea 8, 43
Gregory, Ann 63
Jackson, Fred James 25
Peete, Calvin 11
Powell, Renee 34
Powell, William J. 82
Richmond, Mitch 19
Shippen, John 43
Sifford, Charlie 4, 49, 134
Spiller, Bill 64
Woods, Cheyenne 103
Woods, Tiger 14, 31, 81

Gospel music
Adams, Oleta 18
Adams, Yolanda 17, 67
Andrews, Inez 108
Armstrong, Vanessa Bell 24
Bass, Fontella 104, 109
Baylor, Helen 36
Blind Boys of Alabama, The 99
Bonds, Margaret 39
Bradford, Alex 121
Bradley, J. Robert 65
Brewster, W. Herbert 128
Browne, Tom 136
Caesar, Shirley 19
Cage, Byron 53
Campbell, Lucie E. 118
Clark, Mattie Moss 61
Clark-Cole, Dorinda 66
Clark-Sheard, Karen 22, 114
Clay, Otis 112, 133
Clayton, Merry 112
Cleveland, James 19
Christie, Angella 36
Coates, Dorothy Love 125
Cobbs, Tasha 114
Consolers, The 125
Cooke, Sam 17
Crouch, Andraé 27, 115, 126
Davis, Gary 41
Davis Sisters, The 119
Deep River Boys 131
Dillard, Ricky 134
Dorsey, Thomas 15
Fortune, James 92
Franklin, Aretha 11, 44, 115

Franklin, Kirk 15, 49, 97
Gaynor, Gloria 36
Golden Gate Quartet 104
Green, Al 13, 47, 74
Greene, Travis 134
Haddon, Dietrick 55
Hammond, Fred 23
Hawkins, Edwin 113
Hawkins, Tramaine 16
Hawkins, Walter 87
Higginsen, Vy 65
Highway QC's, The 136
Holloway, Loleatta 115
Houghton, Israel 92
Houston, Cissy 20, 83
Jackson, Mahalia 5
Jeter, Claude 75
Johnson, Blind Willie 136
Johnson, Le'Andria 108
Jones, Bobby 20, 94
Kee, John P. 43, 116
Kenoly, Ron 45
Killings, Debra 57
Knight, Gladys 16, 66
Knight, Marie 80
Lassiter, Roy 24
Lawrence, Donald 99
Little Richard 15
Majors, Jeff 41
Mandisa 119
Mann, Tamela 92
Marrow, Queen Esther 24
Martin, Roberta 58
Martin, Sallie 120
Mary Mary 34, 92
May, Brother Joe 123
Mayfield, Curtis 2, 43
McClendon, Lisa 61
McClurkin, Donnie 25
Mighty Clouds of Joy 110
Mills, Stephanie 36
Monica 21
Moss, J 64
Mullen, Nicole C. 45
Myles, Raymond Anthony 121
Norful, Smokie 127
Peoples, Dottie 22
Phipps, Wintley 59
Pilgrim Travelers, The 129
Preston, Billy 39, 59
Randolph, Robert 132
Reagon, Bernice Johnson 7
Reedy, Jessica 101
Reese, Della 6, 20, 96
Sapp, Marvin 74
Scott, George 55
Sheard, Kierra 61, 114
Soul Stirrers 127
Stampley, Micah 54
Staples, Cleotha 113
Staples, Mavis 50, 88
Staples, "Pops" 32
Staton, Candi 27
Steinberg, Martha Jean "The Queen" 28
Summers, Myrna 129
Swan Silvertones, The 110
Sweet Honey in the Rock 106
Take 6 112
Tharpe, Rosetta 65
Tonex 54
Tribbett, Tye 81
Walker, Albertina 10, 58, 89

Walker, Hezekiah 34
Ward, Willa 105
Washington, Dinah 22
Whalum, Kirk 37, 64
Williams, Deniece 36
Williams, Michelle 73
Wilson, Brian Courtney 94
Wilson, Natalie 38
Winans, Angie 36
Winans, BeBe 14
Winans, CeCe 14, 43
Winans, David 77
Winans, Debbie 36
Winans, Marvin L. 17, 127
Winans, Ronald 54
Winans, Vickie 24
Wright, O. V. 114
Wright, Timothy 74

Graffiti art
Scott, Dread 106
White, Dondi 34

Grammy Awards
Adams, Oleta 18
Adderley, Nat 29
Babyface 10, 31, 82
Badu, Erykah 22, 114
Battle, Kathleen 70
Belafonte, Harry 4, 65
Beyoncé 39, 70, 105
Blade, Brian 88
Blige, Mary J. 20, 34, 60, 97
Blind Boys of Alabama, The 99
Brandy 14, 34, 72
Buckwheat Zydeco 132
Burke, Solomon 31, 86, 129
Caesar, Shirley 19
Cara, Irene 77
Carolina Chocolate Drops 111
Carrington, Terri Lyne 132
Carter, Ron 104
Chapman, Tracy 26
Chenier, Clifton 134
Cleveland, James 19
Cole, Natalie 17, 60, 84, 133
Coleman, Ornette 39, 69, 129
Combs, Sean 17, 43, 92
Coolio 103
Cosby, Bill 7, 26, 59, 125
Cotton, James 123
Cray, Robert 30, 132
Crouch, Andraé 27, 115, 126
D'Angelo 27, 123
Davis, Miles 4
Dee, Ruby 8, 50, 68, 122
Diabaté, Toumani 129
Duke, George 21, 113
Earth, Wind & Fire 98
Edwards, David 122
Ellington, Duke 5
Ellington, Mercer 129
Estelle 75, 133
Évora, Cesária 12, 99
Ferrer, Ibrahim 41
Fitzgerald, Ella 8
Forté, John 74
Franklin, Aretha 11, 44, 115
Fugees 129
Gamble, Kenny 85
Gaye, Marvin 2
Gaynor, Gloria 36
Glover, Corey 34

Goldberg, Whoopi **4, 33, 69**
Gray, Macy **29**
Green, Cee Lo **70, 103**
Guy, Buddy **31**
Harris, Damon **110**
Hart, Alvin Youngblood **61, 132**
Hathaway, Donny **18**
Hawkins, Tramaine **16**
Hawkins, Walter **87**
Hayes, Isaac **20, 58, 73**
Hill, Lauryn **20, 53, 111**
Holland-Dozier-Holland **36**
Hooker, John Lee **30**
Houston, Cissy **20, 83**
Houston, Whitney **7, 28, 83, 100**
Hubbard, Freddie **75**
Isley, Ronald **25, 56**
Jackson, Christopher **136**
Jackson, Janet **6, 30, 68**
Jackson, Michael **19, 53, 76**
James, Etta **13, 52, 100**
Jarreau, Al **21, 65, 105**
Jay-Z **27, 69, 103**
Jean, Wyclef **20, 86**
Jimmy Jam **13**
Johnson, Le'Andria **108**
Jones, Bobby **20, 94**
Jones, Quincy **8, 30**
Keb' Mo' **36, 124**
Kelly, R. **18, 44, 71, 117**
Keys, Alicia **32, 68**
King, B. B. **7, 129**
Knight, Gladys **16, 66**
Knuckles, Frankie **42, 120**
LaBelle, Patti **13, 30**
Lecrae **108**
Lawrence, Donald **99**
Lebo M **109**
Legend, John **67, 116**
Lewis, Terry **13**
Lopes, Lisa **36**
Mahal, Taj **39**
Maitreya, Sananda **85**
Makeba, Miriam **2, 50, 74**
Marley, Ziggy **41**
Marsalis, Branford **34, 103**
M.C. Hammer **20, 80**
McBee, Cecil **123**
McBride, Christian **134**
McClurkin, Donnie **25**
McCoy, Van **123**
McDonald, Audra **20, 62, 128**
Method Man **81**
Mighty Clouds of Joy **110**
Mills, Stephanie **36**
Moore, LeRoi **72**
Murphy, Eddie **4, 20, 61**
Naughty by Nature **124**
Norful, Smokie **127**
Norman, Jessye **5**
Obama, Barack **49, 74, 91**
Odom, Leslie, Jr. **136**
Olatunji, Babatunde **36, 126**
Olusola, Kevin **133**
Paul, Billy **127, 135**
Perkins, Pinetop **70**
Poitier, Sidney **11, 36**
Price, Leontyne **1**
Pride, Charley **26**
Prince **18, 65, 134**
Queen Latifah **1, 16, 58, 119**
?uestlove **74**
Redding, Otis **16**

Reeves, Dianne **32, 119**
Reid, L.A. **28, 129**
Reid, Vernon **34**
Rhymefest **97**
Richie, Lionel **27, 65, 114**
Rihanna **65, 102**
Robinson, Smokey **3, 49**
Rollins, Sonny **37, 94**
Ronettes, The **132**
Roney, Wallace **136**
Roots, The **101**
Ross, Isaiah "Doc" **40**
Rucker, Darius **34, 74, 108**
Sade **15, 92**
Scott, Jill **29, 83**
Seal **14, 75**
Shaggy **31**
Shorter, Wayne **75**
Simon, Joe **109**
Slash **75**
Smith, Will **8, 18**
Stewart, Tricky **98**
Street, Richard **110**
Summer, Donna **25, 102**
Swizz Beatz **108**
Temptations, The **33**
Thundercat **136**
Trammps, The **108**
Turner, Tina **6, 27**
Walker, Hezekiah **34**
Warwick, Dionne **18, 111**
West, Kanye **52, 93**
White, Barry **13, 41**
White, Maurice **29**
Whitfield, Norman **73**
Williams, Deniece **36**
Williams, Joe **5, 25**
Williams, Michelle **73**
Williams, Paul **112**
Williams, Pharrell **47, 82, 119**
Wilson, Nancy **10, 98**
Winans, CeCe **14, 43**
Winans, Marvin L. **17, 127**
Wonder, Stevie **11, 53, 121**
Wooten, Victor **131**
Yusef, Malik **136**

Grand Ole Opry
Bailey, DeFord **33**

Graphic novels
Anderson, Ho Che **54**
Johnson, Mat **31, 105**
Jones, Rashida **101**
McDuffie, Dwayne **62**
Tooks, Lance **62**

Green Bay Packers football team
Brooks, Aaron **33**
Butler, Leroy, III **17**
Driver, Donald **99**
Howard, Desmond **16, 58**
Mann, Bob **126**
Sharper, Darren **32, 118**
White, Reggie **6, 50**
Wood, Willie **111**

Green Party
Clemente, Rosa **74**
McKinney, Cynthia **11, 52, 74**

Grenada government
Bishop, Maurice **39**
Gairy, Eric Matthew **83**

Mitchell, Keith **82**

Guggenheim fellowship
Anderson, T. J. **119**
Braxton, Anthony **128**
Bullins, Ed **25, 121**
Coleman, Ornette **39, 69, 129**
Coleman, Wanda **48, 119**
Dash, Julie **4, 132**
Frazier, LaToya Ruby **131**
Harper, Michael S. **34, 136**
Holder, Geoffrey **78, 124**
Miles, William **112**
Pope.L, William **72**
Rollins, Sonny **37, 94**
Taylor, Cecil **70**
Wilson, Ellis **39**

Guinea government
Camara, Moussa Dadis **76**
Condé, Alpha **95, 131**
Conté, Lansana **7, 76**
Touré, Sekou **6**
Youla, Mamady **133**

Guinea-Bissau government
Cabral, Amílcar **104**
Sanhá Malam Bacai **84, 101**
Vieira, João **14, 84**

Guitar
Ade, King Sunny **41**
Arnold, Kokomo **116**
Baker, Mickey **95**
Banks, Chico **134**
Barker, Danny **32**
Barnes, Roosevelt "Booba" **33**
Bibb, Eric **49, 123**
Brim, John **117**
Brown, Clarence Gatemouth **59**
Butler, Jonathan **28**
Burns, Eddie **44**
Burnside, R. L. **56**
Caymmi, Dorival **72**
Christian, Charlie **136**
Collins, Bootsy **31**
Copeland, Johnny **110**
Cosey, Pete **103**
Cray, Robert **30, 132**
Davis, Gary **41**
Dawkins, Jimmy **111**
Diddley, Bo **39, 72**
Estes, Sleepy John **33**
Fuller, Blind Boy **86**
Fulson, Lowell **118**
Green, Grant **56**
Guitar Slim **125**
Guy, Buddy **31**
Harris, Corey **39, 73**
Hart, Alvin Youngblood **61, 132**
Hemphill, Jessie Mae **33, 59**
Hendrix, Jimi **10**
Homesick James **124**
House, Son **8**
Hooker, John Lee **30**
Hopkins, Lightnin' **83**
Howlin' Wolf **9**
Hutto, J. B. **129**
James, Elmore **114**
Johnson, Blind Willie **136**
Johnson, Robert **2**
Johnson, Syl **97**
Johnson, Tommy **106**
Jordan, Ronny **26**

Killings, Debra **57**
King, B. B. **7, 129**
King, Freddie **92**
Klugh, Earl **59**
Kolosoy, Wendo **73**
Kravitz, Lenny **10, 34**
Leadbelly **82**
Lenoir, J. B. **117**
Lipscomb, Mance **49**
Long, Huey **79**
Loueke, Lionel **88**
Lynn, Barbara **126**
Magic Sam **131**
Magic Slim **110**
Marley, Bob **5**
Mayfield, Curtis **2, 43**
McTell, Blind Willie **89**
Minner, D. C. **133**
Montgomery, Wes **88**
Murphy, Matt **117**
Ndegeocello, Meshell **15, 83**
Nighthawk, Robert **121**
Ongala, Remmy **9, 91**
Parker, Ray, Jr. **85**
Patton, Charley **107**
Pena, Paul **58**
Pitts, Skip **103**
Rachell, Yank **129**
Randolph, Robert **132**
Ranglin, Ernest **78**
Rodríguez, Arsenio **87**
Rush, Bobby **78**
Seals, Son **56**
Shider, Garry **87**
Shines, Johnny **116**
Slash **75**
Spence, Joseph **49**
Sumlin, Hubert **101**
Taylor, Eddie **116**
Taylor, Hound Dog **120**
Ulmer, James **79**
Walker, Joe Louis **118**
Walker, T-Bone **111**
Watson, Johnny "Guitar" **18**
White, Bukka **120**
White, Josh **86**
Williams, Jody **113**

Guyana government
Burnham, Forbes **66**
Jagan, Cheddi **16**

Gymnastics
Biles, Simone **136**
Dawes, Dominique **11, 126**
Hilliard, Wendy **53**
White, Jesse **22, 75**

Hair care
See Beauty salons and products

Haiti government
Aristide, Jean-Bertrand **6, 45**
Duvalier, François **124**
Duvalier, Jean-Claude **124**
Lamothe, Laurent **122**
Manigat, Mirlande **90**
Martelly, Michel **90**
Pascal-Trouillot, Ertha **3**
Paul, Evans **129**
Pierre-Louis, Michèle **75**

Préval, René 87

Harlem Globetrotters
Chamberlain, Wilt 18, 47
Gates, William 97
Haynes, Marques 22
Jackson, Mannie 14
Tatum, Reece 104
Woodard, Lynette 67

Harlem Renaissance
Alexander, Margaret Walker 22
Bennett, Gwendolyn B. 59
Christian, Barbara T. 44
Crichlow, Ernest 75
Cullen, Countee 8
Cuney, William Waring 44
Dandridge, Raymond Garfield 45
Davis, Arthur P. 41
Delaney, Beauford 19
Douglas, Aaron 7
Ellington, Duke 5
Fauset, Jessie 7
Fisher, Rudolph 17
Frazier, E. Franklin 10
Horne, Frank 44
Hughes, Langston 4
Hurston, Zora Neale 3
Imes, Elmer Samuel 39
Johnson, Georgia Douglas 41
Johnson, James Weldon 5
Johnson, William Henry 3
Larsen, Nella 10
Locke, Alain 10
McKay, Claude 6
Mills, Florence 22
Morton, Ferdinand Q. 90
Nail, John E. 92
Nugent, Richard Bruce 39
Payton, Philip A., Jr. 88
Petry, Ann 19
Thurman, Wallace 16
Toomer, Jean 6
VanDerZee, James 6
Waring, Laura Wheeler 99
West, Dorothy 12, 54
Wilson, Ellis 39

Harlem Writers Guild
Guy, Rosa 5
Killens, John O. 54
Wesley, Valerie Wilson 18

Harmonica
Arnold, Billy Boy 112
Bailey, DeFord 33
Barnes, Roosevelt "Booba" 33
Bell, Carey 114
Burns, Eddie 44
Cotton, James 123
Horton, Big Walter 115
Howlin' Wolf 9
Neal, Raful 44, 121
Parker, Junior 116
Pryor, Snooky 119
Ross, Isaiah "Doc" 40
Slim Harpo 120
Terry, Sonny 88
Williamson, Sonny Boy 134

Harp
Coltrane, Alice 70
Majors, Jeff 41

Harvard Law School
Bell, Derrick 6, 98
Dickerson, Debra J. 60
Ogletree, Charles, Jr. 12, 47
Wilkins, David 77

Harvard University
Amaker, Tommy 62
Epps, Archie C., III 45
Ferguson, Ronald F. 75
Gomes, Peter J. 15, 93
Hammonds, Evelynn 69
Huggins, Nathan Irvin 52
Loury, Glenn 36
Poindexter, Hildrus A. 87

Head Start
Edelman, Marian Wright 5, 42
Taylor, Helen 30

Health care reform
Adams-Campbell, Lucille L. 60
Berrysmith, Don Reginald 49
Carroll, L. Natalie 44
Cole, Lorraine 48
Cooper, Edward S. 6
Dirie, Waris 56
Gibson, Kenneth A. 6
Hughes, Dora 88
Hughes, Ebony 57
Kintaudi, Leon 62
Lavizzo-Mourey, Risa 48
Potter, Myrtle 40
Randall, Vernellia R. 95
Richardson, Rupert 67
Tuckson, Reed V. 71
Vaughn, Viola 70
Williams, Daniel Hale 2
Williams, David Rudyard 50

Heart disease
Cooper, Edward S. 6
Grant, Augustus O. 71
Watkins, Levi, Jr. 9

Heisman Trophy
Allen, Marcus 20
Bush, Reggie 59, 88
Campbell, Earl 104
Davis, Ernie 48
George, Eddie 80
Griffin, Robert, III 107
Howard, Desmond 16, 58
Newton, Cam 96
Sanders, Barry 1, 53
Simpson, O. J. 15, 100
Walker, Herschel 1, 69
Ware, Andre 37
Williams, Ricky 85

Heroism
Autrey, Wesley 68
Delaney, Joe 76

HEW
See U.S. Department of Health,
   Education, and Welfare

HHS
See U.S. Department of Health and
   Human Services

Hip-hop music
Akon 68
apl.de.ap 84
Ashanti 37, 96

Banks, Azealia 107
Baraka, Sho 109
Benjamin, Andre 45
Big Freedia 128
Blacc, Aloe 119
Blackman, Toni 86
Blige, Mary J. 20, 34, 60, 97
Blitz the Ambassador 115
B.o.B. 91
Bradley, Adam 101
Budden, Joe 108
Cole, J. 97
Combs, Sean 17, 43, 92
D'banj 107
De La Soul 119
DJ Clue? 111
Elliott, Missy 31, 90
Estelle 75, 133
Fabolous 93
Fat Boys 92
Fiasco, Lupe 64
FKA Twigs 123
Flying Lotus 124
Forté, John 74
Franti, Michael 93
Fresh, Doug E. 93
Fugees 129
Garrett, Sean 57
Ghostface Killah 90
Glasper, Robert 101
Guru 84
Hill, Lauryn 20, 53, 111
Hodge, Derrick 114
Jean, Wyclef 20, 86
Jennings, Lyfe 56, 69
Kid Cudi 83
Kitwana, Bakari 86
K-Swift 73
Kweli, Talib 93
Lighty, Chris 105
Lil Jon 124
Lil Mama 117
Lil Wayne 66, 84
Madlib 88
Mane, Gucci 91
Masta Ace 118
Method Man 81
Miguel 98
Minaj, Nicki 86, 124
Nelly 32, 90
Nate Dogg 92
Patton, Antwan 45
Peterson, James 81
Pharcyde, The 127
Phife Dawg 134
Prince Be 136
Public Enemy 98
?uestlove 74
Rae Sremmurd 126
Rascal, Dizzee 82
Redman 81
Riggins, Karriem 102
Rock, Pete 121
Roots, The 101
Rotimi 130
Run 31, 73
Santana, Juelz 120
Scott-Young, Mona 101
Sermon, Erick 81
Shabazz Palaces 123
Slick Rick 93
Smith, Danyel 40
Swizz Beatz 108

Thundercat 136
Tricky 98
2 Chainz 105
Wale 92
Washington, Kamasi 134
West, Kanye 52, 93
will.i.am 64
Williams, Pharrell 47, 82, 119
Yusef, Malik 136

Hip-hop theater
Power, Will 83

Historians
Blassingame, John Wesley 40
Bogle, Donald 34
Cooper, Afua 53
Crew, Spencer R. 55
Cruse, Harold 54
Fisher, Miles Mark 91
Franklin, John Hope 5, 77
Gates, Henry Louis, Jr. 3, 38, 67
Giddings, Paula 11
Hammonds, Evelynn 69
Harding, Vincent 67, 130
Harris, Jessica B. 91
Harris, Rennie 120
Horton, James Oliver 58
Huggins, Nathan Irvin 52
Logan, Rayford W. 40
Moore, Wes 86
Patterson, Orlando 4, 127
Querino, Manuel Raimundo 84
Reddick, Lawrence Dunbar 20
Rogers, Joel Augustus 30
Sadlier, Rosemary 62
Skinner, Kiron K. 65
Snowden, Frank M., Jr. 67
Washington, James Melvin 50
Williams, George Washington 18
Williams, Rhonda Y. 86

Hockey
Carnegie, Herbert 25
Doig, Jason 45
Grand-Pierre, Jean-Luc 46

Horse racing
Harris, Sylvia 70
Khumalo, S'manga 119
Krigger, Kevin 111
Minor, DeWayne 32
St. Julien, Marlon 29
Winkfield, Jimmy 42

House of Representatives
See U.S. House of Representatives

Houston Astros baseball team
Richard, J. R. 87
Watson, Bob 25

**Houston Rockets basketball
team**
Lucas, John 7
Olajuwon, Hakeem 2, 72
Smith, Kenny 114

Howard University
Adams-Campbell, Lucille L. 60
Benjamin, Tritobia Hayes 53
Branson, Herman 87
Cardozo, Francis L. 33
Childers, Lulu Vere 95

Cobb, W. Montague 39
Davis, Arthur P. 41
Dodson, Owen 38
Gerima, Haile 38, 80
Harris, Gary L. 87
Jenifer, Franklyn G. 2
Johnson, Mordecai Wyatt 79
Ladner, Joyce A. 42
Langston, John Mercer 101
Locke, Alain 10
Logan, Rayford W. 40
Malveaux, Floyd 54
Neal, Larry 38
Payton, Benjamin F. 23
Porter, James A. 11
Reid, Irvin D. 20
Ribeau, Sidney 70
Robinson, Spottswood W., III 22
Snowden, Frank M., Jr. 67
Sowande, Fela 39
Spriggs, William 67
Swygert, H. Patrick 22
Wells, James Lesesne 10
Wesley, Dorothy Porter 19
White, Charles 39
Young, Roger Arliner 29

HUD
See U.S. Department of Housing
   and Urban Development

Hugo Awards
Butler, Octavia 8, 43, 58
Delany, Samuel R., Jr. 9

Human rights
Abiola-Costello, Hafsat 108
Atyam, Angelina 55
Carter, Mandy 11
Dow, Unity 104
Harden, Monique 97
Kato, David 103
Maathai, Wangari 43, 97
McDougall, Gay J. 11, 43
Mugisha, Frank 119
Mukoko, Jestina 75
Stevenson, Bryan 128

Hunter College
DeCarava, Roy 42, 81
Mayhew, Richard 39
Thomas, Michael 69

IBM
Adkins, Rod 41
Blackwell, Robert D., Sr. 52
Dean, Mark 35
Foster, Jylla Moore 45
Thompson, John W. 26
Zollar, Alfred 40

Ice skating
See Figure skating

Illinois state government
Braun, Carol Moseley 4, 42
Burris, Roland W. 25, 75
Colter, Cyrus J. 36
Jones, Emil, Jr. 74
Kelly, Robin 114
Meeks, James T. 92
Obama, Barack 49, 74, 91
Raoul, Kwame 55
Trotter, Donne E. 28
Washington, Harold 6

White, Jesse 22, 75

Illustrations
Anderson, Ho Che 54
Baker, Matt 76
Biggers, John 20, 33
Bryan, Ashley 41, 104
Crichlow, Ernest 75
Dillon, Leo 103
Fax, Elton 48
Honeywood, Varnette P. 54, 88
Hudson, Cheryl 15
Kitt, Sandra 23
Magruder, Nilah 134
Nelson, Kadir 115
Pinkney, Jerry 15, 124
Ransome, James E. 88
Saint James, Synthia 12
Simmons, Gary 58

IMF
See International Monetary Fund

Indiana state government
Carson, Julia 23, 69
Carter, Pamela Lynn 67

**Indianapolis Colts football
team**
Caldwell, Jim 81
Harrison, Marvin 134
Sanders, Bob 72
Wayne, Reggie 131

Indianapolis 500
Ribbs, Willy T. 2

Industrial design
Harrison, Charles 72

Information technology
Blackwell, Robert D., Sr. 52
Coleman, Ken 57
Council, LaVerne 94
Gooden, Linda 94
Hamilton, Vicki 95
Hill, Wyllstyne D. 94
Mayberry-Stewart, Melodie 94
Pinkett, Randal 61
Smith, Joshua 10
Steward, David L. 36
Walker, Tristan 98
Woods, Jacqueline 52
Zollar, Alfred 40

Insurance
Gaston, Arthur George 3, 38, 59
Herndon, Alonzo Franklin 89
Hill, Jesse, Jr. 13
Holstein, Casper 89
James, Donna A. 51
Kidd, Mae Street 39
Killingsworth, Cleve, Jr. 54
Overton, Anthony 128
Procope, Ernesta 23
Procope, John Levy 56
Spaulding, Charles Clinton 9
Thiam, Tidjane 104
Vaughns, Cleopatra 46
Williams, Ronald A. 57
Willie, Louis, Jr. 68

Interior design
Ashford, Calvin, Jr. 74
Bridges, Sheila 36

De' Alexander, Quinton 57
Ham, Cynthia Parker 58
Hayes, Cecil N. 46
King, Robert Arthur 58
Myles, Kim 69
Steave-Dickerson, Kia 57
Taylor, Karin 34

**International Monetary Fund
(IMF)**
Babangida, Ibrahim 4
Chissano, Joaquim 7, 55, 67
Patterson, P. J. 6, 20

Internet
CasSelle, Malcolm 11
Cooper, Barry 33
Ellington, E. David 11
Gilliard, Steve 69
Knowling, Robert 38
Mitchell, Shireen 89
Thomas-Graham, Pamela 29
Thompson, John W. 26
Walker, Tristan 98

Interpol
Noble, Ronald 46

Inventions
Chisholm, Daquan 93
Griffin, Bessie Blount 43, 135
Johnson, Lonnie G. 32, 93
Jones, Frederick McKinley 68
Julian, Percy Lavon 6
Latimer, Lewis H. 4
Matzeliger, Jan 93
McCoy, Elijah 8
Morgan, Garrett 1
Temple, Lewis 102
West, James E. 87
Woods, Granville T. 5

Investment banking
Jones, Clarence B. 114
McGuire, Raymond J. 57

Investment management
Beal, Bernard B. 46
Bryant, John 26
Ford, Wallace 58
Gardner, Chris 65
Goings, Russell 59
Green, Isaac H. 79
Harris, Carla A. 67
Middleton, Reggie 105
Procope, Ernesta 23
Rogers, John W., Jr. 5, 52
Utendahl, John 23

Islam
Ali, Ayaan Hirsi 58, 92
Kalbani, Adil 77
Muhammed, W. Deen 27
Noble Drew Ali 100
Redding, Ann Holmes 77
Simmons, Gwendolyn Zoharah 132

Italy government
Kyenge, Cécile 113

Ivory Coast government
Bedie, Henri Konan 21
Gbagbo, Laurent 43, 90
Guéï, Robert 66
Houphouët-Boigny, Félix 4, 64

Ouattara, Alassane 90
Thiam, Tidjane 104

Jackson State University
Mason, Ronald 27

Jamaica government
Golding, Bruce 78
Holness, Andrew 99
Marks, Audrey 99
Patterson, P. J. 6, 20
Shearer, Hugh 107
Simpson Miller, Portia 62, 100

Jazz
Adderley, Julian "Cannonball" 30
Adderley, Nat 29
Akinmusire, Ambrose 103
Albright, Gerald 23
Ali, Rashied 79
Allen, Geri 92
Allen, Red 129
Allen, Tony 117
Ammons, Albert 112
Ammons, Gene 112
Amy, Curtis 114
Anderson, Carl 48
Anderson, Fred 87
Anderson, Ivie 126
Armenteros, Chocolate 133
Armstrong, Louis 2
Astatke, Mulatu 81
Austin, Lovie 40
Austin, Patti 24
Ayers, Roy 16
Ayler, Albert 104
Baby Laurence 136
Bailey, Buster 38
Bailey, Philip 63
Barker, Danny 32
Barrett, Sweet Emma 130
Barron, Kenny 128
Bassey, Offiong 119
Batiste, Alvin 66
Batiste, Jon 108, 130
Batiste, Lionel 105
Battiste, Harold, Jr. 136
Bechet, Sidney 18
Belgrave, Marcus 77, 129
Belle, Regina 1, 51
Berry, Chu 136
Betts, Keter 85
Bey, Salome 134
Blade, Brian 88
Blake, John, Jr. 123
Blakey, Art 37
Blanchard, Terence 43
Bland, Edward 111
Blanton, Jimmy 108
Bolden, Buddy 39
Bostic, Earl 121
Braxton, Anthony 128
Bridgewater, Dee Dee 32, 92
Brooks, Roy 125
Brooks, Tina 133
Brown, Clifford 86
Browne, Tom 136
Bryant, Ray 95
Buckner, Milt 110
Buika 120
Burbridge, Kofi 120
Burley, Dan 96
Butler, Henry 121
Butler, Jonathan 28

Byas, Don **133**
Byrd, Donald **109**
Cables, George **125**
Callier, Terry **106**
Calloway, Blanche **100**
Calloway, Cab **14**
Campbell, Roy, Jr. **118**
Carrington, Terri Lyne **132**
Carter, Benny **46**
Carter, Regina **23, 131**
Carter, Ron **104**
Carter, Warrick L. **27**
Cartiér, Xam Wilson **41**
Catlett, Sid **133**
Chambers, Paul **121**
Charles, Ray **16, 48**
Cheatham, Doc **17**
Cherry, Don **119**
Christian, Charlie **136**
Christian, Jodie **103**
Clark, Sharón **105**
Clark, Sonny **128**
Clarke, Kenny **27**
Clayton, Gerald **111**
Cobb, Arnett **114**
Cobb, Jimmy **119**
Cobham, Billy **123**
Cole, Cozy **123**
Cole, Freddy **128**
Cole, Maria **104**
Cole, Nat "King" **17**
Cole, Natalie **17, 60, 84, 133**
Coleman, Denardo **122**
Coleman, George **106**
Coleman, Ornette **39, 69, 129**
Coleman, Steve **124**
Collette, Buddy **119**
Coltrane, Alice **70**
Coltrane, John **19**
Coltrane, Ravi **71**
Cook, Charles "Doc" **44**
Cook, Junior **126**
Cooper, Jerome **129**
Cosey, Pete **103**
Counce, Curtis **127**
Count Basie **23**
Crawford, Hank **77**
Crawford, Randy **19**
Criss, Sonny **128**
Crothers, Scatman **19**
Crouch, Stanley **11, 87**
Crowder, Henry **16**
Crusaders, The **116**
Curson, Ted **108**
Daemyon, Jerald **64**
Daniels, Billy **124**
Dara, Olu **35**
Davis, Anthony **11**
Davis, Frank Marshall **47**
Davis, Miles **4**
Davis, Walter, Jr. **134**
Davis, Wild Bill **114**
Day, Andra **132**
Delta Rhythm Boys **133**
Dickenson, Vic **38**
Diehl, Aaron **132**
Dixon, Bill **87**
Doggett, Bill **124**
Donegan, Dorothy **19**
Dorham, Kenny **113**
Downing, Will **19**
Drake, Hamid **121**
Drew, Kenny **123**

Duke, George **21, 113**
Dumas, Henry **41**
Durham, Bobby **73**
Dyett, Walter **113**
Eckstine, Billy **28**
Edison, Harry **114**
Edwards, Teddy **123**
Eldridge, Roy **37**
Ellington, Duke **5**
Ellington, Mercer **129**
Ellison, Ralph **7**
Ervin, Booker **106**
Eubanks, Kevin **15, 108**
Farmer, Art **38**
Favors, Malachi **136**
Ferbos, Lionel **95**
Ferbos, Lionel **95**
Ferrell, Rachelle **29**
Fitzgerald, Ella **8, 18**
Flanagan, Tommy **69**
Foster, Frank **97**
Foster, George "Pops" **40**
Fox, Donal **114**
Freelon, Nnenna **32**
Freeman, Von **104**
Freeman, Yvette **27**
Fuller, Arthur **27**
Garner, Erroll **76**
Garrison, Jimmy **133**
Gillespie, Dizzy **1**
Glasper, Robert **101**
Glenn, Tyree **129**
Golson, Benny **37**
Gonzales, Babs **134**
Gordon, Dexter **25**
Graves, Milford **126**
Gray, Wardell **128**
Green, Bennie **131**
Green, Grant **56**
Greene, Jimmy **74**
Greer, Sonny **127**
Griffin, Johnny **71**
Grimes, Henry **124**
Gryce, Gigi **124**
Güines, Tata **69**
Hall, Adelaide **126**
Hamilton, Chico **117**
Hampton, Lionel **17, 41**
Hancock, Herbie **20, 67**
Handy, John **131**
Hardin Armstrong, Lil **39**
Harris, Barry **68**
Harris, Kevin **120**
Hart, Billy **126**
Hartman, Johnny **109**
Hawes, Hampton **121**
Hawkins, Coleman **9**
Haynes, Roy **87**
Heath, Percy **100**
Henderson, Fletcher **32**
Henderson, Joe **127**
Higginbotham, J. C. **37**
Hill, Andrew **66**
Hines, Earl "Fatha" **39**
Hinton, Milt **30**
Hodge, Derrick **114**
Hodges, Johnny **129**
Holiday, Billie **1**
Horn, Shirley **32, 56**
Hubbard, Freddie **75**
Humes, Helen **128**
Hyman, Phyllis **19**
Jackson, Bobby **119**

Jackson, Milt **26**
Jacquet, Illinois **49**
Jamal, Ahmad **69**
James, Etta **13, 52, 100**
Jarman, Joseph **136**
Jarreau, Al **21, 65, 105**
Jeffries, Herb **122**
Johnson, Buddy **36**
Johnson, Gus **132**
Johnson, J. J. **37**
Johnson, James P. **134**
Johnson, Ken **106**
Johnson, Lonnie **85**
Jones, Elvin **14, 68**
Jones, Etta **35**
Jones, Hank **57, 86**
Jones, Jonah **39**
Jones, Papa Jo **99**
Jones, Philly Joe **121**
Jones, Quincy **8, 30**
Jones, Thad **68**
Jordan, Duke **133**
Jordan, Louis **104**
Jordan, Ronny **26**
Kay, Connie **114**
Kelly, Wynton **121**
Kenyatta, Robin **54**
Kirk, Andy **134**
Klugh, Earl **59**
La Roca, Pete **107**
Lancaster, Byard **105**
Land, Harold **125**
Lateef, Yusef **91, 117**
Laws, Hubert **90**
Lea, Babatunde **124**
Ledisi **73**
Lee, Consuela **84**
Lewis, George **104**
Lewis, George **130**
Lewis, Ramsey **35, 70**
Lincoln, Abbey **3, 88**
Liston, Melba **118**
Little, Booker **105**
Locke, Eddie **44**
Long, Huey **79**
Loueke, Lionel **88**
Lucie, Lawrence **80**
Lucien, Jon **66**
Lunceford, Jimmie **134**
Lutcher, Nellie **130**
Lynne, Gloria **115**
Mance, Junior **132**
Marsalis, Branford **34, 103**
Marsalis, Delfeayo **41**
Marsalis, Ellis **90**
Marsalis, Wynton **16, 90**
McBee, Cecil **123**
McBride, Christian **134**
McBride, James **35, 87**
McDuff, Jack **116**
McGhee, Howard **122**
McGriff, Jimmy **72**
McIntyre, Kalaparusha Maurice **117**
McLean, Jackie **78**
McRae, Carmen **77**
Miley, Bubber **120**
Miller, Marcus **84**
Millinder, Lucky **101**
Mills, Florence **22**
Mingus, Charles **15**
Mitchell, Blue **126**
Mitchell, Dwike **111**
Mitchell, Nicole **66**

Mitchell, Roscoe **134**
Moffett, Charnett **127**
Monk, Thelonious **1**
Montgomery, Little Brother **117**
Montgomery, Wes **88**
Moody, James **83**
Moondoc, Jemeel **119**
Moore, Melba **21**
Moran, Jason **89**
Morgan, Lee **102**
Morton, Jelly Roll **29**
Moye, Famoudou Don **136**
Muse, Clarence Edouard **21**
Nascimento, Milton **2, 64**
Navarro, Fats **104**
Nelson, Oliver **113**
Newborn, Phineas, Jr. **127**
Newman, David **76**
Oliver, Joe "King" **42**
Ory, Kid **118**
Owens, Jimmy **130**
Page, Walter **117**
Parham, Truck **124**
Parker, Charlie **20**
Parker, Maceo **72**
Parlan, Horace **108**
Payne, Freda **58**
Perkins, Carl **128**
Peterson, Marvin "Hannibal" **27**
Peterson, Oscar **52**
Pettiford, Oscar **106**
Powell, Benny **87**
Powell, Bud **24**
Prysock, Arthur **117**
Purdie, Bernard **77**
Ray, Carline **113**
Redman, Don **134**
Redman, Joshua **30**
Reeves, Dianne **32, 119**
Reid, Rufus **130**
Rhyne, Melvin **109**
Riggins, Karriem **102**
Rivers, Sam **95**
Roach, Max **21, 63**
Roberts, Marcus **19, 113**
Rollins, Sonny **37, 94**
Roney, Wallace **136**
Rouse, Charlie **130**
Ruffins, Kermit **85**
Rushing, Jimmy **37**
Sample, Joe **51, 123**
Santamaria, Mongo **81**
Scarlett, Millicent **49**
Scott, Hazel **66**
Scott, Jimmy **48, 122**
Scott, Shirley **133**
Sessoms, Vivian **122**
Shavers, Charlie **131**
Shaw, Marlena **105**
Shepp, Archie **101**
Shipp, Matthew **107**
Shirley, Donald **111**
Shorter, Wayne **75**
Silver, Horace **26, 122**
Simone, Nina **15, 41, 130**
Simpson-Hoffman, N'kenge **52**
Sissle, Noble **29**
Smith, Bessie **3**
Smith, Buster **116**
Smith, Cecilia **102**
Smith, Cladys "Jabbo" **32**
Smith, Dr. Lonnie **49**
Smith, Jimmy **127**

Smith, Lee **136**
Smith, Lonnie Liston **49**
Smith, Stuff **37**
Smith, Willie **107**
Somi **85**
Souza, Carmen **111**
Staton, Dakota **62**
Stewart, Slam **126**
Strayhorn, Billy **31**
Sullivan, Maxine **37**
Sun Ra **60**
Swann, Lynn **28**
Sweatman, Wilbur **125**
Tacuma, Jamaaladeen **124**
Take 6 **112**
Tampa Red **63**
Tapscott, Horace **126**
Tate, Buddy **108**
Tate, Grady **106**
Taylor, Art **132**
Taylor, Billy **23, 92**
Taylor, Cecil **70**
Tchicai, John **102**
Terry, Clark **39, 127**
Thigpen, Ed **110**
Threadgill, Henry **97**
Thundercat **136**
Timmons, Bobby **136**
Tisdale, Wayman **50**
Towles, Nat **128**
Trombone Shorty **97**
Turner, Mark **126**
Turrentine, Stanley **129**
Tyner, McCoy **92**
Ulmer, James **79**
Valdés, Bebo **75**
Valdés, Chucho **89**
Vaughan, Sarah **13**
Vinnegar, Leroy **124**
Vinson, Eddie **112**
Waldron, Mal **109**
Waller, Fats **29**
Walton, Cedar **114**
Ware, David S. **106**
Warren, Butch **116**
Washington, Dinah **22**
Washington, Grover, Jr. **17, 44**
Washington, Kamasi **134**
Washington, Kenny **107**
Waters, Benny **26**
Watson, Johnny "Guitar" **18**
Watts, Reggie **52, 102**
Webb, Chick **105**
Webster, Ben **136**
Webster, Katie **29**
Wein, Joyce **62**
Wess, Frank **116**
Whalum, Kirk **37, 64**
White, Maurice **29**
Wiggins, Gerald **128**
Williams, Buster **131**
Williams, Claude **80**
Williams, Cootie **114**
Williams, Joe **5, 25**
Williams, Mary Lou **15**
Williams, Richard **130**
Williams, Tony **67**
Williamson, Patrice **134**
Wilson, Abram **104**
Wilson, Cassandra **16**
Wilson, Gerald **49, 123**
Wilson, Nancy **10, 98**
Wilson, Teddy **134**

Wooten, Victor **131**
Workman, Reggie **131**
Wright, Eugene **125**
Wright, Leo **131**
York, Vincent **40**
Young, Lee **72**
Young, Lester **37**

Jet magazine
Johnson, John H. **3, 54**

Jewelry
Aire, Chris **117**

Jockeys
Harris, Sylvia **70**
Lewis, Oliver **56**
Winkfield, Jimmy **42**

Johnson C. Smith University
Yancy, Dorothy Cowser **42**

Johnson Products
Johnson, George E. **29**

Johnson Publishing Company, Inc.
Booker, Simeon **23**
Johnson, Eunice W. **83**
Johnson, John H. **3, 54**
Monroe, Bryan **71**
Rice, Linda Johnson **9, 41**
Rogers, Desirée **88**

Joint Center for Political and Economic Studies
Williams, Eddie N. **44**

Joint Chiefs of Staff
See U.S. Joint Chiefs of Staff

Journalism
Abbott, Robert Sengstacke **27**
Abrahams, Peter **39**
Abu-Jamal, Mumia **15**
Als, Hilton **105**
Ansa, Tina McElroy **14**
Aplin-Brownlee, Vivian **96**
Ashley-Ward, Amelia **23**
Asim, Jabari **71**
Aubespin, Mervin **95**
Auguste, Arnold A. **47**
Azikiwe, Nnamdi **13**
Bailey, Chauncey **68**
Baquet, Dean **63, 121**
Barnett, Amy Du Bois **46**
Barrett, Lindsay **43**
Bass, Charlotta Spears **40**
Bates, Karen Grigsby **40**
Bennett, Gwendolyn B. **59**
Bennett, Lerone, Jr. **5, 84**
Best, Carrie **80**
Blair, Jayson **50**
Blake, Asha **26**
Blow, Charles M. **73**
Bolden, Frank E. **44**
Booker, Simeon **23**
Borders, James **9**
Boyd, Gerald M. **32, 59**
Boyd, Suzanne **52**
Bradley, Ed **2, 59**
Britt, Donna **28**
Brower, William **49**
Brown, George Leslie **62**
Brown, Lloyd Louis **42**

Brown, Tony **3**
Bryant, Howard **130**
Buckley, Gail Lumet **39**
Burt-Murray, Angela **59**
Burwell, Bryan **83**
Caldwell, Earl **60**
Campbell, Bebe Moore **6, 24, 59**
Candy, Dana **132**
Cary, Mary Ann Shadd **30**
Cayton, Horace **26**
Chadiha, Jeffri **57**
Chideya, Farai **14, 61**
Chiles, Nick **98**
Churchwell, Robert, Sr. **76**
Ciara, Barbara **69**
Coates, Ta-Nehisi **76, 131**
Cooke, Marvel **31**
Cook-Parrish, Mary Virginia **95**
Cooper, Andrew W. **36**
Cooper, Barry **33**
Cooper, Helene **74**
Cose, Ellis **5, 50**
Croal, N'Gai **76**
Crouch, Stanley **11, 87**
Crump, Steven **96**
Crutchfield, James N. **55**
Cullen, Countee **8**
Cunningham, Evelyn **23, 85**
Dash, Leon **47**
Datcher, Michael **60**
Davis, Belva **61**
Davis, Frank Marshall **47**
Davis, Thulani **61**
Dawkins, Wayne **20**
Deggans, Eric **71**
Douglass, Frederick **87**
Drummond, William J. **40**
Due, Tananarive **30**
Dunnigan, Alice Allison **41**
Duthiers, Vladimir **109**
Eagleson, William Lewis **90**
Edmonds, Terry **17**
Elbagir, Nima **121**
Elder, Larry **25, 120**
Elie, Lolis Eric **97**
Epperson, Sharon **54**
Farley, Christopher John **54**
Faulkner, Harris **131**
Forman, James **7, 51**
Fortune, T. Thomas **6**
Fuller, Hoyt **44**
Gaiter, Dorothy J. **80**
Giddings, Paula **11**
Gilliard, Steve **69**
Givhan, Robin Deneen **72**
Goode, Mal **13**
Gordon, Ed **10, 53**
Granderson, LZ **103**
Grimké, Archibald H. **9**
Gumbel, Bryant **14, 80**
Gumbel, Greg **8**
Hall, Tamron **96**
Hare, Nathan **44**
Harris, Claire **34**
Harris, Jay **19**
Harris, Richard E. **61**
Hatcher, Andrew T. **90**
Haygood, Wil **83**
Haynes, Trudy **44**
Henderson, Angelo **122**
Henriques, Julian **37**
Herbert, Bob **63, 96**
Hickman, Fred **11**

Hill, Jemele **109**
Holmes, T. J. **98**
Holt, Lester **66**
Huggins, Edie **71**
Hunter-Gault, Charlayne **6, 31**
Ifill, Gwen **28**
Jackson, James A. **90**
Jarrett, Vernon D. **42, 135**
Jasper, Kenji **39**
Jealous, Benjamin Todd **70, 113**
Joachim, Paulin **34**
Johnson, Georgia Douglas **41**
Jones, Bomani **121**
Kaufman, Monica **66**
Kearney, Janis **54**
Khanga, Yelena **6**
Killens, John O. **54**
King, Colbert I. **69**
King, Gayle **19, 99**
Kitwana, Bakari **86**
LaGuma, Alex **30**
Lacy, Sam **30, 46**
Lamar, Jake **96**
Lampkin, Daisy **19**
Leavell, Dorothy R. **17**
Lemon, Don **84**
Lewis, Edward T. **21**
Lomax, Louis E. **90**
Lowe, Herbert **57**
Mabrey, Vicki **26**
Mabry, Marcus **70**
Mabuza-Suttle, Felicia **43**
Malveaux, Suzanne **88**
Martin, Louis E. **16**
Martin, Michel **97**
Mason, Felicia **31**
Massaquoi, Hans J. **30, 130**
Maynard, Nancy Hicks **73**
Mbeki, Govan A. **80**
McAlpin, Harry **121**
McBride, James **35, 87**
McCall, Nathan **8**
McGruder, Robert **22, 35**
McKay, Claude **6**
Mickelbury, Penny **28**
Mitchell, Elvis **67**
Mitchell, Russ **21, 73**
Mkapa, Benjamin W. **16, 77**
Monroe, Bryan **71**
Mossell, Gertrude Bustill **40**
Mukoko, Jestina **75**
Murphy, John H. **42**
Murray, Pauli **38**
Nakasa, Nat **123**
Nelson, Jill **6, 54**
Neville, Arthel **53**
Newkirk, Pamela **69**
Njawe, Pius **87**
Nkosi, Lewis **46**
Noble, Gil **76**
Norris, Michele **83**
O'Brien, Soledad **88**
Oliver, Pam **54, 123**
Olojede, Dele **59**
Page, Clarence **4**
Palmer, Everard **37**
Parham, Marjorie B. **71**
Parker, Star **70**
Parks, Gordon **1, 35, 58**
Payne, Ethel L. **28**
Payne, Les **89**
Perez, Anna **1**
Perkins, Tony **24**

Phillips, Joseph C. 73
Pinkston, W. Randall 24
Pitts, Byron 71
Pitts, Leonard, Jr. 54, 85
Plaatje, Sol T. 80
Poussaint, Renee 78
Pressley, Condace L. 41
Price, Hugh B. 9, 54
Prince, Richard E. 71
Pugh, Charles 81
Quarles, Norma 25
Rapier, James T. 82
Raspberry, William 2
Reed, Ishmael 8
Reeves, Rachel J. 23
Rhoden, William C. 67
Riley, Rochelle 50
Robertson, Gil L., IV 85
Robinson, Eugene 77
Robinson, Max 3
Rodgers, Johnathan 6, 51
Ross, Don 27
Rowan, Carl T. 1, 30
Russwurm, John Brown 100
Rust, Art, Jr. 83
Salih, Al-Tayyib 37
Salters, Lisa 71
Sanders, Pharoah 64
Sanneh, Kelefa 96
Schiavocampo, Mara 97
Schuyler, George Samuel 40
Schuyler, Philippa 50
Senior, Olive 37
Sesay, Isha 107
Setmayer, Tara 130
Shaw, Bernard 2, 28
Shipp, E. R. 15
Sidner, Sara 105
Simpson, Carole 6, 30
Smith, Clarence O. 21
Smith, Danyel 40
Smith, Michael 129
Smith, Stephen A. 69
Sowell, Thomas 2, 99
Staples, Brent 8
Stewart, Alison 13
Stokes, Carl 10, 73
Stone, Chuck 9, 120
Syler, Rene 53
Tate, Eleanora E. 20, 55
Tatum, Elinor R. 78
Tatum, Wilbert 76
Taylor, Kristin Clark 8
Teague, Bob 111
Thurman, Wallace 16
Tolson, Melvin B. 37
Trotter, Monroe 9
Tucker, Cynthia 15, 61
Walker, Teshima 114
Wallace, Michele Faith 13
Walton, Lester Aglar 134
Washington, Elsie B. 78
Washington, Harriet A. 69
Watson, Carlos 50
Watts, Rolonda 9
Wells-Barnett, Ida B. 8
Wesley, Valerie Wilson 18
Whitaker, Mark 21, 47
Whitfield, LeRoy 84
Whitlock, Jason 78, 130
Wilbekin, Emil 63
Wilbon, Michael 68, 132
Wiley, Ralph 8, 78

Wilkerson, Isabel 71
Wilkins, Roger 2, 84
Williams, Armstrong 29
Williams, Clarence 70
Williams, Juan 35, 80
Wiwa, Ken 67
Woods, Mattiebelle 63
Yette, Samuel F. 63
Zook, Kristal Brent 62

Judaism
Funnye, Capers C., Jr. 73
Gray, Ahuvah 130
Stanton, Alysa 78

Judiciary
Allen, Macon Bolling 104
Gibbs, Mifflin W. 99
Hatchett, Glenda 32
Hubbard, Arnette 38
Sampson, Edith S. 4
Slater, Duke 125
Spencer, Vaino H. 99
Watt, Garland W. 113

Kansas City Chiefs football team
Allen, Marcus 20
Cherry, Deron 40
Delaney, Joe 76
Smith, Neil 109
Thomas, Derrick 25
Thomas, Emmitt 71

Kansas City Royals baseball team
White, Frank 95

Kansas state government
Haley, George 21, 129

Kansas State University
Prince, Ron 64

Kappa Alpha Psi
Hamilton, Samuel C. 47

Kentucky Derby
Krigger, Kevin 111
Winkfield, Jimmy 42

Kentucky Negro Educational Association
Cotter, Joseph Seamon, Sr. 40

Kentucky state government
Kidd, Mae Street 39

Kenya government
Kariuki, J. M. 67
Kenyatta, Jomo 5
Kenyatta, Uhuru 110
Kibaki, Mwai 60
Maathai, Wangari 43, 97
Mboya, Tom 107
Moi, Daniel Arap 1, 35
Ngilu, Charity 58
Odinga, Raila 67, 110

King Center
See Martin Luther King Jr. Center for Nonviolent Social Change

King Oliver's Creole Band
Armstrong, Louis 2
Hardin Armstrong, Lil 39

Oliver, Joe "King" 42

King's Troop of the Royal Horse Artillery
Scantlebury, Janna 47

Kraft General Foods
Fudge, Ann (Marie) 11, 55
Sneed, Paula A. 18

Kwanzaa
Karenga, Maulana 10, 71

Labour Party
Amos, Valerie 41

Landscape architecture
Williston, David Augustus 99

LAPD
See Los Angeles Police Department

Latin baseball leagues
Kaiser, Cecil 42

Law education
Alexander, Michelle 98
Bell, Derrick 6, 98
Carter, Stephen L. 4
Forman, James, Jr. 89
Guinier, Lani 7, 30
Johnson, Edward Austin 107
Langston, John Mercer 101
Williams, Patricia 11, 54

Law enforcement
Alexander, Joyce London 18
Barrett, Jacquelyn 28
Battle, Samuel J. 130
Batts, Anthony 128
Bolton, Terrell D. 25
Bradley, Thomas 2, 20
Brown, Lee P. 1, 24, 109
Bully-Cummings, Ella 48
Evans, Warren C. 76
Feemster, Herbert 72
Freeman, Charles 19
Gibson, Johnnie Mae 23
Gittens, Charles L. 124
Glover, Nathaniel, Jr. 12
Gomez-Preston, Cheryl 9
Harvard, Beverly 11
Hillard, Terry 25
Holton, Hugh, Jr. 39
Hurtt, Harold 46
Johnson, Norma H. 17, 97
Johnson, Robert T. 17
Johnson, Sterling, Jr. 124
Jordan, Eddie 82
McKinnon, Isaiah 9
Moose, Charles 40
Napoleon, Benny N. 23
Noble, Ronald 46
Oliver, Jerry 37
Parks, Bernard C. 17
Ramsey, Charles H. 21, 69
Reeves, Bass 100
Roberts, Norwell 134
Robinson, Bishop L. 66
Schmoke, Kurt 1, 48
Sealy, Lloyd G. 125
Smith, Richard 51
Thomas, Franklin A. 5, 49
Wainwright, Joscelyn 46
Ward, Benjamin 68

Watkins, Craig 97
Williams, Dennis P. 123
Williams, Willie L. 4
Wilson, Jimmy 45
Wray, Noble 114

LDF
See NAACP Legal Defense and Educational Fund

League of Nations
Haile Selassie 7

Legal Defense Fund
See NAACP Legal Defense and Educational Fund

Lesotho government
Mosisili, Pakalitha 96
Thabane, Thomas 123

Lexicography
Major, Clarence 9

Liberia government
Doe, Samuel K. 100
Henries, A. Doris Banks 44
Roberts, Joseph Jenkins 125
Russwurm, John Brown 100
Sawyer, Amos 2, 123
Sirleaf, Ellen Johnson 71
Tolbert, William R. 100
Tubman, William 99
Weah, George 58

Library science
Bontemps, Arna 8
Franklin, Hardy R. 9, 87
Harsh, Vivian Gordon 14
Hutson, Jean Blackwell 16, 135
Jones, Clara Stanton 51
Josey, E. J. 10
Morrison, Sam 50
Rollins, Charlemae Hill 27
Shockley, Ann Allen 84
Smith, Jessie Carney 35
Wedgeworth, Robert W. 42
Wesley, Dorothy Porter 19

Librettos
Chenault, John 40

Lincoln University (MO)
Page, Inman 82
Randall, Dudley 8, 55

Lincoln University (PA)
Cuney, William Waring 44
Sudarkasa, Niara 4

Linguistics
McWhorter, John 35, 119

Literacy
Amos, Wally 9
Omolewa, Michael 119

Literary criticism
Braithwaite, William Stanley 52
Brown, Sterling Allen 10, 64
Broyard, Anatole 68
Cartey, Wilfred 47
Christian, Barbara T. 44
Cook, Mercer 40
De Veaux, Alexis 44
Emanuel, James A. 46
Fleming, Raymond 48

Ford, Nick Aaron **44**
Joachim, Paulin **34**
Mackey, Nathaniel **75**
Mugo, Micere Githae **32**
Ngugi wa Thiong'o **29, 61, 101**
Redding, J. Saunders **26**
Reed, Ishmael **8**
Smith, Barbara **28**
Wesley, Valerie Wilson **18**
West, Cornel **5, 33, 80**

Litigation
Adegbile, Debo P. **119**
Allen, Lucy **85**
Baldwin, Cynthia **74, 107**
Clark, Ray **122**
Cochran, Johnnie **11, 39, 52**
Gary, Willie E. **12, 117**
Ming, William Robert, Jr. **125**
Mitchell, Juanita Jackson **128**
Ozanne, Ismael R. **129**
Patrick, Deval **12, 61, 127**
Payne, Ulice, Jr. **42**
Payton, John **48, 124**
Plaskett, Stacey **127**
Roberts, Michele **123**
Rock, John S. **113**
Slater, Rodney E. **15, 125**
Sweatt, Heman Marion **114**
Tolbert, James L. **112**
Watt, Garland W. **113**
Worthy, Kym **84**

"Little Rock Nine"
Bates, Daisy **13, 135**
Beals, Melba Pattillo **15, 94**
Thomas, Jefferson **88**

Lobbying
Boyd, John W., Jr. **20, 72**
Brown, Elaine **8**
Brown, Jesse **6, 41**
Christie, Ron **83**
Hart, Thomas A., Sr. **113**
Lee, Canada **8**
Mallett, Conrad, Jr. **16**
Reeves, Gregory **49**
Robinson, Randall **7, 46**
Wynn, Albert R. **25, 77**

Los Angeles Angels baseball team
Baylor, Don **6**
Reagins, Tony **94**

Los Angeles city government
Bradley, Thomas **2, 20**
Brookins, Hamel Hartford **102**
Edwards, Willis **104**
Evers, Myrlie **8**

Los Angeles Clippers basketball team
Baylor, Elgin **93**
Brand, Elton **31**
Griffin, Blake **98**
Parsons, Richard **11, 33, 124**

Los Angeles Dodgers baseball team
Gilliam, Jim **122**
Newcombe, Don **24**
Roseboro, John **123**
Strawberry, Darryl **22**

Wills, Maury **73**

Los Angeles Lakers basketball team
Abdul-Jabbar, Kareem **8**
Baylor, Elgin **93**
Chamberlain, Wilt **18, 47**
Fisher, Derek **97**
Fox, Rick **27**
Green, A. C. **32**
Hazzard, Walt **98**
Johnson, Magic **3, 39, 101**
Odom, Lamar **81**
O'Neal, Shaquille **8, 30, 95**
Thompson, Mychal **126**
Worthy, James **49**

Los Angeles Philharmonic
Lewis, Henry **38**

Los Angeles Police Department (LAPD)
Parks, Bernard C. **17**
Smith, Richard **51**
Williams, Willie L. **4**

Lost-Found Nation of Islam
Ellison, Keith **59**
Farrakhan, Louis **2, 15**
Heard, Nathan C. **45**
Karim, Benjamin **61**
Muhammad, Ava **31**
Muhammad, Elijah **4**
Muhammad, Jabir Herbert **72**
Muhammad, Khallid Abdul **10, 31**
Muhammed, W. Deen **27**
Sutton, Percy E. **42, 82**
Tillard, Conrad **47**
X, Malcolm **1**
X, Marvin **45**

Louisiana state government
Fields, Cleo **13**
Francis, Norman (C.) **60**
Glover, Cedric B. **103**
Jefferson, William J. **25, 72**
Morial, Ernest "Dutch" **26**
Peterson, Karen Carter **90**
Pinchback, P. B. S. **9**
Richardson, Rupert **67**
Richmond, Cedric **93**

Lutheran
Herzfeld, Will L. **132**
Young, Rosa J. **129**

Lynching (anti-lynching legislation)
Moore, Harry T. **29**
Till, Emmett **7**

MacArthur Foundation Fellowship
Abraham, Kyle **116**
Allen, Will **74**
Awuah, Patrick **111, 131**
Benjamin, Regina **20, 75**
Braxton, Anthony **128**
Butler, Octavia **8, 43, 58**
Carter, Majora **77**
Carter, Regina **23, 131**
Coates, Ta-Nehisi **76, 131**
Coleman, Ornette **39, 69, 129**
Coleman, Steve **124**
Cooper, Lisa **73**

Dabiri, John **93**
Danticat, Edwidge **15, 68, 128**
Eberhardt, Jennifer **124**
Frazier, LaToya Ruby **131**
Gordon-Reed, Annette **74**
Hammons, David **69**
Harris, Corey **39, 73**
Hayes, Terrance **124**
Jackson, Mary **73**
Johnson, Angela **52**
Johnson, Charles **1, 82**
Jones, Edward P. **43, 67**
Lee, Raphael C. **87**
Lindsey, Tommie **51**
Lovell, Whitfield **74**
Lowe, Rick **124**
McCraney, Tarell Alvin **116**
Mehretu, Julie **85**
Moran, Jason **89**
Nelson, Stanley **92**
Olopade, Olufunmilayo Falusi **58**
Parks, Suzan-Lori **34, 85**
Robinson, Aminah **50**
Shirley, Aaron **126**
Stevenson, Bryan **128**
Taylor, Cecil **70**
Walcott, Derek **5, 94**
Whitehead, Colson **77**
Williams, Patricia **11, 54**

MacNeil/Lehrer NewsHour
Hunter-Gault, Charlayne **6, 31**

Mad TV
Jones, Orlando **30**
Wilson, Debra **38**

Madame C. J. Walker Manufacturing Company
Joyner, Marjorie Stewart **26**
Walker, A'lelia **14**
Walker, Madame C. J. **7**

Major League Baseball administration
Hill, Michael **95**
Lucas, Bill **97**
Mariner, Jonathan **41**
Solomon, Jimmie Lee **38**
Young, John **111**

Malawi government
Banda, Hastings Kamuzu **6, 54**
Banda, Joyce **101**
Muluzi, Bakili **14, 76**

Mali government
Keïta, Ibrahim Boubacar **113**
Touré, Amadou Toumani **18**
Traore, Dioncounda **103**

Managing, Sports
See Coaching/Managing, Sports

Manhattan Project
Quarterman, Lloyd Albert **4**
Wilkins, J. Ernest, Jr. **43**

March on Washington/Freedom March
Baker, Josephine **3**
Belafonte, Harry **4, 65**
Bunche, Ralph J. **5**
Davis, Ossie **5, 50**
Fauntroy, Walter E. **11**

Forman, James **7, 51**
Franklin, John Hope **5, 77**
Hedgeman, Anna Arnold **22**
Jackson, Mahalia **5**
Jones, Clarence B. **114**
King, Coretta Scott **3, 57**
King, Martin Luther, Jr. **1**
Lewis, John **2, 46, 83**
Meredith, James H. **11**
Randolph, A. Philip **3**
Rustin, Bayard **4**
Sleet, Moneta, Jr. **5, 136**
Wilkins, Roy **4**
Woods, Abraham, Jr. **74**
Young, Whitney M., Jr. **4**

Marketing
DeVard, Jerri **61**
Edwards, Trevor **54**
Fils-Aimé, Reggie **74**
Gaskins, Rudy **74**
Jackson, James A. **90**
Kaigler, Denise **63**
Kendrick, Erika **57**
Leary, Kathryn D. **10**
Miller, Pepper **96**
Moyo, Karega Kofi **36**
Moyo, Yvette Jackson **36**
Rolle, Janet **97**

Martial arts
Barnes, Steven **54**
Copeland, Michael **47**
Kelly, Jim **113**
White, Michael Jai **71, 117**

Martin Luther King Jr. Center for Nonviolent Social Change
Dodson, Howard, Jr. **7, 52**
Farris, Isaac Newton, Jr. **63**
King, Bernice **4, 81**
King, Coretta Scott **3, 57**
King, Dexter **10**
King, Martin Luther, Jr. **1**
King, Yolanda **6**

Martin Luther King Jr. National Memorial Project
Johnson, Harry E. **57**

Marxism
Bishop, Maurice **39**
Jagan, Cheddi **16**
Machel, Samora Moises **8**
Nkrumah, Kwame **3**
Sankara, Thomas **17**

Maryland state government
Brown, Anthony G. **72**
Carter, Jill P. **110**
Currie, Ulysses **73**
Lyons, James E., Sr. **102**
Steele, Michael **38, 73, 91**
Welcome, Verda Freeman **112**

Massachusetts state government
Brooke, Edward W. **8, 88, 126**
Gourdin, Edward O. **93**
Hayden, Lewis **105**
Lewis, William Henry **89**
Patrick, Deval **12, 61, 127**

Masters Golf Tournament
Elder, Lee 6
Woods, Tiger 14, 31, 81

Mathematics
Alcorn, George Edward, Jr. 59
Banneker, Benjamin 93
Blackwell, David 79
Cox, Elbert Frank 111
Deconge-Watson, Lovenia 55
Emeagwali, Philip 30
Falconer, Etta Zuber 59
Granville, Evelyn Boyd 36
Johnson, Katherine 61
Price, Richard 51
Urschel, John 126
Wilkins, J. Ernest, Jr. 43

Maxwell House Coffee Company
Fudge, Ann (Marie) 11, 55

McDonald's Corporation
Thompson, Don 56, 108

McGill University (Canada)
Elliott, Lorris 37

MCP
See Malawi Congress Party

Medical examiners
Carter, Joye Maureen 41
Omalu, Bennet 132

Medicine
Adams-Campbell, Lucille L. 60
Anderson, William G(ilchrist) 57
Atim, Julian 66
Augusta, Alexander T. 111
Banda, Hastings Kamuzu 6, 54
Barnett, Herman 112
Bashir, Halima 73
Benjamin, Regina 20, 75
Black, Keith Lanier 18, 84
Brimm, Charles E. 105
Callender, Clive O. 3
Carroll, L. Natalie 44
Carter, Joye Maureen 41
Chatard, Peter 44
Chinn, May Edward 26
Cobb, W. Montague 39
Cole, Rebecca 38
Comer, James P. 6
Coney, PonJola 48
Cooper, Edward S. 6
Cooper, Lisa 73
Cornwell, Edward E., III 70
Counter, S. Allen 74
Crumpler, Rebecca Lee 89
Dailey, Ulysses Grant 87
Deas, Gerald 85
Dickens, Helen Octavia 14, 64
Drake, Michael V. 122
Drew, Charles Richard 7
Durham, James 90
Edwards, Lena Frances 76
Edwards, Willarda V. 59
Fennoy, Ilene 72
Fisher, Ada M. 76
Fisher, Rudolph 17
Flowers, Sylester 50
Foster, Henry W., Jr. 26
Fraser, Sarah Loguen 100
Freeman, Harold P. 23

French, D. M. 94
Fuller, Solomon Carter, Jr. 15
Gayle, Helene D. 3
Gibbons, Gary 107
Gibson, William F. 6
Giles, Roscoe C. 93
Goodlett, Carlton B. 91
Grant, Augustus O. 71
Grier, Eliza Ann 90
Griffin, Anthony 71
Griffith, Patrick A. 64
Hamburg, Margaret 78
Hansberry, Tony, II 93
Harris, Bernard A. 90
Hinton, William Augustus 8
Holmes, Hamilton E. 82
Hopkins, Donald R. 89
Hutcherson, Hilda Yvonne 54
Jefferson, Mildred Fay 89
Johnson, R. M. 36
Jones, Edith Mae Irby 65
Joseph, Kathie-Ann 56
Keith, Rachel Boone 63
Kenney, John A., Jr. 48
Kintaudi, Leon 62
Kong, B. Waine 50
Kountz, Samuel L. 10
Lacks, Henrietta 101
Lavizzo-Mourey, Risa 48
Lawless, Theodore K. 8
Lee, Raphael C. 87
Leevy, Carroll M. 42
Leffall, Lasalle 3, 64
Logan, Onnie Lee 14
Malveaux, Floyd 54
Maxey, Randall 46
Mossell, Nathan Francis 91
Naki, Hamilton 63
Nour, Nawal M. 56
Okaalet, Peter 58
Olopade, Olufunmilayo Falusi 58
Osman, Said 127
Pace, Betty 59
Pape, Jean William 126
Parker, Willie J. 133
Petioni, Muriel 99
Pinn, Vivian Winona 49
Pitt, David Thomas 10
Rabb, Maurice F., Jr. 58
Randolph, Linda A. 52
Reece, E. Albert 63
Ross-Lee, Barbara 67
Scantlebury-White, Velma 64
Smith, Ian 62
Stewart, Ella 39
Sweet, Ossian 68
Taylor, Susan C. 62
Thomas, Claudia Lynn 64
Thomas, Vivien 9
Thornton, Yvonne S. 69
Tuckson, Reed V. 71
Walker, Joseph Edison 111
Washington, Harriet A. 69
Watkins, Levi, Jr. 9
Welsing, Frances Cress 5
White, Augustus, III 100
White-Hammond, Gloria 61
Williams, Daniel Hale 2
Wilson, Donald E. 88
Witt, Edwin T. 26
Wright, Charles H. 35

Wright, Louis Tompkins 4

Meharry Medical College
Coney, PonJola 48
Foster, Henry W., Jr. 26
Griffith, Patrick A. 64
Lyttle, Hulda Margaret 14

Men's movement
Somé, Malidoma Patrice 10

Merrill Lynch & Co., Inc.
Ford, Harold E(ugene), Jr. 16, 70
Matthews Shatteen, Westina 51
O'Neal, Stanley 38, 67

Meteorology
Anderson, Charles Edward 37
Bacon-Bercey, June 38

Mexican baseball league
Bell, James "Cool Papa" 36
Dandridge, Ray 36

Miami Dolphins football team
Cox, Bryan 83
Greene, Joe 10
Little, Larry 90
Morris, Mercury 114
Williams, Ricky 85

Michigan state government
Brown, Cora 33
Collins, Barbara-Rose 7, 87
Kilpatrick, Carolyn Cheeks 16
Reeves, Triette Lipsey 27
Wisdom, Kimberlydawn 57

Michigan Supreme Court
Archer, Dennis 7, 36
Mallett, Conrad, Jr. 16

Michigan State University
Wharton, Clifton R., Jr. 7

Midwifery
Logan, Onnie Lee 14
Mason, Biddy 89
Robinson, Sharon 22

Military police
Cadoria, Sherian Grace 14

Militia
Kony, Joseph 101
Lubanga, Thomas 104
Nkunda, Laurent 75
Ojukwu, Odumegwu 99

Miller Brewing Company
Colbert, Virgis William 17
Shropshire, Thomas B. 49

Millinery
Bailey, Xenobia 11

Million Man March
Farrakhan, Louis 2, 15
Hawkins, La-Van 17, 54
Worrill, Conrad 12

Milwaukee Brewers baseball team
Aaron, Hank 5
Baylor, Don 6

Milwaukee Bucks basketball team
Abdul-Jabbar, Kareem 8
Bridgeman, Junior 132

Robertson, Oscar 26

Minneapolis city government
Belton, Sharon Sayles 9, 16

Minnesota Supreme Court
Page, Alan 7

Minnesota Timberwolves basketball team
Garnett, Kevin 14, 70, 118

Minnesota Twins baseball team
Baylor, Don 6
Carew, Rod 20
Puckett, Kirby 4, 58

Minnesota Vikings football team
Carter, Cris 21, 109
Culpepper, Daunte 32, 85
Cunningham, Randall 23
Fowler, Reggie 51
Gilliam, Frank 23
Green, Dennis 5, 45
McDaniel, Randall Cornell 81
Moon, Warren 8, 66
Moss, Randy 23, 90
Page, Alan 7
Peterson, Adrian 109
Randle, John 87
Rashad, Ahmad 18
Stringer, Korey 35

Minority Business Enterprise Legal Defense and Education Fund
Mitchell, Parren J. 42, 66

Minstrel shows
Lane, William Henry 90
McDaniel, Hattie 5

Miss America
Dunlap, Ericka 55
Harold, Erika 54
Vincent, Marjorie Judith 2
Williams, Vanessa L. 4, 17

Miss Universe
Lopes, Leila 99

Miss USA
Gist, Carole 1

Miss World
Darego, Agbani 52

Mississippi state government
Anderson, Reuben V. 81
Fleming, Erik R. 75

Missouri state government
Wilson, Margaret Bush 79

Mixed martial arts
Davis, Phil 132
Jackson, Rampage 83
Jones, Jon 121
Silva, Anderson 96
Slice, Kimbo 73, 136

Modeling
Allen-Buillard, Melba 55
Banks, Tyra 11, 50
Beauvais, Garcelle 29, 95

Beckford, Tyson 11, 68
Berry, Halle 4, 19, 57, 91
Campbell, Naomi 1, 31, 120
Darego, Agbani 52
Davis, Mia Amber 94
Dirie, Waris 56
Dobson, Tamara 111
Dunn, Jourdan 130
Ebanks, Selita 67
Gibson, Tyrese 27, 62, 134
Hardison, Bethann 12
Hounsou, Djimon 19, 45
Iman 4, 33, 87
Iman, Chanel 66
Johnson, Beverly 2, 102
Kebede, Liya 59
Kodjoe, Boris 34, 89
Langhart Cohen, Janet 19, 60
Leslie, Lisa 16, 73
LisaRaye 27
Lopes, Leila 99
Marcille, Eva 97
McKenzie, Jaunel 73
Michele, Michael 31
Niane, Katoucha 70
Onwurah, Ngozi 38
Rochon, Lela 16
RuPaul 17, 91
Sarpong, Sam 132
Simmons, Kimora Lee 51, 83
Sims, Naomi 29, 79
Smith, B(arbara) 11
Tamia 24, 55
Taylor, Karin 34
Watley, Jody 54
Webb, Veronica 10, 95
Wek, Alek 18, 63, 105

Modern dance
Ailey, Alvin 8
Allen, Debbie 13, 42
Brown, Ronald K. 91
Byrd, Donald 10
Collins, Janet 33, 64
Davis, Chuck 33
Diggs, Taye 25, 63
Dove, Ulysses 5
Fagan, Garth 18, 98
Faison, George 16
Henson, Darrin 33
Jeune, Vitolio 98
Jones, Bill T. 1, 46, 80
King, Alonzo 38
Kitt, Eartha 16, 75
Miller, Bebe 3
Pomare, Eleo 72
Spears, Warren 52
Vereen, Ben 4
Williams, Dudley 60

Montgomery bus boycott
Abernathy, Ralph David 1
Baker, Ella 5
Burks, Mary Fair 40
Carr, Johnnie 69
Jackson, Mahalia 5
Killens, John O. 54
King, Martin Luther, Jr. 1
Nixon, Edgar Daniel 100
Parks, Rosa 1, 35, 56
Robinson, Joann Gibson 100

Rustin, Bayard 4

Montgomery County (MD) Police Department
Moose, Charles 40

Montreal Expos baseball team
Dawson, Andre 85
Doby, Lawrence Eugene, Sr. 16, 41

Morehouse College
Brown, Uzee 42
Gloster, Hugh Morris, Sr. 90
Hill, Marc Lamont 80, 128
Hope, John 8
Mays, Benjamin E. 7
Satcher, David 7, 57, 111

Motivational speaking
Bahati, Wambui 60
Baisden, Michael 66
Blanchard, Shawn 129
Bozella, Dewey 97
Brown, Les 5
Bunkley, Anita Richmond 39
Creagh, Milton 27
Gardner, Chris 65
Grant, Gwendolyn Goldsby 28
Gray, Farrah 59
Jolley, Willie 28
July, William 27
Kimbro, Dennis 10
LeGrand, Eric 118
Munroe, Myles 125
Russell-McCloud, Patricia 17
Shabazz, Ilyasah 36
Shelton, Trent 122
Tuff, Antoinette 120
Tyson, Asha 39
Yarber, Tony 129

Motorcycle racing
Brown, Antron 85
Showers, Reggie 30
Stewart, James, Jr. 60, 98

Motown Records
Atkins, Cholly 40
Avant, Clarence 19, 86
Ballard, Florence 112
Birdsong, Cindy 113
Bizimungu, Pasteur 19
Busby, Jheryl 3, 74
de Passe, Suzanne 25
Edwards, Esther Gordy 43
Gaye, Anna Gordy 121
Gaye, Marvin 2
Gordy, Berry, Jr. 1
Harrell, Andre 9, 30
Holland-Dozier-Holland 36
Holloway, Brenda 65
Hutch, Willie 62
Jackson, George 19
Jamerson, James 59
Jones, Robert G. 81
Kendricks, Eddie 22
Knight, Gladys 16, 66
Massenburg, Kedar 23, 110
Powell, Maxine 8, 115
Richie, Lionel 27, 65, 114
Robinson, Smokey 3, 49
Ross, Diana 8, 27
Sanders, Angelia 86
Supremes, The 33
Terrell, Jean 116

Terrell, Tammi 32
Wells, Mary 28
Whitfield, Norman 73
Wilson, Frank 106
Wilson, Mary 28
Wonder, Stevie 11, 53, 121

Mount Holyoke College
Tatum, Beverly Daniel 42, 84

Movement for Democratic Change (MDC)
Moyo, Lovemore 76
Tsvangirai, Morgan 26, 72

Mozambique government
Chissano, Joaquim 7, 55, 67
Diogo, Luisa Dias 63
Guebuza, Armando 81
Machel, Graça 16, 102
Machel, Samora Moises 8

Multimedia art
Adkins, Terry 122
Amaki, Amalia 76
Bailey, Xenobia 11
Lovell, Whitfield 74
Owens, Clifford 129
Pinder, Jefferson 77
Robinson, Aminah 50
Simpson, Lorna 4, 36

Muppets, The
Clash, Kevin 14, 93

Museum of Modern Art
Pindell, Howardena 55
Smith, Ming 100

Music Critics Circle
Holt, Nora 38

Music publishing
Avant, Nicole A. 90
Edmonds, Tracey 16, 64
Griffey, Dick 89
Gryce, Gigi 124
Handy, W. C. 8
Holland-Dozier-Holland 36
Humphrey, Bobbi 20
Jackson, George 19
James, Rick 17
Martin, Sallie 120
Mayfield, Curtis 2, 43
Otis, Clyde 67
Pryce, Trevor 89
Redding, Otis 16
Riley, Boots 89
Shorty, Ras, I 47
Strong, Barrett 89

Music Television (MTV)
Bellamy, Bill 12
Chideya, Farai 14, 61
Morton, Frederick A., Jr. 93
Norman, Christina 47
Powell, Kevin 31, 74
Run 31, 73

Musical composition
Anderson, T. J. 119
Armatrading, Joan 32, 133
Ashford, Nickolas 21, 97
Ashford and Simpson 21, 97
Attaway, William 102
Baiocchi, Regina Harris 41

Ballard, Hank 41
Battiste, Harold, Jr. 136
Bebey, Francis 45
Bell, LeRoy 98
Benson, Obie 96
Bland, Edward 111
Blige, Mary J. 20, 34, 60, 97
Bonds, Margaret 39
Bonga, Kuenda 13
Boulogne, Joseph, Chevalier de Saint-Georges 94
Braxton, Anthony 128
Bridgetower, George 78
Brown, Dennis 99
Brown, Patrick "Sleepy" 50
Brown, Uzee 42
Burleigh, Henry Thacker 56
Caesar, Shirley 19
Campbell, Lucie E. 118
Carter, Ron 104
Carter, Warrick L. 27
Castor, Jimmy 100
Chapman, Tracy 26
Charlemagne, Manno 11
Charles, Ray 16, 48
Cleveland, James 19
Cole, J. 97
Cole, Natalie 17, 60, 84, 133
Coleman, Steve 124
Collins, Bootsy 31
Davis, Anthony 11
Davis, Miles 4
Davis, Sammy, Jr. 18
Dawson, William Levi 39
Diddley, Bo 39, 72
Domino, Fats 20
Ellington, Duke 5
Ellington, Mercer 129
Europe, James Reese 10
Evans, Faith 22
Freeman, Paul 39
Fuller, Arthur 27
Gamble, Kenny 85
Garrett, Sean 57
Gaynor, Gloria 36
Gillespie, Dizzy 1
Golson, Benny 37
Grant, Micki 125
Greaves, R. B. 106
Green, Al 13, 47, 74
Gryce, Gigi 124
Hailey, JoJo 22
Hailey, K-Ci 22
Handy, W. C. 8
Harris, Corey 39, 73
Hathaway, Donny 18
Hayes, Isaac 20, 58, 73
Hayes, Teddy 40
Hibbert, Toots 103
Holland-Dozier-Holland 36
Holmes, Clint 57
Holt, Nora 38
Humphrey, Bobbi 20
Hutch, Willie 62
Isley, Ronald 25, 56
Jackson, Christopher 136
Jackson, Fred James 25
Jackson, Michael 19, 53, 76
Jackson, Randy 40
James, Rick 17
Jerkins, Rodney 31
Johnson, Buddy 36
Johnson, Georgia Douglas 41

Johnson, J. Rosamond **121**
Jones, Jonah **39**
Jones, Quincy **8, 30**
Jones, Thad **68**
Joplin, Scott **6**
Jordan, Montell **23**
Jordan, Ronny **26**
Kay, Ulysses **37**
Kelly, R. **18, 44, 71, 117**
Keys, Alicia **32, 68**
Kidjo, Angelique **50**
Killings, Debra **57**
Lebo M **109**
León, Tania **13**
Lewis, George **104**
Little Milton **36, 54**
Little Walter **36**
Mahlasela, Vusi **65**
Majors, Jeff **41**
Martin, Roberta **58**
Maxwell **20, 81**
Mayfield, Curtis **2, 43**
M.C. Hammer **20, 80**
McFerrin, Bobby **68**
Mills, Stephanie **36**
Mitchell, Brian Stokes **21**
Mitchell, Roscoe **134**
Monica **21**
Moore, Dorothy Rudd **46**
Moore, Undine Smith **28**
Muse, Clarence Edouard **21**
Nash, Johnny **40**
Ndegeocello, Meshell **15, 83**
Nelson, Oliver **113**
Osborne, Jeffrey **26, 121**
Otis, Clyde **67**
Parker, Ray, Jr. **85**
Pratt, Awadagin **31**
Price, Florence **37**
Pritchard, Robert Starling **21**
Redding, Otis **16**
Reed, A. C. **36**
Roach, Max **21, 63**
Robinson, Reginald R. **53**
Run-DMC **31, 75**
Russell, Brenda **52**
Santigold **96**
Scott-Heron, Gil **94**
Seal **14, 75**
Shirley, Donald **111**
Shorty, Ras, I **47**
Simpson, Valerie **21, 97**
Smith, Hale **118**
Somi **85**
Sowande, Fela **39**
Stewart, Tricky **98**
Still, William Grant **37**
Strayhorn, Billy **31**
Sundiata, Sekou **66**
Sweat, Keith **19**
Threadgill, Henry **97**
Tillis, Frederick **40**
Toussaint, Allen **60, 132**
Trombone Shorty **97**
Usher **23, 56, 95**
Van Peebles, Melvin **7, 95**
Walker, George **37**
Washington, Grover, Jr. **17, 44**
Williams, Deniece **36**
Williams, Tony **67**
Wilson, Abram **104**
Wilson, Frank **106**
Winans, Angie **36**

Winans, Debbie **36**
Withers, Bill **61**
Wooten, Victor **131**

Musical direction
Barnes, Katreese **97**
Bonds, Margaret **39**
Europe, James Reese **10**
Johnson, Ken **106**
Rushen, Patrice **12**

Musicology
George, Zelma Watson **42**

Mystery/detective fiction
Bates, Karen Grigsby **40**
Bland, Eleanor Taylor **39**
Creagh, Milton **27**
DeLoach, Nora **30**
Hayes, Teddy **40**
Haywood, Gar Anthony **43**
Himes, Chester **8**
Holton, Hugh, Jr. **39**
Mickelbury, Penny **28**
Mosley, Walter **5, 25, 68**
Thomas-Graham, Pamela **29**
Wesley, Valerie Wilson **18**

NAACP
See National Association for the
　Advancement of Colored People

NAACP Image Awards
Alexander, Michelle **98**
Ali, Muhammad **2, 16, 52, 136**
Barclay, Paris **37, 94, 133**
Brandy **14, 34, 72**
Caesar, Adolph **133**
Cannon, Nick **47, 73, 132**
Cole, Natalie **17, 60, 84, 133**
Cosby, Bill **7, 26, 59, 125**
Dyson, Michael Eric **11, 40, 128**
Ejogo, Carmen **126**
Fields, Kim **36**
Freeman, Morgan **2, 20, 62, 100**
Gibson, Tyrese **27, 62, 134**
Glover, Danny **1, 24, 103**
Henson, Taraji P. **58, 77, 127**
Lattimore, Kenny **35, 128**
Lawrence, Martin **6, 27, 60**
Mac, Bernie **29, 61, 72**
McRae, Carmen **77**
Mitchell, Roscoe **134**
Moore, Chanté **26, 130**
Moore, Shemar **21, 112**
Nelson, Kadir **115**
Nyong'o, Lupita **127**
Okonedo, Sophie **67**
Prince **18, 65, 134**
Prince-Bythewood, Gina **31, 77**
Rhimes, Shonda Lynn **67**
Scribner, Marcus **136**
Spencer, Octavia **100**
Taylor, Regina **9, 46, 97**
Tony! Toni! Toné! **127**
Warner, Malcolm-Jamal **22, 36, 110**
Washington, Kerry **46, 107**
Wesley, Richard **73**
Wilson, Charlie **31, 77, 135**

**NAACP Legal Defense and
Educational Fund (LDF)**
Berrien, Jacqueline A. **93**
Chambers, Julius **3**
Coleman, James E., Jr. **79**

Coleman, William T. **76**
Days, Drew S., III **10**
Edelman, Marian Wright **5, 42**
Fisher, Ada Lois Sipuel **76**
Guinier, Lani **7, 30**
Jones, Elaine R. **7, 45**
Marshall, Thurgood **1, 44**
Motley, Constance Baker **10, 55**
Payton, John **48, 124**
Rice, Constance LaMay **60**
Smith, Kemba **70**
Smythe Haith, Mabel **61**

NABJ
See National Association of Black
　Journalists

NACW
See National Association of Col-
　ored Women

Namibia government
Mbuende, Kaire **12**
Nujoma, Samuel **10**
Pohamba, Hifikepunye **95**

NASA
See National Aeronautics and
　Space Administration

NASCAR
See National Association for Stock
　Car Auto Racing

Nation of Islam
See Lost-Found Nation of Islam

**National Aeronautics and
Space Administration (NASA)**
Alexander, Claudia **130**
Anderson, Michael P. **40**
Bluford, Guy **2, 35**
Bolden, Charles Frank, Jr. **7, 78**
Campbell, Donald J. **66**
Carruthers, George R. **40**
Douglas, Donya **97**
Drew, Alvin, Jr. **67**
Easley, Annie J. **61**
Ericsson-Jackson, Aprille **28**
Gregory, Frederick **8, 51**
Harris, Bernard A. **90**
Higginbotham, Joan **124**
Jemison, Mae C. **1, 35, 129**
Johnson, Katherine **61**
Johnson, Lonnie G. **32, 93**
McNair, Ronald **3, 58**
Mills, Joseph C. **51**
Nichols, Nichelle **11**
Sigur, Wanda **44**
Wilson, Stephanie **72**

**National Association for the
Advancement of Colored
People (NAACP)**
Anderson, Reuben V. **81**
Anderson, William G(ilchrist) **57**
Anthony, Wendell **25**
Austin, Junius C. **44**
Ballance, Frank W. **41**
Bond, Julian **2, 35, 106, 130**
Brock, Roslyn McCallister **86**
Brown, Homer S. **47**
Chambers, Julius **3**
Chavis, Benjamin **6**
Cobb, W. Montague **39**
Coleman, Beatrice **120**

Du Bois, W. E. B. **3**
DuBois, Shirley Graham **21**
Dukes, Hazel Nell **56**
Farmer, James **2, 64**
Fuller, S. B. **13**
Grimké, Archibald H. **9**
Hampton, Fred **18**
Hayes, Dennis **54**
Henderson, Wade **14**
Hollowell, Donald L. **57**
Hooks, Benjamin L. **2, 85**
Houston, Charles Hamilton **4**
Jealous, Benjamin Todd **70, 113**
Kidd, Mae Street **39**
Lampkin, Daisy **19**
Law, W. W. **121**
Madison, Joseph E. **17**
Marshall, Thurgood **1, 44**
McKissick, Floyd B. **3**
Meredith, James H. **11**
Mfume, Kweisi **6, 41**
Miller, Lorraine C. **119**
Mitchell, Clarence M., Jr. **88**
Moore, Harry T. **29**
Morgan, Irene **65**
Moses, Robert Parris **11**
Motley, Constance Baker **10, 55**
Moyo, Yvette Jackson **36**
Richardson, Rupert **67**
Rustin, Bayard **4**
Simkins, Modjeska Monteith **112**
Sutton, Percy E. **42, 82**
Talbert, Mary B. **77**
Terrell, Mary Church **9**
Tobias, Channing H. **79**
Tucker, C. Delores **12, 56**
Van Lierop, Robert **53**
White, Walter F. **4**
Wilkins, Roy **4**
Wilson, Margaret Bush **79**
Wright, Louis Tompkins **4**

**National Association of Black
Journalists (NABJ)**
Curry, George E. **23**
Dawkins, Wayne **20**
Harris, Jay T. **19**
Jarrett, Vernon D. **42, 135**
Lowe, Herbert **57**
Payne, Les **89**
Pressley, Condace L. **41**
Rice, Linda Johnson **9, 41**
Shipp, E. R. **15**
Stone, Chuck **9, 120**
Washington, Laura S. **18**

**National Association of
Broadcasters Hall of Fame**
Harvey, Steve **18, 58**
Jackson, Hal **41, 104**
Joyner, Tom **19, 90**

**National Association of Col-
ored Women (NACW)**
Bethune, Mary McLeod **4**
Butler, Selena Sloan **98**
Cook-Parrish, Mary Virginia **95**
Cooper, Margaret J. **4**
Harper, Frances Ellen Watkins **11**
Lampkin, Daisy **19**
Ruffin, Josephine St. Pierre **75**
Stewart, Ella **39**
Talbert, Mary B. **77**
Terrell, Mary Church **9**

Washington, Margaret Murray 119

National Association for Stock Car Auto Racing (NASCAR)
Lester, Bill 42, 85

National Baptist Convention USA
Bradley, J. Robert 65
Jemison, T. J. 119
Jones, E. Edward, Sr. 45
Lyons, Henry 12, 118
Shaw, William J. 30
Thurston, Stephen J. 49

National Bar Association
Alexander, Joyce London 18
Alexander, Sadie Tanner Mossell 22
Archer, Dennis 7, 36
Bailey, Clyde 45
Hubbard, Arnette 38
Pincham, R. Eugene, Sr. 69
Quince, Peggy A. 69
Ray, Charlotte E. 60
Robinson, Malcolm S. 44
Thompson, Larry D. 39
Walker, Cora T. 68

National Basketball Players Association
Fisher, Derek 97
Gourdine, Simon 11
Hunter, Billy 22, 109
Roberts, Michele 123

National Black Farmers Association (NBFA)
Boyd, John W., Jr. 20, 72

National Book Awards
Coates, Ta-Nehisi 76, 131
Ellison, Ralph 7
Haley, Alex 4
Hayes, Terrance 124
Johnson, Charles 1, 82
Mackey, Nathaniel 75
Patterson, Orlando 4, 127
Woodson, Jacqueline 125

National Broadcasting Company (NBC)
Gumbel, Bryant 14, 80
Hinderas, Natalie 5
Holt, Lester 66
Johnson, Rodney Van 28
Madison, Paula 37, 99
Reynolds, Star Jones 10, 27, 61
Roker, Al 12, 49
Schiavocampo, Mara 97
Simpson, Carole 6, 30
Thomas-Graham, Pamela 29
Williams, Montel 4, 57

National Coalition of 100 Black Women (NCBW)
Mays, Leslie A. 41
McCabe, Jewell Jackson 10

National Council of Negro Women (NCNW)
Bethune, Mary McLeod 4
Blackwell, Unita 17
Cole, Johnnetta B. 5, 43
Height, Dorothy I. 2, 23, 78
Lampkin, Daisy 19

Smith, Jane E. 24

National Cowboys of Color Museum and Hall of Fame
Austin, Gloria 63
Austin, Jim 63
Pickett, Bill 11
Pride, Charley 26
Sampson, Charles 13

National Education Association (NEA)
Futrell, Mary Hatwood 33
Koontz, Elizabeth Duncan 101

National Endowment for the Arts (NEA)
Barthé, Earl 78
Bradley, David Henry, Jr. 39
Brown, Chuck 78, 102
Bullins, Ed 25, 121
Coleman, Wanda 48, 119
Edwards, David 122
Hall, Arthur 39
Harper, Michael S. 34, 136
Hemphill, Essex 10
Jackson, Angela 134
Kirk, Andy 134
Pope.L, William 72
Serrano, Andres 3
Williams, John A. 27
Williams, William T. 11

National Football League (NFL)
Alexander, Shaun 58
Allen, Larry 109
Allen, Marcus 20
Anderson, Jamal 22
Asomugha, Nnamdi 100
Barber, Ronde 41
Barber, Tiki 57, 107
Barney, Lem 26
Batch, Charlie 120
Beckham, Odell, Jr. 132
Bell, Le'Veon 132
Berry, Eric 125
Bettis, Jerome 64
Bowles, Todd 128
Bridgewater, Teddy 132
Briscoe, Marlin 37
Brooks, Aaron 33
Brooks, Derrick 43, 119
Brown, Jason 125
Brown, Jerry 117
Brown, Jim 11, 95
Brown, Tim 134
Bruce, Isaac 26
Bryant, Cullen 81
Bryant, Dez 116
Bush, Reggie 59, 88
Butler, Leroy, III 17
Caldwell, Jim 81
Campbell, Earl 104
Carter, Cris 21, 109
Chancellor, Kam 131
Cherry, Deron 40
Cox, Bryan 83
Crennel, Romeo 54, 107
Cromartie, Antonio 115
Croom, Sylvester 50
Cruz, Victor 107
Culp, Curley 110
Culpepper, Daunte 32, 85

Cunningham, Randall 23
Davis, Milt 74
Davis, Terrell 20
Davis, Thomas 132
Davis, Vernon 133
Davis, Wade, Jr. 103
Dean, Fred 98
Delaney, Joe 76
Dent, Richard 97
Dickerson, Eric 27, 108
Driver, Donald 99
Duerson, Dave 93
Dungy, Tony 17, 42, 59, 118
Dunn, Warrick 90
Edwards, Herman 51
Farmer, Ray 133
Farr, Mel 24
Faulk, Marshall 35, 96
Fitzgerald, Larry 133
Foster, Arian 114
Fowler, Reggie 51
George, Eddie 80
Gilliam, Frank 23
Gilliam, Joe 31
Gordon, Josh 120
Gore, Frank 117
Green, Darrell 39, 74
Green, Dennis 5, 45
Greene, Joe 10
Greenwood, L. C. 115
Griffin, Robert, III 107
Haley, Charles 134
Hardy, Greg 118
Harris, Franco 97
Harris, James 79
Harrison, Marvin 134
Harvin, Percy 123
Heyward, Craig 131
Hill, Calvin 19
Holmes, Santonio 87
Howard, Desmond 16, 58
Humphrey, Claude 119
Hurd, Sam 116
Irvin, Michael 64
Jackson, DeSean 120
Jackson, Hue 133
Jackson, Rickey 88
Jackson, Tom 70
Jenkins, Kris 98
Johnson, Andre 127
Johnson, Calvin 108
Johnson, Chad 108
Johnson, Chris 92
Johnson, John Henry 96
Johnson, Keyshawn 91
Johnson, Levi 48
Joiner, Charlie 102
Jones, Adam 103
Jones, Deacon 92, 112
Jones, Jacoby 117
Jones, Julio 131
Jones, Walter 119
Jones-Drew, Maurice 113
Kennedy, Cortez 104
Ladd, Ernie 64
Lane, Dick 92
Lewis, Jamal 115
Lewis, Ray 33, 109
Little, Floyd 86
Little, Larry 90
Lofton, James 42
Lott, Ronnie 9
Lynch, Marshawn 124

Manley, Dexter 116
Mann, Bob 126
Marshall, Brandon 116
Martin, Curtis 104
Martin, Jonathan 119
Mathis, Robert 121
Matson, Ollie 93
May, Mark 117
Mayhew, Martin R. 76
McCoy, LeSean 123
McDaniel, Randall Cornell 81
McNabb, Donovan 29, 119
McNair, Steve 22, 47, 79
Mitchell, Freddie 116
Monk, Art 38, 73
Moon, Warren 8, 66
Morris, Mercury 114
Moss, Randy 23, 90
Motley, Marion 26
Muncie, Chuck 112
Newsome, Ozzie 26, 117
Newton, Cam 96
Ogden, Jonathan 110
Oliver, Paul 115
Owens, Brig 118
Owens, Terrell 53, 106
Pace, Orlando 21, 134
Page, Alan 7
Parker, Jim 64
Payton, Walter 11, 25
Peete, Rodney 60
Perry, Joe 95
Peters, Jason 125
Peterson, Adrian 109
Portis, Clinton 130
Pryce, Trevor 89
Randle, John 87
Rashad, Ahmad 18
Reece, Marcel 114
Reese, Jerry 103
Revis, Darrelle 130
Rhodes, Ray 14
Rice, Jerry 5, 55, 89
Rice, Ray 112
Roaf, Willie 106
Robinson, Dave 110
Rolle, Myron 98
Sam, Michael 121
Sanders, Barry 1, 53
Sanders, Bob 72
Sanders, Charlie 130
Sanders, Deion 4, 31, 96
Sapp, Warren 38, 109
Sayers, Gale 28
Seymour, Richard 101
Sharpe, Shannon 97
Sharper, Darren 32, 118
Shell, Art 1, 66
Shelton, Trent 122
Sherman, Richard 118
Simpson, O. J. 15, 100
Singletary, Mike 4, 76
Slater, Duke 125
Smith, Bubba 96
Smith, Bruce 80
Smith, DeMaurice 92
Smith, Emmitt 7, 87
Smith, Geno 118
Smith, Neil 109
Smith, Rick 72
Smith, Steve 120
Stallworth, John 102
Stewart, Kordell 21, 111

Stingley, Darryl **69**
Strahan, Michael **35, 81, 135**
Stringer, Korey **35**
Strode, Woody **111**
Suggs, Terrell **108**
Swann, Lynn **28**
Tatum, Jack **87**
Taylor, Jason **70**
Taylor, Lawrence **25**
Thomas, Derrick **25**
Thomas, Emmitt **71**
Thomas, Thurman **75**
Thrower, Willie **35**
Tolbert, Mike **125**
Toler, Burl **80**
Tomlin, Mike **123**
Tomlinson, LaDainian **65, 112**
Tunnell, Emlen **54**
Upshaw, Gene **18, 47, 72**
Urschel, John **126**
Vick, Michael **39, 65, 94**
Vincent, Troy **91**
Walker, Herschel **1, 69**
Ward, Hines **84**
Ware, Andre **37**
Ware, DeMarcus **92**
Washington, Kenny **50**
Watson, Benjamin **126**
Wayne, Reggie **131**
White, Reggie **6, 50**
Wilfork, Vince **124**
Williams, Darrent **116**
Williams, Doug **22, 112**
Williams, J. Mayo **83**
Williams, Ricky **85**
Williamson, Fred **67**
Willis, Patrick **99**
Wilson, David **123**
Wilson, Russell **119**
Winslow, Kellen **83**
Wood, Willie **111**
Wright, Rayfield **70**
Wyllie, Tony **131**

National Hockey League (NHL)
Brashear, Donald **39**
Brathwaite, Fred **35**
Brown, Sean **52**
Doig, Jason **45**
Fuhr, Grant **1, 49**
Grand-Pierre, Jean-Luc **46**
Grier, Mike **43**
Iginla, Jarome **35**
Kane, Evander **97**
Laraque, Georges **48**
Mayers, Jamal **39**
McBride, Bryant **18**
McCarthy, Sandy **64**
McKegney, Tony **3**
O'Ree, Willie **5**
Salvador, Bryce **51**
Simmonds, Wayne **121**
Subban, P. K. **121**
Ward, Joel **129**
Weekes, Kevin **67**

National Institutes of Health (NIH)
Anderson, Norman B. **45**
Cargill, Victoria A. **43**
Dunston, Georgia Mae **48**
Gibbons, Gary **107**

Pinn, Vivian Winona **49**

National Inventors Hall of Fame
Carruthers, George R. **40**

National Medical Association
Cole, Lorraine **48**
Giles, Roscoe C. **93**
Maxey, Randall **46**
Ojikutu, Bisola **65**

National Newspaper Publishers Association
Cooper, Andrew W. **36**
Jealous, Benjamin Todd **70, 113**
Oliver, John J., Jr. **48**

National Oceanic and Atmospheric Administration
Bacon-Bercey, June **38**
Fields, Evelyn J. **27**

National Organization for Women (NOW)
Hernandez, Aileen Clarke **13**
Kennedy, Florynce **12, 33**
Murray, Pauli **38**

National Parent Teacher Association
Butler, Selena Sloan **98**

National Public Radio (NPR)
Abu-Jamal, Mumia **15**
Bates, Karen Grigsby **40**
Bowles, Cephas **127**
Drummond, William J. **40**
Early, Gerald **15**
Jackson, Bobby **119**
Lewis, Delano **7**
Martin, Michel **97**
Mitchell, Elvis **67**
Norris, Michele **83**
Smiley, Tavis **20, 68**
Walker, Teshima **114**
Williams, Juan **35, 80**
Zook, Kristal Brent **62**

National Rifle Association (NRA)
Williams, Robert F. **11, 136**

National Science Foundation (NSF)
Jackson, Deborah **94**
Massey, Walter E. **5, 45**

National Security Council
Frazer, Jendayi **68**
Powell, Colin **1, 28, 75**
Rice, Condoleezza **3, 28, 72**
Rice, Susan **74, 103**
Sutphen, Mona **77**

National Union for the Total Independence of Angola (UNITA)
Roberto, Holden **65**
Savimbi, Jonas **2, 34**

National Urban League
Barrow, Willie T. **85, 128**
Berry, Edwin C. **81**
Gordon, Bruce S. **41, 53, 82**
Granger, Lester B. **75**

Greely, M. Gasby **27**
Haynes, George Edmund **8**
Jacob, John E. **2**
Jones, Eugene Kinckle **79**
Jordan, Vernon E. **3, 35**
Price, Hugh B. **9, 54**
Spriggs, William **67**
Young, Whitney M., Jr. **4**

National Wildlife Federation
Osborne, Na'taki **54**

National Women's Hall of Fame
Cary, Mary Ann Shadd **30**
Kelly, Leontine **33**
Talbert, Mary B. **77**

NBC
See National Broadcasting Company

NCBW
See National Coalition of 100 Black Women

NCNW
See National Council of Negro Women

NEA
See National Education Association; National Endowment for the Arts

Nebraska state government
Chambers, Ernie **130**

Nebula Awards
Butler, Octavia **8, 43, 58**
Delany, Samuel R., Jr. **9**

Négritude
Césaire, Aimé **48, 69**
Damas, Léon-Gontran **46**
Ndiaye, Iba **74**

Negro Ensemble Company
Cash, Rosalind **28**
Gordon, Carl **87**
Hooks, Robert **76**
Rolle, Esther **13, 21**
Schultz, Michael A. **6**
Ward, Douglas Turner **42**

Negro Leagues
Barnhill, David **30**
Bell, James "Cool Papa" **36**
Black, Joe **75**
Brown, Raymond **102**
Brown, Willard **36**
Campanella, Roy **25**
Charleston, Oscar **39**
Dandridge, Ray **36**
Davis, Piper **19**
Day, Leon **39**
Dihigo, Martín **103**
Foster, Andrew **79**
Gibson, Josh **22**
Gilliam, Jim **122**
Grant, Frank **100**
Hairston, Sam **88**
Hyde, Cowan F. "Bubba" **47**
Irvin, Monte **31, 134**
Johnson, Clifford "Connie" **52**
Johnson, Judy **105**
Johnson, Mamie "Peanut" **40**

Kaiser, Cecil **42**
Kimbro, Henry A. **25**
Leonard, Buck **67**
Lloyd, John Henry "Pop" **30**
Mackey, Biz **82**
Morton, Ferdinand Q. **90**
O'Neil, Buck **19, 59**
Paige, Satchel **7**
Pride, Charley **26**
Radcliffe, Ted **74**
Smith, Hilton **29**
Stearnes, Norman "Turkey" **31**
Stone, Toni **15**
Suttles, Mule **108**
Wells, Willie **105**
Whitney, Davey L. **110**

Netherlands Antilles government
Liberia-Peters, Maria Philomena **12**

Neurosurgery
Black, Keith Lanier **18, 84**
Canady, Alexa **28**
Carson, Ben **1, 35, 76, 128**
Dennis, Gary C. **91**

Nevada state government
Horsford, Steven **88**

New Jersey state government
Bryant, Wayne R. **6**
Payne, William D. **60**
Watson Coleman, Bonnie **127**

New Negro movement
See Harlem Renaissance

New Orleans city government
Henry, Troy **85**
Mason, Ronald **27**
Nagin, Ray **42, 57, 88**
Perry, James **83**

New Orleans Saints football team
Brooks, Aaron **33**
Mills, Sam **33**

New York City government
Adams, Eric **133**
Barron, Charles **136**
Barron, Inez **136**
Campbell, Mary Schmidt **43**
Davis, Gordon J. **76**
Dinkins, David **4**
Farrell, Herman D., Jr. **81**
Fields, C. Virginia **25**
Ford, Wallace **58**
Hageman, Hans **36**
McCray, Chirlane **134**
Paterson, Basil A. **69, 122**
Spigner, Archie **81**
Sutton, Percy E. **42**
Thompson, William, Jr. **35, 114**
Tolbert, Terence **74**
Walcott, Dennis M. **112**

New York Giants football team
Barber, Tiki **57, 107**
Reese, Jerry **103**
Strahan, Michael **35, 81, 135**
Taylor, Lawrence **25**

New York Jets football team
Jenkins, Kris **98**
Martin, Curtis **104**

Revis, Darrelle **130**
Smith, Geno **118**

New York Knicks basketball team
Ewing, Patrick **17, 73, 130**
Johnson, Larry **28**
Meminger, Dean **114**
Reed, Willis, Jr. **86**
Stith, Tom **93**

New York Mets baseball team
Clendenon, Donn **26, 56**
Manuel, Jerry **94**
Reyes, José **134**

New York Public Library
Baker, Augusta **38**
Dodson, Howard, Jr. **7, 52**

New York Shakespeare Festival
Browne, Roscoe Lee **66**
Gunn, Moses **10**
Wolfe, George C. **6, 43, 127**

New York state government
Adams, Eric **133**
Barron, Charles **136**
Barron, Inez **136**
Brown, Byron W. **72**
Farrell, Herman D., Jr. **81**
Jeffries, Hakeem **118**
Johnson, Edward Austin **107**
McCall, H. Carl **27**
Meeks, Gregory T. **25, 117**
Motley, Constance Baker **10, 55**
Owens, Major **6, 117**
Paterson, Basil A. **69, 122**
Paterson, David A. **59**
Smith, Malcolm A. **75**
Waldon, Alton R., Jr. **98**

New York State Supreme Court
Dudley, Edward R. **58**
Jones, Theodore T., Jr. **108**
Tingling, Milton A. **110**
Wright, Bruce McMarion **3, 52**

New York Stock Exchange
Doley, Harold, Jr. **26**

New York Times
Blair, Jayson **50**
Blow, Charles M. **73**
Boyd, Gerald M. **32, 59**
Broyard, Anatole **68**
Caldwell, Earl **60**
Canedy, Dana **132**
Cooper, Helene **74**
Herbert, Bob **63, 96**
Hunter-Gault, Charlayne **6, 31**
Mabry, Marcus **70**
Price, Hugh B. **9, 54**
Rhoden, William C. **67**
Wilkins, Roger **2, 84**

New York University
Campbell, Mary Schmidt **43**
Newkirk, Pamela **69**

New York Yankees baseball team
Baylor, Don **6**
Cano, Robinson **97**

Howard, Elston **125**
Jackson, Reggie **15**
Jeter, Derek **27, 93, 124**
Sabathia, CC **74**
Strawberry, Darryl **22**
Watson, Bob **25**
Williams, Bernie **128**
Winfield, Dave **5, 91**

Newark (NJ) city government
Baraka, Ras J. **121**
Booker, Cory Anthony **68**
Gibson, Kenneth Allen **6**
James, Sharpe **23, 69**
Payne, Donald M., Jr. **132**

Newbery medal
Alexander, Kwame **98**
Curtis, Christopher Paul **26, 113**
Hamilton, Virginia **10**

NFL
See National Football League

NHL
See National Hockey League

Niagara movement
Du Bois, W. E. B. **3**
Hope, John **8**
Talbert, Mary B. **77**
Trotter, Monroe **9**

Nickelodeon
DJ Lance Rock **94**
Mitchell, Kel **66, 131**
Thompson, Kenan **52**

Niger government
Issoufou, Mahamadou **102**
Tandja, Mamadou **33, 78**

Nigeria government
Abiola, Moshood **70**
Abubakar, Abdulsalami **66**
Akunyili, Dora Nkem **58**
Buhari, Muhammadu **128**
Jonathan, Goodluck **83**
Muhammed, Murtala **119**
Obasanjo, Olusegun **5**
Okonjo-Iweala, Ngozi **101**
Yar'Adua, Umaru **69, 89**

Nigerian military
Abacha, Sani **11, 70**
Abiola, Moshood **70**
Babangida, Ibrahim **4**
Buhari, Muhammadu **128**
Muhammed, Murtala **119**
Obasanjo, Olusegun **5, 22**
Ojukwu, Odumegwu **99**

NIH
See National Institutes of Health

Nike, Inc.
Edwards, Trevor **54**
Miller, Larry G. **72**

Nobel Peace Prize
Annan, Kofi Atta **15, 48**
Bunche, Ralph J. **5**
King, Martin Luther, Jr. **1**
Luthuli, Albert **13**
Maathai, Wangari **43, 97**
Obama, Barack **49, 74, 91**

Tutu, Desmond Mpilo **6, 44**

Nobel Prize in Literature
Morrison, Toni **2, 15, 86**
Soyinka, Wole **4, 93**
Walcott, Derek **5, 94**

Nonfiction
Abrahams, Peter **39**
Adams-Ender, Clara **40**
Ali, Hana Yasmeen **52**
Allen, Debbie **13, 42**
Allen, Robert L. **38**
Andrews, Tina **74**
Atkins, Cholly **40**
Baisden, Michael **66**
Bashir, Halima **73**
Beah, Ishmael **69**
Blassingame, John Wesley **40**
Blockson, Charles L. **42**
Bogle, Donald **34**
Brown, Cecil M. **46**
Brown, Lloyd Louis **42**
Broyard, Bliss **68**
Buckley, Gail Lumet **39**
Carby, Hazel **27**
Carter, Stephen L. **4**
Cashin, Sheryll **63**
Chiles, Nick **98**
Cole, Johnnetta B. **5, 43**
Cook, Mercer **40**
Cox, Joseph Mason Andrew **51**
Cruse, Harold **54**
Curvin, Robert **132**
Danquah, Meri Nana Ama **93**
Datcher, Michael **60**
Davis, Angela J. **88**
Davis, Arthur P. **41**
Davis, George **36**
Davis, Thulani **61**
Dickerson, Debra J. **60**
Dube, John Langalibalele **119**
Dunnigan, Alice Allison **41**
Elder, Larry **25, 120**
Elliott, Lorris **37**
Fine, Sam **60**
Finner-Williams, Paris Michele **62**
Fisher, Antwone **40**
Forna, Aminatta **95**
Foster, Cecil **32**
Gayle, Addison, Jr. **41**
Gladwell, Malcolm **62**
Golden, Marita **19, 99**
Greenwood, Monique **38**
Harrison, Alvin **28**
Harrison, Calvin **28**
Henderson, David **53**
Henries, A. Doris Banks **44**
Henriques, Julian **37**
Hercules, Frank **44**
Hernton, Calvin C. **51**
Horne, Frank **44**
Ilibagiza, Immaculée **66**
Jacobs, George **118**
Jefferson, Margo **108**
Johnson, Sandra K. **94**
Johnson, William **91**
Jolley, Willie **28**
Jordan, Vernon E. **7, 35**
Kayira, Legson **40**
Kearney, Janis **54**
Kennedy, Randall **40**
Kincaid, Jamaica **4, 109**

Ladner, Joyce A. **42**
Lampley, Oni Faida **43, 71**
Lane, Lunsford **93**
Laymon, Kiese **113**
Lee, Jarena **100**
Lincoln, C. Eric **38**
Mabuza-Suttle, Felicia **43**
Malveaux, Julianne **32, 70**
Manley, Ruth **34**
Mathabane, Mark **5, 99**
Matthews Shatteen, Westina **51**
McKenzie, Vashti M. **29**
McKinney Hammond, Michelle **51**
Miller, Pepper **96**
Mossell, Gertrude Bustill **40**
Murray, Pauli **38**
Naylor, Gloria **10, 42**
Neal, Mark Anthony **74**
Newkirk, Pamela **69**
Nissel, Angela **42**
Norton, Meredith **72**
Parks, Rosa **1, 35, 56**
Pearson, Felicia **99**
Petersen, Neal **96**
Pitts, Leonard, Jr. **54, 85**
Reid, Ira De A. **100**
Run **31, 73**
Rusesabagina, Paul **60**
Sadlier, Rosemary **62**
Sancho, Ignatius **133**
Shakur, Yusef **85**
Smith, Jessie Carney **35**
Steele, Shelby **13, 82**
Thornton, Yvonne S. **69**
Wade-Gayles, Gloria Jean **41**
Walker, Rebecca **50**
Wambugu, Florence **42**
Washington-Williams, Essie Mae **118**
Williams, Terrie **35**
Williams, Wendy **62**
Wiwa, Ken **67**
Wright, Nathan, Jr. **56**
Zook, Kristal Brent **62**

North Carolina state government
Adams, Alma **127**
Ballance, Frank W. **41**
Fuller, Thomas O. **90**
Lee, Howard N. **136**
Watt, Mel **26, 105**

North Carolina State University
Lowe, Sidney **64**

North Pole
Counter, S. Allen **74**
Delany, Martin R. **27**
Henson, Matthew **2**
Hillary, Barbara **65**
McLeod, Gus **27**

NOW
See National Organization for Women

NPR
See National Public Radio

NRA
See National Rifle Association

NSF
See National Science Foundation

Nuclear energy
O'Leary, Hazel 6
Packer, Daniel 56
Quarterman, Lloyd Albert 4

Nuclear Regulatory Commission
Jackson, Shirley Ann 12

Nursing
Adams-Ender, Clara 40
Auguste, Rose-Anne 13
Ferguson, Vernice D. 108
Hillary, Barbara 65
Hughes, Ebony 57
Hunter, Alberta 42
Johnson, Hazel 22
Johnson, Mamie "Peanut" 40
Lewis, Daurene 72
Lyttle, Hulda Margaret 14
Richards, Hilda 49
Riley, Helen Caldwell Day 13
Robinson, Rachel 16
Robinson, Sharon 22
Seacole, Mary 54
Shabazz, Betty 7, 26
Staupers, Mabel K. 7
Taylor, Susie King 13

Nutrition
Clark, Celeste 15
Gregory, Dick 1, 54
Smith, Ian 62
Watkins, Shirley R. 17

Oakland Athletics baseball team
Baylor, Don 6
Blue, Vida 122
Henderson, Rickey 28, 78
Jackson, Reggie 15

Oakland Tribune
Bailey, Chauncey 68
Maynard, Nancy Hicks 73
Maynard, Robert C. 7

OAU
See African Union

Obie Awards
Bey, Salome 134
Browne, Roscoe Lee 66
Bullins, Ed 25, 121
Caesar, Adolph 133
Carroll, Vinnette 29, 136
Carter, Nell 39
Cathey, Reg E. 122
De Shields, André 72
Freeman, Morgan 2, 20, 62, 100
Freeman, Yvette 27
Orlandersmith, Dael 42
Sands, Diana 87
Smith, Roger Guenveur 12, 133
Thigpen, Lynne 17, 41
White, Lillias 120
Wolfe, George C. 6, 43, 127

Office of Civil Rights
See U.S. Department of Education

Ohio state government
Beatty, Joyce 117
Brown, Les 5

Ford, Jack 39
Hicks-Hudson, Paula 136
Mallory, William L., Sr. 119
Stokes, Carl 10, 73
White, Michael R. 5
Williams, George Washington 18

Oklahoma state government
Ross, Don 27

Oklahoma Supreme Court
Colbert, Tom 115

Olympics
Abdirahman, Abdi 126
Ali, Muhammad 2, 16, 52, 136
Atkinson, Alia 126
Barksdale, Don 103
Beamon, Bob 30
Bekele, Kenenisa 75
Berian, Boris 136
Biles, Simone 136
Bolt, Usain 73, 104
Bonaly, Surya 7
Bonheur, Yannick 84
Boozer, Bob 103
Bowe, Riddick 6, 107
Brigitha, Enith 126
Campbell, Milt 113
Campbell-Brown, Veronica 102
Carlos, John 97
Christie, Linford 8
Clay, Bryan 57, 74
Coachman, Alice 18, 123
Davis, Anthony 120
Davis, Shani 58, 84
Dawes, Dominique 11, 126
DeFrantz, Anita 37
DeGale, James 74
Devers, Gail 7, 87
Dibaba, Mare 131
Dibaba, Tirunesh 73, 109
Edwards, Teresa 14, 95
Ervin, Anthony 66
Eto'o, Samuel 73
Farah, Mo 104
Felix, Allyson 48, 98
Flowers, Vonetta 35
Fraser-Pryce, Shelly-Ann 113
Frazier, Joe 19, 98
Freeman, Cathy 29
Garrison, Zina 2, 133
Gatlin, Justin 123
Gay, Tyson 114
Gebrselassie, Haile 70
Gourdin, Edward O. 93
Gourdine, Meredith 33
Greene, Maurice 27, 77
Griffith, Yolanda 25
Griffith-Joyner, Florence 28
Harrison, Alvin 28
Harrison, Calvin 28
Harris-Stewart, Lusia 90
Hayes, Bob 77
Hazzard, Walt 98
Hernández, Orlando 96
Hines, Garrett 35
Holmes, Kelly 47
Holyfield, Evander 6
Howard, Sherri 36
Iginla, Jarome 35
James, G. Larry 74
James, Vanessa 84
Jefferson, Richard 136

Jeptoo, Rita 121
Johnson, Ben 1
Johnson, Michael 13
Johnson, Rafer 33
Jones, Cullen 73
Jones, Lou 64
Jones, Randy 35
Jones, Roy, Jr. 22, 134
Joyner-Kersee, Jackie 5
Keflezighi, Meb 49, 121
Kidd, Jason 86
Kipchoge, Eliud 124
Kipsang, Wilson 115
Lewis, Carl 4, 97
Malone, Karl 18, 51, 90
Marion, Shawn 136
Matson, Ollie 93
Metcalfe, Ralph 26
Miller, Cheryl 10, 74
Montgomery, Tim 41
Moses, Edwin 8
Moussambani, Eric 105
Muhammad, Ibtihaj 133
Mutola, Maria 12
Omar, Samia Yusuf 107
Owens, Jesse 2
Pettigrew, Antonio 118
Powell, Mike 7
Quirot, Ana 13
Richards-Ross, Sanya 66, 98
Rudolph, Wilma 4
Savón, Félix 105
Scurry, Briana 27
Simpson, Sherone 120
Smith, Tommie 102
Stevenson, Teófilo 103
Temple, Ed 109
Thomas, Debi 26
Thugwane, Josia 21
Vanessa James and Yannick Bonheur 84
Wade, Dwyane 61, 103
Walker, LeRoy T. 106
Wanjiru, Sammy 94
Ward, Andre 62
Ward, Lloyd 21, 46
Westbrook, Peter 20
Whitaker, Pernell 10, 89
White, Willye 67
Whitfield, Mal 60
Wilder, Deontay 121
Williams, Lauryn 58, 127
Woodruff, John 68

100 Black Men of America
Dortch, Thomas W., Jr. 45
Llewellyn, J. Bruce 13, 85

Ontario Legislature
Curling, Alvin 34

Opera
Adams, Leslie 39
Allen, Betty 83
Anderson, Marian 2, 33
Arroyo, Martina 30
Battle, Kathleen 70
Brown, Angela M. 54
Brown, Anne 76
Brown, Uzee 42
Brownlee, Lawrence 88
Bumbry, Grace 5
Collins, Janet 33, 64
Conrad, Barbara Smith 90

Dale, Clamma 103
Davis, Anthony 11
Dobbs, Mattiwilda 34
Duncan, Todd 76
Elzy, Ruby 119
Estes, Simon 28
Freeman, Paul 39
Graves, Denyce Antoinette 19, 57
Greely, M. Gasby 27
Greenfield, Elizabeth Taylor 116
Grist, Reri 84
Hendricks, Barbara 3, 67
Joplin, Scott 6
Joyner, Matilda Sissieretta 15
Lister, Marquita 65
Matshikiza, Pumeza 115
Matthews, Benjamin 93
Maynor, Dorothy 19
McFerrin, Robert, Sr. 94
Mitchell, Leona 42
Norman, Jessye 5
Phillips, Helen L. 63
Price, Leontyne 1
Ragin, Derek Lee 84
Simpson-Hoffman, N'kenge 52
Still, William Grant 37
Three Mo' Tenors 35
Verrett, Shirley 66, 91
Warfield, William 94
White, Willard 53
Williams, Camilla 116
Yende, Pretty 124

Ophthalmology
Bath, Patricia E. 37

Oracle Corporation
Phillips, Charles E., Jr. 57, 109
Woods, Jacqueline 52

Organ
Bryant, Paul 115
Buckner, Milt 110
Davis, Wild Bill 114
Doggett, Bill 124
McDuff, Jack 116
McGriff, Jimmy 72
Rhyne, Melvin 109
Scott, Shirley 133
Smith, Jimmy 127

Organization executive
Baker, Maxine 28
Edelin, Ramona Hoage 19
Gayle, Helene D. 3, 46
Jackson, Phillip 115
McGhee, Heather C. 106
Meyers, Michael 131
Wright, Antoinette 60

Organization of African Unity
See African Union

Organized crime
Coke, Christopher 108
Holstein, Casper 89
Johnson, Bumpy 102

Osteopathy
Allen, Ethel D. 13
Anderson, William G(ilchrist) 57
Ross-Lee, Barbara 67

Painting
Alston, Charles 33
Amos, Emma 63

Andrews, Benny 22, 59
Bailey, Radcliffe 19
Bannister, Edward Mitchell 88
Barnes, Ernie 16, 78
Barthe, Richmond 15
Basquiat, Jean-Michel 5
Bearden, Romare 2, 50
Beasley, Phoebe 34
Biggers, John 20, 33
Bradford, Mark 89
Brown, Frederick J. 102
Colescott, Robert 69
Collins, Paul 61
Cortor, Eldzier 42
Cowans, Adger W. 20
Crichlow, Ernest 75
Crite, Allan Rohan 29
Davis, Bing 84
Delaney, Beauford 19
Delaney, Joseph 30
Delsarte, Louis 34
Douglas, Aaron 7
Driskell, David C. 7
Duncanson, Robert S. 127
Ferguson, Amos 81
Freeman, Leonard 27
Gilliam, Sam 16
Goodnight, Paul 32
Green, Jonathan 54
Guyton, Tyree 9, 94
Harkless, Necia Desiree 19
Hayden, Palmer 13
Honeywood, Varnette P. 54, 88
Hunter, Clementine 45
Jackson, Earl 31
Johnson, William Henry 3
Jones, Loïs Mailou 13, 136
Knight, Gwendolyn 63
Knox, Simmie 49
Lawrence, Jacob 4, 28
Lee, Annie Frances 22
Lee-Smith, Hughie 5, 22
Lewis, Norman 39
Lewis, Samella 25
Ligon, Glenn 82
Loving, Alvin, Jr. 35, 53
Major, Clarence 9
Marshall, Kerry James 59
Mason, Desmond 127
Mayhew, Richard 39
McGee, Charles 10
Mehretu, Julie 85
Mitchell, Corinne 8
Motley, Archibald, Jr. 30
Mutu, Wangechi 44
Nascimento, Abdias do 93
Ndiaye, Iba 74
Neals, Otto 73
Nugent, Richard Bruce 39
Ofili, Chris 124
Ouattara 43
Pierre, Andre 17
Pindell, Howardena 55
Pippin, Horace 9
Porter, James A. 11
Prince Twins Seven-Seven 95
Ransome, James E. 88
Reid, Senghor 55
Ringgold, Faith 4, 81
Ruley, Ellis 38
Sallee, Charles 38
Sebree, Charles 40
Simpson, Merton D. 110

Smith, Vincent D. 48
Sudduth, Jimmy Lee 65
Tanksley, Ann 37
Tanner, Henry Ossawa 1
Thomas, Alma 14
Thomas, Mickalene 61
Tolliver, Mose 60
Tolliver, William 9
Verna, Gelsy 70
Wagner, Albert 78
Walker, Kara 16, 80
Waring, Laura Wheeler 99
Washington, James, Jr. 38
Wells, James Lesesne 10
White, Charles 39
Wiley, Kehinde 62
Williams, William T. 11
Wilson, Ellis 39
Wilson, John 109
Woodruff, Hale 9

Pan-Africanism
Carmichael, Stokely 5, 26
Clarke, John Henrik 20
Cuffe, Paul 98
Du Bois, David Graham 45, 135
Garvey, Marcus 1
Haile Selassie 7
Kenyatta, Jomo 5
Lee, Robert 112
Logan, Rayford W. 40
Madhubuti, Haki 7, 85
Marshall, Paule 7, 77
Nkrumah, Kwame 3
Nyerere, Julius 5, 136
Touré, Sekou 6
Turner, Henry McNeal 5

Paralympics
Browne, Richard 132

Patents
Jennings, Thomas L. 125

PBS
See Public Broadcasting Service

Peace Corps
See U.S. Peace Corps

Pediatrics
Carson, Ben 1, 35, 76, 128
Elders, Joycelyn 6
Fennoy, Ilene 72
Lawrence, Margaret Morgan 100
Shirley, Aaron 126
Witt, Edwin T. 26

PEN/Faulkner Awards
Bradley, David Henry, Jr. 39
Mayhew, Richard 39
Wideman, John Edgar 5, 87

Pennsylvania state government
Allen, Ethel D. 13
Brown, Homer S. 47
Fattah, Chaka 11, 70, 112, 130
Fauset, Crystal Dreda Bird 100
Irvis, K. Leroy 67
Nix, Robert N. C., Jr. 51

Pennsylvania Supreme Court
Baldwin, Cynthia 74, 107

Pentecostal church
Blake, Charles E. 82
Brazier, Arthur M. 115
DuBois, Joshua 88
Franklin, Robert M. 13
Hayes, James C. 10
Kee, John P. 43, 116
Mason, Charles Harrison 107
Munroe, Myles 125
Patterson, Gilbert Earl 41
Patterson, J. O., Jr. 80
Rivers, Eugene F., III 81
Sapp, Marvin 74
Seymour, William J. 106
Winans, Marvin L. 17, 127
Wright, Timothy 74
Yearwood, Lennox, Jr. 112

People United to Serve Humanity (PUSH)
Barrow, Willie T. 85, 128
Jackson, Jesse 1, 27, 72
Jackson, Jesse, Jr. 14, 45, 81, 108

PepsiCo Inc.
Banks, Paula A. 68
Boyd, Edward 70

PGA of America Hall of Fame
Powell, William J. 82
Sifford, Charlie 4, 49, 134

Pharmaceuticals
Flowers, Sylester 50
Frazier, Kenneth 97
Lewis-Hall, Freda 105
Potter, Myrtle 40

Pharmacist
Akunyili, Dora Nkem 58
Flowers, Sylester 50
Pickett, Cecil 39
Stewart, Ella 39

Philadelphia city government
Allen, Ethel D. 13
Goode, W. Wilson 4
Nutter, Michael 69, 112
Street, John F. 24

Philadelphia Eagles football team
Cunningham, Randall 23
McNabb, Donovan 29, 119
Mitchell, Freddie 116
Rhodes, Ray 14
White, Reggie 6, 50

Philadelphia Flyers hockey team
Brashear, Donald 39
Charleston, Oscar 39

Philadelphia Phillies baseball team
Howard, Ryan 65, 113
Rollins, Jimmy 70

Philadelphia 76ers basketball team
Barkley, Charles 5, 66
Bol, Manute 1
Chamberlain, Wilt 18, 47
Erving, Julius 18, 47

Stackhouse, Jerry 30

Philanthropy
Banks, Paula A. 68
Brown, Eddie C. 35
Bryant, Kimberly 127
Carson, Candy 133
Church, Robert Reed, Sr. 132
Cole, Maria 104
Cooper, Evern 40
Cosby, Camille 14, 80
Dawson, Matel, Jr. 39
Edley, Christopher 2, 48
Gardner, Chris 65
Gray, Willie 46
Ibrahim, Mo 67, 115
Johnson, Sheila Crump 48
Jones, Paul R. 76
Lavizzo-Mourey, Risa 48
Malone, Annie 13
McCarty, Oseola 16, 136
Millines Dziko, Trish 28
Pleasant, Mary Ellen 9
Pyfrom, Estella 127
Reeves, Rachel J. 23
Rolle, Myron 98
Thomas, Franklin A. 5, 49
Waddles, Charleszetta "Mother" 10, 49
Walker, Madame C. J. 7
Washington, Pauletta Pearson 86
Wein, Joyce 62
White, Reggie 6, 50
Williams, Fannie Barrier 27

Philosophy
Appiah, Kwame Anthony 67, 101
Hall, Stuart 78
Piper, Adrian 71
Toomer, Jean 6
West, Cornel 5, 33, 80

Photography
Allah, Khalik 131
Andrews, Bert 13
Barboza, Anthony 10
Bingham, Howard 96
Borders, Marcy 131
Cowans, Adger W. 20
Cox, Renée 67
DeCarava, Roy 42, 81
Farley, James Conway 99
Fosso, Samuel 116
Frazier, LaToya Ruby 131
Hansen, Austin 88
Harris, Lyle Ashton 83
Hinton, Milt 30
Keïta, Seydou 124
Moutoussamy-Ashe, Jeanne 7
Parks, Gordon 1, 35, 58
Pinderhughes, John 47
Robeson, Eslanda Goode 13
Roble, Abdi 71
Serrano, Andres 3
Shakur, Afeni 67, 135
Sidibé, Malick 124
Simpson, Lorna 4, 36
Smith, Marvin 46
Smith, Ming 100
Smith, Morgan 46
Tanner, Henry Ossawa 1
Thomas, Mickalene 61
Taylor, Lonzie Odie 96
VanDerZee, James 6

Weems, Carrie Mae **63, 116**
White, John H. **27**
Williams, Clarence **70**
Willis, Deborah **85**

Photojournalism
Ashley-Ward, Amelia **23**
Cole, Ernest **123**
du Cille, Michel **74**
Jackson, Vera **40**
Moutoussamy-Ashe, Jeanne **7**
Parks, Gordon **1, 35, 58**
Sleet, Moneta, Jr. **5, 136**
Van Lierop, Robert **53**
Wallace, William **75**
White, John H. **27**
Williams, Clarence **70**
Withers, Ernest C. **68, 88**
Yette, Samuel F. **63**

Physical therapy
Griffin, Bessie Blount **43, 135**

Physics
Adkins, Rutherford H. **21**
Branson, Herman **87**
Gates, Sylvester James, Jr. **15, 130**
Gourdine, Meredith **33**
Green, Hadiyah-Nicole **133**
Imes, Elmer Samuel **39**
Jackson, Deborah **94**
Jackson, Shirley Ann **12**
Johnson, Anthony M. **92**
Massey, Walter E. **5, 45**
Mickens, Ronald Elbert **105**
Stith, James H. **116**
Tyson, Neil deGrasse **15, 65**

Piano
Adams, Leslie **39**
Allen, Geri **92**
Ammons, Albert **112**
Austin, Lovie **40**
Barrett, Emma **130**
Barron, Kenny **128**
Batiste, Jon **108, 130**
Bonds, Margaret **39**
Brooks, Hadda **40**
Bryant, Ray **95**
Buckner, Milt **110**
Butler, Henry **121**
Cables, George **125**
Cartiér, Xam Wilson **41**
Christian, Jodie **103**
Clark, Sonny **128**
Clayton, Gerald **111**
Cole, Nat "King" **17**
Coltrane, Alice **70**
Cook, Charles "Doc" **44**
Count Basie **23**
Dameron, Tadd **103**
Davenport, Cow Cow **115**
Davis, Walter, Jr. **134**
Davis, Wild Bill **114**
Diehl, Aaron **132**
Doggett, Bill **124**
Domino, Fats **20**
Donegan, Dorothy **19**
Drew, Kenny **123**
Duke, George **21, 113**
Ellington, Duke **5**
Flanagan, Tommy **69**
Fox, Donal **114**
Garland, Red **115**

Garner, Erroll **76**
Hancock, Herbie **20, 67**
Hardin Armstrong, Lil **39**
Harris, Barry **68**
Harris, Kevin **120**
Hawes, Hampton **121**
Hayes, Isaac **20, 58, 73**
Hinderas, Natalie **5**
Hines, Earl "Fatha" **39**
Horn, Shirley **32, 56**
Jamal, Ahmad **69**
Johnson, James P. **134**
Johnson, Johnnie **56**
Jones, Hank **57, 86**
Joplin, Scott **6**
Jordan, Duke **133**
Kelly, Wynton **121**
Keys, Alicia **32, 68**
Lee, Consuela **84**
Lutcher, Nellie **130**
Mabon, Willie **119**
Mance, Junior **132**
Marsalis, Ellis **90**
McRae, Carmen **77**
McShann, Jay **110**
Merriweather, Big Maceo **109**
Mitchell, Dwike **111**
Monk, Thelonious **1**
Montgomery, Little Brother **117**
Moran, Jason **89**
Newborn, Phineas, Jr. **127**
Parlan, Horace **108**
Perkins, Carl **128**
Perkins, Pinetop **70**
Peterson, Oscar **52**
Powell, Bud **24**
Pratt, Awadagin **31**
Preston, Billy **39, 59**
Price, Florence **37**
Pritchard, Robert Starling **21**
Professor Longhair **109**
Roberts, Marcus **19, 113**
Robinson, Reginald R. **53**
Sample, Joe **51, 123**
Schuyler, Philippa **50**
Scott, Hazel **66**
Scott, Shirley **133**
Shipp, Matthew **107**
Shirley, Donald **111**
Silver, Horace **26, 122**
Simone, Nina **15, 41, 130**
Smith, Willie **107**
Sun Ra **60**
Swann, Lynn **28**
Southern, Eileen **56**
Spann, Otis **107**
Spivey, Victoria **119**
Sunnyland Slim **118**
Sykes, Roosevelt **20**
Tapscott, Horace **126**
Taylor, Billy **23, 92**
Taylor, Cecil **70**
Timmons, Bobby **136**
Tucker, Tommy **127**
Turner, Ike **68**
Tyner, McCoy **92**
Valdés, Bebo **75**
Valdés, Chucho **89**
Vaughan, Sarah **13**
Waldron, Mal **109**
Walker, George **37**
Waller, Fats **29**
Walton, Cedar **114**

Watts, André **42, 101**
Webster, Katie **29**
Wiggins, Gerald **128**
Williams, Mary Lou **15**
Wilson, Teddy **134**
Yancey, Jimmy **116**
Yirga, Samuel **126**

Pittsburgh Pirates baseball team
Bonds, Barry **6, 34, 63, 99**
Clendenon, Donn **26, 56**
Ellis, Dock **78**
Stargell, Willie **29**

Pittsburgh Steelers football team
Batch, Charlie **120**
Gilliam, Joe **31**
Greene, Joe **10**
Greenwood, L. C. **115**
Harris, Franco **97**
Perry, Lowell **30**
Stallworth, John **102**
Stewart, Kordell **21, 111**
Swann, Lynn **28**
Ward, Hines **84**
Woodson, Rod **79**

Planned Parenthood Federation of America Inc.
Wattleton, Faye **9**

Playboy
Brown, Robert **65**
Taylor, Karin **34**

Playwright
Anthony, Trey **63**
Arkadie, Kevin **17**
Armah, Esther **87**
Babatunde, Rotimi **104**
Baldwin, James **1**
Bandele, Biyi **68, 121**
Baraka, Amiri **1, 38, 118**
Barrett, Lindsay **43**
Beckham, Barry **41**
Branch, William Blackwell **39**
Brown, Cecil M. **46**
Brown, Oscar, Jr. **53**
Bullins, Ed **25, 121**
Caldwell, Benjamin **46**
Carroll, Vinnette **29, 136**
Césaire, Aimé **48, 69**
Chenault, John **40**
Childress, Alice **15**
Clark-Bekedermo, J. P. **44**
Clarke, George **32**
Cleage, Pearl **17, 64**
Corthron, Kia **43**
Cotter, Joseph Seamon, Sr. **40**
Cox, Joseph Mason Andrew **51**
Dadié, Bernard **34**
Davis, Eisa **68**
De Veaux, Alexis **44**
Dean, Phillip Hayes **122**
Dent, Thomas C. **50**
Diamond, Lydia R. **101**
Dodson, Owen **38**
Domingo, Colman **94**
Elder, Lonne, III **38**
Evans, Mari **26**
Farah, Nuruddin **27**
Franklin, J. E. **44**

Glover, Keith **79**
Gordone, Charles **15**
Grant, Micki **125**
Gurira, Danai **73**
Hall, Katori **132**
Hansberry, Lorraine **6**
Harris, Bill **72**
Hayes, Teddy **40**
Hill, Errol **40, 135**
Hill, Leslie Pinckney **44**
Holder, Laurence **34**
Hughes, Langston **4**
Jackson, Angela **134**
Johnson, Georgia Douglas **41**
Johnson, Je'Caryous **63**
Jones, Sarah **39**
Kennedy, Adrienne **11**
Kente, Gibson **52**
King, Woodie, Jr. **27**
Kwei-Armah, Kwame **84**
Lampley, Oni Faida **43, 71**
Lee, Leslie **85, 122**
Long, Richard Alexander **65**
Maponya, Maishe **101**
Marechera, Dambudzo **39**
Mason, Judi Ann **112**
McClinton, Marion Isaac **77**
McCraney, Tarell Alvin **116**
McGhee, Sharon K. **113**
Milner, Ron **39**
Mitchell, Loften **31**
Moss, Carlton **17**
Mugo, Micere Githae **32**
Ngugi wa Thiong'o **29, 61, 101**
Nottage, Lynn **66**
Onwueme, Tess Osonye **23**
Orlandersmith, Dael **42**
Parks, Suzan-Lori **34, 85**
Perry, Tyler **40, 54, 103**
Rahman, Aishah **37**
Redwood, John Henry **78**
Rhone, Trevor **80**
Rotimi, Ola **1, 130**
Salter, Nikkole **73**
Sanchez, Sonia **17, 51**
Santiago-Hudson, Ruben **85**
Schuyler, George Samuel **40**
Sebree, Charles **40**
Smith, Anna Deavere **6, 44**
Talbert, David E. **34, 93**
Taylor, Regina **9, 46, 97**
Teer, Barbara Ann **81**
Thurman, Wallace **17**
Tolson, Melvin B. **37**
Walcott, Derek **5, 94**
Walton, Lester Aglar **134**
Ward, Douglas Turner **42**
Wesley, Richard **73**
Williams, Roy **89**
Williams, Samm-Art **21**
Wilson, August **7, 33, 55**
Wilson, Tracey Scott **777**
Wolfe, George C. **6, 43, 127**
Youngblood, Shay **32**

Poet laureate (U.S.)
Dove, Rita **6, 78, 101**
Trethewey, Natasha **103**

Poetry
Abani, Chris **77**
Adams, Jenoyne **60**
Alexander, Elizabeth **75**

Alexander, Kwame **98**
Alexander, Margaret Walker **22**
Allen, Samuel L. **38**
Angelou, Maya **1, 15, 122**
Atkins, Russell **45**
Aubert, Alvin **41**
Ayim, May **126**
Baiocchi, Regina Harris **41**
Bandele, Asha **36**
Baraka, Amiri **1, 38, 118**
Barrax, Gerald William **45**
Barrett, Lindsay **43**
Bass, Holly **134**
Bell, James Madison **40**
Bennett, Gwendolyn B. **59**
Bennett, Louise **69**
Berry, James **41**
Blanco, Mykki **106**
Bontemps, Arna **8**
Boyd, Melba Joyce **86**
Braithwaite, William Stanley **52**
Brand, Dionne **32**
Brathwaite, Kamau **36**
Breeze, Jean "Binta" **37**
Brooks, Gwendolyn **1, 28**
Brown, Cecil M. **46**
Brutus, Dennis **38**
Burgess, Marjorie L. **55**
Carter, Martin **49**
Cartey, Wilfred **47**
Césaire, Aimé **48, 69**
Chenault, John **40**
Cheney-Coker, Syl **43**
Clark-Bekederemo, J. P. **44**
Clarke, Cheryl **32**
Clarke, George **32**
Cleage, Pearl **17, 64**
Cliff, Michelle **42**
Clifton, Lucille **14, 64, 91**
Coleman, Wanda **48, 119**
Cooper, Afua **53**
Cornish, Sam **50**
Cortez, Jayne **43, 109**
Cotter, Joseph Seamon, Sr. **40**
Cox, Joseph Mason Andrew **51**
Cuney, William Waring **44**
Dabydeen, David **48**
Dadié, Bernard **34**
D'Aguiar, Fred **50**
Damas, Léon-Gontran **46**
Dandridge, Raymond Garfield **45**
Danner, Margaret Esse **49**
Datcher, Michael **60**
Davis, Charles T. **48**
Davis, Frank Marshall **47**
Dawes, Kwame **126**
De Veaux, Alexis **44**
Dedeaux, Richard **119**
Dent, Thomas C. **50**
Dodson, Owen **38**
Dove, Rita **6, 78, 101**
Draper, Sharon Mills **16, 43**
Dumas, Henry **41**
Dunbar, Paul Laurence **8**
Dunbar-Nelson, Alice Ruth Moore **44**
Dungy, Camille **86**
Ellis, Thomas Sayers **129**
Emanuel, James A. **46**
Evans, Mari **26**
Fabio, Sarah Webster **48**
Fair, Ronald L. **47**
Figueroa, John J. **40**

Fisher, Antwone **40**
Fleming, Raymond **48**
Forbes, Calvin **46**
Ford, Nick Aaron **44**
Frazier, Oscar **58**
Gabre-Medhin, Tsegaye **64**
Gilbert, Christopher **50**
Goings, Russell **59**
Goodison, Lorna **71**
Hammon, Jupiter **124**
Harkless, Necia Desiree **19**
Harper, Frances Ellen Watkins **11**
Harper, Michael S. **34, 136**
Harris, Bill **72**
Harris, Claire **34**
Hayden, Robert **12**
Hayes, Terrance **124**
Henderson, David **53**
Hernton, Calvin C. **51**
Hill, Leslie Pinckney **44**
Hoagland, Everett H. **45**
Horne, Frank **44**
Horton, George Moses **124**
Hughes, Langston **7**
Jackson, Angela **134**
Jackson, Fred James **25**
Joachim, Paulin **34**
Johnson, Fenton **91**
Johnson, Georgia Douglas **41**
Johnson, Linton Kwesi **37**
Jones, Sarah **39**
Kaufman, Bob **105**
Kay, Jackie **37**
Keene, John **73**
Knight, Etheridge **37**
Lacy, Marc **111**
Laraque, Paul **67**
Letson, Al **39**
Lorde, Audre **6**
Mackey, Nathaniel **75**
Manley, Ruth **34**
Marechera, Dambudzo **39**
Matejka, Adrian **87**
McClellan, George Marion **91**
Moore, Jessica Care **30**
Mugo, Micere Githae **32**
Mullen, Harryette **34**
Naylor, Gloria **10, 42**
Neto, António Agostinho **43**
Nugent, Richard Bruce **39**
Okara, Gabriel **37**
Okigbo, Christopher **102**
Osbey, Brenda Marie **102**
Parker, Pat **19**
Peters, Lenrie **43**
Philip, Marlene Nourbese **32**
Phillips, Carl **111**
Quigless, Helen G. **49**
Randall, Dudley **8, 55**
Redmond, Eugene **23**
Richards, Beah **30**
Sanchez, Sonia **17, 51**
Sapphire **14, 95**
Scott-Heron, Gil **94**
Senghor, Léopold Sédar **12**
Senior, Olive **37**
Smith, Mary Carter **26, 134**
Spencer, Anne **27**
Sundiata, Sekou **66**
Tolson, Melvin B. **37**
Touré, Askia (Muhammad Abu Bakr el) **47**
Trethewey, Natasha **103**

Troupe, Quincy **83**
van Sertima, Ivan **25**
Walker, Margaret **29**
Washington, James, Jr. **38**
Weaver, Afaa Michael **37**
Williams, Saul **31**
Williams, Sherley Anne **25**
Woods, Scott **55**
Young, Al **82**
Yusef, Malik **136**

Poetry Slam, Inc.
Woods, Scott **55**

Political science
Ake, Claude **30**
Cohen, Cathy J. **88**
Dawson, Michael C. **63**
Harris-Lacewell, Melissa **81**
Skinner, Kiron K. **65**
Walters, Ronald **83**
Watson, Carlos **50**

Politics
Adebari, Rotimi **83**
Alexander, Archie Alphonso **14**
Ali, Ayaan Hirsi **58, 92**
Allen, Claude **68**
Austin, Junius C. **44**
Avant, Clarence **19, 86**
Barnes, Melody **75**
Barrow, Dean **69**
Blackwell, Unita **17**
Boye, Madior **30**
Brazile, Donna **25, 70**
Brown, Oscar, Jr. **53**
Burris, Roland W. **25, 75**
Burton, Bill **96**
Buthelezi, Mangosuthu Gatsha **9**
Butler, Jerry **26**
Cain, Herman **15, 92**
Carson, Ben **1, 35, 76, 128**
Césaire, Aimé **48, 69**
Chideya, Farai **14, 61**
Coleman, Mary **46**
Compton, John **65**
Conneh, Sekou Damate, Jr. **51**
Connerly, Ward **14**
Davis, James E. **50**
Edmonds, Terry **17**
Fields, Julia **45**
Foster, Ezola **28**
Frazier, Ryan **89**
Greenlee, Sam **48**
Hatcher, Andrew T. **90**
Henry, Aaron **19**
Holmes, Amy **69**
Ingraham, Hubert A. **19**
Jackson, Mae **57**
Jarrett, Valerie **73**
Kelley, Cliff **75**
Keyes, Alan **11, 105**
Lindsay, Peta **100**
Lynch, William, Jr. **115**
Magloire, Paul Eugène **68**
McGlowan, Angela **64, 86**
Moore, Minyon **45**
Morton, Ferdinand Q. **90**
Nelson, Sophia A. **93**
Obasanjo, Stella **32**
Pereira, Aristides **30, 97**
Perry, Ruth **15**
Pinkney, Arnold R. **122**
Pitta, Celso **17**

Reed, Joe L. **110**
Sankoh, Foday **74**
Simmons, E. Denise **79**
Simmons, Jamal **72**
Sisulu, Sheila Violet Makate **24**
Smith, Jennifer **21**
Smith, Princella **86**
Spencer, Winston Baldwin **68**
Watkins, Joe **86**
Williams, Eddie N. **44**
Williams, Eric Eustace **65**
Williams, Maggie **7, 71**

Pop music
Ashford, Nickolas **21, 97**
Ashford and Simpson **21, 97**
Babyface **10, 31, 82**
Bailey, Pearl **14**
Bailey Rae, Corinne **83**
Bassey, Shirley **25**
Benson, Obie **96**
Birdsong, Cindy **113**
Bleu, Corbin **65**
Brown, Bobby **58, 124**
Brown, Melanie **73**
Butler, Jonathan **28**
Cameo **120**
Carey, Mariah **32, 53, 69**
Chanté, Keshia **50**
Checker, Chubby **28**
Clayton, Merry **112**
Coasters, The **102**
Cole, Nat "King" **17**
Commodores, The **118**
Coppola, Imani Francesca **82**
Cox, Deborah **28**
Cruz, Taio **104**
David, Craig **31, 53**
Derulo, Jason **93, 132**
Dixie Cups, The **109**
Ferrell, Rachelle **29**
Graham, Katerina **99**
Gray, Macy **29**
Hailey, JoJo **22**
Hailey, K-Ci **22**
Harris, Damon **110**
Harris, Major **110**
Hawkins, Screamin' Jay **30**
Hayes, Isaac **20, 58, 73**
Holmes, Clint **57**
Horton, Gladys **92**
Houston, Whitney **7, 28, 83, 100**
Hudson, Jennifer **63, 83**
Humphrey, Bobbi **20**
Ink Spots, The **102**
Isley, Ronald **25, 56**
Jackson, Janet **6, 30, 68**
Jackson, Jermaine **79**
Jackson, LaToya **95**
Jackson, Michael **19, 53, 76**
Jackson 5 **103**
James, Rick **17**
Jones, Booker T. **84**
Jones, Quincy **8, 30**
Jordan, Montell **23**
Kelis **58, 122**
Kendricks, Eddie **22**
Keys, Alicia **32, 68**
Khan, Chaka **12, 50**
Kingston, Sean **94**
Knowles, Mathew **96**
LaBelle, Patti **13, 30**
Lewis, Leona **75**

Little Eva **128**
Luckett, Letoya **61**
Martelly, Michel **90**
Mathis, Johnny **20**
McFerrin, Bobby **68**
Mills Brothers, The **99**
Monica **21**
Mtukudzi, Oliver **109**
Mumba, Samantha **29**
Mvula, Laura **110**
Mya **35**
Naughton, Naturi **97**
Neville, Aaron **21**
New Edition **101**
Ne-Yo **65**
Noah, Yannick **4, 60, 121**
Olusola, Kevin **133**
Osborne, Jeffrey **26, 121**
Otis, Clyde **67**
Palmer, Keke **68, 120**
P.M. Dawn **54**
Preston, Billy **39, 59**
Prince **18, 65, 134**
Raven-Symoné **44, 113**
Reid, Vernon **34**
Richie, Lionel **27, 65, 114**
Rihanna **65, 102**
Robinson, Cynthia **132**
Robinson, Smokey **3, 49**
Rogers, Bobby **110**
Ronettes, The **132**
Rowland, Kelly **100**
Rucker, Darius **34, 74, 108**
Sandé, Emeli **113**
Seal **14, 75**
Secada, Jon **97**
Sessoms, Vivian **122**
Sharp, Dee Dee **130**
Shirelles, The **111**
Short, Bobby **52**
Simpson, Valerie **21, 97**
Sisqo **30**
Smith, Myrna **92**
Smith, Willow **92**
Solange **97**
Staton, Candi **27**
Street, Richard **110**
Streeter, Sevyn **115**
Stromae **121**
Summer, Donna **25, 102**
Supremes, The **33**
Sweat, Keith **19**
Temptations, The **33**
Terrell, Jean **116**
The-Dream **74**
Thomas, Irma **29**
Turner, Tina **6, 27**
Usher **23, 56, 95**
Vanity **67, 134**
Warwick, Dionne **18, 111**
Washington, Dinah **22**
Washington, Grover, Jr. **17, 44**
Washington, Val **12**
Weeknd, The **131**
Welch, Elisabeth **52**
White, Barry **13, 41**
White, Josh, Jr. **52**
will.i.am **64**
Williams, Paul **112**
Wilson, Jackie **60**
Wilson, Mary **28**
Withers-Mendes, Elisabeth **64**

Wonder, Stevie **11, 53, 121**

Portland (OR) Police Department
Moose, Charles **40**

Portland Trail Blazers basketball team
Aldridge, LaMarcus **125**
Drexler, Clyde **4, 61**
Miller, Larry G. **72**
Porter, Terry **75**
Roy, Brandon **98**

Pratt Institute
Mayhew, Richard **39**

Presbyterianism
Callender, Eugene **119**
Cannon, Katie **10**

Princeton University
Appiah, Kwame Anthony **67, 101**
Blanks, Deborah K. **69**
Harris-Lacewell, Melissa **81**
Rouse, Cecilia **93**
Simmons, Ruth **13, 38**

Printmaking
Blackburn, Robert **28**
Burroughs, Margaret Taylor **9, 134**
Crichlow, Ernest **75**
Neals, Otto **73**
Tanksley, Ann **37**
Thrash, Dox **35**
Wells, James Lesesne **10**
Wilson, John **109**

Prison ministry
Bell, Ralph S. **5**

Prison reform
Betts, R. Dwayne **86**

Procter & Gamble
Clement-Holmes, Linda **94**

Professional Women's Club of Chicago
Gray, Ida **41**

Proposition 209
Connerly, Ward **14**

Prosecution
Bensouda, Fatou **103**
Darden, Christopher **13**
Mosby, Marilyn **128**
Ozanne, Ismael R. **129**
Thompson, Ken **131**
Worthy, Kym **84**

Provincial Freeman
Cary, Mary Ann Shadd **30**

Psychiatry
Bell, Carl C. **111**
Cobbs, Price M. **9**
Comer, James P. **6**
Eberhardt, Jennifer **124**
Fanon, Frantz **44**
Fuller, Solomon Carter, Jr. **15**
Hamburg, Beatrix **84**
Johnson-Powell, Gloria **107**
Lawrence, Margaret Morgan **100**
Poussaint, Alvin F. **5, 67**

Welsing, Frances Cress **5**

Psychology
Anderson, Norman B. **45**
Brown, Joyce F. **25**
Clark, Kenneth B. **5, 52**
Clark, Mamie Phipps **79**
Edwards, Harry **2**
Finner-Williams, Paris Michele **62**
Fulani, Lenora **11**
Gardere, Jeffrey **76**
Gilbert, Christopher **50**
Hale, Lorraine **8**
Hare, Nathan **44**
Hilliard, Asa Grant, III **66**
Staples, Brent **8**
Steele, Claude **13, 97**
Sumner, Francis Cecil **112**
Tatum, Beverly Daniel **42, 84**

Psychotheraphy
Berrysmith, Don Reginald **49**
Ford, Clyde W. **40**

Public Broadcasting Service (PBS)
Brown, Les **5**
Brown, Tony **3**
Creagh, Milton **27**
Hampton, Henry **6**
Hunter-Gault, Charlayne **6, 31**
Ifill, Gwen **28**
Lawson, Jennifer **1, 50**
Long, Loretta **58**
Lynch, Shola **61**
Roker, Al **12, 49**

Public housing
Lane, Vincent **5**
Perry, James **83**
Reems, Ernestine Cleveland **27**

Public policy
Douglas, Derek **88**

Public relations
Barrett, Andrew C. **12**
Calhoun, Lillian Scott **87**
Compton-Rock, Malaak **86**
Edmonds, Terry **17**
Graham, Stedman **13**
Jones, Robert G. **81**
McCabe, Jewell Jackson **10**
Perez, Anna **1**
Pritchard, Robert Starling **21**
Rowan, Carl T. **1, 30**
Taylor, Kristin Clark **8**
Tobin, Patricia **75**
Wyllie, Tony **131**

Public schools
Ackerman, Arlene **108**
Baker, Gwendolyn Calvert **9**
Clayton, Constance **1**
Coleman, William F., III **61**
Collins, Marva **3, 71**
Crew, Rudy **16, 113**
Dewitty, Thelma **114**
Lemon, Alton T. **112**
Tyler, Ollie **128**

Public speaking
Bell, James Madison **40**
Brown, Hallie Quinn **100**
Douglass, Frederick **87**

Kennedy, Randall **40**

Publishing
Abbott, Robert Sengstacke **27**
Alexander, Kwame **98**
Ames, Wilmer **27**
Ashley-Ward, Amelia **23**
Aubert, Alvin **41**
Auguste, Arnold A. **47**
Baisden, Michael **25, 66**
Bakewell, Danny **99**
Boston, Lloyd **24**
Boyd, T. B., III **6**
Brown, Jamie Foster **91**
Brown, Marie Dutton **12**
Cary, Mary Ann Shadd **30**
Coombs, Orde M. **44**
Cox, William E. **68**
Dawkins, Wayne **20**
Driver, David E. **11**
Ducksworth, Marilyn **12**
Dumas, Henry **41**
Fuller, Hoyt **44**
Giddings, Paula **11**
Goodlett, Carlton B. **91**
Harris, Jay **19**
Harris, Monica **18**
Hill, Bonnie Guiton **20**
Hudson, Cheryl **15**
Hudson, Wade **15**
James, Juanita **13**
Jones, Quincy **8, 30**
Kunjufu, Jawanza **3, 50**
Lawson, Jennifer **1, 50**
Leavell, Dorothy R. **17**
Lewis, Edward T. **21**
Lorde, Audre **6**
Madhubuti, Haki **7, 85**
Maynard, Nancy Hicks **73**
Maynard, Robert C. **7**
McDonald, Erroll **1**
Moore, Jessica Care **30**
Morgan, Garrett **1**
Murphy, John H. **42**
Overton, Anthony **128**
Parks, Gordon **1, 35, 58**
Perez, Anna **1**
Randall, Dudley **8, 55**
Scott, C. A. **29**
Sengstacke, John **18**
Smith, Clarence O. **21**
Stinson, Denise L. **59**
Stringer, Vickie **58**
Tyree, Omar Rashad **21**
Vanzant, Iyanla **17, 47, 108**
Walker, Alice **1, 43**
Washington, Alonzo **29**
Washington, Laura S. **18**
Wells-Barnett, Ida B. **8**
Williams, Armstrong **29**
Woods, Teri **69**

Pulitzer Prize
Baquet, Dean **63, 121**
Brooks, Gwendolyn **1, 28**
Canedy, Dana **132**
Coleman, Ornette **39, 69, 129**
Dash, Leon **47**
Dove, Rita **6, 78, 101**
du Cille, Michel **74**
Fuller, Charles **8**
Givhan, Robin Deneen **72**
Gordone, Charles **15**

Haley, Alex 4
Henderson, Angelo 122
Jefferson, Margo 108
Jones, Edward P. 43, 67
King, Colbert I. 69
Komunyakaa, Yusef 9
Lewis, David Levering 9
Marable, Manning 10, 102
McPherson, James Alan 70
Morrison, Toni 2, 15, 86
Newkirk, Pamela 69
Page, Clarence 4
Parks, Suzan-Lori 34, 85
Payne, Les 89
Pitts, Leonard, Jr. 54, 85
Raspberry, William 2
Robinson, Eugene 77
Shipp, E. R. 15
Sleet, Moneta, Jr. 5, 136
Tucker, Cynthia 15, 61
Walker, Alice 1, 43
Walker, George 37
White, John H. 27
Wilkerson, Isabel 71
Wilkins, Roger 2, 84
Williams, Clarence 70
Wilson, August 7, 33, 55

Puppetry
Clash, Kevin 14, 93

PUSH
See People United to Serve Humanity

Quiltmaking
Benberry, Cuesta 65
Ringgold, Faith 4, 81

Qwest Records
Jones, Quincy 8, 30

Race car driving
Brown, Antron 85
Hamilton, Lewis 66
Lester, Bill 42, 85
Ribbs, Willy T. 2
Scott, Wendell Oliver, Sr. 19

Race relations
Alexander, Clifford 26
Asante, Molefi Kete 3
Ayim, May 126
Baldwin, James 1
Bethune, Mary McLeod 4
Bobo, Lawrence 60
Booker, Simeon 23
Bosley, Freeman, Jr. 7
Boyd, T. B., III 6
Bradley, David Henry, Jr. 39
Branch, William Blackwell 39
Brown, Elaine 8
Butler, Paul D. 17
Cary, Lorene 3
Cashin, Sheryll 63
Cayton, Horace 26
Chavis, Benjamin 6
Clark, Kenneth B. 5, 52
Clark, Septima 7
Cobbs, Price M. 9
Cochran, Johnnie 11, 39, 52
Cole, Johnnetta B. 5, 43
Comer, James P. 6
Cone, James H. 3, 82
Cook, Suzan D. Johnson 22

Cook, Toni 23
Davis, Angela 5, 114
Davis, Benjamin O., Jr. 2, 43
Davis, Benjamin O., Sr. 4
Delany, Martin R. 27
Diallo, Amadou 27
Dickerson, Debra J. 60
Divine, Father 7
DuBois, Shirley Graham 21
Dunbar-Nelson, Alice Ruth Moore 44
Dyson, Michael Eric 11, 40, 128
Edelman, Marian Wright 5, 42
Ellison, Ralph 7
Farmer, James 2, 64
Farmer-Paellmann, Deadria 43
Farrakhan, Louis 2
Fauset, Jessie 7
Franklin, John Hope 5, 77
Fuller, Charles 8
Gibson, William F. 6
Goode, W. Wilson 4
Graham, Lawrence Otis 12
Gregory, Dick 1, 54
Grimké, Archibald H. 9
Hall, Elliott S. 24
Hampton, Henry 6
Harris, Alice 7
Hastie, William H. 8
Haynes, George Edmund 8
Henry, Aaron 19
Henry, Lenny 9, 52
Hill, Oliver W. 24, 63
Hope, John 8
Howard, M. William, Jr. 26
Hunt, Darnell 92
Ingram, Rex 5
Jeffries, Leonard 8
Jones, Elaine R. 7, 45
Khanga, Yelena 6
King, Bernice 4, 81
King, Coretta Scott 3, 57
King, Martin Luther, Jr. 1
King, Yolanda 6
Lane, Charles 3
Lee-Smith, Hughie 5, 22
Lorde, Audre 6
Mabuza-Suttle, Felicia 43
Martin, Louis E. 16
Martin, Trayvon 105
McDougall, Gay J. 11, 43
McKay, Claude 6
McWhorter, John 35, 119
Meredith, James H. 11
Micheaux, Oscar 7
Moore, Harry T. 29
Mosley, Walter 5, 25, 68
Muhammad, Khallid Abdul 10, 31
Page, Clarence 4
Pitt, David Thomas 10
Poussaint, Alvin F. 5, 67
Price, Frederick K. C. 21
Price, Hugh B. 9, 54
Reid, Ira De A. 100
Robeson, Paul 2
Robinson, Spottswood W., III 22
Shabazz, Attallah 6
Simpson, Carole 6, 30
Sister Souljah 11, 100
Sisulu, Sheila Violet Makate 24
Smith, Anna Deavere 6, 44
Sowell, Thomas 2, 99
Spaulding, Charles Clinton 9

Staples, Brent 8
Steele, Shelby 13, 82
Stradford, J. B. 101
Taulbert, Clifton Lemoure 19
Till, Emmett 7
Tutu, Desmond Mpilo 6, 44
Tutu, Nontombi Naomi 57
Tyree, Omar Rashad 21
Walcott, Derek 5, 94
Walker, Maggie 17
Washington, Booker T. 4
Washington, Harold 6
Wells-Barnett, Ida B. 8
Welsing, Frances Cress 5
Wiley, Ralph 8, 78
Wilkins, Roy 4
Williams, Gregory 11
Williams, Walter E. 4, 133
Wilson, Sunnie 7, 55
Wright, Richard 5
Young, Whitney M., Jr. 4

Radio
Abrahams, Peter 39
Abu-Jamal, Mumia 15
Anderson, Eddie "Rochester" 30
Ashong, Derrick 86
Banks, William 11
Baskett, James 102
Bates, Karen Grigsby 40
Beasley, Phoebe 34
Blayton, Jesse B., Sr. 55
Booker, Simeon 23
Branch, William Blackwell 39
Brewster, W. Herbert 128
CoCo Brother 93
Crocker, Frankie 29
Elder, Larry 25, 120
Fuller, Charles 8
Gibson, Truman K., Jr. 60
Goode, Mal 13
Greene, Petey 65
Gumbel, Greg 8
Hamblin, Ken 10
Haynes, Trudy 44
Holt, Nora 38
Hughes, Cathy 27
Jackson, Hal 41, 104
Joe, Yolanda 21
Joyner, Tom 19, 90
Kelley, Cliff 75
Lewis, Delano 7
Lewis, Ramsey 35, 70
Liggins, Alfred, III 43
Love, Ed 58
Lover, Ed 10
Ludacris 37, 60
Luper, Clara 94
Madison, Joseph E. 17
Majors, Jeff 41
McGhee, Sharon K. 113
Michaux, Solomon Lightfoot 91
Mickelbury, Penny 28
Moss, Carlton 17
Parr, Russ 51
Pressley, Condace L. 41
Pugh, Charles 81
Quivers, Robin 61
Red Alert, Kool DJ 33
Samara, Noah 15
Smiley, Rickey 59
Smiley, Tavis 20, 68
Smith, Greg 28

Steinberg, Martha Jean "The Queen" 28
Stuart, Moira 82
Thomas, Rufus 20, 96
Tirico, Mike 68, 124
Wade, Ernestine 126
Whack, Rita Coburn 36
Whitlock, Jason 78, 130
Williams, Armstrong 29
Williams, Nat D. 91
Williams, Ted 91
Williams, Wendy 62
Woods, Georgie 57
Yarbrough, Camille 40

Radio Hall of Fame
Jackson, Hal 41, 104
Joyner, Tom 19, 90
Williams, Wendy 62

Ragtime
Blake, Eubie 29
Europe, James Reese 10
Johnson, James P. 134
Joplin, Scott 6
Robinson, Reginald R. 53
Sissle, Noble 29

Rap music
A$AP Rocky 109
Bambaataa, Afrika 34
Banks, Lloyd 113
Banner, David 55
Benjamin, Andre 45
Bey, Yasiin 30, 96
Big Daddy Kane 79
Big L 120
Big Sean 96
Birdman 110
Black Thought 63
Blackman, Toni 86
Blow, Kurtis 31, 122
B.o.B. 91
Bonney, Tabi 98
Bow Wow 35
Bradley, Adam 101
Brown, Foxy 25
Bun B 123
Cam'ron 104
Cannon, Nick 47, 73, 132
Chamillionaire 82
Chief Keef 112
Chuck D. 9
C-Murder 99
Combs, Sean 17, 43, 92
Common 31, 63, 98
Coolio 103
Curren$y 114
Da Don, Polow 86
De La Soul 119
Deezer D 53
DJ Jazzy Jeff 32
DJ Screw 110
DMX 28, 64
Dr. Dre 10, 14, 30, 116
Drake 86
Dupri, Jermaine 13, 46
E-40 125
Elliott, Missy 31, 90
Estelle 75, 133
Eve 29
Fabolous 93
Fat Boys 92
Fetty Wap 130

50 Cent **46, 83**
Flavor Flav **67**
Flo Rida **78**
Freestyle Fellowship **122**
Future **109**
Geto Boys **115**
Ghostface Killah **90**
Gibbs, Freddie **125**
Gotti, Irv **39**
Grae, Jean **51**
Grandmaster Flash **33, 60**
Gray, F. Gary **14, 49**
Harrell, Andre **9, 30**
Heavy D **58, 98**
Ice Cube **8, 30, 60**
Ice-T **6, 31, 96**
J Dilla **102**
Ja Rule **35, 91**
Jay Electronica **125**
Jay-Z **27, 69, 103**
Jones, Roy, Jr. **22, 134**
Juicy J **116**
Juvenile **96**
KB **122**
Khalifa, Wiz **96**
Kid Cudi **83**
Killer Mike **117**
K'naan **76**
Knight, Suge **11, 30, 102**
KRS-One **34**
Kweli, Talib **93**
Lamar, Kendrick **105**
Le1f **120**
Lighty, Chris **105**
Lil B **121**
Lil Jon **124**
Lil' Kim **28**
Lil Wayne **66, 84**
LL Cool J **16, 49, 94**
London, Theophilus **95**
Lopes, Lisa **36**
Lord Infamous **117**
Lord Jamar **126**
Lover, Ed **10**
Ludacris **37, 60**
Mac Daddy **111**
Mack Maine **125**
Madlib **88**
Mane, Gucci **91**
Mase **24**
Masta Ace **118**
Master P **21, 115**
MC Breed **75**
M.C. Hammer **20, 80**
MC Lyte **34, 108**
McDaniels, Ralph **79**
Method Man **81**
Migos **126**
Nas **33, 111**
Nate Dogg **92**
Naughty by Nature **124**
Nelly **32, 90**
Notorious B.I.G. **20**
Ol' Dirty Bastard **52**
O'Neal, Shaquille **8, 30, 95**
OutKast **35**
Peterson, James **81**
Prince Be **136**
Proof **101**
Public Enemy **98**
Pusha T **123**
Queen Latifah **1, 16, 58, 119**
?uestlove **74**

Ray J **86**
Red Alert, Kool DJ **33**
Redman **81**
Rhymefest **97**
Rhymes, Busta **31**
Riley, Boots **89**
Roberts, Kimberly Rivers **72**
Rock, Pete **121**
Romeo **98**
Ross, Rick **79, 104**
Royce da 5'9" **134**
Run-DMC **31, 75**
RZA **80, 128**
Santana, Juelz **120**
Sarpong, Sam **132**
ScHoolboyQ **117**
Sermon, Erick **81**
Shakur, Tupac **14**
Shanté, Roxanne **33**
Shmurda, Bobby **123**
Shyne **101**
Simmons, Russell **1, 30**
Sir Mix-A-Lot **82**
Sister Souljah **11, 100**
Slick Rick **93**
Slim Thug **86**
Smith, Will **8, 18, 53**
Snoop Dogg **35, 84**
Speech **82**
Sticky Fingaz **86**
Sugarhill Gang, The **79, 125**
Sweatshirt, Earl **114**
Thundercat **136**
Timbaland **32**
Tinie Tempah **115**
T-Pain **73, 111**
Treacherous Three **128**
Trina **114**
2 Chainz **105**
Tyga **117**
Tyler, the Creator **100**
Waka Flocka Flame **110**
Wale **92**
Wanz **116**
Woolard, Jamal **102**
Xzibit **78**
Yarbrough, Camille **40**
Yayo, Tony **113**
YG **122**
Ying Yang Twins **112**
Young Jeezy **63**
Yusef, Malik **136**
Z-Ro **109**

Rastafarianism
Burning Spear **79**
Dube, Lucky **77**
Haile Selassie **7**
Marley, Bob **5**
Marley, Rita **32, 70**
Tosh, Peter **9**

Reader's Choice Awards
Holton, Hugh, Jr. **39**

Reading Is Fundamental
Trueheart, William E. **49**

Real estate development
Amoudi, Mohammed al- **88**
Bakewell, Danny **99**
Burks, Juanita P. **95**
Chapman, Susan E. **94**
Church, Robert Reed, Sr. **132**

Lane, Vincent **5**
Maponya, Richard **101**
Marshall, Bella **22**
Nail, John E. **92**
Payton, Philip A., Jr. **88**
Russell, Herman Jerome **17**
Toote, Gloria E. A. **64**

Reality television
Anthony, La La **122**
Big Freedia **128**
Braxton, Tamar **134**
Campbell, Naomi **1, 31, 120**
Garrison, Zina **2, 133**
Kandi **83**
Leakes, NeNe **107**
Moore, Chanté **26, 130**
Omarosa **69, 110**
Ray J **86**
RuPaul **17, 91**

Record producer
Albright, Gerald **23**
Ayers, Roy **16**
Babyface **10, 31, 82**
Bambaataa, Afrika **34**
Barnes, Lloyd **77**
Bivins, Michael **72**
Butler, George, Jr. **70**
Carter, Troy **98**
Cole, J. **97**
Da Don, Polow **86**
Danjah, Terror **91**
Davis, Carl **105**
de Passe, Suzanne **25**
DJ Jazzy Jeff **32**
Dodd, Coxsone **99**
Dr. Dre **10, 14, 30, 116**
Duke, George **21, 113**
Dupri, Jermaine **13, 46**
Elliott, Missy **31, 90**
Felix Da Housecat **110**
Flying Lotus **124**
Fuqua, Harvey **90**
Gotti, Irv **39**
Hailey, JoJo **22**
Hailey, K-Ci **22**
Hammond, Fred **23**
Hawkins, Walter **87**
Huff, Leon **86**
Ice Cube **8, 30, 60**
Ja Rule **35, 91**
Jackson, George **19**
Jackson, Joe **78**
Jackson, Michael **19, 53, 76**
Jackson, Randy **40**
Jean, Wyclef **20, 86**
Jerkins, Rodney **31**
Jimmy Jam **13**
Jones, Quincy **8, 30**
Kelly, R. **18, 44, 71, 117**
Knowles, Mathew **96**
Lewis, Terry **13**
Marley, Rita **32, 70**
Marley, Stephen **100**
Mayfield, Curtis **2, 43**
McGregor, Stephen **99**
Minott, Sugar **86**
Mitchell, Willie **114**
Osborne, Jeffrey **26, 121**
Robinson, Sylvia **79**
Sermon, Erick **81**
Sims, Danny **106**

Stewart, Tricky **98**
Sweat, Keith **19**
Thundercat **136**
Timbaland **32**
Turner, Ike **68**
Tyler, the Creator **100**
Vandross, Luther **13, 48, 59**
White, Barry **13, 41**
Whitfield, Norman **73**
Williams, J. Mayo **83**
Williams, Pharrell **47, 82, 119**
Yabby You **83**
Young, Lee **72**

Recording executive
Battiste, Harold, Jr. **136**
Birdman **110**
Brae, C. Michael **61**
Busby, Jheryl **3, 74**
Butler, George, Jr. **70**
Dash, Damon **3, 113**
de Passe, Suzanne **25**
Dupri, Jermaine **13, 46**
Gaye, Anna Gordy **121**
Gordy, Berry, Jr. **1**
Gotti, Irv **39**
Harrell, Andre **9, 30**
Jackson, George **19**
Jackson, Randy **40**
James Bracken and Vivian Bracken **107**
Jimmy Jam **13**
Jones, Quincy **8, 30**
Knight, Suge **11, 30, 102**
Lewis, Terry **13**
Liles, Kevin **42, 99**
Mack Maine **125**
Massenburg, Kedar **23, 110**
Master P **21, 115**
Mayfield, Curtis **2, 43**
McPherson, David **32**
Reid, L.A. **28, 129**
Rhone, Sylvia **2**
Robey, Don **115**
Sanders, Angelia **86**
Simmons, Russell **1, 30**
Spivey, Victoria **119**
Stoute, Steve **38**
Thomas, Tabby **119**
Williams, J. Mayo **83**

Reggae
Afro, Teddy **78**
Banton, Buju **93**
Barnes, Lloyd **77**
Beenie Man **32**
Big Youth **107**
Blondy, Alpha **30**
Brown, Dennis **99**
Burning Spear **79**
Chronixx **123**
Cliff, Jimmy **28, 92**
Dawuni, Rocky **94**
Dekker, Desmond **104**
Dodd, Coxsone **99**
Dube, Lucky **77**
Ellis, Alton **74**
Ellis, Hortense **97**
Ford, Vincent **75**
Griffiths, Marcia **29**
Hammond, Lenn **34**
Hibbert, Toots **103**
Isaacs, Gregory **89**

Johnson, Linton Kwesi 37
Marley, Bob 5
Marley, Rita 32, 70
Marley, Stephen 100
Marley, Ziggy 41
McGregor, Stephen 99
Minott, Sugar 86
Mowatt, Judy 38
Perry, Lee 19, 103
Perry, Ruth 19
Rhoden, Wayne 70
Shaggy 31
Sly & Robbie 34
Steely 80
Tosh, Peter 9
Yabby You 83

Republican Party
Allen, Ethel D. 13
Fisher, Ada M. 76
Howard, Perry Wilbon, Jr. 112
Pierson, Katrina 134
Scott, Tim 87, 125
Steele, Michael 38, 73, 91
Toote, Gloria E. A. 64

Restaurants/Catering/Cooking
Armstrong, Govind 81
Cain, Herman 15, 92
Calabrese, Karyn 89
Crum, George 101
Daniels-Carter, Valerie 23
Dorsey, Thomas J. 90
Downing, George T. 91
Ford, Barney 90
Garvin, Gerry 78
Hawkins, La-Van 17, 54
Henry, Dwight 104
Howell, Ayinde 91
James, Charles H., III 62
Lewis, Aylwin B. 51, 88
Montgomery, Robbie 101
Otis, Clarence, Jr. 55
Ouattara, Morou 74
Pierce, Harold 75
Rodriguez, Jimmy 47
Samuelsson, Marcus 53, 120
Sbraga, Kevin 88
Smith, B(arbara) 11
Terry, Bryant 128
Washington, Regynald G. 44
Williams, Lindsey 75
Woods, Sylvia 34, 104

Rhode Island School of Design
Bannister, Edward Mitchell 88
Prophet, Nancy Elizabeth 42

Rhodes scholar
Booker, Cory Anthony 68
Braxton, Brad 77
Kennedy, Randall 40
Locke, Alain 10
Pinkett, Randal 61
Rice, Susan 74, 103
Rolle, Myron 98
Wideman, John Edgar 5, 87

Rhythm and blues/soul music
Aaliyah 30
Ace, Johnny 36
Acklin, Barbara Jean 107
Adams, Johnny 39

Adams, Oleta 18
Akon 68
Alexander, Arthur 131
Amerie 52
Anderson, Jacob 128
Arrington, Steve 132
Ashanti 37, 96
Ashford, Nickolas 21, 97
Ashford and Simpson 21, 97
Atlantic Starr 122
Austin, Patti 24
Ayers, Roy 16
Babyface 10, 31, 82
Badu, Erykah 22, 114
Bailey, Philip 63
Baker, Anita 21, 48
Baker, LaVern 26
Baker, Mickey 95
Ballard, Florence 112
Ballard, Hank 41
Bar-Kays, The 118
Barrino, Fantasia 53, 94
Bass, Fontella 104, 109
Belgrave, Marcus 77, 129
Bell, LeRoy 98
Bell, Thom 112
Belle, Regina 1, 51
Benét, Eric 28, 77
Benton, Brook 121
Berry, Chuck 29
Beverly, Frankie 25
Beyoncé 39, 70, 105
Big Maybelle 117
Bilal 101
Billy Ward and the Dominoes 105
Bivins, Michael 72
Blacc, Aloe 119
Blige, Mary J. 20, 34, 60, 97
Bostic, Earl 121
Boyz II Men 82
Bradley, Charles 126
Bradshaw, Tiny 102
Brandy 14, 34, 72
Braxton, Tamar 134
Braxton, Toni 15, 61, 91
Bridges, Leon 126
Brooks, Hadda 40
Brothers Johnson 130
Brown, Bobby 58, 124
Brown, Charles 23
Brown, Chris 74, 109
Brown, Chuck 78, 102
Brown, Clarence Gatemouth 59
Brown, James 15, 60
Brown, Nappy 73
Brown, Oscar, Jr. 53
Brown, Ruth 90
Brown, Shirley 132
Browne, Tom 136
Buckwheat Zydeco 132
Burke, Clarence, Jr. 112
Burke, Solomon 31, 86, 129
Busby, Jheryl 3, 74
Butler, Jerry 26
Cadillacs 107
Cameo 120
Carey, Mariah 32, 53, 69
Carr, James 117
Castor, Jimmy 100
Chandler, Gene 105
Chantels, The 128
Charles, Ray 16, 48
Chiffons, The 129

Chi-Lites 106
Ciara 56, 115
Clay, Otis 112, 133
Clinton, George 9, 93
Clovers, The 104
Cole, Keyshia 63, 107
Cole, Natalie 17, 60, 84, 133
Commodores, The 118
Conley, Arthur 129
Contours, The 109
Cooke, Sam 17
Covay, Don 127
Cox, Deborah 28
Crawford, Hank 77
Crown Heights Affair 132
Crusaders, The 116
D'Angelo 27, 123
David, Craig 31, 53
Davis, Thornetta 131
Davis, Tyrone 54
Day, Andra 132
Dazz Band 116
DeBarge, El 89
Deep River Boys 131
Dells, The 109
Delta Rhythm Boys 133
Derulo, Jason 93, 132
DeSanto, Sugar Pie 122
Detroit Emeralds, The 121
DeVaughn, Raheem 91
Diddley, Bo 39, 72
Doggett, Bill 124
Domino, Fats 20
Dorsey, Lee 65
Downing, Will 19
Dramatics, The 106
Drifters, The 121
Dupri, Jermaine 13, 46
Earth, Wind & Fire 98
Emotions, The 125
En Vogue 100
Escobar, Damien 56
Escobar, Tourie 56
Evans, Faith 22
Falcons, The 128
Feemster, Herbert 72
Fiona, Melanie 84
Five Keys, The 104
FKA Twigs 123
Flamingos, The 108
Floyd, Eddie 127
Franklin, Aretha 11, 44, 115
Fuqua, Harvey 90
Gamble, Kenny 85
Gap Band, The 100
Garrett, Sean 57
Gaye, Marvin 2
Gaynor, Gloria 36
Gibson, Tyrese 27, 62, 134
Gill, Johnny 51
Ginuwine 35
Goapele 55
Goodman, Al 87
Gotti, Irv 39
Graham Central Station 123
Gray, Dobie 99
Gray, Macy 29
Greaves, R. B. 106
Green, Al 13, 47, 74
Green, Cee Lo 70, 103
Hailey, JoJo 22
Hailey, K-Ci 22
Hall, Aaron 57

Hamilton, Anthony 61
Harold Melvin & the Blue Notes 105
Harris, Corey 39, 73
Harris, Damon 110
Harris, Major 110
Harris, Thurston 129
Hathaway, Donny 18
Hathaway, Lalah 57, 88
Hayes, Isaac 20, 58, 73
Hendryx, Nona 56
Henry, Clarence "Frogman" 46
Hill, Darryl 128
Hill, Lauryn 20, 53, 111
Hilson, Keri 84
Holloway, Brenda 65
Houston, Cissy 20, 83
Houston, Whitney 7, 28, 83, 100
Huff, Leon 86
Humes, Helen 128
Hunter, Ivory Joe 106
Hyman, Phyllis 19
India.Arie 34
Ingram, James 84
Intruders, The 119
Isley, Marvin 87
Isley, Ronald 25, 56
Jackson, Bull Moose 130
Jackson, Millie 25
Jagged Edge 117
Jaheim 58
Jamelia 51
James, Etta 13, 52, 100
James, Leela 117
James, Rick 17
James & Bobby Purify 131
Jennings, Lyfe 56, 69
Jive Five 131
Johnson, Al 119
Johnson, Robert 2
Johnson, Syl 97
Johnson, Syleena 98
Johnson-George, Tamara 79
Jones, Booker T. 84
Jones, Donell 29
Jones, Quincy 8, 30
Jones, Sharon 86
Jordan, Louis 104
Jordan, Montell 23
Kandi 83
Kay, Connie 114
Kelela 132
Kelly, R. 18, 44, 71, 117
KEM 47, 127
Kendricks, Eddie 22
Keys, Alicia 32, 68
King, B. B. 7, 129
King, Ben E. 128
King, Evelyn 129
King Curtis 92
Kiwanuka, Michael 126
Knight, Gladys 16, 66
Knight, Marie 80
LaBelle, Patti 13, 30
Lakeside 120
Lance, Major 111
Larrieux, Amel 63
LaSalle, Denise 111
Lattimore, Kenny 35, 128
LaVette, Bettye 85
Ledisi 73
Lee, Julia 130
Lee Andrews & the Hearts 134

Legend, John 67, 116
Levert, Eddie 70
Levert, Gerald 22, 59
Little Anthony & the Imperials 107
Little Eva 128
Little Richard 15
Lloyd 99
Lopes, Lisa 36
Love, Darlene 23, 92
Luckett, Letoya 61
Lutcher, Nellie 130
Lynn, Barbara 126
Mabon, Willie 119
Maitreya, Sananda 85
Manhattans, The 123
Mario 71
Marvelettes, The 126
Maxwell 20, 81
Maye, Lee 111
Mayfield, Curtis 2, 43
McCoo, Marilyn 53
McCoy, Van 123
McKnight, Brian 18, 34
Meters, The 118
Midnight Star 110
Miguel 98
Miles, Buddy 69
Millinder, Lucky 101
Mitchell, Willie 114
Monáe, Janelle 86
Monica 21
Montgomery, Robbie 101
Moonglows, The 108
Moore, Chanté 26, 130
Moore, Melba 21
Musiq 37, 84
Mvula, Laura 110
Mya 35
Nash, Johnny 40
Ndegeocello, Meshell 15, 83
Neale, Haydain 52
Neville, Aaron 21
New Birth 124
New Edition 101
Ne-Yo 65
Notorious B.I.G. 20
Ocean, Frank 100
O'Jays, The 98
Omarion 107
Orioles, The 100
Orlons, The 130
Otis, Clyde 67
Parker, Maceo 72
Parker, Ray, Jr. 85
Paul, Billy 127, 135
Peebles, Ann 114
Pendergrass, Teddy 22, 83
Penguins, The 107
Phillips, Esther 107
Pinkney, Fayette 80
Pitts, Skip 103
Platters, The 99
Pleasure P 84
Porter, David 127
Preston, Billy 39, 59
Price, Kelly 23
Price, Lloyd 119
Prince 18, 65, 134
Prysock, Arthur 117
Rare Essence 121
Ravens, The 103
Ray, Goodman & Brown 131
Reagon, Toshi 76

Record, Eugene 60
Redding, Otis 16
Reed, A. C. 36
Reed, Natina 106
Reeves, Martha 85
Richard, Dawn 92
Riley, Teddy 116
Riperton, Minnie 32
Robinson, Cynthia 132
Robinson, Smokey 3, 49
Rogers, Bobby 110
Rose Royce 120
Ross, Diana 8, 27
Ruffin, Jimmy 125
Russell, Brenda 52
Saadiq, Raphael 125
Sade 15, 92
Sam and Dave 102
Scott, Jill 29, 83
Scott, Jimmy 48, 122
Scott-Heron, Gil 94
Shamir 129
Shanice 112
Sharp, Dee Dee 130
Shaw, Marlena 105
Siji 56
Simon, Joe 109
Simpson, Valerie 21, 97
Sisqo 30
Sledge, Percy 39, 128
Songz, Trey 88
S.O.S. Band 136
Spaniels, The 105
Sparks, Jordin 66
Starr, Edwin 122
Staton, Candi 27
Steinberg, Martha Jean "The
Queen" 28
Stewart, Amii 129
Stewart, Billy 112
Stone, Angie 31
Stone, Jesse 98
Street, Richard 110
Streeter, Sevyn 115
Strong, Barrett 89
Stubblefield, Clyde 133
Studdard, Ruben 46
Sullivan, Jazmine 81
Supremes, The 33
Swallows, The 133
Swann, Bettye 109
Sweat, Keith 19
Tamia 24, 55
Taste of Honey, A 115
Tavares 115
T-Boz 108
Temptations, The 33
Terrell, Tammi 32
Tex, Joe 116
The-Dream 74
Thomas, Carla 96
Thomas, Irma 29
Thomas, Rozonda 34, 78
Thomas, Rufus 20, 96
TLC 34
Tony! Toni! Toné! 127
Toussaint, Allen 60, 132
Tresvant, Ralph 57
Tucker, Tommy 127
Turner, Ike 68
Turner, Tina 6, 27
Ulmer, James 79
Usher 23, 56, 95

Valentino, Bobby 62
Vandross, Luther 13, 48, 59
Ward, Anita 118
Warwick, Dionne 18, 111
Watley, Jody 54
Wellington, Valerie 118
Wells, Mary 28
West, Kanye 52, 93
Whispers, The 124
White, Barry 13, 41
Whitney, Marva 109
Williams, Larry 118
Williams, Michelle 73
Williams, Paul 112
Willis, Chuck 132
Wilson, Cassandra 16
Wilson, Charlie 31, 77, 135
Wilson, Mary 28
Wilson, Nancy 10, 98
Withers, Bill 61
Witherspoon, Jimmy 113
Womack, Bobby 60, 92, 123
Wonder, Stevie 11, 53, 121
Woods, Belita 103
Woodson, Ali Ollie 89
Wright, O. V. 114
Yarbrough & Peoples 132

Rock and Roll Hall of Fame
Ballard, Florence 112
Ballard, Hank 41
Bennett, Estelle 77
Berry, Chuck 29
Bland, Bobby 36, 113
Brown, Charles 23
Burke, Solomon 31, 86, 129
Christian, Charlie 136
Clinton, George 9, 93
Cole, Nat "King" 17
Davis, Miles 4
Diddley, Bo 39, 72
Drifters, The 121
Franklin, Aretha 11, 44, 115
Gamble, Kenny 85
Grandmaster Flash 33, 60
Green, Al 13, 47, 74
Guy, Buddy 31
Harris, Damon 110
Hayes, Isaac 20, 58, 73
Holiday, Billie 1
Holland-Dozier-Holland 36
Hooker, John Lee 30
Isley, Marvin 87
Isley, Ronald 25, 56
Jackson, Mahalia 5
Jackson, Michael 19, 53, 76
Jackson, Tito 81
Jackson 5 103
Jamerson, James 59
James, Etta 13, 52, 100
Johnson, Johnnie 56
Jones, Booker T. 84
Jones, Quincy 8, 30
King, B. B. 7, 129
King, Ben E. 128
Knight, Gladys 16, 66
Love, Darlene 23, 92
Mayfield, Curtis 2, 43
Morton, Jelly Roll 29
Orioles, The 100
Price, Lloyd 119
Prince 18, 65, 134
Public Enemy 98

Reeves, Martha 85
Robinson, Cynthia 132
Ronettes, The 132
Ross, Diana 8, 27
Run-DMC 31, 75
Sam and Dave 102
Shider, Garry 87
Sledge, Percy 39, 128
Soul Stirrers 127
Spector, Ronnie 77
Steinberg, Martha Jean "The
Queen" 28
Stone, Jesse 98
Stone, Sly 85
Summer, Donna 25, 102
Supremes, The 33
Toussaint, Allen 60, 132
Turner, Big Joe 92
Turner, Ike 68
Turner, Tina 6, 27
Walker, T-Bone 111
Wilson, Jackie 60
Wilson, Mary 28
Womack, Bobby 60, 92, 123
Wonder, Stevie 11, 53, 121
Yancey, Jimmy 116

Rock music
Adebimpe, Tunde 75
Armatrading, Joan 32, 133
Ballard, Hank 41
Bennett, Estelle 77
Berry, Chuck 29
Blackwell, Otis 98
Burbridge, Kofi 120
Burbridge, Oteil 120
Clemons, Clarence 41
Diddley, Bo 39, 72
Domino, Fats 20
Edwards, Esther Gordy 43
Fishbone 101
Glover, Corey 34
Hendrix, Jimi 10
Johnson, Johnnie 56
King, Chris Thomas 120
King Curtis 92
Kravitz, Lenny 10, 34
Little Richard 15
Lymon, Frankie 22
Mayfield, Curtis 2, 43
Miles, Buddy 69
Moore, LeRoi 72
Porter, Tiran 133
Preston, Billy 39, 59
Prince 18, 65, 134
Reagon, Toshi 76
Reid, Vernon 34
Run-DMC 31, 75
Slash 75
Spector, Ronnie 77
Stew 69
Stone, Jesse 98
Stone, Sly 85
Tait, Michael 57
Tamar-kali 63
Tinsley, Boyd 50
Turner, Ike 68
Turner, Big Joe 92
Turner, Tina 6, 27
will.i.am 64
Williams, Larry 118

Wilson, Jackie 60

Rockefeller Foundation
Price, Hugh B. 9, 54

Rodeo
Nash, Johnny 40
Pickett, Bill 11
Sampson, Charles 13
Turman, Glynn 100
Whitfield, Fred 23

Roman Catholic Church
Akpan, Uwem 70
Arinze, Francis 19
Aristide, Jean-Bertrand 6, 45
Chineworth, Mary Alice 79
Clements, George 2
DeLille, Henriette 30
Fabre, Shelton 71
Gantin, Bernardin 70
Gregory, Wilton D. 37
Guy, Rosa 5
Healy, James Augustine 30
Jean-Juste, Gérard 78
Jones, Alex 64
Marino, Eugene Antonio 30
Otunga, Maurice Michael 55
Rugambwa, Laurean 20
Senghor, Augustin Diamacoune 66
Stallings, George A., Jr. 6

Romance fiction
Bunkley, Anita Richmond 39
Hill, Donna 32
Jackson, Brenda 87
Washington, Elsie B. 78

Royalty
Christophe, Henri 9
Ka Dinizulu, Mcwayizeni 29
Mswati III 56
Mutebi, Ronald 25

Rugby
Mundine, Anthony 56

Rutgers University
Gibson, Donald Bernard 40

Rwanda government
Habyarimana, Juvenal 8
Kagame, Paul 54
Mushikiwabo, Louise 88

Sailing
Petersen, Neal 96
Pinkney, Bill 42
Seymour, Teddy 110

St. Kitts and Nevis government
Douglas, Denzil Llewellyn 53

St. Louis Blues hockey team
Brathwaite, Fred 35
Mayers, Jamal 39

St. Louis Cardinals baseball team
Baylor, Don 6
Brock, Lou 18
Coleman, Vince 128
Flood, Curt 10, 93
Gibson, Bob 33
Lankford, Ray 23

Smith, Ozzie 77

St. Louis city government
Bosley, Freeman, Jr. 7
Harmon, Clarence 26

Salvation Army
Gaither, Israel L. 65

San Antonio Spurs basketball team
Duncan, Tim 20, 91
Elliott, Sean 26
Gervin, George 80
Mohammed, Nazr 64
Parker, Tony 75
Robinson, David 24, 90

San Diego Chargers football team
Barnes, Ernie 16, 78
Joiner, Charlie 102
Oliver, Paul 115
Tomlinson, LaDainian 65, 112
Winslow, Kellen 83

San Diego Padres baseball team
Carter, Joe 30
Gwynn, Tony 18, 83, 122
McGriff, Fred 24
Smith, Ozzie 77
Winfield, Dave 5, 91

San Francisco 49ers football team
Davis, Vernon 133
Gore, Frank 117
Green, Dennis 5, 45
Hayes, Bob 77
Lott, Ronnie 9
Perry, Joe 95
Rice, Jerry 5, 55, 89
Singletary, Mike 4, 76
Washington, Gene 63
Willis, Patrick 99

San Francisco Giants base-ball team
Bonds, Barry 6, 34, 63, 99
Bonds, Bobby 43
Carter, Joe 30
Fuentes, Tito 123
Hart, Jim Ray 136
Mays, Willie 3
McCovey, Willie 103
Strawberry, Darryl 22

Saturday Night Live
Barnes, Katreese 97
Che, Michael 123
Jones, Leslie 136
Meadows, Tim 30
Morgan, Tracy 61, 102, 131
Morris, Garrett 31, 133
Murphy, Eddie 4, 20, 61
Rock, Chris 3, 22, 66
Rudolph, Maya 46, 106
Thompson, Kenan 52

Saxophone
Adderley, Julian "Cannonball" 30
Adkins, Terry 122
Albright, Gerald 23
Ammons, Gene 112

Amy, Curtis 114
Anderson, Fred 87
Ayler, Albert 104
Battiste, Harold, Jr. 136
Bechet, Sidney 18
Berry, Chu 136
Bostic, Earl 121
Braxton, Anthony 128
Brooks, Tina 133
Byas, Don 133
Clemons, Clarence 41
Cobb, Arnett 114
Coleman, George 106
Coleman, Steve 124
Coltrane, John 19
Coltrane, Ravi 71
Cook, Junior 126
Crawford, Hank 77
Criss, Sonny 128
Edwards, Teddy 123
Ervin, Booker 106
Favors, Malachi 136
Foster, Frank 97
Freeman, Von 104
Golson, Benny 37
Gordon, Dexter 25
Gray, Wardell 128
Greene, Jimmy 74
Griffin, Johnny 71
Handy, John 131
Hawkins, Coleman 9
Henderson, Joe 127
Hodges, Johnny 129
Jackson, Bull Moose 130
Jacquet, Illinois 49
Jarman, Joseph 136
Kay, Ulyssess 37
Kenyatta, Robin 54
Kinch, Soweto 108
King Curtis 92
Land, Harold 125
McIntyre, Kalaparusha Maurice 117
McLean, Jackie 78
Mitchell, Roscoe 134
Moody, James 83
Moondoc, Jemeel 119
Moore, LeRoi 72
Moura, Paulo 87
Nelson, Oliver 113
Newman, David 76
Parker, Charlie 20
Parker, Maceo 72
Redman, Joshua 30
Rivers, Sam 95
Rollins, Sonny 37, 94
Rouse, Charlie 130
Sanders, Pharoah 64
Shaw, Eddie 136
Shepp, Archie 101
Shider, Garry 87
Shorter, Wayne 75
Smith, Buster 116
Tate, Buddy 108
Tchicai, John 102
Turner, Mark 126
Turrentine, Stanley 129
Vinson, Eddie 112
Ware, David S. 106
Washington, Grover, Jr. 17, 44
Washington, Kamasi 134
Waters, Benny 26
Webster, Ben 136
Wess, Frank 116

Whalum, Kirk 37, 64
Williams, Richard 130
Wright, Leo 131
York, Vincent 40
Young, Lester 37

Schomburg Center for Re-search in Black Culture
Andrews, Bert 13
Dodson, Howard, Jr. 7, 52
Hutson, Jean Blackwell 16, 135
Morrison, Sam 50
Reddick, Lawrence Dunbar 20
Schomburg, Arthur Alfonso 9

School desegregation
Boulware, Harold R. 109
Bridges, Ruby 77
Brown, Oliver Leon 94
Chestnut, J. L., Jr. 73
DeLaine, Joseph A. 110
Fortune, T. Thomas 6
Hobson, Julius W. 44
Holmes, Hamilton E. 82
Nell, William C. 128
Sweatt, Heman Marion 114

Science fiction
Barnes, Steven 54
Butler, Octavia 8, 43, 58
Delany, Samuel R., Jr. 9
Johnson, Alaya Dawn 129

SCLC
See Southern Christian Leadership Conference

Screenplay writing
Akil, Mara Brock 60, 82
Brown, Cecil M. 46
Clack, Zoanne 73
Davis, Thulani 61
Elder, Lonne, III 38
Ellis, Trey 97
Fisher, Antwone 40
Fletcher, Geoffrey 85
Jones, Orlando 30
Lancaster, Byard 105
Lumet, Jenny 80
Mason, Judi Ann 112
McMillan, Tracy 93
Nissel, Angela 42
Prince-Bythewood, Gina 31, 77
Pryce, Trevor 89
Rhimes, Shonda Lynn 67
Rhone, Trevor 80
Ridley, John 69
Robinson, Matt 69
RZA 80, 128
Singleton, John 2, 30, 122
Talbert, David E. 34, 93
Van Peebles, Melvin 7, 95
Wesley, Richard 73
White, James L. 130
Wilmore, Larry 121

Sculpture
Allen, Tina 22, 75
Amos, Emma 63
Bailey, Radcliffe 19
Barthe, Richmond 15
Biggers, John 20, 33
Biggers, Sanford 62
Billops, Camille 82
Brown, Donald 19

Burke, Selma 16
Catlett, Elizabeth 2, 120
Chanticleer, Raven 91
Chase-Riboud, Barbara 20, 46
Cortor, Eldzier 42
Dwight, Edward 65
Edwards, Melvin 22
Fuller, Meta Vaux Warrick 27
Guyton, Tyree 9, 94
Hammons, David 69
Hathaway, Isaac Scott 33
Hunt, Richard 6
Lewis, Edmonia 10
Lewis, Samella 25
Manley, Edna 26
Marshall, Kerry James 59
McCullough, Geraldine 58, 79
McGee, Charles 10
Moody, Ronald 30
Neals, Otto 73
Perkins, Marion 38
Pierce, Elijah 84
Prophet, Nancy Elizabeth 42
Puryear, Martin 42, 101
Saar, Alison 16
Saar, Betye 80
Savage, Augusta 12
Scott, John T. 65
Shabazz, Attallah 6
Simmons, Gary 58
Stout, Renee 63
Washington, James, Jr. 38
Wilson, John 109

Seattle city government
Rice, Norm 8

Seattle Mariners baseball team
Griffey, Ken, Jr. 12, 73
Reynolds, Harold 77

Seattle SuperSonics basketball team
Payton, Gary 99

Security and defense services
Garrett, James F. 78

Senegal government
Diouf, Abdou 3
Sall, Macky 101
Senghor, Léopold Sédar 66
Wade, Abdoulaye 66

Sesame Street
Byrd, Eugene 64
Clash, Kevin 14, 93
Glover, Savion 14
Long, Loretta 58
Orman, Roscoe 55, 129
Reed Hall, Alaina 83
Robinson, Matt 69

Sexual harassment
Gomez-Preston, Cheryl 9
Hill, Anita 5, 65
McCauley, Gina 76
Thomas, Clarence 2, 39, 65
Auguste, Arnold A. 47

Ship captain
Cuffe, Paul 98

Sickle cell anemia
Edwards, Willarda V. 59
Pace, Betty 59

Sierra Leone government
Kabbah, Ahmad Tejan 23
Koroma, Ernest Bai 84

Skateboarding
Williams, Stevie 71

Skiing
Horton, Andre 33
Horton, Suki 33

Skillman Foundation
Goss, Carol A. 55

Slavery
Albert, Octavia V. R. 100
Allen, Richard 14
Asante, Molefi Kete 3
Bibb, Henry and Mary 54
Blackshear, Leonard 52
Blassingame, John Wesley 40
Brown, William Wells 99
Burns, Anthony 102
Chase-Riboud, Barbara 20, 46
Cooper, Anna Julia 20
Du Bois, W. E. B. 3
Dunbar, Paul Laurence 8
Durham, James 90
Easton, Hosea 91
Equiano, Olaudah 78
Farmer-Paellmann, Deadria 43
Gaines, Ernest J. 7
Garnet, Henry Highland 100
Gordon-Reed, Annette 74
Haley, Alex 4
Harper, Frances Ellen Watkins 11
Hayden, Lewis 105
Henson, Josiah 90
Horton, George Moses 124
Huggins, Nathan Irvin 52
Jacobs, Harriet 104
Johnson, Charles 1, 82
Keckley, Elizabeth 90
Lane, Lunsford 93
Langston, John Mercer 101
Mason, Biddy 89
McWorter, Free Frank 91
Miles, Tiya 116
Minkins, Shadrach 104
Montgomery, Isaiah T. 91
Muhammad, Elijah 4
Nell, William C. 128
Northup, Solomon 115
Pleasant, Mary Ellen 9
Reeves, Bass 100
Ruggles, David 126
Russwurm, John Brown 100
Sharpe, Samuel 103
Stephens, Charlotte Andrews 14
Stewart, Maria W. Miller 19
Tancil, Gladys Quander 59
Taylor, Susie King 13
Tubman, Harriet 9, 135
Vesey, Denmark 100
Walker, David 129
Wall, Orindatus S. B. 92
Yates, Jack 114

Smithsonian Institution
Bunch, Lonnie G., III 91

Smith College
Mayhew, Richard 39
Simmons, Ruth 13, 38

SNCC
See Student Nonviolent Coordinating Committee

Soccer
Adu, Freddy 67
Altidore, Jozy 109
Alves, Dani 121
Anderson, Viv 58
Anelka, Nicolas 118
Antunes, Lúcio 109
Balotelli, Mario 104
Barnes, John 53
Beasley, Jamar 29
Benítez, Christian 113
Bigirimana, Gael 115
Charles, John 108
Chitalu, Godfrey 108
Cole, Ashley 106
Crooks, Garth 53
Davids, Edgar 106
dos Santos, Manuel Francisco 65
Drogba, Didier 78, 132
Eto'o, Samuel 73
Eusebio 118
Evra, Patrice 102
Ferdinand, Rio 82
Gyan, Asamoah 87
Henry, Thierry 66, 127
Ibrahim, Fuad 109
Ince, Paul 83
James, David 84
Johanneson, Albert 129
Jones, Cobi N'Gai 18
Kanouté, Fred 68
Kompany, Vincent 132
Leônidas 96
Mello, Breno 73
Mensah, John 87
Meyiwa, Senzo 124
Milla, Roger 2
Muamba, Fabrice 104
Nakhid, David 25
Okocha, Jay Jay 99
Onyewu, Oguchi 60
Pelé 7
Pelé, Abedi 122
Regis, Cyrille 51
Ronaldinho 69
Scurry, Briana 27
Seedorf, Clarence 121
Smalling, Chris 118
Song, Alex 105
Sono, Jomo 86
Sturridge, Daniel 120
Touré, Yaya 99
Weah, George 58

Social science/social criticism
Austin, Bobby W. 95
Berry, Mary Frances 7
Black, Albert 51
Bobo, Lawrence 60
Cayton, Horace 26
Clark, Kenneth B. 5, 52
Cobbs, Price M. 9
Collins, Patricia Hill 67
Edwards, Harry 2
Frazier, E. Franklin 10
George, Zelma Watson 42

Hall, Stuart 78
Hare, Nathan 44
Harris, Eddy L. 18
Haynes, George Edmund 8
hooks, bell 5, 90
Hunt, Darnell 92
Ladner, Joyce A. 42
Lawrence-Lightfoot, Sara 10
Marable, Manning 10, 102
Reid, Ira De A. 100
Williams, David Rudyard 50
Woodson, Robert L. 10

Social work
Auguste, Rose-Anne 13
Berry, Bertice 8, 55
Berrysmith, Don Reginald 49
Blakely, Delois N. 122
Brown, Cora 33
Canada, Geoffrey 23
Coles, Alice 80
Colston, Hal 72
Compton-Rock, Malaak 86
Dumpson, James R. 108
Dunham, Katherine 4, 59
Fields, C. Virginia 25
Finner-Williams, Paris Michele 62
Gbowee, Leymah 76
Granger, Lester B. 75
Grillo, Evelio 95
Hale, Clara 16
Hale, Lorraine 8
Harris, Alice 7
Haynes, George Edmund 8
Jackson, Judith D. 57
Jackson, Mae 57
King, Barbara 22
Kirk, Clara 95
Lewis, Thomas 19
Little, Robert L. 2
McMurray, Georgia L. 36
Quander, Nellie 102
Robinson, Rachel 16
Sears, Stephanie 53
Smith, Damu 54
Vaughn, Viola 70
Waddles, Charleszetta "Mother" 10, 49
Walker, Bernita Ruth 53
Wallace, Joaquin 49
Wells, Henrietta Bell 69
White-Hammond, Gloria 61
Thrower, Willie 35
Young, Whitney M., Jr. 4

Soledad Brothers
Jackson, George Lester 14

Somalia government
Ahmed, Sharif 80
Ali Mahdi Mohamed 5
Mohamud, Hassan Sheikh 105

Sororities
See Fraternities/sororities

Soul food
Terry, Bryant 128
Williams, Lindsey 75
Woods, Sylvia 34, 104

Soul Train
Cornelius, Don 4, 100
D'Angelo 27, 123

Winans, CeCe 14, 43

South African Communist Party
Hani, Chris 6
Mhlaba, Raymond 55

South Africa government
Dandala, Mvume 77
Dlamini-Zuma, Nkosazana 34, 105
Mhlaba, Raymond 55
Motlanthe, Kgalema 74
Sisulu, Walter 47
Zuma, Jacob 33, 75
Zwelithini, Goodwill 128

South Carolina state government
Cardozo, Francis L. 33
Goggins, Juanita 127
Pinckney, Clementa C. 130
Scott, Tim 87, 125

South Sudan government
Kiir, Salva Mayardit 85, 103
Machar, Riek 117

Southern Christian Leadership Conference (SCLC)
Abernathy, Ralph 1
Barrow, Willie T. 85, 128
Brooks, Tyrone 59
Chavis, Benjamin 6
Hooks, Benjamin L. 2, 85
Jackson, Jesse 1, 27, 72
Jones, William A., Jr. 61
King, Bernice 4, 81
King, Martin Luther, Jr. 1
King, Martin Luther, III 20
Lawson, James M., Jr. 90
Lee, Eric P. 79
Lowery, Joseph 2
Moses, Robert Parris 11
Moss, Otis, Jr. 72
Nash, Diane 72
Orange, James 74
Rustin, Bayard 4
Shuttlesworth, Fred 47, 98
Walker, Wyatt Tee 80
Williams, Hosea 15, 31, 123

Special Olympics
Clairborne, Loretta 34

Speedskating
Davis, Shani 58, 84

Spelman College
Cole, Johnnetta B. 5, 43
Falconer, Etta Zuber 59
Price, Glenda 22
Simmons, Ruth 13, 38
Tatum, Beverly Daniel 42, 84
Wade-Gayles, Gloria Jean 41

Sphinx Organization
Dworkin, Aaron P. 52

Spingarn medal
Aaron, Hank 5
Ailey, Alvin 8
Anderson, Marian 2, 33
Angelou, Maya 1, 15, 122
Bates, Daisy 13, 135
Belafonte, Harry 4, 65
Bethune, Mary McLeod 4

Bond, Julian 2, 35, 106, 130
Bradley, Thomas 2, 20
Braithwaite, William Stanley 52
Brooke, Edward W. 8, 88, 126
Bunche, Ralph J. 5
Burleigh, Henry Thacker 56
Carson, Ben 1, 35, 76, 128
Carter, Robert L. 51, 100
Carver, George Washington 4
Chesnutt, Charles 29
Clark, Kenneth B. 5, 52
Conyers, John, Jr. 4, 45, 111
Cosby, Bill 7, 26, 59, 125
Davis, Sammy, Jr. 18
Dee, Ruby 8, 50, 68, 122
Drew, Charles Richard 7
Du Bois, W. E. B. 3
Ellington, Duke 5
Evers, Medgar 3
Evers, Myrlie 8
Franklin, John Hope 5, 77
Gilpin, Charles Sidney 81
Graves, Earl G. 1, 35
Grimké, Archibald H. 9
Haley, Alex 4
Hastie, William H. 8
Hayes, Roland 4
Height, Dorothy I. 2, 23, 78
Higginbotham, A. Leon, Jr. 13, 25
Hill, Oliver W. 24, 63
Hinton, William Augustus 8
Hooks, Benjamin L. 2, 85
Hope, John 8
Horne, Lena 5, 86
Houston, Charles Hamilton 4
Hughes, Langston 4
Jackson, Jesse 1, 27, 72
Johnson, James Weldon 5
Johnson, John H. 3, 54
Johnson, Mordecai Wyatt 79
Jordan, Barbara 4, 78
Jordan, Vernon E. 3, 35
Julian, Percy Lavon 6
Just, Ernest Everett 3
Keith, Damon J. 16, 74
King, Martin Luther, Jr. 1
Lawless, Theodore K. 8
Lawrence, Jacob 4
Lewis, John 2, 46, 83
Logan, Rayford 40
Marshall, Thurgood 1, 44
Mays, Benjamin E. 7
Mitchell, Clarence M., Jr. 88
Moore, Harry T. 29
Motley, Constance Baker 10, 55
Moton, Robert Russa 83
Overton, Anthony 128
Parks, Gordon 1, 35, 58
Parks, Rosa 1, 35, 56
Patterson, Frederick Douglass 12
Powell, Colin 1, 28, 75
Price, Leontyne 1
Randolph, A. Philip 3
Riles, Wilson C. 79
Robeson, Paul 2
Robinson, Jackie 6
Rowan, Carl T. 1, 30
Staupers, Mabel K. 7
Sullivan, Leon H. 3, 30
Sutton, Percy E. 42, 82
Talbert, Mary B. 77
Tobias, Channing H. 79
Tyson, Cicely 7, 51, 112

Weaver, Robert C. 8, 46
White, Walter F. 4
Wilder, L. Douglas 3, 48
Wilkins, Roy 4
Williams, Paul R. 9
Winfrey, Oprah 2, 15, 61, 106
Woodson, Carter G. 2
Wright, Louis Tompkins 4
Wright, Richard 5
Young, Andrew 3, 48, 110
Young, Charles 77
Young, Coleman 1, 20

Spirituals
Anderson, Marian 2, 33
Carr, Kurt 56
Fisher, Miles Mark 91
Hairston, Jester 88
Hayes, Roland 4
Jackson, Mahalia 5
Johnson, Hall 90
Joyner, Matilda Sissieretta 15
Norman, Jessye 5
Reese, Della 6, 20, 96
Williams, Denise 40
Work, John Wesley, III 133

Sports administration
Bickerstaff, Bernie 21, 133
Dumars, Joe 16, 65, 126
Fuller, Vivian 33
Goss, Tom 23
Kerry, Leon G. 46
Lee, Bertram M., Sr. 46
Littlepage, Craig 35
Mills, Steve 47
Newsome, Ozzie 26, 117
Payne, Ulice, Jr. 42
Phillips, Teresa L. 42
Randolph, Willie 53
Smith, Gene 123
Ujiri, Masai 107
Ussery, Terdema, II 29

Sports agent
Holland, Kimberly N. 62
Owens, Brig 118
Stewart, Dave 117

Stanford University
Bobo, Lawrence 60
Rice, Condoleezza 3, 28, 72
Steele, Claude 13, 97
Walker, Arthur, II 87
Washington, Gene 63

State University of New York
Butts, Calvin O., III 9, 90
Clemente, Rosa 74
Wharton, Clifton R., Jr. 7

Stellar Awards
Baylor, Helen 36
Dillard, Ricky 134
Hawkins, Walter 87
Lawrence, Donald 99
Norful, Smokie 127
Sapp, Marvin 74
Tribbett, Tye 81
Walker, Hezekiah 34

Storytelling
Baker, Augusta 38
Bennett, Louise 69

Hill, Hugh Morgan 83

Student Nonviolent Coordinating Committee (SNCC)
Al-Amin, Jamil Abdullah 6
Anderson, William G(ilchrist) 57
Blackwell, Unita 17
Carmichael, Stokely 5, 26
Clark, Septima 7
Forman, James 7, 51
Hamer, Fannie Lou 6
Moses, Robert Parris 11
Nash, Diane 72
Simmons, Gwendolyn Zoharah 132
Touré, Askia (Muhammad Abu Bakr el) 47

Sudan government
Bashir, Omar al- 77
Cham, Adongo Agada Akway 77
Garang, John 105

Sun Microsystems
Tademy, Lalita 36

Sundance Film Festival
Coogler, Ryan 114
Corinealdi, Emayatzy 133
Dash, Julie 4, 132
DuVernay, Ava 98, 126
Harris, Leslie 6
Nelson, Stanley 92

Supreme Court
See U.S. Supreme Court

Surfing
Corley, Tony 62

Surrealism
Ellison, Ralph 7
Lee-Smith, Hughie 5, 22

Swaziland government
Mswati III 56

Swimming
Atkinson, Alia 126
Brigitha, Enith 126
Ervin, Anthony 66
Jones, Cullen 73
Moussambani, Eric 105

Tampa Bay Buccaneers football team
Barber, Ronde 41
Brooks, Derrick 43, 119
McDaniel, Randall Cornell 81
Morris, Raheem 77
Sapp, Warren 38, 109

Tanzania government
Kikwete, Jakaya Mrisho 73
Mkapa, Benjamin W. 16, 77
Mwinyi, Ali Hassan 1, 77
Nyerere, Julius 5, 136

Tap dancing
Anderson, Maceo 111
Atkins, Cholly 40
Baby Laurence 136
Bates, Peg Leg 14, 135
Brown, Ernest 80
Coles, Honi 128
Glover, Savion 14
Hines, Gregory 1, 42
Lane, William Henry 90

Robinson, LaVaughn 69
Sims, Howard "Sandman" 48
Slyde, Jimmy 70
Walker, Dianne 57

Teaching
Abani, Chris 77
Adams-Ender, Clara 40
Alexander, Margaret Walker 22
Amadi, Elechi 40
Archie-Hudson, Marguerite 44
Aubert, Alvin 41
Baiocchi, Regina Harris 41
Ballard, Allen Butler, Jr. 40
Beals, Melba Pattillo 15, 94
Bibb, Henry and Mary 54
Blackwell, Gloria 127
Blanchard, Shawn 129
Blassingame, John Wesley 40
Branch, William Blackwell 39
Brawley, Benjamin 44
Brown, Charlotte Hawkins 106
Burroughs, Nannie Helen 96
Campbell, Mary Schmidt 43
Cardozo, Francis L. 33
Carter, Joye Maureen 41
Chenault, John 40
Cheney-Coker, Syl 43
Clarke, John Henrik 20
Clemmons, Reginal G. 41
Cobb, Jewel Plummer 42
Cobb, W. Montague 39
Cole, Johnnetta B. 5, 43
Coleman, Beatrice 120
Colescott, Robert 69
Collins, Patricia Hill 67
Cook, Mercer 40
Cooper Cafritz, Peggy 43
Cortor, Eldzier 42
Cotter, Joseph Seamon, Sr. 40
Crouch, Hubert 95
Dailey, Ulysses Grant 87
Davis, Arthur P. 41
Davis, Gary 41
Davis, George 36
Davis, Milt 74
De Veaux, Alexis 44
Delpit, Lisa 101
Dennard, Brazeal 37
Draper, Sharon Mills 16, 43
Drummond, William J. 40
Dumas, Henry 41
Dunnigan, Alice Allison 41
Dyett, Walter 113
Dymally, Mervyn 42
Early, Gerald 15
Everett, Percival 93
Falconer, Etta Zuber 59
Feelings, Muriel 44
Ferguson, Ronald F. 75
Figueroa, John J. 40
Ford, Nick Aaron 44
Forrest, Leon 44
Fuller, A. Oveta 43
Fuller, Arthur 27
Fuller, Howard L. 37
Gayle, Addison, Jr. 41
Gill, Gerald 69
Granville, Evelyn Boyd 36
Graves, Milford 126
Hall, Arthur 39
Hamburg, Beatrix 84
Hammonds, Evelynn 69

Hare, Nathan 44
Harris, Barry 68
Haskins, James 36, 54
Henries, A. Doris Banks 44
Hill, Errol 40, 135
Hill, Leslie Pinckney 44
Horne, Frank 44
Humphries, Frederick 20
Imes, Elmer Samuel 39
Jackson, Fred James 25
Jansen, Jonathan 102
Jarvis, Erich 67
Kennedy, Randall 40
Ladner, Joyce A. 42
Ladson-Billings, Gloria 130
Leevy, Carroll M. 42
Lewis, Norman 39
Lindsey, Tommie 51
Luper, Clara 94
Logan, Rayford W. 40
Mance, Junior 132
McCullough, Geraldine 58, 79
Mckesson, DeRay 133
Mickens, Ronald Elbert 105
Ming, William Robert, Jr. 125
Mitchell, Parren J. 42, 66
Moore, Harry T. 29
Naylor, Gloria 10, 42
Norman, Maidie 20
Oliver, Kimberly 60
Owens, Helen 48
Owens, Jimmy 130
Palmer, Everard 37
Patterson, Mary Jane 54
Perry, Steve 98
Peters, Margaret and Matilda 43
Player, Willa B. 43
Prophet, Nancy Elizabeth 42
Putney, Martha S. 75
Querino, Manuel Raimundo 84
Ray, Charlotte E. 60
Redmond, Eugene 23
Reid, Rufus 130
Reid, Senghor 55
Rhodes, Jewell Parker 84
Ross-Lee, Barbara 67
Shockley, Ann Allen 84
Simpson-Hoffman, N'kenge 52
Smith, Anna Deavere 6, 44
Smith, John L. 22
Spencer, Peter 128
Toler, Burl 80
Turner, Charles Henry 134
Tutu, Nontombi Naomi 57
Twilight, Alexander 125
Wambugu, Florence 42
Watson, Diane 41
Wells, Henrietta Bell 69
Wesley, Richard 73
Yancy, Dorothy Cowser 42
Yarbrough, Camille 40
York, Vincent 40

Teatro Experimental do Negro
Nascimento, Abdias do 93

Telecommunications
Clyburn, Mignon 78
Gordon, Bruce S. 41, 53, 82
Ibrahim, Mo 67, 115
Irvin, Vernon 65
Rapelang Rabana 112

Wilkins, Ray 47

Television
Akil, Mara Brock 60, 82
Allen, Byron 3, 24, 97
Arkadie, Kevin 17
Banks, Tyra 11, 50
Blake, Asha 26
Brown, James 22
Brown, Joe 29
Brown, Vivian 27
Chase, Debra Martin 49, 96
Clack, Zoanne 73
CoCo Brother 93
Corbi, Lana 42
Creagh, Milton 27
de Passe, Suzanne 25
Deezer D 53
Earthquake 55
Ephriam, Mablean 29
Evans, Harry 25
Falana, Lola 42
Fales-Hill, Susan 88
Frazier, Kevin 58
Gardere, Jeffrey 76
George, Nelson 12, 101
Gray, Willie 46
Greely, M. Gasby 27
Greene, Petey 65
Hall, Arsenio 58
Hatchett, Glenda 32
Haynes, Trudy 44
Henriques, Julian 37
Hill, Marc Lamont 80, 128
Jackson, George 19
Jackson, Randy 40
Jackson, Tom 70
Joe, Yolanda 21
Kandi 83
LeFlore, Lyah Beth 96
Lomax, Louis E. 90
Long, Loretta 58
Mabuza-Suttle, Felicia 43
Mathis, Greg 26
McCrary Anthony, Crystal 70
McFarland, Roland 49
McGlowan, Angela 64, 86
McKenzie, Vashti M. 29
Mercado-Valdes, Frank 43
Mitchell, Russ 21, 73
Moss, Carlton 16
Neville, Arthel 53
Nissel, Angela 42
Norman, Christina 47
Pitts, Byron 71
Poussaint, Renee 78
Price, Frederick K. C. 21
Prince-Bythewood, Gina 31, 77
Quarles, Norma 25
Reynolds, Star Jones 10, 27, 61
Ridley, John 69
Roberts, Deborah 35
Roker, Al 12, 49
Russell, Nipsey 66
Salters, Lisa 71
Shepherd, Sherri 55
Simmons, Kimora Lee 51, 83
Smiley, Tavis 20, 68
Stewart, Nzingha 89
Stuart, Moira 82
Taylor, Jason 70
Taylor, Karin 34
Tillman, Deborah 98

Vance, Jim 110
Vaughn, Countess 53
Wainwright, Joscelyn 46
Washington, Hayma 86
Watson, Carlos 50
Wayans, Damien 78
Wayans, Damon 8, 41
Wayans, Marlon 29, 82
Wayans, Shawn 29
Williams, Armstrong 29
Williams, Wendy 62
Wilmore, Larry 121

Television direction
Barclay, Paris 37, 94, 133
Duke, Bill 3, 96
Hemingway, Anthony 107
Johnson, Clark 96
Laneuville, Eric 123
Warner, Malcolm-Jamal 22, 36, 110
Whack, Rita Coburn 36

Television production
Bowser, Yvette Lee 17, 133
Perry, Tyler 40, 54, 103
Rhimes, Shonda Lynn 67

Tennessee state government
DeBerry, Lois M. 115
Ford, Harold E. 42

Tennessee State University
Clark, Yvonne Young 95
Phillips, Teresa L. 42

Tennessee Supreme Court
Birch, Adolpho A., Jr. 85

Tennessee Titans football team
George, Eddie 80
McNair, Steve 22, 47, 79
Rolle, Myron 98

Tennis
Ashe, Arthur 1, 18
Blake, James 43, 131
Garrison, Zina 2, 133
Gibson, Althea 8, 43
Jackson, Jamea 64
McNeil, Lori 1
Noah, Yannick 4, 60, 121
Peters, Margaret and Matilda 43
Rubin, Chanda 37
Stephens, Sloane 105
Washington, MaliVai 8
Washington, Ora Mae 115
Williams, Richard 131
Williams, Samm-Art 21
Williams, Serena 20, 41, 73, 129
Williams, Venus 17, 34, 62
Young, Donald, Jr. 57

Texas Rangers baseball team
Cottrell, Comer 11

Texas state government
Delco, Wilhelmina 33
Gaines, Matthew 95
Johnson, Eddie Bernice 8, 90
Jordan, Barbara 4, 78
Turner, Sylvester 136

Theater administration/ownership
Austin, Lovie 40
Banks, Michelle 59

Borders, James 9
Cox, Ida 42
Dudley, Sherman H. 117
Gibson, John Trusty 87
Hamlin, Larry Leon 49, 62
Leggs, Kingsley 62
LeNoire, Rosetta 37
Leon, Kenny 10, 98
Marsalis, Delfeayo 41
Spears, Warren 52

**Theatrical
direction/production**
Belgrave, Cynthia 75
Campbell, Dick 129
Dixon, Brandon Victor 134
Glover, Keith 79
Hall, Juanita 62
Hayes, Teddy 40
Leon, Kenny 10, 98
McClinton, Marion Isaac 77
Milner, Ron 39
Perry, Tyler 40, 54, 103
Scott, Harold Russell, Jr. 61
Springer, Ashton, Jr. 115
Taylor, Regina 9, 46, 97
Teer, Barbara Ann 81
Thompson, Tazewell 13
Wolfe, George C. 6, 43, 127

Theology
Cone, James H. 3, 82
Harding, Vincent 67, 130
Henderson, George Washington
    101

Time Warner Inc.
Parsons, Richard 11, 33, 124

**TLC Beatrice International
Holdings, Inc.**
Lewis, Reginald F. 6

Togo government
Eyadéma, Gnassingbé 7, 52
Gnassingbé, Faure 67
Olympio, Sylvanus 126

The Tonight Show
Eubanks, Kevin 15, 108

Tony Awards
Allen, Debbie 13, 42
Bailey, Pearl 14
Belafonte, Harry 4, 65
Carroll, Diahann 9
Carter, Nell 39
Clarke, Hope 14
Coles, Honi 128
Cooper, Chuck 75
Davis, Viola 34, 76, 100, 131
Erivo, Cynthia 133
Faison, George 16
Falana, Lola 42
Fishburne, Laurence 4, 22, 70
Glover, Savion 14
Goldberg, Whoopi 4, 33, 69
Hall, Juanita 62
Hines, Gregory 1, 42
Holder, Geoffrey 78, 124
Horne, Lena 5, 86
Hyman, Phyllis 19
Iglehart, James Monroe 129
James, Nikki M. 94
Jones, Bill T. 1, 46, 80

Jones, James Earl 3, 49, 79
Jones, Sarah 39
LaChanze 93
Lenox, Adriane 59
McDonald, Audra 20, 62, 128
Mitchell, Brian Stokes 21
Mokae, Zakes 80
Moore, Melba 21
Odom, Leslie, Jr. 136
Porter, Billy 112
Premice, Josephine 41
Rashad, Phylicia 21
Richards, Lloyd 2
Rose, Anika Noni 70
Santiago-Hudson, Ruben 85
Thigpen, Lynne 17, 41
Tyson, Cicely 7, 51, 112
Uggams, Leslie 23, 114
Vereen, Ben 4
Washington, Denzel 1, 16, 93
White, Lillias 120
Wilson, August 7, 33, 55
Wolfe, George C. 6, 43, 127
Wright, Jeffrey 54, 111

**Toronto Blue Jays baseball
team**
Carter, Joe 30
Gaston, Cito 71
McGriff, Fred 24

**Toronto Raptors basketball
team**
Carter, Butch 27
Carter, Vince 26
Olajuwon, Hakeem 2, 72
Thomas, Isiah 7, 26, 65

Tourism
Edmunds, Gladys 48

Track and field
Ashford, Evelyn 63
Beamon, Bob 30
Bekele, Kenenisa 75
Berian, Boris 136
Bolt, Usain 73, 104
Browne, Richard 132
Campbell, Milt 113
Campbell-Brown, Veronica 102
Carlos, John 97
Christie, Linford 8
Clay, Bryan 57, 74
Coachman, Alice 18, 123
Devers, Gail 7, 87
Dibaba, Genzebe 130
Dibaba, Tirunesh 73, 109
Farah, Mo 104
Felix, Allyson 48, 98
Fraser-Pryce, Shelly-Ann 113
Freeman, Cathy 29
Gatlin, Justin 123
Gay, Tyson 114
Gebrselassie, Haile 70
Graham, Trevor 84
Greene, Maurice 27, 77
Griffith-Joyner, Florence 28
Harrison, Alvin 28
Harrison, Calvin 28
Hayes, Bob 77
Hill, Candace 130
Holmes, Kelly 47
Jacobs, Regina 38
James, G. Larry 74

Johnson, Michael 13
Johnson, Rodney Van 28
Jones, Lou 64
Jones, Marion 21, 66
Joyner-Kersee, Jackie 5
Kearney, Beverly 109
Kipchoge, Eliud 124
Lewis, Carl 4, 97
Matson, Ollie 93
Metcalfe, Ralph 26
Montgomery, Tim 41
Moses, Edwin 8
Mutola, Maria 12
Omar, Samia Yusuf 107
Owens, Jesse 2
Pettigrew, Antonio 118
Pollard, Fritz 53
Powell, Mike 7
Quirot, Ana 13
Richards-Ross, Sanya 66, 98
Rudisha, David 112
Rudolph, Wilma 4
Simpson, Sherone 120
Smith, Tommie 102
Temple, Ed 109
Thugwane, Josia 21
Walker, LeRoy T. 106
White, Willye 67
Whitfield, Mal 60
Williams, Lauryn 58, 127
Wilson, Ajee' 129
Wilson, David 123
Woodruff, John 68

Transplant surgery
Alexander, Joseph L. 95
Callender, Clive O. 3
Hayanga, Jeremiah 118
Kountz, Samuel L. 10

Trombone
Fuller, Curtis 115
Glenn, Tyree 129
Green, Bennie 131
Lewis, George 104
Liston, Melba 118
Marsalis, Delfeayo 41
Ory, Kid 118
Powell, Benny 87
Trombone Shorty 97

Trumpet
Adderley, Nat 29
Akinmusire, Ambrose 103
Allen, Red 129
Armenteros, Chocolate 133
Armstrong, Louis 2
Belgrave, Marcus 77, 129
Blanchard, Terence 43
Brown, Clifford 86
Browne, Tom 136
Byrd, Donald 109
Campbell, Roy, Jr. 118
Cherry, Don 119
Curson, Ted 108
Dara, Olu 35
Davis, Miles 4
Dixon, Bill 87
Dorham, Kenny 113
Edison, Harry 114
Eldridge, Roy 37
Ellison, Ralph 7
Farmer, Art 38
Ferbos, Lionel 95

Gillespie, Dizzy 1
Hubbard, Freddie 75
Jones, Jonah 39
Jones, Thad 68
Little, Booker 105
Marsalis, Wynton 16, 90
Masekela, Hugh 1, 106
McGhee, Howard 122
Miley, Bubber 120
Mitchell, Blue 126
Morgan, Lee 102
Navarro, Fats 104
Owens, Jimmy 130
Roney, Wallace 136
Shavers, Charlie 131
Smith, Cladys "Jabbo" 32
Terry, Clark 39, 127
Williams, Cootie 114
Wilson, Abram 104
Wilson, Gerald 49, 123

Tuskegee Airmen
Archer, Lee, Jr. 79
Bromery, Randolph Wilson 85
Brown, Willa 40
Carter, Herbert E. 108
Chappell, Roy M. 95
Davis, Benjamin O., Jr. 2, 43
Haysbert, Raymond V., Sr. 87
Hoskins, Harold K. 103
James, Daniel, Jr. 16
Plinton, James O., Jr. 98
Proctor, Bernard Shaw 120
Pruitt, Wendell O. 106
Stone, Chuck 9, 120
Young, Perry H. 100

Tuskegee University
Carver, George Washington 4
Dawson, William Levi 39
Gomillion, Charles 90
Moton, Robert Russa 83
Patterson, Frederick Douglass 12
Payton, Benjamin F. 23
Taylor, Robert Robinson 80
Washington, Margaret Murray 119
Williston, David Augustus 99

UCC
See United Church of Christ

Uganda government
Amin, Idi 42
Kisekka, Samson 112
Museveni, Yoweri 4, 119
Obote, Milton 63

UN
See United Nations

UNCF
See United Negro College Fund

Underground Railroad
Blockson, Charles L. 42
Cohen, Anthony 15
Crew, Spencer R. 55
DeBaptiste, George 32
Ruggles, David 126
Shadd, Abraham D. 81
Spencer, Peter 128
Tubman, Harriet 9, 135

UNIA
See Universal Negro Improvement
Association

Unions
Brown, Lloyd Louis **42**
Burrus, William Henry "Bill" **45**
Clay, William Lacy **8**
Ellis-Lamkins, Phaedra **88**
Farmer, James **2, 64**
Fletcher, Benjamin **90**
Fletcher, Bill, Jr. **41**
Holt Baker, Arlene **73**
LeGrand, Naquasia **126**
Lucy, William **50**
McGee, James Madison **46**
Morris, William "Bill" **51**
Ramaphosa, Cyril **3, 117**
Randolph, A. Philip **3**
Roberts, Lillian **83**
Smith, Nate **49**
Tucker, Rosina **14**
Wyatt, Addie L. **56**

UNIP
See United National Independence
Party

UNITA
See National Union for the Total
Independence of Angola

United Church of Christ (UCC)
Chavis, Benjamin **6**
Forbes, James A., Jr. **71**
Miller, Clyde **113**
Moss, Otis, III **72**
Stanley, A. Knighton **117**
Wright, Jeremiah A., Jr. **45, 69, 103**

**United Democratic Front
(UDF; Malawi)**
Muluzi, Bakili **14, 76**

United Methodist Church
Caldwell, Kirbyjon **55**
Cleaver, Emanuel **4, 45, 68, 107**
Lawson, James M., Jr. **90**
Lewis, Shirley A. R. **14**
Muzorewa, Abel **85**
Stith, Charles R. **73**
Williams, Cecil **130**

United Nations (UN)
Annan, Kofi Atta **15, 48**
Ashe, John **131**
Bunche, Ralph J. **5**
Cousin, Ertharin **115**
Frazier, E. Franklin **10**
Juma, Calestous **57**
Lafontant, Jewel Stradford **3, 51**
McDonald, Gabrielle Kirk **20**
McHenry, Donald F. **83**
Mongella, Gertrude **11**
Omolewa, Michael **119**
Osotimehin, Babatunde **107**
Perkins, Edward **5**
Rice, Susan **74, 103**
Sidibé, Michel **133**
Smythe Haith, Mabel **61**
Young, Andrew **3, 48, 110**
Yumkella, Kandeh **105**

**United Negro College Fund
(UNCF)**
Boyd, T. B., III **6**
Bunkley, Anita Richmond **39**
Creagh, Milton **27**
Dawson, Matel, Jr. **39**
Edley, Christopher **2, 48**
Lomax, Michael L. **58**
Patterson, Frederick Douglass **12**

United Parcel Service
Cooper, Evern **40**
Darden, Calvin **38**
Washington, Patrice Clarke **12**

**United States Football League
(USFL)**
White, Reggie **6, 50**
Williams, Doug **22, 112**

**Universal Negro Improvement
Association (UNIA)**
Austin, Junius C. **44**
Garvey, Marcus **1**
McGuire, George Alexander **80**

University administration
See College and university administration

University of Alabama
Davis, Mike **41**
Lucy Foster, Autherine **35**

**University of Californi-
a–Berkeley**
Blackwell, David **79**
Drummond, William J. **40**
Edley, Christopher F., Jr. **48**

**University of Chicago Hospi-
tals**
Lee, Raphael C. **87**

University of Michigan
Amaker, Tommy **62**
Dillard, Godfrey J. **45**
Fuller, A. Oveta **43**
Goss, Tom **23**
Gray, Ida **41**
Imes, Elmer Samuel **39**

Upscale magazine
Bronner, Nathaniel H., Sr. **32**

Urban League (regional)
Adams, Sheila J. **25**
Clayton, Xernona **3, 45**
Jacob, John E. **2**
Layton, William **87**
Walcott, Dennis M. **112**
Young, Whitney M., Jr. **4**

Urban planning/renewal
Blakely, Edward J. **88**
Bosley, Freeman, Jr. **7**
Brown, Aja **115**
Carter, Majora **77**
Gates, Theaster **118**
Harris, Alice **7**
Lane, Vincent **5**
Lowe, Rick **124**

U.S. Air Force
Anderson, Michael P. **40**
Bush, Charles Vernon **125**

Davis, Benjamin O., Jr. **2, 43**
Drew, Alvin, Jr. **67**
Dwight, Edward **65**
Gregory, Frederick **8, 51**
Harris, Marcelite Jordan **16**
James, Daniel, Jr. **16**
Johnson, Lonnie G. **32, 93**
Jones, Wayne **53**
Lyles, Lester **31**

U.S. Army
Adams-Ender, Clara **40**
Allensworth, Allen **129**
Anderson, Marcia **115**
Augusta, Alexander T. **111**
Austin, Lloyd **101**
Baker, Vernon Joseph **65, 87**
Becton, Julius W., Jr. **110**
Brown, Anthony G. **72**
Cadoria, Sherian Grace **14**
Carter, Edward A., Jr. **104**
Clarke, Anna Mac **95**
Clemmons, Reginal G. **41**
Davis, Benjamin O., Sr. **4**
Delany, Martin R. **27**
Ellis, Larry R. **110**
Flipper, Henry O. **3**
Fox, John R. **105**
Greenhouse, Bunnatine "Bunny" **57**
Honoré, Russel L. **64**
Jackson, Fred James **25**
Johnson, Hazel **22**
Johnson, Henry **129**
Johnson, Shoshana **47**
King, Teresa **80**
Matthews, Mark **59**
Morris, Melvin **120**
Perry, Herman **89**
Poindexter, Hildrus A. **87**
Powell, Colin **1, 28, 75**
Rogers, Alan G. **72**
Sidat-Singh, Wilmeth **116**
Snow, Samuel **71**
Stanford, John **20**
Stowers, Freddie **107**
Via, Dennis **108**
Ward, William E. **107**
Watkins, Perry **12**
West, Allen **89**
West, Togo D., Jr. **16**
Young, Charles **77**

U.S. Army Air Corps
Anderson, Charles Edward **37**

**U.S. Atomic Energy Commis-
sion**
Nabrit, Samuel Milton **47**

U.S. Attorney's Office
Johnson, Sterling, Jr. **124**
Jordan, Eddie **82**
Lafontant, Jewel Stradford **3, 51**
Lynch, Loretta E. **103**

**U.S. Bureau of Engraving and
Printing**
Felix, Larry R. **64**

U.S. Cabinet
Kirk, Ron **11, 75, 111**

U.S. Coast Guard
Brown, Erroll M. **23**
Healy, Michael **90**

Rochon, Stephen W. **78**

**U.S. Commission on Civil
Rights**
Berry, Mary Frances **7**
Edley, Christopher **2, 48**
Fletcher, Arthur A. **63**

**U.S. Conference of Catholic
Bishops**
Gregory, Wilton D. **37**

U.S. Court of Appeals
Hastie, William H. **8**
Higginbotham, A. Leon, Jr. **13, 25**
Kearse, Amalya Lyle **12**
Keith, Damon J. **16, 74**
Rawlinson, Johnnie B. **79**
Williams, Ann Claire **82**

**U.S. Department of Agricul-
ture (USDA)**
Espy, Mike **6**
Layton, William **87**
Sherrod, Shirley **87**
Vaughn, Gladys Gary **47**
Watkins, Shirley R. **17**

U.S. Department of Commerce
Brown, Ron **5**
Irving, Larry, Jr. **12**
Morrow, E. Frederic **100**
Shavers, Cheryl **31**

U.S. Department of Defense
Greenhouse, Bunnatine "Bunny" **57**
Johnson, Jeh **76, 125**
Tribble, Israel, Jr. **8**

U.S. Department of Education
Ali, Russlynn H. **92**
Groff, Peter **96**
Hill, Anita **5, 65**
Hill, Bonnie Guiton **20**
Paige, Rod **29**
Purnell, Silas **59**
Thomas, Clarence **2, 39, 65**
Tribble, Israel, Jr. **8**
Velez-Rodriguez, Argelia **56**

U.S. Department of Energy
O'Leary, Hazel **6**

**U.S. Department of Health and
Human Services (HHS)**
See also U.S. Department of
Health, Education, and Welfare
Gaston, Marilyn Hughes **60**
Hamburg, Margaret **78**
Hughes, Dora **88**

**U.S. Department of Health,
Education, and Welfare (HEW)**
Harris, Patricia Roberts **2**
Randolph, Linda A. **52**
Spearman, Leonard H. O., Sr. **81**
Sullivan, Louis **8**

**U.S. Department of Homeland
Security**
Johnson, Jeh **76, 125**

**U.S. Department of Housing
and Urban Development
(HUD)**
Blackwell, J. Kenneth, Sr. **61**
Gaines, Brenda **41**

Harris, Patricia Roberts 2
Jackson, Alphonso R. 48
Weaver, Robert C. 8, 46

U.S. Department of Justice
Campbell, Bill 9, 76
Days, Drew S., III 10
Guinier, Lani 7, 30
Harris, Maya Lakshmi 88
Holder, Eric, Jr. 9, 76, 104
Lafontant, Jewel Stradford 3, 51
Lewis, Delano 7
Patrick, Deval 12, 61, 127
Thompson, Larry D. 39
Williams, Michael L. 86

U.S. Department of Labor
Crockett, George W., Jr. 10, 64
Fletcher, Arthur A. 63
Herman, Alexis M. 15

U.S. Department of State
Baltimore, Richard Lewis, III 71
Bethune, Mary McLeod 4
Bunche, Ralph J. 5
Davis, Ruth 37
Dougherty, Mary Pearl 47
Frazer, Jendayi 68
Ervin, Clark Kent 82
Garrett, Joyce Finley 59
Grimké, Archibald H. 9
Haley, George Williford Boyce 21
Harris, Patricia Roberts 2
Lafontant, Jewel Stradford 3, 51
McGee, James D. 74
Powell, Colin 1, 28, 75
Rice, Condoleezza 3, 28, 72
Rice, Susan 74, 103
Stokes, Carl 10, 73
Sutphen, Mona 77
Thomas-Greenfield, Linda 99
Van Lierop, Robert 53
Walton, Lester Aglar 134
Wharton, Clifton R., Jr. 7
Wharton, Clifton Reginald, Sr. 36

U.S. Department of the Treasury
Morton, Azie Taylor 48

U.S. Department of Transportation
Coleman, William T. 76
Davis, Benjamin O., Jr. 2, 43
Foxx, Anthony 81, 123
Slater, Rodney E. 15, 125

U.S. Department of Veterans Affairs
Brown, Jesse 6, 41

U.S. Diplomatic Corps
See U.S. Department of State

U.S. District Attorney
Harris, Kamala D. 64, 122
Lloyd, Reginald 64
Thompson, Ken 131

U.S. District Court judge
Bryant, William Benson 61
Carter, Robert L. 51, 100
Cooke, Marcia 60
Diggs-Taylor, Anna 20
Henderson, Thelton E. 68

Johnson, Norma H. 17, 97
Johnson, Sterling, Jr. 124
Keith, Damon J. 16, 74
Parker, Barrington D. 92
Parsons, James 14
Perry, Matthew J., Jr. 96
Reeves, Carlton W. 129
Sleet, Gregory M. 109
Tanner, Jack E. 100
Williams, Ann Claire 82
Williams, David W. 110

U.S. Dream Academy
Phipps, Wintley 59

U.S. Environmental Protection Agency
Jackson, Lisa 77

U.S. Foreign Service
See U.S. Department of State

U.S. Geological Survey
Bromery, Randolph Wilson 85
Person, Waverly 9, 51

U.S. House of Representatives
Adams, Alma 127
Archie-Hudson, Marguerite 44
Ballance, Frank W. 41
Beatty, Joyce 117
Bishop, Sanford D., Jr. 24, 111
Brown, Corrine 24, 90
Burke, Yvonne Brathwaite 42
Carson, André 69
Carson, Julia 23, 69
Chisholm, Shirley 2, 50
Christensen, Donna M. 17, 132
Clarke, Yvette 92
Clay, William Lacy 8
Clay, William Lacy, Jr. 95
Clayton, Eva M. 20
Cleaver, Emanuel 4, 45, 68, 107
Clyburn, James E. 21, 71, 118
Collins, Barbara-Rose 7, 87
Collins, Cardiss 10, 80, 120
Conyers, John, Jr. 4, 45, 111
Crockett, George W., Jr. 10, 64
Cummings, Elijah E. 24, 102
Davis, Artur 41
Davis, Danny K. 24, 79
Dawson, William L. 130
De Priest, Oscar Stanton 80
Dellums, Ronald 2, 81
Diggs, Charles C. 21
Dixon, Julian C. 24
Dymally, Mervyn 42
Edwards, Donna 77
Ellison, Keith 59
Espy, Mike 6
Fattah, Chaka 11, 70, 112, 130
Fauntroy, Walter E. 11
Fields, Cleo 13
Flake, Floyd H. 18, 110
Ford, Harold E(ugene) 42
Ford, Harold E(ugene), Jr. 16, 70
Franks, Gary 2
Frazer, Victor O. 98
Fudge, Marcia L. 76
Gray, William H., III 3
Green, Al 118
Hastings, Alcee 16, 119
Hawkins, Augustus F. 68

Hilliard, Earl F. 24
Jackson, Jesse, Jr. 14, 45, 81, 108
Jackson Lee, Sheila 20
Jefferson, William J. 25, 72
Jeffries, Hakeem 118
Johnson, Eddie Bernice 8, 90
Johnson, Hank, Jr. 80
Jordan, Barbara 4, 78
Kelly, Robin 114
Kilpatrick, Carolyn Cheeks 16
Langston, John Mercer 101
Lawrence, Brenda 127
Lee, Barbara 25, 102
Leland, Mickey 2
Lewis, John 2, 46, 83
Love, Mia 96, 125
Majette, Denise 41
McKinney, Cynthia 11, 52, 74
Meek, Carrie 6, 36
Meek, Kendrick 41, 89
Meeks, Gregory T. 25, 117
Menard, John Willis 90
Metcalfe, Ralph 26
Mfume, Kweisi 6, 41
Millender-McDonald, Juanita 21, 61
Miller, Lorraine C. 119
Mitchell, Arthur Wergs 91
Mitchell, Parren J. 42, 66
Moore, Gwendolynne S. 55
Norton, Eleanor Holmes 7, 93
Owens, Major 6, 117
Payne, Donald M. 2, 57, 112
Payne, Donald M., Jr. 132
Pinchback, P. B. S. 9
Plaskett, Stacey 127
Powell, Adam Clayton, Jr. 3
Rangel, Charles B. 3, 52, 85
Rapier, James T. 82
Richardson, Laura 81
Richmond, Cedric 93
Rush, Bobby 26, 76
Scott, David 41, 117
Scott, Robert C. 23
Scott, Tim 87, 125
Sewell, Terri 93
Smalls, Robert 82
Stokes, Louis 3
Thompson, Bennie 26, 119
Towns, Edolphus 19, 75
Tubbs Jones, Stephanie 24, 72
Waldon, Alton R., Jr. 98
Washington, Harold 6
Waters, Maxine 3, 67, 103
Watson, Diane 41
Watson Coleman, Bonnie 127
Watt, Mel 26, 105
Watts, J. C., Jr. 14, 38
West, Allen 89
Wheat, Alan 14
Wilson, Frederica 92
Wynn, Albert R. 25, 77
Young, Andrew 3, 48, 110

U.S. Information Agency
Allen, Samuel 38
Haley, George 21, 129

U.S. Marines
Bennett, Richard 97
Bolden, Charles Frank, Jr. 7, 78
Brown, Jesse 6, 41
Coleman, Ronald S. 110
Petersen, Franke E. 31

Von Lipsey, Roderick K. 11

U.S. Navy
Black, Barry C. 47
Brashear, Carl 29
Brown, Jesse Leroy 31
Brown, Wesley A. 102
Clark, Carl 101
Doby, Lawrence Eugene, Sr. 16, 41
Fields, Evelyn J. 27
Gravely, Samuel L., Jr. 5, 49
Howard, Michelle 28, 125
Miller, Dorie 29
Pinkney, Bill 42
Pruitt, Wendell O. 106
Reason, J. Paul 19
Wright, Lewin 43

U.S. Peace Corps
Days, Drew S., III 10
Johnson, Rafer 33
Lewis, Delano 7

U.S. presidency
Obama, Barack 49, 74, 91

U.S. Register of the Treasury
Bruce, Blanche Kelso 33

U.S. Senate
Black, Barry C. 47
Bowman, Bertie 71
Braun, Carol Moseley 4, 42
Brooke, Edward W. 8, 88, 126
Bruce, Blanche Kelso 33
Burris, Roland W. 25, 75
Obama, Barack 49, 74, 91
Pinchback, P. B. S. 9
Revels, Hiram Rhoades 98
Scott, Tim 87, 125

U.S. State Department
See U.S. Department of State

U.S. Supreme Court
Marshall, Thurgood 1, 44
Thomas, Clarence 2, 39, 65

U.S. surgeon general
Benjamin, Regina 20, 75
Elders, Joycelyn 6
Satcher, David 7, 57, 111

U.S. Virgin Islands government
Christensen, Donna M. 17, 132
DeJongh, John, Jr. 85
Evans, Melvin H. 88
Frazer, Victor O. 98
Hastie, William H. 8
Turnbull, Charles Wesley 62

USDA
See U.S. Department of Agriculture

USFL
See United States Football League

Vancouver Grizzlies basketball team
Abdur-Rahim, Shareef 28

Vaudeville
Anderson, Eddie "Rochester" 30
Austin, Lovie 40
Baby Laurence 136
Bates, Peg Leg 14, 135

Cox, Ida **42**
Davis, Sammy, Jr. **18**
Dudley, Sherman H. **117**
Gilpin, Charles Sidney **81**
Johnson, J. Rosamond **121**
Johnson, Jack **8**
Martin, Sara **38**
McDaniel, Hattie **5**
Mills, Florence **22**
Moore, Tim **124**
Robinson, Bill "Bojangles" **11**
Walker, George **129**
Waters, Ethel **7**
Williams, Bert **18**

Vermont state government
Twilight, Alexander **125**

Veterans's issues
Carr, Keela **74**

Veterinary science
Jawara, Dawda Kairaba **11**
Lushington, Augustus Nathaniel **56**
Thomas, Vivien **9**

Vibe
Jones, Quincy **8, 30**
Smith, Danyel **40**
Wilbekin, Emil **63**

Vibraphone
Hampton, Lionel **17, 41**
Hutcherson, Bobby **115**
Smith, Cecilia **102**

Victim's Bill of Rights
Dee, Merri **55**

Video gaming
Croal, N'Gai **76**
Fils-Aimé, Reggie **74**

Vietnam Veterans of America
Duggins, George **64**

Village Voice
Cooper, Andrew W. **36**
Crouch, Stanley **11**

Violin
Blake, John, Jr. **123**
Boulogne, Joseph, Chevalier de Saint-Georges **94**
Bridgetower, George **78**
Carter, Regina **23, 131**
Daemyon, Jerald **64**
Dworkin, Aaron P. **52**
Escobar, Damien **56**
Escobar, Tourie **56**
Murray, Tai **47**
Smith, Stuff **37**
Tinsley, Boyd **50**
Williams, Claude **80**

Virginia state government
Jones, Dwight C. **122**
Marsh, Henry **32**
Martin, Ruby Grant **49**
Wilder, L. Douglas **3, 48**

Virginia Supreme Court
Hassell, Leroy Rountree, Sr. **41, 116**

Virology
Fuller, A. Oveta **43**

Vogue magazine
Talley, André Leon **56, 106**

Volleyball
Blanton, Dain **29**

Voodoo
Beauvoir, Max **74**
Dunham, Katherine **4, 59**
Guy, Rosa **5**
Hurston, Zora Neale **3**
Pierre, Andre **17**

Voting rights
Boynton Robinson, Amelia **131**
Cary, Mary Ann Shadd **30**
Chestnut, J. L., Jr. **73**
Church, Robert Reed, Sr. **132**
Clark, Septima **7**
Forman, James **7, 51**
Hamer, Fannie Lou **6**
Harper, Frances Ellen Watkins **11**
Hill, Jesse, Jr. **13**
Lampkin, Daisy **19**
Moore, Harry T. **29**
Moses, Robert Parris **11**
Terrell, Mary Church **9**
Touré, Faya Ora Rose **56**
Trotter, Monroe **9**
Wells-Barnett, Ida B. **8**

WAAC (Women's Auxiliary Army Corps)
See Women's Army Corps

WAC
See Women's Army Corps

War criminals
Lubanga, Thomas **104**
Ntaganda, Bosco **111**
Sankoh, Foday **74**

Washington, D.C., city government
Barry, Marion, Jr. **7, 44, 125**
Bowser, Muriel **129**
Brown, Kwame R. **91**
Cooper Cafritz, Peggy **43**
Dixon, Sharon Pratt **1**
Fenty, Adrian **60, 88**
Gray, Vincent C. **88**
Hobson, Julius W. **44**
Jarvis, Charlene Drew **21**
Neal, Larry **38**
Norton, Eleanor Holmes **7, 93**
Washington, Walter **45**
Williams, Anthony **21**

Washington Post
Aplin-Brownlee, Vivian **96**
Britt, Donna **28**
Gaines, Patrice **106**
Givhan, Robin Deneen **72**
Haygood, Wil **83**
King, Colbert I. **69**
McCall, Nathan **8**
Nelson, Jill **6, 54**
Raspberry, William **2**

Washington Redskins football team
Green, Darrell **39, 74**
Manley, Dexter **116**
May, Mark **117**

Monk, Art **38, 73**
Owens, Brig **118**
Portis, Clinton **130**

Washington Wizards basketball team
Heard, Gar **25**
Howard, Juwan **15**
Unseld, Wes **23**

Weather
Brown, Vivian **27**
Christian, Spencer **15**
McEwen, Mark **5**
Roker, Al **12, 49**

Welfare reform
Bryant, Wayne R. **6**
Carson, Julia **23, 69**
Parker, Star **70**
Wallace, Joaquin **49**
Williams, Walter E. **4, 133**

West Indian folk songs
Rhoden, Wayne **70**

West Indian literature
See Caribbean literature/West Indian literature

West Point
Davis, Benjamin O., Jr. **2, 43**
Flipper, Henry O. **3**
Young, Charles **77**

White House
Allen, Eugene **79**
Burton, Bill **96**
Butts, Cassandra **78, 136**
Christie, Ron **83**
Currie, Betty **21**
Gaspard, Patrick **84**
Hatcher, Andrew T. **90**
Jarvis, Kristen **85**
Keckley, Elizabeth **90**
Love, Reggie **77**
McAlpin, Harry **121**
Obama, Michelle **61, 90**
Rochon, Stephen W. **78**
Rogers, Desirée **88**
Rouse, Cecilia **93**
Strautmanis, Michael **87**

Wine/winemaking
Allen-Buillard, Melba **55**
Rideau, Iris **46**
Walker, Ray **109**

Wisconsin Supreme Court
Butler, Louis **70**

Women's Army Corps (WAC)
Adams Earley, Charity **13, 34**
Cadoria, Sherian Grace **14**
Clarke, Anna Mac **95**

Women's Auxiliary Army Corps
See Women's Army Corps

Women's issues
Abiola-Costello, Hafsat **108**
Allen, Ethel D. **13**
Avery, Byllye Y. **66**
Ba, Mariama **30**
Bashir, Halima **73**
Brown, Elaine **8**

Burroughs, Nannie Helen **96**
Campbell, Bebe Moore **6, 24, 59**
Cannon, Katie **10**
Carby, Hazel **27**
Cary, Mary Ann Shadd **30**
Charles, Mary Eugenia **10, 55**
Chinn, May Edward **26**
Christian, Barbara T. **44**
Clark, Septima **7**
Cook-Parrish, Mary Virginia **95**
Cooper, Anna Julia **20**
De Veaux, Alexis **44**
Edwards, Lena Frances **76**
Evans, Diana **72**
Fauset, Jessie **7**
Giddings, Paula **11**
Gomez, Jewelle **30**
Grimké, Archibald H. **9**
Guy-Sheftall, Beverly **13, 92**
Hamer, Fannie Lou **6**
Harper, Frances Ellen Watkins **11**
Harris, Leslie **6**
Haynes, Elizabeth Ross **102**
Height, Dorothy I. **2, 23, 78**
Hernandez, Aileen Clarke **13**
Hill, Anita **5, 65**
Hine, Darlene Clark **24**
Holland, Endesha Ida Mae **3, 57**
hooks, bell **5, 90**
Hughes, Ebony **57**
Hull, Akasha Gloria **45**
Hussein, Lubna **80**
Jackson, Alexine Clement **22**
Joe, Yolanda **21**
Jordan, June **7, 35**
Koontz, Elizabeth Duncan **101**
Lampkin, Daisy **19**
Lorde, Audre **6**
Marshall, Paule **7, 77**
Mbaye, Mariétou **31**
McCabe, Jewell Jackson **10**
McCauley, Gina **76**
McCray, Chirlane **134**
McKenzie, Vashti M. **29**
McMillan, Terry **4, 17, 53**
Millender-McDonald, Juanita **21, 61**
Millner, Denene **76**
Mongella, Gertrude **11**
Mossell, Gertrude Bustill **40**
Naylor, Gloria **10, 42**
Nelson, Jill **6, 54**
Niane, Katoucha **70**
Nichols, Nichelle **11**
Parker, Pat **19**
Parker, Willie J. **133**
Rawlings, Nana Konadu Agyeman **13**
Ruffin, Josephine St. Pierre **75**
Shange, Ntozake **8, 89**
Sherrod, Shirley **87**
Simpson, Carole **6, 30**
Smith, Barbara **28**
Smith, Jane E. **24**
Talbert, Mary B. **77**
Terrell, Mary Church **9**
Vanzant, Iyanla **17, 47, 108**
Villard-Appolon, Malya **106**
Walker, Alice **1, 43**
Walker, Rebecca **50**
Wallace, Michele Faith **13**
Williams, Fannie Barrier **27**

Xuma, Madie Hall **59**

Women's Leadership Forum
Shabazz, Ilyasah **36**

Women's National Basketball Association
Bickerstaff, Bernie **21, 133**
Bolton-Holifield, Ruthie **28**
Cash, Swin **59**
Catchings, Tamika **43**
Cooper, Cynthia **17**
Edwards, Teresa **14, 95**
Ford, Cheryl **45**
Griffith, Yolanda **25**
Griner, Brittney **128**
Holdsclaw, Chamique **24, 110**
Jones, Merlakia **34**
Lennox, Betty **31**
Leslie, Lisa **16, 73**
Madison, Paula **37, 99**
McCray, Nikki **18**
Miller, Cheryl **10, 74**
Milton, DeLisha **31**
Moore, Maya **94**
Palmer, Violet **59**
Parker, Candace **74**
Peck, Carolyn **23**
Perrot, Kim **23**
Staley, Dawn **57**
Swoopes, Sheryl **12, 56**
Thompson, Tina **25, 75**
Williams, Natalie **31**
Woodard, Lynette **67**

Workplace equity
Clark, Septima **7**
Hill, Anita **5, 65**
Nelson, Jill **6, 54**
Simpson, Carole **6, 30**

Works Progress (Projects) Administration (WPA)
Alexander, Margaret Walker **22**
Blackburn, Robert **28**

DeCarava, Roy **42, 81**
Douglas, Aaron **7**
Dunham, Katherine **4, 59**
Fauset, Crystal Dreda Bird **100**
Hall, Juanita **62**
Lawrence, Jacob **4, 28**
Lee-Smith, Hughie **5, 22**
Murray, Pauli **38**
Sallee, Charles **38**
Sebree, Charles **40**
Winkfield, Jimmy **42**
Wright, Richard **5**

World Bank
Okonjo-Iweala, Ngozi **101**
Soglo, Nicéphore **15**

World beat
Fela **1, 42**
Maal, Baaba **66**
N'Dour, Youssou **1, 53, 79**
Okosuns, Sonny **71**
Ongala, Remmy **9, 91**

World Cup
dos Santos, Manuel Francisco **65**
Eusebio **118**
Gyan, Asamoah **87**
Mensah, John **87**
Milla, Roger **2**
Muhammad, Ibtihaj **133**
Pelé **7**
Scurry, Briana **27**
Sturridge, Daniel **120**

World hunger
Iman **4, 33, 87**
Leland, Mickey **2**

World music
Amadou & Mariam **113**
Diabaté, Toumani **129**
Kidjo, Angelique **50**
Kuti, Femi **47, 110**

Nzié, Anne-Marie **136**

WPA
See Works Progress (Projects) Administration

Wrestling
Henry, Mark **116**
Ladd, Ernie **64**
Lashley, Bobby **63**
Lister, Tommy **127**
Rock, The **29, 66**
Young, Darren **114**

Xerox Corp.
Burns, Ursula **60**
Rand, A. Barry **6**

Yale Repertory Theater
Dutton, Charles S. **4, 22**
Richards, Lloyd **2**

Yale University
Blassingame, John Wesley **40**
Carby, Hazel **27**
Davis, Charles T. **48**
Neal, Larry **38**

YMCA
See Young Men's Christian Association

Yoruban folklore
Soyinka, Wole **4, 93**

Young adult literature
Anderson, Ho Che **54**
Bolden, Tonya **32**
Ekwensi, Cyprian **37**
Johnson, Angela **52**
Millner, Denene **76**
Myers, Walter Dean **8, 20, 123**

Young Men's Christian Association (YMCA)
Goode, Mal **13**
Hope, John **8**

Tobias, Channing H. **79**
Yergan, Max **123**

Young Women's Christian Association (YWCA)
Clark, Septima **7**
Claytor, Helen **14, 52**
Height, Dorothy I. **2, 23, 78**
Jackson, Alexine Clement **22**
Jenkins, Ella **15**
Stewart, Ella **39**
Xuma, Madie Hall **59**

YWCA
See Young Women's Christian Association

Zaire government
Mobutu Sese Seko **1, 56**

Zambia government
Chiluba, Frederick **56, 80**
Mwanawasa, Levy **72**
Sata, Michael **102, 125**

Zimbabwe government
Moyo, Lovemore **76**
Mugabe, Robert **10, 71**
Muzorewa, Abel **85**
Nkomo, Joshua **4, 65**
Tsvangirai, Morgan **26, 72**

Zoology
Just, Ernest Everett **3**
Turner, Charles Henry **134**
Young, Roger Arliner **29**

Zydeco
Buckwheat Zydeco **132**
Chenier, C. J. **134**
Chenier, Clifton **134**

Cumulative Name Index

*Volume numbers appear in **bold***

Aaliyah 1979–2001 **30**

Aaron, Hank 1934— **5**

Aaron, Henry Louis *See Aaron, Hank*

Aaron, Quinton 1984— **82**

Abacha, Sani 1943–1998 **11, 70**

Abani, Chris 1966— **77**

Abbott, Diane 1953— **9, 132**

Abbott, Robert Sengstacke 1868–1940 **27**

Abdi, Barkhad 1985— **119**

Abdirahman, Abdi 1977— **126**

Abdirahman, Abdihakem *See Abdirahman, Abdi*

Abdul-Jabbar, Kareem 1947— **8**

Abdullah, Imaam Isa *See York, Dwight D.*

Abdullah, Kazem 1979(?)— **97**

Abdulmajid, Iman Mohamed *See Iman*

Abdul-Rahman, Mahdi *See Hazzard, Walt*

Abdur-Rahim, Shareef 1976— **28**

Abele, Julian 1881–1950 **55**

Abercrumbie, P. Eric 1948— **95**

Abernathy, Ralph David 1926–1990 **1**

Aberra, Amsale 1954— **67**

Abiola, Moshood 1937–1998 **70**

Abiola-Costello, Hafsat 1974— **108**

Abraham, Kyle 1977— **116**

Abrahams, Peter 1919— **39**

Abrahams, Zaraah 1987— **127**

Abubakar, Abdulsalami 1942— **66**

Abudu, Mo 1964— **121**

Abudu, Mosunmola *See Abudu, Mo*

Abu-Jamal, Mumia 1954— **15**

Abune Paulos 1935–2012 **105**

Ace, Johnny 1929–1954 **36**

Aces, The **117**

Aceyalone *See Freestyle Fellowship*

Achebe, Albert Chinualumogu *See Achebe, Chinua*

Achebe, Chinua 1930–2013 **6, 99, 111**

Ackerman, Arlene 1947–2013 **108**

Acklin, Barbara Jean 1943–1998 **107**

Acogny, Germaine 1944— **55**

Adam, Mariam *See Imani Winds*

Adams, Alberta 1917–2014 **133**

Adams, Alma 1946— **127**

Adams, Eric 1960— **133**

Adams, Eula L. 1950— **39, 120**

Adams, Floyd, Jr. 1945–2014 **12, 122**

Adams, Grantley 1898–1971 **82**

Adams, H. Leslie *See Adams, Leslie*

Adams, Jenoyne (?)— **60**

Adams, Johnny 1932–1998 **39**

Adams, Leslie 1932— **39**

Adams, Oleta 19(?)(?)— **18**

Adams, Osceola Macarthy 1890–1983 **31**

Adams, Paul 1977— **50**

Adams, Sheila J. 1943— **25**

Adams, Yolanda 1961— **17, 67**

Adams-Campbell, Lucille L. 1953— **60**

Adams Earley, Charity 1918–2002 **13, 34**

Adams-Ender, Clara 1939— **40**

Adderley, Julian "Cannonball" 1928–1975 **30**

Adderley, Nat 1931–2000 **29**

Adderley, Nathaniel *See Adderley, Nat*

Ade, Sunny King 1946— **41**

Adebari, Rotimi 1963(?)— **83**

Adebimpe, Tunde 1975— **75**

Adegbile, Debo P. 1966— **119**

Adeniyi, Sunday *See Ade, Sunny King*

Adichie, Chimamanda Ngozi 1977— **64, 121**

Adjaye, David 1966— **38, 78**

Adkins, Essie Joseph *See Delta Rhythm Boys*

Adkins, Rod 1958— **41**

Adkins, Rutherford H. 1924–1998 **21**

Adkins, Terry 1953–2014 **122**

Adoboli, Kweku 1980— **106**

Adu, Freddy 1989— **67**

Adu, Fredua Koranteng *See Adu, Freddy*

Adu, Helen Folasade *See Sade*

Aduba, Uzo 1981(?)— **122**

Aduba, Uzoamaka *See Aduba, Uzo*

Afewerki, Isaias 1946— **98**

Afro, Teddy 1976— **78**

Agyeman, Jaramogi Abebe 1911–2000 **10, 63**

Agyeman Rawlings, Nana Konadu 1948— **13**

Ahidjo, Ahmadou 1924–1989 **81**

Ahmed, Mahmoud 1941— **130**

Ahmed, Sharif 1964— **80**

Aidoo, Ama Ata 1942— **38**

Aiken, Loretta Mary *See Mabley, Jackie "Moms"*

Ailey, Alvin 1931–1989 **8**

Ainsworth, Leonard Victor *See Gray, Dobie*

Aire, Chris 1965(?)— **117**

Ake, Claude 1939–1996 **30**

Akil, Mara Brock 1970— **60, 82**

Akinmusire, Ambrose 1982— **103**

Akinnuoye-Agbaje, Adewale 1967— **56**

Akinola, Peter Jasper 1944— **65**

Akinosho, Olurotimi *See Rotimi*

Akintimehin, Olubowale Victor *See Wale*

Akomfrah, John 1957— **37**

Akon 1973(?)— **68**

Akpan, Uwem 1971— **70**

Akunyili, Dora Nkem 1954— **58**

Al-Amin, Jamil Abdullah 1943— **6**

Albert, Octavia V. R. 1853–1890(?) **100**

Albright, Gerald 1947— **23**

Alcindor, Ferdinand Lewis *See Abdul-Jabbar, Kareem*

Alcorn, George Edward, Jr. 1940— **59**

Aldridge, Ira 1807–1867 **99**

Aldridge, LaMarcus 1985— **125**

Alexander, Archie Alphonso 1888–1958 **14**

Alexander, Arthur 1940–1993 **131**

Alexander, Claudia 1959–2015 **130**

Alexander, Clifford 1933— **26**

Alexander, Elizabeth 1962— **75**

Alexander, James *See Bar-Kays, The*

Alexander, James *See Pilgrim Travelers, The*

Alexander, John Marshall *See Ace, Johnny*

Alexander, Joseph L. 1930–2002 **95**

Alexander, Joyce London 1949— **18**

Alexander, Khandi 1957— **43**

Alexander, Kwame 1969(?)— **98**

Alexander, Lincoln 1922–2012 **106**

Alexander, Margaret Walker 1915–1998 **22**

Alexander, Michelle 1967— **98**

Alexander, Sadie Tanner Mossell 1898–1989 **22**

Alexander, Shaun 1977— **58**

Ali, Ayaan Hirsi 1969— **58, 92**

Ali, Hana Yasmeen 1976— **52**

Ali, Laila 1977— **27, 63**

Ali, Mahershala 1974— **122**

Ali, Mohammed Naseehu 1971— **60**

Ali, Muhammad 1942–2016 **2, 16, 52, 136**

Ali, Rashied 1935–2009 **79**

Ali, Russlynn H. 1971(?)— **92**

Ali, Tatyana 1979— **73**

Ali Mahdi Mohamed 1940— **5**

Allah, Khalik 1985— **131**

Allain, Stephanie 1959— **49**

Allen, Betty 1927–2009 **83**

Allen, Byron 1961— **3, 24, 97**

Allen, Claude 1960— **68**

Allen, Debbie 1950— **13, 42**

Allen, Dick 1942— **85**

Allen, Ethel D. 1929–1981 **13**

Allen, Eugene 1919— **79**

Allen, Fulton *See Fuller, Blind Boy*

Allen, Geri 1957— **92**

Allen, Henry *See Allen, Red*

Allen, Larry 1971— **109**

Allen, Lucy 1932— **85**

Allen, Macon Bolling 1816–1894 **104**

Allen, Marcus 1960— **20**

Allen, Ora Denise *See LaSalle, Denise*

Allen, Ray 1975— **82**

Allen, Red 1908–1967 **129**

Allen, Richard 1760–1831 **14**

Allen, Robert L. 1942— **38**

Allen, Samuel W. 1917— **38**

Allen, Tina 1949–2008 **22, 75**

Allen, Tony 1940— **117**

Allen, Will 1949— **74**

Allen-Buillard, Melba 1960— **55**

Allensworth, Allen 1842–1914 **129**

Allison, Luther 1939–1997 **111**

Allison, Verne *See Dells, The*

Almoctar, Goumour *See Bombino*

Alonso, Laz 1974— **87**

Als, Hilton 1961— **105**

Alston, Charles Henry 1907–1977 **33**

Alston, Gerald *See Manhattans, The*

Altidore, Josmer *See Altidore, Jozy*

Altidore, Jozy 1989— **109**

Alves, Dani 1983— **121**

Amadi, Elechi 1934— **40**

Amadou & Mariam **113**

Amaker, Harold Tommy, Jr. *See Amaker, Tommy*

Amaker, Norman 1935–2000 **63**

Amaker, Tommy 1965— **62**

Amaki, Amalia 1949— **76**

Amata, Jeta 1975— **111**

Amerie 1980— **52**

Ames, Wilmer 1950–1993 **27**

Amin, Idi 1925–2003 **42**

Ammons, Albert 1907–1949 **112**

Ammons, Gene 1925–1974 **112**

Ammons, James H. 1952(?)— **81**

Amos, Emma 1938— **63**

Amos, John 1941— **8, 62**

Amos, Valerie 1954— **41**

Amos, Wally 1937— **9**

Amy, Curtis 1927–2002 **114**

Amoudi, Mohammed al- 1946— **88**

Anderson, Alfa *See Chic*

Anderson, Anthony 1970— **51, 77**

Anderson, Bubba *See Crown Heights Affair*

Anderson, Carl 1945–2004 **48**

Anderson, Charles Edward 1919–1994 **37**

Anderson, Eddie "Rochester" 1905–1977 **30**

Anderson, Elmer 1941— **25**

Anderson, Ezzrett 1920— **95**

Anderson, Fred 1929–2010 **87**

Anderson, Ho Che 1969— **54**

Anderson, Ivie 1905(?)–1949 **126**

Anderson, Jacob 1990— **128**

Anderson, Jamal 1972— **22**

Anderson, Katherine *See Marvelettes, The*

Anderson, Kisean *See Kingston, Sean*

Anderson, Lauren 1965— **72**

Anderson, Maceo 1910–2001 **111**

Anderson, Marcia 1958(?)— **115**

Anderson, Marian 1902–1993 **2, 33**

Anderson, Michael P. 1959–2003 **40**

Anderson, Mike 1959— **63**

Anderson, Norman B. 1955— **45**

Anderson, Reuben V. 1942— **81**

Anderson, Sean Michael Leonard *See Big Sean*

Anderson, Sugarfoot *See Anderson, Ezzrett*

Anderson, T. J. 1928— **119**

Anderson, Thomas Jefferson *See Anderson, T. J.*

Anderson, Viv 1956— **58**

Anderson, William *See Drifters, The*

Anderson, William G(ilchrist) 1927— **57**

Andler, Sylvia Brigitte Gertrud *See Ayim, May*

Andre 3000 *See Benjamin, Andre*

Andrews, Benny 1930–2006 **22, 59**

Andrews, Bert 1929–1993 **13**

Andrews, Inez 1929–2012 **108**

Andrews, Lee *See Lee Andrews & the Hearts*

Andrews, Mark *See Sisqo*

Andrews, Raymond 1934–1991 **4**

Andrews, Tina 1951— **74**

Andrews, Troy *See Trombone Shorty*

Anelka, Nicolas 1979— **118**

Angelou, Maya 1928–2014 **1, 15, 122**

Anna Marie *See Lincoln, Abbey*

Annan, Kofi Atta 1938— **15, 48**

Ansa, Tina McElroy 1949— **14**

Anthony, Alani *See Anthony, La La*

Anthony, Carmelo 1984— **46, 94**

Anthony, Crystal *See McCrary Anthony, Crystal*

Anthony, La La 1979— **122**

Anthony, Michael 1930(?)— **29**

Anthony, Trey 1974— **63**

Anthony, Wendell 1950— **25**

Antunes, Lúcio 1966— **109**

apl.de.ap 1974— **84**

Aplin-Brownlee, Vivian 1946–2007 **96**

Appiah, Kwame Anthony 1954— **67, 101**

Arac de Nyeko, Monica 1979— **66**

Arach, Monica *See Arac de Nyeko, Monica*

Archer, Clifford *See Atlantic Starr*

Archer, Dennis (Wayne) 1942— **7, 36**

Archer, Lee, Jr. 1919— **79**

Archer, Michael Eugene *See D'Angelo*

Archer, Osceola *See Adams, Osceola Macarthy*

Archibald, Nathaniel *See Archibald, Tiny*

Archibald, Tiny 1948— **90**

Archie-Hudson, Marguerite 1937— **44**

Ardoin, Alphonse 1915–2007 **65**

Arenas, Gilbert 1982— **84**

Arinze, Francis 1932— **19**

Aristide, Jean-Bertrand 1953— **6, 45**

Arkadie, Kevin 1957— **17**

Armah, Ayi Kwei 1939— **49**

Armah, Esther 1963— **87**

Armatrading, Joan 1950— **32, 133**

Armenteros, Alfredo *See Armenteros, Chocolate*

Armenteros, Chocolate 1928–2016 **133**

Armstrong, Govind 1968— **81**

Armstrong, Henry 1912–1988 **104**

Armstrong, Louis 1900–1971 **2**

Armstrong, Robb 1962— **15**

Armstrong, Vanessa Bell 1953— **24**

Arnez J, 1966(?)— **53**

Arnold, Billy Boy 1935— **112**

Arnold, James *See Arnold, Kokomo*

Arnold, Kokomo 1901–1968 **116**

Arnold, Monica *See Monica*

Arnold, Tichina 1971— **63**

Arnold, William *See Arnold, Billy Boy*

Arnwine, Barbara 1951(?)— **28**

Arrington, Joseph, Jr. *See Tex, Joe*

Arrington, Richard 1934— **24, 100**

Arrington, Steve 1956— **132**

Arroyo, Martina 1936— **30**

Artest, Ron 1979— **52**

Arthur, Owen 1949— **33**

Artist, The *See Prince*

Asante, Molefi Kete 1942— **3**

A$AP Rocky 1988— **109**

Ashanti 1980— **37, 96**

Ashe, Arthur 1943–1993 **1, 18**

Ashe, John 1954— **131**

Ashford, Calvin, Jr. 1935(?)–2008 **74**

Ashford, Emmett 1914–1980 **22**

Ashford, Evelyn 1957— **63**

Ashford, Nickolas 1941–2011 **21, 97**

Ashford and Simpson **21, 97**

Ashley, Maurice 1966— **15, 47**

Ashley & JaQuavis **107**

Ashley-Ward, Amelia 1957— **23**

Ashong, Derrick 1975— **86**

Asim, Jabari 1962— **71**

Asomugha, Nnamdi 1981— **100**

Astatke, Mulatu 1942(?)— **81**

Atim, Julian 1980(?)— **66**

Atkins, Cholly 1930–2003 **40**

Atkins, David *See Sinbad*

Atkins, Erica 1972— *See Mary Mary*

Atkins, Jeffrey *See Ja Rule*

Atkins, Juan 1962— **50**

Atkins, Russell 1926— **45**

Atkins, Tina 1974— *See Mary Mary*

Atkinson, Alia 1988— **126**

Atlantic Starr **122**

Atta Mills, John 1944— **75**

Attaway, William 1911–1986 **102**

Atyam, Angelina 1946— **55**

Aubert, Alvin 1930— **41**

Aubespin, Mervin 1937— **95**

Augusta, Alexander T. 1825–1890 **111**

Auguste, Arnold A. 1946— **47**

Auguste, Donna 1958— **29**

Auguste, (Marie Carmele) Rose-Anne 1963— **13**

Augustine, Jean 1937— **53**

Austin, Bobby W. 1944— **95**

Austin, Gloria 1956— **63**

Austin, Jim 1951— **63**

Austin, Junius C. 1887–1968 **44**

Austin, Lloyd 1953— **101**

Austin, Lovie 1887–1972 **40**

Austin, Patti 1948— **24**

Austin, Wanda M. 1953(?)— **94**

Autrey, Wesley 1956— **68**

Avant, Clarence 1931— **19, 86**

Avant, Nicole A. 1968— **90**

Avery, Byllye Y. 1937— **66**

Avery, James 1945(?)–2013 **118**

Awoonor, Kofi 1935–2013 **37, 115**

Awoonor-Williams, George *See Awoonor, Kofi*

Awoyinka, Adesiji *See Siji*

Awuah, Patrick 1965— **111, 131**

Ayers, Roy 1940— **16**

Ayew, Abedi *See Pelé, Abedi*

Ayim, May 1960–1996 **126**

Ayler, Albert 1936–1970 **104**

Azikiwe, Nnamdi 1904–1996 **13**

Ba, Mariama 1929–1981 **30**

Babangida, Ibrahim (Badamasi) 1941— **4**

Babatunde, Obba 19(?)(?)— **35**

Babatunde, Rotimi 19(?)(?)— **104**

Baby Laurence 1921–1974 **136**

Babyface 1959— **10, 31, 82**

Baca, Susana 1954— **80**

Bacon-Bercey, June 1942— **38**

Badu, Erykah 1971— **22, 114**

Bagayoko, Amadou *See Amadou & Mariam*

Bahati, Wambui 1950(?)— **60**

Bailey, Buddy *See Clovers, The*

Bailey, Buster 1902–1967 **38**

Bailey, Chauncey 1949–2007 **68**

Bailey, Clyde 1946— **45**

Bailey, DeFord 1899–1982 **33**

Bailey, Jimmy *See Cadillacs*

Bailey, Pearl Mae 1918–1990 **14**

Bailey, Philip 1951— **63**

Bailey, Preston 1948(?)— **64**

Bailey, Radcliffe 1968— **19**

Bailey, Shamir *See Shamir*

Bailey, William C. *See Bailey, Buster*

Bailey, Xenobia 1955(?)— **11**

Bailey Rae, Corinne 1979— **83**

Baines, Harold 1959— **32**

Baiocchi, Regina Harris 1956— **41**

Baisden, Michael 1963— **25, 66**

Baker, Anita 1957— **21, 48**

Baker, Arlene Holt *See Holt Baker, Arlene*

Baker, Augusta 1911–1998 **38**

Baker, Constance *See Motley, Constance Baker*

Baker, Delbert W. 1953— **110**

Baker, Dusty 1949— **8, 43, 72, 110**

Baker, Ella 1903–1986 **5**

Baker, George *See Divine, Father*

Baker, Gwendolyn Calvert 1931— **9**

Baker, Houston A(lfred), Jr. 1943— **6**

Baker, James *See New Birth*

Baker, Johnnie B., Jr. *See Baker, Dusty*

Baker, Josephine 1906–1975 **3**

Baker, LaVern 1929–1997 **26**

Baker, Matt 1921–1959 **76**

Baker, Maxine 1952— **28**

Baker, Mickey 1925— **95**

Baker, Thurbert 1952— **22**

Baker, Vernon Joseph 1919–2010 **65, 87**

Bakewell, Danny 1946— **99**

Balance, Frank W. 1942— **41**

Baldwin, Cynthia 1945— **74, 107**

Baldwin, David *See Drifters, The*

Baldwin, James 1924–1987 **1**

Balentino, Umberto Alejandro *See Jeffries, Herb*

Balinton, Umpeylia Marsema *See DeSanto, Sugar Pie*

Ball, Kirshnik *See Migos*

Ballard, Allen Butler, Jr. 1930— **40**

Ballard, Florence 1943–1976 **112**

See also Supremes, The

Ballard, Hank 1927–2003 **41**

Ballard, John 1830–1905 **95**

Balotelli, Mario 1990— **104**

Baltimore, Richard Lewis, III 1946— **71**

Bambaataa, Afrika 1958— **34**

Bambara, Toni Cade 1939— **10**

Banda, Hastings Kamuzu 1898(?)–1997 **6, 54**

Banda, Joyce 1950— **101**

Bandele, Asha 1970(?)— **36**

Bandele, Biyi 1967— **68, 121**

Bandele-Thomas, Biyi *See Bandele, Biyi*

Banks, A. Doris See Henries, A. Doris Banks
Banks, Azealia 1991— **107**
Banks, Chico 1962(?)–2008 **134**
Banks, Ernie 1931–2015 **33, 126**
Banks, Jeffrey 1953— **17**
Banks, Lloyd 1982— **113**
Banks, Michelle 1968(?)— **59**
Banks, Patryce See Graham Central Station
Banks, Paula A. 1950— **68**
Banks, Ron See Dramatics, The
Banks, Tyra 1973— **11, 50**
Banks, Vernon X. See Banks, Chico
Banks, William (Venoid) 1903–1985 **11**
Banneker, Benjamin 1731–1806 **93**
Banner, David 1975(?)— **55**
Bannister, Edward Mitchell 1828–1901 **88**
Banton, Buju 1973— **93**
Baquet, Dean 1956— **63, 121**
Baraka, Amiri 1934–2014 **1, 38, 118**
Baraka, Ras J. 1970— **121**
Baraka, Sho 19(?)(?)— **109**
Barbee, Lloyd Augustus 1925–2002 **71**
Barber, Atiim Kiambu Hakeem-Ah See Barber, Tiki
Barber, Keith See Pilgrim Travelers, The
Barber, Ronde 1975— **41**
Barber, Tiki 1975— **57, 107**
Barboza, Anthony 1944— **10**
Barclay, Paris 1956— **37, 94, 133**
Barden, Donald H. 1943— **9, 20, 89**
Bar-Kays, The **118**
Barker, Danny 1909–1994 **32**
Barkley, Charles 1963— **5, 66**
Barksdale, Chuck See Dells, The
Barksdale, Don 1923–1993 **103**
Barlow, Roosevelt 1917–2003 **49**
Barnes, Ernie 1938–2009 **16, 78**
Barnes, John 1963— **53**
Barnes, Katreese 196(?)— **97**
Barnes, Lloyd 1944— **77**
Barnes, Melody 1964— **75**
Barnes, Prentiss See Moonglows, The
Barnes, Roosevelt "Booba" 1936–1996 **33**
Barnes, Steven 1952— **54**
Barnett, Amy Du Bois 1969— **46**
Barnett, Etta Moten 1901–2004 **18, 56**
Barnett, Herman 1926–1973 **112**
Barnett, Marguerite 1942–1992 **46**
Barnett, Tahliah Debrett See FKA Twigs
Barney, Lem 1945— **26**
Barnhill, David 1914–1983 **30**
Barnwell, Ysaye See Sweet Honey in the Rock
Barrax, Gerald William 1933— **45**
Barrett, Andrew C. 1942(?)— **12**
Barrett, Jacqueline 1950— **28**
Barrett, Lindsay 1941— **43**
Barrett, Marcia See Boney M.
Barrett, Mario Dewar See Mario
Barrett, Sweet Emma 1897–1983 **130**

Barrino, Fantasia 1984— **53, 94**
Barris, Kenya 1974— **135**
Barron, Charles 1950— **136**
Barron, Inez 1946— **136**
Barron, Kenny 1943— **128**
Barrow, Dean 1951— **69**
Barrow, Jamal See Shyne
Barrow, Joseph Louis See Louis, Joe
Barrow, Willie T. 1924–2015 **85, 128**
Barry, Marion, Jr. 1936–2014 **7, 44, 125**
Bartels, Peggielene 1953(?)— **80**
Barthé, Earl 19(?)(?)— **78**
Barthe, Richmond 1901–1989 **15**
Barwuah, Mario See Balotelli, Mario
Bashir, Halima 1979— **73**
Bashir, Omar al- 1944— **77**
Basie, William James See Count Basie
Baskett, James 1904–1948 **102**
Basquiat, Jean-Michel 1960–1988 **5**
Bass, Charlotta Amanda Spears 1874–1969 **40**
Bass, Fontella 1940–2012 **104, 109**
Bass, Holly 1975— **134**
Bass, Karen 1953— **70**
Bassett, Angela 1958— **6, 23, 62**
Bassett, Ebenezer D. 1833–1908 **132**
Bassey, Offiong 1985— **119**
Bassey, Shirley 1937— **25**
Baszile, Jennifer 1969(?)— **79**
Batch, Charlie 1974— **120**
Bates, Clayton See Bates, Peg Leg
Bates, Daisy 1914(?)–1999 **13, 135**
Bates, Elias See Diddley, Bo
Bates, Karen Grigsby 19(?)(?)— **40**
Bates, Peg Leg 1907–1998 **14, 135**
Bath, Patricia E. 1942— **37**
Batie, Cassandra Monique See Day, Andra
Batiste, Alvin 1932–2007 **66**
Batiste, Jon 1986— **108, 130**
Batiste, Lionel 1932(?)–2012 **105**
Batiste, Russell See Meters, The
Battiste, Harold, Jr. 1931–2015 **136**
Battle, Kathleen 1948— **70**
Battle, Samuel J. 1883–1966 **130**
Batts, Anthony 1960— **128**
Baugé, Grégory 1985— **86**
Baugh, David 1947— **23**
Baughn, David See Drifters, The
Baylor, Don(ald Edward) 1949— **6**
Baylor, Elgin 1934— **93**
Baylor, Helen 1953— **36**
Baynard, Ajax See Crown Heights Affair
Baynard, James See Crown Heights Affair
Bazawule, Samuel See Blitz the Ambassador
Beach, Michael 1963— **26, 120**
Beah, Ishmael 1980— **69**
Beal, Bernard B. 1954(?)— **46**
Beals, Jennifer 1963— **12**
Beals, Melba Pattillo 1941— **15, 94**
Beamon, Bob 1946— **30**
Beard, Matthew 1925–1981 **120**
Bearden, Romare 1912–1988 **2, 50**
Beasley, Jamar 1979— **29**
Beasley, Myrlie See Evers, Myrlie

Beasley, Phoebe 1943— **34**
Beaton, Norman Lugard 1934–1994 **14**
Beatty, Joyce 1950— **117**
Beatty, Talley 1923(?)–1995 **35**
Beaty, Zelmo 1939–2013 **115**
Beauty, Ray See Delta Rhythm Boys
Beauvais, Garcelle 1966— **29, 95**
Beauvoir, Max 1936(?)— **74**
Bebey, Francis 1929–2001 **45**
Bechet, Sidney 1897–1959 **18**
Beck, Robert See Iceberg Slim
Beckford, Tyson 1970— **11, 68**
Beckham, Barry 1944— **41**
Beckham, Odell, Jr. 1992— **132**
Beckwith, Naomi 1976— **101**
Becton, Julius W., Jr. 1926— **110**
Bedie, Henri Konan 1934— **21**
Beenie Man 1973— **32**
Bekele, Kenenisa 1982— **75**
Beken 1956(?)— **111**
Belafonte, Harold George, Jr. See Belafonte, Harry
Belafonte, Harry 1927— **4, 65**
Belgrave, Cynthia 1920–1997 **75**
Belgrave, Marcus 1936–2015 **77, 129**
Bell, Carey 1936–2007 **114**
Bell, Carl C. 1947— **111**
Bell, Cool Papa See Bell, James "Cool Papa"
Bell, Darrin 1975— **77**
Bell, Derrick 1930–2011 **6, 98**
Bell, James "Cool Papa" 1901–1991 **36**
Bell, James A. 1948— **50**
Bell, James Madison 1826–1902 **40**
Bell, LeRoy 1951— **98**
Bell, Le'Veon 1992— **132**
Bell, Michael 1955— **40**
Bell, Ralph S. 1934— **5**
Bell, Ricky See New Edition
Bell, Robert Mack 1943— **22**
Bell, Thom 1943— **112**
Bell, Thomas Randolph See Bell, Thom
Bell, W. Kamau 19(?)(?)— **107**
Bell, Walter Kamau See Bell, W. Kamau
Bell, William A., Sr. 1949— **122**
Bellamy, Bill 1967— **12**
Bellamy, Terry 1972— **58**
Bellamy, Walt 1939–2013 **119**
Belle, Albert (Jojuan) 1966— **10**
Belle, Regina 1963— **1, 51**
Below, Fred See Aces, The
Belton, Sharon Sayles 1951— **9, 16**
Benberry, Cuesta 1923–2007 **65**
Benét, Eric 1966— **28, 77**
Benham, Robert 1946— **78**
Ben-Israel, Ben Ami 1940(?)— **11**
Benítez, Christian 1986–2013 **113**
Benjamin, Andre (3000) 1975— **45**
  See also OutKast
Benjamin, Regina 1956— **20, 75**
Benjamin, Steve 1969— **98**
Benjamin, Tritobia Hayes 1944— **53**
Bennett, Estelle 1941–2009 **77** See also Ronettes, The

Bennett, George Harold "Hal" 1930— **45**
Bennett, Gwendolyn B. 1902–1981 **59**
Bennett, Lerone, Jr. 1928— **5, 84**
Bennett, Louise 1919–2006 **69**
Bennett, Patricia See Chiffons, The
Bennett, Richard 1980(?)— **97**
Benson, Angela 19(?)(?)— **34**
Benson, Obie 1936–2005 **96**
Benson, Renaldo See Benson, Obie
Benson, Ricci See Rose Royce
Bensouda, Fatou 1961— **103**
Bentley, Lamont 1973–2005 **53**
Benton, Brook 1931–1988 **121**
Berhe, Ruth See Ruth B
Berian, Boris 1992— **136**
Bernard, Marvin See Yayo, Tony
Berrien, Jacqueline A. 1961— **93**
Berry, Bertice 1960— **8, 55**
Berry, Bill See Berry, Edwin C.
Berry, Charles Edward Anderson See Berry, Chuck
Berry, Chu 1908–1941 **136**
Berry, Chuck 1926— **29**
Berry, Edwin C. 1910–1987 **81**
Berry, Eric 1988— **125**
Berry, Fred "Rerun" 1951–2003 **48**
Berry, Halle 1966— **4, 19, 57, 91**
Berry, James 1925— **41**
Berry, James Eric See Berry, Eric
Berry, Leon Brown See Berry, Chu
Berry, Mary Frances 1938— **7**
Berry, Moses 1950(?)— **84**
Berry, Theodore M. 1905–2000 **31**
Berrysmith, Don Reginald 1936— **49**
Best, Carrie 1903–2001 **80**
Betha, Mason Durrell 1977(?)— **24**
Bethune, Mary (Jane) McLeod 1875–1955 **4**
Beti, Mongo 1932–2001 **36**
Betsch, MaVynee 1935— **28**
Bettis, Jerome 1972— **64**
Betts, Keter 1928–2005 **85**
Betts, R. Dwayne 1979(?)— **86**
Bevel, James L. 1936–2008 **75**
Beverly, Frankie 1946— **25**
Bey, Salome 1944(?)— **134**
Bey, Yasiin 1973— **30, 96**
Beyoncé 1981— **39, 70, 105**
Bibb, Eric 1951— **49, 123**
Bibb, Henry 1815–1854 **54**
Bibb, Leon 1922–2015 **132**
Bibb, Mary 1820–1877 **54**
Bickerstaff, Bernard Tyrone See Bickerstaff, Bernie
Bickerstaff, Bernie 1944— **21, 133**
Bickerstaff, Cydni L. 1968— **133**
Bickerstaff, J. B. 1979— **133**
Bickerstaff, John-Blair See Bickerstaff, J. B.
Big Bank Hank See Sugarhill Gang, The
Big Boi See Patton, Antwan
Big Daddy Kane 1968— **79**
Big Freedia 1981(?)— **128**
Big G See Glover, Anwan
Big L 1974–1999 **120**
Big Maybelle 1924–1972 **117**
Big Sean 1977— **96**
Big Time Sarah 1953-2015 **45, 134**

Big Youth 1949— **107**
Biggers, John 1924–2001 **20, 33**
Biggers, Sanford 1970— **62**
Bigirimana, Gael 1993— **115**
Biko, Stephen *See Biko, Steven (Bantu)*
Biko, Steven (Bantu) 1946–1977 **4**
Bilal 1979— **101**
Biles, Simone 1997— **136**
Billingslea, Joe *See Contours, The*
Billong, Alexandre Dimitri Song *See Song, Alex*
Billops, Camille 1933— **82**
Billy Ward and the Dominoes **105**
bin Wahad, Dhoruba 1943— **85**
Bing, Dave 1943— **3, 59, 78**
Bingham, Howard 1939— **96**
Bingham, Margot 1988— **135**
Birch, Adolpho A., Jr. 1932— **85**
Birch, Glynn R. 195(?)— **61**
Birdman 1969— **110**
Birdsong, Cindy 1939— **113**
Birra, Ali 1948— **113**
Bishop, Eric *See Foxx, Jamie*
Bishop, Maurice 1944–1983 **39**
Bishop, Sanford D., Jr. 1947— **24, 111**
Bishop, Stephen 1820–1857 **95**
Bivins, Edward *See Manhattans, The*
Bivins, Michael 1968— **72** *See also New Edition*
Biya, Chantal 1970— **89**
Biya, Paul 1933— **28, 114**
Biyidi-Awala, Alexandre *See Beti, Mongo*
Bizimungu, Pasteur 1951— **19**
Blacc, Aloe 1979— **119**
Black, Albert 1940— **51**
Black, Barry C. 1948— **47**
Black, Joe 1924–2002 **75**
Black, Keith Lanier 1957— **18, 84**
Black Kold Madina *See Roberts, Kimberly Rivers*
Black Thought 1972— **63**
Blackburn, Robert 1920— **28**
Blackman, Toni 1968— **86**
Blackmon, Brenda 1952— **58**
Blackmon, Larry *See Cameo*
Blackmore, Amos Wells *See Wells, Junior*
Blackshear, Leonard 1943— **52**
Blackwell, David 1919— **79**
Blackwell, Gloria 1927–2010 **127**
Blackwell, Kenneth, Sr. 1948— **61**
Blackwell, Otis 1932–2002 **98**
Blackwell, Robert D., Sr. 1937— **52**
Blackwell, Unita 1933— **17**
Blackwood, Maureen 1960— **37**
Blacque, Taurean 1941— **58**
Blade, Brian 1970— **88**
Blair, Jayson 1976— **50**
Blair, Maxine *See Powell, Maxine*
Blair, Paul 1944— **36**
Blake, Asha 1961(?)— **26**
Blake, Charles E. 1940— **82**
Blake, Eubie 1883–1983 **29**
Blake, James 1979— **43, 131**
Blake, James Hubert *See Blake, Eubie*
Blake, John, Jr. 1947–2014 **123**
Blakely, Delois N. 1942(?)— **122**
Blakely, Edward J. 1938— **88**

Blakely, Queen Mother Dr. Delois *See Blakely, Delois N.*
Blakey, Art 1919–1990 **37**
Blanchard, Shawn 1982— **129**
Blanchard, Terence 1962— **43**
Blanco, Mykki 1986(?)— **106**
Bland, Bobby 1930–2013 **36, 113**
Bland, Bobby "Blue" *See Bland, Bobby*
Bland, Edward 1926–2013 **111**
Bland, Eleanor Taylor 1944–2010 **39**
Blanks, Billy 1955(?)— **22**
Blanks, Deborah K. 1958— **69**
Blanton, Dain 1971— **29**
Blanton, Jimmy 1918–1942 **108**
Blassingame, John Wesley 1940–2000 **40**
Blaylock, Ronald 1960(?)— **86**
Blayton, Jesse B., Sr. 1897–1977 **55**
Bleu, Corbin 1989— **65**
Blige, Mary J. 1971— **20, 34, 60, 97**
Blind Boys of Alabama, The **99**
Blitz the Ambassador 1982— **115**
Blockson, Charles L. 1933— **42**
Blondy, Alpha 1953— **30**
Bloomer, George 1963— **86**
Blow, Charles M. 1968(?)— **73**
Blow, Kurtis 1959— **31, 122**
Blue, Vida 1949— **122**
Bluford, Guion Stewart, Jr. *See Bluford, Guy*
Bluford, Guy 1942— **2, 35**
Bluitt, Juliann Stephanie 1938— **14**
Boateng, Ozwald 1968(?)— **35, 113**
Boateng, Paul Yaw 1951— **56**
B.o.B. 1988— **91**
Bobb, Robert C. 1945— **83**
Bobo, Lawrence 1958— **60**
Bogan, Ann *See New Birth*
Bogle, Donald 19(?)(?)— **34**
Bogues, Tyrone "Muggsy" 1965— **56**
Bol, Manute 1963— **1**
Bolden, Buddy 1877–1931 **39**
Bolden, Charles Frank, Jr. 1946— **7, 78**
Bolden, Charles Joseph *See Bolden, Buddy*
Bolden, Frank E. 1913–2003 **44**
Bolden, Tonya 1959— **32**
Bolin, Jane 1908–2007 **22, 59**
Bolling, Allen Macon *See Allen, Macon Bolling*
Bolt, Usain 1986— **73, 104**
Bolton, Terrell D. 1959(?)— **25**
Bolton-Holifield, Ruthie 1967— **28**
Bombino 1980— **112**
Bonaly, Surya 1973— **7**
Bond, Beverly 1970— **53**
Bond, J. Max, Jr. 1935— **76**
Bond, Julian 1940–2015 **2, 35, 106, 130**
Bonds, Barry 1964— **6, 34, 63, 99**
Bonds, Bobby 1946— **43**
Bonds, Margaret 1913–1972 **39**
Bonet, Lisa 1967— **58, 133**
Boney, Lisa Michelle *See Bonet, Lisa*
Boney M. **133**
Bonga, Kuenda 1942— **13**

Bongo, Albert-Bernard *See Bongo, Omar*
Bongo, Ali Ben 1959— **80**
Bongo, Omar 1935–2009 **1, 79**
Bonheur, Yannick 1982— **84**
Bonner, Leroy 1943–2013 **113**
Bonney, Tabi 1978(?)— **98**
Bontemps, Arna(ud Wendell) 1902–1973 **8**
Booker, Cory Anthony 1969— **68**
Booker, Ernest *See Pilgrim Travelers, The*
Booker, Simeon 1918— **23**
Bootie Brown *See Pharcyde, The*
Boozer, Bob 1937–2012 **103**
Borders, James (Buchanan, IV) 1949— **9**
Borders, Marcy 1973–2015 **131**
Borders, William Holmes 1905–1993 **94**
Boseman, Chadwick 1982— **111**
Bosh, Chris 1984— **85**
Bosley, Freeman (Robertson), Jr. 1954— **7**
Bossard, Henry K. *See Swan Silvertones, The*
Bostic, Earl 1913–1965 **121**
Bostic, Eugene Earl *See Bostic, Earl*
Bostic, Joe 1909–1988 **95**
Boston, Kelvin E. 1955(?)— **25**
Boston, Lloyd 1970(?)— **24**
Boulogne, Joseph, Chevalier de Saint-Georges 1745(?)–1799 **94**
Boulware, Harold R. 1913–1983 **109**
Bow Wow 1987— **35**
Bowe, Riddick 1967— **6, 107**
Bowen, John W. E., Sr. 1855–1933 **89**
Bowen, Ruth 1924–2009 **83**
Bowles, Cephas 1952–2015 **127**
Bowles, Todd 1963— **128**
Bowman, Bertie 1931— **71**
Bowman, Herbert *See Bowman, Bertie*
Bowser, Muriel 1972— **129**
Bowser, Yvette Lee 1965— **17, 133**
Boyd, Edward 1914–2007 **70**
Boyd, Eva Narcissus *See Little Eva*
Boyd, Gerald M. 1950–2006 **32, 59**
Boyd, Gwendolyn 1955— **49**
Boyd, John W., Jr. 1965— **20, 72**
Boyd, Melba Joyce 1950— **86**
Boyd, Steven *See Dramatics, The*
Boyd, Suzanne 1963— **52**
Boyd, T(heophilus) B(artholomew), III 1947— **6**
Boye, Madior 1940— **30**
Boyega, John 1992— **133**
Boykin, Keith 1965— **14**
Boykin, Otis 1920–1982 **92**
Boykin, Phillip 1968— **102**
Boynton Robinson, Amelia 1911–2015 **131**
Boyz II Men **82**
Bozella, Dewey 1959— **97**
Bozizé, François 1946— **96, 117**
Bracken, James 1909–1972 **107**
Bracken, Vivian 1921–1989 **107**
Bradford, Alex 1927–1978 **121**
Bradford, Mark 1961— **89**
Bradley, Adam 1974— **101**

Bradley, Alton *See Golden Gate Quartet*
Bradley, Charles 1948— **126**
Bradley, David Henry, Jr. 1950— **39**
Bradley, Ed 1941–2006 **2, 59**
Bradley, J. Robert 1919–2007 **65**
Bradley, Jennette B. 1952— **40**
Bradley, Thomas 1917–1998 **2, 20**
Bradshaw, Myron C. *See Bradshaw, Tiny*
Bradshaw, Tiny 1907–1958 **102**
Brady, St. Elmo 1884–1966 **107**
Brady, Wayne 1972— **32, 71**
Brae, C. Michael 1963(?)— **61**
Braithwaite, William Stanley 1878–1962 **52**
Bramlett, Joseph 1988— **91**
Branch, William Blackwell 1927— **39**
Brand, Adolph Johannes *See Ibrahim, Abdullah*
Brand, Dionne 1953— **32**
Brand, Dollar *See Ibrahim, Abdullah*
Brand, Elton 1979— **31**
Brandon, Barbara 1960(?)— **3**
Brandon, Thomas Terrell 1970— **16**
Brandy 1979— **14, 34, 72**
Branham, George, III 1962— **50**
Branson, Herman 1914–1995 **87**
Brashear, Carl Maxie 1931— **29**
Brashear, Donald 1972— **39**
Brathwaite, Fred 1972— **35**
Brathwaite, Kamau 1930— **36**
Brathwaite, Lawson Edward *See Kamau Brathwaite*
Braugher, Andre 1962— **13, 58, 91**
Braun, Carol Moseley 1947— **4, 42**
Brawley, Benjamin 1882–1939 **44**
Braxton, Anthony 1945— **128**
Braxton, Brad 1969(?)— **77**
Braxton, Gene *See Herndon, Angelo*
Braxton, Tamar 1977— **134**
Braxton, Toni 1967— **15, 61, 91**
Brazier, Arthur M. 1921–2010 **115**
Brazile, Donna 1959— **25, 70**
Breaux, Christopher *See Ocean, Frank*
Breed, Eric T. *See MC Breed*
Breed, MC *See MC Breed*
Breedlove, Sarah *See Walker, Madame C. J.*
Breeze, Jean "Binta" 1956— **37**
Brembly, Paul *See Golden Gate Quartet*
Brewer, Rosalind 1962— **100**
Brewster, T. L. *See Soul Stirrers*
Brewster, W. Herbert 1897(?)–1987 **128**
Brewster, William Herbert *See Brewster, W. Herbert*
Brickley, Audrey *See Orlons, The*
Brickley, Jean *See Orlons, The*
Brickley, Shirley *See Orlons, The*
Bridgeman, Junior 1953— **132**
Bridgeman, Ulysses Lee *See Bridgeman, Junior*
Bridges, Christopher *See Ludacris*
Bridges, Leon 1990(?)— **126**
Bridges, Ruby 1954— **77**
Bridges, Sheila 1964— **36**
Bridges, Todd 1965— **37**

Bridgetower, George 1780(?)–1860 **78**

Bridgewater, Dee Dee 1950— **32, 92**

Bridgewater, Teddy 1992— **132**

Bridgewater, Theodore Edmond *See Bridgewater, Teddy*

Bridgforth, Glinda 1952— **36**

Briggs, Curtis 1952(?)— **84**

Brigitha, Enith 1955— **126**

Brim, John 1922–2003 **117**

Brimm, Charles E. 1924–2010 **105**

Brimmer, Andrew 1926–2012 **2, 48, 106**

Briscoe, Connie 1952— **15**

Briscoe, Marlin 1946(?)— **37**

Britt, Donna 1954(?)— **28**

Broadbent, Hydeia 1984— **36**

Brock, Lou 1939— **18**

Brock, Michael *See Dramatics, The*

Brock, Roslyn McCallister 1965— **86**

Brodie, Roosevelt *See Harold Melvin & the Blue Notes*

Broil, Arlette B. *See Griffin, Bessie*

Bromery, Randolph Wilson 1926— **85**

Broner, Adrien 1989— **109**

Bronner, Nathaniel H., Sr. 1914–1993 **32**

Brooke, Edward W. 1919–2015 **8, 88, 126**

Brookins, Hamel Hartford 1925–2012 **102**

Brooks, Aaron 1976— **33**

Brooks, Arthur *See Impressions, The*

Brooks, Avery 1948— **9, 98**

Brooks, Danielle 1989— **119**

Brooks, Derrick 1973— **43, 119**

Brooks, Golden 1970— **62**

Brooks, Gwendolyn 1917–2000 **1, 28**

Brooks, Hadda 1916–2002 **40**

Brooks, Harold Floyd *See Brooks, Tina*

Brooks, Mehcad 1980— **62**

Brooks, Orville *See Golden Gate Quartet*

Brooks, Richard *See Impressions, The*

Brooks, Robert Calvin *See Bland, Bobby*

Brooks, Roy 1938–2005 **125**

Brooks, Tina 1932–1974 **133**

Brooks, Tyrone 1945— **59**

Broonzy, Big Bill 1893–1958 **82**

Brother Blue *See Hill, Hugh Morgan*

Brothers Johnson **130**

Brower, William 1916–2004 **49**

Brown, Aaquil *See Rae Sremmurd*

Brown, Aja 1982— **115**

Brown, Alvin 1963— **96**

Brown, Angela M. 1964(?)— **54**

Brown, Anne 1912–2009 **76**

Brown, Anthony G. 1961— **72**

Brown, Antron 1976— **85**

Brown, Beverly *See Dixie Cups, The*

Brown, Bill *See Billy Ward and the Dominoes*

Brown, Billy *See Ray, Goodman & Brown*

Brown, Bobbi Kristina 1993–2015 **130**

Brown, Bobby 1969— **58, 124** *See also New Edition*

Brown, Buck *See Brown, Robert*

Brown, Byrd 1930–2001 **49**

Brown, Byron W. 1958— **72**

Brown, Carlinhos 1962— **81**

Brown, Cecil M. 1943— **46**

Brown, Charles 1922–1999 **23**

Brown, Charlotte Hawkins 1883–1961 **106**

Brown, Chris 1989— **74, 109**

Brown, Chuck 1936–2012 **78, 102**

Brown, Clarence Gatemouth 1924–2005 **59**

Brown, Claude 1937–2002 **38**

Brown, Clifford 1930–1956 **86**

Brown, Cora 1914–1972 **33**

Brown, Corrine 1946— **24, 90**

Brown, Cupcake 1964— **63**

Brown, Dennis 1957–1999 **99**

Brown, Donald 1963— **19**

Brown, Eddie C. 1940— **35**

Brown, Elaine 1943— **8**

Brown, Ernest 1916–2009 **80**

Brown, Erroll M. 1950(?)— **23**

Brown, Foxy 1979— **25**

Brown, Frederick J. 1945–2012 **102**

Brown, George Leslie 1926–2006 **62**

Brown, H. Rap *See Al-Amin, Jamil Abdullah*

Brown, Hallie Quinn 1850(?)–1949 **100**

Brown, Harley *See Dramatics, The*

Brown, Homer S. 1896–1977 **47**

Brown, Hubert Gerold *See Al-Amin, Jamil Abdullah*

Brown, James 1933–2006 **15, 60**

Brown, James 1951— **22**

Brown, James Mack *See Dramatics, The*

Brown, James Nathaniel *See Brown, Jim*

Brown, James Willie, Jr. *See Komunyakaa, Yusef*

Brown, Jamie Foster 19(?)(?)— **91**

Brown, Janice Rogers 1949— **43**

Brown, Jason 1983— **125**

Brown, Jerry 1987–2012 **117**

Brown, Jesse 1944–2003 **6, 41**

Brown, Jesse Leroy 1926–1950 **31**

Brown, Jim 1936— **11, 95**

Brown, Joe 19(?)(?)— **29**

Brown, Joyce F. 1946— **25**

Brown, Kenji *See Rose Royce*

Brown, Khalif *See Rae Sremmurd*

Brown, Kwame R. 1970— **91**

Brown, Lawrence Darrow *See Gray, Dobie*

Brown, Lee *See Gonzales, Babs*

Brown, Lee P. 1937— **1, 24, 109**

Brown, Les(lie Calvin) 1945— **5**

Brown, Lloyd Louis 1913–2003 **42**

Brown, Melanie 1975— **73**

Brown, Mike 1970— **77, 107**

Brown, Nappy 1929–2008 **73**

Brown, Oliver Leon 1918–1961 **94**

Brown, Oscar, Jr. 1926–2005 **53**

Brown, Patrick "Sleepy" 1970— **50**

Brown, Raymond 1908–1965 **102**

Brown, Robert 1936–2007 **65**

Brown, Ron(ald Harmon) 1941–1996 **5**

Brown, Ronald K. 1966— **91**

Brown, Rosemary 1930–2003 **62**

Brown, Ruth 1928–2006 **90**

Brown, Sam *See Intruders, The*

Brown, Sean 1976— **52**

Brown, Shirley 1947— **132**

Brown, Sterling Allen 1901–1989 **10, 64**

Brown, Tim 1966— **134**

Brown, Tony 1933— **3**

Brown, Uzee 1950— **42**

Brown, Vincent *See Naughty by Nature*

Brown, Vivian 1964— **27**

Brown, Warren 1971(?)— **61**

Brown, Wesley 1945— **23**

Brown, Wesley A. 1927–2012 **102**

Brown, Willa Beatrice 1906–1992 **40**

Brown, Willard 1911(?)–1996 **36**

Brown, William *See Ray, Goodman & Brown*

Brown, William Anthony *See Brown, Tony*

Brown, William Wells 1814(?)–1884 **99**

Brown, Willie 1934— **7, 85**

Brown, Zora Kramer 1949— **12**

Brown Bomber, The *See Louis, Joe*

Browne, Richard 1991— **132**

Browne, Roscoe Lee 1925–2007 **66**

Browne, Tom 1954— **136**

Brownlee, Lawrence 1972(?)— **88**

Broyard, Anatole 1920–1990 **68**

Broyard, Bliss 1966— **68**

Bruce, Blanche Kelso 1849–1898 **33**

Bruce, Bruce 19(?)(?)— **56**

Bruce, Isaac 1972— **26**

Bruner, Stephen *See Thundercat*

Brunson, Dorothy 1938— **1, 87**

Brutus, Dennis 1924— **38**

Bryan, Ashley 1923— **41, 104**

Bryant, Cullen 1951–2009 **81**

Bryant, Desmond *See Bryant, Dez*

Bryant, Dez 1988— **116**

Bryant, Howard 1968— **130**

Bryant, Hugh *See Delta Rhythm Boys*

Bryant, Jamal 1971— **128**

Bryant, Jason *See S.O.S. Band*

Bryant, John 1966— **26**

Bryant, John R. 1943— **45**

Bryant, Kimberly 1967— **127**

Bryant, Kobe 1978— **15, 31, 71, 110**

Bryant, Paul 1933–2010 **115**

Bryant, Ray 1931–2011 **95**

Bryant, Sharon *See Atlantic Starr*

Bryant, Wayne R(ichard) 1947— **6**

Bryant, William Benson 1911–2005 **61**

Bryant, William Cullen *See Bryant, Cullen*

Buchanan, Manley Augustus *See Big Youth*

Buchanan, Ray 1971— **32**

Buckley, Gail Lumet 1937— **39**

Buckley, Victoria (Vikki) 1947–1999 **24**

Buckner, Milt 1915–1977 **110**

Buckwheat Zydeco 1947— **132**

Budden, Joe 1980— **108**

Budden, Joseph Anthony, II *See Budden, Joe*

Buery, Richard, Jr. 1972— **97**

Buff Love *See Fat Boys*

Buhari, Muhammadu 1942— **128**

Buika 1972— **120**

Bulawayo, NoViolet 1981— **125**

Bullard, Eugene Jacques 1894–1961 **12**

Bullard, Robert D. 1946— **121**

Bullins, Ed 1935— **25, 121**

Bullock, Anna Mae *See Turner, Tina*

Bullock, Steve 1936— **22**

Bully-Cummings, Ella 1957(?)— **48**

Bumbry, Grace (Ann) 1937— **5**

Bun B 1973— **123**

Bunch, Lonnie G., III 1952— **91**

Bunche, Ralph J(ohnson) 1904–1971 **5**

Bunkley, Anita Richmond 19(?)(?)— **39**

Burbridge, Kofi 1961— **120**

Burbridge, Oteil 1964— **120**

Buress, Hannibal 1983— **101**

Burgess, John 1909–2003 **46**

Burgess, Kevin Elijah *See KB*

Burgess, Marjorie L. 1929— **55**

Burgess, Marlina *See Shaw, Marlena*

Burke, Clarence, Jr. 1949–2013 **112**

Burke, Glenn 1952–1995 **122**

Burke, Selma Hortense 1900–1995 **16**

Burke, Solomon 1940–2010 **31, 86, 129**

Burke, Yvonne Brathwaite 1932— **42**

Burkett, Ben 1951— **123**

Burks, Juanita P. 1920— **95**

Burks, Mary Fair 1920–1991 **40**

Burleigh, Henry Thacker 1866–1949 **56**

Burley, Dan 1907–1962 **96**

Burley, Mary Lou *See Williams, Mary Lou*

Burnett, Charles 1944— **16, 68**

Burnett, Chester Arthur *See Howlin' Wolf*

Burnett, Dorothy 1905–1995 **19**

Burnham, Forbes 1923–1985 **66**

Burnim, Mickey L. 1949— **48**

Burning Spear 194(?)— **79**

Burns, Anthony 1834–1862 **102**

Burns, Eddie 1928— **44**

Burns, Jesse Louis *See Jackson, Jesse*

Burns, Ursula 1958— **60**

Burnside, R. L. 1926–2005 **56**

Burrell, Orville Richard *See Shaggy*

Burrell, Stanley Kirk *See M.C. Hammer*

Burrell, Tom 1939— **21, 51**

Burris, Chuck 1951— **21**

Burris, Roland W. 1937— **25, 75**

Burroughs, Margaret Taylor 1917–2010 **9, 134**

Burroughs, Nannie Helen 1879(?)–1961 **96**

Burrows, Stephen 1943— **31**

Burrus, William Henry "Bill" 1936—
45
Burruss, Kandi See Kandi
Burse, Charlie See Memphis Jug
Band
Burt-Murray, Angela 1970— 59
Burton, Bill 1977— 96
Burton, LeVar 1957— 8
Burton, Tony 1937–2016 135
Burwell, Bryan 1955— 83
Busby, Jheryl 1949–2008 3, 74
Bush, Charles Vernon 1939–2012
125
Bush, Gordon 1942— 82
Bush, Reggie 1985— 59, 88
Bushwick Bill See Geto Boys
Buthelezi, Mangosuthu Gatsha
1928— 9
Butler, George, Jr. 1931–2008 70
Butler, Henry 1949— 121
Butler, Ishmael See Shabazz Pal-
aces
Butler, Jerry 1939— 26 See also
Impressions, The
Butler, Jimmy 1989— 135
Butler, Jonathan 1961— 28
Butler, Leroy, III 1968— 17
Butler, Louis 1952— 70
Butler, Octavia 1947–2006 8, 43,
58
Butler, Paul D. 1961— 17
Butler, Selena Sloan 1872(?)–1964
98
Butts, Calvin O., III 1949— 9, 90
Butts, Cassandra 1965–2016 78,
136
Bwino, Ndiwa See Malawi Mouse
Boys
Byas, Carlos Wesley See Byas,
Don
Byas, Don 1912–1972 133
Bynoe, Peter C. B. 1951— 40
Bynum, Juanita 1959— 31, 71
Byrd, Donald 1932–2013 109
Byrd, Donald 1949— 10
Byrd, Eugene 1975— 64
Byrd, Henry Roeland See Professor
Longhair
Byrd, Marlon 1977— 112
Byrd, Michelle 1965— 19
Byrd, Robert (Oliver Daniel, III)
1952— 11
Byron, JoAnne Deborah See
Shakur, Assata
Cabell, Enos 1949— 102
Cables, George 1944— 125
Cabral, Amílcar 1924–1973 104
Cade, Toni See Bambara, Toni
Cade
Cadillacs 107
Cadoria, Sherian Grace 1940— 14
Caesar, Adolph 1933–1986 133
Caesar, Shirley 1938— 19
Cage, Byron 1965(?)— 53
Cain, Herman 1945— 15, 92
Cain, Lorenzo 1986— 128
Calabrese, Karyn 1947— 89
Caldwell, Benjamin 1937— 46
Caldwell, Earl 1941(?)— 60
Caldwell, Jim 1955— 81
Caldwell, Kirbyjon 1953(?)— 55
Caldwell, Nicholas See Whispers,
The

Caldwell, Ronnie See Bar-Kays,
The
Caldwell, Steve See Orlons, The
Calhoun, Cora See Austin, Lovie
Calhoun, Lillian Scott 1923–2006
87
Calhoun, Roy See Lee Andrews &
the Hearts
Calhoun, Wendell See Lee An-
drews & the Hearts
Callaway, Thomas DeCarlo See
Green, Cee Lo
Callender, Clive O(rville) 1936— 3
Callender, Eugene 1926–2013 119
Callier, Terry 1945–2012 106
Calloway, Blanche 1902–1978 100
Calloway, Cab 1907–1994 14
Calloway, Reggie See Midnight
Star
Calloway, Vincent See Midnight
Star
Camara, Moussa Dadis 1964— 76
Cameo 120
Cameron, Earl 1917— 44
Cameron, James 1914–2006 80
Camp, Georgia Blanche Douglas
See Johnson, Georgia Douglas
Camp, Kimberly 1956— 19
Campanella, Roy 1921–1993 25
Campbell, Bebe Moore 1950–2006
6, 24, 59
Campbell, Bill 1954— 9, 76
Campbell, Charleszetta Lena See
Waddles, Charleszetta
Campbell, Cornelius Coleridge See
Campbell, Dick 1903–1994 129
Campbell, Donald J. 1935— 66
Campbell, E(lmer) Simms
1906–1971 13
Campbell, Earl 1955— 104
Campbell, Lucie E. 1885–1963 118
Campbell, Mary Schmidt 1947— 43
Campbell, Michael Che See Che,
Michael
Campbell, Milt 1933–2012 113
Campbell, Milton See Little Milton
Campbell, Naomi 1970— 1, 31,
120
Campbell, Roy, Jr. 1952–2014 118
Campbell, Tisha See Campbell-
Martin, Tisha
Campbell-Brown, Veronica 1982—
102
Campbell-Martin, Tisha 1969— 8,
42
Campbell-Williams, Lucie E. See
Campbell, Lucie E.
Cam'ron 1976— 104
Canada, Geoffrey 1954— 23
Canady, Alexa 1950— 28
Canedy, Dana 1965(?)— 132
Canegata, Leonard Lionel Corne-
lius See Lee, Canada
Cannon, Katie 1950— 10
Cannon, Nick 1980— 47, 73, 132
Cannon, Park 1991— 134
Cannon, Patrick 1966— 120
Cannon, Reuben 1946— 50
Cannon, Toronzo 1968— 135
Cano, Robinson 1982— 97
Canó Mercedes, Robinson José
See Cano, Robinson
Cara, Irene 1959— 77

Carby, Hazel 1948— 27
Cardozo, Francis L. 1837–1903 33
Carew, Rod 1945— 20
Carey, Jake See Flamingos, The
Carey, Mariah 1970— 32, 53, 69
Carey, Zeke See Flamingos, The
Cargill, Victoria A. 19(?)(?)— 43
Carlos, John 1945— 97
Carmichael, Jerrod 1988(?)— 124
Carmichael, Stokely 1941–1998 5,
26
Carnegie, Herbert 1919— 25
Carney, William H. 1840–1908 104
Carolina Chocolate Drops 111
Carr, James 1942–2001 117
Carr, Johnnie 1911–2008 69
Carr, Keela 1973— 74
Carr, Kurt 196(?)— 56
Carr, Leroy 1905–1935 49
Carrington, Terri Lyne 1965— 132
Carroll, Diahann 1935— 9
Carroll, Earl See Cadillacs
Carroll, L. Natalie 1950— 44
Carroll, Porter, Jr. See Atlantic Starr
Carroll, Rocky 1963— 74
Carroll, Vinnette 1922–2002 29,
136
Carruthers, George R. 1939— 40
Carson, André 1974— 69
Carson, Ben 1951— 1, 35, 76, 128
Carson, Candy 1953— 133
Carson, Johnnie 1943— 85
Carson, Josephine See Baker, Jo-
sephine
Carson, Julia 1938–2007 23, 69
Carson, Lacena Rustin See Car-
son, Candy
Carson, Lisa Nicole 1969— 21
Carter, Anson 1974— 24
Carter, Ben See Ben-Israel, Ben
Ami
Carter, Benny 1907–2003 46
Carter, Betty 1930— 19
Carter, Bo See Mississippi Sheiks
Carter, Butch 1958— 27
Carter, Cris 1965— 21, 109
Carter, Dwayne Michael, Jr. See Lil
Wayne
Carter, Edward A., Jr. 1916–1963
104
Carter, Herbert E. 1919–2012 108
Carter, Hurricane See Carter, Rubin
Carter, Jill P. 1964— 110
Carter, Joe 1960— 30
Carter, Johnny See Dells, The; Fla-
mingos, The
Carter, Joye Maureen 1957— 41
Carter, Kenneth 1959(?)— 53
Carter, Majora 1966— 77
Carter, Mandy 1946— 11
Carter, Martin 1927–1997 49
Carter, Nell 1948–2003 39
Carter, Pamela Lynn 1949— 67
Carter, Regina 1966(?)— 23, 131
Carter, Rob See Dramatics, The
Carter, Robert L. 1917–2012 51,
100
Carter, Ron 1937— 104
Carter, Rubin 1937–2014 26, 121
Carter, Shawn Corey See Jay-Z
Carter, Stephen L(isle) 1954— 4
Carter, Troy 1973(?)— 98
Carter, Vince 1977— 26

Carter, Warrick L. 1942— 27
Cartey, Wilfred 1931–1992 47
Cartiér, Xam Wilson 1949— 41
Carver, George Washington
1861(?)–1943 4
Cary, Lorene 1956— 3
Cary, Mary Ann Shadd 1823–1893
30
Casel, Nitanju Bolade See Sweet
Honey in the Rock
Casey, Brandon See Jagged Edge
Casey, Brian See Jagged Edge
Casey, Dwane 1957— 135
Cash, Nayvadius See Future
Cash, Rosalind 1938–1995 28
Cash, Swin 1979— 59
Cashin, Sheryll 1962— 63
CasSelle, Malcolm 1970— 11
Castor, Jimmy 1940–2012 100
Catchings, Tamika 1979— 43
Cathey, Reg E. 1958— 122
Catlett, Elizabeth 1915–2012 2, 120
Catlett, Sid 1910–1951 133
Catlin, Mamie 1926–2015 131
Catto, Octavius V. 1839–1871 83
Cauley, Ben See Bar-Kays, The
Caymmi, Dorival 1914–2008 72
Cayton, Horace 1903–1970 26
Cedric the Entertainer 1964— 29,
60, 115
Cee Lo See Green, Cee Lo
Celestin, Joe See Celestin,
Josaphat
Celestin, Josaphat 1956— 101
Cenac, Wyatt 1976— 94
Cepeda, Orlando 1937— 98
Cephus, Kiari See Migos
Césaire, Aimé 1913–2008 48, 69
Chadiha, Jeffri 1970— 57
Chaka Chaka, Yvonne 1965— 112
Chalmers, Almario See Chalmers,
Mario
Chalmers, Mario 1986— 122
Cham, Adongo Agada Akway
1954(?)— 77
Chamberlain, Wilt 1936–1999 18,
47
Chambers, Ernest William See
Chambers, Ernie
Chambers, Ernie 1937— 130
Chambers, George See Chambers
Brothers, The
Chambers, James See Cliff, Jimmy
Chambers, Joe See Chambers
Brothers, The
Chambers, Julius (LeVonne)
1936— 3
Chambers, Lester See Chambers
Brothers, The
Chambers, Paul 1935–1969 121
Chambers, Willie See Chambers
Brothers, The
Chambers Brothers, The 116
Chamillionaire 1979— 82
Champion, Betty Jean See Swann,
Bettye
Chancellor, Kam 1988— 131
Chandler, Gene 1937— 105
Chandler, Tyson 1982— 114
Chaney, Don 1946— 98
Chaney, John 1932— 67
Channer, Colin 1963— 36
Chanté, Keshia 1988— 50

Chantels, The **128**

Chanticleer, Raven 1928–2002 **91**

Chapman, Aroldis 1988— **132**

Chapman, Nathan A., Jr. 1957— **21**

Chapman, Susan E. 1968— **94**

Chapman, Tracy 1964— **26**

Chappell, Emma C. 1941— **18**

Chappell, Roy M. 1921–2002 **95**

Chappelle, Dave 1973— **50, 115**

Charlemagne, Emmanuel *See Charlemagne, Manno*

Charlemagne, Manno 1948— **11**

Charles, Ezzard 1921–1975 **95**

Charles, John 1944–2002 **108**

Charles, Mary Eugenia 1919–2005 **10, 55**

Charles, Pierre 1954–2004 **52**

Charles, Ray 1930–2004 **16, 48**

Charleston, Oscar 1896–1954 **39**

Chase, Debra Martin 1956— **49, 96**

Chase, John Saunders, Jr. 1925— **99**

Chase, Leah 1923— **57**

Chase-Riboud, Barbara 1939— **20, 46**

Chatard, Peter 1936— **44**

Chatman, John Len *See Memphis Slim*

Chatmon, Bo *See Mississippi Sheiks*

Chatmon, Lonnie *See Mississippi Sheiks*

Chatmon, Sam *See Mississippi Sheiks*

Chavis, Benjamin (Franklin, Jr.) 1948— **6**

Che, Michael 1983— **123**

Chea, Alvin *See Take 6*

Cheadle, Don 1964— **19, 52**

Cheatham, Doc 1905–1997 **17**

Checker, Chubby 1941— **28**

Cheeks, Julius 1929–1981 **135**

Cheeks, June *See Cheeks, Julius*

Cheeks, Maurice 1956— **47, 106**

Chenault, John 1952— **40**

Chenault, Kenneth 1951— **4, 36, 108**

Cheney-Coker, Syl 1945— **43**

Chenier, C. J. 1957— **134**

Chenier, Clayton Joseph *See Chenier, C. J.*

Chenier, Clifton 1925–1987 **134**

Cheruiyot, Robert 1978— **69**

Cherry, Deron 1959— **40**

Cherry, Don 1936–1995 **119**

Cherry, Nicole *See Marian Anderson String Quartet*

Chesimard, JoAnne (Deborah) *See Shakur, Assata*

Chesnutt, Charles 1858–1932 **29**

Chester, Brenda *See DoHarris, Brenda*

Chestnut, J. L., Jr. 1930–2008 **73**

Chestnut, Morris 1969— **31, 116**

Chew, Robert F. 1960–2013 **109**

Chic **117**

Chideya, Farai 1969— **14, 61**

Chief Black Thunderbird Eagle *See York, Dwight D.*

Chief Keef 1995— **112**

Chiffons, The **129**

Chikoti, Shadreck 1979— **125**

Childers, Lulu Vere 1870–1946 **95**

Childress, Alice 1920–1994 **15**

Childress, Alvin 1907–1986 **114**

Chiles, Nick 1965— **98**

Chi-Lites **106**

Chiluba, Frederick 1943— **56, 80**

Chineworth, Mary Alice 1917— **79**

Chinn, May Edward 1896–1980 **26**

Chisholm, Daquan 1993— **93**

Chisholm, Samuel J. 1942— **32**

Chisholm, Shirley 1924–2005 **2, 50**

Chissano, Joaquim 1939— **7, 55, 67**

Chitalu, Godfrey 1947–1993 **108**

Chong, Rae Dawn 1961— **62**

Christensen, Donna M. 1945— **17, 132**

Christian, Barbara T. 1946–2000 **44**

Christian, Charlie 1916–1942 **136**

Christian, Jodie 1932-2012 **103**

Christian, Spencer 1947— **15**

Christian-Green, Donna M. *See Christensen, Donna M.*

Christie, Angella **36**

Christie, Linford 1960— **8**

Christie, Perry Gladstone 1944— **53**

Christie, Ron 1969(?)— **83**

Christophe, Henri 1767–1820 **9**

Chronixx 1992— **123**

Chuck D 1960— **9** *See also Public Enemy*

Church, Bruce *See Bruce, Bruce*

Church, Robert Reed, Sr. 1839–1912 **132**

Churchill, Tony *See New Birth*

Churchwell, Robert, Sr. 1917–2009 **76**

Chweneyagae, Presley 1984— **63**

Ciara 1985— **56, 115**

Ciara, Barbara 195(?)— **69**

Cissé, Souleymane *See Souleymane, Mahamane*

Clack, Zoanne 1968(?)— **73**

Claiborne, Loretta 1953— **34**

Chancler, Leon *See Chancler, Ndugu*

Chancler, Ndugu 1952— **115**

Clarence 13X 1928–1969 **126**

Clark, Carl 1916— **101**

Clark, Celeste (Clesteen) Abraham 1953— **15**

Clark, Conrad Yeatis *See Clark, Sonny*

Clark, Joe 1939— **1**

Clark, John Pepper *See Clark-Bekedermo, J. P.*

Clark, Kenneth B. 1914–2005 **5, 52**

Clark, Kristin *See Taylor, Kristin Clark*

Clark, Mamie Phipps 1917–1983 **79**

Clark, Mattie Moss 1925–1994 **61**

Clark, Patrick 1955— **14**

Clark, Ray 1931–2014 **122**

Clark, Septima (Poinsette) 1898–1987 **7**

Clark, Sharón 1961— **105**

Clark, Sonny 1931–1963 **128**

Clark, Wahida 19(?)(?)— **107**

Clark, Yvonne Young 1929— **95**

Clark-Bekedermo, J. P. 1935— **44**

Clark-Cole, Dorinda 1957— **66**

Clarke, Anna Mac 1919–1944 **95**

Clarke, Austin C. 1934— **32**

Clarke, Cheryl 1947— **32**

Clarke, George Elliott 1960— **32**

Clarke, Hope 1943(?)— **14**

Clarke, John Henrik 1915–1998 **20**

Clarke, Kenny 1914–1985 **27**

Clarke, Patrice Francise *See Washington, Patrice Clarke*

Clarke, Peter *See Peters, Clarke*

Clarke, Stanley 1951— **115**

Clarke, Yvette 1964— **92**

Clark-Sheard, Karen 1960— **22, 114**

Clash, Kevin 1960— **14, 93**

Clay, Bryan 1980— **57, 74**

Clay, Cassius *See Ali, Muhammad*

Clay, Otis 1942–2016 **112, 133**

Clay, William Lacy 1931— **8**

Clay, William Lacy, Jr. 1956— **95**

Clayton, Constance 1937— **1**

Clayton, Doctor 1898–1947 **120**

Clayton, Eva M. 1934— **20**

Clayton, Gerald 1984— **111**

Clayton, Mayme Agnew 1923–2006 **62**

Clayton, Merry 1948— **112**

Clayton, Peter Joe *See Clayton, Doctor*

Clayton, Xernona 1930— **3, 45**

Claytor, Helen 1907–2005 **14, 52**

Cleage, Albert B., Jr. *See Agyeman, Jaramogi Abebe*

Cleage, Pearl 1948— **17, 64**

Clear, Duval *See Masta Ace*

Cleaver, Eldridge 1935— **5**

Cleaver, Emanuel, II 1944— **4, 45, 68, 107**

Cleaver, Kathleen Neal 1945— **29**

Cleighton, Peter Joe *See Clayton, Doctor*

Clemente, Rosa 1972— **74**

Clement-Holmes, Linda 1962— **94**

Clements, George (Harold) 1932— **2**

Clemmons, Reginal G. 19(?)(?)— **41**

Clemons, Clarence 1942— **41**

Clemons, Michael "Pinball" 1965— **64**

Clendenon, Donn 1935–2005 **26, 56**

Cleveland, James 1932(?)–1991 **19**

Cliff, Jimmy 1948— **28, 92**

Cliff, Michelle 1946— **42**

Clifton, Lucille 1936–2010 **14, 64, 91**

Clifton, Nathaniel "Sweetwater" 1922(?)–1990 **47**

Clinkscale, Aja Lena *See Brown, Aja*

Clinton, George 1941— **9, 93**

Clovers, The **104**

Clyburn, James E. 1940— **21, 71, 118**

Clyburn, Mignon 1962— **78**

C-Murder 1971— **99**

Coachman, Alice 1923–2014 **18, 123**

Coasters, The **102**

Coates, Dorothy Love 1928–2002 **125**

Coates, Ta-Nehisi 1975— **76, 131**

Cobb, Arnett 1918–1989 **114**

Cobb, Jewel Plummer 1924— **42**

Cobb, Jimmy 1929— **119**

Cobb, Monty *See Cobb, W. Montague*

Cobb, W. Montague 1904–1990 **39**

Cobb, William Anthony *See Cobb, William Jelani*

Cobb, William Jelani 1969— **59, 121**

Cobbs, Bill 1934— **101**

Cobbs, Natasha *See Cobbs, Tasha*

Cobbs, Price M(ashaw) 1928— **9**

Cobbs, Tasha 1981— **114**

Cobham, Billy 1944— **123**

Cobham, William Emanuel, Jr.*See Cobham, Billy*

Cochran, Johnnie 1937–2005 **11, 39, 52**

Cockrel, Kenneth V., Jr. 1965— **79**

Cockrel, Kenneth Vern, Sr. 1938–1989 **79**

CoCo Brother 19(?)(?)— **93**

Cody, Radmilla 1975— **99**

Coggins, Danny *See Moonglows, The*

Cohen, Anthony 1963— **15**

Cohen, Cathy J. 1962— **88**

Coke, Christopher 1969— **108**

Colbert, Thomas *See Colbert, Tom*

Colbert, Tom 1949— **115**

Colbert, Virgis William 1939— **17**

Cole, Ashley 1980— **106**

Cole, Cozy 1909–1981 **123**

Cole, Ernest 1940–1990 **123**

Cole, Freddy 1931— **128**

Cole, J. 1985— **97**

Cole, Johnnetta B(etsch) 1936— **5, 43**

Cole, Keyshia 1981— **63, 107**

Cole, Lionel Frederick *See Cole, Freddy*

Cole, Lorraine 195(?)— **48**

Cole, Maria 1922–2012 **104**

Cole, Nat "King" 1919–1965 **17**

Cole, Natalie 1950–2015 **17, 60, 84, 133**

Cole, Rebecca 1846–1922 **38**

Cole, Teju 1975— **120**

Cole, William Randolph *See Cole, Cozy*

Coleman, Ashley Antoinette Snell *See Ashley & JaQuavis*

Coleman, Beatrice 1904–2014 **120**

Coleman, Bessie 1892–1926 **9**

Coleman, Bonnie Watson *See Watson Coleman, Bonnie*

Coleman, Chad L. 196(?)— **128**

Coleman, Denardo 1956— **122**

Coleman, Donald 1952— **24, 62**

Coleman, Gary 1968–2010 **35, 86**

Coleman, George 1935— **106**

Coleman, Herb *See Delta Rhythm Boys*

Coleman, James E., Jr. 1948(?)— **79**

Coleman, JaQuavis Javon *See Ashley & JaQuavis*

Coleman, Ken 1942— **57**

Coleman, Lamont *See Big L*

Coleman, Leonard S., Jr. 1949— **12**

Coleman, Mary 1946— **46**

Coleman, Michael B. 1954— **28, 79**

Coleman, Ornette 1930–2015 **39, 69, 129**

Coleman, Ornette Denardo *See Coleman, Denardo*

Coleman, Ronald S. 1948— **110**

Coleman, Steve 1956— **124**

Coleman, Troy *See Cowboy Troy*

Coleman, Valerie *See Imani Winds*

Coleman, Vince 1961— **128**

Coleman, Wanda 1946–2013 **48, 119**

Coleman, William F., III 1955(?)— **61**

Coleman, William T. 1920— **76**

Colemon, Johnnie 1921(?)— **11**

Coleridge-Taylor, Samuel 1875–1912 **75**

Coles, Alice 1951(?)— **80**

Coles, Charles *See Coles, Honi*

Coles, Dennis *See Ghostface Killah*

Coles, Honi 1911–1992 **128**

Colescott, Robert 1925— **69**

Collette, Buddy 1921–2010 **119**

Collette, William Marcel *See Collette, Buddy*

Collins, Albert 1932–1993 **12**

Collins, Barbara-Rose 1939— **7, 87**

Collins, Bootsy 1951— **31**

Collins, Cardiss 1931–2013 **10, 80, 120**

Collins, Clarence *See Little Anthony & the Imperials*

Collins, Janet 1917–2003 **33, 64**

Collins, Jason 1978— **111**

Collins, Lyn 1948–2005 **53**

Collins, Marva 1936— **3, 71**

Collins, Patricia Hill 1948— **67**

Collins, Paul 1936— **61**

Collins, William *See Collins, Bootsy*

Colston, Hal 1953(?)— **72**

Colter, Cyrus J. 1910–2002 **36**

Coltrane, Alice 1937–2007 **70**

Coltrane, John William 1926–1967 **19**

Coltrane, Ravi 1965— **71**

Combs, Sean 1969— **17, 43, 92**

Comer, James P(ierpont) 1934— **6**

Commodores, The **118**

Common 1972— **31, 63, 98**

Compaore, Blaise 1951— **87**

Compton, John 1925–2007 **65**

Compton-Rock, Malaak 1969— **86**

Concha Buika *See Buika*

Condé, Alpha 1938— **95, 131**

Condrey, Cory *See CoCo Brother*

Cone, James H. 1938— **3, 82**

Coney, PonJola 1951— **48**

Conley, Arthur 1946–2003 **129**

Conley, Nellie *See Madame Sul-Te-Wan*

Conneh, Sekou Damate, Jr. 1960— **51**

Connerly, Ward 1939— **14**

Connor, William *See Swan Silvertones, The*

Conrad, Barbara Smith 1940(?)— **90**

Conrad, Cecilia A. 1955— **94**

Consolers, The **125**

Conté, Lansana 1934(?)–2008 **7, 76**

Contee, Cheryl 1971— **88**

Contours, The **109**

Conyers, John, Jr. 1929— **4, 45, 111**

Conyers, Monica 1964— **85**

Conyers, Nathan G. 1932— **24**

Coogler, Ryan 1986— **114**

Cook, Charles "Doc" 1891–1958 **44**

Cook, Herman *See Cook, Junior*

Cook, Junior 1934–1992 **126**

Cook, (Will) Mercer 1903–1987 **40**

Cook, Samuel DuBois 1928— **14**

Cook, Suzan D. Johnson 1957— **22**

Cook, Toni 1944— **23**

Cook, Victor Trent *See Three Mo' Tenors*

Cook, Wesley *See Abu-Jamal, Mumia*

Cook, Will Marion 1869–1944 **40**

Cooke, Charles L. *See Cook, Charles "Doc"*

Cooke, Marcia 1954— **60**

Cooke, Marvel 1901(?)–2000 **31**

Cooke, Sam 1931–1964 **17** *See also Highway QC's, The; Pilgrim Travelers, The; Soul Stirrers*

Cook-Parrish, Mary Virginia 1862(?)–1945 **95**

Cooks, Patricia 1944–1989 **19**

Coolio 1963— **103**

Cools, Anne 1943— **64**

Coombs, Orde M. 1939–1984 **44**

Cooper, Afua 1957— **53**

Cooper, Andrew Lewis *See Cooper, Andy "Lefty"*

Cooper, Andrew W. 1928–2002 **36**

Cooper, Andy "Lefty" 1898–1941 **63**

Cooper, Anna Julia 1858–1964 **20**

Cooper, Barry 1956— **33**

Cooper, Charles "Chuck" 1926–1984 **47**

Cooper, Charles Theodore *See Cooper, Tarzan*

Cooper, Chuck 1954— **75**

Cooper, Cynthia *See Cooper-Dyke, Cynthia*

Cooper, Edward S(awyer) 1926— **6**

Cooper, Evern 19(?)(?)— **40**

Cooper, Helene 1966— **74**

Cooper, J. California 1931–2014 **12, 85, 125**

Cooper, Jeffrey *See Midnight Star*

Cooper, Jerome 1946–2015 **129**

Cooper, Joan *See Cooper, J. California*

Cooper, Lisa 1963— **73**

Cooper, Marcus *See Pleasure P*

Cooper, Margaret J. 194(?)— **46**

Cooper, Mario 1954–2015 **129**

Cooper, Michael 1956— **31**

Cooper, Tarzan 1907–1980 **96**

Cooper Cafritz, Peggy 1947— **43**

Cooper-Dyke, Cynthia 1963— **17, 89**

Copeland, Creadell *See Highway QC's, The*

Copeland, Johnny 1937–1997 **110**

Copeland, Kenny *See Rose Royce*

Copeland, Michael 1954— **47**

Copeland, Misty 1982— **125**

Copeland, Shemekia 1979— **110**

Coppola, Imani Francesca 1978— **82**

Corbi, Lana 1955— **42**

Corbin, Tyrone 1962— **126**

Cordes, Attrell *See P.M. Dawn; Prince Be*

Corinealdi, Emayatzy 1980— **133**

Corley, Tony 1949— **62**

Cornelius, Don 1936–2012 **4, 100**

Cornish, Sam 1935— **50**

Cornwell, Edward E., III 1956— **70**

Correia, Antoné De'Jaun *See Correia, De'Jaun*

Correia, De'Jaun 1994— **93**

Cortez, Jayne 1934–2012 **43, 109**

Corthron, Kia 1961— **43**

Cortor, Eldzier 1916— **42**

Cosby, Bill 1937— **7, 26, 59, 125**

Cosby, Camille 1945— **14, 80**

Cosby, William Henry, Jr. *See Cosby, Bill*

Cose, Ellis 1951— **5, 50, 118**

Cosey, Pete 1943–2012 **103**

Cosey, Peter Palus *See Cosey, Pete*

Cotter, Joseph Seamon, Sr. 1861–1949 **40**

Cotton, James 1935— **123**

Cottrell, Comer 1931— **11**

Counce, Curtis 1926–1963 **127**

Council, LaVerne 1961(?)— **94**

Count Basie 1904–1984 **23**

Counter, S. Allen 1944— **74**

Courtney, Opal, Jr. *See Spaniels, The*

Cousin, Ertharin 1957— **115**

Cousins, DeMarcus 1990— **108**

Couto, Mia 1955— **45**

Coverley, Louise Bennett *See Bennett, Louise*

Cowans, Adger W. 1936— **20**

Cowboy Troy, 1970— **54**

Cox, Bryan 1968— **83**

Cox, Deborah 1974(?)— **28**

Cox, Donald Lee 1936–2011 **93**

Cox, Elbert Frank 1895–1969 **111**

Cox, Ida 1896–1967 **42**

Cox, Joseph Mason Andrew 1930— **51**

Cox, Laverne 198(?)— **122**

Cox, Renée 1960— **67**

Cox, Roderick Leverne *See Cox, Laverne*

Cox, William E. 1942— **68**

Cozart, Keith *See Chief Keef*

Craig, Carl 1969— **31, 71**

Craig, Judy *See Chiffons, The*

Craig-Jones, Ellen Walker 1906–2000 **44**

Crain, S. R. *See Soul Stirrers*

Crawford, Bud *See Crawford, Terence*

Crawford, Carl 1981— **90**

Crawford, Hank 1934–2009 **77**

Crawford, Randy 1952— **19**

Crawford, Terence 1987— **135**

Crawford, Traverse *See Delta Rhythm Boys*

Crawford, Veronica *See Crawford, Randy*

Cray, Robert 1953— **30, 132**

Creagh, Milton 1957— **27**

Cream, Arnold Raymond *See Walcott, Jersey Joe*

Crennel, Romeo 1947— **54, 107**

Crenshaw, Kimberlé Williams 1959— **88**

Crenshaw, Robert *See Swan Silvertones, The*

Crew, Rudolph F. *See Crew, Rudy*

Crew, Rudy 1950— **16, 113**

Crew, Spencer R. 1949— **55**

Crews, Terrence Alan *See Crews, Terry*

Crews, Terry 1968— **123**

Crichlow, Ernest 1914–2005 **75**

Crisp, Coco 1979— **109**

Crisp, Covelli Loyce *See Crisp, Coco*

Criss, Anthony *See Naughty by Nature*

Criss, Sonny 1927–1977 **128**

Criss, William *See Criss, Sonny*

Crite, Allan Rohan 1910–2007 **29**

Croal, N'Gai 1972— **76**

Crocker, Frankie 1937–2000 **29**

Crockett, George W., Jr. 1909–1997 **10, 64**

Cromartie, Antonio 1984— **115**

Crooks, Garth 1958— **53**

Croom, Sylvester 1954— **50**

Cross, Dolores E. 1938— **23**

Crosthwait, David 1892–1976 **93**

Crothers, Benjamin Sherman *See Crothers, Scatman*

Crothers, Scatman 1910–1986 **19**

Crouch, Andraé 1942–2015 **27, 115, 126**

Crouch, Hubert 1906–1980 **95**

Crouch, Stanley 1945— **11, 87**

Crowder, Henry 1895–1954(?) **16**

Crowdy, William Saunders 1847–1908 **109**

Crown Heights Affair **132**

Crudup, Arthur 1905–1974 **115**

Crudup, Big Boy *See Crudup, Arthur*

Crum, George 1822–1914 **101**

Crume, Arthur *See Soul Stirrers*

Crump, Lavell *See Banner, David*

Crump, Steven 1957— **96**

Crumpler, Rebecca Lee 1831–1895 **89**

Crusaders, The **116**

Cruse, Harold 1916–2005 **54**

Crutchfield, James N. 1947— **55**

Cruz, Taio 1983— **104**

Cruz, Victor 1986— **107**

Cueto, Johnny 1986— **130**

Cuffe, Paul 1759–1817 **98**

Cullen, Countee 1903–1946 **8**

Cullers, Vincent T. 1924(?)–2003 **49**

Culp, Curley 1946— **110**

Culp, Napoleon Brown Goodson *See Brown, Nappy*

Culpepper, Daunte 1977— **32, 85**

Cummings, Elijah E. 1951— **24, 102**

Cuney, William Waring 1906–1976 **44**

Cunningham, Carl *See Bar-Kays, The*

Cunningham, Evelyn 1916–2010 **23, 85**

Cunningham, Randall 1963— **23**

Cunningham, Roy *See Bar-Kays, The*

Curling, Alvin 1939— **34**

Curren$y 1981— **114**

Currie, Betty 1939(?)— **21**

Currie, Ulysses 1937— **73**

Curry, Butch *See Lee Andrews & the Hearts*

Curry, Dell 1964— **126**

Curry, George E. 1947— **23**

Curry, Mark 1964— **17**
Curry, Michael 1968— **85**
Curry, Stephen 1988— **110**
Curry, Thomas *See Lee Andrews & the Hearts*
Curson, Ted 1935–2012 **108**
Curtis, Christopher Paul 1953— **26, 113**
Curtis-Hall, Vondie 1956— **17**
Curvin, Robert 1934–2015 **132**
Da Don, Polow 1978— **86**
da Silva, Benedita 1942— **5**
da Silva, Jorge Mário *See Jorge, Seu*
da Silva, Leônidas *See Leônidas*
da Silva Ferreira, Eusebio *See Eusebio*
Dabiri, John 1980(?)— **93**
Dabydeen, David 1956— **48**
DaCosta, YaYa 1982— **98**
Dacres, Desmond Adolphus *See Dekker, Desmond*
Dadié, Bernard 1916— **34**
Daemyon, Jerald 1970(?)— **64**
D'Aguiar, Fred 1960— **50**
Dailey, Ulysses Grant 1885–1961 **87**
Dale, Clamma 1948— **103**
Daly, Marie Maynard 1921–2003 **37, 134**
Damas, Léon-Gontran 1912–1978 **46**
Dameron, Tadd 1917–1965 **103**
Dance, Kelvin *See Kitwana, Bakari*
Dandala, Mvume 1951— **77**
Dandridge, Dorothy 1922–1965 **3**
Dandridge, Ray 1913–1994 **36**
Dandridge, Raymond Garfield 1882–1930 **45**
D'Angelo 1974— **27, 123**
Dangote, Aliko 1957— **124**
Daniels, Billy 1915–1988 **124**
Daniels, Gertrude *See Haynes, Trudy*
Daniels, Jerry *See Ink Spots, The*
Daniels, Lee 1959— **36, 76**
Daniels, Mel 1944— **106**
Daniels, William Boone *See Daniels, Billy*
Daniels-Carter, Valerie 19(?)(?)— **23**
Danjah, Terror 1977— **91**
Danner, Margaret Esse 1915–1986 **49**
Danquah, Meri Nana Ama 1967— **93**
Danticat, Edwidge 1969— **15, 68, 128**
Dantley, Adrian 1956— **72**
Dara, Olu 1941— **335**
D'Arby, Terence Trent *See Maitreya, Sananda*
Darden, Calvin 1950— **38**
Darden, Christopher 1957— **13**
Darego, Agbani 1982— **52**
Dash, Damon 1971— **31, 113**
Dash, Darien 1972(?)— **29**
Dash, Julie 1952— **4, 132**
Dash, Leon 1944— **47**
Datcher, Michael 1967— **60**
Dathorne, O. R. 1934— **52**
Daughtry, Eugene *See Intruders, The*

Davenport, Arthur *See Fattah, Chaka*
Davenport, Charles Edward *See Davenport, Cow Cow*
Davenport, Cow Cow 1894–1955 **115**
David, Craig 1981— **31, 53**
David, Keith 1954— **27**
Davids, Edgar 1973— **106**
Davidson, Jaye 1967(?)— **5**
Davidson, Quentin *See Rare Essence*
Davidson, Tommy 1963(?)— **21**
Davis, Alfreda *See Davis Sisters, The*
Davis, Allison 1902–1983 **12**
Davis, Altovise 1943–2009 **76**
Davis, Angela 1944— **5, 114**
Davis, Angela J. 1956— **88**
Davis, Anthony 1951— **11**
Davis, Anthony 1993— **120**
Davis, Anthony Moses *See Beenie Man*
Davis, Arthur P. 1904–1996 **41**
Davis, Artur 1967— **41**
Davis, Audrey *See Davis Sisters, The*
Davis, Belva 1932— **61**
Davis, Ben 1912–2013 **115**
Davis, Benjamin O(liver), Jr. 1912–2002 **2, 43**
Davis, Benjamin O(liver), Sr. 1877–1970 **4**
Davis, Bing 1937— **84**
Davis, Carl 1934–2012 **105**
Davis, Charles T. 1918–1981 **48**
Davis, Chuck 1937— **33**
Davis, Danny K. 1941— **24, 79**
Davis, Doris A. 1936(?)— **100**
Davis, Douglas E. *See Fresh, Doug E.*
Davis, Ed 1911–1999 **24**
Davis, Eisa 1971— **68**
Davis, Erellon Benjamin *See Davis, Ben*
Davis, Eric 1962— **116**
Davis, Ernie 1939–1963 **48**
Davis, Erroll B., Jr. 1944— **57**
Davis, Frank Marshall 1905–1987 **47**
Davis, Gary 1896–1972 **41**
Davis, George 1939— **36**
Davis, Gordon J. 1941— **76**
Davis, Guy 1952— **36**
Davis, Jamelia Niela *See Jamelia*
Davis, James E. 1962–2003 **50**
Davis, Lorenzo "Piper" 1917–1997 **19**
Davis, Marlena *See Orlons, The*
Davis, Mary *See S.O.S. Band*
Davis, Mia Amber 1974–2011 **94**
Davis, Mike 1960— **41**
Davis, Miles (Dewey, III) 1926–1991 **4**
Davis, Milt 1929–2008 **74**
Davis, Mtulazaji *See Freestyle Fellowship*
Davis, Nolan 1942— **45**
Davis, Ossie 1917–2005 **5, 50**
Davis, Peylia *See DeSanto, Sugar Pie*
Davis, Phil 1984— **132**
Davis, Rajai 1980— **135**
Davis, Rob *See Dramatics, The*

Davis, Robert Earl, Jr. *See DJ Screw*
Davis, Ruth *See Davis Sisters, The*
Davis, Ruth 1943— **37**
Davis, Sammy, Jr. 1925–1990 **18**
Davis, Shani 1982— **58, 84**
Davis, Terrell 1972— **20**
Davis, Thelma *See Davis Sisters, The*
Davis, Theresa *See Emotions, The*
Davis, Thomas 1983— **132**
Davis, Thornetta 1963— **131**
Davis, Thulani 1948— **61**
Davis, Tyrone 1938–2005 **54**
Davis, Vernon 1984— **133**
Davis, Viola 1965— **34, 76, 100, 131**
Davis, Wade, Jr. 1977— **103**
Davis, Walter, Jr. 1932–1990 **134**
Davis, Wild Bill 1918–1995 **114**
Davis, William Strethen *See Davis, Wild Bill*
Davis Sisters, The **119**
Dawes, Dominique 1976— **11, 126**
Dawes, Kwame 1962— **126**
Dawkins, Darryl 1957–2015 **131**
Dawkins, Egbert Nathaniel, III *See Blacc, Aloe*
Dawkins, James Henry *See Dawkins, Jimmy*
Dawkins, Jimmy 1936–2013 **111**
Dawkins, Wayne 1955— **20**
Dawn, Marpessa 1934–2008 **75**
Dawn, Sandra *See Chantels, The*
Dawson, Andre 1954— **85**
Dawson, Matel "Mat," Jr. 1921–2002 **39**
Dawson, Michael C. 1951— **63**
Dawson, Rosario 1979— **72**
Dawson, William L. 1886–1970 **130**
Dawson, William Levi 1899–1990 **39**
Dawuni, Rocky 1969— **94**
Day, Andra 1984— **132**
Day, Leon 1916–1995 **39**
Days, Drew S(aunders, III) 1941— **10**
Dazz Band **116**
D'banj 1980— **107**
De' Alexander, Quinton 19??— **57**
de Assís Moreira, Ronaldo *See Ronaldinho*
De Bankolé, Isaach 1957— **78**
de Carvalho, Barcelo *See Bonga, Kuenda*
De La Soul **119**
de Lavallade, Carmen 1931— **78**
de Passe, Suzanne 1948(?)— **25**
De Priest, Oscar Stanton 1871–1951 **80**
De Shields, André 1946— **72**
De Veaux, Alexis 1948— **44**
"Deadwood Dick" *See Love, Nat*
Dean, Charles *See Commodores, The*
Dean, Fred 1952— **98**
Dean, Kasseem David *See Swizz Beatz*
Dean, Mark E. 1957— **35**
Dean, Phillip Hayes 1931–2014 **122**
Deas, Gerald 1931— **85**
Deauphin, Jean-Prosper *See Beken*

DeBaptiste, George 1814(?)–1875 **32**
DeBarge, El 1961— **89**
DeBerry, Lois M. 1945–2013 **115**
Déby, Idriss 1952— **30, 125**
DeCarava, Roy 1919–2009 **42, 81**
DeChalus, Lorenzo *See Lord Jamar*
Deconge-Watson, Lovenia 1933— **55**
Dedeaux, Richard 1940–2013 **119**
Dee, Merri 1936— **55**
Dee, Ruby 1924–2014 **8, 50, 68, 122**
Deep River Boys **131**
Deezer D 1965— **53**
DeFrantz, Anita 1952— **37**
DeGale, James 1986— **74**
Deggans, Eric 1965— **71**
Degree, Leaveil *See Whispers, The*
DeJongh, John, Jr. 1957— **85**
Dekker, Desmond 1941–2006 **104**
DeLaine, Joseph A. 1898–1974 **110**
Delaney, Beauford 1901–1979 **19**
Delaney, Joe 1958–1983 **76**
Delaney, Joseph 1904–1991 **30**
Delany, Annie Elizabeth 1891–1995 **12**
Delany, Martin R. 1812–1885 **27**
Delany, Samuel R(ay), Jr. 1942— **9**
Delany, Sarah (Sadie) 1889— **12**
Delco, Wilhelmina R. 1929— **33**
Delice, Ronald 1966— **48**
Delice, Rony 1966— **48**
DeLille, Henriette 1813–1862 **30**
Dells, The **109**
Dellums, Ronald 1935— **2, 81**
DeLoach, Nora 1940–2001 **30**
Delpit, Lisa 1952— **101**
Delsarte, Louis 1944— **34**
Delta Rhythm Boys **133**
Dembélé, Nathanael *See Songhoy Blues*
Demby, William 1922— **51**
Demps, Larry *See Dramatics, The*
DeMudd, Pierre *See Dazz Band*
Denby, Herman *See Swallows, The*
Denby, Junior *See Swallows, The*
Dennard, Brazeal 1929— **37**
Dennis, Gary C. 1950— **91**
Dent, Cedric *See Take 6*
Dent, Richard 1960— **97**
Dent, Thomas C. 1932–1998 **50**
Dent, Tom *See Dent, Thomas C.*
Dentley, Khristian *See Take 6*
DePreist, James 1936–2013 **37, 109**
DePrince, Michaela 1995— **104**
Derham, James *See Durham, James*
DeRozan, DeMar 1989— **125**
Derulo, Jason 1989— **93, 132**
Desalegn, Hailemariam 1965— **105**
DeSanto, Sugar Pie 1935— **122**
Desrouleaux, Jason Joel *See Derulo, Jason*
Detroit Emeralds, The **121**
DeVard, Jerri 1957(?)— **61**
DeVaughn, Raheem 1975— **91**
Devers, Gail 1966— **7, 87**
Devine, Loretta 1953— **24**
Devine, Major J. *See Divine, Father*
DeVoe, Ronnie *See New Edition*

DeVore-Mitchell, Ophelia 1922–2014 120
Dewese, Mohandas See Kool Moe Dee
Dewitty, Thelma 1912–1977 114
Dexter, Felix 1961–2013 129
Di Genius See McGregor, Stephen
Diabaté, Toumani 1965— 129
Dial, Thornton 1928— 114
Diallo, Amadou 1976–1999 27
Diamond, Lydia R. 1969— 101
Diaw, Boris 1982— 122
Diawara, Djeli Moussa 1962— 111
Diawara, Fatoumata 1982— 114
Dibaba, Genzebe 1991— 130
Dibaba, Mare 1989— 131
Dibaba, Tirunesh 1985— 73, 109
Dickens, Helen Octavia 1909–2001 14, 64
Dickenson, Vic 1906–1984 38
Dickerson, Debra J. 1959— 60
Dickerson, Eric 1960— 27, 108
Dickerson, Ernest 1952(?)— 6, 17
Dickerson, Isaac See Fisk Jubilee Singers
Dickey, Eric Jerome 1961— 21, 56
Dickey, Gwen See Rose Royce
Dickey, Robert Lee See James & Purify
Diddley, Bo 1928–2008 39, 72
Diehl, Aaron 1985— 132
Diesel, Vin 1967(?)— 29
Dieudonné 1966— 67, 118
Difda, Kalaparusha Ahrah See McIntyre, Kalaparusha Maurice
Diggs, Charles C. 1922–1998 21
Diggs, Robert Fitzgerald See RZA
Diggs, Scott See Diggs, Taye
Diggs, Taye 1972— 25, 63
Diggs-Taylor, Anna 1932— 20
Dihigo, Martín 1905(?)–1971 103
Dilla, J See J Dilla
Dillard, Godfrey J. 1948— 45
Dillard, Ricky 1965— 134
Dillard, Tramar See Flo Rida
Dilligard, Julius See Crown Heights Affair
Dillon, Leo 1933–2012 103
Dinkins, David 1927— 4
Diogo, Luisa Dias 1958— 63
Diop, Birago 1906–1989 53
Diop, Cheikh Anta 1923–1986 4
Diouf, Abdou 1935— 3
Diouf, Khalif See Le1f
Dirie, Waris 1965(?)— 56
Divine, Father 1877(?)–1965 7
Dixie Cups, The 109
Dixon, Bill 1925–2010 87
Dixon, Brandon Victor 1981— 134
Dixon, Dean 1915–1976 68
Dixon, George 1870–1909 52
Dixon, Ivan 1931–2008 69
Dixon, Julian C. 1934— 24
Dixon, Margaret A. 1923(?)–2011 14, 136
Dixon, Rodrick See Three Mo' Tenors
Dixon, Sharon Pratt 1944— 1
Dixon, Sheila 1953— 68
Dixon, Willie (James) 1915–1992 4
DJ Clue? 1975— 111
DJ Easy Lee See Treacherous Three

DJ Jazzy Jeff 1965— 32
DJ Lance Rock 1965— 94
DJ Rashad 1979–2014 121
DJ Ready Red See Geto Boys
DJ Red Alert See Alert, Kool DJ Red
DJ Screw 1971–2000 110
Djotodia, Michel 1949— 117
Dlamini-Zuma, Nkosazana 1949— 34, 105
DMC See Run-DMC
DMX 1970— 28, 64
do Nascimento, Edson Arantes See Pelé
Dobbs, John Wesley 1882–1961 89
Dobbs, Mattiwilda 1925— 34
Dobson, Tamara 1947–2006 111
Doby, Larry See Doby, Lawrence Eugene, Sr.
Doby, Lawrence Eugene, Sr. 1924–2003 16, 41
Dodd, Clement Seymour See Dodd, Coxsone
Dodd, Coxsone 1932–2004 99
Dodson, Howard, Jr. 1939— 7, 52
Dodson, Larry See Bar-Kays, The
Dodson, Owen 1914–1983 38
Doe, Samuel K. 1951–1990 100
Dogan, Matthew Winifred 1863–1947 91
Doggett, Bill 1916–1996 124
Doggett, William Ballard See Doggett, Bill
DoHarris, Brenda 1946— 116
Doig, Jason 1977— 45
Dokes, Michael 1958— 105
Doley, Harold, Jr. 1947— 26
Dollar, Creflo 1962— 106
Domingo, Colman 1969— 94
Domini, Rey See Lorde, Audre (Geraldine)
Domino, Fats 1928— 20
Donald, Arnold 1954— 36, 126
Donaldson, Jeff 1932–2004 46
Donegan, Dorothy 1922–1998 19
Donovan, Kevin See Bambaataa, Afrika
Dorham, Kenny 1924–1972 113
Dorham, McKinley Howard See Dorham, Kenny
Dorhan, Carlita See Taste of Honey, A
Dorn, Michael 1952— 112
Dorrell, Karl 1963— 52
Dorsey, Lee 1926–1986 65
Dorsey, Thomas Andrew 1899–1993 15
Dorsey, Thomas J. 1812(?)–1875 90
Dortch, Thomas W., Jr. 1950— 45
dos Santos, Isabel 1973— 114
dos Santos, José Eduardo 1942— 43, 114
dos Santos, Manuel Francisco 1933 65
Dougherty, Mary Pearl 1915–2003 47
Douglas, Aaron 1899–1979 7
Douglas, Ashanti Shequoiya See Ashanti
Douglas, Bob 1882–1979 96
Douglas, Buster 1960— 127
Douglas, Denzil Llewellyn 1953— 53

Douglas, Derek 1971— 88
Douglas, Donya 1970(?)— 97
Douglas, Emory 1943— 89
Douglas, James See Douglas, Buster
Douglas, Lizzie See Memphis Minnie
Douglass, Frederick 1817(?)–1895 87
Douglass, Harry See Deep River Boys
Doumbia, Mariam See Amadou & Mariam
Dourdan, Gary 1966— 37
Dove, Rita 1952— 6, 78, 101
Dove, Ulysses 1947— 5
Dow, Unity 1959— 104
Downing, George T. 1819–1903 91
Downing, Will 19(?)(?)— 19
Downs, Bobby See New Birth
Dozier, Lamont See Holland-Dozier-Holland
Dr. Dre 1965— 10, 14, 30, 116
Dr. J See Erving, Julius
Drake 1986— 86
Drake, Hamid 1955— 121
Drake, Lavern See Cadillacs
Drake, Michael V. 1950(?)— 122
Dramatics, The 106
Draper, Sharon Mills 1952— 16, 43
Drayton, William Jonathan, Jr. See Flavor Flav
Dream, The See The-Dream
Drew, Alvin, Jr. 1962— 67
Drew, Charles Richard 1904–1950 7
Drew, Kenneth Sidney, Sr. See Drew, Kenny
Drew, Kenny 1928–1993 123
Drew, Maurice See Jones-Drew, Maurice
Drew, Timothy See Noble Drew Ali
Drew Ali See Noble Drew Ali
Drexler, Clyde 1962— 4, 61
Drifters, The 121
Driskell, David C(lyde) 1931— 7
Driver, David E. 1955— 11
Driver, Donald 1975— 99
D-Roc See Ying Yang Twins
Drogba, Didier 1978— 78, 132
Drummond, Andre 1993— 132
Drummond, William J. 1944— 40
Du Bois, David Graham 1925–2005 45, 135
Du Bois, W(illiam) E(dward) B(urghardt) 1868–1963 3
du Cille, Michel 1955(?)— 74
Dube, John Langalibalele 1871–1946 119
Dube, Lucky 1964–2007 77
DuBois, Joshua 1982— 88
DuBois, Shirley Graham 1907–1977 21
Duchemin, Alamaine See Maxis, Theresa
Duchemin, Marie See Maxis, Theresa
Duchemin, Theresa Maxis See Maxis, Theresa
Ducksworth, Marilyn 1957— 12
Duckworth, Kendrick Lamar See Lamar, Kendrick
Dudley, Edward R. 1911–2005 58

Dudley, Sherman H. 1870(?)–1940 117
Dudus See Coke, Christopher
Due, Patricia Stephens 1939–2012 100
Due, Tananarive 1966— 30
Duerson, Dave 1960–2011 93
Duggins, George 1943–2005 64
Duke, Bill 1943— 3, 96
Duke, George 1946–2013 21, 113
Dukes, Hazel Nell 1932— 56
Dumars, Joe 1963— 16, 65, 126
Dumars, Joseph, III See Dumars, Joe
Dumas, Henry 1934–1968 41
Dumpson, James R. 1909–2012 108
Dunbar, Alice See Dunbar-Nelson, Alice Ruth Moore
Dunbar, Paul Laurence 1872–1906 8
Dunbar, Sly 1952— See Sly & Robbie
Dunbar-Nelson, Alice Ruth Moore 1875–1935 44
Duncan, Cleveland See Penguins, The
Duncan, Michael Clarke 1957–2012 26, 104
Duncan, Tim 1976— 20, 91
Duncan, Todd 1903–1998 76
Duncanson, Robert S. 1821(?)–1872 127
Dungey, Channing 1969— 134
Dungey, Merrin 1971— 62
Dungy, Camille 1972— 86
Dungy, Tony 1955— 17, 42, 59, 118
Dunham, Katherine 1910–2006 4, 59
Dunigan, Ricky See Lord Infamous
Dunlap, Ericka 1982(?)— 55
Dunn, Freddie See Rose Royce
Dunn, Jerry 1953— 27
Dunn, Jourdan 1990— 130
Dunn, Warrick 1975— 90
Dunner, Leslie B. 1956— 45
Dunnigan, Alice Allison 1906–1983 41
Dunston, Georgia Mae 1944— 48
Duplechan, Larry 1956— 55
DuPree, Johnny 1953— 96
Dupri, Jermaine 1972— 13, 46
Dural, Stanley, Jr. See Buckwheat Zydeco
Durant, Kevin 1988— 76, 107
Durham, Bobby 1937–2008 73
Durham, James 1762–1834(?) 90
Durham, Robert Joseph See Durham, Bobby
Duthiers, Vladimir 1969— 109
Dutton, Charles S. 1951— 4, 22
Dutton, Marie Elizabeth 1940— 12
Duvalier, Baby Doc See Duvalier, Jean-Claude
Duvalier, François 1907–1971 124
Duvalier, Jean-Claude 1951–2014 124
Duvalier, Papa Doc See Duvalier, François
DuVernay, Ava 1972— 98, 126
Dwight, Edward 1933— 65
Dworkin, Aaron P. 1970— 52
Dye, Jermaine 1974— 58

Dyett, Walter 1901–1969 **113**
Dymally, Mervyn 1926— **42**
Dyson, Michael Eric 1958— **11, 40, 128**
E-40 1967— **125**
Eagleson, William Lewis 1835–1899 **90**
Early, Deloreese Patricia See Reese, Della
Early, Gerald (Lyn) 1952— **15**
Early, Norman S., Jr. 1945— **124**
Earth, Wind & Fire **98**
Earthquake, 1963— **55**
Easley, Annie J. 1933— **61**
Easton, Hosea 1798–1837 **91**
Ebanks, Michelle 1962— **60**
Ebanks, Selita 1983— **67**
Eberhardt, Jennifer 1965— **124**
Eckstein, William Clarence See Eckstine, Billy
Eckstine, Billy 1914–1993 **28**
Edelin, Ramona Hoage 1945— **19**
Edelman, Marian Wright 1939— **5, 42**
Edgerton, Khia Danielle See K-Swift
Edison, Harry 1915(?)–1999 **114**
Edison, Harry "Sweets" See Edison, Harry
Edley, Christopher 1928–2003 **2, 48**
Edley, Christopher F., Jr. 1953— **48**
Edmonds, Kenneth See Babyface
Edmonds, Terry 1950(?)— **17**
Edmonds, Tracey 1967— **16, 64**
Edmunds, Gladys 1951(?)— **48**
Edugyan, Esi 1978— **98**
Edwards, Bernard See Chic
Edwards, David 1915–2011 **122**
Edwards, Dennis See Contours, The
Edwards, Donna 1958— **77**
Edwards, Eli See McKay, Claude
Edwards, Esther Gordy 1920(?)— **43**
Edwards, Harry 1942— **2**
Edwards, Herman 1954— **51**
Edwards, Honeyboy See Edwards, David
Edwards, Lena Frances 1900–1986 **76**
Edwards, Melvin 1937— **22**
Edwards, Robert See Intruders, The
Edwards, Teddy 1924–2003 **123**
Edwards, Teresa 1964— **14, 95**
Edwards, Theodore Marcus, Sr. See Edwards, Teddy
Edwards, Trevor 1962— **54**
Edwards, Willarda V. 1951— **59**
Edwards, Willis 1946–2012 **104**
Eikerenkoetter, Frederick J., II See Reverend Ike
Ejiofor, Chiwetel 1977— **67, 116**
Ejogo, Carmen 1974— **126**
Ekwensi, Cyprian 1921— **37**
El Wilson, Barbara 1959— **35**
Elam, Keith See Guru
Elba, Idris 1971— **49, 89, 116**
Elbagir, Nima 1978— **121**
Elder, Larry 1952— **25, 120**
Elder, (Robert) Lee 1934— **6**
Elder, Lonne, III 1931–1996 **38**

Elders, Joycelyn (Minnie) 1933— **6**
Eldridge, Roy 1911–1989 **37**
El-Hajj Malik El-Shabazz See X, Malcolm
Elie, Lolis Eric 1985— **97**
Elise, Kimberly 1967— **32, 101**
Ellerbe, Brian 1963— **22**
Ellington, Duke 1899–1974 **5**
Ellington, E. David 1960— **11**
Ellington, Edward Kennedy See Ellington, Duke
Ellington, Mercedes 1939— **34**
Ellington, Mercer 1919–1996 **129**
Ellington, Robert See Dramatics, The
Elliott, Lorris 1931–1999 **37**
Elliott, Missy 1971— **31, 90**
Elliott, Sean 1968— **26**
Ellis, Alton 1938–2008 **74**
Ellis, Aunjanue 1969— **108**
Ellis, Billy See S.O.S. Band
Ellis, Charles H., III 1958(?)— **79**
Ellis, Clarence A. 1943— **38**
Ellis, Dock 1945–2008 **78**
Ellis, Dorothy 1935— **131**
Ellis, Hortense 1941–2000 **97**
Ellis, Jennifer 1963(?)— **135**
Ellis, Jimmy 1940–2014 **44, 127**
Ellis, Jimmy, II See Trammps, The
Ellis, Larry R. 1946— **110**
Ellis, Monica See Imani Winds
Ellis, Nelsan 1981— **105**
Ellis, Thomas Sayers 1963— **129**
Ellis, Trey 1962— **97**
Ellis-Lamkins, Phaedra 1976— **88**
Ellison, Keith 1963— **59**
Ellison, Ralph (Waldo) 1914–1994 **7**
Ellison, Steven See Flying Lotus
Elmore, Ronn 1957— **21**
El-Shabazz, El-Hajj Malik See X, Malcolm
Elumelu, Tony 1963— **116**
Elzy, Ruby 1908–1943 **119**
Emanuel, James A. 1921— **46**
Emeagwali, Dale 1954— **31**
Emeagwali, Philip 1954— **30**
Emecheta, Buchi 1944— **30**
Emmanuel, Alphonsia 1956— **38**
Emotions, The **125**
En Vogue **100**
English, Alvin See Contours, The
Ensley, Carol Denise See Nash, Niecy
Ephriam, Mablean 1949(?)— **29**
Epperson, Sharon 1969(?)— **54**
Epps, Archie C., III 1937–2003 **45**
Epps, Mike 1970— **60**
Epps, Omar 1973— **23, 59**
Epps, Tauheed See 2 Chainz
Equiano, Olaudah 1745(?)–1797 **78**
Ericsson-Jackson, Aprille 19(?)(?)— **28**
Erivo, Cynthia 1987— **133**
Ervin, Anthony 1981— **66**
Ervin, Booker 1930–1970 **106**
Ervin, Clark Kent 1959— **82**
Erving, Julius 1950— **18, 47**
Escobar, Alcides 1986— **130**
Escobar, Damien 1987— **56**
Escobar, Tourie 1985— **56**
Esposito, Giancarlo (Giusseppi Alessandro) 1958— **9**

Espy, Alphonso Michael See Espy, Mike
Espy, Mike 1953— **6**
Estelle 1980— **75, 133**
Esters, Monica Ann See Conyers, Monica
Estes, Rufus 1857–19(?)(?) **29**
Estes, Simon 1938— **28**
Estes, Sleepy John 1899–1977 **33**
Eto'o, Samuel 1981— **73**
Eubanks, Kevin 1957— **15, 108**
Eugene-Richard, Margie 1941— **63**
Europe, (William) James Reese 1880–1919 **10**
Eusebio 1942–2014 **118**
Evans, Darryl 1961— **22**
Evans, Diana 1972(?)— **72**
Evans, Ernest See Checker, Chubby
Evans, Etu 1969— **55**
Evans, Faith 1973(?)— **22**
Evans, Greene See Fisk Jubilee Singers
Evans, Harry 1956(?)— **25**
Evans, Mari 1923— **26**
Evans, Melvin H. 1917–1984 **88**
Evans, Nate See Impressions, The
Evans, Warren C. 1948— **76**
Eve 1979— **29**
Everett, Carl 1971— **103**
Everett, Francine 1917–1999 **23**
Everett, Percival 1956— **93**
Everett, Ronald McKinley See Karenga, Maulana
Evers, Medgar (Riley) 1925–1963 **3**
Evers, Myrlie 1933— **8**
Évora, Cesária 1941–2011 **12, 99**
Evra, Patrice 1981— **102**
Ewing, Patrick 1962— **17, 73, 130**
Eyadéma, Gnassingbé 1937–2005 **7, 52**
Fabio, Sarah Webster 1928–1979 **48**
Fabolous 1977— **93**
Fabre, Shelton 1963— **71**
Fagan, Garth 1940— **18, 98**
Fair, Leroy See Contours, The
Fair, Ronald L. 1932— **47**
Fair, Yvonne See Chantels, The
Fairbanks, Mabel 1915(?)–2001 **117**
Faison, Donald 1974— **50**
Faison, Frankie 1949— **55**
Faison, George William 1946— **16**
Falana, Lola 1942— **42**
Falconer, Etta Zuber 1933–2002 **59**
Falcons, The **128**
Fales-Hill, Susan 1962— **88**
Fanon, Frantz 1925–1961 **44**
Fantasia See Barrino, Fantasia
Farah, Mo 1983— **104**
Farah, Nuruddin 1945— **27**
Fargas, Antonio 1946(?)— **50**
Farley, Christopher John 1966— **54**
Farley, J. J. See Soul Stirrers
Farley, James Conway 1854–1910(?) **99**
Farmer, Art(hur Stewart) 1928–1999 **38**
Farmer, Forest J(ackson) 1941— **1**
Farmer, James 1920–1999 **2, 64**
Farmer, Ray 1974— **133**

Farmer-Paellmann, Deadria 1966— **43**
Farr, Mel 1944— **24**
Farrakhan, Louis 1933— **2, 15**
Farrell, Bobby See Boney M.
Farrell, Herman D., Jr. 1932— **81**
Farris, Isaac Newton, Jr. 1962— **63**
Fat Boys **92**
Father Goose See Rhoden, Wayne
Fatlip See Pharcyde, The
Fattah, Chaka 1956— **11, 70, 112, 130**
Faulk, Marshall 1973— **35, 96**
Faulkner, Harris 1965— **131**
Fauntroy, Walter E(dward) 1933— **11**
Fauset, Crystal Dreda Bird 1893–1965 **100**
Fauset, Jessie (Redmon) 1882–1961 **7**
Favors, Malachi 1927–2004 **136**
Favors, Steve 1948— **23**
Fax, Elton 1909–1993 **48**
Fearman, Eric See Dazz Band
Feaster, Robert Franklin See Sundiata, Sekou
Feelings, Muriel 1938— **44**
Feelings, Tom 1933–2003 **11, 47**
Feemster, Herbert 1942— **72**
Fela 1938–1997 **1, 42**
Felder, Wilton See Crusaders, The
Felix, Allyson 1985— **48, 98**
Felix, Larry R. (?)— **64**
Felix Da Housecat 1971— **110**
Fennoy, Ilene 1947— **72**
Fenton, Kevin 1966(?)— **87**
Fenty, Adrian 1970— **60, 88**
Fenty, Robyn Rihanna See Rihanna
Ferbee, Willie See Drifters, The
Ferbos, Lionel 1911— **95**
Ferdinand, Rio 1978— **82**
Ferguson, Amos 1920–2009 **81**
Ferguson, Kevin See Slice, Kimbo
Ferguson, Roger W., Jr. 1951— **25, 112**
Ferguson, Ronald F. 1950(?)— **75**
Ferguson, Vernice D. 1928–2012 **108**
Ferrell, Rachelle 1961— **29**
Ferrer, Ibrahim 1927— **41**
Fetchit, Stepin 1892–1985 **32**
Fetty Wap 1991— **130**
Fiasco, Lupe 1982— **64**
Fielder, Cecil 1963— **2, 112**
Fielder, Prince 1984— **68**
Fields, C. Virginia 1946— **25**
Fields, Cleo 1962— **13**
Fields, Evelyn J. 1949— **27**
Fields, Felicia P. (?)— **60**
Fields, Julia 1938— **45**
Fields, Kim 1969— **36**
50 Cent 1976— **46, 83**
Figueroa, John J. 1920–1999 **40**
Files, Lolita 1964(?)— **35**
Fils-Aimé, Reggie 1961— **74**
Fine, Sam 1969— **60**
Finley, Ron 1978(?)— **110**
Finner-Williams, Paris Michele 1951— **62**
Finnie, Lance See Falcons, The
Fiona, Melanie 1983— **84**
Fishbone **101**

Fishburne, Larry See Fishburne, Laurence
Fishburne, Laurence 1961— **4, 22, 70**
Fisher, Ada Lois Sipuel 1924–1995 **76**
Fisher, Ada M. 1947— **76**
Fisher, Antwone Quenton 1959— **40**
Fisher, Derek 1974— **97**
Fisher, Gail 1935–2000 **85**
Fisher, George See Peters, Brock
Fisher, Miles Mark 1899–1970 **91**
Fisher, Rudolph John Chauncey 1897–1934 **17**
Fisher, Thelma See Dewitty, Thelma
Fisk Jubilee Singers **112**
Fitzgerald, Ella 1918–1996 **8, 18**
Fitzgerald, Larry 1983— **133**
Five Blind Boys of Alabama, The See Blind Boys of Alabama, The
Five Keys, The **104**
FKA Twigs 1988— **123**
Flack, Roberta 1940— **19**
Flake, Floyd H. 1945— **18, 110**
Flamingos, The **108**
Flanagan, Tommy 1930–2001 **69**
Flash, Grandmaster See Grandmaster Flash
Flavor Flav 1959— **67** See also Public Enemy
Fleming, Erik R. 1965— **75**
Fleming, Raymond 1945— **48**
Flemons, Dom See Carolina Chocolate Drops
Flemons, Wade See Earth, Wind & Fire
Fletcher, Alphonse, Jr. See Fletcher, Buddy
Fletcher, Arthur A. 1924–2005 **63**
Fletcher, Benjamin 1890–1949 **90**
Fletcher, Bill, Jr. 1954— **41**
Fletcher, Buddy 1965— **16, 108**
Fletcher, Geoffrey 1970— **85**
Flipper, Henry O(ssian) 1856–1940 **3**
Flo Rida 1979— **78**
Flood, Curt 1938–1997 **10, 93**
Florence, Kenneth Howard See Norton, Ken
Flowers, Sylester 1935— **50**
Flowers, Vonetta 1973— **35**
Floyd, Eddie 1937— **127**
Floyd, Elson S. 1956— **41**
Flying Lotus 1983— **124**
Folks, Byron See Allen, Byron
Forbes, Audrey Manley 1934— **16**
Forbes, Calvin 1945— **46**
Forbes, James A., Jr. 1935— **71**
Ford, Barney 1822–1902 **90**
Ford, Cheryl 1981— **45**
Ford, Clyde W. 1951— **40**
Ford, Harold E(ugene) 1945— **42**
Ford, Harold E(ugene), Jr. 1970— **16, 70**
Ford, Jack 1947— **39**
Ford, James Lewis Carter See Ford, T-Model
Ford, Johnny 1942— **70**
Ford, Nick Aaron 1904–1982 **44**
Ford, T-Model 1920(?)–2013 **91, 113**
Ford, Vincent 1940(?)–2008 **75**

Ford, Wallace 1950— **58**
Ford, Willie See Dramatics, The
Foreman, George 1948— **1, 15**
Forman, James 1928–2005 **7, 51**
Forman, James, Jr. 1967— **89**
Forna, Aminatta 1964— **95**
Forrest, Leon 1937–1997 **44**
Forrest, Vernon 1971–2009 **40, 79**
Forté, John 1975— **74**
Forte, Linda Diane 1952— **54**
Fortune, James 1977(?)— **92**
Fortune, T(imothy) Thomas 1856–1928 **6**
Fosso, Samuel 1962— **116**
Foster, Andrew 1879–1930 **79**
Foster, Arian 1986— **114**
Foster, Cecil (A.) 1954— **32**
Foster, Ezola 1938— **28**
Foster, Frank 1928–2011 **97**
Foster, George "Pops" 1892–1969 **40**
Foster, Henry W., Jr. 1933— **26**
Foster, Jylla Moore 1954— **45**
Foster, Marie 1917–2003 **48**
Foster, Rube See Foster, Andrew
Foster, William P. 1919–2010 **88**
Four Tops, The See Benson, Obie
Fowler, Reggie 1959— **51**
Fowles, Gloria See Gaynor, Gloria
Fox, Donal 1952— **114**
Fox, John R. 1917–1944 **105**
Fox, Rick 1969— **27**
Fox, Ulrich Alexander See Fox, Rick
Fox, Vivica A. **15, 53**
Foxx, Anthony 1971— **81, 123**
Foxx, Jamie 1967— **15, 48**
Foxx, Kim 1972— **134**
Foxx, Kimberly See Foxx, Kim
Foxx, Redd 1922–1991 **2**
Foye, K'wan 19(?)(?)— **97**
Francis, Norman (C.) 1931— **60**
Francis, Thais 1980— **93**
Francis, Yvette Fay See Francis-McBarnette, Yvette Fay
Francis-McBarnette, Yvette Fay 1926–2016 **135**
Francois, Terry A. 1940–1989 **106**
Franklin, Aretha 1942— **11, 44, 115**
Franklin, C. L. 1915–1984 **68**
Franklin, Carl 1949— **11**
Franklin, Elmo See Mighty Clouds of Joy
Franklin, Hardy R. 1929–2004 **9, 87**
Franklin, J. E. 1937— **44**
Franklin, John Hope 1915–2009 **5, 77**
Franklin, Kirk 1970— **15, 49, 97**
Franklin, Robert M(ichael) 1954— **13**
Franklin, Shante Anthony See Curren$y
Franklin, Shirley 1945— **34, 80**
Franks, Gary 1954(?)— **2**
Franti, Michael 1966— **93**
Fraser, Sarah Loguen 1850–1933 **100**
Fraser, Shelly-Ann See Fraser-Pryce, Shelly-Ann
Fraser-Pryce, Shelly-Ann 1986— **113**
Frazer, Jendayi 196(?)— **68**
Frazer, Victor O. 1943— **98**

Frazier, Edward Franklin 1894–1962 **10**
Frazier, Joe 1944–2011 **19, 98**
Frazier, Kenneth 1954— **97**
Frazier, Kevin 1964— **58**
Frazier, LaToya Ruby 1982— **131**
Frazier, Oscar 1956–2005 **58**
Frazier, Ryan 1977— **89**
Frazier, Walt 1945— **91**
Frazier-Lyde, Jacqui 1961— **31**
Fredericks, Henry Saint Claire See Mahal, Taj
Freelon, Nnenna 1954— **32**
Freeman, Aaron 1956— **52**
Freeman, Al, Jr. 1934–2012 **11, 105**
Freeman, Albert Cornelius, Jr. See Freeman, Al, Jr.
Freeman, Bernard See Bun B
Freeman, Cathy 1973— **29**
Freeman, Charles Eldridge 1933— **19**
Freeman, Harold P. 1933— **23**
Freeman, Leonard 1950— **27**
Freeman, Marianna 1957— **23**
Freeman, Morgan 1937— **2, 20, 62, 100**
Freeman, Paul 1936— **39**
Freeman, Von 1923–2012 **104**
Freeman, Yvette **27**
Freestyle Fellowship **122**
French, Albert 1943— **18**
French, D. M. 1924–2011 **94**
Fresh, Doug E. 1966— **93**
Fresh Prince, The See Smith, Will
Frey, Alan See New Birth
Friday, Jeff 1964(?)— **24**
Fryer, Roland G. 1977— **56**
Fudge, Ann (Marie) 1951— **11, 55**
Fudge, Marcia L. 1952— **76**
Fuentes, Rigoberto See Fuentes, Tito
Fuentes, Tito 1944— **123**
Fugees **129**
Fuhr, Grant 1962— **1, 49**
Fulani, Lenora (Branch) 1950— **11**
Fuller, A. Oveta 1955— **43**
Fuller, Arthur 1972— **27**
Fuller, Blind Boy 1907(?)–1941 **86**
Fuller, Charles (Henry) 1939— **8**
Fuller, Curtis 1934— **115**
Fuller, Howard L. 1941— **37**
Fuller, Hoyt 1923–1981 **44**
Fuller, Meta Vaux Warrick 1877–1968 **27**
Fuller, S. B. 1895–1988 **13**
Fuller, Solomon Carter, Jr. 1872–1953 **15**
Fuller, Thomas O. 1867–1942 **90**
Fuller, Vivian 1954— **33**
Fulson, Lowell 1921–1999 **118**
Funches, Johnny See Dells, The
Funches, Ron 1983— **121**
Funderburg, I. Owen 1924–2002 **38**
Funnye, Capers C., Jr. 1952(?)— **73**
Fuqua, Antoine 1966— **35**
Fuqua, Charlie See Ink Spots, The
Fuqua, Harvey 1927–2010 **90** See also Moonglows, The
Futch, Eddie 1911–2001 **33**
Future 1983— **109**
Gabre-Medhin, Tsegaye 1936–2006 **64**

Gabriel, Athelgra Neville See Dixie Cups, The
Gaines, Brenda 19(?)(?)— **41**
Gaines, Clarence E., Sr. 1923–2005 **55**
Gaines, Ernest J(ames) 1933— **7**
Gaines, Grady 1934— **38**
Gaines, LaDonna Andrea See Summer, Donna
Gaines, Lee See Delta Rhythm Boys
Gaines, Lloyd 1911–19(?)(?) **79**
Gaines, Matthew 1840–1900 **95**
Gaines, Patrice 1950— **106**
Gairy, Eric Matthew 1922–1997 **83**
Gaiter, Dorothy J. 1950(?)— **80**
Gaither, Israel L. 1944— **65**
Gaither, Jake 1903–1994 **14**
Gamble, Kenny 1943— **85**
Gamble, Oscar 1949— **113**
Gans, Joe 1874–1910 **91**
Gant, Kenneth See Midnight Star
Gant, Richard 1944— **105**
Gantin, Bernardin 1922–2008 **70**
Gantt, Harvey (Bernard) 1943— **1**
Gap Band, The **100**
Garang, John 1945–2005 **105**
Gardere, Jeffrey 1956— **76**
Gardner, Carl See Coasters, The
Gardner, Chris 1954— **65**
Gardner, Edward G. 1925— **45**
Gardner, Vernon See Deep River Boys
Garland, Red 1923–1984 **115**
Garland, William M. See Garland, Red
Garner, Erroll 1921–1977 **76**
Garner, Henry See Rose Royce
Garner, Tyron 1967–2006 **99**
Garnet, Henry Highland 1815–1882 **100**
Garnett, Kevin 1976— **14, 70, 118**
Garrett, James F. 1942— **78**
Garrett, Joyce Finley 1931–1997 **59**
Garrett, Sean 1979— **57**
Garrincha See dos Santos, Manuel Francisco
Garrison, Jimmy 1934(?)–1976 **133**
Garrison, Zina 1963— **2, 133**
Gartin, Lydia See Diamond, Lydia R.
Garvey, Marcus 1887–1940 **1**
Garvin, Gerry 1967(?)— **78**
Gary, Willie E. 1947— **12, 117**
Gaskins, Eric 1958— **64**
Gaskins, Rudy 1960(?)— **74**
Gaspard, Patrick 1967— **84**
Gaston, Arthur George 1892–1996 **3, 38, 59**
Gaston, Cito 1944— **71**
Gaston, Clarence Edwin See Gaston, Cito
Gaston, Marilyn Hughes 1939— **60**
Gates, Henry Louis, Jr. 1950— **3, 38, 67**
Gates, Pop See Gates, William
Gates, Rosalind See Brewer, Rosalind
Gates, Sylvester James, Jr. 1950— **15, 130**
Gates, Theaster 1973— **118**
Gates, William 1917–1999 **97**
Gatlin, Justin 1982— **123**

Gatson, Daisy Lee *See Bates, Daisy*

Gay, Council *See Contours, The*

Gay, Marvin Pentz, Jr. *See Gaye, Marvin*

Gay, Roxane 1974— **136**

Gay, Tyson 1982— **114**

Gaye, Anna Gordy 1922–2014 **121**

Gaye, Marvin 1939–1984 **2**

Gaye, Nona 1974— **56**

Gayle, Addison, Jr. 1932–1991 **41**

Gayle, Helene D. 1955— **3, 46**

Gaynor, Gloria 1947— **36**

Gbagbo, Laurent 1945— **43, 90**

Gbowee, Leymah 1971(?)— **76**

Gebrselassie, Haile 1973— **70**

Gee, Kay *See Naughty by Nature*

Gentry, Alvin 1954— **23**

Gentry, Melvin *See Midnight Star*

George, Eddie 1973— **80**

George, Nelson 1957— **12, 101**

George, Paul 1990— **124**

George, Zelma Watson 1903–1994 **42**

Gerima, Haile 1946— **38, 80**

Gervin, George 1952— **80**

Geto Boys **115**

Ghostface Killah 1970— **90**

Gibbons, Gary 1956— **107**

Gibbs, Darryl *See Crown Heights Affair*

Gibbs, Freddie 1982— **125**

Gibbs, Marla 1931— **86**

Gibbs, Mifflin W. 1823–1915 **99**

Gibson, Althea 1927–2003 **8, 43**

Gibson, Bob 1935— **33**

Gibson, Donald Bernard 1933— **40**

Gibson, John Trusty 1878–1937 **87**

Gibson, Johnnie Mae 1949— **23**

Gibson, Josh 1911–1947 **22**

Gibson, Kenneth Allen 1932— **6**

Gibson, Ted 1965— **66**

Gibson, Truman K., Jr. 1912–2005 **60**

Gibson, Tyrese 1978— **27, 62, 134**

Gibson, William F(rank) 1933— **6**

Giddens, Rhiannon *See Carolina Chocolate Drops*

Giddings, Paula (Jane) 1947— **11**

Gidron, Richard D. 1939–2007 **68**

Gil, Gilberto 1942— **53**

Gilbert, Christopher 1949— **50**

Gilbert, John Wesley 1864–1923 **91**

Giles, Cameron *See Cam'ron*

Giles, Roscoe C. 1890–1970 **93**

Gill, Gerald 1948–2007 **69**

Gill, Johnny 1966— **51** *See also New Edition*

Gill, Turner 1962— **83**

Gilles, Ralph 1970— **61**

Gillespie, Dizzy 1917–1993 **1**

Gillespie, John Birks *See Gillespie, Dizzy*

Gilliam, Frank 1934(?)— **23**

Gilliam, Jim 1928–1978 **122**

Gilliam, Joe, Jr. 1950–2000 **31**

Gilliam, Junior *See Gilliam, Jim*

Gilliam, Sam 1933— **16**

Gilliard, Steve 1964–2007 **69**

Gillis, Jesse, Jr. *See Harold Melvin & the Blue Notes*

Gillum, Andrew 1979— **128**

Gilmore, Artis 1949— **101**

Gilmore, Maharshalalhashbaz *See Ali, Maharshala*

Gilmore, Marshall 1931— **46**

Gilpin, Charles Sidney 1878–1930 **81**

Ginuwine 1975(?)— **35**

Ginyard, Caleb J. C. *See Golden Gate Quartet*

Giovanni, Nikki 1943— **9, 39, 85**

Girmazion, Daniel Teklehaimanot *See Teklehaimanot, Daniel*

Gist, Carole 1970(?)— **1**

Gist, Keir *See Naughty by Nature*

Gittens, Charles L. 1928–2011 **124**

Givens, Adele 19(?)(?)— **62**

Givens, Cliff *See Billy Ward and the Dominoes; Golden Gate Quartet*

Givens, Robin 1964— **4, 25, 58**

Givhan, Robin Deneen 1964— **72**

Gladney, Paul *See Mooney, Paul*

Gladwell, Malcolm 1963— **62**

Glanville, Douglas Metunwa 1970— **82**

Glasper, Robert 1978— **101**

Glass, Ron 1945— **111**

Glenn, Ornette *See Freestyle Fellowship*

Glenn, Tyree 1912–1974 **129**

Gloster, Hugh Morris, Sr. 1911–2002 **90**

Glover, Anwan 1973— **123**

Glover, Cedric B. 1965— **103**

Glover, Corey 1964— **34**

Glover, Danny 1948— **1, 24, 103**

Glover, Donald 1983— **85**

Glover, Keith 1966— **79**

Glover, Nathaniel, Jr. 1943— **12**

Glover, Ralph Anwan *See Glover, Anwan*

Glover, Savion 1974— **14**

Gnassingbé, Faure 1966— **67**

Goapele 1977— **55**

"The Goat" *See Manigault, Earl "The Goat"*

Godbolt, James Titus *See Slyde, Jimmy*

Goff, Houston *See Stackhouse, Houston*

Goggins, Juanita 1934–2010 **127**

Goines, Donald 1937(?)–1974 **19**

Goings, Russell 1932(?)— **59**

Goldberg, Whoopi 1955— **4, 33, 69**

Golden, Marita 1950— **19, 99**

Golden, Thelma 1965— **10, 55**

Golden Gate Quartet **104**

Golding, Bruce 1947— **78**

Golding, Meta 1971— **135**

Goldsberry, Ronald 1942— **18**

Golson, Benny 1929— **37**

Golston, Allan C. 1967(?)— **55**

Gomes, Peter J. 1942–2011 **15, 93**

Gomez, Jewelle 1948— **30**

Gomez-Preston, Cheryl 1954— **9**

Gomillion, Charles 1900–1995 **90**

Gonzales, Babs 1919(?)–1980 **134**

Good, Meagan 1981— **117**

Goode, Mal(vin Russell) 1908–1995 **13**

Goode, W(oodrow) Wilson 1938— **4**

Gooden, Dwight 1964— **20**

Gooden, Linda 1953(?)— **94**

Gooden, Lolita *See Shanté, Roxanne*

Gooden, Sam *See Impressions, The*

Gooding, Cuba, Jr. 1968— **16, 62**

Goodison, Lorna 1947— **71**

Goodlett, Carlton B. 1914–1997 **91**

Goodman, Al 1943–2010 **87** *See also Ray, Goodman & Brown*

Goodman, Kim C. 1966— **94**

Goodnight, Paul 1946— **32**

Gorden, W. C. 1930— **71**

Gorden, William C. *See Gorden, W. C.*

Gordon, Billy *See Contours, The*

Gordon, Bruce S. 1946— **41, 53, 82**

Gordon, Carl 1932–2010 **87**

Gordon, Dee 1988— **130**

Gordon, Devaris *See Gordon, Dee*

Gordon, Dexter 1923–1990 **25**

Gordon, Ed 1960— **10, 53**

Gordon, Josh 1991— **120**

Gordon, Pamela 1955— **17**

Gordon, Ronnie *See Bar-Kays, The*

Gordon, Tom 1967— **130**

Gordone, Charles 1925–1995 **15**

Gordon-Reed, Annette 1958— **74**

Gordy, Anna *See Gaye, Anna Gordy*

Gordy, Berry, Jr. 1929— **1**

Gore, Frank 1983— **117**

Goreed, Joseph *See Williams, Joe*

Goring, Sonia *See Chantels, The*

Goss, Carol A. 1947— **55**

Goss, Margaret Taylor *See Burroughs, Margaret Taylor*

Goss, Tom 1946— **23**

Gossett, Louis, Jr. 1936— **7**

Gotti, Irv 1971— **39**

Gourdin, Edward O. 1897–1966 **93**

Gourdine, Anthony *See Little Anthony & the Imperials*

Gourdine, Meredith 1929–1998 **33**

Gourdine, Simon (Peter) 1940— **11**

Graca, Marcelino Manuel da *See Grace, Sweet Daddy*

Grace, Charles Manuel *See Grace, Sweet Daddy*

Grace, George H. 1948— **48**

Grace, Sweet Daddy 1881–1960 **104**

Grae, Jean 1976— **51**

Graham, Aubrey Drake *See Drake*

Graham, David *See Du Bois, David Graham*

Graham, Katerina 1989— **99**

Graham, Larry *See Graham Central Station*

Graham, Lawrence Otis 1962— **12**

Graham, Lorenz 1902–1989 **48**

Graham, Stedman 1951(?)— **13**

Graham, Trevor 1962(?)— **84**

Graham Central Station **123**

Grandberry, Omari Ishmael *See Omarion*

Granderson, Curtis 1981— **66**

Granderson, LZ 1972— **103**

Grandmaster Flash 1958— **33, 60**

Grand-Pierre, Jean-Luc 1977— **46**

Granger, Lester B. 1896–1976 **75**

Grant, Augustus O. 1946(?)— **71**

Grant, Bernie 1944–2000 **57**

Grant, Frank 1865–1937 **100**

Grant, Gwendolyn Goldsby 19(?)(?)— **28**

Grant, Micki 1941(?)— **125**

Grant, Rupert Westmore *See Lord Invader*

Granville, Evelyn Boyd 1924— **36**

Gravely, Samuel L., Jr. 1922–2004 **5, 49**

Graves, Alexander *See Moonglows, The*

Graves, Butch 1962— **77**

Graves, Denyce Antoinette 1964— **19, 57**

Graves, Earl G(ilbert) 1935— **1, 35**

Graves, Earl Gilbert, Jr. *See Graves, Butch*

Graves, Milford 1941— **126**

Gray, Ahuvah 1946(?)— **130**

Gray, Carl Wardell *See Gray, Wardell*

Gray, Darius 1945— **69**

Gray, Delores *See Gray, Ahuvah*

Gray, Dobie 1940(?)–2011 **99**

Gray, F. Gary 1969— **14, 49**

Gray, Farrah 1984— **59**

Gray, Fred Sr. 1930— **37**

Gray, Frizzell *See Mfume, Kweisi*

Gray (Nelson Rollins), Ida 1867–1953 **41**

Gray, Macy 1970— **29**

Gray, Terius *See Juvenile*

Gray, Vincent C. 1942— **88**

Gray, Wardell 1921–1955 **128**

Gray, William H., III 1941— **3**

Gray, Willie 1947— **46**

Gray, Yeshimbra "Shimmy" 1972— **55**

Greaves, R. B. 1943–2012 **106**

Greaves, William 1926–2014 **38, 123**

Greely, M. Gasby 1946— **27**

Greely, Margaret Gasby *See Greely, M. Gasby*

Green, A. C. 1963— **32**

Green, Al 1946— **13, 47, 74**

Green, Al 1947— **118**

Green, Bennie 1923–1977 **131**

Green, Cee Lo 1974— **70, 103**

Green, Darrell 1960— **39, 74**

Green, Dennis 1949— **5, 45**

Green, Draymond 1990— **126**

Green, Grant 1935–1979 **56**

Green, Hadiyah-Nicole 1981— **133**

Green, Henry *See Williams Brothers*

Green, Isaac H. 1959— **79**

Green, Jerry *See Contours, The*

Green, Jonathan 1955— **54**

Green, Nancy 1834–1923 **112**

Greene, Frank S., Jr. 1938–2009 **101**

Greene, Imogene *See Davis Sisters, The*

Greene, Jimmy 1975— **74**

Greene, Joe 1946— **10**

Greene, Mark *See Ray, Goodman & Brown*

Greene, Maurice 1974— **27, 77**

Greene, Petey 1931–1984 **65**

Greene, Ralph Waldo *See Greene, Petey*

Greene, Richard Thaddeus, Sr. 1913–2006 **67**

Greene, Talib Kweli See Kweli, Talib

Greene, Travis 1984— **134**

Greenfield, Elizabeth Taylor 1819(?)–1876 **116**

Greenfield, Eloise 1929— **9**

Greenfield, Ronnie Spector See Spector, Ronnie

Greenhouse, Bunnatine "Bunny" 1944— **57**

Greenlee, Sam 1930— **48**

Greenwood, L. C. 1946–2013 **115**

Greenwood, Monique 1959— **38**

Greer, Hal 1936— **92**

Greer, Sonny 1903(?)–1982 **127**

Greer, William Alexander See Greer, Sonny

Gregg, Eric 1951— **16**

Gregory, Ann 1912–1990 **63**

Gregory, Dick 1932— **1, 54**

Gregory, Frederick 1941— **8, 51**

Gregory, Gerald See Spaniels, The

Gregory, Wilton 1947— **37**

Grice, George See Gryce, Gigi

Grier, Bobby 1933— **95**

Grier, David Alan 1955— **28**

Grier, Eliza Ann 1863(?)–1902 **90**

Grier, Mike 1975— **43**

Grier, Pam 1949— **9, 31, 86**

Grier, Roosevelt (Rosey) 1932— **13**

Griffey, Dick 1938–2010 **89**

Griffey, Ken, Jr. 1969— **12, 73**

Griffin, Angela 1976— **80**

Griffin, Anthony 1960— **71**

Griffin, Bessie 1922–1989 **135**

Griffin, Bessie Blount 1914–2009 **43, 135**

Griffin, Blake 1989— **98**

Griffin, John Arnold, III See Griffin, Johnny

Griffin, Johnny 1928–2008 **71**

Griffin, LaShell 1967— **51**

Griffin, Robert, III 1990— **107**

Griffith, Emile 1938–2013 **113**

Griffith, Mark Winston 1963— **8**

Griffith, Patrick A. 1944— **64**

Griffith, Yolanda 1970— **25**

Griffith-Joyner, Florence 1959–1998 **28**

Griffiths, Marcia 1948(?)— **29**

Grillo, Evelio 1919–2008 **95**

Grimes, Henry 1935— **124**

Grimké, Archibald H(enry) 1849–1930 **9**

Griner, Brittney 1990— **128**

Grist, Reri 1932— **84**

Groff, Peter 1963— **96**

Grooms, Henry R(andall) 1944— **50**

Gryce, George See Gryce, Gigi

Gryce, Gigi 1925–1983 **124**

Guarionex See Schomburg, Arthur Alfonso

Guebuza, Armando 1943— **81**

Guéï, Robert 1941–2002 **66**

Guillaume, Robert 1927— **3, 48**

Güines, Tata 1930–2008 **69**

Guinier, (Carol) Lani 1950— **7, 30**

Guitar Slim 1926(?)–1959 **125**

Gumbel, Bryant 1948— **14, 80**

Gumbel, Greg 1946— **8**

Gunn, Moses 1929–1993 **10**

Gurira, Danai 1978(?)— **73**

Guru 1961–2010 **84**

Guy, Billy See Coasters, The

Guy, (George) Buddy 1936— **31**

Guy, Jasmine 1964(?)— **2**

Guy, Rosa 1925(?)— **5**

Guyot, Lawrence 1939–2012 **108**

Guyse, Etta Drucille See Guyse, Sheila

Guyse, Sheila 1925–2013 **122**

Guy-Sheftall, Beverly 1946— **13, 92**

Guyton, Tyree 1955— **9, 94**

Gwynn, Tony 1960–2014 **18, 83, 122**

Gyan, Asamoah 1985— **87**

Gyasi, Yaa 1989— **136**

Habré, Hissène 1942— **6, 104**

Habyarimana, Juvenal 1937–1994 **8**

Haddon, Dietrick 1973(?)— **55**

Hageman, Hans 19(?)(?)— **36**

Hageman, Ivan 19(?)(?)— **36**

Hagler, Marvelous Marvin 1954— **102**

Haile Selassie 1892–1975 **7**

Hailey, JoJo 1971— **22**

Hailey, K-Ci 1969— **22**

Hairston, Jester 1901–2000 **88**

Hairston, Sam 1920–1997 **88**

Haju, Gerard See Malawi Mouse Boys

Hale, Clara 1902–1992 **16**

Hale, Lorraine 1926(?)— **8**

Hale, Nathaniel Dawayne See Nate Dogg

Haley, Alex (Palmer) 1921–1992 **4**

Haley, Charles 1964— **134**

Haley, George 1925–2015 **21, 129**

Hall, Aaron 1963— **57**

Hall, Adelaide 1901–1993 **126**

Hall, Alvin D. 1952— **86**

Hall, Arsenio 1955— **58**

Hall, Arthur 1943–2000 **39**

Hall, Elliott S. 1938(?)— **24**

Hall, Juanita 1901–1968 **62**

Hall, Katori 1981— **132**

Hall, Kevan 19(?)(?)— **61**

Hall, Lloyd A(ugustus) 1894–1971 **8**

Hall, Regina 1970— **135**

Hall, Stuart 1932— **78**

Hall, Syren See Fiona, Melanie

Hall, Tamron 1970— **96**

Hall, Valerie Eileen See Wellington, Valerie

Hall, Willie See Bar-Kays, The

Halliburton, Warren J. 1924— **49**

Hallim, Melanie Fiona See Fiona, Melanie

Ham, Cynthia Parker 1970(?)— **58**

Hamblin, Ken 1940— **10**

Hamburg, Beatrix 1923— **84**

Hamburg, Margaret 1955— **78**

Hamer, Fannie Lou 1917–1977 **6**

Hamilton, Anthony 1971— **61**

Hamilton, Bernie 1928–2008 **117**

Hamilton, Chico 1921–2013 **117**

Hamilton, Darryl 1964–2015 **130**

Hamilton, Foreststorn See Hamilton, Chico

Hamilton, Lawrence 1954–2014 **122**

Hamilton, Leonard 1948— **100**

Hamilton, Lewis 1985— **66**

Hamilton, Lisa Gay 1964— **71**

Hamilton, Samuel C. 19(?)(?)— **47**

Hamilton, Tanya 1968— **93**

Hamilton, Vicki 1964(?)— **95**

Hamilton, Virginia 1936— **10**

Hamlin, Larry Leon 1948–2007 **49, 62**

Hammer, M. C. See M.C. Hammer

Hammon, Jupiter 1711–1806(?) **124**

Hammond, Fred 1960— **23**

Hammond, Lenn 1970(?)— **34**

Hammond, Paula 1963— **119**

Hammonds, Evelynn 1953— **69**

Hammons, David 1943— **69**

Hampton, Fred 1948–1969 **18**

Hampton, Henry (Eugene, Jr.) 1940— **6**

Hampton, Lionel 1908(?)–2002 **17, 41**

Hancock, Herbie 1940— **20, 67**

Hancock, Michael B. 1969— **123**

Handy, John 1933— **131**

Handy, W(illiam) C(hristopher) 1873–1937 **8**

Haney, Lee 1959— **77**

Hani, Chris 1942–1993 **6**

Hani, Martin Thembisile See Hani, Chris

Hanley, Quincy Matthew See ScHoolboy Q

Hanna, Jerome See Jive Five

Hannah, Marc (Regis) 1956— **10**

Hansberry, Lorraine (Vivian) 1930–1965 **6**

Hansberry, Tony, II 1994— **93**

Hansberry, William Leo 1894–1965 **11**

Hansen, Austin 1910–1996 **88**

Happy Land Jubilee Singers See Blind Boys of Alabama, The

Hardaway, Anfernee 1971— **13, 111**

Hardaway, Penny See Hardaway, Anfernee

Hardaway, Tim 1966— **35**

Harden, James 1989— **116**

Harden, Monique 1968— **97**

Harden, Rashad Hanif See DJ Rashad

Hardin Armstrong, Lil 1898–1971 **39**

Hardin, Lillian Beatrice See Hardin Armstrong, Lil

Harding, Vincent 1931–2014 **67, 130**

Hardison, Bethann 19(?)(?)— **12**

Hardison, Kadeem 1966— **22**

Hardson, Tre See Pharcyde, The

Hardwick, Omari 1974— **122**

Hardy, Antonio See Big Daddy Kane

Hardy, Greg 1988— **118**

Hardy, Nell See Carter, Nell

Hare, Nathan 1934— **44**

Harewood, David 1965— **52**

Harewood, Dorian 1950— **104**

Harkless, Necia Desiree 1920— **19**

Harmon, Clarence 1940(?)— **26**

Harmon, Gordy See Whispers, The

Harold, Erika 1980(?)— **54**

Harold Melvin & the Blue Notes **105**

Harp, Toni 1949— **123**

Harper, Ben 1969— **34, 62**

Harper, Frances E(llen) W(atkins) 1825–1911 **11**

Harper, Frank See Harper, Hill

Harper, Hill 1966— **32, 65, 97**

Harper, Michael S. 1938–2016 **34, 136**

Harper, Rachel M. 1972— **92**

Harrell, Andre (O'Neal) 1962(?)— **9, 30**

Harrington, Carey Bell See Bell, Carey

Harrington, Oliver W. 1912–1995 **9, 136**

Harris, Addie See Shirelles, The

Harris, Alice 1934— **7**

Harris, Barbara 1930— **12**

Harris, Barry 1929— **68**

Harris, Bernard A. 1956— **90**

Harris, Bill See Clovers, The

Harris, Bill 1941— **72**

Harris, Bobby See Dazz Band

Harris, Carla A. 1962— **67**

Harris, Ciara Princess See Ciara

Harris, Claire 1937— **34**

Harris, Corey 1969— **39, 73**

Harris, Damon 1950–2013 **110**

Harris, E. Lynn 1955–2009 **12, 33, 116**

Harris, Eddy L. 1956— **18**

Harris, Franco 1950— **97**

Harris, Gary L. 1953— **87**

Harris, James 1947— **79**

Harris, James, III See Jimmy Jam

Harris, Jay **19**

Harris, Jessica B. 1948— **91**

Harris, Kamala D. 1964— **64, 122**

Harris, Kevin 1975— **120**

Harris, Leslie 1961— **6**

Harris, Lois See Chantels, The

Harris, Lorenzo See Harris, Rennie

Harris, Lyle Ashton 1965— **83**

Harris, Major 1947–2012 **110**

Harris, Marcelite Jordon 1943— **16**

Harris, Mary Styles 1949— **31**

Harris, Maya Lakshmi 1966— **88**

Harris, Monica 1968— **18**

Harris, Naomie 1976— **55, 116**

Harris, Otis Robert, Jr. See Harris, Damon

Harris, Patricia Roberts 1924–1985 **2**

Harris, R. H. See Soul Stirrers

Harris, Rennie 1964— **120**

Harris, Richard See Jive Five

Harris, Richard E. 1912(?)— **61**

Harris, Rhonda See Vanzant, Iyanla

Harris, Robin 1953–1990 **7**

Harris, Shack See Harris, James

Harris, Sherwin David See Harris, Wood

Harris, "Sweet" Alice See Harris, Alice

Harris, Sylvia 1967(?)— **70**

Harris, Thurston 1931–1990 **129**

Harris, Wesley L. 1941— **92**

Harris, William Anthony See Harris, Bill

Harris, Wood 1969— **114**

Harris, Wynonie 1915(?)–1969 **102**

Harris-Lacewell, Melissa 1973— **81**

Harrison, Alvin 1974— **28**

Harrison, Calvin 1974— **28**

Harrison, Charles 1931— **72**

Harrison, Marvin 1972— **134**

Harrison, Mya *See Mya*

Harris-Stewart, Lusia 1955— **90**

Harry, Jackée 1956— **111**

Harsh, Vivian Gordon 1890–1960 **14**

Hart, Alvin Youngblood 1963— **61, 132**

Hart, Billy 1940— **126**

Hart, Gregory Edward *See Hart, Alvin Youngblood*

Hart, Jim Ray 1941–2016 **136**

Hart, Kevin 1980— **103**

Hart, Thomas A., Sr. 1919–2013 **113**

Hartman, Johnny 1923–1983 **109**

Harvard, Beverly (Joyce Bailey) 1950— **11**

Harvey, Steve 1956— **18, 58**

Harvey, William R. 1941— **42**

Harvin, Percy 1988— **123**

Harvin, William Percival, III *See Harvin, Percy*

Haskins, Clem 1943— **23**

Haskins, James 1941–2005 **36, 54**

Hassell, Leroy Rountree, Sr. 1955–2011 **41, 116**

Hastie, William H(enry) 1904–1976 **8**

Hastings, Alcee 1936— **16, 119**

Hatcher, Andrew T. 1923–1990 **90**

Hatcher, Charles Edwin *See Starr, Edwin*

Hatcher, Richard G. 1933— **55**

Hatchett, Glenda 1951(?)— **32**

Hathaway, Donny 1945–1979 **18**

Hathaway, Isaac Scott 1874–1967 **33**

Hathaway, Lalah 1968— **57, 88**

Haughton, Aaliyah *See Aaliyah*

Havens, Richard Pierce *See Havens, Richie*

Havens, Richie 1941–2013 **111**

Hawes, Hampton 1928–1977 **121**

Hawkins, Adrienne Lita *See Kennedy, Adrienne*

Hawkins, Augustus F. 1907–2007 **68**

Hawkins, Barbara Ann *See Dixie Cups, The*

Hawkins, Coleman 1904–1969 **9**

Hawkins, Connie 1942— **91**

Hawkins, Edwin 1943— **113**

Hawkins, Erskine Ramsey 1914–1993 **14**

Hawkins, Jamesetta *See James, Etta*

Hawkins, La-Van 1960— **17, 54**

Hawkins, Rosa Lee *See Dixie Cups, The*

Hawkins, "Screamin'" Jay 1929–2000 **30**

Hawkins, Steven Wayne 1962— **14**

Hawkins, Tramaine Aunzola 1951— **16**

Hawkins, Walter 1949–2010 **87**

Hayanga, Awori *See Hayanga, Jeremiah*

Hayanga, Jeremiah 1974(?)— **118**

Hayden, Carla D. 1952— **47**

Hayden, Lewis 1811–1889 **105**

Hayden, Palmer 1890–1973 **13**

Hayden, Robert Earl 1913–1980 **12**

Haye, David 1980— **82**

Hayes, Bob 1942–2002 **77**

Hayes, Cecil N. 1945— **46**

Hayes, Dennis 1951— **54**

Hayes, Edwin *See Freestyle Fellowship*

Hayes, Elvin 1945— **93**

Hayes, Isaac 1942–2008 **20, 58, 73**

Hayes, James C. 1946— **10**

Hayes, Robert Lee *See Hayes, Bob*

Hayes, Roland 1887–1977 **4**

Hayes, Teddy 1951— **40**

Hayes, Terrance 1971— **124**

Haygood, Wil 1954— **83**

Haynes, Cornell, Jr. *See Nelly*

Haynes, Elizabeth Ross 1883–1953 **102**

Haynes, George Edmund 1880–1960 **8**

Haynes, Marques 1926— **22**

Haynes, Roy 1925— **87**

Haynes, Trudy 1926— **44**

Haynie, Sharon 1955— **94**

Haysbert, Dennis 1954— **42, 106**

Haysbert, Raymond V., Sr. 1920–2010 **87**

Haywood, Gar Anthony 1954— **43**

Haywood, Jimmy 1993(?)— **58**

Haywood, Margaret A. 1912— **24**

Haywood, Spencer 1949— **99**

Hazel, Darryl B. 1949— **50**

Hazzard, Walt 1942–2011 **98**

Hazziez, Joseph *See Tex, Joe*

Hazziez, Jusef *See Tex, Joe*

Hazziez, Yusef *See Tex, Joe*

Head, Bessie 1937–1986 **28**

Healy, James Augustine 1830–1900 **30**

Healy, Michael 1839–1904 **90**

Heard, Gar 1948— **25**

Heard, Nathan C. 1936–2004 **45**

Hearne, John Edgar Caulwell 1926–1994 **45**

Hearns, Thomas 1958— **29**

Heath, Percy 1923–2005 **100**

Heavy D 1967–2011 **58, 98**

Hector, Jamie 1975— **98**

Hedgeman, Anna Arnold 1899–1990 **22**

Hedgeman, Peyton Cole *See Hayden, Palmer*

Hegamin, Lucille 1894–1970 **120**

Height, Dorothy I. 1912— **2, 23, 78**

Hemingway, Anthony 1977— **107**

Hemphill, Essex 1957— **10**

Hemphill, Jessie Mae 1923–2006 **33, 59**

Hemsley, Sherman 1938–2012 **19, 104**

Henderson, Angelo 1962–2014 **122**

Henderson, Cornelius Langston 1888(?)–1976 **26**

Henderson, David 1942— **53**

Henderson, Fletcher 1897–1952 **32**

Henderson, George Washington 1850–1936 **101**

Henderson, Gordon 1957— **5**

Henderson, Harvey *See Bar-Kays, The*

Henderson, Henry Fairfax, Jr. 1928— **89**

Henderson, Jeff 1964— **72**

Henderson, Joe 1937–2001 **127**

Henderson, John William *See Homesick James*

Henderson, Natalie Leota *See Hinderas, Natalie*

Henderson, Rickey 1958— **28, 78**

Henderson, Stephen E. 1925–1997 **45**

Henderson, Thelton E. 1933— **68**

Henderson, Wade 1944(?)— **14**

Henderson, Wayne *See Crusaders, The*

Henderson, Zelma 1920–2008 **71**

Hendricks, Barbara 1948— **3, 67**

Hendrix, James Marshall *See Hendrix, Jimi*

Hendrix, Jimi 1942–1970 **10**

Hendrix, Johnny Allen *See Hendrix, Jimi*

Hendryx, Nona 1944— **56**

Hendy, Francis 195(?)— **47**

Henries, A. Doris Banks 1913–1981 **44**

Henriques, Julian 1955(?)— **37**

Henry, Aaron Edd 1922–1997 **19**

Henry, Clarence "Frogman" 1937— **46**

Henry, Dwight 1963— **104**

Henry, Joshua 1994— **94**

Henry, Lenny 1958— **9, 52**

Henry, Marianne *See Marian Anderson String Quartet*

Henry, Mark 1971— **116**

Henry, Richard Bullock *See Obadele, Imari*

Henry, Thierry 1977— **66, 127**

Henry, Troy 1960(?)— **85**

Henson, Darrin 1970(?)— **33**

Henson, Josiah 1789–1883 **90**

Henson, Matthew (Alexander) 1866–1955 **2**

Henson, Taraji P. 1970— **58, 77, 127**

Herbert, Bob 1945— **63, 96**

Hercules, Frank 1911–1996 **44**

Herenton, Willie W. 1940— **24, 81**

Herman, Alexis Margaret 1947— **15**

Hernandez, Aileen Clarke 1926— **13**

Hernández, Orlando 1965— **96**

Herndon, Alonzo Franklin 1858–1927 **89**

Herndon, Angelo 1913–1997 **90**

Herndon, Charlie *See New Birth*

Hernton, Calvin C. 1932–2001 **51**

Herzfeld, Will L. 1937–2002 **132**

Heyward, Craig 1966–2006 **131**

Heyward, Ironhead *See Heyward, Craig*

Hibbert, Frederick Nathaniel *See Hibbert, Toots*

Hibbert, Toots 1946— **103**

Hickman, Fred(erick Douglass) 1951— **11**

Hicks, Ulysses *See Five Keys, The*

Hicks-Hudson, Paula 1951— **136**

Hicks Maynard, Nancy *See Maynard, Nancy Hicks*

Higginbotham, A. Leon, Jr. 1928–1998 **13, 25**

Higginbotham, Jack *See Higginbotham, Jay C.*

Higginbotham, Jay C. 1906–1973 **37**

Higginbotham, Joan 1963— **124**

Higginbotham, Robert *See Tucker, Tommy*

Higginsen, Vy 1945(?)— **65**

Hightower, Dennis F(owler) 1941— **13**

Hightower, Rosetta *See Orlons, The*

Highway QC's, The **136**

Hill, Andrew 1931–2007 **66**

Hill, Anita 1956— **5, 65**

Hill, Beatrice *See Moore, Melba*

Hill, Bonnie Guiton 1941— **20**

Hill, Calvin 1947— **19**

Hill, Candace 1999— **130**

Hill, Darryl 1990— **128**

Hill, Donna 1955— **32**

Hill, Dulé 1975— **29, 129**

Hill, Errol 1921–2003 **40, 135**

Hill, Gil 1931–2016 **135**

Hill, Grant 1972— **13, 94**

Hill, Hugh Morgan 1921–2009 **83**

Hill, Janet 1947— **19**

Hill, Jemele 1975— **109**

Hill, Jesse, Jr. 1927— **13**

Hill, Lamar *See Treacherous Three*

Hill, Lauryn 1975— **20, 53, 111** *See also Fugees*

Hill, Leslie Pinckney 1880–1960 **44**

Hill, Marc Lamont 1978— **80, 128**

Hill, Michael 1971— **95**

Hill, Oliver W. 1907–2007 **24, 63**

Hill, Peter 1767–1829 **92**

Hill, Tamia *See Tamia*

Hill, Wyllstyne D. 1949(?)— **94**

Hillard, Terry 1954— **25**

Hillary, Barbara 1923(?)— **65**

Hilliard, Asa Grant, III 1933–2007 **66**

Hilliard, David 1942— **7, 105**

Hilliard, Earl F. 1942— **24**

Hilliard, Wendy 196(?)— **53**

Hilson, Keri 1982— **84**

Himes, Chester 1909–1984 **8**

Hinderas, Natalie 1927–1987 **5**

Hine, Darlene Clark 1947— **24**

Hines, Earl "Fatha" 1905–1983 **39**

Hines, Garrett 1969— **35**

Hines, Gregory (Oliver) 1946–2003 **1, 42**

Hinton, Milt 1910–2000 **30**

Hinton, William Augustus 1883–1959 **8**

Hoagland, Everett H. 1942— **45**

Hoagland, Jaheim *See Jaheim*

Hobson, Julius W. 1919–1977 **44**

Hobson, Mellody 1969— **40**

Hodge, Aldis 1986— **124**

Hodge, Derrick 1979— **114**

Hodges, Johnny 1907–1970 **129**

Hogan, Beverly Wade 1951— **50**

Hoggs, Billy *See Contours, The*

Holden, Kip 1952— **120**

Holden, Melvin *See Holden, Kip*

Holder, Eric, Jr. 1951— **9, 76, 104**

Holder, Geoffrey 1930–2014 **78, 124**

Holder, Laurence 1939— **34**

Holdsclaw, Chamique 1977— **24, 110**

Holiday, Billie 1915–1959 **1**

Holiday, Jrue 1990— **115**

Holland, Brian *See Holland-Dozier-Holland*

Holland, Clinton See Delta Rhythm Boys

Holland, Eddie See Holland-Dozier-Holland

Holland, Endesha Ida Mae 1944–2006 **3, 57**

Holland, Kimberly N. 19(?)(?)— **62**

Holland, Robert, Jr. 1940— **11**

Holland-Dozier-Holland **36**

Hollins, Lionel 1953— **133**

Holloway, Brenda 1946— **65**

Holloway, Loleatta 1946–2011 **115**

Hollowell, Donald L. 1917–2004 **57**

Holmes, Amy 1973— **69**

Holmes, Benjamin See Fisk Jubilee Singers

Holmes, Clint 1946— **57**

Holmes, De'Angelo See Ying Yang Twins

Holmes, Hamilton E. 1941–1995 **82**

Holmes, Kelly 1970— **47**

Holmes, Larry 1949— **20, 68**

Holmes, Loutelious Ann, Jr. See Holmes, T. J.

Holmes, Santonio 1984— **87**

Holmes, Shannon 1973(?)— **70**

Holmes, T. J. 1977— **98**

Holness, Andrew 1972— **99**

Holsey, Lucius Henry 1842–1920 **92**

Holstein, Casper 1876–1944 **89**

Holt, Lester 1959— **66**

Holt, Morris See Magic Slim

Holt, Nora 1885(?)–1974 **38**

Holt Baker, Arlene 1951— **73**

Holte, Patricia Louise See LaBelle, Patti

Holton, DeShaun Dupree See Proof

Holton, Hugh, Jr. 1947–2001 **39**

Holyfield, Evander 1962— **6**

Homesick James 1910(?)–2006 **124**

Honeywood, Varnette P. 1950–2010 **54, 88**

Honoré, Russel L. 1947— **64**

Hood, James Walker 1831–1918 **91**

Hooker, John Lee 1917–2000 **30**

hooks, bell 1952— **5, 90**

Hooks, Benjamin L. 1925–2010 **2, 85**

Hooks, Robert 1937— **76**

Hooper, Stix See Crusaders, The

Hope, Elmo 1923–1967 **135**

Hope, John 1868–1936 **8**

Hope, Lugenia Burns 1871–1947 **89**

Hope, St. Elmo Sylvester See Hope, Elmo

Hopgood, Hadda See Brooks, Hadda

Hopkins, Bernard 1965— **35, 69, 105**

Hopkins, Donald R. 1941— **89**

Hopkins, Lightnin' 1912–1982 **83**

Hopkins, Sam See Hopkins, Lightnin'

Horford, Al 1988— **107**

Horford Reynoso, Alfred Joel See Horford, Al

Horn, Shirley 1934–2005 **32, 56**

Horne, Frank 1899–1974 **44**

Horne, Lena 1917–2010 **5, 86**

Horsford, Steven 1973— **88**

Horsley, Richie See Ray, Goodman & Brown

Horton, Andre 1979— **33**

Horton, Big Walter 1918(?)–1981 **115** See also Memphis Jug Band

Horton, George Moses 1798(?)–1883(?) **124**

Horton, Gladys 1945–2011 **92** See also Marvelettes, The

Horton, James Oliver 1943— **58**

Horton, (Andreana) Suki 1982— **33**

Horton, Walter See Horton, Big Walter

Horton, Willie 1942— **104**

Hoskins, Harold K. 1927–2012 **103**

Houghton, Israel 1971— **92**

Hounsou, Djimon 1964— **19, 45**

Houphouët, Dia See Houphouët-Boigny, Félix

Houphouët-Boigny, Félix 1905–1993 **4, 64**

House, Eddie James, Jr. See House, Son

House, Eugene See House, Son

House, Son 1902–1988 **8**

Houston, Charles Hamilton 1895–1950 **4**

Houston, Cissy 1933— **20, 83**

Houston, Jordan Michael See Juicy J

Houston, Whitney 1963–2012 **7, 28, 83, 100**

Howard, Ayanna 1972— **65**

Howard, Corinne See Mitchell, Corinne

Howard, Desmond 1970— **16, 58**

Howard, Dwight 1985— **113**

Howard, Elston 1929–1980 **125**

Howard, Juwan Antonio 1973— **15**

Howard, M. William, Jr. 1946— **26**

Howard, Michelle 1960— **28, 125**

Howard, Perry Wilbon, Jr. 1877–1961 **112**

Howard, Ryan 1979— **65, 113**

Howard, Sherri 1962— **36**

Howard, Terrence 1969— **59, 94**

Howard, William See Dramatics, The

Howell, Ayinde 1978— **91**

Howlin' Wolf 1910–1976 **9**

Howroyd, Janice Bryant 1953— **42**

Hoyte, Lenon 1905–1999 **50**

Hrabowski, Freeman A., III 1950— **22**

Hubbard, Arnette 19(?)(?)— **38**

Hubbard, Freddie 1948–2008 **75**

Hubbard, Frederick DeWayne See Hubbard, Freddie

Huddleston, William Emanuel See Lateef, Yusef

Hudlin, Reginald 1961— **9, 86**

Hudlin, Warrington, Jr. 1953(?)— **9**

Hudson, Cheryl 19(?)(?)— **15**

Hudson, Ernie 1945— **72, 131**

Hudson, James See Spaniels, The

Hudson, Jennifer 1981— **63, 83**

Hudson, Lou 1944–2014 **121**

Hudson, Louis Clyde See Hudson, Lou

Hudson, Saul See Slash

Hudson, Wade 1946— **15**

Huff, Leon 1942— **86**

Huggins, Edie 1935–2008 **71**

Huggins, Larry 1950— **21**

Huggins, Nathan Irvin 1927–1989 **52**

Hughes, Albert 1972— **7**

Hughes, Allen 1972— **7**

Hughes, Cathy 1947(?)— **27**

Hughes, Dora 1970(?)— **88**

Hughes, Ebony 1948— **57**

Hughes, (James Mercer) Langston 1902–1967 **4**

Hughes, Leon See Coasters, The

Hughley, D. L. 1963— **23, 76**

Hughley, Darryl Lynn See Hughley, D. L.

Hull, Akasha Gloria 1944— **45**

Humes, Helen 1913–1981 **128**

Humphrey, Bobbi 1950— **20**

Humphrey, Claude 1944— **119**

Humphries, Frederick 1935— **20**

Hundley, Mandisa Lynn See Mandisa

Hunt, Darnell 1962— **92**

Hunt, Richard (Howard) 1935— **6**

Hunter, Alberta 1895–1984 **42**

Hunter, Billy 1942— **22, 109**

Hunter, Charlayne See Hunter-Gault, Charlayne

Hunter, Clementine 1887–1988 **45**

Hunter, George William See Hunter, Billy

Hunter, Ivory Joe 1914–1974 **106**

Hunter, Lindsey 1970— **110**

Hunter, Torii 1975— **43, 109**

Hunter-Gault, Charlayne 1942— **6, 31**

Hurd, Sam 1985— **116**

Hurley, Earl See Swallows, The

Hurst, Michelle 1942— **135**

Hurston, Zora Neale 1891–1960 **3**

Hurt, Byron 1970— **61**

Hurt, Mississippi John 1892(?)–1966 **84**

Hurtt, Harold 1947(?)— **46**

Hussein, Lubna 1970(?)— **80**

Hutch, Willie 1944–2005 **62**

Hutcherson, Bobby 1941— **115**

Hutcherson, Hilda Yvonne 1955— **54**

Hutchinson, Earl Ofari 1945— **24**

Hutchinson, Jeanette See Emotions, The

Hutchinson, Pamela See Emotions, The

Hutchinson, Sheila See Emotions, The

Hutchinson, Wanda See Emotions, The

Hutson, Jean Blackwell 1914–1998 **16, 135**

Hutson, Leroy See Impressions, The

Hutson, Marcus See Whispers, The

Hutto, J. B. 1926–1983 **129**

Hutto, Joseph Benjamin See Hutto, J. B.

Hyde, Cowan F. "Bubba" 1908–2003 **47**

Hyman, Earle 1926— **25, 79**

Hyman, Phyllis 1949(?)–1995 **19**

Ibrahim, Abdullah 1934— **131**

Ibrahim, Fuad 1991— **109**

Ibrahim, Ibee See Ibrahim, Fuad

Ibrahim, Mo 1946— **67, 115**

Ice Cube 1969— **8, 30, 60**

Iceberg Slim 1918–1992 **11**

Ice-T 1958— **6, 31, 96**

Ifill, Gwen 1955— **28**

Iginla, Jarome 1977— **35**

Iglehart, James Monroe 1974— **129**

Iguodala, Andre 1984— **129**

Ilibagiza, Immaculée 1972(?)— **66**

Iluobe, Christopher Airemiokhai See Aire, Chris

Iman 1955— **4, 33, 87**

Iman, Chanel 1989— **66**

Imani See Pharcyde, The

Imani Winds **113**

Imes, Elmer Samuel 1883–1941 **39**

Impressions, The **135**

Ince, Paul 1967— **83**

India.Arie 1975— **34**

Ingraham, Hubert A. 1947— **19**

Ingram, James 1952— **84**

Ingram, Raphael See Five Keys, The

Ingram, Rex 1895–1969 **5**

Ingram, Ripley See Five Keys, The

Ink Spots, The **102**

Innis, Niger 1968— **135**

Innis, Roy (Emile Alfredo) 1934— **5**

Intruders, The **119**

Irvin, Hubert Merrill See Irvin, Monte

Irvin, Michael 1966— **64**

Irvin, Monford Merrill See Irvin, Monte

Irvin, Monte 1919–2016 **31, 134**

Irvin, Vernon 1961— **65**

Irving, Barrington, Jr. 1983— **112**

Irving, Clarence (Larry) 1955— **12**

Irving, Kyrie 1992— **102**

Irvis, K. Leroy 1917(?)–2006 **67**

Isaac, Julius 1928— **34**

Isaacs, Cheryl Boone 1949— **113**

Isaacs, Gregory 1951–2010 **89**

Isaacs, John 1915–2009 **76**

Isles, Bill See O'Jays, The

Isley, Marvin 1953–2010 **87**

Isley, Ronald 1941— **25, 56**

Issoufou, Mahamadou 1952— **102**

Iverson, Allen 1975— **24, 46, 129**

Iverson, Johnathan Lee 1976— **22, 100**

Ivey, Artis, Jr. See Coolio

Ivey, Phil 1976— **72, 106**

Iweala, Uzodinma 1982— **131**

J Dilla 1974–2006 **102**

Ja Rule 1976— **35, 91**

Jackée See Harry, Jackée

Jackson, Alexine Clement 1936— **22**

Jackson, Angela 1951— **134**

Jackson, Alphonso R. 1946— **48**

Jackson, Benjamin Clarence See Jackson, Bull Moose

Jackson, Bobby 1956–2013 **119**

Jackson, Brenda 1953— **87**

Jackson, Bull Moose 1919–1989 **130**

Jackson, Christopher 1975— **136**

Jackson, Deborah 1952— **94**

Jackson, DeSean 1986— **120**

Jackson, Earl 1948— **31**

Jackson, Edison O. 1943(?)— **67**

Jackson, Eric 1959— **127**

Jackson, Eric, Jr. See Ying Yang Twins

Jackson, Frank G. 1946— **76**

Jackson, Fred James 1950— **25**

Jackson, George 1960(?)— **19**

Jackson, George Lester 1941–1971 **14**

Jackson, Hal 1915–2012 **41, 104**

Jackson, Henry Melody, Jr. *See Armstrong, Henry*

Jackson, Hue 1965— **133**

Jackson, Isaiah (Allen) 1945— **3**

Jackson, Jackie *See Jackson 5*

Jackson, Jamea 1986— **64**

Jackson, James A. 1878–1960 **90**

Jackson, James Curtis, III *See 50 Cent*

Jackson, Janet 1966— **6, 30, 68**

Jackson, Jennie *See Fisk Jubilee Singers*

Jackson, Jermaine 1954— **79** *See also Jackson 5*

Jackson, Jesse 1941— **1, 27, 72**

Jackson, Jesse, Jr. 1965— **14, 45, 81, 108**

Jackson, Jimmie Lee 1938–1965 **126**

Jackson, Joe 1929— **78**

Jackson, John 1924–2002 **36**

Jackson, John David *See Fabolous*

Jackson, Judith D. 1950— **57**

Jackson, Keenon Daequan Ray *See YG*

Jackson, Laurence Donald *See Baby Laurence*

Jackson, Lisa 1962— **77**

Jackson, Mae 1941–2005 **57**

Jackson, Mahalia 1911–1972 **5**

Jackson, Mannie 1939— **14**

Jackson, Mark 1965— **121**

Jackson, Marlon *See Jackson 5*

Jackson, Mary 1945— **73**

Jackson, Maynard 1938–2003 **2, 41**

Jackson, Michael 1958–2009 **19, 53, 76** *See also Jackson 5*

Jackson, Millie 1944— **25**

Jackson, Milt 1923–1999 **26**

Jackson, O'Shea *See Ice Cube*

Jackson, Otis, Jr. *See Madlib*

Jackson, Phillip 1950— **115**

Jackson, Quinton *See Jackson, Rampage*

Jackson, Rampage 1978— **83**

Jackson, Randy 1956— **40**

Jackson, Reginald Martinez 1946— **15**

Jackson, Rickey 1958— **88**

Jackson, Robert *See New Birth*

Jackson, Samuel L. 1948— **8, 19, 63, 102**

Jackson, Sandi 1963— **108**

Jackson, Sheneska 1970(?)— **18**

Jackson, Shirley Ann 1946— **12**

Jackson, Stephen 1978— **118**

Jackson, Tito 1953— **81** *See also Jackson 5*

Jackson, Tom 1951— **70**

Jackson, Vera 1912— **40**

Jackson, Vivian *See Yabby You*

Jackson, Willie *See Spaniels, The*

Jackson, Zelda Mavin *See Ormes, Jackie*

Jackson 5 **103**

Jackson Lee, Sheila 1950— **20**

Jaco, Wasalu Muhammad *See Fiasco, Lupe*

Jacob, John E(dward) 1934— **2**

Jacobs, George 1927–2013 **118**

Jacobs, Harriet 1813–1897 **104**

Jacobs, Marion Walter *See Little Walter*

Jacobs, Regina 1963— **38**

Jacquet, Illinois 1922(?)–2004 **49**

Jagan, Cheddi 1918–1997 **16**

Jagged Edge **117**

Jaheim 1978— **58**

Jakes, T. D. 1957— **17, 43, 116**

Jakes, Thomas Dexter *See Jakes, T. D.*

Jalade-Ekeinde, Omotola 1978— **118**

Jam, Jimmy *See Jimmy Jam*

Jam Master Jay *See Run-DMC*

Jamal, Ahmad 1930— **69**

Jamelia 1981— **51**

Jamerson, James 1936–1983 **59**

James, Charles H., III 1959(?)— **62**

James, Daniel "Chappie," Jr. 1920–1978 **16**

James, David 1970— **84**

James, Donna A. 1957— **51**

James, Elmo *See James, Elmore*

James, Elmore 1918–1963 **114**

James, Etta 1938–2012 **13, 52, 100**

James, G. Larry 1947–2008 **74**

James, Juanita (Therese) 1952— **13**

James, LaRon Louis *See Santana, Juelz*

James, LeBron 1984— **46, 78, 105**

James, Leela 1983— **117**

James, Marlon 1970— **85, 124**

James, Nikki M. 1981— **94**

James, Sharpe 1936— **23, 69**

James, Skip 1902–1969 **38**

James, Sly 1951— **107**

James, Sylvester, Jr. *See James, Sly*

James, Vanessa 1987— **84**

James & Bobby Purify **131**

James Bracken and Vivian Bracken **107**

Jamison, Judith 1943— **7, 67, 96**

Jammeh, Yahya 1965— **23, 104**

Jansen, Jonathan 1956— **102**

Jaojoby 1955— **130**

Jarman, Joseph 1937— **136**

Jarreau, Al 1940— **21, 65, 105**

Jarreau, Alwyn Lopez *See Jarreau, Al*

Jarrett, Valerie 1956— **73**

Jarrett, Vernon D. 1918–2004 **42, 135**

Jarvis, Charlene Drew 1941— **21**

Jarvis, Erich 1965— **67**

Jarvis, Kristen 1981(?)— **85**

Jasper, John J. 1812–1901 **91**

Jasper, Kenji 1976(?)— **39**

Jawara, Dawda Kairaba 1924— **11**

Jawara, Jali Musa *See Diawara, Djeli Moussa*

Jay Electronica 1976— **125**

Jay-Z 1969— **27, 69, 103**

Jazz Crusaders, The *See Crusaders, The*

Jealous, Benjamin Todd 1973— **70, 113**

Jean, Michaëlle 1957— **70**

Jean, Wyclef 1970— **20, 86** *See also Fugees*

Jean-Baptiste, Kyle 1993–2015 **131**

Jean-Baptiste, Marianne 1967— **17, 46**

Jean-Juste, Gérard 1946–2009 **78**

Jean-Louis, Jimmy 1968— **76**

Jeffers, Eve Jihan *See Eve*

Jefferson, Blind Lemon 1893(?)–1929 **81**

Jefferson, Denise 1944–2010 **87**

Jefferson, Margo 1947— **108**

Jefferson, Mildred Fay 1927–2010 **89**

Jefferson, Richard 1980— **136**

Jefferson, William J. 1947— **25, 72**

Jeffrey, Herbert *See Jeffries, Herb*

Jeffries, Hakeem 1970— **118**

Jeffries, Herb 1913(?)–2014 **122**

Jeffries, Leonard 1937— **8**

Jemison, Mae C. 1956— **1, 35, 129**

Jemison, Major L. 1955(?)— **48**

Jemison, T. J. 1918–2013 **119**

Jemison, Theodore Judson *See Jemison, T. J.*

Jenifer, Franklyn G(reen) 1939— **2**

Jenkins, Beverly 1951— **14**

Jenkins, Chad 1975— **132**

Jenkins, Ella 1924— **15**

Jenkins, Fergie 1943— **46**

Jenkins, Hubby *See Carolina Chocolate Drops*

Jenkins, Jay *See Young Jeezy*

Jenkins, Kris 1979— **98**

Jenkins, Ray 1920–2009 **77**

Jenkins, Terrence *See Terrence J*

Jenkins, Tomi *See Cameo*

Jennings, Chester *See Jennings, Lyfe*

Jennings, Lyfe 1973— **56, 69**

Jennings, Thomas L. 1791–1859 **125**

Jeptoo, Rita 1981— **121**

Jerkins, Rodney 1978(?)— **31**

Jesu, Kunjoya Mwa *See Malawi Mouse Boys*

Jeter, Claude 1914–2009 **75** *See also Swan Silvertones*

Jeter, Derek 1974— **27, 93, 124**

Jeune, Vitolio 1982— **98**

Jim, Songezo 1990— **111**

Jimmy Jam 1959— **13**

Jive Five **131**

Joachim, Paulin 1931— **34**

Jobe, Duke *See Rose Royce*

Jobe, Lequeint *See Rose Royce*

Joe, Yolanda 19(?)(?)— **21**

Johanneson, Albert 1940(?)–1995 **129**

John, Daymond 1969— **23, 114**

Johns, Vernon 1892–1965 **38**

Johnson, Al 1948–2013 **119**

Johnson, Alaya Dawn 1982— **129**

Johnson, Alfred Orlando, Jr. *See Johnson, Al*

Johnson, Andre *See Rare Essence*

Johnson, Andre 1981— **127**

Johnson, Angela 1961— **52**

Johnson, Anthony M. 1954— **92**

Johnson, Arnez *See Arnez J*

Johnson, Avery 1965— **62**

Johnson, Ben 1961— **1**

Johnson, Beverly 1952— **2, 102**

Johnson, Blind Willie 1897(?)–1945 **136**

Johnson, Buddy 1915–1977 **36**

Johnson, Bumpy 1905(?)–1968 **102**

Johnson, Calvin 1985— **108**

Johnson, Camará DaCosta *See DaCosta, YaYa*

Johnson, Carol Diann *See Carroll, Diahann*

Johnson, Caryn E. *See Goldberg, Whoopi*

Johnson, Chad 1978— **108**

Johnson, Charles 1948— **1, 82**

Johnson, Charles Arthur *See St. Jacques, Raymond*

Johnson, Charles Spurgeon 1893–1956 **12**

Johnson, Chris 1985— **92**

Johnson, Clarence *See Chi-Lites*

Johnson, Clark 1954— **96**

Johnson, Clifford "Connie" 1922–2004 **52**

Johnson, Conrad O. 1915–2008 **97**

Johnson, Dennis 1954–2007 **89**

Johnson, Donald Ray *See Taste of Honey, A*

Johnson, Dwayne *See Rock, The*

Johnson, Earvin *See Johnson, Magic*

Johnson, Eddie Bernice 1935— **8, 90**

Johnson, Edward Austin 1860–1944 **107**

Johnson, Ellsworth Raymond *See Johnson, Bumpy*

Johnson, Eunice W. 1916–2010 **83**

Johnson, Fenton 1888–1958 **91**

Johnson, Frederick *See Swallows, The*

Johnson, George *See Brothers Johnson*

Johnson, George E. 1927— **29**

Johnson, Georgia Douglas 1880–1966 **41**

Johnson, Gus 1913–2000 **132**

Johnson, Gus 1938–1987 **92**

Johnson, Hall 1888–1970 **90**

Johnson, Hank, Jr. 1954— **80**

Johnson, Harry E. 1954— **57**

Johnson, Harvey, Jr. 1947(?)— **24, 82**

Johnson, Hazel 1927— **22**

Johnson, Henry 1897(?)–1929 **129**

Johnson, Hubert *See Contours, The*

Johnson, J. J. 1924–2001 **37**

Johnson, J. Rosamond 1873–1954 **121**

Johnson, Jack 1878–1946 **8**

Johnson, James *See Drifters, The*

Johnson, James Louis *See Johnson, J. J.*

Johnson, James P. 1894–1955 **134**

Johnson, James Weldon 1871–1938 **5**

Johnson, James William *See Johnson, James Weldon*

Johnson, Janice Marie *See Taste of Honey, A*

Johnson, Je'Caryous 1977— **63**

Johnson, Jeh 1957— **76, 125**

Johnson, Jeh Vincent 1931— **44**

Johnson, Joan Marie *See Dixie Cups, The*

Johnson, Joe *See Golden Gate Quartet*

Johnson, Joe 1981— **94**

Johnson, John Arthur *See Johnson, Jack*

Johnson, John H. 1918–2005 **3, 54**

Johnson, John Henry 1929–2011 **96**

Johnson, John Rosamond *See Johnson, J. Rosamond*

Johnson, Johnnie 1924–2005 **56**

Johnson, Judy 1899–1989 **105**

Johnson, Katherine (Coleman Goble) 1918— **61**

Johnson, Ken 1914–1941 **106**

Johnson, Kevin 1966— **70, 132**

Johnson, Keyshawn 1972— **91**

Johnson, Larry 1969— **28**

Johnson, Le'Andria 1983— **108**

Johnson, Leroy R. 1928— **89**

Johnson, Levi 1950— **48**

Johnson, Linton Kwesi 1952— **37**

Johnson, Lonnie 1899(?)–1970 **85**

Johnson, Lonnie G. 1949— **32, 93**

Johnson, Louis *See Brothers Johnson*

Johnson, Louis *See Swan Silvertones, The*

Johnson, Magic 1959— **3, 39, 101**

Johnson, Mamie "Peanut" 1932— **40**

Johnson, Marguerite *See Angelou, Maya*

Johnson, Marques 1956— **133**

Johnson, Mat 1970— **31, 105**

Johnson, Michael (Duane) 1967— **13**

Johnson, Michelle *See Ndegeocello, Meshell*

Johnson, Money *See Swallows, The*

Johnson, Mordecai Wyatt 1890–1976 **79**

Johnson, Norma H. 1932–2011 **17, 97**

Johnson, Norman *See Jive Five*

Johnson, R. M. 1968— **36**

Johnson, Rafer 1934— **33**

Johnson, Ralph *See Impressions, The*

Johnson, Robert 1911–1938 **2**

Johnson, Robert L. 1946— **3, 39, 121**

Johnson, Robert T. 1948— **17**

Johnson, Rodney Van 19(?)(?)— **28**

Johnson, Sandra K. 1960(?)— **94**

Johnson, Sheila Crump 1949(?)— **48**

Johnson, Shoshana 1973— **47**

Johnson, Stan *See Crown Heights Affair*

Johnson, Sterling, Jr. 1934— **124**

Johnson, Syl 1938— **97**

Johnson, Syleena 1977— **98**

Johnson, Taalib *See Musiq*

Johnson, Tommy 1896–1956 **106**

Johnson, Virginia (Alma Fairfax) 1950— **9**

Johnson, William 1809–1851 **91**

Johnson, William Henry 1901–1970 **3**

Johnson, William Julius *See Johnson, Judy*

Johnson, Willie *See Golden Gate Quartet*

Johnson, Woodrow Wilson *See Johnson, Buddy*

Johnson, Wycliffe *See Steely*

Johnson-Brown, Hazel W. *See Johnson, Hazel*

Johnson-George, Tamara 1971— **79**

Johnson-Powell, Gloria 1937— **107**

Joiner, Alvin Nathaniel *See Xzibit*

Joiner, Charlie 1947— **102**

Jolicoeur, David Jude *See De La Soul*

Jolley, Willie 1956— **28**

Jonathan, Goodluck 1957— **83**

Jones, Absalom 1746–1818 **52**

Jones, Adam 1983— **103**

Jones, Adam 1985— **114**

Jones, Alex 1941— **64**

Jones, Andruw 1977— **98**

Jones, Anthony *See Jones, Van*

Jones, Bill T. 1952— **1, 46, 80**

Jones, Bob *See Jones, Robert G.*

Jones, Bobby 1938— **20, 94**

Jones, Bomani 1980— **121**

Jones, Booker T. 1944— **84**

Jones, Carl *See Delta Rhythm Boys*

Jones, Carl 1955(?)— **7**

Jones, Caroline R. 1942— **29**

Jones, Charles *See Highway QC's, The*

Jones, Clara Stanton 1913–2012 **51**

Jones, Clarence B. 1931— **114**

Jones, Cobi N'Gai 1970— **18**

Jones, Creadel *See Chi-Lites*

Jones, Cullen 1984— **73**

Jones, Daron *See* **112**

Jones, David D. *See Jones, Deacon*

Jones, Deacon 1938–2013 **92, 112**

Jones, Donell 1973— **29**

Jones, Doris W. 1914(?)–2006 **62**

Jones, Dwight C. 1948— **122**

Jones, E. Edward, Sr. 1931— **45**

Jones, Ed "Too Tall" 1951— **46**

Jones, Eddie Lee *See Guitar Slim*

Jones, Edith Mae Irby 1927— **65**

Jones, Edward P. 1950— **43, 67**

Jones, Elaine R. 1944— **7, 45**

Jones, Elvin 1927–2004 **14, 68**

Jones, Emil, Jr. 1935— **74**

Jones, Etta 1928–2001 **35**

Jones, Eugene Kinckle 1885–1954 **79**

Jones, Frederick McKinley 1893–1961 **68**

Jones, Frederick Russell *See Jamal, Ahmad*

Jones, Gayl 1949— **37**

Jones, Genevieve 1975(?)— **101**

Jones, Hank 1918–2010 **57, 86**

Jones, Ingrid Saunders 1945— **18**

Jones, Jacoby 1984— **117**

Jones, James Earl 1931— **3, 49, 79**

Jones, James Earl, III *See S.O.S. Band*

Jones, James Yancy *See Tail Dragger*

Jones, Jo *See Jones, Papa Jo*

Jones, John *See Rare Essence*

Jones, John 1816–1879 **89**

Jones, Jon 1987— **121**

Jones, Jonah 1909–2000 **39**

Jones, Jonathan David Samuel *See Jones, Papa Jo*

Jones, Joseph Rudolph *See Jones, Philly Joe*

Jones, Julio 1989— **131**

Jones, K. C. 1932— **83**

Jones, Kelis *See Kelis*

Jones, Kimberly Denise *See Lil' Kim*

Jones, Kirk *See Sticky Fingaz*

Jones, LeRoi *See Baraka, Amiri*

Jones, Leslie 1967— **136**

Jones, Lillie Mae *See Carter, Betty*

Jones, Loïs Mailou 1905–1998 **13, 136**

Jones, Lou 1932–2006 **64**

Jones, Malik Yusef *See Yusef, Malik*

Jones, Marion 1975— **21, 66**

Jones, Marvin *See Highway QC's, The*

Jones, Merlakia 1973— **34**

Jones, Monty 1951(?)— **66**

Jones, Nasir bin Olu Dara *See Nas*

Jones, Ollie *See Ravens, The*

Jones, Orlando 1968— **30**

Jones, Orville *See Ink Spots, The*

Jones, Papa Jo 1911–1985 **99**

Jones, Paul R. 1928— **76**

Jones, Phalon *See Bar-Kays, The*

Jones, Philly Joe 1923–1985 **121**

Jones, Quincy 1933— **8, 30**

Jones, Quintorris Lopez *See Jones, Julio*

Jones, Randy 1969— **35**

Jones, Rashida 1976— **101**

Jones, Robbie 1977— **113**

Jones, Robert Elijah 1872–1960 **90**

Jones, Robert Elliott *See Jones, Jonah*

Jones, Robert G. 1936–2008 **81**

Jones, Roy, Jr. 1969— **22, 134**

Jones, Russell *See Ol' Dirty Bastard*

Jones, Ruth Lee *See Washington, Dinah*

Jones, Sam 1933— **85**

Jones, Sarah 1974— **39**

Jones, Sharon 1955(?)— **86**

Jones, Sissieretta *See Joyner, Matilda Sissieretta*

Jones, Star *See Reynolds, Star Jones*

Jones, Tayari 1970— **96**

Jones, Thad 1923–1986 **68**

Jones, Theodore T., Jr. 1944–2012 **108**

Jones, Thomas W. 1949— **41**

Jones, Van 1968— **70**

Jones, Walter 1974— **119**

Jones, Wayne 1952— **53**

Jones, William A., Jr. 1934–2006 **61**

Jones-Drew, Maurice 1985— **113**

Joplin, Scott 1868–1917 **6**

Jordan, Barbara 1936–1996 **4, 78**

Jordan, Charles 1937–2014 **122**

Jordan, Deloris 1941— **108**

Jordan, Duke 1922–2006 **133**

Jordan, Eddie 1952— **82**

Jordan, Eddie 1955— **83**

Jordan, Eric Benét *See Benét, Eric*

Jordan, Irving Sidney *See Jordan, Duke*

Jordan, June 1936— **7, 35**

Jordan, Louis 1908–1975 **104**

Jordan, Michael 1963— **6, 21**

Jordan, Michael B. 1987— **97**

Jordan, Montell 1968(?)— **23**

Jordan, Ronny 1962— **26**

Jordan, Vernon E(ulion, Jr.) 1935— **3, 35**

Jorge, Seu 1970— **73**

Joseph, Edward *See Joseph, Jamal*

Joseph, Jamal 1953— **101**

Joseph, Kathie-Ann 1970(?)— **56**

Joseph, Paterson 1964— **126**

Josey, E. J. 1924— **10**

Joyce, Dru 1955— **81**

Joyner, Jacqueline *See Joyner-Kersee, Jackie*

Joyner, Marjorie Stewart 1896–1994 **26**

Joyner, Matilda Sissieretta 1869(?)–1933 **15**

Joyner, Tom 1949(?)— **19, 90**

Joyner-Kersee, Jackie 1962— **5**

J-Swift *See Pharcyde, The*

Juicy J 1975— **116**

Julian, Hubert 1897–1983 **90**

Julian, Percy Lavon 1899–1975 **6**

Julien, Isaac 1960— **3**

July, William, II 19(?)(?)— **27**

Juma, Calestous 1953— **57**

Junior, Marvin *See Dells, The*

Just, Ernest Everett 1883–1941 **3**

Justice, David Christopher 1966— **18**

Juvenile 1975— **96**

Ka Dinizulu, Israel *See Ka Dinizulu, Mcwayizeni*

Ka Dinizulu, Mcwayizeni 1932–1999 **29**

Kabbah, Ahmad Tejan 1932— **23**

Kabera, Eric 1970— **104**

Kabila, Joseph 1971— **30, 126**

Kabila, Laurent 1939— **20**

Kaboré, Roch Marc Christian 1957— **132**

Kachinwe, Zondiwe *See Malawi Mouse Boys*

Kafando, Michel 1942— **131**

Kagame, Paul 1957— **54**

Kahlil, Aisha *See Sweet Honey in the Rock*

Kahora, Billy 197(?)— **125**

Kaigler, Denise 1962— **63**

Kaine *See Ying Yang Twins*

Kaiser, Cecil 1916–2011 **42**

Kaka, Luthando 1986— **118**

Kalbani, Adil 1959(?)— **77**

Kamau, Johnstone *See Kenyatta, Jomo*

Kamau, Kwadwo Agymah 1960(?)— **28**

Kamworor, Geoffrey 1992— **134**

Kandi 1976— **83**

Kane, Evander 1991— **97**

Kani, Karl 1968(?)— **10**

Kanouté, Fred 1977— **68**

Karenga, Maulana 1941— **10, 71**

Karim, Benjamin 1932–2005 **61**

Karim-Ali, Mahershalalhashbaz *See Ali, Mahershala*

Kariuki, J. M. 1929–1975 **67**

Kassahun, Tewodros *See Afro, Teddy*

Kato, David 1964–2011 **103**

Katoucha *See Niane, Katoucha*

Katumbi, Moïse 1964— **135**

Kaufman, Bob 1925–1986 **105**

Kaufman, Monica 1948(?)— **66**

Kaufman, Robert Garnell *See Kaufman, Bob*

Kaunda, Kenneth (David) 1924— **2**

Kay, Connie 1927–1994 **114**

Kay, Jackie 1961— **37**

Kay, Ulysses 1917–1995 **37**

Kayira, Legson 1942— **40**

KB 1988— **122**

Kearney, Beverly 1958— **109**

Kearney, Janis 1953— **54**

Kearse, Amalya Lyle 1937— **12**

Keaton, Kevin *See Treacherous Three*

Keb' Mo', 1951— **36, 124**

Kebede, Liya 1978— **59**

Keckley, Elizabeth 1818–1907 **90**

Kee, John P. 1962— **43, 116+**

Keenan, Brian *See Chambers Brothers, The*

Keene, John 1965— **73**

Keflezighi, Meb 1975— **49, 121**

Keïta, Ibrahim Boubacar 1945— **113**

Keita, Salif 1949— **83**

Keïta, Seydou 1921(?)–2001 **124**

Keith, Damon J. 1922— **16, 74**

Keith, Floyd A. 1948— **61**

Keith, Michael *See 112*

Keith, Rachel Boone 1924–2007 **63**

Kelela 1983— **132**

Kelis 1979— **58, 122**

Kelley, Cliff 1941— **75**

Kelley, Elijah 1986— **65**

Kelley, Kenny *See Manhattans, The*

Kelley, Malcolm David 1992— **59**

Kellogg, Clark 1961— **64**

Kelly, Chris *See Mac Daddy*

Kelly, Jim 1946–2013 **113**

Kelly, Leontine 1920— **33**

Kelly, Patrick 1954(?)–1990 **3**

Kelly, R. 1967— **18, 44, 71, 117**

Kelly, Robert *See Kelly, R.*

Kelly, Robin 1956— **114**

Kelly, Sharon Pratt *See Dixon, Sharon Pratt*

Kelly, Winzell *See Dramatics, The*

Kelly, Wynton 1931–1971 **121**

KEM 1969— **47, 127**

Kemp, Herb 1941–2011 **94**

Kendrick, Erika 1975— **57**

Kendricks, Eddie 1939–1992 **22**

Kennard, William Earl 1957— **18**

Kennedy, Adrienne 1931— **11**

Kennedy, Cortez 1968— **104**

Kennedy, Florynce Rae 1916–2000 **12, 33**

Kennedy, Hershall *See Graham Central Station*

Kennedy, Lelia McWilliams Robinson 1885–1931 **14**

Kennedy, Randall 1954— **40**

Kennedy-Overton, Jayne Harris 1951— **46**

Kenner-Jackson, Doris *See Shirelles, The*

Kenney, John A., Jr. 1914–2003 **48**

Kenoly, Ron 1944— **45**

Kente, Gibson 1932–2004 **52**

Kenyatta, Jomo 1891(?)–1978 **5**

Kenyatta, Robin 1942–2004 **54**

Kenyatta, Uhuru 1961— **110**

Kérékou, Ahmed *See Kérékou, Mathieu*

Kérékou, Mathieu 1933–2015 **1, 131**

Kerry, Leon G. 1949(?)— **46**

Key, Keegan-Michael *See Key & Peele*

Key & Peele **107**

Keyes, Alan 1950— **11, 105**

Keys, Alicia 1981— **32, 68**

Kgositsile, Thebe Neruda *See Sweatshirt, Earl*

Khalifa, Wiz 1987— **96**

Khama, Ian 1953— **95**

Khan, Chaka 1953— **12, 50**

Khanga, Yelena 1962— **6**

Khumalo, Leleti 1970— **51**

Khumalo, S'manga 1985— **119**

Kibaki, Mwai 1931— **60**

Kibble, Joey *See Take 6*

Kibble, Mark *See Take 6*

Kid Cudi 1984— **83**

Kidd, Jason 1973— **86**

Kidd, Mae Street 1904–1995 **39**

Kidjo, Angelique 1960— **50**

Kiir, Salva Mayardit 1951— **85, 103**

Kikumba, Jules Shungu Wembadio Pene *See Papa Wemba*

Kikwete, Jakaya Mrisho 1950— **73**

Killebrew, Sonny *See S.O.S. Band*

Killebrew, Willie *See S.O.S. Band*

Killens, John O. 1967–1987 **54**

Killer Mike 1975— **117**

Killings, Debra 196(?)— **57**

Killingsworth, Cleve, Jr. 1952— **54**

Kilpatrick, Carolyn Cheeks 1945— **16**

Kilpatrick, Kwame 1970— **34, 71, 116**

Kimble, Perry *See Taste of Honey, A*

Kimbro, Dennis (Paul) 1950— **10**

Kimbro, Henry A. 1912–1999 **25**

Kimbro, Warren 1934–2009 **76**

Kimetto, Dennis 1984— **125**

Kincaid, Bernard 1945— **28**

Kincaid, Jamaica 1949— **4, 109**

Kinch, Soweto 1978— **108**

King, Alonzo 19(?)(?)— **38**

King, B. B. 1925–2015 **7, 129**

King, Barbara 19(?)(?)— **22**

King, Ben E. 1938–2015 **128** See also Drifters, The

King, Bernice 1963— **4, 81**

King, Chris Thomas 1964— **120**

King, Colbert I. 1939— **69**

King, Coretta Scott 1927–2006 **3, 57**

King, Dexter (Scott) 1961— **10**

King, Don 1931— **14, 128**

King, Evelyn 1960— **129**

King, Evelyn "Champagne" *See King, Evelyn*

King, Freddie 1934–1976 **92**

King, Gayle 1954— **19, 99**

King, Jimmie *See Bar-Kays, The*

King, Martin Luther, III 1957— **20**

King, Martin Luther, Jr. 1929–1968 **1**

King, Martin Luther, Sr. 1899–1984 **89**

King, Oona 1967— **27**

King, Preston 1936— **28**

King, Reatha Clark 1938— **65**

King, Regina 1971— **22, 45**

King, Riley B. *See King, B. B.*

King, Robert Arthur 1945— **58**

King, Robert Hillary 1942— **84**

King, Rodney 1965–2012 **103**

King, Teresa 1961— **80**

King, William *See Commodores, The*

King, Woodie Jr. 1937— **27**

King, Yolanda (Denise) 1955— **6**

King Curtis 1934–1971 **92**

Kingston, Sean 1990— **94**

Kinsman Dazz *See Dazz Band*

Kintaudi, Leon 1949(?)— **62**

Kintaudi, Ngoma Miezi *See Kintaudi, Leon*

Kipchoge, Eliud 1984— **124**

Kiprotich, Wilson Kipsang *See Kipsang, Wilson*

Kipsang, Wilson 1982— **115**

Kirby, George 1924–1995 **14**

Kirk, Andy 1898–1992 **134**

Kirk, Clara 1941— **95**

Kirk, Ron 1954— **11, 75, 111**

Kirkland, Eddie 1923–2011 **99**

Kirkland, Niatia Jessica *See Lil Mama*

Kirnan, Conrad Henry *See Kay, Connie*

Kisekka, Samson 1912–1999 **112**

Kisule, David Kato *See Kato, David*

Kitt, Eartha 1927–2008 **16, 75**

Kitt, Sandra 1947— **23**

Kittles, Rick 1976(?)— **51**

Kitwana, Bakari 19(?)(?)— **86**

Kiwanuka, Michael 1987— **126**

Klugh, Earl 1953— **59**

K'naan 1978— **76**

Knight, Etheridge 1931–1991 **37**

Knight, Gladys 1944— **16, 66**

Knight, Gwendolyn 1913–2005 **63**

Knight, Marie 1925(?)–2009 **80**

Knight, Marion Hugh, Jr. *See Knight, Suge*

Knight, Suge 1965— **11, 30, 102**

Knowles, Beyoncé *See Beyoncé*

Knowles, Mathew 1952— **96**

Knowles, Solange *See Solange*

Knowles, Tina 1954(?)— **61**

Knowling, Robert Jr. 1955(?)— **38**

Knox, Simmie 1935— **49**

Knuckles, Frankie 1955–2014 **42, 120** See also Roots, The

Kobia, Samuel 1947— **43**

Kodjoe, Boris 1973— **34, 89**

Kole, Ernest Levi Tsoloane *See Cole, Ernest*

Kolosoy, Wendo 1925–2008 **73**

Kompany, Vincent 1986— **132**

Komunyakaa, Yusef 1941— **9**

Kone, Seydou *See Blondy, Alpha*

Kong, B. Waine 1943— **50**

Kony, Joseph 1961(?)— **101**

Kool DJ Red Alert *See Alert, Kool DJ Red*

Kool Moe Dee 1963— **37**

Kool Rock Ski *See Fat Boys*

Koontz, Elizabeth Duncan 1919–1989 **101**

Koroma, Ernest Bai 1953— **84**

Kotto, Yaphet (Fredrick) 1944— **7**

Kountz, Samuel L(ee) 1930–1981 **10**

Kravitz, Lenny 1964— **10, 34**

Kravitz, Leonard *See Kravitz, Lenny*

Krigger, Kevin 1983— **111**

KRS-One 1965— **34**

Krute, Fred *See Alert, Kool DJ Red*

K-Swift 1978–2008 **73**

Kufuor, John Agyekum 1938— **54, 82**

Kunjufu, Jawanza 1953— **3, 50**

Kuti, Fela Anikulapo *See Fela*

Kuti, Femi 1962— **47, 110**

Kuzwayo, Ellen 1914–2006 **68**

Kwei-Armah, Kwame 1967— **84**

Kweli, Talib 1975— **93**

Kyenge, Cécile 1964— **113**

Kyles, Cedric Antonio *See Cedric the Entertainer*

La Beaux, W. L. *See Soul Stirrers*

La Menthe, Ferdinand Joseph *See Morton, Jelly Roll*

La Roca, Pete 1938–2012 **107**

La Salle, Eriq 1962— **12**

L.A. Sunshine *See Treacherous Three*

LaBelle, Patti 1944— **13, 30**

Labrinth 1989— **135**

LaChanze 1961— **93**

Lacks, Henrietta 1921–1951 **101**

Lacy, Marc 1969— **111**

Lacy, Sam 1903–2003 **30, 46**

Lacy, Walter Marcellus *See Lacy, Marc*

Ladd, Ernie 1938–2007 **64**

Ladner, Joyce A. 1943— **42**

Ladson-Billings, Gloria 1947— **130**

Ladysmith Black Mambazo **103**

Laferriere, Dany 1953— **33**

Lafontant, Jewel Stradford 1922–1997 **3, 51**

Lafontant-MANkarious, Jewel Stradford *See Lafontant, Jewel Stradford*

LaGuma, Alex 1925–1985 **30**

Lakeside **120**

Lamar, Jake 1961— **96**

Lamar, Kendrick 1987— **105**

Lamming, George 1927— **35**

Lamont, William Joseph *See Billy Ward and the Dominoes*

Lamothe, Laurent 1972— **122**

Lampkin, Daisy 1883(?)–1965 **19**

Lampley, Oni Faida 1959–2008 **43, 71**

Lampley, Vera *See Lampley, Oni Faida*

Lancaster, Byard 1942–2012 **105**

Lance, Major 1939–1994 **111**

Land, Harold 1928–2001 **125**

Lander, Austin *See New Birth*

Landry, Jackie *See Chantels, The*

Lane, Charles 1953— **3**

Lane, Dick 1927–2002 **92**

Lane, Lunsford 1803–18(?)(?) **93**

Lane, Vincent 1942— **5**

Lane, William Henry 1825(?)–1852(?) **90**

Laneuville, Eric 1952— **123**

Langford, Larry P. 1948— **74**

Langford, William See Golden Gate Quartet

Langhart Cohen, Janet 1941— **19, 60**

Langston, John Mercer 1829–1897 **101**

Lanier, Bob 1948— **47**

Lanier, Willie 1945— **33**

Lankford, Raymond Lewis 1967— **23**

LaPread, Ronald See Commodores, The

Laraque, Georges 1976— **48**

Laraque, Paul 1920–2007 **67**

Larkin, Barry 1964— **24**

Laroche, Joseph Philippe Lemercier 1889–1912 **85**

Larrieux, Amel 1973(?)— **63**

Lars, Byron 1965— **32**

Larsen, Nella 1891–1964 **10**

LaRue, Dione See Sharp, Dee Dee

Laryea, Thomas Davies, III 1979— **67**

LaSalle, Denise 1939— **111**

Lashley, Bobby 1976— **63**

Lashley, Franklin Roberto See Lashley, Bobby

Lassiter, Roy 1969— **24**

Lateef, Yusef 1920–2013 **91, 117**

Lathan, Sanaa 1971— **27**

Latiker, Diane 1957— **132**

Latimer, Lewis H(oward) 1848–1928 **4**

Lattany, Kristin Hunter 1931–2008 **88**

Lattimore, Kenny 1970— **35, 128**

LaVette, Bettye 1946— **85**

Lavizzo-Mourey, Risa 1954— **48**

Law, W. W. 1923–2002 **121**

Law, Westley Wallace See Law, W. W.

Lawal, Kase L. 19(?)(?)— **45**

Lawless, Theodore K(enneth) 1892–1971 **8**

Lawrence, Brenda 1954— **127**

Lawrence, Diedra See Marian Anderson String Quartet

Lawrence, Donald 1958— **99**

Lawrence, Jacob (Armstead) 1917–2000 **4, 28**

Lawrence, Margaret Morgan 1914— **100**

Lawrence, Martin 1965— **6, 27, 60**

Lawrence, Robert Henry, Jr. 1935–1967 **16**

Lawrence-Lightfoot, Sara 1944— **10**

Laws, Hubert 1939— **90**

Lawson, George See Deep River Boys

Lawson, James M., Jr. 1928— **90**

Lawson, Jennifer 1946— **1, 50**

Laymon, Kiese 197(?)— **113**

Layton, William 1915–2007 **87**

Lazare, Palaceer See Shabazz Palaces

Le Loka, Tsidii 1968(?)— **116**

Le1f 1989— **120**

Lea, Babatunde 1948(?)— **124**

Lea, Michael See Lea, Babatunde

Leadbelly 1885–1949 **82**

Leakes, NeNe 1967— **107**

Leary, Kathryn D. 1952— **10**

Leavell, Dorothy R. 1944— **17**

Lebo M 1964— **109**

Lecrae 1979— **108**

Ledbetter, Hudson William See Leadbelly

Ledisi 197(?)— **73**

Lee, Annie Frances 1935— **22**

Lee, Barbara See Chiffons, The

Lee, Barbara 1946— **25, 102**

Lee, Bertram M., Sr. 1939–2003 **46**

Lee, Beverly See Shirelles, The

Lee, Canada 1907–1952 **8**

Lee, Consuela 1926–2009 **84**

Lee, Debra L. 1954— **62**

Lee, Don Luther See Madhubuti, Haki R.

Lee, Eric P. 1958— **79**

Lee, Gabby See Lincoln, Abbey

Lee, Howard N. 1934— **136**

Lee, Jarena 1783–1855(?) **100**

Lee, Joe A. 1946(?)— **45**

Lee, Joie 1962(?)— **1**

Lee, Julia 1902–1958 **130**

Lee, Leslie 1930–2014 **85, 122**

Lee, Malcolm D. 1970— **75**

Lee, Raphael C. 1949— **87**

Lee, Robert 1920–2010 **112**

Lee, Shelton Jackson See Lee, Spike

Lee, Spike 1957— **5, 19, 86**

Lee Andrews & the Hearts **134**

Lee-Smith, Hughie 1915–1999 **5, 22**

Leevy, Carroll M. 1920— **42**

Lefel, Edith 1963–2003 **41**

Leffall, Lasalle, Jr. 1930— **3, 64**

LeFlore, Lyah Beth 1970— **96**

Leftenant, Nathan See Cameo

Legend, John 1978— **67, 116**

Legendary Orioles, The See Orioles, The

Leggs, Kingsley 196(?)— **62**

LeGrand, Eric 1990— **118**

LeGrand, Naquasia 1991— **126**

Leibowitz, Helen See Chantels, The

Leland, George Thomas See Leland, Mickey

Leland, Mickey 1944–1989 **2**

Lemmons, Kasi 1961— **20**

Lemon, Alton T. 1928–2013 **112**

Lemon, Don 1966— **94**

Lennox, Betty 1976— **31**

Lenoir, J. B. 1929–1967 **117**

LeNoire, Rosetta 1911–2002 **37**

Lenox, Adriane 1956— **59**

Leon, Kenny 1956— **10, 98**

León, Tania 1943— **13**

Leonard, Buck 1907–1997 **67**

Leonard, Kawhi 1991— **122**

Leonard, Sugar Ray 1956— **15**

Leonard, Walter Fenner See Leonard, Buck

Leônidas 1913–2004 **96**

Leslie, Lisa 1972— **16, 73**

Lester, Adrian 1968— **46**

Lester, Bill 1961— **42, 85**

Lester, Bobby See Moonglows, The

Lester, Julius 1939— **9, 115**

Lester, Robert See Chi-Lites

Lesure, James 1975— **64**

LeTang, Henry 1915–2007 **66**

Letson, Al 1972— **39**

Levert, Eddie 1942— **70** See also O'Jays, The

Levert, Gerald 1966–2006 **22, 59**

Levi, Moses See Shyne

Lewis, Amisho Baraka See Baraka, Sho

Lewis, Aubrey 1935–2001 **133**

Lewis, Aylwin B. 1954— **51, 88**

Lewis, Butch 1946–2011 **71, 99**

Lewis, Byron E(ugene) 1931— **13**

Lewis, Carl 1961— **4, 97**

Lewis, Daurene 194(?)— **72**

Lewis, David See Atlantic Starr

Lewis, David Levering 1936— **9**

Lewis, Delano (Eugene) 1938— **7**

Lewis, Denise 1972— **33**

Lewis, Earl See Flamingos, The

Lewis, (Mary) Edmonia 1845(?)–1911(?) **10**

Lewis, Edward T. 1940— **21**

Lewis, Emmanuel 1971— **36**

Lewis, Frederick Carlton See Lewis, Carl

Lewis, George 1900–1968 **130**

Lewis, George 1952— **104**

Lewis, Henry 1932–1996 **38**

Lewis, Jamal 1979— **115**

Lewis, John 1940— **2, 46, 83**

Lewis, Jonathan See Atlantic Starr

Lewis, Lennox 1965— **27**

Lewis, Leona 1985— **75**

Lewis, Marvin 1958— **51, 87**

Lewis, Norman 1909–1979 **39**

Lewis, Oliver 1856–1924 **56**

Lewis, Ramsey 1935— **35, 70**

Lewis, Ray 1975— **33, 109**

Lewis, Reginald F. 1942–1993 **6**

Lewis, Ronald See Lewis, Butch

Lewis, Samella 1924— **25**

Lewis, Shirley Ann Redd 1937— **14**

Lewis, Terry 1956— **13**

Lewis, Thomas 1939— **19**

Lewis, Wayne See Atlantic Starr

Lewis, William Henry 1868–1949 **89**

Lewis, William M., Jr. 1956— **40**

Lewis-Hall, Freda 1955(?)— **105**

Lewis-Thornton, Rae 1962— **32**

Liggins, Alfred, III 1965— **43**

Lighty, Chris 1968–2012 **105**

Lighty, Darrell Steven See Lighty, Chris

Ligon, Glenn 1960— **82**

Ligon, Joe See Mighty Clouds of Joy

Lil B 1989— **121**

Lil' Bow Wow See Bow Wow

Lil Jon 1971— **124**

Lil' Kim 1975— **28**

Lil Mama 1989— **117**

Lil' Romeo See Romeo

Lil Wayne 1982— **66, 84**

Lilakoi Moon See Bonet, Lisa

Liles, Kevin 1968— **42, 99**

Lillard, Damian 1990— **117**

Lincoln, Abbey 1930–2010 **3, 88**

Lincoln, C(harles) Eric 1924–2000 **38**

Lindo, Allen Pineda See apl.de.ap

Lindo, Delroy 1952— **18, 45**

Lindsay, Peta 1984— **100**

Lindsey, Tommie 1951— **51**

Lipscomb, Belinda See Midnight Star

Lipscomb, Mance 1895–1976 **49**

LisaRaye 1967— **27**

Lister, Marquita 1965(?) **65**

Lister, Tiny See Lister, Tommy

Lister, Tommy 1958— **127**

Liston, Melba 1926–1999 **118**

Liston, Sonny 1928(?)–1970 **33**

Little, Benilde 1958— **21**

Little, Booker 1938–1961 **105**

Little, Cleavon 1939–1992 **117**

Little, Floyd 1942— **86**

Little, Larry 1945— **90**

Little, Malcolm See X, Malcolm

Little, Robert L(angdon) 1938— **2**

Little Anthony See Little Anthony & the Imperials

Little Anthony & the Imperials **107**

Little Chronicle See Chronixx

Little Eva 1943–2003 **128**

Little Milton 1934–2005 **36, 54**

Little Richard 1932— **15**

Little Walter 1930–1968 **36** See also Aces, The

Little Warrior See Barrow, Willie T.

Littlepage, Craig 1951— **35**

LL Cool J 1968— **16, 49, 94**

Llewellyn, J. Bruce 1927–2010 **13, 85**

Lloyd 1986— **99**

Lloyd, Christopher See Banks, Lloyd

Lloyd, Earl 1928–2015 **26, 127**

Lloyd, John Henry "Pop" 1884–1965 **30**

Lloyd, Reginald 1967— **64**

Locke, Alain 1886–1954 **10**

Locke, Attica 1974— **85**

Locke, Eddie 1930— **44**

Lockwood, Robert, Jr. 1915–2006 **120**

Lofton, James 1956— **42**

Lofton, Kenneth 1967— **12**

Lofton, Ramona See Sapphire

Logan, Onnie Lee 1910(?)–1995 **14**

Logan, Rayford W. 1897–1982 **40**

Loguen, J. W. 1813–1872 **91**

Lomax, Louis E. 1922–1970 **90**

Lomax, Michael L. 1947— **58**

London, Theophilus 1987— **95**

Long, Eddie L. 1953— **29, 89**

Long, Huey 1904–2009 **79**

Long, Loretta 1940— **58**

Long, Nia 1970— **17, 95**

Long, Richard Alexander 1927— **65**

Loper, Ramon See Five Keys, The

Lopes, Davey 1945— **92**

Lopes, Leila 1986— **99**

Lopes, Lisa 1971–2002 **36** See also TLC

Lord, Tracy See Little Anthony & the Imperials

Lord Infamous 1973–2013 **117**

Lord Invader 1914–1961 **117**

Lord Jamar 1968— **126**

Lord Kitchener 1922–2000 **110**

Lord Pitt of Hampstead See Pitt, David Thomas

Lorde, Audre (Geraldine) 1934–1992 **6**

Lorenzo, Irving *See Gotti, Irv*

Loroupe, Tegla 1973— **59**

Lott, Ronnie 1959— **9**

Loueke, Lionel 1973(?)— **88**

Louis, Errol T. 1962— **8**

Louis, Joe 1914–1981 **5**

Louis, Willie 1937–2013 **113**

Loury, Glenn 1948— **36**

Love, Darlene 1941— **23, 92**

Love, Ed 1932(?)— **58**

Love, Laura 1960— **50**

Love, Loni 1971— **113**

Love, Ludmya Bourdeau *See Love, Mia*

Love, Mia 1975— **96, 125**

Love, Nat 1854–1921 **9**

Love, Reggie 1982— **77**

Lovelace, Bobby *See Midnight Star*

Lovell, Whitfield 1959— **74**

Lover, Ed **10**

Lovett, Winfred *See Manhattans, The*

Loving, Alvin, Jr., 1935–2005 **35, 53**

Loving, Mildred 1939–2008 **69**

Lowe, Herbert 1962— **57**

Lowe, Kenny *See Lee Andrews & the Hearts*

Lowe, Rick 1961— **124**

Lowe, Sidney 1960— **64**

Lowery, Evelyn Gibson 1925–2013 **115**

Lowery, Joseph E. 1924— **2**

Lowery, Myron 1946(?)— **80**

Lowry, A. Leon 1913–2005 **60**

Lowry, Kyle 1986— **135**

Luandrew, Albert *See Sunnyland Slim*

Lubanga, Thomas 1960— **104**

Lucas, Bill 1936–1979 **97**

Lucas, Harold *See Clovers, The*

Lucas, John 1953— **7**

Lucas, William DeVaughn *See Lucas, Bill*

Lucie, Lawrence 1907–2009 **80**

Lucien, Jon 1942–2007 **66**

Luckett, Letoya 1981— **61**

Lucy, William 1933— **50**

Lucy Foster, Autherine 1929— **35**

Ludacris, 1978— **37, 60**

Lue, Tyronn 1977— **136**

Lufeyo, Jameson *See Malawi Mouse Boys*

Luke, Derek 1974— **61**

Lumbly, Carl 1952— **47**

Lumet, Jenny 1967— **80**

Lumpkin, Elgin Baylor *See Ginuwine*

Lumumba, Chokwe 1947–2014 **118**

Lumumba, Patrice 1925–1961 **33**

Luna, Donyale 1946–1979 **88**

Lunceford, Jimmie 1902–1947 **134**

Luper, Clara 1923–2011 **94**

Lushington, Augustus Nathaniel 1869–1939 **56**

Lutcher, Nellie 1912(?)–2007 **130**

Luter, Fred, Jr. 1956— **103**

Luthuli, Albert (John Mvumbi) 1898(?)–1967 **13**

Lyfe *See Jennings, Lyfe*

Lyle, Marcenia *See Stone, Toni*

Lyle, Ron 1941–2011 **125**

Lyles, Lester Lawrence 1946— **31**

Lymon, Frankie 1942–1968 **22**

Lynch, Bill *See Lynch, William, Jr*

Lynch, Loretta E. 1959— **103**

Lynch, Marshawn 1986— **124**

Lynch, Shola 1969— **61**

Lynch, William, Jr. 1941–2013 **115**

Lynn, Barbara 1942— **126**

Lynn, Lonnie Rashid, Jr. *See Common*

Lynne, Gloria 1929(?)–2013 **115**

Lyons, Henry 1942— **12, 118**

Lyons, James E., Sr. 1944(?)— **102**

Lyttle, Hulda Margaret 1889–1983 **14**

Maal, Baaba 1953— **66**

Maathai, Wangari 1940–2011 **43, 97**

Mabior, John Garang de *See Garang, John*

Mabley, Jackie "Moms" 1897(?)–1975 **15**

Mabon, Willie 1925–1985 **119**

Mabrey, Vicki 1957(?)— **26**

Mabry, Marcus 1967— **70**

Mabuza, Lindiwe 1938— **18**

Mabuza-Suttle, Felicia 1950— **43**

Mac, Bernie 1957–2008 **29, 61, 72**

Mac Daddy 1978–2013 **111**

Maceo, Antonio 1845–1896 **82**

Machado de Assis 1839–1908 **74**

Machaka, Yvonne *See Chaka Chaka, Yvonne*

Machar, Riek 1952— **117**

Machel, Graça 1945— **16, 102**

Machel, Samora Moises 1933–1986 **8**

Mack, Bunky *See Swallows, The*

Mack, Iris 1955(?)— **105**

Mack, Norris *See Swallows, The*

Mack, Tony 1966— **104**

Mack Maine 1982— **125**

Mackey, Biz 1897–1965 **82**

Mackey, Nathaniel 1947— **75**

Mackie, Anthony 1979— **102**

Madame Sul-Te-Wan 1873–1959 **95**

Madhubuti, Haki R. 1942— **7, 85**

Madikizela-Mandela, Winnie 1934— **2, 35, 112**

Madison, Joseph E. 1949— **17**

Madison, Paula 1952— **37, 99**

Madison, Romell 1952— **45**

Madlib 1973— **88**

Magan, Ayaan Hirsi *See Ali, Ayaan Hirsi*

Maghett, Samuel *See Magic Sam*

Magic Sam 1937–1969 **131**

Magic Slim 1937–2013 **110**

Magloire, Paul Eugène 1907–2001 **68**

Magruder, Nilah 1988(?)— **134**

Mahal, Taj 1942— **39**

Mahama, John Dramani 1958— **103**

Mahlasela, Vusi 1965— **65**

Mahorn, Rick 1958— **60**

Maillard, Carol *See Sweet Honey in the Rock*

Mainor, Dorothy Leigh 1910(?)–1996 **19**

Maitreya, Sananda 1962— **85**

Majette, Denise 1955— **41**

Major, Clarence 1936— **9**

Majors, Jeff 1960(?)— **41**

Makeba, Miriam 1932–2008 **2, 50, 74**

Malawi Mouse Boys **114**

Malco, Romany 1968— **71**

Malcolm X *See X, Malcolm*

Malema, Julius 1981— **98**

Mallett, Conrad, Jr. 1953— **16**

Mallory, Mark 1962— **62**

Mallory, William L., Sr. 1931–2013 **119**

Malone, Annie (Minerva Turnbo Pope) 1869–1957 **13**

Malone, Karl 1963— **18, 51, 90**

Malone, Maurice 1965— **32**

Malone, Moses 1955–2015 **79, 131**

Malone Jones, Vivian 1942–2005 **59**

Malonga, Eric Moussambani *See Moussambani, Eric*

Malphurs, Juaquin James *See Waka Flocka Flame*

Malveaux, Floyd 1940— **54**

Malveaux, Julianne 1953— **32, 70**

Malveaux, Suzanne 1966— **88**

Manardo, Bob *See Falcons, The*

Mance, Julian Clifford, Jr. *See Mance, Junior*

Mance, Junior 1928— **132**

Mandela, Nelson 1918–2013 **1, 14, 77, 117**

Mandela, Winnie *See Madikizela-Mandela, Winnie*

Mandisa 1976— **119**

Mane, Gucci 1980— **91**

Manhattans, The **123**

Manigat, Mirlande 1940— **90**

Manigault, Earl "The Goat" 1943— **15**

Manigault, Omarosa *See Omarosa*

Manigault-Stallworth, Omarosa *See Omarosa*

Manka, Hashim Thabit *See Thabeet, Hasheem*

Manley, Audrey Forbes 1934— **16**

Manley, Dexter 1959— **116**

Manley, Edna 1900–1987 **26**

Manley, Ruth 1947— **34**

Mann, Bob 1924–2006 **126**

Mann, Robert *See Mann, Bob*

Mann, Tamela 1966— **92**

Manning, Frankie 1914–2009 **78**

Manning, Marva Ann *See Whitney, Marva*

Manson, John *See Swan Silvertones, The*

Manuel, Jerry 1953— **94**

Maponya, Maishe 1951— **101**

Maponya, Richard 1926— **101**

Marable, Manning 1950–2011 **10, 102**

Maraire, Tendai *See Shabazz Palaces*

Maraj, Onika Tanya indexref See Minaj, Nicki

March, William Carrington 1923–2002 **56**

Marchand, Inga *See Foxy Brown*

Marcille, Eva 1984— **97**

Marechera, Charles William *See Marechera, Dambudzo*

Marechera, Dambudzo 1952–1987 **39**

Marechera, Tambudzai *See Marechera, Dambudzo*

Margot B. *See Bingham, Margot*

Marian Anderson String Quartet **111**

Mariner, Jonathan 1954(?)— **41**

Marino, Eugene Antonio 1934–2000 **30**

Mario 1986— **71**

Marion, Shawn 1978— **136**

Markham, Dewey *See Markham, Pigmeat*

Markham, E(dward) A(rchibald) 1939— **37**

Markham, Pigmeat 1904–1981 **106**

Marks, Audrey 19(?)(?)— **99**

Marks, John R., III 1947(?)— **123**

Marle, Milton *See Billy Ward and the Dominoes*

Marley, Bob 1945–1981 **5**

Marley, David *See Marley, Ziggy*

Marley, Rita 1947— **32, 70**

Marley, Robert Nesta *See Marley, Bob*

Marley, Stephen 1972— **100**

Marley, Ziggy 1968— **41**

Marrow, Queen Esther 1943(?)— **24**

Marrow, Tracy *See Ice-T*

Marsalis, Branford 1960— **34, 103**

Marsalis, Delfeayo 1965— **41**

Marsalis, Ellis 1934— **90**

Marsalis, Wynton 1961— **16, 90**

Marsh, Henry L., III 1934(?)— **32**

Marshall, Bella 1950— **22**

Marshall, Brandon 1984— **116**

Marshall, Gloria *See Sudarkasa, Niara*

Marshall, Kerry James 1955— **59**

Marshall, Paule 1929— **7, 77**

Marshall, Quavious *See Migos*

Marshall, Thurgood 1908–1993 **1, 44**

Marshall, Valenza Pauline Burke *See Marshall, Paule*

Marshall, William 1924–2003 **107**

Marte, Starling 1988— **117**

Martelly, Michel 1961— **90**

Martha Jean "The Queen" *See Steinberg, Martha Jean*

Martin, Cuonzo 1971— **121**

Martin, Curtis 1973— **104**

Martin, Darnell 1964— **43, 78**

Martin, Duane 1965— **108**

Martin, Helen 1909–2000 **31**

Martin, Jesse L. 19(?)(?)— **31**

Martin, Johnny *See Mighty Clouds of Joy*

Martin, Jonathan 1989— **119**

Martin, Louis Emanuel 1912–1997 **16**

Martin, Luci *See Chic*

Martin, Michel 19(?)(?)— **97**

Martin, Porscha *See Atlantic Starr*

Martin, Roberta 1907–1969 **58**

Martin, Roland S. 1968— **49, 84**

Martin, Ruby Grant 1933–2003 **49**

Martin, Sallie 1895(?)–1988 **120**

Martin, Sara 1884–1955 **38**

Martin, Skip, III *See Dazz Band*

Martin, Trayvon 1995–2012 **105**

Martinez, Juan *See Pharcyde, The*

Martínez, Pedro 1971— **81, 126**

Martin-Green, Sonequa 1985— **133**

Marvelettes, The **126**

Marvin X *See X, Marvin*

Mary Mary **34, 92**

Mase 1977(?)— **24**

Masekela, Barbara 1941— **18**

Masekela, Hugh 1939— **1, 106**

Masekela, Sal 1971— **106**

Masire, Quett (Ketumile Joni) 1925— **5**

Mason, Anthony 1966–2015 **128**

Mason, Biddy 1818–1891 **89**

Mason, Charles Harrison 1866–1961 **107**

Mason, Derek 1970— **120**

Mason, Desmond 1977— **127**

Mason, Felicia 1963(?)— **31**

Mason, Herman, Jr. 1962— **83**

Mason, Judi Ann 1955–2009 **112**

Mason, Ronald 1949— **27**

Mason, Vincent *See De La Soul*

Massaquoi, Hans J. 1926–2013 **30, 130**

Massenburg, Kedar 1963(?)— **23, 110**

Massey, Bobby *See O'Jays, The*

Massey, Brandon 1973— **40**

Massey, Walter E(ugene) 1938— **5, 45**

Massie, Samuel Proctor, Jr. 1919— **29**

Masta Ace 1966— **118**

Master Gee *See Sugarhill Gang, The*

Master P 1970— **21, 115**

Matejka, Adrian 1971(?)— **87**

Mathabane, Johannes *See Mathabane, Mark*

Mathabane, Mark 1960— **5, 99**

Mathis, Greg 1960— **26**

Mathis, Johnny 1935— **20**

Mathis, Robert 1981— **121**

Matshikiza, Pumeza 1979(?)— **115**

Matson, Ollie 1930–2011 **93**

Matta, Adam *See Carolina Chocolate Drops*

Matthews, Ameena 19(?)(?)— **105**

Matthews, Benjamin 1932–2006 **93**

Matthews, Denise Katrina *See Vanity*

Matthews, Mark 1894–2005 **59**

Matthews Shatteen, Westina 1948— **51**

Matzeliger, Jan 1852–1889 **93**

Mauldin, Jermaine Dupri *See Dupri, Jermaine*

Maupin, John E., Jr. 1946— **92**

Maxey, Randall 1941— **46**

Maxis, Theresa 1810–1892 **62**

Maxwell 1973— **20, 81**

Maxwell, Willie *See Fetty Wap*

May, Brother Joe 1912–1972 **123**

May, Derrick 1963— **41**

May, Joseph W. *See May, Brother Joe*

May, Mark 1959— **117**

Mayberry-Stewart, Melodie 1948— **94**

Maye, Arthur Lee *See Maye, Lee*

Maye, Lee 1934–2002 **111**

Mayers, Jamal 1974— **39**

Mayers, Rakim *See A$AP Rocky*

Mayes, Lenny *See Dramatics, The*

Mayfield, Curtis 1942–1999 **2, 43**

See also Impressions, The

Mayhew, Martin R. 1965— **76**

Mayhew, Richard 1924— **39**

Maynard, Nancy Hicks 1946–2008 **73**

Maynard, Robert C(lyve) 1937–1993 **7**

Maynor, Dorothy 1910–1996 **19**

Mayo, Whitman 1930–2001 **32**

Mays, Benjamin E(lijah) 1894–1984 **7**

Mays, Leslie A. 19(?)(?)— **41**

Mays, William G. 1946— **34**

Mays, William Howard, Jr. *See Mays, Willie*

Mays, Willie 1931— **3**

Mayweather, Floyd 1977— **57, 104**

Mazrui, Ali 1933–2014 **12, 124**

M'bala M'bala, Dieudonné *See Dieudonné*

Mbabazi, Esther 1988(?)— **122**

Mbatha-Raw, Gugu 1983— **89**

Mbaye, Mariétou 1948— **31**

Mbeki, Govan A. 1910–2001 **80**

Mbeki, Thabo 1942— **14, 73**

Mboup, Souleymane 1951— **10**

Mboya, Thomas Joseph Odhiambo *See Mboya, Tom*

Mboya, Tom 1930–1969 **107**

Mbuende, Kaire Munionganda 1953— **12**

MC Breed 1971–2008 **75**

M.C. Hammer 1963— **20, 80**

MC Lyte 1971— **34, 108**

McAdoo, Bob 1951— **75**

McAlpin, Harry 1906–1985 **121**

McAnulty, William E., Jr. 1947–2007 **66**

McBay, Henry C. 1914–1995 **91**

McBee, Cecil 1935— **123**

McBride, Bryant Scott 1965— **18**

McBride, Chi 1961— **73**

McBride, Christian 1972— **134**

McBride, James 1957— **35, 87**

McCabe, Jewell Jackson 1945— **10**

McCain, Franklin 1941–2014 **119**

McCalister, Jimmy *See Lee Andrews & the Hearts*

McCall, H. Carl 1938(?)— **27**

McCall, Nathan 1955— **8**

McCalla, Leyla *See Carolina Chocolate Drops*

McCann, Renetta 1957(?)— **44**

McCarthy, Sandy 1972— **64**

McCartney, Brandon *See Lil B*

McCarty, Oseola 1908–1999 **16, 136**

McCary, Michael S. *See Boyz II Men*

McCauley, Gina 1976(?)— **76**

McClary, Thomas *See Commodores, The*

McClellan, George Marion 1860–1934 **91**

McClendon, Forrest 1965— **94**

McClendon, Lisa 1975(?)— **61**

McClendon, Lloyd 1959— **123**

McClinton, Marion Isaac 1954— **77**

McClurkin, Donnie 1961— **25**

McCollum, Robert Lee *See Nighthawk, Robert*

McCoo, Marilyn 1943— **53**

McCovey, Willie 1938— **103**

McCowin, Michael *See Mighty Clouds of Joy*

McCoy, Elijah 1844–1929 **8**

McCoy, LeSean 1988— **123**

McCoy, Robert Lee *See Nighthawk, Robert*

McCoy, Van 1940–1979 **123**

McCracklin, Jimmy 1921–2012 **108**

McCraney, Tarell Alvin 1980— **116**

McCrary, Crystal *See McCrary Anthony, Crystal*

McCrary, Darius 1976— **111**

McCrary Anthony, Crystal 1969— **70**

McCray, Chirlane 1954— **134**

McCray, Nikki 1972— **18**

McCullough, Bernard Jeffrey *See Mac, Bernie*

McCullough, DeAndre 1977–2012 **106**

McCullough, Geraldine 1917–2008 **58, 79**

McCullum, Robert Lee *See Nighthawk, Robert*

McCutchen, Andrew 1986— **116**

McDaniel, Hattie 1895–1952 **5**

McDaniel, Prudence *See Marian Anderson String Quartet*

McDaniel, Randall Cornell 1964— **81**

McDaniel, Rudy *See Tacuma, Jamaaladeen*

McDaniels, Darryl *See DMC*

McDaniels, Ralph 19(?)(?)— **79**

McDonald, Audra 1970— **20, 62, 128**

McDonald, Butch *See New Birth*

McDonald, Charles J. 1931— **120**

McDonald, Erroll 1954(?)— **1**

McDonald, Gabrielle Kirk 1942— **20**

McDougall, Gay J. 1947— **11, 43**

McDuff, Jack 1926–2001 **116**

McDuffie, Dwayne 1962— **62**

McDuffy, Eugene *See McDuff, Jack*

McElroy, Sollie *See Flamingos, The*

McEwen, Mark 1954— **5**

McFadden, Bernice L. 1966— **39**

McFarlan, Tyron 1971(?)— **60**

McFarland, Roland 1940— **49**

McFerrin, Bobby 1950— **68**

McFerrin, Robert, Jr. *See McFerrin, Bobby*

McFerrin, Robert, Sr. 1921–2006 **94**

McGee, Charles 1924— **10**

McGee, James D. 1949— **74**

McGee, James Madison 1940— **46**

McGee, Vonetta 1945–2010 **95**

McGhee, Heather C. 1981— **106**

McGhee, Howard 1918–1987 **122**

McGhee, Maggie *See McGhee, Howard*

McGhee, Sharon K. 1957–2012 **113**

McGill, Anthony 1979— **76**

McGill, Lucius *See Dells, The*

McGill, Mickey *See Dells, The*

McGlowan, Angela 1970— **64, 86**

McGrady, Tracy 1979— **80**

McGrath, Pat 1970— **72**

McGregor, Stephen 1990— **99**

McGriff, Dorothy *See Coates, Dorothy Love*

McGriff, Fred 1963— **24**

McGriff, James Harrell *See McGriff, Jimmy*

McGriff, Jimmy 1936–2008 **72**

McGruder, Aaron 1974— **28, 56, 120**

McGruder, Robert 1942— **22, 35**

McGuire, George Alexander 1866–1934 **80**

McGuire, Raymond J. 1957(?)(—) **57**

McHenry, Donald F. 1936— **83**

McIntosh, Winston Hubert *See Tosh, Peter*

McIntyre, Kalaparusha Maurice 1936–2013 **117**

McIntyre, Maurice Benford *See McIntyre, Kalaparusha Maurice*

McIntyre, Natalie *See Gray, Macy*

McJunkin, George 1851–1922 **93**

McKay, Claude 1889–1948 **6**

McKay, Festus Claudius *See McKay, Claude*

McKay, Nellie Yvonne 19(?)(?)–2006 **17, 57**

McKee, Lonette 1954— **12, 119**

McKegney, Tony 1958— **3**

McKenzie, Jaunel 1986— **73**

McKenzie, Timothy Lee *See Labrinth*

McKenzie, Vashti M. 1947— **29**

Mckesson, DeRay 1985— **133**

McKinney, Cynthia 1955— **11, 52, 74**

McKinney, Nina Mae 1912–1967 **40**

McKinney Hammond, Michelle 1957— **51**

McKinney-Whetstone, Diane 1954(?)— **27**

McKinnon, Ike *See McKinnon, Isaiah*

McKinnon, Isaiah 1943— **9**

McKissack, Leatrice 1930— **80**

McKissick, Floyd B(ixler) 1922–1981 **3**

McKnight, Brian 1969— **18, 34**

McKnight, Claude V., III *See Take 6*

McLean, Jackie 1931–2006 **78**

McLendon, John B., Jr. 1915–1999 **89**

McLeod, Gus 1955(?)— **27**

McMillan, Rosalynn A. 1953— **36**

McMillan, Terry 1951— **4, 17, 53**

McMillan, Tracy 1964— **93**

McMurray, Georgia L. 1934–1992 **36**

McNabb, Donovan 1976— **29, 119**

McNair, Ronald 1950–1986 **3, 58**

McNair, Steve 1973–2009 **22, 47, 79**

McNaughton, Jamar Rolando *See Chronixx*

McNeil, David *See Billy Ward and the Dominoes*

McNeil, Lori 1964(?)— **1**

McPhail, Sharon 1948— **2, 119**

McPhatter, Clyde *See Billy Ward and the Dominoes; Drifters, The*

McPherson, David 1968— **32**

McPherson, James Alan 1943— **70**

McQuater, Matthew *See Clovers, The*

McQueen, Butterfly 1911–1995 **6, 54**

McQueen, Steve 1969— **84**
McRae, Carmen 1920–1994 77
McRae, Hal 1945— **84**
McShann, Jay 1916–2006 110
McTell, Blind Willie 1901–1959 89
McVea, Jack 1914–2000 135
McVea, John *See McVea, Jack*
McVey, Joseph Wayne *See Z-Ro*
McWhorter, John 1965— **35, 119**
McWorter, Free Frank 1777–1854
91
Meadows, Tim 1961— **30**
Meek, Barbara 1934–2015 131
Meek, Carrie (Pittman) 1926— **6,
36**
Meek, Kendrick 1966— **41, 89**
Meeks, Gregory W. 1953— **25, 117**
Meeks, James T. 1956— **92**
Mehretu, Julie 1970— **85**
Mèkurya, Gétatchèw 1935–2016
135
Meles Zenawi *See Zenawi, Meles*
Mell, Patricia 1953— **49**
Mello, Breno 1931–2008 73
Melton, Frank 1949–2009 81
Melton, Harold D. 1966— **79**
Melvin, Harold *See Harold Melvin &
the Blue Notes*
Meminger, Dean 1948–2013 114
Memmi, Albert 1920— **37**
Memphis Jug Band 130
Memphis Minnie 1897–1973 33
Memphis Slim 1915–1988 105
Menard, John Willis 1838–1893 90
Mengestu, Dinaw 1978— **66, 114**
Mengistu, Haile Mariam 1937— **65**
Mensah, John 1982— **87**
Mensah, Thomas 1950— **48**
Mercado-Valdes, Frank 1962— **43**
Mercer, Kelvin *See De La Soul*
Meredith, James H(oward) 1933—
11
Merkerson, S. Epatha 1952— **47,
83**
Merriweather, Big Maceo
1905–1953 **109**
Merriweather, Major *See Merri-
weather, Big Maceo*
Mescudi, Scott Ramon Seguro *See
Kid Cudi*
Messenger, The *See Divine, Father*
Metcalfe, Ralph 1910–1978 26
Meters, The **118**
Method Man 1971— **81**
Meyer, June *See Jordan, June*
Meyers, Michael 1950— **131**
Meyiwa, Senzo 1984–2014 124
Mfume, Kweisi 1948— **6, 41**
Mhinga, Yvonne *See Chaka Chaka,
Yvonne*
Mhlaba, Raymond 1920–2005 55
Michaux, Solomon Lightfoot
1884–1968 91
Micheaux, Oscar (Devereaux)
1884–1951 7
Michel, Pras *See Fugees*
Michele, Michael 1966— **31**
Mickelbury, Penny 1948— **28**
Mickens, Ronald Elbert 1943— **105**
Mickle, Dale *See Dixie Cups, The*
Middleton, Reggie 1967— **105**
Midnight Star **110**
Mighty Clouds of Joy **110**

Migos **126**
Miguel 1986(?)— **98**
Miles, Buddy 1947–2008 69
Miles, George Allen, Jr. *See Miles,
Buddy*
Miles, Tiya 1970— **116**
Miles, William 1931–2013 112
Miley, Bubber 1903–1932 120
Miley, James Wesley *See Miley,
Bubber*
Milla, Roger 1952— **2**
Millender-McDonald, Juanita
1938–2007 21, 61
Miller, Bebe 1950— **3**
Miller, Cheryl 1964— **10, 74**
Miller, Clyde 1927–2011 113
Miller, Corey *See C-Murder*
Miller, Dorie 1919–1943 29
Miller, Doris *See Miller, Dorie*
Miller, Elmaurice *See Delta Rhythm
Boys*
Miller, Larry G. 1950(?)— **72**
Miller, Lorraine C. 1948— **119**
Miller, Marcus 1959— **84**
Miller, Maria 1803–1879 19
Miller, Omar Benson 1978— **93**
Miller, Patina 1984— **94**
Miller, Pepper 1953— **96**
Miller, Percy *See Master P*
Miller, Percy Romeo, Jr. *See Ro-
meo*
Miller, Portia Simpson *See Simpson
Miller, Portia*
Miller, Reggie 1965— **33**
Miller, Rice *See Williamson, Sonny
Boy*
Miller, Romeo *See Romeo*
Miller, Tangi 1975— **116**
Miller, Warren F., Jr. 1943— **53**
Miller, Wentworth 1972— **75**
Miller-Travis, Vernice 1959— **64**
Millinder, Lucius Venable *See
Millinder, Lucky*
Millinder, Lucky 1900–1966 101
Millines Dziko, Trish 1957— **28**
Millner, Denene 1969(?)— **76**
Mills, Dylan Kwabena *See Rascal,
Dizzee*
Mills, Florence 1896–1927 22
Mills, Joseph C. 1946— **51**
Mills, Sam 1959— **33**
Mills, Stephanie 1957— **36**
Mills, Steve 1960(?)— **47**
Mills Brothers, The **99**
Milner, Ron 1938— **39**
Milton, DeLisha 1974— **31**
Minaj, Nicki 1984— **86, 124**
Ming, Bob *See Ming, William Rob-
ert, Jr.*
Ming, Mel 1944— **106**
Ming, William Robert, Jr.
1911–1973 125
Mingo, Frank L. 1939–1989 32
Mingus, Charles Jr. 1922–1979 15
Minkins, Shadrach 1814(?)–1875
104
Minner, D. C. 1935–2008 133
Minor, DeWayne 1956— **32**
Minoso, Minnie 1925–2015 89, 127
Minott, Sugar 1956–2010 86
Minus, Rene *See Chantels, The*
Mississippi Sheiks 122
Mitchell, Arthur 1934— **2, 47**

Mitchell, Arthur Wergs 1883–1968
91
Mitchell, Blue 1930–1979 126
Mitchell, Brian Stokes 1957— **21**
Mitchell, Clarence M., Jr.
1911–1984 88
Mitchell, Corinne 1914–1993 8
Mitchell, Dwike 1930–2013 111
Mitchell, Elvis 1958— **67**
Mitchell, Freddie 1978— **116**
Mitchell, Ivory, Jr. *See Mitchell,
Dwike*
Mitchell, James *See Detroit Emer-
alds, The*
Mitchell, Juanita Jackson
1913–1992 128
Mitchell, Keith 1946— **82**
Mitchell, Kel 1978— **66, 131**
Mitchell, Leona 1949— **42**
Mitchell, Liz *See Boney M.*
Mitchell, Loften 1919–2001 31
Mitchell, Nicole 1967(?)— **66**
Mitchell, Parren J. 1922–2007 42,
66
Mitchell, Richard Allen *See Mitchell,
Blue*
Mitchell, Roscoe 1940— **134**
Mitchell, Russ 1960— **21, 73**
Mitchell, Sam 1963— **82**
Mitchell, Sharon 1962— **36**
Mitchell, Shireen 1970— **89**
Mitchell, Willie 1928–2010 114
Mizanekristos, Kelela *See Kelela*
Mizell, Jason *See Run-DMC*
Mkapa, Benjamin W. 1938— **16, 77**
Mo', Keb' *See Keb' Mo'*
Mobutu Sese Seko 1930–1997 1,
56
Moctar, Omara *See Bombino*
Modeliste, Joseph *See Meters, The*
Moffett, Charnett 1967— **127**
Mofolo, Thomas (Mokopu)
1876–1948 37
Mogae, Festus Gontebanye 1939—
19, 79
Mohamed, Ali Mahdi *See Ali Mahdi
Mohamed*
Mohammed, Nazr 1977— **64**
Mohammed, W. Deen 1933— **27**
Mohammed, Warith Deen *See Mo-
hammed, W. Deen*
Mohamud, Hassan Sheikh 1955—
105
Mohlabane, Goapele *See Goapele*
Moi, Daniel Arap 1924— **1, 35**
Mokae, Zakes 1934–2009 80
Mollel, Tololwa 1952— **38**
Moments, The *See Ray, Goodman
& Brown*
Monáe, Janelle 1985— **86**
Mongella, Gertrude 1945— **11**
Monica 1980— **21**
Mo'Nique 1967— **35, 84**
Monk, Art 1957— **38, 73**
Monk, Thelonious 1917–1982 1
Monroe, Bryan 1965— **71**
Monroe, Earl 1944— **89**
Monroe, Mary 19(?)(?)— **35**
Monteith, Mary Modjeska *See Sim-
kins, Modjeska Monteith*
Montgomery, Eurreal Wilford *See
Montgomery, Little Brother*
Montgomery, Isaiah T. 1847–1924
91

Montgomery, Little Brother
1906–1985 **117**
Montgomery, Robbie 1940— **101**
Montgomery, Ryan Daniel *See
Royce da 5'9"*
Montgomery, Tim 1975— **41**
Montgomery, Wes 1923–1968 88
Moody, Anne 1940–2015 127
Moody, James 1925— **83**
Moody, Ronald 1900–1984 30
Moody-Adams, Michele 1956— **76**
Moon, Warren 1956— **8, 66**
Moondoc, Jemeel 1951— **119**
Mooney, Paul 1941— **37, 120**
Moonglows, The **108**
Moore, Alice Ruth *See Dunbar-
Nelson, Alice Ruth Moore*
Moore, Anthony *See Romanthony*
Moore, Archie 1916(?)–1998 120
Moore, Barbara C. 1949— **49**
Moore, Ben *See James & Bobby
Purify*
Moore, Bobby *See Rashad, Ahmad*
Moore, Chanté 1967— **26, 130**
Moore, Davey 1933–1963 105
Moore, David Schultz *See Moore,
Davey*
Moore, Dorothy Rudd 1940— **46**
Moore, Gwendolynne S. 1951— **55**
Moore, Harry Roscoe *See Moore,
Tim*
Moore, Harry T. 1905–1951 29
Moore, James Isaac *See Slim
Harpo*
Moore, Jessica Care 1971— **30**
Moore, Johnny *See Drifters, The*
Moore, Johnny *See Ray, Goodman
& Brown*
Moore, Johnny B. 1950— **38**
Moore, Juanita 1922– 201483, 124
Moore, Kermit 1929–2013 116
Moore, Kevin *See Mo', Keb'*
Moore, Lecrae *See Lecrae*
Moore, LeRoi 1961–2008 72
Moore, Maya 1989— **94**
Moore, Melba 1945— **21**
Moore, Michael *See Rose Royce*
Moore, Minyon 19(?)(?)— **45**
Moore, Richard *See bin Wahad,
Dhoruba*
Moore, Sam *See Sam and Dave*
Moore, Shemar 1970— **21, 112**
Moore, Tim 1887–1958 124
Moore, Undine Smith 1904–1989
28
Moore, Wes 1978— **86**
Moorer, Lana *See MC Lyte*
Moorer, Michael 1967— **19, 132**
Moose, Charles 1953— **40**
Morake, Lebohang *See Lebo M*
Morales, Mark 1960— *See Fat
Boys*
Moran, Jason 1975— **89**
Moreland, Mantan 1902–1973 117
Morgan, Garrett (Augustus)
1877–1963 1
Morgan, Gertrude 1900–1986 63
Morgan, Irene 1917–2007 65
Morgan, Joe 1943— **9, 96**
Morgan, John *See Ray, Goodman
& Browne*
Morgan, Lee 1938–1972 102
Morgan, Rose (Meta) 1912(?)— **11**

Morgan, Tracy 1968— **61, 102, 131**

Morgan Lawrence, Margaret *See Lawrence, Margaret Morgan*

Morganfield, McKinley *See Muddy Waters*

Morial, Ernest "Dutch" 1929–1989 **26**

Morial, Marc H. 1958— **20, 51**

Morón, Alonzo G. 1909–1971 **91**

Morris, Eugene Edward *See Morris, Mercury*

Morris, Garrett 1937— **31, 133**

Morris, Greg 1934–1996 **28**

Morris, Lamorne 1983— **135**

Morris, Melvin 1942— **120**

Morris, Mercury 1947— **114**

Morris, Nathan *See Boyz II Men*

Morris, Raheem 1976— **77**

Morris, Wanya *See Boyz II Men*

Morris, William "Bill" 1938— **51**

Morris, Stevland Judkins *See Wonder, Stevie*

Morrison, Keith 1942— **13**

Morrison, Mary Thelma *See Washington, Mary T.*

Morrison, Sam 1936— **50**

Morrison, Toni 1931— **2, 15, 86**

Morrison, Vanessa 1969(?)— **84**

Morrow, E. Frederic 1909–1994 **100**

Morton, Azie Taylor 1936–2003 **48**

Morton, Ferdinand Q. 1881–1949 **90**

Morton, Frederick A., Jr. 1967(?)— **93**

Morton, Jelly Roll 1885(?)–1941 **29**

Morton, Joe 1947— **18**

Mos Def *See Bey, Yasiin*

Mosby, Marilyn 1980— **128**

Moseley-Braun, Carol *See Braun, Carol Moseley*

Moses, Edwin 1955— **8**

Moses, Gilbert, III 1942–1995 **12**

Moses, Robert Parris 1935— **11**

Mosisili, Pakalitha 1945— **96**

Mosley, "Sugar" Shane 1971— **32**

Mosley, Tim *See Timbaland*

Mosley, Walter 1952— **5, 25, 68**

Moss, Bryant *See Moss, Preacher*

Moss, Carlton 1909–1997 **17**

Moss, J. (?)— **64**

Moss, Otis, Jr. 1935— **72**

Moss, Otis, III 1971(?)— **72**

Moss, Preacher 1967— **63**

Moss, Randy 1977— **23, 90**

Moss, Shad Gregory *See Lil' Bow Wow*

Mossell, Gertrude Bustill 1855–1948 **40**

Mossell, Nathan Francis 1856–1946 **91**

Moten, Bennie 1894–1935 **135**

Moten, Etta *See Barnett, Etta Moten*

Motlanthe, Kgalema 1949— **74**

Motley, Archibald, Jr. 1891–1981 **30**

Motley, Constance Baker 1921–2005 **10, 55**

Motley, Marion 1920–1999 **26**

Moton, Robert Russa 1867–1940 **83**

Moura, Paulo 1932–2010 **87**

Mourning, Alonzo 1970— **17, 44, 131**

Moussambani, Eric 1978— **105**

Moutoussamy-Ashe, Jeanne 1951— **7**

Mowatt, Judy 1952(?)— **38**

Mowry, Jess 1960— **7**

Mowry, Tamera 1978— **79**

Mowry, Tia 1978— **78**

Moye, Famoudou Don 1946— **136**

Moy'e, Theodore *See Treacherous Three*

Moyo, Dambisa 1970(?)— **76**

Moyo, Karega Kofi 19(?)(?)— **36**

Moyo, Lovemore 1965— **76**

Moyo, Yvette Jackson 1953— **36**

Mphahlele, Es'kia 1919— **40**

Mswati III 1968— **56**

Mtukudzi, Oliver 1952— **109**

Muamba, Fabrice 1988— **104**

Mudimbe, V. Y. 1941— **61**

Mugabe, Robert 1924— **10, 71**

Mugisha, Frank 1979— **119**

Mugo, Madeleine *See Mugo, Micere Githae*

Mugo, Micere Githae 1942— **32**

Muhajir, El *See X, Marvin*

Muhammad, Ava 1951— **31**

Muhammad, Elijah 1897–1975 **4**

Muhammad, Ibtihaj 1985— **133**

Muhammad, Jabir Herbert 1929–2008 **72**

Muhammad, Khallid Abdul 1951(?)— **10, 31**

Muhammed, Murtala 1938–1976 **119**

Mukoko, Jestina 1957(?)— **75**

Mullen, Harryette 1953— **34**

Mullen, Nicole C. 1967— **45**

Muluzi, Bakili 1943— **14, 76**

Mumba, Samantha 1983— **29**

Mumford, Eugene *See Billy Ward and the Dominoes; Golden Gate Quartet*

Muncie, Chuck 1953–2013 **112**

Muncie, Harry Vance *See Muncie, Chuck*

Mundine, Anthony 1975— **56**

Munroe, Myles 1954–2014 **125**

Munsey, Harry Vance *See Muncie, Chuck*

Mupuya, Andrew 1992— **118**

Murphy, Charles 1959— **95**

Murphy, Charlie *See Murphy, Charles*

Murphy, Eddie 1961— **4, 20, 61**

Murphy, Edward Regan *See Murphy, Eddie*

Murphy, Guitar *See Murphy, Matt*

Murphy, John H. 1916— **42**

Murphy, Laura M. 1955— **43**

Murphy, Matt 1929(?)— **117**

Murphy, Taylonn 1969— **131**

Murphy McKenzie, Vashti *See McKenzie, Vashti M.*

Murray, Albert L. 1916— **33**

Murray, Cecil 1929— **12, 47**

Murray, Eddie 1956— **12**

Murray, Lenda 1962— **10**

Murray, Margaret James *See Washington, Margaret Murray*

Murray, Pauli 1910–1985 **38**

Murray, Tai 1982— **47**

Murrell, Sylvia Marilyn 1947— **49**

Musa, Ali, Mohammed *See Birra, Ali*

Muse, Clarence Edouard 1889–1979 **21**

Museveni, Yoweri 1944— **4, 119**

Mushikiwabo, Louise 1961— **88**

Musiq 1977— **37, 84**

Muslim, Saalim *See Storyboard P*

Mutebi, Ronald 1956— **25**

Mutola, Maria de Lurdes 1972— **12**

Mutombo, Dikembe 1966— **7, 107**

Mutu, Wangechi 19(?)(?)— **44**

Muzorewa, Abel 1925–2010 **85**

Mvula, Laura 1987— **110**

Mwanawasa, Levy 1948–2008 **72**

Mwangi, Meja 1948— **40**

Mwinyi, Ali Hassan 1925— **1, 77**

Mya 1979— **35**

Myers, Dave *See Aces, The*

Myers, Dwight *See Heavy D*

Myers, Lewis Eddy *See Myers, Lou*

Myers, Lou 1935(?)–2013 **110**

Myers, Louis *See Aces, The*

Myers, Walter Dean 1937–2014 **8, 70, 123**

Myka 9 *See Freestyle Fellowship*

Myles, John H. *See Swan Silvertones, The*

Myles, Kim 1974— **69**

Myles, Raymond Anthony 1958(?)–1998 **121**

Myrie, Mark Anthony *See Banton, Buju*

Nabagesera, Kasha Jacqueline 1980— **130**

Nabrit, Samuel Milton 1905–2003 **47**

Nagin, Ray 1956— **42, 57, 88**

Nail, John E. 1883–1947 **92**

Najm, Faheem Rasheed *See T-Pain*

Nakasa, Nat 1937–1965 **123**

Nakasa, Ndazana Nathaniel *See Nakasa, Nat*

Nakhid, David 1964— **25**

Naki, Hamilton 1926–2005 **63**

Nance, Cynthia 1958— **71**

Nanula, Richard D. 1960— **20**

Napoleon, Benny N. 1956(?)— **23**

Nas 1973— **33, 111**

Nascimento, Abdias do 1914–2011 **93**

Nascimento, Milton 1942— **2, 64**

Nash, Diane 1938— **72**

Nash, Joe 1919–2005 **55**

Nash, Johnny 1940— **40**

Nash, Michael *See Rose Royce*

Nash, Niecy 1970— **66, 115**

Nash, Shannon King 1971— **84**

Nash, Terius Youngdell *See The-Dream*

Nate Dogg 1969–2011 **92**

Naughton, Naturi 1984— **97**

Naughty by Nature **124**

Navarro, Fats 1923–1950 **104**

Navarro, Theodore, Jr. *See Navarro, Fats*

Naylor, Gloria 1950— **10, 42**

Nazario, Zoe Yadira Zaldaña *See Saldana, Zoe*

Ndadaye, Melchior 1953–1993 **7**

Ndegeocello, Meshell 1968— **15, 83**

Ndiaye, Adama Amanda *See Paris, Adama*

Ndiaye, Iba 1928–2008 **74**

N'Dour, Youssou 1959— **1, 53, 79**

Ndungane, Winston Njongonkulu 1941— **16**

Neal, Elise 1970— **29**

Neal, Kenny 1957— **123**

Neal, Larry 1937–1981 **38**

Neal, Mark Anthony 1965(?)— **74**

Neal, Michael *See Rare Essence*

Neal, Raful 1936–2014 **44, 121**

Neale, Haydain 1970— **52**

Neals, Otto 1930— **73**

Negga, Ruth 1982— **135**

Nell, William C. 1816–1874 **128**

Nelly 1974— **32, 90**

Nelson, Benjamin Earl *See King, Ben E.*

Nelson, Jill 1952— **6, 54**

Nelson, Kadir 1974— **115**

Nelson, Lucille *See Hegamin, Lucille*

Nelson, Oliver 1932–1975 **113**

Nelson, Prince Rogers *See Prince*

Nelson, Sophia A. 1967— **93**

Nelson, Stanley 1951— **92**

Nelson Meigs, Andrea 1968— **48**

Neto, António Agostinho 1922–1979 **43**

Nettles, Marva Deloise *See Collins, Marva*

Neverson, Tremaine Aldon *See Songz, Trey*

Neville, Aaron 1941— **21**

Neville, Art *See Meters, The*

Neville, Arthel 1962— **53**

Neville, Cyril *See Meters, The*

Neville, Ian *See Meters, The*

New Birth **124**

New Day Express *See Crown Heights Affair*

New Edition **101**

Newborn, Phineas, Jr. 1931–1989 **127**

Newcombe, Don 1926— **24**

Newkirk, Pamela 1957— **69**

Newman, David 1933–2009 **76**

Newman, Lester C. 1952— **51**

Newsome, Ozzie 1956— **26, 117**

Newton, Cam 1989— **96**

Newton, Huey (Percy) 1942–1989 **2**

Newton, Thandie 1972— **26, 114**

Newton, Thandiwe *See Newton, Thandie*

Ne-Yo 1982— **65**

Ngaujah, Sahr 1976— **86**

Ngengi, Kamau wa *See Kenyatta, Jomo*

Ngilu, Charity 1952— **58**

Ngubane, (Baldwin Sipho) Ben 1941— **33**

Nguema Mbasogo, Teodoro Obiang *See Obiang, Teodoro*

Ngugi, James T. *See Ngugi wa Thiong'o*

Ngugi wa Thiong'o 1938— **29, 61, 101**

Nguyen-Stevenson, Michael Ray *See Tyga*

Niane, Katoucha 1960–2008 **70**

Nicholas, Denise 1944— **82**

Nicholas, Fayard 1914–2006 **20, 57, 61**

Nicholas, Harold 1921— **20**

Nicholas, J. D. See Commodores, The

Nicholls, Frankie Warren, Jr. See Knuckles, Frankie

Nichols, Grace See Nichols, Nichelle

Nichols, James Thomas See Bell, James "Cool Papa"

Nichols, Nichelle 1933(?)— 11

Nickel Nine See Royce da 5'9"

Nighthawk, Robert 1909–1967 121

Nissel, Angela 1974— 42

Nix, Robert N. C., Jr. 1928–2003 51

Nix, Victor See Rose Royce

Nixon, Edgar Daniel 1899–1987 100

Nixon, Otis 1959— 111

Njawe, Pius 1957–2010 87

Njongonkulu, Winston Ndungane 1941— 16

Nkoli, Simon 1957–1998 60

Nkomo, Joshua 1917–1999 4, 65

Nkosi, Lewis 1936— 46

Nkrumah, Kwame 1909–1972 3

Nkunda, Laurent 1967— 75

Nkurunziza, Pierre 1963(?)— 78, 130

N'Namdi, George R. 1946— 17

Noah, Trevor 1984— 128

Noah, Yannick 1960— 4, 60, 121

Noble, Gil 1932— 76

Noble, Reginald See Redman

Noble, Ronald 1957— 46

Noble Drew Ali 1886–1929 100

Nocentelli, Leo See Meters, The

Norful, Smokie 1975— 127

Norful, Willie Ray, Jr. See Norful, Smokie

Norman, Christina 1960(?)— 47

Norman, Jessye 1945— 5

Norman, Kyle See Jagged Edge

Norman, Maidie 1912–1998 20

Norman, Pat 1939— 10

Norris, Michele 1961— 83

Northup, Solomon 1808–1863(?) 115

Norton, Eleanor Holmes 1937— 7, 93

Norton, Ken 1943–2013 101, 115

Norton, Meredith 1970(?)— 72

Norwood, Brandy See Brandy

Norwood, William Raymond, Jr. See Ray J

Notorious B.I.G. 1972–1997 20

Nottage, Cynthia DeLores See Tucker, C. DeLores

Nottage, Lynn 1964— 66

Nour, Nawal M. 1965(?)— 56

Ntaganda, Bosco 1972— 111

Ntaryamira, Cyprien 1955–1994 8

Nteff, Alain 1992— 127

Ntshona, Winston 1941— 52

Nugent, Richard Bruce 1906–1987 39

Nujoma, Samuel 1929— 10

Nunez, Elizabeth 1944— 62, 112

Nunez-Harrell, Elizabeth See Nunez, Elizabeth

Nunn, Annetta 1959— 43

Nunn, Bobby See Coasters, The

Nutter, Michael 1957— 69, 112

Nuttin' but Stringz See Escobar, Tourie, and Escobar, Damien

Nyanda, Siphiwe 1950— 21

Nyerere, Julius 1922–1999 5, 136

Nyerere, Kambarage See Nyerere, Julius

Nyong'o, Lupita 1983— 127

Nzié, Anne-Marie 1932–2016 136

Nzo, Alfred (Baphethuxolo) 1925— 15

Obadele, Imari 1930–2010 84

Obama, Barack 1961— 49, 74, 91

Obama, Michelle 1964— 61, 90

Obasanjo, Olusegun 1937— 5, 22

Obasanjo, Stella 1945–2005 32, 56

Obiang, Teodoro 1942— 103

Obote, Milton 1925–2005 63

Oboth, Isaac 1990(?)— 117

O'Brien, Soledad 1966— 88

Ocean, Frank 1987— 100

Ochocinco, Chad See Johnson, Chad

ODB See Ol' Dirty Bastard

Odetta 1930— 37, 74

Odinga, Raila 1945— 67, 110

Odom, Lamar 1979— 81

Odom, Leslie, Jr. 1981— 136

Odumegwu-Ojukwu, Chukwuemeka See Ojukwu, Odumegwu

Offset See Migos

Ofili, Chris 1968— 124

Ogden, Jonathan 1974— 110

Oglesby, Zena 1947— 12

Ogletree, Charles, Jr. 1952— 12, 47

O'Grady, Lorraine 1934— 73

Ogunlesi, Adebayo O. 19(?)(?)— 37

Ojikutu, Bayo 1971— 66

Ojikutu, Bisola 1974— 65

Ojukwu, Emeka See Ojukwu, Odumegwu

Ojukwu, Odumegwu 1933–2011 99

Okaalet, Peter 1953— 58

Okara, Gabriel 1921— 37

Okigbo, Christopher 1932–1967 102

Okogwu, Patrick Chukwuemeka See Tinie Tempah

Okonedo, Sophie 1969— 67

Okonjo-Iweala, Ngozi 1954— 101

Okonma, Tyler See Tyler, the Creator

Okosuns, Sonny 1947–2008 71

Okocha, Augustine Azuka See Okocha, Jay Jay

Okocha, Jay Jay 1973— 99

Ol' Dirty Bastard 1968–2004 52

Olagundoye, Olatokunbo Susan Olasobunmi Abeke See Olagundoye, Toks

Olagundoye, Toks 1975— 113

Olajuwon, Akeem See Olajuwon, Hakeem

Olajuwon, Hakeem 1963— 2, 72

Olatunji, Babatunde 1927–2003 36, 126

Olden, Georg(e) 1920–1975 44

O'Leary, Hazel (Rollins) 1937— 6

Oliver, Bilal Sayeed See Bilal

Oliver, Garrett 1962— 95

Oliver, Jerry 1947— 37

Oliver, Joe "King" 1885–1938 42

Oliver, John J., Jr. 1945— 48

Oliver, Kimberly 1976— 60

Oliver, Pam 1961— 54, 123

Oliver, Paul 1984–2013 115

Oliver, Rachel See Atlantic Starr

Olojede, Dele 1961— 59

Olopade, Olufunmilayo Falusi 1957(?)— 58

Olusola, Kevin 1988— 133

Olympio, Sylvanus 1902–1963 126

Omalu, Bennet 1968— 132

Omar, Samia Yusuf 1991–2012 107

Omarion 1984— 107

Omarosa 1974— 69, 110

Omolewa, Michael 194(?)— 119

Omotola See Jalade-Ekeinde, Omotola

O'Neal, Frederick 1905–1992 99

O'Neal, Patrice 1969–2011 99

O'Neal, Rodney 1954— 88

O'Neal, Ron 1937–2004 46

O'Neal, Shaquille 1972— 8, 30, 95

O'Neal, Stanley 1951— 38, 67

O'Neil, Buck 1911–2006 19, 59

O'Neil, John Jordan See O'Neil, Buck

Ongala, Ramadhani Mtoro See Ongala, Remmy

Ongala, Remmy 1947–2010 9, 91

Onile-Ere, Adetayo Ayowale See Cruz, Taio

Onwueme, Tess Osonye 1955— 23

Onwurah, Ngozi 1966(?)— 38

Onyewu, Oguchi 1982— 60

Opitz, May See Ayim, May

Orange, James 1942–2008 74

Orange, Walter See Commodores, The

O'Ree, William Eldon See O'Ree, Willie

O'Ree, Willie 1935— 5

Orioles, The 100

Orlandersmith, Dael 1959— 42

Orlons, The 130

Orman, Roscoe 1944— 55, 129

Ormes, Jackie 1911–1985 73

Orr, Kevyn 1958— 118

Ortiz, Ami See Chantels, The

Ortiz, David 1975— 52, 82

Ortiz, Luis 1979— 134

Ory, Edward See Ory, Kid

Ory, Kid 1886–1973 118

Osbey, Brenda Marie 1957— 102

Osborne, Jeffrey 1948— 26, 121

Osborne, Na'taki 1974— 54

Osborne, Roberta Louise See Adams, Alberta

Osman, Said 1952(?)— 127

Osotimehin, Babatunde 1949— 107

Otis, Clarence, Jr. 1956— 55

Otis, Clyde 1924–2008 67

Otunga, Maurice Michael 1923–2003 55

Ouattara 1957— 43

Ouattara, Alassane 1942— 90

Ouattara, Morou 1966— 74

Ousley, Curtis See King Curtis

Ousmane, Sembène See Sembène, Ousmane

OutKast 35

Outler, Jimmy See Soul Stirrers

Overton, Anthony 1865–1946 128

Owens, Brig 1943— 118

Owens, Brigman See Owens, Brig

Owens, Clifford 1971— 129

Owens, Dana See Queen Latifah

Owens, Helen 1937— 48

Owens, Henry See Golden Gate Quartet

Owens, J. C. See Owens, Jesse

Owens, Jack 1904–1997 38

Owens, James Cleveland See Owens, Jesse

Owens, James Robert, Jr. See Owens, Jimmy

Owens, Jesse 1913–1980 2

Owens, Jimmy 1943— 130

Owens, Kevin See Ray, Goodman & Brown

Owens, Kim Lamont See KEM

Owens, Major 1936–2013 6, 117

Owens, Paul See Swan Silvertones, The

Owens, Terrell 1973— 53, 106

Oyebanjo, Dapo Daniel See D'banj

Oyelowo, David 1976— 82, 126

Oyewale, Taiwo Bamidele Olaniyi See Prince Twins Seven-Seven

Oyeyemi, Helen 1984— 135

Oyono, Ferdinand 1929— 38

Ozanne, Ismael R. 1971(?)— 129

Ozen, Barbara Lynn See Lynn, Barbara

P. Diddy See Combs, Sean

Pace, Betty 1954— 59

Pace, Judy 1942— 119

Pace, Orlando 1975— 21, 134

Packer, Daniel 1947— 56

Packer, Will 1974(?)— 71

Packer, Z. Z. 1973— 64

Page, Alan (Cedric) 1945— 7

Page, Clarence 1947— 4

Page, Greg 1958–2009 78

Page, Inman 1853–1935 82

Page, Walter 1900–1957 117

Paige, Leroy Robert See Paige, Satchel

Paige, Rod 1933— 29

Paige, Satchel 1906–1982 7

Painter, Nell Irvin 1942— 24, 88

Palacio, Andy 1960–2008 96

Palcy, Euzhan 1958— 94

Palmer, Everard 1930— 37

Palmer, Keke 1993— 68, 120

Palmer, Lauren Keyana See Palmer, Keke

Palmer, Rissi 1981— 65

Palmer, Violet 1964— 59

Papa Wemba 1949–2016 135

Papa Wendo See Kolosoy, Wendo

Pape, Jean William 1946— 126

Parham, Charles Valdez See Parham, Truck

Parham, Marjorie B. 1918— 71

Parham, Truck 1911–2002 124

Paris, Adama 1976— 120

Parish, Robert 1953— 43

Parker, Barrington D. 1915–1993 92

Parker, Candace 1986— 74

Parker, Charlie 1920–1955 20

Parker, Herman, Jr. See Parker, Junior

Parker, Jim 1934–2005 64

Parker, Junior 1932–1971 116

Parker, Kellis E. 1942–2000 **30**

Parker, (Lawrence) Kris(hna) *See KRS-One*

Parker, LarStella Irby *See Parker, Star*

Parker, Maceo 1943— **72**

Parker, Nicole Ari 1970— **52**

Parker, Q *See 112*

Parker, Quinnes *See 112*

Parker, Ray, Jr. 1954— **85**

Parker, Star 1956— **70**

Parker, Tony 1982— **75**

Parker, Vernon 1959— **97**

Parker, Willie J. 1963(?)— **133**

Parks, Bernard C. 1943— **17**

Parks, Gordon 1912–2006 **1, 35, 58**

Parks, Henry Green, Jr. 1916–1989 **89**

Parks, Rosa 1913–2005 **1, 35, 56**

Parks, Suzan-Lori 1963— **34, 85**

Parlan, Horace 1931— **108**

Parr, Russ 196(?)— **51**

Parris, Teyonah 1987(?)— **131**

Parsons, James Benton 1911–1993 **14**

Parsons, Richard 1948— **11, 33, 124**

Pascal-Trouillot, Ertha 1943— **3**

Paterson, Basil A. 1926–2014 **69, 122**

Paterson, David A. 1954— **59**

Patillo, Melba Joy 1941— **15**

Patrick, Deval 1956— **12, 61, 127**

Patterson, Chuck 1945–2013 **124**

Patterson, Don 1936–1988 **135**

Patterson, Floyd 1935–2006 **19, 58**

Patterson, Frederick Douglass 1901–1988 **12**

Patterson, Gilbert Earl 1939— **41**

Patterson, J. O., Jr. 1935— **80**

Patterson, Louise 1901–1999 **25**

Patterson, Mary Jane 1840–1894 **54**

Patterson, Orlando 1940— **4, 127**

Patterson, P(ercival) J(ames) 1936(?)— **6, 20**

Patterson, Robert, Jr. *See Ali, Rashied*

Patton, Antwan 1975— **45** *See also OutKast*

Patton, Charley 1891(?)–1934 **107**

Patton, Paula 1975— **62**

Patton, Venetria K. 1968— **125**

Paul, Billy 1934–2016 **127, 135**

Paul, Chris 1985— **84, 100**

Paul, Evans 1955— **129**

Paulk, Marcus T. 1986— **127**

Payne, Allen 1962(?)— **13**

Payne, Donald M. 1934–2012 **2, 57, 112**

Payne, Donald M., Jr. 1958— **132**

Payne, Ethel L. 1911–1991 **28**

Payne, Freda 1942— **58**

Payne, Hazel *See Taste of Honey, A*

Payne, Les 1941— **89**

Payne, Ulice, Jr. 1955— **42**

Payne, William D. 1932— **60**

Payton, Benjamin F. 1932— **23**

Payton, Gary 1968— **99**

Payton, John 1946–2012 **48, 124**

Payton, Philip A., Jr. 1876–1917 **88**

Payton, Walter 1954–1999 **11, 25**

P.E.A.C.E. *See Freestyle Fellowship*

Peake, Tadley Ewing *See Dameron, Tadd*

Peaker, Franklin *See Harold Melvin & the Blue Notes*

Pearman, Raven-Symoné Christina *See Raven-Symoné*

Pearson, Felicia 1980— **99**

Peck, Carolyn 1966(?)— **23**

Peck, Raoul 1953— **32**

Peebles, Ann 1947— **114**

Peebles, Annie Murray *See Peebles, Ann*

Peele, Jordan *See Key & Peele*

Peete, Calvin 1943— **11**

Peete, Holly Robinson 1965— **20**

Peete, Rodney 1966— **60**

Pelé 1940— **7**

Pelé, Abedi 1964— **122**

Pena, Paul 1950–2005 **58**

Pendergrass, Teddy 1950–2010 **22, 83**

Penguins, The **107**

Penniman, Richard Wayne *See Little Richard*

Peoples, Alisa *See Yarbrough & Peoples*

Peoples, Dottie 19(?)(?)— **22**

Pereira, Aristides 1923–2011 **30, 97**

Perez, Anna 1951— **1**

Perez, Pascual 1957–2012 **108**

Perkins, Anthony 1959(?)— **24**

Perkins, Carl 1928–1958 **128**

Perkins, Eddie 1937–2012 **103**

Perkins, Edward (Joseph) 1928— **5**

Perkins, James, Jr. 1953(?)— **55**

Perkins, Joe Willie *See Perkins, Pinetop*

Perkins, Marion 1908–1961 **38**

Perkins, Minnie *See Grant, Micki*

Perkins, Pinetop 1913— **70**

Perren, Freddie 1943–2004 **60**

Perrineau, Harold, Jr. 1968— **51**

Perrot, Kim 1967–1999 **23**

Perry, Emmitt, Jr. *See Perry, Tyler*

Perry, Herman 1922–1945 **89**

Perry, James 1975— **83**

Perry, Joe 1927–2011 **95**

Perry, Laval 195(?)— **64**

Perry, Lee 1936— **19, 103**

Perry, Lincoln *See Fetchit, Stepin*

Perry, Lowell 1931–2001 **30**

Perry, Matthew J., Jr. 1921–2011 **96**

Perry, Rainford Hugh *See Perry, Lee*

Perry, Ruth 1936— **19**

Perry, Ruth Sando 1939— **15**

Perry, Scratch *See Perry, Lee*

Perry, Steve 1970— **98**

Perry, Tyler 1969— **40, 54, 103**

Perry, Warren 1942(?)— **56**

Person, Sandy *See Orlons, The*

Person, Waverly 1927— **9, 51**

Peters, Brock 1927–2005 **96**

Peters, Clarke 1952— **103**

Peters, Jason 1982— **125**

Peters, Lenrie 1932— **43**

Peters, Margaret 1915— **43**

Peters, Maria Philomena 1941— **12**

Peters, Matilda 1917— **43**

Petersen, Frank E. 1932— **31**

Petersen, Neal 1967— **96**

Peterson, Adrian 1985— **109**

Peterson, Hannibal *See Peterson, Marvin*

Peterson, James 19(?)(?)— **81**

Peterson, James 1937— **38**

Peterson, Jesse Lee 1949— **81**

Peterson, Karen Carter 1969— **90**

Peterson, Marvin 1948— **27**

Peterson, Oscar 1925— **52**

Peterson, Sylvia *See Chiffons, The*

Petioni, Muriel 1914 –2011 **99**

Petry, Ann 1909–1997 **19**

Pettiford, Oscar 1922–1960 **106**

Pettigrew, Antonio 1967–2010 **118**

Pettus, Kenny *See Dazz Band*

Pharcyde, The **127**

Pharr, Kelsey *See Delta Rhythm Boys*

Phife Dawg 1970–2016 **134**

Phifer, Mekhi 1974— **25, 103**

Philip, M. Nourbese *See Philip, Marlene Nourbese*

Philip, Marlene Nourbese 1947— **32**

Phillips, Arthur *See Dramatics, The*

Phillips, Bobby *See Cadillacs*

Phillips, Brandon 1981— **116**

Phillips, Carl 1959— **111**

Phillips, Charles E., Jr. 1959— **57, 109**

Phillips, Esther 1935–1984 **107**

Phillips, Helen L. 1919–2005 **63**

Phillips, Joseph *See Atlantic Starr*

Phillips, Joseph C. 1962— **73**

Phillips, Peter *See Rock, Pete*

Phillips, Teresa L. 1958— **42**

Phillips, Tony 1959–2016 **135**

Phipps, Wintley 1955— **59**

Pickens, James, Jr. 1954— **59**

Pickett, Bill 1870–1932 **11**

Pickett, Cecil 1945— **39**

Pickett, Wilson *See Falcons, The*

Pierce, Elijah 1892–1984 **84**

Pierce, Harold 1917-1988 **75**

Pierce, Maryland *See Five Keys, The*

Pierce, Paul 1977— **71**

Pierce, Wendell 1962— **90**

Pierre, Andre 1915— **17**

Pierre, Percy Anthony 1939— **46**

Pierre-Louis, Michèle 1947— **75**

Pierson, Katrina 1976— **134**

Pigford, Eva *See Marcille, Eva*

Pilgrim Travelers, The **129**

Pimentel, Miguel Jontel *See Miguel*

Pincham, R. Eugene, Sr. 1925–2008 **69**

Pinchback, P(inckney) B(enton) S(tewart) 1837–1921 **9**

Pinckney, Clementa C. 1973–2015 **130**

Pinckney, Sandra 194(?)— **56**

Pindell, Howardena 1943— **55**

Pinder, Jefferson 1970— **77**

Pinderhughes, John 1946— **47**

Pindling, Lynden 1930–2000 **81**

Pineda, Michael 1989— **121**

Pinkett, Jada *See Pinkett Smith, Jada*

Pinkett, Randal 1971— **61**

Pinkett Smith, Jada 1971— **10, 41, 95**

Pinkney, Arnold R. 1931–2014 **122**

Pinkney, Bill *See Drifters, The*

Pinkney, Bill 1935— **42**

Pinkney, Fayette 1948–2009 **80**

Pinkney, Jerry 1939— **15, 124**

Pinkston, W. Randall 1950— **24**

Pinn, Vivian Winona 1941— **49**

Piper, Adrian 1948— **71**

Pippen, Scottie 1965— **15, 89**

Pippin, Horace 1888–1946 **9**

Pitchford, Lonnie 1955–1998 **133**

Pitt, David Thomas 1913–1994 **10**

Pitt, Eugene *See Jive Five*

Pitta (do Nascimento), Celso (Roberto) 19(?)(?)— **17**

Pitts, Byron 1960— **71**

Pitts, Charles *See Pitts, Skip*

Pitts, Derrick 1956(?)— **77**

Pitts, Leonard, Jr. 1957— **54, 85**

Pitts, Robb 1941— **84**

Pitts, Robert Lee *See Pitts, Robb*

Pitts, Skip 1947–2012 **103**

Plaatje, Sol T. 1876–1932 **80**

Plaskett, Stacey 1966— **127**

Platters, The **99**

Player, Willa B. 1909–2003 **43**

Pleasant, Loretta *See Lacks, Henrietta*

Pleasant, Mary Ellen 1814–1904 **9**

Pleasure P 1984— **84**

Plessy, Homer Adolph 1862–1925 **31**

Plinton, James O., Jr. 1914–1996 **98**

Plummer, Glenn 1961— **120**

P.M. Dawn **54**

Pohamba, Hifikepunye 1935— **95**

Poindexter, Hildrus A. 1901–1987 **87**

Poitier, Sidney 1927— **11, 36**

Poitier, Sydney Tamiia 1973— **65**

Polite, Carlene Hatcher 1932–2009 **82**

Polite, Lloyd, Jr. *See Lloyd*

Pollard, Ackquille Jean *See Shmurda, Bobby*

Pollard, Fritz 1894–1986 **53**

Pollard, William L. 1945(?)— **91**

Pomare, Eleo 1937–2008 **72**

Poole, Elijah *See Muhammad, Elijah*

Pope.L, William 1955— **72**

Porter, Billy 1969— **112**

Porter, Bo 1972— **123**

Porter, Countee Leroy *See Cullin, Countee*

Porter, David 1941— **127**

Porter, Dorothy *See Wesley, Dorothy Porter*

Porter, George, Jr. *See Meters, The*

Porter, James A(mos) 1905–1970 **11**

Porter, Maggie *See Fisk Jubilee Singers*

Porter, Marquis Donnell *See Porter, Bo*

Porter, Terry 1963— **75**

Porter, Tiran 1948— **133**

Portis, Clinton 1981— **130**

Portuondo, Omara 1930— **53**

Potter, Myrtle 1958— **40**

Potts, Sylvester *See Contours, The*

Pough, Terrell 1987(?)–2005 **58**

Pounder, Carol Christine Hilaria *See Pounder, CCH*
Pounder, CCH 1952— **72**
Poussaint, Alvin F. 1934— **5, 67**
Poussaint, Renee 1944— **78**
Powell, Adam Clayton, Jr. 1908–1972 **3**
Powell, Benny 1930–2010 **87**
Powell, Bud 1924–1966 **24**
Powell, Colin 1937— **1, 28, 75**
Powell, Debra A. 1964— **23**
Powell, Keith 1979(?)— **101**
Powell, Kevin 1966— **31, 74**
Powell, Maxine 1915–2013 **8, 115**
Powell, Michael Anthony *See Powell, Mike*
Powell, Michael K. 1963— **32**
Powell, Mike 1963— **7**
Powell, Renee 1946— **34**
Powell, William *See O'Jays, The*
Powell, William J. 1916–2009 **82**
Power, Will 1970— **83**
Powers, Alton Adelbert *See Powers, Ben*
Powers, Ben 1950–2015 **132**
Prater, Dave *See Sam and Dave*
Pratt, Awadagin 1966— **31**
Pratt, Elmer *See Pratt, Geronimo*
Pratt, Geronimo 1947–2011 **18, 95**
Pratt, Kyla 1986— **57**
Pratt Dixon, Sharon *See Dixon, Sharon Pratt*
Pree, Dawn *See New Birth*
Preer, Evelyn 1896–1932 **82**
Premice, Josephine 1926–2001 **41**
Pressley, Condace L. 1964— **41**
Preston, Billy 1946–2006 **39, 59**
Preston, William Everett *See Preston, Billy*
Préval, René 1943— **87**
Preyan, Jermaine *See Mack Maine*
Price, David 1985— **101**
Price, Florence 1887–1953 **37**
Price, Frederick K. C. 1932— **21**
Price, Glenda 1939— **22**
Price, Hugh B. 1941— **9, 54**
Price, Kelly 1973(?)— **23**
Price, Leontyne 1927— **1**
Price, Lisa 1962— **97**
Price, Lloyd 1933— **119**
Price, McKinley L. 1949— **136**
Price, Richard 1930(?)— **51**
Pride, Charley 1938(?)— **26**
Primas, Randy 1949–2012 **106**
Primus, Pearl 1919–1994 **6, 125**
Prince 1958–2016 **18, 65, 134**
Prince, Richard E. 1947— **71**
Prince, Ron 1969— **64**
Prince, Tayshaun 1980— **68**
Prince Be 1970–2016 **136** *See also P.M. Dawn*
Prince Johnny C *See Geto Boys*
Prince Markie Dee *See Fat Boys*
Prince Twins Seven-Seven 1944–2011 **95**
Prince-Bythewood, Gina 1969— **31, 77**
Pritchard, Robert Starling 1927— **21**
Procope, Ernesta 19(?)(?)— **23**
Procope, John Levy 1925–2005 **56**
Proctor, Bernard Shaw 1921–2013 **120**

Professor Griff *See Public Enemy*
Professor Longhair 1918–1980 **109**
Proof 1973–2006 **101**
Prophet, Billy *See Jive Five*
Prophet, Nancy Elizabeth 1890–1960 **42**
Prothrow, Deborah Boutin *See Prothrow-Stith, Deborah*
Prothrow-Stith, Deborah 1954— **10**
Pruitt, Wendell O. 1920–1945 **106**
Pryce, Trevor 1975— **89**
Pryor, James Edward *See Pryor, Snooky*
Pryor, Rain 1969— **65**
Pryor, Richard 1940–2005 **3, 24, 56**
Pryor, Snooky 1921–2006 **119**
Prysock, Arthur 1929–1997 **117**
Public Enemy **98**
Puckett, Kirby 1960–2006 **4, 58**
Puff Daddy *See Combs, Sean*
Pugh, Charles 1971— **81**
Pugh, Iola Lewis *See Consolers, The*
Pugh, Sullivan *See Consolers, The*
Puig, Yasiel 1990— **113**
Purdie, Bernard 1939— **77**
Purifoy, Noah 1917–2004 **135**
Purify, Bobby *See James & Bobby Purify*
Purify, James *See James & Bobby Purify*
Purnell, Silas 1923–2003 **59**
Puryear, Martin 1941— **42, 101**
Pusha T 1977— **123**
Putney, Martha S. 1916–2008 **75**
Puzey, Leonard *See Ravens, The*
Pyfrom, Estella 1936— **127**
Quander, Nellie 1880–1961 **102**
Quarles, Benjamin Arthur 1904–1996 **18**
Quarles, Norma 1936— **25**
Quarterman, Lloyd Albert 1918–1982 **4**
Quattlebaum, Michael David, Jr. *See Blanco, Mykki*
Quavno *See Migos*
Queen Latifah 1970— **1, 16, 58, 119**
Querino, Manuel Raimundo 1851–1923 **84**
?uestlove 1971— **74** *See Roots, The*
Quigless, Helen G. 1944–2004 **49**
Quince, Peggy A. 1948— **69**
Quirot, Ana 1963— **13**
Quisim, Basheer *See Gryce, Gigi*
Quivers, Robin 1952— **61**
Qusim, Basheer *See Gryce, Gigi*
Rabb, Maurice F., Jr. 1932–2005 **58**
Rabia, Aliyah *See Staton, Dakota*
Rachell, James *See Rachell, Yank*
Rachell, Yank 1910–1997 **129**
Rackley, Gloria *See Blackwell, Gloria*
Radcliffe, Ted 1902–2005 **74**
Radcliffe, Theodore Roosevelt *See Radcliffe, Ted*
Rae Sremmurd **126**
Ragin, Derek Lee 1958— **84**
Rahman, Aishah 1936— **37**
Raines, Franklin 1949— **14, 107**
Raines, Rock *See Raines, Tim*
Raines, Tim 1959— **107**

Rainey, Ma 1886–1939 **33**
Raleigh Ritchie *See Anderson, Jacob*
Ralph, Sheryl Lee 1956— **18, 108**
Ramaphosa, Cyril 1952— **3, 117**
Rambough, Lori Ann *See Sommore*
Ramírez, Hanley 1983— **135**
Ramphele, Mamphela 1947— **29**
Ramsey, Charles H. 1948— **21, 69**
Rand, A(ddison) Barry 1944— **6**
Randall, Alice 1959— **38**
Randall, Dudley 1914–2000 **8, 55**
Randall, Vernellia R. 1948— **95**
Randle, John 1967— **87**
Randle, Theresa 1967— **16**
Randolph, A(sa) Philip 1889–1979 **3**
Randolph, Donald James *See Covay, Don*
Randolph, Linda A. 1941— **52**
Randolph, Robert 1980— **132**
Randolph, Willie 1954— **53**
Rangel, Charles B. 1930— **3, 52, 85**
Ranglin, Ernest 1932— **78**
Rankin Don *See Rhoden, Wayne*
Ransome, James E. 1961— **88**
Ra'oof, Abdul *See S.O.S. Band*
Raoul, Kwame 1964— **55**
Rapelang Rabana 198(?)— **112**
Rapier, James T. 1837–1883 **82**
Rare Essence **121**
Ras Tafari *See Haile Selassie*
Rascal, Dizzee 1985— **82**
Rashad, Ahmad 1949— **18**
Rashad, Phylicia 1948— **21**
Raspberry, William 1935— **2**
Raven *See Raven-Symoné*
Ravens, The **103**
Raven-Symoné 1985— **44, 113**
Rawlings, Jerry (John) 1947— **9**
Rawlings-Blake, Stephanie 1970— **93, 128**
Rawlinson, Johnnie B. 1952— **79**
Rawls, Johnny 1951— **135**
Rawls, Lou 1936–2006 **17, 57** *See also Highway QC's, The; Pilgrim Travelers, The*
Ray, Carline 1925–2013 **113**
Ray, Charlotte E. 1850–1911 **60**
Ray, Gene Anthony 1962–2003 **47**
Ray, Goodman & Brown **131**
Ray, Harry *See Ray, Goodman & Brown*
Ray J 1981— **86**
Raymond, Usher *See Usher*
Razaf, Andy 1895–1973 **19**
Razafkeriefo, Andreamentania Paul *See Razaf, Andy*
Ready, Stephanie 1975— **33**
Reagins, Tony 1967— **94**
Reagon, Bernice Johnson 1942— **7**
Reagon, Toshi 1964— **76**
Reason, Joseph Paul 1943— **19**
Reaves, Donald J. 1946— **102**
Record, Eugene 1940–2005 **60** *See also Chi-Lites*
Red Alert, Kool DJ 19(?)(?)— **33**
Redd, Dana 1968— **93**
Reddick, Lance 1962— **52, 128**
Reddick, Lawrence Dunbar 1910–1995 **20**
Redding, Ann Holmes 1951— **77**

Redding, J. Saunders 1906–1988 **26**
Redding, Louis L. 1901–1998 **26**
Redding, Otis, Jr. 1941— **16**
Redman 1970— **81**
Redman, Dewey 1931–2006 **135**
Redman, Don 1900–1964 **134**
Redman, Joshua 1969— **30**
Redmond, Eugene 1937— **23**
Redwood, John Henry 1942–2003 **78**
Reece, E. Albert 1950— **63**
Reece, Marcel 1985— **114**
Reed, A. C. 1926— **36**
Reed, Alaina *See Reed Hall, Alaina*
Reed, Ishmael 1938— **8**
Reed, Jimmy 1925–1976 **38**
Reed, Joe L. 1939(?)— **110**
Reed, Kasim 1969— **82**
Reed, Larry *See Dramatics, The*
Reed, Natina 1979–2012 **106**
Reed, Willie *See Louis, Willie*
Reed, Willis, Jr. 1942— **86**
Reed Amini, Alaina *See Reed Hall, Alaina*
Reed Hall, Alaina 1946–2009 **83**
Reeder, Joyce *See Beatty, Joyce*
Reedy, Jessica 1988— **101**
Reems, Ernestine Cleveland 1932— **27**
Rees, Dee 197(?)— **100**
Reese, Calvin *See Reese, Pokey*
Reese, Della 1931— **6, 20, 96**
Reese, Jerry 1963— **103**
Reese, Milous J., Jr. 1904— **51**
Reese, Pokey 1973— **28**
Reese, Tracy 1964— **54**
Reeves, Bass 1838–1910 **100**
Reeves, Carlton W. 1964— **129**
Reeves, Dianne 1956— **32, 119**
Reeves, Gregory 1952— **49**
Reeves, Martha 1941— **85**
Reeves, Rachel J. 1950(?)— **23**
Reeves, Shirley Alston *See Shirelles, The*
Reeves, Triette Lipsey 1963— **27**
Regis, Cyrille 1958— **51**
Reid, Antonio *See Reid, L.A.*
Reid, Ira De A. 1901–1968 **100**
Reid, Irvin D. 1941— **20**
Reid, L.A. 1956— **28, 129**
Reid, Rufus 1944— **130**
Reid, Senghor 1976— **55**
Reid, Tim 1944— **56**
Reid, Vernon 1958— **34**
Reivers, Corbin Bleu *See Corbin Bleu*
Render, Michael *See Killer Mike*
Retta 1970— **131**
Reuben, Gloria 19(?)(?)— **15**
Rev Run *See Run; Run-DMC*
Revels, Hiram Rhoades 1827–1901 **98**
Reverend Ike 1935–2009 **79**
Revis, Darrelle 1985— **130**
Reyes, José 1983— **134**
Reynolds, Harold 1960— **77**
Reynolds, L. J. *See Dramatics, The*
Reynolds, Star Jones 1962(?)— **10, 27, 61**
Rhames, Ving 1959— **14, 50**
Rhimes, Shonda Lynn 1970— **67**
Rhoden, Dwight 1962— **40**

Rhoden, Wayne 1966— **70**
Rhoden, William C. 1950(?)— **67**
Rhodes, Jewell Parker 1954— **84**
Rhodes, Ray 1950— **14**
Rhone, Sylvia 1952— **2**
Rhone, Trevor 1940–2009 **80**
Rhymefest 1977— **97**
Rhymes, Busta 1972— **31**
Rhyne, Melvin 1936–2013 **109**
Ribbs, William Theodore, Jr. See Ribbs, Willy T.
Ribbs, Willy T. 1956— **2**
Ribeau, Sidney 1947(?)— **70**
Ribeiro, Alfonso 1971— **17**
Rice, Condoleezza 1954— **3, 28, 72**
Rice, Constance LaMay 1956— **60**
Rice, Emmett J. 1920–2011 **94**
Rice, Jerry 1962— **5, 55, 89**
Rice, Jim 1953— **75**
Rice, Linda Johnson 1958— **9, 41**
Rice, Louise Allen 1941— **54**
Rice, Mack See Falcons, The
Rice, Norm(an Blann) 1943— **8**
Rice, Ray 1987— **112**
Rice, Susan 1964— **74, 103**
Rich, Eddie See Swallows, The
Richard, Dawn 1983— **92**
Richard, J. R. 1950— **87**
Richards, Beah 1926–2000 **30**
Richards, Hilda 1936— **49**
Richards, Lloyd 1923(?)— **2**
Richards, Sanya See Richards-Ross, Sanya
Richardson, Curtis See Highway QC's, The
Richardson, Desmond 1969— **39**
Richardson, Donna 1962— **39**
Richardson, Elaine Potter See Kincaid, Jamaica
Richardson, Julieanna 1954— **81**
Richardson, LaTanya 1949— **71**
Richardson, Laura 1962— **81**
Richardson, Lee See Highway QC's, The
Richardson, Nolan 1941— **9**
Richardson, Pat See Norman, Pat
Richardson, Rupert 1930–2008 **67**
Richardson, Salli 1967— **68**
Richards-Ross, Sanya 1985— **66, 98**
Richie, Leroy C. 1941— **18**
Richie, Lionel 1949— **27, 65, 114**
See also Commodores, The
Richmond, Cedric 1973— **93**
Richmond, Mitchell James 1965— **19**
Ricks, Jimmy See Ravens, The
Riddick, Clyde See Golden Gate Quartet
Rideau, Iris 1940(?)— **46**
Ridenhour, Carlton See Chuck D.
Ridley, John 1965— **69**
Riggins, Karriem 1975— **102**
Riggs, Marlon 1957–1994 **5, 44**
Rihanna 1988— **65, 102**
Riles, Wilson C. 1917–1999 **79**
Riley, Amber 1986— **97**
Riley, Ben 1933— **130**
Riley, Boots 1971— **89**
Riley, Helen Caldwell Day 1926— **13**
Riley, Rochelle 1959(?)— **50**

Riley, Teddy 1967— **116**
Riley, Timothy Christian See Tony! Toni! Toné!
Rillieux, Norbert 1806–1894 **92**
Ringgold, Faith 1930— **4, 81**
Riperton, Minnie 1947–1979 **32**
Rivers, Doc 1961— **25, 81**
Rivers, Eugene F., III 1950— **81**
Rivers, Glenn See Rivers, Doc
Rivers, Kim See Roberts, Kimberly Rivers
Rivers, Sam 1923— **95**
Roach, Max 1924–2007 **21, 63**
Roaf, Andrée Layton 1941–2009 **106**
Roaf, William Layton See Roaf, Willie
Roaf, Willie 1970— **106**
Roberto, Holden 1923–2007 **65**
Roberts, Aldwyn See Lord Kitchener
Roberts, Darryl 1962(?)— **70**
Roberts, Dave 1972— **132**
Roberts, Deborah 1960— **35**
Roberts, Ian See Kwei-Armah, Kwame
Roberts, James See Lover, Ed
Roberts, Joseph Jenkins 1809–1876 **125**
Roberts, Kimberly Rivers 1981(?)— **72**
Roberts, Kristina LaFerne See Zane
Roberts, Lee See Conley, Art
Roberts, Lillian 1928— **83**
Roberts, Marcus 1963— **19, 113**
Roberts, Marthaniel See Roberts, Marcus
Roberts, Michele 1956— **123**
Roberts, Mike 1948— **57**
Roberts, Norwell 1946— **134**
Roberts, Robin 1960— **16, 54, 113**
Roberts, Roy S. 1939(?)— **14**
Roberts, William Leonard, II See Ross, Rick
Robertson, Cardiss Hortense See Collins, Cardiss
Robertson, Gil L., IV 1964— **85**
Robertson, Lance See DJ Lance Rock
Robertson, Oscar 1938— **26**
Robeson, Eslanda Goode 1896–1965 **13**
Robeson, Paul (Leroy Bustill) 1898–1976 **2**
Robey, Don 1903–1975 **115**
Robinson, Amelia Boynton See Boynton Robinson, Amelia
Robinson, Aminah 1940— **50**
Robinson, Arnett See Falcons, The
Robinson, Bill "Bojangles" 1878–1949 **11**
Robinson, Bishop L. 1927— **66**
Robinson, Cleo Parker 1948(?)— **38**
Robinson, Craig 1962— **107**
Robinson, Craig 1971— **103**
Robinson, Cynthia 1944(?)–2015 **132**
Robinson, Darren 1967–1995 See Fat Boys
Robinson, Dave 1941— **110**
Robinson, David 1965— **24, 90**

Robinson, Eddie G. 1919–2007 **10, 61**
Robinson, Eugene 1955— **77**
Robinson, Fatima 19(?)(?)— **34**
Robinson, Fenton 1935–1997 **38**
Robinson, Flynn 1941–2013 **112**
Robinson, Frank 1935— **9, 87**
Robinson, Ida B. 1891–1946 **106**
Robinson, Jack Roosevelt See Robinson, Jackie
Robinson, Jackie 1919–1972 **6**
Robinson, Joann Gibson 1912–1992 **100**
Robinson, Justin See Carolina Chocolate Drops
Robinson, LaVaughn 1927–2008 **69**
Robinson, Louise See Sweet Honey in the Rock
Robinson, Luther See Robinson, Bill "Bojangles"
Robinson, Malcolm S. 1948— **44**
Robinson, Matt 1937–2002 **69**
Robinson, Matthew, Jr. See Robinson, Matt
Robinson, Max 1939–1988 **3**
Robinson, Patrick 1966— **19, 71**
Robinson, Rachel 1922— **16**
Robinson, Randall 1941— **7, 46**
Robinson, Reginald R. 1972— **53**
Robinson, Romye See Pharcyde, The
Robinson, Sharon 1950— **22**
Robinson, Shaun 19(?)(?)— **36**
Robinson, Smokey 1940— **3, 49**
Robinson, Spottswood W., III 1916–1998 **22**
Robinson, Sugar Ray 1921–1989 **18**
Robinson, Sylvia 1936— **79**
Robinson, Will 1911–2008 **51, 69**
Robinson, William, Jr. See Robinson, Smokey
Robinson-Berry, Joan 19(?)(?)— **94**
Roble, Abdi 1964— **71**
Roby, Kimberla Lawson 1965— **86**
Roche, Joyce M. 1947— **17**
Rochereau, Tabu Ley 1937(?)–2013 **117**
Rochester See Anderson, Eddie "Rochester"
Rochon, Lela 1965(?)— **16**
Rochon, Stephen W. 1950(?)— **78**
Rock, Chris 1967(?)— **3, 22, 66**
Rock, John S. 1825–1866 **113**
Rock, John Sweat See Rock, John S.
Rock, John Swett See Rock, John S.
Rock, Pete 1970— **121**
Rock, Sugar Ray See Crown Heights Affair
Rock, The 1972— **29, 66**
Rock, Tony 1974— **108**
Rock, Vin See Naughty by Nature
Rodgers, Johnathan 1946— **6, 51**
Rodgers, Nile See Chic
Rodgers, Rod 1937–2002 **36**
Rodman, Dennis 1961— **12, 44, 96, 118**
Rodney, Winston See Burning Spear
Rodrigues, Percy 1918–2007 **68**
Rodríguez, Arsenio 1911–1970 **87**
Rodriguez, Cheryl 1952— **64**

Rodriguez, Jimmy 1963(?)— **47**
Rogers, Alan G. 1967–2008 **72**
Rogers, Bobby 1940–2013 **110**
Rogers, Desirée 1959— **88**
Rogers, Jimmy 1924–1997 **38**
Rogers, Joe 1964— **27**
Rogers, Joel Augustus 1883(?)–1996 **30**
Rogers, John W., Jr. 1958— **5, 52**
Rogers, Kelis See Kelis
Rogers, Nat See Little Anthony & the Imperials
Rogers, Rodney Ray 1971— **106**
Rogers, Willie See Soul Stirrers
Rojas, Don 1949— **33**
Roker, Al 1954— **12, 49**
Roker, Roxie 1929–1995 **68**
Rolle, Esther 1920–1998 **13, 21**
Rolle, Janet 1961— **97**
Rolle, Myron 1986— **98**
Rollins, Billy See Contours, The
Rollins, Charlemae Hill 1897–1979 **27**
Rollins, Howard E., Jr. 1950–1996 **16**
Rollins, Ida Gray Nelson See Gray (Nelson Rollins), Ida
Rollins, James Calvin, III See Rollins, Jimmy
Rollins, Jimmy 1978— **70**
Rollins, Sonny 1930— **37, 94**
Rollins, Theodore Walter See Rollins, Sonny
Romanthony 1967–2013 **115**
Romeo 1989— **98**
Ronaldinho 1980— **69**
Rondo, Rajon 1986— **111**
Ronettes, The **132**
Roney, Wallace 1960— **136**
Rooakhptah, Amunnubi See York, Dwight D.
Rooks, Sean 1969–2016 **136**
Roots, The **101**
Rose, Anika Noni 1972— **70**
Rose, Derrick 1988— **82**
Rose, Harold M. 1930–2016 **134**
Rose, Jalen 1973— **108**
Rose, Lionel 1948— **56**
Rose Royce **120**
Roseboro, John 1933–2002 **123**
Ross, Araminta See Tubman, Harriet
Ross, Charles 1957— **27**
Ross, Diana 1944— **8, 27**
Ross, Don 1941— **27**
Ross, Freddie See Big Freedia
Ross, Isaiah "Doc" 1925–1993 **40**
Ross, Rick 1976— **79, 104**
Ross, Tracee Ellis 1972— **35**
Rosser, Frederick Douglas, III See Young, Darren
Ross-Lee, Barbara 1942— **67**
Rotimi 1988(?)— **130**
Rotimi, Emmanuel Gladstone Olawale See Rotimi, Ola
Rotimi, Ola 1938–2000 **1, 130**
Roundfield, Danny 1953–2012 **109**
Roundtree, Dovey 1914— **80**
Roundtree, Richard 1942— **27**
Rouse, Cecilia 1963— **93**
Rouse, Charlie 1924–1988 **130**
Rowan, Carl T(homas) 1925— **1, 30**

Rowe-Adams, Jackie 194(?)— **109**
Rowell, Victoria 1960— **13, 68**
Rowland, Kelly 1981— **100**
Roy, Brandon 1984— **98**
Roy, Kenny 1990(?)— **51**
Royce 5'9" *See Royce da 5'9"*
Royce da 5'9" 1977— **134**
Royo, Andre 1968— **136**
Rubin, Chanda 1976— **37**
Rucker, Darius 1966— **34, 74, 108**
Rudder, David 1953— **79**
Rudisha, David 1988— **112**
Rudolph, Maya 1972— **46, 106**
Rudolph, Wilma (Glodean) 1940—
4
Ruffin, Jimmy 1936–2014 **125**
Ruffin, Joseph Lee *See Shakur,
Yusef*
Ruffin, Josephine St. Pierre
1842–1924 **75**
Ruffins, Kermit 1964— **85**
Rugambwa, Laurean 1912–1997 **20**
Ruggles, David 1810–1849 **126**
Ruley, Ellis 1882–1959 **38**
Run 1964— **31, 73, 75**
Run-DMC **31, 75**
RuPaul 1960— **17, 91**
Rusesabagina, Paul 1954— **60**
Rush, Bobby 1940— **78**
Rush, Bobby 1946— **26, 76**
Rush, Otis 1934— **38**
Rushen, Patrice 1954— **12**
Rushing, Jimmy 1903–1972 **37**
Russell, Bill 1934— **8**
Russell, Brenda 1944(?)— **52**
Russell, Herman Jerome 1931(?)—
17
Russell, Nipsey 1924–2005 **66**
Russell, Robin *See New Birth*
Russell, William Felton *See Rus-
sell, Bill*
Russell-McCloud, Patricia 1946—
17
Russwurm, John Brown 1799–1851
100
Rust, Art, Jr. 1927–2010 **83**
Rustin, Bayard 1910–1987 **4**
Ruth B 1995— **135**
Rutling, Thomas *See Fisk Jubilee
Singers*
RZA 1969— **80, 128**
Saadiq, Raphael 1966— **125** *See
also See Tony! Toni! Toné!*
Saar, Alison 1956— **16**
Saar, Betye 1926— **80**
Sabathia, Carsten Charles, Jr. *See
Sabathia, CC*
Sabathia, CC 1980— **74**
Sade 1959— **15, 92**
Sadler, Joseph *See Grandmaster
Flash*
Sadlier, Rosemary 19(?)(?)— **62**
St. Jacques, Raymond 1930–1990
8
Saint James, Synthia 1949— **12**
St. John, Kristoff 1966— **25**
St. Julien, Marlon 1972— **29**
St. Louis, David 1974(?)— **126**
St. Patrick, Mathew 1969— **48**
Saint-Georges, Chevalier de *See
Boulogne, Joseph, Chevalier de
Saint-Georges*

Saint-Georges, Joseph Boulogne
*See Boulogne, Joseph, Chevalier
de Saint-Georges*
Saldana, Zoe 1978— **72, 118**
Sales, Ruby 1948— **133**
Salih, Al-Tayyib 1929— **37**
Sall, Macky 1961— **101**
Sallee, Charles 1911— **38**
Salley, Sam *See Harold Melvin &
the Blue Notes*
Salter, Nikkole 1979(?)— **73**
Salters, Alisia *See Salters, Lisa*
Salters, Lisa 1966(?)— **71**
Salvador, Bryce 1976— **51**
Sam, Michael 1990— **121**
Sam, Robert *See Graham Central
Station*
Sam and Dave **102**
Samara, Noah 1956— **15**
SAMO *See Basquiat, Jean-Michel*
Sample, Joe 1939–2014 **51, 123**
See also Crusaders, The
Sampson, Charles 1957— **13**
Sampson, Edith S(purlock)
1901–1979 **4**
Samuel, Sealhenry Olumide *See
Seal*
Samuelsson, Marcus 1970— **53,
120**
Sanchez, Sonia 1934— **17, 51**
Sancho, Charles Ignatius *See San-
cho, Ignatius*
Sancho, Ignatius 1729–1780 **133**
Sandé, Emeli 1987— **113**
Sanders, Angelia 1961(?)— **86**
Sanders, Barry 1968— **1, 53**
Sanders, Bob 1981— **72**
Sanders, Charlie 1946–2015 **130**
Sanders, Deion 1967— **4, 31, 96**
Sanders, Demond *See Sanders,
Bob*
Sanders, Dori(nda) 1935— **8**
Sanders, Joseph R(ichard, Jr.)
1954— **11**
Sanders, Malika 1973— **48**
Sanders, Pharoah 1940— **64**
Sanders, Rose M. *See Touré, Faya
Ora Rose*
Sanders, Satch 1938— **77**
Sanders, Thomas Ernest *See
Sanders, Satch*
Sands, Diana 1934–1973 **87**
Sané, Pierre Gabriel 1948–1998 **21**
Sanford, Isabel 1917–2004 **53**
Sanford, John Elroy *See Foxx,
Redd*
Sangare, Oumou 1968— **18, 99**
Sangho, Awa 1972— **127**
Sanhá Malam Bacai 1947–2012 **84,
101**
Sankara, Thomas 1949–1987 **17**
Sankoh, Foday 1937–2003 **74**
Sanneh, Kelefa 1975— **96**
Santamaria, Mongo 1917–2003 **81**
Santana, Juelz 1982— **120**
Santiago-Hudson, Ruben 1956—
85
Santiel, Terral *See Rose Royce*
Santiel, Terry *See Rose Royce*
Santigold 1976— **96**
Santogold *See Santigold*
Santos de Freitas, Antonio Carlos
See Brown, Carlinhos

Sapp, Marvin 1966(?)— **74**
Sapp, Rhonda LaChanze *See
LaChanze*
Sapp, Warren 1972— **38, 109**
Sapphire 1950— **14, 95**
Saro-Wiwa, Kenule 1941–1995 **39**
Sarpong, Sam 1975–2015 **132**
Sasser, Sean 1968–2013 **113**
Sassou-Nguesso, Denis 1943—
103
Sata, Michael 1937–2014 **102, 125**
Satcher, David 1941— **7, 57, 111**
Satchmo *See Armstrong, (Daniel)
Louis*
Saunders, Mahalia *See Ellis,
Hortense*
Savage, Augusta Christine
1892(?)–1962 **12**
Savimbi, Jonas (Malheiro)
1934–2002 **2, 34**
Savón, Félix 1967— **105**
Sawyer, Amos 1945— **2, 123**
Sawyer, Eugene 1934–2008 **81**
Saxton, Shirley Childress *See
Sweet Honey in the Rock*
Sayers, Gale 1943— **28**
Sayles Belton, Sharon *See Belton,
Sharon Sayles*
Sbraga, Kevin 1979(?)— **88**
Scandrick, Marvin *See 112*
Scandrick, Slim *See 112*
Scantlebury, Janna 1984(?)— **47**
Scantlebury-White, Velma 1955—
64
Scarface *See Geto Boys*
Scarlett, Millicent 1971— **49**
Schiavocampo, Mara 1979— **97**
Schmoke, Kurt 1949— **1, 48**
Schofield, Willie *See Falcons, The*
Schomburg, Arthur Alfonso
1874–1938 **9**
Schomburg, Arturo Alfonso *See
Schomburg, Arthur Alfonso*
ScHoolboy Q 1986— **117**
Schultz, Michael A. 1938— **6**
Schuyler, George Samuel
1895–1977 **40**
Schuyler, Philippa 1931–1967 **50**
Scott, Byron 1961— **125**
Scott, C. A. 1908–2000 **29**
Scott, Coretta *See King, Coretta
Scott*
Scott, Cornelius Adolphus *See
Scott, C. A.*
Scott, David 1946— **41, 117**
Scott, Dread 1965— **106**
Scott, George 1929–2005 **55** *See
also Blind Boys of Alabama, The*
Scott, George 1944–2013 **113**
Scott, Harold Russell, Jr.
1935–2006 **61**
Scott, Hazel 1920–1981 **66**
Scott, Jeff *See Imani Winds*
Scott, Jill 1972— **29, 83**
Scott, Jimmy 1925–2014 **48, 122**
Scott, John T. 1940–2007 **65**
Scott, "Little" Jimmy *See Scott,
Jimmy*
Scott, Milton 1956— **51**
Scott, Robert C. 1947— **23**
Scott, Shirley 1934–2002 **133**
Scott, Stuart 1965— **34, 126**
Scott, Tim 1965–2015 **87, 125**
Scott, Wallace *See Whispers, The*

Scott, Walter *See Whispers, The*
Scott, Wendell Oliver, Sr.
1921–1990 **19**
Scott-Heron, Gil 1949–2011 **94**
Scott-Young, Mona 1967(?)— **101**
Scribner, Marcus 2000— **136**
Scruggs, Mary Elfrieda *See Wil-
liams, Mary Lou*
Scurry, Briana 1971— **27**
Seacole, Mary 1805–1881 **54**
Seal **14, 75**
Seale, Bobby 1936— **3**
Seale, Robert George *See Seale,
Bobby*
Seals, Frank *See Seals, Son*
Seals, Son 1942–2004 **56**
Sealy, Lloyd G. 1917–1985 **125**
Sealy, Malik 1970–2000 **118**
Sears, Leah Ward 1955— **5, 79**
Sears, Stephanie 1964— **53**
Sears-Collins, Leah J(eanette) *See
Sears, Leah Ward*
Sebree, Charles 1914–1985 **40**
Secada, Jon 1962— **97**
Secada, Juan Francisco *See
Secada, Jon*
Seedorf, Clarence 1976— **121**
Seele, Pernessa 1954— **46**
Sefolosha, Thabo 1984— **121**
Selasi, Taiye 1979— **125**
Selassie, Haile *See Haile Selassie*
Self Jupiter *See Freestyle Fellow-
ship*
Sembène, Ousmane 1923–2007
13, 62
Senghor, Augustin Diamacoune
1928–2007 **66**
Senghor, Léopold Sédar
1906–2001 **12, 66**
Sengstacke, John Herman Henry
1912–1997 **18**
Senior, Olive 1941— **37**
Senna, Danzy 1970— **93**
Sentamu, John 1949— **58**
Sermon, Erick 1968— **81**
Serrano, Andres 1951(?)— **3**
Sesay, Isha 1976— **107**
Sessoms, Vivian 198(?)— **122**
Setmayer, Tara 1975— **130**
Seven-Seven, Prince Twins *See
Prince Twins Seven-Seven*
Sewell, Terri 1965— **93**
Seymour, Richard 1979— **101**
Seymour, Teddy 1941(?)— **110**
Seymour, William J. 1879–1922
106
Shabazz, Attallah 1958— **6**
Shabazz, Betty 1936–1997 **7, 26**
Shabazz, Ilyasah 1962— **36**
Shabazz Palaces **123**
Shadd, Abraham D. 1801–1882 **81**
Shaddix, Katrina Lanette *See Pier-
son, Katrina*
Shade, Will *See Memphis Jug
Band*
Shaggy 1968— **31**
Shakespeare, Robbie 1953— *See
Sly & Robbie*
Shakur, Afeni 1947–2016 **67, 135**
Shakur, Assata 1947— **6**
Shakur, Meshell Suihailia Bashir
See Ndegeocello, Meshell
Shakur, Tupac Amaru 1971–1996
14

Shakur, Yusef 1973— **85**

Shamir 1974— **129**

Shange, Ntozake 1948— **8, 89**

Shanice 1973— **112**

Shank, Suzanne F. 1962(?)— **77**

Shannon, Randy 1966— **82**

Shanté, Roxanne 1969— **33**

Sharp, Dee Dee 1945— **130**

Sharpe, Samuel 1801(?)–1832 **103**

Sharpe, Shannon 1968— **97**

Sharper, Darren 1975— **32, 118**

Sharpton, Al 1954— **21, 97**

Shaver, Earnie Dee *See Shavers, Earnie*

Shavers, Charlie 1920–1971 **131**

Shavers, Cheryl 19(?)(?)— **31**

Shavers, Earnie 1944— **127**

Shaw, Bernard 1940— **2, 28**

Shaw, Brian 1966— **127**

Shaw, Eddie 1937— **136**

Shaw, Ernesto D., Jr. *See DJ Clue?*

Shaw, Marlena 1942— **105**

Shaw, William J. 1934— **30**

Sheard, Kierra 1987— **61, 114**

Sheard, Kiki *See Sheard, Kierra*

Shearer, Hugh 1923–2004 **107**

Sheffey, Asa Bundy *See Hayden, Robert Earl*

Sheffield, Gary 1968— **16, 108**

Shelby, Thomas *See Lakeside*

Shell, Art 1946— **1, 66**

Shelton, Billy *See Clovers, The*

Shelton, Paula Young 1961— **86**

Shelton, Trent 1984— **122**

Shepherd, Sherri 1970— **55**

Shepp, Archie 1937— **101**

Sheppard, Ella *See Fisk Jubilee Singers*

Sherman, Richard 1988— **118**

Sherrod, Clayton 1944— **17**

Sherrod, Shirley 1948— **87**

Shetler, Tom *See Falcons, The*

Shider, Garry 1953–2010 **87**

Shines, John Ned *See Shines, Johnny*

Shines, Johnny 1915–1992 **116**

Shinhoster, Earl 1950(?)–2000 **32**

Shipp, E. R. 1955— **15**

Shipp, Matthew 1960— **107**

Shippen, John 1879–1968 **43**

Shirelles, The **111**

Shirley, Aaron 1933–2014 **126**

Shirley, Donald 1927–2013 **111**

Shirley, George I. 1934— **33**

Shmurda, Bobby 1994— **123**

Shocklee, Hank *See Public Enemy*

Shockley, Ann Allen 1927— **84**

Shockley, Stephen *See Lakeside*

Shonibare, Yinka 1962— **58**

Shores, Arthur D. 1904–1996 **99**

Short, Bobby 1924–2005 **52**

Short, Columbus 1982— **79**

Shorter, Wayne 1933— **75**

Shorty, Ras, I 1941–2000 **47**

Showers, Reggie 1964— **30**

Shropshire, Thomas B. 1925–2003 **49**

Shuttlesworth, Fred 1922–2011 **47, 98**

Shyne 1978— **101**

Sidat-Singh, Wilmeth 1918–1943 **116**

Sidibe, Gabourey 1983— **84**

Sidibé, Malick 1936(?)— **124**

Sidibé, Michel 1952— **133**

Sidner, Sara 1972— **105**

Sifford, Charles Luther *See Sifford, Charlie*

Sifford, Charlie 1922–2015 **4, 49, 134**

Sigur, Wanda 1958— **44**

Siji 1971(?)— **56**

Silas, Paul 1943— **24, 129**

Silva, Anderson 1975— **96**

Silva, Marina 1958— **80**

Silver, Horace 1928–2014 **26, 122**

Siméus, Dumas M. 1939— **25, 110**

Simkins, Modjeska Monteith 1899–1992 **112**

Simmonds, Wayne 1988— **121**

Simmons, Bill *See Midnight Star*

Simmons, Bob 1948— **29**

Simmons, E. Denise 19(?)(?)— **79**

Simmons, Gary 1964— **58**

Simmons, Gwendolyn Zoharah 1944(?)— **132**

Simmons, Henry 1970— **55**

Simmons, Jamal 1971— **72**

Simmons, Joseph *See Run; Run-DMC*

Simmons, Kimora Lee 1975— **51, 83**

Simmons, Russell 1957(?)— **1, 30**

Simmons, Ruth J. 1945— **13, 38**

Simms, Margaret 1946— **94**

Simon, Joe 1943— **109**

Simon, Lateefah 1977— **95**

Simone, Nina 1933–2003 **15, 41, 130**

Simpson, Carole 1940— **6, 30**

Simpson, John *See S.O.S. Band*

Simpson, Lorna 1960— **4, 36**

Simpson, Merton D. 1928–2013 **110**

Simpson, O. J. 1947— **15, 100**

Simpson, Sherone 1984— **120**

Simpson, Valerie 1946— **21, 97**

Simpson-Hoffman, N'kenge 1975(?)— **52**

Simpson Miller, Portia 1945— **62, 100**

Sims, Danny 1936–2012 **106**

Sims, Howard "Sandman" 1917–2003 **48**

Sims, Lowery Stokes 1949— **27**

Sims, Naomi 1948–2009 **29, 79**

Sims, Peter *See La Roca, Pete*

Sinbad 1957(?)— **1, 16**

Sinclair, Floyd *See Mayweather, Floyd*

Sinclair, Madge 1938–1995 **78**

Singletary, Mike 1958— **4, 76**

Singleton, John 1968— **2, 30, 122**

Sinkford, Jeanne C. 1933— **13**

Sir Mix-A-Lot 1963— **82**

Sirleaf, Ellen Johnson 1938— **71**

Sirleaf, Marietta Sangai *See Retta*

Sisqo 1976— **30**

Sissako, Abderrahmane 1961— **127**

Sissle, Noble 1889–1975 **29**

Sister Souljah 1964— **11, 100**

Sisulu, Albertina 1918–2011 **57, 95**

Sisulu, Sheila Violet Makate 1948(?)— **24**

Sisulu, Walter 1912–2003 **47**

Sizemore, Barbara A. 1927–2004 **26, 110**

Sizemore, Grady 1982— **96**

Skerrit, Roosevelt 1972— **72**

Skinner, Kiron K. 1962(?) **65**

Sklarek, Norma Merrick 1926–2012 **25, 101**

Slash 1975— **75**

Slater, Duke 1898–1966 **125**

Slater, Frederick Wayman *See Slater, Duke*

Slater, Rodney E. 1955— **15, 125**

Slaughter, John Brooks 1934— **53**

Sledge, Percy 1940–2015 **39, 128**

Sleet, Gregory M. 1951— **109**

Sleet, Moneta, Jr. 1926–1996 **5, 136**

Slice, Kimbo 1974–2016 **73, 136**

Slick Rick 1965— **93**

Slim *See 112*

Slim Harpo 1924–1970 **120**

Slim Jimmy *See Rae Sremmurd*

Slim Jxmmi *See Rae Sremmurd*

Slim Jukebox, The *See Geto Boys*

Slim Thug 1980— **86**

Slimkid3 *See Pharcyde, The*

Slocumb, Jonathan 19(?)(?)— **52**

Sly & Robbie **34**

Slyde, Jimmy 1927–2008 **70**

Smalling, Chris 1989— **118**

Smalls, Robert 1839–1915 **82**

Smaltz, Audrey 1937(?)— **12**

Smiley, Rickey 1968— **59**

Smiley, Tavis 1964— **20, 68**

Smith, Amanda Berry 1837–1915 **109**

Smith, Anjela Lauren 1973— **44**

Smith, Anna Deavere 1950— **6, 44**

Smith, Annette *See Chantels, The*

Smith, Arlene *See Chantels, The*

Smith, Arthur Lee, *See Asante, Molefi Kete*

Smith, B. *See Smith, B(arbara)*

Smith, B(arbara) 1949(?)— **11**

Smith, Barbara 1946— **28**

Smith, Bessie 1894–1937 **3**

Smith, Bruce 1984— **80**

Smith, Bruce W. 19(?)(?)— **53**

Smith, Bubba 1945–2011 **96**

Smith, Buster 1904–1991 **116**

Smith, Carl Reginald *See Smith, Reggie*

Smith, Cecilia 1960(?)— **102**

Smith, Charles Aaron *See Smith, Bubba*

Smith, Che *See Rhymefest*

Smith, Cladys "Jabbo" 1908–1991 **32**

Smith, Clarence 1904–1929 **113**

Smith, Clarence Edward *See Clarence 13X*

Smith, Clarence O. 1933— **21**

Smith, Clifford *See Method Man*

Smith, Damu 1951— **54**

Smith, Dante Terrell *See Bey, Yasiin*

Smith, Danyel 1966(?)— **40**

Smith, DeMaurice 1964— **92**

Smith, Dickie *See Five Keys, The*

Smith, Dr. Lonnie 1942— **49**

Smith, Emmitt 1969— **7, 87**

Smith, Eugene *See Smith, Gene*

Smith, Eugene Cyril, III *See Smith, Geno*

Smith, Gene 1955— **123**

Smith, Geno 1990— **118**

Smith, George *See Manhattans, The*

Smith, Greg 1964— **28**

Smith, Hale 1925–2009 **118**

Smith, Henry *See Smith, Buster*

Smith, Hezekiah Leroy Gordon *See Smith, Stuff*

Smith, Hilton 1912–1983 **29**

Smith, Ian 1970(?)— **62**

Smith, Jabbo *See Smith, Cladys "Jabbo"*

Smith, Jaden 1998— **82**

Smith, James Oscar *See Smith, Jimmy*

Smith, James Todd *See LL Cool J*

Smith, Jane E. 1946— **24**

Smith, Jennifer 1947— **21**

Smith, Jessie Carney 1930— **35**

Smith, Jimmy 1928–2005 **127**

Smith, John L. 1938— **22**

Smith, Jonathan Mortimer *See Lil Jon*

Smith, Joshua (Isaac) 1941— **10**

Smith, Kemba 1971— **70**

Smith, Kenneth *See Smith, Kenny*

Smith, Kenny 1965— **114**

Smith, LaQuan 1988— **113**

Smith, Lee 195(?)— **136**

Smith, Lee 1957— **101**

Smith, Lenithia Bonita *See Leakes, NeNe*

Smith, Lonnie Liston 1940— **49**

Smith, Lovie 1958— **66, 107**

Smith, Mabel Louise *See Big Maybelle*

Smith, Malcolm A. 1956— **75**

Smith, Mamie 1883–1946 **32**

Smith, Marie F. 1939— **70**

Smith, Marvin 1910–2003 **46**

Smith, Mary Carter 1919–2007 **26, 134**

Smith, Michael 1979— **129**

Smith, Ming 19(?)(?)— **100**

Smith, Morgan 1910–1993 **46**

Smith, Myrna 1941–2010 **92**

Smith, Nate 1929— **49**

Smith, Neil 1966— **109**

Smith, Orlando *See Smith, Tubby*

Smith, Ozzie 1954— **77**

Smith, Pinetop *See Smith, Clarence*

Smith, Princella 1983— **86**

Smith, Randy 1948–2009 **81**

Smith, Reggie 1945— **113**

Smith, Richard 1957— **51**

Smith, Rick 1969— **72**

Smith, Roger Guenveur 1959— **12, 133**

Smith, Shaffer Chimere *See Ne-Yo*

Smith, Stephen A. 1967— **69**

Smith, Steve 1979— **120**

Smith, Stuff 1909–1967 **37**

Smith, Tasha 1971— **73**

Smith, Tommie 1944— **102**

Smith, Trevor, Jr. *See Rhymes, Busta*

Smith, Trixie 1895–1943 **34**

Smith, Tubby 1951— **18, 83**

Smith, Vincent D. 1929–2003 **48**

Smith, Walker, Jr. See Robinson, Sugar Ray
Smith, Will 1968— **8, 18, 53**
Smith, Will 1981–2016 **135**
Smith, Willi (Donnell) 1948–1987 **8**
Smith, Willie 1897(?)–1973 **107**
Smith, Willow 2000— **92**
Smith, Zadie 1975— **51**
Smyre, Calvin 1947— **90**
Smythe Haith, Mabel 1918–2006 **61**
Sneed, Paula A. 1947— **18**
Snipes, Wesley 1962— **3, 24, 67**
Snoop Dogg 1971— **35, 84**
Snow, Samuel 1923–2008 **71**
Snow, Valada See Snow, Valaida
Snow, Valaida 1904(?)–1956 **135**
Snowden, Frank M., Jr. 1911–2007 **67**
Snowden, Gail 1945— **108**
Soglo, Nicéphore 1935— **15**
Sohn, Sonja 1964— **100**
Solange 1986— **97**
Solomon, Jimmie Lee 1947(?)— **38**
Somé, Malidoma Patrice 1956— **10**
Somi 1979— **85**
Sommore, 1966— **61**
Song, Alex 1987— **105**
Songhoy Blues **135**
Songz, Trey 1984— **88**
Sono, Jomo 1955— **86**
S.O.S. Band **136**
Sosa, Sammy 1968— **21, 44**
Soto Alejo, Federico Arístides See Güines, Tata
Soul Stirrers **127**
Soulchild, Musiq See Musiq
Souleymane, Mahamane 1940— **78**
Southern, Eileen 1920–2002 **56**
Southgate, Martha 1960(?)— **58**
Souza, Carmen 1981— **111**
Sowande, Fela 1905–1987 **39**
Sowande, Olufela Obafunmilayo See Sowande, Fela
Sowell, Thomas 1930— **2, 99**
Soyinka, Wole 1934— **4, 93**
Spaniels, The **105**
Spann, Otis 1930(?)–1970 **107**
Sparks, Corinne Etta 1953— **53**
Sparks, Jordin 1989— **66**
Sparks, Willie See Graham Central Station
Spaulding, Charles Clinton 1874–1952 **9**
Spearman, Leonard H. O., Sr. 1929–2008 **81**
Spearman, Ollie See Tyler, Ollie
Spears, Warren 1954–2005 **52**
Special K See Treacherous Three
Speck, George See Crum, George
Spector, Ronnie 1943— **77** See also Ronettes, The
Speech 1968— **82**
Speight, Bruno See S.O.S. Band
Spellman-Diaz, Toyin See Imani Winds
Spence, Joseph 1910–1984 **49**
Spencer, Anne 1882–1975 **27**
Spencer, Michael G. 1952— **87**
Spencer, Octavia 1972— **100**
Spencer, Peter 1782(?)–1843 **128**
Spencer, Vaino H. 1920— **99**

Spencer, Winston Baldwin 1948— **68**
Spigner, Archie 1928— **81**
Spikes, Dolores Margaret Richard 1936— **18**
Spiller, Bill 1913–1988 **64**
Spivey, Victoria 1906–1976 **119**
Sprewell, Latrell 1970— **23**
Spriggs, William 195(?)— **67**
Springer, Ashton, Jr. 1930–2013 **115**
Stackhouse, Houston 1910–1980 **122**
Stackhouse, Jerry 1974— **30**
Staley, Dawn 1970— **57**
Stallings, Felix, Jr. See Felix Da Housecat
Stallings, George A(ugustus), Jr. 1948— **6**
Stallworth, John 1952— **102**
Stampley, Micah 1971— **54**
Stanford, John 1938— **20**
Stanford, Olivia Lee Dilworth 1914–2004 **49**
Stanley, A. Knighton 1937–2013 **117**
Stanley, Knighton See Stanley, A. Knighton
Stanley, Tony See Stanley, A. Knighton
Stanton, Alysa 1963— **78**
Stanton, Robert 1940— **20**
Staples, Brent 1951— **8**
Staples, Cleotha 1934–2013 **113**
Staples, Mavis 1939(?)— **50, 88**
Staples, "Pops" 1915–2000 **32**
Staples, Roebuck See Staples, "Pops"
Staples, Ron See Mighty Clouds of Joy
Stargell, Willie 1940(?)–2001 **29**
Starks, Jabo 1938— **135**
Starks, John See Starks, Jabo
Starr, Bobby See Intruders, The
Starr, Edwin 1942–2003 **122**
Staton, Candi 1940(?)— **27**
Staton, Dakota 1930(?)–2007 **62**
Staupers, Mabel K(eaton) 1890–1989 **7**
Stearnes, Norman "Turkey" 1901–1979 **31**
Steave-Dickerson, Kia 1970— **57**
Steele, Claude 1946— **13, 97**
Steele, Lawrence 1963— **28**
Steele, Michael 1958— **38, 73, 91**
Steele, Sage 1972— **115**
Steele, Shelby 1946— **13, 82**
Steely 1962–2009 **80**
Steinberg, Martha Jean 1930(?)–2000 **28**
Stephens, Charlotte Andrews 1854–1951 **14**
Stephens, John See Legend, John
Stephens, Myrtle See Potter, Myrtle
Stephens, Sloane 1993— **105**
Stephenson, Lance 1990— **118**
Stevens, Earl See E-40
Stevens, Yvette See Khan, Chaka
Stevenson, Bryan 1959— **128**
Stevenson, Teófilo 1952–2012 **103**
Stew 1961— **69**
Steward, David L. 19(?)(?)— **36**
Steward, Emanuel 1944–2012 **18, 106**
Stewart, Alison 1966(?)— **13**

Stewart, Amii 1956— **129**
Stewart, Amy Paulette See Stewart, Amii
Stewart, Billy 1937–1970 **112**
Stewart, Bubba See Stewart, James, Jr.
Stewart, Christopher Alan See Stewart, Tricky
Stewart, Dave 1957— **117**
Stewart, Derrick See Pharcyde, The
Stewart, Ella 1893–1987 **39**
Stewart, James, Jr. 1985— **60, 98**
Stewart, Kordell 1972— **21, 111**
Stewart, Leroy See Stewart, Slam
Stewart, Mark See Stew
Stewart, Nzingha 1974— **89**
Stewart, Paul Wilbur 1925— **12**
Stewart, Slam 1914–1987 **126**
Stewart, Sylvester See Stone, Sly
Stewart, Tonea Harris 1947— **78**
Stewart, Tricky 1974— **98**
Stickney, Phyllis Yvonne 19(?)(?)— **108**
Sticky Fingaz 1970— **86**
Still, William Grant 1895–1978 **37**
Stingley, Darryl 1951–2007 **69**
Stinson, Denise L. 1954— **59**
Stith, Charles R. 1949— **73**
Stith, James H. 1941— **116**
Stith, Tom 1939–2010 **93**
Stiverne, Bermane 1978— **128**
Stockman, Shawn See Boyz II Men
Stokes, Carl 1927–1996 **10, 73**
Stokes, Louis 1925— **3**
Stokes, Otis See Lakeside
Stoltz, Brian See Meters, The
Stone, Angie 1965(?)— **31**
Stone, Charles Sumner, Jr. See Stone, Chuck
Stone, Chuck 1924–2014 **9, 120**
Stone, Jesse 1901–1999 **98** See also Drifters, The
Stone, Sly 1943— **85**
Stone, Toni 1921–1996 **15**
Stoney, Michael 1969— **50**
Storyboard P 1990(?)— **118**
Stott, Dorothy M. See Stout, Renee
Stott, Dot See Stout, Renee
Stoudemire, Amar'e 1982— **59, 106**
Stout, Juanita Kidd 1919–1998 **24**
Stout, Renee 1958— **63**
Stoute, Steve 1971(?)— **38**
Stoutt, H. Lavity 1929–1995 **83**
Stowers, Freddie 1896–1918 **107**
Stradford, J. B. 1861–1935 **101**
Strahan, Michael 1971— **35, 81, 135**
Strain, Sammy See Little Anthony & the Imperials
Strautmanis, Michael 1969— **87**
Strawberry, Darryl 1962— **22**
Strayhorn, Billy 1915–1967 **31**
Street, John F. 1943(?)— **24**
Street, Richard 1942–2013 **110**
Streeter, Amber Denise See Streeter, Sevyn
Streeter, Sarah See Big Time Sarah
Streeter, Sevyn 1986— **115**
Stringer, C. Vivian 1948— **13, 66**
Stringer, Korey 1974–2001 **35**
Stringer, Vickie 196(?)— **58**

Strode, Woodrow Wilson Woolwine See Strode, Woody
Strode, Woody 1914–1994 **111**
Stromae 1985— **121**
Stroman, Nathaniel See Earthquake
Strong, Barrett 1941— **89**
Strong, Charlie 1960— **118**
Stuart, Moira 1949— **82**
Stubblefield, Clyde 1943— **133**
Stubbs, Joe See Contours, The
Studdard, Ruben 1978— **46**
Sturridge, Daniel 1989— **120**
Subban, P. K. 1989— **121**
Subban, Pernell Karl See Subban, P. K
Sudarkasa, Niara 1938— **4**
Sudduth, Jimmy Lee 1910–2007 **65**
Sugarhill Gang, The **79, 125**
Suggs, Terrell 1982— **108**
Sullivan, Jazmine 1987— **81**
Sullivan, Leon H. 1922–2001 **3, 30**
Sullivan, Louis (Wade) 1933— **8**
Sullivan, Maxine 1911–1987 **37**
Sul-Te-Wan, Madame See Madame Sul-Te-Wan
Sumlin, Hubert 1931–2011 **101**
Summer, Donna 1948–2012 **25, 102**
Summers, Myrna 1949— **129**
Sumner, Francis Cecil 1926–1973 **112**
Sun Ra, 1914–1993 **60**
Sundiata, Sekou 1948–2007 **66**
Sunnyland Slim 1907(?)–1995 **118**
Supremes, The **33**
Surrell, Maurice See Williams Brothers
Sutphen, Mona 1967— **77**
Suttles, George See Suttles, Mule
Suttles, Mule 1900–1966 **108**
Suttles, Warren See Ravens, The
Sutton, Percy E. 1920–2009 **42, 82**
Swae Lee See Rae Sremmurd
Swallows, The **133**
Swan Silvertones, The **110**
Swann, Bettye 1944— **109**
Swann, Lynn 1952— **28**
Swaray, Fanta Estelle See Estelle
Sweat, Keith 1961(?)— **19**
Sweatman, Wilbur 1882–1961 **125**
Sweatshirt, Earl 1994— **114**
Sweatt, Heman Marion 1912–1982 **114**
Sweet, Ossian 1895–1960 **68**
Sweet Honey in the Rock **106**
Swizz Beatz 1978— **108**
Swoopes, Sheryl 1971— **12, 56**
Swygert, H. Patrick 1943— **22**
Sy, Omar 1978— **109**
Sy, Oumou 1952— **65**
Sykes, Roosevelt 1906–1984 **20**
Sykes, Wanda 1964— **48, 81**
Syler, Rene 1963— **53**
Tabu Ley See Rochereau, Tabu Ley
Tacuma, Jamaaladeen 1956— **124**
Tademy, Lalita 1948— **36**
Tafari Makonnen See Haile Selassie
Tail Dragger 1940— **112**
Tait, Michael 1966— **57**
Take 6 **112**
Takeoff See Migos

Talbert, David E. 1966(?)— **34, 93**
Talbert, Mary B. 1866–1923 **77**
Taliaferro, Edwin See Lumumba, Chokwe
Talley, André Leon 1949— **56, 106**
Talley, Nedra See Ronettes, The
Tamar-kali 1973(?)— **63**
Tamia 1975— **24, 55**
Tampa Red 1904(?)–1980 **63**
Tancil, Gladys Quander 1921–2002 **59**
Tandja, Mamadou 1938— **33, 78**
Tanksley, Ann (Graves) 1934— **37**
Tanner, Henry Ossawa 1859–1937 **1**
Tanner, Jack E. 1919–2006 **100**
Tapscott, Horace 1934–1999 **126**
Taste of Honey, A **115**
Tate, Bruce See Penguins, The
Tate, Buddy 1913–2001 **108**
Tate, Eleanora E. 1948— **20, 55**
Tate, George Holmes See Tate, Buddy
Tate, Grady 1932— **106**
Tate, John 1955–1998 **107**
Tate, Larenz 1975— **15**
Tate, Minnie See Fisk Jubilee Singers
Tatum, Art 1909–1956 **28**
Tatum, Beverly Daniel 1954— **42, 84**
Tatum, Elinor R. 197(?)— **78**
Tatum, Jack 1948— **87**
Tatum, Reece 1921–1967 **104**
Tatum, Wilbert 1933–2009 **76**
Tau, Mpho Parks 1970— **124**
Taubira, Christiane 1952— **117**
Taulbert, Clifton Lemoure 1945— **19**
Tavares **115**
Tavares, Butch See Tavares
Tavares, Chubby See Tavares
Tavares, Pooch See Tavares
Tavares, Ralph See Tavares
Tavares, Tiny See Tavares
Taylor, Art 1929–1995 **132**
Taylor, Arthur S., Jr. See Taylor, Art
Taylor, Bennie See Dramatics, The
Taylor, Billy 1921–2010 **23, 92**
Taylor, Bo 1966–2008 **72**
Taylor, Cecil 1929— **70**
Taylor, Charles 1948— **20**
Taylor, Darren See Taylor, Bo
Taylor, Eddie 1923–1985 **116**
Taylor, Ephren W., II 1982— **61**
Taylor, Gardner C. 1918— **76**
Taylor, Helen (Lavon Hollingshed) 1942–2000 **30**
Taylor, Hound Dog 1917(?)–1975 **120**
Taylor, Jason 1974— **70**
Taylor, Jermain 1978— **60**
Taylor, John (David Beckett) 1952— **16**
Taylor, Johnnie See Highway QC's, The; Soul Stirrers
Taylor, Karin 1971— **34**
Taylor, Katrina Laverne See Trina
Taylor, Koko 1928–2009 **40, 80**
Taylor, Kristin Clark 1959— **8**
Taylor, Lawrence 1959— **25**
Taylor, Leroy See New Birth
Taylor, Lonzie Odie 1899–1977 **96**

Taylor, Malik Isaac See Phife Dawg
Taylor, Marshall Walter "Major" 1878–1932 **62**
Taylor, Meshach 1947(?)— **4**
Taylor, Mildred D. 1943— **26**
Taylor, Natalie 1959— **47**
Taylor, Raphael See Pilgrim Travelers, The
Taylor, Recy 1919— **92**
Taylor, Regina 1960— **9, 46, 97**
Taylor, Richard See Manhattans, The
Taylor, Robert Robinson 1868–1942 **80**
Taylor, Robert Rochon 1899–1957 **104**
Taylor, Ron 1952–2002 **35**
Taylor, Spencer, Jr. See Highway QC's, The
Taylor, Susan C. 1957— **62**
Taylor, Susan L. 1946— **10, 86**
Taylor, Susie King 1848–1912 **13**
Taylor, Theodore Roosevelt See Taylor, Hound Dog
T-Boz 1970— **108** See also TLC
Tchicai, John 1936— **102**
Teague, Bob 1929–2013 **111**
Teasley, Lisa 1962— **92**
Teer, Barbara Ann 1937–2008 **81**
Teklehaimanot, Daniel 1988— **130**
Temple, Collis, Jr. 1952— **119**
Temple, Ed 1927— **109**
Temple, Lewis 1800–1854 **102**
Temptations, The **33**
Tergat, Paul 1969— **59**
Terrell, Dorothy A. 1945— **24**
Terrell, Ernie 1939— **118**
Terrell, Jean 1944— **116**
Terrell, Mary (Elizabeth) Church 1863–1954 **9**
Terrell, Tammi 1945–1970 **32**
Terrell, Velma Jean See Terrell, Jean
Terrell-Kearney, Kim 1965— **83**
Terrence J 1982— **108**
Terrill, Saunders See Terry, Sonny
Terry, Bryant 1976— **128**
Terry, Clark 1920–2015 **39, 127**
Terry, Phil See Intruders, The
Terry, Sonny 1911–1986 **88**
Tesfaye, Abel Makkonen See Weeknd, The
Tex, Joe 1933(?)–1982 **116**
Thabane, Motsoahae Thomas See Thabane, Thomas
Thabane, Thomas 1939— **123**
Thabeet, Hasheem 1987— **123**
Tharpe, Rosetta 1915–1973 **65**
Thaws, Adrian Nicholas Matthews See Tricky
The Artist See Prince
Thedford, Timothy Elpadaro See Jay Electronica
The-Dream 1982— **74**
Thiam, Aliaune Akon See Akon
Thiam, Tidjane 1962— **104**
Thigpen, Ed 1930–2010 **110**
Thigpen, Lynne 1948–2003 **17, 41**
Thomas, Alma Woodsey 1891–1978 **14**
Thomas, Arthur Ray 1951— **52**
Thomas, Carla 1942— **96**

Thomas, Chris See King, Chris Thomas
Thomas, Clarence 1948— **2, 39, 65**
Thomas, Claudia Lynn 1950— **64**
Thomas, David See Take 6
Thomas, Debi 1967— **26**
Thomas, Derrick 1967–2000 **25**
Thomas, Emmitt 1943— **71**
Thomas, Ernest Joseph See Thomas, Tabby
Thomas, Frank 1968— **12, 51**
Thomas, Franklin A. 1934— **5, 49**
Thomas, Irma 1941— **29**
Thomas, Isiah 1961— **7, 26, 65**
Thomas, Jefferson 1942–2010 **88**
Thomas, Michael 1967— **69**
Thomas, Mickalene 1971— **61**
Thomas, Philip See Crown Heights Affair
Thomas, Rozonda 1971— **78** See also TLC
Thomas, Rufus 1917–2001 **20, 96**
Thomas, Sean Patrick 1970— **35**
Thomas, Stayve Jerome See Slim Thug
Thomas, Tabby 1929–2014 **119**
Thomas, Thurman 1966— **75**
Thomas, Todd See Speech
Thomas, Trisha R. 1964— **65**
Thomas, Vivien (T.) 1910–1985 **9**
Thomas-Graham, Pamela 1963(?)— **29**
Thomas-Greenfield, Linda 1952— **99**
Thomason, Marsha 1976— **47**
Thomaz, Cameron Jibril See Khalifa, Wiz
Thompson, Ahmir See ?uestlove
Thompson, Bennie 1948— **26, 119**
Thompson, Cynthia Bramlett 1949— **50**
Thompson, Dearon See Deezer D
Thompson, Don 1963— **56, 108**
Thompson, Gerald See Lee Andrews & the Hearts
Thompson, John Douglas 1964— **81**
Thompson, John W. 1949— **26**
Thompson, Ken 1966— **131**
Thompson, Kenan 1978— **52**
Thompson, Klay 1990— **126**
Thompson, Larry D. 1945— **39**
Thompson, Marshall See Chi-Lites
Thompson, Mychal 1955— **126**
Thompson, Sylvester See Johnson, Syl
Thompson, Tazewell (Alfred, Jr.) 1954— **13**
Thompson, Tina 1975— **25, 75**
Thompson, Tony See Chic
Thompson, Tristan 1991— **131**
Thompson, William C., Jr. 1953— **35, 114**
Thoms, Tracie 1975— **61**
Thornton, Big Mama 1926–1984 **33**
Thornton, Terrence See Pusha T
Thornton, Yvonne S. 1947— **69**
Thrash, Dox 1893–1965 **35**
Thrasher, Andrew See Drifters, The
Thrasher, Gerhart See Drifters, The
Threadgill, Henry 1944— **97**
Three Mo' Tenors **35**
Thrower, Willie 1930–2002 **35**

Thugwane, Josia 1971— **21**
Thundercat 1984— **136**
Thurman, Howard 1900–1981 **3**
Thurman, Wallace Henry 1902–1934 **16**
Thurmond, Nate 1941— **88**
Thurston, Baratunde 1977— **79, 101**
Thurston, Stephen J. 1952— **49**
Tiant, Luis 1940— **102**
Till, Emmett (Louis) 1941–1955 **7**
Tillard, Conrad 1964— **47**
Tillis, Frederick 1930— **40**
Tillman, Deborah 1962(?)— **98**
Tillman, Dorothy 1947— **76**
Tillman, George, Jr. 1968— **20**
Tillman, Georgeanna See Marvelettes, The
Tilmon, Abe See Detroit Emeralds, The
Tilmon, Cleofas See Detroit Emeralds, The
Tilmon, Ivory See Detroit Emeralds, The
Tilmon, Raymond See Detroit Emeralds, The
Timbaland 1971— **32**
Timmons, Bobby 1935–1974 **136**
Tingling, Milton A. 1953— **110**
Tinie Tempah 1988— **115**
Tinsley, Boyd 1964— **50**
Tipton, Fredrick See Gibbs, Freddie
Tirico, Michael See Tirico, Mike
Tirico, Mike 1966— **68, 124**
Tisby, Dexter See Penguins, The
Tisdale, Wayman 1964— **50**
TLC **34**
Tobias, Channing H. 1882–1961 **79**
Tobin, Patricia 1943–2008 **75**
Todd, Franck See Golden Gate Quartet
Todman, Terence A. 1926— **55**
Tolbert, James L. 1926–2013 **112**
Tolbert, Mike 1985— **125**
Tolbert, Terence 1964— **74**
Tolbert, William Michael See Tolbert, Mike
Tolbert, William R. 1913–1980 **100**
Toler, Burl 1928–2009 **80**
Toles, Michael See Bar-Kays, The
Toivola, Jani 1977— **118**
Tolliver, Mose 1915(?)–2006 **60**
Tolliver, William (Mack) 1951— **9**
Tolson, Melvin B(eaunorus) 1898–1966 **37**
Tolton, Augustine 1854–1897 **62**
Tomlin, Michael Pettaway See Tomlin, Mike
Tomlin, Mike 1972— **123**
Tomlinson, LaDainian 1979— **65, 112**
Tonex, 1978(?)— **54**
Toney, James 1968— **89**
Tony! Toni! Toné! **127**
Tooks, Lance 1962— **62**
Toomer, Jean 1894–1967 **6**
Toomer, Nathan Pinchback See Toomer, Jean
Toote, Gloria E. A. 1931— **64**
Toots and the Maytals See Hibbert, Toots
Torian, Reggie See Impressions, The

Torres, Gina 1969— **52**

Torry, Guy 19(?)(?)— **31**

Tosh, Peter 1944–1987 **9**

Touré, Aliou *See Songhoy Blues*

Touré, Amadou Toumani 1948(?)— **18**

Touré, Askia (Muhammad Abu Bakr el) 1938— **47**

Touré, Faya Ora Rose 1945— **56**

Touré, Garba *See Songhoy Blues*

Touré, Oumar *See Songhoy Blues*

Touré, Sekou 1922–1984 **6**

Touré;, Yaya 1983— **99**

Toussaint, Allen 1938–2015 **60, 132**

Toussaint, Lorraine 1960— **32**

Towles, Nat 1905–1963 **128**

Townes, Jeffrey Allan *See DJ Jazzy Jeff*

Towns, Edolphus 1934— **19, 75**

Towns, Karl-Anthony 1995— **136**

Townsend, Robert 1957— **4, 23**

T-Pain 1985— **73, 111**

Trammell, Kimberly N. *See Holland, Kimberly N.*

Trammell, Walter *See Delta Rhythm Boys*

Trammps, The **108**

Traore, Dioncounda 1942— **103**

Travis, Tracey T. 1962— **94**

Treach *See Naughty by Nature*

Treacherous Three **128**

Tresvant, Ralph 1968— **57** *See also New Edition*

Trethewey, Natasha 1966— **103**

Tribbett, Tye 1977— **81**

Tribble, Israel, Jr. 1940— **8**

Tricky 1967— **98**

Trina 1974— **114**

Trombone Shorty 1986— **97**

Trotter, Donne E. 1950— **28**

Trotter, Lloyd G. 1945(?)— **56**

Trotter, (William) Monroe 1872–1934 **9**

Trotter, Tariq Luqmaan *See Black Thought; Roots, The*

Trouillot, Ertha Pascal *See Pascal-Trouillot, Ertha*

Troupe, Quincy 1943— **83**

Trouppe, Quincy Thomas, Sr. 1912–1993 **84**

Troy, Michael *See Freestyle Fellowship*

True, Rachel 1966— **82**

Trueheart, William E. 1942— **49**

Truesdale, Yanic 1970— **133**

Tshele, Elizabeth Zandile *See Bulawayo, NoViolet*

Tsvangirai, Morgan 1952— **26, 72**

Tuakli-Wosornu, Taiye *See Selasi, Taiye*

Tubbs Jones, Stephanie 1949–2008 **24, 72**

Tubman, Harriet 1820(?)–1913 **9, 135**

Tubman, William 1895–1971 **99**

Tucker, C. Delores 1927–2005 **12, 56**

Tucker, Chris 1972— **13, 23, 62**

Tucker, Cynthia 1955— **15, 61**

Tucker, Rosina Budd Harvey Corrothers 1881–1987 **14**

Tucker, Tommy 1933–1982 **127**

Tuckson, Reed V. 1951(?)— **71**

Tuff, Antoinette 1966— **120**

Tuku *See Mtukudzi, Oliver*

Tunie, Tamara 1959— **63**

Tunnell, Emlen 1925–1975 **54**

Ture, Kwame *See Carmichael, Stokely*

Turman, Glynn 1947— **100**

Turnbull, Charles Wesley 1935— **62**

Turnbull, Walter 1944–2007 **13, 60**

Turner, Big Joe 1911–1985 **92**

Turner, Charles Henry 1867–1923 **134**

Turner, Henry McNeal 1834–1915 **5**

Turner, Ike 1931–2007 **68**

Turner, Irving *See Swallows, The*

Turner, Izear *See Turner, Ike*

Turner, Kylo *See Pilgrim Travelers, The*

Turner, Mark 1965— **126**

Turner, Morrie 1923–2014 **122**

Turner, Morris Nolten *See Turner, Morrie*

Turner, Sylvester 1954— **136**

Turner, Tina 1939— **6, 27**

Turrentine, Stanley 1934–2000 **129**

Tutu, Desmond (Mpilo) 1931— **6, 44**

Tutu, Nontombi Naomi 1960— **57**

Tutuola, Amos 1920–1997 **30**

Twiggs, Leo 1934— **127**

Twilight, Alexander 1795–1857 **125**

Twitty, Michael 1978(?)— **134**

2 Chainz 1976— **105**

Tyga 1989— **117**

Tyler, Aisha N. 1970— **36**

Tyler, Ollie 1945— **128**

Tyler, the Creator 1991— **100**

Tyner, McCoy 1938— **92**

Tyree, Omar Rashad 1969— **21**

Tyrese *See Gibson, Tyrese*

Tyson, Andre 1960— **40**

Tyson, Asha 1970— **39**

Tyson, Cicely 1924(?)— **7, 51, 112**

Tyson, Mike 1966— **28, 44, 93**

Tyson, Neil deGrasse 1958— **15, 65**

Uggams, Leslie 1943— **23, 114**

Ujiri, Masai 1970— **107**

Ukpabio, Helen 1969— **86**

Ulmer, James 1942— **79**

Underwood, Blair 1964— **7, 27, 76**

Union, Gabrielle 1972— **31, 92**

Unseld, Wes 1946— **23**

Upshaw, Gene 1945–2008 **18, 47, 72**

Upton, B. J. *See Upton, Melvin, Jr.*

Upton, Justin 1987— **124**

Upton, Melvin, Jr. 1984— **124**

Uribe, Juan 1979— **122**

Urschel, John 1991— **126**

Usher 1977— **23, 56, 95**

Usry, James L. 1922–2002 **23, 134**

Usher, Jessie T. 1992— **136**

Ussery, Terdema Lamar, II 1958— **29**

Utendahl, John 1956— **23**

Uys, Ashley 1983— **125**

Valdés, Bebo 1918— **75**

Valdés, Chucho 1941— **89**

Valdés, Dionisio Ramón Emilio *See Valdés, Bebo*

Valentine, Johnny *See Mighty Clouds of Joy*

Valentino, Bobby 1980— **62**

Van Haver, Paul *See Stromae*

Van Lierop, Robert 1939— **53**

Van Loan, James *See Billy Ward and the Dominoes*

Van Peebles, Mario 1957— **2, 51**

Van Peebles, Melvin 1932— **7, 95**

van Sertima, Ivan 1935— **25**

Vance, Courtney B. 1960— **15, 60**

Vance, Jim 1942— **110**

VanDerZee, James (Augustus Joseph) 1886–1983 **6**

Vandross, Luther 1951–2005 **13, 48, 59**

Vanessa James and Yannick Bonheur **84**

Vanity 1959–2016 **67, 134**

Vann, Harold Moore *See Muhammad, Khallid Abdul*

Vanzant, Iyanla 1953— **17, 47, 108**

Vaughan, Sarah (Lois) 1924–1990 **13**

Vaughn, Countess 1978— **53**

Vaughn, Gladys Gary 1942(?)— **47**

Vaughn, Jacque 1975— **127**

Vaughn, Mo 1967— **16**

Vaughn, Viola 1947— **70**

Vaughns, Cleopatra 1940— **46**

Vega, David *See Graham Central Station*

Vega, Marta Moreno 1942(?)— **61**

Velez-Rodriguez, Argelia 1936— **56**

Vera, Yvonne 1964— **32**

Verdell, Jackie *See Davis Sisters, The*

Verdelle, A. J. 1960— **26**

Vereen, Ben(jamin Augustus) 1946— **4**

Verna, Gelsy 1961–2008 **70**

Verrett, Shirley 1931–2010 **66, 91**

Vesey, Denmark 1767(?)–1822 **100**

Via, Dennis 1958(?)— **108**

Vibra-Naires, The *See Orioles, The*

Vick, Michael 1980— **39, 65, 94**

Vieira, João Bernardo 1939–2009 **14, 84**

Villard-Appolon, Malya 1959(?)— **106**

Villarosa, Clara 1930(?)— **85**

Vincent, Marjorie Judith 1965(?)— **2**

Vincent, Mark *See Diesel, Vin*

Vincent, Troy 1971— **91**

Vinnegar, Leroy 1928–1999 **124**

Vinson, Cleanhead *See Vinson, Eddie*

Vinson, Eddie 1917–1988 **112**

Vinson, Walter *See Mississippi Sheiks*

Virgil, Ozzie 1933— **48**

Vogue, En *See En Vogue*

Von Lipsey, Roderick 1959— **11**

wa Ngengi, Kamau *See Kenyatta, Jomo*

Waddles, Charleszetta 1912–2001 **10, 49**

Waddles, Mother *See Waddles, Charleszetta*

Wade, Abdoulaye 1926— **66**

Wade, Dwyane 1982— **61, 103**

Wade, Ernestine 1906–1983 **126**

Wade, Harold *See Trammps, The*

Wade, Stanley *See Trammps, The*

Wade-Gayles, Gloria Jean 1937(?)— **41**

Wagner, Albert 1924–2006 **78**

Wagner, Annice 1937— **22**

Wainwright, Joscelyn 1941— **46**

Waka Flocka Flame 1986— **110**

Walcott, Dennis M. 1951— **112**

Walcott, Derek 1930— **5, 94**

Walcott, Jersey Joe 1914–1994 **102**

Waldon, Alton R., Jr. 1936— **98**

Waldron, Mal 1925–2002 **109**

Wale 1984— **92**

Walker, Aaron Thibeaux *See Walker, T-Bone*

Walker, Albertina 1929–2010 **10, 58, 89**

Walker, Alice 1944— **1, 43**

Walker, Antoine 1976— **132**

Walker, Arthur, II 1936–2001 **87**

Walker, Bernita Ruth 1946— **53**

Walker, Cedric "Ricky" 1953— **19**

Walker, Chet 1940— **106**

Walker, Cora T. 1922–2006 **68**

Walker, David 179(?)–1830 **129**

Walker, Dianne 1951— **57**

Walker, Eamonn 1961(?)— **37**

Walker, Eliza *See Fisk Jubilee Singers*

Walker, George 1873–1911 **129**

Walker, George 1922— **37**

Walker, Greg *See Taste of Honey, A*

Walker, Herschel 1962— **1, 69**

Walker, Hezekiah 1962— **34**

Walker, Joe Louis 1949— **118**

Walker, John T. 1925–1989 **50**

Walker, Joseph Edison 1880–1958 **111**

Walker, Kara 1969— **16, 80**

Walker, Kurtis *See Blow, Kurtis*

Walker, LeRoy T. 1918–2012 **106**

Walker, Lucius, Jr. 1930–2010 **88**

Walker, Madame C. J. 1867–1919 **7**

Walker, Maggie Lena 1867(?)–1934 **17**

Walker, Margaret 1915–1998 **29**

Walker, Nellie Marian *See Larsen, Nella*

Walker, Ray 1981— **109**

Walker, Rebecca 1969— **50**

Walker, T. J. 1961(?)— **7**

Walker, T-Bone 1910–1975 **111**

Walker, Teshima 1968–2013 **114**

Walker, Thomas *See Walker, T. J.*

Walker, Tristan 1984— **98**

Walker, Wyatt Tee 1929— **80**

Wall, John 1990— **129**

Wall, Orindatus S. B. 1825–1891 **92**

Wallace, Ben 1974— **54**

Wallace, Joaquin 1965— **49**

Wallace, Michele Faith 1952— **13**

Wallace, Perry E. 1948— **47**

Wallace, Phyllis A(nn) 1920(?)–1993 **9**

Wallace, Rasheed 1974— **56**

Wallace, Richard *See Mighty Clouds of Joy*

Wallace, Ruby Ann *See Dee, Ruby*

Wallace, Sippie 1898–1986 **1**

Wallace, William 1939–2008 **75**

Waller, Fats 1904–1943 **29**

Waller, Thomas Wright *See Waller, Fats*

Wallis, Quvenzhané 2003— **109**

Walters, Richard *See Slick Rick*

Walters, Ronald 1938— **83**

Walton, Alex *See Moonglows, The*

Walton, Cedar 1934–2013 **114**

Walton, Cora *See Taylor, Koko*

Walton, Lester Aglar 1882–1965 **134**

Wambugu, Florence 1953— **42**

Wamutombo, Dikembe Mutombo Mpolondo Mukamba Jean Jacque *See Mutombo, Dikembe*

Wanjiru, Sammy 1986–2011 **94**

Wansley, Michael *See Wanz*

Wanz 1961— **116**

Ward, Andre 1984— **62**

Ward, Anita 1957(?)— **118**

Ward, Benjamin 1926–2002 **68**

Ward, Billy *See Billy Ward and the Dominoes*

Ward, Douglas Turner 1930— **42**

Ward, Eugene *See Commodores, The*

Ward, Hines 1976— **84**

Ward, Joel 1980— **129**

Ward, Lloyd 1949— **21, 46**

Ward, Willa 1920–2012 **105**

Ward, William E. 1949— **107**

Ware, Andre 1968— **37**

Ware, Carl H. 1943— **30**

Ware, David S. 1949–2012 **106**

Ware, DeMarcus 1982— **92**

Ware, Edward *See Deep River Boys*

Warfield, Marsha 1955— **2**

Warfield, William 1920–2002 **94**

Waring, Laura Wheeler 1887–1948 **99**

Warner,. Malcolm-Jamal 1970— **22, 36, 110**

Warren, Butch 1939–2013 **116**

Warren, Edward Rudolph, Jr. *See Warren, Butch*

Warren, Ernest *See Spaniels, The*

Warren, Lovely 1977— **136**

Warren, Mervyn *See Take 6*

Warren, Michael 1946— **27**

Warrick, Marie Dionne *See Warwick, Dionne*

Warsame, Keinan Abdi *See K'naan*

Warwick, Dionne 1940— **18, 111**

Washington, Alonzo 1967— **29**

Washington, Booker T(aliaferro) 1856–1915 **4**

Washington, Denzel 1954— **1, 16, 93**

Washington, Dinah 1924–1963 **22**

Washington, Ebonya 1973(?)— **79**

Washington, Elsie B. 1942–2009 **78**

Washington, Essie Mae *See Washington-Williams, Essie Mae*

Washington, Fred(er)i(cka Carolyn) 1903–1994 **10**

Washington, Gene 1947— **63**

Washington, Grover, Jr. 1943–1999 **17, 44**

Washington, Harold 1922–1987 **6**

Washington, Harriet A. 1951— **69**

Washington, Hayma 19(?)(?)— **86**

Washington, Isaiah 1963— **62**

Washington, James, Jr. 1909(?)–2000 **38**

Washington, James Melvin 1948–1997 **50**

Washington, Kamasi 1981— **134**

Washington, Karen 1958(?)— **117**

Washington, Kenny 1918–1971 **50**

Washington, Kenny 1958— **107**

Washington, Kerry 1977— **46, 107**

Washington, Laura S. 1956(?)— **18**

Washington, MaliVai 1969— **8**

Washington, Margaret Murray 1865–1925 **119**

Washington, Mary T. 1906–2005 **57**

Washington, Ora Mae 1899(?)–1971 **115**

Washington, Patrice Clarke 1961— **12**

Washington, Pauletta Pearson 1950— **86**

Washington, Regynald G. 1954(?)— **44**

Washington, Ron 1952— **119**

Washington, Tamia Reneé *See Tamia*

Washington, Valores James 1903–1995 **12**

Washington, Walter 1915–2003 **45**

Washington-Williams, Essie Mae 1925–2013 **118**

Wasow, Omar 1970— **15**

Waters, Benny 1902–1998 **26**

Waters, Ethel 1895–1977 **7**

Waters, Maxine 1938— **3, 67, 103**

Waters, Muddy 1915–1983 **34**

Watkins, Craig 1967— **97**

Watkins, Donald 1948— **35**

Watkins, Frances Ellen *See Harper, Frances Ellen Watkins*

Watkins, Gloria Jean *See hooks, bell*

Watkins, Joe 1953— **86**

Watkins, Levi, Jr. 1945— **9**

Watkins, Perry James Henry 1948–1996 **12**

Watkins, Shirley R. 1938— **17**

Watkins, Ted 1923(?)–1993 **104**

Watkins, Tionne *See T-Boz; TLC*

Watkins, Walter C. 1946— **24**

Watley, Jody 1959— **54**

Watson, Benjamin 1980— **126**

Watson, Bo *See Midnight Star*

Watson, Bob 1946— **25**

Watson, Carlos 1970— **50**

Watson, Diane 1933— **41**

Watson, Ivory *See Ink Spots, The*

Watson, Johnny "Guitar" 1935–1996 **18**

Watson Coleman, Bonnie 1945— **127**

Watt, Garland W. 1932–2013 **113**

Watt, Mel 1945— **26, 105**

Wattleton, (Alyce) Faye 1943— **9**

Watts, André 1946— **42, 101**

Watts, J(ulius) C(aesar), Jr. 1957— **14, 38**

Watts, Reggie 1972— **52, 102**

Watts, Rolonda 1959— **9**

Wayans, Damien 198(?)— **78**

Wayans, Damon 1961— **8, 41**

Wayans, Keenen Ivory 1958— **18**

Wayans, Kim 1961— **80**

Wayans, Marlon 1972— **29, 82**

Wayans, Shawn 1971— **29**

Waymon, Eunice Kathleen *See Simone, Nina*

Wayne, Reggie 1978— **131**

Weah, George 1966— **58**

Weathers, Barbara *See Atlantic Starr*

Weathers, Carl 1948— **10, 117**

Weaver, Afaa Michael 1951— **37**

Weaver, Karen 1959(?)— **134**

Weaver, Michael S. *See Weaver, Afaa Michael*

Weaver, Mike 1951— **109**

Weaver, Robert C. 1907–1997 **8, 46**

Webb, Chick 1909–1939 **105**

Webb, Sheyann *See Webb-Christburg, Sheyann*

Webb, Veronica 1965— **10, 95**

Webb, Wellington 1941— **3, 81**

Webb, William Henry *See Webb, Chick*

Webb, Wilmeth *See Sidat-Singh, Wilmeth*

Webb-Christburg, Sheyann 1956— **110**

Webber, Chris 1973— **15, 30, 59, 118**

Webber, Mayce Edward Christopher, III *See Webber, Chris*

Webster, Ben 1909–1973 **136**

Webster, Katie 1936–1999 **29**

Wedgeworth, Robert W. 1937— **42**

Weekes, Kevin 1975— **67**

Weeknd, The 1990— **131**

Weeks, Thomas, III 1967— **70**

Weems, Carrie Mae 1953— **63, 116**

Weems, Renita J. 1954— **44**

Weems, Ted *See Lee Andrews & the Hearts*

Wein, Joyce 1928–2005 **62**

Wek, Alek 1977— **18, 63, 105**

Welburn, Edward T. 1950— **50**

Welch, Elisabeth 1908–2003 **52**

Welcome, Verda Freeman 1907–1990 **112**

Welles, Rosalind *See Washington, Elsie B.*

Wellington, Valerie 1959–1993 **118**

Wells, Henrietta Bell 1912–2008 **69**

Wells, James Lesesne 1902–1993 **10**

Wells, Junior 1934–1998 **102** *See also Aces, The*

Wells, Mary 1943–1992 **28**

Wells, Vernon 1978— **91**

Wells, Willie 1906–1989 **105**

Wells-Barnett, Ida B(ell) 1862–1931 **8**

Welsing, Frances (Luella) Cress 1935— **5**

Wendo *See Kolosoy, Wendo*

Wesley, Dorothy Porter 1905–1995 **19**

Wesley, Richard 1945— **73**

Wesley, Rutina 1979— **97**

Wesley, Valerie Wilson 194(?)— **18**

Wess, Frank 1922–2013 **116**

West, Allen 1961— **89**

West, Bernie *See Five Keys, The*

West, Cornel 1953— **5, 33, 80**

West, Dorothy 1907–1998 **12, 54**

West, James E. 1931— **87**

West, Kanye 1977— **52, 93**

West, Rudy *See Five Keys, The*

West, Togo Dennis, Jr. 1942— **16**

Westbrook, Kelvin 1955— **50**

Westbrook, Peter 1952— **20**

Westbrook, Russell 1988— **116**

Westbrooks, Bobby 1930(?)–1995 **51**

Whack, Rita Coburn 1958— **36**

Whalum, Kirk 1958— **37, 64**

Wharton, A. C., Jr. 1944— **110**

Wharton, Clifton R(eginald), Jr. 1926— **7**

Wharton, Clifton Reginald, Sr. 1899–1990 **36**

Wheat, Alan Dupree 1951— **14**

Wheaton, James 1924–2002 **103**

Whispers, The **124**

Whitaker, Forest 1961— **2, 49, 67**

Whitaker, Jesse *See Pilgrim Travelers, The*

Whitaker, Mark 1957— **21, 47**

Whitaker, Pernell 1964— **10, 89**

Whitaker, "Sweet Pea" *See Whitaker, Pernell*

White, Armond 1953— **80, 118**

White, Augustus, III 1936— **100**

White, Barry 1944–2003 **13, 41**

White, Bill 1933(?)— **1, 48**

White, Booker T. Washington *See White, Bukka*

White, Bukka 1906(?)–1977 **120**

White, Charles 1918–1979 **39**

White, Charlie *See Billy Ward and the Dominoes*

White, (Donald) Dondi 1961–1998 **34**

White, Frank 1950— **95**

White, James L. 1947–2015 **130**

White, Jesse 1934— **22, 75**

White, Jessica 1984— **83**

White, Jo Jo 1946— **112**

White, John H. 1945— **27**

White, Joseph Henry *See White, Jo Jo*

White, Josh 1914(?)–1969 **86**

White, Josh, Jr. 1940— **52**

White, Lillias 1951— **120**

White, Linda M. 1942— **45**

White, Lois Jean 1938— **20**

White, Maurice 1941— **29** *See also Earth, Wind & Fire*

White, Michael Jai 1967— **71, 117**

White, Michael R(eed) 1951— **5**

White, Reggie 1961–2004 **6, 50**

White, Reginald Howard *See White, Reggie*

White, Santi *See Santigold*

White, Sylvain 1971— **96**

White, Terri 1948— **82**

White, Walter F(rancis) 1893–1955 **4**

White, Willard 1946— **53**

White, William DeKova *See White, Bill*

White, Willye 1939— **67**

White-Hammond, Gloria 1951(?)— **61**

Whitehead, Colson 1969— **77**

Whitehead, Don *See Earth, Wind & Fire*

Whiteside, Hassan 1989— **127**

Whitfield, Fred 1967— **23**

Whitfield, LeRoy 1969–2005 **84**

Whitfield, Lynn 1954— **18**

Whitfield, Mal 1924— **60**

Whitfield, Norman 1940–2008 **73**

Whitfield, Van 1960(?)— **34**
Whitlock, Jason 1967— **78, 130**
Whitmore, George 1944–2012 **106**
Whitney, Davey L. 1930— **110**
Whitney, Marva 1944–2012 **109**
Whittaker, Hudson *See Tampa Red*
Wideman, John Edgar 1941— **5, 87**
Widener, Warren 1938— **99**
Wiggins, Andrew 1995— **128**
Wiggins, Charles Ray *See Saadiq, Raphael; Tony! Toni! Toné!*
Wiggins, D'Wayne *See Tony! Toni! Toné!*
Wiggins, Gerald 1922–2008 **128**
Wiggins, Londee *See New Birth*
Wiggins, Raphael *See Saadiq, Raphael; Tony! Toni! Toné!*
Wilbekin, Emil 1968— **63**
Wilbon, Michael 1958— **68, 132**
Wilburn, Nayvadius *See Future*
Wilcox, Emandu *See Pharcyde, The*
Wilder, Deontay 1985— **121**
Wilder, L. Douglas 1931— **3, 48**
Wiley, Isaac *See Dazz Band*
Wiley, Kehinde 1977— **62**
Wiley, Michael *See Dazz Band*
Wiley, Ralph 1952–2004 **8, 78**
Wiley, Samira 1987— **131**
Wilfork, Vince 1981— **124**
Wilkens, Lenny 1937— **11, 88**
Wilkens, Leonard Randolph *See Wilkens, Lenny*
Wilkerson, Isabel 1961— **71**
Wilkerson, Robert King *See King, Robert Hillary*
Wilkins, David 1956— **77**
Wilkins, Dominique 1960— **74**
Wilkins, Elbert *See Dramatics, The*
Wilkins, J. Ernest, Jr. 1923— **43**
Wilkins, Ray 1951— **47**
Wilkins, Roger 1932— **2, 84**
Wilkins, Roy 1901–1981 **4**
Wilkins, Thomas Alphonso 1956— **71**
will.i.am 1975— **64**
Williams, Albert Cecil *See Williams, Cecil*
Williams, Alice Faye *See Shakur, Afeni*
Williams, Ann Claire 1949— **82**
Williams, Anthony 1951— **21**
Williams, Anthony Charles *See Tonex*
Williams, Armstrong 1959— **29**
Williams, Bernard *See Harold Melvin & the Blue Notes*
Williams, Bernie 1968— **128**
Williams, Bert 1874–1922 **18**
Williams, Billy 1938— **86**
Williams, Billy Dee 1937— **8, 105**
Williams, Bryan *See Birdman*
Williams, Buster 1942— **131**
Williams, Calvin *See Golden Gate Quartet*
Williams, Camilla 1919–2012 **116**
Williams, Carl *See Kani, Karl*
Williams, Cecil 1929— **130**
Williams, Charles Anthony, Jr. *See Williams, Buster*
Williams, Charles Melvin *See Williams, Cootie*

Williams, Clarence 1893(?)–1965 **33**
Williams, Clarence 1967— **70**
Williams, Clarence, III 1939— **26**
Williams, Claude 1908–2004 **80**
Williams, Cootie 1908(?)–1985 **114**
Williams, Curtis *See Penguins, The*
Williams, Daniel Hale (III) 1856–1931 **2**
Williams, Darrent 1982–2007 **116**
Williams, David Rudyard 1954— **50**
Williams, David W. 1910–2000 **110**
Williams, Deniece 1951— **36**
Williams, Denise 1958— **40**
Williams, Dennis P. 1953— **123**
Williams, Deron 1984— **92**
Williams, Doug *See Williams Brothers*
Williams, Doug 1955— **22, 112**
Williams, Dudley 1938— **60**
Williams, Eddie N. 1932— **44**
Williams, Eric Eustace 1911–1981 **65**
Williams, Evelyn 1922(?)— **10**
Williams, Fannie Barrier 1855–1944 **27**
Williams, Frederick (B.) 1939–2006 **63**
Williams, George Washington 1849–1891 **18**
Williams, Gertrude *See Morgan, Gertrude*
Williams, Gregory (Howard) 1943— **11**
Williams, Hosea 1926–2000 **15, 31, 123**
Williams, J. Mayo 1894–1980 **83**
Williams, Jody 1935— **113**
Williams, Joe 1918–1999 **5, 25**
Williams, John A. 1925— **27**
Williams, Joseph Leon *See Williams, Jody*
Williams, Juan 1954— **35, 80**
Williams, Ken 1964— **68**
Williams, Larry 1935–1980 **118**
Williams, Lauryn 1983— **58, 127**
Williams, Leonard *See Williams Brothers*
Williams, Lil' Ed 1955— **135**
Williams, Lindsey 1966— **75**
Williams, Maggie 1954— **7, 71**
Williams, Maizie *See Boney M.*
Williams, Malinda 1975— **57**
Williams, Marco 1956— **53**
Williams, Margaret Ann *See Williams, Maggie*
Williams, Mary Lou 1910–1981 **15**
Williams, Melvin *See Williams Brothers*
Williams, Michael Kenneth 1966— **97**
Williams, Michael L. 1953— **86**
Williams, Michelle 1980— **73**
Williams, Milan *See Commodores, The*
Williams, Montel 1956— **4, 57**
Williams, Monty 1971— **125**
Williams, Nat D. 1907–1983 **91**
Williams, Natalie 1970— **31**
Williams, O(swald) S. 1921— **13**
Williams, Patricia 1951— **11, 54**
Williams, Paul *See Paul, Billy*
Williams, Paul 1939–1971 **112** *See also Temptations, The*

Williams, Paul R(evere) 1894–1980 **9**
Williams, Paulette Linda *See Shange, Ntozake*
Williams, Pharrell 1973— **47, 82, 119**
Williams, Preston Warren, II 1939(?)— **64**
Williams, Rhonda Y. 1967(?)— **86**
Williams, Richard 1931–1985 **130**
Williams, Richard 1942— **131**
Williams, Ricky 1977— **85**
Williams, Robert F. 1925–1996 **11, 136**
Williams, Robert Peter *See Guillaume, Robert*
Williams, Ronald A. 1949— **57**
Williams, Roy 1968— **89**
Williams, Russell, II 1952— **70**
Williams, Samuel Arthur 1946— **21**
Williams, Saul 1972— **31**
Williams, Serena 1981— **20, 41, 73, 129**
Williams, Sherley Anne 1944–1999 **25**
Williams, Spencer 1893–1969 **126**
Williams, Stanley "Tookie" 1953–2005 **29, 57**
Williams, Stevie 1979— **71**
Williams, Taiye *See Selasi, Taiye*
Williams, Ted 1957— **91**
Williams, Terrie M. 1954— **35**
Williams, Tony 1945–1997 **67**
Williams, Vanessa A. 1963— **32, 66**
Williams, Vanessa L. 1963— **4, 17**
Williams, Venus 1980— **17, 34, 62**
Williams, Walt 1943–2016 **133**
Williams, Walter *See O'Jays, The*
Williams, Walter E. 1936— **4, 133**
Williams, Wendy 1964— **62**
Williams, Wilbert *See Mighty Clouds of Joy*
Williams, William December *See Williams, Billy Dee*
Williams, William T(homas) 1942— **11**
Williams, Willie L(awrence) 1943— **4**
Williams Brothers **135**
Williamson, Fred 1938— **67**
Williamson, Homesick James *See Homesick James*
Williamson, James *See Homesick James*
Williamson, John Lee Curtis *See Williamson, Sonny Boy 1914–1948*
Williamson, Lisa *See Sister Souljah*
Williamson, Mykelti 1957— **22**
Williamson, Patrice 1967(?)— **134**
Williamson, Sonny Boy 1899(?)–1965 **84**
Williamson, Sonny Boy 1914–1948 **134**
Williamson, Sonny Boy, I *See Williamson, Sonny Boy 1914–1948*
Willie, Louis, Jr. 1923–2007 **68**
Willie D *See Geto Boys*
Willingham, Tyrone 1953— **43**
Willis, Bill 1921–2007 **68**
Willis, Cheryl *See Hudson, Cheryl*
Willis, Chuck 1928(?)–1958 **132**
Willis, Deborah 1948— **85**
Willis, Dontrelle 1982— **55**

Willis, Patrick 1985— **99**
Willis, William Karnet *See Willis, Bill*
Williston, David Augustus 1868–1962 **99**
Wills, Harry 1889(?)–1958 **80**
Wills, Maury 1932— **73**
Wilmore, Larry 1961— **121**
Wilson, Abram 1973–2012 **104**
Wilson, Ajee' 1994— **129**
Wilson, August 1945–2005 **7, 33, 55**
Wilson, Brian Courtney 19(?)(?)— **94**
Wilson, Cassandra 1955— **16**
Wilson, Chandra 1969— **57**
Wilson, Charlie 1953— **31, 77, 135** *See also Gap Band, The*
Wilson, David 1991— **123**
Wilson, Debra 1970(?)— **38**
Wilson, Demond 1946— **102**
Wilson, Donald E. 1936(?)— **88**
Wilson, Dorien 1962(?)— **55**
Wilson, Ellis 1899–1977 **39**
Wilson, Frank 1940–2012 **106**
Wilson, Frederica 1942— **92**
Wilson, Flip 1933–1998 **21**
Wilson, Gerald 1918–2014 **49, 123**
Wilson, Gloria Mai *See Lynne, Gloria*
Wilson, Grady Demond *See Wilson, Demond*
Wilson, Jackie 1934–1984 **60** *See also Billy Ward and the Dominoes*
Wilson, Jimmy 1946— **45**
Wilson, John 1922— **109**
Wilson, Leslie *See New Birth*
Wilson, Lionel 1915–1998 **99**
Wilson, Margaret Bush 1919–2009 **79**
Wilson, Mary 1944 **28**
Wilson, Melvin *See New Birth*
Wilson, Muki *See Crown Heights Affair*
Wilson, Nancy 1937— **10, 98**
Wilson, Natalie 1972(?)— **38**
Wilson, Orlandus *See Golden Gate Quartet*
Wilson, Paul *See Flamingos, The*
Wilson, Phill 1956— **9, 104**
Wilson, Reggie 1967— **116**
Wilson, Robert *See Gap Band, The*
Wilson, Ronnie *See Gap Band, The*
Wilson, Russell 1988— **119**
Wilson, Shanice Lorraine *See Shanice*
Wilson, Stephanie 1966— **72**
Wilson, Sunnie 1908–1999 **7, 55**
Wilson, Teddy 1912–1986 **134**
Wilson, Theodore Shaw *See Wilson, Teddy*
Wilson, Tracey Scott 1967(?)— **77**
Wilson, William Julius 1935— **22**
Wilson, William Nathaniel *See Wilson, Sunnie*
Wimbley, Damon 1966— *See Fat Boys*
Winans, Angie 1968— **36**
Winans, Benjamin 1962— **14**
Winans, CeCe 1964— **14, 43**
Winans, David 1934–2009 **77**
Winans, Debbie 1972— **36**
Winans, Marvin L. 1958— **17, 127**

Winans, Ronald 1956–2005 **54**
Winans, Vickie 1953(?)— **24**
Winburn, Anna Mae 1913–1999 **135**
Winfield, Dave 1951— **5, 91**
Winfield, David Mark *See Winfield, Dave*
Winfield, Paul (Edward) 1941–2004 **2, 45**
Winfree, Larry *See Ray, Goodman & Brown*
Winfrey, Oprah 1954— **2, 15, 61, 106**
Wingo, Richard *See Jagged Edge*
Winkfield, Jimmy 1882–1974 **42**
Winley, Harold *See Clovers, The*
Winslow, Kellen 1957— **83**
Wisdom, Kimberlydawn 1956— **57**
Withers, Bill 1938— **61**
Withers, Ernest C. 1922–2007 **68, 88**
Withers-Mendes, Elisabeth 1973(?)— **64**
Witherspoon, Jimmy 1920(?)–1997 **113**
Witherspoon, John 1942— **38**
Witt, Edwin T. 1920— **26**
Wiwa, Ken 1968— **67**
Wiz Khalifa *See Khalifa, Wiz*
Wofford, Chloe Anthony *See Morrison, Toni*
Wolde Yohannes, Gebre Medhin *See Abune Paulos*
Wolfe, Ann 1971— **82**
Wolfe, George C. 1954— **6, 43, 127**
Womack, Bobby 1944–2014 **60, 92, 123**
Womack, Solomon *See Swan Silvertones, The*
Wonder, Stevie 1950— **11, 53, 121**
Wonder Mike *See Sugarhill Gang, The*
Wood, Mark Adam, Jr. *See Lakeside*
Wood, William Vernell *See Wood, Willie*
Wood, Willie 1936— **111**
Woodard, Alfre 1953— **9, 108**
Woodard, Lynette 1959— **67**
Woodbridge, Hudson *See Tampa Red*
Woodruff, Hale (Aspacio) 1900–1980 **9**
Woodruff, John 1915–2007 **68**

Woods, Abraham, Jr. 1928–2008 **74**
Woods, Belita 1948–2012 **103**
Woods, Cheyenne 1990— **103**
Woods, Eldrick *See Woods, Tiger*
Woods, Georgie 1927–2005 **57**
Woods, Granville T. 1856–1910 **5**
Woods, Jacqueline 1962— **52**
Woods, Mattiebelle 1902–2005 **63**
Woods, Renn 1958— **110**
Woods, Scott 1971— **55**
Woods, Sylvia 1926–2012 **34, 104**
Woods, Teri 1968— **69**
Woods, Thomas *See Clovers, The*
Woods, Tiger 1975— **14, 31, 81**
Woodson, Ali Ollie 1951–2010 **89**
Woodson, Carter G(odwin) 1875–1950 **2**
Woodson, Jacqueline 1963— **125**
Woodson, Mike 1958— **78**
Woodson, Robert L. 1937— **10**
Woodson, Rod 1965— **79**
Woolard, Jamal 1975— **102**
Wooldridge, Anna Marie *See Lincoln, Abbey*
Wooten, Victor 1964— **131**
Work, John Wesley, III 1901–1967 **133**
Workman, Reggie 1937— **131**
Worrill, Conrad 1941— **12**
Worthy, James 1961— **49**
Worthy, Kym 1956— **84**
Wosornu, Taiye *See Selasi, Taiye*
Wray, Noble 1960— **114**
Wright, Albert *See Wright, Chalky*
Wright, Antoinette 195(?)— **60**
Wright, Archibald Lee *See Moore, Archie*
Wright, Beverly 1947— **97**
Wright, Bruce McMarion 1918–2005 **3, 52**
Wright, Chalky 1912–1957 **103**
Wright, Charles H. 1918–2002 **35**
Wright, Clyde *See Golden Gate Quartet*
Wright, Deborah C. 1958— **25**
Wright, Erica *See Badu, Erykah*
Wright, Ernest, Jr. *See Little Anthony & the Imperials*
Wright, Eugene 1923— **125**
Wright, Jeffrey 1965— **54, 111**
Wright, Jeremiah A., Jr. 1941— **45, 69, 103**
Wright, Leo 1933–1991 **131**

Wright, Lewin 1962— **43**
Wright, Louis Tompkins 1891–1952 **4**
Wright, Nathan, Jr. 1923–2005 **56**
Wright, Norma Jean *See Chic*
Wright, O. V. 1939–1980 **114**
Wright, Overton Vertis *See Wright, O. V.*
Wright, Rayfield 1945— **70**
Wright, Richard 1908–1960 **5**
Wright, Richard Robert, Sr. 1855–1947 **100**
Wright, Sarah E. 1928–2009 **95**
Wright, Timothy 1947— **74**
Wyatt, Addie L. 1924— **56**
Wylie, Mary T. Washington *See Washington, Mary T.*
Wyllie, Hubert Anthony *See Wyllie, Tony*
Wyllie, Tony 1967— **131**
Wynn, Albert R. 1951— **25, 77**
X, Malcolm 1925–1965 **1**
X, Marvin 1944— **45**
Xuma, Madie Hall 1894–1982 **59**
Xzibit 1974— **78**
Yabby You 1946–2010 **83**
Yancey, James DeWitt *See J Dilla*
Yancey, Jimmy 1898(?)–1951 **116**
Yancy, Dorothy Cowser 1944— **42**
Yar'Adua, Umaru 1951–2010 **69, 89**
Yarber, Tony 1978— **129**
Yarbrough, Camille 1938— **40**
Yarbrough, Cavin *See Yarbrough & Peoples*
Yarbrough, Cedric 1971— **51**
Yarbrough & Peoples **132**
Yasiin *See Bey, Yasiin*
Yates, Jack 1828–1897 **114**
Yates, John Henry *See Yates, Jack*
Yayi, Boni T. 1952— **84**
Yayo, Tony 1978— **113**
Yearwood, Lennox, Jr. 1969— **112**
Yeboah, Emmanuel Ofosu 1977— **53**
Yende, Pretty 1985— **124**
Yerby, Frank 1916–1991 **96**
Yergan, Max 1892–1975 **123**
Yette, Samuel F. 1929— **63**
YG 1990— **122**
Ying Yang Twins`**112**
Yirga, Samuel 1985(?)— **126**
Yoba, (Abdul-)Malik (Kashie) 1967— **11**
York, Dwight D. 1945— **71**

York, Malachi Z. *See York, Dwight D.*
York, Vincent 1952— **40**
Youla, Mamady 1961— **133**
Young, Al 1939— **82**
Young, Andre Romelle *See Dr. Dre*
Young, Andrew 1932— **3, 48, 110**
Young, Charles 1864–1922 **77**
Young, Coleman 1918–1997 **1, 20**
Young, Darren 1979— **114**
Young, Dewey *See Swan Silvertones, The*
Young, Donald, Jr. 1989— **57**
Young, Earl *See Trammps, The*
Young, Jean Childs 1933–1994 **14**
Young, Jimmy 1948–2005 **54**
Young, John *See Lee Andrews & the Hearts*
Young, John 1949— **111**
Young, Johnny 1917(?)–1974 **120**
Young, Ledisi Anibade *See Ledisi*
Young, Lee 1914–2008 **72**
Young, Lee Thompson 1984–2013 **114**
Young, Leonidas Raymond *See Young, Lee*
Young, Perry H. 1919–1998 **100**
Young, Roger Arliner 1899–1964 **29**
Young, Rosa J. 1890–1971 **129**
Young, Thomas *See Three Mo' Tenors*
Young, Wanda *See Marvelettes, The*
Young, Whitney M(oore), Jr. 1921–1971 **4**
Young, Yvonne *See Orlons, The*
Young, Zora 1948— **129**
Young Jeezy 1977— **63**
Youngblood, Johnny Ray 1948— **8**
Youngblood, Shay 1959— **32**
Yumkella, Kandeh 1959— **105**
Yusef, Malik 1971— **136**
Zane 1967(?)— **71**
Zenawi, Meles 1955)— **3, 99**
Zeno, George Louis Francis *See Lewis, George*
Zollar, Alfred 1955(?)— **40**
Zollar, Jawole Willa Jo 1950— **28**
Zook, Kristal Brent 1966(?)— **62**
Z-Ro 1977— **109**
Zulu, Princess Kasune 1977— **54**
Zuma, Jacob 1942— **33, 75**
Zuma, Nkosazana Dlamini *See Dlamini-Zuma, Nkosazana*
Zwelithini, Goodwill 1948— **128**